CODE OF VIRGINIA

1950

With Provisions for Subsequent Pocket Parts

ANNOTATED

Prepared under the Supervision of

The Virginia Code Commission

BY

The Editorial Staff of the Publishers

VOLUME 1

2008 Replacement Volume

Includes acts adopted at the 2008 Regular Session, Acts 2008, cc. 1 to 884, and 2008 Special Session I, cc. 1 and 2, of the General Assembly

LexisNexis

P.O. Box 7587, Charlottesville, VA 22906-7587

4900814

ISBN 978-1-4224-5073-4

www.lexisnexis.com

Customer Service: 1-800-833-9844

(Pub.49005)

Scope of Volume

Scope of Annotations

To better serve our customers, by making our annotations more current, LexisNexis has changed the sources that are read to create annotations for this publication. Rather than waiting for cases to appear in printed reporters, we now read court decisions as they are released by the courts. A consequence of this more current reading of cases, as they are posted online on LEXIS, is that the most recent cases annotated may not yet have print reporter citations. These will be provided, as they become available, through later publications.

This publication contains annotations taken from decisions of the Virginia Supreme Court posted on LEXIS as of April 1, 2008, decisions of the Virginia Court of Appeals posted as of April 1, 2008, and decisions of the appropriate federal courts posted as of April 1, 2008. These cases will be printed in the following reports:

South Eastern Reporter, Second Series.
Supreme Court Reporter.
Federal Reporter, Third Series.
Federal Supplement, Second Series.
Federal Rules Decisions.
Bankruptcy Reporter.

Additionally, annotations have been taken from the following sources:

Virginia Law Review, through Volume 93, p. 1175.
Washington and Lee Law Review, through Volume 64, p. 625.
William and Mary Law Review, through Volume 48, p. 2401.
University of Richmond Law Review, through Volume 41, p. 1063.
George Mason University Law Review, through Volume 14, p. 829.

Circuit Court Opinions, 1999 Va. Cir. LEXIS 727 (6/25/99) through 73 Va. Cir. 515 (8/13/07).
Opinions of the Attorney General through September 2005.

Unpublished Opinions of Court of Appeals

Some of the annotations contained in this supplement are derived from unpublished opinions of the Court of Appeals of Virginia. These opinions will not appear in the Court of Appeals Reports or any other court reporter. The unpublished opinions can be identified by their citation, which gives the parties' names, a case number, "Ct. of Appeals," and a date.

The Court of Appeals has placed the following footnote on all unpublished opinions: "Pursuant to Code § 17.1-413, recodifying § 17-116.010, this opinion is not designated for publication."

"Although an unpublished opinion of the Court has no precedential value, a court or commission does not err by considering the rationale and adopting it to the extent it is persuasive." Fairfax County School Board v. Rose, 29 Va. App. 32, 509 S.E.2d 525 (Va. App. 1999).

A copy of the full text of any unpublished opinion can be obtained by contacting: Court of Appeals of Virginia, Attention: Clerk's Assistant (Opinions), 109 North Eighth Street, Richmond, Virginia 23219.

Foreword

The first legislatively adopted Code of Virginia was published as two volumes in 1819, with statutes grouped by subject matter in sequentially numbered chapters. The General Assembly, by specific legislative enactment, subsequently recodified the entire body of statutory law in 1849, 1887, 1919 and 1950. Interim Codes incorporating Acts of Assembly during the intervening years were privately edited and published, occasionally under legislative authority. Notable among these are the Code of Virginia, 1904, in two volumes, by West Publishing Company; and, the Code of Virginia, 1942, in one volume, by The Michie Company.

The body of statutory law recodified by Act of Assembly in 1950 was contained in ten volumes as published by The Michie Company. All original ten volumes have been have been replaced and, with the exception of Volume 10, divided into additional lettered volumes with previous supplements incorporated therein. This 2008 Replacement Volume 1 replaces the 2005 Replacement Volume 1, and separates out the Constitutions of the Commonwealth of Virginia and the United States into a single unnumbered Volume styled "Constitutions."

In 1946, the General Assembly created the Commission on Code Recodification and continued it in 1948 as a permanent agency of the legislative branch designated the Virginia Code Commission. Since previous revisors of the Code exited at the conclusion of their work, the establishment of the Commission represents a significant and historical change in prior practice. Revision of the Code is now an ongoing and accelerated process, particularly following advent of regular annual sessions of the General Assembly under the Constitution of 1971, and the marked increase in legislative activity.

Responsibility for incorporating the Acts of Assembly into a compilation of existing statutory laws is vested in the Virginia Code Commission. Under authority set forth in §§ 30-145 through 30-155 of the Code of Virginia, the Commission has discretion to fix the number of volumes of the Code and to decide the form, makeup and arrangement of same. The Commission is further empowered to renumber, rename and rearrange any Code titles, chapters, articles and sections.

In a number of instances existing statutes have been amended two or more times by separate acts passed at the same session, the second or subsequent act not taking account of the earlier amendments. In such instances the acts have been combined by the Commission so as to give effect to all amendments unless there is a conflict in the language. Where an actual conflict existed, the last amendment is controlling and has been used in the Code.

The Commission is also has the task of proposing code revisions. This duty has been discharged by periodic revisions of separate titles which have, by Commission practice, been submitted to the General Assembly for enactment. Chapters or articles from other titles are occasionally incorporated into the revised titles. This piecemeal revision has extended the existence of the Code of 1950 beyond the approximate thirty year life of its predecessors.

Changes in the condition of Virginia over the past 58 years have rendered some Code titles obsolete or of diminished importance, while concepts and technologies unknown in 1950 now affect virtually all legislation. The Commission recognizes, and the history of the Code has demonstrated, that alterations, deletions and additions to statutes over time will eventually render any title and numbering system obsolete. It is with this reality that the Commission determined to reorganize the Code in 2007, and utilized the passage of Senate Joint Resolution 388 in the 2005 Session to provide public notice of this intent.

Concern over costs expressed by some state agencies, particularly where Code numbers are integral to electronic systems, caused the General Assembly to waiver in its support of this project. In the immediate future the Commission will continue separate title revisions while pressing the inevitability of a comprehensive reorganization of the Code. We also acknowledge the Code of 1950 enjoys a familiarity over generations that makes change uncomfortable. Deference to time honored tradition is a long recognized trait of Virginians.

Pursuant to statutory mandate only those Acts of a general or permanent nature are included in the Code. Acts affecting only one or a few localities have typically not been codified. The Commission recognizes that this important body of law, which can dramatically impact the people of the subject localities, is not accessible through the Code. We are accordingly considering the publication of local acts in a separate volume.

The full activities of the Commission are most readily accessible through the internet at http://legis.state.va.us/codecomm/codehome.htm. As an agency of the legislative branch, public comment is invited at every meeting of the Commission.

R. Steven Landes, *Chairman*
John S. Edwards, *Vice-Chairman*
William R. Janis
Ryan T. McDougle
Robert L. Calhoun
Thomas M. Moncure, Jr.
James F. Almand
Frank S. Ferguson
E. M. Miller, Jr.

July 2008

Members of the Virginia Code Commission and the predecessor Commission on Code Recodification

---

Almand, James F. (Judge) 2006- .
Almond, J. Lindsay Jr. (Attorney General) 1948-1957.
Ames, E. Almer Jr. (Senate) 1964-1967 (Vice-Chairman 1966-1967).
Apperson, Harvey B. (Attorney General) 1947.
Bateman, Fred W. (Senate) 1966-1967.
Battle, John S. (Senate) 1946-1949 (Chairman 1947-1949).
Banks, John A. Jr. (Director, Division of Legislative Services) 1973-1988.
Boatwright, John B. (Director, Statutory Research and Drafting) 1952-1965.
Boothe, Armistead L. (House & Senate) 1947-1963 (Chairman 1950-1963).
Broaddus, William G. (Attorney General designee) 1982-1985.
Button, Robert Y. (Attorney General) 1962-1963).
Calhoun, Robert L. (Former Senate) 1996- .
Carneal, Russell M. (House & Judge) 1973, 1975-1998.
Chichester, Cassius M. (Director, Statutory Research and Drafting) 1946-1951.
Cohen, Bernard S. (House & Former House) 1992-1999.
Cohoon, Willis E. (House) 1946.
Coleman, J. Marshall (Attorney General) 1978-1981.
DeBoer, Jay W. (House) 1996-2000.
Edwards, John. S. (Senate) 2001- (Vice-Chairman 2006-).
Emick, Dudley J., Jr. (Senate) 1981-1991 (Chairman 1988-1991, Vice-Chairman 1984-1987).
Ferguson, Frank S. (Attorney General designee) 1994- .
Forbes, J. Randy (Senate) 1999-2000 (Vice Chairman 2000).
Gartlan, Joseph V., Jr. (Senate) 1988-1999 (Chairman 1992-1999).
Glasscock, J. Samuel (House) 1988-1991 (Vice-Chairman 1988-1991).
Goodwyn, S. Bernard (Judge) 2004-2007.
Gray, Frederick T. (House & Senate) 1968-1983 (Chairman 1981-1983).
Harrison, Albertis S. (Attorney General) 1958-1960.
Hobson, Haskins (Judge) 1953.
Hodges, William H. (Senate) 1968-1971 (Vice-Chairman 1968-1971).
Howell, William J. (House) 2000-2003 (Chairman 2000-2002).
Huntley, W. Moscoe (Judge) 1960-1965.
Hurt, Robert (House) 2004-2008.
Janis, William R. (House) 2008- .
Johnson, Randall G. (Judge) 2003-2004.
Jones, James P. (Senate) 1984-1987.
Kneedler, H. Lane (Attorney General designee) 1986-1988.
Knowles, John Wingo (Judge) 1966-1991.
Kulp, Kames E. (Judge) 1999-2002.
Lamb, Brokenbrough (Judge) 1947-1952.
Landes, R. Steven (House) 2000- (Chairman 2006- , Vice-Chairman 2003-2006).
Lapsley, G. McIver (Director, Statutory Research and Drafting) 1966-1969.
Manning, L. Cleaves (Judge) 1994.
Marshall, Gail Starling (Attorney General designee) 1989-1993.
McDougle, Ryan T. (Senate) 2006- .
Michael, J. Harry, Jr. (Senate) 1972-1980 (Chairman 1980, Vice-Chairman 1972-1979).
Miller, Andrew P. (Attorney General) 1970-1976.
Miller, E.M., Jr. (Director, Division of Legislative Services) 1989- .
Miller, Willis D. (Judge) 1946.

Mims, William C. (Senate) 2000-2006 (Chairman 2003-2006, Vice-Chairman 2000-2002).
Moncure, Thomas M., Jr. (Former House) 2000- .
Morrison, Theodore V., Jr. (House & Former House) 1974-1995 (Chairman 1984-1987, Vice-Chairman 1980-1983).
Murphy, W. Tayloe, Jr. (House) 1992-1999 (Vice-Chairman 1994-1999).
Norris, Robert O. Jr. (Senate) 1952-1955.
Parkerson, William F., Jr. (Former Senate) 1988-1995.
Patty, Kenneth C. (Atttorney General designee) 1964-1967.
Philpott, A.L. (House) 1966-1991 (Chairman 1968-1979).
Powell, Cleo E. (Judge) 2008-2008.
Reasor, Jackson E., Jr. (Senate) 1992-1998.
Snead, Harold F. (Judge) 1954-1957.
Staples, Abraham P. (Attorney General) 1946.
Strickland, Diane McQuade (Judge) 2002-2006.
Thompson, W. Carrington (Senate) 1970-1971.
Thomson, James M. (House) 1961-1967 (Chairman 1964-1967).
Troy, Anthony F. (Attorney General) 1977.
Wilkinson, James B. (Judge) 1995-2003.

THE GREAT SEAL OF THE COMMONWEALTH

Virginia's great seal was adopted by the Virginia Convention on July 5, 1776. Its design was the work of a committee chaired by George Mason, who was the principal author of both the Virginia Declaration of Rights and the first Virginia Constitution. George Wythe, Richard Henry Lee and Robert Carter Nicholas also served as members of the committee.

The committee report of 1776 described the two sides of the Seal in detail and various renderings came into use over time. In 1930, a committee was named to prepare an "accurate and faithful description of the great seal of this Commonwealth." The now official design of the Seal is both remarkably true to that set forth by the Virginia Convention and deferential to its classical origins. The colors of the Seal were officially established in 1949.

The obverse, or front, side of the seal depicts the Roman goddess Virtus representing the genius of the Commonwealth. She is dressed as an Amazon, a sheathed sword in one hand and a spear in the other and one foot on the dead body of Tyranny who is presented with a broken chain in his left hand, a scourage in his right and a fallen crown nearby. Virginia's motto, Sic Semper Tyrannis (Thus Always to Tyrants) is intended as a caption spelling out the triumph of Virtue over Tyranny.

The reverse, or back, side of the seal depicts three Roman goddess, Libertas (Liberty) in the center holding a wand and pileus in her right hand, Aeternitas (Eternity) with a globe and phoenix in her right hand, and Ceres (Fruitfulness) with a cornucopia in her left hand and an ear of wheat in her right. At the top is the word Perservando (by Preserving). A border of Virginia creeper encircles the design on each side.

The representation of civic or public Virtue dominates the obverse of the great seal. The Latin root of Virtue is "vir," meaning "man," and the classical Amazons were a race of female warriors. Virtus, clothed as an Amazon, harkens to those qualities. It is also notable that Libertas appears on the reverse of the great seal as a visual reminder that Liberty is the result of Virtue defeating Tyranny.

The great seal, imprinted on two metallic discs two and one-fourth inches in diameter, is affixed to documents signed by the Governor and intended for use before tribunals or for purposes outside the jurisdiction of Virginia. The lesser seal, a smaller version of the obverse side of the seal and measuring one and nine-sixteenth inches in diameter, is used on commissions for gubernatorial appointees and to authenticate the signature of the Secretary of the Commonwealth.

VIRGINIA AS THE COMMONWEALTH

There is no "State" of Virginia. While generically categorized as a state within the federal union, Virginia has been the "Commonwealth" since independence from the British Crown. Virginia is the first of four states that are commonwealths, to include our daughter Commonwealth of Kentucky, which was formed from Virginia in 1792.

Our first Constitution, adopted on June 29, 1776, directed that "Commissions and Grants shall run, In the Name of the Commonwealth of Virginia, and bear teste by the Governor with the Seal of the Commonwealth annexed." The Constitution furthermore dictated that criminal indictments were to conclude "against the peace and dignity of the commonwealth."

It is the Virginia Declaration of Rights, adopted on June 12, 1776, that sets forth our rights and philosophy of government. Virginia's founders viewed government as a contract between people who are "created equally free and independent." The underlying ideal was that personal sovereignty was given over in order to create a society, which then in turn facilitated individual pursuits. As "all Power is . . . vested in, and consequently derived from the People," government was created to the benefit of its citizens.

Of greatest importance, Virginia's founders envisioned that the people should possess certain traits, namely, "a firm Adherence to Justice, Moderation, Temperance, Frugality and Virtue." No concept was more central than that of public or civic virtue. The civically virtuous citizen was self-determinative and self-reliant while recognizing a duty to the general welfare, and the common good, of the community at large.

Virginians, as members of the Commonwealth, enjoy a higher degree of sovereignty. The continuing existence of the Commonwealth requires that each citizen be an active participant in government. All citizens must likewise be practitioners of civic virtue, dedicated to conducting themselves in a socially responsible manner.

A state may or may not reflect the will of the people, but a commonwealth simply cannot exist without the people's express consent. The commonwealth is an extraordinary form of government based upon the collective genius of its citizens. The Commonwealth is distinguished from, and superior to, a mere state by the greatness of the good people of Virginia.

User's Guide

The following guide contains comments on a few of the time-saving features to be found in the Code of Virginia. See also the Preface at the beginning of the Cumulative Supplements to each volume.

If you have questions or suggestions concerning the Code of Virginia, please write, call toll free at 1-800-833-9844, or send a fax at 1-518-487-3584. Direct written inquiries to:

LexisNexis
Attn: Code of Virginia
P.O. Box 7587
Charlottesville, Virginia 22906-7587

This guide is designed to help both the lawyer and the layperson get the most out of the Code of Virginia. It gives brief information on how to use each of the following features most effectively:

—Administrative Law Appendix
—Advance Code Service
—Amendment Notes
—Analyses
—Annotations
—Applied
—Compacts
—Cross References
—Editor's Notes
—Effective Dates
—Headings, Catchlines and Preambles
—Historical Citations
—Indexes
—Law Reviews
—Legal Ethics Opinions
—Organization and Numbering of Code
—Repealed Sections
—Retention of Obsolete Volumes and Supplements
—Tables

ADMINISTRATIVE LAW APPENDIX

The Administrative Law Appendix is a finding guide to existing regulations and forms of administrative agencies of the Commonwealth. It is published annually in a separate soft-bound volume. It describes the powers of each agency, availability of its regulations, and a list of its regulations. It does not contain the text of regulations, but does provide information on where to obtain copies thereof.

ADVANCE CODE SERVICE

The Advance Code Service updates the Cumulative Supplement to the Code and contains more recent annotations from cases and law reviews. Statutory material is sometimes set out in the Advance Code Service, as, for instance, when the General Assembly holds a special session.

The Advance Code Service is published in three cumulative pamphlets, approximately quarterly. Its contents are included in the following year's supplement, when published.

AMENDMENT NOTES

Amendment notes show without editorial comment changes made in a statute by the legislature. If the changes are extensive and a detailed comparison would be impractical or confusing, the note may simply indicate that the amendment "rewrote this section." In those instances, the user should consult the Acts of Assembly to determine the changes made by the amendment.

Amendment notes have been separated from other notes to enable the user to identify more easily the information that each type of note contains.

Amendment notes are carried in the annual supplements until the volume is next replaced. In replaced volumes, such notes are retained for sections amended within the two preceding years, or, in the case of amendments with delayed effective dates, for two years after the effective date. In order to know what changes were made to a section before the two-year cutoff, the user should retain all replaced volumes and supplements.

ANALYSES

Each title and chapter is preceded by an analysis, which is a table of contents for that title or chapter. Use of the analyses can provide a quick understanding of the scope of the title or chapter.

ANNOTATIONS

All reported state and federal cases which arise in Virginia and construe Virginia law have been read and fully annotated under pertinent statutes. All case notes have been read and edited to guarantee their continuing accuracy. Where a decision has undergone subsequent review, the reviewing court's action is noted in the case citation if it affects the annotated point. Where two or more decisions apply the same rule in essentially identical terms, their citations are cumulated under the case note stating the rule. If a more recent case applying the same rule appears in the supplement or Advance Code Service, its full text is not repeated there, but is referred to by repeating all or part of its catchline and the location of the full text, using the words "In accord with ..."

Case notes are given catchlines briefly summarizing the note(s) thereunder, to assist the user in identifying the notes which will be most helpful to him. These are arranged by subject matter. Notes pertaining to the section's constitutionality appear first because of their relative importance. Notes of general applicability usually precede those of more narrow application. Where there is a large number of case notes, they are often further grouped into larger units with broad headings. These headings are printed in an analysis immediately preceding the case notes.

Where a section has been substantially amended or repealed and the subject matter reenacted in a comparable new section, the publisher has retained those case notes which, while construing the former law, may also construe or contribute to the user's understanding of the new provision.

All annotations are intended as source material, and the user is urged to review the actual case itself rather than relying wholly on an annotation.

APPLIED

A decision which refers to a Code section as the basis for a ruling, but without construing the section, is listed under the section under the "Applied" heading. Since some decisions frequently construe related points of law, consulting "Applied" cases can help the user see the sections before him in perspective.

COMPACTS

Compacts to which the Commonweath is a party are set forth in a single unnumbered Volume styled "Compacts." Where a compact is integral to the understanding of related statutes it is also included in the Code.

CROSS REFERENCES

Cross references refer the user to other statutes or rules of court that may modify or supplement a statutory provision or place it in context. They are not included for sections immediately preceding or following the section at hand within the same chapter and do not cite all related statutes. The general index should be used to locate all of the law on a subject.

EDITOR'S NOTES

These notes immediately follow the section to which they pertain and inform the user about special circumstances connected with the section, such as its effective date, applicability, expiration date, and other noncodified sections affecting the interpretation or operation of an act. Usually, these notes will cite the act which contains this information so that the user may trace the information to the Acts of Assembly. The following is an example of how an act is cited: Acts 1995, c. 171, cl. 4. Following the word "Acts" is the year of the legislative session which passed the act. The number after "c." indicates the chapter of the act. Finally, the numbered divisions of an act are called "clauses," and following "cl." is the clause number.

The General Assembly has sometimes assigned Code section numbers to acts which, in the opinion of the Commission, are not of such a general and permanent nature to warrant inclusion in the Code. The Commission has usually not codified such acts, but has set out the assigned section number followed by the words "not set out." Where codified statutes contain provisions, such as severability clauses or repealing clauses, which are not normally codified but which have been assigned Code sections numbers by the General Assembly, such provisions have been likewise "not set out."

EFFECTIVE DATES

Most of the acts adopted by the General Assembly do not contain express effective date provisions. Sections added, amended, or repealed by such acts become effective in accordance with Article IV, Section 13 of the Constitution of Virginia. For the effective date of such acts from the most recent session, see the Preface in the supplement.

Where the act does contain an effective date provision, the date will be noted in an effective date note, amendment note, or in a repeal line, as appropriate. Delayed effective dates are also noted by inclusion of the date in the section catchline, set off by parentheses.

Effective date notes are carried in the annual supplements until the volume is next replaced. In replaced volumes, such notes are retained for sections enacted within the two preceding years, or, in the case of delayed effective dates, for two years after the effective date.

HEADINGS, CATCHLINES AND PREAMBLES

Every title, article, chapter, and individual Code section contains a topical word or phrase which precedes the text of that statutory unit. Such language, which indicates the subject matter of the unit, is called a heading when referring to a title, chapter, or article and a catchline when referring to a single section. By necessity, title, article, and chapter headings are less specific than section catchlines since they express the overall contents of a larger division. These headings and catchlines are reviewed and amended whenever necessary to reflect the textual contents more accurately. Preambles have usually been omitted, but if of sufficient importance they have been mentioned in notes.

HISTORICAL CITATION

The material appearing in parentheses immediately following the text of a statute is the historical citation. The citation includes, in chronological order, all session laws and official Code citations that enact or amend that Code section. The following is an example of how an act is cited: Acts 1995, c. 171, cl. 4. Following the word "Acts" is the year of the legislative session which passed the act. The number after "c." indicates the chapter of the act. Finally, the numbered divisions of an act are called "clauses," and following "cl." is the clause number.

INDEXES

The general index for the Code of Virginia is published in soft cover volumes which are updated and replaced annually. In addition, a separate index to the Rules of the Supreme Court is included in Volume 11.

For some basic principles concerning index use, consult the Foreword to the Index in the front of the first volume of the general index.

LAW REVIEWS

Law reviews published in Virginia have been examined for relevancy to Code sections, and are cited when some relationship is found. These citations appear under the catchline "Law Reviews."

LEGAL ETHICS OPINIONS

Unauthorized Practice Opinions and Legal Ethics Opinions as rendered by the Virginia State Bar are set forth in two unnumbered Volumes. Opinions are numbered sequentially, and an index to the Opinions is contained in the second Volume.

ORGANIZATION AND NUMBERING OF CODE

The Code of Virginia is organized into Titles by general subject matter. The Titles are arranged alphabetically and are numbered 1 through 66. Titles may be further divided into chapters and articles. A Table of Titles is found at the beginning of each Code volume. Rules of the Supreme Court of Virginia are set out in Volume 11 pursuant to § 8.01-3 of the Code.

Code sections are identified by two-part, hyphenated numbers. The first part of the number identifies the Title in which the section if found. The second part identifies the section within that Title. For example, § 4.1-100 is the first section in Title 4.1. When new Code provisions are inserted between existing provisions, it is often necessary to further divide the Title or section number with periods or colons so as to accommodate the new provision while preserving the numbering system.

The more recent practice of the Commission in recodifications has been to "imbed" chapters and, as appropriate, articles in numbering sections. For example, all section numbers in Chapter 5 of Title 1 begin with the 5, §§ 1-500 through 1-512.

REPEALED SECTIONS

Where a section is repealed, its section number is retained in its former location, with a citation to the repealing act and the effective date thereof, if stated in the act. A cross reference to new provisions covering the same subject as the repealed section, if any, is also provided.

RETENTION OF OBSOLETE VOLUMES AND SUPPLEMENTS

Retention of obsolete Code volumes and supplements is recommended, since these may be useful for historical research or for pending matters governed by a former statute.

TABLES

Volume 10 of the Code of Virginia contains tables which will help the user locate material in the Code.

The Table of Comparative Sections shows the relationship between sections of the Michie Code of 1942 and sections of the Code of 1950. The Table of Acts shows where acts of the legislature may be found in the Code. The Table of Sections Amended or Repealed cites all acts which have amended or repealed a given Code section. The Table of Comparable Sections for Certain Repealed and Revised Titles shows, for each section of the repealed title, the comparable section (if any) in the revised title which supersedes the repealed title.

Table of Titles

TITLE

In addition, this publication contains

Table of Contents

VOLUME 1

CODE OF VIRGINIA

Title 1.

General Provisions.

CHAPTER 1.

CODE OF VIRGINIA.

§ **1-1. Contents and designation of Code.** — The laws embraced in this and the following titles, chapters, articles and sections of this act shall constitute, and be designated and cited as the "Code of Virginia," hereinafter referred to as "the Code" or "this Code." (Code 1919, § 1; R. P. 1948, § 1-1.)

Cross references. — As to rules of construction, see §§ 1-200 through 1-257 and notes thereto.

History of Code of 1950 and cumulative supplement. — The proposed Code of Virginia, submitted by the then Commission on Code Recodification to the 1948 session of the General Assembly, with certain amendments fully explained in the preface and known as the "Reorganization Provisions of the Code of Virginia," was adopted as the Code of Virginia, to be effective as provided in §§ 1-2 and 1-2.1, by an act approved April 6, 1948.

Under authority and direction of chapter 262 of the Acts of 1948, codified as former §§ 9-66 through 9-77 (see now § 30-152 et seq.), the Commission, now styled the Virginia Code Commission, prepared and had published an annotated edition, in ten volumes including the index, of the Code so adopted, with the reorganization provisions and the general acts of the 1948 session incorporated therein.

This edition was submitted to the General Assembly for approval at its 1950 session and was adopted by an act approved January 27, 1950.

The final paragraph of that act, which has not been codified, read in part: "... the body of the statute law contained in the foregoing ten volumes is to take effect February one, nineteen hundred fifty as the official Code of Virginia, sometimes for brevity called the Code of 1950."

The general acts of the 1950 through 2008 sessions have been codified and published, under authority of § 30-152 et seq., in the supplements and in the added and replacement volumes.

CASE NOTES

The 1948 enactment of the Code submitted to that session of the General Assembly was a valid enactment and did not violate Va. Const., Art. IV, § 11, or § 12, which provides that no law shall embrace more than one object, which shall be expressed in its title. Article IV, § 12, was not intended to apply to a general code revision, and adoption of a code by general title is broad enough to cover any lawful enactment. McClain v. Commonwealth, 189 Va. 847, 55 S.E.2d 49 (1949). See notes to Va. Const., Art. IV, §§ 11 and 12.

§ **1-2. Effective date of Code.** — All the provisions of this Code shall be in force on and after February 1, 1950, except as provided in § 1-2.1. (Code 1919, § 6567; R. P. 1948, § 1-2.)

Cross references. — As to rules of construction, see §§ 1-200 through 1-257 and notes thereto.

CASE NOTES

Applied in Fauver v. Bell, 192 Va. 518, 65 S.E.2d 575 (1951).

§ **1-2.1. Effective date of certain provisions.** — The following provisions of this Code shall become effective July 1, 1948, namely:

Chapter 1 of Title 1; Chapters 1, 8, 9, 12, 14, 15, and 16 of Title 2; Chapter 13 of Title 3; Chapter 11 of Title 6; Chapters 2 and 5 of Title 9; all of Title 10; Article 7 of Chapter 1 of Title 14; Article 3 of Chapter 6 of Title 18; Chapter 2 of Title 19; Chapter 3 of Title 24; Chapter 3 of Title 27; Chapters 15 and 19 of Title 32; all of Title 41; Article 4 of Chapter 6 of Title 42; Articles 2 and 12 of Chapter 1 of Title 44 and all of Chapter 2 of Title 44; Chapter 3 of Title 51; Chapter 1 of Title 52; Chapters 1 through 14, inclusive, of Title 53; Chapter 24 of Title 54; Chapters 12 and 13 of Title 59; Chapter 7 of Title 62; all of Title 63 except Chapter 13. (R. P. 1948, § 1-2.1.)

Cross references. — As to rules of construction, see §§ 1-200 through 1-257 and notes thereto.

Editor's note. — Title 2, referred to above, was repealed by Acts 1966, c. 677. Title 3, referred to above, was repealed by Acts 1966, c. 702. Title 6, referred to above, was repealed by Acts 1966, c. 584. Chapter 2 of Title 9, referred to above, was repealed by Acts 1970, c. 463; Acts 1978, c. 580. Title 10, referred to above, was repealed by Acts 1988, c. 891. Title 14, referred to above, was repealed by Acts 1964, c. 386. Title 18, referred to above, was repealed by Acts 1960, c. 358. Title 19, referred to above, was repealed by Acts 1960, c. 366. Title 24, referred to above, was repealed by Acts 1970, c. 462. Chapter 15 of Title 32, referred to above, was repealed by Acts 1968, c. 578. Chapter 19 of Title 32, referred to above, was repealed by Acts 1979, c. 711. Title 41, referred to above, was repealed by Acts 1970, c. 291. Title 42, referred to above, was repealed by Acts 1970, c. 606. Chapter 3 of Title 51, referred to above, was repealed by Acts 1952, c. 1. Chapter 1 of Title 53, referred to above, was repealed by Acts 1956, c. 386; Acts 1970, c. 648; Acts 1972, c. 175; Acts 1974, cc. 44, 45. Chapters 2 through 14 of Title 53, referred to above, were repealed by Acts 1982, c. 636. Chapter 24 of Title 54, referred to above, was repealed by Acts 1974, c. 534; Acts 1976, c. 651; Acts 1977, c. 640; Acts 1979, c. 408. Title 59, referred to above, was repealed by Acts 1968, c. 439. Title 62, referred to above, was repealed by Acts 1968, c. 659. Title 63, referred to above, was repealed by Acts 1968, c. 578.

§ **1-3. Repeal of acts of a general nature.** — All acts and parts of acts of a general nature, in force at the time of the adoption of this Code, shall be repealed from and after February 1, 1950, with such limitations and exceptions as are hereinafter expressed; and all acts and parts of acts of a general nature in force at the time of the adoption of this Code, and in conflict with any of the provisions of this Code which by virtue of § 1-2.1 become effective on July 1, 1948, shall be repealed from and after July 1, 1948, with such limitations and exceptions as are hereinafter expressed. (Code 1919, § 6567; R. P. 1948, § 1-3.)

CASE NOTES

Special act not repealed. — The Code of 1919 was a revision of the general statutes of the Commonwealth, and it did not repeal a special act of 1910 establishing a road law for Augusta County. Hamilton v. Commonwealth, 143 Va. 572, 130 S.E. 383 (1925).

Omission of acts of a general nature. — An act providing a different rule of ejectment procedure in three named counties, being a general law, was held repealed by being omitted from the Code of 1887. Carter's Heirs v. Edwards, 88 Va. 205, 13 S.E. 352 (1891).

An act authorizing the voluntary incorporation of building fund associations, being an act of a general nature, was repealed by being omitted from the Code of 1887. Crabtree v. Old Dominion Bldg. & Loan Ass'n, 95 Va. 670, 29 S.E. 741 (1898).

§ 1-4. Effect of such repeal generally; effect of revision or amendment of state Constitution. — No such repeal nor any amendment or revision of the Constitution of Virginia shall affect any offense or act committed or done, or any penalty or forfeiture incurred, or any right established, accrued, or accruing before the day upon which such repeal, amendment or revision takes effect, or any prosecution, suit, or proceeding pending on that day, except that the proceedings thereafter had shall conform, so far as practicable, to the provisions of this Code; and where any penalty, forfeiture, or punishment is mitigated by those provisions, such provisions may, with the consent of the party affected, be applied to any judgment to be pronounced after that day; and such repeal, amendment or revision as to any statute of limitations, under which the bar of a right of action or remedy is complete at the time the repeal, amendment or revision takes effect, shall not be deemed a removal of such bar, but the bar shall continue, notwithstanding such repeal, amendment or revision. (Code 1919, § 6569; R. P. 1948, § 1-4; 1971, Ex. Sess., c. 14.)

Michie's Jurisprudence. — For related discussion, see 3B M.J. Carriers, § 2.

CASE NOTES

Acts done under a statute while in force remain valid, though the statute may afterwards be repealed, but the rule goes no farther than to render valid things actually done. Crawford v. Halsted & Putnam, 61 Va. (20 Gratt.) 211 (1871).

An election held under an act subsequently repealed by being omitted from the Code of 1887 was not invalidated by such repeal. Thomas v. Commonwealth, 90 Va. 92, 17 S.E. 788 (1893).

Section not controlling in action arising under federal act. — This section is not expressly controlling or directly in point on a legal question presented in an action arising under the Federal Housing and Rent Act of 1947 to recover damages and attorney's fees for rentals charged in excess of the maximum rent that could be charged, where such act is later repealed, because the alleged right of action asserted arose under a federal act. Levinson v. Bott, 193 Va. 47, 67 S.E.2d 923 (1951).

As to change of mode of procedure in a pending case to conform to the then new Code of 1887, see Edmunds' Ex'r v. Bruce, 88 Va. 1007, 14 S.E. 840 (1892).

Applied in Southworth v. Sullivan, 162 Va. 325, 173 S.E. 524 (1934).

§ 1-5. Effect of such repeal as to persons in office. — All persons who, at the time when such repeal takes effect, shall hold any office under any of the acts hereby repealed, shall continue to hold the same according to the tenure thereof, except those offices which may have been abolished, and those as to which a different provision is made by this Code. (Code 1919, § 6571; R. P. 1948, § 1-5.)

§ 1-6. Effect of repeal of validating statutes. — The repeal by any provisions of this Code of a statute validating previous acts, contracts or transactions shall not affect the validity of such acts, contracts or transactions, but the same shall remain as valid as if there had been no such repeal, but no further. (Code 1919, § 8; R. P. 1948, § 1-6.)

§ 1-7. Acts passed between certain dates not affected. — The enactment of this Code shall not affect any act passed by the General Assembly, which shall have become a law after January 14, 1948, and before February 1, 1950; but every such act shall have full effect, and so far as the same varies from or conflicts with any provision contained in this Code it shall have effect as a subsequent act, and as repealing any part of this Code inconsistent therewith; provided, however, that any such act which becomes a law between said dates and which amends and reenacts, or reenacts any previously existing provisions of law conferring any power or imposing any duty upon any department, board, commission, agency or officer of the state government whose functions, powers and duties are affected by any of the provisions of this Code becoming effective July 1, 1948, shall be construed as conferring the powers and imposing the duties specified therein upon the department, board, commission, agency or officer of the state government to which or to whom the duties and powers imposed or conferred by such previously existing provisions of law were transferred by the provisions of this Code becoming effective July 1, 1948. (Code 1919, § 6568; R. P. 1948, § 1-7.)

CASE NOTES

Under former Codes. — As to application of similar provisions of the Codes of 1887 and 1919, see Virginia Dev. Co. v. Crozer Iron Co., 90 Va. 126, 17 S.E. 806 (1893), aff'd on rehearing, 90 Va. 126, 19 S.E. 782 (1894); Somers v. Commonwealth, 97 Va. 759, 33 S.E. 381 (1899); Southern Ry. v. Russell, 133 Va. 292, 112 S.E. 700 (1922); Campbell v. City of Danville, 138 Va. 817, 122 S.E. 120 (1924).

§ 1-8. Notice, recognizance or process given, taken or issued before Code in force. — Although a notice, recognizance or process shall have been given, taken or issued before the day prescribed for the commencement of this Code, or of any provisions of this Code, it may, nevertheless, be given, taken or returnable to a day after such commencement, or to a court established by this Code or the clerk's office of such court, in like manner as if this Code had commenced before the same was given, taken, or issued. (Code 1919, § 6570; R. P. 1948, § 1-8.)

§ 1-9. Pending cases; parties; where books, records and papers to remain. — Nothing in this Code shall operate to discontinue any cause or matter, civil or criminal, which shall be pending and undetermined in any court on the day before this Code, or any provision of this Code, takes effect; but every such cause and matter shall be proceeded in, tried and determined in such court, or in the court which succeeds to or has its jurisdiction, and in the names of the same parties, or in the names of any officers, boards, commission, or other persons or bodies who may have succeeded under the provisions of this Code to the rights or obligations of such parties, or any of them. The papers and records of such causes and matters, and all books, records and papers whatever which on such day may be in the custody of any clerk of a court shall remain in custody of the clerk of the same, or of such court as succeeds to or has its jurisdiction. (Code 1919, § 6570; R. P. 1948, § 1-9.)

CHAPTER 2.

COMMON LAW, STATUTES AND RULES OF CONSTRUCTION.

§§ 1-10 through 1-17.2: Repealed by Acts 2005, c. 839, cl. 10, effective October 1, 2005.

Editor's note. — Acts 2005, c. 839, recodified Chapters 2 and 3 of Title 1, and all of Title 7.1, as Chapters 2.1 through 5 of Title 1, effective October 1, 2005. In addition to revision by Acts 2005, c. 839, Titles 1 and 7.1 were also amended by other acts passed at the 2005 Session. As required by § 30-152, the Code Commission has incorporated the majority of these amendments into the new sections. Where appropriate, the historical citations to former sections have been added to corresponding new sections. For tables of corresponding former and new sections, see the tables in Volume 10.

Former § 1-13.4 was repealed by Acts 1986, c. 155. Former § 1-13.11 was repealed by Acts 1981, c. 228. Former § 1-13.39 was repealed by Acts 1983, c. 260. Former § 1-14 was repealed by Acts 1975, c. 547.

CHAPTER 3.

CITIZENSHIP.

§§ 1-18 through 1-21: Repealed by Acts 2005, c. 839, cl. 10, effective October 1, 2005.

Editor's note. — Acts 2005, c. 839, recodified Chapters 2 and 3 of Title 1, and all of Title 7.1 as Chapters 2.1 through 5 of Title 1, effective October 1, 2005. In addition to revision by Acts 2005, c. 839, Titles 1 and 7.1 were also amended by other acts passed at the 2005 Session. As required by § 30-152, the Code Commission has incorporated the majority of these amendments into the new sections. Where appropriate, the historical citations to former sections have been added to corresponding new sections. For tables of corresponding former and new sections, see the tables in Volume 10.

CHAPTER 2.1.

COMMON LAW AND RULES OF CONSTRUCTION.

Article 1.

Common Law and Acts of Parliament.

§ **1-200. The common law.** — The common law of England, insofar as it is not repugnant to the principles of the Bill of Rights and Constitution of this Commonwealth, shall continue in full force within the same, and be the rule of decision, except as altered by the General Assembly. (Code 1919, § 2, § 1-10; 2005, c. 839.)

Editor's note. — Chapters 2 and 3 of Title 1 and Title 7 have been rewritten, primarily as new Chapters 2.1 through 5 of Title 1, by Acts 2005, c. 839, effective October 1, 2005.

In addition to revision by Acts 2005, c. 839, §§ 1-13.23:1 [see now § 1-237] and 7.1-40.7:1 [see now § 1-510] were also amended by other acts passed at the 2005 Session. As required by § 30-152, the Code Commission has incorporated these amendments into the new sections.

Where appropriate, the historical citations to former sections have been added to corresponding new sections.

The case notes appearing under new sections were decided under corresponding former sections or under prior law.

For tables of corresponding former and new sections, see the tables in Volume 10.

Acts 2005, c. 839, cl. 2, provides: "That whenever any of the conditions, requirements, provisions or contents of any section or chapter of Titles 1 and 7.1 or any other title of the Code of Virginia as such titles existed prior to October 1, 2005, are transferred in the same or modified form to a new section or chapter of Title 1 or any other title of the Code and whenever any such former section or chapter is given a new number in Title 1 or any other title, all references to any such former section or chapter of Title 1 or other title appearing in this Code shall be construed to apply to the new or renumbered section or chapter containing such conditions, requirements, provisions, contents or portions thereof."

Acts 2005, c. 839, cl. 3, provides: "That the regulations of any department or agency affected by the revision of Titles 1 or 7.1 or such other titles in effect on the effective date of this act shall continue in effect to the extent that they are not in conflict with this act and shall be deemed to be regulations adopted under this act."

Acts 2005, c. 839, cl. 4, provides: "That the title revisions of Titles 1 and 7.1 as Chapters 2.1, 3.1, 4, and 5 of Title 1 shall not be construed to require the reappointment of any officer or any member of a board, council, committee or other appointed body referred to in

Titles 1 and 7.1 and each such officer and member shall continue to serve for the term for which appointed pursuant to the provisions of Chapter 2 and Chapter 3 of Title 1 and Title 7.1."

Acts 2005, c. 839, cl. 5, provides: "That the provisions of § 30-152 of the Code of Virginia shall apply to the revision of Titles 1 and 7.1 so as to give effect to other laws enacted by the 2005 session of the General Assembly notwithstanding the delay in the effective date of this act."

Acts 2005, c. 839, cl. 6, provides: "That the repeal of Chapters 2 and 3 of Title 1 and Title 7.1, effective as of October 1, 2005, shall not affect any act or offense done or committed, or any penalty incurred, or any right established, accrued or accruing on or before such date, or any proceeding, prosecution, suit or action pending on that day. Except as otherwise provided in this act, neither the repeal of Chapters 2 and 3 of Title 1 and Title 7.1 nor the enactment of Chapters 2.1, 3.1, 4 and 5 of Title 1 shall apply to offenses committed prior to October 1, 2005, and prosecution for such offenses shall be governed by the prior law, which is continued in effect for that purpose. For the purpose of this enactment, an offense was committed prior to October 1, 2005, if any of the essential elements of the offense occurred prior thereto."

Acts 2005, c. 839, cl. 7, provides: "That any notice given, recognizance taken, or process or writ issued before October 1, 2005, shall be valid although given, taken or to be returned to a day after such date, in like manner as if Chapters 2.1, 3.1, 4 and 5 of Title 1 had been effective before the same was given, taken or issued."

Acts 2005, c. 839, cl. 8, provides: "That if any clause, sentence, paragraph, subdivision or section of Chapters 2.1, 3.1, 4 and 5 of Title 1 shall be adjudged in any court of competent jurisdiction to be invalid, the judgment shall not affect, impair or invalidate the remainder thereof, but shall be confined in its operation to the clause, sentence, paragraph, subdivision or section thereof directly involved in the controversy in which the judgment shall have been rendered, and to this end the provisions of Title 1 are declared severable."

Acts 2005, c. 839, cl. 9, provides: "All actions of any county, city or town or political subdivision of the Commonwealth or any combination thereof identified by population classification under an act of the Assembly enacted prior to July 1, 1960, and of the officers thereof and of the clerks of courts thereof in the operation of their respective offices either on a fee or salary basis for the calendar year of 1961, and until March 30, 1962, are hereby ratified, validated and confirmed."

Law Review. — For article, "A Century of Tort Immunities in Virginia," see 4 U. Rich. L. Rev. 238 (1970). For survey of Virginia law on torts for the year 1970-71, see 57 Va. L. Rev. 1501 (1971). For note on law revision and reform in the common-law countries, see 13 Wm. & Mary L. Rev. 253 (1971). For survey of Virginia law on taxation for the year 1972-73, see 59 Va. L. Rev. 1584 (1973). For survey of Virginia criminal procedure for the year 1977-1978, see 64 Va. L. Rev. 1419 (1978). For a re-examination of sovereign tort immunity in Virginia, see 15 U. Rich. L. Rev. 247 (1981). For article on discovery penalties, see 15 U. Rich. L. Rev. 283 (1981).

Michie's Jurisprudence. — For related discussion, see 3C M.J. Common Law, §§ 5, 6; 12A M.J. Licenses, § 10; 13B M.J. Municipal Corporations, §§ 1, 4.

CASE NOTES

Editor's note. — Most of the cases annotated below were decided under former law.

The common law of England is in force in Virginia in conformity to the terms of this section. Wiseman v. Commonwealth, 143 Va. 631, 130 S.E. 249 (1925); Elliott v. Commonwealth, 172 Va. 595, 1 S.E.2d 273 (1939); Brown v. Brown, 183 Va. 353, 32 S.E.2d 79 (1944); Needam v. Needam, 183 Va. 681, 33 S.E.2d 288 (1945); Rosenberger v. Rosenberger, 184 Va. 1024, 37 S.E.2d 55 (1946); Carter v. Hinkle, 189 Va. 1, 52 S.E.2d 135 (1949).

Insofar as applicable to our circumstances. — Such of the doctrines and principles of the common law as are repugnant to the nature and character of our political system, or which the different and varied circumstances of our country render inapplicable to us, are either not in force here or must be so modified in their application as to adapt them to our condition. It is a reasonable and substantial compliance with the common law, rather than a literal one, which is exacted by its adoption. Foster v. Commonwealth, 96 Va. 306, 31 S.E. 503 (1898). See Baring v. Reeder, 11 Va. (1 Hen. & M.) 154 (1806); Coleman v. Moody, 14 Va. (4 Hen. & M.) 1 (1809); Findlay v. Smith, 20 Va. (6 Munf.) 134 (1818); Stout v. Jackson, 23 Va. (2 Rand.) 132 (1823); Stokes & Smith v. Upper Appomattox Co., 30 Va. (3 Leigh) 318 (1831).

Such of English common-law doctrines and principles as are repugnant to the nature and character of the political system, or which the different and varied circumstances of the country render inapplicable to the State, are either not in force here, or must be so modified in their application as to adapt them to the condition.

Weishaupt v. Commonwealth, 227 Va. 389, 315 S.E.2d 847 (1984).

Except where modified by statute. — Virginia is a common-law State, except where modified by statute. Carey v. Foster, 221 F. Supp. 185 (E.D. Va. 1963), aff'd, 345 F.2d 772 (4th Cir. 1965).

Although the General Assembly can abrogate the common law, its intent to do so must be plainly manifested. Wackwitz v. Roy, 244 Va. 60, 418 S.E.2d 861 (1992).

Legislative intent to change the common law must be clear or plainly manifested. Chandler v. National R.R. Passenger Corp., 882 F. Supp. 533 (E.D. Va. 1995).

This section does not mean that common-law rules are forever chiseled in stone, never changing. The common law is dynamic, evolves to meet developing societal problems, and is adaptable to society's requirements at the time of its application by the court. Williamson v. Old Brogue, Inc., 232 Va. 350, 350 S.E.2d 621 (1986).

But the common law cannot be enlarged by judicial decision in the absence of authority. — Virginia law, including the common law of England incorporated into the Virginia Code by § 1-10 [now § 1-200], does not provide a basis for recognizing a common law right to use force to resist an illegal detention; in the absence of authority requiring such a right, there was no reason for enlarging, by judicial decision, the scope of the common law on the subject. Commonwealth v. Hill, 264 Va. 541, 570 S.E.2d 805, 2002 Va. LEXIS 170 (2002).

Virginia courts have applied this section to justify reliance on contemporary as well as preenactment common-law doctrines. Long v. Vlasic Food Prods. Co., 439 F.2d 229 (4th Cir. 1971).

Before English common law can be applied in Virginia it must be analyzed in light of this section and the cases interpreting it. Weishaupt v. Commonwealth, 227 Va. 389, 315 S.E.2d 847 (1984).

Rule that wife may not unilaterally revoke implied consent to marital intercourse is rejected. — So much of the English common-law rule regarding a husband's marital exemption from a charge of raping his wife and the implied consent to marital intercourse as provides that a wife cannot unilaterally revoke her implied consent to marital intercourse is rejected. Weishaupt v. Commonwealth, 227 Va. 389, 315 S.E.2d 847 (1984).

Illustrative cases. — This section was applied as to embracery in Wiseman v. Commonwealth, 143 Va. 631, 130 S.E. 249 (1925); as to right of political subdivision to preference in payment of debts, in United States Fid. & Guar. Co. v. Carter, 161 Va. 381, 170 S.E. 764 (1933); as to owner keeping fowls on his own land, in Graeme v. Adams, 64 Va. (23 Gratt.) 225 (1873); as to bastardy, in State Hwy. & Transp. Comm'r v. Cardinal Realty Co., 232 Va. 434, 350 S.E.2d 660 (1986); as to single tort, resulting in damage to both person and property, giving rise to two distinct causes of action, in Dodson v. Remco Enters., Inc., 504 F. Supp. 540 (E.D. Va. 1980); as to ownership of beds of streams granted prior to 1802, in Brockenbrough's Ex'rs v. Spindle's Adm'rs, 58 Va. (17 Gratt.) 21 (1866).

This section was applied as to suicide as a common law crime, in Wackwitz v. Roy, 244 Va. 60, 418 S.E.2d 861 (1992).

This section was applied to prevent a grantor from reserving an interest in real property for the benefit of a stranger to the deed. Shirley v. Shirley, 259 Va. 513, 525 S.E.2d 274 (2000).

Supreme Court of Virginia rejected defendant's argument that § 1-10 [now § 1-200] required the Commonwealth of Virginia to prove that she knew she had a firearm in her possession when she carried the firearm onto school property, in violation of subsection B of § 18.2-308.1, and found that subsection B of § 18.2-308.1 created strict criminal liability. Esteban v. Commonwealth, 266 Va. 605, 587 S.E.2d 523, 2003 Va. LEXIS 106 (2003).

In a negligence action, a tenant could not recover damages for personal injuries resulting from a landlord's alleged noncompliance with duties imposed by § 55-248.13 of the Virginia Residential Landlord and Tenant Act, §§ 55-248.2 through 55-248.40, because the Act does not, either through the express language of §§ 55-248.40, 55-248.21, and 55-248.4 or by necessary implication, abrogate the common-law rule that a landlord was not liable in tort for a tenant's personal injuries caused by the landlord's failure to repair premises under the tenant's control and possession. Sections 55-248.3:1, 55-248.4, 55-248.21, and 55-248.40 revealed that the Act provided a comprehensive scheme governing contractual relationships between landlords and tenants instead of creating a statutory cause of action allowing a tenant to recover damages for personal injuries resulting from a landlord's noncompliance with the Act. Isbell v. Commercial Inv. Assocs., 273 Va. 605, 644 S.E.2d 72, 2007 Va. LEXIS 52 (2007).

CIRCUIT COURT OPINIONS

Illustrative cases. — In holding that the crime of conspiracy to commit a misdemeanor existed in Virginia, the court noted that, under the common law of England, a conspiracy to commit a misdemeanor was an offense. Commonwealth v. Howlett, 61 Va. Cir. 509, 2003 Va. Cir. LEXIS 136 (Norfolk 2003).

§ 1-201. Acts of Parliament. — The right and benefit of all writs, remedial and judicial, given by any statute or act of Parliament, made in aid of the common law prior to the fourth year of the reign of James the First, of a general nature, not local to England, shall still be saved, insofar as the same are consistent with the Bill of Rights and Constitution of this Commonwealth and the Acts of Assembly. (Code 1919, § 3, § 1-11; 2005, c. 839.)

Law Review. — For note on law revision and reform in the common-law countries, see 13 Wm. & Mary L. Rev. 253 (1971).

Michie's Jurisprudence. — For related discussion, see 12A M.J. Licenses, § 6; 18 M.J. Taxation, § 198.

CASE NOTES

Scire facias. — As to preservation by this section of scire facias in personal actions, see Dykes & Co. v. Woodhouse's Adm'r, 24 Va. (3 Rand.) 287 (1825) (decided under prior law).

ARTICLE 2.

Rules of Construction and Definitions.

§ 1-202. General rule of construction. — The rules and definitions set forth in this chapter shall be used in the construction of this Code and the acts of the General Assembly, unless the construction would be inconsistent with the manifest intention of the General Assembly. (Code 1919, § 5; Code 1950, § 1-13; 1950, p. 20; 2005, c. 839.)

Law Review. — For article, "Legislative History and the Interpretation of Statutes: Toward a Fact-Finding Model of Statutory Interpretation," see 76 Va. L. Rev. 1295 (1990).

Michie's Jurisprudence. — For related discussion, see 17 M.J. Statutes, §§ 36, 80, 109; 18 M.J. Taxation, § 10; 18 M.J. Time, § 2.

CASE NOTES

Editor's note. — The cases annotated below were decided under prior law.

Section applies to statutes, not to deeds, wills, etc. — This section applies only "in the construction of this Code and of all statutes." It says nothing about deeds, contracts, wills, or other documents, but is restricted to statutes, and in reference to the latter, it applies to all statutes. Kelly v. Trehy, 133 Va. 160, 112 S.E. 757 (1922).

Code is one act and construed as a whole. — The Code of 1887 was held to be one act, which must be construed as a whole. Gaines' Adm'r v. Marye, 94 Va. 225, 26 S.E. 511 (1897); First Nat'l Bank v. Holland, 99 Va. 495, 39 S.E. 126 (1901); South & N.W. Ry. v. Commonwealth, 104 Va. 314, 51 S.E. 824 (1905); Bertram v. Commonwealth, 108 Va. 902, 62 S.E. 969 (1908).

The Code of 1919 was held a single act, and its different sections were regarded, not as prior and subsequent acts, but as simultaneous expressions of the legislative will. It was further held that all provisions therein dealing with the same subject should be construed together and reconciled whenever possible. Shepherd v. F.J. Kress Box Co., 154 Va. 421, 153 S.E. 649 (1930), citing Piedmont Fin. Corp. v. Commonwealth, 146 Va. 287, 135 S.E. 673 (1926).

Resort to original statutes. — Notwithstanding the fact that the Codes of 1887 and 1919 were revisions of the statute law, if the various sections of one of the Codes were harmonious and their meaning plain, resort could not be had in construing them to the original statutes to see if any error was committed in the revision. If, however, there was a substantial doubt as to the meaning of the sections, the law which was the subject of the revision could be looked to in ascertaining their meaning. If they were inconsistent and could not stand together, the original statutes, and the respective dates of their enactment, could be examined to see what was the last expression of the will of the legislature on the subject. Gaines' Adm'r v. Marye, 94 Va. 225, 26 S.E. 511 (1897); W.S. Forbes & Co. v. Southern Cotton Oil Co., 130 Va. 245, 108 S.E. 15 (1921); Xippas v. Commonwealth, 141 Va. 497, 126 S.E. 207 (1925). And see Shepherd v. F.J. Kress Box Co., 154 Va. 421, 153 S.E. 649 (1930).

Intention to alter old law by revision must plainly appear. — The settled rule in construing the Code is that the old law was not intended to be altered, unless such intention plainly appears. Durrett v. Davis, 65 Va. (24 Gratt.) 302 (1874); Hamilton v. Commonwealth, 143 Va. 572, 130 S.E. 383 (1925). See Parramore v. Taylor, 52 Va. (11 Gratt.) 220 (1854); Davis v. Commonwealth, 58 Va. (17 Gratt.) 617 (1867); Owners of Steamboat Wenonah v. Bragdon, 62 Va. (21 Gratt.) 685 (1872); Vaughan v. Jones, 64 Va. (23 Gratt.) 444 (1873); Thomas' Adm'r v. Lewis, 89 Va. 1, 15 S.E. 389 (1892); Harrison v. Wissler, 98 Va. 597, 36 S.E. 982 (1900); Puckett v. Mullins' Adm'r, 106 Va. 248, 55 S.E. 676 (1906); Wright v. Collins' Adm'r, 111 Va. 806, 69 S.E. 942 (1911); Chapman v. Richardson, 123 Va. 388, 96 S.E. 776 (1918).

Change in phraseology is not important. Code revisors often make such changes and shorten statutes with no intention to change their substance, and no change in substance will be construed as intended unless it plainly appears. Keister's Adm'r v. Keister's Ex'rs, 123 Va. 157, 96 S.E. 315 (1918); Norfolk & Portsmouth Bar Ass'n v. Drewry, 161 Va. 833, 172 S.E. 282 (1934).

Revised or substituted statute omitting provisions in original. — It is a general rule that when a revised statute, or one reenacted for another, omits provisions contained in original act, the omitted part cannot be supplied by construction. Richmond-Ashland Ry. v. Commonwealth ex rel. City of Richmond, 162 Va. 296, 173 S.E. 892 (1934).

When a statute is revised, or when one act is framed from another, and portions of the former are omitted, the missing part will not be revived by statutory construction but will be considered as annulled and revoked. Godlewski v. Gray, 221 Va. 1092, 277 S.E.2d 213 (1981).

Construction of one section considered in construing similar sections. — The construction placed upon language used in one section of the Code may be considered in determining the meaning of similar or the same language used in other sections. First Nat'l Bank v. Holland, 99 Va. 495, 39 S.E. 126 (1901).

That the section of a Code last adopted in sequence will prevail where the difference in language is irreconcilable, see Building Supplies Corp. v. Willcox, 284 F. 113 (4th Cir. 1922).

If there is conflict between the body of a statute and a proviso, then the proviso must prevail, as the later expression of the legislative intent. Loyd Corp. v. Commonwealth, 126 Va. 39, 100 S.E. 833 (1919).

When a statute has been construed by the courts and is then reenacted by the legislature, the construction given to it is presumed to be sanctioned by the legislature and therefore becomes obligatory upon the courts. Kelly v. Trehy, 133 Va. 160, 112 S.E. 757 (1922).

When the General Assembly enacts a statute in language with a long history of definition by the Supreme Court, it intends that the words carry their historical construction. Quintana v. Commonwealth, 224 Va. 127, 295 S.E.2d 643 (1982), cert. denied, 460 U.S. 1029, 103 S. Ct. 1280, 75 L. Ed. 2d 501, rehearing denied, 461 U.S. 940, 103 S. Ct. 2113, 77 L. Ed. 2d 316 (1983).

Subsequent legislation is enacted in the light of and with knowledge of an interpretative statute, such as this section, and hence the latter controls unless there be a clear legislative intent to substitute a different interpretation. Alphonse Custodis Chimney Constr. Co. v. Molina, 183 Va. 512, 32 S.E.2d 726 (1945). See Kelly v. Trehy, 133 Va. 160, 112 S.E. 757 (1922).

The rule that taxing statutes must be construed liberally in favor of the taxpayer when they are doubtful or ambiguous remains unaffected by this section. Williams v. City of Richmond, 177 Va. 477, 14 S.E.2d 287 (1941).

CIRCUIT COURT OPINIONS

Illustrative cases. — In holding that the crime of conspiracy to commit a misdemeanor existed in Virginia, the court noted that, under the common law of England, a conspiracy to commit a misdemeanor was an offense. Commonwealth v. Howlett, 61 Va. Cir. 509, 2003 Va. Cir. LEXIS 136 (Norfolk 2003).

§ 1-203. Adult. — *"Adult"* means a person 18 years of age or more. (1972, cc. 824, 825, § 1-13.42; 2005, c. 839.)

CASE NOTES

Applied in McDonald v. Commonwealth, 274 Va. 249, 645 S.E.2d 918, 2007 Va. LEXIS 87 (2007).

§ 1-204. Age of majority. — For the purposes of all laws of the Commonwealth including common law, case law, and the acts of the General Assembly, unless an exception is specifically provided in this Code, a person shall be an adult, shall be of full age, and shall reach the age of majority when he becomes 18 years of age. (1972, cc. 824, 825, § 1-13.42; 2005, c. 839.)

CASE NOTES

Editor's note. — Most of the cases annotated below were decided under prior law.

Minority is a legal status subject to change by the legislature rather than a vested right. For cases under prior law, see Mack v. Mack, 217 Va. 534, 229 S.E.2d 895 (1976); Hurdle v. Prinz, 218 Va. 134, 235 S.E.2d 354 (1977).

Application to plaintiffs under age 21 when causes of action accrued prior to enactment of section. — There was no retroactive application of this section where the statute was applied to plaintiffs, both of whom were under the age of 21 at the time their causes of action accrued prior to the enactment of the statute, causing the statute of limitations to run from the time plaintiffs reached 18 rather than from the age of 21 as at common law. Hurdle v. Prinz, 218 Va. 134, 235 S.E.2d 354 (1977).

Application of the age of majority statute to the plaintiff's, both of whom were under the age of 21 at the time their causes of action accrued prior to the enactment of the statute, causing the statute of limitations to run from the time plaintiff's reached the age of 18 rather than from the age of 21 as at common law, was not error. Hurdle v. Prinz, 218 Va. 134, 235 S.E.2d 354 (1977).

Former § 8-30 in no event could properly be read to delay until age 21 the running of the statute of limitations in cases where causes of action for personal injury accrued while plaintiffs were under 21 years of age, but where this section, changing the age of majority and therefore changing the status of plaintiffs, was enacted before plaintiffs reached 21. Hurdle v. Prinz, 218 Va. 134, 235 S.E.2d 354 (1977).

Attorney's claim for fees barred by client's infancy. — Trial court properly determined that an attorney's claim for legal services was barred by the client's infancy; the attorney's services to the client concerning his potential inheritance were not actually necessary to the client's position and condition, as any distribution from the estate of the client's grandfather would not have come until several years after the client turned 18. Zelnick v. Adams, 269 Va. 117, 606 S.E.2d 843, 2005 Va. LEXIS 4 (2005).

Child support payments. — When contract provisions as to child support entered into prior to the change in the age of majority were supplanted by a later court order in a divorce suit entered after the change in majority, the court order controls and support payments were not owing for children over 18 despite contract's provision for payments until age 21. Eaton v. Eaton, 215 Va. 824, 213 S.E.2d 789 (1975).

Where a divorce decree incorporated the terms of a property settlement contract, by which the husband agreed to make child support payments until his child reached the age of 21, where the chancellor subsequently ordered a consent decree awarding the husband custody of the child and reduced child support payments until further order of the court, and where custody of the child was subsequently restored to the wife by court order and monthly payment required for the child's support was reinstated for the same period fixed in the property settlement contract, the consent decree did not supplant the child support provisions of the contract and did not deprive the court of jurisdiction to order support beyond 18, despite the statutory reduction of the age of majority from 21 to 18 enacted subsequently. Gazale v. Gazale, 219 Va. 775, 250 S.E.2d 365 (1979).

Where no specific age for termination was set forth, but support payments were required until the child reached his majority, the parties intended not to extend the duty of child support beyond the period within which, in the absence of an agreement, the father would have been liable under Virginia law for such support. Meredith v. Meredith, 216 Va. 636, 222 S.E.2d 511 (1976).

The parties intended that the father's duty to support his "minor" children terminated on the day when, in the absence of any agreement, his legal liability for such support under Virginia law ended and that was his child's eighteenth birthday. Mack v. Mack, 217 Va. 534, 229 S.E.2d 895 (1976).

Applied in McDonald v. Commonwealth, 274 Va. 249, 645 S.E.2d 918, 2007 Va. LEXIS 87 (2007).

§ 1-205. Bond with surety. — "Bond with surety" includes the payment in cash of the full amount of the required bond and, in such case, no surety shall be required. (1977, c. 156, § 1-13.1:1; 2005, c. 839.)

§ 1-206. Certified mail equivalent to registered mail. — If any mail or notice is required to be sent by registered mail, it shall constitute compliance with this requirement if such mail or notice is sent by certified mail. (1956, c. 647, § 1-15.1; 2005, c. 839.)

§ 1-207. Child; juvenile; minor; infant. — *"Child," "juvenile," "minor," "infant,"* or any combination thereof means a person less than 18 years of age. (1972, cc. 824, 825, § 1-13.42; 2005, c. 839.)

CASE NOTES

Minority is a legal status subject to change by the legislature rather than a vested right. For cases under prior law, see Mack v. Mack, 217 Va. 534, 229 S.E.2d 895 (1976); Hurdle v. Prinz, 218 Va. 134, 235 S.E.2d 354 (1977).

Attorney's claim for fees barred by client's infancy. — Trial court properly determined that an attorney's claim for legal services was barred by the client's infancy; the attorney's services to the client concerning his potential inheritance were not actually necessary to the client's position and condition, as any distribution from the estate of the client's grandfather would not have come until several years after the client turned 18. Zelnick v. Adams, 269 Va. 117, 606 S.E.2d 843, 2005 Va. LEXIS 4 (2005) (decided under prior law).

Sodomy statute constitutional as applied where defendant is adult and victim is minor. — As defendant's victims, 16 and 17, were "minors" as defined by § 1-207, his as-applied constitutional challenge to the sodomy statute, § 18.2-361, failed because nothing in *Lawrence v. Texas,* 539 U.S. 558 (2003), or *Martin v. Ziherl,* 607 S.E.2d 367 (2005), prohibited the application of the sodomy statute to conduct between adults and minors. McDonald v. Commonwealth, 274 Va. 249, 645 S.E.2d 918, 2007 Va. LEXIS 87 (2007).

§ 1-208. City. — *"City"* means an independent incorporated community which became a city as provided by law before noon on July 1, 1971, or which has within defined boundaries a population of 5,000 or more and which has become a city as provided by law. (Code 1919, § 5; Code 1950, § 1-13; 1950, p. 21; 1971, Ex. Sess., c. 49, § 1-13.2; 1995, c. 155; 2005, c. 839.)

Cross references. — As to local government, see Va. Const., Art. VII and § 15.2-100 et seq.

Law Review. — For note, "Securing a Valid Annexation in Virginia," see 10 U. Rich. L. Rev. 557 (1976).

§ 1-209. Collegial body. — *"Collegial body"* means a governmental entity whose power or authority is vested within its membership. (2004, c. 651, § 1-13.4:1; 2005, c. 839.)

§ 1-210. Computation of time. — A. When an act of the General Assembly or rule of court requires that an act be performed a prescribed amount of time before a motion or proceeding, the day of such motion or proceeding shall not be counted against the time allowed, but the day on which such act is performed may be counted as part of the time. When an act of the General Assembly or rule of court requires that an act be performed within a prescribed amount of time after any event or judgment, the day on which the event or judgment occurred shall not be counted against the time allowed.

B. When the last day for performing an act during the course of a judicial proceeding falls on a Saturday, Sunday, legal holiday, or any day or part of a day on which the clerk's office is closed as authorized by an act of the General Assembly, the act may be performed on the next day that is not a Saturday,

Sunday, legal holiday, or day or part of a day on which the clerk's office is closed as authorized by an act of the General Assembly.

C. When an act of the General Assembly specifies a maximum period of time in which a legal action may be brought and the last day of that period falls on a Saturday, Sunday, legal holiday, or day or part of a day on which the clerk's office is closed as authorized by an act of the General Assembly, the action may be brought on the next day that is not a Saturday, Sunday, legal holiday, or day or part of a day on which the clerk's office is closed as authorized by an act of the General Assembly.

D. Any court or proceeding authorized to be adjourned from day to day shall not be required to meet on a Sunday or legal holiday. (Code 1919, § 5; 1932, p. 24; Code 1950, § 1-13; 1950, pp. 21, 23, §§ 1-13.3, 1-13.27; 1962, cc. 104, 284, § 1-13.3:1; 1977, c. 93; 1986, c. 166; 1987, c. 92; 2005, c. 839; 2008, c. 816.)

The 2008 amendments. — The 2008 amendment by c. 816 added subsection C and redesignated former subsection C as subsection D.

Michie's Jurisprudence. — For related discussion, see 1B M.J. Appeal and Error, § 127; 12A M.J. Limitation of Actions, § 2; 13A M.J. Motions for Judgment, § 18; 14B M.J. Process, § 16; 18 M.J. Sundays and Holidays, § 3; 18 M.J. Time, § 5.

CASE NOTES

Editor's note. — Most of the cases annotated below were decided under prior law.

In general. — Acts 1932, p. 24, added the latter part of the section [now subsection A of this section], relating to notice or act required by statute within a certain time after an event or judgment. With this exception, this rule of construction as to computation of time has been on the statute books of the State, with a brief intermission, for over a century. Acts 1916, ch. 290, p. 508, made radical changes in the language of this provision, and extended the rule of construction to contracts, but the language of the old section was restored by the Code of 1919, which went into effect January 8, 1920. Kelly v. Trehy, 133 Va. 160, 112 S.E. 757 (1922). See School Bd. v. Alexander, 126 Va. 407, 101 S.E. 349 (1919).

Excluding day on which event or judgment occurred. — Hence, where a final decree, from which an appeal was obtained, was entered on April 24, the period for executing the appeal bond did not begin to run until April 25. Hurley v. Bennett, 163 Va. 241, 176 S.E. 171 (1934).

Prior to 1932, a different holding prevailed. See Kelly v. Trehy, 133 Va. 160, 112 S.E. 757 (1922) (time for filing bill of exceptions); Swift & Co. v. Wood, 103 Va. 494, 49 S.E. 643 (1905) (time for return of notice of motion for judgment); Jennings v. Pocahontas Consol. Collieries Co., 114 Va. 213, 76 S.E. 298 (1912) (time for filing declaration).

Under this section, when a statute or rule of court requires a notice to be given or any other act to be done within a certain time after any event or judgment, that time shall be in addition to the day on which the event or judgment took place; thus here, the five month speedy trial time allowance under § 19.2-243 did not begin to run until the day after defendant's probable cause hearing. Randolph v. Commonwealth, 22 Va. App. 334, 470 S.E.2d 132 (1996).

Trustee's objection to debtors' claim of exemptions, under 11 U.S.C.S. § 522(b)(2)(A), was overruled as debtors timely filed their amended homestead deeds on November 16, 2005, pursuant to § 34-17, because: (1) a legal proceeding was not in ordinary parlance considered to have been "held" until it was over; (2) a meeting of creditors had not "occurred," pursuant to subsection A of § 1-210, until it actually concluded; and (3) the original meeting of creditors was not concluded on October 17, 2005, but was continued to November 23, 2005, at which time the meeting was concluded according to trustee. In re Shelton, 343 B.R. 545, 2006 Bankr. LEXIS 1401 (W.D. Va. Feb. 24, 2006).

In matters of private contract, such as the notice of sale required by a deed of trust, this section does not now apply; but it is the rule in Virginia that if a contract is to be performed or some act is to be done within a certain number of days from a specified date, the first or specified day is not to be counted. Dickerson v. McNulty, 142 Va. 559, 129 S.E. 242 (1925).

Sections govern how time period in § 34-17 should be calculated. — This section and former § 1-13.3:1 [now subsections A and B of this section], and not the Federal Rules of Bankruptcy Procedure, govern how the five-day period provided for in § 34-17 should be calculated to determine whether debtors failed to file their homestead deed in a timely fashion. In re Haynesworth, 145 Bankr. 222 (Bankr. E.D. Va. 1992).

Sunday being dies non juridicus, it is not one of the days of the term of a court. Michie v. Michie's Adm'rs, 58 Va. (17 Gratt.) 109 (1866); Read v. Commonwealth, 63 Va. (22 Gratt.) 924 (1872); Bowles v. Brauer, 89 Va. 466, 16 S.E. 356 (1892).

An entry of a vacation decree on Sunday was held void. Lee v. Willis, 99 Va. 16, 37 S.E. 826 (1900).

Computation of time. — When a statute prescribes a certain number of days within which an act is to be done, and says nothing about Sunday, it is to be included, unless the last day falls on Sunday, in which case the act may generally be on the succeeding day. But, if the act may be lawfully done on Sunday, and the last day falls on Sunday, then Sunday is not to be excluded. Bowles v. Brauer, 89 Va. 466, 16 S.E. 356 (1892). See Harris v. Sparrow, 146 Va. 747, 132 S.E. 694 (1926), with reference to computation of time within which bill of exception must be filed.

Saturday and Sunday counted. — Virginia law was to be applied in determining whether a debtor had set apart homestead property within the number of days required by statute and Saturday and Sunday were to be included in counting those days. Mayer v. Quy Van Nguyen, 211 F.3d 105, 2000 U.S. App. LEXIS 8271 (4th Cir. 2000).

Saturday is not a legal holiday for the purpose of exclusion in the computation of time in which a procedural act should be done. Cousins v. Commonwealth, 187 Va. 506, 47 S.E.2d 391 (1948).

Section not intended to remedy unauthorized closing of clerk's office. — See Hutchins v. Carrillo, 27 Va. App. 595, 500 S.E.2d 277 (1998).

Discretion to accept statement filed after due date. — It was within the commission's discretion to accept the employer's written statement, which was due on a Saturday, but was filed on the following Monday. James v. Tarmac Mid-Atlantic, Inc., No. 2115-93-1 (Ct. of Appeals May 10, 1994).

Plaintiff could still file her motion for judgment recommencing her action on the following Monday, where six months from her voluntary nonsuit fell on a Saturday. Ward v. Insurance Co. of N. Am., 253 Va. 232, 482 S.E.2d 795 (1997).

CIRCUIT COURT OPINIONS

Applicability. — Where the Virginia Property Owner's Association Act, § 55-508 et seq., expressly required that notice of the cancellation of a real estate sales contract actually be received within three days after the prospective purchasers received an association disclosure packet, the time for receiving actual notice could not be extended even though the third day was a legal holiday; this section cannot be applied to extend a contractual period of cancellation between two private parties such as the prospective purchasers and the sellers. Taylor v. Boehm, 58 Va. Cir. 229, 2002 Va. Cir. LEXIS 6 (Albemarle County 2002).

§ **1-211. Constitutional references.** — Whenever any act of the General Assembly in effect at noon on July 1, 1971, refers to any section, article, or provision of the prior Constitution of Virginia, such reference shall apply to any comparable section, article, or provision of the Constitution of Virginia then in effect unless the construction would be contrary to the legislative intent of the act. (1971, Ex. Sess., c. 49, § 1-13.41; 2005, c. 839.)

§ **1-211.1. Courthouse; posting of notices.** — If any notice, summons, order, or other official document of any type is required to be posted on or at the front door of a courthouse or on a public bulletin board at a courthouse, it shall constitute compliance with this requirement if the notice, summons, order, or other official document is posted with other such documents at or near the principal public entrance to the courthouse in a location that is conspicuous to the public and approved by the chief judge of the circuit in which the courthouse is situated. (2007, c. 734.)

§ **1-212. Courts of record.** — *"Courts of record"* means the Supreme Court of Virginia, the Court of Appeals of Virginia, and the circuit courts. (1971, Ex. Sess., c. 49, § 1-13.5:1; 2005, c. 839.)

Law Review. — For survey of Virginia law on practice and pleading for the year 1970-71, see 57 Va. L. Rev. 1561 (1971).

§ 1-213. Delegation of duties assigned to political subdivision. — The governing body of a political subdivision shall be responsible for any duty or responsibility imposed upon its political subdivision. (1986, c. 239, § 1-17.2; 1987, c. 471; 1988, c. 273; 2005, c. 839.)

§ 1-214. Effective dates. — A. All laws enacted at a regular session of the General Assembly, including laws which are enacted by reason of actions taken during the reconvened session following a regular session, but excluding general appropriation acts, decennial reapportionment acts, and emergency acts, shall take effect on the first day of July following the adjournment of the regular session at which they were enacted, unless a subsequent date is specified.

B. All laws enacted at a special session of the General Assembly, including laws which are enacted by reason of actions taken during the reconvened session following a special session, but excluding general appropriations acts, decennial reapportionment acts, and emergency acts, shall take effect on the first day of the fourth month following the month of adjournment of the special session at which they were enacted, unless a subsequent date is specified.

C. A general appropriation act shall take effect from its passage, unless another effective date is specified in the act.

D. An emergency act shall take effect from its passage, or on a subsequent date if specified in the act, provided that the emergency shall be expressed in the body of the act and that the emergency shall be approved by a four-fifths vote of the members voting in each house of the General Assembly. The name of each member voting and how he voted shall be recorded in the journal.

E. A decennial reapportionment act to reapportion the Commonwealth into electoral districts shall take effect immediately. (Code 1919, § 4; 1971, Ex. Sess., c. 49, § 1-12; 1981, c. 329; 2005, c. 839.)

Cross references. — For implementation of changes to Title 24.2, see § 24.2-101.1. See Va. Const., Art. IV, § 13.

CASE NOTES

Editor's note. — The cases annotated below were decided under prior law.

As to what constitutes a case of emergency referred to in this section, see Couk v. Skeen, 109 Va. 6, 63 S.E. 11 (1908).

Act without emergency clause under former law. — An act which contained no emergency clause did not take effect until the lapse of 90 days after the adjournment of the General Assembly, but became effective immediately upon the expiration of the suspension period. Burks v. Commonwealth, 126 Va. 763, 101 S.E. 230 (1919), decided under § 53 of the Constitution of 1902 and a prior version of this section as it stood before the 1971 amendment.

Computation of effective date under former law. — An event which took place June 1, 1914, occurred "seventeen days before " an act approved March 20, 1914, "took effect, " the session of the General Assembly having adjourned sine die March 20, 1914. Burks v. Commonwealth, 126 Va. 763, 101 S.E. 230 (1919), decided under § 53 of the Constitution of 1902 and a prior version of this section as it stood before the 1971 amendment.

An act approved March 3, 1932, the 1932 session of the Assembly having adjourned sine die March 22, 1932, became law on June 21, 1932. Allen v. Mottley Constr. Co., 160 Va. 875, 170 S.E. 412 (1933), decided under § 53 of the Constitution of 1902 and a prior version of this section as it stood before the 1971 amendment.

§ **1-215. Ex officio.** — *"Ex officio"* means service by virtue of one's office and includes voting privileges for ex officio members unless otherwise provided. (2005, c. 839.)

§ **1-216. Gender.** — A word used in the masculine includes the feminine and neuter. (Code 1919, § 5; Code 1950, § 1-13; 1950, p. 21, § 1-13.7; 1997, c. 406; 2005, c. 839.)

§ **1-217. Headlines of sections.** — The headlines of the sections printed in black-face type are intended as mere catchwords to indicate the contents of the sections and do not constitute part of the act of the General Assembly. (Code 1919, § 5; Code 1950, § 1-13; 1950, p. 21, § 1-13.9; 2005, c. 839.)

CASE NOTES

Editor's note. — Some of the cases annotated below were decided under prior law.

Statute heading just informative convenience. — It is well-settled that the words of the statute, not its heading, carry the force of law. The heading of the statute is purely a matter of informative convenience. The court must construe the body of the statute. Jones v. Division of Child Support Enforcement ex rel. Owens, 19 Va. App. 184, 450 S.E.2d 172 (1994); Foster v. Commonwealth, 271 Va. 235, 623 S.E.2d 902, 2006 Va. LEXIS 6 (2006).

Related to titles of acts. — In the construction of an act, its title is entitled to its due share of consideration, and while a headline is not strictly a title, it occupies a closely related position. It contains catchwords which are intended to indicate the contents of a section. Jordan v. Town of South Boston, 138 Va. 838, 122 S.E. 265 (1924). See Chambers v. Higgins, 169 Va. 345, 193 S.E. 531 (1937).

Retaining a heading after an amendment similar to that which appeared prior to the amendment does not control the classification of the section or take precedence over the language adopted by the legislature. Shaw v. Commonwealth, 9 Va. App. 331, 387 S.E.2d 792 (1990).

Not applicable to federal law. — Parental rights of a mother were properly terminated where the mother was convicted in federal court of abusive sexual contact, a felony, as felony sexual assault in Virginia included all felonies proscribed by the article within the Virginia Code captioned "Criminal Sexual Assault"; unlike the contents of § 1-13.9 [now § 1-217] regarding the "headlines" of Virginia Code "sections," the federal law contained no provision stating that captions of subtitles, chapters, or articles were intended as mere catchwords, and it expressly provided that a subtitle, chapter, or article could be cited by its caption where no section or provision established or authorized a short title citation for such subtitle, chapter, or article. M. G. v. Albemarle County Dep't of Soc. Servs., 41 Va. App. 170, 583 S.E.2d 761, 2003 Va. App. LEXIS 406 (2003).

§ **1-218. Includes.** — *"Includes"* means includes, but not limited to. (2005, c. 839.)

§ **1-219. Land; real estate.** — *"Land," "lands,"* or *"real estate"* includes lands, tenements and hereditaments, and all rights and appurtenances thereto and interests therein, other than a chattel interest. (Code 1919, § 5; Code 1950, § 1-13; 1950, p. 22, § 1-13.12; 2005, c. 839.)

CASE NOTES

Editor's note. — The cases annnotated below were decided under prior law.

Leasehold is not real property. — At common law, an estate for years was considered personalty. Absent statutory modification, this remains the law in Virginia. There is no statutory modification of this common-law rule. Therefore, leasehold interests are not considered to be real estate. CSB, Inc. v. Cradle of Democracy Broadcasting Co., 547 F. Supp. 106 (E.D. Va. 1982).

A chattel real or leasehold is intangible personal property and not real property. CSB, Inc. v. Cradle of Democracy Broadcasting Co., 547 F. Supp. 106 (E.D. Va. 1982).

"Real estate" does not include unat-

tached building. — The words used in this section to define "real estate" plainly do not encompass a building that is unattached to land. Pardoe & Graham Real Estate, Inc. v. Schulz Homes Corp., 259 Va. 398, 525 S.E.2d 284 (2000).

"Land" embraces underlying minerals. — Land sold without reservation of any kind embraces the underlying minerals. Steinman v. Vicars, 99 Va. 595, 39 S.E. 227 (1901).

And includes ground rents. — The word "land" as defined in this section is sufficient to include ground rents. Willis's Ex'r v. Commonwealth, 97 Va. 667, 34 S.E. 460 (1899).

Water mains, gates, hydrants and pipes of a city water system were to be regarded as fixtures and taxable as "land" under § 183 (g) of the Constitution of 1902, notwithstanding the statutory definition of "land" contained herein. City of Newport News v. Warwick County, 159 Va. 571, 166 S.E. 570 (1932).

§ 1-219.1. Limitations on eminent domain. — A. The right to private property being a fundamental right, the General Assembly shall not pass any law whereby private property shall be taken or damaged for public uses without just compensation. The term "public uses" mentioned in Article I, Section 11 of the Constitution of Virginia is hereby defined as to embrace only the acquisition of property where: (i) the property is taken for the possession, ownership, occupation, and enjoyment of property by the public or a public corporation; (ii) the property is taken for construction, maintenance, or operation of public facilities by public corporations or by private entities provided that there is a written agreement with a public corporation providing for use of the facility by the public; (iii) the property is taken for the creation or functioning of any public service corporation, public service company, or railroad; (iv) the property is taken for the provision of any authorized utility service by a government utility corporation; (v) the property is taken for the elimination of blight provided that the property itself is a blighted property; or (vi) the property taken is in a redevelopment or conservation area and is abandoned or the acquisition is needed to clear title where one of the owners agrees to such acquisition or the acquisition is by agreement of all the owners.

B. For purposes of this section:

"Blighted property" means any property that endangers the public health or safety in its condition at the time of the filing of the petition for condemnation and is (i) a public nuisance or (ii) an individual commercial, industrial, or residential structure or improvement that is beyond repair or unfit for human occupancy or use.

"Government utility corporation" means any county or municipality, or entity or agency thereof, which provides or operates one or more of the following authorized utility services: gas, pipeline, electric light, heat, power, water supply, sewer, telephone, or telegraph.

"Public corporation" means the Commonwealth of Virginia or any political subdivision thereof or any incorporated municipality therein or any public agency of the Commonwealth or of any political subdivision thereof or of any municipality therein.

"Public facilities" means (i) airports, landing fields, and air navigation facilities; (ii) educational facilities; (iii) flood control, bank and shore protection, watershed protection, and dams; (iv) hospital facilities; (v) judicial and court facilities; (vi) correctional facilities, including jails and penitentiaries; (vii) library facilities; (viii) military installations; (ix) parks so designated by the Commonwealth or by the locality in its comprehensive plan; (x) properties of historical significance so designated by the Commonwealth; (xi) law enforcement, fire, emergency medical, and rescue facilities; (xii) sanitary sewer, water or stormwater facilities; (xiii) transportation facilities including highways, roads, streets, and bridges, traffic signals, related easements and rights-of-way, mass transit, ports, and any components of federal, state, or local transportation facilities; (xiv) waste management facilities for hazardous, radioactive, or other waste; (xv) office facilities occupied by a public corpora-

tion; and (xvi) such other facilities that are necessary to the construction, maintenance, or operation of a public facility as listed in clauses (i) through (xv) and directly related thereto.

C. No more private property may be taken than that which is necessary to achieve the stated public use.

D. Except where property is taken (i) for the creation or functioning of a public service corporation, public service company, or railroad; or (ii) for the provision of any authorized utility service by a government utility corporation, property can only be taken where: (a) the public interest dominates the private gain and (b) the primary purpose is not private financial gain, private benefit, an increase in tax base or tax revenues, or an increase in employment.

E. During condemnation proceedings, the property owner may challenge whether the taking or damaging is for a public use, the stated public use is a pretext for an unauthorized use, or the taking or damaging of property is a violation of subsection D. Nothing in this section shall be construed as abrogating any defenses or rights otherwise available to the property owner independently of this section.

F. Subject to the provisions of subsection D, the limitations contained in this section shall not abrogate any other provision of law that authorizes a condemnor to dispose of property taken for a public use as surplus property, as otherwise provided by law.

G. If the acquisition of only part of a property would leave its owner with an uneconomic remnant, the condemnor shall offer to acquire the entire property for its fair market value as otherwise provided by law, but the condemnor shall not acquire an uneconomic remnant if the owner objects and desires to maintain ownership of the excess property.

H. The provisions of this section shall control to the extent there are any inconsistencies between this section and any other general or special law; otherwise, nothing herein shall be construed as abrogating the power of eminent domain delegated independently of this section.

I. The provisions of this section shall not apply to the forfeiture of property under Chapters 22 (§ 19.2-369 et seq.), 22.1 (§ 19.2-386.1 et seq.), and 22.2 (§ 19.2-386.15 et seq.) of Title 19.2.

J. The provisions of this section shall not apply to real property that is subject to a certificate of take or a certificate of deposit recorded prior to July 1, 2007, in the circuit court clerk's office for the circuit where the real property is located or real property that is the subject of a petition for condemnation filed prior to July 1, 2007. (2007, cc. 882, 901, 926.)

The number of this section was assigned by the Virginia Code Commission, the number in the 2007 acts having been § 1-237.1.

Editor's note. — Acts 2007, cc. 882, 901, and 926, cl. 3, provides: "That, until July 1, 2010, the provisions of this act shall not affect the ability of a redevelopment and housing authority organized pursuant to Title 36 of the Code of Virginia to acquire property pursuant to any redevelopment or conservation plan adopted prior to January 1, 2007. However, the provisions of this act shall be applicable to all redevelopment and conservation plans adopted after January 1, 2007."

Acts 2007, cc. 882, 901, and 926, cl. 4, provides: "Nothing contained in this act shall prohibit the Norfolk Redevelopment and Housing Authority or the City of Norfolk to acquire property through the use of eminent domain for the location of a recreational facility open to the public to be owned or operated by a not-for-profit entity, provided such acquisitions are instituted prior to July 1, 2010."

§ 1-220. Local ordinances incorporating state law by reference. — When counties, cities and towns are empowered to incorporate by reference provisions of the Code, acts of the General Assembly, or state regulations into a local ordinance, any ordinance incorporating by reference provisions of the Code, acts of the General Assembly or state regulations may include future amendments to the provisions of the Code, acts of the General Assembly or state regulations provided such intent is specifically stated in such ordinance. (1993, c. 710, § 1-13.39:2; 2001, c. 771; 2005, c. 839.)

§ 1-221. Locality. — *"Locality"* means a county, city, or town as the context may require. (2005, c. 839.)

§ 1-222. Majority authority. — Whenever authority is conferred by law to three or more persons, a majority of such persons shall have the power to exercise such authority, unless otherwise provided. (Code 1919, § 5; Code 1950, § 1-13; 1950, p. 21, § 1-13.1; 2005, c. 839.)

CASE NOTES

Editor's note. — The cases annotated below were decided under prior law.

This section is a rule of construction which only confers power on a majority of a valid commission when acting pursuant to their authority. Dillon v. Davis, 201 Va. 514, 112 S.E.2d 137 (1960).

Persons deriving authority from statutory source. — This subsection refers only to the construction of statutes and to public officers or other persons deriving their authority from a statutory source. It has no application to arbitrators acting under a private agreement of submission. Fraley v. Nickels, 121 Va. 377, 93 S.E. 636 (1917).

Bank directors. — If a majority of a board of bank directors be present and qualified to vote and do vote, an election may be made by a majority of the votes given, although they be not a majority of the whole board; and this although others of the directors be present, but do not vote. Booker v. Young, 53 Va. (12 Gratt.) 303 (1855).

§ 1-223. Month; year. — *"Month"* means a calendar month and *"year"* means a calendar year. (Code 1919, § 5; Code 1950, § 1-13; 1950, pp. 22, 24, §§ 1-13.13, 1-13.33; 2005, c. 839.)

Michie's Jurisprudence. — For related discussion, see 18 M.J. Time, § 2; 21A M.J. Words and Phrases.

CASE NOTES

The word "month" in a statute means a month as designated in the calendar without regard to the number of days it may contain, and is to be computed not by counting the days but by looking at the calendar. It runs from a given day in one month to a corresponding number in the next month, except where the last month has not so many days, in which event it expires on the last day of that month. Cousins v. Commonwealth, 187 Va. 506, 47 S.E.2d 391 (1948) (decided under prior law).

And not 30 days. — Where the minimum punishment for an offense is confinement in jail for not less than one month, it is error for the jury, in view of this section, to fix the punishment at 30 days in jail when the calendar month consists of 31 days. But as the error is in the accused's favor it is harmless. Barrack v. Commonwealth, 142 Va. 596, 128 S.E. 638 (1925) (decided under prior law).

Courts are required to employ calendar years and not "365-day periods" when computing whether a statute of limitations has expired. Ward v. Insurance Co. of N. Am., 253 Va. 232, 482 S.E.2d 795 (1997) (decided under prior law).

§ 1-224. Municipality; incorporated communities; municipal corporation. — *"Municipality," "incorporated communities," "municipal corporation,"* and words or terms of similar import mean cities and towns. (2005, c. 839.)

§ 1-225. Nonlegislative citizen member. — *"Nonlegislative citizen member"* means any natural person who is not a member of the General Assembly of Virginia. (2004, c. 709, § 1-13.13:1; 2005, c. 839.)

Editor's note. — Acts 2004, c. 709, cl. 2, provides: "That this act shall not be construed to affect existing appointments for which the terms have not expired. However, any new appointments or appointments to fill vacancies made after the effective date of this act [April 12, 2004] shall be made in accordance with the provisions of this act."

§ 1-226. Notary. — *"Notary"* means notary public. (Code 1919, § 5; Code 1950, § 1-13; 1950, p. 22, § 1-13.14; 2005, c. 839.)

§ 1-227. Number. — A word used in the singular includes the plural and a word used in the plural includes the singular. (Code 1919, § 5; Code 1950, § 1-13; 1950, p. 22, § 1-13.15; 2005, c. 839.)

CASE NOTES

The article "a" does not necessarily denote the singular. Wolfe v. Commonwealth, 167 Va. 486, 189 S.E. 320 (1937) (decided under prior law).

§ 1-228. Oath. — *"Oath"* includes affirmation. (Code 1919, § 5; Code 1950, § 1-13; 1950, p. 22, § 1-13.16; 2005, c. 839.)

Michie's Jurisprudence. — For related discussion, see 14A M.J. Oath, § 2.

§ 1-229. Optional form of county government; effect of change in form. — Whenever any county, city, town, political subdivision, or combination thereof is identified in an act of the General Assembly by reference to its proximity to a county that has adopted an optional form of government provided in Title 15.2, and that county changes its form of government, the act shall continue to apply to such county, city, town, political subdivision, or combination thereof and shall cease to apply only upon the subsequent enactment by the General Assembly of a measure in which such intent clearly is stated. (1990, c. 253, § 1-13.35:1; 2005, c. 839.)

§ 1-230. Person. — *"Person"* includes any individual, corporation, partnership, association, cooperative, limited liability company, trust, joint venture, government, political subdivision, or any other legal or commercial entity and any successor, representative, agent, agency, or instrumentality thereof. (Code 1919, § 5; Code 1950, § 1-13; 1950, p. 22, § 1-13.19; 1988, c. 36; 2005, c. 839.)

Law Review. — For survey of Virginia law on business associations for the year 1971-72, see 58 Va. L. Rev. 1172 (1972).

Michie's Jurisprudence. — For related discussion, see 4B M.J. Corporations, § 6; 17 M.J. Statutes, § 60; 21A M.J. Words and Phrases.

CASE NOTES

Editor's note. — The cases annotated below were decided under prior law.

Corporations. — Corporations are included under the term "persons" as used in a statute, unless they are exempted by its terms or by the nature of the subject to which the statute relates. Miller's Ex'r v. Commonwealth, 68 Va. (27 Gratt.) 110 (1876). See Portsmouth Gas Co. v. Sanford, 97 Va. 124, 33 S.E. 516 (1899).

When the word "person" is used in a statute, corporations as well as natural persons are included for civil purposes. B & O R.R. v.

Gallahue's Adm'rs, 53 Va. (12 Gratt.) 655 (1855). See Sun Life Assurance Co. v. Bailey, 101 Va. 443, 44 S.E. 692 (1903).

The word "person" in a former statute relating to persons paying taxes on real estate was held to include "corporations." Crafford v. Board of Supvrs., 87 Va. 110, 12 S.E. 147 (1890).

In support of the rule that corporations are to be deemed and taken as persons when the circumstances in which they are placed are identical with those of natural persons, see Stribling v. Bank of Valley, 26 Va. (5 Rand.) 132 (1827); Bank of United States v. Merchants' Bank, 40 Va. (1 Rob.) 573 (1843); B & O R.R. v. Gallahue's Adm'rs, 53 Va. (12 Gratt.) 655 (1855).

But it has been held that a city charter giving authority to impose a license tax upon persons engaged in certain enumerated callings, and "upon any other person or employment," did not empower the city to impose such tax upon a railroad corporation, which is neither a person nor employment within the ordinary acceptation of these words. City of Lynchburg v. Norfolk & W.R.R., 80 Va. 237 (1885).

Counties and cities may be included in the word "person." Commonwealth v. Schmelz, 116 Va. 62, 81 S.E. 45 (1914). See Portsmouth Gas Co. v. Sanford, 97 Va. 124, 33 S.E. 516 (1899).

A city is a "person" whose rights may be prejudiced by a forgery. Hanbury v. Commonwealth, 203 Va. 182, 122 S.E.2d 911 (1961).

Municipal corporations have a dual identity, existing both as a body politic and a body corporate; in the latter identity, a municipal corporation may be a "person" just as any corporation or other legal entity is a person. City of Va. Beach v. Flippen, 251 Va. 358, 467 S.E.2d 471 (1996).

Board of public welfare (now board of social services) held person aggrieved for appeal purposes. — See Board of Pub. Welfare v. Blackburn, 214 Va. 425, 201 S.E.2d 777 (1974).

Sanctions error where issue as to whether city was person undetermined. — Where district judge awarded sanctions to city since plaintiffs should have known that the city was incapable of forming the criminal intent necessary for liability under the Virginia Conspiracy Act, where the Virginia Conspiracy Act itself does not clearly state whether cities can be subjected to liability, where the Virginia Supreme Court has not been confronted directly with whether a city is a person within the meaning of the Virginia Conspiracy Act, and where a recent pronouncement of the Supreme Court in a Virginia Conspiracy Act case seemed to have left open the possibility that a city could be sued under that act, the district court abused its discretion in sanctioning plaintiffs since the court of appeals was unable to say that plaintiffs had "absolutely no chance of success" in bringing a Virginia Conspiracy Act claim against the city. Brubaker v. City of Richmond, 943 F.2d 1363 (4th Cir. 1991).

§ 1-231. When "person" includes business trust and limited liability company. — Whenever the term "person" is defined to include both "corporation" and "partnership," such term shall also include "business trust and limited liability company." (2002, c. 621, § 1-13.19:1; 2005, c. 839.)

Cross references. — For the Virginia Business Trust Act, see § 13.1-1200 et seq.

§ 1-232. Person under disability. — *"Person under disability"* includes a person less than 18 years of age. (1972, cc. 824, 825, § 1-13.42; 2005, c. 839.)

§ 1-233. Personal estate. — *"Personal estate"* includes chattels real and such other estate as, upon the death of the owner intestate, would devolve upon his personal representative. (Code 1919, § 5; Code 1950, § 1-13; 1950, p. 22, § 1-13.20; 2005, c. 839.)

CASE NOTES

Bank stock is personal property. West v. City of Newport News, 104 Va. 21, 51 S.E. 206 (1905).

§ 1-234. Personal representative. — *"Personal representative"* includes the executor of a will or the administrator of the estate of a decedent, the administrator of such estate with the will annexed, the administrator of such estate unadministered by a former representative, whether there is a will or not, any person who is under the order of a circuit court to take into his possession the estate of a decedent for administration, and every other curator of a decedent's estate, for or against whom suits may be brought for causes of action that accrued to or against the decedent. (Code 1919, § 5; Code 1950, § 1-13; 1950, p. 22, § 1-13.21; 1971, Ex. Sess., c. 49; 2005, c. 839.)

Michie's Jurisprudence. — For related discussion, see 8A M.J. Executors and Administrators, § 13.

CASE NOTES

The primary sense of the word "representatives," when used in a bequest of personal property, is the same as that of "legal representatives" or "personal representatives." Each of them is equivalent to executors or administrators. But this primary sense of the word "representatives" may be controlled, where an intention is clearly indicated to employ it in a different sense. Brent v. Washington's Adm'rs, 59 Va. (18 Gratt.) 526 (1868) (decided under prior law).

An administrator with the will annexed — that is, an ancillary administratrix — is among those who can be a "personal representative" under this section. Higgins v. Washington Metro. Area Transit Auth., 507 F. Supp. 984 (D.D.C. 1981) (decided under prior law).

§ 1-235. Population; inhabitants. — *"Population"* or *"inhabitants"* means with reference to any county, city, town, political subdivision of the Commonwealth or any combination thereof, the natural persons in such county, city, town, political subdivision or combination as shown by the unadjusted United States decennial census last preceding the time at which any provision dependent upon population is being applied or the time as of which it is being construed. Where two or more political subdivisions are consolidated, the population of the consolidated county or city or other political subdivision shall be the combined population of the consolidating subdivisions, under the last preceding unadjusted United States decennial census. (1942, p. 668; Michie Code 1942, § 5a; Code 1950, § 1-13; 1950, p. 23, § 1-13.22; 1954, c. 295, § 1-13.10:1; 1958, c. 330; 1966, c. 78; 2005, c. 839.)

Cross references. — See Va. Const., Art. VII, § 1. For effect of population changes on statutes containing population classifications, see § 1-236.

CIRCUIT COURT OPINIONS

Relevant evidence. — A census report was properly admitted, pursuant to §§ 1-13.22 and 1-13.35 [now § 1-236], as evidence to establish that a city was large enough to use laser speed devices. Commonwealth v. Fagin, 61 Va. Cir. 428, 2003 Va. Cir. LEXIS 225 (Charlottesville 2003) (decided under prior law).

§ 1-236. Population classifications. — Any act of the General Assembly with a population classification applicable to any county, city, town, or subdivision of the Commonwealth or any combination thereof shall continue to apply to any such body notwithstanding any subsequent change in population and shall apply to any county, city, town, or political subdivision of the Commonwealth or any combination thereof subsequently falling within such population classification. The provisions of this section shall not apply to, or limit, the distribution of any state funds, grants-in-aid, or other allocation from the state treasury, to any county, city, town, or other political subdivision of the Commonwealth. (1950, pp. 464, 465, §§ 1-13.35, 1-13.36; 1960, cc. 251, 307; 1962, c. 315; 1964, c. 404; 1966, c. 78; 2005, c. 839.)

CIRCUIT COURT OPINIONS

Relevant evidence. — A census report was properly admitted, pursuant to §§ 1-13.22 and 1-13.35 [now §§ 1-235 and 1-236], as evidence to establish that a city was large enough to use laser speed devices. Commonwealth v. Fagin, 61 Va. Cir. 428, 2003 Va. Cir. LEXIS 225 (Charlottesville 2003) (decided under prior law).

§ 1-237. Process. — *"Process"* includes subpoenas, the summons and complaint in a civil action, and process in statutory actions. (1954, c. 543, § 1-13.23:1; 1986, c. 155; 2005, cc. 681, 839.)

Editor's note. — Acts 2005, c. 681, effective January 1, 2006, amended former § 1-13.23:1, from which this section is derived. Pursuant to § 30-152 and Acts 2005, c. 839, cl. 5, the 2005 amendment by c. 681 has been given effect in this section as set out above. The phrase "the summons and complaint in a civil action" was substituted for "in chancery, notices to commence actions at law."

§ 1-238. Reenacted. — *"Reenacted,"* when used in the title or enactment of a bill or act of the General Assembly, means that the changes enacted to a section of the Code of Virginia or an act of the General Assembly are in addition to the existing substantive provisions in that section or act, and are effective prospectively unless the bill expressly provides that such changes are effective retroactively on a specified date.

The provisions of this section are declaratory of existing public policy and law. (2001, c. 720, § 1-13.39:3; 2005, c. 839.)

Editor's note. — Acts 2001, c. 720, cl. 2 provides: "That the provisions of this act are intended to reverse the ruling in Rubio v. Rubio, 33 Va. App. 74, 531 S.E. 2nd 612 (2000)."

CASE NOTES

Declaratory of existing law. — Amendments to the law surrounding the Virginia Birth-Related Neurological Injury Compensation Act were effective prospectively, as the phrase "declaratory of existing law" did not state retroactive intent and the language of the amended laws did not support retroactivity. Berner v. Mills, 265 Va. 408, 579 S.E.2d 159, 2003 Va. LEXIS 52 (2003) (decided under prior law).

Retrospective application of reenacted laws. — Trial court properly denied defendant's motion to be sentenced under a version of § 18.2-308.4 that became effective after the crime was committed; the language of the statute did not clearly allow for retroactive application of the amendment, and the statute also could not be applied retroactively pursuant to this section. Taylor v. Commonwealth, 44 Va. App. 179, 604 S.E.2d 103, 2004 Va. App. LEXIS 512 (2004) (decided under prior law).

§ 1-239. Repeal not to affect liabilities; mitigation of punishment. — No new act of the General Assembly shall be construed to repeal a former law, as to any offense committed against the former law, or as to any act done, any penalty, forfeiture, or punishment incurred, or any right accrued, or claim arising under the former law, or in any way whatever to affect any such offense or act so committed or done, or any penalty, forfeiture, or punishment so incurred, or any right accrued, or claim arising before the new act of the General Assembly takes effect; except that the proceedings thereafter held shall conform, so far as practicable, to the laws in force at the time of such proceedings; and if any penalty, forfeiture, or punishment be mitigated by any provision of the new act of the General Assembly, such provision may, with the consent of the party affected, be applied to any judgment pronounced after the new act of the General Assembly takes effect. (Code 1919, § 6, § 1-16; 2005, c. 839.)

Cross references. — As to proceedings pending when Code takes effect, see §§ 1-4, 8.01-1.

Michie's Jurisprudence. — For related discussion, see 5B M.J. Criminal Procedure, §§ 4, 84; 17 M.J. Statutes, §§ 73, 91, 96, 105; 18 M.J. Taxation, § 12.

CASE NOTES

Editor's note. — Most of the cases annotated below were decided under prior law.

General comment. — This section or a predecessor has been the law of Virginia for more than 100 years and has long been held to apply to civil as well as criminal cases. Pursuant to it, both substantive and vested rights are protected from retroactive application of statutes. Garraghty v. Virginia, Dep't of Cors., 52 F.3d 1274 (4th Cir. 1995).

Under the former law the rule was different in Virginia. See Scutt v. Commonwealth, 4 Va. (2 Va. Cas.) 54 (1817); Commonwealth v. Leftwich, 26 Va. (5 Rand.) 657 (1827); Pitman v. Commonwealth, 41 Va. (2 Rob.) 800 (1843).

When rights and claims are subject to protection of due process. — It is only when a right has accrued or a claim has arisen that it is subject to the protection of the due process clause. Hess v. Snyder Hunt Corp., 240 Va. 49, 392 S.E.2d 817 (1990).

Application to both criminal and civil cases. — A former statute corresponding to this section was held to apply to forfeitures in civil as well as criminal cases. White's Adm'x v. Freeman, 79 Va. 597 (1884), citing Mosby v. St. Louis Mut. Ins. Co., 72 Va. (31 Gratt.) 629 (1879).

Substantive rights and vested rights protected from retroactive application of statutes. — "Substantive" rights, as well as "vested" rights, are included within those interests protected from retroactive application of statutes. City of Norfolk v. Kohler, 234 Va. 341, 362 S.E.2d 894 (1987); Brushy Ridge Coal Co. v. Blevins, 6 Va. App. 73, 367 S.E.2d 204 (1988).

After obtaining a judgment relieving appellant of quarterly reregistration requirements under former § 19.2-298.4 for sex offenders, appellant was not entitled to enjoin the reposting of his information on a sex offender internet registry after the 2006 amendment to § 9.1-909 as appellant did not have an accrued right under § 1-239 affected by the statute's retroactive application as the removal remedy under § 9.1-909 was self-executing and could be altered "at will" by the legislature. Morency v. Commonwealth, 274 Va. 569, 649 S.E.2d 682, 2007 Va. LEXIS 114 (2007).

Prospective construction approved by section. — The general principle that statutes should be given a prospective rather than a retrospective construction has been given statutory approval by this section. Ferguson v. Ferguson, 169 Va. 77, 192 S.E. 774 (1937).

New laws generally presumed prospective in operation. — New laws, except as to matters of remedy which may be applied retrospectively, are usually presumed to be prospective and not retrospective in their operation. Paul v. Paul, 214 Va. 651, 203 S.E.2d 123 (1974).

Consistent with § 64.1-62, requiring that wills be construed as if the testator died immediately before death, unless the will showed a contrary intent, inter vivos trusts were to be construed according to the law in effect at the time the trust was executed, absent language showing a contrary intent, as such a rule recognized that the interests of trust beneficiaries accrued when the trust was executed and protected those interests, and such a rule was compelled by § 1-16 [a former version of this section], mandating that no new law should be construed in any way whatever to affect any right accrued, or claim arising before the new law took effect. McGehee v. Edwards, 268 Va. 15, 597 S.E.2d 99, 2004 Va. LEXIS 96 (2004).

What procedural provisions control. — The procedural provisions of the statute in effect on the date of trial control the conduct of trial insofar as practicable. Smith v. Commonwealth, 219 Va. 455, 248 S.E.2d 135 (1978), cert. denied, 441 U.S. 967, 99 S. Ct. 2419, 60 L. Ed. 2d 1074 (1979).

The procedural provisions of the statute in effect on the date of trial control the conduct of trial insofar as practicable. Riley v. Commonwealth, 21 Va. App. 330, 464 S.E.2d 508 (1995).

Sentencing discretion with trial court. — Where statute changed the status of the offense charged from a felony to a misdemeanor after entry of the defendants' guilty plea but prior to his sentencing and the Commonwealth agreed to pursue misdemeanor sentencing, it was discretionary with the trial court, and not with the Commonwealth, whether misdemeanor or felony punishment should be imposed. Awkard v. Commonwealth, 21 Va. App. 40, 461 S.E.2d 419 (1995).

Instances of prospective operation. — A deposition of a party, to be read in a pending cause at law, commenced before the passage of the statute which required that parties should testify, ore tenus, but which was not completed until that law went into effect, is inadmissible as evidence. Crawford v. Halsted & Putnam, 61 Va. (20 Gratt.) 211 (1871).

A statute which amended the former law as to payment of decedents' debts by inserting in the third class "debts of trustee for persons under disabilities," was only prospective in its operation and did not authorize the placing of a debt as trustee in the third class, though the estate was not distributed until the act went into operation. Price's Ex'r v. Harrison's Ex'r, 72 Va. (31 Gratt.) 114 (1878).

Where a provision of a curative act amending a former law with reference to the assessment of land for taxes, if construed retrospectively, would deprive a citizen of the opportunity to be heard as to the correctness and justice of an assessment made under the original act, which opportunity was afforded by the original act, such provision will, if possible, be construed prospectively only, and the remedy given under the original act as to acts done prior to the passage of the curative act will be preserved. Whitlock v. Hawkins, 105 Va. 242, 53 S.E. 401 (1906).

Subdivision ordinance without "grandfather" clause. — Local government body could not, after amending subdivision ordinance without making any provision to "grandfather" pending applications, lawfully invoke unwritten "practice" of applying prior law to pending application and thereafter approve subdivision prohibited by the amendment. Parker v. County of Madison, 244 Va. 39, 418 S.E.2d 855 (1992).

A local governing body's obligation to act in accordance with the new law, not the former, is not reduced by the mere filing of a subdivision application before the new law becomes effective, unless the new law expressly so provides. Parker v. County of Madison, 244 Va. 39, 418 S.E.2d 855 (1992).

Repealing statute referring solely to matters of remedy and procedure. — This section prescribes a rule of construction of a new law repealing a former law where rights have accrued or arise under the former law. It has no application to a repealing statute referring solely to matters of remedy and procedure where the legislature expressly declares it shall have retroactive operation. Appellants are given no right in the strict sense to a particular mode of procedure unless they avail themselves of it while the statute is in force. Phipps v. Sutherland, 201 Va. 448, 111 S.E.2d 422 (1959); Virginia & W. Va. Coal Co. v. Charles, 251 F. 83 (W.D. Va. 1917), aff'd, 254 F. 379 (4th Cir. 1918), appeal dismissed, 252 U.S. 569, 40 S. Ct. 345, 64 L. Ed. 720 (1920).

Statute repealing rule of evidence. — This section saves from the operation of a repealing statute substantive claims and rights, but has no application to a change by repeal of a mere rule of evidence; and it cannot bind a future legislature which expressed a contrary intention in a repealing statute. Virginia & W. Va. Coal Co. v. Charles, 254 F. 379 (4th Cir. 1918), appeal dismissed, 252 U.S. 569, 40 S. Ct. 345, 64 L. Ed. 720 (1920).

The intention of the legislature to repeal Act March 13, 1912, relating to the effect to be given as evidence to deeds recorded prior to 1865, as shown by Act March 14, 1914, cannot be overthrown by this section, prescribing a rule for the construction of statutes in case of repeals. Virginia & W. Va. Coal Co. v. Charles, 251 F. 83 (W.D. Va. 1917), aff'd, 254 F. 379 (4th Cir. 1918), appeal dismissed, 252 U.S. 569, 40 S. Ct. 345, 64 L. Ed. 720 (1920).

Since rules of evidence are procedural, rather than substantive rights or claims, they are not protected from the effect of a repealing statute. Wyatt v. Virginia Dep't of Social Servs., 11 Va. App. 225, 397 S.E.2d 412 (1990).

When there is no ambiguity in the repealing statute, this section, prescribing a rule of construction in the case of repeals, has no application. Virginia & W. Va. Coal Co. v. Charles, 251 F. 83 (W.D. Va. 1917), aff'd, 254 F. 379 (4th Cir. 1918), appeal dismissed, 252 U.S. 569, 40 S. Ct. 345, 64 L. Ed. 720 (1920).

Election to accept mitigation of punishment. — Although the punishment for murder of the first degree was mitigated by the 1914 amendment to former § 18.1-22, a prisoner who committed the offense prior to the amendment but was tried subsequent thereto was not obliged to accept the mitigation provided by the amendment. This section was to be read in connection with former § 18.1-22. Conaway v. Commonwealth, 118 Va. 792, 88 S.E. 75 (1916).

Where a defendant commits an offense before a new, mitigatory statute goes into effect but comes to trial after the new statute goes into effect, the penalty in existence at the time of the offense should be applied unless the Commonwealth first elects to proceed under the new statute and obtains the consent of the defendant to do so. Ruplenas v. Commonwealth, 221 Va. 972, 275 S.E.2d 628 (1981).

Legislative reduction of penalty after prisoner sentenced. — The fact that the legislature reduces the penalty for a crime after a prisoner is sentenced, and he does not benefit from that mitigation of punishment, does not constitute an arbitrary classification or deny the prisoner equal protection of the law. Abdo v. Commonwealth, 218 Va. 473, 237 S.E.2d 900 (1977).

This section did not mandate that the trial court mitigate the defendant's punishment in accordance with a new law which became effective after final judgment of conviction, where the defendant's motion for reduction of sentence was filed after the effective date of the new law and prior to completion of appellate review. Abdo v. Commonwealth, 218 Va. 473, 237 S.E.2d 900 (1977).

The election of the Commonwealth to prosecute under a new law which mitigates punishment and the privilege of an accused to consent to be tried thereunder, must be exercised before judgment is pronounced. Abdo v. Commonwealth, 218 Va. 473, 237 S.E.2d 900 (1977).

Application of former § 1-13.42. — There was no retroactive application of § 1-13.42 [see now § 1-204], specifying the age of majority, where the statute was applied to plaintiffs, both of whom were under the age of 21 at the time their causes of action accrued prior to the enactment of the statute, causing the statute of limitations to run from the time plaintiffs reached 18 rather than from the age of 21 as at common law. Hurdle v. Prinz, 218 Va. 134, 235 S.E.2d 354 (1977).

Retroactive application of § 18.2-23.1. — Since the effect of § 18.2-23.1 is to mitigate punishment by barring conviction for the underlying conspiracy if a defendant has been convicted of the completed substantive offense, the Commonwealth's consent was necessary for application of § 18.2-23.1 to a defendant's trial on offenses that occurred prior to the effective date thereof. Naito v. Commonwealth, No. 1421-86-4 (Ct. of Appeals Nov. 22, 1988).

Retroactive application of former § 2.1-116 (see now § 2.2-2905). — Of course, a state official who simply enforces a presumptively valid state statute will rarely lose his immunity from suit. However, two defendants in the instant case did not simply enforce a presumptively valid state statute. Rather, totally disregarding long-standing Virginia law prohibiting new legislation from being construed to eliminate pre-existing substantive rights, they attempted to apply the 1985 amendment to § 2.1-116 retroactively to do precisely this. Moreover, they did this in the face of several holdings of this court that the act established a property interest in continued public employment, and a holding of the Virginia Supreme Court that the right to continued public employment is substantive and cannot be retroactively eliminated. Garraghty v. Virginia, Dep't of Cors., 52 F.3d 1274 (4th Cir. 1995).

Retroactive application of § 65.2-602. — Because the statute created a new substantive right through the use of the 1991 amending language, the commission erred in applying retroactively amended § 65.2-602. B.E. & K. Constr. Co. v. Stanley, No. 1863-94-2 (Ct. of Appeals April 4, 1995).

Trial court properly denied defendant's motion to be sentenced under a version of § 18.2-308.4 which became effective after the crime was committed; the language of the statute did not clearly allow for retroactive application of the amendment. Taylor v. Commonwealth, 44 Va. App. 179, 604 S.E.2d 103, 2004 Va. App. LEXIS 512 (2004).

Burden of proof in paternity action. — The statutory provisions establishing the burden of proof in a paternity proceeding as set forth in § 20-49.4 are procedural provisions. Accordingly, the trial court did not err in determining the defendant's paternity in accordance with the clear and convincing standard set forth in § 20-49.4, the standard in effect on the date of trial. Wyatt v. Virginia Dep't of Social Servs., 11 Va. App. 225, 397 S.E.2d 412 (1990).

Rights of employees in classified service could not be affected by new law excluding certain persons from such service. — Provisions in city charter conferring upon selected city employees a package of job guarantees that no employee in the classified service could be discharged except for cause and upon written charges, and after an opportunity to be heard, created a substantive right, and in the language of this section, a right accrued under the former law which could not be repealed or in any way whatever affected by the enactment of a new law providing that assistant heads of administrative departments except for the departments of fire and police shall not be included in classified service. City of Norfolk v. Kohler, 234 Va. 341, 362 S.E.2d 894 (1987).

CIRCUIT COURT OPINIONS

Editor's note. — Some of the cases annotated below were decided under prior law.

Applicability of amendments. — Pursuant to the second clause of former § 1-16 [see now § 1-239], the 2004 amendment to § 8.01-262(3) applied to a product liability personal injury case; venue in Norfolk was thus improper since neither the manufacturer nor the distributor had any facility there. Spruill v. Jugs, Inc., 66 Va. Cir. 75, 2004 Va. Cir. LEXIS 348 (Norfolk Sept. 29, 2004).

Rights of city employees not vested. — Plaintiffs, active or retired firefighters and police officers, had no vested right to retirement benefits provided under a 1972 city ordinance since their rights to benefits vested only after they performed all requirements completely; the city's enactment of an ordinance in 1996 which modified plaintiffs' employment benefits could not be set aside under former § 1-16 [now this section] since the city could reasonably modify such benefits as long as it had no punitive purpose. Avery v. City of Norfolk, 61 Va. Cir. 453, 2003 Va. Cir. LEXIS 139 (Norfolk 2003).

Sex offender registry. — Defendants who had previously reported to the sex offender registry and were thereafter excused from the 90-day reporting requirement pursuant to § 9.1-909 and a court order did not have a substantial and vested right under § 1-239 to be permanently removed from the State Police registry on the Internet based on the police's removal of their names therefrom after the court order was issued, as the trial court's order did not require the State Police to remove their names from the registry; such removal was not a vested property right and accordingly, amendments to § 9.1-909 allowed the police to record defendants' names on the Internet registry, and defendants' declaratory relief request under § 8.01-184 to be permanently removed from the registry failed. Doe v. Commonwealth, — Va. Cir. —, 2007 Va. Cir. LEXIS 130 (Fairfax County June 7, 2007).

§ **1-240. Repeal not to revive former act.** — When an act of the General Assembly that has repealed another act shall itself be repealed, the previous act shall not be revived without express words to that effect, unless the act repealing it be passed during the same session. (Code 1919, § 7, § 1-17; 2005, c. 839.)

CASE NOTES

This section applies to statutes and not to the common law. For cases under prior law, see Booth v. Commonwealth, 57 Va. (16 Gratt.) 519 (1861); Insurance Co. v. Barley's Adm'r, 57 Va. (16 Gratt.) 363 (1863).

Omitted portions annulled. — When a statute is revised, or one act framed from another, and some parts are omitted, the omitted parts are not revived by construction, but are annulled. Combined Saw & Planer Co. v. Flournoy, 88 Va. 1029, 14 S.E. 976 (1892) (decided under prior law).

§ **1-241. Seal.** — "Seal," when required to be affixed by any court or public office to any paper, includes an impression or print of such official seal made upon the paper. When the seal of any natural person is required, it shall be sufficient for the person to place a mark intended as a seal. (Code 1919, § 5; Code 1950, § 1-13; 1950, p. 23, § 1-13.25; 1975, c. 500; 2005, c. 839.)

§ **1-242. Senate Committee on Privileges and Elections.** — *"Senate Committee on Privileges and Elections,"* whenever the Committee is referred to as an appointing authority, means the Senate Committee designated under the Rules of the Senate to make Senate appointments to study committees and commissions. (2004, c. 709, § 1-13.25:1; 2005, c. 839.)

Editor's note. — Acts 2004, c. 709, cl. 2, provides: "That this act shall not be construed to affect existing appointments for which the terms have not expired. However, any new appointments or appointments to fill vacancies made after the effective date of this act [April 12, 2004] shall be made in accordance with the provisions of this act."

§ **1-243. Severability.** — The provisions of acts of the General Assembly or the application thereof to any person or circumstances that are held invalid shall not affect the validity of other acts, provisions, or applications that can be given effect without the invalid provisions or applications. The provisions of all acts, except for the title of the act, are severable unless (i) the act specifically provides that its provisions are not severable; or (ii) it is apparent that two or more acts or provisions must operate in accord with one another. (1986, c. 239, § 1-17.1; 1987, c. 56; 2005, c. 839.)

Law Review. — For 2003/2004 survey of criminal law and procedure, see 39 U. Rich. L. Rev. 133 (2004).

CASE NOTES

Editor's note. — The cases annotated below were decided under prior law.

The test of severability in the commonwealth of Virginia is whether the legislature would be satisfied with what remains after the invalid part has been eliminated. Sons of Confederate Veterans, Inc. v. Holcomb, 129 F. Supp. 2d 941, 2001 U.S. Dist. LEXIS 538 (W.D. Va. 2001), aff'd sub nom. Sons of Confederate Veterans, Inc. v. Comm'r, Va. DMV, 288 F.3d 610 (4th Cir. 2002).

Provision is not inextricably intertwined with the rest of the statute. — The fact that the prima facie evidence provision is not inextricably intertwined with the rest of the statute is illustrated by the fact that the cross burning statute, now codified at § 18.2-423, existed for 16 years, from 1952 to 1968, without the prima facie evidence provision. Elliott v. Commonwealth, 267 Va. 464, 593 S.E.2d 263, 2004 Va. LEXIS 41 (2004).

The General Assembly impermissibly delegated taxing power to the local area transportation authority through enactment of Acts 2007, c. 896, because it did not have the constitutional power to delegate taxing authority to an unelected political subdivision, pursuant to Va. Const., Art. I, § 6. However, the parts of the enactment that were unconstitutional could be severed from the rest of the enactment because the enactment's provisions did not have to operate with regard to each other and enactment did not state that its provisions could not be severed. Marshall v. N. Va. Transp. Auth., 275 Va. 419, 657 S.E.2d 71, 2008 Va. LEXIS 25 (2008).

Ordinance held not severable. — Where ordinance's restrictions on commercial and noncommercial speech were inextricably intertwined, severability provision within the ordinance could not save any part, section, or clause of the ordinance as it applied to billboards where its restrictions on noncommercial speech were found unconstitutional. Adams Outdoor Adv. v. City of Newport News, 236 Va. 370, 373 S.E.2d 917 (1988).

§ **1-244. Short title citations.** — Whenever a subtitle, chapter, or article does not have a section or provision establishing or authorizing a short title citation for such subtitle, chapter or article, such subtitle, chapter or article may be cited by its caption. The caption is that word or group of words appearing directly below the numerical designation given the subtitle, chapter or article. Captions are intended as mere catchwords to indicate the contents of the subtitles, chapters, and articles and do not constitute part of the act of the General Assembly. (1993, c. 308, § 1-13.9:1; 2005, c. 839.)

§ **1-245. State.** — "State," when applied to a part of the United States, includes any of the 50 states, the District of Columbia, the Commonwealth of Puerto Rico, Guam, the Northern Mariana Islands, and the United States Virgin Islands. (Code 1919, § 5; Code 1950, § 1-13; 1950, p. 23, § 1-13.26; 1971, Ex. Sess., c. 49; 2005, c. 839.)

§ **1-246. Stricken language or italics.** — Stricken language for deletions and italics for additions or changes may be used in legislative drafts, printed bills, enrolled bills, and printed Acts of Assembly, in an attempt to call attention to amendments to existing acts of the General Assembly. The stricken language and italics shall not be construed as evidence of amendments to acts of the General Assembly. (1950, p. 24, § 1-13.34; 1986, c. 155; 2005, c. 839.)

§ **1-247. Summaries of legislation.** — Any legislative summary associated with a bill, joint resolution or resolution, including any summary appearing on the face of such legislation, shall not constitute a part of the legislation considered, agreed to, or enacted, and shall not be used to indicate or infer legislative intent. (1997, c. 375, § 30-19.03:2; 2005, c. 839.)

§ **1-248. Supremacy of federal and state law.** — The Constitution and laws of the United States and of the Commonwealth shall be supreme. Any ordinance, resolution, bylaw, rule, regulation, or order of any governing body or any corporation, board, or number of persons shall not be inconsistent with the Constitution and laws of the United States or of the Commonwealth. (Code 1919, § 5; Code 1950, § 1-13; 1950, p. 22, § 1-13.17; 2005, c. 839.)

Michie's Jurisprudence. — For related discussion, see 13B M.J. Municipal Corporations, §§ 60, 61.

CASE NOTES

Editor's note. — The cases annotated below were decided under prior law.

An ordinance may not conflict with state law. Board of Supvrs. v. Pumphrey, 221 Va. 205, 269 S.E.2d 361 (1980).

It is, of course, fundamental that local ordinances must conform to and not be in conflict with the public policy of the state as embodied in its statutes. Blanton v. Amelia County, 261 Va. 55, 540 S.E.2d 869, 2001 Va. LEXIS 16 (2001).

Municipal ordinances must be consistent with the general law and policy of the State. National Linen Serv. Corp. v. City of Norfolk, 196 Va. 277, 83 S.E.2d 401 (1954). See Allen v. City of Norfolk, 196 Va. 177, 83 S.E.2d 397 (1954).

The provision of the Norfolk City Code making possession of certain indicia of a lottery prima facie evidence of guilt was contrary to state policy and void because inconsistent with former § 18.1-340, in that it prescribed a different method of proof, imposing on accused a burden not contemplated by the legislature. Allen v. City of Norfolk, 196 Va. 177, 83 S.E.2d 397 (1954). See Allen v. City of Norfolk, 195 Va. 844, 80 S.E.2d 605, modified, 196 Va. 177, 83 S.E.2d 397 (1954).

Under § 15.2-1429, no punishment for violation of an ordinance may exceed the penalties prescribed by general law for like offenses; Virginia Beach, Va., Code § 23-38, which punished destruction of property by fine of up to $2,500 and up to 12 months in jail, manifested a conflict with state law because the penalty that attached exceeded the penalty under the state code destruction of property statute, § 18.2-137, a violation of which was punishable only by a fine not exceeding $500, and defendants' convictions for violations of Virginia Beach, Va., Code § 23-38 were reversed. Strout v. City of Va. Beach, 43 Va. App. 99, 596 S.E.2d 529, 2004 Va. App. LEXIS 240 (2004).

But may enlarge thereon. — The fact that an ordinance enlarges upon statutory provisions does not necessarily create an inconsistency therewith, since some state statutes are not sufficiently comprehensive to cover local exigencies. Allen v. City of Norfolk, 196 Va. 177, 83 S.E.2d 397 (1954).

The mere fact that the State, in the exercise of the police power, has made certain regulations does not prohibit a municipality from exacting additional requirements, so long as there is no conflict. King v. County of Arlington, 195 Va. 1084, 81 S.E.2d 587 (1954).

The fact that an ordinance enlarges upon the provisions of a statute by requiring more than the statute requires creates no conflict therewith, unless the statute limits the requirement for all cases to its own prescription. Blanton v. Amelia County, 261 Va. 55, 540 S.E.2d 869, 2001 Va. LEXIS 16 (2001).

Where both an ordinance and a statute are prohibitory and the only difference between them is that the ordinance goes further in its prohibition, but not counter to the prohibition under the statute, and the municipality does not attempt to authorize by the ordinance what the legislature has forbidden or forbid what the legislature has expressly licensed, authorized, or required, there is nothing contradictory between the provisions of the statute and the ordinance because of which they cannot coexist and be effective. Blanton v. Amelia County, 261 Va. 55, 540 S.E.2d 869, 2001 Va. LEXIS 16 (2001).

And provide greater penalty than statute. — The fact that the penalty for the violation of an ordinance prohibiting the use of common towels is greater than that provided for in the statute on the subject does not invalidate the ordinance. National Linen Serv. Corp. v. City of Norfolk, 196 Va. 277, 83 S.E.2d 401 (1954).

Ordinance held not invalid because it enlarged on the statute by prescribing a heavier penalty for the second offense. Allen v. City of Norfolk, 196 Va. 177, 83 S.E.2d 397 (1954).

If both the statute and ordinance can stand together, courts are obliged to harmonize them, rather than nullifying the ordinance. Board of Supvrs. v. Pumphrey, 221 Va. 205, 269 S.E.2d 361 (1980); Granny's Cottage, Inc. v. Town of Occoquan, 3 Va. App. 577, 352 S.E.2d 10 (1987).

There can be no conflict between a statute and an ordinance where there is no statute dealing with the same subject matter. Kisley v. City of Falls Church, 212 Va. 693, 187 S.E.2d 168, appeal dismissed, 409 U.S. 907, 93 S. Ct. 237, 34 L. Ed. 2d 169 (1972).

An ordinance may forbid an act not prohibited by state law. — A local legislative body, in the exercise of its police powers, may forbid the doing of an act where state legislation is silent on the subject. Kisley v. City of Falls Church, 212 Va. 693, 187 S.E.2d 168, appeal dismissed, 409 U.S. 907, 93 S. Ct. 237, 34 L. Ed. 2d 169 (1972).

An ordinance may prohibit an act upon which state law is silent or proscribe conduct already proscribed by state law where the ordinance is not inconsistent with state law. Board of Supvrs. v. Pumphrey, 221 Va. 205, 269 S.E.2d 361 (1980); Granny's Cottage, Inc. v. Town of Occoquan, 3 Va. App. 577, 352 S.E.2d 10 (1987).

Powers of condominium owners limited. — While the Condominium Act, § 55-79.39 et seq., is designed to and does permit the exercise of wide powers by an association of unit owners, these powers are limited by general law and the Act itself. Unit Owners Ass'n of Buildamerica-1 v. Gillman, 223 Va. 752, 292 S.E.2d 378 (1982).

Public nudity ordinances. — State laws do not prevent a local governing body, under its police power, from enacting public nudity ordinances not inconsistent with the state law prohibiting conduct which the local governing body reasonably deems to be contrary to the morals, health, safety and general welfare of the community. Wayside Restaurant, Inc. v. City of Virginia Beach, 215 Va. 231, 208 S.E.2d 51 (1974).

County ordinance prohibiting the keeping of a dog addicted to attacking human beings was held valid and not in conflict with the state law which prohibits the keeping of a dog addicted to attacking livestock and poultry. King v. County of Arlington, 195 Va. 1084, 81 S.E.2d 587 (1954).

Statute governing use of biosolids. — The general assembly, by its enactment former § 32.1-164.5 [see now § 62.1-44.19:3 et seq.], has expressly authorized the land application of biosolids conditioned upon the issuance of a permit and a county's ordinances were inconsistent with that section and invalid because the ordinances forbid certain plaintiffs from using biosolids on their farmland even though those plaintiffs had obtained licenses to use biosolids pursuant to the statutory and regulatory scheme established by the general assembly. Blanton v. Amelia County, 261 Va. 55, 540 S.E.2d 869, 2001 Va. LEXIS 16 (2001).

An ordinance punishing forgery of city cigarette tax stamp was a nullity. This was not a case where a specific statute takes precedence over a general statute relating to the same offense, but a case where a general state statute (former § 18.1-96) controlled as against a later city ordinance in conflict with it. Hanbury v. Commonwealth, 203 Va. 182, 122 S.E.2d 911 (1961).

CIRCUIT COURT OPINIONS

Public expenditure of funds. — Trial court found that the taxpayers had standing to bring their claims against the town and county, as the taxpayers claimed that the town and county were violating state, federal, and local laws by creating and operating with public funds a site for temporary day workers involving some people who entered and were in the United States illegally. Karunakarum v. Town of Herndon, 70 Va. Cir. 208, 2006 Va. Cir. LEXIS 33 (Fairfax County 2006).

State health commissioner's issuance of certificate did not deprive county of ability to make land use decisions. — That the Virginia State Heath Commissioner issued a hospital owner a certificate of public need to build an acute care hospital did not prevent a county board of supervisors from denying the owner's application to build it in a specific location. Pursuant to former § 1-13.17, the board could exercise its authority to make land use decisions without undermining the Commissioner's authority to evaluate health needs and to authorize the construction of health care facilities where needed. N. Va. Cmty. Hosp., L.L.C. v. Loudoun County Bd. of Supervisors, 70 Va. Cir. 283, 2006 Va. Cir. LEXIS 168 (Loudoun County 2006).

Tattooing ban. – City ordinance's total ban on tattooing violated § 1-248, as it conflicted with Virginia's policy of restricting but not banning tattooing, as expressed in §§ 15.2-912 and 18.2-371.3. Thus, the city's demurrer to petitioner's claim that the ordinance was inconsistent with state law was denied. Blue Horseshoe Tattoo, V, Ltd. v. City of Norfolk, 72 Va. Cir. 388, 2007 Va. Cir. LEXIS 151 (Norfolk 2007).

§ **1-249. Supreme Court.** — *"Supreme Court"* means the Supreme Court of Virginia. (1975, c. 36, § 1-13.27:2; 2005, c. 839.)

Michie's Jurisprudence. — For related discussion, see 1B M.J. Appeal and Error, § 1.

§ 1-250. Swear; sworn. — *"Swear"* or *"sworn"* means "affirm" or "affirmed." (Code 1919, § 5; Code 1950, § 1-13; 1950, p. 23, § 1-13.28; 2005, c. 839.)

§ 1-251. Systems of state highways. — *"Systems of state highways"* means all systems of highways within the Commonwealth over which the Commonwealth Transportation Board exercises jurisdiction and control. In context, such words shall apply to the extent, but only to the extent, that the Commonwealth Transportation Board exercises such jurisdiction and control. (1970, c. 136, § 1-13.40; 2005, c. 839.)

Michie's Jurisprudence. — For related discussion, see 17 M.J. Streets and Highways, § 2.

§ 1-252. Tier-city. — *"Tier-city"* means an incorporated community within a consolidated county that (i) has within defined boundaries a population of 5,000 or more, (ii) has been designated as a tier-city by the General Assembly, and (iii) has both the powers of a town and such additional powers as may be granted tier-cities by the General Assembly. All references in this Code and the acts of the General Assembly to towns shall be deemed references to tier-cities, except to the extent tier-cities may be specifically excluded or where the context requires otherwise. (1984, c. 695, §§ 1-13.28:1, 1-13.28:2; 1989, c. 493; 2005, c. 839.)

§ 1-253. Time zone. — The United States Eastern Standard Time shall be in effect in all parts of the Commonwealth except during the period when the United States Eastern Daylight Time shall be in effect as provided by federal law. This section shall not be construed to be in contravention of federal law, or duly authorized orders of the United States Secretary of Transportation with respect to the time zones of the United States and the application of standard time to interstate commerce and other matters within such zones.

In all laws, statutes, orders, decrees, rules and regulations relating to the time of performance of any act by any officer or agency of the Commonwealth, or any political subdivision thereof, or relating to the time in which any rights shall accrue or determine, or within which any act shall or shall not be performed by any person subject to the jurisdiction of the Commonwealth, and in all public schools, institutions of the Commonwealth or its political subdivisions, and contracts or choses in action made or to be performed in the Commonwealth, it shall be understood and intended that the time applicable thereto or referred to or implied therein shall be the United States Eastern Standard Time, or the United States Eastern Daylight Time, when and during such is in effect. (1946, p. 103; Michie Suppl. 1946, § 5b; 1952, c. 637, § 1-15; 1962, c. 617; 1964, c. 646; 1966, c. 581; 1988, c. 177; 2005, c. 839.)

Michie's Jurisprudence. — For related discussion, see 18 M.J. Time, § 2.

§ 1-254. Town. — *"Town"* means any existing town or an incorporated community within one or more counties which became a town before noon, July 1, 1971, as provided by law or which has within defined boundaries a population of 1,000 or more and which has become a town as provided by law. (Code 1919, § 5; Code 1950, § 1-13; 1950, p. 24, § 1-13.29; 1971, Ex. Sess., c. 49; 1995, c. 155; 2005, c. 839.)

Cross references. — For definition of "town" under article relating to local government, see Va. Const., Art. VII, § 1.

Law Review. — For note, "Securing a Valid

Annexation in Virginia," see 10 U. Rich. L. Rev. 557 (1976).

§ 1-255. United States. — "United States" includes the 50 states, the District of Columbia the Commonwealth of Puerto Rico, Guam, the Northern Mariana Islands and the United States Virgin Islands. (Code 1919, § 5; Code 1950, § 1-13; 1950, p. 24, § 1-13.31; 2005, c. 839.)

CASE NOTES

Applies to all statutes. — The definition of "United States" herein applies to all statutes. Alphonse Custodis Chimney Constr. Co. v. Molina, 183 Va. 512, 32 S.E.2d 726 (1945).

Puerto Rico was one of the "territories" referred to as a part of the "United States" and its citizens and residents were citizens and residents of the United States within former § 65-62. Alphonse Custodis Chimney Constr. Co. v. Molina, 183 Va. 512, 32 S.E.2d 726 (1945) (decided under prior law).

"So-called" means "commonly named." For case construing "the several territories so-called" under former law, see Alphonse Custodis Chimney Constr. Co. v. Molina, 183 Va. 512, 32 S.E.2d 726 (1945).

§ 1-256. Weights and measurements; metric equivalents. — Words or terms relating to the customary system of weights and measurements include their International System (SI) metric equivalents, but shall not require the posting or publishing of the equivalents along with the customary system of weights and measurements. (1980, c. 465. § 1-15.2; 2005, c. 839.)

§ 1-257. Written; writing; in writing. — "Written," "writing," and "in writing" include any representation of words, letters, symbols, numbers, or figures, whether (i) printed or inscribed on a tangible medium or (ii) stored in an electronic or other medium and retrievable in a perceivable form and whether an electronic signature authorized by Chapter 42.1 (§ 59.1-479 et seq.) of Title 59.1 is or is not affixed. (Code 1919, § 5; Code 1950, § 1-13; 1950, p. 24, § 1-13.32; 1999, c. 145; 2000, c. 995; 2005, c. 839.)

CHAPTER 3.1.

BOUNDARIES OF THE COMMONWEALTH.

§ 1-300. Boundaries. — The territory and boundaries of the Commonwealth shall be and remain the same as they were after the Constitution of Virginia was adopted on June 29, 1776, except for the territory that constitutes

West Virginia and its boundaries, and other boundary adjustments as provided in this chapter. (Code 1950, § 7-1; 1966, c. 102, § 7.1-1; 2005, c. 839.)

CASE NOTES

The Code asserts jurisdiction over the Virginia shores and strands of the Potomac, in accordance with the claim in the Virginia Constitution; and it is admitted that these terms include the lands between high and low water mark. Washington Airport, Inc. v. Smoot Sand & Gravel Corp., 44 F.2d 342 (4th Cir. 1930), rev'd, 283 U.S. 348, 51 S. Ct. 474, 75 L. Ed. 1109 (1931) (decided under prior law). The majority opinion in the reversing case, which actually dealt with the boundary line between Virginia and the District of Columbia, declared that the original boundary of Maryland was the high-water mark on the southern bank of the Potomac, and that the compact of 1785 between Maryland and Virginia and the case of *Maryland v. West Virginia*, 217 U.S. 577, 30 S. Ct. 630, 54 L. Ed. 888 (1910), settling a controversy between those states, could not affect the rights of the District of Columbia. The decision was in effect a holding that the boundary between Virginia and the District of Columbia was the high-water mark on the southern bank of the Potomac. But see dissenting opinion. And see provisions of § 1-312 establishing present boundary between Virginia and the District.

§ 1-301. Extent of territory of the Commonwealth after the Constitution of 1776. — The authorities in determining the extent of the territory of the Commonwealth after the adoption of the Constitution of 1776 shall consist of:

1. The charter of April 10, 1606, granted by James the First, in the fourth year of his reign, that authorized the first plantation at any place upon the coast of the Commonwealth between the thirty-fourth and forty-first degrees of north latitude; and granted the territory from the seat of the plantation (which under this charter was begun at Jamestown), for 50 miles along the coast towards the west and southwest, as the coast lay, and for 50 miles along the coast, towards the east and northeast, or towards the north, as the coast lay, together with all the islands within 100 miles directly over against the seacoast, and all the territory from the same 50 miles every way on the seacoast, directly into the mainland for the space of 100 miles.

2. The second charter of James, dated May 23, 1609, in the seventh year of his reign, that granted all the territory from the point of land called Cape or Point Comfort, all along the seacoast to the northward 200 miles, and from the point of Cape Comfort all along the seacoast to the southward 200 miles, and all that space and circuit of land lying from the seacoast of the precinct, up into the land, throughout from sea to sea, west and northwest, and also all the islands lying within 100 miles along the coast of both seas of the precinct aforesaid.

3. The third charter of James, dated March 12, 1611-12, in the ninth year of his reign, that granted all the islands in any part of the seas within 300 leagues of any territory granted in the former patents.

4. The 1763 treaty of peace between Great Britain and France that established a line along the middle of the river Mississippi and became the Commonwealth's western boundary.

5. Section 21 of the Constitution of Virginia adopted June 29, 1776, that ceded, released, and confirmed to the people of Maryland, Pennsylvania, North and South Carolina, such parts of the territory of the Commonwealth as were contained within the charters erecting those colonies, with all the rights in those parts that might have been claimed by the Commonwealth, except the free navigation of the Rivers Potomac and Pocomoke, with the property of the Commonwealth shore or strands bordering on either of the rivers, and all improvements thereon; and that at the same time laid down in the section that the western and northern extent of the Commonwealth should in all other respects stand as fixed by the charter of James the First, granted in 1609, and

by the treaty of peace between Great Britain and France in 1763, unless by act of the legislature one or more territories should thereafter be laid off, and governments established, westward of the Alleghany mountains. (Code 1950, § 7-1; 1966, c. 102, § 7.1-1; 2005, c. 839.)

CASE NOTES

The Code asserts jurisdiction over the Virginia shores and strands of the Potomac, in accordance with the claim in the Virginia Constitution; and it is admitted that these terms include the lands between high and low water mark. Washington Airport, Inc. v. Smoot Sand & Gravel Corp., 44 F.2d 342 (4th Cir. 1930), rev'd, 283 U.S. 348, 51 S. Ct. 474, 75 L. Ed. 1109 (1931) (decided under prior law). The majority opinion in the reversing case, which actually dealt with the boundary line between Virginia and the District of Columbia, declared that the original boundary of Maryland was the high-water mark on the southern bank of the Potomac, and that the compact of 1785 between Maryland and Virginia and the case of *Maryland v. West Virginia*, 217 U.S. 577, 30 S. Ct. 630, 54 L. Ed. 888 (1910), settling a controversy between those states, could not affect the rights of the District of Columbia. The decision was in effect a holding that the boundary between Virginia and the District of Columbia was the high-water mark on the southern bank of the Potomac. But see dissenting opinion. And see provisions of § 1-312 establishing present boundary between Virginia and the District.

§ 1-302. Jurisdiction and ownership of Commonwealth over offshore waters and submerged lands. — A. The jurisdiction of the Commonwealth shall extend to and over, and be exercisable with respect to, waters offshore from the coasts of the Commonwealth as follows:

1. The marginal sea and the high seas to the extent claimed in the Virginia Constitution of 1776 and not thereafter ceded by action of the General Assembly.

2. All submerged lands, including the subsurface thereof, lying under the waters listed in subdivision 1 of this subsection.

B. The ownership of the waters and submerged lands enumerated or described in subsection A of this section shall be in the Commonwealth unless it shall be, with respect to any given parcel or area, in any other person or entity by virtue of a valid and effective instrument of conveyance or by operation of law.

C. Nothing contained herein shall be construed to limit or restrict in any way:

1. The jurisdiction of the Commonwealth over any person or with respect to any subject within or without the Commonwealth which jurisdiction is exercisable by reason of citizenship, residence, or for any other reason recognized by law.

2. The jurisdiction or ownership of or over any other waters or submerged lands, within or forming part of the boundaries of the Commonwealth. Nor shall anything in this section be construed to impair the exercise of legislative jurisdiction by the United States over any area to which such jurisdiction has been validly ceded by the Commonwealth and that remains in the ownership of the United States.

D. Nothing in this section shall alter the geographic area to which any act of the General Assembly applies if the act specifies the area precisely in miles or by some other numerical designation of distance or position. However, nothing in the act or in this section shall be construed as a waiver or relinquishment of jurisdiction or ownership by the Commonwealth over or in any area to which such jurisdiction or ownership extends by virtue of this section or any other provision or rule of law. (Code 1950, § 7-1.1; 1960, c. 518; 1966, c. 102, § 7.1-2; 1972, c. 689; 2005, c. 839.)

§ 1-303. Cession of territory northwest of Ohio River. — A. The territory northwest of the Ohio River ceded by the Commonwealth shall be and remain the same as provided by:

1. An act of the General Assembly passed on January 2, 1781, that resolved that this Commonwealth would on certain conditions yield for the benefit of the United States all her right to the territory northwest of the Ohio River.
2. An act of the General Assembly passed on December 20, 1783, that authorized the transfer to the United States, subject to the terms and conditions contained in the act of the United States Congress passed on September 13, 1783 and the deed of cession that was made accordingly.
3. An act of the General Assembly passed on December 30, 1788, whereby, after referring to an ordinance for the government of the territory, passed by the United States Congress on July 13, 1787, and reciting a particular article declared in the ordinance to be part of the compact between the original states and the people and states in the territory, the article of compact was ratified and confirmed.

B. Such cession shall be deemed and taken according to the true intent and meaning of the acts and deed, and subject to all the terms and conditions therein expressed. (Code 1950, § 7-2; 1966, c. 102, § 7.1-3; 2005, c. 839.)

Editor's note. — For historical purposes, the text of the original acts have been set out in the Compacts volume.

§ 1-304. Boundary with North Carolina. — The boundary line between the Commonwealth and North Carolina shall be and remain the same as the line run by Fry and Jefferson, and afterwards extended by Walker and Smith and approved on December 7, 1791, by an act of the General Assembly. (Code 1950, § 7-3; 1966, c. 102, § 7.1-4; 2005, c. 839.)

§ 1-305. Boundary with North Carolina eastward from low-water mark of Atlantic Ocean. — The boundary line between the Commonwealth and North Carolina eastward from the low-water mark of the Atlantic Ocean shall be and remains the line beginning at the intersection with the low-water mark of the Atlantic Ocean and the existing North Carolina-Virginia boundary line; thence due east to the seaward jurisdictional limit of Virginia; such boundary line to be extended on the true 90 degree bearing as far as a need for further delimitation may arise. (1970, c. 343, § 7.1-4.1; 2005, c. 839.)

§ 1-306. Boundary with Tennessee. — The boundary line between the Commonwealth and Tennessee shall be and remain the same as established by the Supreme Court of the United States in the case of Tennessee v. Virginia, 190 U.S. 64 (1903), and the compact between the Commonwealth and Tennessee approved on February 9, 1901, by an act of the General Assembly. (Code 1950, § 7-4; 1966, c. 102, § 7.1-5; 2005, c. 839.)

§ 1-307. Compact and boundary with Kentucky. — A. Except such part as may constitute the boundary line between West Virginia and the Commonwealth of Kentucky, the boundary between this Commonwealth and the Commonwealth of Kentucky, shall be and remain as the line approved on January 13, 1800, by an act of the General Assembly.

B. The articles set forth in the act of separation of the Commonwealth of Kentucky from this Commonwealth adopted by the General Assembly on December 18, 1789, shall be and remain a solemn compact mutually binding on the Commonwealths of Virginia and Kentucky, and unalterable by either without the consent of the other. (Code 1950, § 7-5; 1966, c. 102, § 7.1-6; 2005, c. 839.)

Editor's note. — The text of the original acts have been set out in the Compacts volume for historical purposes.

§ 1-308. Boundary with Maryland. — The Black-Jenkins Award, which established the boundary line between the Commonwealth and Maryland and was ratified on March 14, 1878, by an act of the General Assembly shall be and remain obligatory on this Commonwealth and the citizens thereof, and shall be forever observed and kept by the Commonwealth and all of its citizens according to the true intent and meaning of the same, and to that end the faith of the Commonwealth stands pledged. (Code 1950, § 7-6; 1966, c. 102, § 7.1-7; 2005, c. 839.)

Editor's note. — The text of the original act has been set out in the Compacts volume for historical purposes.

CASE NOTES

Editor's note. — The cases annotated below were decided under the original acts, now set out in the Compacts volume for reference.

Maryland has a uniform southern boundary along Virginia and West Virginia at low-water mark on the south bank of the Potomac River to the intersection of the north and south line between Maryland and West Virginia. Maryland v. West Virginia, 217 U.S. 577, 30 S. Ct. 630, 54 L. Ed. 888 (1910). But see Smoot Sand & Gravel Corp. v. Washington Airport, Inc., 283 U.S. 348, 51 S. Ct. 474, 75 L. Ed. 1109 (1931).

Article 4 of the compact precluded regulation by Maryland of Virginia's sovereign riparian rights. — Portion of a binding arbitration award set out at § 7.1-7 [now § 1-308], Fourth, clearly established Virginia's dominion over the soil to the low-water mark on the Virginia shore of the Potomac River by prescription, and clearly established Virginia's sovereign riparian right to use the river beyond the low water mark without regulation by Maryland. Virginia v. Maryland, 540 U.S. 56, 124 S. Ct. 598, 157 L. Ed. 2d 461, 2003 U.S. LEXIS 9192 (2003).

Rights granted under Article 7 of the Compact are not subject to regulation by Maryland. — Plain language of § 7.1-7 [now § 1-308], Seventh, grants to the citizens of Maryland and Virginia full property rights in the shores of the Potomac River and the privilege of building improvements from the shore and, especially since the scope of Maryland's sovereignty over the river was vigorously disputed both before and after ratification of the interstate compact, there was no grant or recognition of sovereign authority to permit Maryland to regulate the exercise of this privilege by Virginia citizens. Virginia v. Maryland, 540 U.S. 56, 124 S. Ct. 598, 157 L. Ed. 2d 461, 2003 U.S. LEXIS 9192 (2003).

Article 8 of the compact gives Virginia concurrent jurisdiction with Maryland, over the Potomac River from shore to shore, and over that part of the Pocomoke River which is within the limits of Virginia, to enact such laws, with the consent and approval of Maryland, as may be deemed necessary and proper for the preservation of fish in said waters. Hendricks v. Commonwealth, 75 Va. 934 (1882), criticized. Wharton v. Wise, 153 U.S. 155, 14 S. Ct. 783, 38 L. Ed. 669 (1894).

Article 10 of the compact refers only to offenses against the citizen or individual. When the offense is against the state, and not against an individual or citizen, there is no declaration as to the court of which state shall take cognizance of it. Hendricks v. Commonwealth, 75 Va. 934 (1882). And see Wharton v. Wise, 153 U.S. 155, 14 S. Ct. 783, 38 L. Ed. 669 (1894), holding that such article of the compact does not forbid the State of Virginia from trying and convicting citizens of Maryland for offenses committed in Virginia against its laws regulating oyster fisheries.

Mutual rights of fishery. — The provisions of articles 7 and 8 of the compact, which give mutual rights of fishery to the citizens of the two states, refer only to the Potomac River, and do not operate to give such rights in the Pocomoke river and sound. Wharton v. Wise, 153 U.S. 155, 14 S. Ct. 783, 38 L. Ed. 669 (1894), criticizing, Hendricks v. Commonwealth, 75 Va. 934 (1882).

Determination of location of murder

victim's body. — The exact physical location of a murder victim's body within river constituted a factual question which the jury could appropriately decide. However, the exact location of the boundary between Virginia and Maryland involves an interpretation of this section and represents a legal question outside the jury's province. If it were impossible for the jurors to interpret the evidence concerning the body's exact placement so as to conclude under this section that the body lay in Virginia, the trial court should not have submitted the issue of venue to the jury. Traverso v. Commonwealth, 6 Va. App. 172, 366 S.E.2d 719 (1988).

Where body of murder victim was found six to seven and one-half feet from Virginia shoreline, and the only evidence introduced concerning the low water mark showed that, on the day the body was found, the river level was at the actual low water mark, unless a line could be drawn between two headlands in order to form a new low water mark, the body's placement would have been six to seven and one-half feet beyond the Virginia border. Since victim's body lay six to seven and one-half feet from the Commonwealth of Virginia, venue did not lie in Loudoun County and the appellant's conviction would be reversed. Traverso v. Commonwealth, 6 Va. App. 172, 366 S.E.2d 719 (1988).

§ 1-309. Boundary with Maryland eastward from Assateague Island. — The boundary line between the Commonwealth and Maryland eastward from Assateague Island shall be and remain as follows: Beginning at a point on the Maryland-Virginia line located on Assateague Island designated as station "Pope Island Life Saving Station (1907)" defined by latitude 38°01′36.93″ and longitude 75°14′47.105″; thence running N 84°05′43.5″ E (true) - 1,100.00 feet to station "Atlantic"; thence due east (true) to the Maryland-Virginia jurisdictional limit. (1970, c. 342, § 7.1-7.1; 2005, c. 839.)

§ 1-310. Boundary with Maryland in upper reaches of Pocomoke sound and lower reaches of Pocomoke River. — A. The boundary line between the Commonwealth and Maryland in the previously undescribed portion of the Maryland-Virginia line in the upper reaches of the Pocomoke sound and lower reaches of the Pocomoke River shall be and remain as follows:

Beginning at a point which is corner D defined by latitude 37°56′28.00″ and longitude 75°45′43.56″; which is the last point on the Maryland-Virginia line that was defined by the "joint report of engineers on relocating and remarking Maryland-Virginia boundary line across Tangier and Pocomoke sounds December 1916"; thence running N 73°34′31.9″ E about 17,125.11 feet to corner H a point defined by latitude 37°57′115.82″ and longitude 75°42′18.48″; thence running N 85°39′33.9″ E about 3,785.82 feet to corner J a point defined by latitude 37°57′18.65″ and longitude 75°41′31.25″; thence running S 74°16′00.8″ E about 7,278.41 feet to corner K a point defined by latitude 37°56′59.13″ and longitude 75°40′03.89″; thence running S 61°57′55.7″ E about 3,664.73 feet to corner L a point defined by latitude 37°56′42.10″ and longitude 75°39′23.51″; thence running N 76°15′24.5″ E about 2,263.49 feet to corner M a point defined by latitude 37°56′47.65″ and longitude 75°38′54.85″; thence running N 00°49′51.5″ W about 7,178.56 feet to corner N a point defined by latitude 37°57′58.61″ and longitude 75°38′56.15″; thence northeasterly about 3 ½ miles following the middle thread of the meandering Pocomoke river to corner P a point defined by latitude 37°59′39.37″ and longitude 75°37′26.52″, which is at or near the point of intersection with the Scarborough and Calvert boundary line of May 28, 1668; corners N and P are connected by a line running N 35°08′33.5″ E about 12,465.32 feet; thence N 83°45′59.9″ E about 24,156.95 feet to the boundary monument near triangulation station Davis on the Scarborough and Calvert boundary line of May 28, 1668. Geographic positions are based on 1927 datum.

B. No vested right of any individual, partnership or corporation within the area affected by this section shall in any wise be impaired, restricted or affected thereby. This section shall not be retrospective in its operation nor shall it in any way affect the rights of any individual, partnership or corporation in any suit now pending in any of the courts of this Commonwealth or of the United States wherein such cause of action arose over, or is in any way based upon, the area affected. This section shall in no wise preclude the Commonwealth from prosecuting any individual, partnership or corporation for violation of any of the criminal laws of this Commonwealth within such area until this section shall become effective. (1970, c. 315, § 7.1-7.2; 2005, c. 839.)

§ 1-311. Recession of portion of District of Columbia. — That portion of the District of Columbia which, by an act of the General Assembly, passed December 3, 1789, was ceded to the United States and receded and forever relinquished to this Commonwealth by an act of Congress approved July 9, 1846, and accepted by the Commonwealth by an act of the General Assembly adopted on February 3, 1846, shall be and remain reannexed to this Commonwealth and constitutes a portion thereof, subject to such reservation and provisions respecting the public property of the United States, as the United States Congress has enacted in its act of recession. (Code 1950, § 7-8; 1966, c. 102, § 7.1-9; 2005, c. 839.)

Editor's note. — The text of the original act has been set out in the Compacts volume for historical purposes.

CASE NOTES

Act making cession of territory. — See Suckley v. Rotchford, 53 Va. (12 Gratt.) 60 (1855) (decided under prior law).

§ 1-312. Boundary with District of Columbia. — The boundary line between the Commonwealth and the District of Columbia shall be and remain as described by the United States Public Law 208, Seventy-Ninth Congress, approved October 31, 1945, and amended by Chapter 772 of the 1968 Acts of Assembly and Chapter 94 of the 2002 Acts of Assembly. (Code 1950, § 7-9; 1966, c. 102, § 7.1-10; 1968, c. 772; 2002, c. 94; 2005, c. 839.)

CASE NOTES

Virginia has ceded to the United States exclusive jurisdiction over the territory embraced within the Washington National Airport, reserving, however, the power to levy a tax on the sale of oil and gasoline sold on the airport for use in vehicles. This reservation does not include the power to levy taxes for the privilege of doing business on the airport. Hence one whose business is the sale of oil and gasoline there is not properly assessed under Arlington County's business privilege tax ordinance or the state's merchants' license tax, since they are not taxes on the sale of the products. Floyd v. Fischer, 199 Va. 363, 99 S.E.2d 612 (1957) (decided under prior law).

Under the grant from Virginia to the United States in § 107 of the act of Congress set out in this section, the Commonwealth is presumed to have specifically reserved all taxing rights which it intended to reserve, and the Virginia retail merchants' license tax and the county's business privilege license tax, not having been reserved, are necessarily excluded. Floyd v. Fischer, 199 Va. 363, 99 S.E.2d 612 (1957) (decided under prior law).

Grant of exclusive jurisdiction over Washington National Airport to the federal government does not exclude all state jurisdiction relating to the federal area. Bartsch v. Washington Metro. Area Transit Comm'n, 357 F.2d 923 (4th Cir. 1966) (decided under prior law).

Virginia law governs employment relationships. — At Washington National Airport, Virginia law governs employment relationships between private employers and their employees. Singleton v. International Ass'n of Machinists, Dist. 141, Local Lodge No. 1747, 240 Va. 403, 397 S.E.2d 856 (1990) (decided under prior law).

§ 1-313. Boundary line between Loudoun County, Virginia, and Jefferson County, West Virginia. — A. The boundary line between Loudoun County, Virginia, and Jefferson County, West Virginia shall be the watershed line of the top of the ridge of the Blue Ridge Mountains as established by the survey approved by the Commission on April 29, 1997, and recorded in the land books in the courthouses of Loudoun County, Virginia, and Jefferson County, West Virginia.

B. No vested right of any individual, partnership, or corporation within the territory affected by this act shall in any wise be impaired, restricted, or affected by this act. This act shall not be retrospective in its operation nor shall it in any way affect the rights of any individual, partnership, or corporation in any suit now pending in any of the courts of this Commonwealth or of the United States wherein the cause of action arose over, or is in any way based upon, the territory affected. (1993, c. 141, § 7.1-10.1; 1998, c. 123; 2005, c. 839.)

CHAPTER 4.

Jurisdiction Over Lands Acquired by the United States.

§ 1-400. Conditional consent given to acquisition of lands by United States; concurrent jurisdiction ceded. — A. On and after July 1, 1981, the conditional consent of the Commonwealth is hereby given in accordance with clause 17, § 8, Article 1 of the United States Constitution to the acquisition by the United States, or under its authority, by purchase, lease, condemnation, or otherwise, of any lands in the Commonwealth, whether under water or not, required for customhouses, post offices, arsenals, forts, magazines, dockyards, military reserves, or for needful public buildings.

B. The acquisition by condemnation of any property within the Commonwealth, not expressly consented to in subsection A of this section, shall require the prior approval of the General Assembly.

C. Over all lands hereafter acquired by the United States, the Commonwealth hereby cedes to the United States concurrent governmental, judicial, executive and legislative power and jurisdiction.

D. There is hereby expressly reserved in the Commonwealth, over all lands so acquired by the United States the following:

1. Tax on motor vehicle fuels and lubricants. — The Commonwealth shall have the jurisdiction and power to levy a tax on oil, gasoline and all other motor fuels and lubricants thereon owned by others than the United States and a tax on the sale thereof, on such lands, except sales to the United States for use in the exercise of essentially governmental functions.

2. Service of civil and criminal process. — The Commonwealth shall have the jurisdiction and power to serve criminal and civil process on such lands.

3. Sale of intoxicating liquors. — The Commonwealth shall have the jurisdiction and power to license and regulate, or to prohibit, the sale of intoxicating liquors on any such lands.

4. Tax on property and businesses. — The Commonwealth shall have the jurisdiction and power to tax all property, including buildings erected thereon, not belonging to the United States, and to require licenses and impose license taxes upon any business or businesses conducted thereon.

E. For all purposes of taxation and of the jurisdiction of the courts of the Commonwealth over persons, transactions, matters and property on such lands, the lands shall be deemed to be a part of the county or city in which they are situated.

F. Any such acquisition by or conveyance or lease to the United States, as provided in this section, shall be deemed to have been secured or made upon the express condition that the reservations of power and limitations provided in this section are recognized as valid by the United States and, in the event the United States shall deny the validity of the reservations, as to all or any part of such lands, then and in that event, the title and possession of all or any such part of such lands, conveyed to the United States by the Commonwealth, shall immediately revert to the Commonwealth.

G. Nothing contained in this section shall affect any special act adopted ceding jurisdiction to the United States, nor any deeds executed pursuant to § 1-401. (1976, c. 211, § 7.1-18.1; 1981, c. 533; 2005, c. 839.)

CASE NOTES

Editor's note. — The cases annotated below were decided under prior law.

The question whether a federal area within a state is subject to exclusive jurisdiction of the United States is complicated and often difficult to decide. A determination depends upon many factors, jurisdiction being subject to the terms, conditions, restrictions, limitations and provisions of the acquisition by the United States, including the consent of the State and acceptance by the United States. Western Union Tel. Co. v. Commonwealth ex rel. SCC, 204 Va. 421, 132 S.E.2d 407 (1963).

The presumption prevails that the State has jurisdiction over land which is owned by United States unless a defendant shows that the United States was deeded the land and accepted jurisdiction over it. Smith v. Commonwealth, 219 Va. 455, 248 S.E.2d 135 (1978), cert. denied, 441 U.S. 967, 99 S. Ct. 2419, 60 L. Ed. 2d 1074 (1979).

Jurisdiction may be transferred to the general government by cession. The terms of cession, to the extent that they may lawfully be prescribed, determine the extent of the federal jurisdiction. United States v. Schuster, 220 F. Supp. 61 (E.D. Va. 1963).

The argument that a state is powerless to surrender its jurisdiction to the United States over privately owned lands is without merit. United States v. Schuster, 220 F. Supp. 61 (E.D. Va. 1963).

The reservation in an act of cession of concurrent jurisdiction with the United States over land, so that the courts and officers of the State may take such cognizance, execute such process and discharge such legal functions within the same as may not be incompatible with the consent given, is subject to the provisions of Article 1, § 8 of the federal Constitution, that is, as may not be incompatible with the exclusive jurisdiction of the United States, and may operate to authorize the service by the officers of the State of the civil and criminal process of its courts, with reference to acts done within the acknowledged territory of the State outside of the ceded lands. This reservation is valid and is intended to prevent such places from becoming harbors of refuge for debtors and criminals. Foley v. Shriver, 81 Va. 568 (1886).

Retention of right to serve process does not prevent cession of jurisdiction. — The mere fact that the State has retained the right to serve criminal and civil process on land described in this section is not effective to prevent cession of exclusive or concurrent criminal jurisdiction to the federal government. The purpose of this reservation is to prevent the land involved from becoming an asylum for fugitives from justice. United States v. Schuster, 220 F. Supp. 61 (E.D. Va. 1963).

And practice is to permit federal government to prosecute. — The practice which exists in this area with respect to crimes committed on lands "acquired" in any manner by the United States is to permit — indeed, to require — the federal government to prosecute. The State adopts a "hands off" policy. United States v. Schuster, 220 F. Supp. 61 (E.D. Va. 1963).

Reservation of right to execute process. — See Western Union Tel. Co. v. Chiles, 214 U.S. 274, 29 S. Ct. 613, 53 L. Ed. 994 (1909) (Norfolk Navy Yard); Norfolk & Portsmouth Belt Line R.R. v. Parker, 152 Va. 484, 147 S.E. 461 (1929).

Does not affect personal status of resident. — The right of the State to serve process in territory ceded to the United States does not affect the personal status of a resident in such territory. Such person does not thereby acquire a residence in this State so as to defeat the right of a creditor to attach his property in this State on the ground that he is a nonresident. Bank of Phoebus v. Byrum, 110 Va. 708, 67 S.E. 349 (1910).

State ceded concurrent jurisdiction to prosecute crimes committed on lands transferred to the federal government. — Virginia consented to cede only "concurrent jurisdiction" to the United States to prosecute crimes committed on lands transferred to the federal government; the presumption in favor of concurrent jurisdiction was rebuttable, but only by a clear manifestation of a specific intent to do so. Campbell v. Commonwealth, 39 Va. App. 180, 571 S.E.2d 906, 2002 Va. App. LEXIS 681 (2002).

State has ceded concurrent jurisdiction of crimes committed on private property leased for naval base. — Virginia has ceded concurrent jurisdiction to the federal government for crimes committed on private property leased by the United States for purposes of the operation of a naval base. United States v. Schuster, 220 F. Supp. 61 (E.D. Va. 1963).

Virginia laws in force at Old Point Comfort. — The general laws of Virginia, other than criminal, which are not in conflict with those of the United States relating to forts, and which do not interfere with the military control, discipline, and use by the United States of Fortress Monroe as a military post, are in force at Old Point Comfort, and are especially in force in those parts and places at Old Point Comfort which have been appropriated to other than the military purposes of the United States. Crook, Horner & Co. v. Old Point Comfort Hotel Co., 54 F. 604 (E.D. Va. 1893).

§ 1-401. Ceding additional jurisdiction to United States. — A. Whenever the head or other authorized officer of any department or independent establishment or agency of the United States shall deem it desirable that additional jurisdiction or powers be ceded over any lands in the Commonwealth acquired or proposed to be acquired by the United States under his immediate jurisdiction, custody or control, and whenever the Governor and Attorney General of the Commonwealth shall agree to the same, the Governor and Attorney General shall execute and acknowledge a deed in the name of and under the lesser seal of the Commonwealth ceding such additional jurisdiction. The deed shall accurately and specifically describe the area and location of the land over which the additional jurisdiction and powers are ceded and shall set out specifically what additional jurisdiction and powers are ceded, and may set out any reservations in the Commonwealth of jurisdiction which may be deemed proper in addition to those referred to in subsection D.

B. No such deed shall become effective or operative until the jurisdiction therein provided for is accepted on behalf of the United States as required by 40 U.S.C. § 255. The head or other authorized officer of a department or independent establishment or agency of the United States shall indicate such acceptance by executing and acknowledging such deed and admitting it to record in the office of the clerk of the court in which deeds conveying the lands affected would properly be recorded.

C. When such deed has been executed and acknowledged on behalf of the Commonwealth and the United States, and admitted to record as provided in subsection B, it shall have the effect of ceding to and vesting in the United States the jurisdiction and powers therein provided for and none other.

D. Every such deed as is provided for in this section shall reserve in the Commonwealth over all lands therein referred to the jurisdiction and power to serve civil and criminal process on such lands and in the event that the lands or any part thereof shall be sold or leased to any person, under the terms of which sale or lease the vendee or lessee shall have the right to conduct thereon any private industry or business, then the jurisdiction ceded to the United States over any such lands so sold or leased shall cease and determine, and thereafter the Commonwealth shall have all jurisdiction and power she would have had if no jurisdiction or power had been ceded to the United States. This provision, however, shall not apply to post exchanges, officers' clubs and similar activities on lands acquired by the United States for purposes of national defense. It is further provided that the reservations provided for in this subsection shall remain effective even though they should be omitted from any deed executed pursuant to this section.

E. Nothing contained in this section shall be construed as repealing any special acts ceding jurisdiction to the United States to acquire any specific tract of land. (Code 1950, § 7-24; 1966, c. 102, § 7.1-21; 1972, c. 597; 1976, c. 211; 2005, c. 839.)

CASE NOTES

The presumption prevails that the State has jurisdiction over land which is owned by United States unless a defendant shows that the United States was deeded the land and accepted jurisdiction over it. Smith v. Commonwealth, 219 Va. 455, 248 S.E.2d 135 (1978), cert. denied, 441 U.S. 967, 99 S. Ct. 2419, 60 L. Ed. 2d 1074 (1979) (decided under prior law).

§ **1-402. Shenandoah National Park.** — The respective jurisdiction and powers of the Commonwealth and the United States over all lands within the Shenandoah National Park, as it is now constituted or may hereafter be extended, shall be as follows:

1. Criminal and police jurisdiction. — The United States shall have exclusive jurisdiction, legislative, executive and judicial, with respect to the commission of crimes, and the arrest, trial and punishment therefor, and exclusive general police jurisdiction thereover.

2. Sale of alcoholic beverages. — The United States shall have the power to regulate or prohibit the sale of alcoholic beverages on such lands; provided, that, if the sale of alcoholic beverages is prohibited by general law in the Commonwealth outside of such lands, no such alcoholic beverages shall be sold on the lands contained in the Park area; and provided further, that if the general laws of the Commonwealth permit the sale of alcoholic beverages, then the regulations of the United States relating to such sales on such lands shall conform as nearly as possible to the regulatory provisions in accordance with which such sales are permitted in the Commonwealth outside of such Park lands. Nothing in this subsection shall be construed as reserving in the Commonwealth power to require licenses of persons engaged in the sale of intoxicating beverages on such lands, nor the power to require that any sales be made through official liquor stores.

3. Service of civil and criminal process. — The Commonwealth shall have jurisdiction to serve civil process within the limits of the Park in any suits properly instituted in any of the courts of the Commonwealth and to serve criminal process within such limits in any suits or prosecutions for or on account of crimes committed in the Commonwealth but outside of the Park.

4. Tax on alcoholic beverages. — The Commonwealth shall have jurisdiction and power to levy a nondiscriminatory tax on all alcoholic beverages possessed or sold on such lands.

5. Tax on motor vehicle fuels and lubricants. — The Commonwealth shall have jurisdiction and power to tax the sales of oil and gasoline, and other motor vehicle fuels and lubricants for use in motor vehicles. This subsection shall not be construed as a consent by the United States to the taxation by the Commonwealth of such sales for the exclusive use of the United States.

6. Tax on businesses. — The Commonwealth shall have jurisdiction and power to levy nondiscriminatory taxes on private individuals, associations and corporations, their franchises and properties, on such lands, and on their businesses conducted thereon.

7. Jurisdiction of courts. — The courts of the Commonwealth shall have concurrent jurisdiction with the courts of the United States of all civil causes of action arising on such lands to the same extent as if the cause of action had arisen in the county or city in which the land lies outside the Park area, and the state officers shall have jurisdiction to enforce on such lands the judgments of the state courts and the collection of taxes by appropriate process.

8. Voting residence. — Persons residing in or on any of the lands embraced in the Park shall have the right to establish a voting residence in the Commonwealth by reason thereof, and the consequent right to vote at all elections within the county or city in which the land or lands upon which they reside are located upon like terms and conditions, and to the same extent as they would be entitled to vote in such county or city if the lands on which they reside had not been deeded or conveyed to the United States.

9. Fugitives. — All fugitives from justice taking refuge in the Park shall be subject to the same laws as refugees from justice found in the Commonwealth. (Code 1950, § 7-22; 1966, c. 102, § 7.1-19; 2005, c. 839.)

CASE NOTES

Section merely preserves traditional jurisdiction of State. — Having no power to confer jurisdiction on federal courts, Virginia, in enacting this section, intended only to preserve its traditional jurisdiction, and Congress, in adopting the very language of subdivision (g) of this section in a subsequent statute, intended no more. Fowler v. Dodson, 159 F. Supp. 101 (E.D. Pa. 1958) (decided under prior law).

Jurisdiction of action arising from automobile collision in Park. — Absent diversity of citizenship, a federal district court had no jurisdiction of an action arising from an automobile collision occurring in Shenandoah National Park. Fowler v. Dodson, 159 F. Supp. 101 (E.D. Pa. 1958) (decided under prior law).

Jurisdiction to serve process within the limits of the Park was not reserved by the Commonwealth in Chapter 371 of the Acts of 1928, under which lands in the Park were conveyed to the United States; and the jurisdiction was denied in Buttery v. Robbins, 177 Va. 368, 14 S.E.2d 544 (1941) (decided under prior law). But such jurisdiction is now reserved by subdivision 3 of this section.

§ 1-403. Conveyances of certain waste and unappropriated lands and marshlands to the United States. — A. The Governor is authorized to execute in the name of the Commonwealth deeds conveying, subject to the jurisdictional and other limitations and reservations contained in §§ 1-400 and 1-405, to the United States such title as the Commonwealth may have in waste and unappropriated lands entirely surrounded by lands owned by the United States, when the same are certified as being vacant and unappropriated by a duly authorized agent of the United States and are described by metes and bounds descriptions filed with the Secretary of the Commonwealth and with the clerk of the court in the county wherein such unappropriated land is situated.

B. The Governor is authorized to execute, in the name and on behalf of the Commonwealth, a deed or other appropriate instrument conveying to the United States, without any consideration but subject to the jurisdictional limitations and reservations contained in §§ 1-400 and 1-405, such right, title and interest in or easement over and across the marshes lying along the seaside of the Counties of Accomack and Northampton as may be necessary and proper for the construction, operation and maintenance of a canal or channel for small boats over and through such marshlands. (Code 1950, § 7-23; 1966, c. 102, § 7.1-20; 1976, c. 211; 2005, c. 839.)

§ 1-404. Licensing sale of mixed alcoholic beverages on lands ceded to or owned by United States. — The Virginia Alcoholic Beverage Control Board may license the sale of mixed alcoholic beverages as defined in Chapter 1 (§ 4.1-100 et seq.) of Title 4.1 at places primarily engaged in the sale of meals on lands ceded by the Commonwealth to the United States or owned by the government of the United States or any agency thereof provided that such lands are used as ports of entry or egress to and from the United States, and provided that such lands lie within or partly within the boundaries of any county in this Commonwealth which permits the lawful dispensing of mixed alcoholic beverages. The Board is hereby authorized to adopt rules and regulations governing the sale of such spirits, and to fix the fees for such licenses, within the limits fixed by general law. (1968, c. 511, § 7.1-21.1; 1993, c. 866; 2005, c. 839.)

§ 1-405. Reversion to Commonwealth; recorded title prerequisite to vesting jurisdiction. — A. As used in this section, unless the context requires otherwise:

"Corrective action" means the response and remediation to environmental contamination to the extent required by any applicable environmental law or regulation applicable to the property.

"Environmental contamination" means any hazardous waste, substance or toxic material, or its discharge or release, that is regulated under any environmental law or regulation applicable to the property, and shall include petroleum (including crude oil), natural gas, liquefied natural gas, ordnance, unexploded munitions, and asbestos.

B. If the United States shall cease to be the owner of any lands, or any part thereof, granted or conveyed to it by the Commonwealth; if the purposes of any such grant or conveyance to the United States shall cease; or if the United States shall for five consecutive years fail to use any such land for the purposes of the grant or conveyance, then, and in that event, the right and title to such land, or such part thereof, shall immediately revert to the Commonwealth unless such land, or part thereof, contains environmental contamination. No land containing environmental contamination shall be transferred or revert to the Commonwealth, unless and until all corrective action necessary to protect human health and the environment with respect to any environmental contamination on the lands, or portion thereof, has been completed to the satisfaction of the Commonwealth and approved by the Governor pursuant to § 2.2-1149, and the United States has executed and delivered a transfer instrument including covenants warranting that (i) all corrective action necessary to protect human health and the environment with respect to any environmental contamination on the land or any portion thereof has been taken, and (ii) any corrective action for environmental contamination occurring before the date of transfer found to be necessary after the date of the transfer of the title of the land or any portion thereof shall be conducted by the United States.

In cases where the Defense Base Closure and Realignment Commission (BRAC Commission) established pursuant to P.L. 101-510 (1990), as amended, identifies United States military bases located in the Commonwealth for closure, the Commonwealth shall have, in addition to the foregoing, the right to enter upon such lands so identified for the purpose of inspection for environmental contamination. Upon completion of such inspection, the Commonwealth shall report its findings to the Governor and the appropriate federal agencies.

C. All deeds, conveyances or title papers for the transfer of title of lands to the United States shall be recorded in the county or city wherein the land or the greater part thereof lies, but no tax shall be required on any such instrument made to the United States by which they acquire lands for public purposes.

D. The jurisdiction ceded by § 1-400 shall not vest until the United States shall have acquired the title of record to such lands, or rights or interest therein, by purchase, condemnation, lease or otherwise. So long as the lands, or any rights or interest therein, are held in fee simple by the United States, and no longer, such lands, rights or interest, as the case may be, shall continue exempt and exonerated, from all state and local taxes which may be levied or imposed under the authority of the Commonwealth. (Code 1950, § 7-25; 1966, c. 102, § 7.1-22; 1975, c. 449; 1976, c. 211; 1994, c. 23; 2005, c. 839.)

Editor's note. — Acts 2007, c. 490, provides: "§ 1. Notwithstanding the limitation on the transfer or reversion of lands to the Commonwealth contained in subsection B of § 1-405 of the Code of Virginia, lands located within the Northern Virginia Planning District that contain environmental contamination may revert or transfer to the Commonwealth if the United States enters into a written agreement with the Commonwealth pursuant to § 2.2-1149 to indemnify the Commonwealth against all costs and liabilities associated with such environmental contamination and related corrective action or otherwise provides satisfactory assurances that all corrective action necessary to protect human health and the environment will be taken at the sole expense of the United States. The written agreement shall be in a form approved by the Attorney General of Virginia.

"§ 2. In addition to the requirements set forth in § 1, such transfer or reversion shall not occur unless and until the United States has agreed, and provides assurances satisfactory to the Commonwealth, to provide all transportation infrastructure improvements required to accommodate the development of any property owned by the United States and contiguous or adjacent to the property subject to the transfer or reversion.

"§ 3. Except as provided in § 1, the provisions of § 1-405 of the Code of Virginia shall apply mutatis mutandis to this act.

"§ 4. As used in this act, 'corrective action' and 'environmental contamination' shall mean the same as those terms are defined in § 1-405 of the Code of Virginia."

§ 1-406. Conveyances to political subdivisions of lands ceded to and no longer used by United States. — Whenever any land in the Commonwealth has been or is conveyed to the United States with a provision in the deed that upon abandonment or use for any purpose other than that stated in the deed such land shall revert to the Commonwealth, and if any such land is abandoned or is no longer used for the purpose for which conveyed, the Governor is hereby authorized to convey to the political subdivision in which such land is situated, all right, title and interest of the Commonwealth in and to such land. This section shall not affect any lease made under Chapter 321 of the Acts of 1952. (Code 1950, § 7-25.1; 1954, c. 170; 1966, c. 102, § 7.1-23; 2005, c. 839.)

Editor's note. — Acts 2007, cc. 707 and 740, cl. 1, effective March 21, 2007, provides: "§ 1. Notwithstanding the provisions of § 1-406 of the Code of Virginia or any other provision of law to the contrary, the Governor, on behalf of the Commonwealth and at such time as the Governor deems appropriate, may convey all right, title, and interest of the Commonwealth in and to certain real property located within the City of Hampton commonly referred to as 'Fort Monroe,' including any right of the Commonwealth to receive such property in the event of a reversion or the triggering of a possibility of a reverter, to the Fort Monroe Federal Area Development Authority created pursuant to § 15.2-6302 of the Code of Virginia."

§ 1-407. Concurrent jurisdiction of Commonwealth and United States over certain lands leased to political subdivisions. — Whenever the United States government has exclusive jurisdiction over property located in the Commonwealth of Virginia, and leases the property, or part thereof, to any political subdivision to be used by it for a public purpose, the exclusive jurisdiction shall cease as to the property so leased and the Commonwealth and the United States government shall have concurrent jurisdiction over the property so long as the lease continues. At the termination of the lease the jurisdiction of the Commonwealth shall cease and the United States shall have exclusive jurisdiction thereof. (Code 1950, § 7-25.2; 1964, c. 362; 1966, c. 102, § 7.1-24; 2005, c. 839.)

§ 1-408. Relinquishment by United States of jurisdiction over lands in the Commonwealth. — Whenever a duly authorized official or agent of the United States, acting pursuant to authority conferred by the United States Congress, notifies the Governor that the United States desires or is willing to relinquish to the Commonwealth the jurisdiction, or a portion thereof, held by the United States over lands located in the Commonwealth, as designated in such notice, the Governor may, in his discretion, accept such relinquishment. Such acceptance shall be made by sending a notice of acceptance to the official or agent designated by the United States to receive such notice of acceptance. The Governor shall send a signed copy of the notice of acceptance, together with the notice of relinquishment received from the United States, to the Secretary of the Commonwealth, who shall maintain a permanent file of said notices.

Upon the sending of the notice of acceptance to the designated official or agent of the United States, the Commonwealth shall immediately have such jurisdiction over the lands designated in the notice of relinquishment as the notice shall specify.

Upon receipt of a copy of the notice of relinquishment and a copy of the notice of acceptance, the Secretary of the Commonwealth shall immediately give written notice of such change in jurisdiction to the Attorney General and the attorney for the Commonwealth of the city or county in which such lands are located. The Secretary of the Commonwealth shall also certify a copy of each of the notices to the clerk of court in which deeds are admitted to record for the city or county in which such lands are located. The clerk shall record the notices in his deed book and index them in the name of the United States and the Commonwealth. (1975, c. 411, § 7.1-25.1; 2005, c. 839.)

CHAPTER 5.

EMBLEMS.

Article 1.

Symbols of Sovereignty.

Article 2.

Emblems, Designations, and Honors.

ARTICLE 1.

Symbols of Sovereignty.

§ **1-500. The great seal.** — The great seal of the Commonwealth shall consist of two metallic discs, two and one-fourth inches in diameter, with an ornamental border one fourth of an inch wide, with such words and figures engraved as follows: On the obverse, Virtus, the genius of the Commonwealth, dressed as an Amazon, resting on a spear in her right hand, point downward, touching the earth; and holding in her left hand, a sheathed sword, or parazonium, pointing upward; her head erect and face upturned; her left foot on the form of Tyranny represented by the prostrate body of a man, with his head to her left, his fallen crown nearby, a broken chain in his left hand, and a scourge in his right. Above the group and within the border conforming therewith, shall be the word "Virginia," and, in the space below, on a curved line, shall be the motto, "Sic Semper Tyrannis." On the reverse, shall be placed a group consisting of Libertas, holding a wand and pileus in her right hand; on her right, Aeternitas, with a globe and phoenix in her right hand; on the left of Libertas, Ceres, with a cornucopia in her left hand, and an ear of wheat in her right; over this device, in a curved line, the word "Perseverando." (Code 1950, § 7-26; 1966, c. 102, § 7.1-26; 2005, c. 839.)

§ **1-501. The lesser seal.** — The lesser seal of the Commonwealth shall be one and nine sixteenths inches in diameter, and be engraved with the device and inscriptions contained in the obverse of the great seal. (Code 1950, § 7-27; 1966, c. 102, § 7.1-27; 2005, c. 839.)

§ **1-502. Custody; impressions displayed in The Library of Virginia.** — The seals of the Commonwealth described in §§ 1-500 and 1-501 shall be kept by the Secretary of the Commonwealth and used as provided by law, and at least three clear impressions of the seals shall be kept and displayed by the Librarian of Virginia in some suitable place in The Library of Virginia, for public inspection. (Code 1950, § 7-28; 1966, c. 102, § 7.1-28; 1994, c. 64; 1998, c. 427; 2005, c. 839.)

§ **1-503. Uses and tax on great seal.** — The great seal shall be affixed to documents, signed by the Governor, which are to be used before tribunals, or for purposes outside of the jurisdiction of the Commonwealth; and in every such case, except where the Commonwealth is a party concerned in the use to be made of the document, the tax imposed by § 58.1-1725 on the seal of the Commonwealth shall be collected and accounted for by the Secretary of the Commonwealth. (Code 1950, § 7-30; 1966, c. 102, § 7.1-30; 2005, c. 839.)

§ **1-504. Uses and tax on lesser seal.** — The lesser seal shall be affixed to all grants for lands and writs of election issued by the Governor; to all letters of pardon and reprieve; to all commissions, civil and military, signed by the Governor, and to all other papers, requiring a seal, authorized to be issued by the Governor for the purpose of carrying the laws into effect within the Commonwealth; and also, when deemed necessary by the Secretary of the Commonwealth, may be used by him as an authentication of his official signature. No tax shall be imposed on the use of such lesser seal, except upon commissions appointing notaries, and commissioners in other states for taking acknowledgments, and upon certificates of the Secretary of the Commonwealth, when, at the request of the parties desiring such certificates, the seal is attached. In all such cases the tax shall be the same as upon the great seal, and shall be collected and accounted for in the same manner. (Code 1950, § 7-31; 1966, c. 102, § 7.1-31; 2005, c. 839.)

§ 1-505. Seals deemed property of Commonwealth; unauthorized use; penalty. — The seals of the Commonwealth shall be deemed the property of the Commonwealth; and no persons shall exhibit, display, or in any manner utilize the seals or any facsimile or representation of the seals of the Commonwealth for nongovernmental purposes unless such use is specifically authorized by law.

Except for the authorized commercial use of the seal as provided in § 2.2-122, any person violating the provisions of this section shall be punished by a fine of not more than $100, or by imprisonment for not more than 30 days or both. (1966, c. 102, § 7.1-31.1; 1995, c. 295; 2005, c. 839.)

§ 1-506. Flag of the Commonwealth. — The flag of the Commonwealth shall be a deep blue field, with a circular white centre of the same material. Upon this circle shall be painted or embroidered, to show on both sides alike, the coat of arms of the Commonwealth, as described in § 1-500 for the obverse of the great seal of the Commonwealth; and there may be a white fringe on the outer edge, furthest from the flagstaff. This shall be known and respected as the flag of the Commonwealth. (Code 1950, § 7-32; 1966, c. 102, § 7.1-32; 2005, c. 839.)

§ 1-507. Governor to prescribe size of flag. — The Governor shall regulate the size and dimensions of the flag proper for forts, arsenals and public buildings, for ships-of-war and merchant marine, for troops in the field, respectively, and for any other purpose, according to his discretion by proclamation. (Code 1950, § 7-33; 1966, c. 102, § 7.1-33; 2005, c. 839.)

§ 1-508. Director of General Services to have available flags of the Commonwealth for sale. — The Director of the Department of General Services shall have available at all times flags of the Commonwealth, to be offered for sale to the public in such manner as the Director may determine.

Such flags shall be of good quality, shall conform to the specifications prescribed in § 1-506, and shall be offered in the various sizes prescribed by the Governor pursuant to § 1-507.

The prices to be charged for such flags shall be at cost as determined by the Director. (Code 1950, § 7-33.1; 1958, c. 553; 1960, c. 347; 1966, c. 102, § 7.1-34; 2005, c. 839.)

§ 1-509. When flag to be suspended over Capitol. — During the sessions of either house of the General Assembly the flag of the Commonwealth shall be kept raised over the respective chambers of the Capitol, or other place of session, if practicable, as directed by the Director of the Department of General Services and the Chief of the Virginia Capitol Police in consultation with the Clerk of the House of Delegates and the Clerk of the Senate. (Code 1950, § 7-34; 1966, c. 102, § 7.1-35; 1970, c. 561; 2005, c. 839.)

ARTICLE 2.

Emblems, Designations, and Honors.

§ 1-510. Official emblems and designations. — The following are hereby designated official emblems and designations of the Commonwealth:

Artisan Center — "Virginia Artisans Center," located in the City of Waynesboro.

Bat — Virginia Big-eared bat (*Corynorhinos townsendii virginianus*).

Beverage — Milk.

Blue Ridge Folklore State Center — Blue Ridge Institute located in the village of Ferrum.

Boat — "Chesapeake Bay Deadrise."

Covered Bridge Capital of the Commonwealth — Patrick County.

Covered Bridge Festival — Virginia Covered Bridge Festival held in Patrick County.

Dog — American Foxhound.

Emergency medical services museum — "To The Rescue," located in the City of Roanoke.

Fish — Brook Trout.

Fleet — Replicas of the three ships, Susan Constant, Godspeed, and Discovery, which comprised the Commonwealth's founding fleet that brought the first permanent English settlers to Jamestown in 1607, and which are exhibited at the Jamestown Settlement in Williamsburg.

Flower — American Dogwood (*Cornus florida*).

Folk dance — Square dancing, the American folk dance that traces its ancestry to the English Country Dance and the French Ballroom Dance, and is called, cued, or prompted to the dancers, and includes squares, rounds, clogging, contra, line, the Virginia Reel, and heritage dances.

Fossil — Chesapecten jeffersonius.

Gold mining interpretive center — Monroe Park, located in the County of Fauquier.

Insect — Tiger Swallowtail Butterfly (*Papilio glaucus Linne*).

Motor sports museum — "Wood Brothers Racing Museum and Virginia Motor Sports Hall of Fame," located in Patrick County.

Outdoor drama — "The Trail of the Lonesome Pine Outdoor Drama," adapted for the stage by Clara Lou Kelly and performed in the Town of Big Stone Gap.

Outdoor drama, historical — "The Long Way Home" based on the life of Mary Draper Ingles, adapted for the stage by Earl Hobson Smith, and performed in the City of Radford.

Shell — Oyster shell (*Crassostrea virginica*).

Song emeritus — "Carry Me Back to Old Virginia," by James A. Bland, as set out in the House Joint Resolution 10, adopted by the General Assembly of Virginia at the Session of 1940.

Sports hall of fame — "Virginia Sports Hall of Fame," located in the City of Portsmouth.

War memorial museum — "Virginia War Museum," (formerly known as the War Memorial Museum of Virginia), located in the City of Newport News. (Code 1950, §§ 7-35, 7-36, 7-37; 1966, cc. 102, 547, §§ 7.1-37, 7.1-38, 7.1-39; 1974, c. 24, § 7.1-40; 1982, c. 191, § 7.1-40.1; 1986, c. 138, § 7.1-40.2; 1988, c. 317, § 7.1-40.3; 1991, cc. 71, 575, §§ 7.1-40.4, 7.1-40.5; 1993, cc. 251, 509, § 7.1-40.6; 1994, cc. 33, 134, 220, 464, §§ 7.1-40.2:1, 7.1-40.8; 1995, cc. 12, 180, § 7.1-40.2:2; 1996, c. 52, § 7.1-40.9; 1997, cc. 66, 576, § 7.1-40.10; 1999, cc. 69, 336, § 7.1-40.11; 2001, cc. 97, 134, § 7.1-40.12; 2001, c. 228, § 7.1-40.13; 2005, cc. 557, 839; 2006, c. 128; 2007, cc. 391, 685; 2008, c. 262.)

Editor's note. — Acts 2005, c. 557, enacted former § 7.1-40.7:1 designating the Virginia big-eared bat as the official bat of the Commonwealth. The substance of the provisions were included in § 1-510 as enacted by Acts 2005, c. 839.

The 2007 amendments. — The 2007 amendments by cc. 391 and 685 are identical, and inserted "Covered Bridge Festival — Virginia Covered Bridge Festival held in Patrick County."

The 2008 amendments. — The 2008

amendment by c. 262 inserted "Covered Bridge Festival — Virginia Covered Bridge Festival held in Patrick County."

§ 1-511. English designated the official language of the Commonwealth. — English shall be designated as the official language of the Commonwealth. Except as provided by law, no state agency or local government shall be required to provide and no state agency or local government shall be prohibited from providing any documents, information, literature or other written materials in any language other than English. (1996, c. 829, § 7.1-42; 2005, c. 839.)

Law Review. — For comment, "The Fiber of the Common Bond," see 13 Geo. Mason L. Rev. 367 (2005).

§ 1-512. Poet laureate. — The honorary position of Poet Laureate of Virginia is hereby created. The Governor may appoint a poet laureate from a list of nominees submitted by the Poetry Society of Virginia. Each poet laureate shall serve a term of two years with no restrictions on reappointment. (1997, c. 299, § 7.1-43; 2005, c. 839.)

Title 2.

Administration of the Government Generally.

[Repealed.]

§§ 2-1 through 2-309: Repealed by Acts 1966, c. 677.

Cross references. — For present provisions relating to administration of government, see § 2.2-100 et seq.

Title 2.1.

Administration of the Government Generally.

[Repealed.]

§§ **2.1-1 through 2.1-819:** Repealed by Acts 2001, c. 844, cl. 11, effective October 1, 2001.

Cross references. — For note regarding the recodification of Titles 2.1 and 9 as new Titles 2.2 and 9.1, and accompanying revisions of other material, see Editor's note under § 2.2-100.

Title 2.2.
Administration of Government.

Subtitle I.
Organization of State Government.

Part A.
Office of the Governor.

Part B.

Part C.
State Agencies Related to the General Operation of Government.

Part D.
State Authorities, Boards, Commissions, Councils, Foundations and Other Collegial Bodies.

SUBTITLE I.

ORGANIZATION OF STATE GOVERNMENT.

PART A.

OFFICE OF THE GOVERNOR.

CHAPTER 1.

GOVERNOR.

Article 1.

General Provisions.

Article 1.

General Provisions.

§ 2.2-100. Salaries of Governor and other officers; administrative assistants. — A. The Governor and all officers of the Commonwealth shall receive annually for their services such salaries as are fixed by law.

B. The Governor may employ the necessary administrative assistants, including a chief of staff, and fix their salaries within the limitation of funds appropriated for executive control of the Commonwealth. Any chief of staff appointed by the Governor shall be confirmed by a majority of the members in each house of the General Assembly.

C. The Governor may employ the staff required to perform necessary services in the operation of the Executive Mansion. (Code 1950, §§ 2-34, 14-9 to 14-16, 14-18 to 14-26; 1962, c. 356; 1964, c. 386, § 14.1-12; 1966, cc. 55, 677, § 2.1-38; 1968, cc. 223, 562; 1970, cc. 262, 759; 1977, c. 672; 1984, cc. 104, 750, 779; 1998, c. 872; 2001, c. 844.)

Cross references. — For constitutional provision as to compensation of Governor, see Va. Const., Art. V, § 4. For requirement that state agencies, boards, commissions, etc., submit environmental impact reports on major state projects, see § 10.1-1188.

Editor's note. — In accordance with § 9-77.10 (now § 30-149), the Virginia Code Commission, in 1998, undertook a three-year recodification of Titles 2.1 and 9. Title 2.1 had last been recodified in 1966 and Title 9 had never been recodified. The Commission's draft of this revision, which was published as House Document 51 of the 2001 Session, was sent to the Governor and General Assembly in January, 2001. The revision, as amended by the General Assembly, became Acts 2001, c. 844, effective October 1, 2001.

Title 2.1 was rewritten primarily as new Title 2.2, with certain material now incorporated into Titles 6.1, 9.1, 17.1, 30, 37.1 and 51.1, and Title 9 was rewritten primarily as new Title

9.1, with certain material now incorporated into Titles 3.1, 2.2, and 30. In addition, the Virginia Public Procurement Act, §§ 11-35 to 11-80, was rewritten as § 2.2-4300 et seq., and §§ 53.1-180 to 53.1-185.3, the Comprehensive Community Corrections Act for Local-Responsible Offenders, was rewritten as § 9.1-173 to 9.1-183.

In addition to revision by Acts 2001, c. 844, Titles 2.1 and 9, § 11-35 et seq. and § 53.1-183 [see now § 9.1-178] were also amended by other acts passed at the 2001 Session. As required by § 9-77.11 (see new § 30-152), the Code Commission has incorporated the majority of these amendments into the new sections.

Where appropriate, the historical citations to former sections have been added to corresponding new sections.

The case notes appearing under new sections were decided under corresponding former sections or under prior law.

For tables of corresponding former and new sections, see the tables in Volume 10.

Acts 2001, c. 844, cl. 2, provides: "That whenever any of the conditions, requirements, provisions or contents of any section or chapter of Title 2.1 or Title 9 or any other title of the Code of Virginia as such titles existed prior to October 1, 2001, are transferred in the same or modified form to a new section or chapter of Title 2.2 or Title 9.1 or any other title of the Code and whenever any such former section or chapter is given a new number in Title 2.2 or Title 9.1 or any other title, all references to any such former section or chapter of Title 2.1 or Title 9 or other title appearing in this Code shall be construed to apply to the new or renumbered section or chapter containing such conditions, requirements, provisions, contents or portions thereof."

Acts 2001, c. 844, cl. 3, provides: "That the regulations of any department or agency affected by the revision of Title 2.1, Title 9 or such other titles in effect on the effective date of this act shall continue in effect to the extent that they are not in conflict with this act and shall be deemed to be regulations adopted under this act."

Acts 2001, c. 844, cl. 4, provides: "That this title revision of Title 2.1 as Title 2.2 and Title 9 as Title 9.1 and the repeal of Chapter 7 (§ 11-35 et seq.) of Title 11 shall not be construed to require the reappointment of any officer or any member of a board, council, committee or other appointed body referred to in Title 2.2 or Title 9.1 and each such officer and member shall continue to serve for the term for which appointed pursuant to the provisions of Title 2.1, Title 9, or Chapter 7 (§ 11-35 et seq.) of Title 11. The revision of Title 2.1 as Title 2.2 and Title 9 as Title 9.1 in this act shall not affect the classification or assignment of any state agency, institution, board, commission, council or other collegial body within the executive branch currently in effect pursuant to Title 2.1 or Title 9; such classifications and assignments within the executive branch which existed prior to the effective date of this act shall continue unless reclassified or reassigned by a later enactment of the General Assembly and signed by the Governor."

Acts 2001, c. 844, cl. 5, provides: "That this title revision of Title 2.1 as Title 2.2 or Title 9 as Title 9.1 shall not be construed to affect the term of office of any elected officeholder holding office on October 1, 2001."

Acts 2001, c. 844, cl. 6, provides: "That the provisions of § 30-152, formerly § 9-77.11, of the Code of Virginia shall apply to the codification of Title 2.2 and Title 9.1 so as to give effect to other laws enacted by the 2001 Session of the General Assembly notwithstanding the delay in the effective date of this act."

Acts 2001, c. 844, cl. 7, provides: "That the repeal of Title 2.1, Title 9, and Chapter 7 (§ 11-35 et seq.) of Title 11 effective as of October 1, 2001, shall not affect any act or offense done or committed, or any penalty incurred, or any right established, accrued or accruing on or before such date, or any proceeding, prosecution, suit or action pending on that day. Except as otherwise provided in this act, neither the repeal of Title 2.1, Title 9 or Chapter 7 (§ 11-35 et seq.) of Title 11 nor the enactment of Title 2.2 or the enactment of Title 9.1, shall apply to offenses committed prior to October 1, 2001, and prosecution for such offenses shall be governed by the prior law, which is continued in effect for that purpose. For the purpose of this enactment, an offense was committed prior to October 1, 2001, if any of essential elements of the offense occurred prior thereto."

Acts 2001, c. 844, cl. 8, provides: "That any notice given, recognizance taken, or process or writ issued before October 1, 2001, shall be valid although given, taken or to be returned to a day after such date, in like manner as if Title 2.2 and Title 9.1 had been effective before the same was given, taken or issued."

Acts 2001, c. 844, cl. 9, provides: "That if any clause, sentence, paragraph, subdivision, section or part of Title 2.2 and Title 9.1 shall be adjudged in any court of competent jurisdiction to be invalid, the judgment shall not affect, impair or invalidate the remainder thereof, but shall be confined in its operation to the clause, sentence, paragraph, subdivision, section or part thereof directly involved in the controversy in which the judgment shall have been rendered, and to this end the provisions of Title 2.2 and Title 9.1 are declared severable."

Acts 2001, c. 844, cl. 10, provides: "That any reference in the Code of Virginia or the Acts of Assembly to the Privacy Protection Act of 1976 shall be construed to mean the Government

Data Collection and Dissemination Practices Act."

Law Review. — For survey of Virginia administrative law and utility regulation for the year 1978-1979, see 66 Va. L. Rev. 193 (1980). For an article, "Agency Adjudication, the Importance of Facts, and the Limitation of Labels," see 57 Wash. & Lee L. Rev. 351 (2000).

Michie's Jurisprudence. — For related discussion, see 2A M.J. Attorney General, § 3; 9A M.J. Governor, § 3.

CASE NOTES

Editor's note. — The cases below were decided under former Title 2.1 or prior provisions.

The Virginia Department of Health is not a "corporate citizen" of the State, maintaining a separate identity from the State. Medicenters of Am., Inc. v. Virginia, 373 F. Supp. 305 (E.D. Va. 1974).

Rather, it is merely an "arm of the State," i.e., the State's alter ego. Medicenters of Am., Inc. v. Virginia, 373 F. Supp. 305 (E.D. Va. 1974).

And does not have certain powers apart from State. — The Virginia Department of Health has not the power to raise capital, engage in other financial and contractual relationships, or sue and be sued, in its own right, as an entity separate and distinct from the State. Medicenters of Am., Inc. v. Virginia, 373 F. Supp. 305 (E.D. Va. 1974).

Legislature cannot withhold from Attorney General the salary prescribed by law, nor can it delegate such power to the Auditor of Public Accounts (now Comptroller), and he may recover his salary by mandamus. Blair v. Marye, 80 Va. 485 (1885).

Attorney General's salary not subject to attachment, detention for debt, etc. — The salary of the Attorney General is of constitutional grant, and of public official right, and the doctrine of offset cannot be applied to it. It is not liable to attachment, garnishment, nor assignment in bankruptcy, and upon principles of public policy it has absolute immunity from detention for debt or counterclaims. Blair v. Marye, 80 Va. 485 (1885).

But the State may recover fees paid him by mistake. — The Commonwealth may recover from the Attorney General fees paid him by the Auditor of Public Accounts (now Comptroller) under the mistaken belief that he was entitled thereto as part of his compensation. Commonwealth v. Field, 84 Va. 26, 3 S.E. 882 (1887).

§ 2.2-101. Clerical forces and office expenses of Governor. — The Governor may appoint the clerical force necessary to the efficient operation of his office, but the aggregate amount paid such clerks shall not exceed the sum provided by law. The Governor may expend for the contingent expenses of his office such sums as are provided by law. (Code 1950, §§ 14-11, 14-25; 1964, c. 386, § 14.1-13; 1970, c. 260; 1998, c. 872, § 2.1-38.3; 2001, c. 844.)

§ 2.2-102. Personal staff as commander in chief. — The personal staff of the Governor and commander in chief shall consist of the Adjutant General of the Commonwealth and any additional aides detailed by the Governor from the commissioned personnel of the National Guard of Virginia, the officers reserve corps or the naval reserve corps, or officers of the army or navy of the United States, retired or former officers of the army or navy of the United States, which detail shall operate for the time being as a commission to each officer so detailed as aide-de-camp. Commissions as military aides to the Governor shall be issued by the Secretary of the Commonwealth with the rank the Governor deems appropriate and shall continue in effect at the pleasure of the Governor during his term in office. The commissions shall be honorary in nature and shall not constitute a commission in the militia of the Commonwealth or entitle the recipient to any pay or benefits. The insignia to be worn by aides when performing their duties shall be prescribed by the Governor. No officer so detailed shall be compelled to serve. Officers so detailed shall not be relieved from their ordinary duties, except when actually on duty with the Governor. No officer shall be detailed under this section unless he is a qualified voter of the Commonwealth. In addition, the Governor may appoint and commission with the rank of colonel as a personal aide, the Clerk of the House of Delegates. (Code 1950, § 2-36; 1958, c. 119; 1966, c. 677, § 2.1-40; 1984, c. 17; 2001, c. 844.)

§ 2.2-103. Authority to formulate executive branch policies; chief officer for personnel administration and planning and budget. — A. Except as otherwise provided by the Constitution or law, the Governor shall have the authority and responsibility for the formulation and administration of the policies of the executive branch, including resolution of policy and administrative conflicts between and among agencies.

B. The Governor shall be the Chief Personnel Officer of the Commonwealth. He shall direct the execution of Chapter 29 (§ 2.2-2900 et seq.). The Governor may employ personnel assistants and employees necessary to carry out Chapter 29 (§ 2.2-2900 et seq.). The Governor shall have the following powers and duties relating to state personnel administration:

1. Establish and maintain a classification plan for the service of the Commonwealth, and from time to time, make such amendments as may be necessary. The classification plan shall provide for the grouping of all positions in classes based upon the respective duties, authority, and responsibilities. Each position in the service of the Commonwealth shall be allocated to the appropriate class title.

2. Establish and administer a compensation plan for all employees, and from time to time make such amendments as may be necessary. The compensation plan shall be uniform; and for each class of positions there shall be set forth a minimum and a maximum rate of compensation and any necessary or equitable intermediate rates.

3. Adopt necessary rules, not in conflict with Chapter 29 (§ 2.2-2900 et seq.), to provide for the administration of the duties imposed by Chapter 29 (§ 2.2-2900 et seq.), and to govern minimum hours of work, attendance regulations, leaves of absences for employees and the order and manner in which layoffs shall be made.

C. The Governor shall be the chief planning and budget officer of the Commonwealth. (Code 1950, §§ 2-46, 2-81; 1966, cc. 55, 677, §§ 2.1-52, 2.1-113; 1975, c. 390; 1976, cc. 725, 760, 761 §§ 2.1-41.1, 2.1-114.2, 2.1-387; 1978, c. 846; 1984, c. 720; 2001, c. 844.)

§ 2.2-104. Delegation of powers. — The Governor may designate and empower any secretary or other officer in the executive branch of state government who is required to be confirmed by the General Assembly or either house thereof, to perform without approval, ratification, or other action by the Governor any function that is vested in the Governor by law, or which such officer is required or authorized by law to perform only with or subject to the approval, ratification of the Governor; however nothing contained in this section shall relieve the Governor of his responsibility in office for the acts of any secretary or officer designated by him to perform such functions. Any designation or authorization under this section shall be (i) in the form of a written executive order, (ii) subject to the terms, conditions, and limitations the Governor deems advisable, and (iii) revocable in whole or in part at any time by the Governor. (1976, c. 731, § 2.1-39.1; 2001, c. 844.)

§ 2.2-105. Appointments to office; effect of refusal to confirm by the General Assembly. — No person appointed to any office by the Governor, whose appointment is subject to confirmation by the General Assembly, shall enter upon, or continue in, office after the General Assembly has refused to confirm his appointment. Nor shall such person be eligible for reappointment during the recess of the General Assembly to fill the vacancy caused by the refusal to confirm. (Code 1950, § 2-35; 1966, c. 677, § 2.1-39; 2001, c. 844.)

§ 2.2-106. Appointment of agency heads; severance. — A. Notwithstanding any provision of law to the contrary, the Governor shall appoint the administrative head of each agency of the executive branch of state government except the:

1. Executive Director of the Virginia Port Authority;
2. Director of the State Council of Higher Education for Virginia;
3. Executive Director of the Department of Game and Inland Fisheries;
4. Executive Director of the Jamestown-Yorktown Foundation;
5. Executive Director of the Motor Vehicle Dealer Board;
6. Librarian of Virginia;
7. Administrator of the Commonwealth's Attorneys' Services Council;
8. Executive Director of the Virginia Housing Development Authority;
9. Executive Director of the Board of Accountancy; and
10. Chief Information Officer of the Commonwealth.

However, the manner of selection of those heads of agencies chosen as set forth in the Constitution of Virginia shall continue without change. Each administrative head and Secretary appointed by the Governor pursuant to this section shall (i) be subject to confirmation by the General Assembly, (ii) have the professional qualifications prescribed by law, and (iii) serve at the pleasure of the Governor.

B. As part of the confirmation process for each administrative head and Secretary, the Secretary of the Commonwealth shall provide copies of the resumes and statements of economic interests filed pursuant to § 2.2-3117 to the chairs of the House of Delegates and Senate Committees on Privileges and Elections. For appointments made before January 1, copies shall be provided to the chairs within 30 days of the appointment or by January 7 whichever time is earlier; and for appointments made after January 1 through the regular session of that year, copies shall be provided to the chairs within seven days of the appointment. Each appointee shall be available for interviews by the Committees on Privileges and Elections or other applicable standing committee. For the purposes of this section and § 2.2-107, here shall be a joint subcommittee of the House of Delegates and Senate Committees on Privileges and Elections consisting of five members of the House Committee and three members of the Senate Committee appointed by the respective chairs of the committees to review the resumes and statements of economic interests of gubernatorial appointees. The members of the House of Delegates shall be appointed in accordance with the principles of proportional representation contained in the Rules of the House of Delegates. No appointment confirmed by the General Assembly shall be subject to challenge by reason of a failure to comply with the provisions of this paragraph pertaining to the confirmation process.

C. For the purpose of this section, "agency" includes all administrative units established by law or by executive order that are not (i) arms of the legislative or judicial branches of government; (ii) institutions of higher education as classified under §§ 23-253.7, 22.1-346, 23-14, 23-252, and; (iii) regional planning districts, regional transportation authorities or districts, or regional sanitation districts; and (iv) assigned by law to other departments or agencies, not including assignments to secretaries under Article 7 (§ 2.2-215 et seq.) of Chapter 2 of this title.

D. Severance benefits provided to any departing agency head, whether or not appointed by the Governor, shall be publicly announced by the appointing authority prior to such departure. (1977, c. 542, § 2.1-41.2; 1979, c. 294; 1981, c. 589; 1983, c. 298; 1984, c. 104; 1986, c. 565; 1994, c. 661; 1995, cc. 767, 816; 1996, c. 812; 1998, c. 427; 2000, cc. 382, 400; 2001, cc. 832, 844; 2003, cc. 981, 1021; 2005, cc. 803, 938; 2006, c. 254.)

Editor's note. — Acts 2001, c. 832 amended § 2.1-41.2, from which this section is derived. Pursuant to § 30-152, Acts 2001, c. 832 has been given effect in this section as set out above. The 2001 amendment by c. 832, inserted subdivision 9.

For provisions of Acts 2003, cc. 981 and 1021, cls. 4 to 16, reflecting the intent of the General Assembly to provide for the consolidation of the procurement and operational functions of information technology for state agencies in a single agency, and related transitional and other provisions, see the Editor's note at § 2.2-2005.

§ 2.2-107. Appointment of members of commissions, boards, and other collegial bodies. — Except as provided in the Constitution of Virginia, or where the manner of selection of members of boards and commissions is by election by the General Assembly, or as provided in Title 3.1 or § 54.1-901, but notwithstanding any other provision of law to the contrary, the Governor shall appoint all members of boards, commissions, councils or other collegial bodies created by the General Assembly in the executive branch of state government to terms of office as prescribed by law. Each member appointed pursuant to this section shall be subject to confirmation by the General Assembly and shall have the professional qualifications prescribed by law.

As part of the confirmation process for each gubernatorial appointee, the Secretary of the Commonwealth shall provide copies of the resume and statement of economic interests filed pursuant to § 2.2-3117 or 2.2-3118, as appropriate, to the chairs of the House of Delegates and Senate Committees on Privileges and Elections. For the purposes of this section and § 2.2-106, there shall be a joint subcommittee of the House of Delegates and Senate Committees on Privileges and Elections consisting of five members of the House Committee and three members of the Senate Committee appointed by the respective chairs of the committees to review the resumes and statements of economic interests of gubernatorial appointees. The members of the House of Delegates shall be appointed in accordance with the principles of proportional representation contained in the Rules of the House of Delegates. No appointment confirmed by the General Assembly shall be subject to challenge by reason of a failure to comply with the provisions of this paragraph pertaining to the confirmation process. (1977, c. 447, § 2.1-42.1; 1978, c. 834; 2001, c. 844; 2005, cc. 803, 938.)

Cross references. — See Va. Const., Art. V, § 8.

Editor's note. — Effective October 1, 2008, the reference to "Title 3.1" in the first paragraph should read "Title 3.2."

§ 2.2-108. Removal of members of certain boards, commissions, etc. — A. Notwithstanding any provision of law to the contrary, the Governor may remove from office for malfeasance, misfeasance, incompetence, or gross neglect of duty any member of the board of any public institution of higher education or other educational institution in Virginia, and fill the vacancy resulting from the removal. Each appointment to fill a vacancy shall be subject to confirmation by the General Assembly.

B. Notwithstanding any provision of law to the contrary, the Governor may remove from office for malfeasance, misfeasance, incompetence, misconduct, neglect of duty, absenteeism, conflict of interests, failure to carry out the policies of the Commonwealth as established in the Constitution or by the General Assembly, or refusal to carry out a lawful directive of the Governor any member of any board, commission, council or other collegial body established by the General Assembly in the executive branch of state government except those boards provided for in subsection A, and fill the vacancy resulting from the removal subject to confirmation by the General Assembly.

C. The Governor shall set forth in a written public statement his reasons for removing any member pursuant to this section at the time the removal occurs.

The Governor shall be the sole judge of the sufficiency of the cause for removal as set forth in this section. (Code 1950, § 2-39; 1966, c. 677, § 2.1-43; 1977, c. 446; 1988, c. 765; 2001, c. 844.)

§ 2.2-109. Requiring appearances by officers, etc., and production of records, etc.; issuance of subpoenas and other writs; employment of accountants. — Whenever the Governor deems it necessary and proper, he may require any state officer, superintendent, board, or employee to appear before him, and he may also require the production of any official books, accounts, vouchers, and other papers relating to their offices and duties. The Governor may issue subpoenas or other writs for the purpose of enforcing the provisions of this section. The Governor may employ accountants to properly inspect such records, vouchers, or other papers. (Code 1950, § 2-40; 1956, c. 424; 1966, c. 677, § 2.1-44; 2001, c. 844.)

Cross references. — See Va. Const., Art. V, § 8.

§ 2.2-109.01. Signed statements required from appointees. — For purposes of this section:

"Appointed position" means a position appointed by the Governor or other appointing authority in accordance with law.

"Covered appointee" means any person serving in an appointed position who is eligible for severance benefits under the Workforce Transition Act of 1995 (§ 2.2-3200 et seq.), including but not limited to, any (i) officer, (ii) agency head, or (iii) member of a board, commission, council, or other collegial body.

Upon initial appointment or reappointment, the Governor or other appointing authority, or their designee, shall obtain a signed statement from each covered appointee providing that such person has read and understands the severance benefits for which he is eligible under the Workforce Transition Act of 1995. The Governor or other appointing authority, or their designee shall provide all such statements to the Secretary of the Commonwealth. The Secretary shall provide for such statements to be retained in the records of the Commonwealth. (2006, cc. 813, 902.)

§ 2.2-110. Officers of Commonwealth and its institutions to make reports to Governor. — The officers of the executive branch of state government and superintendents and boards of state institutions, shall make to the Governor written reports at the times prescribed by law or at any time the Governor may require on any subject relating to their offices and institutions. The reports shall be in a form and contain such information as the Governor may require. The reports shall be filed in the office of the Secretary of the Commonwealth, and under his supervision, summarized and recorded in books kept for the purpose. (Code 1950, § 2-38; 1966, c. 677, § 2.1-42; 2001, c. 844.)

§ 2.2-111. Suits, actions, etc., by Governor. — A. In order to protect or preserve the interests or legal rights of the Commonwealth and its citizens, the Governor may, by and with the advice of the Attorney General, institute any action, suit, motion or other proceeding, in the name of the Commonwealth, in the Supreme Court of the United States or any other court or tribunal in which such action, suit, motion or other proceeding may be properly commenced and prosecuted.

B. In accordance with subsection A and pursuant to his duty to protect or preserve the general welfare of the citizens of the Commonwealth, the Governor may institute any action, suit, motion or other proceeding on behalf of its citizens, in the name of the Commonwealth acting in its capacity as parens patriae, where he has determined that existing legal procedures fail to adequately protect existing legal rights and interests of such citizens. (Code 1950, § 2-43; 1966, c. 677, § 2.1-49; 1975, c. 241; 2001, c. 844.)

CASE NOTES

Editor's note. — The case below was decided under former Title 2.1 or prior provisions.

Standing to challenge discontinuation of artificially administered hydration and nutrition. — A challenge to the Governor's standing to file an action to prevent the discontinuation of the artificial administration of hydration and nutrition to an individual in a persistent vegetative state was totally without merit, as this section and § 54.1-2986 provided that standing. Gilmore v. Finn, 259 Va. 448, 527 S.E.2d 426 (2000).

§ 2.2-112. To whom return on warrant of Governor to be made. — Any officer to whom any order or warrant of the Governor is directed shall make return to the Secretary of the Commonwealth, who shall preserve it in his office. (Code 1950, § 2-44; 1966, c. 677, § 2.1-50; 2001, c. 844.)

§ 2.2-113. Temporary suspension of state mandates. — A. The Governor may suspend, temporarily and for a period not to exceed one year, any mandate, or portion thereof, prescribed by any unit of the executive branch of state government on a county, city, town, or other unit of local government upon a finding that it faces fiscal stress and the suspension of the mandate or portion thereof would help alleviate the fiscal hardship.

B. No application shall be made by the locality until approved by resolution of the governing body.

C. At the time of application, the following information shall be published in the Virginia Register: (i) the name of the petitioning locality, (ii) the mandate or portion thereof requested to be suspended, (iii) the impact of the suspension of the mandate on the ability of the local government to deliver services, (iv) the estimated reduction in current budget from the suspension, and (v) the time period requested for suspension. Publication in the Virginia Register shall occur at least 20 days in advance of any suspension by the Governor.

D. No later than January 1 of each year, the Governor shall submit to the General Assembly a report that identifies each petitioning locality, the mandate or portion thereof for which suspension was sought, and the response provided to the locality.

E. Nothing in this section shall apply to the Department of Education.

In making a determination of fiscal stress, the Governor may consider, but is not limited to, the following factors: any changes in anticipated revenue, income distribution of residents, revenue effort, revenue capacity, and changes in local population and employment levels. (1991, c. 638, § 2.1-51.5:1; 1993, c. 230; 1994, c. 158; 2001, c. 844; 2003, c. 169.)

§ 2.2-114. Coordination of official communications with federal and foreign governments. — The Governor may adopt regulations for coordination of official communications on behalf of the Commonwealth by any officer, agency or employee of the Commonwealth with the government of the United States, another state or foreign nation. Subject to the ultimate authority of the General Assembly to prescribe the policies of the Commonwealth and within the framework of policy established by the General Assembly, all communications shall be at the policy direction of the Governor; however, communications by the General Assembly or the Supreme Court of Virginia with the legislature or the judiciary, respectively, of the United States, another state or foreign nation, shall be at the discretion of the General Assembly and the Supreme

Court of Virginia. Actions taken under § 2.2-611 shall be subject to the provisions of this section. (1976, c. 704, § 2.1-38.2; 2001, c. 844.)

§ 2.2-115. Governor's Development Opportunity Fund. — As used in this section, unless the context requires otherwise:

"New job" means employment of an indefinite duration, created as the direct result of the private investment, for which the firm pays the wages and standard fringe benefits for its employee, requiring a minimum of either (i) 35 hours of the employee's time a week for the entire normal year of the firm's operations, which "normal year" must consist of at least 48 weeks or (ii) 1,680 hours per year.

Seasonal or temporary positions, positions created when a job function is shifted from an existing location in the Commonwealth to the location of the economic development project, positions with suppliers, and multiplier or spin-off jobs shall not qualify as new jobs. The term "new job" shall include positions with contractors provided that all requirements included within the definition of the term are met.

"Prevailing average wage" means that amount determined by the Virginia Employment Commission to be the average wage paid workers in the city or county of the Commonwealth where the economic development project is located. The prevailing average wage shall be determined without regard to any fringe benefits.

"Private investment" means the private investment required under this section.

A. There is created the Governor's Development Opportunity Fund (the Fund) to be used by the Governor to attract economic development prospects and secure the expansion of existing industry in the Commonwealth. The Fund shall consist of any funds appropriated to it by the general appropriation act and revenue from any other source, public or private. The Fund shall be established on the books of the Comptroller, and any funds remaining in the Fund at the end of a biennium shall not revert to the general fund but shall remain in the Fund. Interest earned on the Fund shall be credited to the Fund. The Governor shall report to the chairmen of the House Committees on Appropriations and Finance, and the Senate Committee on Finance as funds are awarded in accordance with this section.

B. Funds shall be awarded from the Fund by the Governor as grants or loans to political subdivisions. Loans shall be approved by the Governor and made in accordance with guidelines established by the Virginia Economic Development Partnership and approved by the Comptroller. Loans shall be interest-free unless otherwise determined by the Governor and shall be repaid to the Fund. The Governor may establish the interest rate to be charged; otherwise, any interest charged shall be at market rates as determined by the State Treasurer and shall be indicative of the duration of the loan. The Virginia Economic Development Partnership shall be responsible for monitoring repayment of such loans and reporting the receivables to the Comptroller as required.

Beginning with the five fiscal years from fiscal year 2006-2007 through fiscal year 2010-2011, and for every five fiscal years' period thereafter, in general, no less than one-third of the moneys appropriated to the Fund in every such five-year period shall be awarded to counties and cities having an annual average unemployment rate that is greater than the final statewide average unemployment rate for the calendar year that immediately precedes the calendar year of the award. However, if such one-third requirement will not be met because economic development prospects in such counties and cities are unable to fulfill the applicable minimum private investment and new jobs requirements set forth in this section, then any funds remaining in the Fund at the end of the five-year period that would have otherwise been awarded to such counties and cities shall be made available for awards in the next five fiscal years' period.

C. Funds may be used for public and private utility extension or capacity development on and off site; public and private installation, extension, or capacity development of high-speed or broadband Internet access, whether on or off site; road, rail, or other transportation access costs beyond the funding capability of existing programs; site acquisition; grading, drainage, paving, and any other activity required to prepare a site for construction; construction or build-out of publicly owned buildings; training; or grants or loans to an industrial development authority, housing and redevelopment authority, or other political subdivision for purposes directly relating to any of the foregoing. However, in no case shall funds from the Fund be used, directly or indirectly, to pay or guarantee the payment for any rental, lease, license, or other contractual right to the use of any property.

It shall be the policy of the Commonwealth that moneys in the Fund shall not be used for any economic development project in which a business relocates or expands its operations in one or more Virginia localities and simultaneously closes its operations or substantially reduces the number of its employees in another Virginia locality. The Secretary of Commerce and Trade shall enforce this policy and for any exception thereto shall promptly provide written notice to the Chairmen of the Senate Finance and House Appropriations Committees, which notice shall include a justification for any exception to such policy.

D. 1. Except as provided in this subsection, no grant or loan shall be awarded from the Fund unless the project involves a minimum private investment of $10,000,000 and creates 100 new jobs for which the average wage, excluding fringe benefits, is no less than the prevailing average wage. In localities with a population between 50,000 and 100,000, the minimum private investment shall be $5,000,000, creating 50 new jobs for which the average wage, excluding fringe benefits, is no less than the prevailing average wage. In localities with a population of 50,000 or less, the minimum private investment shall be $2,500,000, creating 25 new jobs for which the average wage, excluding fringe benefits, is no less than the prevailing average wage. Central cities or urban cores shall be treated for eligibility purposes the same as communities with a population between 50,000 and 100,000. For projects for which the average wage of the new jobs created, excluding fringe benefits, is at least twice the prevailing average wage for that locality or region, the Governor shall have the discretion to require no less than one-half the number of new jobs as set forth for that locality in this subsection.

2. Notwithstanding the provisions of subdivision D 1, if a project is to be located in a county or city whose annual average unemployment rate for the most recent calendar year is greater than the final statewide average unemployment rate for the most recent calendar year, a grant or loan may be awarded from the Fund if the average wage of the new jobs, excluding fringe benefits, will be no less than 85% of the prevailing average wage. In addition, for projects in such counties and cities, the Governor may award a grant or loan for a project paying less than 85% of the prevailing average wage but still providing customary employee benefits, only after the Secretary of Commerce and Trade has made a written finding that the economic circumstances in the area are sufficiently distressed (i.e., high unemployment or underemployment and negative economic forecasts) that assistance to the locality to attract the project is nonetheless justified. However, the minimum private investment and number of new jobs required to be created as set forth in this subsection shall still be a condition of eligibility for an award from the Fund. Such written finding shall promptly be provided to the Chairmen of the Senate Finance and House Appropriations Committees.

3. Notwithstanding the provisions of subdivision 1, if a project is to be located in a locality whose unemployment rate is one and one half times or more the state average, the minimum private investment shall be adjusted to $7,500,000 and the minimum number of new jobs created shall be adjusted to 75 jobs for which the average wage, excluding fringe benefits, is no less than the prevailing average wage. In localities with a population between 50,000 and 100,000, the minimum private investment shall be $3,500,000, creating 35 new jobs for which the average wage, excluding fringe benefits, is no less than the prevailing average wage. In localities with a population of 50,000 or less, the minimum private investment shall be $1,500,000, creating 15 new jobs for which the average wage, excluding fringe benefits, is no less than the prevailing average wage. Localities qualifying under this subdivision that have created Regional Industrial Facilities Authorities pursuant to § 15.2-6402, shall be eligible at the lowest investment and job creation threshold of any locality in that Authority.

E. 1. The Virginia Economic Development Partnership shall assist the Governor in developing objective guidelines and criteria that shall be used in awarding grants or making loans from the Fund. The guidelines and criteria shall include provisions for geographic diversity and a cap on the amount of funds to be provided to any individual project. In developing the guidelines and criteria, the Virginia Economic Development Partnership shall use the measure for Fiscal Stress published by the Commission on Local Government of the Department of Housing and Community Development for the locality in which the project is located or will be located as one method of determining the amount of assistance a locality shall receive from the Fund.

2. a. Notwithstanding any provision in this section or in the guidelines, each political subdivision that receives a grant or loan from the Fund shall enter into a contract with each business beneficiary of funds from the Fund. A person or entity shall be a business beneficiary of funds from the Fund if grant or loan moneys awarded from the Fund by the Governor are paid to a political subdivision and (i) subsequently distributed by the political subdivision to the person or entity or (ii) used by the political subdivision for the benefit of the person or entity but never distributed to the person or entity.

b. The contract between the political subdivision and the business beneficiary shall provide in detail (i) the fair market value of all funds that the Commonwealth has committed to provide, (ii) the fair market value of all matching funds (or in-kind match) that the political subdivision has agreed to provide, (iii) how funds committed by the Commonwealth (including but not limited to funds from the Fund committed by the Governor) and funds that the political subdivision has agreed to provide are to be spent, (iv) the minimum private investment to be made and the number of new jobs to be created agreed to by the business beneficiary, (v) the average wage (excluding fringe benefits) agreed to be paid in the new jobs, (vi) the prevailing average wage, and (vii) the formula, means, or processes agreed to be used for measuring compliance with the minimum private investment and new jobs requirements.

The contract shall state the date by which the agreed upon private investment and new job requirements shall be met by the business beneficiary of funds from the Fund and may provide for the political subdivision to grant up to a 15-month extension of such date if deemed appropriate by the political subdivision subsequent to the execution of the contract. Any extension of such date granted by the political subdivision shall be in writing and promptly delivered to the business beneficiary, and the political subdivision shall simultaneously provide a copy of the extension to the Virginia Economic Development Partnership.

The contract shall provide that if the private investment and new job contractual requirements are not met by the expiration of the date stipulated in the contract, including any extension granted by the political subdivision, the business beneficiary shall be liable to the political subdivision for repayment of a portion of the funds provided under the contract. The contract shall include a formula for purposes of determining the portion of such funds to be repaid. The formula shall, in part, be based upon the fair market value of all funds that have been provided by the Commonwealth and the political subdivision and the extent to which the business beneficiary has met the private investment and new job contractual requirements. Any such funds repaid to the political subdivision that relate to the award from the Governor's Development Opportunity Fund shall promptly be paid over by the political subdivision to the Commonwealth by payment remitted to the State Treasurer. Upon receipt by the State Treasurer of such payment, the Comptroller shall deposit such repaid funds into the Governor's Development Opportunity Fund.

c. The contract shall be amended to reflect changes in the funds committed by the Commonwealth or agreed to be provided by the political subdivision.

3. Notwithstanding any provision in this section or in the guidelines, prior to executing any such contract with a business beneficiary, the political subdivision shall provide a copy of the proposed contract to the Attorney General. The Attorney General shall review the proposed contract (i) for enforceability as to its provisions and (ii) to ensure that it is in appropriate, legal form. The Attorney General shall provide any written suggestions to the political subdivision within seven days of his receipt of the copy of the contract. The Attorney General's suggestions shall be limited to the enforceability of the contract's provisions and the legal form of the contract.

4. Notwithstanding any provision in this section or in the guidelines, a political subdivision shall not expend, distribute, pledge, use as security, or otherwise use any award from the Fund unless and until such contract as described herein is executed with the business beneficiary.

F. Within the 30 days immediately following June 30 and December 30 of each year, the Governor shall provide a report to the chairmen of the House Committees on Appropriations and Finance and the Senate Committee on Finance which shall include, but is not limited to, the following information regarding grants and loans awarded from the Fund during the immediately preceding six-month period for economic development projects: the name of the company that is the business beneficiary of the grant or loan and the type of business in which it engages; the location (county, city, or town) of the project; the amount of the grant or loan committed from the Fund and the amount of all other funds committed by the Commonwealth from other sources and the purpose for which such grants, loans, or other funds will be used; the amount of all moneys or funds agreed to be provided by political subdivisions and the purposes for which they will be used; the number of new jobs agreed to be created by the business beneficiary; the amount of investment in the project agreed to be made by the business beneficiary; the timetable for the completion of the project and new jobs created; the prevailing average wage; and the average wage (excluding fringe benefits) agreed to be paid in the new jobs.

G. The Governor shall provide grants and commitments from the Fund in an amount not to exceed the dollar amount contained in the Fund. If the Governor commits funds for years beyond the fiscal years covered under the existing appropriation act, the State Treasurer shall set aside and reserve the funds the Governor has committed, and the funds shall remain in the Fund for those future fiscal years. No grant or loan shall be payable in the years beyond the existing appropriation act unless the funds are currently available in the Fund. (1996, cc. 590, 598, 859, § 2.1-51.6:5; 1999, cc. 787, 816; 2001, c. 844; 2006, cc. 251, 890; 2007, c. 654.)

Editor's note. — Acts 2006, c. 890, cl. 2, provides: "That the Virginia Economic Development Partnership shall assist the Governor in updating the current guidelines for the Governor's Development Opportunity Fund to incorporate the provisions of this act. The Governor shall provide a copy of the updated guidelines to the House Committees on Appropriations and Finance and the Senate Committee on Finance by November 1, 2006."

Acts 2006, c. 890, cl. 3, provides: "That, by August 1, 2006, the Virginia Economic Development Partnership shall develop the legal form of the contract described under this act, which shall include standard provisions, as appropriate, for the provisions of subdivision E 2 b of § 2.2-115 of the Code of Virginia. A copy of the contract form shall be provided to the Attorney General by such date. The Attorney General shall review the contract form and shall make any written recommendations to the Partnership by August 15, 2006.

"The Partnership shall develop the final legal form by August 31, 2006, and shall provide a copy of the same to the House Committees on Appropriations and Finance and the Senate Committee on Finance by such date. The final legal form, including standard provisions, shall be used in economic development contracts between political subdivisions and business beneficiaries of funds from the Governor's Development Opportunity Fund."

Acts 2006, c. 890, cl. 4, provides: "That the Virginia Economic Development Partnership shall develop and implement a plan with a primary objective of attracting economic development prospects to Southside and Southwestern Virginia. The plan shall promote such areas to economic development prospects. The Partnership shall update the plan as needed."

Acts 2006, c. 890, cl. 5, provides: "That the provisions of this act shall be applicable to economic development projects initially approved by the Governor for an award from the Governor's Development Opportunity Fund on or after July 1, 2006."

The 2007 amendments. — The 2007 amendment by c. 654 added subdivision D 3.

§ 2.2-116. Service on board of national tobacco trust entity. — The Governor may serve in his official capacity on the board of directors of any entity established to ensure the implementation in the Commonwealth of a national tobacco trust established to provide payments to tobacco growers and tobacco quota owners to ameliorate adverse economic consequences resulting from a national settlement of states' claims against tobacco manufacturers. (2000, c. 1048, § 2.1-41.3; 2001, c. 844.)

§ 2.2-117. Governor to administer anti-crime partnership program. — It shall be the responsibility of the Governor to establish and administer an anti-crime partnership program within the Commonwealth and to authorize, direct, and coordinate existing and future activities of agencies of the Commonwealth in such program. The Governor, in addition to all other duties and responsibilities conferred on him by the Constitution and laws of the Commonwealth, may enter into written anti-crime partnership agreements with political subdivisions of the Commonwealth to assist and enhance their ability to reduce the incidence of violent and drug-related crime and fear of crime.

In addition to such other terms and conditions to which the parties agree, each partnership agreement shall (i) provide for the creation of a partnership committee to advise and direct the partnership, (ii) enumerate the responsibilities of the Commonwealth and the political subdivisions involved, and (iii) state the duration of the partnership, providing for dates on which the partnership will begin and end.

The Governor may provide to anti-crime partnerships established pursuant to this section such technical and personnel resources of the Commonwealth as he determines and such financial resources as provided in the general appropriation act. (1992, c. 663, § 2.1-51.6:3; 2001, c. 844.)

§ 2.2-118. Governor to administer substance abuse prevention program. — It shall be the responsibility of the Governor to administer the substance abuse prevention program within the Commonwealth and to authorize, direct, and coordinate activities of agencies of the Commonwealth in such program. The Governor is hereby empowered to establish an office of substance abuse prevention within the office of the Governor to assist in the coordination of the substance abuse prevention activities of the Commonwealth, review substance abuse prevention program expenditures by agencies of the Commonwealth, and determine the direction and appropriateness of such expenditures. The Governor shall cooperate with federal, state and local agencies, private and public agencies, interested organizations, and individuals in order to prevent substance abuse within the Commonwealth. The Governor shall report annually by December 1 of each year to the General Assembly on the activities of the office. (2000, cc. 90, 249, § 2.1-51.6:6; 2001, c. 844.)

§ 2.2-119. Governor to administer highway safety program and secure benefits to Commonwealth under federal Highway Safety Act of 1966. — It shall be the responsibility of the Governor to administer the highway safety program within the Commonwealth and to authorize, direct and coordinate existing and future activities of agencies of the Commonwealth and its political subdivisions in such program. The Governor, in addition to all other duties and responsibilities conferred on him by the Constitution and laws of the Commonwealth, may contract and do all other things necessary on behalf of the Commonwealth to secure the full benefits available to the Commonwealth under the federal Highway Safety Act of 1966, and any amendments thereto, and in so doing, cooperate with federal and state agencies, private and public agencies, interested organizations, and individuals, to effectuate the purposes of that act and any amendments thereto, and the highway safety program within the Commonwealth.

The Governor shall be the official having the ultimate responsibility for dealing with the United States government with respect to programs and activities pursuant to the federal Highway Safety Act of 1966 and any amendments thereto. To that end he shall be responsible for related activities of any and all departments and agencies of the Commonwealth and its political subdivisions. He may designate such persons, agencies and commissions to assist him in coordinating the activities contemplated under the federal act, this section, and the state's highway safety program. (1968, c. 160, § 2.1-51.6; 2001, c. 844.)

§ 2.2-120. Powers with respect to state-owned motor vehicles. — A. The Governor may prescribe, by general or special executive orders, regulations for the purchase, use, storage, maintenance and repair of all motor vehicles owned by the Commonwealth, and in the possession of any state department, institution or agency where his supervision is not forbidden by the Constitution.

B. The Governor may use any building or land owned by the Commonwealth, and not required to be used for other purposes, for storing and garaging state-owned motor vehicles. He may employ watchmen or guards, mechanics and other labor to repair and service such vehicles, and provide for the purchase of gasoline, oil and other supplies for such vehicles, and allocate among the various departments and agencies using such vehicles their proportionate part of the cost of repairs, servicing, gasoline, oil, and other supplies.

C. The Governor may create in the State Treasurer's office a special fund to be reflected on the books of the Comptroller, out of which all costs and expenses incurred pursuant to this section shall be paid. All allocations of costs and charges for repairing and servicing motor vehicles made against any institution, agency, or department shall, when approved by the department head, be paid into the special fund by interdepartmental transfers on the Comptroller's books. All funds so paid or transferred into the special fund are appropriated for the purposes of this section and shall be paid out on warrants of the

Comptroller issued upon vouchers signed by the state officer or employee designated by the Governor.

D. The Governor may, by executive order or regulation, impose upon the Director of the Department of Planning and Budget, or any other agency of the executive branch of the state government, any or all administrative duties pertaining to the administration of this section.

E. If any state officer, agent or employee fails to comply with any rule, regulation or order of the Governor made pursuant to this section, the Comptroller shall, upon order of the Governor, refuse to issue any warrant on account of expenses incurred, or to be incurred in the purchase, operation, maintenance, or repair of any motor vehicle now or to be in the possession or under the control of such officer, agent or employee, or the Governor may order some state officer or agent to take possession of the vehicle and transfer it to some other department, institution, agency, officer, agent or employee, or to make such other disposition as the Governor may direct. (Code 1950, § 2-42; 1966, c. 677, § 2.1-47; 2001, c. 844.)

§ **2.2-121. Approval of purchase of passenger-type automobile; transfer and valuation of surplus vehicles.** — No passenger-type automobile shall be purchased by the Commonwealth or any officer or employee on behalf of the Commonwealth without the prior written approval of the Governor. The Governor may transfer surplus motor vehicles among the departments, institutions and agencies, and the Director of the Department of Accounts shall determine the value of the surplus equipment for the purpose of maintaining the financial accounts of the departments, agencies and institutions affected by such transfers. (1954, c. 365, § 2-42.1; 1966, c. 677, § 2.1-48; 2001, c. 844.)

§ **2.2-122. Commercial use of seals of the Commonwealth.** — A. Notwithstanding the provisions of § 1-505, the Governor may authorize the use of the seals of the Commonwealth for commercial purposes upon a finding that such use promotes an appropriate image of the Commonwealth, its heritage and its history, and that such use is carried out in accordance with the laws of the Commonwealth. In considering whether the use of the seals in association with a product promotes an appropriate image of the Commonwealth, preference shall be given to products that (i) preserve traditional methods of production, including handcrafting techniques, (ii) enhance public appreciation of the Commonwealth's aesthetic values, and (iii) incorporate workmanship and materials of the highest quality. A prospective licensee shall be deemed qualified to protect and promote the image of the Commonwealth if it holds licenses to produce products associated with museums and sites of major historical importance in the Commonwealth, including but not limited to homes of Presidents of the United States and restored historical areas.

B. The Secretary of the Commonwealth and the Director of the Division of Purchases and Supply shall assist the Governor in determining the appropriateness of (i) any contract entered into for the commercial use of the seals of the Commonwealth, (ii) the product intended to be sold, (iii) any marketing activities undertaken to promote the sale of the product, and (iv) the pricing structure, including royalties to be paid to the Commonwealth for such use and sale. Any such royalties paid to the Commonwealth shall be deposited in the general fund. (1995, c. 295, § 2.1-51.6:4; 2001, c. 844; 2005, c. 839.)

§ **2.2-123. Authority over rooms and space in public buildings.** — Rooms and space in public buildings at the seat of government, other than the Capitol, whether the rooms or space are occupied, may be vacated, assigned, and reassigned by the Governor to such departments, divisions, agencies, and officers of the Commonwealth as the Governor deems proper. The Governor shall not vacate, assign or reassign any rooms or space occupied by the Supreme Court, the General Assembly, the State Corporation Commission or other independent agencies, without the consent and approval of such bodies. (Code 1950, § 2-41; 1966, c. 677, § 2.1-46; 2001, c. 844.)

§ **2.2-124. Regulation of athletic leaves of absence.** — A. The Governor shall establish rules to provide for the regulation of athletic leaves of absence for state employees as follows:

1. A public employee who qualifies as a member of the United States team for athletic competition on the Pan American or Olympic level in a sport contested in such competition may be granted leave of absence upon approval of the appropriate cabinet secretary without loss or reduction of pay, time, annual leave, or efficiency rating for the purpose of preparing for and engaging in competition on such levels. In no event shall the paid leave under this subdivision exceed the period of the official training camp and competition combined or ninety calendar days a year, whichever is less. A public employee who qualifies and applies as a member of the United States team for athletic competition on the international level other than the Pan American or Olympic games may be granted a leave of absence without pay.

2. A public employee who qualifies and applies for an athletic leave of absence under the provisions of this subdivision shall notify his employer of his desire for such leave at least thirty days before the effective date of the leave; however, if the official training camp for international or Olympic games commences less than thirty days after the employee's selection as a member of the United States team, the employee shall notify his employer of his desire for athletic leave immediately upon his selection as a member of such team.

3. All or any portion of the approved athletic leave of absence provided for in this subdivision may be canceled retroactively by the employer if the employee does not participate in the training or competition for approved reasons or for reasons that are unrelated to the physical and/or mental ability to compete.

4. If the absence of a state employee necessitates the hiring of a substitute during the employee's absence, the Commonwealth shall reimburse the governmental branch, department, agency, board, institution, or commission of the Commonwealth for actual costs incurred in employing the substitute.

B. As used in this section, unless the context requires a different meaning:

"Public employee" means any full-time employee of the Commonwealth or of any branch of the state government, of any executive department of the Commonwealth, or of any agency, board, institution or commission of the State; however, no elected official shall be considered a public employee for purposes of this section.

"Athlete" means an individual who is dedicated to improving a skill or skills in a particular physical exercise, sport, or game requiring strength, agility, or stamina and for whom this effort does not result in financial gain or remuneration.

"International or Olympic competition" means any athletic competition involving athletes from two or more nation-states. (1981, c. 335, § 2.1-114.2:1; 2001, c. 844.)

§ **2.2-125. Governor authorized to accept certain property from Confederate Memorial Literary Society.** — The Governor may accept, in the name of the Commonwealth, the property known as The White House of the Confederacy, any building that may be erected by the Confederate Memorial Literary Society, and the property known as The Lee House, located at 707 East Franklin Street in the City of Richmond, together with any moneys or other assets, including items being housed and displayed in such buildings or any of them, belonging to the Confederate Memorial Literary Society. The buildings and their contents thereof shall thereafter be preserved and maintained for historic purposes by the Commonwealth. Upon the transfer of title to the property to the Commonwealth, the Governor shall appoint a board of trustees consisting of thirteen persons appointed from the Commonwealth at large, which shall thereafter be charged with the preservation and maintenance of the properties and the administration of any funds that may be received or donated by the Confederate Memorial Literary Society or from any other source. The members of the board first appointed shall be appointed as follows: four for terms of four years, four for terms of three years, four for terms of two years, and one for a term of one year. Subsequent appointments shall be for terms of four years except appointments to fill vacancies, which shall be for the unexpired terms.

The board shall appoint a treasurer, who shall have custody of its funds and shall be bonded in such amount as the board may determine. Expenditures from such funds shall be made by the treasurer as the board directs, for any purpose, in the discretion of the board, consonant with the purpose for which the same are donated.

The board may fix, charge and collect admission fees to the buildings under its custody and control, and expend moneys so received in the upkeep, maintenance and operation of such buildings as historic shrines. (1966, c. 412, §§ 9-84.1, 9-84.2, 9-84.3, 9-84.4; 2001, c. 844.)

§ **2.2-126. Disposition of official correspondence.** — A. Before the end of his term of office, the Governor shall have delivered to The Library of Virginia for safekeeping all correspondence and other records of his office during his term. This section shall not apply to correspondence or other records of a strictly personal or private nature, or active files necessary for the transaction of business by the Office of the Governor, the decision thereon to be made by the Governor after consultation with the Librarian of Virginia. Records delivered to The Library of Virginia shall be made accessible to the public, once cataloging has been completed.

B. Should any subsequent Governor need such records for the transaction of business of the Office of the Governor, the records may be reviewed at the Library and copied, if necessary, but the Governor and his staff shall ensure that the original records are preserved intact and remain in The Library of Virginia. (Code 1950, § 2-40.1; 1966, c. 677, § 2.1-45; 1988, c. 476; 1994, c. 64; 2001, c. 844; 2003, c. 590.)

Article 2.

Executive Reorganization.

§ **2.2-127. Purpose.** — The Governor shall from time to time examine the organization of all executive agencies and shall determine what changes therein are necessary to:

1. Promote better execution of the laws, the more effective management of the executive branch of state government and of its agencies and functions, and the expeditious administration of the public business;
2. Reduce expenditures and promote economy to the fullest extent consistent with the efficient operation of state government;
3. Increase the efficiency of the operations of state government to the fullest extent practicable;
4. Group, coordinate, and consolidate agencies and functions of state government, as nearly as may be, according to major purposes;
5. Reduce the number of agencies by consolidating those having similar functions under a single head, and to abolish such agencies or functions thereof that are not necessary for the efficient conduct of the state government; and

6. Eliminate overlapping and duplication of effort. (1977, c. 505, § 2.1-8.1; 2001, c. 844.)

§ **2.2-128. Definitions.** — For the purpose of this chapter:

"Agency" means an administrative unit of state government, including any department, institution, commission, board, council, authority, or other body, however designated.

"Board" means any collegial body in the executive branch of state government created by the General Assembly.

"Function" means an activity, assignment or set of operations.

"Reorganization" means a transfer, consolidation, coordination, or abolition of a function, or the assignment or reassignment of responsibility and authority for the execution of a function. (1977, c. 505, § 2.1-8.2; 2001, c. 844.)

§ **2.2-129. Reorganization plans.** — When the Governor, after investigation, finds that the:

1. Transfer of the whole or a part of an agency, or of the whole or a part of the functions thereof, to the jurisdiction and control of another agency;
2. Abolition of all or a part of the functions of an agency;
3. Transfer or abolition of the whole or a part of the responsibilities of a board;
4. Abolition of a board;
5. Consolidation or coordination of the whole or a part of an agency, or of the whole or a part of the functions thereof, with the whole or a part of another agency or the functions thereof;
6. Consolidation or coordination of a part of an agency or the functions thereof with another part of the same agency or the functions thereof;
7. Abolition of the whole or a part of an agency which agency or part does not have, or on the taking effect of the reorganization plan will not have, any functions; or
8. Authorization for the exercise of functions or responsibilities by an agency, board, or officer to whom such functions or responsibilities have been transferred; is necessary to accomplish one or more of the purposes of § 2.2-127, he shall prepare a plan for reorganization and transmit the plan to each house of the General Assembly at least forty-five days prior to the commencement of a regular or special session of the General Assembly. (1977, c. 505, § 2.1-8.3; 2001, c. 844.)

§ **2.2-130. Contents of reorganization plans.** — A reorganization plan transmitted by the Governor under § 2.2-129:

1. May change the name or title of any agency, agency head, or board, council, commission or other collegial body affected by a reorganization, and shall designate the name or title of any new agency, agency head, or collegial body resulting from a reorganization;
2. May provide for the appointment of the head of any agency affected by, or resulting from, a reorganization, for an initial term not to exceed the balance of the term of the incumbent Governor, and for four-year terms thereafter;
3. May provide for the compensation of the head of an agency, not to exceed the rate found by the Governor to be applicable to comparable officers in the executive branch;
4. Shall provide for the transfer or other disposition of the records, property, and personnel affected by a reorganization;
5. Shall provide for the transfer of such unexpended balances of appropriations, and other funds, available for use in connection with a function or agency affected by a reorganization, or for the use of the agency that has the functions after the reorganization plan is effective. However, the unexpended balances so

transferred may be used only for the purposes for which the appropriation was originally made; and

6. Shall provide for terminating the affairs of an agency that is abolished. (1977, c. 505, § 2.1-8.4; 2001, c. 844.)

§ 2.2-131. Limitation on powers. — A reorganization plan may not provide for, and a reorganization under this chapter shall not have the effect of, authorizing an agency to exercise a function that is not authorized by law at the time the plan is transmitted to the General Assembly. (1977, c. 505, § 2.1-8.5; 2001, c. 844.)

§ 2.2-132. Approval by the General Assembly; effective date; publication. — A. A reorganization plan transmitted by the Governor to the General Assembly under this chapter shall become effective only if the Senate and the House of Delegates each approve the reorganization plan by a resolution by a majority of the members present and voting in each house. Any portion of the reorganization plan may be deleted by either the Senate or the House of Delegates in the resolution approving the plan. The Governor may withdraw a reorganization plan transmitted to the General Assembly under this chapter at any time before its effective date. A reorganization plan or portions thereof as approved by the Senate and the House of Delegates shall become effective on the first day of the fourth month following the adjournment of the General Assembly at which such plan was approved, unless a different date is specified in the plan.

B. A reorganization plan that is adopted pursuant to this section shall be printed in the Acts of Assembly and in the Code of Virginia. (1977, c. 505, §§ 2.1-8.6, 2.1-8.7; 2001, c. 844.)

§ 2.2-133. Effect on other laws, pending legal proceedings, and unexpended appropriations. — A. A statute enacted, and a regulation or other action made, prescribed, issued, granted, or performed in respect of or by an agency or function affected by a reorganization under this chapter, before the effective date of the reorganization, has, except to the extent rescinded, modified, superseded, or made inapplicable by or under authority of law or by the abolition of a function, the same effect as if the reorganization had not been made. However, if the statute, regulation or other action has vested the functions in the agency from which it is removed under the reorganization plan, the function, insofar as it is to be exercised after the plan becomes effective, shall be deemed as vested in the agency under which the function is placed by the plan.

B. For the purpose of subsection A, *"regulation or other action"* means a regulation, rule, order, policy, determination, directive, authorization, permit, privilege, requirement, designation, or other action.

C. A suit, action, or other proceeding lawfully commenced by or against the head of an agency or other officer of the Commonwealth or member of a state board, council, commission or other collegial body, in his official capacity or in relation to the discharge of his official duties, shall not abate by reason of the taking effect of a reorganization plan under this chapter.

D. The appropriations or portions of appropriations unexpended by reason of the operation of this chapter shall not be used for any purpose, but shall revert to the state treasury. (1977, c. 505, § 2.1-8.8; 2001, c. 844.)

Article 3.

Gubernatorial Commissions.

§ **2.2-134. Authority to create gubernatorial commissions.** — A. The Governor may create gubernatorial commissions for purposes related to his authority and responsibility. These entities shall be referred to as "Commissions."

B. For the purpose of this chapter, "gubernatorial commission" includes any temporary study group, task force, blue ribbon panel or any similar collegial body created by the Governor. (1984, c. 615, §§ 2.1-51.35, 2.1-51.36; 2001, c. 844.)

§ **2.2-135. Limitations and requirements.** — A. Each gubernatorial commission shall be created by executive order. The executive order shall specify (i) the specific duties of the commission, (ii) the date of creation, (iii) the date of expiration, (iv) the sources from which staff support are to be provided and a reasonable estimate of the amount of staff support expected over the lifetime of the commission, (v) an estimate of the costs to be incurred, and (vi) the source of funding.

B. Funding for gubernatorial commissions shall be provided only from funds (i) appropriated for the Governor's discretionary use, (ii) appropriated for the purposes for which the task force was established, or (iii) contributed by the private sector for the purposes for which the task force was established. Staff support for gubernatorial commissions may be provided by agencies or institutions with related purposes.

C. Gubernatorial commissions shall be created for a period not to exceed one year. Upon reevaluation, a commission may be extended one time by issuance of a new executive order for a period not to exceed one additional year. A commission shall not extend beyond the term of the Governor under whom it is created.

D. The Governor shall make a report every six months to the Senate Committee on Finance and House Committee on Appropriations specifying for each gubernatorial commission the amount and costs of staff support provided and the sources of the staff support. (1984, c. 615, § 2.1-51.37; 2001, c. 844.)

Article 4.

Security of Government Databases.

§§ **2.2-136 through 2.2-138:** Repealed by Acts 2002, c. 247, effective July 1, 2002.

Cross references. — As to security of government databases, see now § 2.2-2009.

CHAPTER 2.

Governor's Secretaries.

Article 1.

General Provisions.

§ 2.2-200. Appointment of Governor's Secretaries; general powers; severance. — A. The Governor's Secretaries shall be appointed by the Governor, subject to confirmation by the General Assembly if in session when the appointment is made, and if not in session, then at its next succeeding session. Each Secretary shall hold office at the pleasure of the Governor for a term coincident with that of the Governor making the appointment or until a successor is appointed and qualified. Before entering upon the discharge of duties, each Secretary shall take an oath to faithfully execute the duties of the office.

B. Each Secretary shall be subject to direction and supervision by the Governor. Except as provided in Article 5 (§ 2.2-208 et seq.) of this chapter, the agencies assigned to each Secretary shall:

1. Exercise their respective powers and duties in accordance with the general policy established by the Governor or by the Secretary acting on behalf of the Governor;

2. Provide such assistance to the Governor or the Secretary as may be required; and

3. Forward all reports to the Governor through the Secretary.

C. Unless the Governor expressly reserves such power to himself and except as provided in Article 5 (§ 2.2-208 et seq.) of this chapter, each Secretary may:

1. Resolve administrative, jurisdictional, operational, program, or policy conflicts between agencies or officials assigned;

2. Direct the formulation of a comprehensive program budget for the functional area identified in § 2.2-1508 encompassing the services of agencies assigned for consideration by the Governor;

3. Hold agency heads accountable for their administrative, fiscal and program actions in the conduct of the respective powers and duties of the agencies;

4. Direct the development of goals, objectives, policies and plans that are necessary to the effective and efficient operation of government;

5. Sign documents on behalf of the Governor that originate with agencies assigned to the Secretary; and

6. Employ such personnel and to contract for such consulting services as may be required to perform the powers and duties conferred upon the Secretary by law or executive order.

D. Severance benefits provided to any departing Secretary shall be publicly announced by the Governor prior to such departure.

E. As used in this chapter, *"Governor's Secretaries"* means the Secretary of Administration, the Secretary of Agriculture and Forestry, the Secretary of Commerce and Trade, the Secretary of Education, the Secretary of Finance, the Secretary of Health and Human Resources, the Secretary of Natural Resources, the Secretary of Public Safety, the Secretary of Technology, and the

Secretary of Transportation. (1972, c. 641, § 2.1-51.7; 1975, c. 390; 1976, cc. 729, 730, 732, 733, 734, 743, §§ 2.1-51.8:1, 2.1-51.13, 2.1-51.14, 2.1-51.16, 2.1-51.17, 2.1-51.26; 1984, c. 720, § 2.1-51.33; 1986, c. 492, § 2.1-51.39; 1998, c. 646; 1990, cc. 1, 317, §§ 2.1-51.41, 2.1-51.42; 1993, c. 699; 1996, cc. 500, 617; 1998, c. 793; 1999, cc. 412, 421, 433, §§ 2.1-51.44, 2.1-51.45; 2000, c. 937; 2001, c. 844; 2004, cc. 940, 963; 2006, c. 254.)

Editor's note. — The amendments to this section by Acts 2004, cc. 940 and 963 are effective no later than the beginning of the term of the Governor elected November 8, 2005. However, if funding for the position and expenses of the Secretary of Agriculture and Forestry is included in the 2004 Appropriation Act, the amendments shall become effective on the date set out in that act. The funding was provided in the 2004 appropriation act. See Acts 2004, Sp. Sess. 1, c. 4, Item 94.10. The provisions of Acts 2004, cc. 940 and 963, became effective July 1, 2004.

Acts 2004, cc. 940 and 963, cl. 2, provide: "That except as provided in the third enactment of this act, the provisions of this act shall become effective no later than the beginning of the term of the Governor elected November 8, 2005."

Acts 2004, cc. 940 and 963, cl. 3, provide: "That if funding for the position and expenses of the Secretary of Agriculture and Forestry created by this act is included in the 2004 Appropriation Act passed by the General Assembly, the provisions of this act shall become effective beginning on the date set out in the appropriation act."

§ 2.2-201. Secretaries; general; compensation. — A. Each Secretary shall be considered an extension of the Governor in the management coordination and cohesive direction of the executive branch of state government ensuring that the laws are faithfully executed.

B. Each Secretary shall be paid the compensation fixed by law. (1972, c. 641, § 2.1-51.10; 1984, c. 720, § 2.1-51.10:1; 2001, c. 844.)

§ 2.2-202. Payment of expenses of office. — The expenses of the offices of the Governor's Secretaries shall be paid from funds provided for the purpose by law; however, in addition, the Governor may supplement such funds from appropriations made to his office for the executive control of the Commonwealth or for discretionary purposes. (1972, c. 641, § 2.1-51.12; 2001, c. 844.)

Law Review. — For an article reviewing key environmental developments at the federal and state levels during the period from June, 1996 to June, 1998, see 32 U. Rich. L. Rev. 1217 (1998).

Article 2.

Secretary of Administration.

§ 2.2-203. Position established; agencies for which responsible. — The position of Secretary of Administration (the Secretary) is created. The Secretary shall be responsible to the Governor for the following agencies and boards: Department of Human Resource Management, Department of General Services, Compensation Board, Secretary of the Commonwealth, Department of Employment Dispute Resolution, and Virginia Public Broadcasting Board. The Governor may, by executive order, assign any other state executive agency to the Secretary, or reassign any agency listed above to another Secretary. (1976, c. 743, §§ 2.1-51.25, 2.1-51.27; 1978, c. 84; 1980, c. 620; 1981, c. 315; 1984, cc. 720, 746; 1985, c. 447; 1988, cc. 424, 839; 1993, c. 542; 1994, cc. 4, 85; 1995, c. 837; 1997, c. 858; 1999, cc. 412, 421, 433; 2000, cc. 66, 657, 947, 1006; 2001, c. 844; 2002, c. 572; 2003, cc. 197, 657, 670, 884; 2006, c. 150; 2008, cc. 387, 689.)

Cross references. — For transition of property and powers of the Department of Veterans' Affairs to the Department of Veterans Services, see Editor's note under § 2.2-2000.

Editor's note. — Acts 2008, cc. 387 and 689, cl. 3 provides: "That as of July 1, 2008, the Department of Agriculture and Consumer Services shall be deemed successor in interest to the Department of Charitable Gaming to the extent that this act transfers powers and duties. All right, title, and interest in and to any real or tangible personal property vested in the Department of Charitable Gaming shall be transferred to and taken as standing in the name of the Department of Agriculture and Consumer Services."

Acts 2008, cc. 387 and 689, cl. 4 provides: "That the Governor may transfer an appropriation or any portion thereof within a state agency established, abolished, or otherwise affected by the provisions of this act, or from one such agency to another, to support the changes in organization or responsibility resulting from or required by the provisions of this act."

Acts 2008, cc. 387 and 689, cl. 5 provides: "That all rules and regulations adopted by the Department of Charitable Gaming or the Charitable Gaming Board that are in effect as of July 1, 2008, and that pertain to the subject of this act, shall remain in full force and effect until altered, amended, or rescinded by the Department of Agriculture and Consumer Services or the Charitable Gaming Board."

The 2008 amendments. — The 2008 amendments by cc. 387 and 689 are identical, and deleted "Department of Charitable Gaming" following "Department of Employment Dispute Resolution" in the first sentence.

§ **2.2-203.1. Secretary to establish telecommuting policy.** — A. The Secretary, in cooperation with the Secretary of Technology and in consultation with the Council on Technology Services, shall establish a comprehensive statewide telecommuting and alternative work schedule policy under which eligible employees of state agencies, as determined by state agencies, may telecommute or participate in alternative work schedules, and the Secretary shall periodically update such policy as necessary.

B. The telecommuting and alternative work schedule policy described in subsection A shall include, but not be limited to, model guidelines, rules and procedures for telecommuting and participation in alternative work schedules, and identification of the broad categories of positions determined to be ineligible to participate in telecommuting and the justification for such a determination. Such policy may also include an incentive program, to be established and administered by the Department of Human Resources Management, that may encourage state employees to telecommute or participate in alternative work schedules and that may encourage the state agencies' management personnel to promote telecommuting and alternative work schedules for eligible employees. (2001, c. 405, § 2.1-51.31:1; 2004, cc. 701, 755; 2005, c. 421.)

Editor's note. — Acts 2001, c. 405 enacted § 2.1-51.31:1, from which this section is derived. Pursuant to § 30-152, Acts 2001, c. 405 has been given effect in this section as set out above.

§ **2.2-203.2. Secretary to advise and assist public and private sectors regarding telecommuting; report to the General Assembly.** — A. The Secretary shall advise and assist state agencies, and upon request of the localities, the Secretary may advise and assist localities in planning, developing and administering programs, projects, plans, policies and other activities to promote telecommuting by employees of state agencies or localities.

B. The Secretary, upon request, may advise and assist private sector employers in the Commonwealth in planning, developing and administering programs, projects, plans, policies and other activities for telecommuting by private sector employees and in developing incentives provided by the private sector to encourage private sector employers in the Commonwealth to utilize employee telecommuting.

C. The Secretary shall report annually to the General Assembly on the status and efficiency of telecommuting in the Commonwealth. (2001, c. 405, § 2.1-51.31:2.)

Editor's note. — Acts 2001, c. 405 enacted § 2.1-51.31:2, from which this section is derived. Pursuant to § 30-152, Acts 2001, c. 405 has been given effect in this section as set out above.

§ 2.2-203.2:1. Secretary to report state job elimination due to privatization. — On or before November 30 of each year, the Secretary shall report to the Governor and the General Assembly on the number of state jobs eliminated in the immediately preceding fiscal year due to the privatization of commercial activities to a commercial source. As used in this section, *"commercial activities"* and *"commercial source"* shall mean the same as those terms are defined in § 2.2-2620. (2005, c. 476.)

Article 2.1.

Secretary of Agriculture and Forestry.

§ 2.2-203.3. (Effective until October 1, 2008) Position established; agencies for which responsible; additional duties. — The position of Secretary of Agriculture and Forestry (the Secretary) is created. The Secretary shall be responsible to the Governor for the following agencies: Department of Forestry, Department of Agriculture and Consumer Services, Virginia Agricultural Council, and Virginia Marine Products Board. The Governor, by executive order, may assign any state executive agency to the Secretary, or reassign any agency listed in this section to another Secretary. (2004, cc. 940, 963.)

Section set out twice. — The section above is effective until October 1, 2008. For the version of this section effective October 1, 2008, see the following section, also numbered 2.2-203.3.

Editor's note. — The enactment of this section by Acts 2004, cc. 940 and 963 is effective no later than the beginning of the term of the Governor elected November 8, 2005. However, if funding for the position and expenses of the Secretary of Agriculture and Forestry is included in the 2004 Appropriation Act, the enactments shall become effective on the date set out in that act. The funding was provided in the 2004 appropriation act. See Acts 2004, Sp. Sess. 1, c. 4, Item 94.10. The provisions of Acts 2004, cc. 940 and 963, became effective July 1, 2004.

Acts 2004, cc. 940 and 963, cl. 2, provide: "That except as provided in the third enactment of this act, the provisions of this act shall become effective no later than the beginning of the term of the Governor elected November 8, 2005."

Acts 2004, cc. 940 and 963, cl. 3, provide: "That if funding for the position and expenses of the Secretary of Agriculture and Forestry created by this act is included in the 2004 Appropriation Act passed by the General Assembly, the provisions of this act shall become effective beginning on the date set out in the appropriation act."

§ 2.2-203.3. (Effective October 1, 2008) Position established; agencies for which responsible; additional duties. — The position of Secretary of Agriculture and Forestry (the Secretary) is created. The Secretary shall be responsible to the Governor for the following agencies: Department of Forestry, Department of Agriculture and Consumer Services, and Virginia Agricultural Council. The Governor, by executive order, may assign any state executive agency to the Secretary, or reassign any agency listed in this section to another Secretary. (2004, cc. 940, 963; 2008, c. 860.)

Section set out twice. — The section above is effective October 1, 2008. For the version of this section effective until October 1, 2008, see the preceding section, also numbered 2.2-203.3.

Editor's note. — The enactment of this section by Acts 2004, cc. 940 and 963 is effective no later than the beginning of the term of the Governor elected November 8, 2005. However, if funding for the position and expenses of the Secretary of Agriculture and Forestry is included in the 2004 Appropriation Act, the enactments shall become effective on the date set out in that act. The funding was provided in the 2004 appropriation act. See Acts 2004, Sp. Sess. 1, c. 4, Item 94.10. The provisions of Acts 2004, cc. 940 and 963, became effective July 1, 2004.

Acts 2004, cc. 940 and 963, cl. 2, provide: "That except as provided in the third enactment of this act, the provisions of this act shall become effective no later than the beginning of the term of the Governor elected November 8, 2005."

Acts 2004, cc. 940 and 963, cl. 3, provide: "That if funding for the position and expenses of the Secretary of Agriculture and Forestry created by this act is included in the 2004 Appropriation Act passed by the General Assembly, the provisions of this act shall become effective beginning on the date set out in the appropriation act."

The 2008 amendments. — The 2008 amendment by c. 860, effective October 1, 2008, deleted "and Virginia Marine Products Board" at the end of the second sentence and made related changes.

Article 3.

Secretary of Commerce and Trade.

§ 2.2-204. Position established; agencies for which responsible; additional duties. — The position of Secretary of Commerce and Trade (the Secretary) is created. The Secretary shall be responsible to the Governor for the following agencies: Department of Business Assistance, Virginia Economic Development Partnership Authority, Virginia Tourism Authority, Department of Labor and Industry, Department of Mines, Minerals and Energy, Virginia Employment Commission, Department of Professional and Occupational Regulation, Department of Housing and Community Development, Department of Minority Business Enterprise, Virginia Housing Development Authority, Virginia Resources Authority, Virginia Racing Commission, Tobacco Indemnification and Community Revitalization Commission, and Board of Accountancy. The Governor, by executive order, may assign any state executive agency to the Secretary, or reassign any agency listed in this section to another Secretary.

The Secretary shall implement the provisions of the Virginia Biotechnology Research Act (§ 2.2-5500 et seq.). (1986, c. 492, §§ 2.1-51.38, 2.1-51.40; 1988, cc. 67, 173; 1989, c. 165; 1991, c. 337; 1993, cc. 499, 699; 1994, c. 472, § 2.1-51.39:2; 1995, c. 89; 1996, cc. 589, 590, 598, 599, 702; 1999, cc. 412, 421, 433; 2001, cc. 832, 844; 2004, cc. 57, 940, 963.)

Editor's note. — Acts 2001, c. 832 amended § 2.1-51.40, from which this section is derived. Pursuant to § 30-152, Acts 2001, c. 832 has been given effect in this section as set out above. The 2001 amendment by c. 832, inserted "Board of Accountancy" preceding "and Virginia Marine Products Board" in the second sentence of the first paragraph.

The amendments to this section by Acts 2004, cc. 940 and 963 are effective no later than the beginning of the term of the Governor elected November 8, 2005. However, if funding for the position and expenses of the Secretary of Agriculture and Forestry is included in the 2004 Appropriation Act, the amendments shall become effective on the date set out in that act. The funding was provided in the 2004 appropriation act. See Acts 2004, Sp. Sess. 1, c. 4, Item 94.10. The provisions of Acts 2004, cc. 940 and 963, became effective July 1, 2004.

Acts 2004, cc. 940 and 963, cl. 2, provide: "That except as provided in the third enactment of this act, the provisions of this act shall become effective no later than the beginning of the term of the Governor elected November 8, 2005."

Acts 2004, cc. 940 and 963, cl. 3, provide: "That if funding for the position and expenses of the Secretary of Agriculture and Forestry created by this act is included in the 2004 Appropriation Act passed by the General Assembly, the provisions of this act shall become effective beginning on the date set out in the appropriation act."

Acts 2008, c. 879, effective for the biennium ending June 30, 2010, in Item 106 B, provides: "The Secretary shall report to the Chairmen of the Senate Finance and the House Appropriations and Finance Committees by October 30 of each year, on the use and efficacy of state incentives in creating investments and jobs in Virginia in the prior fiscal year. The two-part report shall identify, by planning districts, the following items using the most recent data available: (1) the number of companies receiving business incentives; (2) the dollar amounts received by each company for each incentive; (3) the number of jobs to be created; (4) the average salary; and (5) the amount of investment agreed upon by the state and the company as a condition for receiving the incentives. For the purposes of this report, the incentives to be reviewed in the study are those incentives included in the Virginia Economic Development Partnership publication, 'Virginia Business Incentives 1997-98' as well as business incentive programs authorized and funded by the General Assembly since the 1999 Session. The first part of the study shall not identify by name the companies participating in the state's incentive programs. In the second part of the report, organized by planning district, the Secretary shall include the actual number of jobs created, average salary, and level of investments made by each company awarded incentives in the prior fiscal year; if not prohibited by state law or by memorandum of agreement or understanding between the Commonwealth and the company, the names of the companies awarded incentives shall be included. In addition, the report shall also identify the specific actions taken by the state as part of its business incentive program to create private investments and jobs in rural areas of the state and the success of these actions."

§ 2.2-205. Economic development policy for the Commonwealth. — A. During the first year of each new gubernatorial administration, the Secretary, with the assistance of a cabinet-level committee appointed in accordance with subsection B, shall develop and implement a written comprehensive economic development policy for the Commonwealth. In developing this policy, the Secretary and the committee shall review the economic development policy in effect at the commencement of the Governor's term of office. The Secretary shall make such revisions to the existing policy as the Secretary deems necessary to ensure that it is appropriate for the Commonwealth. Once the policy has been adopted by the Secretary and the committee and approved by the Governor, it shall be submitted to the General Assembly for its consideration.

B. During the first year of each new gubernatorial administration, the Governor shall issue an executive order creating a cabinet-level committee to assist the Secretary in the development of the comprehensive economic development policy for the Commonwealth. The Secretary shall be the chairman of the committee, and the Secretaries of Administration, Education, Health and Human Resources, Natural Resources, Technology and Transportation shall serve as committee members. The Governor may also appoint members of regional and local economic development groups and members of the business community to serve on the committee. (1991, c. 562, § 2.1-51.39:1; 1993, c. 699; 2001, c. 844; 2004, c. 989.)

§ 2.2-205.1. Economic Crisis Strike Force. — A. There is hereby established the Economic Crisis Strike Force (Strike Force) for the purpose of serving as a working group to respond as needed to economic disasters in Virginia communities by (i) immediately providing a single point of contact for citizens in affected communities to assist with accessing available government and private sector services and resources, (ii) assisting localities in developing short-term and long-term strategies for addressing the economic crisis, and (iii) identifying opportunities for workforce retraining, job creation, and new investment.

B. The Strike Force shall be chaired by the Secretary of Commerce and Trade and be deployed at the direction of the Governor. Membership shall include high level representatives designated by the Secretaries of Education and Health and Human Resources and by the respective heads of the following agencies: the Department of Agriculture and Consumer Services, the Department of Business Assistance, the Department of Education, the Department of Housing and Community Development, the Department of Labor and Industry, the Department of Medical Assistance Services, the Department of Minority Business Enterprise, the Department of Social Services, the Virginia

Community College System, the Virginia Employment Commission, the Virginia Economic Development Partnership, and the Virginia Tourism Authority. The Strike Force shall also include representatives from such other agencies as may be designated by the Governor to meet the needs of a particular affected community. In addition, the Governor may designate such citizens as he deems appropriate to advise the Strike Force.

C. Staff support for the Strike Force shall be provided by the Office of the Governor and the Secretary of Commerce and Trade. All agencies of the Commonwealth shall assist the Strike Force upon request.

D. On or before December 1 of each year, the Strike Force shall report to the Governor and the General Assembly on its activities.

E. For the purposes of this section, *"economic disaster"* means an employment loss of at least 5% during the immediately preceding six-month period, the closure or downsizing of a major regional employer in an economically distressed area, a natural disaster or act of terrorism for which the Governor has declared a state of emergency, or other economic crisis situations, which in the opinion of the Governor adversely affect the welfare of the citizens of the Commonwealth. (2006, cc. 79, 80.)

Editor's note. — Acts 2006, cc. 79 and 80, cl. 2, provides: "That an emergency exists and this act shall be in force upon its passage [March 21, 2006]."

§ 2.2-206. Urban issues; report; responsibilities of the Secretary. — A. In order to evaluate and promote the economic potential and development of the urban areas in the Commonwealth, during the first year of each new gubernatorial administration, the Secretary, with the assistance of a cabinet-level committee appointed in accordance with subsection B, shall develop a report on the condition of the state's urban areas and establishing priorities for addressing those conditions. The report shall include the following components:

1. A review of economic and social conditions in the cities of the Commonwealth;

2. The identification of inequities between those urban areas experiencing economic growth and relatively low fiscal stress and those urban areas experiencing economic decline and relatively high levels of fiscal stress;

3. The establishment of specific and quantifiable benchmarks for addressing economic and social conditions and inequities within urban areas;

4. Prioritized recommendations for specific actions by state agencies intended to meet the established performance benchmarks within a prescribed schedule; and

5. A system for tracking agency progress in meeting the benchmarks during the succeeding biennia.

B. During the first year of each new gubernatorial administration, the Governor shall issue an executive order creating a cabinet-level committee to assist the Secretary in the development of an urban policy vision and priorities for the Commonwealth. The Secretary shall be the chairman of the committee, and the Secretaries of Education, Health and Human Resources, Natural Resources and Transportation shall serve as committee members. The Governor may also appoint representatives of local government from Virginia's urban areas to serve as committee members. During the third year of each new gubernatorial administration the Secretary shall review and report on the performance of each agency in meeting the established benchmarks. (1999, c. 519, § 2.1-51.39:3; 2001, c. 844; 2004, c. 238.)

§ 2.2-207. Annual legislative report. — Within sixty days prior to the beginning of each regular legislative session, the Secretary and the Secretary of Education shall jointly present a report to the General Assembly summarizing private sector and education partnership programs and recommendations to promote efficiency and growth in business and education partnerships. (1993, cc. 248, 752, § 2.1-51.40:1; 2001, c. 844.)

ARTICLE 4.

Secretary of Education.

§ **2.2-208. Position established; agencies for which responsible; powers and duties.** — The position of Secretary of Education (the "Secretary") is created. The Secretary shall be responsible to the Governor for the following agencies: Department of Education, State Council of Higher Education, Virginia Museum of Fine Arts, The Science Museum of Virginia, Frontier Culture Museum of Virginia, The Library of Virginia, Jamestown-Yorktown Foundation, Board of Regents of Gunston Hall, and the Commission for the Arts. The Governor may, by executive order, assign any other state executive agency to the Secretary, or reassign any agency listed above to another Secretary.

Unless the Governor expressly reserves such a power to himself, the Secretary is empowered to resolve administrative, jurisdictional or policy conflicts between any agencies or officers for which he is responsible and to provide policy direction for programs involving more than a single agency. He is authorized to direct the preparation of alternative policies, plans and budgets for education for the Governor and, to that end, may require the assistance of the agencies for which he is responsible. He shall direct the formulation of a comprehensive program budget for cultural affairs encompassing the programs and activities of the agencies involved in cultural affairs. (1976, c. 733, §§ 2.1-51.19, 2.1-51.20, 2.1-51.21; 1977, c. 413; 1979, c. 314; 1985, cc. 193, 447, 505; 1986, cc. 335, 603; 1987, c. 458; 1992, c. 630; 1993, cc. 653, 665; 1994, c. 64; 1998, cc. 701, 899; 1999, cc. 840, 855; 2001, c. 844; 2003, c. 452.)

§§ **2.2-209, 2.2-210:** Repealed by Acts 2004, c. 37.

ARTICLE 5.

Secretary of Finance.

§ **2.2-211. Position established; agencies for which responsible; additional powers.** — A. The position of Secretary of Finance (the "Secretary") is created. The Secretary shall be responsible for the following agencies: Department of Accounts, Department of Planning and Budget, Department of Taxation, Department of the Treasury and Department of the State Internal Auditor. The Governor, by executive order, may assign any other state executive agency to the Secretary of Finance, or reassign any agency listed.

B. To the greatest extent practicable, the agencies assigned to the Secretary shall pay all amounts due and owing by the Commonwealth through electronic transfers of funds from the general fund or appropriate special fund to the bank account of the payee or a party identified by law to receive funds on behalf of the payee. All wire transfer costs associated with the electronic transfer shall be paid by the payee subject to exemptions authorized by the State Treasurer affecting the investment, debt, and intergovernmental transactions of the Commonwealth and its agencies, institutions, boards, and authorities. (1984, c. 720, §§ 2.1-51.32, 2.1-51.33, 2.1-51.34; 1985, c. 72; 1996, c. 500; 2001, c. 844.)

Article 6.

Secretary of Health and Human Resources.

§ 2.2-212. Position established; agencies for which responsible; additional powers. — The position of Secretary of Health and Human Resources (the Secretary) is created. The Secretary of Health and Human Resources shall be responsible to the Governor for the following agencies: Department of Health, Department for the Blind and Vision Impaired, Department of Health Professions, Department for the Aging, Department of Mental Health, Mental Retardation and Substance Abuse Services, Department of Rehabilitative Services, Department of Social Services, Department of Medical Assistance Services, Child Day-Care Council, Virginia Department for the Deaf and Hard-of-Hearing, the Office of Comprehensive Services for Youth and At-Risk Youth and Families, and the Assistive Technology Loan Fund Authority. The Governor may, by executive order, assign any other state executive agency to the Secretary of Health and Human Resources, or reassign any agency listed above to another Secretary.

Unless the Governor expressly reserves such power to himself, the Secretary shall (i) serve as the lead Secretary for the coordination and implementation of the long-term care policy of the Commonwealth, working with the Secretaries of Transportation, Commerce and Trade, and Education, and the Commissioner of Insurance, to facilitate interagency service development and implementation, communication and cooperation, (ii) serve as the lead Secretary for the Comprehensive Services Act for At-Risk Youth and Families, working with the Secretary of Education and the Secretary of Public Safety to facilitate interagency service development and implementation, communication and cooperation, and (iii) coordinate the disease prevention activities of agencies in the Secretariat to ensure efficient, effective delivery of health related services and financing. (1976, c. 729, §§ 2.1-51.13, 2.1-51.14, 2.1-51.15; 1978, c. 635; 1982, cc. 345, 459; 1983, c. 20; 1984, cc. 720, 781; 1985, cc. 447, 448; 1987, cc. 219, 698; 1988, cc. 646, 765; 1989, cc. 614, 695; 1990, c. 458; 1991, c. 563; 1994, c. 755; 1996, cc. 492, 902; 1998, c. 793; 2000, c. 937; 2001, cc. 577, 844; 2004, cc. 14, 142; 2006, cc. 344, 380; 2007, cc. 10, 399, 534, 581.)

Editor's note. — Acts 2001, cc. 577 and 777 amended § 2.1-51.15, from which this section is derived. Pursuant to § 30-152, Acts 2001, cc. 577 and 777 have been given effect in this section as set out above.

This section is set out above as it read without the entry for the Advisory Council on the Future of Nursing in Virginia, which was added by Acts 2001, c. 777, and expired July 1, 2006, pursuant to Acts 2001, c. 777, cl. 2.

Acts 2004, c. 142, cl. 2, provides: "That the provisions of this act shall not be construed to affect existing members of the Council on Indians whose terms have not expired as of July 1, 2004. However, any new appointments made after July 1, 2004, shall be made in accordance with the provisions of this act."

Acts 2005, cc. 199 and 235, cl. 1 provides: "§ 1. Publication of clinical drug trial results.

"The Secretary of Health and Human Resources shall make available, on the appropriate state health-related websites, information directing citizens of the Commonwealth to publicly available information on clinical drug trials and other clinical studies including those sponsored by the National Institutes of Health and those sponsored by the private sector, such as the Pharmaceutical Research and Manufacturers of America."

The 2007 amendments. — The 2007 amendments by cc. 10 and 399 are identical, and rewrote clause (i) of the second paragraph which had read: "coordinate the work of state agencies to implement the long-term care policy of the Commonwealth."

The 2007 amendments by cc. 534 and 581 are identical, and in the last paragraph, added clause (iii) and made related changes.

Research References. — Bender's Health Care Law Monthly (Matthew Bender).

Foley, Lardner, Weissburg, and Aronson, Health Care Law Sourcebook: A Compendium of Federal Laws, Regulations and Documents Relating to Health Care (Matthew Bender).

Macdonald, Kaufman, etc., Treatise on Health Care Law (Matthew Bender).

Macdonald, Meyer, and Essig, Health Care law: A Practical Guide (Matthew Bender).

§ 2.2-213. Secretary of Health and Human Resources to develop certain criteria. — In order to respond to the needs of substance abusing women and their children, the Secretary shall develop criteria for (i) enhancing access to publicly funded substance abuse treatment programs in order to effectively serve pregnant substance abusers; (ii) determining when a drug-exposed child may be referred to the early intervention services and tracking system available through Part C of the Individuals with Disabilities Education Act, 20 U.S.C. § 1431 et seq.; (iii) determining the appropriate circumstances for contact between hospital discharge planners and local departments of social services for referrals for family-oriented prevention services, when such services are available and provided by the local social services agency; and (iv) determining when the parent of a drug-exposed infant, who may be endangering a child's health by failing to follow a discharge plan, may be referred to the child protective services unit of a local department of social services.

The Secretary shall consult with the Commissioner of Mental Health, Mental Retardation and Substance Abuse Services, the Commissioner of Social Services, the Commissioner of Health, community services boards, behavioral health authorities local departments of social services, and local departments of health in developing the criteria required by this section. (1992, c. 428, § 2.1-51.15:1; 2001, c. 844.)

§ 2.2-213.1. Secretary of Health and Human Resources and Commissioner of Insurance to develop long-term care public information campaign. — A. In order to respond to the burgeoning population of seniors in the Commonwealth, the Secretary of Health and Human Resources and the Commissioner of Insurance shall develop a public information campaign to inform the citizens of the Commonwealth of (i) the impending crisis in long-term care, (ii) the effect of the impending crisis on the Virginia Medicaid program and on the finances of families and their estates, (iii) innovative alternatives and combinations of institutional and community-based long-term care services, and (iv) the requirements for long-term care insurance certificates and policies and the meaning of terminology used in such certificates and policies.

B. The Secretary of Health and Human Resources and the Commissioner of Insurance shall enlist the assistance of the Board of Health and the Commissioner of Health, in the exercise of their responsibilities set forth in Title 32.1 to protect, implement, and preserve the public health, in disseminating the information concerning long-term care to the public. (2005, c. 92.)

§ 2.2-213.2. Secretary to coordinate system for children with incarcerated parents. — The Secretary of Health and Human Resources, in consultation with the Secretary of Public Safety, shall establish an integrated system for coordinating the planning and provision of services for children with incarcerated parents among state, local, nonprofit agencies, and faith-based organizations in order to provide such children with services needed to continue parental relationships with the incarcerated parent, where appropriate, and encourage healthy relationships in the family and community. (2006, c. 366.)

§ 2.2-214. Responsibility of certain agencies within the Secretariat; review of regulations. — The Boards of Health, Mental Health, Mental Retardation and Substance Abuse Services, Social Services, and Medical Assistance Services and the Department of Rehabilitative Services shall review their regulations and policies related to service delivery in order to ascertain and eliminate any discrimination against individuals infected with human immunodeficiency virus. (1989, c. 613, § 2.1-51.14:1; 1992, c. 755; 2001, c. 844.)

§ 2.2-214.1. Healthy Lives Prescription Fund; nonreverting; purposes; report. — A. There is hereby created in the Department of the Treasury a special nonreverting fund that shall be known as the Healthy Lives Prescription Fund.

B. The Fund shall be established on the books of the Comptroller. The Fund shall consist of such moneys appropriated by the General Assembly and any funds available from the federal government, donations, grants, and in-kind contributions made to the Fund for the purposes stated herein. Interest earned on moneys in the Fund shall remain in the Fund and be credited to it. Any moneys remaining in the Fund, including interest thereon, at the end of each fiscal year shall not revert to the general fund but shall remain in the Fund.

C. Moneys in the Fund shall be available to develop and implement programs that will enhance current prescription drug programs for citizens of the Commonwealth who are without insurance or ability to pay for prescription drugs and to develop innovative programs to make such prescription drugs more available.

D. The Secretary shall provide an annual report on the status of the Fund and efforts to meet the goals of the Fund. (2003, cc. 661, 674.)

Article 7.

Secretary of Natural Resources.

§ 2.2-215. Position established; agencies for which responsible. — The position of Secretary of Natural Resources (the Secretary) is created. The Secretary shall be responsible to the Governor for the following agencies: Department of Conservation and Recreation, Department of Historic Resources, Marine Resources Commission, Department of Game and Inland Fisheries, Chippokes Plantation Farm Foundation, Virginia Museum of Natural History, Council on Indians, and the Department of Environmental Quality. The Governor may, by executive order, assign any state executive agency to the Secretary of Natural Resources, or reassign any agency listed above to another Secretary. (1972, c. 641, §§ 2.1-51.7, 2.1-51.9; 1974, cc. 44, 45, 354, 420; 1975, c. 390; 1976, cc. 729, 732, 733, 734, 743, 767; 1978, c. 32; 1979, c. 294; 1982, c. 459; 1984, cc. 590, 720, 739, 750; 1985, cc. 193, 447, 448; 1986, cc. 335, 492, 567, 492; 1988, cc. 608, 707, 891; 1989, c. 656; 1992, c. 887; 2001, c. 844; 2004, c. 142; 2005, c. 41.)

§ 2.2-216. Coordination of water quality information; monitoring the quality of the waters, habitat, and living resources of Chesapeake Bay and its tributaries. — The Secretary shall:

1. Serve as the lead Secretary for the coordination of technical assistance, information, and training to ensure that consistent water quality information is provided to all citizens of the Commonwealth; and

2. Consult with the Secretary of Agriculture and Forestry and the Secretary of Health and Human Resources and cooperate with appropriate state and federal agencies in the development and implementation of a comprehensive program to monitor the quality of the waters, habitat, and the living resources of the Chesapeake Bay and its tributaries. (1984, c. 183, § 2.1-51.8:2; 1986, c. 492; 2001, c. 844; 2004, c. 58; 2008, c. 368.)

The 2008 amendments. — The 2008 amendment by c. 368 rewrote the section, which read: "The Secretary shall cooperate with appropriate state and federal agencies in the development and implementation of a comprehensive program to monitor the quality of the waters, habitat, and the living resources of the Chesapeake Bay and its tributaries."

§ **2.2-217. Friend of the Bay Award.** — The Secretary shall establish the "Friend of the Bay Award" program. The program shall annually recognize those individuals, businesses, organizations and other entities that have made significant efforts to preserve and enhance the Chesapeake Bay and its tributaries. The program shall make such awards on a noncompetitive basis, using criteria to be developed by the Secretary, in consultation with those agencies within the Secretariat, the Virginia delegation to the Chesapeake Bay Commission and the Citizens Advisory Committee to the Chesapeake Executive Council. (1994, c. 392, § 2.1-51.8:3; 2001, c. 844.)

§ **2.2-218. Development of strategies to restore the water quality and living resources of the Chesapeake Bay and its tributaries.** — The Secretary shall coordinate the development of tributary plans designed to improve water quality and restore the living resources of the Chesapeake Bay and its tributaries. Each plan shall be tributary-specific in nature and prepared for the Potomac, Rappahannock, York, and James River Basins as well as the western coastal basins (comprising the small rivers on the western Virginia mainland that drain to the Chesapeake Bay, not including the Potomac, Rappahannock, York and James Rivers) and the eastern coastal basin (encompassing the creeks and rivers of the Eastern Shore of Virginia that are west of U.S. Route 13 and drain to the Chesapeake Bay). Each plan shall (i) address the reduction of nutrients and suspended solids, including sediments, entering the Chesapeake Bay and its tributaries and (ii) summarize other existing programs, strategies, goals and commitments for reducing toxics; the preservation and protection of living resources; and the enhancement of the amount of submerged aquatic vegetation, for each tributary basin and the Bay. The plans shall be developed in consultation with affected stakeholders, including, but not limited to, local government officials; wastewater treatment operators; seafood industry representatives; commercial and recreational fishing interests; developers; farmers; local, regional and statewide conservation and environmental interests; and the Virginia delegation to the Chesapeake Bay Commission. (1996, c. 1031, § 2.1-51.12:1; 1999, c. 548; 2001, c. 844; 2003, c. 885.)

Editor's note. — Acts 2003, c. 885, cl. 7, provides: "That all current members of the collegial bodies whose terms have been modified by this act shall be eligible, if reappointed, to the full number of terms provided by this act regardless of prior service."

§ **2.2-219. Tributary plan content; development timelines.** — A. Each tributary plan developed pursuant to § 2.2-218 shall include the following:

1. Recommended specific strategies, goals, commitments and methods of implementation designed to achieve the nutrient goals of the 1987 Chesapeake Bay Agreement and the 1992 amendments to that agreement signed by the Governors of Virginia, Maryland, and Pennsylvania, the Mayor of the District of Columbia, the Administrator of the United States Environmental Protection Agency and the Chairman of the Chesapeake Bay Commission, collectively known as the Chesapeake Executive Council.

2. Recommended specific strategies, goals, commitments and methods of implementation to achieve sediment and suspended solids reductions from nonpoint sources sufficient to achieve living resource goals, particularly those related to habitat conditions necessary to support submerged aquatic vegetation.

3. A report on progress made pursuant to the "Chesapeake Bay Basinwide Toxics Reduction and Prevention Strategy" signed by the Chesapeake Executive Council on October 14, 1994, that is applicable to the tributary for which the plan is prepared.

4. A report on progress on the "Submerged Aquatic Vegetation Restoration Goals" signed by the Chesapeake Executive Council on September 15, 1993, that is applicable to the tributary for which the plan is prepared.

5. A report on progress related to the objectives of the "Local Government Partnership Initiative" signed by the Chesapeake Executive Council on November 30, 1995.

6. Specifically identified recommended state, local and private responsibilities and actions, with associated timetables, for implementation of the plan, to include the (i) person, official, governmental unit, organization or other responsible body; (ii) specific programmatic and environmental benchmarks and indicators for tracking and evaluating implementation and progress; (iii) opportunities, if appropriate, to achieve nutrient reduction goals through nutrient trading; (iv) estimated state and local benefits derived from implementation of the proposed alternatives in the plan; (v) state funding commitments and specifically identified sources of state funding as well as a method for considering alternative or additional funding mechanisms; (vi) state incentives for local and private bodies for assisting with implementation of the plans; and (vii) estimate and schedule of costs for the recommended alternatives in each plan.

7. Scientific documentation to support the recommended actions in a plan and an analysis supporting the documentation if it differs from the conclusions used by the Chesapeake Bay Program.

8. An analysis and explanation of how and when the plan is expected to achieve the elements of subdivisions 1, 2, 3 and 4.

9. A process for and schedule of adjustment of the plan if reevaluation concludes that the specific nutrient reduction goals will not be met.

10. An analysis of the cost effectiveness and equity of the recommended nutrient reduction alternatives.

11. An opportunity for public comment and a public education and information program that includes but is not limited to information on specific assignments of responsibility needed to execute the plan.

B. Tributary plans shall be developed by the following dates for the:

1. Potomac River Basin, January 1, 1997.
2. Rappahannock River Basin, January 1, 1999.
3. York River Basin, July 1, 1998.
4. James River Basin, July 1, 1998.
5. Eastern and western coastal basins, January 1, 1999.

C. In developing tributary plans, the Secretary shall consider, among other factors: (i) studies relevant to the establishment of nutrient, sediment and suspended solids reduction goals; (ii) the relative contributions and impacts of point and nonpoint sources of nutrients; (iii) the scientific relationship between nutrient, sediment and suspended solids controls and the attainment of water quality goals; and (iv) estimates of costs for each publicly owned treatment works affected by point source nutrient reduction goals and estimates of costs for nonpoint source nutrient, sediment and suspended solids reduction goals.

D. In any tributary plan reevaluation, the Secretary shall consider, among other factors: (i) whether all publicly owned treatment works in the basin under consideration have either installed biological nutrient removal technology or achieved equivalent nutrient reduction by other means; (ii) total nutrient reductions achieved by nonpoint sources to the tributary; (iii) the need for additional nutrient controls for the attainment of water quality goals; (iv) a comparison between nutrient reductions achieved by point source controls and nonpoint source controls in order to equitably allocate any additional reductions; and (v) the cost effectiveness, including nutrient trading options, of any additional nutrient reduction controls. (1996, c. 1031, § 2.1-51.12:2; 1997, c. 22; 1999, c. 548; 2001, c. 844.)

Editor's note. — Acts 2008, c. 879, effective for the biennium ending June 30, 2010, in Item 360 A, provides: "The Secretary of Natural Resources shall report to the Chairmen of the Senate Committees on Finance and Agriculture, Conservation, and Natural Resources, and the House Committees on Appropriations and Conservation and Natural Resources, by November 4 of each year on implementation of the Chesapeake Bay nutrient reduction strategies. The report shall include and address the progress and costs of point source and nonpoint source pollution strategies. The report shall include, but not be limited to, information on levels of dissolved oxygen, acres of submerged aquatic vegetation, computer modeling, variety and numbers of living resources, and other relevant measures for the General Assembly to evaluate the progress and effectiveness of the tributary strategies. In addition, the Secretary shall include information on the status of all of Virginia's commitments to the Chesapeake Bay Agreements."

§ **2.2-220. Annual reporting.** — The Secretary shall report by November 1 of each year to the House Committee on Agriculture, Chesapeake and Natural Resources, the Senate Committee on Agriculture, Conservation and Natural Resources, the House Committee on Appropriations, the Senate Committee on Finance, and the Virginia delegation to the Chesapeake Bay Commission on progress made in the development and implementation of each plan. This annual report may be incorporated as part of the report required by § 62.1-44.118. The annual report shall include, but not be limited to:

1. An analysis of actions taken and proposed and their relation to the timetables and programmatic and environmental benchmarks and indicators.
2. The results and analyses of quantitative or qualitative tests or studies, including but not limited to water quality monitoring and submerged aquatic vegetation surveys, which relate to actual resource improvements in each tributary. The results and analyses are to be clearly related to designated portions of each tributary.
3. A complete summary of public comments received on each plan.
4. The current or revised cost estimates for implementation of the plans.
5. The status of Virginia's strategies as compared to the development, content and implementation of tributary strategies by the other jurisdictions that are signatories to the Chesapeake Bay Agreement. (1996, c. 1031, § 2.1-51.12:3; 2001, c. 844; 2003, c. 885; 2007, c. 637.)

Editor's note. — Acts 2003, c. 885, cl. 7, provides: "That all current members of the collegial bodies whose terms have been modified by this act shall be eligible, if reappointed, to the full number of terms provided by this act regardless of prior service."

The 2007 amendments. — The 2007 amendment by c. 637 added the present second sentence in the introductory paragraph.

§ **2.2-220.1. Chesapeake Bay 2000 Agreement; annual report.** — By November 1 of each year, the Secretary of Natural Resources, in consultation with appropriate state and federal agencies, shall report to the House Committee on Chesapeake and Its Tributaries, the Senate Committee on Agriculture, Conservation, and Natural Resources, the House Committee on Appropriations, the Senate Committee on Finance, the Virginia delegation to the Chesapeake Bay Commission, and the Virginia Chesapeake Bay Partnership Council on specific progress made in implementing the provisions of the Chesapeake Bay 2000 Agreement. The report shall include, but not be limited to, a description of the programs, activities, and initiatives developed and implemented by state and local government agencies to meet each of the goals and commitments contained in the Agreement and an assessment of projected state funding necessary to meet the goals and commitments. (2001, c. 259, § 2.1-51.12:4.)

Editor's note. — Acts 2001, c. 259 enacted § 2.1-51.12:4, from which this section is derived. Pursuant to § 30-152, Acts 2001, c. 259 has been given effect in this section as set out above.

The Virginia Chesapeake Bay Partnership Council, referred to in this section, has been abolished. See Acts 2001, c. 577, which repealed Chapter 43 (§§ 9-334, 9-335) of Title 9.

Article 8.

Secretary of Public Safety.

§ 2.2-221. Position established; agencies for which responsible. — The position of Secretary of Public Safety (the Secretary) is created. The Secretary shall be responsible to the Governor for the following agencies: Department of Alcoholic Beverage Control, Department of Corrections, Department of Juvenile Justice, Department of Correctional Education, Department of Criminal Justice Services, Department of Forensic Science, Virginia Parole Board, Department of Emergency Management, Department of Military Affairs, Department of Veterans Services, Virginia Veterans Services Foundation, Department of State Police, Department of Fire Programs and the Commonwealth's Attorneys' Services Council. The Governor may, by executive order, assign any other state executive agency to the Secretary, or reassign any agency listed above to another Secretary. (1976, c. 732, §§ 2.1-51.16, 2.1-51.18; 1978, cc. 455, 606, 607, 820; 1984, cc. 720, 779; 1985, cc. 447, 448; 1986, c. 60; 1988, cc. 67, 173, 888; 1989, c. 733; 1990, cc. 1, 317; 1992, c. 81; 1996, c. 503; 2001, c. 844; 2006, cc. 150, 326.)

§ 2.2-221.1. Secretary to coordinate system for offender transition and reentry services. — The Secretary of Public Safety shall establish an integrated system for coordinating the planning and provision of offender transitional and reentry services among and between state, local, and nonprofit agencies in order to prepare inmates for successful transition into their communities upon release from incarceration and for improving opportunities for treatment, employment, and housing while on subsequent probation, parole, or post-release supervision.

It is the intent of the General Assembly that funds used for the purposes of this section be leveraged to the fullest extent possible and that direct transitional and reentry employment and housing assistance for offenders be provided in the most cost effective means possible, including through agreements with local nonprofit pre- and post-release service organizations. (2005, c. 153.)

Editor's note. — Acts 2008, c. 879, effective for the biennium ending June 30, 2010, in Item 381 B, provides: "The Secretary shall provide a status report on actions taken to improve offender transitional and reentry services, as provided in § 2.2-221.1, Code of Virginia, including improvements to the preparation and provision for employment, treatment, and housing opportunities for those being released from incarceration. The report shall be provided to the Governor and the Chairmen of the House Appropriations and Senate Finance Committees no later than November 15 of each year."

§ 2.2-222. Secretary to provide annual reports on juvenile offenders. — The Secretary shall provide annual reports to the Governor and the General Assembly on juvenile offender demographics by offense, age, committing court, previous court contacts of offenders, and, beginning in July 1998, recidivism rates of juveniles committed to agencies within the Secretariat. The annual report shall also include summaries of any juvenile program evaluations completed in the previous year on programs operated by the Departments of Juvenile Justice, Corrections or Criminal Justice Services and whose evaluation was directed by the General Assembly or the Secretary. (1976, c. 732, § 2.1-51.17; 1984, c. 720; 1990, cc. 1, 317; 1996, c. 617; 2001, c. 844.)

§ 2.2-223. Interagency Drug Offender Screening and Assessment Committee. — The Secretary shall establish and chair an Interagency Drug Offender Screening and Assessment Committee to oversee the drug screening, assessment and treatment provisions of §§ 16.1-273, 16.1-278.1, 16.1-278.8, 18.2-251.01, 18.2-251, 18.2-252, 19.2-299 and 19.2-299.2 for defendants convicted in the criminal courts of the Commonwealth. The Committee shall include the Directors or Commissioners of the Department of Corrections; Department of Criminal Justice Services; Department of Juvenile Justice; Department of Mental Health, Mental Retardation and Substance Abuse Services; the Virginia Alcohol Safety Action Program; and the Virginia Criminal Sentencing Commission. The Committee shall have the responsibility to: (i) assist and monitor agencies in implementing the above-listed Code of Virginia sections, (ii) ensure quality and consistency in the screening and assessment process, (iii) promote interagency coordination and cooperation in the identification and treatment of drug abusing or drug dependent offenders, (iv) implement an evaluation process and conduct periodic program evaluations, and (v) make recommendations to the Governor and General Assembly regarding proposed expenditures from the Drug Assessment Fund. The Committee shall report on the status and effectiveness of offender drug screening, assessment and treatment to the Virginia State Crime Commission and the House Committees on Courts of Justice and Appropriations, and the Senate Committees on Courts of Justice and Finance by January 1 of each year. (1999, cc. 891, 913, § 2.1-51.18:3; 2001, c. 844.)

§ 2.2-224. Secretary of Public Safety to publish certain list. — The Secretary shall publish annually a list of those localities that have acquired any aircraft through forfeiture procedures. The list shall include a description of each aircraft so acquired. The Secretary shall develop a program to encourage the use of such aircraft for travel associated with law-enforcement purposes, including but not limited to, extradition of prisoners and arrestees within and without the Commonwealth. (1995, c. 464, § 2.1-51.17:01; 2001, c. 844.)

ARTICLE 9.

Secretary of Technology.

§ 2.2-225. Position established; agencies for which responsible; additional powers. — The position of Secretary of Technology (the Secretary) is created. The Secretary shall be responsible to the Governor for the following agencies and boards: Information Technology Investment Board, Innovative Technology Authority, Virginia Information Technologies Agency, Virginia Geographic Information Network Advisory Board, the Wireless E-911 Services Board, and the Virginia Research and Technology Advisory Commission. The Governor, by executive order, may assign any other state executive agency to the Secretary, or reassign any agency listed in this section to another Secretary.

Unless the Governor expressly reserves such power to himself, the Secretary may, with regard to strategy development, planning and budgeting for technology programs in the Commonwealth:

1. Monitor trends and advances in fundamental technologies of interest and importance to the economy of the Commonwealth and direct and approve a stakeholder-driven technology strategy development process that results in a comprehensive and coordinated view of research and development goals for industry, academia and government in the Commonwealth. This strategy shall be updated biennially and submitted to the Governor, the Speaker of the House of Delegates and the President Pro Tempore of the Senate.

2. Work closely with the appropriate federal research and development agencies and program managers to maximize the participation of Commonwealth industries and universities in these programs consistent with agreed strategy goals.

3. Direct the development of plans and programs for strengthening the technology resources of the Commonwealth's high technology industry sectors and for assisting in the strengthening and development of the Commonwealth's Regional Technology Councils.

4. Direct the development of plans and programs for improving access to capital for technology-based entrepreneurs.

5. Assist the Joint Commission on Technology and Science created pursuant to § 30-85 in its efforts to stimulate, encourage, and promote the development of technology in the Commonwealth.

6. Continuously monitor and analyze the technology investments and strategic initiatives of other states to ensure the Commonwealth remains competitive.

7. Strengthen interstate and international partnerships and relationships in the public and private sectors to bolster the Commonwealth's reputation as a global technology center.

8. Develop and implement strategies to accelerate and expand the commercialization of intellectual property created within the Commonwealth.

9. Ensure the Commonwealth remains competitive in cultivating and expanding growth industries, including life sciences, advanced materials and nanotechnology, biotechnology, and aerospace.

10. Monitor the trends in the availability and deployment of and access to broadband communications services, which include, but are not limited to, competitively priced, high-speed data services and Internet access services of general application, throughout the Commonwealth and advancements in communications technology for deployment potential. The Secretary shall report annually by December 1 to the Governor and General Assembly on those trends. (1999, cc. 412, 421, 433, §§ 2.1-51.44, 2.1-51.45, 2.1-51.46; 2001, c. 844; 2003, cc. 981, 1021; 2004, c. 989.)

Cross references. — As to the establishment of the Council on Technology Services, see § 2.2-2651.

Editor's note. — For provisions of Acts 2003, cc. 981 and 1021, cls. 4 to 16, reflecting the intent of the General Assembly to provide for the consolidation of the procurement and operational functions of information technology for state agencies in a single agency, and related transitional and other provisions, see the Editor's note at § 2.2-2005.

§ 2.2-225.1. (Expires July 1, 2018) Office of Telework Promotion and Broadband Assistance. — A. There is hereby established the Office of Telework Promotion and Broadband Assistance in the office of the Secretary of Technology, consisting of a director, appointed by the Secretary of Technology, and such additional telework and broadband professionals as deemed necessary. The goals of the Office are to encourage telework as a family-friendly, business-friendly public policy that promotes workplace efficiency and reduces strain on transportation infrastructure. In conjunction with efforts to promote telework, the Office shall work with public and private entities to develop widespread access to broadband services. It shall be the duty of the director of the Office to advise the Secretary and the Board of Directors of the Innovative Technology Authority, generally.

B. The director shall have the following duties:

1. Promote and encourage use of telework alternatives for public and private employees, including but not limited to appropriate policy and legislative initiatives.

2. Assist state agencies in establishing telework policies.

3. Support the efforts of both public and private entities within the Commonwealth to enhance or facilitate the deployment of, and access to competitively priced, advanced electronic communications services (commonly known as broadband) and Internet access services of general application throughout the Commonwealth.

4. Specifically work towards establishing affordable, accessible broadband services to unserved areas of the Commonwealth and monitor advancements in communication that will facilitate this goal.

5. Advocate for, and facilitate the development and deployment of, applications, programs, and services including, but not limited to telework, telemedicine, and e-learning that will bolster the usage of and demand for broadband level telecommunications.

6. Serve as a broadband information and applications clearinghouse for the Commonwealth and a coordination point for broadband-related services and programs in the Commonwealth.

7. Advise the Secretary on broadband adoption, deployment, and application issues.

8. Coordinate activities regarding telework with, and regularly report to, a panel consisting of the Secretaries of Administration, Commerce and Trade, Finance, Technology, and Transportation. The Secretary of Technology shall serve as chair of the panel. Additional members may be designated by the Governor. Staff support for the panel shall be provided by the offices of the Secretaries of Technology and Transportation and the Governor shall designate additional agencies to provide staff support as necessary.

C. The Office shall not have the power to consolidate or otherwise have authority over advanced communications projects being conducted by public or private bodies outside of the executive branch of government. (2008, c. 444.)

Editor's note. — Acts 2008, c. 444, cl. 2, provides: "That the provisions of this act shall expire on July 1, 2018."

§§ **2.2-226 through 2.2-227:** Repealed by Acts 2003, cc. 981 and 1021.

Cross references. — For current provisions concerning Virginia Information Technologies Agency, see § 2.2-2005 et seq.

Editor's note. — Repealed § 2.2-226 was amended by Acts 2003, c. 888.

For provisions of Acts 2003, cc. 981 and 1021, cls. 4 to 16, reflecting the intent of the General Assembly to provide for the consolidation of the procurement and operational functions of information technology for state agencies in a single agency, and related transitional and other provisions, see the Editor's note at § 2.2-2005.

Article 10.

Secretary of Transportation.

§ 2.2-228. Position established; agencies for which responsible. — The position of Secretary of Transportation (the "Secretary") is created. The Secretary shall be responsible to the Governor for the following agencies: Department of Transportation, Department of Rail and Public Transportation, Department of Aviation, Department of Motor Vehicles, the Virginia Port

Authority, and the Motor Vehicle Dealer Board. The Governor, by executive order, may assign any state executive agency to the Secretary, or reassign any agency listed in this section to another Secretary. (1990, cc. 1, 317, §§ 2.1-51.41, 2.1-51.43; 1992, c. 167; 1993, c. 757; 2001, c. 844.)

Editor's note. — Acts 2008, c. 879, effective for the biennium ending June 30, 2010, in Item 436 A, provides: "A. The transportation policy goals enumerated in this Act shall be implemented by the Secretary of Transportation, including the Secretary acting as Chairman of the Commonwealth Transportation Board.

"1. The maintenance of existing transportation assets to ensure the safety of the public shall be the first priority in budgeting, allocation, and spending. The highway share of the Transportation Trust Fund shall be used for highway maintenance and operation purposes prior to its availability for new development, acquisition, and construction.

"2. The efficient and cost-effective movement of people and goods will consider the needs in, and connectivity of, all modes of transportation, including bicycling, walking, public transportation, highways, freight and passenger rail, ports, and airports. The planning, development, construction, and operations of Virginia's transportation facilities will reflect this goal.

"3. Stewardship of the environment will be a priority in the allocation of resources and the planning and evaluation of projects and activities by transportation agencies.

"4. To the greatest extent possible, the appropriation of transportation revenues shall reflect planned spending of such revenues by agency and by program. The maximization of all federal transportation funds available to the Commonwealth shall be paramount in the budgetary, spending, and allocation processes. The Secretary is hereby authorized to take all actions necessary to ensure that federal transportation funds are allocated and utilized for the maximum benefit of the Commonwealth, whether such funds are authorized under P.L. 109-59 of the 109th Congress, or any successor or related federal transportation legislation."

§ 2.2-229. Office of Intermodal Planning and Investment of the Secretary of Transportation. — There is hereby established the Office of Intermodal Planning and Investment of the Secretary of Transportation, consisting of a director, appointed by the Secretary of Transportation, and such additional transportation professionals as the Secretary of Transportation shall determine. The goals of the Office are to provide solutions that link existing systems; reduce congestion; improve safety, mobility, and accessibility; and provide for greater travel options. It shall be the duty of the director of the office to advise the Secretary and the Commonwealth Transportation Board on intermodal issues, generally.

The purpose of the Office shall be:

1. To coordinate and oversee major multimodal corridor studies as directed by the Secretary;

2. To assist the Commonwealth Transportation Board in the Development of the Statewide Transportation Plan pursuant to § 33.1-23.03;

3. To advocate multimodal planning solutions as part of the six-year improvement program;

4. To work with and coordinate action of the Virginia Department of Transportation, the Virginia Department of Rail and Public Transportation, the Virginia Port Authority, and the Virginia Department of Aviation to promote intermodal and multimodal solutions in each agency's strategic and long-range plans;

5. To work with and review plans of regional transportation agencies and authorities to promote intermodal and multimodal solutions;

6. To assess implementation of intermodal planning, including periodic comparisons between and among statewide and regional multimodal plans;

7. To work with and coordinate actions of the agencies of the transportation Secretariat to assess freight movements and promote intermodal and multimodal solutions to address freight needs;

8. To assess and coordinate transportation safety needs related to passenger and freight movements by all transportation modes;

9. To coordinate the adequate accommodation of pedestrian, bicycle, and other forms of nonmotorized transportation in the six-year improvement program and other state and regional transportation plans;

10. To develop transportation performance measures and prepare an annual performance report on state and regional efforts;

11. To inventory and assess intermodal facilities of statewide importance, prioritize new facilities, and recommend facilities for consideration in the six-year improvement program; and

12. To identify and facilitate public and private partnerships to achieve the goals of state and regional plans. (2002, c. 361; 2006, c. 942; 2007, cc. 80, 219.)

The 2007 amendments. — The 2007 amendments by cc. 80 and 219 are identical, and in the first paragraph, substituted "Office of Intermodal Planning and Investment" for "Intermodal Office"; transferred the former last paragraph to the second sentence in the first paragraph; added subdivisions 1, 2, 7 through 9 and 12; and redesignated former subdivisions 1 through 6 as present subdivisions 3 through 6, 10 and 11.

CHAPTER 3.

VIRGINIA LIAISON OFFICE.

§ **2.2-300. Office created; appointment of Director.** — There is created in the Office of the Governor, the Virginia Liaison Office, as ("the Office"). The Office shall consist of a Director who shall be appointed by the Governor, subject to confirmation by the General Assembly as provided in § 2.2-106. The Director shall preferably, by reason of professional experience, be familiar with the structure and operations of the federal government and of the Commonwealth. (1978, c. 515, § 2.1-564; 1979, c. 429; 1981, c. 315; 1982, c. 421; 2001, c. 844.)

§ **2.2-301. Duties of Director; staff; office location.** — A. The Director shall be responsible for the general management of the Office and for the tasks assigned to it by law or by the Governor.

B. The Director may hire staff, and accept offers of service from volunteers on a full- or part-time basis.

C. The Director may obtain, either in the City of Washington, D. C., or at some location within the Commonwealth within twenty-five miles of Washington, D. C., such office space as he deems necessary for carrying out the duties imposed on him by this chapter. (1978, c. 515, §§ 2.1-565, 2.1-566; 1981, c. 315; 2001, c. 844.)

§ **2.2-302. Responsibilities of Office.** — It shall be the responsibility of the Office, through its Director, generally, to serve as an institutional and organizational link between the government of the Commonwealth and those agencies, bureaus, departments, offices, and entities of the United States government located in the City of Washington, D. C., and its immediate environs. The responsibilities of the Office shall include, but not necessarily be limited to:

1. Monitoring and tracking the development of federal legislation which is of interest to the Commonwealth;
2. Conducting in-depth analyses of federal legislation and regulations as to their impact upon the Commonwealth;
3. Providing state agencies with up-to-date information on the status of federal legislation and regulations;
4. Influencing the development of federal legislation by keeping the State Congressional Delegation informed about the Governor's priorities;
5. Alerting state agencies and local governments to early opportunities for federal grants;
6. Joining in cooperative efforts with other states, through their Washington offices, on issues of mutual concern;
7. Maintaining personal contacts with Congressional staffs, key federal agency officials, public interest groups, etc.;
8. Writing, or advising upon, testimony to be presented by the Governor or state agency heads before Congressional committees;
9. Assisting state agency officials in resolving administrative problems which occur between the state and federal agencies;
10. Monitoring and tracking the status of federal grant applications submitted by state agencies;
11. Assisting state agencies in obtaining needed information from the federal government;
12. Serving as a base office for state officials traveling to Washington;
13. Arranging meetings between federal and state officials;
14. Serving as an information source about the Commonwealth when called upon by another state's Congressional delegate's staff;
15. Preparing analyses of legislation and initiatives which originate with the federal government, other states and interstate groups, including preparing statements of their potential impact on the Commonwealth, and coordinating state positions on such legislation and initiatives;
16. Maintaining liaison with other states and interstate groups;
17. Supporting state agencies in monitoring and influencing the development of federal regulations of interest to the Commonwealth; and
18. Reporting twice yearly to the members of the Senate Committee on Finance, the House Committee on Appropriations, and the Governor all federal mandates and regulations that may have an effect on the Commonwealth. These reports shall be presented by January 15 and July 15 of each year and shall contain the names of those Virginia congressional members who voted for the legislation resulting in the mandates. (1978, c. 515, § 2.1-567; 1981, c. 315; 1994, c. 479; 1997, c. 67; 2001, c. 844.)

§ 2.2-302.1. Support for enactment of pooled purchasing of health insurance efforts. — It is the public policy of the Commonwealth to support federal efforts to encourage pooling of health insurance by small businesses, provided any such health insurance plans remain subject to state law. (2006, c. 910.)

§ 2.2-303. Cooperation with Department of Planning and Budget; supplemental assistance. — The Office shall be charged with the coordination of its work with that of the Virginia Department of Planning and Budget. The Department of Planning and Budget shall provide the Office with such support, beyond that provided for in § 2.2-301, as may prove necessary. (1978, c. 515, § 2.1-568; 1981, c. 315; 2001, c. 844.)

CHAPTER 3.1.

Office of Commonwealth Preparedness.

§ **2.2-304. Office created; purpose; appointment of Assistant to the Governor for Commonwealth Preparedness; staff.** — A. There is created in the Office of the Governor, the Office of Commonwealth Preparedness (the Office). The purpose of the Office is to work with and through others, including federal, state, and local officials, as well as the private sector, to develop a seamless, coordinated security and preparedness strategy and implementation plan. The Office shall serve as the liaison between the Governor and the federal Department of Homeland Security.

B. The Office shall consist of an Assistant to the Governor for Commonwealth Preparedness (the Assistant to the Governor) who shall be appointed by the Governor, for a term commencing on the Monday after the third Wednesday in January, after the Governor's inauguration. The Assistant to the Governor shall be appointed for a term of four years. The appointment shall be subject to confirmation by the General Assembly as provided in § 2.2-106. After the Assistant to the Governor is confirmed by the General Assembly, the Governor shall fill vacancies only in the event of the Assistant to the Governor's resignation, death, disability, or upon removal by the Governor after notification to the Speaker of the House of Delegates and the President pro tempore of the Senate of the reason for removal. Upon such vacancy, the Governor shall appoint a successor for the remainder of the unexpired term that shall be effective until 30 days after the next meeting of the ensuing General Assembly and, if confirmed, thereafter for the remainder of the term.

The Assistant to the Governor shall, by reason of professional background have knowledge of military, law enforcement, public safety, or emergency management and preparedness issues, in addition to familiarity with the structure and operations of the federal government and of the Commonwealth. The Assistant to the Governor shall be responsible for the general management of the Office and shall perform such duties as may be provided by law or assigned by the Governor. The Assistant to the Governor may appoint such persons as he deems necessary for the efficient conduct of the Office, and apportion, out of the appropriation for the Office, such salaries among such persons as he deems proper, but the aggregate amount paid them shall not exceed the amount provided by law. The Assistant to the Governor shall appoint an interoperability coordinator to review all communications-related grant requests from state agencies and localities to ensure federal grants are used to enhance interoperability. (2006, cc. 860, 901.)

§ **2.2-305. Duties of the Office.** — It shall be the responsibility of the Office, through the Assistant to the Governor, to:

1. Provide oversight, coordination, and review of all disaster, emergency management, and terrorism management plans for the state and its agencies.
2. Work with federal officials to obtain additional federal resources and coordinate policy development and information exchange.
3. Coordinate working relationships between state agencies and the Governor's Cabinet.
4. Serve as the point of contact with the federal Department of Homeland Security.

5. Serve as the Governor's representative on regional efforts to develop a coordinated security and preparedness strategy, including the National Capitol Region security group organized as part of the federal Urban Areas Security Initiative.

6. Serve as a direct liaison between the Governor and local governments and first responders on issues of emergency prevention, preparedness, response, and recovery.

7. Educate the public on homeland security and overall preparedness issues.

8. Serve as chairman of the Secure Commonwealth Panel.

9. Encourage public safety volunteer efforts throughout the state.

10. Serve as vice-chairman of the Virginia Military Advisory Council to establish a working relationship with Virginia's active duty military bases.

11. Coordinate the development of a formula for allocation of State Homeland Security Program funds to localities and state agencies in compliance with federal grant guidance and constraints and which formula shall be, to the extent permissible under federal constraints, based on actual risk and threat.

12. Establish regional working groups to meet regularly and focus on regional initiatives in training, equipment, and strategy to ensure ready access to response teams in times of emergency and facilitate testing and training exercises for emergencies and mass casualty preparedness.

13. Provide oversight and review of the Virginia Department of Emergency Management's annual statewide assessment of local and regional capabilities, including equipment, training, personnel, response times, and other factors.

14. Do all acts necessary to ensure that available federal and state resources are directed toward safeguarding Virginia and its citizens. (2006, cc. 860, 901.)

§ 2.2-306. Secure Commonwealth Panel; membership; duties; compensation; staff. — A. The Secure Commonwealth Panel (the Panel), is established as an advisory board, within the meaning of § 2.2-2100, in the executive branch of state government. The Panel shall consist of 34 members as follows: three members of the House of Delegates and two nonlegislative citizens to be appointed by the Speaker of the House of Delegates; three members of the Senate of Virginia and two nonlegislative citizens to be appointed by the Senate Committee on Rules; the Lieutenant Governor; the Attorney General; the Executive Secretary of the Supreme Court of Virginia; the Assistant to the Governor for Commonwealth Preparedness, the Secretary of Commerce and Trade, the Secretary of Health and Human Resources, the Secretary of Public Safety, the Secretary of Technology and the Secretary of Transportation or their designees; two local first responders; three local government representatives; two physicians with knowledge of public health; four members from the business or industry sector; and four additional members from the private sector. Except for appointments made by the Speaker of the House of Delegates and the Senate Committee on Rules, all other appointments shall be made by the Governor. Additional ex officio members may be appointed to the Panel by the Governor at his discretion. Legislative members shall serve terms coincident with their terms of office or until their successors shall qualify. Nonlegislative citizen members shall serve for terms of four years. The Assistant to the Governor of the Office shall be the chairman of the Panel.

B. The Panel shall monitor and assess the implementation of statewide prevention, preparedness, response, and recovery initiatives and where necessary to review, evaluate, and make recommendations relating to the emergency preparedness of government at all levels in the Commonwealth. Additionally, the Panel shall facilitate cabinet-level coordination among the various agencies of state government related to emergency preparedness and shall facilitate private sector preparedness and communication. The Panel shall make quarterly reports to the Governor concerning the state's emergency preparedness, response, recovery, and prevention efforts.

C. Members of the Panel shall serve without compensation but shall be reimbursed for all reasonable and necessary expenses incurred in the discharge of their duties as provided in § 2.2-2825.

D. Staff support for the Panel and funding for the costs of expenses of the members shall be provided by the Office of Commonwealth Preparedness. (2006, cc. 860, 901; 2007, cc. 714, 729, 742.)

The 2007 amendments. — The 2007 amendment by c. 714, in subsection A, inserted "the Executive Secretary of the Supreme Court of Virginia" and made related changes.

The 2007 amendments by cc. 729 and 742 are nearly identical, and in subsection A, in the second sentence, substituted "34 members" for "29 members" and inserted "the Executive Secretary of the Supreme Court of Virginia" following "Attorney General" and "four members from the business or industry sector" following "public health" and made minor stylistic changes.

Subsection A has been set out in the form above at the direction of the Virginia Code Commission.

CHAPTER 4.

SECRETARY OF THE COMMONWEALTH.

Article 1.

General Provisions.

Article 2.

Registration of Names or Insignia of Certain Organizations.

Article 3.

Registration of Lobbyists.

Article 1.

General Provisions.

§ 2.2-400. Appointment and term of office; filling vacancies; oath. — A. The Governor shall appoint, subject to confirmation by the General Assembly, a Secretary of the Commonwealth for a term commencing on the Monday after the third Wednesday in January after his inauguration. The appointment shall be for a term of four years. Vacancies shall be filled by appointment by the Governor for the unexpired term and shall be effective until thirty days after the next meeting of the ensuing General Assembly and, if confirmed, thereafter for the remainder of the term.

B. The Secretary of the Commonwealth, before he acts as such, shall, in addition to the other oaths prescribed by law, take an oath to keep secret such matters as he may be required by the Governor to conceal. (Code 1950, § 2-59; 1958, c. 1, § 2-57.1; 1966, c. 677, §§ 2.1-65, 2.1-67; 2001, c. 844.)

Cross references. — As to the application process and administration of the Virginia Respite Care Grant Program, see § 2.2-717.

Michie's Jurisprudence. — For related discussion, see 17 M.J. State, § 4.

§ 2.2-401. Ex officio Secretary to Governor; in charge of division of records. — The Secretary of the Commonwealth, who shall be ex officio Secretary to the Governor, shall be in direct charge of the division of records. (Code 1950, § 2-58; 1966, c. 677, § 2.1-66; 2001, c. 844.)

CASE NOTES

Editor's note. — The case below was decided under former Title 2.1 or prior provisions.

Office of Secretary of Commonwealth not abolished. — So much of Acts 1927, p. 105, as provided for the abolition of the office of Secretary of the Commonwealth was unconstitutional, and Acts 1930, p. 82, was inconsistent with any intent to abolish the office. Nor did the fact that for several years after 1930 the General Assembly made no direct appropriation to the office evidence any intent to abolish it by implication pursuant to the power given by § 80 of the Virginia Constitution of 1902. Jackson v. Hodges, 176 Va. 89, 10 S.E.2d 566 (1940).

No increase in salary during term of office. — The Governor had no authority to increase the salary of the Secretary of the Commonwealth as ex officio Secretary to the Governor because of additional duties imposed upon him. Such increase was within the restriction of § 83 of the Virginia Constitution of 1902, prohibiting increase of salaries of officers of the executive department during term of office. Jackson v. Hodges, 176 Va. 89, 10 S.E.2d 566 (1940).

§ 2.2-402. Keeper of seals of Commonwealth; duties generally. — The Secretary of the Commonwealth shall (i) be keeper of the seals of the Commonwealth; (ii) keep a record of all executive acts, arrange and preserve all records and papers belonging to the executive branch of state government; (iii) be charged with the clerical duties of that department; and (iv) render to the Governor, in the dispatch of executive business, such services as he requires. The Secretary of the Commonwealth shall record or register all papers or documents required by law to be registered or recorded in his office, and, when required, furnish a copy of any record in his office under the seal of the Commonwealth.

The Secretary of the Commonwealth may authenticate records of any court of the Commonwealth and of any department of the government. He shall keep a register of all city, incorporated town, county, and district officers, and, when required, give a certificate of the election and qualification of any such officer.

The Secretary of the Commonwealth shall make an annual report to the Governor, identifying the following: (a) the boards of visitors of all public institutions, and other boards appointed by the Governor; (b) all commissions issued under appointments made by the Governor, except commissions to notaries public; (c) all departments, boards, councils, commissions, and other collegial bodies created in the executive branch of state government; and (d) such other matters as the Governor requires. The reports shall be transmitted by the Governor to the General Assembly, printed as other annual reports are printed, bound in a separate volume, and disposed of according to law.

The Secretary of the Commonwealth shall collect all fees described in § 2.2-409, and all other fees of office and commissions, accruing and pay them into the state treasury.

The Secretary of the Commonwealth shall include information and photographs of the members of the General Assembly in such annual report; these materials shall be maintained for the Secretary's use in the annual report by the Clerks of the House of Delegates and the Senate. (Code 1950, §§ 2-60, 14-13; 1956, c. 217; 1964, c. 386, § 14.1-14; 1966, c. 677, § 2.1-68; 1998, c. 872; 1999, c. 51; 2001, c. 844.)

§ 2.2-403. Compilation of compacts and related records and reports. — The Secretary of the Commonwealth shall conserve a copy of each of the compacts to which the Commonwealth is now or has been a party, commencing with the compact entered into with the state of North Carolina that is referenced in chapter XXIX of the October Session of the 1778 Acts of the General Assembly. The record shall contain the dates on which the compacts were confirmed by the Commonwealth.

In accordance with § 30-154.1, beginning July 1, 2001, the Virginia Code Commission shall annually forward to the Secretary of the Commonwealth any newly enacted, amended or repealed compact as it was adopted by the Commonwealth.

The Secretary of the Commonwealth shall also maintain all records relating to the appointment of persons in accordance with compacts confirmed by the Commonwealth.

The Secretary of the Commonwealth shall report to the Governor and the Virginia Commission on Interstate Cooperation within fifteen days after the convening of each legislative session, and at such other times as deemed appropriate, on appointments and vacancies to the interstate boards, commissions and committees established for the purposes of such compacts. (1976, c. 198, § 2.1-68.1; 2001, cc. 100, 844.)

Editor's note. — Acts 2001, c. 100 amended § 2.1-68.1, from which this section is derived. Pursuant to § 30-152, Acts 2001, c. 100 has been given effect in this section as set out above. The 2001 amendment by c. 100, in the first paragraph, substituted "conserve a copy of each" for "prepare and maintain a compilation of all" in the first sentence, and in the second sentence, substituted "record" for "compilation" and deleted "and the complete texts of the terms of such compacts" at the end; and added the present second paragraph.

§ 2.2-404. Certifying records for use in other states. — Whenever any record of any court in the Commonwealth or of any department of the government is to be used in another state in the United States, the Secretary of the Commonwealth shall authenticate the same in the manner and give the certificates required by the laws of the state when such record is to be used, as far as practicable. (Code 1950, § 2-61; 1966, c. 677, § 2.1-69; 2001, c. 844.)

§ 2.2-405. Secretary of Commonwealth to present list of vacancies to arise on commissions, boards, etc. — The Secretary of the Commonwealth shall prepare by the fifteenth of January in each year a list of all vacancies that are scheduled to arise during that year on all boards, commissions, councils or other collegial bodies appointed by the Governor. The list shall be presented to the Governor and the General Assembly as soon as practicable following its preparation, and the Secretary of the Commonwealth shall make copies of the list available to the public at cost. (1979, c. 141, § 2.1-42.2; 2001, c. 844.)

§ 2.2-406. Secretary of Commonwealth to report list of interim appointments requiring confirmation; other appointments. — A. The Secretary of the Commonwealth shall periodically, during the interim between sessions of the General Assembly, present to the chairmen of the Senate and House Committees on Privileges and Elections a list of the names of all persons appointed by the Governor that require confirmation by the General Assembly. A list shall be presented by June 1, August 1, October 1, and December 1, and shall include the names of all persons so appointed since adjournment or since the last required report, the position to which appointed, and the person whom the appointee will succeed.

B. The Secretary of the Commonwealth shall report to the General Assembly by December 1 of each year, the number of persons appointed to any state board, commission, agency or authority, categorized by race, gender and national origin. Information on the race, gender and national origin of appointees shall be obtained through voluntary self-identification following appointment. Such information shall be used solely for the purpose of compiling the statistical information required under this section and any personally identifiable information collected under this section shall be confidential and shall be exempt from disclosure under the Freedom of Information Act (§ 2.2-3700 et seq.). (1994, c. 846, § 2.1-42.3; 1995, c. 579; 2001, c. 844.)

§ 2.2-406.1. Secretary of Commonwealth to maintain and transfer records on collegial bodies to the Governor-elect. — A. The Secretary of the Commonwealth shall maintain an electronic database of collegial bodies to which the Governor makes appointments. The database shall be organized by collegial body and include the following information:

1. Authority for each appointment;
2. Term length and term expiration dates for each appointee;
3. Eligibility requirements or other restrictions affecting the next appointment;
4. Name, address, and telephone number of each appointee;
5. Identity of the chairman and vice-chairman and the method of their election; and
6. Name of the affiliated agency or entity that provides staff support and the name and telephone number of the contact person within such agency or entity.

B. Agencies and entities of the Commonwealth that provide staff support to a collegial body shall notify the Secretary of the Commonwealth of an appointee's death or resignation and any changes to the contact information for an appointee or staff or a appointee's eligibility status.

C. The electronic database or copy thereof shall be transferred to each Governor-elect upon request. (2003, cc. 532, 556.)

§ **2.2-407:** Reserved.

§ **2.2-408. Collection of information relevant to boundary changes from governmental subdivisions of Commonwealth.** — The Secretary of the Commonwealth shall be responsible for the collection from the governmental subdivisions of the Commonwealth of information relevant to their boundary changes and the dissemination of such information to the appropriate departments of state government. (1978, c. 641, § 2.1-71.1; 2001, c. 844.)

§ **2.2-409. Secretary of the Commonwealth.** — A. The Secretary of the Commonwealth shall charge the following fees for services rendered in his office to be paid by the person for whom the service is rendered at the time it is done:

For a testimonial, including seal tax	$10.00
For each authentication after the first testimonial for documents bearing the testament by the same person on the same date, including seal tax	5.00
For a copy of any paper, if on one sheet	1.00
And for each sheet after the first	.75
For issuing a commission to a commissioner in another state	7.00
For power of attorney for nonresident insurers, contractors	3.00
For service of process on parties, each defendant	19.00
For service of process on reciprocal insurers	7.00
For registration of name, badge and insignia	7.50
For affixing the Seal of the Commonwealth	2.00
For issuing a commission to a notary for the Commonwealth at large, including seal tax	35.00
For issuing a commission to an electronic notary public	35.00

And for filing in his office any paper required by law to be filed, the same fee as is allowed by law for recording similar papers.

B. Notwithstanding any other provision of law, the Secretary shall charge a technology fee of $10 in addition to the fees set out in subsection A for commissioning of a notary public or electronic notary public, which funds shall be deposited into the Secretary of the Commonwealth's Technology Trust Fund established by the comptroller and used only to obtain and update office automation and information technology equipment including software and conversion services; to preserve, maintain, and enhance records, including but not limited to the costs of repairs, maintenance, service contracts, and system upgrades; and to improve public access to records. There shall be no transfers out of the fund, including transfers to the general fund. (Code 1950, § 14-114; 1964, c. 386, § 14.1-103; 1966, c. 272; 1976, c. 559; 1979, c. 14; 1984, c. 362; 1987, cc. 449, 459; 1998, cc. 259, 872, § 2.1-71.2; 2001, c. 844; 2007, cc. 269, 362, 590.)

Editor's note. — Acts 2007, cc. 269 and 590, cl. 3, provides: "That the provisions of this Act relating to electronic notaries public and electronic notarization shall become effective July 1, 2008."

Acts 2008, c. 879, effective for the biennium ending June 30, 2010, in Item 61, provides: "A. Notwithstanding the provisions of § 2.2-409, Code of Virginia, or any other law to the contrary, the Secretary of the Commonwealth shall charge a fee of $35.00 for issuing a commission to a notary for the Commonwealth at large, including seal tax.

"B. The fee charged by the Secretary of the Commonwealth under the provisions of §2.2-409, Code of Virginia, for a Service of Process shall be $28.00."

The 2007 amendments. — The 2007 amendments by cc. 269 and 590 are identical, and designated the existing provisions of the section as subsection A and added subsection B; in present subsection A, substituted "35.00" for "25.00," increased the fee "For issuing a commission to a notary" by $10 and added the fee "For issuing a commission to an electronic notary public."

The 2007 amendments by cc. 269 and 590, effective July 1, 2008, are identical, and inserted "or electronic notary public" in the first sentence of subsection B. See Acts 2007, cc. 269 and 590, cl. 3.

The 2007 amendment by c. 362 added the fee "For each authentication after ..." in subsection A.

§ 2.2-410. Appointment of assistants; deputy to act in absence of Secretary; notice to Governor. — A. The Secretary of the Commonwealth shall appoint in his office the assistants allowed by law.

B. During the absence of the Secretary of the Commonwealth from his office his duties shall be performed by the Deputy Secretary, but when such absence is for more than five days at a time, notice thereof shall be given to the Governor. (Code 1950, §§ 2-63, 2-64; 1966, c. 677, §§ 2.1-72, 2.1-73; 2001, c. 844.)

Article 2.

Registration of Names or Insignia of Certain Organizations.

§ 2.2-411. Registration of names or insignia of certain societies, organizations or associations; alteration or cancellation of name. — Any association, lodge, order, fraternal society, beneficial association, or fraternal and beneficial society or association, historical, military, or veterans' organization, labor union, foundation, federation, or any other society, organization or association, degree, branch, subordinate lodge, or auxiliary thereof, whether incorporated or unincorporated, the principles and activities of which are not repugnant to the Constitution and laws of the United States or the Commonwealth, may register, in the office of the Secretary of the Commonwealth, a facsimile, duplicate, or description of its name, badge, motto, button, declaration, charm, emblem, rosette or other insignia, and may, by reregistration, alter or cancel the name. (Code 1950, § 38-308; 1952, c. 225, § 2-64.1; 1966, c. 677, § 2.1-74; 2001, c. 844.)

Cross references. — As to illegal use of the insignia of any association or organization mentioned in this section, see § 18.2-177.

Michie's Jurisprudence. — For related discussion, see 3A M.J. Beneficial and Benevolent Associations, § 9.

§ 2.2-412. Application for such registration, alteration or cancellation. — Application for registration, alteration, or cancellation under this article shall be made by the chief officer of the association, lodge, order, fraternal society, beneficial association, or fraternal and beneficial society or association, historical, military, or veterans' organization, labor union, foundation, federation, or other society, organization, or association, degree, branch, subordinate lodge, or auxiliary thereof, upon blanks to be provided by the Secretary of the Commonwealth. (Code 1950, § 38-309; 1952, c. 225, § 2-64.2; 1966, c. 677, § 2.1-75; 2001, c. 844.)

§ 2.2-413. Registration for benefit of associated branches, etc. — Registration shall be for the use, benefit, and on behalf of all associations, degrees, branches, subordinate lodges, and auxiliaries of such associations, lodge, order, fraternal society, beneficial association, or fraternal and beneficial society or association, historical, military, or veterans' organization, labor union, foundation, federation, or other society, organization, or association, degree, branch, subordinate lodge, or auxiliary thereof, and the individual members of such organizations, throughout the Commonwealth. (Code 1950, § 38-310; 1952, c. 225, § 2-64.3; 1966, c. 677, § 2.1-76; 2001, c. 844.)

§ **2.2-414. Record of registration; certification of registration; fees.** — A. The Secretary of the Commonwealth shall keep a properly indexed record of the registration provided for by § 2.2-411, which record shall also show any altered or canceled registration.

B. Upon granting registration provided in § 2.2-411, the Secretary of the Commonwealth shall issue his certificate to the petitioners, setting forth the fact of such registration.

C. The fees of the Secretary of the Commonwealth for registration, alteration, cancellation, searches, and certificates issued pursuant to this article shall be the same as provided by law for similar services. (Code 1950, § 38-311; 1952, c. 225, § 2-64.4; 1966, c. 677, §§ 2.1-77, 2.1-79, 2.1-81; 2001, c. 844.)

§ **2.2-415. Names or insignia not to be imitative.** — No registration shall be granted or alteration permitted to any association, lodge, order, fraternal society, beneficial association, or fraternal and beneficial society or association, historical, military, or veterans' organization, labor union, foundation, federation, or other society, organization, or association, degree, branch, subordinate lodge, or auxiliary thereof, having a name, badge, motto, button, decoration, charm, emblem, rosette, or other insignia, similar to, imitating, or so nearly resembling as to be calculated to deceive, any other name, badge, button, decoration, charm, emblem, rosette, or other insignia whatsoever, already registered pursuant to the provisions of § 2.2-411. (Code 1950, § 38-312; 1952, c. 225, § 2-64.5; 1966, c. 677, § 2.1-78; 2001, c. 844.)

§ **2.2-416. Registration of mottoes or slogans of state departments; exemptions.** — Any state department, division, board, commission, agency or facility owned and operated by the Commonwealth, which develops or creates, or commissions the development or creation of a motto or slogan for its use pursuant to or in furtherance of the programs or business of the department, division, agency or facility, shall without delay register the motto or slogan with the Secretary of the Commonwealth, who shall maintain a record of such registration to be open to public inspection during normal office hours.

However, public institutions of higher education in Virginia and units of the Virginia National Guard shall be exempt from the requirements of this section. (1972, c. 403, § 2.1-81.1; 2001, c. 844.)

§ **2.2-417. Use of registered motto or slogan or recognizable variation thereof; penalty for violation.** — A. Upon registration of a motto or slogan as provided in § 2.2-416, no individual, partnership, association or corporation shall employ such motto or slogan or a recognizable variation thereof on any article offered for sale to the public at a price above the actual cost of production of the article without the express consent of the registrant, which, if it approved of such use, may require payment of a reasonable fee or royalty for the use of its motto or slogan and, in addition, may impose restrictions upon such use.

B. No individual, partnership, association or corporation shall otherwise publicly use a recognizable variation of a registered motto or slogan for any purpose without the express consent of the registrant. Such consent may in any event be revoked by the registrant upon thirty days' written notice to the licensee. All fees or royalties collected pursuant to this section shall be paid into the general fund of the state treasury.

Public use of a registered motto or slogan or a recognizable variation of a registered motto or slogan for any purpose without the express consent of the registrant or the continued use of a registered motto or slogan or recognizable variation thereof following withdrawal of consent to such use by the registrant shall be punishable by a fine of no more than $1,000. Each day of violation shall constitute a separate offense. (1972, c. 403, §§ 2.1-81.2, 2.1-81.3; 2001, c. 844.)

Michie's Jurisprudence. — For related discussion, see 3A M.J. Beneficial and Benevolent Associations, § 9.

Article 3.

Registration of Lobbyists.

§ **2.2-418. Statement of intent and purposes.** — The General Assembly finds and declares the following:

1. The operation of open and responsible government requires the fullest opportunity to be afforded to the people to petition their government for the redress of grievances and to express freely their opinions on legislative and executive actions.

2. The identity and expenditures of certain persons who attempt to influence legislative and executive actions with respect to legislation and executive orders should be publicly identified to preserve and maintain the integrity of government. (1994, cc. 857, 937, § 2.1-779; 2001, c. 844.)

§ **2.2-419. Definitions.** — As used in this article, unless the context requires a different meaning:

"Anything of value" means:

1. A pecuniary item, including money, or a bank bill or note;
2. A promissory note, bill of exchange, order, draft, warrant, check, or bond given for the payment of money;
3. A contract, agreement, promise, or other obligation for an advance, conveyance, forgiveness of indebtedness, deposit, distribution, loan, payment, gift, pledge, or transfer of money;
4. A stock, bond, note, or other investment interest in an entity;
5. A receipt given for the payment of money or other property;
6. A right in action;
7. A gift, tangible good, chattel, or an interest in a gift, tangible good, or chattel;
8. A loan or forgiveness of indebtedness;
9. A work of art, antique, or collectible;
10. An automobile or other means of personal transportation;
11. Real property or an interest in real property, including title to realty, a fee simple or partial interest, present or future, contingent or vested within realty, a leasehold interest, or other beneficial interest in realty;
12. An honorarium or compensation for services;
13. A rebate or discount in the price of anything of value unless the rebate or discount is made in the ordinary course of business to a member of the public without regard to that person's status as an executive or legislative official, or the sale or trade of something for reasonable compensation that would ordinarily not be available to a member of the public;
14. A promise or offer of employment; or
15. Any other thing of value that is pecuniary or compensatory in value to a person.

"Anything of value" does not mean a campaign contribution properly received and reported pursuant to Chapter 9.3 (§ 24.2-945 et seq.) of Title 24.2.

"Compensation" means:

1. An advance, conveyance, forgiveness of indebtedness, deposit, distribution, loan, payment, gift, pledge, or transfer of money or anything of value; or
2. A contract, agreement, promise or other obligation for an advance, conveyance, forgiveness of indebtedness, deposit, distribution, loan, payment, gift, pledge, or transfer of money or anything of value, for services rendered or to be rendered.

"Compensation" does not mean reimbursement of expenses if the reimbursement does not exceed the amount actually expended for the expenses and it is substantiated by an itemization of expenses.

"Executive action" means the proposal, drafting, development, consideration, amendment, adoption, approval, promulgation, issuance, modification, rejection, or postponement by an executive agency or official of legislation or executive orders issued by the Governor.

"Executive agency" means an agency, board, commission, or other body in the executive branch of state government. *"Executive agency"* includes the State Corporation Commission, the Virginia Department of Workers' Compensation, and the State Lottery Department.

"Executive official" means:

1. The Governor;
2. The Lieutenant Governor;
3. The Attorney General;
4. Any officer or employee of the office of the Governor or Lieutenant Governor other than a clerical or secretarial employee;
5. The Governor's Secretaries, the Deputy Secretaries, and the chief executive officer of each executive agency; or
6. Members of supervisory and policy boards, commissions and councils, as defined in § 2.2-2100, however selected.

"Expenditure" means:

1. A purchase, payment, distribution, loan, forgiveness of a loan or payment of a loan by a third party, advance, deposit, transfer of funds, a promise to make a payment, or a gift of money or anything of value for any purpose;
2. A payment to a lobbyist for salary, fee, reimbursement for expenses, or other purpose by a person employing, retaining, or contracting for the services of the lobbyist separately or jointly with other persons;
3. A payment in support of or assistance to a lobbyist or the lobbyist's activities, including the direct payment of expenses incurred at the request or suggestion of the lobbyist;
4. A payment that directly benefits an executive or legislative official or a member of the official's immediate family;
5. A payment, including compensation, payment, or reimbursement for the services, time, or expenses of an employee for or in connection with direct communication with an executive or legislative official;
6. A payment for or in connection with soliciting or urging other persons to enter into direct communication with an executive or legislative official; or
7. A payment or reimbursement for categories of expenditures required to be reported pursuant to this chapter.

"Expenditure" does not mean a campaign contribution properly received and reported pursuant to Chapter 9.3 (§ 24.2-945 et seq.) of Title 24.2.

"Fair market value" means the price that a good or service would bring between a willing seller and a willing buyer in the open market after negotiations. If the fair market value cannot be determined, the actual price paid for the good or service shall be given consideration.

"Gift" means anything of value to the extent that a consideration of equal or greater value is not received.

"Gift" does not mean:

1. Printed informational or promotional material;

2. A gift that is not used and, no later than sixty days after receipt, is returned to the donor or delivered to a charitable organization and is not claimed as a charitable contribution for federal income tax purposes;

3. A gift, devise, or inheritance from an individual's spouse, child, parent, grandparent, brother, sister, parent-in-law, brother-in-law, sister-in-law, nephew, niece, aunt, uncle, or first cousin or the spouse of that individual, if the donor is not acting as the agent or intermediary for someone other than a person covered by this subdivision; or

4. A gift of a value of $25 or less.

"Immediate family" means (i) the spouse and (ii) any other person who resides in the same household as the executive or legislative official and is the dependent of the official.

"Legislative action" means:

1. Preparation, research, drafting, introduction, consideration, modification, amendment, approval, passage, enactment, tabling, postponement, defeat, or rejection of a bill, resolution, amendment, motion, report, nomination, appointment, or other matter by the General Assembly or a legislative official;

2. Action by the Governor in approving, vetoing, or recommending amendments for a bill passed by the General Assembly; or

3. Action by the General Assembly in overriding or sustaining a veto by the Governor, considering amendments recommended by the Governor, or considering, confirming, or rejecting an appointment of the Governor.

"Legislative official" means:

1. A member or member-elect of the General Assembly;

2. A member of a committee, subcommittee, commission, or other entity established by and responsible to the General Assembly or either house of the General Assembly; or

3. Persons employed by the General Assembly or an entity established by and responsible to the General Assembly.

"Lobbying" means:

1. Influencing or attempting to influence executive or legislative action through oral or written communication with an executive or legislative official; or

2. Solicitation of others to influence an executive or legislative official.

"Lobbying" does not mean:

1. Requests for appointments, information on the status of pending executive and legislative actions, or other ministerial contacts if there is no attempt to influence executive or legislative actions;

2. Responses to published notices soliciting public comment submitted to the public official designated in the notice to receive the responses;

3. The solicitation of an association by its members to influence legislative or executive action; or

4. Communications between an association and its members and communications between a principal and its lobbyists.

"Lobbyist" means:

1. An individual who is employed and receives payments, or who contracts for economic consideration, including reimbursement for reasonable travel and living expenses, for the purpose of lobbying;

2. An individual who represents an organization, association, or other group for the purpose of lobbying; or

3. A local government employee who lobbies.

"Lobbyist's principal" or *"principal"* means the entity on whose behalf the lobbyist influences or attempts to influence executive or legislative action. An organization whose employees conduct lobbying activities on its behalf is both a principal and an employer of the lobbyists. In the case of a coalition or

association that employs or retains others to conduct lobbying activities on behalf of its membership, the principal is the coalition or association and not its individual members.

"Local government" means:

1. Any county, city, town, or other local or regional political subdivision;
2. Any school division;
3. Any organization or entity that exercises governmental powers that is established pursuant to an interstate compact; or
4. Any organization composed of members representing entities listed in subdivisions 1, 2, or 3 of this definition.

"Local government employee" means a public employee of a local government.

"Person" means an individual, proprietorship, firm, partnership, joint venture, joint stock company, syndicate, business trust, estate, company, corporation, association, club, committee, organization, or group of persons acting in concert.

"Value" means the actual cost or fair market value of an item or items, whichever is greater. If the fair market value cannot be determined, the actual amount paid for the item or items shall be given consideration. (1994, cc. 857, 937, § 2.1-780; 2001, c. 844; 2006, cc. 787, 843, 892.)

§ 2.2-420. Exemptions. — The registration and reporting provisions of this article shall not apply to:

1. The Governor, Lieutenant Governor, Attorney General, and their immediate staffs or the Governor's Secretaries and their immediate staffs, acting in an official capacity;
2. Members of the General Assembly and other legislative officials and legislative employees acting in an official capacity;
3. Local elected officials acting in an official capacity;
4. Any employee of a state executive agency acting in an official capacity;
5. A duly elected or appointed official or employee of the United States acting in an official capacity;
6. An individual who limits lobbying solely to (i) formal testimony before a public meeting of an executive agency or legislative body and registers the appearance in the records of the agency or body and (ii) testimony and information compelled by action of an executive agency or legislative body;
7. A person who receives $500 or less in compensation and reimbursements, excluding personal living and travel expenses that are not reimbursed from any other source, in a calendar year for his lobbying activities;
8. A person who receives no compensation or anything of value for lobbying, and does not expend more than $500, excluding personal living and travel expenses that are not reimbursed from any other source, in lobbying in the calendar year; or
9. An employee of a business, other entity, or local government whose job duties do not regularly include influencing or attempting to influence legislative or executive action. (1994, cc. 857, 937, § 2.1-781; 2001, c. 844; 2006, c. 843.)

§ 2.2-421. Reporting requirements for certain state agencies. — A. The chief administrative officer of each board, department, institution, or agency of the Commonwealth shall file a registration statement with the Secretary of the Commonwealth on behalf of the officers and employees who will be engaged in lobbying as defined in § 2.2-419 and shall comply with the provisions of this article that require lobbyists to register with the Secretary of the Commonwealth. No fee shall be collected for registrations required by this section.

B. Any state governmental body required to file a registration under this section shall comply with the provisions of this article relating to registration.

C. The registration requirements of this section shall not apply to:

1. The Governor, Lieutenant Governor, Attorney General and their immediate staffs, or the Governor's Secretaries and their deputies and immediate staffs, acting in an official capacity;

2. Members of the General Assembly and other legislative officials and legislative employees acting in an official capacity;

3. The chief administrative officer of each department or division in the executive branch of state government;

4. The chief administrative officer of each division of the State Corporation Commission; or

5. Any state government employee acting in an official capacity. (1994, c. 915, § 2.1-781.1; 2001, c. 844.)

§ **2.2-422. Registration requirements.** — A. A lobbyist shall register with the Secretary of the Commonwealth prior to engaging in lobbying. A lobbyist who engages in lobbying entirely outside the capital city shall comply with this section by registering with the Secretary within fifteen days after first engaging in lobbying. Registration shall be required annually and expire May 1 of each year.

B. The chief administrative officer of each local government shall register with the Secretary of the Commonwealth and file a statement pursuant to § 2.2-423 if any local government employees will act as lobbyists on its behalf. No registration fee shall be required. Each local government shall file a consolidated report in accordance with the reporting requirements of § 2.2-426 and shall maintain locally a copy of the report that is available for inspection and copying during regular business hours. (1994, cc. 857, 937, § 2.1-782; 2001, c. 844.)

§ **2.2-423. Contents of registration statement.** — A. The registration statement shall be on a form provided by the Secretary of the Commonwealth and include the following information:

1. The name and business address and telephone number of the lobbyist;

2. The name and business address and telephone number of the person who will keep custody of the lobbyist's and the lobbyist's principal's accounts and records required to comply with this article, and the location and telephone number for the place where the accounts and records are kept;

3. The name and business address and telephone number of the lobbyist's principal;

4. The kind of business of the lobbyist's principal;

5. For each principal, the full name of the individual to whom the lobbyist reports;

6. For each principal, a statement whether the lobbyist is employed or retained and whether exclusively for the purpose of lobbying;

7. The position held by the lobbyist if he is a part-time or full-time employee of the principal;

8. The full name and business address and telephone number of each lobbyist employed by or representing the lobbyist's principal;

9. An identification of the subject matter (with as much specificity as possible) with regard to which the lobbyist or lobbyist's principal will engage in lobbying; and

10. The signed statement by the lobbyist that the information contained on the registration statement is true and correct.

B. Whenever any change, modification or addition to his status as a lobbyist is made, the lobbyist shall, within one week of such change, modification or addition, furnish full information regarding the same to the Secretary of the Commonwealth on forms provided by the Secretary.

C. The Secretary of the Commonwealth shall furnish a copy of this article to any individual offering to register as a lobbyist and shall mail by certified mail a copy of this article and a copy of the information furnished by the lobbyist to the person whom the lobbyist represents to be his principal.

D. If the principal to whom the information is sent under subsection C does not, within ten days of such mailing, file an affidavit, signed by the person or duly authorized agent of the person, denying that the lobbyist appears on his behalf, such person shall be deemed to have appointed the Secretary of the Commonwealth his agent for service of process in any prosecution arising for violation of this article. If such affidavit is filed, the Secretary shall notify the attorney for the Commonwealth of the City of Richmond. (1994, cc. 857, 937, § 2.1-783; 2001, c. 844.)

§ **2.2-424. Registration fees.** — The Secretary shall collect an annual registration fee of fifty dollars from the lobbyist for each principal for whom, or on whose behalf, the lobbyist will act. (1994, cc. 857, 937, § 2.1-784; 2001, c. 844.)

§ **2.2-425. Registration information to be recorded in legislative docket; list of executive officials.** — A. The Secretary of the Commonwealth shall maintain in a legislative docket the information filed under § 2.2-423 pertaining to lobbying involving legislative actions during any session of the General Assembly. The Secretary shall furnish current, complete lists thereof to the clerk of each house and to each member of the General Assembly once every two weeks during the session of the General Assembly beginning with the convening of the General Assembly.

B. The Secretary of the Commonwealth shall prepare a list of executive officials, their positions and names, to be revised at least semi-annually and made available to lobbyists to assist them in complying with the provisions of this article. (1994, cc. 857, 937, § 2.1-785; 2001, c. 844.)

§ **2.2-426. Lobbyist reporting; penalty.** — A. Each lobbyist shall file a separate annual report of expenditures, including gifts, for each principal for whom he lobbies by July 1 for the preceding 12-month period complete through April 30.

B. Each principal who expends more than $500 to employ or compensate multiple lobbyists shall be responsible for filing a consolidated lobbyist report pursuant to this section in any case in which the lobbyists are each exempt under the provisions of subdivision 7 or 8 of § 2.2-420 from the reporting requirements of this section.

C. The report shall be on a form provided by the Secretary of the Commonwealth, which shall be substantially as follows and shall be accompanied by instructions provided by the Secretary.

LOBBYIST'S DISCLOSURE STATEMENT

PART I:

(1) PRINCIPAL: ....

In Part I, item 2a, provide the name of the individual authorizing your employment as a lobbyist. The lobbyist filing this statement MAY NOT list his name in item 2a. THE INDIVIDUAL LISTED IN PART I, ITEM 2A, MUST SIGN THE PRINCIPAL'S STATEMENT.

(2a) Name: ....

(2b) Permanent Business Address: ....

(2c) Business Telephone: ....

(3) Provide a list of executive and legislative actions (with as much specificity as possible) for which you lobbied and a description of activities conducted.
....
....
....

(4) INCORPORATED FILINGS: If you are filing an incorporated disclosure statement, please complete the following:
Individual filing financial information: ....
Individuals to be included in the filing: ....
....

(5) Please indicate which schedules will be attached to your disclosure statement:
[ ] Schedule A: Entertainment Expenses
[ ] Schedule B: Gifts
[ ] Schedule C: Other Expenses

(6) EXPENDITURE TOTALS:
a) ENTERTAINMENT .... $ ....
b) GIFTS .... $ ....
c) OFFICE EXPENSES .... $ ....
d) COMMUNICATIONS .... $ ....
e) PERSONAL LIVING AND TRAVEL EXPENSES .... $ ....
f) COMPENSATION OF LOBBYISTS .... $ ....
g) HONORARIA .... $ ....
h) REGISTRATION COSTS .... $ ....
i) OTHER .... $ ....
TOTAL .... $ ....

PART II:
(1a) NAME OF LOBBYIST: ....
(1b) Permanent Business Address: ....
(1c) Business Telephone: ....
(2) As a lobbyist, you are (check one)
[ ] EMPLOYED (on the payroll of the principal)
[ ] RETAINED (not on the payroll of the principal, however compensated)
[ ] NOT COMPENSATED (not compensated; expenses may be reimbursed)
(3) List all lobbyists other than yourself who registered to represent your principal.
....
....
....
(4) If you selected "EMPLOYED" as your answer to Part II, item 2, provide your job title.
....

PLEASE NOTE: Some lobbyists are not individually compensated for lobbying activities. This may occur when several members of a firm represent a single principal. The principal, in turn, makes a single payment to the firm. If this describes your situation, do not answer Part II, items 5a and 5b. Instead, complete Part III, items 1 and 2.

(5a) What was the DOLLAR AMOUNT OF YOUR COMPENSATION as a lobbyist? (If you have job responsibilities other than those involving lobbying, you may have to prorate to determine the part of your salary attributable to your lobbying activities.) Transfer your answer to this item to Part I, item 6f.
(5b) Explain how you arrived at your answer to Part II, item 5a.
....
....
....

PART III:
PLEASE NOTE: If you answered Part II, items 5a and 5b, you WILL NOT complete this section.

(1) List all members of your firm, organization, association, corporation, or other entity who furnished lobbying services to your principal.
....
....
....

(2) Indicate the total amount paid to your firm, organization, association, corporation or other entity for services rendered. Transfer your answer to this item to Part I, item 6f..

SCHEDULE A
ENTERTAINMENT EXPENSES

PLEASE NOTE: Any single entertainment event included in the expense totals of the principal, with a value greater than $50, should be itemized below. Transfer any totals from this schedule to Part I, item 6a. (Please duplicate as needed.)

Date and Location of Event:
....
....

Description of Event:
....
....

Total Number of Persons Attending:
....

Names of Legislative and Executive Officials Attending: (List names only if the average value for each person attending the event was greater than $50.)
....
....
....
....

Food ....$ ....
Beverages ....$ ....
Transportation of Legislative and Executive Officials ....$ ....
Lodging of Legislative and Executive Officials ....$ ....
Performers, Speakers, Etc. ....$ ....
Displays ....$ ....
Rentals ....$ ....
Service Personnel ....$ ....
Miscellaneous ....$ ....
TOTAL ....$ ....

SCHEDULE B
GIFTS

PLEASE NOTE: Any single gift reported in the expense totals of the principal, with a value greater than $50, should be itemized below. (Report meals, entertainment and travel under Schedule A.) Transfer any totals from this schedule to Part I, item 6b. (Please duplicate as needed.)

Date of gift:	Description of gift:	Name of each legislative or executive official who is a recipient of a gift:	Cost of individual gift:
....	....	....	$ ....

....	....	....	$ ....
....	....	....	$ ....
....	....	....	$ ....
TOTAL COST TO PRINCIPAL		....	$ ....

SCHEDULE C
OTHER EXPENSES

PLEASE NOTE: This section is provided for any lobbying-related expenses not covered in Part I, items 6a — 6h. An example of an expenditure to be listed on schedule C would be the rental of a bill box during the General Assembly session. Transfer the total from this schedule to Part I, item 6i. (Please duplicate as needed.)

DATE OF EXPENSE	DESCRIPTION OF EXPENSE	AMOUNT
....	....	$ ....
....	....	$ ....
....	....	$ ....
....	....	$ ....
....	....	$ ....
....	....	$ ....
....	....	$ ....
....	....	$ ....
....	....	$ ....
TOTAL "OTHER" EXPENSES	....	$ ....

PART IV: STATEMENTS
Both the lobbyist and principal officer must sign the disclosure statement, attesting to its completeness and accuracy. The following items are mandatory and if they are not properly completed, the entire filing will be rejected and returned to the lobbyist:

(1) All signatures on the statement must be ORIGINAL in the format specified in the instructions provided by the Secretary that accompany this form. No stamps, or other reproductions of the individual's signature will be accepted.
(2) An individual MAY NOT sign the disclosure statement as lobbyist and principal officer.

STATEMENT OF LOBBYIST

I, the undersigned registered lobbyist, do state that the information furnished on this disclosure statement and on all accompanying attachments required to be made thereto is, to the best of my knowledge and belief, complete and accurate.

....
Signature of lobbyist

....
Date

STATEMENT OF PRINCIPAL

I, the undersigned principal (or an authorized official thereof), do state that the information furnished on this disclosure statement and on all accompanying attachments required to be made thereto is, to the best of my knowledge and belief, complete and accurate.

....
Signature of principal

....
Date

D. A person who signs the disclosure statement knowing it to contain a material misstatement of fact shall be guilty of a Class 5 felony.

E. Each lobbyist shall send to each legislative and executive official who is required to be identified by name on Schedule A or B of the Lobbyist's Disclosure Form a copy of Schedule A or B or a summary of the information pertaining to that official. Copies or summaries shall be provided to the official by December 15 for the preceding 12-month period complete through November 30. (1994, cc. 857, 937, § 2.1-786; 1997, cc. 616, 635, 843; 1998, c. 732; 2000, c. 297; 2001, c. 844; 2002, cc. 248, 491; 2005, c. 90; 2006, c. 843.)

Cross references. — As to punishment for Class 5 felonies, see § 18.2-10.

Editor's note. — Acts 2005, c. 90, cl. 2, provides: "That information required to be filed by subsection E of § 2.2-426 to certain officials by December 15, 2005, shall cover the preceding 11 month period complete through November 30, 2005."

§ **2.2-427. Filings; inspection.** — Registration statements and lobbying reports shall be open to public inspection and copying during the regular business hours of the office of the Secretary of the Commonwealth.

Such statements and reports shall be deemed to have been filed only when actually received in the office of the Secretary or mailed to the Secretary by registered, certified, or regular mail with the sender retaining sufficient proof of mailing, which may be a United States Postal Certificate of Mailing. (1994, cc. 857, 937, § 2.1-787; 2001, c. 844.)

§ **2.2-428. Standards for automated preparation and transmittal of lobbyists' disclosure statements; database.** — A. The Secretary shall accept any lobbyist's disclosure statement required by § 2.2-426 filed by computer or electronic means in accordance with the standards approved by the Secretary and using software meeting standards approved by the Secretary. The Secretary may provide software to filers without charge or at a reasonable cost. The Secretary may prescribe the method of execution and certification of electronically filed statements and the procedures for receiving statements in the office of the Secretary.

B. The Secretary shall establish a lobbyist disclosure database, available to the public, from required disclosure statements filed electronically and may enter into that database information from required disclosure statements filed by other methods. (1997, cc. 364, 392, § 2.1-787.1; 2001, c. 844.)

§ **2.2-429. Retention of records by a lobbyist or lobbyist's principal.** — A lobbyist and a lobbyist's principal shall preserve for a period of two years all accounts, bills, books, papers, receipts, and other documents and records necessary to substantiate the expenditure reports submitted under this article. (1994, cc. 857, 937, § 2.1-788; 2001, c. 844.)

§ **2.2-430. Termination.** — A lobbyist may terminate a lobbyist registration by filing a report required under § 2.2-426 including information through the last day of lobbying activity. A termination report shall indicate that the lobbyist intends to use the report as the final accounting of lobbying activity. (1994, cc. 857, 937, § 2.1-789; 2001, c. 844.)

§ **2.2-431. Penalties; filing of substituted statement.** — A. Every lobbyist failing to file the statement prescribed by § 2.2-426 within the time prescribed therein shall be assessed a civil penalty of fifty dollars, and every individual failing to file the statement within ten days after the time prescribed herein shall be assessed an additional civil penalty of fifty dollars per day from the eleventh day of such default until the statement is filed. The penalties shall be assessed and collected by the Secretary. The Attorney General shall assist the Secretary in collecting the penalties, upon request.

B. Every lobbyist's principal whose lobbyist fails to file the statement prescribed by § 2.2-426 shall be assessed a civil penalty of fifty dollars, and shall be assessed an additional civil penalty of fifty dollars per day from the eleventh day of such default until the statement is filed. The penalty shall be assessed and collected by the Secretary. The Attorney General shall assist the Secretary in collecting the penalties, upon request.

C. No individual who has failed to file the statement required by § 2.2-426 or who has failed to pay all penalties assessed pursuant to this section, shall register or act as a lobbyist as long as he remains in default.

D. Whenever any lobbyist is or will be in default under § 2.2-426, and the reasons for such default are or will be beyond his control, or the control of his principal, or both, the Secretary may suspend the assessment of any penalty otherwise assessable and accept a substituted statement, upon the submission of sworn proofs that shall satisfy him that the default has been beyond the control of the lobbyist or his principal, and that the substituted statement contains the most accurate and complete information available after the exercise of due diligence.

E. Penalties collected pursuant to this section shall be payable to the State Treasurer for deposit to the general fund. (1994, cc. 857, 937, § 2.1-790; 2001, c. 844.)

§ 2.2-432. Contingent compensation prohibited. — It shall be unlawful for any individual to lobby for compensation that is dependent in any manner upon the outcome of any legislative or executive action. (1994, cc. 857, 937, § 2.1-791; 2001, c. 844.)

§ 2.2-433. Prohibited acts; violation a misdemeanor. — A. No lobbyist shall:

1. Lobby in violation of the provisions of this article;
2. Make any expenditure, or obligate himself to do so, in connection with lobbying, unless he fully discloses the expenditure as required in this article; or
3. Misrepresent in any material respect or omit any information required to be reported pursuant to this article.

B. No lobbyist's principal shall:

1. Fail to file any statement required to be filed by the provisions of this article;
2. Misrepresent in any material respect or omit any information required to be reported pursuant to this article; or
3. Violate any of the provisions of this article.

C. Except as provided in subsection D of § 2.2-426, any lobbyist or lobbyist's principal violating any provision of this article shall be guilty of a Class 1 misdemeanor. However, a lobbyist who receives no compensation or anything of value for lobbying shall not be subject to the criminal penalties prescribed by this section. (1994, cc. 857, 937, § 2.1-792; 2001, c. 844.)

Cross references. — As to punishment for Class 1 misdemeanors, see § 18.2-11.

§ 2.2-434. Employment of lobbyists prohibited; exceptions. — Employment of a lobbyist for compensation by an officer, board, institution or agency of the Commonwealth, is expressly prohibited; however, this section shall not apply to any individual who is a full-time or part-time employee of such office, board, department, institution or agency of the Commonwealth. (1994, cc. 857, 937, § 2.1-793; 2001, c. 844.)

§ 2.2-435. Prohibition for state party chairman. — The chairman or any full-time paid employee of a state political party, as defined in § 24.2-101, or a member of his immediate family, as defined in § 2.2-3101, shall not be employed as a lobbyist by any principal. (1994, cc. 857, 937, § 2.1-794; 2001, c. 844.)

CHAPTER 4.1.

Special Advisor for Workforce Development.

§§ 2.2-435.1 through 2.2-435.5: Repealed by Acts 2006, cc. 696 and 751, cl. 4.

CHAPTER 4.2.

Coordination of Workforce Development.

§ 2.2-435.6. Chief Workforce Development Officer. — A. The Governor shall serve as Chief Workforce Development Officer for the Commonwealth.

B. The Governor may designate a senior staff member from the immediate staff of the Governor's Office to be responsible for the responsibilities assigned to the Governor pursuant to this chapter and Article 25 (§ 2.2-2669 et seq.) of Chapter 26 of this title or other tasks as may be assigned to such person by the Governor. (2006, cc. 696, 751.)

Editor's note. — Acts 2006, cc. 696 and 751, cl. 2, provides: "That by December 1, 2006, the Governor shall develop a statewide strategic plan addressing the need for reforms in workforce policy, including the implementation of workforce development and training initiatives and policies. The statewide strategic plan shall address, among such other issues as may be deemed appropriate, (i) the potential advantages and disadvantages of instituting a single statewide local workforce investment board, (ii) the need for reforms at the local workforce investment board level, (iii) concerns of rural communities, (iv) measures to maintain the active participation of local business interests in local workforce investment boards, and (v) means of reducing the amount of time expended by members of local workforce investment boards on administrative matters. The strategic plan shall be provided to the Chairmen of the House Appropriations and Senate Finance Committees for review prior to final adoption."

Acts 2006, cc. 696 and 751, cl. 3, provides: "That by December 1, 2006, the Governor, in conjunction with his development of the statewide strategic plan addressing the need for reforms in workforce policy, shall identify and implement strategies to optimize the role of the Virginia Community College System in workforce development. The Governor shall identify and implement the strategies in consultation with the Chancellor of the Virginia Community College System and the Board of the Virginia Community College System. The strategies shall include, but not be limited to, opportunities for cooperative curricula between secondary and postsecondary educational entities to improve workforce development. The Governor shall report to the chairmen of the House Committee on Appropriations and the Senate Committee on Finance on the identified strategies prior to implementation."

§ 2.2-435.7. Responsibilities of the Chief Workforce Development Officer. — A. The Governor's responsibilities as Chief Workforce Development Officer shall include:

1. Developing a strategic plan for the statewide delivery of workforce development and training programs and activities. The strategic plan shall be developed in coordination with the development of the comprehensive economic development policy required by § 2.2-205. The strategic plan shall include performance measures that link the objectives of such programs and activities to the record of state agencies, local workforce investment boards, and other relevant entities in attaining such objectives;

2. To the extent permissible under applicable federal law, determining the appropriate allocation of funds and other resources that have been appropriated or are otherwise available for disbursement by the Commonwealth for workforce development programs and activities;

3. Ensuring that the Commonwealth's workforce development efforts are implemented in a coordinated and efficient manner by, among other activities, taking appropriate executive action to this end and recommending to the General Assembly necessary legislative actions to streamline and eliminate duplication in such efforts;

4. Facilitating efficient implementation of workforce development and training programs by cabinet secretaries and agencies responsible for such programs;

5. Developing, in coordination with the Virginia Workforce Council, (i) certification standards for programs and providers and (ii) uniform policies and procedures, including standardized forms and applications, for one-stop centers;

6. Monitoring, in coordination with the Virginia Workforce Council, the effectiveness of each one-stop center and recommending actions needed to improve their effectiveness;

7. Establishing measures to evaluate the effectiveness of the local workforce investment boards and conducting annual evaluations of the effectiveness of each local workforce investment board. As part of the evaluation process, the Governor shall recommend to such boards specific best management practices;

8. Conducting annual evaluations of the performance of workforce development and training programs and activities and their administrators and providers, using the performance measures developed through the strategic planning process described in subdivision 1. The evaluations shall include, to the extent feasible, (i) a comparison of the per-person costs for each program or activity, (ii) a comparative rating of each program or activity based on its success in meeting program objectives, and (iii) an explanation of the extent to which each agency's appropriation requests incorporate the data reflected in the cost comparison described in clause (i) and the comparative rating described in clause (ii). These evaluations, including the comparative rankings, shall be considered in allocating resources for workforce development and training programs;

9. Monitoring federal legislation and policy, in order to maximize the Commonwealth's effective use of and access to federal funding available for workforce development programs;

10. Submitting biennial reports, which shall be included in the Governor's executive budget submissions to the General Assembly, on improvements in the coordination of workforce development efforts statewide. The reports shall identify (i) program success rates in relation to performance measures established by the Virginia Workforce Council, (ii) obstacles to program and resource coordination, and (iii) strategies for facilitating statewide program and resource coordination. In addition, the reports shall provide information on the implementation of the Memorandum of Understanding among the Governor's

Office, the Secretaries of Education and Commerce and Trade, the Virginia Community College System, and the Virginia Employment Commission, which Memorandum of Understanding establishes transition plans for moving certain Workforce Investment Act responsibilities from the Virginia Employment Commission to the Virginia Community College System. Upon completion of the transfer of Workforce Investment Act responsibilities from the Virginia Employment Commission to the Virginia Community College System, the reports shall analyze the effectiveness of the Virginia Community College System in carrying out its Workforce Investment Act responsibilities; and

11. Submitting to the chairs of the House and Senate Commerce and Labor Committees copies of (i) all evaluations by the Chief Workforce Development Officer of the accountability and performance of the Commonwealth's workforce programs and (ii) all reports by the Office of the Chancellor of the Virginia Community College System on accomplishments and recommendations relating to regional cooperation on workforce, education, and economic development issues.

B. The Governor may delegate any of his responsibilities enumerated in subsection A to a senior staff member within his immediate office. (2006, cc. 696, 751; 2008, cc. 269, 388.)

The 2008 amendments. — The 2008 amendments by cc. 269 and 388 are nearly identical, and in subsection A, inserted the present second sentence in subdivision A 1; deleted subdivision A 5, which read: "Providing independent staffing for the Workforce Council"; redesignated former subdivisions A 6 through A 11 as subdivisions A 5 through A 10; deleted "and" at the end of subdivision A 9; added the third and fourth sentences to subdivision A 10; and added subdivision A 11.

PART B.

CHAPTER 5.

DEPARTMENT OF LAW.

Article 1.

General Provisions.

Michie's Jurisprudence. — For related discussion, see 2A M.J. Attorney General, §§ 1, 2.

ARTICLE 1.

General Provisions.

§ 2.2-500. Attorney General to be chief executive officer; duties generally. — The Attorney General shall be the chief executive officer of the Department of Law, and shall perform such duties as may be provided by law. (Code 1950, § 2-85; 1966, c. 677, § 2.1-117; 2001, c. 844.)

Cross references. — For general constitutional provision concerning Attorney General, see Va. Const., Art. V, § 15. As to the powers of the Virginia Economic Development Partnership Authority, see § 2.2-2237. As to the purchase of legal services or expert witnesses or other services associated with litigation or regulatory proceedings authorized under this section being exempt from the Virginia Public Procurement Act, see § 2.2-4344. As to the Attorney General's duty to defend the law providing for the daily observation of one minute of silence is the public schools, see § 22.1-203.

CASE NOTES

Editor's note. — The case below was decided under former Title 2.1 or prior provisions.

Attorney generals not proper parties in prison condition suit. — Where plaintiff failed to state what legal duties attorney generals owed him and how those duties were breached, all claims against them were properly dismissed in suit complaining of correctional facilities for morbidly obese inmate. Torcasio v. Murray, 862 F. Supp. 1482 (E.D. Va. 1994), aff'd in part, rev'd in part, 57 F.3d 1340 (4th Cir. 1995), cert. denied, 516 U.S. 1071, 116 S. Ct. 772, 133 L. Ed. 2d 724 (1996).

§ 2.2-501. Assistant and deputy Attorneys General. — The Attorney General shall appoint a chief deputy Attorney General and may appoint the necessary deputy Attorneys General and assistant Attorneys General and fix their salaries within the limitation of the funds provided for the purpose in the general appropriation act.

If a vacancy occurs in the office of Attorney General for any reason, the chief deputy Attorney General shall serve as acting Attorney General until such time as the vacancy is filled pursuant to § 24.2-213. The acting Attorney General shall exercise all the powers, and duties, and enjoy all the perquisites of the office of Attorney General as are provided by law. (Code 1950, § 2-94; 1966, c. 677, § 2.1-130; 1977, c. 596; 2001, c. 844.)

CASE NOTES

Construction with other law. — Circuit court properly sustained a demurrer filed by defendant, the Office of the Attorney General who employed a group of former employees, which was filed in response to the employees' amended motion for judgment, as the employees were not covered by the Virginia Personnel Act, § 2.2-2900 et seq., because they were exempt under subdivision 1 of § 2.2-2905; hence, in utilizing the interpretive guidance of both §§ 2.2-501 and 2.2-502, the employees were ineligible to receive Workforce Transition Act benefits under § 2.2-3202. Boynton v. Kilgore, 271 Va. 220, 623 S.E.2d 922, 2006 Va. LEXIS 2 (2006).

§ **2.2-502. Support staff.** — The Attorney General may appoint such persons as he deems necessary for the efficient conduct of his office, and apportion, out of the appropriation for his office, such salaries among such persons as he deems proper, but the aggregate amount paid them shall not exceed the amount provided by law. (Code 1950, § 2-95; 1966, c. 677, § 2.1-131; 2001, c. 844.)

CASE NOTES

Construction with other law. — Circuit court properly sustained a demurrer filed by defendant, the Office of the Attorney General who employed a group of former employees, which was filed in response to the employees' amended motion for judgment, as the employees were not covered by the Virginia Personnel Act, § 2.2-2900 et seq., because they were exempt under § 2.2-2905; hence, in utilizing the interpretive guidance of both §§ 2.2-501 and 2.2-502, the employees were ineligible to receive Workforce Transition Act benefits under § 2.2-3202. Boynton v. Kilgore, 271 Va. 220, 623 S.E.2d 922, 2006 Va. LEXIS 2 (2006).

§ **2.2-503. Office space.** — The Governor shall assign to the Attorney General office space for the Attorney General, his assistants and employees suitable for the transaction of the legal business of the Commonwealth. (Code 1950, § 2-96; 1966, c. 677, § 2.1-132; 1994, c. 64; 2001, c. 844.)

§ **2.2-504. Contingent and traveling expenses.** — The Attorney General may expend for the contingent expenses of his office the sums appropriated for his office by the General Assembly. The Attorney General, the deputy and assistant Attorneys General, and other employees of the office shall be reimbursed for actual travel expenses in the performance of their duties in accordance with § 2.2-2823. (Code 1950, § 2-97; 1966, c. 677, § 2.1-133; 2001, c. 844.)

§ **2.2-505. Official opinions of Attorney General.** — A. The Attorney General shall give his advice and render official advisory opinions in writing only when requested in writing so to do by one of the following: the Governor; a member of the General Assembly; a judge of a court of record or a judge of a court not of record; the State Corporation Commission; an attorney for the Commonwealth; a county, city or town attorney in those localities in which such office has been created; a clerk of a court of record; a city or county sheriff; a city or county treasurer or similar officer; a commissioner of the revenue or similar officer; a chairman or secretary of an electoral board; or the head of a state department, division, bureau, institution or board.

B. Except in cases where an opinion is requested by the Governor or a member of the General Assembly, the Attorney General shall have no authority to render an official opinion unless the question dealt with is directly related to the discharge of the duties of the official requesting the opinion. Any opinion request to the Attorney General by an attorney for the Commonwealth or county, city or town attorney shall itself be in the form of an opinion embodying a precise statement of all facts together with such attorney's legal conclusions. (Code 1950, § 2-86; 1966, c. 677, § 2.1-118; 1968, c. 414; 1971, Ex. Sess., c. 155; 1976, c. 715; 1999, c. 14; 2001, c. 844.)

Cross references. — As to request of Governor, see Va. Const., Art. V, § 8.

Law Review. — For article, "The Newsman's Confidential Source Privilege in Virginia," see 22 U. Rich. L. Rev. 377 (1988). For annual survey commentary, "Constitutional Crisis in the Commonwealth: Resolving the Conflict between Governors and Attorney General," see 41 U. Rich. L. Rev. 43 (2006). For annual survey article, "Real Estate Law," see 41 U. Rich. L. Rev. 257 (2006).

CASE NOTES

Editor's note. — The case below was decided under former Title 2.1 or prior provisions.

General Assembly is not bound by opinions of the Attorney General. Forest Hills Early Learning Ctr., Inc. v. Lukhard, 540 F. Supp. 1046 (E.D. Va. 1982), aff'd in part, vacated in part and remanded, 728 F.2d 230 (4th Cir. 1984).

OPINIONS OF THE ATTORNEY GENERAL

Attorney General could not issue official advisory opinion on question requiring factual determination. — Whether law enforcement officers employed pursuant to § 15.2-1712 are considered to be performing "law enforcement activities" for purposes of workers' compensation and personal and property damage liability coverage under a local government risk management insurance program is a question requiring a factual determination rather than an interpretation of law and, therefore, the Attorney General could not issue an official advisory opinion on the question. See opinion of Attorney General to The Honorable William C. Mims, Member, Senate of Virginia, 01-047 (12/27/01).

§ 2.2-506. Legal services to attorneys for the Commonwealth in certain proceedings; costs. — The Attorney General shall at the request of an attorney for the Commonwealth, provide legal service to such attorney for the Commonwealth in any proceedings brought against him seeking to restrain the enforcement of any state law.

Any costs chargeable against the defendant in any such case shall be paid by the Commonwealth from the appropriation for the payment of criminal charges. (1962, c. 235, § 2-86.2; 1966, c. 677, § 2.1-120; 2001, c. 844.)

§ 2.2-507. Legal service in civil matters. — A. All legal service in civil matters for the Commonwealth, the Governor, and every state department, institution, division, commission, board, bureau, agency, entity, official, court, or judge, including the conduct of all civil litigation in which any of them are interested, shall be rendered and performed by the Attorney General, except as provided in this chapter and except for any litigation concerning a justice or judge initiated by the Judicial Inquiry and Review Commission. No regular counsel shall be employed for or by the Governor or any state department, institution, division, commission, board, bureau, agency, entity, or official. The Attorney General may represent personally or through one or more of his assistants any number of state departments, institutions, divisions, commissions, boards, bureaus, agencies, entities, officials, courts, or judges that are parties to the same transaction or that are parties in the same civil or administrative proceeding and may represent multiple interests within the same department, institution, division, commission, board, bureau, agency, or entity. The soil and water conservation district directors or districts may request legal advice from local, public, or private sources; however, upon request of the soil and water conservation district directors or districts, the Attorney General shall provide legal service in civil matters for such district directors or districts.

B. The Attorney General may represent personally or through one of his assistants any of the following persons who are made defendant in any civil action for damages arising out of any matter connected with their official duties:

1. Members, agents or employees of the Alcoholic Beverage Control Board;
2. Agents inspecting or investigators appointed by the State Corporation Commission;
3. Agents, investigators, or auditors employed by the Department of Taxation;
4. Members, agents or employees of the State Mental Health, Mental Retardation and Substance Abuse Services Board, the Department of Mental Health, Mental Retardation and Substance Abuse Services, the State Board of Health, the State Department of Health, the Department of General Services, the State Board of Social Services, the Department of Social Services, the State Board of Corrections, the Department of Corrections, the State Board of Juvenile Justice, the Department of Juvenile Justice, the Virginia Parole Board, or the Department of Agriculture and Consumer Services;
5. Persons employed by the Commonwealth Transportation Board;
6. Persons employed by the Commissioner of Motor Vehicles;
7. Persons appointed by the Commissioner of Marine Resources;
8. Police officers appointed by the Superintendent of State Police;
9. Conservation police officers appointed by the Department of Game and Inland Fisheries;
10. Third impartial panel members appointed to hear a teacher's grievance pursuant to § 22.1-312;
11. Staff members or volunteers participating in a court-appointed special advocate program pursuant to Article 5 (§ 9.1-151 et seq.) of Chapter 1 of Title 9.1;
12. Any emergency medical service agency that is a licensee of the Department of Health in any civil matter and any guardian ad litem appointed by a court in a civil matter brought against him for alleged errors or omissions in the discharge of his court-appointed duties; or
13. Conservation officers of the Department of Conservation and Recreation.

Upon request of the affected individual, the Attorney General may represent personally or through one of his assistants any basic or advanced emergency medical care attendant or technician possessing a valid certificate issued by authority of the State Board of Health in any civil matter in which a defense of immunity from liability is raised pursuant to § 8.01-225.

C. If, in the opinion of the Attorney General, it is impracticable or uneconomical for such legal service to be rendered by him or one of his assistants, he may employ special counsel for this purpose, whose compensation shall be fixed by the Attorney General. The compensation for such special counsel shall be paid out of the funds appropriated for the administration of the board, commission, division or department being represented or whose members, officers, inspectors, investigators, or other employees are being represented pursuant to this section. Notwithstanding any provision of this section to the contrary, the Supreme Court may employ its own counsel in any matter arising out of its official duties in which it, or any justice, is a party. (Code 1950, § 2-87; 1958, c. 542; 1966, cc. 222, 677, § 2.1-121; 1974, cc. 44, 45, 432; 1975, c. 372; 1976, cc. 580, 726; 1978, c. 96; 1979, c. 450; 1980, c. 255; 1981, c. 427; 1982, c. 636; 1984, cc. 703, 742; 1987, c. 326; 1988, c. 435; 1989, c. 733; 1990, cc. 637, 752, 791; 2001, c. 844; 2005, c. 236; 2007, cc. 248, 595; 2008, c. 577.)

The 2007 amendments. — The 2007 amendment by c. 248, in subsection C, inserted "being represented or" and substituted "being represented" for "defended" in the second sentence.

The 2007 amendment by c. 595 added subdivision A 13 and made related changes.

The 2008 amendments. — The 2008 amendment by c. 577 rewrote the last sentence in subsection A, which read: "Upon request of the local attorney for the Commonwealth, the Attorney General may provide legal service in civil matters for soil and water conservation district directors or districts."

Law Review. — For annual survey commentary, "Constitutional Crisis in the Commonwealth: Resolving the Conflict between Governors and Attorney General," see 41 U. Rich. L. Rev. 43 (2006).

CASE NOTES

Editor's note. — Most of the cases below were decided under former Title 2.1 or prior provisions.

Assistance to hearing officer in case against medical provider. — The Attorney General complied with mandate to render all legal service in civil matters for the Commonwealth and all its agencies by assigning separate assistants to prosecute and to advise the hearing officer on procedure in case against doctor whose medical provider contract was terminated. Hladys v. Commonwealth, 235 Va. 145, 366 S.E.2d 98 (1988).

Doctor's right in a medical license revocation proceeding to a neutral decision maker was not improperly infringed when one assistant attorney general advised the board while another assistant attorney general prosecuted the case against the doctor. The doctor had not show the required bias or improper conduct and the General Assembly had directed the Attorney General to conduct legal services for every state board. Vuyyuru v. Va. Bd. of Med., — Va. App. —, — S.E.2d —, 2008 Va. App. LEXIS 30 (Jan. 15, 2008).

Scope of inquiry. — While Supreme Court recognized that the Attorney General vigorously disputed the existence of any conflict of interests between her office and the Virginia Retirement System, it was not the province of the judicial branch of government to question the motives or judgment of the head of the executive branch; rather, inquiry for the Supreme Court was limited to whether the Governor exceeded the scope of authority vested in his office by his appointment of a "special counsel" and whether, in the exercise of that grant of power, the Governor's acts were arbitrary and capricious. Wilder v. Attorney Gen., 247 Va. 119, 439 S.E.2d 398 (1994).

Finding not binding on Supreme Court. — Where trial court's finding that the Governor appointed regular counsel was not merely a finding of fact, but a mixed question of law and fact, such finding was not binding on the Supreme Court. Wilder v. Attorney Gen., 247 Va. 119, 439 S.E.2d 398 (1994).

Arising from official duties. — Under subsection B of § 2.2-507, the Attorney General may represent members, agents, or employees of the Department of Corrections who are made defendant in any civil action for damages arising out of any matter connected with their official duties and, contrary to an inmate's contention, the statute does not require that an individual be a member, agent, or employee of the relevant department at the time the counterclaim is filed; all that is required is that the civil litigation for which damages are sought arise from the individual's official duties. Douglas v. McCarty, — F.3d —, 2003 U.S. App. LEXIS 23585 (4th Cir. Nov. 19, 2003).

Attorney generals not proper parties in prison condition suit. — Where plaintiff failed to state what legal duties attorney generals owed him and how those duties were breached, all claims against them were properly dismissed in suit complaining of correctional facilities for morbidly obese inmate. Torcasio v. Murray, 862 F. Supp. 1482 (E.D. Va. 1994), aff'd in part, rev'd in part, 57 F.3d 1340 (4th Cir. 1995), cert. denied, 516 U.S. 1071, 116 S. Ct. 772, 133 L. Ed. 2d 724 (1996).

Legal services for Social Services Department mandatory. — This section provides that the Office of the Attorney General shall provide all legal services for the Department of Social Services in civil matters; the term "shall" is mandatory and reflects the General Assembly's intention that there be no discretion in complying with the statute, except as provided in the statute itself, an issue not raised on these facts. Brunty v. Smith, 22 Va. App. 191, 468 S.E.2d 161 (1996).

§ 2.2-507.1. Authority of Attorney General regarding charitable assets. — A. The assets of a charitable corporation incorporated in or doing any business in Virginia shall be deemed to be held in trust for the public for such purposes as are established by the governing documents of such charitable corporation, the gift or bequest made to such charitable corporation, or other applicable law. The Attorney General shall have the same authority to act on behalf of the public with respect to such assets as he has with respect to assets held by unincorporated charitable trusts and other charitable entities, including the authority to seek such judicial relief as may be necessary to protect the public interest in such assets.

B. Nothing contained in this section is intended to modify the standard of conduct applicable under existing law to the directors of charitable corporations incorporated in or doing any business in Virginia. (2002, c. 792; 2004, c. 289.)

Law Review. — For 2003/2004 survey of the law of wills, trusts and estates, see 39 U. Rich. L. Rev. 447 (2004).

CASE NOTES

Suits filed prior to July 1, 2002. — Trial court had jurisdiction to decide a lawsuit that a fraternity filed against a foundation it created in 1966 seeking an order declaring that the foundation held title to property it owned in trust for the benefit of the fraternity, even though the Attorney General of Virginia was not a party to the lawsuit, because the suit was filed before July 1, 2002. Kappa Sigma Fraternity, Inc. v. Kappa Sigma Fraternity, 266 Va. 455, 587 S.E.2d 701, 2003 Va. LEXIS 105 (2003).

§ 2.2-507.2. Youth Internet Safety Fund established. — There is hereby created in the state treasury a special nonreverting fund to be known as the Youth Internet Safety Fund, hereafter referred to as "the Fund." The Fund shall be established on the books of the Comptroller. All money as may be appropriated by the General Assembly and any gifts, bequests, grants, or donations shall be paid into the state treasury and credited to the Fund. Interest earned on moneys in the Fund shall remain in the Fund and be credited to it. Any moneys remaining in the Fund, including interest thereon, at the end of each fiscal year shall not revert to the general fund but shall remain in the Fund. Moneys in the Fund shall be used solely for the purposes of education, public awareness, and other activities to promote the safe and secure use of the Internet. Unless otherwise restricted by the terms of the gift or bequest, the Attorney General may direct the sale, exchange, or other disposition of such gifts and bequests. Expenditures and disbursements from the Fund shall be made by the State Treasurer on warrants issued by the Comptroller upon written request signed by the Attorney General. (2007, c. 309.)

Editor's note. — Acts 2007, c. 309, cl. 2, provides: "That an emergency exists and this act is in force from its passage [March 12, 2007]."

Acts 2007, c. 309, cl. 3, provides: "That the provisions of the Virginia Public Procurement Act (§ 2.2-4300 et seq.) shall not apply to expenditures from the fund created by this act."

§ 2.2-508. Legal service in certain redistricting proceedings. — Upon notification by a county, city or town of a pending civil action challenging the legality of its election district boundaries as required by § 24.2-304.5, the Attorney General shall review the papers in the civil action and may represent the interests of the Commonwealth in developing an appropriate remedy that is consistent with requirements of law, including but not limited to Article VII, Section 5 of the Constitution of Virginia, Chapter 3 (§ 24.2-302.1 et seq.) of Title 24.2, or Chapter 39 (§ 30-263 et seq.) of Title 30. (1989, c. 112, § 2.1-121.1; 1995, c. 249; 2001, c. 844; 2004, c. 1000.)

§ 2.2-509. Representation in administrative proceedings. — Notwithstanding any other provision of law, if the Attorney General finds after consultation with the head of the affected department that it is in the best interests of the Commonwealth to do so, the Attorney General may authorize any employee of his office or any employee of a department to represent that department or an affiliated body in any administrative proceedings before the department, an affiliated body or before any hearing officer or examiner appointed or employed by the department or affiliated body. (1991, c. 227, § 2.1-121.2; 2001, c. 844.)

CASE NOTES

City attorney's representation in an administrative proceeding. — Although the record did not indicate the Attorney General specifically authorized a city attorney to represent the Virginia ABC Board in an administrative proceeding regarding suspension of a liquor license, any error in the process by which the city attorney presented evidence at the hearing was harmless; § 2.2-509 contemplated that a substitute could represent the Board in administrative proceedings. Supermarket Express, L.L.C. v. Dep't of Alcoholic Beverage Control, No. 1389-04-1, 2005 Va. App. LEXIS 118 (Ct. of Appeals Mar. 22, 2005).

§ 2.2-509.1. Powers of investigators; enforcement of certain tobacco laws. — Investigators with the Office of the Attorney General as designated by the Attorney General shall be authorized to seize cigarettes as defined in § 3.1-336.1, which are sold, possessed, distributed, transported, imported, or otherwise held in violation of § 3.1-336.6 or 58.1-1037. In addition, such investigators shall be authorized to accompany and participate with special agents of the Alcoholic Beverage Control Board or other law-enforcement officials engaging in an enforcement action under § 3.1-336.6 or 58.1-1037. (2006, c. 695.)

Editor's note. — Effective October 1, 2008, the reference to "3.1-336.1" should read "3.2-4200" and the references to "3.1-336.6" should read "3.2-4207."

§ 2.2-510. Employment of special counsel generally. — No special counsel shall be employed for or by the Governor or any state department, institution, division, commission, board, bureau, agency, entity, official, justice of the Supreme Court, or judge of any circuit court or district court except in the following cases:

1. When the Governor determines that, because of the nature of the legal service to be performed, the Attorney General's office is unable to render such service, then the Governor shall issue an exemption order stating with particularity the facts and reasons leading to the conclusion that the Attorney General's office is unable to render such service. The Governor may then employ special counsel to render such service as he may deem necessary and proper. The compensation for such special counsel shall be paid out of the funds appropriated for the administration of the board, commission, division, or department to be represented or whose members, officers, inspectors, investigators, or other employees are to be represented pursuant to this section.

2. In cases of legal services in civil matters to be performed for the Commonwealth, where it is impracticable or uneconomical for the Attorney General to render such service, he may employ special counsel whose compensation shall be paid out of the appropriation for the Attorney General's office.

3. In cases of legal services in civil matters to be performed for any state department, institution, division, commission, board, bureau, agency, entity, official, justice of the Supreme Court, or judge of any circuit court or district court where it is impracticable or uneconomical for the Attorney General's office to render such service, special counsel may be employed but only as set

forth in subsection C of § 2.2-507, upon the written recommendation of the Attorney General, who shall approve all requisitions drawn upon the Comptroller for warrants as compensation for such special counsel before the Comptroller shall have authority to issue such warrants.

4. In cases where the Attorney General certifies to the Governor that it would be improper for the Attorney General's office to render legal services due to a conflict of interests, or that he is unable to render certain legal services, the Governor may employ special counsel or other assistance to render such services as may be necessary.

5. In cases of legal services in civil matters to be performed by the Virginia Office for Protection and Advocacy pursuant to Chapter 8.1 (§ 51.5-39.1 et seq.) of Title 51.5. (Code 1950, § 2-88; 1966, c. 677, § 2.1-122; 1975, c. 372; 1976, c. 726; 2001, c. 844; 2002, c. 572; 2007, c. 248.)

The 2007 amendments. — The 2007 amendment by c. 248, rewrote subdivision 1, which read: "Where because of the nature of the service to be performed, the Attorney General's office is unable to render such service, the Governor after issuing an exemption order stating with particularity the facts and reasons upon which he bases his conclusion that the Attorney General's office is unable to render such service, may employ special counsel to render such service as the Governor may deem necessary and proper" and inserted "as set forth in subsection C of § 2.2-507" in subdivision 3.

Law Review. — For annual survey commentary, "Constitutional Crisis in the Commonwealth: Resolving the Conflict between Governors and Attorney General," see 41 U. Rich. L. Rev. 43 (2006).

§ 2.2-510.1. Open negotiation for employment of special counsel. — No state agency or state agent shall enter into a contingency fee contract for legal services in which contingency fees and expenses are reasonably anticipated to exceed $100,000 until an open and competitive negotiation process has been undertaken in accordance with the provisions of the Public Procurement Act (§ 2.2-4300 et seq.), applied mutatis mutandis. The contract shall be awarded to the attorney or firm that submits the most competitive proposal to provide such services considering the cost of the services, the qualifications of the attorney or firm to provide the services, the experience of the attorney or firm with similar legal matters, legal expertise generally, and such other relevant factors as may be identified by the Attorney General.

The provisions of this section shall not apply to any contracts for legal fees entered into pursuant to § 2.2-507 for the purpose of implementing the Virginia Debt Collection Act (§ 2.2-4800 et seq.). (2002, c. 196.)

§ 2.2-511. Criminal cases. — A. Unless specifically requested by the Governor to do so, the Attorney General shall have no authority to institute or conduct criminal prosecutions in the circuit courts of the Commonwealth except in cases involving (i) violations of the Alcoholic Beverage Control Act (§ 4.1-100 et seq.), (ii) violation of laws relating to elections and the electoral process as provided in § 24.2-104, (iii) violation of laws relating to motor vehicles and their operation, (iv) the handling of funds by a state bureau, institution, commission or department, (v) the theft of state property, (vi) violation of the criminal laws involving child pornography and sexually explicit visual material involving children, (vii) the practice of law without being duly authorized or licensed or the illegal practice of law, (viii) with the concurrence of the local attorney for the Commonwealth, violations of the Virginia Computer Crimes Act (§ 18.2-152.1 et seq.), (ix) with the concurrence of the local attorney for the Commonwealth, violations of the Air Pollution Control Law (§ 10.1-1300 et seq.), the Virginia Waste Management Act (§ 10.1-1400 et seq.), and the State Water Control Law (§ 62.1-44.2 et seq.), (x) with the concurrence of the local attorney for the Commonwealth, violations of Chapters 2 (§ 18.2-18 et seq.), 3 (§ 18.2-22 et seq.), and 10 (§ 18.2-434 et seq.) of Title 18.2, if such crimes relate to violations of law listed in clause (ix) of this subsection, (xi) with the concurrence of the local attorney for the Commonwealth, criminal violations by Medicaid providers or their employees in the course of doing business, or violations of Chapter 13 (§ 18.2-512 et seq.) of Title 18.2, in which cases the Attorney General may leave the prosecution to the local attorney for the Commonwealth, or he may institute proceedings by information, presentment or indictment, as appropriate, and conduct the same, (xii) with the concurrence of the local attorney for the Commonwealth, violations of Article 9 (§ 18.2-246.1 et seq.) of Chapter 6 of Title 18.2, (xiii) with the concurrence of the local attorney for the Commonwealth, assisting in the prosecution of violations of §§ 18.2-186.3 and 18.2-186.4, and (xiv) with the concurrence of the local attorney for the Commonwealth, assisting in the prosecution of violations of § 18.2-46.2, 18.2-46.3, or 18.2-46.5 when such violations are committed on the grounds of a state correctional facility.

In all other criminal cases in the circuit courts, except where the law provides otherwise, the authority of the Attorney General to appear or participate in the proceedings shall not attach unless and until a petition for appeal has been granted by the Court of Appeals or a writ of error has been granted by the Supreme Court. In all criminal cases before the Court of Appeals or the Supreme Court in which the Commonwealth is a party or is directly interested, the Attorney General shall appear and represent the Commonwealth. In any criminal case in which a petition for appeal has been granted by the Court of Appeals, the Attorney General shall continue to represent the Commonwealth in any further appeal of a case from the Court of Appeals to the Supreme Court.

B. The Attorney General shall, upon request of a person who was the victim of a crime and subject to such reasonable procedures as the Attorney General may require, ensure that such person is given notice of the filing, of the date, time and place and of the disposition of any appeal or habeas corpus proceeding involving the cases in which such person was a victim. For the purposes of this section, a victim is an individual who has suffered physical, psychological or economic harm as a direct result of the commission of a crime; a spouse, child, parent or legal guardian of a minor or incapacitated victim; or a spouse, child, parent or legal guardian of a victim of a homicide. Nothing in this subsection shall confer upon any person a right to appeal or modify any decision in a criminal, appellate or habeas corpus proceeding; abridge any right guaranteed by law; or create any cause of action for damages against the Commonwealth or any of its political subdivisions, the Attorney General or any of his employees or agents, any other officer, employee or agent of the Commonwealth or any of its political subdivisions, or any officer of the court. (Code 1950, § 2-90; 1958, c. 235; 1966, c. 677, § 2.1-124; 1974, c. 490; 1975, c. 42; 1984, c. 703; 1993, c. 866; 1995, cc. 565, 839; 1997, c. 801; 1998, cc. 507, 510; 2000, c. 239; 2001, c. 844; 2002, cc. 588, 623; 2003, c. 103; 2004, cc. 450, 883, 996; 2007, c. 409.)

Editor's note. — Acts 2007, c. 409, cl. 2, provides: "That the provisions of this act may result in a net increase in periods of imprisonment or commitment. Pursuant to § 30-19.1:4, the estimated amount of the necessary appropriation cannot be determined for periods of imprisonment in state adult correctional facilities and is $0 for periods of commitment to the custody of the Department of Juvenile Justice."

The 2007 amendments. — The 2007 amendment by c. 409 in subsection A, deleted "and" at the end of clause (xii), substituted "assisting" for "assist" and added "and" at the end of clause (xiii), and added clause (xiv).

CASE NOTES

Editor's note. — The case below was decided under former Title 2.1 or prior provisions.

Proceedings conducted on motions to vacate orders releasing defendants from custody were civil in nature, and this section and Va. Const., Art. VI, § 1 and U.S. Const., Amend. 5 were inapplicable. Appeals from denial of such motions were properly before the Supreme Court. Virginia Dep't of Cors. v. Crowley, 227 Va. 254, 316 S.E.2d 439 (1984).

§ 2.2-512. Employment of special counsel to prosecute persons illegally practicing law. — Notwithstanding any other provision of law, the Attorney General may expend funds appropriated to his office for the purpose of employing special counsel to investigate and prosecute a complaint that any person is engaged in the practice of law without being duly authorized or licensed so to do or is practicing law in violation of law. The compensation of the special counsel shall be paid out of the appropriation for the Attorney General's office. No special counsel shall be employed and paid except upon the request of the Executive Committee of the Virginia State Bar. (1958, c. 235, § 2-90.1; 1966, c. 677, § 2.1-125; 1980, c. 269; 2001, c. 844.)

§ 2.2-513. Counsel for Commonwealth in federal matters. — The Attorney General shall represent the interests of the Commonwealth, its departments, boards, institutions and commissions in matters before or controversies with the officers and several departments of the government of the United States. (Code 1950, § 2-91; 1966, c. 677, § 2.1-126; 2001, c. 844.)

§ 2.2-514. Compromise and settlement of disputes. — A. Except as provided in this section or subsection B of § 23-38.33:1, the Attorney General may compromise and settle disputes, claims and controversies involving all interests of the Commonwealth including, but not limited to the Virginia Tort Claims Act (§ 8.01-195.1 et seq.), and may discharge any such claims, but only after the proposed compromise, settlement or discharge, together with the reasons therefor, have been submitted in writing to the Governor and approved by him. Where any dispute, claim or controversy involves the interests of any department, institution, division, commission, board, authority or bureau of the Commonwealth, the Attorney General may compromise and settle or discharge the same provided the action is approved both by the Governor, as provided in this section, and by the head, or his designee, of the department, institution, division, board, authority or bureau that is interested. However, when any dispute, claim or controversy arises under the Virginia Tort Claims Act (§ 8.01-195.1 et seq.) or otherwise involves the interests of any department, institution, division, commission, board, authority or bureau of the Commonwealth, and the settlement amount does not exceed $250,000, the Attorney General or an assistant Attorney General assigned to such department, institution, division, commission, board, authority or bureau, or such other designee of the Attorney General, may compromise and settle or discharge the same provided the action is approved by the head, or his designee, of the department, institution, division, board or bureau whose interests are in issue. When the dispute, claim or controversy involves a case in which the Commonwealth has a claim for sums due it as the result of hospital, medical or dental care furnished by or on behalf of the Commonwealth, the Attorney General or such assistant Attorney General may compromise and settle and discharge the same when the settlement amount does not exceed $250,000.

B. No settlement under subsection A shall be made subject to a confidentiality agreement that prohibits the Commonwealth, a state agency, officer or employee from disclosing the amount of such settlement except where such confidentiality agreement is imposed by a court of competent jurisdiction or otherwise is required by law.

C. No settlement under subsection A shall be made subject to a confidentiality agreement if such settlement requires that a matter or issue shall be the subject of (i) regulatory action pursuant to Article 2 (§ 2.2-4006 et seq.) of Chapter 40 of this title, or (ii) legislation proposed to be introduced in the General Assembly. (Code 1950, § 2-92; 1956, c. 387; 1966, c. 677, § 2.1-127; 1973, c. 219; 1979, c. 266; 1986, c. 180; 1989, c. 75; 1995, cc. 359, 384; 2001, cc. 118, 844; 2004, c. 729; 2007, c. 217.)

Cross references. — As to the Attorney General's authority to engage in alternative dispute resolution, see § 2.2-4366. As to civil charges issued by the Virginia Soil and Water Conservation Board as exempt from this section, see § 10.1-603.2:1.

Editor's note. — Acts 2001, c. 118 amended § 2.1-127, from which this section is derived. Pursuant to § 30-152, Acts 2001, c. 118 has been given effect in this section as set out above. The 2001 amendment by c. 118 inserted "authority" preceding "or bureau" in four places; in the first sentence, substituted "all" for "the," and inserted "including, but not limited to the Virginia Tort Claims Act (§ 8.01-195.1 et seq.)"; in the second sentence, inserted "or his designee," and substituted "that" for "which"; and in the third sentence, inserted "arises under the Virginia Tort Claims Act (§ 8.01-195.1 et seq.) or otherwise," inserted "or such other designee of the Attorney General," and inserted "or his designee."

Section 23-38.33:1, referred to in the first sentence of subsection A, was repealed by Acts 1998, cc. 39 and 784.

The 2007 amendments. — The 2007 amendment by c. 217 substituted "and the settlement amount does not exceed $250,000" for "and the amount in dispute does not exceed $50,000" in the third and fourth sentences of subsection A.

Law Review. — For note on the abrogation of sovereign immunity in Virginia, The Virginia Tort Claims Act, see 7 G.M.U. L. Rev. 291 (1984).

CASE NOTES

Authority of Attorney General to reduce or eliminate lien. — Under the authority of this section, the Attorney General may reduce or eliminate a claim of the Commonwealth, and the amount of the Commonwealth's lien created by § 8.01-66.9 would be reduced or eliminated correspondingly. Commonwealth Dep't of Med. Assistance Servs. v. Huynh, 262 Va. 165, 546 S.E.2d 677, 2001 Va. LEXIS 68 (2001) (decided under prior law).

Amendment to § 8.01-66.9 vested judge with authority vested in department head. — The effect of the 1981 amendment of § 8.01-66.9 was to vest in the trial judge, in the circumstances specified by the statute, the authority, otherwise vested in the Attorney General, the Governor, and the appropriate department head by former § 2.1-127 (now § 2.2-514), to compromise and reduce the Commonwealth's lien. The purpose of the amendment was to reduce expense and delay, to avoid litigation, and to promote settlements. Commonwealth v. Smith, 239 Va. 108, 387 S.E.2d 767 (1990) (decided under prior law).

Offer of judgment was not ultra vires contract. — Where the amount in dispute in claim was well under $50,000, and the Commonwealth had not argued that the head of the institution involved did not approve the settlement, the assistant Attorney General involved had the statutory authority to enter into this settlement, and her offer of judgment was not an ultra vires contract that was void ab initio. Said v. Virginia Commonwealth University/Medical College, 130 F.R.D. 60 (E.D. Va. 1990) (decided under prior law).

CIRCUIT COURT OPINIONS

Authority to reduce Medicaid lien and apportion settlement proceeds. — In a medical malpractice case, where the patient's attorney had made a good faith effort to negotiate a compromise, the court had the authority to, and did reduce the amount of Medicaid lien and apportion the balance of the settlement recovery between the patient and his attorney. Diaz v. Arlington Anesthesia, Inc., 56 Va. Cir. 329, 2001 Va. Cir. LEXIS 466 (Arlington County 2001).

Department of Transportation's motion for judgment did not impair contractor's rights. — Department of Transportation could recover on a performance bond it had on a project to be completed by its contractor, as: (1) nothing within a contract, or the resulting settlement, served as an alteration discharging the surety; (2) its settlement with its contractor reduced the amount the contractor owed, which benefitted the surety; and (3) the contractor retained its rights under § 33.1-386. Commonwealth, DOT v. Selective Ins. Co., 68 Va. Cir. 451, 2005 Va. Cir. LEXIS 225 (Loudoun County Sept. 12, 2005).

§ 2.2-515. Service on board of national tobacco trust entity. — The Attorney General may serve in his official capacity on the board of directors of any entity established to ensure the implementation in the Commonwealth of a national tobacco trust established to provide payments to tobacco growers and tobacco quota owners to ameliorate adverse economic consequences resulting from a national settlement of states' claims against tobacco manufacturers. (2000, c. 1048, § 2.1-127.1; 2001, c. 844.)

§ 2.2-515.1. (Contingent expiration — see Editor's notes) Statewide Facilitator for Victims of Domestic Violence. — The Attorney General shall establish a Statewide Facilitator for Victims of Domestic Violence within the Office of the Attorney General. The Statewide Facilitator shall have the responsibility to assist agencies in implementing domestic violence programs and shall report on the status of such programs to the House Committee on Courts of Justice and the Senate Committee on Courts of Justice and the Virginia State Crime Commission by January 1 of each year. (2002, cc. 810, 818.)

Section set out twice. — The section above does not include amendments made by Acts 2007, c. 599, which have a limited scope of application. For the version of this section including the amendments by Acts 2007, c. 599, see the following section, also numbered 2.2-515.1.

Editor's note. — Acts 2002, cc. 810 and 818, cl. 2, provide: "That the Supreme Court shall establish reasonable judicial training regarding domestic violence and the resources available for victims in the Commonwealth of Virginia."

Acts 2002, cc. 810 and 818, cl. 3, provide: "That the Commonwealth Attorney's Services Council shall provide training to attorneys for the Commonwealth regarding the prosecution of domestic violence cases."

§ 2.2-515.1. (Contingent scope of application — see Editor's notes) Statewide Facilitator for Victims of Domestic Violence. — The Attorney General shall establish a Statewide Facilitator for Victims of Domestic Violence within the Office of the Attorney General. The Statewide Facilitator shall have the responsibility to (i) establish an address confidentiality program in accordance with § 2.2-515.2, (ii) assist agencies in implementing domestic violence programs, and (iii) report on the status of such programs to the House Committee on Courts of Justice and the Senate Committee on Courts of Justice and the Virginia State Crime Commission by January 1 of each year. (2002, cc. 810, 818; 2007, c. 599.)

Section set out twice. — The section above is amended by Acts 2007, c. 599 with a limited scope of application. For this section as in effect without the Acts 2007, c. 599 amendments, see the preceding section, also numbered 2.2-515.1.

Editor's note. — Acts 2007, c. 599, cl. 2, as amended by Acts 2008, c. 649, cl. 2, provides: "That the provisions of this act shall be limited to and implemented solely within the Counties of Albemarle, Arlington, Augusta, Dickenson, Fairfax, Henry, Lee, Rockbridge, Russell, Scott, Washington, and Wise as well as the Cities of Buena Vista, Charlottesville, Lexington, Martinsville, Norfolk, and Roanoke. An evaluation of the program shall be prepared by the Office of the Attorney General and the results forwarded to the members of the Senate Committee on General Laws and the House Committee on General Laws by December 31, 2010."

Acts 2007, c. 599, cl. 3, as amended by Acts 2008, c. 649, cl. 2, provides: "That following the evaluation of the program by the Office of the Attorney General in accordance with the second enactment of this act, the continuation of the address confidentiality program on a statewide basis shall be conditioned upon an appropriation effectuating the purposes of this act passed during the 2011 Session of the General Assembly and signed into law by the Governor."

The 2007 amendments. — The 2007 amendment by c. 599 inserted (i) and made related changes. See Acts 2007, c. 599, cls. 2 and 3, for applicability.

§ 2.2-515.2. (Contingent scope of application — See Editor's notes) Address confidentiality program established; victims of domestic violence; application; disclosure of records. — A. As used in this section:

"Address" means a residential street address, school address, or work address of a person as specified on the person's application to be a program participant.

"Applicant" means a person who is a victim of domestic violence or is a parent or guardian of a minor child or incapacitated person who is the victim of domestic violence.

"Domestic violence" means an act as defined in § 38.2-508 and includes threat of such acts committed against an individual in a domestic situation, regardless of whether these acts or threats have been reported to law-enforcement officers. Such threat must be a threat of force which would place any person in reasonable apprehension of death or bodily injury.

"Domestic violence programs" means public and not-for-profit agencies the primary mission of which is to provide services to victims of sexual or domestic violence.

"Program participant" means a person certified by the Office of the Attorney General as eligible to participate in the Address Confidentiality Program.

B. The Statewide Facilitator for Victims of Domestic Violence shall establish a program to be known as the "Address Confidentiality Program" to protect victims of domestic violence by authorizing the use of designated addresses for such victims. An individual who is at least 18 years of age, a parent or guardian acting on behalf of a minor, a guardian acting on behalf of an incapacitated person, or an emancipated minor may apply in person, at domestic violence programs that provide services where the role of the services provider is (i) to assist the eligible person in determining whether the address confidentiality program should be part of such person's overall safety plan; (ii) to explain the address confidentiality program services and limitations; (iii) to explain the program participant's responsibilities; and (iv) to assist the person eligible for participation with the completion of application materials. The Office of the Attorney General shall approve an application if it is filed in the manner and on the form prescribed by the Attorney General and if the application contains the following:

1. A sworn statement by the applicant declaring to be true and correct under penalty of perjury that the applicant has good reason to believe that:

a. The applicant, or the minor or incapacitated individual on whose behalf the application is made, is a victim of domestic violence;

b. The applicant fears further violent acts from the applicant's assailant; and

c. The applicant is not on active parole or probation supervision requirements under federal, state, or local law.

2. A designation of the Office of the Attorney General as agent for the purpose of receiving mail on behalf of the applicant;

3. The applicant's actual address to which mail can be forwarded and a telephone number where the applicant can be called;

4. A listing of any minor children residing at the applicant's actual address, each minor child's date of birth, and each minor child's relationship to the applicant; and

5. The signature of the applicant and any person who assisted in the preparation of the application and the date.

C. Upon approval of a completed application, the Office of the Attorney General shall certify the applicant as a program participant. An applicant shall be certified for one year following the date of the institution of the program, unless the certification is withdrawn or invalidated before that date. A program participant may apply to be recertified every year.

D. Upon receipt of first-class mail addressed to a program participant, the Attorney General or his designee shall forward the mail to the actual address of the program participant. The actual address of a program participant shall be available only to the Attorney General and to those employees involved in the operation of the Address Confidentiality Program and to law-enforcement officers. A program participant's actual address may be entered into the Virginia Criminal Information Network (VCIN) system so that it may be made known to law-enforcement officers accessing the VCIN system for law-enforcement purposes.

E. The Office of the Attorney General may cancel a program participant's certification if:

1. The program participant requests withdrawal from the program;

2. The program participant obtains a name change through an order of the court;

3. The program participant changes his residence address and does not provide seven days' notice to the Office of the Attorney General prior to the change of address;

4. The mail forwarded by the Office of the Attorney General to the address provided by the program participant is returned as undeliverable;

5. Any information contained in the application is false;

6. The program participant has been placed on parole or probation while a participant in the address confidentiality program; and

7. The applicant is required to register as a sex offender pursuant to Chapter 9 (§ 9.1-900 et seq.) of Title 9.1.

For purposes of the address confidentiality program, residents of temporary housing for 30 days or less are not eligible to enroll in the address confidentiality program until a permanent residential address is obtained.

The application form shall contain a statement notifying each applicant of the provisions of this subsection.

F. A program participant may request that any state or local agency use the address designated by the Office of the Attorney General as the program participant's address, except when the program participant is purchasing a firearm from a dealer in firearms. The agency shall accept the address designated by the Office of the Attorney General as a program participant's address, unless the agency has received a written exemption from the Office of the Attorney General demonstrating to the satisfaction of the Attorney General that:

1. The agency has a bona fide statutory basis for requiring the program participant to disclose to it the actual location of the program participant;

2. The disclosed confidential address of the program participant will be used only for that statutory purpose and will not be disclosed or made available in any way to any other person or agency; and

3. A state agency may request an exemption by providing in writing to the Office of the Attorney General identification of the statute or administrative rule that demonstrates the agency's bona fide requirement and authority for the use of the actual address of an individual. A request for a waiver from an agency may be for an individual program participant, a class of program participants, or all program participants. The denial of an agency's exemption request shall be in writing and include a statement of the specific reasons for the denial. Acceptance or denial of an agency's exemption request shall constitute final agency action.

Any state or local agency that discloses the program participant's confidential address provided by the Office of the Attorney General shall be immune from civil liability unless the agency acted with gross negligence or willful misconduct.

A program participant's actual address shall be disclosed pursuant to a court order.

G. Records submitted to or provided by the Office of the Attorney General in accordance with this section shall be exempt from disclosure under the Virginia Freedom of Information Act (§ 2.2-3700 et seq.) to the extent such records contain information identifying a past or current program participant, including such person's name, actual and designated address, telephone number, and any email address. However, access shall not be denied to the person who is the subject thereof, or the parent or legal guardian of a program participant in cases where the program participant is a minor child or an incapacitated person, except when the parent or legal guardian is named as the program participant's assailant.

H. Neither the Office of the Attorney General, its officers or employees, or others who have a responsibility to a program participant under this section shall have any liability nor shall any cause of action arise against them in their official or personal capacity from the failure of a program participant to receive any first class mail forwarded to him by the Office of the Attorney General pursuant to this section. Nor shall any such liability or cause of action arise from the failure of a program participant to timely receive any first class mail forwarded by the Office of the Attorney General pursuant to this section. (2007, c. 599; 2008, c. 649.)

Editor's note. — Acts 2007, c. 599, cl. 2, as amended by Acts 2008, c. 649, cl. 2, provides: "That the provisions of this act shall be limited to and implemented solely within the Counties of Albemarle, Arlington, Augusta, Dickenson, Fairfax, Henry, Lee, Rockbridge, Russell, Scott, Washington, and Wise as well as the Cities of Buena Vista, Charlottesville, Lexington, Martinsville, Norfolk, and Roanoke. An evaluation of the program shall be prepared by the Office of the Attorney General and the results forwarded to the members of the Senate Committee on General Laws and the House Committee on General Laws by December 31, 2010."

Acts 2007, c. 599, cl. 3, as amended by Acts 2008, c. 649, cl. 2, provides: "That following the evaluation of the program by the Office of the Attorney General in accordance with the second enactment of this act, the continuation of the address confidentiality program on a statewide basis shall be conditioned upon an appropriation effectuating the purposes of this act passed during the 2011 Session of the General Assembly and signed into law by the Governor."

The 2008 amendments. — The 2008 amendment by c. 649, in subsection A, added definition for "Domestic violence programs"; rewrote subsection B; in subsection D, deleted "for law enforcement purposes" at the end of the second sentence, added the last sentence; added subdivisions E 6 and E 7 and made related changes; and in subsection F, rewrote the introductory paragraph, added subdivision F 3 and added the last paragraph.

§ 2.2-516. Annual report. — The Attorney General shall annually, on or before May 1, deliver to the Governor a report of the state and condition of all important matters in which he has represented the Commonwealth during the preceding year. He shall also include in his report the official opinions rendered by him that he believes to be of general interest or helpful in promoting uniformity in the construction of the laws of the Commonwealth. (Code 1950, § 2-93; 1966, c. 677, § 2.1-128; 1988, c. 122; 2001, c. 844.)

ARTICLE 2.

Division of Consumer Counsel.

§ 2.2-517. Division of Consumer Counsel created; duties. — A. There is created in the Department of Law a Division of Consumer Counsel (the "Division") that shall represent the interests of the people as consumers.

B. The duties of the Division shall be to:

1. Appear before governmental commissions, agencies and departments, including the State Corporation Commission, to represent and be heard on behalf of consumers' interests, and investigate such matters relating to such appearance.

2. Make such studies related to enforcing consumer laws of the Commonwealth as deemed necessary to protect the interests of the consumer and recommend to the Governor and General Assembly the enactment of such legislation deemed necessary to promote and protect the interests of the people as consumers.

C. The Division, in all investigations connected with enforcing consumer laws and appearances before governmental bodies shall, on behalf of the interests of the consumer, cooperate and coordinate its efforts with such commissions, agencies and departments in ensuring that any matters adversely affecting the interests of the consumer are properly controlled and regulated. The appearance of a representative of the Division before any governmental body shall in no way limit or alter the duties of such governmental body.

D. The Attorney General may employ and fix the salaries of such attorneys, employees and consultants, within the amounts appropriated to the Attorney General for providing legal service for the Commonwealth, and other services as may be provided for by law, as he may deem necessary in the operation of the Division of Consumer Counsel to carry out its functions. (1970, c. 781, §§ 2.1-133.1, 2.1-133.3; 2001, c. 844.)

Law Review. — For article analyzing the financial barriers to public participation in the regulatory activities of the SCC, see 14 Wm. & Mary L. Rev. 567 (1973). For article, "Regulation of Electric Utilities by the State Corporation Commission," see 14 Wm. & Mary L. Rev. 589 (1973). For article analyzing rate-making issues under the SCC, see 14 Wm. & Mary L. Rev. 601 (1973).

CASE NOTES

Editor's note. — The case below was decided under former Title 2.1 or prior provisions.

The procedures prescribed for protecting consumers' interests satisfy the requirements of the due process clause of the Virginia Constitution and the due process and equal protection clauses of the Fourteenth Amendment to the Constitution of the United States. Howell v. SCC, 214 Va. 128, 198 S.E.2d 611 (1973).

ARTICLE 3.

Division of Debt Collection.

§ 2.2-518. Division of Debt Collection. — There is created in the Department of Law a Division of Debt Collection that shall provide all legal services and advice related to the collection of funds owed to the Commonwealth, pursuant to § 2.2-507 and the Virginia Debt Collection Act (§ 2.2-4800 et seq.).

The Attorney General may appoint and fix the salaries of such attorneys and employees as may be necessary to carry out the functions of the Division, within the amounts appropriated to the Division, and may supplement such funds from appropriations made to his office for the provision of legal services to the Commonwealth.

The Division may retain as special revenue up to 30 percent of receivables collected on behalf of state agencies and may contract with private collection agents for the collection of debts amounting to less than $15,000, as provided in the appropriation act. (1990, c. 71, § 2.1-133.4; 2001, c. 844; 2004, c. 919.)

Editor's note. — Acts 2008, c. 879, effective for the biennium ending June 30, 2010, in Item 60, provides: "A. All agencies and institutions shall follow the procedures for collection of funds owed the Commonwealth as specified in §§ 2.2-518 and 2.2-4806 of the Code of Virginia, except as provided otherwise therein or in this act.

"B.1. The Division of Debt Collection is entitled to retain as fees up to 30 percent of any revenues generated by it pursuant to paragraph A. to pay operating costs supported by the appropriation in this item.

"2. Upon closing its books at the end of the fiscal year, after the execution of all transfers to state agencies having claims collected by the Division of Debt Collection, the Division may retain up to a $400,000 balance in its operating accounts. Any amounts contained in the operating accounts that exceed $400,000 on the final day of the fiscal year shall be deposited to the credit of the general fund no later than September 1 of the succeeding fiscal year.

"3. The Director, Department of Planning and Budget, may grant an exception to the provisions in paragraph B.2. if the Division of Debt Collection can show just cause.

"C. The Division of Debt Collection may contract with private collection agents for the collection of debts amounting to less than $15,000."

Acts 2008, c. 879, effective for the biennium ending June 30, 2010, in Item 63 B 1, provides: "The amounts provided in this Item include funds to support the Enterprise Applications Master Services Interim Agreement between the Commonwealth of Virginia and CGI Technologies & Solutions, Inc. (CGI). Notwithstanding any other provision of law except the limitations imposed by § 2.2-518, § 2.2-4803 and § 2.2-4806, Code of Virginia, Executive Department agencies and institutions may enter into management agreements with CGI for debt collection and cost recovery services pursuant to Statements of Work 6 and 7 of the Enterprise Applications Master Services Agreement. Work on enhanced collections and recoveries shall not proceed if they commit the Commonwealth to expanding or significantly altering any existing federal or state program without the review and approval of the Governor and General Assembly."

§ 2.2-519. Prompt collection of accounts receivable. — A. The Division shall oversee and ensure prompt delivery of the Commonwealth's accounts receivable in accordance with the Virginia Debt Collection Act (§ 2.2-4800 et seq.). The Division shall enforce the policies and procedures as set forth in § 2.2-4806 for reporting, accounting for, and collecting the Commonwealth's delinquent accounts receivable.

B. All agencies and institutions of the Commonwealth shall comply with all requirements established pursuant to § 2.2-4806 and by the Department of Law regarding the collection of the Commonwealth's accounts receivable. (2008, c. 637.)

PART C.

STATE AGENCIES RELATED TO THE GENERAL OPERATION OF GOVERNMENT.

CHAPTER 6.

GENERAL PROVISIONS.

ARTICLE 1.

In General.

§ 2.2-600. Standard nomenclature to be employed. — Every independent administrative entity established by law and every collegial body established by law or executive order within the executive branch of state government shall be designated according to a standard nomenclature system. The following definitions shall be applied:

"Department" means an independent administrative agency within the executive branch.

"Board" means a permanent collegial body affiliated with an agency.

"Commission" or *"Council"* means a permanent collegial body either affiliated with more than one agency or independent of an agency within the executive branch.

"Division," "Bureau," "Section," "Unit" or other similar titles shall be reserved for internal groupings within agencies.

"Office" means an administrative office of the Governor, Lieutenant Governor, Attorney General or a governor's secretary.

Exceptions to this standard nomenclature shall be used only for agencies and entities with unique characteristics requiring unique descriptive titles, including museums, libraries and historic or commemorative attractions. (1984, c. 393, § 2.1-1.2; 2001, c. 844.)

Cross references. — As to classification of executive branch boards, commissions, and councils, see § 2.2-2100.

§ 2.2-601. General powers of the departments established in this title. — Each department established in this title shall have the following general powers to:

1. Employ such personnel as may be required to carry out the respective purposes for which such department was created;
2. Make and enter into contracts and agreements necessary or incidental to the performance of its duties and execution of its powers under this title;
3. Accept grants from the United States government and agencies and instrumentalities thereof and any other source. To these ends, each department shall have the power to comply with the conditions and execute the agreements necessary, convenient, or desirable; and
4. Do all acts necessary or convenient to carry out the respective purposes for which the department was created. (1968, c. 223, § 2.1-63.2; 1974, c. 420, § 2.1-372; 1976, cc. 760, 761, §§ 2.1-114.4, 2.1-390; 1982, c. 345; 1984, cc. 728, 746, §§ 2.1-563.16, 2.1-708; 1985, cc. 72, 265, § 2.1-234.31; 1988, c. 839, § 2.1-738; 1995, c. 357; 1996, c. 727; 1997, c. 858; 1998, c. 808; 1999, cc. 342, 412, 421, 433; 2000, cc. 483, 491; 2001, c. 844.)

§ 2.2-602. Duties of agencies and their appointing authorities. — The heads of state agencies shall be the appointing authorities of the respective agencies, and shall establish and maintain within their agencies methods of administration relating to the establishment and maintenance of personnel standards on a merit basis that are approved by the Governor for the proper and efficient enforcement of the Virginia Personnel Act (§ 2.2-2900 et seq.). But the Governor shall exercise no authority with respect to the selection or tenure of office of any individual employed in accordance with such methods, except when the Governor is the appointing authority.

Appointing authorities may assign to the personnel officers or to other officers and employees of their agencies such personnel duties as they see fit.

Agencies shall establish and maintain rosters of their employees that shall set forth, as to each employee, the class title, pay and status and such other data as they may deem desirable to produce significant facts pertaining to personnel administration.

Agencies shall establish and maintain such promotion and employment lists, rated according to merit and fitness, as they deem desirable. Agencies may make use of the employment list kept by the Department of Human Resource Management in lieu of keeping employment lists for their agencies.

Agencies shall supply the Governor with any information he deems necessary for the performance of his duties in connection with the administration of Virginia Personnel Act (§ 2.2-2900 et seq.). (1976, c. 761, § 2.1-114.7; 2000, cc. 66, 657; 2001, c. 844.)

§ 2.2-603. Authority of agency directors. — A. Notwithstanding any provision of law to the contrary, the agency director of each agency in the executive branch of state government shall have the power and duty to (i) supervise and manage the department or agency and (ii) prepare, approve, and submit to the Governor all requests for appropriations and to be responsible for all expenditures pursuant to appropriations.

B. The director of each agency in the executive branch of state government, except those that by law are appointed by their respective boards, shall not proscribe any agency employee from discussing the functions and policies of the agency, without prior approval from his supervisor or superior, with any person unless the information to be discussed is protected from disclosure by the Virginia Freedom of Information Act (§ 2.2-3700 et seq.) or any other provision of state or federal law.

C. Subsection A shall not be construed to restrict any other specific or general powers and duties of executive branch boards granted by law.

D. This section shall not apply to those agency directors that are appointed by their respective boards or by the Board of Education. Directors appointed in this manner shall have the powers and duties assigned by law or by the board.

E. In addition to the requirements of subsection C of § 2.2-619, the director of each agency in any branch of state government shall, at the end of each fiscal year, report to (i) the Secretary of Finance and the Chairmen of the House Committee on Appropriations and the Senate Committee on Finance a listing and general description of any federal contract, grant, or money in excess of $1,000,000 for which the agency was eligible, whether or not the agency applied for, accepted, and received such contract, grant, or money, and, if not, the reasons therefore and the dollar amount and corresponding percentage of the agency's total annual budget that was supplied by funds from the federal government and (ii) the Chairmen of the House Committees on Appropriations and Finance, and the Senate Committee on Finance any amounts owed to the agency from any source that are more than six months delinquent, the length of such delinquencies, and the total of all such delinquent amounts in each six-month interval. Clause (i) shall not be required of public institutions of higher education.

F. The director of every department in the executive branch of state government shall report to the Chief Information Officer as described in § 2.2-2005, all known incidents that threaten the security of the Commonwealth's databases and data communications resulting in exposure of data protected by federal or state laws, or other incidents compromising the security of the Commonwealth's information technology systems with the potential to cause major disruption to normal agency activities. Such reports shall be made to the Chief Information Officer within 24 hours from when the department discovered or should have discovered their occurrence. (1985, c. 212, § 2.1-20.01:1; 1992, c. 672; 1995, c. 219; 1996, c. 98; 1997, c. 491; 1999, cc. 70, 892; 2001, c. 844; 2004, cc. 488, 638.)

Editor's note. — Acts 2004, c. 638, which added subsection G [now F], in cl. 2, provides: "That the provisions of this act shall become effective on January 1, 2005."

§ **2.2-604. Performance of duties assigned to an agency.** — The chief executive officer shall be responsible for any duty or task imposed upon his agency. The chief executive officer may delegate or assign to any officer or employee of his agency any tasks required to be performed by him or the agency and, in the case of an agency with a supervisory board, such board may delegate or assign the tasks. Except as otherwise provided by law, the chief executive officer may also delegate to any officer or employee of any state or quasi-state agency nondiscretionary duties conferred or imposed upon the chief executive officer or his agency by law where the delegation of duties is necessary to achieve efficiency and economy in the administration of government. The chief executive officer or supervisory board delegating or assigning tasks shall remain responsible for the performance of such tasks.

Any delegation pursuant to this section shall, where appropriate, be accompanied by written guidelines for the exercise of the tasks delegated. Where appropriate, the guidelines shall require that agency heads receive summaries of actions taken. Such delegation shall not relieve the chief executive officer or supervisory board of the responsibility to ensure faithful performance of the duties and tasks. (1988, c. 273, § 2.1-20.01:2; 2001, c. 844; 2005, c. 839.)

§ 2.2-604.1. Designation of officials; interests of senior citizens and adults with disabilities. — The head of each state agency shall designate an existing employee who shall be responsible for reviewing policy and program decisions under consideration by the agency in light of the effect of such decisions on senior citizens and adults with disabilities. The designated employee shall advise and alert the agency head of opportunities to make policies, programs, and regulations senior-friendly and disability-friendly. (2006, c. 345.)

§ 2.2-605. Appointment of acting officer in case of temporary disability. — When any officer in charge of or at the head of any division or department of the state government shall, because of sickness or for any other reason, be unable to perform the duties of his office and no provision is made for someone, or for the appointment of someone, to exercise the powers and perform the duties of such office while the officer is sick or unable to act, the Governor may appoint some person temporarily to fill such office as acting head or in charge of such division or department, who shall after qualifying exercise the powers and perform the duties of such office until the incumbent returns or the office is otherwise filled. (Code 1950, § 2-16; 1966, c. 677, § 2.1-20; 2001, c. 844.)

§ 2.2-606. Consideration of certain issues in policy development. — In the formulation and implementation of policies and regulations, each department and division of the executive branch and those boards affiliated with a state agency within the executive branch of state government shall consider the impact of the policies and regulations on family formation, stability, and autonomy. This section shall not be construed to confer a right or benefit, substantive or procedural, enforceable at law or in equity by any party against the Commonwealth, its agencies, officers, or any other person. (1995, c. 530, § 2.1-7.2; 2001, c. 844.)

§ 2.2-607. Reporting transfers of personnel; granting reports. — A. Whenever a state employee is transferred for a limited period of time from one state agency to another without transferring appropriations, as may be provided by law, the transfer shall be reported by the transferring agency to the Department of Human Resource Management, including the name and classification of the employee, the name of the transferring and receiving agencies and the length of time of transfer. If, at a subsequent time, the length of time is shortened or extended, a subsequent report of that fact shall also be submitted.

B. A consolidated report of all current transfers and all that have begun and ended within the preceding three-month period shall be prepared as of the first day of each January, April, July and October. A copy of each report shall be submitted to the Chairmen of the House Committee on Appropriations and the Senate Committee on Finance and the Director of the Department of Planning and Budget no later than three working days after the effective date of the report. (1982, c. 414, § 2.1-114.7:1; 2000, cc. 66, 657; 2001, c. 844.)

§ 2.2-608. Furnishing reports; Governor authorized to require reports. — A. Agencies, institutions, collegial bodies, and other governmental entities that are specifically required by the Code of Virginia to report annually or biennially to the Governor and General Assembly shall submit their reports on or before October 1 of each year, unless otherwise specified. The Governor may require any agency to furnish an annual or biennial report.

B. Any agency, institution, collegial body, or other governmental entity outside of the legislative branch of government required to submit a report to the General Assembly or any committee, subcommittee, commission, agency, or other body within the legislative branch or to the chairman or agency head of such entity shall distribute a hard copy of such report to each member of the General Assembly who requests a copy in accordance with the provisions of § 30-34.4:1. The cost of printing and distributing reports shall be borne by the reporting entity or its supporting agency. (1984, c. 734, § 2.1-2.1; 2001, c. 844; 2004, c. 650.)

§ 2.2-609. Copies of state publications furnished to Librarian of Virginia. — A. Pursuant to the State Publications Depository Program (§ 42.1-92 et seq.), every agency, institution, collegial body, or other state governmental entity of any branch of government shall furnish a maximum of 20 copies of each of its publications, as defined in § 42.1-93, or, if authorized by the Library, other publication information as may be designated by the Library to facilitate the acquisition and distribution of publications, regardless of physical form or characteristics.

B. Every agency, institution, collegial body, or other state governmental entity of any branch of government shall provide information requested by the Library to assist in the publication of an annual catalog of state agency publications as required by § 42.1-95 of the State Publications Depository Program.

C. For purposes of this section, *"Library"* means The Library of Virginia. (1977, c. 672, §§ 2.1-467.2, 2.1-467.4; 1979, c. 403; 1981, c. 234; 1992, c. 181; 1994, c. 64; 1998, c. 427; 2001, c. 844; 2004, cc. 28, 152; 2006, c. 59.)

§ 2.2-610. Furnishing copies of documents at no cost to law enforcement officials. — All agencies and instrumentalities of the Commonwealth shall provide, at no cost, copies of documents requested by the Department of State Police or other law-enforcement officers as part of an active criminal investigation.

"Law-enforcement officer" means the same as that term is defined in § 9.1-101. (1997, c. 44, § 2.1-2.2; 2001, c. 844.)

§ 2.2-611. Acceptance by departments, etc., of funds from United States; application of funds. — A. Any department, agency, bureau or institution of the Commonwealth may (i) accept grants of funds made by the United States government or any department or agency thereof, to be applied to purposes within the functions of such state department, agency, bureau or institution, and (ii) administer and expend such funds for the purposes for which they are granted.

B. The State Treasurer is appointed custodian of all such funds, and shall disburse them on warrants issued by the Comptroller for the department, agency, bureau or institution for whose use they are granted. (Code 1950, §§ 2-3, 2-4; 1966, c. 677, §§ 2.1-3, 2.1-4; 2001, c. 844.)

Cross references. — As to coordination of official communications with the federal government and governments of other states or foreign nations, see § 2.2-114.

§ 2.2-612. Notification to localities of reduction or discontinuation of service. — A. No agency, board, commission or other entity of the Commonwealth shall take any action to reduce or discontinue a service that it performs for a local government or reduce or discontinue any form of financial assistance to a local government without first notifying all affected local governments at least 90 days in advance of the proposed action. However, in emergencies, certified by the Governor for executive branch agencies or by the chief administrative officer for any other entity of the Commonwealth, such action may be taken immediately following the notice.

B. The provisions of subsection A shall not apply to any action taken by an executive branch agency or other entity of the Commonwealth pursuant to a specific legislative requirement, agreement or contract negotiated with a local government, the application of a statute prescribing periodic adjustments in state financial assistance, workforce reduction resulting from diminished appropriation or legislated early retirement provisions, or judicial decree.

C. Nothing in subsection A shall apply to any officer who receives funding under § 15.2-1636.7 or who may appeal Compensation Board budget decisions under § 15.2-1636.9 or § 15.2-1636.10, or to those payments made to localities in accordance with §§ 53.1-20.1, 53.1-83.1, 53.1-84, or § 53.1-85. (1997, c. 859, § 2.1-7.3; 2001, c. 844; 2004, cc. 34, 155.)

§ 2.2-613. Agency mandates on localities; assessment. — Pursuant to § 15.2-2903, all agencies, as defined in § 2.2-128, shall conduct an assessment of all mandates imposed on local governments administered by the agency to determine which mandates, if any, may be altered or eliminated. (1993, c. 652, § 2.1-7.1; 2001, c. 844.)

§ 2.2-614. Purebred livestock raised by state institutions and agencies may be sold instead of slaughtered. — The person in charge of any state institution or agency that raises purebred livestock may, when any of the livestock are to be slaughtered, sell the same to any person desiring to acquire the livestock for breeding purposes, provided the interests of the institution or agency will not be adversely affected by the sale. (1958, c. 586, § 2-4.3; 1966, c. 677, § 2.1-7; 2001, c. 844.)

§ 2.2-614.1. Authority to accept revenue by commercially acceptable means; service charge; bad check charge. — A. Subject to § 19.2-353.3, any public body that is responsible for revenue collection, including, but not limited to, taxes, interest, penalties, fees, fines or other charges, may accept payment of any amount due by any commercially acceptable means, including, but not limited to, checks, credit cards, debit cards, and electronic funds transfers.

B. The public body may add to any amount due a sum, not to exceed the amount charged to that public body for acceptance of any payment by a means that incurs a charge to that public body or the amount negotiated and agreed to in a contract with that public body, whichever is less. Any state agency imposing such additional charges shall waive them when the use of these means of payment reduces processing costs and losses due to bad checks or other receivable costs by an amount equal to or greater than the amount of such additional charges.

C. If any check or other means of payment tendered to a public body in the course of its duties is not paid by the financial institution on which it is drawn, because of insufficient funds in the account of the drawer, no account is in the name of the drawer, or the account of the drawer is closed, and the check or other means of payment is returned to the public body unpaid, the amount thereof shall be charged to the person on whose account it was received, and his liability and that of his sureties, shall be as if he had never offered any such payment. A penalty of $35 or the amount of any costs, whichever is greater, shall be added to such amount. This penalty shall be in addition to any other penalty provided by law, except the penalty imposed by § 58.1-12 shall not apply. (2002, c. 719; 2004, c. 565.)

Cross references. — As to use of penalties received under this section by the State Corporation Commission, see § 12.1-17. As to collection of fees, etc., by court clerks in lieu of money, see § 17.1-222.1. As to collection of license and permit fees by the Director of the Department of Game and Inland Fisheries, see § 29.1-112. As to penalty for uncollected checks and electronic payments tendered for license fees or taxes to the Department of Motor Vehicles, see § 46.2-207. As to service charge for payment of taxes by certain means to the Virginia Employment Commission, see § 60.2-519.2.

Article 2.

Implementation Of Federal Mandates Act.

§ 2.2-615. Short title. — This chapter shall be known and may be cited as the "Implementation of Federal Mandates Act". (1995, c. 604, § 2.1-795; 2001, c. 844.)

§ 2.2-616. Legislative declaration. — A. In enacting this chapter, the General Assembly employs its legislative authority to establish that the people of Virginia, acting through their elected officials in Virginia government, have the responsibility and authority to establish policy in and for Virginia pertaining to federal programs mandated in federal statutes.

B. The intent of the General Assembly is to assure the primacy of the Commonwealth's legal and political authority to implement in and for Virginia the policy mandated by federal statutes and to vigorously challenge and scrutinize the extent and scope of authority asserted by federal executive branch agencies when federal agency actions and interpretations are inconsistent with Virginia policy and exceed the lawful authority of the federal government or are not required by federal law.

C. In this connection the General Assembly finds and declares that:

1. The power to implement federal policies in and for Virginia is central to the ability of the people of Virginia to govern themselves under a federal system of government; and

2. Any implementation of federal policies in and for Virginia by federal executive branch agencies that is contrary to fundamental notions of federalism and self-determination must be identified and countered.

D. The General Assembly further finds and declares that:

1. There is an urgent need to modify federal mandates because the implementation of these mandates by the Commonwealth wastes the financial resources of local governments, the citizens of Virginia and the Commonwealth and does not properly respect the rights of the Commonwealth, local governments, and citizens.

2. The state government has an obligation to the public to do what is necessary to protect the rights of Virginia citizens under federal law while minimizing or eliminating any additional cost or regulatory burden on any citizen of the Commonwealth.

3. The Tenth Amendment to the United States Constitution directs that powers that are not delegated to the United States are reserved to the states or to the people. Virginia, as one of the sovereign states within the Union, has constitutional authority to enact laws protecting the environment of the Commonwealth and safeguarding the public health, safety, and welfare of the citizens of Virginia. However, this authority has too often been ignored by the federal government, as the federal government has intruded more and more into areas that must be left to the states. It is essential that the dilution of the

authority of state and local governments be halted and that the provisions of the Tenth Amendment be accorded proper respect.

4. Current federal regulatory mandates, as reflected in federal administrative regulations, guidelines, and policies, often do not reflect the realities of Virginia and federal regulators frequently do not understand the needs and priorities of the citizens of Virginia.

5. The citizens of the Commonwealth can create and wish to create innovative solutions to Virginia's problems, but the current manner in which legal challenges to state policies and federal programmatic substitutions of state programs are handled does not allow the Commonwealth the flexibility it needs. It is not possible for the Commonwealth of Virginia to effectively and efficiently implement the provisions of federal statutes unless the burden to prove the insufficiency of the Commonwealth's efforts to implement federal requirements is shifted to the person or agency who asserts such insufficiency.

6. The provisions of this chapter will better balance the exercise of the powers of the federal government and the powers reserved to the states. In addition, the application of this chapter ultimately will bring about greater protection for the Commonwealth and the nation because it will direct the Commonwealth to implement federal statutes at the least possible cost, thereby freeing more moneys for other needs.

7. The purpose of this chapter is to ensure that federal mandates implemented in Virginia comply with state policy as established by the General Assembly. (1995, c. 604, § 2.1-796; 2001, c. 844.)

§ 2.2-617. Definitions. — As used in this chapter, unless the context requires otherwise:

"Federal statute" means a federal statute that is in accord with the United States Constitution imposing mandates on state or local governments, which may include, but is not limited to, the following:

1. The Safe Drinking Water Act, 42 U.S.C. § 300f, et seq., as amended;
2. The Clean Air Act, 42 U.S.C. § 7401, et seq., as amended;
3. The Federal Water Pollution Control Act, 33 U.S.C. § 1251, et seq., as amended;
4. The Solid Waste Disposal Act, 42 U.S.C. § 3251, et seq., as amended;
5. The Resource Conservation and Recovery Act of 1976, 42 U.S.C. § 6901, et seq., as amended;
6. The Comprehensive Environmental Response, Compensation, and Liability Act of 1980, 42 U.S.C. § 9601, et seq., as amended;
7. The Superfund Amendments and Reauthorization Act of 1986, P.L. 99-499, as amended;
8. The Endangered Species Act of 1973, 16 U.S.C. § 1531, et seq., as amended;
9. The Asbestos School Hazard Abatement Statute, 20 U.S.C. § 4011, et seq., as amended;
10. The Brady Handgun Violence Prevention Act of 1993, P.L. 101-336, as amended;
11. The Commercial Motor Vehicle Safety Act of 1986, 49 U.S.C. § 2501, et seq., as amended;
12. The Family and Medical Leave Act of 1993, P.L. 103-3, as amended;
13. The Emergency Planning and Community Right-to-Know Act, P.L. 99-145 and 99-499, as amended;
14. The Federal, State, and Local Partnership for Education Improvement Program, 20 U.S.C. § 1751, et seq., as amended;
15. The National Voter Registration Act of 1993, P.L. 103-31, as amended;
16. The Federal School Lunch Program and School Breakfast Program, 42 U.S.C. §§ 1751 and 1773, P.L. 101-336, as amended;

17. The Federal Social Services and Medicaid Requirements, 42 U.S.C. § 1396, et seq., as amended;

18. The Federal Highway Safety Programs; and

19. The Intermodal Surface Transportation Efficiency Act of 1991, P.L. 102-240, as amended. (1995, c. 604, § 2.1-797; 2001, c. 844.)

§ 2.2-618. State programs to implement federal statutes. — Any agency of the executive branch of state government that is authorized to develop a state program to implement any mandates contained in a federal statute shall develop the state program and adopt any necessary regulations using the following criteria:

1. State programs shall be developed by the agency to meet the requirements of federal statutes in good faith with a critical view toward any federal regulations, guidelines, or policies.

2. State programs shall be developed with due consideration of the financial restraints of the Commonwealth, local governments, and the citizens of Virginia.

3. Any state program that implements the goals of the federal statute shall use the most efficient method possible with careful consideration given to cost of the program and the impact of the program on Virginia citizens and local governments, and the long-range public health, safety, and welfare of citizens of the Commonwealth. (1995, c. 604, § 2.1-798; 2001, c. 844.)

§ 2.2-619. Governor to report to the General Assembly. — A. The Governor shall report to the General Assembly regarding the proposed implementation of this section.

B. If any state program is authorized or mandated by a federal statute, no state funds for the program shall be appropriated unless:

1. The state program is necessary to protect the public health, safety, and welfare;

2. The state program is necessary to implement the federal statute;

3. The operation of the state program benefits the state by providing a cost-effective implementation of the federal statute by the Commonwealth, local government, and business; or

4. The state program benefits the Commonwealth, local government, and business by providing a cost-effective means to meet a higher public health, safety, and welfare standard established under state law.

C. Each agency making a budget request for state appropriations for a state program authorized or mandated by federal statute shall include in its budget request citations to the federal constitutional provisions and the state constitutional or statutory provisions that authorize the state program. The Governor shall review the budget request and determine whether additional state statutory authority is required in order to implement the state program and shall make recommendations to the General Assembly.

D. The General Assembly, after receiving a recommendation from the Governor, shall determine whether a state program is necessary and whether federal constitutional authority and state constitutional or statutory authority exist. The General Assembly shall review toward the interpretation of the federal statute found in federal regulations, guidelines, or policies. Appropriation of state funds for a state program shall constitute the General Assembly's determination that the state program is necessary and that federal constitutional authority and state constitutional or statutory authority exist. State appropriations may not be based solely on requirements found in regulations, guidelines, or policies of a federal agency.

E. Prior to recommending to the General Assembly any budget for an agency that is charged with implementing federal mandates, the Governor shall request that the agency provide information to the Department of Planning and Budget regarding any monetary savings for the state and any reduction in regulatory burdens on the public and on local governments that could be or have been achieved through the development of state policies that meet the intent of the federal statute but do not necessarily follow all applicable federal regulations, guidelines, or policies. The agency shall also provide advice to the Department of Planning and Budget regarding any changes in law that are necessary to provide the agency with the authority to implement state policies in such a way as to create additional savings or greater reductions in regulatory burdens. The Department of Planning and Budget shall review and compile the information received from agencies pursuant to this section and shall include recommendations in the executive budget.

F. For purposes of this section, "state program" shall not include any portion of a program that is funded with nontax or nonfee revenue, or both, which state authorities are required to administer in a trusteeship or custodial capacity and that are not subject to appropriation by the General Assembly. (1995, c. 604, § 2.1-799; 2001, c. 844.)

§ 2.2-620. Establishment of the Capitol District as the seat of government of the Commonwealth. — A. For administrative purposes, the area that encompasses the seat of government of the Commonwealth shall be referred to as the "Capitol District."

B. The term "Capitol District" shall be geographically defined as the area in Richmond, Virginia, contained within the centerline of East Broad Street between its intersections with the centerline of Eighth Street and the Interstate 95 overpass, the centerline of Eighth Street between its intersections with the centerlines of East Broad Street and Main Street, the centerline of Main Street between its intersections with the centerline of Eighth Street and the Interstate 95 overpass, and the overpass of Interstate 95 between its intersections with the centerlines of East Broad Street and Main Street, and all buildings and property owned or leased by the Commonwealth within such area.

C. Nothing in this section shall be construed to restrict (i) the authority of the legislative, executive, or judicial branch of state government in the administration of its employees or facilities within the Capitol District or to grant any additional authority or responsibility to any government agency or entity (ii) the law-enforcement authority of the police department of the City of Richmond within the Department's jurisdiction. (2008, c. 548.)

CHAPTER 7.

Department for the Aging.

Article 1.

General Provisions.

Article 2.

Virginia Public Guardian and Conservator Program.

Article 3.

Virginia Respite Care Grant Program.

Article 4.

Alzheimer's Disease and Related Disorders.

Article 1.

General Provisions.

§ 2.2-700. Department created; appointment of Commissioner; powers and duties. — A. There is created a Department for the Aging (the Department), which shall be headed by a Commissioner appointed by the Governor to serve at his pleasure.

B. The Commissioner of the Department shall, under the direction and control of the Governor, exercise the powers and perform the duties conferred or imposed upon him by law and perform such other duties as may be required by the Governor.

C. In cooperation with the Commonwealth Council on Aging, the Commissioner shall serve as the Governor's principal advisor on aging issues, and recommend to the Governor and the General Assembly such policies, legislation, and other actions appropriate to meet the needs of an aging society and to improve aging services in the Commonwealth. In addition, the Commissioner shall serve as special assistant to the Governor for Aging Policy and shall report directly to the Governor as necessary on aging policies. (1974, c. 420, § 2.1-371; 1982, c. 345; 2001, c. 844; 2004, c. 694.)

§ 2.2-701. Nature of long-term care services. — A. The long-term care services shall include, but not be limited to, the following:

1. A balanced range of health, social, and supportive services to deliver long-term care services to persons aged 60 and older with chronic illnesses or functional impairments;

2. Meaningful choice, increased functional ability, and affordability as determining factors in defining long-term care service needs, which needs shall be determined by a uniform system for comprehensively assessing the needs and preferences of individuals requiring such services;

3. Service delivery, consistent with the needs and preferences of individuals requiring such services, that occurs in the most independent, least restrictive, and most appropriate living situation possible; and

4. Opportunities for self-care and independent living, as appropriate, by encouraging all long-term care programs to maximize self-care and independent living within the mainstream of life in the community.

B. Such services shall include, but not be limited to, the following categories: socialization services, health care services, nutrition services, daily living services, educational services, housing services, transportation services, and supportive services.

C. As used in this section:

"Daily living services" includes homemaker, companion, personal care and chore services, home repair, weatherization and adult day care.

"Educational services" includes information on the long-term care services provided by agencies of the Commonwealth, its localities and private sector agencies, and public information as provided in § 2.2-213.1.

"Health care services" includes home health care and community medical care.

"Housing services" includes community-based residential opportunities and retrofitting existing housing as needed.

"Nutrition services" includes home-delivered meals, food stamps, and congregate meals.

"Socialization services" includes telephone reassurance, friendly visiting, and congregate meals.

"Supportive services" includes adult protective services, mental health and mental retardation services, counseling services and legal aid.

"Transportation services" includes readily available access to public transportation or area coordinated para-transit systems. (1982, c. 346, § 2.1-373.8; 2001, c. 844; 2007, c. 747.)

The 2007 amendments. — The 2007 amendment by c. 747 inserted subsection A and redesignated remaining subsections accordingly; in subsection B, substituted "Such services" for "The long-term care services" and inserted "educational services, housing services, transportation services"; and rewrote subsection C to put definitions in alphabetical order and adding definitions for educational, housing and transportation services."

§ 2.2-702. Administrative responsibilities of Department regarding long-term care. — The administrative responsibilities of the Department regarding long-term care shall be to:

1. Develop appropriate fiscal and administrative controls over public long-term care services in the Commonwealth.

2. Develop a state long-term care plan to guide the coordination and delivery of services by the human resources agencies, including transportation services. The plan shall ensure the development of a continuum of long-term care programs and services for the impaired elderly population in need of services.

3. Identify programmatic resources and assure the equitable statewide distribution of these resources.

4. Perform ongoing evaluations of the cost-effective utilization of long-term care resources. (1982, c. 346, § 2.1-373.6; 1983, c. 411; 2001, c. 844.)

§ 2.2-703. Powers and duties of Department with respect to aging persons; area agencies on aging. — A. The mission of the Department shall be to improve the quality of life for older Virginians and to act as a focal point among state agencies for research, policy analysis, long-range planning, and education on aging issues. The Department shall also serve as the lead agency in coordinating the work of state agencies on meeting the needs of an aging society. The Department's policies and programs shall be designed to enable older persons to be as independent and self-sufficient as possible. The Department shall promote local participation in programs for older persons, evaluate and monitor the services provided for older Virginians and provide information to the general public. In furtherance of this mission, the Department shall have, without limitation, the following duties to:

1. Study the economic and physical condition of the residents in the Commonwealth whose age qualifies them for coverage under Public Law 89-73 or any law amendatory or supplemental thereto of the Congress of the United States, and the employment, medical, educational, recreational and housing facilities available to them, with the view of determining the needs and problems of such persons;

2. Determine the services and facilities, private and governmental and state and local, provided for and available to older persons and to recommend to the appropriate persons such coordination of and changes in such services and facilities as will make them of greater benefit to older persons and more responsive to their needs;

3. Act as the single state agency, under Public Law 89-73 or any law amendatory or supplemental thereto of the Congress of the United States, and as the sole agency for administering or supervising the administration of such plans as may be adopted in accordance with the provisions of such laws. The Department may prepare, submit and carry out state plans and shall be the agency primarily responsible for coordinating state programs and activities related to the purposes of, or undertaken under, such plans or laws;

4. Apply, with the approval of the Governor, for and expend such grants, gifts or bequests from any source that becomes available in connection with its duties under this section, and may comply with such conditions and requirements as may be imposed in connection therewith;

5. Hold hearings and conduct investigations necessary to pass upon applications for approval of a project under the plans and laws set out in subdivision 3, and shall make reports to the Secretary of the United States Department of Health and Human Services as may be required;

6. Designate area agencies on aging pursuant to Public Law 89-73 or any law amendatory or supplemental thereto of the Congress of the United States and to adopt regulations for the composition and operation of such area agencies on aging;

7. Provide information to consumers and their representatives concerning the recognized features of special care units. Such information shall educate consumers and their representatives on how to choose special care and may include brochures and electronic bulletin board notices;

8. Provide staff support to the Commonwealth Council on Aging;

9. Assist state, local, and nonprofit agencies, including, but not limited to, area agencies on aging, in identifying grant and public-private partnership opportunities for improving services to elderly Virginians;

10. Contract with a not-for-profit Virginia corporation granted tax-exempt status under § 501(c)(3) of the Internal Revenue Code with statewide experience in Virginia in conducting a state long-term care ombudsman program or designated area agencies on aging for the administration of the ombudsman program. Such contract shall provide a minimum staffing ratio of one ombudsman to every 2,000 long-term care beds, subject to sufficient appropriations by the General Assembly. The Department may also contract with such entities for the administration of elder rights programs as authorized under Public Law 89-73, such as insurance counseling and assistance, and to create an elder information/elder rights center;

11. Serve as the focal point for the rights of older Virginians and their families by establishing, maintaining and publicizing a toll-free number to provide resource and referral information, and to provide such other assistance and advice as may be requested; and

12. Develop and maintain a four-year plan for aging services in the Commonwealth, pursuant to § 2.2-703.1.

B. The governing body of any county, city or town may appropriate funds for support of area agencies on aging designated pursuant to subdivision A 6.

C. All agencies of the Commonwealth shall assist the Department in effectuating its functions in accordance with its designation as the single state agency as required in subdivision A 3.

D. As used in this chapter, *"older Virginians"* or *"older persons"* mean persons aged 60 years or older. (1974, c. 420, § 2.1-373; 1976, c. 299; 1978, c. 271; 1979, c. 678; 1982, c. 345; 1983, cc. 165, 215; 1997, c. 320; 1998, c. 665; 1999, cc. 712, 1021; 2000, cc. 307, 313; 2001, c. 844; 2004, c. 694; 2005, cc. 610, 924; 2008, c. 361.)

Cross references. — As to the participation by the Department in the budget development process of other agencies dealing with related matters, see § 2.2-1507.

Editor's note. — Acts 2005, cc. 610 and 924, cl. 5 provides: "That the Board of Long-Term Care Administrators shall convene a task force to develop licensing regulations for assisted living facility administrators and submit an initial progress report by November 1, 2005, and a follow-up progress report by November 1, 2006, on such regulations to the chairmen of the Joint Commission on Health Care, the House Committee on Health, Welfare and Institutions, and the Senate Committee on Rehabilitation and Social Services."

Acts 2005, cc. 610 and 924, cl. 6 provides: "That the Board of Long-Term Care Administrators shall adopt final regulations to implement the provisions of this act to be effective on or before July 1, 2007."

The 2008 amendments. — The 2008 amendment by c. 361 substituted "pursuant to § 2.2-703.1" for "including but not limited to identifying collaborative opportunities with other state and local agencies and programs to better serve the needs of an aging society. This plan shall be developed by the Department in consultation with relevant stakeholders" at the end of subdivision A 12.

§ 2.2-703.1. Powers and duties of Department relating to four-year plan; report. — A. The Department shall develop and maintain a four-year plan for aging services in the Commonwealth. Such a plan shall also serve as the State Plan for Aging Services as required by the federal Administration on Aging. In developing the plan, the Department shall consult various state and local agencies, including, but not limited to, Virginia's Area Agencies on Aging, the Commonwealth's Health and Human Resources agencies, the Virginia Department of Transportation, the Virginia Department of Housing and Community Development, the Virginia Housing Development Authority, and the Virginia Department of Corrections, as well as the Commonwealth Council on Aging, the Virginia Alzheimer's Disease and Related Disorders Commission, and the Virginia Public Guardianship and Conservator Program Advisory Board. The Department shall also consult with businesses, nonprofit organizations, and stakeholders as the Department deems appropriate.

B. The four-year plan shall include a description of Virginia's aging population, its impact on the Commonwealth, and issues related to providing services to this population at both the state and local levels. The plan shall include factors for the Department to consider in determining when additional funding may be required for certain programs or services. The following shall be included in the plan:

1. Information on changes in the aging population, with particular attention to the growing diversity of this population including low-income, minority, and non-English speaking older individuals;

2. Unmet needs and waiting list data for aging-related services as reported by Virginia's Area Agencies on Aging and those state agencies that may maintain and provide this information;

3. The results of periodic needs surveys and customer satisfaction surveys targeted to older Virginians that may be conducted by the Department, the Area Agencies on Aging, or any other state or local agency;

4. An analysis by those state agencies listed in subsection A of how the aging of the population impacts their agency and how the agency is responding. This

analysis shall be provided to the Department every four years on a schedule and in a format determined by the Department;

5. The impact of changes in federal and state funding for aging services; and

6. Any other factors the Department deems appropriate.

C. In carrying out the above duties, the Commissioner shall submit the plan to the Governor and the General Assembly by November 30 of 2009 and every four years thereafter.

D. The Commissioner shall also submit an annual report by November 30 of each year to the Governor and the General Assembly on the status of aging services in the Commonwealth. (2008, c. 361.)

§ 2.2-704. Responsibility of Department for complaints regarding long-term care services. — The Department or its designee shall investigate complaints regarding community services that are designed to provide long-term care to older persons and are rendered by the Department of Health, the Department of Social Services, the Department of Mental Health, Mental Retardation and Substance Abuse Services, the area agencies on aging or any private nonprofit or proprietary agency.

Nothing in this section shall affect the services provided by local departments of welfare or social services pursuant to § 63.2-1605. (1982, c. 346, § 2.1-373.3; 2001, c. 844.)

§ 2.2-705. Access to residents, facilities and patients' records by Office of State Long-Term Care Ombudsman. — The entity designated by the Department to operate the programs of the Office of the State Long-Term Care Ombudsman pursuant to the Older Americans Act, Public Law 100-175, shall, in the investigation of complaints referred to the program, have the same access to (i) residents, facilities and patients' records of licensed adult care residences in accordance with § 63.2-1706 and (ii) patients, facilities and patients' records of nursing facilities or nursing homes in accordance with § 32.1-25, and shall have access to the patients, residents and patients' records of state hospitals operated by the Department of Mental Health, Mental Retardation and Substance Abuse Services. However, if a patient is unable to consent to the review of his medical and social records and has no legal guardian, such representatives shall have appropriate access to such records in accordance with this section. Notwithstanding the provisions of § 32.1-125.1, the entity designated by the Department to operate the programs of the Office of the State Long-Term Care Ombudsman shall have access to nursing facilities and nursing homes and state hospitals in accordance with this section. Access to residents, facilities and patients' records shall be during normal working hours except in emergency situations. (1980, c. 477, § 2.1-373.1; 1982, c. 345; 1989, c. 160; 1993, cc. 333, 957, 993; 1996, cc. 113, 341; 2001, c. 844.)

Editor's note. — Acts 1993, cc. 957 and 993, which amended § 2.1-373.1, from which this section was derived, provided in cl. 4: "That the provisions of this act shall be implemented to the extent funds are appropriated therefor." See Acts 1993, c. 994, item 381 B, relating to the extent funds were appropriated for Acts 1993, cc. 957 and 993.

Law Review. — For an article, "Reform of Adult Guardianship Law," see 32 U. Rich. L. Rev. 1273 (1998).

§ 2.2-706. Confidentiality of records of Office of the State Long-Term Care Ombudsman. — All documentary and other evidence received or maintained by the Department or its agents in connection with specific complaints or investigations under any program of the Office of the State Long-Term Care Ombudsman conducted by or under the Commissioner of that

Department shall be confidential and not subject to the Virginia Freedom of Information Act (§ 2.2-3700 et seq.), except that such information may be released on a confidential basis in compliance with regulations adopted by the Department and consistent with provisions of subdivision 4 of § 2.2-601 and with the requirements of the Older Americans Act (42 U.S.C. § 3001 et seq.).

The Commissioner of the Department shall release information concerning completed investigations of complaints made under the programs of the Office of the State Long-Term Care Ombudsman, but shall in no event release the identity of any complainant or resident of a long-term care facility unless (i) the complainant or resident or his legal representative consents in writing to disclosure, or (ii) disclosure is required by court order. The Commissioner of the Department shall establish procedures to notify long-term care facilities of the nature of complaints and their findings. (1980, c. 478, § 2.1-373.2; 1982, c. 345; 1988, c. 41; 1989, c. 160; 2001, c. 844.)

§ 2.2-707. Protection for representatives of the Office of the State Long-Term Care Ombudsman. — Any designated representative of the Office of the State Long-Term Care Ombudsman who, in good faith with reasonable cause and without malice, performs the official duties of ombudsman, including acting to report, investigate or cause any investigation to be made regarding a long-term care provider, shall be immune from any civil liability that might otherwise be incurred or imposed as the result of the making of the report or investigation. (1989, c. 160, § 2.1-373.2:1; 2001, c. 844.)

§ 2.2-708. Coordination of local long-term care services. — The governing body of each county or city, or a combination thereof, shall designate a lead agency and member agencies to accomplish the coordination of local long-term care services. The agencies shall establish a long-term care coordination committee composed of, but not limited to, representatives of each agency. The coordination committee shall guide the coordination and administration of public long-term care services in the locality. The membership of the coordination committee shall be comprised of, but not limited to, representatives of the local department of public health, the local department of social services, the community services board or community mental health clinic, the area agency on aging, the local nursing home pre-admission screening team, and representatives of housing, transportation, and other appropriate local organizations that provide long-term care services. A plan shall be implemented that ensures the cost-effective utilization of all funds available for long-term care services in the locality. Localities are encouraged to provide services within each category of service in the continuum and to allow one person to deliver multiple services, when possible. (1982, c. 346, § 2.1-373.7; 2001, c. 844; 2008, cc. 391, 419.)

Cross references. — As to participation by local board of social services in long-term care service coordination pursuant to § 2.2-708, see § 63.2-1602.

The 2008 amendments. — The 2008 amendments by cc. 391 and 419 are identical, and in the fourth sentence, deleted "and" following "the area agency on aging" and inserted "and representatives of housing, transportation, and other appropriate local organizations that provide long-term care services" at the end.

§ 2.2-709. Contracts between area agency and Campbell County. — Notwithstanding any contrary provision of law, Campbell County may, under contract with the Area Agency on Aging designated to serve Campbell County, provide directly any and all services specified in Public Law 89-73, as amended. (1985, c. 112, § 2.1-373.01; 2001, c. 844.)

§ **2.2-710:** Repealed by Acts 2003, cc. 749 and 766, cl. 2.

Cross references. — For present provisions regarding Alzheimer's and Related Diseases Research Award Fund, see § 2.2-719.

ARTICLE 2.

Virginia Public Guardian and Conservator Program.

§ 2.2-711. Policy statement; Virginia Public Guardian and Conservator Program established; definitions. — A. The General Assembly declares that it is the policy of the Commonwealth to ensure that persons who cannot adequately care for themselves because of incapacity (in this article, also referred to as "clients") are able to meet essential requirements for physical and emotional health and management of financial resources with the assistance of a guardian or conservator, as appropriate, in circumstances where (i) the incapacitated person's financial resources are insufficient to fully compensate a private guardian or conservator and pay court costs and fees associated with the appointment proceeding and (ii) there is no other proper and suitable person willing and able to serve in such capacity or there is no guardian or conservator appointed within one month of adjudication pursuant to § 37.2-1015. In order to ensure that the protection and assistance of a guardian or conservator are available to all incapacitated persons in the Commonwealth, there is established the statewide Virginia Public Guardian and Conservator Program (the Program) within the Department to (i) facilitate the creation of local or regional programs to provide services as public guardians or conservators and (ii) fund, coordinate, administer and manage such programs.

B. The definitions found in § 37.2-1000 shall apply to this article. (1998, c. 787, §§ 2.1-373.10, 2.1-373.11; 2001, c. 844; 2005, c. 712.)

§ 2.2-712. Powers and duties of the Department with respect to public guardian and conservator program. — A. The Department shall fund from appropriations received for such purpose a statewide system of local or regional public guardian and conservator programs.

B. The Department shall:

1. Make and enter into all contracts necessary or incidental to the performance of its duties and in furtherance of the purposes as specified in this article in conformance with the Public Procurement Act (§ 2.2-4300 et seq.).

2. Contract with local or regional public or private entities to provide services as guardians and conservators operating as local or regional Virginia Public Guardian and Conservator Programs in those cases in which a court, pursuant to §§ 37.2-1010 and 37.2-1015, determines that a person is eligible to have a public guardian or conservator appointed.

3. Adopt reasonable regulations in accordance with the Administrative Process Act (§ 2.2-4000 et seq.) as appropriate to implement, administer and manage the state and local or regional programs authorized by this article, including, but not limited to the adoption of:

a. Minimum training and experience requirements for volunteers and professional staff of the local and regional programs;

b. An ideal range of staff to client ratios for the programs; adoption of procedures to be followed whenever a local or regional program falls below or exceeds the ideal range of staff to client ratios, which shall include, but not be limited to, procedures to ensure that services shall continue to be available to those in need and that appropriate notice is given to the courts, sheriffs, where appropriate, and the Department; and

c. Procedures governing disqualification of any program falling below or exceeding the ideal range of staff to client ratios, which shall include a process for evaluating any program that has exceeded the ratio to assess the effects falling below or exceeding the ideal range of ratios has had or is having upon the program and upon the incapacitated persons served by the program.

The regulations shall require that evaluations occur no less frequently than every six months and shall continue until the staff to client ratio returns to within the ideal range.

4. Establish procedures and administrative guidelines to ensure the separation of local or regional Virginia Public Guardian and Conservator Programs from any other guardian or conservator program operated by the entity with whom the Department contracts, specifically addressing the need for separation in programs that may be fee-generating.

5. Establish record-keeping and accounting procedures to ensure that each local or regional program (i) maintains confidential, accurate and up-to-date records of the personal and property matters over which it has control for each incapacitated person for whom it is appointed guardian or conservator and (ii) files with the Department an account of all public and private funds received.

6. Establish criteria for the conduct of and filing with the Department and as otherwise required by law: values history surveys, annual decisional accounting and assessment reports, the care plan designed for the incapacitated person and such other information as the Department may by regulation require.

7. Establish criteria to be used by the local and regional programs in setting priorities with regard to services to be provided.

8. Take such other actions as are necessary to ensure coordinated services and a reasonable review of all local and regional programs.

9. Maintain statistical data on the programs and report to the General Assembly on or before January 1 of each year as provided in the procedures of the Division of Legislative Automated Systems for the processing of legislative documents regarding the status of the Virginia Public Guardian and Conservator Program and the developing trends with regard to the need for guardians, conservators and other types of surrogate decision-making services. In addition, the Department shall enter into a contract with an appropriate research entity with expertise in gerontology, disabilities and public administration to conduct an evaluation of local public guardian and conservator programs from funds specifically allocated for this purpose, and the evaluator shall provide a report with recommendations to the Department and to the Public Guardian and Conservator Advisory Board by December 1, 2003. Trends identified in the report shall be presented to the General Assembly. The Department shall request such a report from an appropriate research entity every four years, provided the General Assembly appropriates funds for that purpose.

10. Recommend appropriate legislative or executive actions.

C. Nothing in this article shall prohibit the Department from contracting pursuant to subdivision B 2 with an entity that may also provide privately funded surrogate decision-making services, including guardian and conservator services funded with fees generated by the estates of incapacitated persons, provided such private programs are administered by the contracting entity entirely separately from the local or regional Virginia Public Guardian and Conservator Programs, in conformity with regulations established by the Department in that respect.

D. In accordance with the Public Procurement Act (§ 2.2-4300 et seq.) and recommendations of the Public Guardian and Conservator Advisory Board, the Department may contract with a not-for-profit private entity that does not provide services to incapacitated persons as guardian or conservator to administer the program, and, if it does, the term "Department" when used in this article shall refer to the contract administrator. (1998, c. 787, § 2.1-373.12; 2000, c. 463; 2001, c. 844; 2005, c. 712.)

Law Review. — For an article, "Reform of Adult Guardianship Law," see 32 U. Rich. L. Rev. 1273 (1998).

§ 2.2-713. Minimum requirements for local programs; authority. — Every local or regional program with which the Department contracts to provide services as a public guardian or conservator shall (i) furnish bond with corporate surety in an amount deemed sufficient by the Department to afford adequate financial protection to the maximum number of incapacitated persons to be served by the program; (ii) have in place a multi-disciplinary panel to (a) screen cases for the purpose of ensuring that appointment of a guardian or conservator is appropriate under the circumstances and is the least restrictive alternative available to assist the incapacitated person and (b) continually review cases being handled by the program as required by the Department; (iii) accept only appointments as guardian or conservator that generate no fee or would generate a minimal fee as defined by regulation payable from a public source of funds and not from the estate of the incapacitated person; (iv) have a direct service staff to client ratio that is consistent with that specified by regulation of the Department; and (v) develop a plan, in consultation with the local circuit court and sheriffs where appropriate, to provide advance notice to the court when the program falls below or exceeds the ideal range of staff to client ratios in order to assure continuity of services. Volunteers shall not be counted for purposes of ascertaining compliance with the staff to client ratio specified by the Department.

A local or regional program that exceeds the specified staff to client ratio shall not be disqualified from serving as a guardian or conservator except as provided by regulation or if the court or the Department finds that there is an immediate threat to the person or property of any incapacitated person or that exceeding the specified ratio is having or will have a material and adverse effect on the ability of the program to properly serve all of the incapacitated persons it has been designated to serve.

A local or regional program appointed as a guardian or conservator shall have all the powers and duties specified in Article 2 (§ 37.2-1019 et seq.) of Chapter 10 of Title 37.2, except as otherwise specifically limited by the court. In addition, a public guardian or conservator shall have a continuing duty to seek a proper and suitable person who is willing and able to serve as guardian or conservator for the incapacitated person. A public guardian or conservator shall have authority to make funeral, cremation, or burial arrangements if the public guardian or conservator is not aware of any person that has been otherwise designated to make arrangements for disposition of remains as set forth in § 54.1-2825 of the Code of Virginia. A public guardian or conservator shall have authority to make funeral, cremation, or burial arrangements after the death of an incapacitated person if the next of kin of the incapacitated does not wish to make the arrangements and the public guardian or conservator has made a good faith effort to locate the next of kin to determine if the next of kin wishes to make the burial, cremation or funeral arrangements. Good faith effort shall include contacting the next of kin identified in the petition for appointment of a guardian or conservator. The funeral service licensee, funeral service establishment, registered crematory, public guardian or conservator shall be immune from civil liability for any act, decision, or omission resulting from acceptance of any dead body for burial, cremation or other disposition when the provisions of this section are met, unless such acts, decisions or omissions resulted from bad faith or malicious intent.

A public guardian shall not have authority to admit an incapacitated person to a psychiatric hospital or mental health facility without a civil commitment proceeding, or to approve or authorize a sterilization procedure except when specific authority has been given pursuant to a proceeding in the circuit court. A public guardian may authorize mental health treatment, including the administration of psychotropic medication, unless the appointing court specifically provides otherwise.

A local or regional program appointed as a guardian or conservator may delegate the powers, duties and responsibilities to individual volunteers or professional staff as authorized in the contract with the Department.

In addition to funds received from the Department, a local or regional program may accept private funds solely for the purposes of providing public education, supplemental services for incapacitated persons and support services for private guardians and conservators, consistent with the purposes of this article. (1998, c. 787, § 2.1-373.14; 2001, c. 844; 2006, c. 854.)

Law Review. — For 2006 survey article, "Wills, Trusts, and Estates," see 41 U. Rich. L. Rev. 321 (2006).

Article 3.

Virginia Respite Care Grant Program.

§ 2.2-714. Definitions. — As used in this article, unless the context requires otherwise:

"Adult day care services" means the provision of supplementary care and protection during a part of the day only to aged, infirm, or disabled adults. Such services may be in or away from the residence of the aged, infirm, or disabled adult.

"Community respite care organization" means a local subdivision of the Commonwealth, a combination of political subdivisions, a separate public agency or a private nonprofit agency exempt under § 501 (c) (3) of the Internal Revenue Code, which has the authority under its applicable charter, laws or articles of organization to receive funds to support respite care activities.

"Department" means the Department for the Aging.

"Fund" means the Virginia Respite Care Grant Fund established by § 2.2-716.

"Respite care" means the provision of supplementary care and protection for aged, infirm, or disabled adults. Respite care includes, but is not limited to, adult day care services. (2000, cc. 877, 896, § 2.1-373.15; 2001, c. 844.)

Editor's note. — Acts 2000, c. 877, one of the two acts which enacted § 2.1-373.15, from which this section was derived, provided in cl. 2: "That the provisions of this act shall not become effective unless an appropriation effectuating the purposes of this act is included in the 2000 Appropriation Act, passed during the 2000 Session of the General Assembly and signed into law by the Governor." Acts 2000, c. 896, the other act from which § 2.1-373.15 was derived, did not contain a contingency clause. An appropriation for Individual Care Services was made in the 2000 Appropriation Act, c. 1073. See Item 295.

§ 2.2-715. Respite Care Grant Program established. — Beginning January 1, 2001, any community respite care organization shall be eligible to receive an annual respite care grant in the amount of up to $100,000 for the development, expansion, or start-up operation of adult day care services or other services that provide respite care to aged, infirm, or disabled adults. The grants under this article shall be paid from the Fund, as provided in this article, to the community respite care organization. As a condition of a grant, money appropriated from such fund shall be matched by community respite care organization funds (in-kind or cash) earmarked for the development or expansion of respite care services. The total amount of grants to be paid under this chapter for any year shall not exceed the amount appropriated by the General Assembly to the Fund for payment to community respite care organizations for such year. Only one grant shall be allowed annually for each community respite care organization under the provisions of this section. (2000, cc. 877, 896, § 2.1-373.16; 2001, c. 844.)

§ **2.2-716. Virginia Respite Care Grant Fund established.** — There is hereby established a special fund in the state treasury to be known as the Virginia Respite Care Grant Fund, which shall be administered by the Department. The Fund shall include such moneys as may be appropriated by the General Assembly from time to time and designated for the Fund. The Fund shall be used solely for the payment of grants to community respite care organizations pursuant to this article. Unallocated moneys in the Fund in any year shall remain in the Fund and be available for allocation for grants under this article in ensuing fiscal years. (2000, cc. 877, 896, § 2.1-373.17; 2001, c. 844.)

§ **2.2-717. Grant application process; administration.** — A. Grant applications shall be submitted by community respite care organizations to the Department between December 1 and March 1. Failure to meet the application deadline shall render the community respite care organization ineligible to receive a grant during such calendar year. For filings by mail, the postmark cancellation shall govern the date of the filing determination.

B. Applications for grants shall include (i) identification of the community respite care organization, (ii) identification of the matching funds, and (iii) such other relevant information as the Department may require. As a condition of receipt of a grant, a community respite care organization shall agree to make available to the Department for inspection, upon request, all relevant and applicable documents to determine whether the community respite care organization meets the requirements for the receipt of grants as set forth in this article, and to consent to the use by the Department, for official purposes, of all relevant information relating to eligibility for the requested grant.

C. The Department shall review applications for grants and determine the amount of the grant to be allocated to each community respite care organization in accordance with the Virginia Public Procurement Act (§ 2.2-4300 et seq.).

D. A community respite care organization shall have no claim against the Commonwealth with respect to any grant authorized by this article.

E. The Department shall certify to the Comptroller the amount of grant to be allocated to eligible applicants. Payments shall be made by check issued by the State Treasurer on warrant of the Comptroller. The Comptroller shall not draw any warrants to issue checks for this program without a specific legislative appropriation as specified in conditions and restrictions on expenditures in the appropriation act.

F. Actions of the Department relating to the review, allocation and awarding of grants shall be exempt from the provisions of the Administrative Process Act (§ 2.2-4000 et seq.) pursuant to subdivision B 4 of § 2.2-4002. Decisions of the Department shall be final and not subject to review or appeal.

G. The Department may examine the records, books, and other applicable documents to determine whether the community respite care organization has satisfied the requirements for grants as set forth in this section. (2000, cc. 877, 896, § 2.1-373.18; 2001, c. 844.)

ARTICLE 4.

Alzheimer's Disease and Related Disorders.

§ 2.2-718. Powers and duties of the Department with respect to Alzheimer's disease and related disorders. — The Department for the Aging shall serve as a referral point for linking families caring for persons with Alzheimer's disease and related disorders with Virginia's chapters of the Alzheimer's Disease and Related Disorders Association. The Department shall provide information, counseling and referral about services and programs that may support individuals and families dealing with Alzheimer's disease and related disorders. (2003, cc. 749, 766.)

§ 2.2-719. Alzheimer's and Related Diseases Research Award Fund. — There is established a fund to be known as the Alzheimer's and Related Diseases Research Award Fund, hereafter referred to as "the Fund." The Fund shall be administered by the Virginia Center on Aging and the awards shall be made through an awards committee consisting of representatives from the scientific and medical community and the general public. The awards shall be given annually to scientists in Virginia in order to support research into the causes of Alzheimer's disease and related disorders, methods of treatment, ways that families can cope with the stresses of the disease, and the impact of the disease on the citizens of the Commonwealth. (2003, cc. 749, 766.)

§ 2.2-720. (Expires July 1, 2009) Alzheimer's Disease and Related Disorders Commission. — A. The Alzheimer's Disease and Related Disorders Commission (Commission) is established as an advisory commission in the executive branch of state government. The purpose of the entity is to assist people with Alzheimer's disease and related disorders and their caregivers.

B. The Commission shall consist of 15 nonlegislative citizen members. Members shall be appointed as follows: three members to be appointed by the Speaker of the House of Delegates; two members to be appointed by the Senate Committee on Rules; and 10 members to be appointed by the Governor, of whom seven shall be from among the boards, staffs, and volunteers of the Virginia chapters of the Alzheimer's Disease and Related Disorders Association and three shall be from the public at large.

After the initial staggering of terms, nonlegislative citizen members shall be appointed for a term of four years. Appointments to fill vacancies, other than by expiration of a term, shall be for the unexpired terms. All members may be reappointed. However, no nonlegislative citizen member shall serve more than two consecutive four-year terms. The remainder of any term to which a member is appointed to fill a vacancy shall not constitute a term in determining the member's eligibility for reappointment. Vacancies shall be filled in the same manner as the original appointments.

The Commission shall elect a chairman and vice-chairman from among its membership. A majority of the voting members shall constitute a quorum. The Commission shall meet at least four times each year. The meetings of the Commission shall be held at the call of the chairman or whenever the majority of the voting members so request.

C. Members shall receive such compensation for the discharge of their duties as provided in § 2.2-2813. All members shall be reimbursed for reasonable and necessary expenses incurred in the performance of their duties as provided in §§ 2.2-2813 and 2.2-2825. Funding for the costs of compensation and expenses of the members shall be provided by the Department for the Aging.

D. The Commission shall have the following powers and duties:

1. Examine the needs of persons with Alzheimer's disease and related disorders, as well as the needs of their caregivers, and ways that state government can most effectively and efficiently assist in meeting those needs;

2. Advise the Governor and General Assembly on policy, funding, regulatory and other issues related to persons suffering from Alzheimer's disease and related disorders and their caregivers;

3. Develop the Commonwealth's plan for meeting the needs of patients with Alzheimer's disease and related disorders and their caregivers, and advocate for such plan;

4. Submit a report, including an executive summary, by October 1 of each year to the Governor and General Assembly regarding the activities and recommendations of the Commission; and

5. Establish priorities for programs among state agencies related to Alzheimer's disease and related disorders and criteria to evaluate these programs.

E. The Department for the Aging shall provide staff support to the Commission. All agencies of the Commonwealth shall provide assistance to the Commission, upon request.

F. The Commission may apply for and expend such grants, gifts or bequests from any source as may become available in connection with its duties under this section, and may comply with such conditions and requirements as may be imposed in connections therewith.

G. This section shall expire on July 1, 2009. (2003, cc. 749, 766; 2005, cc. 633, 758; 2006, cc. 347, 381.)

Editor's note. — Acts 2003, cc. 749 and 766, cl. 3, as amended by Acts 2004, c. 1000, cl. 2, provide: "Notwithstanding § 2.2-720, current members of the Alzheimer's Disease and Related Disorders Commission shall continue to serve until July 1, 2004. Thereafter, terms established by § 2.2-720 shall apply."

Acts 2005, c. 758, cl. 2, provides: "That this act shall not be construed to affect existing appointments, made by the Senate Committee on Privileges and Elections, for which the terms have not expired. However, any new appointments made after July 1, 2005 shall be made in accordance with the provisions of this act."

CHAPTER 8.

Department of Accounts.

Article 1.

General Provisions.

ARTICLE 1.

General Provisions.

§ 2.2-800. Department of Accounts created; appointment of Comptroller; oath. — A. There is created a Department of Accounts (the "Department"). The Director of the Department shall be known as the Comptroller. He shall be appointed by the Governor to serve at his pleasure.

B. The Comptroller shall, under the direction and control of the Governor, exercise the powers and perform the duties conferred or imposed upon him by law and perform such other duties as may be required by the Governor.

C. The Comptroller, before entering upon the discharge of his duties, shall take an oath that he will faithfully and honestly execute the duties of his office. (Code 1950, §§ 2-160, 2-161; 1958, c. 124; 1966, c. 677, §§ 2.1-192, 2.1-194; 1976, c. 728; 1984, c. 720; 2001, c. 844.)

Editor's note. — Acts 2008, c. 879, effective for the biennium ending June 30, 2010, in Item 259, provides: "A.1. The Department of Accounts shall operate a payroll service center to support the salaried and wage employees of all agencies identified by the Department of Planning and Budget. The agencies so identified shall cooperate with the Department of Accounts in transferring such records and functions as may be required. The service center shall provide services to employees to include, but not be limited to, payroll, benefit enrollment and leave accounting. The Department of Accounts shall be responsible for all accounting reconciliations for these services; however, each employing agency shall remain fully responsible for certifying the accuracy of each payroll paid to its employees. This certification shall be in such form as the Comptroller directs.

"2. The Department of Accounts shall recover the cost of services provided by the payroll service center for nongeneral fund employees through interagency transactions as determined by the State Comptroller. The amounts determined by the State Comptroller to be payable by those agencies listed in § 3-1.01 L. shall be net of the amounts so designated for transfer to the general fund.

"B.1. The Department of Accounts shall operate a fiscal service center to support the operations of all agencies identified by the Department of Planning and Budget. The agencies so identified shall cooperate with the Department of Accounts in transferring such records and functions as may be required. The service center shall provide services to agencies to include accounts payable processing, travel voucher processing, related reconciliations, and such other fiscal services as may be appropriate.

"2. The Department of Accounts shall recover the cost of services provided by the fiscal service center through interagency transactions as determined by the State Comptroller.

"C. Nothing in this section shall prohibit additional agencies from using the services of the centers; however, such additions shall be subject to approval by the affected cabinet secretary and the Secretary of Finance."

§ 2.2-801. Comptroller to appoint administrative assistants, etc. — A. The Comptroller shall appoint the administrative assistants, deputies and clerks allowed by law.

B. The Comptroller shall appoint administrative assistants, who shall have authority to act for and perform the duties of the Comptroller under his direction, supervision and control, and in the absence of the Comptroller to perform all the duties of the office. Of such absence, the others shall be informed. When the absence of the Comptroller is to be for more than five days at a time, notice thereof shall be given to the Governor.

C. In the event the administrative assistant is incapacitated from performing his duties during the absence of the Comptroller, the Governor shall designate some other person in the office to act during the absence of the Comptroller, and in the event of the removal, resignation or death of the Comptroller, the administrative assistant shall perform all the duties of the office until the vacancy is filled in the manner prescribed by law.

D. Such officers and their sureties shall be liable for any default or breach of duty of their administrative assistants respectively during their absence. (1950, §§ 2-145, 2-146, 2-147, 2-148; 1966, c. 677, §§ 2.1-173, 2.1-174, 2.1-175, 2.1-176; 2001, c. 844.)

§ 2.2-802. General accounting and clearance through Comptroller. — In the Department the Comptroller shall maintain a complete system of general accounting to comprehend the financial transactions of every state department, division, officer, board, commission, institution or other agency owned or controlled by the Commonwealth, whether at the seat of government or not. All transactions in public funds shall clear through the Comptroller's office. (Code 1950, § 2-162; 1958, c. 124; 1966, c. 677, § 2.1-195; 2001, c. 844.)

§ 2.2-803. Financial accounting and control. — A. Unified financial accounting and control shall be established through the departments and agencies of the Commonwealth, in the manner prescribed in this chapter.

The Comptroller shall prescribe what accounts shall be kept by each state agency in addition to the system of general accounting maintained in the Comptroller's office. In prescribing what accounts shall be kept by each state agency, the Comptroller shall take care that there shall be no unnecessary duplication.

B. The Comptroller shall direct the development of a modern, effective and uniform system of bookkeeping and accounting, to include (i) an efficient system of checks and balances between the officers at the seat of the government entrusted with the collection and receipt, custody and disbursement of the revenues of the Commonwealth; and (ii) a system of accounting, applicable to all state officers, departments, boards, commissions, agencies, and penal, educational and eleemosynary institutions maintained in whole or in part by the Commonwealth, which shall be suitable to their respective needs, considering their relation to each other and their relation to subordinate officers and officials. All systems so developed shall require the approval and certification of the Auditor of Public Accounts that they are adequate for purposes of audit and financial control.

As to the collection of debts owed, the system of bookkeeping and accounting shall permit any state agency to refrain from collecting any amount owed to it if the administrative cost of collection likely would exceed the amount owed. The Comptroller shall develop other policies and procedures to reduce the costs of collecting debts owed to state agencies.

As to the operation of merchandising activities, or other centralized support services provided by one state agency to other state agencies for which charges are made, the system of accounting shall be designed to reflect all charges properly allocable so that the net profit or loss therefrom shall be reflected. In the furtherance of this objective the Joint Legislative Audit and Review Commission may direct the Comptroller to establish under such terms and conditions as they may determine internal service fund accounts on his books and record therein the receipts and expenditures of these several functions. The Comptroller shall provide the agencies responsible for the operations of these functions with working capital advances with which to finance the operations pursuant to appropriations made by law. The Joint Legislative Audit and Review Commission may direct the Comptroller to transfer excess fund balances to the general fund or to remove from his books internal service fund accounts that are no longer considered appropriate and record the necessary transfer of funds.

Unit prices of services rendered by internal service funds shall be fixed so that all costs properly allocable to providing the service shall be fully recoverable.

C. The Comptroller shall maintain a full explanation of all systems of accounting devised and adopted in furtherance of this section, but no copyright system shall be adopted that shall entail additional cost upon the Commonwealth by reason of such copyright. The systems of accounting shall be communicated by the Comptroller to the officials affected thereby, and he shall as soon as possible instruct the officials as to the systems of accounting.

D. Should any of the state offices, departments, boards, commissions, agencies, or institutions refuse or neglect to adopt the systems of accounting developed by the Comptroller, then upon suit of the Attorney General a writ of mandamus will lie to the Supreme Court to compel the adoption. It shall be the duty of the Attorney General to promptly institute such suit in any such case. (1975, c. 323, § 2.1-196.1; 1976, c. 533; 1984, c. 612; 2001, c. 844; 2006, c. 340.)

Editor's note. — Acts 2008, c. 879, effective for the biennium ending June 30, 2010, in Item 259, provides: "A.1. The Department of Accounts shall operate a payroll service center to support the salaried and wage employees of all agencies identified by the Department of Planning and Budget. The agencies so identified shall cooperate with the Department of Accounts in transferring such records and functions as may be required. The service center shall provide services to employees to include, but not be limited to, payroll, benefit enrollment and leave accounting. The Department of Accounts shall be responsible for all accounting reconciliations for these services; however, each employing agency shall remain fully responsible for certifying the accuracy of each payroll paid to its employees. This certification shall be in such form as the Comptroller directs.

"2. The Department of Accounts shall recover the cost of services provided by the payroll service center for nongeneral fund employees through interagency transactions as determined by the State Comptroller. The amounts determined by the State Comptroller to be payable by those agencies listed in § 3-1.01 L. shall be net of the amounts so designated for transfer to the general fund.

"B.1. The Department of Accounts shall operate a fiscal service center to support the operations of all agencies identified by the Department of Planning and Budget. The agencies so identified shall cooperate with the Department of Accounts in transferring such records and functions as may be required. The service center shall provide services to agencies to include accounts payable processing, travel voucher processing, related reconciliations, and such other fiscal services as may be appropriate.

"2. The Department of Accounts shall recover the cost of services provided by the fiscal service center through interagency transactions as determined by the State Comptroller.

"C. Nothing in this section shall prohibit additional agencies from using the services of the centers; however, such additions shall be subject to approval by the affected cabinet secretary and the Secretary of Finance."

§ 2.2-803.1. Processing of payroll and other transactions by certain institutions of higher education. — A. The College of William and Mary; George Mason University; James Madison University; Old Dominion University; the University of Virginia, including the College at Wise; Virginia Commonwealth University; Virginia Military Institute; and Virginia Polytechnic Institute and State University shall each process the payroll of its respective college or university employees as provided in the memoranda of understanding between the Department of Accounts and each such institution implementing a pilot program granting relief from rules, regulations, and reporting requirements pursuant to subdivision E 1 of Item 330 of Chapter 966 of the Acts of Assembly of 1994 as continued in effect by subsection B of Item 271 of Chapter 899 of the Acts of Assembly of 2002.

B. The College of William and Mary; George Mason University; James Madison University; Old Dominion University; Radford University; the University of Virginia, including the College at Wise; Virginia Commonwealth University; Virginia Military Institute; and Virginia Polytechnic Institute and State University shall each process its respective nonpayroll disbursements, receipts, and expenditures as provided in the memoranda of understanding between the Department of Accounts and each such institution implementing a pilot program granting relief from rules, regulations, and reporting requirements pursuant to subdivision E 1 of Item 330 of Chapter 966 of the Acts of Assembly of 1994 as continued in effect by subsection B of Item 271 of Chapter 899 of the Acts of Assembly of 2002. "Nonpayroll disbursements, receipts, and expenditures" shall include all disbursements, receipts, and expenditures, other than payroll as described in subsection A. Such disbursements, receipts, and expenditures shall include, but are not limited to, travel reimbursements, revenue refunds, cash receipts, disbursements for vendor payments, petty cash, and interagency payments. (2003, c. 457.)

§ **2.2-804. Recovery of certain improper payments to state employees.** — If any officer or employee of the Commonwealth, whether or not exempt from the provisions of Chapter 29 (§ 2.2-2900 et seq.) of this title, contrary to any applicable statute, regulation or written policy of the Commonwealth, obtains or authorizes any other officer or employee to obtain any compensation or other payment to which an employee is not entitled, and upon the written request of his employer, fails or refuses to return or reimburse such compensation or payment, then both the employee who received the payment to which he was not entitled and the employee who authorized the payment shall be liable for repayment to the employer. Liability shall not attach unless such authorization was given with actual or constructive knowledge that the recipient employee was not entitled to such compensation or payment.

As long as he remains an officer or employee of the Commonwealth, and liability is admitted, his employer may recover the compensation or payment from any compensation or other payments to which the officer or employee is entitled as an administrative offset pursuant to § 2.2-4806. However, the offset shall not exceed the amount allowed pursuant to § 8.01-512.3. If the officer or employee leaves state service, liability is disputed or recovery cannot be accomplished, the employer may request the Attorney General to bring an action for restitution pursuant to this section, and the court may award the prevailing party costs and reasonable attorneys' fees.

The provisions of this section shall not apply to good faith disbursements made to beneficiaries of the Virginia Retirement System. (1998, c. 876, § 2.1-196.2; 2001, c. 844.)

§ **2.2-805. Fiscal year.** — The fiscal year shall commence on the first day of July and end on the thirtieth day of June. (Code 1950, § 2-165; 1966, c. 677, § 2.1-197; 2001, c. 844.)

§ **2.2-806. Reports and payments by city and county treasurers, and clerks of court; deposits of state income tax payments.** — A. All county and city treasurers receiving state income tax payments, whether from taxpayers or from the commissioner of the revenue, shall deposit the payments, within one banking day of receipt, into an account of the state treasury. The treasurers shall maintain a record of the date on which the payments are received and the date on which the payments are deposited into the state treasury. The Auditor of Public Accounts shall either prescribe or approve the treasurer's record-keeping system and shall audit such records as provided for in Chapter 14 (§ 30-130 et seq.) of Title 30. Reporting of the deposits shall be in accordance with subsection B.

B. All county and city treasurers and clerks of courts receiving state moneys shall deposit promptly all state moneys and, in the manner directed by the State Treasurer, shall transfer state moneys into an account of the state treasury twice each week and submit a report of state moneys being transferred. However, except for state income tax payments that shall be controlled by subsection A, state moneys received amounting to less than $5,000 may be transferred into an account of the state treasury once each week. (Code 1950, § 2-166; 1966, c. 677, § 2.1-198; 1982, c. 292; 1987, c. 511; 1991, c. 485; 2001, c. 844.)

§ 2.2-807. Monthly reports of state departments, divisions, etc., receiving public funds. — Every state department, division, officer, board, commission, institution or other agency owned or controlled by the Commonwealth, whether at the seat of government or not, including county and city treasurers and clerks of courts, collecting or receiving public funds, or moneys from any source whatever, belonging to or for the use of the Commonwealth, or for the use of any state agency, and paying the same to the State Treasurer, or depositing the same to his credit in pursuance of law, shall, on or before the tenth day of each month, or oftener if so directed by the Comptroller, report to the Comptroller in such manner as he may direct, the amount collected or received and paid into the state treasury for the preceding calendar month or other period designated by the Comptroller. The report shall show also the dates of payments to or deposits to the credit of the State Treasurer. (Code 1950, § 2-167; 1966, c. 677, § 2.1-199; 2001, c. 844.)

§ 2.2-808. Collection of delinquent taxes. — Whenever, by any section of this Code, the Comptroller is required or is authorized to collect any delinquent taxes, he shall refer the matter to the Tax Commissioner, who shall at once proceed to collect the same and may employ such legal process as may be necessary for that purpose. When so collected the Tax Commissioner shall pay the same into the state treasury. (Code 1950, § 2-167.1; 1966, c. 677, § 2.1-200; 2001, c. 844.)

§ 2.2-809. When accounts on Comptroller's books to be balanced; general ledger of accounts. — All unsettled accounts on the books of the Comptroller shall be balanced on the last day of each fiscal year, and the balances brought forward on the first day of the new fiscal year. For this purpose there shall be a general ledger of accounts, which shall be kept to show the balances due to or from the Commonwealth. (Code 1950, § 2-169; 1966, c. 677, § 2.1-202; 2001, c. 844.)

§ 2.2-810. Judges and clerks to certify to Supreme Court lists of all allowances made by courts. — The judge of every court of the Commonwealth making an allowance for the payment of any sum out of the state treasury shall certify to the Supreme Court a list of all allowances at least monthly, the date of the making and the amount of such allowance, and to whom made. A certificate of all allowances made by such court shall be made up by the clerk of the court and forwarded to the Supreme Court. The form of the certificate shall be prescribed by the Supreme Court, and it shall be made on blanks prepared by them and furnished the judges and clerks of the several courts of the Commonwealth. The Comptroller shall not draw any warrant on the State Treasurer in satisfaction of any allowance made by any court of the Commonwealth until the Supreme Court has received notification of the allowance by the court of the claim and approved the allowance for payment. (Code 1950, § 2-172; 1966, c. 677, § 2.1-204; 1978, c. 195; 1979, c. 509; 2001, c. 844.)

§ 2.2-811. Cancellation of state bonds received in settlement of claims. — All bonds of the Commonwealth that are received by the Comptroller in the settlement of claims of the Commonwealth against the sureties of treasurers, sheriffs, or other officers, or in settlement of any other claim, shall be turned over by him to the Treasury Board, who shall cancel the bonds according to law. (Code 1950, § 2-173; 1966, c. 677, § 2.1-205; 2001, c. 844.)

§ 2.2-812. What Comptroller may do with old books and papers. — The Comptroller may dispense with all noncurrent books, papers, invoices, financial documents, and similar papers belonging to his office in a manner prescribed by the Virginia Public Records Act (§ 42.1-76 et seq.) in coordination with the needs of the Auditor of Public Accounts. (Code 1950, § 2-174; 1960, c. 240; 1966, c. 677, § 2.1-206; 1981, c. 514; 2001, c. 844.)

§ 2.2-813. Annual report of Comptroller to Governor. — The Comptroller shall make a preliminary annual report to the Governor on or before August 15. The Governor shall submit the preliminary report to the General Assembly within thirty days of its receipt. The Comptroller shall provide a final annual report on or before December 15. The report shall include (i) financial statements that are prepared, insofar as practical as determined by the Comptroller and the Auditor of Public Accounts, in accordance with generally accepted accounting principles; (ii) supplementary statements prepared on the budgetary basis of accounting; (iii) information provided by the State Treasurer on the status of bonded debt in the Commonwealth and the future general fund requirements for such debt; and (iv) other information deemed necessary by the State Treasurer. The Comptroller and the State Treasurer shall also make other reports at such times as the Governor may require. (Code 1950, § 2-175; 1960, c. 84; 1966, c. 677, § 2.1-207; 1984, c. 378; 1992, c. 327; 2001, c. 844.)

§ 2.2-813.1. Biannual disclosure by Comptroller of revenue sources collected. — The Comptroller shall post on the Internet website for the Department of Accounts the following information according to the following schedule: (i) no later than October 1 of each year, the total amount of each revenue source collected by the Commonwealth for the most recent six-month period ending June 30, and (ii) no later than April 1 of each year, the total amount of each revenue source collected by the Commonwealth for the most recent six-month period ending December 30. The Comptroller shall include in the information posted any Auditor of Public Accounts control findings that any revenue source was used for any purpose other than the purpose originally established in law for such revenue source.

This section may be referred to as the Virginia Truth in Revenue Source Reporting Act. (2003, c. 174.)

§ 2.2-813.2. Biannual disclosure by Comptroller of other obligations of the Commonwealth. — To assist in the managing, planning, and budgeting of the state's financial resources, the Comptroller, in conjunction with the Secretary of Finance, shall report biannually to the Governor and the members of the General Assembly each off-balance sheet financial obligation of the Commonwealth, itemized by agency, board, institution, or authority of the Commonwealth, and such other obligations of the Commonwealth that are estimated by the Comptroller to be incurred. (2007, c. 62.)

ARTICLE 2.

Claims Against Commonwealth.

§ 2.2-814. To whom claims presented; Comptroller to furnish forms. — A. Any person having any pecuniary claim against the Commonwealth upon any legal ground shall present the same to the head of the department, division, institution or agency of the Commonwealth responsible for the alleged act or omission which, if proved, gives rise to the claim. If, however, the claimant cannot identify the alleged act or omission with any single department, division, institution or agency of the Commonwealth, then the claim shall be presented to the Comptroller.

B. The Comptroller shall supply the several clerks of record and, upon request, each head of a department, division, institution or agency mentioned in subsection A with the necessary forms to be used by them for accounts payable out of the state treasury. (Code 1950, §§ 2-193, 2-194; 1960, c. 240; 1966, c. 677, §§ 2.1-223.1, 2.1-223.2; 2001, c. 844.)

Cross references. — As to how claims against the Commonwealth are to be prosecuted, see § 8.01-192. As to time for presenting claims against the Commonwealth, see § 8.01-255.

Law Review. — For article reviewing recent developments and changes in legislation, case law, and Virginia Supreme Court Rules affecting civil litigation, "Civil Practice and Procedure," see 40 U. Rich. L. Rev. 95 (2005).

CASE NOTES

Editor's note. — Most of the cases below were decided under former Title 2.1 or prior provisions.

For discussion of doctrine of sovereign immunity, see Hinchey v. Ogden, 226 Va. 234, 307 S.E.2d 891 (1983).

Former § 14.1-52 (see now § 15.2-1636.9) and this section clearly speak to the same subject and are in conflict. To allow the plaintiff to sue under the general statute would render the specific statute meaningless. Thus, former § 14.1-52 (see now § 15.2-1636.9) would prevail in plaintiff's case and act to deny her any due process remedy. The defendant's argument that the plaintiff had a state procedure in which to seek a remedy and that their defense of sovereign immunity did not deny due process did not, as a result, apply to the case because the plaintiff did not have an opportunity to raise her salary claims in state court. Brewster v. Pike, 608 F. Supp. 1163 (W.D. Va. 1985), aff'd in part, rev'd in part and remanded sub nom. Brewster v. Barnes, 788 F.2d 985 (4th Cir. 1986).

This section and former §§ 8-38 (9), 8-40 and 8-752 dealt with claims payable out of the state treasury in pursuance of appropriations made by law. Hence, these sections were not applicable to a claim against a tunnel district which would not have been payable out of the state treasury. Morris v. Elizabeth River Tunnel Dist., 203 Va. 196, 123 S.E.2d 398 (1962).

Procurement act prevails over this section. — The procurement act (see § 2.2-4300 et seq.) is a specific statute relating to the acquisition of services by public bodies and prevails over the more general statutes relating to the presentation of pecuniary claims against the commonwealth, such as those found in this section. Dr. William E.S. Flory Small Bus. Dev. Ctr., Inc. v. Commonwealth, 261 Va. 230, 541 S.E.2d 915, 2001 Va. LEXIS 39 (2001).

Quasi-contractual claims barred. — Neither this section nor § 8.01-192 establishes a claimant's right to lodge a claim against the sovereign or the sovereign's liability for claims based on quasi-contract, quantum meruit and contract implied in law. Regardless of the requirements of the procurement act, a claimant cannot recover against the commonwealth on these theories in the absence of a statute abrogating the commonwealth's sovereign immunity. Dr. William E.S. Flory Small Bus. Dev. Ctr., Inc. v. Commonwealth, 261 Va. 230, 541 S.E.2d 915, 2001 Va. LEXIS 39 (2001).

Claim presentation. — Professor's breach of contract claim against a state university and its provost for failure to reappoint him as department chair was barred by the Eleventh Amendment and the university, as a branch of the state, did not waive its sovereign immunity to such suit because the professor failed to comply with the procedures set forth in § 2.2-814 for pursuit of a pecuniary claim against the Commonwealth. Amaram v. Va. State Univ., 476 F. Supp. 2d 535, 2007 U.S. Dist. LEXIS 15389 (E.D. Va. 2007).

Applied in Mid-Atlantic Bus. Communs., Inc. v. Va. DMV, 269 Va. 51, 606 S.E.2d 835, 2005 Va. LEXIS 6 (2005).

CIRCUIT COURT OPINIONS

Claim presentation. — Although a student alleged fraud, a loss of property, and an actual contract, and the Commonwealth waived its sovereign immunity, a community college was not an independent legal entity and the student failed to comply with the procedures for presenting a contract claim against the Commonwealth; therefore, sovereign immunity did not bar the student's tort claim, but did bar the student's contract claim. Goff v. J. Sargeant Reynolds Cmty. College, 68 Va. Cir. 382, 2005 Va. Cir. LEXIS 245 (Richmond Aug. 16, 2005).

University's plea in bar was overruled as the developers complied with the basic statutory requirements for filing a pecuniary claim against the Commonwealth of Virginia; while a demand failed to make a demand for damages, an affiant averred that the developers discussed their damages claims with the university's president, who disallowed the claims. The developers' motion to amend their complaint to add the Virginia Comptroller as a necessary party was granted. Geographic Network Affiliates-International, Inc. v. Enter. for Empowerment Found., 69 Va. Cir. 428, 2006 Va. Cir. LEXIS 94 (Norfolk 2006).

Students' claims against the Commonwealth for the negligence of its employees did not fail, even though the students did not give a § 2.2-814 notice as § 2.2-814 was inapplicable since the Virginia Tort Claims Act, specifically § 8.01-195.6 contained its own notice provision. Long v. Commonwealth, — Va. Cir. —, 2007 Va. Cir. LEXIS 78 (Norfolk Apr. 13, 2007).

§ 2.2-815. Claims to be examined and forwarded to Comptroller; what Comptroller may allow. — A. Every claim authorized to be presented to the Comptroller or to the head of a department, division, institution or agency shall be examined by the person to whom it is presented and forwarded with appropriate supporting papers and recommendations without unreasonable delay to the Comptroller, who shall promptly allow the amount that appears to be due.

B. No allowance made by order of any court of record shall be paid out of the state treasury, unless presented to the Comptroller for payment within two years from the date of the allowance. (Code 1950, §§ 2-196, 2-197; 1966, c. 677, §§ 2.1-223.3, 2.1-223.4; 2001, c. 844.)

CASE NOTES

Finality of judgment. — Contractor's breach of contract action filed against the Virginia Department of Motor Vehicles based on a contract awarded under the Virginia Public Procurement Act was properly dismissed as untimely, moreover: (1) the Department's recommendation to the Comptroller regarding the contractor's claim was a task required under § 2.2-815 and had no effect on the finality of the Department's previous rejection of the claim; (2) if the contractor did not believe that said letter was the final denial of its claim, it was free to file an action 30 days after it failed to receive a response to its letter seeking a determination on its claim; and (3) the tolling provisions of subsection D of § 8.01-229 were not available to the contractor. Mid-Atlantic Bus. Communs., Inc. v. Va. DMV, 269 Va. 51, 606 S.E.2d 835, 2005 Va. LEXIS 6 (2005).

CIRCUIT COURT OPINIONS

Basic statutory requirements for filing pecuniary claim against Commonwealth met. — University's plea in bar was overruled as the developers complied with the basic statutory requirements for filing a pecuniary claim against the Commonwealth of Virginia; while a demand failed to make a demand for damages, an affiant averred that the developers discussed their damages claims with the university's president, who disallowed the claims. The developers' motion to amend their complaint to add the Virginia Comptroller as a necessary party was granted. Geographic Network Affiliates-International, Inc. v. Enter. for Empowerment Found., 69 Va. Cir. 428, 2006 Va. Cir. LEXIS 94 (Norfolk 2006).

§ **2.2-816. When Comptroller may refer claim to Governor.** — Whenever a claim cannot be allowed solely because it was not presented within the time prescribed by § 8.01-255, the Comptroller may, within three years after the claim might have been presented, refer the same to the Governor, who may direct payment of all or any part of the claim. (Code 1950, § 2-199; 1966, c. 677, § 2.1-223.6; 1977, c. 624; 2001, c. 844.)

CHAPTER 9.

Department of Business Assistance.

§ **2.2-900. Creation of Department; appointment of Director; powers and duties.** — A. There is created a Department of Business Assistance (the "Department") that shall be headed by a Director appointed by the Governor to serve at his pleasure.

B. The Director of the Department shall, under the direction and control of the Governor, exercise the powers and perform the duties conferred or imposed upon him by law and perform such other duties as may be required by the Governor. (1996, cc. 589, 599, §§ 2.1-548.44, 2.1-548.45; 2001, c. 844.)

§ **2.2-901. Additional power of Department.** — The Department or, with the approval of the Director, a division of the Department shall have the power to adopt regulations and issue guidelines necessary or incidental to the performance of the duties or execution of the powers conferred under this title and other relevant chapters, which regulations shall be adopted by the Department in accordance with the provisions of Article 2 (§ 2.2-4006 et seq.) of the Administrative Process Act. (1996, cc. 589, 599, § 2.1-548.46; 2001, c. 844.)

§ **2.2-902. Duties of the Department; state agencies to furnish information.** — A. The Department shall serve as the liaison between the Commonwealth's existing business and state government in order to promote the development of Virginia's economy. To that end, the Department shall:

1. Provide for training or retraining of individuals for specific employment opportunities at new or expanding business facilities in the Commonwealth;
2. Develop and implement programs to assist small businesses in the Commonwealth in order to promote their growth and the creation and retention of jobs for Virginians;
3. Establish an industry program that is the principal point of communication between basic employers in the Commonwealth and the state government that will address issues of significance to business;
4. Make available to existing businesses, in conjunction and cooperation with localities, chambers of commerce, and other public and private groups, basic information and pertinent factors of interest and concern to such businesses; and
5. Develop statistical reports on job creation and the general economic conditions in the Commonwealth.

B. All agencies of the Commonwealth shall assist the Department upon request and furnish such information and assistance as the Department may require in the discharge of its duties. (1996, cc. 589, 599, §§ 2.1-548.47, 2.1-548.48; 2001, c. 844.)

Cross references. — As to Aerospace Engine Manufacturer Workforce Training Grant Fund, see § 59.1-284.22.

§ **2.2-903. Nonstock corporation to assist small businesses.** — The Department may establish a nonstock corporation under Chapter 10 (§ 13.1-801 et seq.), Title 13.1 as an instrumentality to assist the Department in providing support to the small business segment of the economy of the Commonwealth. The Department may do all things necessary to qualify such corporation as a certified development company under Subchapter V of the Small Business Investment Act of 1958 (15 U.S.C. § 695 et seq.), or any amendment or successor statute thereto, as well as regulations adopted thereunder by the United States Small Business Administration. Any action by the Department to establish such a corporation prior to July 1, 1986, is ratified and approved. (1986, c. 297, § 9-249.1; 1996, cc. 589, 599; 2001, c. 844.)

§ **2.2-904. Workforce Retraining Program.** — A. The Department shall develop a program to provide consulting services and funding to assist companies and businesses with retraining their existing workforces to increase productivity.

B. There is hereby established in the state treasury a special nonreverting fund to be known as the Workforce Retraining Fund. The Fund shall consist of any moneys appropriated thereto by the General Assembly from time to time and designated for the Fund. Any moneys deposited to or remaining in the Fund during or at the end of each fiscal year or biennium, including interest thereon, shall not revert to the general fund but shall remain in the Fund and be available for allocation under this article in ensuing fiscal years.

C. To be eligible for moneys from the Fund, a company shall:

1. Demonstrate that it is undergoing integration of new technology into its production process, a change of product line in keeping with marketplace demands, or substantial change to its service delivery process that would require assimilation of new skills and technological capabilities by the firm's existing labor force;

2. Demonstrate that, for each such integration of new technology into its production process, change of product line in keeping with marketplace demands, or substantial change to its service delivery process:

a. No less than 10 and no more than 200 full-time employees are involved; and

b. A minimum capital investment of $500,000 is committed within a 12-month period;

3. Certify that:

a. The company has not received moneys from the Fund in the previous 24 months;

b. The company counted only full-time employees to qualify for the program; and

c. Such full-time employees carry a minimum pay rate of $8 per hour; and

4. Meet such additional criteria as may be promulgated by the Department.

D. As used in this section:

"Capital investment" means an investment in real property, personal property, or both, at a manufacturing or basic nonmanufacturing facility within the Commonwealth that is capitalized by the company and that increases the

productivity of the manufacturing facility, results in the utilization of a more advanced technology than is in use immediately prior to such investment, or both. In order to qualify as a capital investment, an investment in technology shall result in a measurable increase in capacity or productivity, a measurable decrease in the production of flawed product, or both.

"Full-time employee" means a natural person employed for indefinite duration, requiring a minimum of either (i) 35 hours of the employee's time per week for the entire normal year, which "normal year" must consist of at least 48 weeks or (ii) 1,680 hours per year. Seasonal or temporary employees shall not qualify as new full-time employees under this section.

E. Moneys in the Fund shall be used solely for grants to eligible businesses as provided in this section. The total amount of funds provided to eligible businesses under this section for any year shall not exceed the amount appropriated by the General Assembly to the Fund for such year. Expenditures and disbursements from the Fund shall be made by the State Treasurer on warrants issued by the Comptroller upon written request signed by the Director or his designee. The Fund shall be administered by the Director. (2003, c. 338.)

§ 2.2-904.1. One-stop small business permitting program. — A. As used in this section:

"Business Permitting Center" or *"Center"* means the business registration and permitting center established by this section and located in and under the administrative control of the Department.

"Comprehensive application" means a document incorporating pertinent data from existing applications for permits covered under this section.

"Comprehensive permit" means the single document designed for public display issued by the Business Permitting Center that certifies state agency permit approval and that incorporates the endorsements for individual permits included in the comprehensive permitting program.

"Comprehensive permitting program" or *"Program"* means the mechanism by which comprehensive permits are issued and renewed, permit and regulatory information is disseminated, and account data are exchanged by state agencies.

"Department" means the Department of Business Assistance or any division of the Department to which the Director has delegated or assigned the duties and responsibilities of administering the comprehensive permitting program.

"Permit" means the whole or part of any state agency permit, license, certificate, approval, registration, charter, or any form or permission required by law, to engage in activity associated with or involving the establishment of a small business in the Commonwealth.

"Permit information packet" means a collection of information about permitting requirements and application procedures custom assembled for each request.

"Regulatory" means all permitting and other governmental or statutory requirements establishing a small business or professional activities associated with establishing a small business.

"Regulatory agency" means any state agency, board, commission, or division that regulates one or more professions, occupations, industries, businesses, or activities.

"Renewal application" means a document used to collect pertinent data for renewal of permits covered under this section.

"Small business" means an independently owned and operated business that, together with affiliates, has 250 or fewer employees or average annual gross receipts of $10 million or less averaged over the previous three years.

B. There is created within the Department the comprehensive permitting program (the Program). The Program is established to serve as a single access point to aid entrepreneurs in filling out the various permit applications associated with establishing a small business in Virginia. The Program in no way supersedes or supplants any regulatory authority granted to any state agency with permits covered by this section. As part of the Program, the Department shall coordinate with the regulatory agency, and the regulatory agency shall determine consistent with applicable law, what types of permits are appropriate for inclusion in the Program as well as the rules governing the submission of and payment for those permits. The website of the Department shall provide access to information regarding the Program. The Department shall have the power and duty to:

1. Create a comprehensive application that will allow an entrepreneur, or an agent thereof, seeking to establish a small business, to create accounts that will allow them to acquire the appropriate permits required in the Commonwealth. The comprehensive application shall:

a. Allow the business owner to choose a business type and to provide common information, such as name, address, and telephone number, on the front page, eliminating the need to repeatedly provide common information on each permit application;

b. Allow the business owner to preview and answer questions related to the operation of the business;

c. Provide business owners with a customized to-do agency checklist, which checklist shall provide the permit applications pertinent to each business type and provide the rules, regulations, and general laws applicable to each business type as well as local licensing information;

d. Allow the business owner to submit permit applications by electronic means as authorized by § 59.1-496 and to affix thereto his electronic signature as defined in § 59.1-480;

e. Allow the business owner to check on the status of applications online and to receive information from the permitting agencies electronically; and

f. Allow a business owner to submit electronic payment for application or permitting fees for applications that have been accepted by the permitting agency.

2. Develop and administer a computerized system program capable of storing, retrieving, and exchanging permit information, while protecting the confidentiality of information submitted to the Department to the extent allowable by law. Information submitted to the Department shall be subject to the provisions of the Virginia Freedom of Information Act (§ 2.2-3700 et seq.) as the same would apply were the information submitted directly to the Department or to any permitting agency.

3. Issue and renew comprehensive permits in an efficient manner.

4. Identify the types of permits appropriate for inclusion in the Program. The Department shall coordinate with the regulatory agency, and the regulatory agency shall determine consistent with applicable law, what types of permits are appropriate for inclusion in the Program.

5. Incorporate permits into the Program.

6. Do all acts necessary or convenient to carry out the purposes of this chapter.

C. The Business Permitting Center shall compile information regarding the regulatory programs associated with each of the permits obtainable under the Program. This information shall include, at a minimum, a listing of the statutes and administrative rules requiring the permits and pertaining to the regulatory programs that are directly related to the permit. The Center shall provide information governed by this section to any person requesting it. Materials used by the Center to describe the services provided by the Center shall indicate that this information is available upon request.

D. Each state agency shall cooperate and provide reasonable assistance to the Department in the implementation of this section.

E. Any person requiring permits that have been incorporated into the Program may submit a comprehensive application to the Department requesting the issuance of the permits. The comprehensive application form shall contain in consolidated form information necessary for the issuance of the permits.

F. The applicant shall include with the application the handling fee established by the Department. The amount of the handling fee assessed against the applicant shall be set by the Department at a level necessary to cover the costs of administering the comprehensive permitting program.

G. The authority for approving the issuance and renewal of any requested permit that requires an investigation, inspection, testing, or other judgmental review by the regulatory agency otherwise legally authorized to issue the permit shall remain with that agency. The Center may issue those permits for which proper fee payment and a completed application form have been received and for which no approval action is required by the regulatory agency.

H. Upon receipt of the application and proper fee payment for any permit for which issuance is subject to regulatory agency action under subsection G, the Department shall immediately notify the regulatory agency with authority to approve the permit issuance or renewal requested by the applicant. Each regulatory agency shall advise the Department within a reasonable time after receiving the notice of one of the following:

1. That the regulatory agency approves the issuance of the requested permit and will advise the applicant of any specific conditions required for issuing the permit;

2. That the regulatory agency denies the issuance of the permit and gives the applicant reasons for the denial;

3. That the application is pending; or

4. That the application is incomplete and further information from or action by the applicant is necessary.

I. The Department shall issue a comprehensive permit endorsed for all the approved permits to the applicant and advise the applicant of the status of other requested permits. The applicant shall be responsible for contesting any decision regarding conditions imposed or permits denied through the normal process established by statute or by the regulatory agency with the authority for approving the issuance of the permit.

J. Regulatory agencies shall be provided information from the comprehensive application for their permitting and regulatory functions.

K. The Department shall be responsible for directing the applicant to make all payments for applicable fees established by the regulatory agency directly to the proper agency.

L. There is hereby created in the state treasury a special nonreverting fund to be known as the Comprehensive Permitting Fund, hereafter referred to as "the Fund." The Fund shall be established on the books of the Comptroller. The Fund shall consist of all moneys collected from the handling fee established by the Department pursuant to subsection F and such other funds as may be appropriated by the General Assembly. Interest earned on moneys in the Fund shall remain in the Fund and be credited to it. Any moneys remaining in the Fund, including interest thereon, at the end of each fiscal year shall not revert to the general fund but shall remain in the Fund. Moneys in the Fund shall be used solely to administer the Program. Expenditures and disbursements from the Fund shall be made by the State Treasurer on warrants issued by the Comptroller upon written request signed by Director of the Department.

M. Unless otherwise directed by the regulatory agency, the Department shall not issue or renew a comprehensive permit to any person under any of the following circumstances:

1. The person does not have a valid tax registration, if required.

2. The person is a corporation, limited liability company, business trust, limited partnership or registered limited liability partnership that (i) is delinquent in the payment of fees or penalties collected by the State Corporation Commission pursuant to the business entity statutes it administers; (ii) does not exist; or (iii) is not authorized to transact business in the Commonwealth pursuant to one of the business entity statutes administered by the State Corporation Commission.

3. The person has not submitted the sum of all fees and deposits required for the requested individual permit endorsements, any outstanding comprehensive permit delinquency fee, or other fees and penalties to be collected through the comprehensive permitting program.

N. The Department may adopt regulations in accordance with § 2.2-901 as may be necessary to carry out the purposes of this section. (2007, c. 706.)

CHAPTER 9.1.

Department of Charitable Gaming.

§§ **2.2-905, 2.2-906:** Repealed by Acts 2008, cc. 387 and 689, cl. 2.

Editor's note. — Acts 2008, cc. 387 and 689, cl. 3 provides: "That as of July 1, 2008, the Department of Agriculture and Consumer Services shall be deemed successor in interest to the Department of Charitable Gaming to the extent that this act transfers powers and duties. All right, title, and interest in and to any real or tangible personal property vested in the Department of Charitable Gaming shall be transferred to and taken as standing in the name of the Department of Agriculture and Consumer Services."

Acts 2008, cc. 387 and 689, cl. 4 provides: "That the Governor may transfer an appropriation or any portion thereof within a state agency established, abolished, or otherwise affected by the provisions of this act, or from one such agency to another, to support the changes in organization or responsibility resulting from or required by the provisions of this act."

Acts 2008, cc. 387 and 689, cl. 5 provides: "That all rules and regulations adopted by the Department of Charitable Gaming or the Charitable Gaming Board that are in effect as of July 1, 2008, and that pertain to the subject of this act, shall remain in full force and effect until altered, amended, or rescinded by the Department of Agriculture and Consumer Services or the Charitable Gaming Board."

CHAPTER 10.

Department of Employment Dispute Resolution.

§ **2.2-1000. Creation of Department; appointment of Director; powers and duties.** — A. There is created a Department of Employment Dispute Resolution (the "Department") that shall be headed by a Director appointed by the Governor to serve at his pleasure.

B. The Director of the Department shall, under the direction and control of the Governor, exercise the powers and perform the duties conferred or imposed upon him by law and perform such other duties as may be required by the Governor. (1995, cc. 770, 818, §§ 2.1-116.01, 2.1-116.02; 2000, cc. 947, 1006; 2001, c. 844.)

Cross references. — As to limitations on the use of polygraph evidence in proceedings conducted under this section, see § 40.1-51.4:4.

Editor's note. — Acts 2000, cc. 947 and 1006, cl. 2, provide: "That wherever in the Code of Virginia the term 'Department of Employee Relations Counselors' is used, it shall be deemed to mean the Department of Employment Dispute Resolution."

§ 2.2-1001. Director to administer Department; powers and duties. — The Director shall, under the direction and control of the Governor, administer and supervise the Department and shall:

1. Establish a comprehensive program of employee relations management that includes alternative processes for resolving employment disputes;
2. Establish the grievance procedure and a statewide mediation program;
3. Adopt rules and set hearing officer fees for grievance hearings;
4. For employees who are covered by the grievance procedure, (i) provide forms necessary for the proper use of the grievance procedure; (ii) direct full compliance with the grievance procedure process; (iii) investigate allegations of retaliation as the result of use of or participation in the grievance procedure or of reporting, in good faith, an allegation of fraud, waste or abuse to the State Employee Fraud, Waste and Abuse Hotline and advise the agency head of the findings; and (iv) rule on the qualification of a grievance or the question of access to the grievance procedure;
5. Render final decisions, containing the reasons for such decision, on all matters related to procedural compliance with the grievance procedure;
6. Establish a process to select, on a rotating basis, hearing officers for grievance hearings from (i) the list maintained by the Executive Secretary of the Supreme Court or (ii) attorneys hired as classified employees by the Department through a competitive selection process; train and assign such hearing officers to conduct grievance hearings; evaluate the quality of their services to determine eligibility for continued selection; and, if deemed ineligible for continued selection, establish policies for removing such hearing officers from consideration for future selection;
7. Publish hearing officer decisions and Department rulings;
8. Establish, in conjunction with the Department of Human Resource Management, a training program for human resources personnel on employee relations management and employment rights and responsibilities;
9. Implement a comprehensive training and instructional program for all supervisory personnel that includes the role of the grievance procedure in harmonious employee relations management. The training program shall also include methods for supervisors to instruct nonsupervisory personnel in the use of the grievance procedure. Use of the grievance procedure to resolve disputes shall be encouraged. In-house resources shall be developed to allow the Department and its personnel to conduct on-site training of this nature for units and agencies of state government throughout Virginia. The Department shall assist agencies in establishing performance criteria for such supervisory personnel;
10. Provide information upon the request of any employee concerning personnel policies, regulations, and law applicable to the grievance procedure and counsel employees in the resolution of conflict in the workplace;
11. Establish and maintain a toll-free telephone number to facilitate access by employees to the services of the Department;
12. Collect information and statistical data regarding the use of the grievance procedure and the effectiveness of employee relations management in the various state agencies;
13. Make recommendations to the Governor and the General Assembly to improve the grievance procedure and employee relations management;
14. Exercise such other powers and perform such other duties as may be requested by the Governor; and

15. Perform all acts and employ such personnel as may be required, necessary, or convenient to carry out the provisions of this chapter. (1995, cc. 16, 646, 770, 818, § 2.1-116.03; 1996, cc. 164, 869; 1998, c. 263; 2000, cc. 66, 657, 947, 1006; 2001, c. 844.)

Cross references. — As to the effect of the Virginia Administrative Dispute Resolution Act, § 2.2-4115 et seq., on mediation programs administered by the Department of Employment Dispute Resolution, see § 2.2-4117. As to immunity from civil liability for mediators and mediation services established under this section, see § 8.01-581.23.

CASE NOTES

Editor's note. — Most of the cases below were decided under former Title 2.1 or prior provisions.

Authority of grievance panel to promote should be left to General Assembly. — The determination whether a grievance panel has the authority to promote clearly is best left to the wisdom of the General Assembly and the state officials charged with the administration of the grievance procedure. Therefore, the board was without authority to award a policeman, denied promotion, a retroactive promotion and compensation for back pay. Jones v. Carter, 234 Va. 621, 363 S.E.2d 921 (1988).

Legislative intent to preclude judicial review. — The "final authority" language in former subdivision (7) of former § 2.1-114.5:6, which stated: 'To make and disseminate interpretations of the grievance procedure," supported and was consistent with a legislative intent shown throughout the act to preclude judicial review in certain areas. Murray v. Stokes, 237 Va. 653, 378 S.E.2d 834 (1989).

Judicial review of the interpretation of a personnel policy regarding employee compensation by the Director of the Department of Personnel and Training (now Department of Human Resource Management) is precluded under the Virginia Personnel Act, and therefore, the trial court had no jurisdiction to entertain a bill of complaint seeking review of the interpretation of Rule 8.3(d) of the Department's rules by the director of that department. Murray v. Stokes, 237 Va. 653, 378 S.E.2d 834 (1989).

Court lacked authority to treat petition as notice of grievance. — Where the trial court correctly determined that the employee's demotion upon reinstatement was an issue that had to be grieved separately and was not enforceable as part of the panel's reinstatement decision without exhausting the administrative grievance procedure, the trial court lacked authority to treat the petition filed pursuant to subsection F of former § 2.1-114.5:1 as filing notice of a grievance with an agency. Commonwealth, Dep't of Taxation v. Hogan, 11 Va. App. 306, 397 S.E.2d 902 (1990).

Reversal of hearing officer's decision in error. — Upon judicial review of a hearing officer's decision to amend a disciplinary notice against two penitentiary employees, the trial court erred by concluding that the hearing officer had no authority to amend the disciplinary notice and, therefore, dismissed the Group II disciplinary notice. Because the hearing officer's amendment of the disciplinary notice did not violate any statute, judicial precedent, or accepted legal principal, it was proper and should have been upheld. Commonwealth v. Doyle, — Va. App. —, — S.E.2d —, 2005 Va. App. LEXIS 255 (July 5, 2005).

Agency decision not subject to review. — In a case involving Virginia's State Grievance Procedure, specifically §§ 2.2-3003, 2.2-3004, and 2.2-3006, the Department of Employment Dispute Resolution's decision was not subject to review by the circuit court because it involved an interpretation of agency procedures created pursuant to subdivision 2 of § 2.2-1001 rather than an issue of law; also, the delay by the Department of Human Resource Management (DHRM) in rendering its decision on the request for review did not nullify its ruling because subsection A of § 2.2-3006 contained no prohibitory or limiting language preventing the DHRM from ruling after the expiration of 60 days. Va. Dep't of Taxation v. Brailey, — Va. App. —, — S.E.2d —, 2008 Va. App. LEXIS 19 (Jan. 15, 2008).

CIRCUIT COURT OPINIONS

Burden shifting proper. — Director of the Department of Employment Dispute Resolution had the authority under § 2.2-1001 to establish the grievance procedure, adopt rules for grievance hearings, and perform all acts as were necessary to carry out the provisions of the disciplining of a university employee, such that the use of the McDonnell Douglas burden-shifting analysis by a hearing officer regarding the employee's grievance over his termination, wherein the employee asserted racial discrimination, was not contrary to law. Old Dominion

Univ. v. Birkmeyer, 73 Va. Cir. 341, 2007 Va. Cir. LEXIS 131 (Norfolk 2007).

CHAPTER 11.

Department of General Services.

Article 1.

General Provisions.

Article 2.

Division Of Consolidated Laboratory Services.

Article 3.

Division Of Purchases And Supply.

Article 4.

Division Of Engineering And Buildings.

Article 5.

Abatement Of Risk Of Asbestos In State-Owned And Public School Buildings.

Article 6.

Division Of Support Services.

Article 1.

General Provisions.

§ 2.2-1100. Creation of Department; appointment of Director; duties. — A. There is created a Department of General Services (the Department), which shall be headed by a Director appointed by the Governor to serve at his pleasure.

B. The Director of the Department shall, under the direction and control of the Governor, exercise the powers and perform the duties conferred or imposed upon him by law and perform such other duties as may be required by the Governor. The Director shall be responsible for the overall supervision of the Department's divisions, programs and personnel. Under his direction the Department shall serve as an agency whose services are primarily for the support of other state agencies in carrying out their programs. The head of each division shall, under the direction and control of the Director, exercise the powers and perform the duties conferred by this chapter as they pertain to his division and perform such other duties as required by the Director.

C. Whenever in this title and in the Code of Virginia, reference is made to a division, department or agency transferred to this Department, it shall mean the Department of General Services, through the division to which the powers and duties of that division, department or agency are assigned. Notwithstanding anything in this section to the contrary, the Director shall have the authority to create new divisions within the Department and to assign or reassign the duties of the Department's divisions to whatever divisions as may best perform them. (1977, c. 672, §§ 2.1-422, 2.1-423, 2.1-425; 1978, c. 255; 1984, c. 720; 2001, c. 844; 2005, c. 385.)

Editor's note. — Acts 2004, c. 129, cl. 1, provides: The Department of General Services shall, in coordination with the Secretary of Health and Human Services, establish a statewide contract for telephonic language interpretation services and other interpretation and translation services to Virginia's limited English-speaking residents, if it determines that such a contract is cost-effective."

Acts 2006, c. 124, provides: "§ 1. That the Department of General Services, in cooperation with the Virginia Information Technologies Agency, shall establish and publish in the vendor's manual a procedure for refunding the relevant eVa transaction fees in the event of a change order or cancellation of a contract by a vendor."

§ 2.2-1101. Creation of internal service fund accounts. — Upon written request of the Director of the Department, the Joint Legislative Audit and Review Commission may direct the Comptroller to establish internal service fund accounts on his books and record the receipts and expenditures for appropriate functions of the Department. The Comptroller shall provide the Department with working capital advances with which to finance these operations pursuant to appropriations made by law. Charges for services rendered sufficient to offset costs involved in these operations shall be established. (1977, c. 672, § 2.1-425; 1978, c. 255; 2001, c. 844.)

§ **2.2-1102. Additional powers of Department.** — A. The Department shall have the following additional powers, all of which, with the approval of the Director of the Department, may be exercised by a division of the Department with respect to matters assigned to that division:

1. Prescribe regulations necessary or incidental to the performance of duties or execution of powers conferred under this chapter; and

2. Establish fee schedules that may be collectible from users when general fund appropriations are not applicable to the services rendered.

B. All statewide contracts and agreements made and entered into by the Department for the purchase of computers, software, supplies, and related peripheral equipment and services shall provide for the inclusion of counties, cities, and towns in such contracts and agreements. For good cause shown, the Secretary of Administration may disapprove the inclusion from a specific contract or agreement.

C. The Department may operate or provide for the operation of hazardous waste management facilities. (1977, c. 672, § 2.1-424; 1986, c. 492, § 2.1-425.2; 1995, c. 357; 2001, c. 844.)

Article 2.

Division Of Consolidated Laboratory Services.

§ **2.2-1103. Division of Consolidated Laboratory Services.** — Within the Department shall be created the Division of Consolidated Laboratory Services (the "Division"), which shall provide certain laboratory services, including research and scientific investigations, for various agencies of the Commonwealth in an efficient, effective and professional manner. The provisions of this article shall in no manner limit the authority and responsibilities of institutions of higher education from conducting laboratory services, research and scientific investigations independently of the Division. (Code 1950, § 32-31.1; 1972, c. 741; 1977, c. 672, § 2.1-426; 1990, c. 825; 2001, c. 844.)

§ **2.2-1104. Laboratory, testing, and analytical functions.** — A. The Division shall provide, but is not limited to, the following specific laboratory, testing and analytical functions:

1. Maintain laboratories for the examination of clinical material and pathological specimens submitted by members of the medical profession of the Commonwealth and for which the Division may charge fees to recover full costs.

2. Provide laboratory services for the testing and analysis of various products, foods, drinks, economic poisons and other materials regulated or controlled by the Commonwealth.

3. Provide laboratory services for the analysis and examination of samples and materials related to environmental control.

4. Establish and conduct programs of inspection and certification of other laboratories in the Commonwealth as mandated by the federal Safe Drinking Water Act (P.L. 93-523) and state requirements pursuant to that Act.

B. No fee shall be charged for the analyses of water samples that are required by regulations of the Department of Health or for feed and fertilizer samples that are required by regulations of the Department of Agriculture and Consumer Services.

C. The Division may provide, upon request of any law-enforcement agency, chemical and microbiological testing and analytical functions related to any criminal investigation. Nothing in this section shall be construed to limit or preclude the Department of Forensic Science from conducting all necessary testing and analytical functions associated with any criminal investigation.

D. Upon request of a bidder on any state contract that requires the Division to test or analyze the product being offered by the bidder, the Director of the Division of Purchases and Supply may allow such bidder or his representative to witness the test or analysis.

E. The Division shall provide for security and protection of evidence, official samples and all other samples submitted to the Division for analysis or examination. (1977, c. 672, §§ 2.1-429, 2.1-430; 1984, c. 275; 1986, c. 610; 1989, cc. 53, 409; 1990, c. 825; 1992, cc. 747, 873; 1996, c. 355; 2001, c. 844; 2005, cc. 868, 881.)

Editor's note. — Acts 2008, c. 879, effective for the biennium ending June 30, 2010, in Item 78 A and C, provides: "A. The provisions of § 2.2-1104, Code of Virginia, notwithstanding, the Division of Consolidated Laboratory Services shall ensure that no individual is denied the benefits of laboratory tests mandated by the Department of Health for reason of inability to pay for such services.

"C. The provisions of § 2.2-1104 B, Code of Virginia, notwithstanding, the Division of Consolidated Laboratories may charge a fee for the limited and specific purpose of analyses of water samples where:

"1. testing is required by Department of Health regulations pursuant to Phase II and Phase V regulations of the federal Safe Drinking Water Act, and

"2. funding to support such testing is not otherwise provided for in this act."

§ 2.2-1105. Environmental laboratory certification program. — A. The Division shall by regulation establish a program for the certification of laboratories conducting any tests, analyses, measurements, or monitoring required pursuant to Chapter 13 (§ 10.1-1300 et seq.) of Title 10.1, the Virginia Waste Management Act (§ 10.1-1400 et seq.), or the State Water Control Law (§ 62.1-44.2 et seq.). The program shall include, but need not be limited to, minimum criteria for (i) laboratory procedures, (ii) performance evaluations, (iii) supervisory and personnel requirements, (iv) facilities and equipment, (v) analytical quality control and quality assurance, (vi) certificate issuance and maintenance, (vii) recertification and decertification, and (viii) granting partial and full exemptions from the program based on compliance and performance. The regulations shall be promulgated only after adoption of national accreditation standards by the National Environmental Laboratory Accreditation Conference sponsored by the United States Environmental Protection Agency. The purpose of the program shall be to ensure that laboratories provide accurate and consistent tests, analyses, measurements and monitoring so that the goals and requirements of Chapter 13 of Title 10.1, the Virginia Waste Management Act, and the State Water Control Law may be met.

B. Once the certification program has been established, laboratory certification shall be required before any tests, analyses, measurements or monitoring performed by a laboratory after the effective date of such program may be used for the purposes of Chapter 13 (§ 10.1-1300 et seq.) of Title 10.1, the Virginia Waste Management Act, and the State Water Control Law.

C. The Division shall by regulation establish a fee system to offset the costs of the certification program. The regulations shall establish fee categories based upon the types of substances for which tests, analyses, measurements or monitoring are performed. The fees shall be used solely for offsetting the costs of the laboratory certification program.

D. The Division shall develop procedures for determining the qualifications of laboratories located in jurisdictions outside of Virginia to conduct tests, analyses, measurements or monitoring for use in Virginia. Laboratories located outside of Virginia that are certified or accredited under a program determined by the Division to be equivalent to the program established under this section shall be deemed to meet the certification requirements.

E. In addition to any other penalty provided by law, laboratories found to be falsifying any data or providing false information to support certification shall be decertified or denied certification.

F. Any laboratory subject to this section may petition the Director of the Division for a reasonable variance from the requirements of the regulations promulgated under this section. The Division may grant a reasonable variance if the petitioner demonstrates to the Director's satisfaction that (i) the proposed variance will meet the goals and purposes of the provisions of this section or regulation promulgated under this section, and (ii) the variance does not conflict with federal or state law or regulations. Any petition submitted to the Director is subject to the Administrative Process Act (§ 2.2-4000 et seq.). (1997, c. 652, § 2.1-429.01; 2001, c. 844; 2003, c. 580.)

§ **2.2-1106. Consolidation of other laboratories.** — The Director of the Department may take in and absorb within the Division any laboratory activity that is owned and operated by a political subdivision of the Commonwealth that will conform to the duties and responsibilities of the Division. Any costs that may accrue to the Commonwealth as a result of the consolidation shall be paid out of funds specifically appropriated for this purpose by the appropriation act. (1987, c. 369, § 2.1-429.4; 1996, cc. 366, 447; 2001, c. 844.)

§ **2.2-1107. Disposal of certain hazardous materials.** — Any material seized in a criminal investigation and deemed to be hazardous to health and safety, may be disposed of upon written application of the Division to the attorney for the Commonwealth in the city or county where the material is seized or where any criminal prosecution in which such material is proposed to be evidence is pending. Upon receipt, the attorney for the Commonwealth shall file the application in the circuit court of such county or city. A sworn analysis report signed by a person designated by the Director of the Division shall accompany the application for disposal and shall clearly identify and designate the material for disposal. The application shall state the nature and quantity of the hazardous materials, the location where seized, the person from whom the materials were seized, and the manner in which the material shall be destroyed. Where the ownership of the hazardous material is known, notice shall be given to the owner at least three days prior to any hearing relating to the destruction, and, if any criminal charge is pending in any court as a result of the seizure, notice shall be given to the accused if other than the owner. Upon receipt of the analysis report and the application, the court may order the destruction of all, or a part of, the material; however, a sufficient and representative quantity of the material shall be retained to permit an independent analysis when a criminal prosecution may result from the seizure. A return under oath, reporting the time, place and manner of destruction shall be made to the courts. Copies of the analysis report, application, order and return shall be made a part of the record of any criminal prosecution. The sworn analysis report shall be admissible as evidence to the same extent as the disposed-of material would have been admissible. (Code 1950, § 32-31.6:1; 1976, c. 576; 1977, c. 672, § 2.1-432; 1990, c. 825; 2001, c. 844.)

§ **2.2-1108. Disposal of certain other property.** — Personal property, including drugs, not subject to be disposed of under § 2.2-1107, which has been submitted to the Division for analysis or examination and that has not been reclaimed by the agency submitting the property for analysis or examination, may be disposed of by the Division in accordance with this section if, after the expiration of 120 days after the receipt by the Division of the property, (i) the Director notifies the circuit court of the county or city from which the property was taken, in writing, that the analysis or examination has been completed and (ii) a report is given to the submitting agency that the property has not been reclaimed by the agency and the Division proposes to dispose of the property. The notice shall state the nature and quantity of the property, the location where seized, the name of the accused, if known, and the proposed method of disposing of the property. When the ownership of the property is known, a copy of the notice shall be sent simultaneously with the notice to the court to the owner, or, if any criminal charge is pending in any court relating to the property, the copy shall be sent to the accused at his last known address. Notice shall be by certified mail. The court, within thirty days after receipt of the notice, may direct that the property be disposed of by the Division by an alternative method designed to preserve the property, at the expense of the agency submitting the property to the Division. If the court does not so direct within such thirty-day period, then the Division may dispose of the property by the method set out in the notice. Copies of the analysis report and notice shall be made a part of the record of any criminal prosecution. The report, if sworn to, shall be admissible as evidence to the same extent as the disposed of property would have been admissible. (1978, c. 317, § 2.1-432.1; 1990, c. 825; 2001, c. 844.)

Article 3.

Division Of Purchases And Supply.

§ 2.2-1109. Division of Purchases and Supply established. — Within the Department shall be created a Division of Purchases and Supply (the "Division"), which shall exercise the powers and duties described in this article. (1977, c. 672, § 2.1-435; 2001, c. 844.)

Cross references. — As to inapplicability of provisions of this article to contracts for advertising or publishing entered into by the Virginia Wine Board, see § 3.1-1064.7. For provision that this article shall not apply to contracts for the printing of ballots, statements of results, or other material essential to the conduct of an election, see § 24.2-602.

§ 2.2-1110. Using agencies to purchase through Division of Purchases and Supply; exception. — A. Except as provided by § 2.2-2012 or otherwise directed and authorized by the Division or in the Code of Virginia, every department, division, institution, officer and agency of the Commonwealth, hereinafter called the using agency, shall purchase through the Division all materials, equipment, supplies, printing and nonprofessional services of every description, whenever the whole or a part of the costs is to be paid out of the state treasury. The Division shall make such purchases in conformity with this article.

B. The provisions of subsection A shall not apply to the purchase of materials, equipment, supplies, printing and nonprofessional services of every description by the Virginia Retirement System; however, the Board of Trustees of the Virginia Retirement System shall adopt regulations made in accordance with the Virginia Public Procurement Act (§ 2.2-4300 et seq.) that specify policies and procedures that are based on competitive principles and that are generally applicable to procurement of such goods and services by comparably situated state agencies. The exemption provided by this subsection shall apply for only as long as such regulations, or other regulations meeting the requirements of this subsection, remain in effect at the Virginia Retirement System. (Code 1950, § 2-249; 1958, c. 124; 1966, c. 677, § 2.1-273; 1977, c. 672,

§ 2.1-440; 1980, c. 357; 1988, c. 140; 1995, c. 788; 2001, c. 844; 2003, cc. 981, 1021.)

Editor's note. — For provisions of Acts 2003, cc. 981 and 1021, cls. 4 to 16, reflecting the intent of the General Assembly to provide for the consolidation of the procurement and operational functions of information technology for state agencies in a single agency, and related transitional and other provisions, see the Editor's note at § 2.2-2005.

§ 2.2-1111. Purchases to be made in accordance with the Virginia Public Procurement Act (§ 2.2-4300 et seq.) and regulations of Division; exempt purchases. — A. All purchases made by any department, division, officer or agency of the Commonwealth shall be made in accordance with the Virginia Public Procurement Act (§ 2.2-4300 et seq.) and such regulations as the Division may prescribe.

B. The regulations adopted by the Division shall:

1. Include a purchasing plan that shall be on file at the Division and shall be available to the public upon request;

2. Require that before any public body procures any computer system, equipment or software, it shall consider whether the proposed system, equipment or software is capable of producing products that facilitate the rights of the public to access official records under the Freedom of Information Act (§ 2.2-3700 et seq.) or other applicable law;

3. Require state public bodies to procure only shielded outdoor light fixtures and provide for waivers of this requirement when the Division determines that a bona fide operational, temporary, safety or specific aesthetic need is indicated or that such fixtures are not cost effective over the life cycle of the fixtures. For the purposes of this subdivision, "shielded outdoor light fixture" means an outdoor light fixture that is (i) fully shielded so that no light rays are emitted by the installed fixture above the horizontal plane or (ii) constructed so that no more than two percent of the total luminaire lumens in the zone of 90 to 180 degrees vertical angle is permitted, if the related output of the luminaire is greater than 3200 lumens. In adopting regulations under this subdivision, the Division shall consider national standards for outdoor lighting as adopted by the Illuminating Engineering Society of North America (IESNA).

For any project initiated on or after July 1, 2003, the Virginia Department of Transportation shall design all lighting systems in accordance with current IESNA standards and recommended practices. The lighting system shall utilize fixtures that minimize glare, light trespass, and skyglow, all as defined by the IESNA, while still providing a comfortable, visually effective, safe, and secure outdoor environment in a cost-effective manner over the life cycle of the lighting system.

4. Establish the conditions under which a public body may use, as a basis for the procurement of goods and nonprofessional services, a particular vendor's contract-pricing that has been negotiated and accepted by the U.S. General Services Administration;

5. Establish procurement preferences for products containing recycled oil (including reprocessed and rerefined oil products) and recycled antifreeze no later than December 31, 2002;

6. Establish conditions under which a public body shall demonstrate a good faith effort to ensure that state contracts or subcontracts for goods or services that involve the manual packaging of bulk supplies or the manual assemblage of goods where individual items weigh less than 50 pounds be offered to nonprofit sheltered workshops or other nonprofit organizations that offer transitional or supported employment services serving the handicapped; and

7. Require that on or before October 1, 2009, and every two years thereafter, the Director of the Department of General Services shall solicit from each state

agency and public institution of higher education a list of procurements falling under the Department's authority that were competed with the private sector that appear on the Commonwealth Competition Council's commercial activities list and were, until that time, being performed by each state agency and public institution of higher education during the previous two years, and the outcome of that competition. The Director shall make the lists available to the public on the Department of General Services' website.

C. The Division may make, alter, amend or repeal regulations relating to the purchase of materials, supplies, equipment, nonprofessional services, and printing, and may specifically exempt purchases below a stated amount or particular agencies or specified materials, equipment, nonprofessional services, supplies and printing. (Code 1950, § 2-251; 1958, c. 124; 1966, c. 677, § 2.1-275; 1977, c. 672, § 2.1-442; 1979, c. 508; 1980, c. 357; 1982, c. 647; 1996, c. 435; 1997, c. 907; 2001, cc. 569, 844; 2002, c. 504; 2003, c. 294; 2005, c. 817; 2007, c. 630.)

Cross references. — As to the use of cooperative procurement agreements under the Virginia Public Procurement Act, see § 2.2-4304.

Editor's note. — Acts 2001, c. 569 amended § 2.1-442, from which this section is derived. Pursuant to § 30-152, Acts 2001, c. 569 has been given effect in this section as set out above. The 2001 amendment by c. 569, in subsection B, deleted "and" at the end of subdivision 2, inserted "and" at the end of subdivision 3, and added subdivision 4.

The 2007 amendments. — The 2007 amendment by c. 630 added subdivision B 6 [now B 7] and made related changes.

Law Review. — For article, "Environmental Law," see 35 U. Rich. L. Rev. 601 (2001).

§ 2.2-1112. Standardization of materials, equipment and supplies. — So far as practicable, all materials, equipment and supplies, purchased by or for the officers, departments, agencies or institutions of the Commonwealth, shall be standardized by the Division, and no variation shall be allowed from any established standard without the written approval of the Division. The standard shall be determined upon the needs of all using agencies, so far as their needs are in common, and for groups of using agencies or single using agencies so far as their needs differ. When changes or alterations in equipment are necessary in order to permit the application of any standard, the changes and alterations shall be made as rapidly as possible.

The Division shall determine the proper equipment or electrical devices used to monitor the speed of any motor vehicle pursuant to § 46.2-882 and shall so advise the respective law-enforcement officials. Police chiefs and sheriffs shall ensure that all such equipment and devices meet or exceed the standards established by the Division. This provision shall apply only to equipment and devices purchased on or after July 1, 1986. (Code 1950, §§ 2-255, 2-256; 1958 c. 124; 1966, c. 677, §§ 2.1-279, 2.1-280; 1972, c. 494; 1977, c. 672, § 2.1-446; 1986, c. 530; 1991, c. 345; 2001, c. 844.)

CASE NOTES

Editor's note. — The case below was decided under former Title 2.1 or prior provisions.

Presumptions. — Radar results of a machine that has been calibrated are entitled by statute to a presumption of correctness, and are admissible regardless of whether Commonwealth proves that the specific machine met or exceeded standards established by Division of Purchases and Supplies. White v. Commonwealth, No. 2991-98-3, 2000 Va. App. LEXIS 103 (Ct. of Appeals Feb. 15, 2000).

§ 2.2-1113. Printing management coordination; uniform standards for state forms. — A. The Division may establish criteria and procedures to obtain more economical operation of state printing facilities, provide guidelines to agencies regarding the most beneficial utilization of duplicating and reproduction equipment, and to centralize printing, duplicating and reproduction equipment and services.

B. The Division may set uniform standards for the design, utilization, procurement and inventory of state forms. (1972, c. 503, § 2.1-243.1; 1976, c. 759; 1977, c. 672, §§ 2.1-464, 2.1-465; 2001, c. 844.)

§ 2.2-1114. Regulations as to estimates and requisitions; submission of estimates. — The Division shall prescribe and enforce regulations under which estimates of the needs of the using agencies shall be submitted and requisitions made, and under which contracts for purchases may be made. Estimates of the amount and quality of materials, equipment, supplies, and printing needed by the using agencies shall be submitted at such periods as may be prescribed by the Division. (Code 1950, § 2-250; 1958, c. 124; 1966, c. 677, § 2.1-274; 1977, c. 672, § 2.1-441; 1980, c. 357; 2001, c. 844.)

§ 2.2-1115. Execution of contracts; payment for purchases; violations. — A. All contracts entered into by the Division shall be executed in the name of the Commonwealth.

B. All purchases made by or through the Division shall be paid for in the same manner and out of the same funds as if the purchase had not been made by or through it.

C. The Division shall maintain a system of accounting prescribed by the State Comptroller. All moneys collected by the Division shall be paid promptly into the state treasury and reported to the State Comptroller for appropriate credit.

D. The Comptroller shall not issue any warrant upon any voucher issued by any using agency covering the purchase of any material, equipment or supplies, when such purchases are made in violation of any provision of this article.

E. Intentional violations of the centralized purchasing provisions of this article by any using agency, continued after notice from the Governor to desist, shall constitute malfeasance in office, and shall subject the officer responsible for violation to suspension or removal from office, as may be provided by law in other cases of malfeasance. (Code 1950, §§ 2-215, 2-216, 2-253, 2-263, 2-264; 1958, c. 124; 1966, c. 677, §§ 2.1-240, 2.1-241, 2.1-277, 2.1-289, 2.1-290; 1977, c. 672, §§ 2.1-438, 2.1-444, 2.1-455, 2.1-456; 1984, c. 612; 2001, c. 844.)

§ 2.2-1116. Purchase of products and services of state correctional facilities. — The provisions of this article shall be subject to the provisions of Title 53.1 relating to the products and services of state correctional facilities required by state departments, institutions, and agencies, and the purchase of the same through the Division. (Code 1950, § 2-268; 1958, c. 124; 1966, c. 677, § 2.1-294; 1977, c. 672, § 2.1-453; 2001, c. 844.)

§ 2.2-1117. Purchases from Department for the Blind and Vision Impaired; violation. — Unless exempted by the Division, all such services, articles and commodities as (i) are required for purchase by the Division or by any person authorized to make purchases on behalf of the Commonwealth and its departments, agencies and institutions; (ii) are performed or produced by persons, or in schools or workshops, under the supervision of the Virginia Department for the Blind and Vision Impaired; (iii) are available for sale by such Department; and (iv) conform to the standards established by the Division shall be purchased from such Department at the fair market price without competitive procurement. When convenience or emergency requires it the Commissioner of the Department for the Blind and Vision Impaired may, upon request of the purchasing officer, release the purchasing officer from the obligations of this section. Any purchasing officer convicted of a violation of this section shall be guilty of a Class 1 misdemeanor. (Code 1950, § 2-259.2; 1954, c. 71; 1958, c. 124; 1966, c. 677, § 2.1-285; 1977, c. 672, § 2.1-450; 1982, c. 647; 1984, c. 498; 2001, c. 844.)

Cross references. — As to punishment for Class 1 misdemeanors, see § 18.2-11.

§ 2.2-1118. Purchases from nonprofit sheltered workshops of Virginia serving the handicapped. — A. The Division shall publish annually a list of materials, supplies, services and equipment which, in the opinion of the Division, would be beneficial to the Commonwealth to procure from a sheltered workshop. The list shall exclude items currently produced by schools or workshops under the supervision of the Virginia Department for the Blind and Vision Impaired or by inmates confined in state correctional institutions.

B. Any item or service included on the list required by subsection A may be purchased by the Division from nonprofit sheltered workshops serving the handicapped without competitive procurement, if the Division is satisfied that the items and services (i) can be purchased within ten percent of their fair market value, (ii) will be of acceptable quality, and (iii) can be produced in sufficient quantities within the time required.

C. Nothing in this section shall prohibit the Division from amending the list required under subsection A by adding categories to the list after it has been published. (1978, c. 24, § 2.1-450.1; 1982, c. 647; 1987, c. 72; 2001, c. 844.)

§ 2.2-1119. Cases in which purchasing through Division not mandatory. — A. Unless otherwise ordered by the Governor, the purchasing of materials, equipment, supplies and nonprofessional services through the Division shall not be mandatory in the following cases:

1. Materials, equipment and supplies incident to the performance of a contract for labor or for labor and materials;
2. Manuscripts, maps, audiovisual materials, books, pamphlets and periodicals purchased for the use of The Library of Virginia or any other library in the Commonwealth supported in whole or in part by state funds;
3. Perishable articles, provided that no article except fresh vegetables, fish, eggs or milk shall be considered perishable within the meaning of this subdivision, unless so classified by the Division;
4. Materials, equipment and supplies needed by the Commonwealth Transportation Board; however, this exception may include, office stationery and supplies, office equipment, janitorial equipment and supplies, and coal and fuel oil for heating purposes shall not be included except when authorized in writing by the Division;
5. Materials, equipment and supplies needed by the Virginia Alcoholic Beverage Control Board; however, this exception may include, office stationery and supplies, office equipment, janitorial equipment and supplies, and coal and fuel oil for heating purposes shall not be included except when authorized in writing by the Division;
6. Binding and rebinding of the books and other literary materials of libraries operated by the Commonwealth or under its authority;
7. Printing of the records of the Supreme Court; and
8. Financial services, including without limitation, underwriters, financial advisors, investment advisors and banking services.

B. Telecommunications and information technology goods and services of every description shall be procured as provided by § 2.2-2012. (Code 1950, § 2-260; 1958, c. 124; 1966, c. 677, § 2.1-286; 1970, c. 225; 1977, c. 672,

§ 2.1-451; 1982, c. 647; 1988, c. 140; 1994, c. 64; 2001, c. 844; 2003, cc. 895, 981, 1021.)

Editor's note. — Acts 2003, c. 895, cl. 3, provides: "That the provisions of this act shall not in any way amend or affect existing delegations of telecommunications procurement authority granted by the Department of Information Technology to public bodies or inhibit the ability of the Department to grant future delegations of such authority."

For provisions of Acts 2003, cc. 981 and 1021, cls. 4 to 16, reflecting the intent of the General Assembly to provide for the consolidation of the procurement and operational functions of information technology for state agencies in a single agency, and related transitional and other provisions, see the Editor's note at § 2.2-2005.

§ 2.2-1120. Direct purchases by using agencies and certain charitable corporations and private nonprofit institutions of higher education. — A. The Division shall have the power, by general rule or special order, to permit purchases of any material, equipment, supplies, printing or nonprofessional services of every description to be made by any using agency directly, and not through the Division, whenever it appears to the satisfaction of the Division that by reason of the excess transportation costs, a lower price with equal quality can be obtained by the using agency, or for any other reason, which in the judgment of the Division warrants an exemption.

B. The Division shall allow corporations operating in Virginia and granted tax exempt status under § 501(c)(3) of the Internal Revenue Code and operating as clinics for the indigent and uninsured that are organized for the delivery of primary health care services (i) as federally qualified health centers designated by the Health Care Financing Administration or (ii) at a reduced or sliding fee scale or without charge, to purchase directly from contracts established for state agencies and public bodies by the Division or, provided it is not prohibited by the terms of the procurement, through participation by the Division in other cooperative procurements.

C. The Division shall allow organizations that provide transportation services in Virginia and receive funding from the Federal Transit Administration or the Commonwealth Transportation Fund to purchase directly from contracts established for state agencies and public bodies by the Division. The Department of Rail and Public Transportation shall assist the Division in establishing and maintaining a list of organizations that shall be authorized to make purchases pursuant to this subsection.

D. The Division shall allow private institutions of higher education chartered in Virginia and granted tax-exempt status under § 501(c)(3) of the Internal Revenue Code to purchase directly from contracts established for state agencies and public bodies by the Division. (Code 1950, § 2-257; 1958, c. 124; 1966, c. 677, § 2.1-281; 1977, c. 672, § 2.1-447; 1980, c, 357; 1988, c. 140; 2001, c. 844; 2002, c. 491; 2003, c. 225; 2004, c. 484; 2006, c. 582.)

Editor's note. — Acts 2006, c. 582, cl. 2, provides: "That the Division shall seek the assistance of the Council of Independent Colleges in Virginia in establishing and maintaining a list of private educational institutions authorized to make purchases pursuant to the provisions of this act."

§ **2.2-1121:** Repealed by Acts 2002, c. 579.

Cross references. — As to procurement of telecommunications goods and services and information technology goods and services, see § 2.2-2012.

§ 2.2-1122. Aid and cooperation of Division may be sought by any public body or public broadcasting station in making purchases; use

of facilities of Virginia Distribution Center; Board to furnish list of public broadcasting stations to Division; services to certain volunteer organizations. — A. Virginia public broadcasting stations as defined in § 2.2-2427, and public bodies as defined in § 2.2-4300 who are empowered to purchase material, equipment, and supplies of any kind, may purchase through the Division. When any such public body, public broadcasting station, or duly authorized officer requests the Division to obtain bids for any materials, equipment and supplies, and the bids have been obtained by the Division, the Division may award the contract to the lowest responsible bidder, and the public body or public broadcasting station shall be bound by the contract. The Division shall set forth in the purchase order that the materials, equipment and supplies be delivered to, and that the bill be rendered and forwarded to, the public body or public broadcasting station. Any such bill shall be a valid and enforceable claim against the public body or public broadcasting station requesting the bids.

B. The Division may make available to any public body or public broadcasting station the facilities of the Virginia Distribution Center maintained by the Division; however, the furnishing of any such services or supplies shall not limit or impair any services or supplies normally rendered any department, division, institution or agency of the Commonwealth.

C. The Virginia Public Broadcasting Board shall furnish to the Division a list of public broadcasting stations in Virginia for the purposes of this section.

D. The services or supplies authorized by this section shall extend to any volunteer fire company or volunteer rescue squad that is recognized by an ordinance to be a part of the safety program of a county, city or town when the services or supplies are sought through and approved by the governing body of such county, city or town. (1982, c. 647, § 2.1-454.1; 1984, c. 746; 1997, c. 858; 2001, c. 844.)

§ 2.2-1123. Acquisition of surplus materials from the United States government. — The Division is designated as the agency of state government responsible for acquiring surplus personal property, including but not limited to materials, supplies, and equipment, by purchase, gift, or otherwise, from the United States government or any of its agencies for distribution to departments, agencies, institutions and political subdivisions of the Commonwealth and to eligible, nonprofit, nongovernmental organizations for use in the organizations' activities within the Commonwealth. The acquisitions shall be made, when in the judgment of the Division, it is advantageous to the Commonwealth to do so. The property may be acquired for storage and subsequent distribution or for immediate distribution. The Division may collect the purchase price of any such property, if applicable, and service charges sufficient to defray the costs of carrying out this program from entities to which it distributes the property. The Division shall publish a plan that meets the requirements of the Federal Property and Administrative Services Act of 1949, as it may be amended from time to time, and any similar federal statutes requiring such plan.

The Division may, by general rule or special order, delegate to any using department, agency, institution, political subdivision, or eligible, nonprofit, nongovernmental organization the authority to acquire such property directly from the federal government rather than through the Division, whenever the Division determines that it is advantageous to do so. The Division may prescribe regulations for the acquisition of such property by entities to which it delegates its authority. (1984, c. 746, § 2.1-445.1; 2001, c. 844.)

§ 2.2-1124. Disposition of surplus materials. — A. "Surplus materials" means personal property including, but not limited to, materials, supplies, equipment, and recyclable items, but shall not include property as defined in § 2.2-1147 that is determined to be surplus. Surplus materials shall not include finished products that a mental health or mental retardation facility sells for the benefit of its patients or residents, provided that (i) most of the supplies, equipment, or products have been donated to the facility; (ii) the patients or residents of the facility have substantially altered the supplies, equipment, or products in the course of occupational or other therapy; and (iii) the substantial alterations have resulted in a finished product.

B. The Department shall establish procedures for the disposition of surplus materials from departments, divisions, institutions, and agencies of the Commonwealth. Such procedures shall:

1. Permit surplus materials to be transferred between or sold to departments, divisions, institutions, or agencies of the Commonwealth;

2. Permit surplus materials to be sold to Virginia charitable corporations granted tax-exempt status under § 501(c)(3) of the Internal Revenue Code and operating as clinics for the indigent and uninsured that are organized for the delivery of primary health care services (i) as federally qualified health centers designated by the Health Care Financing Administration or (ii) at a reduced or sliding fee scale or without charge;

3. Permit public sales or auctions, including online public auctions, provided that the procedures provide for sale to all political subdivisions and any volunteer rescue squad or volunteer fire department established pursuant to § 15.2-955 any surplus materials prior to such public sale or auction;

4. Permit surplus motor vehicles to be sold prior to public sale or auction to local social service departments for the purpose of resale at cost to TANF recipients;

5. Permit surplus materials to be sold to Virginia charitable corporations granted tax-exempt status under § 501(c)(3) of the Internal Revenue Code and operating as children's homes;

6. Permit donations to political subdivisions of the Commonwealth under the circumstances specified in this section;

7. Permit other methods of disposal when (a) the cost of the sale will exceed the potential revenue to be derived therefrom or (b) the surplus material is not suitable for sale;

8. Permit any dog especially trained for police work to be sold at an appropriate price to the handler who last was in control of the dog, which sale shall not be deemed a violation of the State and Local Government Conflict of Interests Act (§ 2.2-3100 et seq.);

9. Permit the transfer of surplus clothing to an appropriate department, division, institution, or agency of the Commonwealth for distribution to needy individuals by and through local social services boards;

10. Encourage the recycling of paper products, beverage containers, electronics, and used motor oil;

11. Require the proceeds from any sale or recycling of surplus materials be promptly deposited into the state treasury in accordance with § 2.2-1802 and report the deposit to the State Comptroller;

12. Permit donations of surplus computers and related equipment to public schools in the Commonwealth and Virginia charitable corporations granted tax-exempt status under § 501(c)(3) of the Internal Revenue Code and providing services to persons with disabilities, at-risk youths, or low-income families. For the purposes of this subdivision, "at-risk youths" means school-age children approved eligible to receive free or reduced price meals in the federally funded lunch program;

13. Permit surplus materials to be transferred or sold, prior to public sale or auction, to public television stations located in the state and other nonprofit organizations approved for the distribution of federal surplus materials;

14. Permit a public institution of higher education to dispose of its surplus materials at the location where the surplus materials are held and to retain any proceeds from such disposal, provided that the institution meets the conditions prescribed in subsection B of § 23-38.88 and § 23-38.112 (regardless of whether or not the institution has been granted any authority under Subchapter 3 (§ 23-38.91 et seq.) of Chapter 4.10 of Title 23); and

15. Require, to the extent practicable, the recycling and disposal of computers and other information technology assets. Additionally, for computers or information technology assets that may contain confidential state data or personal identifying information of citizens of the Commonwealth, the Department shall ensure all policies for the transfer or other disposition of computers or information technology assets are consistent with data and information security policies developed by the Virginia Information Technologies Agency.

C. The Department shall dispose of surplus materials pursuant to the procedures established in subsection B or permit any department, division, institution, or agency of the Commonwealth to dispose of its surplus materials consistent with the procedures so established. No surplus materials shall be disposed of without prior consent of the head of the department, division, institution, or agency of the Commonwealth in possession of such surplus materials or the Governor.

D. Departments, divisions, institutions, or agencies of the Commonwealth or the Governor may donate surplus materials only under the following circumstances:

1. Emergencies declared in accordance with § 44-146.18:2 or 44-146.28;

2. As set forth in the budget bill as defined by § 2.2-1509, provided that (a) the budget bill contains a description of the surplus materials, the method by which the surplus materials shall be distributed, and the anticipated recipients, and (b) such information shall be provided by the Department to the Department of Planning and Budget in sufficient time for inclusion in the budget bill;

3. When the market value of the surplus materials, which shall be donated for a public purpose, is less than $500; however, the total market value of all surplus materials so donated by any department, division, institution, or agency shall not exceed 25 percent of the revenue generated by such department's, division's, institution's, or agency's sale of surplus materials in the fiscal year, except these limits shall not apply in the case of surplus computer equipment and related items donated to Virginia public schools; or

4. During a local emergency, upon written request of the head of a local government or a political subdivision in the Commonwealth to the head of a department, division, institution, or agency.

E. On or before October 1 of each year, the Department shall prepare, and file with the Secretary of the Commonwealth, a plan that describes the expected disposition of surplus materials in the upcoming fiscal year pursuant to subdivision B 6. (1996, cc. 935, 978, § 2.1-457.2; 1999, cc. 159, 578, 629, 911; 2000, cc. 615, 636, 661; 2001, c. 844; 2004, c. 670; 2005, cc. 933, 945; 2006, cc. 468, 493; 2007, c. 701.)

Cross references. — As to exemption of certain motor vehicles acquired from the centralized fleet of motor vehicles controlled by the Commonwealth Transportation Commissioner and sold or transferred to TANF recipients or former recipients from the provisions of §§ 2.2-4300 et seq., 2.2-1124, 2.2-1153, 2.2-1156, and 2.2-1177, see § 63.2-611 D.

The 2007 amendments. — The 2007 amendment by c. 701 inserted "electronics" following "containers" in subdivision B 10; and added subdivision B 15.

§ 2.2-1125. Proceeds from the sale or recycling of surplus materials. — A. The proceeds from the sale or recycling of surplus materials pursuant to

§ 2.2-1124 shall promptly be deposited into the state treasury and the deposit reported to the State Comptroller, along with a statement of total proceeds and the amount of the proceeds derived from the sale or recycling of surplus materials purchased in whole or in part from general fund appropriations.

B. At the end of each fiscal quarter, the State Comptroller shall (i) determine the total proceeds derived from the sale of surplus materials purchased in whole or in part from general fund appropriations and direct the State Treasurer to transfer fifty percent of the total of such proceeds to the Conservation Resources Fund and (ii) provide copies of the reports furnished to him pursuant to subsection A, or summaries thereof, to the Department of Planning and Budget.

C. Based on such reports, or summaries, the Department of Planning and Budget, pursuant to its authority in the appropriation act, may increase general fund appropriations to any department, division, institution, or agency of the Commonwealth by the amount of available proceeds derived from the sale or recycling of surplus materials pursuant to § 2.2-1124. The department, division, institution, or agency of the Commonwealth may use the additional appropriations to purchase materials, supplies, or equipment, or to defray the cost of disposing of surplus materials to the extent permitted pursuant to § 2.2-1124.

D. Departments, divisions, institutions, or agencies may retain the full net profits from the sale of recycled materials provided that a report is filed with the State Comptroller on or before October 1 of each year.

E. Departments, divisions, institutions, or agencies meeting management standards prescribed by the Governor may retain the net proceeds from the surplus materials sold pursuant to § 2.2-1124. Such retention shall be effective on July 1 following the determination that the department, division, institution, or agency meets the management standards. (1996, cc. 935, 978, § 2.1-457.3; 2001, c. 844.)

§§ **2.2-1126, 2.2-1127:** Repealed by Acts 2004, c. 650.

Editor's note. — Acts 2004, c. 650, cl. 3, provides: "That the Division of Legislative Automated Systems shall notify the Governor, the Lieutenant Governor, the Clerk of the House of the Delegates, the Clerk of the Senate, and the Law Librarian of the University of Virginia that the automatic distribution of hard copies of annual and biennial reports pursuant to § 2.2-1127 has been replaced by an on-demand electronic notification and report retrieval system available from the General Assembly's website. The Division shall also notify the members of the General Assembly of the availability of the electronic notification and report retrieval system and the additional option of receiving hardcopies of reports by request."

§ **2.2-1128. Sale of state flag.** — The Division shall have available at all times flags of the Commonwealth, to be offered for sale to the public in such manner and cost as the Division may determine. (1977, c. 672, § 2.1-468; 2001, c. 844.)

Article 4.

Division Of Engineering And Buildings.

§ **2.2-1129. Division of Engineering and Buildings.** — A. Within the Department shall be established the Division of Engineering and Buildings (the "Division"), which shall exercise the powers and duties described in this article.

B. The Division shall have charge of all public buildings, grounds and all other property at the seat of government not placed in the charge of others, and shall protect such properties from depredations and injury.

C. Except as provided in § 2.2-1130, the Division shall have custody, control and supervision of the Virginia War Memorial Carillon.

D. To execute the duties imposed by this article, the Division may obtain information and assistance from other state agencies and institutions. (Code 1950, § 2-77.6; 1966, cc. 55, 677, §§ 2-65.1, 2.1-82.1, 2.1-103; 1970, c. 202; 1974, c. 27; 1976, c. 125; 1977, c. 672, §§ 2.1-480, 2.1-481, 2.1-492; 2000, cc. 599, 612; 2001, c. 844.)

§ 2.2-1130. Care of Virginia War Memorial Carillon. — A. Notwithstanding the provisions of subsections B and C of § 2.2-1129, the Director of the Department and the City of Richmond shall enter into an agreement that would allow the City to permit the use of or access to the Virginia War Memorial Carillon for such short-term events as the City deems appropriate. The agreement (i) may allow the City to charge and collect a fee for such use and to retain any such fee, and (ii) shall require the City to provide a report by December 1 of each year to the Director of the Department, in a form approved by the Director, detailing (a) the funds collected by the City for use of the Carillon for the preceding year; (b) the funds made available to the City from all sources; and (c) the City's expenditures for upkeep, maintenance, and improvement of the facility.

B. Notwithstanding the provisions of subsection D of § 2.2-1156 or any other law to the contrary, the proceeds from the lease or other conveyance of an interest in the Virginia War Memorial Carillon by the Department shall be paid to the City to be applied with other City funds for the cost of upkeep, maintenance, and improvement of the Virginia War Memorial Carillon. The proceeds are hereby appropriated and shall be paid by the Comptroller to the City as soon as practicable after receipt by the Commonwealth.

C. All funds retained by the City or transferred to the City in accordance with this section and all fees collected by the City from use of or access to the Virginia War Memorial Carillon shall be paid into the City's treasury to the credit of a special fund that shall be used by the City solely for the upkeep, maintenance, and improvement of the Virginia War Memorial Carillon. Use of the special fund for any other purpose is prohibited.

D. Nothing in this section shall abrogate the obligations of the City of Richmond to provide for the upkeep and maintenance of the Carillon. (1966, c. 55, §§ 2-65.1, 2.1-82.1; 1970, c. 202; 1974, c. 27; 1976, c. 125; 1977, c. 672, § 2.1-481; 2000, cc. 599, 612; 2001, c. 844.)

§ 2.2-1131. Maintenance and utilization standards. — The Division may develop, in cooperation with state institutions and agencies concerned, maintenance and utilization standards for state buildings, and provide functional direction and service to institutions and agencies of the state government with respect to their policies, practices and administration of buildings and grounds. The standards shall include, but are not limited to, advice and appropriate provisions for the installation and utilization of approved water-conservation devices throughout the facilities owned by the Commonwealth. The Division shall review all maintenance and utilization standards and plans of state institutions and agencies. (1966, c. 55, §§ 2-65.1, 2.1-82.1; 1970, c. 202; 1974, c. 27; 1976, c. 125; 1977, c. 672, § 2.1-482; 1978, cc. 139, 770; 2001, c. 844.)

§ 2.2-1131.1. Establishment of performance standards for the use of property. — A. The Division shall establish performance standards for the acquisition, lease and disposition of property and for the management and utilization of such property at the individual agency and statewide levels to maximize the use of property for which it is held. For the purposes of this section *"property"* means the same as that term is defined in § 2.2-1147.

B. The head of each state agency or institution shall ensure that property assets held by the agency on behalf of the Commonwealth are managed in accordance with the standards set by the Division. State public institutions of higher education that have delegated authority to manage aspects of their real property usage and have signed a memorandum of understanding with the Secretary of Administration related to such delegated authority shall be deemed in compliance with the standards set by the Division as long as they abide by the terms of the memorandum of understanding. Standards established in accordance with the memorandum of understanding shall be reported to the Division by October 1 of each year.

C. The Division may take appropriate actions, including assuring compliance with the standards set by the Division and entering into leasing arrangements or other contracts, to ensure that asset usage by each state agency is proper and cost effective.

D. By December 1, 2004, the Division shall submit a report to the Governor and the General Assembly on the performance standards established pursuant to subsection A. Thereafter, the Division shall prepare, no later than November 30 of each year, reports to the Governor and the General Assembly on the implementation and effectiveness of this program. (2004, cc. 684, 750.)

§ **2.2-1132. Administration of capital outlay construction; exception for certain educational institutions.** — A. The Division shall provide assistance in the administration of capital outlay construction projects set forth in the appropriation act, other than highway construction undertaken by the Department of Transportation and the acquisition or improvement of specialized cargo-handling equipment and related port infrastructure including, but not limited to, port construction, renovation, and demolition that is required in a timely manner to meet market demands to enhance commerce through the Virginia Port Authority, the review and approval of plans and specifications, and acceptance of completed projects.

B. The Division may establish standards, as needed, for construction by the Commonwealth and may, with the advice of the Attorney General, establish standard contract provisions and procedures for the procurement and administration of construction and for the procurement and administration of architectural and engineering services relating to construction, which shall be used by all departments, agencies and institutions of the Commonwealth. All departments, agencies and institutions of the Commonwealth shall ensure that the design and construction of state-owned buildings comply with the standards governing energy use and efficiency established by the Division. The standards may provide for incentive contracting that offers a contractor whose bid is accepted the opportunity to share in any cost savings realized by the Commonwealth when project costs are reduced by the contractor, without affecting project quality, during construction of the project. The fee, if any, charged by the project engineer or architect for determining the cost savings shall be paid as a separate cost and shall not be calculated as part of any cost savings.

C. Notwithstanding any standards established by the Division or law to the contrary except as provided in this subsection, any public institution of higher education that has in effect a signed memorandum of understanding with the Secretary of Administration regarding participation in the nongeneral fund decentralization program as set forth in the appropriation act may enter into contracts for specific construction projects without the preliminary review and approval of the Division, provided such institutions are in compliance with the requirements of the Virginia Public Procurement Act (§ 2.2-4300 et seq.) and utilize the general terms and conditions for those forms of procurement approved by the Division and the Office of the Attorney General. The authority granted in this subsection shall only become effective if the institution meets the conditions prescribed in subsection B of § 23-38.88. The Secretary of Administration shall establish guidelines to assist institutions in evaluating alternative project delivery methods prior to entering into a contract. For projects constructed pursuant to this subsection, the responsibility of the Division of Engineering and Buildings shall be as set forth in subsection C of § 36-98.1.

For purposes of this section, "construction" shall include new construction, reconstruction, renovation, restoration, major repair, demolition and all similar work upon buildings and ancillary facilities owned or to be acquired by the Commonwealth. It shall not include buildings or other facilities ancillary to the use of state highways that are located within the right-of-way of any state highway, or assets for use by the Virginia Port Authority within the boundaries of property owned or leased by the Virginia Port Authority. (1982, c. 647, § 2.1-483.1; 1984, c. 641; 1994, c. 924; 1997, c. 488; 2001, c. 844; 2005, cc. 933, 945; 2006, c. 939.)

Editor's note. — Acts 2006, c. 939, cl. 3, provides: "That the Department of Mines, Minerals and Energy, working with the Department of General Services, the State Council on Higher Education, and representatives of other agencies and institutions that construct and operate facilities shall analyze current energy performance standards that agencies and institutions use in facility design, make recommendations for changes to the current design and construction practices that will enhance energy performance and efficiency, and research facility energy performance and efficiency benchmarks and metrics that may be used to measure facility performance."

Acts 2006, c. 939, cl. 4, provides: "That the State Corporation Commission and Secretary of Natural Resources shall develop a proposal for a coordinated review of permits for an energy facility requiring (i) an environmental permit that is subject to issuance by any agency or board within the Secretariat of Natural Resources and (ii) a certificate of public convenience and necessity that is subject to issuance by the Commission. The State Corporation Commission and Secretary of Natural Resources shall submit their proposal for a coordinated review process, together with a listing of the types of projects and permits to be reviewed under the coordinated process, an analysis of the potential costs and benefits of such a process, and any legislation required to establish the coordinated review process, to the Governor and the chairmen of the House Committee on Commerce and Labor, the House Committee on Agriculture, Chesapeake and Natural Resources, the Senate Committee on Commerce and Labor, and the Senate Committee on Agriculture, Conservation and Natural Resources by December 1, 2006."

§ 2.2-1133. Use of value engineering. — A. The Division shall ensure that value engineering is employed for any capital project costing more than five million dollars. Value engineering may also be used for any project costing five million dollars or less. For purposes of this section, "value engineering" means a systematic process of review and analysis of a capital project by a team of persons not originally involved in the project. Such team, which shall include appropriate professionals licensed in accordance with Chapter 4 (§ 54.1-400 et seq.) of Title 54.1, may offer suggestions that would improve project quality and reduce total project cost by combining or eliminating inefficient or expensive parts or steps in the original proposal or by totally redesigning the project using different technologies, materials, or methods.

B. The review developed pursuant to subsection A shall be compiled in a value engineering report and submitted to the Division. Each item included in the value engineering report shall have a status designation of accepted, declined, or accepted as modified. The Division, within 45 days, must approve the value engineering report before the project may move to the next phase of design. For projects that (i) are designed utilizing either the design-build or construction manager at risk construction delivery method, (ii) have the value engineering process as an integral component, and (iii) have been granted an appropriate waiver by the Director of the Department of General Services, a representative designated by the Director shall participate in all cost savings decisions before modifications to the design may be finalized.

C. The Director of the Department may waive the requirements of this section for any proposed capital project for compelling reasons. Any waiver shall be in writing, state the reasons for the waiver, and apply only to a single capital project. On or before September 15 of each year, the Director of the Department shall report to the Governor and the General Assembly on the (i) number and value of the capital projects where value engineering was employed and (ii) identity of the capital projects for which a waiver of the requirements of this section was granted, including a statement of the compelling reasons for granting the waiver. The report shall cover projects completed or for which a waiver was granted within the previous fiscal year.

D. Notwithstanding any law to the contrary, the provisions of this section shall apply to public institutions of higher education in Virginia. (1994, cc. 442, 829, § 2.1-483.1:1; 1996, c. 553; 1997, c. 230; 1998, c. 207; 2001, c. 844; 2008, c. 370.)

The 2008 amendments. — The 2008 amendment by c. 370 added subsection B and redesignated former subsections B and C as subsections C and D.

§ **2.2-1134. Assistance to the Design-Build/Construction Management Review Board.** — The Director of the Division or his designee shall serve as a member of the Design-Build/Construction Management Review Board (the Review Board) created pursuant to § 2.2-2404. The Division shall provide staff support to the Review Board in the conduct of its duties in accordance with § 2.2-2405. (1996, c. 962, § 2.1-483.1:2; 2001, c. 844.)

§ **2.2-1135. Information on equipment utilizing wood wastes.** — The Division shall assemble and maintain information relevant to a determination by any department, agency, or institution regarding the suitability of using a central boiler or other heating equipment that is fueled by wood wastes, including but not limited to the (i) identity of manufacturers and suppliers of wood waste handling and burning equipment, (ii) capital and operating costs of such equipment, (iii) associated air emissions and solid waste disposal requirements, and (iv) fuel storage requirements. The information shall be distributed to any department, agency, or institution with a construction project specifying a central boiler or heating plant, and to personnel involved in the procurement and administration of architectural and engineering services relating to such construction project. For purposes of this section, *"wood wastes"* means raw wood by-products from wood processing and wood product manufacturing industries, including sawdust, chips, bark, and planer shavings. (1993, c. 691, § 2.1-483.2; 2001, c. 844.)

§ **2.2-1136. Review of easements; maintenance of real property records.** — A. The Division shall review all deeds, leases and contractual agreements with utilities to serve state institutions or agencies that require the approval of the Governor, as well as all easements and rights-of-way granted by institutions and agencies to public and private utilities.

B. The Division shall be responsible for the maintenance of real property records of all state institutions and agencies, except records of real property acquired by the Department of Transportation for the construction of highways, and may have such boundary, topographic and other maps prepared as may be necessary. (1966, c. 55, §§ 2-65.1, 2.1-82.1; 1970, c. 202; 1974, c. 27; 1976, c. 125; 1977, c. 672, § 2.1-484; 1978, c. 770; 2001, c. 844.)

§ 2.2-1137. Location, construction or lease of state consolidated office buildings. — Subject to the authority of the Virginia Public Buildings Board, the Division shall be responsible for the location and construction or lease of state consolidated office buildings at the seat of government and throughout the Commonwealth for joint use by state agencies, departments and institutions. (1966, c. 55, §§ 2-65.1, 2.1-82.1; 1970, c. 202; 1974, c. 27; 1976, c. 125; 1977, c. 672, § 2.1-485; 2001, c. 844.)

§ 2.2-1138. Planning and construction by Division; exemption. — A. The Division of Engineering and Buildings shall, subject to written approval of the Governor:

1. Prepare and, when necessary to meet changing conditions, amend a long-range site plan for the location of all state buildings, and related improvements, in Capitol Square and its immediate environs, and for such other areas providing comparable facilities for the seat of government in or adjacent to the City of Richmond as the Governor shall direct;
2. Acquire with funds appropriated for that purpose the necessary land for effectuation of the plan; and
3. Direct and control the execution of all authorized projects for the construction of state buildings and related improvements in or adjacent to the City of Richmond.

B. The Governor may exempt from the provisions of subsection A those buildings and improvements that, in his opinion, should be planned and constructed under the direction of other state agencies or institutions or included in site plans prepared by such other agencies or institutions.

C. No building for state use shall be erected or acquired nor other property acquired for state use, in Capitol Square and its immediate environs, or in such other areas as may be included in the site plan required by subsection A unless it has been approved by the Governor as conforming to the site plan. (Code 1950, §§ 2-77.2, 2-77.3, 2-77.4; 1966, cc. 55, 677, §§ 2.1-99, 2.1-100, 2.1-102; 1977, c. 672, §§ 2.1-489, 2.1-490, 2.1-491; 1979, c. 234; 2001, c. 844.)

Cross references. — As to the Capitol Square Preservation Council, see § 30-193 et seq.

§ 2.2-1139. Transfer of funds; acceptance of donations. — The Governor may transfer to the Department for use by the Division funds appropriated to any state department, agency or institution for the construction, alteration, reconstruction and repair of any building to be erected or acquired for the use of such department, institutional agency, or for the acquisition of land for such building, or for planning, architectural, engineering or other studies in connection therewith, and may accept funds donated for such purposes. (Code 1950, § 2-77.7; 1966, cc. 55, 677, § 2.1-104; 1977, c. 672, § 2.1-493; 2001, c. 844.)

§ 2.2-1140. Assignment of office space. — The Division shall be responsible for the assignment of office space to agencies at the seat of government and buildings under control of the Division, and for the establishment of standards for the utilization and furnishing of such space. (1966, c. 55, § 2-65.1, 2.1-82.1; 1970, c. 202; 1974, c. 27; 1976, c. 125; 1977, c. 672, § 2.1-495; 2001, c. 844.)

§ 2.2-1141. Purchase of furniture for state buildings; repairs to buildings and furniture; surplus furniture. — The Division shall cause to be purchased through the Division of Purchases and Supply with the approval of the Governor, all furniture required for the buildings within the master site plan of Capitol Square, except those assigned for use by agencies and departments. The Division shall have all repairs made to either buildings or furniture thereof, as may be approved by the Governor. The cost of the repairs and furniture shall be paid with funds approved by the Governor. The Division shall declare surplus that furniture that may no longer be satisfactorily used. (Code 1950, § 2-67; 1966, c. 677, § 2.1-85; 1972, c. 763; 1977, c. 672, § 2.1-496; 2001, c. 844.)

§ 2.2-1142. Furniture for Executive Mansion. — The Division shall requisition for the Executive Mansion the furniture required by the Governor, and cause to be sold such old furniture as the Governor may direct, taking care not to exceed appropriated sums therefor, in addition to the proceeds of old furniture sold. An account both of the sales and purchases shall be returned to the Comptroller before any warrant shall issue for any part of the sum appropriated. The warrant shall be only so much as by the account appears to be proper. (Code 1950, § 2-69; 1966, c. 677, § 2.1-87; 1970, c. 260; 1977, c. 672, § 2.1-497; 2001, c. 844.)

§ 2.2-1143. Services for Capitol and other state facilities. — The Division shall contract for water, electricity, gas, sewer service, fuel for heating, and such other services required to serve the facilities within the master site plan of Capitol Square and for such other facilities as the Governor may designate. The cost of the services shall be paid out of funds appropriated for that purpose. (Code 1950, § 2-70; 1966, c. 677, § 2.1-88; 1972, c. 763; 1974, c. 27; 1977, c. 672, § 2.1-498; 2001, c. 844.)

§ 2.2-1144. Control of Capitol Square and other property at seat of government. — A. The Division, under the direction and control of the Governor, shall have control of the Capitol Square with the expense of the maintenance and control to be paid out of the fund appropriated for that purpose. The Division shall keep the keys of the Capitol Building and shall take charge of all the rooms in the Capitol Building, except in those areas under the control of the legislature, the public grounds and all other property at the seat of government not placed in specific charge of others. The Division shall have no control or responsibility with respect to the old and new Senate chambers, the old and new halls of the House of Delegates, the Rotunda, the offices of the Clerks of the Senate and House of Delegates, the legislative committee rooms, the enrolling office, or any other area specifically designated as legislative space. The Division shall do such work and make such repairs for the respective bodies of the General Assembly requested by the clerks thereof with appropriate reimbursement of expenses to the Division.

B. The Division shall have all the furniture and the rooms in the Capitol, other than the rooms excepted in subsection A, the open parts of the Capitol, the public grounds, and all other property at the seat of government not placed in the charge of others, kept in proper order at all times. (Code 1950, §§ 2-71, 2-73; 1966, c. 677, §§ 2.1-89, 2.1-91; 1974 c. 27; 1977, c. 672, §§ 2.1-499, 2.1-500; 2001, c. 844.)

Cross references. — As to the Capitol Square Preservation Council, see § 30-193 et seq.

§ 2.2-1145. Inventory of property and Governor's house; custody of house and property pending election of Governor. — When the term of office of any Governor expires, or he shall die or resign, the Division shall take an inventory of all the public property and furniture in the Governor's house and outbuildings and deliver the inventory to the Comptroller, to be preserved in his office. The Division shall, unless the house is occupied by the Lieutenant Governor, have charge of the house, furniture, and other public property, until a Governor is elected and takes possession. (Code 1950, § 2-68; 1966, c. 677, § 2.1-86; 1977, c. 672, § 2.1-501; 2001, c. 844.)

§ 2.2-1146. Division may lease certain state property; preparation of leases by Attorney General; disposition of rentals. — The Division, with the prior written approval of the Governor, may lease property owned by the Commonwealth and acquired for the development of the state site plan for permanent state office buildings and related structures and facilities lying near the Capitol Square. All such leases shall be prepared by the Attorney General. The leases may run for such time as prescribed by the Governor and shall be for appropriate rental. All rentals received shall be paid into the general fund of the state treasury. (1962, c. 262, § 2-66.2; 1966, cc. 55, 677, § 2.1-84; 1977, c. 672, § 2.1-503; 2001, c. 844.)

§ 2.2-1147. Definitions. — As used in §§ 2.2-1147.1 through 2.2-1156, unless the context requires a different meaning:

"Institutions" shall include, but not be limited to, any corporation owned by the Commonwealth and subject to the control of the General Assembly.

"Property" shall mean an interest in land and any improvements thereon held by the Commonwealth and under the control of or occupied by any of its departments, agencies or institutions, but shall not include (i) real estate or rights-of-way acquired by the Department of Transportation for the construction of highways and (ii) ungranted shores of the sea, marsh and meadowlands as defined in § 28.2-1500.

"Recommend," "recommended," or *"recommendation,"* when used with reference to a recommendation by the Department of General Services to the Governor, means to advise either for or against a proposed action. (1968, c. 717, § 2.1-106.1; 1977, c. 672, § 2.1-504; 1978, c. 770; 1984, c. 641; 1995, c. 850; 2001, c. 844; 2002, c. 561.)

§ 2.2-1147.1. Right to breast-feed. — Notwithstanding any other provision of law, a woman may breast-feed her child at any location where that woman would otherwise be allowed on property that is owned, leased or controlled by the Commonwealth as defined in § 2.2-1147. (2002, c. 561.)

§ 2.2-1147.2. Equal access to state-owned or controlled property; Boy Scouts of America and Girl Scouts of the USA. — Notwithstanding any contrary provision of law, general or special, no state department, agency, or institution providing access and opportunity to use real property that is owned, leased, or controlled by the Commonwealth as defined in § 2.2-1147, may deny equal access or a fair opportunity to use such real property to, or otherwise discriminate against, the Boy Scouts of America or the Girl Scouts of the USA. Nothing in this paragraph shall be construed to require any state department, agency, or institution to sponsor the Boy Scouts of America or the Girl Scouts of the USA, or to exempt any such groups from policies governing access to and use of the real property. (2006, c. 57.)

§ 2.2-1148. Approval of actions; conveyances in name of the Commonwealth. — A. All actions to be taken or approvals to be given by the Governor or the Attorney General pursuant to §§ 2.2-1149 through 2.2-1156 may be taken or given by the Governor or his designee, or by the Attorney General or one of his deputies or assistant attorneys general.

B. All conveyances of any interest in property to or from the Commonwealth or any state department or agency or any state institution that is not a corporation, shall be in the name of the Commonwealth and shall designate the department, agency or institution in control or possession of the property in the following manner: "Commonwealth of Virginia, Department of (name of department, agency or institution, or other appropriate name)." All interests in property conveyed to any department, agency or institution of the Commonwealth, whether past or future, is and shall be the property of the Commonwealth. Conveyance of an interest in property on behalf of the Commonwealth by a department, agency or institution other than that which acquired title on behalf of the Commonwealth shall not create a cloud upon the title. (1984, c. 641, § 2.1-504.1; 2001, c. 844.)

§ **2.2-1149. Department to review proposed acquisitions of real property; approval by the Governor; exceptions.** — Notwithstanding any provision of law to the contrary, no state department, agency or institution shall acquire real property by gift, lease, purchase or any other means without following the guidelines adopted by the Department and obtaining the prior approval of the Governor. The Department shall review every proposed acquisition of real property by gift, lease, purchase or any other means by any department, agency or institution of the Commonwealth and recommend either approval or disapproval of the transactions to the Governor based on cost, demonstrated need, and compliance with the Department's guidelines.

The provisions of this section shall not apply to the:

1. Acquisition of real property for open space preservations pursuant to the purposes of § 10.1-1800 and subdivision A 4 of § 10.1-2204, if it does not require as a condition of acceptance, an appropriation of any state funds for the continued maintenance of such property;

2. Acquisition of easements pursuant to the purposes of §§ 10.1-1020 and 10.1-1021 or §§ 10.1-1700, 10.1-1702, and 10.1-1702;

3. Acquisition through the temporary lease or donation of real property for a period of six months or less duration;

4. Acquisition of easements by public institutions of higher education provided that the particular institution meets the conditions prescribed in subsection B of § 23-38.88;

5. Entering into an operating/income lease or a capital lease by a public institution of higher education, for real property to be used for academic purposes, or for real property owned by the institution or a foundation related to the institution to be used for non-academic purposes, in accordance with the institution's land use plan pursuant to § 2.2-1153 provided that (i) the capital lease does not constitute tax-supported debt of the Commonwealth, (ii) the institution meets the conditions prescribed in subsection B of § 23-38.88, and (iii) for purposes of entering into a capital lease, the institution shall have in effect a signed memorandum of understanding with the Secretary of Administration regarding participation in the nongeneral fund decentralization program as set forth in the appropriation act. For the purposes of this subdivision, an operating/income lease or a capital lease shall be determined using generally accepted accounting principles; or

6. Acquisition of real property for the construction, improvement or maintenance of highways and transportation facilities and purposes incidental thereto by the Department of Transportation; however, acquisitions of real property by the Department of Transportation for office space, district offices, residencies, area headquarters, or correctional facilities shall be subject to the Department's review and the Governor's approval. (1984, c. 641, § 2.1-504.2; 1994, c. 474; 2000, c. 748; 2001, c. 844; 2005, cc. 933, 945.)

Editor's note. — Acts 1998, c. 433, cl. 1 provided: "That in the event the Commonwealth Transportation Commissioner determines that an affiliated university foundation of a public college or university can efficiently, effectively, or economically carry out a transportation or development project on behalf of the Department of Transportation on a highway right-of-way which is owned by the Department, the Commissioner may lease, sell, or otherwise exchange the needed right-of-way to an affiliated university foundation on such terms and conditions as the Commissioner determines to be in the public interest.

"That any such project which is carried out by such an affiliated foundation that is related to the construction, improvement, operation, research or maintenance of highway and transportation facilities and purposes incidental thereto is exempt from the capital appropriations process and requirements of § 2.1-504.2 [now § 2.2-1149]."

Acts 2008, c. 879, effective for the biennium ending June 30, 2010, in Item 208 K 4, provides: "Notwithstanding Section 2.2-1149 of the Code of Virginia, Virginia Commonwealth University is authorized to approve operating, income and capital leases in Qatar under policies and procedures developed by the University."

Acts 2008, c. 879, effective for the biennium ending June 30, 2010, in § 4-2.01 a, provides: "a. SOLICITATION AND ACCEPTANCE OF DONATIONS, GIFTS, GRANTS, AND CONTRACTS:

"1. No state agency shall solicit or accept any donation, gift, grant, or contract without the written approval of the Governor except under written guidelines issued by the Governor which provide for the solicitation and acceptance of nongeneral funds.

"2. The Governor may issue policies in writing for procedures which allow state agencies to solicit and accept nonmonetary donations, gifts, grants, or contracts except that donations, gifts and grants of real property shall be subject to § 4-4.00 of this act and § 2.2-1149, Code of Virginia. This provision shall apply to donations, gifts and grants of real property to endowment funds of institutions of higher education, when such endowment funds are held by the institution in its own name and not by a separately incorporated foundation or corporation.

"3. The preceding subdivisions shall not apply to property and equipment acquired and used by a state agency or institution through a lease purchase agreement and subsequently donated to the state agency or institution during or at the expiration of the lease purchase agreement, provided that the lessor is the Virginia College Building Authority.

"4. The use of endowment funds for property, plant or equipment for state-owned facilities is subject to §§ 4-2.03 Indirect Costs, 4-4.01 Capital Projects-General and 4-5.03 Services and Clients of this act."

§ 2.2-1150. Conveyance and transfers of real property by state agencies; approval of Governor and Attorney General; notice to members of General Assembly. — A. When it is deemed to be in the public interest.

1. Property owned by the Commonwealth may be sold, leased, or other interests therein conveyed to political subdivisions, public authorities, or the federal government, for such consideration as is deemed proper; and

2. Property owned by the Commonwealth and held in the possession of a department, agency or institution of the Commonwealth may be transferred to the possession of another department, agency or institution of the Commonwealth by the execution of an agreement between the heads of such departments, agencies or institutions.

B. No transaction authorized by this section shall be made without the prior written recommendation of the Department to the Governor, the written approval of the Governor of the transaction itself, and the approval of the Attorney General as to the form of the instruments prior to execution.

Prior to entering into any negotiations for the conveyance or transfer of any portion of Camp Pendleton or any military property that has been or may be conveyed to the Commonwealth pursuant to a recommendation by the Defense Base Closure Realignment Commission, the Department shall give written notice to all members of the General Assembly within the planning district in which such property is located. If, within 30 days of receipt of the Department's notice, 25 percent of such members of the General Assembly give notice to the Department that they object to such conveyance or that they require additional information, the Department shall conduct a meeting, with written notice thereof to all members of the General Assembly within that planning district, at which the Department and such members shall discuss the proposed transaction. Members of the General Assembly objecting to the proposed transaction after the meeting shall convey their objections in detail to the Governor, who shall consider the objections. Certification of compliance with the foregoing requirements by the Governor in a deed or other instrument conveying or transferring any portion of Camp Pendleton or any such military property, absent knowledge by the purchaser or transferee to the contrary, shall serve as prima facie evidence of compliance with this subsection.

C. Notwithstanding the provisions of subsection B, a public institution of higher education may convey an easement pertaining to any property such institution owns or controls provided that the institution meets the conditions prescribed in subsection B of § 23-38.88 and § 23-38.112 (regardless of whether or not the institution has been granted any authority under Subchapter 3 (§ 23-38.91 et seq.) of Chapter 4.10 of Title 23). (1984, c. 641, §§ 2.1-504.3, 2.1-504.4; 1986, c. 536; 1989, c. 710; 1996, c. 442; 2001, c. 844; 2005, cc. 933, 945; 2007, c. 624.)

The 2007 amendments. — The 2007 amendment by c. 624 added the second paragraph of subsection B.

Michie's Jurisprudence. — For related discussion, see 17 M.J. State, § 12.

§ 2.2-1150.1. Lease or conveyance of any interest in State Police communication tower. — In-kind goods or services received from lease agreements or conveyances of any interest in Department of State Police communication towers received pursuant to §§ 2.2-1150.2 and 2.2-1151, above the costs of the transaction, shall be retained by the department pursuant to § 2.2-1150 and used in the operation, acquisition, maintenance, construction or replacement of communication towers and systems of the department. The provisions of § 2.2-1156 as they apply to lease agreements or conveyances of any interest shall not apply to any transaction undertaken pursuant to this section. (2002, c. 477; 2008, cc. 676, 690.)

Editor's note. — The section above is codified as directed by the Virginia Code Commission.

The 2008 amendments. — The 2008 amendments by cc. 676 and 690 are identical, and deleted "or sites" preceding "received pursuant," inserted "§ 2.2-1150.2 and" preceding "2.2-1151," and deleted "sites" preceding "and systems of the department."

Law Review. — For article surveying developments in real estate and land use law in Virginia from June 1, 2001 through June 1, 2002, see 37 U. Rich. L. Rev. 271 (2002).

§ 2.2-1150.2. Use of communication towers for deployment of wireless broadband services in unserved areas of the Commonwealth. — A. As used in this section:

"Qualified provider" means a provider of wireless broadband service that has obtained all governmental approvals required for the provision of wireless broadband service in the unserved area in which it seeks to provide such service.

"Unserved area" means any area within the Commonwealth that is demonstrated not to have access to terrestrial broadband or radio frequency Internet service.

"Wireless broadband service" means an Internet connection service capable of transmitting information at a rate that is not less than 256 kilobits per second in at least one direction using a wireless link between a fixed location and the Internet service provider's facility. It does not include wireless fidelity technology used in conjunction with dedicated subscriber line service or cable service to connect devices within a facility to the Internet via a broadband connection.

B. Notwithstanding any provision of § 2.2-1156 to the contrary, any state department, agency, or institution having responsibility for a state-owned communication tower in an unserved area, subject to guidelines adopted by the Department, shall lease or convey a license or other interest in the communication tower to a qualified provider in order to permit the use of the communication tower by the qualified provider in its deployment of wireless broadband service within the unserved area or portion thereof. This requirement is subject to the qualified provider presenting to the Department:

1. A spectrum and certified structural analysis of the tower that demonstrates that:

a. The new service will not interfere with current equipment;

b. No structural element is beyond 85 percent capacity based on current and previously documented future loads; and

c. The tower meets the industry standards set forth by ANSI/TIA/EIA 222-F; and

2. Proof that the tower satisfies all applicable local government requirements.

C. The Department shall adopt guidelines for (i) determining whether a provider of wireless broadband service is qualified to provide such service and (ii) requesting a state department, agency, or institution to enter into a lease or other conveyance of an interest in a communication tower or site pursuant to this section.

D. The lease or other conveyance shall be for such consideration as the Director of the Department deems appropriate, which consideration shall be commensurate with the consideration paid for use of comparable space on similar towers. The lease or other conveyance may include shared use of the facilities by other political subdivisions or persons providing the same or similar services, and by departments, agencies, or institutions of the Commonwealth.

E. The provisions of § 2.2-1156 as they apply to lease agreements or conveyances of any interest shall not apply to any transaction undertaken pursuant to this section.

F. No transaction authorized by this section shall be made without the prior approval of the Director of the Department and the approval of the Attorney General as to the form of any conveyancing instrument prior to execution. (2008, cc. 676, 690.)

§ 2.2-1151. Conveyance of easements and appurtenances thereto to cable television companies, utility companies, public service companies, political subdivisions by state departments, agencies or institutions; communication towers. — A. When it is deemed to be in the public interest and subject to guidelines adopted by the Department:

1. Any state department, agency or institution, through its executive head or governing board may convey to public utility companies, public service corporations or companies, political subdivisions or cable television companies, right-of-way easements over property owned by the Commonwealth and held in its possession and any wires, pipes, conduits, fittings, supports and appurtenances thereto for the transmission of electricity, telephone, cable television, water, gas, steam, or sewage placed on, over or under the property.

2. Any state department, agency or institution having responsibility for a state-owned office building, through its executive head or governing board, may lease space to a credit union in the building for the purpose of providing credit union services that are readily accessible to state employees. The lease shall be for a term of not more than five years, with annual renewals or new leases permitted thereafter. Such lease may be granted for no consideration or for less than the fair market value.

3. Property owned by the Commonwealth may be sold or leased or other interests or rights therein granted or conveyed to political subdivisions or persons providing communication or information services for the purpose of erecting, operating, using or maintaining communication towers, antennas, or other radio distribution devices. If any tower proposed to be erected on property owned by the Commonwealth is to be used solely by private persons providing communication or information services, and there is no immediate use planned or anticipated by any department, agency or institution of the Commonwealth or political subdivision, the guidelines shall provide a means to obtain comments from the local governing body where the property is located. The conveyances shall be for such consideration as the Director of the Department deems appropriate, and may include shared use of the facilities by other political subdivisions or persons providing the same or similar services, and by departments, agencies, or institutions of the Commonwealth.

B. No transaction authorized by this section shall be made without the prior written recommendation by the Department to the Governor, the written approval by the Governor of the transaction itself, and the approval by the Attorney General as to the form of the instruments prior to execution.

C. This section shall not (i) apply to any lease or conveyance of a license or other interest in a communication tower for use in the deployment of wireless broadband service within an unserved area of the Commonwealth made pursuant to § 2.2-1150.2 or (ii) be construed to alter the control or ownership of towers currently maintained by other agencies of the Commonwealth. (1984, c. 641, § 2.1-504.4; 1986, c. 536; 1989, c. 710; 1996, c. 442; 2001, c. 844; 2008, cc. 356, 676, 690.)

The 2008 amendments. — The 2008 amendment by c. 356 rewrote this section.

The 2008 amendments by cc. 676 and 690 are identical and added subsection E [now C].

§ 2.2-1151.1. Conveyances of right-of-way usage to certain nonpublic service companies by the Department of Transportation. — A. As used in this section:

"Department" means the Virginia Department of Transportation.

"Developer" means a person who undertakes to develop real estate.

B. No land use permit shall be issued by the Department to any company other than a public service company as defined in § 56-76, a company owning or operating an interstate natural gas pipeline, or a franchised cable television systems operator owning or operating a utility line as defined in § 56-265.15, unless such company has (i) registered as an operator with the appropriate notification center as defined by § 56-265.15 and (ii) notified the commercial and residential developer, owner of commercial, multifamily or residential real estate, or local government entities with a property interest in any parcel of land located adjacent to the property over which the land use is being requested, that application for the permit has been made. Any permit application approved by the Department shall include an affidavit indicating compliance with the registration and notification requirements provided by this subsection.

C. No performance surety held by the Department in association with a land use permit issued to a company pursuant to subsection B to perform work within the Department's right-of-way shall be released until such time as all claims against the company associated with the work have been resolved, provided a claimant has notified the Department of a claim against such company within 30 days after completion of the work. A claimant shall have no more than one year after the notification is received by the Department to complete any action against the company associated with the work for which the claim has been made. After the expiration of the one-year period, the Department may release the performance surety.

D. Nothing in this section shall be construed or interpreted to create a cause of action or administrative claim against the Department. (2003, c. 330; 2004, c. 636.)

Law Review. — For survey article on judicial decisions in real estate law from June 1, 2002, through June 1, 2003, see 38 U. Rich. L. Rev. 223 (2003).

§ 2.2-1152. Conveyances to Department of Transportation by state institutions or public corporations owned by Commonwealth. — Any state institution or public corporation whose funds and property are owned solely by the Commonwealth may through its governing board convey to the Virginia Department of Transportation the lands necessary for highway purposes or other incidental uses, either for such consideration deemed proper or in exchange for other lands, and to execute the instruments necessary to effectuate the conveyance.

No transaction authorized by this section shall be made without the prior written recommendation of the Department to the Governor, the written approval of the Governor of the transaction itself, and the approval of the Attorney General as to the form of the instruments prior to execution.

The proceeds from the sale, with the written approval of the Governor, may be used by the state institution or public corporation for the purchase of other property or for capital improvements. (1984, c. 641, § 2.1-504.5; 2001, c. 844.)

§ 2.2-1153. State agencies and institutions to notify Division of property not used or required; criteria. — A. Whenever any department, agency or institution of state government possesses or has under its control state-owned property that is not being used or is not required for the programs of the department, agency or institution, it shall so notify the Division. Each department, agency and institution shall submit to the Division a land use plan for property it possesses or has under its control showing present and planned uses of such property. Such plan shall be approved by the cognizant board or governing body of the department, agency or institution holding title to or otherwise controlling the state-owned property or the agency head in the absence of a board or governing body, with a recommendation on whether any property should be declared surplus by the department, agency or institution. Development of such land use plans shall be based on guidelines promulgated by the Division. The guidelines shall provide that each land use plan shall be updated and copies provided to the Division by September 1 of each year. The Division may exempt properties that are held and used for conservation purposes from the requirements of this section. The Division shall review the land use plans and determine whether the property or any portion thereof should be declared surplus to the needs of the Commonwealth. By October 1 of each year, the Division shall provide a report to the Chairmen of the House Appropriations and Senate Finance Committees setting forth the Division's findings, the sale or marketing of properties identified pursuant to this section, and recommending any actions that may be required by the Governor and the General Assembly to identify and dispose of property not being efficiently and effectively utilized.

Until permanent disposition of the property determined to be surplus is effected, the property shall continue to be maintained by the department, agency or institution possessing or controlling it, unless upon the recommendation of the Department, the Governor authorizes the transfer of the property to the possession or control of the Department. In this event, the department, agency or institution formerly possessing or controlling the property shall have no further interest in it.

B. The Division shall establish criteria for ascertaining whether property under the control of a department, agency or institution should be classified as "surplus" to its current or proposed needs. Such criteria shall provide that the cognizant board or governing body, if any, of the department, agency or institution holding the title to or otherwise controlling the state-owned property, or the agency head in the absence of a board or governing body, shall approve the designation of the property as surplus.

C. Notwithstanding the provisions of subsection A:

1. The property known as College Woods, which includes Lake Matoaka and is possessed and controlled by a college founded in 1693, regardless of whether such property has been declared surplus pursuant to this section, shall not be transferred or disposed of without the approval of the board of visitors of such college by a two-thirds vote of all board members at a regularly scheduled board meeting. The General Assembly shall also approve the disposal or transfer.

2. Surplus real property valued at less than $5 million that is possessed and controlled by a public institution of higher education may be sold by such institution, provided that (i) at least 45 days prior to executing a contract for the sale of such property, the institution gives written notification to the Governor and the Chairmen of the House Appropriations and Senate Finance Committees; and (ii) the Governor may postpone the sale at any time up to 10 days prior to the proposed date of sale. Such sale may be effected by public auction, sealed bids, or by marketing through one or more Virginia licensed real estate brokers after satisfying the public notice provisions of subsection A of § 2.2-1156. The terms of all negotiations resulting in such sale shall be public information. The public institution of higher education may retain the proceeds from the sale of such property if the property was acquired by nongeneral funds. If the institution originally acquired the property through a mix of general and nongeneral funds, 50 percent of the proceeds shall be distributed to the institution and 50 percent shall be distributed to the State Park Conservation Resources Fund established under subsection A of § 10.1-202. The authority of a public institution of higher education to sell surplus real property described under this subdivision or to retain any proceeds from the sale of such property shall be subject to the institution meeting the conditions prescribed in subsection B of § 23-38.88 and § 23-38.112 (regardless of whether or not the institution has been granted any authority under Subchapter 3 (§ 23-38.91 et seq.) of Chapter 4.10 of Title 23). (1968, c. 717, § 2.1-106.2; 1972, c. 763; 1977, c. 672, § 2.1-505; 1978, c. 545; 1984, c. 641; 1995, c. 774; 2001, c. 844; 2004, c. 997; 2005, cc. 933, 945.)

Cross references. — As to exemption of certain motor vehicles acquired from the centralized fleet of motor vehicles controlled by the Commonwealth Transportation Commissioner and sold or transferred to TANF recipients or former recipients from the provisions of §§ 2.2-4300 et seq., 2.2-1124, 2.2-1153, 2.2-1156, and 2.2-1177, see § 63.2-611 D.

Editor's note. — Acts 2004, c. 997, cl. 2, provides: "That the Division of Engineering and Buildings of the Department of General Services, in developing the guidelines required by the provisions of the first enactment of this act, shall seek input from state institutions of higher education enumerated in § 23-14 of the Code of Virginia, and other departments, agencies, and institutions that own real property or that have real property under their control."

§ 2.2-1154. State agencies, institutions, to inquire of Division before acquiring land for capital improvements. — A. Any state department, agency or institution shall, before purchasing or otherwise acquiring land for any capital improvement, inquire of the Department whether there is available any suitable land under the control of the Division or any other state department, agency or institution that may be authorized for the purpose for which the additional land is needed.

B. The Department shall require every state department, agency or institution responsible for the construction, operation or maintenance of public facilities within the Commonwealth, when siting state facilities and programs, to evaluate the feasibility of siting such facilities and programs in the Commonwealth's urban centers. In making such evaluation, the agency shall consider (i) the fiscal advantages of utilizing the existing infrastructure available in urban centers as compared to the construction of new infrastructure in less developed areas, (ii) the potential savings associated with leasing facilities from the private sector in urban centers as compared to purchasing or constructing new facilities in other areas, (iii) the convenience to employees and citizen users of state facilities and programs of placing such facilities and programs in close proximity to the road and transportation systems and other amenities found in the Commonwealth's urban centers, and (iv) whether the local governing body is supportive of the location as a desirable use of available land resources.

This subsection shall not be construed to limit the ability of a state department, agency or institution to locate facilities based on other factors such as a rural locality's desire to stimulate economic development or the need to have regionally dispersed services.

C. The provisions of subsection B shall not apply to any facility or program to be located on the campus of any public institution of higher education in Virginia. (1968, c. 717, § 2.1-106.4; 1977, c. 672, § 2.1-508; 2000, c. 704; 2001, c. 844.)

§ 2.2-1155. Temporary transfer of use of property between state agencies and institutions; lease to private entities. — A. Whenever any department, agency, or institution of state government possesses or has under its control property for which there is an anticipated future use, but for which there is no immediate use, the department, agency, or institution of the Commonwealth may effect, subject to the written recommendation of the Department to the Governor and the written approval by the Governor, an agreement in writing with any other department, agency, or institution of state government for the use of the property by the other department, agency, or institution during a period not to exceed fifteen years. The agreement may be extended beyond the fifteen-year period on an annual basis in accordance with the procedures prescribed in this subsection. In the event no other department, agency, or institution of state government has use for the property, the department, agency, or institution may lease the property to private individuals, firms, corporations or other entities in accordance with the procedures and subject to the term limitations prescribed in this subsection.

B. The provisions of subsection A notwithstanding, public institutions of higher education in Virginia, subject to the approval of the General Assembly, may enter into written agreements with university-related foundations, private individuals, firms, corporations, or other entities to lease property in the possession or control of the institution. Any such agreement and proposed development or use of property shall (i) be for a purpose consistent with the educational and general mission, auxiliary enterprises, and sponsored program activities of the institution, or such other purpose as the General Assembly may authorize, and (ii) comply with guidelines adopted by the Department. The term of any agreement shall be based upon, among other things, the useful life of the improvements to the property and shall not exceed fifty years; however, any agreement may be extended upon the written recommendation of the Governor and the approval of the General Assembly. Agreements with private individuals, firms, corporations, or other entities shall also be subject to guidelines adopted by the Secretary of Finance. In the event that any public institution of higher education in Virginia enters into any written agreement with a university-related foundation, private individual, firm, corporation, or other entity to lease property in the possession or control of the institution pursuant to this subsection, neither the real property that is the subject of the lease nor any improvements or personal property located on the real property that is the subject of the lease shall be subject to taxation by any local government authority pursuant to § 58.1-3203 or § 58.1-3502 or any other applicable law during the term of the lease, regardless of the ownership of the property, improvements or personal property, provided the real property, improvements or personal property shall be used for a purpose consistent with the educational and general mission, auxiliary enterprises, and sponsored program activities of the institution.

For the purposes of this section, *"university-related foundation"* means any foundation affiliated with an institution of higher education. (1971, Ex. Sess., c. 239, § 2.1-106.6:1; 1977, c. 672, § 2.1-511; 1981, c. 112; 1984, c. 641; 1988, c. 57; 1990, cc. 53, 688; 1992, c. 331; 2001, c. 844.)

Cross references. — As to applicability of this section to the Pelham Chapel, as configured as of July 1, 2002, see § 57-5.

Editor's note. — Acts 2008, c. 879, effective for the biennium ending June 30, 2010, in § 4-4.01 t, provides: "t.1. Facility Lease Agreements Involving Institutions of Higher Education: In the case of any lease agreement involving state-owned property controlled by an institution of higher education, where the lease has been entered into consistent with the provisions of § 2.2-1155, Code of Virginia, the Governor may amend, adjust or waive any project review and reporting procedures of Executive agencies as may reasonably be required to promote the property improvement goals for which the lease agreement was developed.

"2. This section shall not apply to public institutions of higher education governed by Chapters 933 and 943 of the 2006 Acts of Assembly."

§ **2.2-1156. Sale or lease of surplus property.** — Except when a department, agency or institution notifies the Department of a need for property which has been declared surplus, and the Department finds that stated need to be valid and best satisfied by the use of the property, the Department may dispose of the property as provided in this section.

A. After it determines the property to be surplus to the needs of the Commonwealth, the Department shall request the written opinion of the Secretary of Natural Resources as to whether the property to be sold is a significant component of the Commonwealth's natural or historic resources, and if so how those resources should be protected in the sale of the property. The Secretary of Natural Resources shall provide this review within 15 business days of receipt of full information from the Department. Within 120 days of receipt of the Secretary's review, the Department shall, with the prior written approval of the Governor, proceed to sell the property. The sale shall be by public auction, or sealed bids, or by marketing through one or more real estate brokers licensed by the Commonwealth. Notice of the date, time and place of sale, if by public auction or sealed bids shall be given by advertisement in at least two newspapers published and having general circulation in the Commonwealth, at least one of which shall have general circulation in the county or city in which the property to be sold is located. At least thirty days shall elapse between publication of the notice and the auction or the date on which sealed bids will be opened.

In instances where the appraised value of property proposed to be sold is determined to be a nominal amount or an amount insufficient to warrant statewide advertisement, but in no event in excess of $50,000, the notice of sale may be placed in only one newspaper having general circulation in the county or city in which the property to be sold is located.

B. The Department shall have the right to reject any and all bids or offers when, in the opinion of the Department, the price is inadequate in relation to the value of the property or if a need has been found for the property. If the Department deems the bid or offer fair and adequate in relation to the value of the property, and if no other need for the property has been found, the Department shall recommend acceptance of the bid or offer to the Governor for approval. In lieu of the sale of any such property, the Department may, with the approval of the Governor, lease it to any responsible person, firm or corporation on such terms as are fair and adequate in relation to the value of the property. The provisions of this section requiring disposition of property through the medium of sealed bids, public auction, or marketing through licensed real estate brokers shall not apply to any lease thereof, although such procedures may be followed in the discretion of the Department. The deed or lease to the property shall be executed in the name of the Commonwealth and shall be in a form approved by the Attorney General. Notwithstanding any law to the contrary and notwithstanding how title to the property was acquired, the deed or lease may be executed on behalf of the Commonwealth by the Director of the Department or his designee, and such action shall not create a cloud on the title to the property. The terms of the sale or lease shall be subject to the written approval of the Governor.

C. An exception to sale by sealed bids, public auction, or listing the property with a licensed real estate broker may be granted by the Governor if the property is landlocked and inaccessible from a public road or highway. In such cases, the Department shall notify all adjacent landowners of the Commonwealth's desire to dispose of the property. After the notice has been given, the Department may begin negotiations for the sale of the property with each interested adjacent landowner. The Department, with the approval of the Governor, may accept any offer which it deems to be fair and adequate consideration for the property. In all cases, the offer shall be the best offer made by any adjacent landowner. The terms of all negotiations shall be public information.

D. Fifty percent of the proceeds from all sales or leases, or from the conveyance of any interest in property under the provisions of this article, above the costs of the transaction, which costs shall include fees or commissions, if any, negotiated with and paid to auctioneers or real estate brokers, shall be paid, subject to any contrary provisions of law, into the Conservation Resources Fund, so long as the sales or leases pertain to general fund agencies or the property involved was originally acquired through the general fund, except as provided in Chapter 180 of the Acts of Assembly of 1966. The remaining 50 percent of proceeds involving general fund sales or leases, less a pro rata share of any costs of the transactions, shall be deposited in the general fund of the state treasury. The Department of Planning and Budget shall develop guidelines which allow, with the approval of the Governor, any portion of the deposit in the general fund to be credited to the agency, department or institution having control of the property at the time it was determined surplus to the Commonwealth's needs. Any amounts so credited to an agency, department or institution may be used, upon appropriation, to supplement maintenance reserve funds or capital project appropriations, or for the acquisition, construction or improvement of real property or facilities. Net proceeds from sales or leases of special fund agency properties or property acquired through a gift for a specific purpose shall be retained by the agency or used in accordance with the original terms of the gift.

E. When the Department deems it to be in the best interests of the Commonwealth, it may, with the approval of the Governor, authorize the department, institution or agency in possession or control of the property to dispose of surplus property in accordance with the procedures set forth in this section. (1968, c. 717, § 2.1-106.7; 1970, c. 202; 1972, c. 763; 1977, c. 672, § 2.1-512; 1978, c. 545; 1981, c. 104; 1984, c. 641; 1989, c. 687; 1991, c. 679; 1995, c. 399; 1998, c. 466; 2001, c. 844; 2002, c. 281; 2004, c. 997.)

Cross references. — As to exemption of certain motor vehicles acquired from the centralized fleet of motor vehicles controlled by the Commonwealth Transportation Commissioner and sold or transferred to TANF recipients or former recipients from the provisions of §§ 2.2-4300 et seq., 2.2-1124, 2.2-1153, 2.2-1156, and 2.2-1177, see § 63.2-611 D.

Editor's note. — Acts 2004, c. 997, cl. 2, provides: "That the Division of Engineering and Buildings of the Department of General Services, in developing the guidelines required by the provisions of the first enactment of this act, shall seek input from state institutions of higher education enumerated in § 23-14 of the Code of Virginia, and other departments, agencies, and institutions that own real property or that have real property under their control."

Acts 2008, c. 879, effective for the biennium ending June 30, 2010, in Item 315 C, provides: "Notwithstanding § 4-5.12 of this act and paragraph C of § 2.2-1156, Code of Virginia, the Department of Mental Health, Mental Retardation and Substance Abuse Services is hereby authorized to deposit the entire proceeds of the sales of surplus land at state-owned mental health and mental retardation facilities into a revolving trust fund. The trust fund may initially be used for expenses associated with restructuring such facilities. Remaining proceeds after such expenses shall be dedicated to continuing services for current patients as facility services are restructured. The trust fund will receive any savings resulting from facility restructuring. Thereafter, the fund will be used to enhance services to individuals with mental illness, mental retardation and substance abuse problems."

Acts 2008, c. 879, effective for the biennium ending June 30, 2010, in Item 374 F, provides: "The Department of Historic Resources is authorized to accept a devise of certain real property under the will of Elizabeth Rust Williams known as Clermont Farm located on Route 7 east of the town of Berryville in Clarke County. If, after due consideration of options, the department determines that the property should be sold or leased to a different public or private entity, and notwithstanding the provisions of § 2.2-1156, Code of Virginia, the department is further authorized to sell or lease such property, provided such sale or lease is not in conflict with the terms of the will. The proceeds of any such sale or lease shall be deposited to the Historic Resources Fund established under § 10.1-2202.1, Code of Virginia."

Acts 2008, c. 879, effective for the biennium ending June 30, 2010, in § 4-4.01 s, provides: "s.1. The Governor may authorize the conveyance of any interest in property or improvements thereon held by the Commonwealth to the educational or real estate foundation of any institution of higher education where he finds that such property was acquired with local or private funds or by gift or grant to or for the use of the institution, and not with funds appropriated to the institution by the General Assembly. Any approved conveyance shall be exempt from § 2.2-1156, Code of Virginia, and any other statute concerning conveyance, transfer or sale of state property. If the foundation conveys any interest in the property or any improvements thereon, such conveyance shall likewise be exempt from compliance with any statute concerning disposition of state property. Any income or proceeds from the conveyance of any interest in the property shall be deemed to be local or private funds and may be used by the foundation for any foundation purpose.

"2. This section shall not apply to public institutions of higher education governed by Chapters 933 and 943 of the 2006 Acts of Assembly."

Acts 2008, c. 879, effective for the biennium ending June 30, 2010, in § 4-5.09, provides: "a. Notwithstanding the provisions of §2.2-1156, Code of Virginia, the departments, divisions, institutions, or agencies of the Commonwealth, or the Governor, shall sell or lease surplus real property only under the following circumstances:

"1. Any emergency declared in accordance with §§44-146.18:2 or 44-146.28, Code of Virginia, or

"2. Not less than thirty days after the Governor notifies, in writing, the Chairmen of the House Appropriations and Senate Finance Committees regarding the planned conveyance, including a statement of the proceeds to be derived from such conveyance and the individual or entity taking title to such property.

"3. Surplus property valued at less than $5,000,000 that is possessed and controlled by a public institution of higher education, pursuant to §§2.2-1149 and 2.2-1153, Code of Virginia.

"b. In any circumstance provided for in subsection a of this section, the cognizant board or governing body of the agency or institution holding title or otherwise controlling the state-owned property shall approve, in writing, the proposed conveyance of the property."

Law Review. — For article surveying developments in real estate and land use law in Virginia from June 1, 2001 through June 1, 2002, see 37 U. Rich. L. Rev. 271 (2002).

§ 2.2-1157. Exploration for and extraction of minerals on state-owned uplands. — A. The Department of Mines, Minerals and Energy, in cooperation with the Division, shall develop, with the assistance of affected state agencies, departments, and institutions, a State Minerals Management Plan (the "Plan"). The Plan shall include provisions for the holding of public hearings and the public advertising for competitive bids or proposals for mineral exploration, leasing, and extraction activities on state-owned uplands. Sales of mineral exploration permits and leases for these lands shall be administered by the Division, with the advice of the Department of Mines, Minerals and Energy.

B. Upon receiving the recommendation of both the Director of the Department of General Services and the Director of the Department of Mines, Minerals and Energy, the Governor shall determine whether the proposed mineral exploration, leasing, or extraction of minerals on state-owned uplands is in the public interest. No state-owned uplands shall be approved for mineral exploration, leasing, or extraction without a public hearing in the locality where the affected land or the greater portion thereof is located and a competitive bid or proposal process as described in the Plan. The provisions of this section shall not apply to the extraction of minerals on state-owned uplands pursuant to an oil or gas pooling order unless the well through which the extraction will occur is situated on such land.

For purposes of this section, *"state-owned uplands"* means lands owned by the Commonwealth that (i) lie landward of the mean low water mark in tidal areas or (ii) have an elevation above the average surface water level in nontidal areas.

C. The agencies, departments, or institutions proposing or receiving applications for mineral exploration, leasing or extraction on state-owned uplands shall, through their boards or commissions, recommend as specified in subsection B of § 2.2-1156 all such activities to the Division following guidelines set forth in the Plan. The Division and the Department of Mines, Minerals and Energy shall review and recommend to the Governor such proposed activities. Such agencies, departments or institutions, through their boards or commissions, may execute the leases or contracts that have been approved by the Governor.

D. The proceeds from all such sales or leases above the costs of the sale to the Department of Mines, Minerals and Energy or to the agency, department or institution sponsoring the sale shall be paid into the general fund of the state treasury, so long as the sales or leases pertain to general fund agencies or the property involved was originally acquired through the general fund. Net proceeds from sales or leases of special-fund agency properties or property acquired through a gift shall be retained by such agency or institution or used in accordance with the original terms of the gift if so stated.

E. Mining, leasing, and extraction activities in state-owned submerged lands shall be authorized and administered by the Virginia Marine Resources Commission pursuant to § 28.2-100 et seq. (1982, c. 238, § 2.1-512.1; 1984, c. 750; 1986, c. 488; 2001, c. 844.)

§ 2.2-1158. Management, harvesting and sale of timber on lands under control of Division. — The Division may manage and harvest timber on lands placed under its control in accordance with the best timber management practices, after receiving the advice of the State Forester. The Division may also sell the timber, but before the sale is made, the State Forester or his deputy shall furnish the Division with an estimate of the value of the timber. In the event of sale, the proceeds shall first be used to defray the cost of the sale and the cost of maintenance of the property from which the timber is removed and the remainder, if any, of the funds shall be deposited in the Forest Management of State-owned Lands Fund created in § 10.1-1120. (1968, c. 717, § 2.1-106.8; 1977, c. 672, § 2.1-513; 1980, c. 525; 2001, c. 844.)

§ 2.2-1159. Facilities for persons with physical disabilities in certain buildings; definitions; construction standards; waiver; temporary buildings. — A. For the purposes of this section and § 2.2-1160:

"Building" means any building or facility, used by the public, which is constructed in whole or in part or altered by the use of state, county or municipal funds, or the funds of any political subdivision of this Commonwealth. "Building" shall not include public school buildings and facilities, which shall be governed by standards established by the Board of Education pursuant to § 22.1-138.

"Persons with physical disabilities" means persons with:

1. Impairments that, regardless of cause or manifestation, for all practical purposes, confine individuals to wheelchairs;
2. Impairments that cause individuals to walk with difficulty or insecurity;
3. Total blindness or impairments affecting sight to the extent that the individual functioning in public areas is insecure or exposed to dangers;
4. Deafness or hearing handicaps that might make an individual insecure in public areas because he is unable to communicate or hear warning signals;
5. Faulty coordination or palsy from brain, spinal, or peripheral nerve injury; or
6. Those manifestations of the aging processes that significantly reduce mobility, flexibility, coordination and perceptiveness but are not accounted for in the aforementioned categories.

B. The Division shall prescribe standards for the design, construction, and alteration of buildings constructed in whole or in part or altered by the use of state funds, other than school funds, necessary to ensure that persons with physical disabilities will have ready access to, and use of, such buildings.

C. The governing body of a county, city or town or other political subdivision shall prescribe standards for the design, construction and alteration of buildings, not including public school facilities, constructed in whole or in part or altered by the use of the funds of such locality or political subdivision necessary to ensure that persons with physical disabilities will have ready access to, and use of, such buildings. The Division shall consult with the governing bodies upon request.

D. The Division, with respect to standards issued by it, and the governing body of any county, city or town or other political subdivision with respect to standards issued by it may:

1. Modify or waive any such standard, on a case-by-case basis, upon application made by the head of the department, agency or other instrumentality concerned, upon determining that a modification or waiver is clearly necessary; and
2. Conduct necessary surveys and investigations to ensure compliance with such standards.

E. The provisions of this section and § 2.2-1160 shall apply to temporary and emergency construction as well as permanent buildings. (1970, c. 539, §§ 2.1-109.01, 2.1-109.02, 2.1-109.03, 2.1-109.04, 2.1-109.06, 2.1-109.07; 1972, c. 223; 1977, c. 672, §§ 2.1-514, 2.1-515, 2.1-516, 2.1-517, 2.1-519, 2.1-520, 2.1-521; 1993, c. 226; 2001, c. 844.)

§ 2.2-1160. Facilities for persons with physical disabilities; what buildings to be constructed in accordance with standards. — Every building or facility designed, constructed or substantially altered after the effective date of a standard issued under subsection B of § 2.2-1159, which is applicable to such building shall be designed, constructed or altered in accordance with such standard. (1970, c. 539, § 2.1-109.05; 1977, c. 672, § 2.1-519; 2001, c. 844.)

Cross references. — As to asbestos inspection requirements for child day centers, see § 63.2-1811.

§ 2.2-1161. Buildings not in conformance with standards for persons with physical disabilities. — The Division, upon a determination that a building or facility is not in conformance with the applicable standards for persons with physical disabilities, shall immediately take all necessary steps to ensure such building or facility is in conformance within three months of the date of its determination. The three-month period may be extended for an additional minimum period of time required to obtain funding and complete construction, where the Division determines an extension is necessary. This section shall apply only to those state buildings or facilities designed, constructed or substantially modified after July 1, 1977. (1977, c. 588, § 2.1-521.1; 1979, c. 243; 2001, c. 844.)

§ 2.2-1161.1. Code Adam alerts in public buildings. — Each state building that is open to the public shall have in place a Code Adam or similar program for the prevention of child abduction. Code Adam is a protocol used as a preventive tool against child abductions and for locating lost children in public buildings. The Department of General Services shall develop model plans and ensure that each building covered by this section is prepared to activate Code Adam or a similar program under appropriate circumstances. All state agencies shall render assistance to the Department, upon request, in implementing this statute and the Department's plan within their buildings. (2003, cc. 83, 86.)

ARTICLE 5.

Abatement Of Risk Of Asbestos In State-Owned And Public School Buildings.

§ 2.2-1162. Definitions. — As used in this article.

"Asbestos" means any material containing more than one percent of the asbestiform varieties of:

1. chrysotile (serpentine),
2. crocidolite (riebeckite),
3. amosite (cummingtonite-grunerite),
4. anthophyllite,
5. tremolite, or
6. actinolite.

"Director" means the Director of the Department of General Services.

"Friable" means material that is capable of being crumbled, pulverized or reduced to powder by hand pressure or which under normal use or maintenance emits or can be expected to emit asbestos fibers into the air.

"Local education agency" or *"LEA"* means the same as that term is defined in the United States Environmental Protection Agency Asbestos Hazard and Emergency Response Act regulations set forth in 40 CFR 763.

"Operations and maintenance program" means work practices to maintain asbestos-containing material in good condition and to minimize and control disturbance or damage to such materials.

"Response actions" means any action, including removal, encapsulation, enclosure, repair, method of operation, maintenance, record keeping or notification that protects human health from building materials containing asbestos.

"Secretary" means the Secretary of Administration. (1986, cc. 288, 560, § 2.1-526.12; 1988, c. 723; 1989, c. 398; 1990, c. 50; 2001, c. 844.)

Law Review. — For comment, "Recovering Asbestos Abatement Cost," see 10 G.M.U. L. Rev. 451 (1988).

§ **2.2-1163. Inspection of state-owned buildings; marking locations where asbestos found; risk abatement and estimate of cost thereof.** — The Director at the direction of the Secretary and in cooperation with any other appropriate agencies including but not limited to the Department of Education shall ensure that every building owned by the Commonwealth or any agency of the Commonwealth which has not previously been inspected by competent personnel as provided below is inspected as soon as practical by competent personnel who have the training and equipment necessary to identify (i) the presence of asbestos, and (ii) to the extent practicable the relative hazard or hazards to health and safety posed at each location at which asbestos is identified. Every location at which asbestos is identified shall be clearly marked with suitably designed signs or labels. The Director shall prepare an accurate estimate of the cost of abating the risk of all asbestos so identified. The Director shall also establish a list of abatement priorities, which shall include the estimated cost of abating the risk at each location on the list. To the extent that funds are available, and in accordance with the priorities established by the Director, the agency or institution of the Commonwealth responsible for the maintenance of buildings at any such location shall proceed to abate the risk at such locations. (1985, c. 534, § 2.1-526.13; 1986, cc. 288, 560; 2001, c. 844.)

§ **2.2-1164. Standards for inspection of buildings for asbestos.** — The Director, at the direction of the Secretary and in cooperation with any other appropriate agencies including, but not limited to, the Department of Education shall adopt standards for the inspection of state-owned and local education agency buildings of all types and the ancillary facilities used in connection therewith for the purpose of identifying the presence of asbestos and to the extent practicable the relative hazard to health or safety posed by any asbestos identified. The Administrative Process Act (§ 2.2-4000 et seq.) shall not apply to the adoption of standards under this section.

A. The standards shall include:

1. Inspection for the presence, location and condition of asbestos-containing materials;

2. Development of a building asbestos profile for each building inspected and found to contain asbestos-containing material, which profile shall:

(a) Include information regarding product type (surfacing material, thermal system insulation, or miscellaneous material), specific location, estimated quantity (in square or linear feet), type and percentage of asbestos content, and physical condition;

(b) Be kept in possession of the person designated pursuant to subsection E, at a location in the building where it is readily accessible to building employees or their designated representatives;

(c) Be updated as surveillance, test results and/or response actions are undertaken in the building.

B. The following standards are established for state-owned buildings:

1. When air monitoring is used for building assessment, it shall be used in conjunction with comprehensive visual assessment techniques for determining the priority and nature of response action.

2. The airborne asbestos reoccupancy level, to be measured upon completion of response actions, shall be equal to the reoccupancy standards established for buildings pursuant to subsection C.

C. The Director, in conjunction with the state Departments of Professional and Occupational Regulation, Health, Labor and Industry, Education, and

Environmental Quality, shall adopt standards governing aggressive air sampling after completion of an asbestos project for airborne asbestos for local education agencies and public colleges and universities.

D. Asbestos management plans for state-owned buildings shall include:

1. Operation and maintenance programs, including procedures for the notification of maintenance and housekeeping personnel of the location of asbestos-containing materials likely to be disturbed during routine building operations; the labeling of asbestos-containing materials in routine maintenance areas; and work practices, engineering controls or personal protective measures to minimize asbestos exposure to such personnel and other building occupants;

2. Training requirements for maintenance workers and maintenance supervisory personnel;

3. Assurance of compliance by contractors with licensing under applicable state laws and regulations; and

4. Provisions for setting priorities of buildings for response actions.

E. Each person responsible for such management plans shall designate one member of the maintenance personnel in or responsible for each building containing asbestos-containing materials to serve as the liaison to coordinate the specific efforts of such program within the particular building to which the liaison is assigned. (1985, c. 534, § 2.1-526.14; 1986, cc. 288, 560; 1988, c. 723; 1993, c. 660; 2001, c. 844.)

§ 2.2-1165. Inspection of public school buildings; certification of inspection; certain inspections made before July 1, 1986, deemed in compliance. — A. Every public school division in the Commonwealth shall ensure that every school building owned or operated by it, which has not previously been inspected in compliance with this article, is inspected. Inspection shall conform to the standards developed pursuant to § 2.2-1164.

B. The superintendent of schools for each public school division shall certify to the Superintendent of Public Instruction and the Secretary that the public schools in the division have been inspected in compliance with this article.

C. Inspections completed prior to July 1, 1986, shall be deemed in compliance with this article if the Superintendent of Public Instruction and the Secretary determine that they conform substantially to the standards referenced in § 2.2-1164, or to the inspection procedures contained in 40 CFR 763. (1985, c. 534, § 2.1-526.15; 1986, cc. 288, 560; 2001, c. 844.)

§ 2.2-1166. Marking locations where asbestos found in public school buildings; estimate of cost of risk abatement; list of priorities based on risk. — Each public school division shall ensure that every location at which asbestos is identified following inspections conducted pursuant to subsection A or C of § 2.2-1165 is clearly marked with suitably designed signs or labels. Each division shall prepare an accurate estimate of the cost of abating the risk of asbestos at each location so identified. Each division shall also establish a list of priorities, based upon its determination of the risk to public health and safety posed by asbestos at each such location, which shall include the estimated cost of abating the risk at each location on the list. (1986, cc. 288, 560, § 2.1-526.16; 2001, c. 844.)

§ 2.2-1167. Commonwealth immune from civil liability. — The Commonwealth and its officers, agents and employees shall be immune from civil liability for actions (i) arising from the establishment and implementation of asbestos inspection standards developed pursuant to § 2.2-1164 and (ii) undertaken pursuant to the provisions of this article, Chapter 5 of Title 54.1, and §§ 32.1-126.1 and 63.2-1811. (1988, c. 723, § 2.1-526.17:1; 2001, c. 844.)

ARTICLE 6.

Division Of Support Services.

§ **2.2-1168. Division of Support Services may be established.** — The Director of the Department may establish a Division of Support Services (the "Division") and assign to this Division or to any other division any or all of the duties described in this article or otherwise imposed upon the Department. (1977, c. 672, § 2.1-527; 2001, c. 844.)

§ **2.2-1169. Mail handling, messenger and parcel service.** — The Division shall operate a central service unit to provide all state departments, divisions, institutions and agencies in the Richmond area with mail handling, messenger and parcel service. These services may, if deemed appropriate, be extended to state departments, divisions, institutions and agencies in other areas of the Commonwealth. (1972, c. 503, § 2.1-243.1; 1976, c. 759; 1977, c. 672, § 2.1-528; 2001, c. 844.)

§ **2.2-1170. Office equipment pool; repair.** — The Division may establish a general office equipment pool and central repair shop for such equipment, and may provide guidelines for the utilization of such equipment. For the purposes of this section, computers, software, supplies, and related peripheral equipment shall not be considered general office equipment. (1977, c. 672, § 2.1-529; 2001, c. 844.)

§ **2.2-1171. Printing and duplicating facilities.** — The Division may operate a printing and duplicating facility in the Richmond area, and may establish criteria for its use, subject to the provisions of § 2.2-1113. (1977, c. 672, § 2.1-530; 2001, c. 844.)

§ **2.2-1172. Parking of vehicles in Capitol Square; parking facilities for state officers and employees; violations.** — A. Except as provided in this section, all parking in the Capitol Square of motor vehicles and animal-drawn vehicles is prohibited. However, during the recess of the General Assembly, the Division may cause to be marked off certain portions of the driveways in the Capitol Square and permit vehicles to be parked there under such regulations as may be prescribed. Parking areas on the west of the Capitol shall be reserved at all times for parking by members of the General Assembly.

B. During sessions of the General Assembly, parking in the Capitol Square shall be subject to rules and regulations adopted jointly by the Speaker of the House of Delegates and the chairman of the Senate Committee on Rules.

C. The Division may, with the approval of the Governor, utilize any property owned by the Commonwealth and located in the Richmond area for the purpose of providing parking facilities for officers and employees of the Commonwealth, and to allocate spaces therein. The Division may fix and collect fees for the use of the parking facilities. The Division may adopt regulations for the parking facilities, which regulations shall include the enforcement provisions required by §§ 46.2-1225 through 46.2-1229.

D. Any person parking any vehicle contrary to the rules and regulations referred to in subsection B or contrary to the other provisions of this section, or contrary to any parking sign or "No Parking" sign erected by the Division pursuant to regulations adopted by it, shall be subject to a fine of not less than one dollar nor more than twenty-five dollars for each offense. (Code 1950, § 2-75.1; 1958, c. 2; 1966, c. 677, § 2.1-94; 1970, c. 202; 1977, c. 672, § 2.1-531; 2001, c. 844.)

Cross references. — As to the Capitol Square Preservation Council, see § 30-193 et seq.

ARTICLE 7.

Centralized Fleet Management.

§ **2.2-1173. Definitions.** — As used in this article:

"Centralized fleet" means those passenger-type vehicles assigned to the Department of General Services and available for use by state agencies.

"Contract rental" means a contract for the use of motor vehicles by employees for official state business within the confines of their normal work locations. This does not include rental vehicles used by travelers after reaching their destination.

"Director" means the Director of the Department of General Services.

"Lease" means a contract for the use of a passenger-type vehicle for a term of more than thirty days.

"Passenger-type vehicle" means any automobile, including sedans and station wagons, or van used primarily for the transportation of the operator and no more than fifteen passengers. (1989, c. 479, § 33.1-400; 1998, c. 329; 2001, cc. 815, 842, § 2.1-548.01.)

Cross references. — As to exemption of certain motor vehicles acquired from the centralized fleet of motor vehicles controlled by the Commonwealth Transportation Commissioner and sold or transferred to TANF recipients or former recipients from the provisions of §§ 2.2-4300 et seq., 2.2-1124, 2.2-1153, 2.2-1156, and 2.2-1177, see § 63.2-611 D.

Editor's note. — Acts 2001, cc. 815 and 842 enacted §§ 2.1-548.01 to 2.1-548.09, from which the sections in this article are derived. Pursuant to § 30-152, Acts 2001, cc. 815 and 842 have been given effect in this article as set out above. The historical citations from the former provisions have been placed under the corresponding new sections.

§ **2.2-1174. Vehicles assigned to the centralized fleet.** — Passenger-type vehicles purchased with public funds by any department, agency, institution, or commission of the Commonwealth, or any officer or employee on behalf of the Commonwealth, shall be assigned to the centralized fleet with the following exceptions:

1. Vehicles that have special equipment or performance requirements related to use by law-enforcement officers;
2. Vehicles for use by any elected official of the people of the Commonwealth; and
3. Such other special category of vehicles as may be excepted by the Director. (1989, c. 479, § 33.1-401; 2001, cc. 815, 842, § 2.1-548.02.)

Editor's note. — Acts 2001, cc. 815 and 842 enacted § 2.1-548.02, from which this section is derived. Pursuant to § 30-152, Acts 2001, cc. 815 and 842 have been given effect in this section as set out above.

§ **2.2-1175. Responsibilities of Director.** — The Director shall establish an appropriate administrative unit within the Department to manage the centralized fleet. The Director's responsibilities for the centralized fleet shall include, but not be limited to, the following:

1. Administering the assignment of vehicles to officers and employees of the Commonwealth;
2. Managing a pool of vehicles for short-term use;
3. Purchasing vehicles necessary to the operation of the centralized fleet;
4. Repairing and maintaining vehicles;

5. Monitoring the use of vehicles and enforcing regulations regarding their proper use; and

6. Maintaining records related to the operation and maintenance of vehicles, and the administration of the centralized fleet. (1989, c. 479, § 33.1-402; 2001, cc. 815, 842, § 2.1-548.03.)

Editor's note. — Acts 2001, cc. 815 and 842 enacted § 2.1-548.03, from which this section is derived. Pursuant to § 30-152, Acts 2001, cc. 815 and 842 have been given effect in this section as set out above.

§ 2.2-1176. Approval of purchase, lease, or contract rental of motor vehicle. — No motor vehicle shall be purchased, leased, or subject to a contract rental with public funds by the Commonwealth or by any officer or employee on behalf of the Commonwealth without the prior written approval of the Director. No lease or contract rental shall be approved by the Director except upon demonstration that the cost of such lease or contract rental plus operating costs of the vehicle shall be less than comparable costs for a vehicle owned by the Commonwealth.

Notwithstanding the foregoing provisions of this section, the Virginia Department of Transportation shall be exempted from the approval of purchase, lease, or contract rental of motor vehicles used directly in carrying out its maintenance, operations, and construction programs. (1989, c. 479, § 33.1-403; 1997, c. 48; 1998, c. 329; 2001, cc. 815, 842, § 2.1-548.04.)

Editor's note. — Acts 2001, cc. 815 and 842 enacted § 2.1-548.04, from which this section is derived. Pursuant to § 30-152, Acts 2001, cc. 815 and 842 have been given effect in this section as set out above.

§ 2.2-1177. Transfer of surplus motor vehicles. — The Director may transfer surplus motor vehicles among state agencies, and determine the value of such surplus equipment for the purpose of maintaining the financial accounts of the state agencies affected by such transfers. (1989, c. 479, § 33.1-404; 2001, cc. 815, 842, § 2.1-548.05.)

Cross references. — As to exemption of certain motor vehicles acquired from the centralized fleet of motor vehicles controlled by the Commonwealth Transportation Commissioner and sold or transferred to TANF recipients or former recipients from the provisions of §§ 2.2-4300 et seq., 2.2-1124, 2.2-1153, 2.2-1156, and 2.2-1177, see § 63.2-611 D.

Editor's note. — Acts 2001, cc. 815 and 842 enacted § 2.1-548.05, from which this section is derived. Pursuant to § 30-152, Acts 2001, cc. 815 and 842 have been given effect in this section as set out above.

§ 2.2-1178. Use of passenger-type vehicles on an assigned basis. — A. Passenger-type vehicles assigned to the centralized fleet may be assigned to persons performing state duties only if deemed necessary by the head of the agency or institution requesting such vehicle and approved in writing by the Director. Request for such vehicle shall be made in writing on forms prepared by the Department of General Services by the head of the agency or institution explaining in detail the purpose of or reason for such assignment.

B. Assignments shall be approved by the Director only on the basis of one of the following criteria:

1. The vehicle shall be driven not less than an annual minimum of mileage to be calculated by dividing the most recently approved annual replacement charge for the use of a state-owned vehicle by the remainder of the state reimbursement rate per mile for personal vehicles minus the cost per mile for operating a state-owned vehicle;

2. The vehicle shall be used by an employee whose duties are routinely related to public safety or response to life-threatening situations:

a. A law-enforcement officer as defined in § 9.1-101, with general or limited police powers;

b. An employee whose job duties require the constant use or continuous availability of specialized equipment directly related to their routine functions; or

c. An employee on twenty-four-hour call who must respond to emergencies on a regular or continuing basis, and emergency response is normally to a location other than the employee's official work station; or

3. The vehicle shall be used for essential travel related to the transportation of clients or wards of the Commonwealth on a routine basis, or for essential administrative functions of the agency for which it is demonstrated that use of a temporary assignment or personal mileage reimbursement is neither feasible nor economical.

C. No assignment shall be for a period exceeding two years except upon review by the Director as to the continued need for the assignment.

D. The use of such vehicle shall be limited to official state business. (1989, c. 479, § 33.1-405; 2001, cc. 815, 842, § 2.1-548.06.)

Editor's note. — Acts 2001, cc. 815 and 842 enacted § 2.1-548.06, from which this section is derived. Pursuant to § 30-152, Acts 2001, cc. 815 and 842 have been given effect in this section as set out above.

§ **2.2-1179. Use of vehicles for commuting.** — No passenger-type vehicle purchased or leased with public funds shall be used to commute between an employee's home and official work station without the prior written approval of the agency head and, in the case of vehicles assigned to the centralized fleet, the Director. The Director shall issue regulations governing such use of vehicles and shall ensure that costs associated with such use shall be recovered from employees. Employees who do not report to an official work station shall not be required to pay for travel between their homes and field sites. Regulations promulgated by the Director and recovery of costs shall not apply to use of vehicles by law-enforcement officers. By executive order of the Governor, such rules and regulations may extend to all motor vehicles of any type owned by the Commonwealth, or such of them as the Governor may designate. (1989, c. 479, § 33.1-406; 2001, cc. 815, 842, § 2.1-548.07.)

Editor's note. — Acts 2001, cc. 815 and 842 enacted § 2.1-548.07, from which this section is derived. Pursuant to § 30-152, Acts 2001, cc. 815 and 842 have been given effect in this section as set out above.

§ **2.2-1180. Regulations governing state-owned passenger-type vehicles.** — The Director may promulgate regulations for the purchase, use, storage, maintenance, repair and disposal of all passenger-type vehicles owned by the Commonwealth and assigned to the centralized fleet. By executive order of the Governor, such regulations may extend to all motor vehicles of any type owned by the Commonwealth, or such of them as the Governor may designate.

If any state officer, agent, or employee fails to comply with any regulation of the Director made pursuant to the provisions of this section, the Secretary of Administration shall be so notified, and the Comptroller shall, upon request of the Secretary, refuse to issue any warrant or warrants on account of expenses incurred, or to be incurred in the purchase, operation, maintenance, or repair of any motor vehicle now or to be in the possession or under the control of such officer, agent or employee, or the Secretary of Administration may order the Director to take possession of any such vehicle and to return or transfer it to the centralized fleet for assignment or use as prescribed by this chapter. Regulations previously promulgated by the Commonwealth Transportation Board under the authority granted by § 33.1-407 concerning the purchase, use, storage, maintenance, repair and disposal of all passenger-type vehicles owned by the Commonwealth and assigned to the centralized fleet shall remain in effect until the Director promulgates replacement regulations under the authority granted by this article. (1989, c. 479, § 33.1-407; 1990, cc. 1, 317; 2001, cc. 815, 842, § 2.1-548.08.)

Editor's note. — Acts 2001, cc. 815 and 842 enacted § 2.1-548.08, from which this section is derived. Pursuant to § 30-152, Acts 2001, cc. 815 and 842 have been given effect in this section as set out above.

Section 33.1-407, referred to above, was repealed by Acts 2001, cc. 815, 842, cl. 2, and is the precursor to this section.

§ 2.2-1181. Fleet Management Internal Service Fund. — There is hereby established a Fleet Management Internal Service Fund to be used exclusively to finance the operations of the centralized fleet. (1989, c. 479, § 33.1-408; 2001, cc. 815, 842, § 2.1-548.09.)

Editor's note. — Acts 2001, cc. 815 and 842 enacted § 2.1-548.09, from which this section is derived. Pursuant to § 30-152, Acts 2001, cc. 815 and 842 have been given effect in this section as set out above.

CHAPTER 12.

Department of Human Resource Management.

§ 2.2-1200. Department of Human Resource Management created; Director. — A. There is created a Department of Human Resource Management (the "Department"), which shall be headed by a Director appointed by the Governor to serve at his pleasure.

B. The Director of the Department shall, under the direction and control of the Governor, exercise such powers and perform such duties as are delegated to him by the Governor or conferred or imposed upon him by law and perform such other duties as may be required by the Governor. (Code 1950, § 2-81; 1966, cc. 55, 677, § 2.1-113; 1975, c. 390; 1976, c. 761, § 2.1-114.3; 1978, c. 846; 1984, c. 720; 2000, cc. 66, 657; 2001, c. 844.)

Cross references. — For present provisions as to the Virginia Council on Human Resources, see § 2.2-2675 et seq.

CASE NOTES

Editor's note. — The case below was decided under former Title 2.1 or prior provisions.

Legislative intent to preclude judicial review. — The "final authority" language in former § 2.1-114.5:6 (7) supported and was consistent with a legislative intent shown throughout the act to preclude judicial review in certain areas. Murray v. Stokes, 237 Va. 653, 378 S.E.2d 834 (1989).

Judicial review of the interpretation of a personnel policy regarding employee compensation by the Director of the Department of Personnel and Training (now Department of Human Resource Management) is precluded under the Virginia Personnel Act, and therefore, the trial court had no jurisdiction to entertain a bill of complaint seeking review of the interpretation of Rule 8.3 (d) of the Department of Personnel and training's rules by the director of that department. Murray v. Stokes, 237 Va. 653, 378 S.E.2d 834 (1989).

§ 2.2-1201. Duties of Department. — The Department shall have the following duties:

1. Make recommendations to the Governor regarding the establishment and maintenance of a classification plan for the service of the Commonwealth, and recommend necessary amendments thereto.

2. Make recommendations to the Governor regarding the establishment and administration of a compensation plan for all employees, and recommend necessary amendments thereto.

3. Design and maintain a personnel information system that shall support the operational needs of the Department and of state agencies, and that shall provide for the management information needs of the Governor, his secretaries, and the General Assembly. The system shall provide at a minimum a roster of all employees in the service of the Commonwealth, in which there shall be set forth as to each employee, the employing agency, the class title, pay, status and such other data as may be deemed desirable to produce significant facts pertaining to personnel administration.

4. Establish and direct a program of employee-management relations designed to improve communications between employees and agencies of the Commonwealth.

5. Establish and administer a system of performance evaluation for all employees in the service of the Commonwealth, based on the quality of service rendered, related where practicable to specific standards of performance. In no event shall workers' compensation leave affect the total number of hours credited during a performance cycle for purposes of calculating incentive increases in salary based on such performance evaluations.

6. Establish and administer a system of recruitment designed to attract high quality employees to the service of the Commonwealth. In administering this system, applicants shall be rated on the basis of relative merit and classified in accordance with their suitability for the various classes of positions in the service of the Commonwealth, and a record thereof shall be maintained in the open register.

7. Design and utilize an application form which shall include, but not be limited to, information on prior volunteer work performed by the applicant.

8. Establish and administer a comprehensive and integrated program of employee training and management development.

9. Establish and administer a program of evaluation of the effectiveness of performance of the personnel activities of the agencies of the Commonwealth.

10. Establish and administer a program to ensure equal employment opportunity to applicants for state employment and to state employees in all incidents of employment.

11. Establish and administer regulations relating to disciplinary actions; however, no disciplinary action shall include the suspension without pay for more than 10 days of any state employee who is under investigation without a

hearing conducted either by a level of supervision above the employee's immediate supervisor or by his agency head.

12. Adopt and implement a centralized program to provide awards to employees who propose procedures or ideas that are adopted and that will result in eliminating or reducing state expenditures or improving operations, provided such proposals are placed in effect. The centralized program shall be designed to (i) protect the identity of the individual making the proposal while it is being evaluated for implementation by a state agency, (ii) publicize the acceptance of proposals and financial awards to state employees, and (iii) include a reevaluation process that individuals making proposals may access if their proposals are rejected by the evaluating agency. The reevaluation process must include individuals from the private sector. State employees who make a suggestion or proposal under this section shall receive initial confirmation of receipt within 30 days. A determination of the feasibility of the suggestion or proposal shall occur within 60 days of initial receipt.

13. Develop state personnel policies and, after approval by the Governor, disseminate and interpret state personnel policies and procedures to all agencies. Such personnel policies shall permit an employee, with the written approval of his agency head, to substitute (i) up to 33 percent of his accrued paid sick leave, (ii) up to 100 percent of any other paid leave, or (iii) any combination of accrued paid sick leave and any other paid leave for leave taken pursuant to the Family and Medical Leave Act of 1993 (29 U.S.C. § 2601 et seq.). On and after December 1, 1999, such personnel policy shall include an acceptable use policy for the Internet. At a minimum, the Department's acceptable use policy shall contain provisions that (i) prohibit use by state employees of the Commonwealth's computer equipment and communications services for sending, receiving, viewing, or downloading illegal material via the Internet and (ii) establish strict disciplinary measures for violation of the acceptable use policy. An agency head may supplement the Department's acceptable use policy with such other terms, conditions, and requirements as he deems appropriate. The Director of the Department shall have the final authority to establish and interpret personnel policies and procedures and shall have the authority to ensure full compliance with such policies. However, unless specifically authorized by law, the Director of the Department shall have no authority with respect to the state grievance procedures.

13a. Develop state personnel policies, with the approval of the Governor, that permit any full-time state employee who is also a member of the organized reserve forces of any of the armed services of the United States or of the Virginia National Guard to carry forward from year to year the total of his accrued annual leave time without regard to the regulation or policy of his agency regarding the maximum number of hours allowed to be carried forward at the end of a calendar year. Any amount over the usual amount allowed to be carried forward shall be reserved for use only as leave taken pursuant to active military service as provided by § 2.2-2903.1. Such leave and its use shall be in addition to leave provided under § 44-93. Any leave carried forward for the purposes described remaining upon termination of employment with the Commonwealth or any department, institution or agency thereof that has not been used in accordance with § 2.2-2903.1 shall not be paid or credited in any way to the employee.

14. Ascertain and publish on an annual basis, by agency, the number of employees in the service of the Commonwealth, including permanent full-time and part-time employees, those employed on a temporary or contractual basis, and constitutional officers and their employees whose salaries are funded by the Commonwealth. The publication shall contain the net gain or loss to the agency in personnel from the previous fiscal year and the net gains and losses in personnel for each agency for a three-year period.

15. Submit a report to the members of the General Assembly on or before September 30 of each year showing (i) the total number of full- and part-time employees, (ii) contract temporary employees, (iii) hourly temporary employees, and (iv) the number of employees who voluntarily and involuntarily terminated their employment with each department, agency or institution in the previous fiscal year.

16. Administer the workers' compensation insurance plan for state employees in accordance with § 2.2-2821.

17. Work jointly with the Department of General Services and the Virginia Information Technologies Agency to develop expedited processes for the procurement of staff augmentation to supplement salaried and wage employees of state agencies. Such processes shall be consistent with the Virginia Public Procurement Act (§ 2.2-4300 et seq.). The Department may perform contract administration duties and responsibilities for any resulting statewide augmentation contracts. (1976, c. 761, § 2.1-114.5; 1978, cc. 844, 845; 1979, c. 482; 1980, c. 198; 1988, c. 208; 1989, c. 254; 1992, c. 424; 1993, c. 561; 1994, cc. 17, 954; 1997, c. 856; 1999, c. 384; 2000, cc. 66, 633, 657, 697; 2001, c. 844; 2002, c. 780; 2003, cc. 685, 789; 2005, c. 386; 2006, c. 474; 2008, c. 576.)

Editor's note. — Acts 1994, c. 954, cl. 2, which amended former § 2.1-114.5, from which this section was derived, provides: "That eligibility under the provisions of this act shall be retroactive to January 1, 1993, for any employee of the Virginia State Police."

Acts 1997, c. 856, cl. 2, provides: "That any personnel policy of the Department of Personnel and Training [now Department of Human Resource Management] which is inconsistent with this act shall be null and void on the effective date of this act [January 1, 1996]."

Acts 1997, c. 856, cl. 3, provides: "That an emergency exists and this act [which amended former § 2.1-114.5, from which this section was derived] is effective retroactive to January 1, 1996."

Acts 2005, c. 386, cl. 2, provides: "That the Department of Human Resource Management shall report annually to the Governor and the General Assembly on (i) the number of proposals received and what, if any, actions were taken on them, (ii) the number of proposals that were implemented and the results of those efforts in eliminating or reducing state expenditures or improving operations, (iii) the number of dollars and awards made to employees for adopted proposals, (iv) the actual cost savings realized as a result of implementing such proposals, and (v) the number of proposals that were not implemented or acted upon with an explanation or justification for inaction."

The 2008 amendments. — The 2008 amendment by c. 576 added subdivision 17.

§ 2.2-1201.1. Criminal background checks for certain positions. — The Department shall develop a statewide personnel policy for designating positions within each state agency as sensitive. Such policy shall provide for a state agency to require any final candidate for a position that has been designated as sensitive to submit to fingerprinting and to provide personal descriptive information to be forwarded along with the applicant's fingerprints through the Central Criminal Records Exchange to the Federal Bureau of Investigation for the purpose of obtaining criminal history information regarding such applicant.

For purposes of this section, *"sensitive positions"* shall mean those positions generally described as directly responsible for the health, safety and welfare of the general populace or protection of critical infrastructures. (2003, c. 731.)

§ 2.2-1202. Employee compensation; annual review. — It is a goal of the Commonwealth that its employees be compensated at a rate comparable to the rate of compensation for employees in the private sector of the Commonwealth in similar occupations. In determining comparability, consideration shall be given to the economic value of fringe benefits in addition to direct compensation. An annual review shall be conducted by the Director of the Department to determine where discrepancies in compensation exist as between the public and private sectors of the Commonwealth. The results of the review shall be reported by December 15 of each year to the Governor and the General Assembly. (1976, c. 761, § 2.1-114.6; 2001, c. 844.)

§ 2.2-1203. Certain information not to be made public. — Notwithstanding the provisions of the Freedom of Information Act (§ 2.2-3700 et seq.), the Department shall not disclose lists of home addresses of state employees except in accordance with regulations adopted by the Department pursuant to the Administrative Process Act (§ 2.2-4000 et seq.). (1994, c. 892, § 2.1-114.5:01; 2001, c. 844.)

§ 2.2-1204. Health insurance program for employees of local governments, local officers, teachers, etc.; definitions. — A. The Department shall establish a plan or plans, hereinafter "plan" or "plans", subject to the approval of the Governor, for providing health insurance coverage for employees of local governments, local officers, teachers, and retirees, and the dependents of such employees, officers, teachers and retirees. The plan or plans shall be rated separately from the plan established pursuant to § 2.2-2818 to provide health and related insurance coverage for state employees. Participation in such insurance plan or plans shall be (i) voluntary, (ii) approved by the participant's respective governing body, or by the local school board in the case of teachers, and (iii) subject to regulations adopted by the Department. In addition, at the option of a governing body or school board that has elected to participate in the health insurance plan or plans offered by the Department, the governing body or school board may elect to participate in the long-term care or other benefit program that the Department may make available to the governing body or school board.

B. The plan established by the Department shall satisfy the requirements of the Virginia Public Procurement Act (§ 2.2-4300 et seq.), shall consist of a flexible benefits structure that permits the creation of multiple plans of benefits and may provide for separate rating groups based upon criteria established by the Department. The Department shall adopt regulations regarding the establishment of such a plan or plans, including, but not limited to, requirements for eligibility, participation, access and egress, mandatory employer contributions and financial reserves, and the administration of the plan or plans. The Department may engage the services of other professional advisors and vendors as necessary for the prudent administration of the plan or plans. The assets of the plan or plans, together with all appropriations, premiums and other payments, shall be deposited in the employee health insurance fund, from which payments for claims, premiums, cost containment programs and administrative expenses shall be withdrawn from time to time. The assets of the fund shall be held for the sole benefit of the employee health insurance fund. The fund shall be held in the state treasury. Any interest on unused balances in the fund shall revert back to the credit of the fund. The State Treasurer shall charge reasonable fees to recover the actual costs of investing the assets of the plan or plans.

In establishing the participation requirements, the Department may provide that those employees, officers, and teachers without access to employer-sponsored health care coverage may participate in the plan. It shall collect all premiums directly from the employers of such employees, officers, and teachers.

C. In the event that the financial reserves of the plan fall to an unacceptably low level as determined by the Department, it shall have the authority to secure from the State Treasurer a loan sufficient to raise the reserve level to one that is considered adequate. The State Treasurer may make such a loan, to be repaid on such terms and conditions as established by him.

D. For the purposes of this section:

"Employees of local governments" shall include all officers and employees of the governing body of any county, city or town, and the directing or governing body of any political entity, subdivision, branch or unit of the Commonwealth or of any commission or public authority or body corporate created by or under an act of the General Assembly specifying the power or powers, privileges or authority capable of exercise by the commission or public authority or body corporate, as distinguished from § 15.2-1300, 15.2-1303, or similar statutes, provided that the officers and employees of a social services department, welfare board, mental health, mental retardation and substance abuse services board, center for independent living funded in whole or in part by the Department of Rehabilitative Services pursuant to the provisions of Chapter 6 (§ 51.5-23 et seq.) of Title 51.5, or library board of a county, city, or town shall be deemed to be employees of local government.

"Governing body," with regard to a center for independent living, means the governing board of an applicant established to operate the center for independent living as required by subsection B of § 51.5-23.

"Local officer" means the treasurer, registrar, commissioner of the revenue, attorney for the Commonwealth, clerk of a circuit court, sheriff, or constable of any county or city or deputies or employees of any of the preceding local officers.

"Teacher" means any employee of a county, city, or other local public school board.

E. Any stock and cash distributed to the Commonwealth pursuant to the conversion of Blue Cross and Blue Shield of Virginia, doing business as Trigon Blue Cross Blue Shield, from a mutual insurance company to a stock corporation known as Trigon Healthcare, Inc., that is directly attributable to the health insurance plan or plans established for employees of local governments, local officers, teachers, and retirees, and the dependents of such employees, officers, teachers and retirees, pursuant to subsection A (hereinafter referred to as the local choice plan distribution) shall be deposited in the state treasury to the credit of the employee health insurance fund to be used as provided in this subsection. Such distribution shall not include any cash paid by Blue Cross and Blue Shield of Virginia or its successor to the Commonwealth in connection with such conversion that was assumed as general fund revenue in Chapter 912 of the 1996 Acts of Assembly. All other stock and cash received by the Commonwealth pursuant to such conversion of Blue Cross and Blue Shield of Virginia to a stock corporation shall be allocated as provided in subsection B of § 23-284.

The State Treasurer shall sell any stock received pursuant to the local choice plan distribution as soon as practicable following its receipt, subject to any lockup period or other restriction on its sale, and the proceeds therefrom shall be deposited in the state treasury to the credit of the employee health insurance fund. Notwithstanding any other provision of law to the contrary, the State Treasurer shall not be liable for any losses incurred from the sale or distribution of such stock.

The Department of Human Resource Management shall use any stock, or the proceeds therefrom, and cash received pursuant to the local choice plan distribution to reduce premiums payable by employers participating in a plan or plans established pursuant to subsection A. In setting health insurance premiums for such plan or plans, the Director of the Department of Human Resource Management shall allocate the value of such stock, or proceeds therefrom, and cash among each participating employer. Such allocation shall be based on the proportionate amounts of premiums previously paid by each participating employer. If a participating employer withdraws from such plan or plans before all of the value allocated to it has been used for the benefit of the participating employer, the remaining value shall be transferred to such participating employer upon his withdrawal. (1989, c. 475, § 2.1-20.1:02; 1997, cc. 803, 888, 891; 2000, cc. 66, 620, 649, 657; 2001, cc. 520, 806, 844; 2008, c. 403.)

Editor's note. — Acts 2001, cc. 520 and 806 amended § 2.1-20.1:02, from which this section is derived. Pursuant to § 30-152, Acts 2001, cc. 520 and 806 have been given effect in this section as set out above. The 2001 amendments by cc. 520 and 806 are identical, and deleted former subsection C, pertaining to the administration of the health insurance plan or plans and recommendations made by an advisory committee, and redesignated former subsections D, E and F as present subsections C, D and E.

Acts 2008, c. 879, effective for the biennium ending June 30, 2010, in Item 262, provides: "In the event of default by any employer participating in the health insurance program authorized by §2.2-1204, Code of Virginia, in the remittance of premiums or other fees and costs of the program, the State Comptroller is hereby authorized to pay such premiums and costs and to recover such payments from any funds appropriated and payable by the Commonwealth to the employer for any purpose. The State Comptroller shall make such payments upon receipt of notice from the Director, Department of Human Resource Management, that such payments are due and unpaid from the employer."

The 2008 amendments. — The 2008 amendment by c. 403, in subsection D, deleted "§" preceding "15.2-1300" and inserted "center for independent living funded in whole or in part by the Department of Rehabilitative Services pursuant to the provisions of Chapter 6 (§ 51.5-23 et seq.) of Title 51.5" in the definition of "Employees of local governments" and added the definition of "Governing body."

OPINIONS OF THE ATTORNEY GENERAL

Certain individuals entitled to health benefits under the Line of Duty Act may receive those benefits through the state health benefits program. See opinion of Attorney General to Ms. Sara Redding Wilson, Director, Department of Human Resource Management, 03-090 (12/18/03).

§ 2.2-1205. Purchase of continued health insurance coverage by the surviving spouse and any dependents of an active or retired local law-enforcement officer, firefighter, etc., through the Department. — A. The surviving spouse and any dependents of an active or retired law-enforcement officer of any county, city, or town of the Commonwealth; a jail officer; a regional jail or jail farm superintendent; a sheriff, deputy sheriff, or city sergeant or deputy city sergeant of the City of Richmond; a member of any fire company or department or rescue squad that has been recognized by an ordinance or a resolution of the governing body of any county, city, or town of this Commonwealth as an integral part of the official safety program of such county, city or town; or a member of an emergency medical services department, whose death occurs as the direct or proximate result of the performance of his duty, including the presumptions under §§ 27-40.1, 27-40.2, 51.1-813, and 65.2-402, shall be entitled, upon proper application to the Department, to purchase continued health insurance coverage on the following conditions: (i) on the date of death, the deceased participated in a health insurance plan administered by the Department pursuant to § 2.2-1204 and (ii) on the date of the deceased's death, the applicants were included in the health insurance plan in condition (i) of this subsection. The health insurance plan administered by the Department pursuant to § 2.2-1204 shall provide means whereby coverage for the spouse and any dependents of the deceased as provided in this section may be purchased. The spouse and any dependents of the deceased who purchase continued health insurance coverage pursuant to this section shall pay the same portion of the applicable premium as active employees pay for the same class of coverage, and the local government employer that employed the deceased shall pay the remaining portion of the premium.

B. Any application to purchase continued health insurance coverage hereunder shall be made in writing to the Department within sixty days of the date of the deceased's death. The time for making application may be extended by the Department for good cause shown.

C. In addition to any necessary information requested by the Department, the application shall state whether conditions (i) and (ii) set forth in subsection A of this section have been met. If the Department states that such conditions have not been met, the Department shall conduct an informal fact-finding conference or consultation with the applicant pursuant to § 2.2-4019 of the Administrative Process Act. Upon scheduling the conference or consultation, the provisions of the Administrative Process Act (§ 2.2-4000 et seq.) shall apply thereafter.

D. Upon payment of any required premiums, coverage shall automatically be extended during the period for making application and shall be effective retroactive to the date of the deceased's death.

E. The terms, conditions, and costs of continued health insurance coverage purchased hereunder shall be subject to administration by the Department. The Department may increase the cost of coverage consistent with its administration of health insurance plans under § 2.2-1204. However, at no time shall a surviving spouse or dependents pay more for continued health insurance coverage than active employees pay under the same plan for the same class of coverage.

F. For the surviving spouse, continued health insurance coverage purchased hereunder shall automatically terminate upon occurrence of any of the following: (i) death, (ii) remarriage, (iii) alternate health insurance coverage being obtained, or (iv) any applicable condition outlined in the policies and procedures of the Department governing health insurance plans administered pursuant to § 2.2-1204.

G. For any surviving dependents, continued health insurance coverage purchased hereunder shall automatically terminate upon occurrence of any of the following: (i) death; (ii) marriage; (iii) alternate health insurance coverage being obtained; (iv) attaining the age of twenty-one, unless the dependent is (a) a full-time college student, in which event coverage shall not terminate until such dependent has either attained the age of twenty-five or until such time as the dependent ceases to be a full-time college student, whichever occurs first, or (b) under a mental or physical disability, in which event coverage shall not terminate until three months following cessation of the disability; or (v) any applicable condition outlined in the policies and procedures of the Department governing health insurance plans administered pursuant to § 2.2-1204. (1997, c. 886, § 2.1-20.1:04; 1998, c. 699; 2000, cc. 66, 657; 2001, c. 844.)

§ 2.2-1206. Purchase of continued health insurance coverage by the surviving spouse and any dependents of an active local law-enforcement officer, firefighter, etc., through a plan sponsor. — A. For the purposes of this section, *"plan sponsor"* means a local government employer that has established a plan of health insurance coverage for its employees, retirees and dependents of employees as are described in subsection B.

B. The surviving spouse and any dependents of an active law-enforcement officer of any county, city, or town of this Commonwealth; a jail officer; a regional jail or jail farm superintendent; a sheriff, deputy sheriff, or city sergeant or deputy city sergeant of the City of Richmond; a member of any fire company or department or rescue squad that has been recognized by an ordinance or a resolution of the governing body of any county, city, or town of this Commonwealth as an integral part of the official safety program of such county, city or town; or a member of an emergency medical services department; whose death occurs as the direct or proximate result of the performance of his duty shall be entitled, upon proper application to the appropriate plan sponsor, to purchase continued health insurance coverage on the following conditions: (i) on the date of death, the deceased participated in a health insurance plan administered by the plan sponsor and (ii) on the date of the deceased's death, the applicants were included in the health insurance plan in condition (i) of this subsection. The health insurance plan administered by the plan sponsor shall provide means whereby coverage for the spouse and any dependents of the deceased as provided in this section may be purchased.

C. Any application to purchase continued health insurance coverage hereunder shall be made in writing to the plan sponsor within sixty days of the date of the deceased's death. The time for making application may be extended by the plan sponsor for good cause shown.

D. In addition to any necessary information requested by the plan sponsor, the application shall state whether conditions (i) and (ii) set forth in subsection B have been met. If the plan sponsor states that such conditions have not been met, the plan sponsor, notwithstanding the provisions of §§ 2.2-4002, 2.2-4006, or § 2.2-4011, shall conduct an informal fact-finding conference or consultation with the applicant pursuant to § 2.2-4019 of the Administrative Process Act. Upon scheduling the conference or consultation, the provisions of the local government's grievance procedure for nonprobationary, permanent employees shall apply thereafter.

E. Upon payment of any required premiums, coverage shall automatically be extended during the period for making application and shall be effective retroactive to the date of the deceased's death.

F. The terms, conditions, and costs of continued health insurance coverage purchased hereunder shall be subject to administration by the plan sponsor. The plan sponsor may increase the cost of coverage consistent with its administration of health insurance plans under § 2.2-1204. However, at no time shall the surviving spouse or dependents pay more for continued health insurance coverage than the active employee rate under the same plan for the same class of coverage.

G. For the surviving spouse, continued health insurance coverage purchased hereunder shall automatically terminate upon occurrence of any of the following: (i) death, (ii) remarriage, (iii) alternate health insurance coverage being obtained, or (iv) any applicable condition outlined in the policies and procedures of the plan sponsor governing health insurance plans administered for its active employees.

H. For any surviving dependents, continued health insurance coverage purchased hereunder shall automatically terminate upon occurrence of any of the following: (i) death; (ii) marriage; (iii) alternate health insurance coverage being obtained; (iv) attaining the age of twenty-one, unless the dependent is (a) a full-time college student, in which event coverage shall not terminate until such dependent has either attained the age of twenty-five or until such time as the dependent ceases to be a full-time college student, whichever occurs first, or (b) under a mental or physical disability, in which event coverage shall not terminate until three months following cessation of the disability; or (v) any applicable condition outlined in the policies and procedures of the plan sponsor governing health insurance plans administered for its active employees. (1998, c. 698, § 2.1-20.1:05; 2001, c. 844.)

§ 2.2-1207. Long-term care insurance program for employees of local governments, local officers, and teachers. — A. The Department shall establish a plan or plans, hereinafter "plan" or "plans," subject to the approval of the Governor, for providing long-term care insurance coverage for employees of local governments, local officers, and teachers. The plan or plans shall be rated separately from the plan developed pursuant to § 51.1-513.1 to provide long-term care insurance coverage for state employees. Participation in such insurance plan or plans shall be (i) voluntary, (ii) approved by the participant's respective governing body, or by the local school board in the case of teachers, and (iii) subject to regulations adopted by the Department.

B. The Department shall adopt regulations regarding the establishment of such a plan or plans, and the administration of the plan or plans.

C. For the purposes of this section:

"Employees of local governments" shall include all officers and employees of the governing body of any county, city or town, and the directing or governing body of any political entity, subdivision, branch or unit of the Commonwealth or of any commission or public authority or body corporate created by or under an act of the General Assembly specifying the power or powers, privileges or authority capable of exercise by the commission or public authority or body corporate, as distinguished from §§ 15.2-1300, 15.2-1303, or similar statutes, provided that the officers and employees of a social services department, welfare board, mental health, mental retardation and substance abuse services board, or library board of a county, city, or town shall be deemed to be employees of local government.

"Local officer" means the treasurer, registrar, commissioner of the revenue, attorney for the Commonwealth, clerk of a circuit court, sheriff, or constable of any county or city or deputies or employees of any of the preceding local officers.

"Teacher" means any employee of a county, city, or other local public school board.

D. The Department shall not carry out the provisions of this section if and when the Virginia Retirement System assumes responsibility for the plan or plans pursuant to § 51.1-513.3. (2002, c. 280; 2008, c. 568.)

The 2008 amendments. — The 2008 amendment by c. 568 added subsection D.

§ **2.2-1208. Long-term care insurance.** — A. The Department of Human Resource Management shall develop, implement, and administer a long-term care insurance program for state employees and for any person who has five or more years of creditable service with any retirement plan administered by the Virginia Retirement System. The Department of Human Resource Management is authorized to contract for and purchase such coverage or use other actuarially sound funding necessary to effectuate this provision.

B. Any person eligible to participate in the long-term care insurance program established pursuant to § 2.2-1207 will not be eligible for this plan.

C. The Department shall adopt regulations regarding the establishment and the administration of the plan or plans.

D. The Department shall not carry out the provisions of this section if and when the Virginia Retirement System assumes responsibility for the long-term care coverage program pursuant to § 51.1-513.2. (2004, c. 312; 2008, c. 568.)

The 2008 amendments. — The 2008 amendment by c. 568 deleted "emergency" preceding "regulations" in subsection C; and added subsection D.

CHAPTER 13.

Department of Information Technology.

§§ **2.2-1300 through 2.2-1304:** Repealed by Acts 2003, cc. 981 and 1021.

Editor's note. — For provisions of Acts 2003, cc. 981 and 1021, cls. 4 to 16, reflecting the intent of the General Assembly to provide for the consolidation of the procurement and operational functions of information technology for state agencies in a single agency, and related transitional and other provisions, see the Editor's note at § 2.2-2005.

The amendments to repealed § 2.2-1303 by Acts 2003, cc. 352 and 895, were given effect in § 2.2-2012.

CHAPTER 14.

Department of Minority Business Enterprise.

§ 2.2-1400. Creation of Department of Minority Business Enterprise; appointment of Director; offices; personnel. — A. There is created within the Office of the Governor a Department of Minority Business Enterprise (the "Department"), which shall be headed by a Director appointed by the Governor to serve at his pleasure. The Director shall also serve as a special assistant to the Governor for minority enterprise.

B. The Director of the Department shall, under the direction and control of the Governor, exercise the powers and perform the duties conferred or imposed upon him by law and perform such other duties as may be required by the Governor.

C. The Department shall have its main office in Richmond and may have branch offices as may be necessary, as determined by the Director subject to the approval of the Secretary of Commerce and Trade. (1975, c. 509, §§ 2.1-64.32, 2.1-64.33; 1979, c. 147; 1983, c. 41; 1985, c. 447; 1986, c. 492; 1989, c.268; 1993, c. 699; 2001, c. 844.)

§ 2.2-1401. Definitions. — As used in this chapter unless the context requires a different meaning:

"Certification" means the process by which a business is determined to be a small, women- or minority-owned business for the purpose of reporting small, women-owned, and minority-owned business participation in state contracts and purchases pursuant to §§ 2.2-1404 and 2.2-1405.

"Disadvantaged business enterprise" means a small business concern, as defined in 49 CFR Parts 23 and 26, that is at least 51% owned by one or more socially and economically disadvantaged individuals, or, in the case of any corporation, partnership, or limited liability company or other entity, at least 51% of the equity ownership is owned by one or more socially and economically disadvantaged individuals and the management and daily business operations are controlled by one or more of the socially and economically disadvantaged individuals who own it.

"Minority individual" means an individual who is a citizen of the United States or a non-citizen who is in full compliance with United States immigration law and who satisfies one or more of the following definitions:

1. *"African American"* means a person having origins in any of the original peoples of Africa and who is regarded as such by the community of which this person claims to be a part.

2. *"Asian American"* means a person having origins in any of the original peoples of the Far East, Southeast Asia, the Indian subcontinent, or the Pacific Islands, including but not limited to Japan, China, Vietnam, Samoa, Laos, Cambodia, Taiwan, Northern Mariana, the Philippines, a U.S. territory of the Pacific, India, Pakistan, Bangladesh, or Sri Lanka and who is regarded as such by the community of which this person claims to be a part.

3. *"Hispanic American"* means a person having origins in any of the Spanish-speaking peoples of Mexico, South or Central America, or the Caribbean Islands or other Spanish or Portuguese cultures and who is regarded as such by the community of which this person claims to be a part.

4. *"Native American"* means a person having origins in any of the original peoples of North America and who is regarded as such by the community of which this person claims to be a part or who is recognized by a tribal organization.

"Minority-owned business" means a business concern that is at least 51% owned by one or more minority individuals or in the case of a corporation, partnership, or limited liability company or other entity, at least 51% of the equity ownership interest in the corporation, partnership, or limited liability company or other entity is owned by one or more minority individuals and both the management and daily business operations are controlled by one or more minority individuals.

"Small business" means an independently owned and operated business which, together with affiliates, has 250 or fewer employees, or average annual gross receipts of $10 million or less averaged over the previous three years.

"State agency" means any authority, board, department, instrumentality, institution, agency, or other unit of state government. *"State agency"* shall not include any county, city, or town.

"Women-owned business" means a business concern that is at least 51% owned by one or more women who are U.S. citizens or legal resident aliens, or in the case of a corporation, partnership, or limited liability company or other entity, at least 51% of the equity ownership interest is owned by one or more women who are citizens of the United States or non-citizens who are in full compliance with the United States immigration law, and both the management and daily business operations are controlled by one or more women who are U.S. citizens or legal resident aliens. (1989, c. 268, § 2.1-64.32:1; 2001, c. 844; 2006, cc. 831, 921.)

§ 2.2-1402. Additional powers and duties of Department. — The Department shall have the following additional powers and duties:

1. Coordinate as consistent with prevailing law the plans, programs and operations of the state government that affect or may contribute to the establishment, preservation, and strengthening of small, women- and minority-owned businesses.

2. Promote the mobilization of activities and resources of state and local governments, businesses and trade associations, universities, foundations, professional organizations, and volunteer and other groups towards the growth of small businesses and businesses owned by women and minorities, and facilitate the coordination of the efforts of these groups with those of state departments and agencies.

3. Establish a center for the development, collection, summarization, and dissemination of information that will be helpful to persons and organizations throughout the nation in undertaking or promoting procurement from small, women- and minority-owned businesses.

4. Consistent with prevailing law and availability of funds, and according to the Director's discretion, provide technical and management assistance to small, women- and minority-owned businesses, and defray all or part of the

costs of pilot or demonstration projects that are designed to overcome the special problems of small, women- and minority-owned businesses.

5. Manage the Capital Access Fund for Disadvantaged Businesses created pursuant to § 2.2-2311, and, in cooperation with the Small Business Financing Authority, determine the qualifications, terms, and conditions for the use of such Fund.

6. Implement any remediation or enhancement measure for small, women- or minority-owned businesses as may be authorized by the Governor pursuant to subsection C of § 2.2-4310 and develop regulations, consistent with prevailing law, for program implementation. Such regulations shall be developed in consultation with the state agencies with procurement responsibility and promulgated by those agencies in accordance with applicable law. (1975, c. 509, § 2.1-64.34; 2001, c. 844; 2006, cc. 831, 921.)

§ **2.2-1403. Powers of Director.** — As deemed necessary or appropriate to better fulfill the duties of the Department, the Director may:

1. With the participation of other state departments and agencies, develop comprehensive plans and specific program goals for the small, women- and minority-owned business programs; establish regular performance monitoring and reporting systems to assure that goals of state agencies and institutions are being achieved; and evaluate the impact of federal and state support in achieving objectives.

2. Employ the necessary personnel and/or subcontract according to his discretion, with localities to supplement the functions of business development organizations.

3. Assure the coordinated review of all proposed state training and technical assistance activities in direct support of the small, women- and minority-owned business programs to ensure consistency with program goals and to avoid duplication.

4. Convene, for purposes of coordination, meetings of the heads of departments and agencies, or their designees, whose programs and activities may affect or contribute to the purposes of this chapter.

5. Convene business leaders, educators, and other representatives of the private sector who are engaged in assisting the development of small, women- and minority-owned business programs or who could contribute to its development, for the purpose of proposing, evaluating or coordinating governmental and private activities in furtherance of the objectives of this chapter.

6. Provide the managerial and organizational framework through which joint undertakings with state departments or agencies or private organizations can be planned and implemented.

7. Recommend appropriate legislative or executive actions.

8. Adopt regulations to implement certification programs for small, women- and minority-owned businesses, which regulations shall be exempt from the Administrative Process Act (§ 2.2-4000 et seq.) pursuant to subdivision B 2 of § 2.2-4002. Such certification programs shall deny certification to vendors from states that deny like certifications to Virginia-based small, women- or minority-owned businesses or that provide a preference for small, women- or minority-owned businesses based in that state that is not available to Virginia-based businesses. The regulations shall (i) establish minimum requirements for certification of small, women- and minority-owned businesses; (ii) provide a process for evaluating existing local, state, private sector, and federal certification programs that meet the minimum requirements; and (iii) mandate certification, without any additional paperwork or fee, of any prospective state vendor that has obtained certification under any certification program that is determined to meet the minimum requirements established in the regulations.

9. Establish an interdepartmental board in accordance with § 2.2-1404 to supply the Director with information useful in promoting minority business activity. (1975, c. 509, § 2.1-64.35; 1989, c. 268; 1996, c. 630; 2001, c. 844; 2006, cc. 831, 921.)

§ 2.2-1404. Interdepartmental Board; cooperation with Department. — A. The Interdepartmental Board established by the Director shall be composed of heads of the several departments and agencies of state government or their respective designees, whose functions affect small, women- and minority-owned businesses. The participating departments and agencies shall be determined by the Director of the Department. The Interdepartmental Board shall meet at the call of the Director and shall supply the Director with information useful in promoting small, women- and minority-owned business activity.

B. The head of each participating state department and agency or their designees shall furnish information, assistance, and reports to, and shall otherwise cooperate with, the Director in the performance of his duties as needed.

C. The head of each participating state department or agency shall, when so requested by the Director, designate an assistant or such other similar official to have primary and continuing responsibility for the participation and cooperation of that department or agency in matters concerning small, women- and minority-owned businesses.

D. Each participating state department or agency shall, within constraints of law and availability of funding, continue all current efforts to foster and promote minority business enterprises and to support the small, women- and minority-owned business programs, and shall cooperate with the Director in increasing the total state effort. (1975, c. 509, §§ 2.1-64.36, 2.1-64.37; 1985, c. 448; 2001, c. 844; 2006, cc. 831, 921.)

§ 2.2-1404.1. Use of vendors identified by public institutions of higher education as small, women-, and minority-owned business enterprises. — For purposes of compliance with § 2.2-4310, a public institution of higher education that meets the conditions prescribed in subsection B of § 23-38.88 may procure goods, services, and construction from vendors identified by such public institutions of higher education as small, women-, and minority-owned business enterprises that the institution has certified as such based on criteria approved by the Department. An institution exercising the authority granted by this section shall establish and follow internal procedures and processes designed to verify whether or not a vendor qualifies to be certified as a small, women-, and minority-owned business enterprise under the Department approved criteria and the certification requirements. The institution shall notify the Department promptly of the certification, and shall provide the Department with a copy of its written certification identifying the vendor as a small, women-, and minority-owned business enterprise and all application materials submitted by the vendor to the institution. Such certification shall remain in effect unless and until the Department notifies the institution that the vendor does not meet the certification requirements.

An institution exercising authority granted under this section shall promptly make available to the Department, upon request, copies of its procurement records, receipts, and transactions in regard to procurement from small, women-, and minority-owned business enterprises in order for the Department to ensure institution compliance with its approved criteria and the certification requirements. (2005, cc. 933, 945.)

§ 2.2-1405. Reports and recommendations; collection of data. — The Director shall, from time to time, submit directly or through an assistant to the

Governor his recommendations for legislation or other action as he deems desirable to promote the purposes of this chapter.

The Director shall report, on or before November 1 of each year, to the Governor and the General Assembly the identity of the state departments and agencies failing to submit annual progress reports on small, women- and minority-owned business procurement required by § 2.2-4310, and the nature and extent of such lack of compliance. The annual report shall include recommendations on the ways to improve compliance with the provisions of § 2.2-4310 and such other related matters as the Director deems appropriate.

The Director, with the assistance of the Comptroller, shall develop and implement a systematic data collection process that will provide information for a report to the Governor and General Assembly on state expenditures to small, women- and minority-owned businesses during the previous fiscal year. (1975, c. 509, § 2.1-64.38; 1983, c. 41; 1984, c. 734; 1996, c. 335; 2001, c. 844; 2003, c. 435; 2006, cc. 831, 921.)

CHAPTER 15.

Department of Planning and Budget.

§ 2.2-1500. Department of Planning and Budget created; appointment of Director; powers and duties. — A. There is created a Department of Planning and Budget (the "Department"), which shall be headed by a Director appointed by the Governor to serve at his pleasure.

B. The Director of the Department shall, under the direction and control of the Governor, exercise the powers and perform the duties conferred or imposed upon him by law and perform such other duties as may be required by the Governor. (Code 1950, § 2-47; 1964, c. 302; 1966, cc. 55, 677, § 2.1-53; 1968, c.

223, § 2.1-63.1; 1972, c. 574; 1974, c. 23; 1975, c. 390; 1976, c. 760, §§ 2.1-388, 2.1-389; 1984, c. 720; 2001, c. 844.)

§ 2.2-1501. Duties of Department. — The Department shall have the following duties:

1. Development and direction of an integrated policy analysis, planning, and budgeting process within state government.
2. Review and approval of all sub-state district systems boundaries established or proposed for establishment by state agencies.
3. Formulation of an executive budget as required in this chapter. In implementing this provision, the Department shall utilize the resources and determine the manner of participation of any executive agency as the Governor may determine necessary to support an efficient and effective budget process notwithstanding any contrary provision of law. The budget shall include reports, or summaries thereof, provided by agencies of the Commonwealth pursuant to subsection E of § 2.2-603.
4. Conduct of policy analysis and program evaluation for the Governor.
5. Continuous review of the activities of state government focusing on budget requirements in the context of the goals and objectives determined by the Governor and the General Assembly and monitoring the progress of agencies in achieving goals and objectives.
6. Operation of a system of budgetary execution to ensure that agency activities are conducted within fund limitations provided in the appropriation act and in accordance with gubernatorial and legislative intent. The Department shall make an appropriate reduction in the appropriation and maximum employment level of any state agency or institution in the executive branch of government that reports involuntary separations from employment with the Commonwealth due to budget reductions, agency reorganizations, or workforce down-sizings, or voluntary separations from employment with the Commonwealth as provided in the second and third enactments of the act of the General Assembly creating the Workforce Transition Act of 1995 (§ 2.2-3200). In the event an agency reduces its workforce through privatization of certain functions, the funds associated with such functions shall remain with the agency to the extent of the savings resulting from the privatization of such functions.
7. Development and operation of a system of standardized reports of program and financial performance for management.
8. Coordination of statistical data by reviewing, analyzing, monitoring, and evaluating statistical data developed and used by state agencies and by receiving statistical data from outside sources, such as research institutes and the federal government.
9. Assessment of the impact of federal funds on state government by reviewing, analyzing, monitoring, and evaluating the federal budget, as well as solicitations, applications, and awards for federal financial aid programs on behalf of state agencies.
10. Review and verify the accuracy of agency estimates of receipts from donations, gifts or other nongeneral fund revenue.
11. **(Effective until July 1, 2013)** Development, coordination and implementation of a performance management system involving strategic planning, performance measurement, evaluation, and performance budgeting within state government. The Department shall ensure that information generated from these processes is useful for managing and improving the efficiency and effectiveness of state government operations, and is available to citizens and public officials.
11. **(Effective July 1, 2013)** Development, coordination and implementation of a performance management system involving strategic planning,

performance measurement, evaluation, and performance budgeting within state government. The Department shall ensure that information generated from these processes is useful for managing and improving the efficiency and effectiveness of state government operations, and is available to citizens and public officials. The Department shall submit annually on or before the second Tuesday in January to the Chairman of the House Appropriations Committee and the Chairman of the Senate Finance Committee a report that sets forth state agencies' strategic planning information and performance measurement results pursuant to this subdivision for the immediately preceding fiscal year.

12. Development, implementation and management of an Internet-based information technology system to ensure that citizens have access to performance information.

13. Development, implementation and management of an Internet-based information technology system to ensure that citizens have access to meeting minutes and information pertaining to the development of regulatory policies.

14. Development, coordination and management of a school efficiency review program. (1976, c. 760, § 2.1-391; 1979, cc. 672, 678; 1981, c. 315; 1984, c. 720; 1985, c. 114; 1989, c. 108; 1992, cc. 270, 381; 1995, cc. 152, 219, 811; 2000, c. 424; 2001, cc. 43, 844; 2002, cc. 580, 618; 2003, c. 900; 2005, c. 620.)

Subdivision 11 set out twice. — The first version of subdivision 11 above is effective until July 1, 2013. The second version of subdivision 11 is effective July 1, 2013.

Cross references. — For a provision requiring the participation by certain agencies in the budget development process of other agencies dealing with related matters, see § 2.2-1507. As to the duties of Department of Human Resource Management and executive branch agencies to involuntarily separated employees, see § 2.2-3201. As to review of information required under this section by the Auditor of Public Accounts, see § 30-133.

Editor's note. — The reference to the second and third enactments of the act of the General Assembly creating the Workforce Transition Act of 1995 (§ 2.2-3200), found in subdivision 6 of this section, refers to Acts 1995, cc. 152, 811 cls. 2 and 3. These provisions provided for a program of voluntary resignation from employment with the Commonwealth.

Acts 2001, c. 43 amended § 2.1-391, from which this section is derived. Pursuant to § 30-152, Acts 2001, c. 43 has been given effect in this section as set out above. The 2001 amendment by c. 43 added the last sentence in subdivision 11.

Acts 2003, c. 900, cl. 3, as amended by Acts 2008, c. 240, provides: "That the provisions of this act shall expire on July 1, 2013." Acts 2003, c. 900 deleted the last sentence in subdivision 11.

§ 2.2-1502. Establishing regulations for preplanning of capital outlay projects. — A. The Director of the Department or his designee shall adopt regulations requiring a preplanning justification or a preplanning study, or both, for all capital outlay projects undertaken by any department, agency or institution of the Commonwealth. A preplanning study shall be required for any project of construction, renovation, or other capital outlay involving a structure of 20,000 or more square feet or that is estimated to cost one million dollars or more. For projects of lesser size or cost, the regulations may require only a preplanning justification of the project. The Director or his designee may waive the requirement for a preplanning justification or preplanning study for such projects of lesser size and cost when, a preplanning justification or preplanning study is not needed or would not be warranted by the cost of making one. Preplanning studies for projects estimated to cost less than $2 million shall be done at a cost not exceeding $25,000. Preplanning studies for projects estimated to cost $2 million or more shall be done at a cost not exceeding $50,000. Exceptions to these limitations upon the cost of preplanning studies may be authorized by the House Committee on Appropriations and the Senate Committee on Finance.

B. The regulations shall (i) provide for the content and scope of preplanning justifications and preplanning studies, including the definition of the terms "capital outlay project"; (ii) require consideration of locally available fuels, including wood wastes, for use in new and replacement central heating plants in any proposed or existing public buildings or other facilities; and (iii) shall be exempt from the provisions of the Administrative Process Act (§ 2.2-4000 et seq.). (1983, c. 497, § 2.1-51.31; 1984, c. 720; 1993, c. 29; 2001, c. 844.)

§ **2.2-1502.1. School efficiency review program.** — A. From such funds as may be appropriated or otherwise received for such purpose, and upon written request by a local school board or the division superintendent, the Director shall initiate a review of the relevant school division's central operations. Such review shall examine noninstructional expenditures and identify opportunities to improve operational efficiencies and reduce costs for the division and include but not be limited to examinations of (i) overhead, (ii) human resources, (iii) procurement, (iv) facilities use and management, (v) financial management, (vi) transportation, (vii) technology planning, and (viii) energy management. Such review shall not address the effectiveness of the educational services being delivered by the division.

B. School divisions shall pay 25 percent of the cost of the school efficiency review in the fiscal year immediately following the completion of the final school efficiency review report. Additionally, commencing with reviews completed in fiscal year 2007, partial recovery of the cost of individual reviews shall be made in the fiscal year beginning not less than 12 months and not more than 24 months following the release of a final efficiency review report for an individual school division. Such additional recovery may occur if the affected school division superintendent or superintendent's designee has not certified that at least half the recommendations have been initiated or at least half of the equivalent savings of such efficiency review have been realized. Lacking such certification the school division shall reimburse the state for 25 percent of the cost of the school efficiency review. Such reimbursement shall be paid into the general fund of the state treasury. The Department of Planning and Budget shall provide the format for such certification.

C. All agencies, authorities, and institutions of the Commonwealth shall cooperate and provide assistance as the Director may request. (2005, c. 620; 2006, c. 596.)

Editor's note. — Acts 2008, c. 879, effective for the biennium ending June 30, 2010, in Item 135 C, provides: "Notwithstanding the provisions of § 2.2-1502.1, Code of Virginia, the Board of Education, in cooperation with the Department of Planning and Budget, is authorized to invite a school division to participate in the school efficiency review program described in § 2.2-1502.1, Code of Virginia, as a component of a division level academic review pursuant to § 22.1-253.13:3, Code of Virginia. Commencing in fiscal year 2006, when a school division elects to undergo a school efficiency review pursuant to this provision, the school division shall not be charged the 25 percent for the costs of such review. However, a school division shall pay a separate 25 percent of the total costs of such review if the school division's superintendent or superintendent's designee has not certified that at least half of the recommendations have been initiated within 24 months after the completion of the review."

§ **2.2-1503. Filing of six-year revenue plan by Governor.** — In every year, the Governor shall by December 15 prepare and submit to the members of the General Assembly an estimate of anticipated general fund revenue, an estimate of anticipated transportation fund revenues, and estimates of anticipated revenues for each of the remaining major nongeneral funds, for a prospective period of six years.

The Governor's estimates of anticipated general, transportation, and other nongeneral fund revenues shall be based on the following:

1. Forecasts of economic activity in the Commonwealth.

2. Review by an advisory board of economists with respect to economic assumptions and technical econometric methodology. The Advisory Board of Economists (the Board) is established as an advisory board, within the meaning of § 2.2-2100, in the executive branch of state government for such purpose. The Board shall consist of 15 nonlegislative citizen members appointed by the Governor. Members of the Board shall be economists from either the public or private sector and shall serve at the pleasure of the Governor. All members shall be citizens of the Commonwealth. Vacancies shall be filled in the same manner as the original appointments. Members shall not receive compensation for their services, but shall be reimbursed for all reasonable and necessary expenses for the performance of their duties as provided in §§ 2.2-2813 and 2.2-2825. Funding for the costs of expenses of the members shall be provided by the Department of Taxation. The Department of Taxation shall provide staff support. A majority of the members of the Board shall constitute a quorum. Meetings of the Board shall be held upon the call of the chairman or whenever a majority of the members so request.

3. Review by an advisory council of revenue estimates with respect to economic assumptions and the general economic climate of the Commonwealth. The Advisory Council on Revenue Estimates (the Council) is established as an advisory council, within the meaning of § 2.2-2100, in the executive branch of state government for such purpose. The Council shall include the Speaker and Majority Leader of the House of Delegates, the President pro tempore and Majority Leader of the Senate, the Chairmen of the House Committee on Appropriations, the House Committee on Finance, and the Senate Committee on Finance or their designees, and nonlegislative citizen members representing the private sector appointed by the Governor. Legislative members appointed shall serve terms coincident with their terms of office and nonlegislative citizen members shall serve at the pleasure of the Governor. All members shall be citizens of the Commonwealth. Vacancies shall be filled in the same manner as the original appointments. Members shall not receive compensation for their services, but shall be reimbursed for all reasonable and necessary expenses for the performance of their duties as provided in §§ 2.2-2813 and 2.2-2825. Funding for the costs of expenses of the members shall be provided by the Department of Taxation. The Department of Taxation shall provide staff support. A majority of the members of the Council shall constitute a quorum. Meetings of the Council shall be held upon the call of the chairman or whenever a majority of the members so request.

4. Any such other advisory bodies as the Governor may desire. (1975, c. 501, § 2.1-63.02; 1976, c. 760, § 2.1-393; 1978, c. 802; 1981, c. 83; 1984, c. 473; 1985, c. 448; 2001, c. 844; 2003, c. 612; 2004, c. 1000.)

Editor's note. — Acts 2004, c. 1000, cl. 5, provides: "That this act shall not be construed to affect existing appointments for which the terms have not expired. However, any new appointments or appointments to fill vacancies made after the effective date of this act shall be made in accordance with the provisions of this act."

§ **2.2-1503.1. Filing of six-year financial outline by Governor.** — On or before the first day of each regular session of the General Assembly held in an even-numbered year, the Governor shall prepare and submit to the members of the General Assembly a financial plan for a prospective period of six years. The plan shall consist of (i) the Governor's biennial budget submitted pursuant to subsection A of § 2.2-1508, (ii) estimates of anticipated general fund and nongeneral fund revenue prepared for an additional period of four years pursuant to § 2.2-1503, and (iii) estimates of the general and nongeneral fund appropriations required for each major program for an additional period of four years. In preparing such financial plan, the Governor may utilize the estimate prepared by each agency pursuant to § 2.2-1504, or such other information as he may deem necessary. (2002, cc. 480, 486.)

§ **2.2-1503.2:** Repealed by Acts 2008, Sp. Sess. I, cc. 1, 2, cl. 20, effective May 21, 2008.

Editor's note. — Acts 2008, Sp. Sess. I, cc. 1 and 2, in cl. 21 provide: "That an emergency exists and this act is in force from its passage [May 21, 2008]."

§ **2.2-1503.3. Reestimate of general fund revenues.** — Within five business days after the preliminary close of the Commonwealth's accounts at the end of each fiscal year, the State Comptroller shall submit to the Governor a comparison of the total of individual income, corporate income, and sales taxes collected for the fiscal year, with the totals of such taxes included in the official budget estimate for the fiscal year. If the comparison indicates that the total collection of such taxes as shown in the preliminary close is 1.0 percent or more below the total amount of such taxes as included in the official budget estimate for the fiscal year, the Governor shall prepare a reestimate of general fund revenues for the current biennium and the next biennium in accordance with the provisions of § 2.2-1503. The Governor's reestimate shall be reported to the chairman of the Senate Committee on Finance and the chairmen of the Finance and Appropriation Committees of the House of Delegates not later than September 1 following the close of the fiscal year. (2003, c. 14.)

§ **2.2-1504. Estimates by state agencies of amounts needed.** — A. Biennially in the odd-numbered years, on a date established by the Governor, each of the several state agencies and other agencies and undertakings receiving or asking financial aid from the Commonwealth shall report to the Governor, through the responsible secretary designated by statute or executive order, in a format prescribed for such purpose, an estimate in itemized form in accordance with the expenditure classification adopted by the Governor, showing the amount needed for each year of the ensuing biennial period beginning with the first day of July. The Governor may prescribe targets that shall not be exceeded in the official estimate of each agency; however, an agency may submit to the Governor a request for an amount exceeding the target as an addendum to its official budget estimate.

B. Each agency or undertaking required to submit a biennial estimate pursuant to subsection A shall simultaneously submit an estimate of the amount that will be needed for the two succeeding biennial periods beginning July 1 of the third year following the year in which the estimate is submitted. The Department shall provide, within thirty days following receipt, copies of all agency estimates provided under this subsection to the chairmen of the House Committee on Appropriations and the Senate Committee on Finance.

C. The format used in making these estimates shall (i) be prescribed by the Governor, shall (ii) be uniform for all agencies, and (iii) clearly designate the kind of information to be given. The Governor may prescribe a different format for estimates from institutions of higher education, which format shall be uniform for all such institutions and shall clearly designate the kind of information to be provided. (Code 1950, § 2-48; 1964, c. 125; 1966, c. 677, § 2.1-54; 1968, c. 683; 1975, c. 325; 1976, c. 760, § 2.1-394; 1979, c. 283; 1992, c. 582; 1993, c. 724; 1998, c. 467; 2001, c. 844.)

Cross references. — For requirement that in any odd-numbered year in which the Board of Education proposes changes to the standards of quality, the budget estimates reported pursuant to § 2.2-1504 take into consideration the Board's standards of quality, see § 22.1-18.01.

§ 2.2-1505. Estimates by nonstate agencies of amounts needed. — A. Except as provided in §§ 10.1-2211, 10.1-2212, and 10.1-2213, no state funds shall be appropriated or expended for, or to, nonstate agencies unless:

1. A request for state aid is filed by the organization with the Department of Planning and Budget, as required by § 2.2-1504.

2. The nonstate agency certifies to the satisfaction of the Department that matching funds are available in cash from local or private sources in an amount at least equal to the amount of the request. These matching funds shall be concurrent with the purpose for which state funds are requested. Contributions received and spent prior to the state grant shall not be considered in satisfying the requirements of this subdivision.

3. The nonstate agency provides documentation of its tax exempt status under § 501 (c) (3) of the United States Internal Revenue Code.

B. Except as provided in §§ 23-38.11 through 23-38.18, no state funds shall be appropriated to, or expended for, a private institution of higher education or religious organization.

C. For the purposes of this section, a *"nonstate agency"* means any public or private foundation, authority, institute, museum, corporation or similar organization that is not a unit of state government or a political subdivision of the Commonwealth as established by general law or special act. It shall not include any such entity that receives state funds as a subgrantee of a state agency or through a state grant-in-aid program authorized by law. (1989, c. 711, § 2.1-394.1; 1998, c. 467; 2001, c. 844.)

Editor's note. — Acts 2008, c. 879, effective for the biennium ending June 30, 2010, in Item 253, provides: "A. This appropriation represents the Commonwealth of Virginia's contribution to the Jefferson Science Associates, LLC, for the support of the Thomas Jefferson National Accelerator Facility (Jefferson Lab) located at Newport News, Virginia. This contribution includes funds to support faculty positions and industry-led research that will promote economic development opportunities in the Commonwealth.

"B. This nonstate agency is exempt from the match requirement of § 2.2-1505, Code of Virginia and § 4-5.05 of this act."

Acts 2008, c. 879, effective for the biennium ending June 30, 2010, in Item 437 C, provides: "The department is authorized to pay to the Civil Air Patrol from Aviation Special Funds $100,000 the first year and $100,000 the second year. The provisions of § 2.2-1505, Code of Virginia, and § 4-5.05 of this act shall not apply to the Civil Air Patrol."

§ 2.2-1506. Estimates of financial needs of General Assembly and judiciary. — On or before the first day of September biennially in the odd-numbered years the Committees on Rules of the House of Delegates and the Senate shall furnish the Governor an estimate of the financial needs of the General Assembly for each year of the ensuing biennial period beginning with the first day of July thereafter; and the Supreme Court of Virginia shall furnish to the Governor an estimate of the financial needs of the judiciary for each year of the ensuing biennial period beginning with the first day of July thereafter. The Committees on Rules of the House of Delegates and the Senate and the Supreme Court shall transmit to the Governor the estimates of all increases or decreases. (Code 1950, § 2-49; 1958, c. 370; 1966, c. 677, § 2.1-55; 1968, c. 683; 1974, c. 91; 1976, c. 760, § 2.1-395; 2001, c. 844.)

§ 2.2-1507. Participation of certain agencies in budget development process of other agencies. — Agencies having responsibilities granted under §§ 2.2-703, 2.2-2011, and 2.2-2696 shall participate in the budget development process of relevant agencies and receive from these agencies, prior to submission to the Department their proposed programs and budgets. Recommendations to the appropriate agencies and the secretaries of the Governor on related matters shall be made prior to budget submissions. (1979, c. 678, § 2.1-397.1; 1991, c. 563; 1998, c. 467; 2001, c. 844.)

§ 2.2-1508. Submission of executive budget to General Assembly. — A. On or before December 20 in the year immediately prior to the beginning of each regular session of the General Assembly held in an even-numbered year, the Governor shall submit to the presiding officer of each house of the General Assembly printed copies of a budget document, which shall be known as "The Executive Budget," based on his own conclusions and judgment, containing the following:

1. For each agency, the amount and number of positions appropriated for the current appropriation year and the amount and number of positions recommended for each year of the ensuing biennial period beginning with the first day of July thereafter, accompanied by an explanation of the recommended amount and number of positions.

2. A statement of historical and projected trends that influence the general economic conditions in the Commonwealth and a statement of the economic assumptions upon which revenue projections are based.

3. A statement of the Governor's proposed goals, objectives, and policies in the areas of:

a. Administration of justice;

b. Education, including intellectual and cultural development;

c. Individual and family services;

d. Resources and economic development, including specific references to economic development and management of natural resources;

e. Transportation; and

f. General government, including therein or as separate categories areas of multiple impact, such as telecommunications, energy, and urban development.

4. A statement organized by function, primary agency, and proposed appropriation item that sets forth:

a. Identification of common programs and services;

b. Service attainments or lack of attainments and service terminations or reductions for the biennium;

c. Major goals, objectives, and specific outcomes related to expenditures for programs;

d. Program measures and performance standards to be used in monitoring and evaluating services; and the development of appropriate evaluation cycles, within available resources;

e. The amount of each primary agency's budget that is direct aid to localities.

5. A statement of proposed capital appropriations organized by the primary agency that sets forth the program need for the project and the proposed source of funding.

6. A listing of all activity, program-related, agency or departmental evaluations performed in the previous two years with guidance indicating the manner in which the public can gain access to the full text of such studies.

7. A schedule and description of all data processing or other projects in which the Commonwealth has entered into or plans to enter into a contract, agreement or other financing agreement or such other arrangement that requires that the Commonwealth either pay for the contract by foregoing revenue collections, or allows or assigns to another party the collection on behalf of or for the Commonwealth any fees, charges, or other assessment or revenues to pay for the project. Such schedule shall include by agency and project (i) a summary of the terms, (ii) the anticipated duration, and (iii) cost or charges to any user, whether a state agency or institutions or other party not directly a party to the project arrangements. The description shall also include any terms or conditions that bind the Commonwealth or restrict the Commonwealth operations and the methods of procurement employed to reach such terms.

B. On or before December 20 of the year immediately prior to the beginning of the regular session of the General Assembly held in odd-numbered years, the Governor shall submit to the presiding officer of each house of the General Assembly printed copies of a budget document, which shall be known as "Executive Amendments to the Appropriation Act," describing all gubernatorial amendments proposed to the general appropriation act enacted in the immediately preceding even-numbered session.

C. The Department of Planning and Budget shall prepare "The Executive Budget" and the "Executive Amendments to the Appropriation Act" in a manner and with language that can be easily understood by the citizens of the Commonwealth and that provides, to the extent practical, a cross-reference to the Governor's recommended budget bill or amendments to the Appropriation Act. Such documents shall also be placed on the Internet to provide easy access by the public. (Code 1950, § 2-54; 1954, c. 673; 1966, c. 677, § 2.1-60; 1968, c. 683; 1971, Ex. Sess., c. 57; 1975, c. 325; 1976, c. 760, § 2.1-398; 1977, c. 656; 1978, c. 570; 1979, cc. 319, 320; 1981, c. 114; 1992, c. 582; 2001, c. 844; 2003, cc. 190, 888.)

Cross references. — As to general duties and powers of the Auditor of Public Accounts, see § 30-133.

Editor's note. — Acts 2008, c. 879, effective for the biennium ending June 30, 2010, in Item 268 C 1, provides: "Notwithstanding § 2.2-1508, Code of Virginia, or any other provisions of law, on or before December 20, the Department of Planning and Budget shall deliver to the presiding officer of each house of the General Assembly a copy of the budget document containing the explanation of the Governor's budget recommendations. This copy may be in electronic format."

§ **2.2-1509. Budget bill.** — A. **(Effective until July 1, 2013)** On or before December 20 of the year immediately prior to the beginning of each regular session of the General Assembly held in an even-numbered year, the Governor also shall submit to the presiding officer of each house of the General Assembly, at the same time he submits "The Executive Budget," copies of a tentative bill for all proposed appropriations of the budget, for each year in the ensuing biennial appropriation period, which shall be known as "The Budget Bill." "The Budget Bill" shall be organized by function, primary agency, and proposed appropriation item and shall include (i) an identification of, and authorization for, common programs and (ii) the appropriation of funds according to programs. Strategic plan information and performance measurement results developed by each agency shall be made available to the General Assembly as it considers "The Budget Bill." Except as expressly provided in an appropriation act, whenever the amounts in a schedule for a single appropriation item are shown in two or more lines, the portions of the total amount shown on separate lines are for information purposes only and are not limiting. No such bill shall contain any appropriation the expenditure of which is contingent upon the receipt of revenues in excess of funds unconditionally appropriated.

A. **(Effective July 1, 2013)** On or before December 20 of the year immediately prior to the beginning of each regular session of the General Assembly held in an even-numbered year, the Governor also shall submit to the presiding officer of each house of the General Assembly, at the same time he submits "The Executive Budget," copies of a tentative bill for all proposed appropriations of the budget, for each year in the ensuing biennial appropriation period, which shall be known as "The Budget Bill." "The Budget Bill" shall be organized by function, primary agency, and proposed appropriation item and shall include an identification of, and authorization for, common programs and the appropriation of funds according to programs. Except as expressly provided in an appropriation act, whenever the amounts in a schedule for a single appropriation item are shown in two or more lines, the portions of the total amount shown on separate lines are for information purposes only and are not limiting. No such bill shall contain any appropriation the expenditure of which is contingent upon the receipt of revenues in excess of funds unconditionally appropriated.

B. The salary proposed for payment for the position of each cabinet secretary and administrative head of each agency and institution of the executive branch of state government shall be specified in "The Budget Bill," showing the salary ranges and levels proposed for such positions.

C. "The Budget Bill" shall include all proposed capital appropriations, including each capital project to be financed through revenue bonds or other debt issuance, the amount of each project, and the identity of the entity that will issue the debt.

D. Concurrently with the submission of "The Budget Bill," the Governor shall submit a tentative bill involving a request for authorization of additional bonded indebtedness if its issuance is authorized by, or its repayment is proposed to be made in whole or in part, from revenues or appropriations contained in "The Budget Bill."

E. On or before December 20 of the year immediately prior to the beginning of each regular session held in an odd-numbered year of the General Assembly, the Governor shall submit to the presiding officer of each house printed copies of all gubernatorial amendments proposed to the general appropriation act adopted in the immediately preceding even-numbered year session. In preparing the amendments, the Governor may obtain estimates in the manner prescribed in §§ 2.2-1504, 2.2-1505, and 2.2-1506. On the same date he shall also submit a tentative bill during the second year of the appropriation period, a request for authorization of additional bonded indebtedness if its issuance is authorized by, or its repayment is proposed to be made in whole or in part, from revenues or appropriations contained in the proposed gubernatorial amendments.

F. The proposed capital appropriations or capital projects described in, or for which proposed appropriations are made pursuant to, this section shall include the capital outlay projects required to be included in "The Budget Bill" pursuant to § 2.2-1509.1. The Governor shall propose appropriations for such capital outlay projects in "The Budget Bill" in accordance with the minimum amount of funding and the designated sources of funding for such projects as required under § 2.2-1509.1. (Code 1950, § 2-55; 1952, c. 150; 1966, c. 677, § 2.1-61; 1975, c. 325; 1976, c. 760, § 2.1-399; 1979, c. 319; 1992, c. 582, § 2.1-399.1; 1994, c. 621; 1998, cc. 118, 467, 591; 2001, c. 844; 2002, cc. 839, 888; 2003, c. 900.)

Subsection A set out twice. — The first version of subsection A above is effective until July 1, 2013. The second version of subsection A is effective July 1, 2013.

Cross references. — As to general duties and powers of the Auditor of Public Accounts, see § 30-133.

Editor's note. — Acts 2003, c. 900, cl. 3, as amended by Acts 2008, c. 240, provides: "That the provisions of this act shall expire on July 1, 2013." Acts 2003, c. 900, amended subsection A.

The 2003 amendments. — The 2003 amendment by c. 900, in subsection A, added clause (i) and (ii) designations in the second sentence, and inserted the third sentence. For expiration date, see Editor's note.

§ 2.2-1509.1. Budget bill to include appropriations for capital outlay projects. — A. For purposes of this section:

"Projected general fund revenues" for a fiscal year means the estimated general fund revenues for such year as contained in the six-year revenue plan submitted in the prior calendar year pursuant to § 2.2-1503.

"Capital outlay project" means the same as that term is defined in § 2.2-1515.

B. In "The Budget Bill" submitted pursuant to § 2.2-1509, the Governor shall provide for the funding of capital outlay projects, as specified herein.

Such funding recommendations shall be in addition to any appropriation for capital outlay projects from the Central Maintenance Reserve of the general appropriation act.

1. The Governor shall include in "The Budget Bill" submitted pursuant to § 2.2-1509 a biennial appropriation for the capital outlay plan described in § 2.2-1518. The biennial appropriation shall not be less than two percent of the projected general fund revenues for the biennium.

a. When the projected general fund revenues for a fiscal year or years are eight percent or greater than the projected general fund revenues for the immediately preceding fiscal year the amount of the biennial appropriation for the capital outlay plan that the Governor shall provide from general fund revenues shall not be less than two percent of the projected general fund revenues for each fiscal year.

b. When the projected general fund revenues for a fiscal year or years are at least five percent but less than eight percent greater than the projected general fund revenues for the immediately preceding fiscal year, the Governor may recommend funding of up to one-half of the required biennial appropriation from alternative financing mechanisms, including, but not limited to, bonded indebtedness. The Governor shall submit such bill or bills for consideration by the General Assembly as are necessary to implement such alternative financings, and shall include in "The Budget Bill" submitted pursuant to § 2.2-1509 proposed appropriations from general fund revenues for the remaining one-half of the required biennial appropriation.

c. When the projected general fund revenues for a fiscal year or years are less than five percent greater than the projected general fund revenues for the immediately preceding fiscal year, the Governor may recommend funding of up to the entire required biennial appropriation from alternative financing mechanisms, including, but not limited to, bonded indebtedness. The Governor shall submit such bill or bills for consideration by the General Assembly as are necessary to implement such alternative financings.

2. In implementing the provisions of this section, the amount of general funds to be included in the biennial appropriation for the capital outlay plan shall be calculated on a year-to-year basis, but may be apportioned on a biennial basis; provided, however, that the combined total of general fund appropriations and alternative financing mechanisms for the capital outlay plan included in "The Budget Bill" submitted pursuant to § 2.2-1509 shall equal at least two percent of the projected general fund revenues for the biennium.

C. The capital outlay projects proposed under this section and to be included in "The Budget Bill" submitted pursuant to § 2.2-1509 shall be consistent, as far as practicable, with those capital outlay projects included in the corresponding fiscal year of the current six-year capital outlay plan described in § 2.2-1518. (2002, cc. 839, 888; 2008, Sp. Sess. I, cc. 1, 2.)

Editor's note. — Acts 2008, Sp. Sess. I, cc. 1 and 2, in cl. 21 provide: "That an emergency exists and this act is in force from its passage [May 21, 2008]."

The 2008 amendments. — The 2008 amendments by Sp. Sess. I, cc. 1 and 2, effective May 21, 2008, substituted "capital outlay plan" for "capital improvement plan" throughout the section; substituted "§ 2.2-1515" for "§ 2.2-1503.2" in the paragraph defining "Capital outlay project" in subsection A; substituted "described in § 2.2-1518" for "required by § 2.2-1503.2" at the end of the first sentence of subdivsion B 1; and rewrote subsection C.

§ 2.2-1509.2. Budget Bill to include amounts diverted from Transportation Trust Fund and Highway Maintenance and Operating Fund. — If any money in the Highway Maintenance and Operating Fund or the Transportation Trust Fund established pursuant to § 33.1-23.03:1 is proposed to be used for any purpose other than administering, planning, constructing, improving, and maintaining the roads embraced in the systems of highways for the Commonwealth and its localities and/or furthering the interests of the Commonwealth in the areas of public transportation, railways, seaports, and/or airports, then the Governor, if such diversion is proposed by the Governor, shall include with any such proposal a plan for repayment of funds diverted within three years of such use in "The Budget Bill" submitted pursuant to § 2.2-1509.

If such diversion of funds from the Highway Maintenance and Operating Fund or the Transportation Trust Fund is proposed by the General Assembly as an amendment to the Budget Bill, such amendment shall include language setting out the plan for repayment of such funds within three years. (2003, c. 970.)

§ 2.2-1510. Publication of budget highlights; public hearings. — A. The Governor shall ensure that a summary of the highlights of each budget submitted pursuant to § 2.2-1508 and set of amendments submitted pursuant to subsection E of § 2.2-1509 are sent to a newspaper of general circulation in the following geographical areas of the Commonwealth: Northern Virginia, Hampton Roads, Richmond/Petersburg, Central Virginia, Shenandoah Valley, Roanoke Valley, Southside, and Southwest Virginia prior to the convening of each session of the General Assembly.

B. The House Committee on Appropriations and the Senate Committee on Finance shall hold at least four regional public hearings on the budget bill submitted by the Governor. The four public hearings shall be held prior to the convening of such session of the General Assembly, at hearing sites and times as selected by the chairmen of the two committees. (1998, c. 467, § 2.1-399.2; 2001, c. 844.)

§ 2.2-1511. (Effective until July 1, 2013) Consideration of budget by committees. — The standing committees of the House of Delegates and of the Senate in charge of appropriation measures shall begin consideration of the budget within five calendar days after the convening of the regular session of the General Assembly to which the budget is submitted. The committees or subcommittees thereof, may meet jointly on matters concerning the budget at such times as the chairmen of the two committees deem appropriate. The committees or subcommittees may cause the attendance of heads or responsible representatives of the departments, institutions and all other agencies of the Commonwealth to furnish such information and answer such questions as they require. The committees shall consider strategic plan information and performance-measurement results developed by each agency pursuant to Chapter 55.1 (§ 2.2-5510 et seq.) of this title and submitted by the Governor pursuant to § 2.2-1509. All persons interested in the matters under consideration shall be admitted to the meetings and shall have the right to be heard. (Code 1950, § 2-56; 1966, c. 677, § 2.1-62; 1976, c. 760, § 2.1-400; 1987, c. 138; 2001, c. 844; 2003, c. 900.)

Section set out twice. — The section above is effective until July 1, 2013. For the version of this section effective July 1, 2013, see the following section, also numbered 2.2-1511.

Editor's note. — Acts 2003, c. 900, cl. 3, as amended by Acts 2008, c. 240, provides: "That the provisions of this act shall expire on July 1, 2013."

The 2003 amendments. — The 2003 amendment by c. 900 inserted the next-to-last sentence. See Editor's note for expiration date.

§ 2.2-1511. (Effective July 1, 2013) Consideration of budget by committees. — The standing committees of the House of Delegates and of the Senate in charge of appropriation measures shall begin consideration of the budget within five calendar days after the convening of the regular session of the General Assembly to which the budget is submitted. The committees or subcommittees thereof, may meet jointly on matters concerning the budget at such times as the chairmen of the two committees deem appropriate. The committees or subcommittees may cause the attendance of heads or responsible representatives of the departments, institutions and all other agencies of the Commonwealth to furnish such information and answer such questions as they require. All persons interested in the matters under consideration shall be admitted to the meetings and shall have the right to be heard. (Code 1950, § 2-56; 1966, c. 677, § 2.1-62; 1976, c. 760, § 2.1-400; 1987, c. 138; 2001, c. 844.)

Section set out twice. — The section above is effective July 1, 2013. For this section as in effect until July 1, 2013, see the preceding section, also numbered 2.2-1511.

Editor's note. — Acts 2003, c. 900, cl. 3, as amended by Acts 2008, c. 240, provides: "That the provisions of this act shall expire on July 1, 2013."

§ 2.2-1512. Financial statements by Comptroller. — On or before August 15 annually, the Comptroller shall furnish to the Department the following statements, classified and itemized in strict accordance with the budget classifications adopted by the Governor:

1. A statement showing the balance standing to the credit of the several appropriations for each department, bureau, division, office, board, commission, institution, or other agency or undertaking of the Commonwealth at the end of the last preceding appropriation year.
2. A statement showing the monthly expenditures from each appropriation account, and the total monthly expenditures from all the appropriation accounts, including special and all other appropriations, in the twelve months of the last preceding appropriation year.
3. A statement showing the annual revenues and expenditures in each fund.
4. An itemized and complete financial balance sheet for the Commonwealth at the close of the last preceding fiscal year ending June 30.
5. Such other statements as requested by the Governor. (Code 1950, § 2-50; 1966, c. 677, § 2.1-56; 1968, cc. 121, 683; 1976, c. 760, § 2.1-402; 1984, c. 612; 2001, c. 844.)

§ 2.2-1513. Submission of additional information to legislative committees. — To enable the House Committee on Appropriations and the Senate Committee on Finance to perform their prescribed duties, all departments, agencies and institutions of the Commonwealth, their staff and employees shall, upon request, provide such committees with any additional information, as may be deemed necessary, and allow such committees ample opportunity to observe the department's, agency's or institution's daily operations. (1975, c. 501, § 2.1-63.03; 1976, c. 760, § 2.1-404; 1997, c. 182; 2000, cc. 66, 657; 2001, c. 844.)

§ 2.2-1514. (Contingent expiration date — see Editor's notes) Designation of general fund for nonrecurring expenditures. — A. As used in this section:

"The Budget Bill" means the "The Budget Bill" submitted pursuant to § 2.2-1509, including any amendments to a general appropriation act pursuant to such section.

"Nonrecurring expenditures" means the acquisition or construction of capital outlay projects as defined in § 2.2-1518, the acquisition or construction of capital improvements, the acquisition of land, the acquisition of equipment, or other expenditures of a one-time nature as specified in the general appropri-

ation act. Such term shall not include any expenditures relating to transportation, including but not limited to transportation maintenance.

B. At the end of each fiscal year, the Comptroller shall designate within his annual report pursuant to § 2.2-813 as follows: one-third of the remaining amount of the general fund balance that is not otherwise reserved or designated shall be designated by the Comptroller for nonrecurring expenditures, and two-thirds shall be designated for deposit into the Transportation Trust Fund. No such designation shall be made unless the full amounts required for other reserves or designations including, but not limited to, (i) the Revenue Stabilization Fund deposit pursuant to § 2.2-1829, (ii) the Virginia Water Quality Improvement Fund deposit pursuant to § 10.1-2128, but excluding any deposits provided under the Virginia Natural Resources Commitment Fund established under § 10.1-2128.1, (iii) capital outlay reappropriations pursuant to the general appropriation act, (iv) (a) operating expense reappropriations pursuant to the general appropriation act, and (b) reappropriations of unexpended appropriations to certain public institutions of higher education pursuant to § 2.2-5005, (v) pro rata rebate payments to certain public institutions of higher education pursuant to § 2.2-5005, (vi) the unappropriated balance anticipated in the general appropriation act for the end of such fiscal year, and (vii) interest payments on deposits of certain public institutions of higher education pursuant to § 2.2-5005 are set aside. The Comptroller shall set aside amounts required for clauses (iv) (b), (v), and (vii) beginning with the initial fiscal year as determined under § 2.2-5005 and for all fiscal years thereafter.

C. The Governor shall include in "The Budget Bill" pursuant to § 2.2-1509 recommended appropriations from the general fund or recommended amendments to general fund appropriations in the general appropriation act in effect at that time an amount for nonrecurring expenditures and an amount for deposit into the Transportation Trust Fund equal to the amounts designated by the Comptroller for such purposes pursuant to the provisions of subsection B. Such deposit to the Transportation Trust Fund shall not preclude the appropriation of additional amounts from the general fund for transportation purposes. (2002, cc. 839, 888; 2005, cc. 933, 945; 2007, c. 896; 2008, cc. 643, 701; 2008, Sp. Sess. I, cc. 1, 2.)

Section set out twice. — This section is effective until December 31 of any year revenues designated for the Highway Maintenance and Operating Fund and the Transportation Trust Fund are appropriated for non-transportation related purposes. For this section if such an appropriation is made, see the following section.

Cross references. — For non-collection and refund of civil remedial fees authorized under Acts 2007, c. 896, see former § 46.2-206.1 and the Editor's notes thereunder.

Editor's note. — Acts 2007, c. 896, cl. 3, provides: "That the revenues generated by the provisions of this act shall not be used to calculate or reduce the share of local, federal, and state revenues otherwise available to participating jurisdictions. Further, such revenues and moneys shall not be included in any computation of, or formula for, a locality's ability to pay for public education, upon which appropriations of state revenues to local governments for public education are determined."

Acts 2007, c. 896, cl. 21, provides: "That the revenue generated by this act shall be used solely for transportation purposes."

Acts 2007, c. 896, cl. 22, provides: "That the provisions of this act which generate additional revenue for the Transportation Trust Fund, established under § 33.1-23.03:1 of the Code of Virginia, or the Highway Maintenance and Operating Fund shall expire on December 31 of any year in which the General Assembly appropriates any of the revenues designated under general law to the Highway Maintenance and Operating Fund or the Transportation Trust Fund for any non-transportation related purpose."

Acts 2007, c. 896, cl. 23 contains a severability clause.

Acts 2008, Sp. Sess. I, cc. 1 and 2, in cl. 21 provide: "That an emergency exists and this act is in force from its passage [May 21, 2008]."

The 2007 amendments. — The 2007 amendment by c. 896 inserted the second sentence in the definition of "Nonrecurring expenditures"; in subsection B, substituted the language beginning "as follows: one-third of the remaining" at the end of the first sentence for "an amount for nonrecurring expenditures, which shall equal the remaining amount of the general fund balance that is not otherwise reserved or designated"; and in subsection C, inserted "and an amount for deposit into the Transportation Trust Fund" following "nonrecurring expenditures," substituted "amounts" for "amount" and "purposes" for "purpose," and deleted "of this section" following "subsection B" in the first sentence and added the second sentence. For contingent expiration, see Acts 2007, c. 896, cl. 22.

The 2008 amendments. — The 2008 amendments by cc. 643 and 701 are identical, and inserted "but excluding any deposits provided under the Virginia Natural Resources Commitment fund established under § 10.1-2128.1" in subsection B.

The 2008 amendments by Sp. Sess. I, cc. 1 and 2, effective May 21, 2008, in subsection A, substituted "§ 2.2-1518" for "§ 2.2-1503.2" in the paragraph defining "Nonrecurring expenditures."

§ 2.2-1514. (Contingent effective date — see Editor's notes) Designation of general fund for nonrecurring expenditures. — A. As used in this section:

"The Budget Bill" means the "The Budget Bill" submitted pursuant to § 2.2-1509, including any amendments to a general appropriation act pursuant to such section.

"Nonrecurring expenditures" means the acquisition or construction of capital outlay projects as defined in § 2.2-1518, the acquisition or construction of capital improvements, the acquisition of land, the acquisition of equipment, or other expenditures of a one-time nature as specified in the general appropriation act.

B. At the end of each fiscal year, the Comptroller shall designate within his annual report pursuant to § 2.2-813 an amount for nonrecurring expenditures, which shall equal the remaining amount of the general fund balance that is not otherwise reserved or designated. No such designation shall be made unless the full amounts required for other reserves or designations including, but not limited to, (i) the Revenue Stabilization Fund deposit pursuant to § 2.2-1829, (ii) the Virginia Water Quality Improvement Fund deposit pursuant to § 10.1-2128, but excluding any deposits provided under the Virginia Natural Resources Commitment Fund established under § 10.1-2128.1, (iii) capital outlay reappropriations pursuant to the general appropriation act, (iv) (a) operating expense reappropriations pursuant to the general appropriation act, and (b) reappropriations of unexpended appropriations to certain public institutions of higher education pursuant to § 2.2-5005, (v) pro rata rebate payments to certain public institutions of higher education pursuant to § 2.2-5005, (vi) the unappropriated balance anticipated in the general appropriation act for the end of such fiscal year, and (vii) interest payments on deposits of certain public institutions of higher education pursuant to § 2.2-5005 are set aside. The Comptroller shall set aside amounts required for clauses (iv) (b), (v), and (vii) beginning with the initial fiscal year as determined under § 2.2-5005 and for all fiscal years thereafter.

C. The Governor shall include in "The Budget Bill" pursuant to § 2.2-1509 recommended appropriations from the general fund or recommended amendments to general fund appropriations in the general appropriation act in effect at that time an amount for nonrecurring expenditures equal to the amount designated by the Comptroller for such purpose pursuant to the provisions of subsection B of this section. (2002, cc. 839, 888; 2005, cc. 933, 945; 2008, cc. 643, 701; 2008, Sp. Sess. I, cc. 1, 2.)

Section set out twice. — The section above is effective December 31 of any year revenues designated for the Highway Maintenance and Operating Fund or the Transportation Trust Fund are used for non-transportation related purposes according to Acts 2007, c. 896. See the preceding section also numbered 2.2-1514.

Cross references. — For non-collection and refund of civil remedial fees authorized under Acts 2007, c. 896, see former § 46.2-206.1 and the Editor's notes thereunder.

Editor's note. — Acts 2008, Sp. Sess. I, cc. 1 and 2, in cl. 21 provide: "That an emergency exists and this act is in force from its passage [May 21, 2008]."

The 2008 amendments. — The 2008 amendments by cc. 643 and 701 are identical, and inserted "but excluding any deposits provided under the Virginia Natural Resources Commitment fund established under § 10.1-2128.1" in subsection B.

The 2008 amendments by Sp. Sess. I, cc. 1 and 2, effective May 21, 2008, in subsection A, substituted "§ 2.2-1518" for "§ 2.2-1503.2" in the paragraph defining "Nonrecurring expenditures."

CHAPTER 15.1.

SIX-YEAR CAPITAL OUTLAY PLAN.

§ 2.2-1515. Definitions. — As used in this chapter, unless the context clearly shows otherwise, the term or phrase:

"Advisory Committee" means the Six-Year Capital Outlay Plan Advisory Committee established pursuant to § 2.2-1516.

"Capital outlay project" means acquisition of real property, including buildings or plant or machinery or equipment, or new construction or improvements related to state-owned real property, buildings, plant, or machinery or equipment including plans therefor. It shall include any improvements to real property leased for use by a state agency or public educational institution and not owned by the Commonwealth, when such improvements are financed by public funds and become state property upon the expiration of the lease. Capital outlay projects do not include projects that have been included in the Commonwealth Transportation Board's Six-Year Improvement Program.

"Construction phase" means the following steps, as set out in the Construction and Professional Services Manual of the Department of General Services: preparation of final working drawings and specifications, advertising for a sealed bid or proposal, awarding a contract pursuant to law, and actual construction of a project.

"Detailed planning" means the preparation of architectural and engineering documents up to the preliminary design stage, as defined in the Construction and Professional Services Manual of the Department of General Services.

"Pre-planning" means a process meant to obtain a more detailed definition and cost estimate of a project. It may include the following elements, as appropriate:

1. Statement of program definition including functional space requirements, estimates of gross and net square footage, and functional adjacency requirements;

2. Analysis of program execution options, including review of new construction versus renovation alternatives, necessary phasing or sequencing of the project, and coordination with other ongoing or proposed capital projects;

3. Site analysis, including options considered and, for the site chosen, any specific issues related to topography, utilities, or environment;

4. Presentation, including site plan, conceptual floor plans and elevations, and conceptual exterior;

5. Identification of any Uniform Statewide Building Code compliance or permit requirements unique to the project; or

6. Cost estimate for the project to include total cost of the project, construction cost for the project, total cost per square foot, construction cost per square foot, costing methodology, and identification of any factors unique to the project that may impact overall project cost.

"Project" means a capital outlay project included in the six-year capital outlay plan described in § 2.2-1518.

"Value engineering" means a systematic process of review and analysis of a project by a team of appropriate professionals licensed in accordance with Chapter 4 (§ 54.1-400 et seq.) of Title 54.1. As a result of such review and analysis, the team may recommend changes to improve the project's quality or to reduce the total project cost without reducing the overall quality or function of the project. (2008, Sp. Sess. I, cc. 1, 2.)

Editor's note. — Acts 2008, Sp. Sess. I, cc. 1 and 2, in cl. 19 provide: "That nothing in this act shall be construed or interpreted as limiting any authority granted under Chapter 4.10 (§ 23-38.88 et seq.) of Title 23 of the Code of Virginia, or under any management agreement executed pursuant to the provisions of such chapter, provided that, for any capital outlay project of a public institution of higher education included in the capital outlay plan described in § 2.2-1518 of the Code of Virginia (that is enacted into law) for which the general fund supported resources for the project will exceed 100 percent of the general fund-supported resources allocated for that project pursuant to law, such capital outlay project shall be subject to the provisions of subsection E of § 2.2-1519 of the Code of Virginia. For purposes of this enactment, the term 'capital outlay project' means the same as such term is defined § 2.2-1515 of the Code of Virginia."

Acts 2008, Sp. Sess. I, cc. 1 and 2, cl. 21 provides: "That an emergency exists and this act is in force from its passage [May 21, 2008]."

§ 2.2-1516. Six-Year Capital Outlay Plan Advisory Committee. — A. There is hereby established the Six-Year Capital Outlay Plan Advisory Committee. The Advisory Committee shall consist of the following, or their designees: the Secretary of Finance, the Director of the Department of Planning and Budget, the Director of the Department of General Services, the Executive Director of the State Council of Higher Education for Virginia, and the staff directors of the House Appropriations Committee and the Senate Finance Committee.

B. 1. On or before November 1, 2008, the Advisory Committee shall submit to the Governor and the Chairmen of the House Appropriations and Senate Finance Committees a proposed list of new capital outlay projects (and previously planned or authorized capital outlay projects) to be funded entirely or partially from general fund-supported resources for the six fiscal years beginning July 1, 2009.

2. The list shall include projects by agency, in priority order for each agency. In determining priorities, the Advisory Committee shall consider, but not be limited to, the following:

a. Projects that address safety, health, regulatory, security, environmental requirements, or accreditation;

b. Projects to upgrade or replace major mechanical systems and utility infrastructure;

c. Projects to renovate or maintain existing facilities;

d. Projects to construct, expand, or acquire facilities in order to meet programmatic needs;

e. For public institutions of higher education, projects that meet State Council of Higher Education for Virginia recommendations or guideline parameters;

f. Projects that improve energy efficiency;

g. Projects that are listed on, or eligible to be listed on, the Virginia Landmarks Register;

h. Renovation projects for which a facility condition assessment has been completed; and

i. Projects previously planned.
3. The list shall:
a. Identify each capital outlay project;
b. Describe the scope and nature of the project; and
c. Include any other information that the Advisory Committee deems useful.
C. Beginning in 2009, on or before October 1 of each year, the Advisory Committee shall make recommendations to the Governor and the Chairmen of the House Appropriations and the Senate Finance Committees of any changes to the current six-year capital outlay plan (described in § 2.2-1518) and of project funding, including adjusting the fiscal years covered by the plan so that the plan will cover the six fiscal years beginning July 1 of the following year. (2008, Sp. Sess. I, cc. 1, 2.)

§ **2.2-1517. Agency submission of information.** — In addition to all other reporting requirements imposed upon state agencies and public educational institutions provided under law, state agencies and public educational institutions shall submit to the Advisory Committee information requested by the Advisory Committee in the format and on the schedule established by the Advisory Committee for the initial development of the capital outlay project list as described in § 2.2-1516, as well as for the annual modifications to the six-year capital outlay plan described in § 2.2-1518. The information for the annual modifications shall include, but not be limited to, changes in cost estimates. (2008, Sp. Sess. I, cc. 1, 2.)

§ **2.2-1518. Governor to submit a tentative bill for a capital outlay plan; gubernatorial amendments proposed to the plan.** — A. 1. No later than January 13, 2009, the Governor shall submit to the General Assembly a tentative bill establishing a capital outlay plan that includes new capital outlay projects (and previously planned or authorized capital outlay projects) that the Governor proposes to be funded entirely or partially from general fund-supported resources for the six fiscal years beginning July 1, 2009. Projects included in the capital outlay plan shall be in addition to any projects for which funds are appropriated from the Central Maintenance Reserve of the general appropriation act.

2. The capital outlay plan submitted by the Governor shall list capital outlay projects in different tiers. Each tier shall be a grouping of capital outlay projects with the total estimated cost of each project in the tier falling within a minimum and a maximum project cost assigned to the tier, provided that no estimated project costs shall be set out in the plan. The minimum and maximum range assigned to a tier shall be mutually exclusive of all other minimum and maximum ranges assigned to other tiers in order that no capital outlay project shall be reported in more than one tier.

For each capital outlay project listed in the plan the Governor shall provide the following information: (i) the agency or public educational institution to which the project is related, (ii) a description of the project, and (iii) a ranking number assigned to the project, which number shall signify the priority of the project when compared to all other projects of the agency or institution listed in the plan.

B. In 2010 and each year thereafter, the Governor shall, by no later than the day that immediately precedes the first day of the regular session of the applicable General Assembly, submit to the General Assembly a tentative bill proposing amendments to the current capital outlay plan enacted into law, including adjusting the fiscal years covered by the plan so that the plan will cover the six fiscal years beginning on the immediately following July 1. Any such tentative bill shall be submitted using the format described in subsection A.

C. In submitting to the General Assembly tentative bills for the initial capital outlay plan and for plan amendments, the Governor shall consider the capital outlay project list submitted by the Advisory Committee pursuant to § 2.2-1516 and any amendments to the six-year capital outlay plan recommended by the Advisory Committee pursuant to such section. (2008, Sp. Sess. I, cc. 1, 2.)

§ **2.2-1519. Implementation of certain capital outlay projects.** — A. 1. The Central Capital Planning Fund, the State Agency Capital Account, and the Public Educational Institution Capital Account established pursuant to § 2.2-1520 shall be used to fund capital outlay projects included in the six-year capital outlay plan enacted into law.

2. In addition, public educational institutions and state agencies may request authority and appropriation to conduct pre-planning for any such project using nongeneral fund sources. Such costs may be reimbursed up to the lesser of $250,000 or one percent of the project construction costs.

B. A Virginia-based contractor who does not have the same number of years of comparable experience under construction management or design-build shall not be penalized for having less comparable experience in construction management or design-build projects, provided such contractor does have significant experience in constructing comparable projects under design-bid-build. The procuring entity shall consider the experience and quality of work that a contractor has done on projects comparable to the project being procured, whether under construction management, design-build, or design-bid-build. These factors shall be considered by the procuring entity in making its decisions in a pre-qualification or a contractor selection process.

C. If at any time during the detailed planning phase the total cost of a capital outlay project is estimated to exceed a threshold amount set forth in the general appropriation act for the required use of value engineering, then value engineering shall be utilized for such project. Each agency and public educational institution shall retain documentation of the value engineering process conducted for any project, including documentation relating to (i) recommendations offered to the agency or institution, (ii) recommendations accepted and rejected by the agency or institution, and (iii) any savings to the agency or institution resulting from the adoption of each recommendation.

D. For capital outlay projects for which an appropriation is made to the State Agency Capital Account or the Public Educational Institution Capital Account, after an agency or public educational institution has received authorization to move to the construction phase of a project, the Director of the Department of Planning and Budget shall transfer sufficient appropriation from the State Agency Capital Account or the Public Educational Institution Capital Account, as appropriate.

E. 1. Prior to an agency or public educational institution awarding a construction contract for a project, the Director of the Department of General Services shall review the lowest bid or best proposal for the project. If the total amount of such bid or proposal, plus previously expended funds and a reasonable allowance for contingencies, does not exceed 105 percent of the general fund-supported resources for the project as determined during the detailed planning phase, the Director of the Department of General Services and the Director of the Department of Planning and Budget may approve the contract. If the total amount of such bid or proposal, plus previously expended funds and a reasonable allowance for contingencies, exceeds 105 percent of the general fund-supported resources for the project, the Directors shall not approve the contract unless funding of that portion of such total project cost in excess of 105 percent of the general fund-supported resources allocated to the project is from nongeneral fund sources such as private funds, gifts, grants, auxiliary funds, or federal funds as appropriate.

2. If an agency or public educational institution is unable to procure funding from nongeneral fund sources for that portion of such total project cost in excess of 105 percent of the general fund-supported resources allocated to the project, then the agency or institution may reduce the size or scope of the project as necessary to remain within 105 percent of the general fund-supported resources allocated to the project, provided that (i) it has completed a value engineering review by or in collaboration with the Department of General Services, (ii) it has provided a written, detailed analysis of the proposed reduction to the Governor and to the Chairmen of the House Appropriations and Senate Finance Committees, and (iii) the project after such reduction in size or scope is substantially similar in quality and functionality to the original project.

3. An agency or public educational institution may request a supplemental allocation of general fund-supported resources through the budget process only if it submits a written certification to the Chairmen of the House Appropriations and Senate Finance Committees, the Director of the Department of General Services, the Director of the Department of Planning and Budget, and, for public institutions of higher education only, the Executive Director of the State Council of Higher Education, which certification (i) states that additional funding from nongeneral fund sources as described in subdivision 1 will be insufficient to pay for the full amount of the project cost that is in excess of 105 percent of the general fund-supported resources allocated to the project and (ii) provides a detailed analysis and description of the project as modified for a reduction in size or scope as described in subdivision 2 as well as a justification for why such modifications in size or scope cannot be achieved.

4. Nothing in this section shall preclude an agency or public educational institution from providing for re-design or additional value engineering of projects or re-bidding or re-submitting of proposals.

5. No construction contract for a capital outlay project included in the six-year capital outlay plan enacted into law shall be awarded unless first approved by the Director of the Department of General Services and the Director of the Department of Planning and Budget.

F. After a project has been approved by the Director of the Department of General Services and the Director of the Department of Planning and Budget, the Director of the Department of Planning and Budget shall transfer to the project the remaining funds needed for construction from the State Agency Capital Account or the Public Educational Institution Capital Account, as appropriate. (2008, Sp. Sess. I, cc. 1, 2.)

§ **2.2-1520. Certain funds established.** — A. There is hereby established a special, nonreverting fund in the state treasury to be known as the Central Capital Planning Fund, hereafter referred to as the Fund. The Fund shall include such moneys as may be appropriated by the General Assembly from time to time and designated for the Fund. The Fund shall be established on the books of the Comptroller and shall be administered by the Director of the Department of Planning and Budget. Any moneys remaining in the Fund at the end of each fiscal year shall not revert to the general fund but shall remain in the Fund. Moneys in the Fund shall be used solely to pay the pre-planning or detailed planning costs of capital outlay projects that have been approved for pre-planning or detailed planning by the General Assembly.

B. The State Agency Capital Account shall be established in the general appropriation act as a separate item for appropriation purposes. The State Agency Capital Account shall consist of appropriations of the proceeds from the sale of certain bonds by the Virginia Public Building Authority that are designated for the Account and any other moneys as may be appropriated by the General Assembly. The Account shall be administered by the Director of the Department of Planning and Budget consistent with the provisions of this chapter. The Account shall be used to finance the construction of projects, as defined in § 2.2-2260, that have been approved for construction by the General Assembly. In addition, it is required that the Account reimburse the Central Capital Planning Fund for payments made for pre-planning or detailed planning of all such projects that have been approved for construction by the General Assembly.

C. The Public Educational Institution Capital Account shall be established in the general appropriation act as a separate item for appropriation purposes. The Public Educational Institution Capital Account shall consist of appropriations of the proceeds from the sale of certain bonds by the Virginia College Building Authority that are designated for the Account and any other moneys as may be appropriated by the General Assembly. The Account shall be administered by the Director of the Department of Planning and Budget consistent with the provisions of this chapter. The Account shall be used to finance the construction of projects, as defined in § 23-15, that have been approved for construction by the General Assembly. In addition, it is required that the Account reimburse the Central Capital Planning Fund for payments made for pre-planning or detailed planning of all such projects that have been approved for construction by the General Assembly. (2008, Sp. Sess. I, cc. 1, 2.)

CHAPTER 16.

DEPARTMENT OF THE STATE INTERNAL AUDITOR.

§ **2.2-1600. Department created; appointment of State Internal Auditor; staff support.** — There is created a Department of the State Internal Auditor (the "Department"). The Department shall be an agency under the direction of the Secretary of Finance. The State Internal Auditor shall be selected by and report directly to the Secretary of Finance. The State Internal Auditor shall be either a certified public accountant or a certified internal auditor. The State Internal Auditor, in order to provide continuity to the state's internal audit program, shall be a classified position subject to the provisions of the Virginia Personnel Act (§ 2.2-2900 et seq.).

The Secretary of Finance shall assign responsibility for the Department's administrative support services to one or more state agencies within responsibility of his Secretariat.

The Department shall provide for the development and maintenance of internal audit programs in state agencies in order to ensure that the Commonwealth's assets are subject to appropriate internal management controls. Appropriate internal management controls assist in safeguarding assets, ensuring accurate accounting and reporting of financial transactions, and in providing effective and efficient management. (1985, c. 72, §§ 2.1-234.29, 2.1-234.30, 2.1-234.33; 2001, c. 844.)

§ **2.2-1601. Duties of the Department.** — A. The Department shall have the following duties to:

1. Establish state policies, standards, and procedures that will ensure an effective internal audit program in all state agencies;

2. Provide technical information to state agencies concerning trends and new techniques in internal auditing;
3. Develop evaluative tools and other modern methods to assist agency internal auditors in performing audits;
4. Assist state agencies in developing and implementing automated data processing internal audit programs in the Commonwealth;
5. Provide general technical and audit assistance to agency internal auditors and to the Auditor of Public Accounts and the Governor on request;
6. Assist agency heads and collegial bodies in establishing and operating internal audit organizations;
7. Assist in the professional development of agency internal auditors by developing and conducting training programs;
8. Examine the adequacy of agency internal audit programs through periodic assessments of such programs and provide the Governor, Governor's Secretaries, the State Comptroller, the Director of the Department of Planning and Budget, and agency heads with the results of such assessments;
9. Develop, in conjunction with the State Comptroller, the Auditor of Public Accounts, the Joint Legislative Audit and Review Commission, and other appropriate state officials, a plan for accommodating the internal audit needs of agencies that do not require full-time internal auditors; and
10. Prepare a biennial report for the Governor, Governor's Secretaries, Auditor of Public Accounts, and appropriate agency heads on the status of agency internal audit programs generally, and on agency adherence to other legislative requirements on internal auditing.

B. The provisions of subsection A shall not infringe upon responsibilities assigned to the Comptroller, the Auditor of Public Accounts, or the Joint Legislative Audit and Review Commission by other provisions of the Code of Virginia. (1985, c. 72, § 2.1-234.32; 1990, c. 467; 2001, c. 844.)

§ 2.2-1602. Review of Department; report to Governor and General Assembly. — Every four years the duties of the Department shall be reviewed by the Secretary of Finance to determine whether they should be restructured or eliminated. A report of the Secretary of Finance's determination shall be provided to the Governor and the General Assembly. (1985, c. 72, § 2.1-234.34; 1990, c. 467; 2001, c. 844.)

CHAPTER 17.

Department of Technology Planning.

§§ 2.2-1700 through 2.2-1710: Repealed by Acts 2003, cc. 981 and 1021.

Editor's note. — For provisions of Acts 2003, cc. 981 and 1021, cls. 4 to 16, reflecting the intent of the General Assembly to provide for the consolidation of the procurement and operational functions of information technology for state agencies in a single agency, and related transitional and other provisions, see the Editor's note at § 2.2-2005.

CHAPTER 18.

Department of the Treasury.

Article 1.

General Provisions.

§ 2.2-1800. Department of the Treasury; State Treasurer. — A. There is created a Department of the Treasury ("the Department"), which shall be under the direct control and supervision of the State Treasurer. The State Treasurer shall be appointed by the Governor to serve at his pleasure or until a successor is appointed and qualified.

B. The State Treasurer shall, under the direction and control of the Governor, exercise the powers and perform the duties conferred or imposed by law upon him and shall perform such other duties as may be required by the Governor. (Code 1950, § 2-149; 1966, c. 677, § 2.1-177; 1971, Ex. Sess., c. 125; 1976, c. 728; 1984, c. 720; 2000, cc. 25, 275; 2001, c. 844.)

§ 2.2-1801. State Treasurer to appoint administrative assistants, etc. — A. The State Treasurer shall appoint the administrative assistants, deputies and clerks allowed by law.

B. The State Treasurer shall appoint administrative assistants, who shall have authority to act for and perform the duties of the State Treasurer under his direction, supervision and control, and in the absence of the State Treasurer to perform all the duties of the office. Of such absence, the others shall be informed. When the absence of the State Treasurer is to be for more than five days at a time, notice thereof shall be given to the Governor.

C. In the event the administrative assistant is incapacitated from performing his duties during the absence of the State Treasurer, the Governor shall designate some other administrative assistant n the office to act during the absence of the State Treasurer, and in the event of the removal, resignation or death of the State Treasurer, the administrative assistant shall perform all the duties of the office until the vacancy is filled in the manner prescribed by law.

D. Such officers and their sureties shall be liable for any default or breach of duty of their administrative assistants respectively during their absence. (1950, §§ 2-145, 2-146, 2-147, 2-148; 1966, c. 677, §§ 2.1-173, 2.1-174, 2.1-175, 2.1-176; 2001, c. 844.)

§ 2.2-1802. Payment of state funds into state treasury; deposits in state depositories; credit of fund not paid into general fund; exceptions as to endowments and gifts to institutions; appropriations by federal government. — Every state department, division, officer, board, commission, institution or other agency owned or controlled by the Commonwealth, whether at the seat of government or not, collecting or receiving public funds, or moneys from any source, belonging to or for the use of the Commonwealth, or for the use of any state agency, shall hereafter pay the same promptly into the state treasury. All fees of office and commissions accruing to the State Treasurer shall be paid into the state treasury.

Any state department, division, officer, board, commission, institution or other agency at the seat of government shall deposit such moneys to the credit of the State Treasurer upon communicating with him and receiving instructions from him as to what state depository may be used for the purpose. In every such case the depositor shall retain a deposit receipt or a deposit certificate form certified by the bank receiving the deposit for every such deposit to the State Treasurer and send to the Comptroller a copy of the deposit receipt, certificate, or other documentation supporting the deposit, as prescribed by the Comptroller.

Any state department, division, officer, board, commission, institution or other agency not at the seat of government, other than county and city treasurers and clerks of courts, depositing such moneys to its or his credit in local banks shall deposit such moneys to the credit of the State Treasurer in a state depository duly designated in accordance with this chapter, and in every such case the depositor shall retain a deposit receipt or a deposit certificate form certified by the bank receiving the deposit for every deposit to the State Treasurer and send to the Comptroller a copy of the deposit receipt, certificate, or other documentation supporting the deposit, as prescribed by the Comptroller. Moneys deposited into such state depositories shall be transferred to a concentration bank as prescribed by the State Treasurer.

Moneys paid into the state treasury that are not now payable into the general fund of the state treasury shall be placed to the credit of the respective accounts that are required by law to be kept on the books of the Comptroller or to the credit of new accounts to be opened on the books of the Comptroller with such agencies so paying such moneys into the state treasury, respectively.

This chapter shall not apply to the endowment funds or gifts to institutions owned or controlled by the Commonwealth, or to the income from such endowment funds or gifts, or to private funds belonging to the students or inmates of state institutions. The cash as well as the notes of student loan funds shall be held by the respective institutions.

Appropriations made by the government of the United States to or for the benefit of any state institution or agency, however, shall be paid into the state treasury and used for the purposes for which such appropriations were made. (Code 1950, §§ 2-150, 14-16; 1964, c. 386, § 14.1-15; 1966, c. 677, § 2.1-180; 1988, c. 260; 1992, c. 326; 1998, c. 872; 2001, c. 844.)

Cross references. — For exception of institutional fund held by the Board for the Blind and Vision Impaired from this section, see § 51.5-63.

Editor's note. — Acts 2008, c. 879, effective for the biennium ending June 30, 2010, in Item 208 K 2 and 3, provides: "2. Notwithstanding § 2.2-1802 of the Code of Virginia, Virginia Commonwealth University is authorized to maintain a local bank account in Qatar and non-U.S. countries to facilitate business operations the VCU Qatar Campus. These accounts are exempt from the Securities for Public Deposits Act, Title 2.2, Chapter 44 of the Code of Virginia.

"3. Procurements and expenditures from the local bank account(s) are not subject to the Virginia Public Procurement Act and the Commonwealth Accounting Policies and Procedures (CAPP) Manual. Virginia Commonwealth University will institute procurement policies based on competitive procurement principles, except as otherwise stated within these policies. Expenditures from the local bank account will be recorded in the Commonwealth Accounting and Reporting System by Agency Transaction Vouchers, as appropriated herewith with revenue recognized as equal to the expenditures."

§ 2.2-1803. State Treasurer; regulation procedures for depositing money. — The State Treasurer may adopt regulations or other directives establishing procedures for depositing moneys in depository banks and for reporting the deposits. The regulations may address, by way of explanation and not limitation: (i) the form of the required reports; (ii) the frequency of reports and deposits; (iii) the disposition of checks; and (iv) the establishment of banking relationships. All agencies and entities depositing moneys to the credit of the Treasurer of Virginia, including judicial and legislative service agencies, clerks of court, local treasurers or other officials performing similar duties, and political subdivisions, shall comply with the State Treasurer's regulations or other directives. (1982, c. 109, § 2.1-180.1; 2001, c. 844.)

§ 2.2-1804. Payment by delivery of checks, etc., to State Treasurer; liability when not paid on presentation. — Any public officer, or any firm or corporation, or any other person having to pay money into the treasury may make payment by delivering to the State Treasurer a check, draft or electronic transfer of funds, drawn or endorsed, payable to the State Treasurer, or his order, or may make payment by delivering to the State Treasurer the proper amount of lawful money. Should any check or draft not be paid on presentation, the amount thereof, with all costs, shall be charged to the person on whose account it was received, and his liability and that of his sureties, except the additional liability for costs, shall be as if he had never offered any such check, draft, or certificate of deposit. (Code 1950, § 2-152; 1966, c. 677, § 2.1-182; 2001, c. 844.)

§ 2.2-1805. Records of receipts of such checks, etc.; reports to Comptroller. — A. The State Treasurer shall keep a record of every such check, draft, or electronic transfer of funds, and of all such moneys received by him, and upon receipt shall cause the same to be placed to the credit of the Commonwealth with some state depository. If any check or draft is not paid on presentation, the State Treasurer shall immediately notify the Comptroller, who shall proceed to collect the amount from the person from whom the same was received by the Treasurer. The State Treasurer shall daily transmit to the Comptroller a detailed record of all receipts.

B. The State Treasurer shall not collect any money on a check or draft; but the same shall, in every case, be properly endorsed as required and deposited with some state depository for the credit of the Commonwealth. (Code 1950, §§ 2-153, 2-154; 1966, c. 677, §§ 2.1-183, 2.1-184; 2001, c. 844.)

§ 2.2-1806. Investment of current funds in state treasury; withdrawals and transfers of moneys to be invested. — The Governor and State Treasurer, acting jointly may whenever in their opinion there are funds in the state treasury in excess of the amount required to meet the current needs and demands of the Commonwealth, invest the excess funds in securities that are legal investments under the laws of the Commonwealth for public funds. The funds shall be invested in such of said securities as, in their judgment, will be readily convertible into money. Notwithstanding the provisions of § 2.2-1821 or any other provision relating to the withdrawal of state moneys in a state depository, withdrawals and transfers of state moneys to be so invested may be made by state depositories pursuant to oral including telephonic or electronic instructions of the State Treasurer or his duly authorized deputies. Written confirmations of the withdrawals and transfers shall be provided by the state depository no later than the close of business on the day following the withdrawal and transfer. Payment of state moneys pursuant to this procedure shall be valid against the Commonwealth. (Code 1950, § 2-154.1; 1956, c. 184; 1966, c. 677, § 2.1-185; 1981, c. 36; 2001, c. 844.)

§ 2.2-1807. Investments, etc., in custody of State Treasurer. — The State Treasurer shall be charged with the custody of all investments and invested funds of the Commonwealth or in possession of the Commonwealth in a fiduciary capacity, and shall keep the accounts of such investments. The State Treasurer shall also be charged with the custody of all bonds and certificates of the state debts, whether unissued or canceled, and with the receipt and delivery of state bonds and certificates for transfer, registration or exchange. (Code 1950, § 2-155; 1966, c. 677, § 2.1-186; 2001, c. 844.)

§ 2.2-1808. State Treasurer may sell securities in general fund; exceptions; disposition of proceeds. — The Treasurer may sell, transfer, and convey any notes, bonds, obligations or certificates of stock held in the general fund of the state treasury. The proceeds from any such sale or disposition shall immediately be paid into the general fund. This section shall apply to any present or future holdings. (Code 1950, p. 632, § 2-155.1; 1966, c. 677, § 2.1-187; 1970, c. 687; 1989, c. 28; 1991, cc. 349, 366; 2001, c. 844.)

§ 2.2-1809. Warrants on state treasury to be listed and numbered. — The State Treasurer shall keep a list of all warrants drawn upon the state treasury, numbered consecutively.

No information contained in the list of warrants shall be released for any purpose except as a means of establishing the status of a claim previously reported as having been paid when a person legally entitled to the funds presents evidence that a previously submitted claim has not been paid. (Code 1950, § 2-156; 1966, c. 677, § 2.1-188; 1993, c. 155; 2001, c. 844.)

§ 2.2-1810. State Treasurer to keep accounts with depositories. — The State Treasurer shall keep accounts on the books of his office with the different depositories, on which accounts balances shall be struck monthly, showing the amount in bank to the credit of the State Treasurer at the end of each month. (Code 1950, § 2-157; 1966, c. 677, § 2.1-189; 2001, c. 844.)

§ 2.2-1811. Unpresented checks drawn by State Treasurer; replacement and payment. — The State Treasurer shall report and remit, pursuant to the provisions of §§ 55-210.9, 55-210.12 and 55-210.14, all checks drawn by him on state depositories that have not been presented for payment within one year from the date of issuance. (Code 1950, § 2-158; 1966, c. 677, § 2.1-190; 1983, c. 190; 2001, c. 844.)

Editor's note. — Section 55-210.14, referred to above, was repealed by Acts 1988, c. 378.

§ 2.2-1812. Admissibility of reproductions of checks in evidence; compliance with subpoena. — A. A reproduction of any check or draft or an enlargement of such reproduction drawn by the State Treasurer, when satisfactorily identified, shall be admissible in evidence as the original itself in any judicial or administrative proceeding whether the original is in existence. The introduction of a reproduced check or draft or of an enlargement thereof shall not preclude admission of the original. Any such check or draft, reproduction or enlargement purporting to be sealed, sealed and signed, or signed alone by the State Treasurer or on his behalf by his designee, may be considered satisfactorily identified and admitted as evidence, without any proof of the seal or signature, or of the official character of the person whose name is signed to it.

B. The State Treasurer or his designee, when served with any summons, subpoena, subpoena duces tecum or order, directing him to produce any check or draft kept by or in the possession of any agency or institution of the Commonwealth, may comply by certifying a reproduction or enlargement in accordance with subsection A and mailing the reproduction or enlargement in a sealed envelope to the clerk of court. Upon good cause shown, any court may direct the Treasurer or his designee to appear personally, notwithstanding any other provision of this section. (1979, c. 173, § 2.1-190.1; 1994, c. 16; 2001, c. 844.)

Article 2.

State Depositories.

§ 2.2-1813. Deposits in banks and savings institutions designated as state depositories. — Moneys to be paid into the state treasury shall be deposited in the banks and savings institutions designated as state depositories by the State Treasurer. (Code 1950, § 2-177; 1966, c. 677, § 2.1-209; 1974, c. 517; 1979, c. 215; 1996, c. 77; 2001, c. 844.)

§ 2.2-1814. Amount and time limit of deposits. — The State Treasurer may arrange for and make state deposits in such amounts and for such time as in his judgment the condition of the state treasury permits; however, no state deposit shall be made for a period in excess of five years. The money deposited in a bank or savings institution in excess of the amount insured by the Federal Deposit Insurance Corporation or other federal insurance agency shall be fully collateralized by eligible collateral as defined in § 2.2-4401. (Code 1950, § 2-178; 1966, c. 677, § 2.1-210; 1971, Ex. Sess., cc. 139, 245; 1974, c. 517; 1978, c. 52; 1979, c. 215; 1984, c. 374; 1990, c. 3; 1996, c. 77; 2001, c. 844.)

§ 2.2-1815. Security to be given by depositories holding state funds. — No state funds shall be deposited in any depository unless it is a "qualified public depository" as defined in § 2.2-4401. For purposes of this article, "state funds" means public funds or moneys from any source, belonging to or for the use of the Commonwealth, or for the use of any state department, division, officer, board, commission, institution, or other agency or authority owned or controlled by the Commonwealth. All state funds shall be secured pursuant to the Virginia Security for Public Deposits Act (§ 2.2-4400 et seq.). (Code 1950, § 2-179; 1966, c. 677, § 2.1-211; 1996, cc. 364, 390; 2001, c. 844.)

§ 2.2-1816. How public moneys transferred to depositories. — All transfers of public moneys from one depository to another for any purpose shall be made by electronic funds transfer at the direction of the State Treasurer or his duly authorized deputies who shall order the transferor bank to make payment to the transferee bank for deposit to the credit of the State Treasurer. (Code 1950, § 2-188; 1966, c. 677, § 2.1-219; 1974, c. 232; 2001, c. 844.)

§ 2.2-1817. Commonwealth shall not be liable for loss in collection of checks, etc. — The Commonwealth shall not be liable for any loss resulting from lack of diligence on the part of any depository in forwarding, or in failing to collect, any check, draft, or electronic transfer of funds as is referred to in § 2.2-1804, or for the loss of any check, draft, or electronic transfer of funds in transmission through the mails or otherwise. (Code 1950, § 2-189; 1966, c. 677, § 2.1-220; 2001, c. 844.)

§ 2.2-1818. Responsibility of Commonwealth for securities deposited with Commonwealth Transportation Board. — The Commonwealth shall be responsible for the safekeeping of all bonds or other securities deposited with the Commonwealth Transportation Commissioner or the Commonwealth Transportation Board as surety on account of funds deposited in banks by division engineers of the Department of Transportation. If such bonds or securities or any of them are lost, destroyed or misappropriated, the Commonwealth shall make good such loss to the bank making the deposit of its bonds or other securities.

Upon the closing of accounts of district engineers with banks, its bonds and other securities then on deposit shall be returned to the bank. (Code 1950, § 2-192; 1966, c. 677, § 2.1-223; 2001, c. 844.)

ARTICLE 3.

Disbursement From State Treasury.

§ 2.2-1819. Payments to be made in accordance with appropriations; submission and approval of quarterly estimates. — No money shall be paid out of the state treasury except in accordance with appropriations made by law.

No appropriation to any department, institution or other agency of the state government, except the General Assembly and the judiciary, shall become available for expenditure until the agency submits an annual estimate of the amounts required for each activity to the Director of the Department of Planning and Budget and Governor for approval by the Governor. (Code 1950, § 2-200; 1966, c. 677, § 2.1-224; 1992, c. 582; 2001, c. 844.)

Cross references. — For provision requiring appropriations, see Va. Const., Art. X, § 7.

Editor's note. — Acts 2008, c. 879, effective for the biennium ending June 30, 2010, in § 4-1.07, provides: "Except when otherwise directed by the Governor within the limits prescribed in §§ 4-1.02 Withholding of Spending Authority, 4-1.03 Appropriation Transfers, and 4-1.04 Appropriation Increases of this act, the Director, Department of Planning and Budget, shall prepare and act upon the allotment of appropriations required by this act, and by § 2.2-1819, Code of Virginia, and the authorizations for rates of pay required by this act. Such allotments and authorizations shall have the same effect as if the personal signature of the Governor were subscribed thereto. This section shall not be construed to prohibit an appeal by the head of any state agency to the Governor for reconsideration of any action taken by the Director, Department of Planning and Budget, under this section."

§ 2.2-1820: Reserved.

§ 2.2-1821. Deposits to be to credit of State Treasurer; how money withdrawn. — All state moneys in a state depository shall stand on the books of such depository to the credit of the State Treasurer. The State Treasurer shall have authority to draw any of the money by his check, by electronic funds transfer, or by any means deemed appropriate and sound by the State Treasurer and approved by the Governor, drawn upon a warrant issued by the Comptroller. If any money to his credit shall be knowingly paid otherwise than upon his check, electronic funds transfer or by alternative means specifically approved by the State Treasurer and the Governor, drawn upon such warrant, the payment shall not be valid against the Commonwealth. (Code 1950, § 2-201; 1966, c. 677, § 2.1-226; 1974, c. 231; 1984, c. 374; 2001, c. 844.)

§ 2.2-1822. Conditions to issuance of disbursement warrants. — The Comptroller shall not issue a disbursement warrant unless and until he has audited, through the use of statistical sampling or other acceptable auditing techniques the bill, invoice, account, payroll or other evidence of the claim, demand or charge and satisfied himself as to the regularity, legality and correctness of the expenditure or disbursement, and that the claim, demand or charge has not been previously paid. If he is so satisfied, he shall approve the same; otherwise, he shall withhold his approval. In order that such regularity and legality may appear, the Comptroller may, by general rule or special order, require the certification or other evidence as the circumstances may demand. (Code 1950, § 2-202; 1966, c. 677, § 2.1-227; 1972, c. 205; 2001, c. 844.)

§ 2.2-1822.1. Recovery audits of state contracts. — The Department of Accounts shall procure the services of one or more private contractors, in accordance with the Virginia Public Procurement Act (§ 2.2-4300 et seq.), to conduct systematic recovery audits of state agency contracts. Such recovery audit contracts shall be performance-based and shall contain a provision that authorizes the contractor to be paid a percentage of any payment error that is recovered by such contractor. Individual recovery audits shall consist of the review of contracts to identify payment errors made by state agencies to vendors and other entities resulting from (i) duplicate payments, (ii) invoice errors, (iii) failure to apply applicable discounts, rebates, or other allowances, or (iv) any other errors resulting in inaccurate payments. The Department of Accounts shall report on the status and effectiveness of recovery audits, including any savings realized, to the Chairs of the House Committee on Appropriations and the Senate Committee on Finance by January 1 of each year. (2004, c. 644; 2005, c. 109.)

§ 2.2-1823. Lump-sum transfers prohibited. — Lump-sum transfers of appropriations to state departments, divisions, offices, boards, commissions, institutions and other agencies owned or controlled by the Commonwealth, whether at the seat of government or not, shall be prohibited except for the payment to or distribution among the political subdivisions of the Commonwealth of any appropriations made to them by law. (Code 1950, § 2-203; 1966, c. 677, § 2.1-228; 2001, c. 844.)

§ 2.2-1824. Petty cash, payroll and other funds. — A reasonable petty cash, payroll or other imprest fund may be allowed each state department, institution, board, commission or other agency. The amount of such fund shall be fixed by the Comptroller in each case, but these funds shall be reimbursed only upon vouchers audited by the Comptroller. (Code 1950, § 2-204; 1966, c. 677, § 2.1-229; 1972, c. 240; 2001, c. 844.)

§ 2.2-1825. Issuance of warrants for payment of claims; Comptroller to keep and sign register of warrants issued; signing of checks drawn on such warrants; electronic payment systems. — After the allowance of any claim that is payable out of the state treasury, under any of the provisions of this title, a warrant shall be issued for the sum to be paid. A register of all warrants so issued shall be kept by the Comptroller, which register and a duplicate register shall, from time to time, be signed by the Comptroller or by such deputy he may designate for that purpose. The Comptroller shall not be required to sign the warrants.

All checks drawn upon warrants shown by the register and duplicate register, signed by the Comptroller or his deputy, shall be signed by the State Treasurer, or by such deputy as he may designate for that purpose. The signature may be made by means of a mechanical or electrical device selected by the State Treasurer. The device shall be safely kept so that no one will have access to it except the State Treasurer and his deputies authorized to sign warrants.

However, when deemed appropriate, the State Treasurer may utilize various electronic payment systems in lieu of issuing checks drawn upon warrants. (Code 1950, § 2-206; 1966, c. 677, § 2.1-231; 1984, c. 374; 2001, c. 844.)

§ 2.2-1826. Issuance of replacement warrants generally. — Upon satisfactory proof presented to the Comptroller or to the State Treasurer that any warrant drawn by either the Comptroller or the State Treasurer, or by a predecessor, upon the state treasury has been lost or destroyed before having been paid, the Comptroller or State Treasurer who issued, or from whose office was issued, the original warrant shall issue a replacement of the original warrant. The Comptroller or the State Treasurer may require a bond to be executed, with such security as is approved by him, payable to the Commonwealth, in the amount of the warrant and conditioned to save harmless the Commonwealth from any loss occasioned by issuing the replacement warrant. Every replacement warrant shall show upon its face that it is a replacement.

In the discretion of the State Treasurer, state warrants in payment and redemption of previously lost or otherwise unpaid warrants may be issued directly to the person entitled to the money as the owner, heir, legatee, or as fiduciary of the estate of the deceased owner, heir, or legatee, and in such cases shall not be issued to a named attorney-in-fact, agent, assignee, or any other person regardless of a written instruction to the contrary. In such circumstances, the State Treasurer may refuse to recognize and is not bound by any terms of a power of attorney or assignment that may be presented as having been executed by a person as the purported owner, heir, legatee or fiduciary of the estate of a deceased owner of such warrants. (Code 1950, § 2-207; 1966, c. 677, § 2.1-232; 1982, c. 409; 1993, c. 155; 2001, c. 844.)

§ 2.2-1827. When replacement warrant issued without bond. — No bond shall be required where an original warrant was issued to (i) any eleemosynary or educational institution of the Commonwealth for money appropriated to the institution, (ii) the treasurer of any county or city in the Commonwealth for money apportioned to it out of the school fund and to be disbursed by the treasurer in payment of school warrants, or to be issued to any district school board of any county for money to be disbursed by the board in payment and settlement of any claims lawfully contracted in the operation of the public schools in the district, or in the construction of graded school buildings, or (iii) the treasurer of any county or city in the Commonwealth for money apportioned to it from the gas tax, and such warrant has been lost or destroyed without having been paid. The Comptroller or the State Treasurer who issued the original warrant, or from whose office it was issued, or if issued by his predecessor, shall issue a replacement warrant. The replacement warrant shall show on its face that it is a replacement and shall be issued within thirty days from the date of issuing the original warrant, upon satisfactory proof of the loss or destruction of the original warrant. (Code 1950, § 2-208; 1966, c. 677, § 2.1-233; 2001, c. 844.)

Michie's Jurisprudence. — For related discussion, see 12A M.J. Lost Instruments and Records, § 9.

ARTICLE 4.

Revenue Stabilization Fund.

§ 2.2-1828. Creation of Revenue Stabilization Fund. — There is established a fund to be known as the Revenue Stabilization Fund (the "Fund") for the stabilization of the expected revenues of the Commonwealth. The Fund shall be available to offset, in part, anticipated shortfalls in revenues when appropriations based on previous forecasts exceed expected revenues in subsequent forecasts. (1992, c. 316, § 2.1-191.1; 2001, c. 844.)

Editor's note. — Acts 1992, c. 316, which enacted former Article 2.1 of Chapter 14 of Title 2.1 (see now this article), in cl. 2 provided: "That this act shall become effective upon the approval by the General Assembly of an amendment to the Constitution of Virginia as contained in Chapter 642 of the Acts of Assembly of 1991 and the subsequent ratification of such proposed amendment by the voters as provided in Article XII, Section 1 of the Constitution of Virginia." The amendment to Va. Const., Art. X, § 8, as contained in Acts 1991, c. 642, was approved by the General Assembly and was ratified by the people on November 7, 1992.

§ 2.2-1829. Reports of Auditor of Public Accounts; Fund deposits and withdrawals. — A. On or before December 1 of each year, the Auditor of Public Accounts shall report to the General Assembly the certified tax revenues collected in the most recently ended fiscal year. The Auditor shall, at the same time, (i) provide his report on the 10 percent limitation and the amount that could be paid into the Fund and (ii) the amount necessary for deposit for the next fiscal year into the Fund in order to satisfy the mandatory deposit requirement of Article X, Section 8 of the Constitution of Virginia. The Governor shall include any such amount in his budget bill submitted to the General Assembly pursuant to § 2.2-1509. A schedule of deposits may be provided for in the Appropriation Act.

B. If the report of the Auditor of Public Accounts, pursuant to subsection A, indicates that the annual percentage increase in the certified tax revenues collected in the most recently ended fiscal year is eight percent or greater than the certified tax revenues collected for the immediately preceding fiscal year and that such annual percentage increase in the certified tax revenues for the most recently ended fiscal year is also equal to or greater than 1.5 times the average annual percentage increase in the certified tax revenues collected in the six fiscal years immediately preceding the most recently ended fiscal year, the Governor shall include in his budget recommendations, submitted to the General Assembly in the subsequent session pursuant to § 2.2-1509, an additional amount for deposit to the Fund in excess of any mandatory deposit to the Fund required by Article X, Section 8 of the Constitution of Virginia. Such additional amount shall be equal to at least 25 percent of the product of the certified tax revenues collected in the most recently ended fiscal year multiplied by the difference between the annual percentage increase in the certified tax revenues collected for the most recently ended fiscal year and the average annual percentage increase in the certified tax revenues collected in the six fiscal years immediately preceding the most recently ended fiscal year. Any such additional deposits to the Fund shall be included in the Governor's budget recommendations submitted to the General Assembly in the subsequent session pursuant to § 2.2-1509 only if the estimate of general fund revenues prepared in accordance with § 2.2-1503 for the fiscal year in which the deposit is to be made is at least five percent greater than the actual general fund revenues for the immediately preceding fiscal year.

C. The State Comptroller shall draw such warrants as appropriated and the State Treasurer shall deposit such warrants into the Fund. No amounts shall be withdrawn from the Fund except pursuant to appropriations made by the General Assembly in accordance with § 2.2-1830. However, if any amounts accrue, such as through interest or dividends, to the credit of the Fund in excess of the 10 percent limitation calculated by the Auditor of Public Accounts, any excess shall be paid into the general fund pursuant to Article X, Section 8 of the Constitution of Virginia.

D. For the purposes of the Comptroller's preliminary and final annual reports as required by § 2.2-813, all balances remaining in the Fund on June 30 of each fiscal year shall be considered to be a portion of the fund balance of the general fund of the state treasury. (1992, c. 316, § 2.1-191.2; 1993, c. 26; 2001, c. 844; 2003, cc. 755, 759.)

Editor's note. — Acts 2008, c. 879, effective for the biennium ending June 30, 2010, in Item 265 B, provides: "On or before November 1 of each year, the Auditor of Public Accounts shall report to the General Assembly the certified tax revenues collected in the most recently ended fiscal year. The Auditor shall, at the same time, provide his report on the 10 percent limitation and the amount that could be paid into the Fund in order to satisfy the mandatory deposit requirement of Article X, Section 8 of the Constitution of Virginia as well as the additional deposit requirement of § 2.2-1829, Code of Virginia."

§ 2.2-1830. Decline in forecasted revenues. — In the event that a revised general fund forecast presented to the General Assembly reflects a decline when compared to total general fund revenues appropriated, and the decrease is more than two percent of certified tax revenues collected in the most recently ended fiscal year, the General Assembly may appropriate an amount for transfer from the Fund to the general fund to stabilize the revenues of the Commonwealth. However, in no event shall the transfer exceed more than one-half of the forecasted shortfall in revenues. (1992, c. 316, § 2.1-191.3; 2001, c. 844.)

§ 2.2-1831. Sources or components of "general fund revenues." — Any revised general fund revenue forecast presented to the General Assembly for purposes of this article shall consist of the same revenue sources or components as those on which the total general fund revenues appropriated are based. (1992, c. 316, § 2.1-191.4; 2001, c. 844.)

ARTICLE 5.

Division Of Risk Management.

§ 2.2-1832. Division of Risk Management. — The Division of Risk Management (the "Division"), formerly within the Department of General Services, is hereby transferred to the Department (the "Department") of the Treasury and shall exercise the powers and duties described in this article. (1980, c. 488, § 2.1-526.1; 1988, c. 848; 2000, cc. 618, 632, § 2.1-191.5; 2001, c. 844.)

Cross references. — As to records which are excluded from the provisions of the Virginia Freedom of Information Act, see § 2.2-3705.1 et seq.

Editor's note. — Acts 2000, cc. 618 and 632, which repealed former Article 5.1 of Chapter 32 of Title 2.1, § 2.1-526.1 et seq., and added former Article 2.2 of Chapter 14 of Title 2.1 (see now this article), provide in cl. 3: "That the Governor may transfer an appropriation, or any portion thereof, or any employees within an agency established, abolished or otherwise affected by the provisions of this act, or from one such agency to another, to support the changes in organization or responsibility resulting from or required by the provisions of this act."

Acts 2000, cc. 618 and 632, cl. 4 provide: "That, as of the effective date of this act, the Department of the Treasury shall be deemed successor in interest to the Department of General Services to the extent that this act transfers powers and duties. All right, title and interest in and to any real or tangible personal property vested in the Department of general Services to the extent that this act transfers powers and duties as of the effective date of this act shall be transferred to and taken as standing in the name of the Department of the Treasury."

§ 2.2-1833. Property and insurance records to be maintained. — The Division shall establish and maintain a file of state-owned buildings and contents, hereinafter inclusively referred to as buildings or properties, and the actual cash value or replacement cost value if insured or replacement cost basis thereof, and the amount of fire and extended coverage, vandalism and malicious mischief, optional perils or all risk insurance coverage thereon. All agencies of the Commonwealth shall keep the Division informed as to the status of all properties under their control. (1980, c. 488, § 2.1-526.2; 1982, c. 318; 1988, c. 848; 2000, cc. 618, 632, § 2.1-191.6; 2001, c. 844.)

§ 2.2-1834. Inspection of state-owned properties for insurance purposes; determination of coverage; procurement, discontinuance, etc., of insurance. — A. The Division may inspect or administer a program of self-inspection for all state-owned properties and confer with the proper officials or employees of the several agencies of the Commonwealth for the purpose of determining (i) insurance coverages that are necessary with respect to properties under their control and (ii) the manner whereby savings and costs of such insurance may be made. It may seek the assistance of insurance companies and their representatives, and the State Fire Marshal, in devising means by which hazards may be reduced or eliminated. The Division shall have final responsibility with respect to coverage, noncoverage, provisions of policies, quantity and type of fire and extended coverage, vandalism and malicious mischief, and optional perils or all risk insurance coverage. The Governor may exempt any agency, institution of higher education, or part thereof from any part of the risk management and insurance program.

B. The Division may change or discontinue fire and extended coverage, vandalism and malicious mischief, optional perils or all risk insurance coverage carried pursuant to bond indentures and other contractual requirements, provided the change or discontinuance meets with the written approval of the trustee of the bond indenture and those signatory to the contracts.

C. As its programs are implemented, the Division shall assume the sole responsibility, with the approval of the Governor, for purchasing insurance, self-insuring or combining insurance and self-insurance (i) on all properties of the Commonwealth or (ii) for protection of liabilities or other casualties. (1980, c. 488, § 2.1-526.3; 1982, c. 318; 1988, c. 848; 1996, cc. 475, 510; 2000, cc. 618, 632, § 2.1-191.7; 2001, c. 844.)

§ 2.2-1835. State Insurance Reserve Trust Fund. — A. The State Insurance Reserve Trust Fund (the "Fund") is established and shall consist of the payments required by subsection B. The Fund shall be under the management and control of the Division, and any claims for losses payable out of the Fund shall be at the direction of the Division. The Fund shall be invested as provided in § 2.2-1806 and interest shall be added to the fund as earned.

B. Each agency, department, division, or institution of state government having control over any state structure and contents thereof, or that participates in any program of insurance operated by the Division, shall pay each year into the Fund or any trust fund established pursuant to the provisions of this article amounts necessary to maintain the trusts at levels of funding deemed adequate by the Division. The Division shall set the premium and administrative costs to be paid to it for providing an insurance plan established pursuant to this section. The premiums and administrative costs set by the Division shall be payable in the amounts, at the time and in the manner that the Division in its sole discretion requires. Premiums and administrative costs need not be uniform among participants, but shall be set to best ensure the financial stability of the plan. Whenever any building or structure is under the control of two or more agencies, departments, divisions or institutions of the Commonwealth, the payment required shall be prorated upon the basis of percentage of the area controlled.

C. In the event of loss or damage exceeding $1000 to property on which there is no insurance recovery or limited insurance recovery as a consequence of any action by the Division resulting in noncoverage, reduced insurance, elimination of insured perils or otherwise, the Division shall determine the amount, if any, payable out of the Fund, and such amount, when approved by the Governor, shall be final. The amount payable shall be used for the purpose of restoring the damaged structure or rebuilding it, as the circumstances may require, but in no event shall the amount payable on account of such loss exceed the actual cash value or the replacement cost value of the property in accordance with the basis of insurance, nor shall the amount payable when added to the insurance recovered exceed the actual cash value or the replacement cost value of the property, as recorded in the property and insurance records of the Division.

D. In addition to the amounts payable under subsection C, the costs of operating the Division that are properly allocated to its functions concerning the Fund and other administrative and contractual costs of the Division not otherwise provided for shall be paid out of the Fund, for which purposes such funds are appropriated. (1980, c. 488, § 2.1-526.5; 1982, c. 318; 1988, c. 848; 1996, cc. 475, 510; 2000, cc. 618, 632, § 2.1-191.8; 2001, c. 844.)

§ 2.2-1836. Insurance plan for state-owned buildings and state-owned contents of buildings. — A. Subject to the approval of the Governor, the Division shall establish a risk management plan that may be self-insurance or a combination of self-insurance and purchased insurance to provide coverage on (i) state-owned buildings and (ii) state-owned contents of buildings owned by the Commonwealth or of buildings not owned by the Commonwealth that are occupied in whole or in part by an agency of the Commonwealth.

B. Any insurance plan established pursuant to this section may provide, but not be limited to, physical damage coverage against the perils of (i) fire and lightning; (ii) extended coverage for windstorm, hail, smoke, explosion, other than that caused by steam pressure vessels, riot, riot attending a strike, civil commotion, aircraft and vehicles not owned by the Commonwealth; (iii) vandalism and malicious mischief; (iv) optional perils; and (v) all risk insurance.

C. Any insurance plan established pursuant to this section shall provide for the establishment of a trust fund or contribution to the State Insurance Reserve Trust Fund for the payment of claims covered under such a plan, which are not recoverable from purchased insurance. The funds shall be invested as provided in § 2.2-1806 and interest shall be added to the fund as earned. The trust fund shall also provide for payment of administrative costs, contractual costs and other expenses related to the administration of the plan.

D. The insurance plan for state-owned buildings and state-owned contents of buildings shall be submitted to the Governor for approval prior to implementation. (1980, c. 488, § 2.1-526.7; 1982, c. 318; 1988, c. 848; 2000, cc. 618, 632, § 2.1-191.10; 2001, c. 844.)

§ 2.2-1837. Risk management plan for public liability. — A. Subject to the approval of the Governor, the Division shall establish a risk management plan, which may be purchased insurance, self-insurance or a combination of self-insurance and purchased insurance to provide:

1. Protection against liability imposed by law for damages resulting from any claim:

a. Made against any state department, agency, institution, board, commission, officer, agent, or employee for acts or omissions of any nature while acting in an authorized governmental or proprietary capacity and in the course and scope of employment or authorization;

b. Made against participants, other than professional counsel, in student disciplinary proceedings at public institutions of higher education for nonmalicious acts or omissions of any nature in the course and scope of participation in the proceedings; or

c. Resulting from an authorized indemnification agreement entered into by a Virginia public institution of higher education, which agreements the institutions may execute if the Governor (i) considers in advance of execution (a) the institution's analysis of the relevant public benefit and risk of liability, (b) the Division's charge to be assessed against the institution for providing insurance or self-insurance coverage for the claims resulting from the indemnification agreement, and (c) the Office of the Attorney General's comments, and (ii) determines that execution is necessary to further the public's best interests. The indemnification agreement shall limit the institution's total liability to a stated dollar amount and shall notify the contractor that the full faith and credit of the Commonwealth are not pledged or committed to payment of the institution's obligation under the agreement;

2. Protection against tort liability and incidental medical payments arising out of the ownership, maintenance or use of buildings, grounds or properties owned or leased by the Commonwealth or used by state employees or other authorized persons in the course of their employment;

3. For the payment of attorneys' fees and expenses incurred in defending such persons and entities concerning any claim that (i) arises from their governmental employment or authorization, that (ii) arises from their participation in such student disciplinary proceedings, or (iii) is described in any such indemnification agreement, where the Division is informed by the Attorney General's office that it will not provide a defense due to a conflict or other appropriate reason; and

4. For the payment of attorney's fees and expenses awarded to any individual or entity against the Commonwealth, or any department, agency, institution, board, commission, officer, agent, or employee of the Commonwealth for acts or omissions of any nature while acting in an authorized governmental or proprietary capacity, or in reliance upon any constitutional provision, or law of the Commonwealth. It is the obligation of the Division to provide for such indemnification regardless of whether there is a request for or an award of damages associated with the award of such fees and expenses.

a. As a condition of coverage for the payment of attorney's fees and expenses, the department, agency, institution, board, commission, officer, agent, or employee of the Commonwealth shall (i) promptly notify the Division of the commencement of any claim, suit, action or other proceeding prior to its settlement, (ii) provide the Division with full nonprivileged information on the matter as requested, and (iii) permit the Division to participate in the investigation of such claim, suit, action or other proceeding. Failure to promptly notify the Division or to reasonably cooperate may, at the Division's discretion, result in no payment or a reduced payment being made.

b. The Division shall set the premium and administrative costs to be paid to it for providing payment of attorney fees and expenses awarded pursuant to this section. The premiums and administrative costs set by the Division shall be payable in the amounts, at the time and in the manner that the Division in its sole discretion requires. Premiums and administrative costs shall be set to best ensure the financial stability of the plan.

B. Any risk management plan established pursuant to this section shall provide for the establishment of a trust fund or contribution to the State Insurance Reserve Trust Fund for the payment of claims covered under the plan. The funds shall be invested as provided in § 2.2-1806 and interest shall be added to the fund as earned. The trust fund shall also provide for payment of administrative costs, contractual costs, and other expenses related to the administration of such plan.

C. The risk management plan for public liability shall be submitted to the Governor for approval prior to implementation.

D. The risk management plan established pursuant to this section shall provide protection against professional liability imposed by law as provided in § 24.2-121, resulting from any claim made against a local electoral board, any of its members, any general registrar, or any employee of or paid assistant to a registrar for acts or omissions of any nature while acting in an authorized governmental or proprietary capacity and in the course and scope of employment or authorization, regardless of whether or not the civil action requests monetary damages, subject to the limitations of the risk management plan.

E. The risk management plan established pursuant to this section shall provide protection against any claim made against any soil and water conservation district, director, officer, agent or employee thereof, (i) arising out of the ownership, maintenance or use of buildings, grounds or properties owned, leased or maintained by any such district or used by district employees or other authorized persons in the course of their employment, or (ii) arising out of acts or omissions of any nature while acting in an authorized governmental or proprietary capacity and in the course and scope of employment or authorization.

F. The risk management plan established pursuant to this section shall provide protection against professional liability imposed by law for damages resulting from any claim made against a local school board selection commission or local school board selection commission members for acts or omissions of any nature while acting in an authorized governmental or proprietary capacity and in the course and scope of authorization, subject to the limitations of the risk management plan.

G. The risk management plan established pursuant to this section shall provide coverage for any matter that involves or could involve an action or proceeding against a judge, the nature of which is designed to determine whether discipline or other sanction of the judge for malfeasance or misfeasance is appropriate or to otherwise determine the fitness of the judge to hold office or to continue his employment. No coverage or indemnification shall be made pursuant to this subsection when the Supreme Court of Virginia finds that the judge should be censured or removed from office pursuant to Section 10 of Article VI of the Constitution of Virginia or statutes enacted pursuant thereto.

H. The risk management plan established pursuant to this section shall provide protection against claims made against chaplains by persons incarcerated in a state correctional facility, a juvenile correctional center, or a facility operated pursuant to the Corrections Private Management Act (§ 53.1-261 et seq.) arising out of volunteer services provided by the chaplains to such incarcerated persons. For the purposes of this subsection, chaplains shall include only those persons, who, at the time any claim may arise, were acting pursuant to, and in compliance with, an agreement between the chaplain or an organization to which the chaplain belongs, and the Department of Corrections, the Department of Juvenile Justice, or an operator of a facility operated pursuant to the Corrections Private Management Act. (1980, c. 488, § 2.1-526.8; 1982, c. 318; 1986, cc. 554, 558; 1988, cc. 763, 780, 848; 1990, c. 484; 1995, c. 794; 2000, cc. 618, 632, § 2.1-191.11; 2001, c. 844; 2002, c. 765; 2003, c. 828; 2005, cc. 492, 548.)

CASE NOTES

Editor's note. — The case below was decided under former Title 2.1 or prior provisions.

Eleventh Amendment immunity not waived. — The statutes governing the state's insurance plan do not waive the state's Eleventh Amendment immunity. McConnell v. Adams, 829 F.2d 1319 (4th Cir. 1987), cert. denied, 486 U.S. 1006, 108 S. Ct. 1731, 100 L. Ed. 2d 195 (1988).

Injunctive relief governing future conduct of state officials. — The state's Eleventh Amendment immunity does not protect it from suits for injunctive relief governing its officials' future conduct. McConnell v. Adams, 829 F.2d 1319 (4th Cir. 1987), cert. denied, 486 U.S. 1006, 108 S. Ct. 1731, 100 L. Ed. 2d 195 (1988).

§ **2.2-1838. Insurance of state motor vehicles.** — A. Subject to the approval of the Governor, the Division shall establish a risk management plan, which may be purchased insurance, self-insurance or a combination of self-insurance and purchased insurance to provide (i) protection for the Commonwealth, its officers and employees and other authorized persons against tort liability and incidental medical payments arising out of the ownership, maintenance or use of motor vehicles owned or leased by the Commonwealth or used by state employees or other authorized persons in the course of their employment; and (ii) for payment of attorneys' fees and expenses incurred in defending such persons and entities concerning any claim that arises from their governmental employment or authorization where the Division is informed by the Attorney General's office that it will not provide a defense due to a conflict or other appropriate reason.

B. The risk management plan shall provide for the establishment of a trust fund or a contribution to the State Insurance Reserve Trust Fund for the payment of claims covered under the plan arising out of the ownership, maintenance or use of motor vehicles owned or leased by the Commonwealth or used by state employees or other authorized persons in the course of their employment. The funds shall be invested as provided in § 2.2-1806 and interest shall be added to the fund as earned. The plan shall also provide for payment of the expenses related to the administration of a motor vehicle insurance program for the Commonwealth. The risk management plan shall be submitted to the Governor for approval prior to implementation.

C. Any risk management plan for state motor vehicles established pursuant to this section shall provide (i) protection against the uninsured motorist at limits not less than those provided in § 46.2-100, (ii) incidental medical payments of not less than $5,000 per person to state employees and other authorized persons, and (iii) recovery of damages for loss of use of a motor vehicle, as provided in § 8.01-66. (1980, c. 488, § 2.1-526.6; 1982, c. 318; 1988, c. 848; 2000, cc. 618, 632, § 2.1-191.9; 2001, c. 844.)

§ 2.2-1839. Risk management plans administered by the Department of the Treasury's Risk Management Division for political subdivisions, constitutional officers, etc. — A. The Division shall establish one or more risk management plans specifying the terms and conditions for coverage, subject to the approval of the Governor, and which plans may be purchased insurance, self-insurance or a combination of self-insurance and purchased insurance to provide protection against liability imposed by law for damages and against incidental medical payments resulting from any claim made against any county, city or town; authority, board, or commission; sanitation, soil and water, planning or other district; public service corporation owned, operated or controlled by a locality or local government authority; constitutional officer; state court-appointed attorney; any attorney for any claim arising out of the provision of pro bono legal services for custody and visitation to an eligible indigent person under a program approved by the Supreme Court of Virginia or the Virginia State Bar; any receiver for an attorney's practice appointed under § 54.1-3900.01 or 54.1-3936; affiliate or foundation of a state department, agency or institution; any clinic that is organized in whole or primarily for the delivery of health care services without charge; any local chapter or program of the Meals on Wheels Association of America or any area agency on aging, providing meal and nutritional services to persons who are elderly, homebound, or disabled; any individual serving as a guardian or limited guardian as defined in § 37.2-1000 for any consumer of a community services board or behavioral health authority or any patient or resident of a state facility operated by the Department of Mental Health, Mental Retardation and Substance Abuse Services; or the officers, agents or employees of any of the foregoing for acts or omissions of any nature while in an authorized governmental or proprietary capacity and in the course and scope of employment or authorization.

For the purposes of this section, "delivery of health care services without charge" shall be deemed to include the delivery of dental, medical or other health services when a reasonable minimum fee is charged to cover administrative costs.

B. Participation in the risk management plan shall be voluntary and shall be approved by the participant's respective governing body or by the State Compensation Board in the case of constitutional officers, by the office of the Executive Secretary of the Virginia Supreme Court in the case of state court-appointed attorneys, including attorneys appointed to serve as receivers under § 54.1-3900.01 or 54.1-3936, or attorneys under Virginia Supreme Court or Virginia State Bar approved programs, by the Commissioner of the Department of Mental Health, Mental Retardation and Substance Abuse Services for any individual serving as a guardian or limited guardian for any patient or resident of a state facility operated by such Department or by the executive director of a community services board or behavioral health authority for any individual serving as a guardian or limited guardian for a consumer of such board or authority, and by the Division. Upon such approval, the Division shall assume sole responsibility for plan management, compliance, or removal. The Virginia Supreme Court shall pay the cost for coverage of eligible persons performing services in approved programs of the Virginia Supreme Court or the Virginia State Bar. The Department of Mental Health, Mental Retardation and Substance Abuse Services shall be responsible for paying the cost of coverage for eligible persons performing services as a guardian or limited guardian for any patient or resident of a state facility operated by the Department. The applicable community services board or behavioral health authority shall be responsible for paying the cost of coverage for eligible persons performing services as a guardian or limited guardian for consumers of such board or authority.

C. The Division shall provide for the legal defense of participating entities and shall reserve the right to settle or defend claims presented under the plan. All prejudgment settlements shall be approved in advance by the Division.

D. The risk management plan established pursuant to this section shall provide for the establishment of a trust fund for the payment of claims covered under such plan. The funds shall be invested in the manner provided in § 2.2-1806 and interest shall be added to the fund as earned.

The trust fund shall also provide for payment of legal defense costs, actuarial costs, administrative costs, contractual costs and all other expenses related to the administration of such plan.

E. The Division shall, in its sole discretion, set the premium and administrative cost to be paid to it for providing a risk management plan established pursuant to this section. The premiums and administrative costs set by the Division shall be payable in the amounts at the time and in the manner that the Division in its sole discretion shall require. The premiums and administrative costs need not be uniform among participants, but shall be set so as to best ensure the financial stability of the plan.

F. Notwithstanding any provision to the contrary, a sheriff's department of any city or county, or a regional jail shall not be precluded from securing excess liability insurance coverage beyond the coverage provided by the Division pursuant to this section. (1986, c. 82, § 2.1-526.8:1; 1988, c. 848; 1995, c. 30; 2000, cc. 618, 632, § 2.1-191.12; 2001, c. 844; 2003, cc. 23, 49; 2004, cc. 121, 529; 2005, cc. 184, 212; 2006, c. 713; 2007, c. 773.)

Editor's note. — Acts 2004, c. 822, cl. 3, as amended by Acts 2006, c. 580, provides: "That the provisions of this act establishing the authority and requirements for the purchase of general liability or medical malpractice insurance shall be effective July 1, 2008."

Acts 2004, c. 822, which amended this section, in cl. 4, as added by Acts 2006, c. 580, cl. 1, provides: "That the provisions of this act shall not become effective unless an appropriation of funds effectuating the purpose of this act is included in the general appropriation act for the period of July 1, 2008, through June 30, 2010, passed during the 2008 Session of the General Assembly and signed into law by the Governor." An appropriation was not made.

§ **2.2-1839.1:** Not in effect.

Editor's note. — Acts 2004, c. 822, which enacted this section in cl. 4, as added by Acts 2006, c. 580, cl. 1, provides: "That the provisions of this act shall not become effective unless an appropriation of funds effectuating the purpose of this act is included in the general appropriation act for the period of July 1, 2008, through June 30, 2010, passed during the 2008 Session of the General Assembly and signed into law by the Governor." The funds were not appropriated and therefore this section has been deleted.

§ **2.2-1840. Blanket surety bond plan for state and local employees.** — A. Subject to the approval of the Governor, the Division shall establish a program of blanket surety bonding to provide surety for the faithful performance of duty for all state employees required by statute to be bonded, and for other agency employees handling funds or having access to funds whose function, in the opinion of the agency head and the Division, should be bonded.

B. Local employees, including superintendents and jail officers of regional jail facilities as described in § 53.1-110, local constitutional officers, and those employees of the Supreme Court for whom the Commonwealth pays all or part of the costs of surety bonds shall be required to participate in the blanket surety bond program adopted by the Division through the Comptroller and the Compensation Board. The Division shall exclude clerks of the circuit court with respect to the moneys they hold pursuant to § 8.01-582 insofar as coverage is provided under § 2.2-1841 for their faithful performance concerning those moneys. Before implementing the program, the Division shall determine that the program will be of less cost to the Commonwealth than the aggregate of individual bonds costs.

C. The blanket surety bonding plan for state employees shall be submitted to the Governor for approval prior to implementation.

D. Employees or officers of a public service authority created under the Virginia Water and Sewer Authorities Act (§ 15.2-5100 et seq.) may participate in the blanket surety bond program adopted by the Division through the Comptroller and the Compensation Board whenever any federal or state agency lends or guarantees funds to a public service authority created under the Virginia Water and Sewer Authorities Act where the funds are utilized in the construction or capitalization of projects authorized under the Act, and there is a condition of the loan or guarantee that those employees or officers of the authority who have access to the funds be bonded. Participation by such employees or officers shall be approved by the governing body of the county or city that created the authority or is a member of the authority, with approval of the Division. (1982, c. 318, § 2.1-526.9; 1984, c. 324; 1988, cc. 841, 848; 1993, c. 939; 1995, c. 5; 2000, cc. 618, 632, § 2.1-191.13; 2001, c. 844.)

§ **2.2-1841. Blanket surety bond plan for moneys under control of court.** — The Division shall establish a program of blanket surety bonding to provide surety for the faithful discharge of duty with respect to moneys held pursuant to §§ 8.01-582 and 8.01-600 by all general receivers and clerks. General receivers and clerks shall participate in the program. The Division's cost of obtaining and administering the blanket surety bond shall be paid from those moneys covered by the bond. (1988, c. 841, § 2.1-526.9:1; 2000, cc. 618, 632, § 2.1-191.14; 2001, c. 844.)

§ **2.2-1842. Sovereign immunity.** — Although the provisions of this article are subject to those of Article 18.1 (§ 8.01-195.1 et seq.) of Chapter 3 of Title 8.01, nothing in this article shall be deemed an additional expressed or implied waiver of the Commonwealth's sovereign immunity. (1982, c. 318, § 2.1-526.11; 2000, cc. 618, 632, § 2.1-191.15; 2001, c. 844.)

CASE NOTES

Editor's note. — The case below was decided under former Title 2.1 or prior provisions.

Eleventh Amendment immunity not waived. — The statutes governing the state's insurance plan do not waive the state's Eleventh Amendment immunity. McConnell v. Adams, 829 F.2d 1319 (4th Cir. 1987), cert. denied, 486 U.S. 1006, 108 S. Ct. 1731, 100 L. Ed. 2d 195 (1988).

Injunctive relief governing future conduct of state officials. — The state's Eleventh Amendment immunity does not protect it from suits for injunctive relief governing its officials' future conduct. McConnell v. Adams, 829 F.2d 1319 (4th Cir. 1987), cert. denied, 486 U.S. 1006, 108 S. Ct. 1731, 100 L. Ed. 2d 195 (1988).

§ **2.2-1843. Loss prevention.** — The Division may develop and implement risk management and loss prevention programs related to risk management plans established pursuant to the provisions of this article. The Division may confer with the proper officials or employees of all agencies and institutions of the Commonwealth and of participating entities and persons pursuant to § 2.2-1839, for the purpose of determining risk management and loss prevention programs that shall be carried on with respect to properties and governmental operations under their control and may determine the manner in which the programs may be developed, implemented and enforced. The Division may seek the assistance of risk management consulting companies, insurance companies, loss prevention engineering companies, and their representatives, the State Fire Marshal, and the Division of Engineering and Buildings in devising means by which causes of loss may be reduced or eliminated. The Division shall have the final responsibility with respect to implementation or nonimplementation of a plan by an agency or institution of the Commonwealth and by a participating entity or person pursuant to § 2.2-1839. Information contained in investigative reports of any state or local police department, sheriff's office, fire department or fire marshal relevant to risk management plans established pursuant to the provisions of this article shall be made available to the Division upon request. The relevant information requested shall be furnished within a reasonable time, not to exceed thirty days. (1988, c. 848, § 2.1-526.11:1; 1996, cc. 475, 510; 2000, cc. 618, 632, § 2.1-191.16; 2001, c. 844.)

CHAPTER 19.

Department of Veterans' Affairs.

§§ **2.2-1900 through 2.2-1905:** Repealed by Acts 2003, cc. 657 and 670.

Cross references. — For current provisions as to Department of Veterans Services, see § 2.2-2000 et seq.

CHAPTER 20.

Department of Veterans Services.

§ 2.2-2000. Department created; appointment of Commissioner. — A. There shall be a Department of Veterans Services (the Department), which shall be headed by a Commissioner appointed by the Governor subject to confirmation by the General Assembly. The Commissioner shall be a veteran who has received an honorable discharge from the armed forces of the United States. He shall report directly to the Governor and shall hold his office at the pleasure of the Governor for a term of five years.

B. The Commissioner of the Department shall, under the direction and control of the Governor, exercise powers and perform duties conferred or imposed upon him by law and perform such other duties as may be required by the Governor. (2003, cc. 657, 670; 2004, c. 697.)

Editor's note. — Acts 2003, cc. 657 and 670, cl. 3, provide: "That as of the effective date of this act, the Department of Veterans Services shall be deemed the successor in interest to the Department of Veterans' Affairs. All right, title, and interest in and to any real or tangible personal property vested in the Department of Veterans' Affairs as of the effective date of this act shall be transferred to and taken as standing in the name of the Department of Veterans Services."

Acts 2003, cc. 657 and 670, cl. 4, provide: "That all rules and regulations adopted by the Department of Veterans' Affairs that are in effect as of the effective date of this act and that pertain to the subject of this act shall remain in full force and effect until altered, amended or rescinded by the Department of Veterans Services."

§ 2.2-2001. Administrative responsibilities of the Department. — A. The Department shall be responsible for the establishment, operation, administration, and maintenance of offices and programs related to services for Virginia-domiciled veterans of the armed forces of the United States and their eligible spouses, orphans, and dependents. Such services shall include, but not be limited to, benefits claims processing and all medical care centers and cemeteries for veterans owned and operated by the Commonwealth.

B. The Department shall establish guidelines for the determination of eligibility for Virginia-domiciled veterans and their spouses, orphans, and dependents for participation in programs and benefits administered by the Department. Such guidelines shall meet the intent of the federal statutes and regulations pertaining to the administration of federal programs supporting U.S. Armed Forces veterans and their spouses, orphans, and dependents.

C. The Department shall adopt reasonable regulations to implement a program to certify, upon request of the small business owner, that he holds a "service disabled veteran" status.

D. As used in this chapter:

"Service disabled veteran" means a veteran who (i) served on active duty in the United States military ground, naval, or air service, (ii) was discharged or released under conditions other than dishonorable, and (iii) has a service-connected disability rating fixed by the United States Department of Veterans Affairs.

"Service disabled veteran business" means a business concern that is at least 51% owned by one or more service disabled veterans or, in the case of a corporation, partnership, or limited liability company or other entity, at least 51% of the equity ownership interest in the corporation, partnership, or limited liability company or other entity is owned by one or more individuals who are

service disabled veterans and both the management and daily business operations are controlled by one or more individuals who are service disabled veterans.

"Veteran" means an individual who has served in the active military, naval or air service, and who was discharged or released therefrom under conditions other than dishonorable. (2003, cc. 657, 670; 2007, c. 787; 2008, cc. 467, 521, 767, 768.)

The 2007 amendments. — The 2007 amendment by c. 787 added subsection B.

The 2008 amendments. — The 2008 amendments by cc. 467 and 768 are identical, and in subsection A, inserted "Virginia-domiciled" and substituted "eligible spouses" for "Virginia domiciled surviving spouses" in the first sentence; inserted subsection B and redesigned former subsection B as subsections C and D; in subsection D, inserted the introductory paragraph and added the definition of "Veteran."

The 2008 amendments by cc. 521 and 767 are identical, and substituted "United States Department of Veterans Affairs" for "United States Veterans Administration of (a) 50% or greater or (b) 10% or greater if the service-connected disability is combat related" in the definition of "Service disabled veteran."

§ **2.2-2001.1. Program for mental health and rehabilitative services.** — The Department, in cooperation with the Department of Mental Health, Mental Retardation and Substance Abuse Services and the Department of Rehabilitative Services, shall establish a program to monitor and coordinate mental health and rehabilitative services support for Virginia veterans and members of the Virginia National Guard and Virginia residents in the Armed Forces Reserves not in active federal service. The program shall also support family members affected by covered military members' service and deployments. The purpose of the program is to ensure that adequate and timely assessment, treatment, and support are available to veterans, service members, and affected family members.

The program shall facilitate support for covered individuals to provide timely assessment and treatment for stress-related injuries and traumatic brain injuries resulting from service in combat areas, and subject to the availability of public and private funds appropriated for them, case management services, outpatient, family support, and other appropriate behavioral health and brain injury services necessary to provide individual services and support to military service members and their family members covered by this section. (2008, cc. 584, 754.)

Editor's note. — Acts 2008, cc. 584 and 754, cl. 2 provides: "That the Commissioner of the Department of Veterans Services shall (i) actively pursue all means available to secure federal funding for the program established by this act, including federal grants and earmarked funds and (ii) ensure the maximization of federal and private funds to support the program. Additionally, the Veterans Services Foundation shall support the program established by this act as a top priority of its fund-raising efforts."

§ **2.2-2002. Department offices.** — The Commissioner shall maintain an office in the vicinity of the State Capitol in Richmond. He may maintain service offices in the Commonwealth in whatever locations he determines to be necessary to carry out the provisions of this chapter. (2003, cc. 657, 670; 2005, c. 888.)

§ **2.2-2002.1. Department personnel.** — The Commissioner shall be responsible for appointing the personnel assigned to each service office and determining the compensation to be paid to such personnel. In determining the number of personnel assigned to each service office, the Commissioner shall ensure the number of employees assigned to the processing of benefit claims is sufficient to maintain a ratio of one staff person for every 26,212 veterans residing in the Commonwealth. The Commissioner shall also ensure that the personnel assigned to processing benefit claims provide these services to veterans in locations other than the service office at least one day per week. (2005, c. 888.)

§ **2.2-2003. General powers of Commissioner.** — The Commissioner shall have the following general powers to carry out the purposes of this chapter:

1. Employ required personnel;
2. Enter into all contracts and agreements necessary or incidental to the performance of the Department's duties and the execution of its powers under this chapter, including, but not limited to, contracts with the United States, other states, and agencies and governmental subdivisions of the Commonwealth;
3. Accept grants from the United States government and its agencies and instrumentalities and any other source. To these ends, the Department shall have the power to comply with conditions and execute agreements necessary, convenient, or desirable; and
4. Do all acts necessary or convenient to carry out the purposes of this chapter. (2003, cc. 657, 670.)

§ **2.2-2004. Additional powers and duties of Commissioner.** — The Commissioner shall have the following powers and duties related to veterans services:

1. Perform cost-benefit and value analysis of (i) existing programs and services, and (ii) new programs and services before establishing and implementing them;
2. Seek alternative funding sources for the Department's veterans service programs;
3. Cooperate with all relevant entities of the federal government, including, but not limited to, the United States Department of Veterans Affairs, the United States Department of Housing and Urban Development, and the United States Department of Labor in matters concerning veterans benefits and services;
4. Appoint a full-time coordinator to collaborate with the Joint Leadership Council of Veteran Service Organizations created in § 2.2-2681 on ways to provide both direct and indirect support of ongoing veterans programs, and to determine and address future veterans needs and concerns;
5. Initiate, conduct, and issue special studies on matters pertaining to veterans needs and priorities, as determined necessary by the Commissioner;
6. Evaluate veterans service efforts, practices, and programs of the agencies, political subdivisions or other entities and organizations of the government of the Commonwealth and make recommendations to the Secretary of Public Safety, the Governor, and the General Assembly on ways to increase awareness of the services available to veterans or improve veterans services;
7. Assist entities of state government and political subdivisions of the Commonwealth in enhancing their efforts to provide services to veterans, those members of the Virginia National Guard, Virginia residents in the Armed Forces Reserves who qualify for veteran status, and their immediate family members, including the dissemination of relevant materials and the rendering of technical or other advice;
8. Assist counties, cities, and towns of the Commonwealth in the development, implementation, and review of local veterans services programs as part of the state program and establish as necessary, in consultation with the Board of Veterans Services and the Joint Leadership Council of Veterans Service

Organizations, volunteer local and regional advisory committees to assist and support veterans service efforts;

9. Review the activities, roles, and contributions of various entities and organizations to the Commonwealth's veterans services programs and report on or before December 1 of each year in writing to the Governor and General Assembly on the status, progress, and prospects of veterans services in the Commonwealth, including performance measures and outcomes of veterans services programs;

10. Recommend to the Secretary of Public Safety, the Governor, and the General Assembly any corrective measures, policies, procedures, plans, and programs to make service to Virginia-domiciled veterans and their eligible spouses, orphans, and dependents as efficient and effective as practicable;

11. Design, implement, administer, and review special programs or projects needed to promote veterans services in the Commonwealth;

12. Integrate veterans services activities into the framework of economic development activities in general;

13. Manage operational funds using accepted accounting principles and practices in order to provide for a sum sufficient to ensure continued, uninterrupted operations;

14. Engage Department personnel in training and educational activities aimed at enhancing veterans services;

15. Develop a strategic plan to ensure efficient and effective utilization of resources, programs, and services; and

16. Certify eligibility for the Virginia Military Survivors and Dependents Education Program and perform other duties related to such Program as outlined in § 23-7.4:1. (2003, cc. 657, 670; 2008, cc. 467, 768.)

The 2008 amendments. — The 2008 amendments by cc. 467 and 768 are identical, and substituted "Secretary of Public Safety" for "Secretary of Administration" in subdivision 6; inserted "those members of the Virginia National Guard, Virginia residents in the Armed Forces Reserves who qualify for veteran status, and their immediate family members" in subdivision 7; in subdivision 10, substituted "Secretary of Public Safety" for "Secretary of Administration" near the beginning, inserted "Virginia-domiciled" preceding "veterans and their" and substituted "eligible spouses" for "surviving spouses" near the end; added subdivision 16 and made related changes.

§ 2.2-2004.1. Advisory committees for veterans care centers. — The Commissioner shall establish an advisory committee for the purpose of advising him on any and all matters pertaining to the administration of any veterans care center established in the Commonwealth. (2004, c. 697.)

CHAPTER 20.1.

Virginia Information Technologies Agency.

Article 1.

General Provisions.

The number of this chapter was assigned by the Virginia Code Commission, the chapter having been enacted as Chapter 20.

Article 1.

General Provisions.

§ 2.2-2005. Creation of Agency; appointment of Chief Information Officer. — A. There is hereby created the Virginia Information Technologies Agency (VITA), which shall serve as the agency responsible for administration and enforcement of the provisions of this Chapter and the rules and policies of the Board.

B. The Board shall appoint a Chief Information Officer (the CIO) as the chief administrative officer of the Board to oversee the operation of VITA. The CIO shall be employed under special contract for a term of five years and shall, under the direction and control of the Board, exercise the powers and perform the duties conferred or imposed upon him by law and perform such other duties as may be required by the Board. (2003, cc. 981, 1021.)

The numbers for the sections contained in this article, §§ 2.2-2005 through 2.2-2015, were assigned by the Virginia Code Commission, the numbers in the 2003 act having been 2.2-2000 through 2.2-2010.

Cross references. — As to the Information

Technology Investment Board, see §§ 2.2-2457 et seq. As to exemption of Sex Offender and Crimes Against Minors Registry information systems from provisions related to the Virginia Information Technologies Agency, see § 9.1-921.

Editor's note. — Acts 1997, c. 483, cl. 1, provides: "The Department of Motor Vehicles and the Department of State Police, in conjunction with the Department of Information Technology, shall work together toward using bar code technology, as well as all other types of emerging technology, to improve the operation of the agencies whenever feasible and effective."

Acts 2003, cc. 981 and 1021, cl. 4, provide: "That it is the intent of the General Assembly that the provisions of this act provide for the consolidation of the procurement and operational functions of information technology, including but not limited to servers and networks, for state agencies in a single agency. The Governor may transfer appropriations or portions thereof within any state agency established or otherwise affected by the provisions of this act, or from such agency to another, to support changes in organization or responsibility resulting from or required by the provisions of this act. For the purposes of this clause, "state agency" means any administrative unit of state government in the executive branch, including any department, institution, commission, board, council, authority, or other body, however designated. The term "state agency" shall not include public institutions of higher education as set forth in § 23-9.5 of the Code of Virginia and the Virginia Housing Development Authority."

Acts 2003, cc. 981 and 1021, cl. 5, provide: "That the Secretary of Technology shall continue to serve as the Chief Information Officer of the Commonwealth for six months after the effective date of this act or until such time as the Information Technology Investment Board has hired the Chief Information Officer as provided by the first enactment of this act."

Acts 2003, cc. 981 and 1021, cl. 6, provide: "That on or before January 1, 2004, the Chief Information Officer shall consolidate within the Virginia Information Technologies Agency (i) state network management, and (ii) server and other operation functions, along with appropriate staff, for state agencies with a position level of 100 employees or less. For the purposes of this clause, "state agency" means any administrative unit of state government in the executive branch, including any department, institution, commission, board, council, authority, or other body, however designated. The term "state agency" shall not include public institutions of higher education as set forth in § 23-9.5 of the Code of Virginia and the Virginia Housing Development Authority."

Acts 2003, cc. 981 and 1021, cl. 7, provide: "That on or before July 1, 2004, the Chief Information Officer shall consolidate within the Virginia Information Technologies Agency the server and other operational functions, along with appropriate staff, of state agencies with a position level of between 100 and 400 employees. For the purposes of this clause, "state agency" means any administrative unit of state government in the executive branch, including any department, institution, commission, board, council, authority, or other body, however designated. The term "state agency" shall not include public institutions of higher education as set forth in § 23-9.5 of the Code of Virginia and the Virginia Housing Development Authority."

Acts 2003, cc. 981 and 1021, cl. 8, provide: "That on or before January 1, 2005, the Chief Information Officer shall (i) fully implement the systems development standards, policies, and methodologies required by this act and (ii) consolidate within the Virginia Information Technologies Agency the server and other operational functions, along with appropriate staff, of state agencies with a position level in excess of 400 employees. For the purposes of this clause, "state agency" means any administrative unit of state government in the executive branch, including any department, institution, commission, board, council, authority, or other body, however designated. The term "state agency" shall not include public institutions of higher education as set forth in § 23-9.5 of the Code of Virginia and the Virginia Housing Development Authority."

Acts 2003, cc. 981 and 1021, cl. 9, provide: "That the Information Technology Investment Board may, by a vote of a majority of its members, accelerate the implementation schedule set forth in the sixth, seventh, and eighth enactments of this act."

Acts 2003, cc. 981 and 1021, cl. 10, provide: "That on or before December 1, 2003, the Secretary of Technology shall submit a report to the General Assembly on the progress of implementation of the provisions of this act. The report shall be delivered to the chairs of the House and Senate General Laws Committees, the House Appropriations and Senate Finance Committees, and the House Science and Technology Committee."

Acts 2003, cc. 981 and 1021, cl. 11, provide: "That the gubernatorial appointees to the Council on Technology Services holding office on July 1, 2003 shall continue to serve until such time as appointments are made by the Chief Information Officer in accordance with the provisions of this act."

Acts 2003, cc. 981 and 1021, cl. 12, provide: "That as of the effective date of this act, the Virginia Information Technologies Agency shall be deemed the successor in interest to the

Department of Information Technology, the Department of Technology Planning and the Virginia Information Providers Network Authority. Without limiting the foregoing, all right, title and interest in and to any real or tangible personal property vested in the Department of Information Technology, the Department of Technology Planning and the Virginia Information Providers Network Authority as of the effective date of this act shall be transferred to and taken as standing in the name of the Virginia Information Technologies Agency."

Acts 2003, cc. 981 and 1021, cl. 13, provide: "That the Virginia Information Technologies Agency shall promulgate regulations to implement the provisions of this act to be effective within 280 days of its enactment."

Acts 2003, cc. 981 and 1021, cl. 14, provide: "That all rules and regulations adopted by the Department of Information Technology and the Department of Technology Planning that are in effect as of the effective date of this act and that pertain to the subject of this act shall remain in full force and effect until altered, amended or rescinded by the Virginia Information Technologies Agency."

Acts 2003, cc. 981 and 1021, cl. 15, provide: "That the provisions of this act shall not in any way amend or affect the Commonwealth's institutions of higher education as such institutions may be delegated the authority for the purchase of information technology facilities and services pursuant to any appropriation act adopted by the General Assembly."

Acts 2003, cc. 981 and 1021, cl. 16, provide: "That the provisions of this act shall not in any way amend or affect the existing delegations of telecommunications procurement granted by the Department of Information Technology or the Virginia Information Technologies Agency, as its successor in interest, to public bodies or inhibit the ability of the Department of Information Technology or the Virginia Information Technologies Agency as its successor in interest, to grant future delegations of such authority."

Acts 2006, c. 124, provides: "§ 1. That the Department of General Services, in cooperation with the Virginia Information Technologies Agency, shall establish and publish in the vendor's manual a procedure for refunding the relevant eVa transaction fees in the event of a change order or cancellation of a contract by a vendor."

Acts 2008, c. 879, effective for the biennium ending June 30, 2010, in Item 434 B and D, provides: "B. The provisions of Title 2.2, Chapter 20.1 of the Code of Virginia shall not apply to the Virginia Port Authority.

"D.1. The Department of Human Resource Management shall review all compensation actions for VITA employees for proper application of the Commonwealth's classification and compensation policies or procedures. Subject to a memorandum of agreement between these two agencies, such review shall be undertaken in a timely manner and the results reported back to VITA within five business days of completion.

"2. No later than November 1 of each year the department shall report its findings of any material deviations from such policies or procedures and the corrective actions that have been taken to the Virginia Information Technologies Investment Board, the Governor, the Chairmen of the House Appropriations and Senate Finance Committees, and the Joint Legislative Audit and Review Commission."

Acts 2008, c. 879, effective for the biennium ending June 30, 2010, in § C-177.20 A. 1., provides: "Out of this appropriation, $250,000 the first year from the general fund is designated but not limited to determining the technical and functional requirements and acquisition, provided the appropriation is sufficient for purchase, of a capital project electronic information management solution by the Department of General Services to implement the provisions of HB 5001 and SB 5001 of the 2008 Special Session I of the General Assembly. The Department of General Services shall determine the procurement processes, pursuant to §2.2-4300 et seq. of the Code of Virginia, that result in the most cost efficient and timely means to satisfy the requirements of this provision and in doing so, may determine that such procurement processes specifically related to information technology goods and services not be subject to § 2.2-2005 et seq. of the Code of Virginia. The Department of General Services shall also have the authority to determine if the software solution is best hosted by the provider or the Virginia Information Technologies Agency. The Director, Department of Planning and Budget, shall transfer this amount to the Department of General Services on July 1, 2008."

§ 2.2-2006. Definitions. — As used in this chapter:

"Board" means the Information Technology Investment Board created in § 2.2-2457.

"Communications services" includes telecommunications services, automated data processing services, and management information systems that serve the needs of state agencies and institutions.

"Confidential data" means information made confidential by federal or state law that is maintained by a state agency in an electronic format.

"Information technology" means telecommunications, automated data processing, databases, the Internet, management information systems, and related information, equipment, goods, and services. It is in the interest of the Commonwealth that its public institutions of higher education in Virginia be in the forefront of developments in technology. Therefore, the provisions of this chapter shall not be construed to hamper the pursuit of the missions of the institutions in instruction and research.

"Major information technology project" means any state agency information technology project that (i) is mission-critical, (ii) has statewide application, or (iii) has a total estimated cost of more than $1 million.

"Noncommercial telecommunications entity" means any public broadcasting station as defined in § 2.2-2427.

"Public telecommunications entity" means any public broadcasting station as defined in § 2.2-2427.

"Public telecommunications facilities" means all apparatus, equipment and material necessary for or associated in any way with public broadcasting stations or public broadcasting services as those terms are defined in § 2.2-2427, including the buildings and structures necessary to house such apparatus, equipment and material, and the necessary land for the purpose of providing public broadcasting services, but not telecommunications services.

"Public telecommunications services" means public broadcasting services as defined in § 2.2-2427.

"Secretary" means the Secretary of Technology.

"State agency" or *"agency"* means any agency, institution, board, bureau, commission, council, or instrumentality of state government in the executive branch listed in the appropriation act. However, the terms "state agency," "agency," "institution," "public body," and "public institution of higher education," shall not include the University of Virginia Medical Center.

"Technology asset" means hardware and communications equipment not classified as traditional mainframe-based items, including personal computers, mobile computers, and other devices capable of storing and manipulating electronic data.

"Telecommunications" means any origination, transmission, emission, or reception of signs, signals, writings, images, and sounds or intelligence of any nature, by wire, radio, television, optical, or other electromagnetic systems.

"Telecommunications facilities" means apparatus necessary or useful in the production, distribution, or interconnection of electronic communications for state agencies or institutions including the buildings and structures necessary to house such apparatus and the necessary land. (1984, c. 746, § 2.1-563.13; 1997, c. 858; 2001, c. 844, § 2.2-1301; 2003, cc. 981, 1021; 2004, c. 145; 2007, c. 769.)

Cross references. — As to exemption of Sex Offender and Crimes Against Minors Registry information systems from provisions related to the Virginia Information Technologies Agency, see § 9.1-921.

Editor's note. — Acts 2007, c. 769, cl. 2, provides: "That the provisions of this act shall become effective on July 1, 2008."

The 2007 amendments. — The 2007 amendment by c. 769, effective July 1, 2008, inserted the paragraphs defining "confidential data" and "technology asset."

§ **2.2-2007. Powers of the CIO.** — A. In addition to such other duties as the Board may assign, the CIO shall:

1. Monitor trends and advances in information technology; develop a comprehensive, statewide, four-year strategic plan for information technology to include specific projects that implement the plan; and plan for the acquisition, management, and use of information technology by state agencies. The statewide plan shall be updated annually and submitted to the Board for approval. In developing and updating the plan, the CIO shall consider the

advice and recommendations of the Council on Technology Services created pursuant to § 2.2-2651.

2. Direct the formulation and promulgation of policies, guidelines, standards, and specifications for the purchase, development, and maintenance of information technology for state agencies, including, but not limited to, those (i) required to support state and local government exchange, acquisition, storage, use, sharing, and distribution of geographic or base map data and related technologies, (ii) concerned with the development of electronic transactions including the use of electronic signatures as provided in § 59.1-496, and (iii) necessary to support a unified approach to information technology across the totality of state government, thereby assuring that the citizens and businesses of the Commonwealth receive the greatest possible security, value, and convenience from investments made in technology.

3. Direct the development of policies and procedures, in consultation with the Department of Planning and Budget, that are integrated into the Commonwealth's strategic planning and performance budgeting processes, and that state agencies and public institutions of higher education shall follow in developing information technology plans and technology-related budget requests. Such policies and procedures shall require consideration of the contribution of current and proposed technology expenditures to the support of agency and institution priority functional activities, as well as current and future operating expenses, and shall be utilized by all state agencies and public institutions of higher education in preparing budget requests.

4. Review budget requests for information technology from state agencies and public institutions of higher education and recommend budget priorities to the Information Technology Investment Board.

Review of such budget requests shall include, but not be limited to, all data processing or other related projects for amounts exceeding $100,000 in which the agency or institution has entered into or plans to enter into a contract, agreement or other financing agreement or such other arrangement that requires that the Commonwealth either pay for the contract by foregoing revenue collections, or allows or assigns to another party the collection on behalf of or for the Commonwealth any fees, charges, or other assessments or revenues to pay for the project. For each project, the agency or institution, with the exception of public institutions of higher education that meet the conditions prescribed in subsection B of § 23-38.88, shall provide the CIO (i) a summary of the terms, (ii) the anticipated duration, and (iii) the cost or charges to any user, whether a state agency or institution or other party not directly a party to the project arrangements. The description shall also include any terms or conditions that bind the Commonwealth or restrict the Commonwealth's operations and the methods of procurement employed to reach such terms.

5. Direct the development of policies and procedures for the effective management of information technology investments throughout their entire life cycles, including, but not limited to, project definition, procurement, development, implementation, operation, performance evaluation, and enhancement or retirement. Such policies and procedures shall include, at a minimum, the periodic review by the CIO of agency and public institution of higher education information technology projects estimated to cost $1 million or more or deemed to be mission-critical or of statewide application by the CIO. The CIO shall provide technical guidance to the Department of General Services in the development of policies and procedures for the recycling and disposal of computers and other technology assets. Such policies and procedures shall include the expunging, in a manner as determined by the CIO, of all state confidential data and personal identifying information of citizens of the Commonwealth prior to such sale, disposal, or other transfer of computers or other technology assets.

6. Oversee and administer the Virginia Technology Infrastructure Fund created pursuant to § 2.2-2023.

7. Periodically evaluate the feasibility of outsourcing information technology resources and services, and outsource those resources and services that are feasible and beneficial to the Commonwealth.

8. Have the authority to enter into contracts, and with the approval of the Board for any contracts over $1 million, with one or more other public bodies, or public agencies or institutions or localities of the several states, of the United States or its territories, or the District of Columbia for the provision of information technology services.

9. Report annually to the Governor and the Joint Commission on Technology and Science created pursuant to § 30-85 on the use and application of information technology by state agencies and public institutions of higher education to increase economic efficiency, citizen convenience, and public access to state government.

10. Direct the development of policies and procedures that require VITA to review information technology projects proposed by state agencies and institutions exceeding $100,000, and recommend whether such projects be approved or disapproved. The CIO shall disapprove projects between $100,000 and $1 million that do not conform to the statewide information plan or to the individual plans of state agencies or institutions of higher education.

B. Consistent with § 2.2-2012, the CIO may enter into public-private partnership contracts to finance or implement information technology programs and projects. The CIO may issue a request for information to seek out potential private partners interested in providing programs or projects pursuant to an agreement under this subsection. The compensation for such services shall be computed with reference to and paid from the increased revenue or cost savings attributable to the successful implementation of the program or project for the period specified in the contract. The CIO shall be responsible for reviewing and approving the programs and projects and the terms of contracts for same under this subsection. The CIO shall determine annually the total amount of increased revenue or cost savings attributable to the successful implementation of a program or project under this subsection and such amount shall be deposited in the Virginia Technology Infrastructure Fund created in § 2.2-2023. The CIO is authorized to use moneys deposited in the Fund to pay private partners pursuant to the terms of contracts under this subsection. All moneys in excess of that required to be paid to private partners, as determined by the CIO, shall be reported to the Comptroller and retained in the Fund. The CIO shall prepare an annual report to the Governor and General Assembly on all contracts under this subsection, describing each information technology program or project, its progress, revenue impact, and such other information as may be relevant. (1999, cc. 412, 421, 433, § 2.1-51.47; 2000, c. 995; 2001, c. 844, § 2.2-226; 2002, c. 424; 2003, cc. 981, 1021; 2005, cc. 933, 945; 2007, cc. 276, 701.)

The 2007 amendments. — The 2007 amendment by c. 276 added present subdivision A 8 and redesignated former subdivisions A 8 and A 9 as present subdivisions A 9 and A 10.

The 2007 amendment by c. 701 added the next-to-last and last sentences in subdivision A 5.

§ 2.2-2008. Additional duties of the CIO relating to project management. — The CIO shall have the following duties relating to the management of information technology projects:

1. Develop an approval process for proposed major information technology projects by state agencies to ensure that all such projects conform to the

statewide information management plan and the information management plans of agencies and public institutions of higher education.

2. Establish a methodology for conceiving, planning, scheduling and providing appropriate oversight for information technology projects including a process for approving the planning, development and procurement of information technology projects. Such methodology shall include guidelines for the establishment of appropriate oversight for information technology projects.

3. Establish minimum qualifications and training standards for project managers.

4. Review and approve all procurement solicitations involving major information technology projects.

5. Direct the development of any statewide or multiagency enterprise project.

6. Develop and update a project management methodology to be used by agencies in the development of information technology.

7. Establish an information clearinghouse that identifies best practices and new developments and contains detailed information regarding the Commonwealth's previous experiences with the development of major information technology projects. (2003, cc. 981, 1021.)

§ 2.2-2009. Additional duties of the CIO relating to security of government information. — A. To provide for the security of state government electronic information from unauthorized uses, intrusions or other security threats, the CIO shall direct the development of policies, procedures and standards for assessing security risks, determining the appropriate security measures and performing security audits of government electronic information. Such policies, procedures, and standards will apply to the Commonwealth's executive, legislative, and judicial branches, and independent agencies and institutions of higher education. The CIO shall work with representatives of the Chief Justice of the Supreme Court and Joint Rules Committee of the General Assembly to identify their needs.

B. The CIO shall also develop policies, procedures, and standards that shall address the scope of security audits and the frequency of such security audits. In developing and updating such policies, procedures, and standards, the CIO shall designate a government entity to oversee, plan and coordinate the conduct of periodic security audits of all executive branch and independent agencies and institutions of higher education. The CIO will coordinate these audits with the Auditor of Public Accounts and the Joint Legislative Audit and Review Commission. The Chief Justice of the Supreme Court and the Joint Rules Committee of the General Assembly shall determine the most appropriate methods to review the protection of electronic information within their branches.

C. The CIO shall report to the Governor and General Assembly by December 2008 and annually thereafter, those executive branch and independent agencies and institutions of higher education that have not implemented acceptable policies, procedures, and standards to control unauthorized uses, intrusions, or other security threats. For any executive branch and independent agency or institution of higher education whose security audit results and plans for corrective action are unacceptable, the CIO shall report such results to the (i) Information Technology Investment Board, (ii) affected cabinet secretary, (iii) Governor, and (iv) Auditor of Public Accounts. Upon review of the security audit results in question, the Information Technology Investment Board may take action to suspend the public bodies information technology projects pursuant to subdivision 3 of § 2.2-2458, limit additional information technology investments pending acceptable corrective actions, and recommend to the Governor any other appropriate actions.

D. All public bodies subject to such audits as required by this section shall fully cooperate with the entity designated to perform such audits and bear any associated costs. Public bodies that are not required to but elect to use the entity designated to perform such audits shall also bear any associated costs.

E. The provisions of this section shall not infringe upon responsibilities assigned to the Comptroller, the Auditor of Public Accounts, or the Joint Legislative Audit and Review Commission by other provisions of the Code of Virginia.

F. To ensure the security and privacy of citizens of the Commonwealth in their interactions with state government, the CIO shall direct the development of policies, procedures, and standards for the protection of confidential data maintained by state agencies against unauthorized access and use. Such policies, procedures, and standards shall include, but not be limited to:

1. Requirements that any state employee or other authorized user of a state technology asset provide passwords or other means of authentication to (i) use a technology asset and (ii) access a state-owned or operated computer network or database; and

2. Requirements that a digital rights management system or other means of authenticating and controlling an individual's ability to access electronic records be utilized to limit access to and use of electronic records that contain confidential data to authorized individuals.

G. The CIO shall promptly receive reports from directors of departments in the executive branch of state government made in accordance with § 2.2-603 and shall take such actions as are necessary, convenient or desirable to ensure the security of the Commonwealth's electronic information and confidential data. (2000, c. 961, §§ 2.1-563.42 — 2.1-563.44; 2001, c. 844, §§ 2.2-136 — 2.2-138; 2002, c. 247, § 2.2-226.1; 2003, cc. 981, 1021; 2004, c. 638; 2007, cc. 769, 775.)

Editor's note. — Acts 2004, c. 638, which added subsection E, in cl. 2 provides: "That the provisions of this act shall become effective on January 1, 2005."

Acts 2007, c. 769, cl. 2, provides: "That the provisions of this act shall become effective on July 1, 2008."

The 2007 amendments. — The 2007 amendment by c. 769, effective July 1, 2008, inserted subsection E [now subsection F] and redesignated the remaining subsections accordingly; and added "and confidential data" to the end of subsection F [now subsection G] and made related changes.

The 2007 amendment by c. 775 rewrote subsections A and B; inserted subsection C and redesignated the remaining subsections accordingly; in subsection D, added "and bear any associated costs" to the end of the first sentence, and added the second sentence; and substituted "electronic information" for "databases and data communications" in subsection F.

§ **2.2-2010. Additional powers of VITA.** — VITA shall have the following additional powers which, with the approval of the CIO, may be exercised by a division of VITA with respect to matters assigned to that division:

1. Prescribe regulations necessary or incidental to the performance of duties or execution of powers conferred under this chapter.

2. Plan and forecast future needs for information technology and conduct studies and surveys of organizational structures and best management practices of information technology systems and procedures.

3. Assist state agencies and public institutions of higher education in the development of information management plans and the preparation of budget requests for information technology that are consistent with the policies and procedures developed pursuant to § 2.2-2007.

4. Develop and adopt policies, standards, and guidelines for managing information technology by state agencies and institutions.

5. Develop and adopt policies, standards, and guidelines for the procurement of information technology and telecommunications goods and services of every description for state agencies.

6. Direct the establishment of statewide standards for the efficient exchange of electronic information and technology, including infrastructure, between the public and private sectors in the Commonwealth.

7. Direct the compilation and maintenance of an inventory of information technology, including, but not limited to, personnel, facilities, equipment, goods, and contracts for services.

8. Develop statewide technical and data standards for information technology and related systems to promote efficiency and uniformity.

9. Evaluate the needs of agencies in the Commonwealth with regard to (i) a consistent, reliable, and secure information technology infrastructure, (ii) existing capabilities with regard to building and supporting that infrastructure, and (iii) recommended approaches to ensure the future development, maintenance, and financing of an information technology infrastructure befitting the needs of state agencies and the service level requirements of its citizens.

10. Establish fee schedules that shall be collectible from users when general fund appropriations are not applicable to the services rendered.

11. Provide for the centralized marketing, provision, leasing, and executing of license agreements for electronic access to public information and government services through the Internet, wireless devices, personal digital assistants, kiosks, or other such related media on terms and conditions as may be determined to be in the best interest of the Commonwealth. VITA may fix and collect fees and charges for (i) public information, media, and other incidental services furnished by it to any private individual or entity, notwithstanding the charges set forth in § 2.2-3704 and (ii) such use and services it provides to any state agency or local government. Nothing in this subdivision authorizing VITA to fix and collect fees for providing information services shall be construed to prevent access to the public records of any public body pursuant to the provisions of the Virginia Freedom of Information Act (§ 2.2-3700 et seq.). (1999, cc. 412, 421, 433, § 2.1-563.35:3; 2001, c. 844, § 2.2-1701; 2003, cc. 981, 1021; 2005, c. 939.)

§ 2.2-2011. Additional powers and duties relating to communications services and telecommunications facilities. — A. VITA shall have the following additional powers and duties concerning the planning, budgeting, acquiring, using, and disposing of communications goods and services:

1. Formulate specifications for telecommunications, automated data processing, and management information systems;

2. Analyze and approve all procurements of interconnective telecommunications facilities, telephones, automated data processing, and other communications equipment and goods;

3. Review and approve all agreements and contracts for communications services prior to execution between a state agency and another public or private agency;

4. Develop and administer a system to monitor and evaluate executed contracts and billing and collection systems; and

5. Exempt from review requirements, but not from the Commonwealth's competitive procurement process, any state agency that establishes, to the satisfaction of VITA, (i) its ability and willingness to administer efficiently and effectively the procurement of communications services or (ii) that it has been subjected to another review process coordinated through or approved by VITA.

B. VITA shall have the following powers and duties concerning the development, operation and management of communications services:

1. Manage and coordinate the various telecommunications facilities and communications services, centers, and operations used by the Commonwealth;

2. Acquire, lease, or construct such facilities and equipment as necessary to deliver comprehensive communications services, and to maintain such facilities and equipment owned or leased;

3. Provide technical assistance to state agencies in such areas as: (i) designing management information systems; (ii) performing systems development services, including design, application programming, and maintenance; (iii) conducting research and sponsoring demonstration projects pertaining to all facets of telecommunications and communications services; (iv) effecting economies in telephone systems and equipment; and (v) planning and forecasting for future needs in communications services; and

4. Develop and implement information, billing, and collections systems that will aid state agencies in forecasting their needs and managing their operations. (1984, c. 746, §§ 2.1-563.16, 2.1-563.17, 2.1-563.18; 1985, c. 265; 1995, c. 357; 1997, c. 858; 1999, cc. 412, 421, 433; 2001, c. 844, § 2.2-1303; 2002, c. 579; 2003, cc. 981, 1021.)

§ 2.2-2012. Procurement of information technology and telecommunications goods and services; computer equipment to be based on performance-based specifications. — A. Information technology and telecommunications goods and services of every description shall be procured by (i) VITA for its own benefit or on behalf of other state agencies and institutions or (ii) such other agencies or institutions to the extent authorized by VITA. Such procurements shall be made in accordance with the Virginia Public Procurement Act (§ 2.2-4300 et seq.), regulations that implement the electronic and information technology accessibility standards of the Rehabilitation Act of 1973 (29 U.S.C. § 794d), as amended, and any regulations as may be prescribed by VITA. In no case shall such procurements exceed the requirements of the regulations that implement the electronic and information technology accessibility standards of the Rehabilitation Act of 1973, as amended.

The CIO shall disapprove any procurement that does not conform to the statewide information technology plan or to the individual plans of state agencies or public institutions of higher education.

B. All statewide contracts and agreements made and entered into by VITA for the purchase of communications services, telecommunications facilities, and information technology goods and services shall provide for the inclusion of counties, cities, and towns in such contracts and agreements. Notwithstanding the provisions of § 2.2-4301, VITA may enter into multiple vendor contracts for the referenced services, facilities, and goods and services.

B1. The Department may establish contracts for the purchase of personal computers and related devices by licensed teachers employed in a full-time teaching capacity in Virginia public schools or in state educational facilities for use outside the classroom. The computers and related devices shall not be purchased with public funds, but shall be paid for and owned by teachers individually provided that no more than one such computer and related device per year shall be so purchased.

C. If VITA, or any agency or institution authorized by VITA, elects to procure personal computers and related peripheral equipment pursuant to any type of blanket purchasing arrangement under which public bodies, as defined in § 2.2-4301, may purchase such goods from any vendor following competitive procurement but without the conduct of an individual procurement by or for the using agency or institution, it shall establish performance-based specifications for the selection of equipment. Establishment of such contracts shall emphasize performance criteria including price, quality, and delivery without regard to "brand name." All vendors meeting the Commonwealth's performance requirements shall be afforded the opportunity to compete for such contracts.

D. This section shall not be construed or applied so as to infringe upon, in any manner, the responsibilities for accounting systems assigned to the Comptroller under § 2.2-803.

E. The CIO of VITA shall, on or before October 1, 2009, and every two years thereafter, solicit from each state agency and public institution of higher education a list of procurements that were competed with the private sector that appear on the Commonwealth Competition Council's commercial activities list and were, until that time, being performed by each state agency and public institution of higher education during the previous two years, and the outcome of that competition. The CIO shall make the lists available to the public on VITA's website. (1984, c. 746, §§ 2.1-563.16, 2.1-563.17, 2.1-563.18; 1985, c. 265; 1995, c. 357; 1997, c. 858; 1999, cc. 412, 421, 433; 2001, c. 844, § 2.2-1303; 2002, c. 579; 2003, cc. 352, 895, 981, 1021; 2004, cc. 237, 278; 2007, c. 630.)

Cross references. — As to exception from requirement of approval by the Director of the Division of Purchases and Supply for procurement arrangements made under § 2.2-2012, see § 2.2-4304. For exception of purchases of information technology and telecommunications goods and services as provided in § 2.2-2012 from purchase procedure provided by the Division of Purchases and Supply of the Department of General Services, see § 53.1-52.

Editor's note. — Acts 2003, c. 352 amended § 2.2-1303, from which this section is derived. Pursuant to § 30-152, Acts 2003, c. 352 has been given effect in this section as set out above. The 2003 amendment by c. 352, added subsection B1.

Acts 2003, c. 895, amended § 2.2-1303, from which this section is derived. The 2003 amendment by c. 895 deleted "goods and services of every description" after telecommunications and deleted a reference to the Administrative Process Act in subsection A.

Acts 2003, c. 895, cl. 3, provides: "That the provisions of this act shall not in any way amend or affect existing delegations of telecommunications procurement authority granted by the Department of Information Technology to public bodies or inhibit the ability of the Department to grant future delegations of such authority."

The 2007 amendments. — The 2007 amendment by c. 630 added subsection E.

§ 2.2-2013. Internal service funds; Automated Services Internal Service Fund; Computer Services Internal Service Fund; Telecommunication Services Internal Service Fund. — A. There are established the following internal service funds to be administered by VITA:

1. The Automated Services Internal Service Fund to be used to finance automated systems design, development and testing services and staff of VITA;

2. The Computer Services Internal Service Fund to be used to finance computer operations and staff of VITA; and

3. The Telecommunication Services Internal Service Fund to be used to finance telecommunications operations and staff of VITA.

B. There is established the Acquisition Services Special Fund to be administered by VITA and used to finance procurement and contracting activities and programs unallowable for federal fund reimbursement.

C. All users of services provided for in this chapter administered by VITA shall be assessed a surcharge, which shall be deposited in the appropriate fund. This charge shall be an amount sufficient to allow VITA to finance the operations and staff of the services offered.

D. Additional moneys necessary to establish these funds or provide for the administration of the activities of VITA may be advanced from the general account of the state treasury. (1984, c. 746, §§ 2.1-563.19, 2.1-563.20, 2.1-563.21, 2.1-563.22; 2001, c. 844, § 2.2-1304; 2003, cc. 981, 1021.)

§ 2.2-2014. Submission of information technology plans by state agencies and public institutions of higher education; designation of technology resource. — A. All state agencies and public institutions of higher education shall prepare and submit information technology plans to the CIO for review and approval. All state agencies and public institutions of higher education shall maintain current information technology plans that have been approved by the CIO.

B. The head of each state agency shall designate an existing employee to be the agency's information technology resource who shall be responsible for compliance with the procedures, policies, and guidelines established by the CIO. (1999, cc. 412, 421, 433, § 2.1-51.47; 2000, c. 995; 2001, c. 844, § 2.2-226; 2002, c. 424; 2003, cc. 981, 1021.)

§ 2.2-2015. Authority of CIO to modify or suspend major information technology projects; project termination. — The CIO may direct the modification or suspension of any major information technology project that, as the result of a periodic review authorized by subdivision A 5 of § 2.2-2007, has not met the performance measures agreed to by the CIO and the sponsoring agency or public institution of higher education or if he otherwise deems such action appropriate and consistent with the terms of any affected contracts. The CIO may recommend to the Board the termination of such project. Nothing in this section shall be construed to supersede the responsibility of a board of visitors for the management and operation of a public institution of higher education.

The provisions of this section shall not apply to research projects, research initiatives or instructional programs at public institutions of higher education. However, technology investments in research projects, research initiatives or instructional programs at such institutions estimated to cost $1 million or more of general fund appropriations may be reviewed as provided in subdivision A 5 of § 2.2-2007 if the projects are deemed mission-critical by the institution or of statewide application by the CIO. The CIO and the Secretary of Education, in consultation with public institutions of higher education, shall develop and provide to such institution criteria to be used in determining whether projects are mission-critical. (1999, cc. 412, 421, 433, § 2.1-51.47; 2000, c. 995; 2001, c. 844, § 2.2-226; 2002, c. 424; 2003, cc. 981, 1021.)

ARTICLE 2.

Division of Project Management.

§ 2.2-2016. Division of Project Management established. — There is established within VITA a Division of Project Management (the Division). The Division shall exercise the powers and duties conferred in this article. (2003, cc. 981, 1021.)

The numbers for the sections contained in this article, §§ 2.2-2016 through 2.2-2021, were assigned by the Virginia Code Commission, the numbers in the 2003 act having been 2.2-2011 through 2.2-2016.

Editor's note. — For provisions of Acts 2003, cc. 981 and 1021, cls. 4 to 16, reflecting the intent of the General Assembly to provide for the consolidation of the procurement and operational functions of information technology for state agencies in a single agency, and related transitional and other provisions, see the Editor's note at § 2.2-2005.

§ 2.2-2017. Powers and duties of the Division. — The Division shall have the power and duty to:

1. Implement the approval process for information technology projects developed in accordance with § 2.2-2008;

2. Assist the CIO in the development and implementation of a project management methodology to be used in the development of and implementation of information technology projects in accordance with this article;

3. Provide ongoing assistance and support to state agencies and public institutions of higher education in the development of information technology projects;

4. Establish a program providing cost-effective training to agency project managers;

5. Review information management and information technology plans submitted by agencies and public institutions of higher education and recommend to the CIO the approval of such plans and any amendments thereto;

6. Monitor the implementation of information management and information technology plans and periodically report its findings to the CIO;

7. Assign project management specialists to review and recommend information technology proposals based on criteria developed by the Division based on the (i) degree to which the project is consistent with the Commonwealth's overall strategic plan; (ii) technical feasibility of the project; (iii) benefits to the Commonwealth of the project, including customer service improvements; (iv) risks associated with the project; (v) continued funding requirements; and (vi) past performance by the agency on other projects; and

8. Provide oversight for state agency information technology projects. (2003, cc. 981, 1021.)

§ **2.2-2018. Project planning approval.** — A. Prior to proceeding with any major information technology project, an agency shall submit to the Division a project proposal, outlining the business need for the project, the proposed technology solution, if known, and an explanation of how the project would support the agency's business objectives and the Commonwealth's information technology plan. The project management specialist may require the submission of additional information if needed to adequately review any such proposal.

B. The project management specialist shall review the proposal and recommend its approval or rejection to the CIO. (2003, cc. 981, 1021.)

§ **2.2-2019. Project development approval.** — A. Upon approval of the CIO of the project plan, an agency shall submit to the Division a project development proposal containing (i) a detailed business case including a cost-benefit analysis; (ii) a business process analysis, if applicable; (iii) system requirements, if known; (iv) a proposed development plan and project management structure; and (v) a proposed resource or funding plan. The project management specialist may require the submission of additional information necessary to meet the criteria developed by the Division.

B. The project management specialist assigned to review the project development proposal shall recommend its approval or rejection to the CIO. If the CIO determines that the proposal be approved, he shall recommend such approval to the Board. (2003, cc. 981, 1021.)

§ **2.2-2020. Procurement approval for major information technology projects.** — Upon approval of the Board of the project development proposal involving a major information technology project that requires the procurement of goods or services, the agency shall submit a copy of any Invitation for Bid (IFB) or Request for Proposal (RFP) to the Division. The project management specialist shall review the IFB or RFP and recommend its approval or rejection to the CIO. The CIO shall have the final authority to approve the IFB or RFP prior to its release and shall approve the proposed contract for the award of the project. (2003, cc. 981, 1021.)

§ 2.2-2021. Project oversight. — A. Whenever an agency has received approval from the Board to proceed with the development and acquisition of a major information technology project, an internal agency oversight committee shall be established by the CIO. The internal agency oversight committee shall provide ongoing oversight for the project and have the authority to approve or reject any changes in the project's scope, schedule, or budget. The CIO shall ensure that the project has in place adequate project management and oversight structures for addressing major issues that could affect the project's scope, schedule or budget and shall address issues that cannot be resolved by the internal agency oversight committee.

B. Whenever a statewide or multiagency project has received approval from the Board, the primary project oversight shall be conducted by a committee composed of representatives from agencies impacted by the project, which shall be established by the CIO. (2003, cc. 981, 1021.)

ARTICLE 3.

Virginia Technology Infrastructure Fund.

§ 2.2-2022. Definitions; purpose. — A. As used in this article, unless the context requires a different meaning:

"Costs" means the reasonable and customary charges for goods and services incurred or to be incurred in major information technology projects.

"Technology infrastructure" means telecommunications, automated data processing, word processing and management information systems, and related information, equipment, goods and services.

B. In order for the Commonwealth to take advantage of technological applications in providing services and solving problems of Virginia's citizens, there is a need to reinvest savings that accrue from increased usage of technology into new and emerging technologies that will provide for both greater efficiencies and better responsiveness. The purpose of this article is to create the Virginia Technology Infrastructure Fund (the Fund). The Fund shall make moneys available to state agencies and institutions of higher education for major information technology projects. (1996, cc. 94, 823, §§ 9-145.52, 9-145.53; 1999, cc. 412, 421, 433; 2001, c. 844, § 2.2-1702; 2003, cc. 981, 1021.)

The numbers for the sections contained in this article, §§ 2.2-2022 through 2.2-2024, were assigned by the Virginia Code Commission, the numbers in the 2003 act having been 2.2-2017 through 2.2-2019.

Editor's note. — For provisions of Acts 2003, cc. 981 and 1021, cls. 4 to 16, reflecting the intent of the General Assembly to provide for the consolidation of the procurement and operational functions of information technology for state agencies in a single agency, and related transitional and other provisions, see the Editor's note at § 2.2-2005.

§ 2.2-2023. Virginia Technology Infrastructure Fund created; contributions. — A. The Virginia Technology Infrastructure Fund (the Fund) is created in the state treasury. The Fund is to be used to fund major information technology projects or to pay private partners as authorized in subsection B of § 2.2-2007.

B. The Fund shall consist of: (i) the transfer of general and nongeneral fund appropriations from state agencies which represent savings that accrue from reductions in the cost of information technology and communication services, (ii) the transfer of general and nongeneral fund appropriations from state agencies which represent savings from the implementation of information technology enterprise projects, (iii) funds identified pursuant to subsection B of § 2.2-2007, (iv) such general and nongeneral fund fees or surcharges as may be assessed to agencies for enterprise technology projects, (v) gifts, grants, or donations from public or private sources, and (vi) such other funds as may be appropriated by the General Assembly. Savings shall be as identified by the CIO through a methodology approved by the Board and the Secretary of Finance. The Auditor of Public Accounts shall certify the amount of any savings identified by the CIO. For public institutions of higher education, however, savings shall consist only of that portion of total savings that represent general funds. The State Comptroller is authorized to transfer cash consistent with appropriation transfers. Appropriated funds from federal sources are exempted from transfer. Except for funds to pay private partners as authorized in subsection B of § 2.2-2007, moneys in the Fund shall only be expended as provided by the appropriation act.

Interest earned on the Fund shall be credited to the Fund. The Fund shall be permanent and nonreverting. Any unexpended balance in the Fund at the end of the biennium shall not be transferred to the general fund of the state treasury. (1996, cc. 94, 823, §§ 9-145.54, 9-145.55; 2001, c. 844, § 2.2-1703; 2003, cc. 981, 1021.)

§ 2.2-2024. Annual plan; allowable uses of Fund. — The CIO, with advice from the Council on Technology Services, shall prepare a plan that identifies the projects in which the Fund will participate. The plan shall be consistent with the statewide plan for information technology and shall consider the use of existing resources and long-term operation and maintenance costs. Projects having the greatest benefit to state government as a whole shall have the highest priority in the plan. (1996, cc. 94, 823, § 9-145.56; 1999, cc. 412, 421, 433; 2001, c. 844, § 2.2-1704; 2003, cc. 981, 1021.)

Article 4.

Virginia Geographic Information Network.

§ 2.2-2025. Definitions. — As used in this article, unless the context requires a different meaning:

"Base map data" means the digitized common geographic data that are used by most geographic information systems applications to reference or link attribute or other geographic data.

"Division" means the Geographic Information Network Division.

"Geographic data" means data that contain either coordinates that reference a geographic location or area or attribute data that can be related to a geographic area or location.

"Geographic information system (GIS)" means a computerized system that stores and links geographic data to allow a wide range of information processing and display operations, as well as map production, analysis, and modeling. (1997, c. 817, § 2.1-563.36; 1999, cc. 412, 421, 433; 2001, c. 844, § 2.2-1705; 2003, cc. 981, 1021.)

The numbers for the sections contained in this article, §§ 2.2-2025 through 2.2-2030, were assigned by the Virginia Code Commission, the numbers in the 2003 act having been 2.2-2020 through 2.2-2025.

Editor's note. — For provisions of Acts 2003, cc. 981 and 1021, cls. 4 to 16, reflecting the intent of the General Assembly to provide for the consolidation of the procurement and operational functions of information technology for state agencies in a single agency, and related transitional and other provisions, see the Editor's note at § 2.2-2005.

§ 2.2-2026. Geographic Information Network Division established. — There is established within VITA a Geographic Information Network Division (the Division), which shall foster the creative utilization of geographic information and oversee the development of a catalog of GIS data available in the Commonwealth. The Division shall be headed by a coordinator who shall be under the supervision of and report to the CIO. The Division shall exercise the powers and duties conferred in this article. (1997, c. 817, § 2.1-563.37; 1999, cc. 412, 421, 433; 2001, c. 844, § 2.2-1706; 2003, cc. 981, 1021.)

§ 2.2-2027. Powers and duties of the Division; Division coordinator. — A. The powers and duties of the Division shall include:

1. Requesting the services, expertise, supplies and facilities of VITA from the CIO on issues concerning the Division;

2. Accepting grants from the United States government and agencies and instrumentalities thereof and any other source. To those ends, the Division shall have the power to comply with such conditions and execute such agreements as may be necessary or desirable;

3. Fixing, altering, charging, and collecting rates, rentals, and other charges for the use or sale of products of, or services rendered by, the Division, at rates which reflect the fair market value;

4. Soliciting, receiving, and considering proposals for funding projects or initiatives from any state or federal agency, local or regional government, public institution of higher education, nonprofit organization, or private person or corporation;

5. Soliciting and accepting funds, goods and in-kind services that are part of any accepted project proposal;

6. Establishing ad hoc committees or project teams to investigate related technology or technical issues and providing results and recommendations for Division action; and

7. Establishing such bureaus, sections or units as the Division deems appropriate to carry out its powers and duties.

B. The Coordinator shall:

1. Oversee the development of and recommend to VITA the promulgation of those policies and guidelines required to support state and local government exchange, acquisition, storage, use, sharing and distribution of geographic or base map data and related technologies;

2. Foster the development of a coordinated comprehensive system for providing ready access to electronic state government geographic data products for individuals, businesses, and other entities;

3. Initiate and manage projects or conduct procurement activities relating to the development or acquisition of geographic data or statewide base map data or both;

4. Plan for and coordinate the development or procurement of priority geographic base map data;

5. Develop, maintain, and provide, in the most cost-effective manner, access to the catalog of Virginia geographic data and governmental geographic data users;

6. Provide, upon request, advice and guidance on all agreements and contracts from all branches of state government for geographic data acquisition and design and the installation and maintenance of geographic information systems;

7. Compile a data catalog consisting of descriptions of GIS coverages maintained by individual state and local government agencies;

Nothing in this article shall be construed to require that GIS data be physically delivered to the Division. All state agencies that maintain GIS databases shall report to the Division the details of the data that they develop, acquire, and maintain. Each agency shall submit quarterly reports to the Division specifying all updates to existing data as well as all data development and acquisition currently in progress. Data exempt from the Virginia Freedom of Information Act (§ 2.2-3700 et seq.) need not be reported to the Division.

8. Identify and collect information and technical requirements to assist the Division in setting priorities for the development of state digital geographic data and base maps that meet the needs of state agencies, institutions of higher education, and local governments;

9. Provide services, geographic data products, and access to the repository at rates established by the Division; and

10. Ensure the compliance of those policies, standards, and guidelines developed by VITA required to support and govern the security of state and local government exchange, acquisition, storage, use, sharing, and distribution of geographic or base map data and related technologies. (1997, c. 817, § 2.1-563.38; 1999, cc. 412, 421, 433; 2001, c. 844, § 2.2-1707; 2003, cc. 981, 1021.)

§ **2.2-2028. GIS Fund created.** — There is hereby created in the state treasury a special, nonreverting fund to be known as the GIS Fund, hereafter referred to as the Fund. The Fund shall be established on the books of the Comptroller. All moneys collected pursuant to subsection A of § 2.2-2027 shall be paid into the state treasury and credited to the Fund. Interest earned on moneys in the Fund shall remain in the Fund and be credited to it. Any moneys remaining in the Fund, including interest thereon, at the end of each fiscal year shall not revert to the general fund but shall remain in the Fund. Moneys in the Fund shall be used solely for the purposes set forth in this article. Expenditures and disbursements from the Fund shall be made by the State Treasurer on warrants issued by the Comptroller upon written request signed by the CIO. (1997, c. 817, § 2.1-563.39; 2001, c. 844, § 2.2-1708; 2003, cc. 981, 1021.)

§ **2.2-2029. Additional powers and duties of the CIO.** — The CIO shall have the power and duty, on the recommendation of the Coordinator, to (i) receive and disburse funds; (ii) enter into contracts for the purpose of carrying out the provisions of this article; and (iii) rent office space and procure equipment, goods, and services that are necessary to carry out the provisions of this article. (1997, c. 817, § 2.1-563.40; 1999, cc. 412, 421, 433; 2001, c. 844, § 2.2-1709; 2003, cc. 981, 1021.)

§ **2.2-2030. Nonstock corporation to assist in the development of GIS data.** — VITA is hereby authorized to establish a nonstock corporation under Chapter 10 (§ 13.1-801 et seq.) of Title 13.1 as an instrumentality to assist VITA and the Division in the development and acquisition of geographic data and statewide base map data. On or before December 1 of each year, VITA shall report on the activities of the nonstock corporation to the Governor and the General Assembly. (2001, c. 709, § 2.2-1709.1; 2003, cc. 981, 1021.)

Article 5.

Division of Public Safety Communications.

§ **2.2-2031. Division of Public Safety Communications established; appointment of Virginia Public Safety Communications Coordinator; duties of Division.** — A. There is established within VITA, a Division of Public Safety Communications (the Division), which shall be headed by a Virginia Public Safety Communications Coordinator, appointed by the CIO with the advice and consent of the Wireless E-911 Services Board. The Division shall consist of such personnel as the CIO deems necessary. The salaries of the employees of the Division shall be paid from the Wireless E-911 Fund created pursuant to § 56-484.17.

B. The Division shall provide staff support to the Wireless E-911 Services Board and encourage, promote, and assist in the development and deployment of statewide enhanced emergency telecommunications systems. (2000, c. 1064, § 2.1-563.35:4; 2001, c. 844, § 2.2-1710; 2003, cc. 981, 1021.)

The number of this section was assigned by the Virginia Code Commission, the number in the 2003 act having been 2.2-2026.

Editor's note. — For provisions of Acts 2003, cc. 981 and 1021, cls. 4 to 16, reflecting the intent of the General Assembly to provide for the consolidation of the procurement and operational functions of information technology for state agencies in a single agency, and related transitional and other provisions, see the Editor's note at § 2.2-2005.

Acts 2008, c. 879, effective for the biennium ending June 30, 2010, in Item 419 D 2, provides: "The Secretary of Public Safety, in conjunction with the STARS Management Group and the Superintendent of State Police, shall provide a status report on (1) projected total costs for the system, including project management costs and expected annual operating costs; (2) the status of site acquisition to support the system; (3) the activities related to in-house and contract project management; (4) the project timelines for implementing the system; and (5) other matters as the Secretary may deem appropriate. This report shall be provided to the Governor and the Chairmen of the House Appropriations and Senate Finance Committees no later than October 1 of each year."

Article 6.

Virginia Information Providers Network.

§ **2.2-2032:** Repealed by Acts 2005, c. 939, cl. 2.

Part D.

State Authorities, Boards, Commissions, Councils, Foundations and Other Collegial Bodies.

CHAPTER 21.

General Provisions.

Sec.

§ **2.2-2100. Classification of executive branch boards, commissions and councils.** — A. Effective July 1, 1986, every collegial body established by law or executive order within the executive branch of state government shall be classified according to its level of authority as follows:

"Advisory" — A board, commission or council shall be classified as advisory when its purpose is to provide advice and comment to an executive branch agency or office. An advisory board, commission or council serves as a formal liaison between the agency or office and the public to ensure that the agency or office understands public concerns and that the activities of the agency or office are communicated to the public. An advisory board, commission or council does not serve a regulatory or rule-making purpose. It may participate in the development of public policy by providing comment and advice.

"Policy" — A board, commission or council shall be classified as policy if it is specifically charged by statute to promulgate public policies or regulations. It may also be charged with adjudicating violations of those policies or regulations. Specific functions of the board, commission or council may include, but are not limited to, rate setting, distributing federal funds, and adjudicating regulatory or statutory violations, but each power shall be enumerated by law. Policy boards, commissions or councils are not responsible for supervising agencies or employing personnel. They may review and comment on agency budget requests.

"Supervisory" — A board, commission, or council shall be classified as supervisory if it is responsible for agency operations including approval of requests for appropriations. A supervisory board, commission, or council appoints the agency director and ensures that the agency director complies with all board and statutory directives. The agency director is subordinate to the board. Notwithstanding the foregoing, the Board of Education shall be considered a supervisory board.

B. Each executive branch board, commission or council shall be assigned only one of the above classifications. The classification for boards and councils that are created by law shall be designated by the enabling legislation. The classification for commissions that are created by executive order shall be designated by the executive order. (1985, c. 419, § 9-6.25; 2001, c. 844.)

Cross references. — As to standard nomenclature for independent administrative entities and collegial bodies, see § 2.2-600.

§ 2.2-2101. (Effective until July 1, 2013) Prohibition against service by legislators on boards, commissions, and councils within the executive branch; exceptions. — Members of the General Assembly shall be ineligible to serve on boards, commissions, and councils within the executive branch of state government who are responsible for administering programs established by the General Assembly. Such prohibition shall not extend to boards, commissions, and councils engaged solely in policy studies or commemorative activities. If any law directs the appointment of any member of the General Assembly to a board, commission, or council in the executive branch of state government that is responsible for administering programs established by the General Assembly, such portion of such law shall be void, and the Governor shall appoint another person from the Commonwealth at large to fill such a position.

The provisions of this section shall not apply to members of the Board for Branch Pilots, who shall be appointed as provided for in § 54.1-901; to members of the Board of Trustees of the Southwest Virginia Higher Education Center, who shall be appointed as provided for in § 23-231.3; to members of the Board of Trustees of the Southern Virginia Higher Education Center, who shall be appointed as provided for in § 23-231.25; to members of the Board of Directors of the New College Institute who shall be appointed as provided for in § 23-231.31; to members of the Virginia Interagency Coordinating Council who shall be appointed as provided for in § 2.2-5204; to members of the Board of Veterans Services, who shall be appointed as provided for in § 2.2-2452; to members appointed to the Board of Trustees of the Roanoke Higher Education Authority pursuant to § 23-231.15; to members of the Commonwealth Competition Commission, who shall be appointed as provided for in § 2.2-2621; to members of the Virginia Geographic Information Network Advisory Board, who shall be appointed as provided for in § 2.2-2423; to members of the Advisory Commission on the Virginia Schools for the Deaf and the Blind, who shall be appointed as provided for in § 22.1-346.1; to members of the Substance Abuse Services Council, who shall be appointed as provided for in § 2.2-2696; to members of the Criminal Justice Services Board, who shall be appointed as provided in § 9.1-108; to members of the Council on Virginia's Future, who shall be appointed as provided for in § 2.2-2685; to members of the State Executive Council for Comprehensive Services for At-Risk Youth and Families, who shall be appointed as provided in § 2.2-2648; to members of the Virginia Workforce Council, who shall be appointed as provided for in § 2.2-2669; to members of the Commission on Civics Education, who shall be appointed as provided for in § 22.1-212.18; to members of the Volunteer Firefighters' and Rescue Squad Workers' Service Award Fund Board, who shall be appointed as provided for in § 51.1-1201; to members of the Secure Commonwealth Panel, who shall be appointed as provided for in § 2.2-306; to members of the Forensic Science Board, who shall be appointed as provided for in § 9.1-1109; or to members of the Southwest Virginia Cultural Heritage Commission, who shall be appointed as provided in § 2.2-2533. (1977, c. 629, § 9-6.23; 1978, c. 834; 1988, cc. 839, 888; 1989, c. 198; 1991, c. 627; 1992, cc. 407, 771; 1993, cc. 248, 726, 751, 752, 757; 1994, cc. 486, 843, 858, 951; 1994, 2nd Sp. Sess., c. 7; 1995, cc. 361, 814, 815; 1996, c. 932; 1997, cc. 360, 361, 813, 817; 1998, cc. 622, 724; 1999, cc. 412, 421, 433, 512, 840, 855; 2001, cc. 577, 844; 2003, cc. 94, 451, 657, 670, 854, 900; 2004, c. 37; 2005, cc. 774, 786, 799, 868, 881, 930; 2006, cc. 707, 808, 842, 860, 901; 2007, c. 915; 2008, cc. 654, 659.)

Section set out twice. — The section above is effective until July 1, 2013. For the version of this section effective July 1, 2013, see the following section also numbered § 2.2-2101.

Editor's note. — Acts 2003, c. 900, cl. 3, as amended by Acts 2008, c. 240, provides: "That the provisions of this act shall expire on July 1, 2013."

Acts 2001, c. 577 amended § 9-6.23, from which this section is derived. Pursuant to § 30-152, Acts 2001, c. 577 has been given effect in this section as set out above. The 2001 amendment by c. 577, near the end of the last sentence, deleted "to members of the Council on Coordinating Prevention, who shall be appointed as provided for in § 9-268" following "provided for in § 22.1-346.1," and deleted "or" following "in § 37.1-207."

For provisions of Acts 2003, cc. 657 and 670, relating to transition of Department of Veterans Services to Department of Veterans Affairs, see Editor's note at § 2.2-2000.

Acts 2005, c. 786, cl. 2, provides: "That the initial appointments of the nonlegislative citizen members appointed by the Governor shall be staggered as follows: two nonlegislative citizen members appointed for initial terms of one year; two nonlegislative citizen members, including the one representative from the Virginia Press Association, appointed for initial terms of two years; and two nonlegislative citizen members, including the one representative of a public policy center with one of the Commonwealth's public institutions of higher education, appointed for initial terms of three years."

Acts 2007, c. 849, cl. 2, provides: "For its first year of existence, if the Commission is not funded by a separate appropriation in the Appropriation Act, compensation and reimbursement of expenses for legislative members of the Commission may be funded from the operating budgets of the Clerk of the House of Delegates and the Clerk of the Senate upon the approval of the Joint Rules Committee. If the Commission is not funded by a separate appropriation in the Appropriation Act for any year thereafter, this chapter shall expire on July 1 of the fiscal year that the Commission fails to receive such funding." The funding was not provided. Therefore, the section has been set out above without amendments by Acts 2007, c. 849.

Acts 2007, c. 849, cl. 3, provides: "That the provisions of this act shall expire on August 1, 2009."

The 2003 amendments. — The 2003

amendment by c. 900 inserted "to members of the Council on Virginia's Future, who shall be appointed as provided in § 2.2-2685" near the end of the last paragraph. For expiration date, see Editor's note.

The 2007 amendments. — The 2007 amendment by c. 849 added "or to members of the Virginia Commission on Immigration, who shall be appointed as provided in § 2.2-2530" to the end of the second paragraph and made related changes. Expires August 1, 2009, or earlier if funding is not received. See Editor's note.

The 2007 amendment by c. 915 deleted "to members of the Council on Indians, who shall be appointed as provided for in § 2.2-2628" near the beginning of the second paragraph.

The 2008 amendments. — The 2008 amendments by cc. 654 and 659, effective March 27, 2008, are identical, and added "or to members of the Southwest Virginia Cultural Heritage Commission, who shall be appointed as provided in § 2.2-2533" to the end of the second paragraph and made a related change.

OPINIONS OF THE ATTORNEY GENERAL

Members of the General Assembly are not prohibited from serving on an authority that is established by the General Assembly whose members are appointed by the Governor. See opinion of Attorney General to The Honorable Robert S. Bloxom, Member, House of Delegates, 99-099 (1/12/00).

§ 2.2-2101. (Effective July 1, 2013) Prohibition against service by legislators on boards, commissions, and councils within the executive branch; exceptions. — Members of the General Assembly shall be ineligible to serve on boards, commissions, and councils within the executive branch of state government who are responsible for administering programs established by the General Assembly. Such prohibition shall not extend to boards, commissions, and councils engaged solely in policy studies or commemorative activities. If any law directs the appointment of any member of the General Assembly to a board, commission, or council in the executive branch of state government that is responsible for administering programs established by the General Assembly, such portion of such law shall be void, and the Governor shall appoint another person from the Commonwealth at large to fill such a position.

The provisions of this section shall not apply to members of the Board for Branch Pilots, who shall be appointed as provided for in § 54.1-901; to members of the Board of Trustees of the Southwest Virginia Higher Education Center, who shall be appointed as provided for in § 23-231.3; to members of the Board of Trustees of the Southern Virginia Higher Education Center, who shall be appointed as provided for in § 23-231.25; to members of the Board of Directors of the New College Institute who shall be appointed as provided for in § 23-231.31; to members of the Virginia Interagency Coordinating Council who shall be appointed as provided for in § 2.2-5204; to members of the Board of Veterans Services, who shall be appointed as provided for in § 2.2-2452; to members appointed to the Board of Trustees of the Roanoke Higher Education Authority pursuant to § 23-231.15; to members of the Commonwealth Competition Commission, who shall be appointed as provided for in § 2.2-2621; to members of the Virginia Geographic Information Network Advisory Board, who shall be appointed as provided for in § 2.2-2423; to members of the Advisory Commission on the Virginia Schools for the Deaf and the Blind, who shall be appointed as provided for in § 22.1-346.1; to members of the Substance Abuse Services Council, who shall be appointed as provided for in § 2.2-2696; to members of the Criminal Justice Services Board, who shall be appointed as provided in § 9.1-108; to members of the State Executive Council for Comprehensive Services for At-Risk Youth and Families, who shall be appointed as provided in § 2.2-2648; to members of the Virginia Workforce Council, who shall be appointed as provided for in § 2.2-2669; to members of the Commission on Civics Education, who shall be appointed as provided for in

§ 22.1-212.18; to members of the Volunteer Firefighters' and Rescue Squad Workers' Service Award Fund Board, who shall be appointed as provided for in § 51.1-1201; to members of the Secure Commonwealth Panel, who shall be appointed as provided for in § 2.2-306; to members of the Forensic Science Board, who shall be appointed as provided for in § 9.1-1109; or to members of the Southwest Virginia Cultural Heritage Commission, who shall be appointed as provided in § 2.2-2533. (1977, c. 629, § 9-6.23; 1978, c. 834; 1988, cc. 839, 888; 1989, c. 198; 1991, c. 627; 1992, cc. 407, 771; 1993, cc. 248, 726, 751, 752, 757; 1994, cc. 486, 843, 858, 951; 1994, 2nd Sp. Sess., c. 7; 1995, cc. 361, 814, 815; 1996, c. 932; 1997, cc. 360, 361, 813, 817; 1998, cc. 622, 724; 1999, cc. 412, 421, 433, 512, 840, 855; 2001, cc. 577, 844; 2003, cc. 94, 451, 657, 670, 854; 2004, c. 37; 2005, cc. 774, 786, 799, 868, 881, 930; 2006, cc. 707, 808, 842, 860, 901; 2007, c. 915; 2008, cc. 654, 659.)

Section set out twice. — The section above is effective July 1, 2013. For the version of this section effective until July 1, 2013, see the preceding section, also numbered 2.2-2101.

The 2007 amendments. — The 2007 amendment by c. 915 deleted "to members of the Council on Indians, who shall be appointed as provided for in § 2.2-2628" near the beginning of the second paragraph.

The 2008 amendments. — The 2008 amendments by cc. 654 and 659, effective March 27, 2008, are identical, and added "or to members of the Southwest Virginia Cultural Heritage Commission, who shall be appointed as provided in § 2.2-2533" and made related change.

§ 2.2-2102. "Citizen member" appointments to executive branch boards and commissions. — Positions on boards and commissions designated for "citizen members," "consumer members," and "representatives of the public" are intended to ensure that the composition of a particular board or commission reflects citizen as well as professional interests. Except as otherwise provided by law, the Governor shall, when making an appointment to an executive branch board or commission specifically designated for a "citizen member," "consumer member," or "representative of the public," appoint a person who (i) is not by training or experience a practitioner in the subject area of concern to the board or commission, (ii) is not the spouse, parent, child or sibling of such a practitioner, and (iii) has no direct or indirect financial interest, except as a consumer, in the subject area of concern to the board or commission. (1984, c. 579, § 9-6.24; 2001, c. 844.)

§ 2.2-2103. Cooperation of other agencies with authorities, boards, commissions, councils, and other collegial bodies. — Upon request, all agencies and political subdivisions of the Commonwealth shall assist any authority, board, commission, council or other collegial body established in this title in carrying out the respective duties for which each was created. (1968, c. 567, § 9-84.05; 1973, c. 431, § 9-84.9; 1978, c. 103, § 2.1-335.3; 1991, cc. 44, 594, § 9-145.20; 1992, c. 609, § 9-145.34; 1993, c. 162, § 9-145.49; 1995, cc. 638, 815, §§ 2.1-548.42, 9-344; 1996, cc. 97, 589, 599, §§ 2.1-548.52, 9-153; 1999, c. 976, § 9-304.5; 2001, c. 844.)

§ 2.2-2104. Compensation and expenses. — Compensation and expenses to members of state boards, commissions, councils and other similar bodies shall be paid in accordance with Chapter 28 (§ 2.2-2800 et seq.) of this title. (1980, c. 728, § 2.1-20.3; 1981, c. 181; 1998, c. 790; 2001, c. 844.)

§ 2.2-2105. Investigation of management of institutions or conduct of officers or employees. — Whenever any board of visitors to any of the institutions of the Commonwealth deem it necessary or expedient to investigate the management of their institution or the conduct of any of its officers or employees, such board, or a committee of its members selected by the board, shall have such power and authority to send for persons and papers or to order the attendance of witnesses and compel their attendance as is now conferred upon a committee appointed by the General Assembly or either branch thereof by § 30-10. The oath to be taken by any witness examined by such board or committee may be administered by the president or the presiding officer of the board, chairman of its committee, or the clerk or secretary of the board or committee. All expenses incurred in summoning or in the attendance of such witness shall be paid out of the funds of the institution whose boards made or ordered the investigation. (Code 1919, § 1096, § 9-13; 2001, c. 844.)

§ 2.2-2106. Expenses of certain boards; appearances before General Assembly. — A. The board of directors of the several state hospitals and the boards of directors of the various institutions of learning receiving aid from the Commonwealth shall receive their actual, itemized expenses incurred in the discharge of their duties in attending the meetings of the boards or committees.

B. No officer of any university, college, school, hospital, or other institution or board maintained in part or in whole by the Commonwealth shall spend or appropriate any money for the purpose of sending any member of the board or officials of such institution or other person to appear before the General Assembly, or any committee thereof, for the purpose of advocating in any way any appropriation for any institution supported in whole or in part by the Commonwealth. However, when any committee of the General Assembly desires information in regard to the needs of any state institution it may by proper resolution so determine, and request that any institution or board thereof send one or more competent persons to give the information desired, and the expense thereof may be paid out of the funds appropriated by the Commonwealth for the support of that institution. (Code 1919, §§ 1097, 1098, §§ 9-14, 9-15; 1998, c. 790; 2001, c. 844.)

CHAPTER 22.

AUTHORITIES.

Article 3.

Innovative Technology Authority.

Article 4.

Virginia Economic Development Partnership Authority.

Article 5.

Virginia Information Providers Network Authority.

Article 6.

Virginia Public Building Authority.

Article 7.

Virginia Small Business Financing Authority.

Article 8.

Virginia Tourism Authority.

Article 9.

Virginia National Defense Industrial Authority.

ARTICLE 1.

General Provisions.

§ **2.2-2200. Definitions.** — As used in this chapter, unless the context requires a different meaning:

"Authority" means the respective political subdivisions of the Commonwealth created in this subpart.

"Board" means the respective boards of directors for the authorities created in this subpart.

"Bonds" means any bonds, refunding bonds, notes, debentures, interim certificates, or any bond, grant, revenue anticipation notes or any other evidences of indebtedness or obligation of an authority, whether in temporary or definitive form and whether the interest thereon is exempt from federal income taxation.

"Commonwealth" or *"state"* means the Commonwealth of Virginia or any of its agencies or departments.

"Federal agency" means the United States; the President of the United States; and any department, corporation, agency, or instrumentality heretofore or hereafter created, designated, or established by the United States. (1995, c. 638, § 2.1-548.27; 1999, cc. 852, 881, § 2.1-548.55; 2001, c. 844; 2005, c. 839.)

ARTICLE 2.

Commercial Space Flight Authority.

§ **2.2-2201. Short title; definitions.** — A. This article shall be known and may be cited as the "Virginia Commercial Space Flight Authority Act".

B. As used in this article, unless the context requires a different meaning:

"Project" means the construction, improvement, furnishing, maintenance, acquisition or operation of any facility or the provision for or funding of any activity that will further the purposes described in § 2.2-2202. (1995, c. 758, §§ 9-266.1, 9-266.2; 2001, c. 844.)

§ **2.2-2202. Declaration of public purpose; Authority created.** — A. The General Assembly has determined that there exists in the Commonwealth a need to (i) disseminate knowledge pertaining to scientific and technological research and development among public and private entities, including but not limited to knowledge in the area of commercial space flight, and (ii) promote industrial and economic development. In order to facilitate and coordinate scientific and technological research and development and to promote the industrial and economic development of the Commonwealth, which purposes are declared to be public purposes.

B. To achieve the objectives of subsection A, there is created a political subdivision of the Commonwealth to be known as the "Virginia Commercial Space Flight Authority" (the "Authority"). The Authority's exercise of powers conferred by this article shall be deemed to be the performance of an essential governmental function and matters of public necessity for which public moneys may be spent and private property acquired. (1995, c. 758, § 9-266.3; 2001, c. 844.)

§ **2.2-2203. Board of directors; members and officers; Executive Director.** — The Authority shall be governed by a board of directors consisting of twelve members, four of whom shall be the President of the Center for Innovative Technology, the President of Old Dominion University, the Secretary of Commerce and Trade, and the Secretary of Technology, who shall serve as members of the Board for terms coincident with their terms of office. The remaining eight members shall be appointed by the Governor as follows: three members representing the commercial space flight industry; two members representing the telecommunications industry; one member representing the County of Accomack, one member representing the County of Northampton, and one at-large member. Of the members appointed by the Governor, two shall be appointed for terms of one year, three for terms of two years, and three for terms of three years, from the effective date of their appointment. Thereafter, the members of the Board shall be appointed for terms of three years. All members of the Board appointed by the Governor shall be confirmed by each house of the General Assembly. Vacancies in the membership of the Board shall be filled by appointment for the unexpired portion of the term. Members of the Board shall be subject to removal from office in like manner as are state, county, town and district officers under the provisions of §§ 24.2-230 through 24.2-238. Immediately after appointment, the members of the Board shall enter upon the performance of their duties.

The Board shall annually elect one of its members as chairman and another as vice-chairman, a secretary, and a treasurer who need not be a member of the Board. The Board may also elect other subordinate officers, who need not be members of the Board, as it deems proper. The chairman or, in his absence, the vice-chairman shall preside at all meetings of the Board. In the absence of both the chairman and vice-chairman, the Board shall appoint a chairman pro tempore, who shall preside at such meetings. Seven members shall constitute a quorum for the transaction of the Authority's business, and no vacancy in the membership shall impair the right of a quorum to exercise all the rights and perform all the duties of the Authority.

The members of the Board shall be entitled to reimbursement for their reasonable travel, meal and lodging expenses incurred in attending the meetings of the Board or while otherwise engaged in the discharge of their duties. Such expenses shall be paid out of the treasury of the Authority upon vouchers signed by the chairman of the Board or by such other person designated by the Board for this purpose.

The Board may employ an Executive Director of the Authority, who shall serve at the pleasure of the Board, to direct the day-to-day operations and activities of the Authority and carry out the powers and duties conferred upon him by the Board. The Executive Director and employees of the Authority shall be compensated in the manner provided by the Board and shall not be subject to the provisions of the Virginia Personnel Act (§ 2.2-2900 et seq.) of this title. (1995, c. 758, § 9-266.4; 1999, cc. 412, 421, 433; 2001, c. 844.)

§ **2.2-2204. Powers of the Authority.** — The Authority is granted all powers necessary or convenient for the carrying out of its statutory purposes, including, but not limited to, the power to:

1. Sue and be sued, implead and be impleaded, complain and defend in all courts;
2. Adopt, use, and alter at will a common seal;
3. Acquire any project and property, real, personal or mixed, tangible or intangible, or any interest therein, by purchase, gift or devise and to sell, lease (whether as lessor or lessee), transfer, convey or dispose of any project or property, real, personal or mixed, tangible or intangible or any interest therein, at any time acquired or held by the Authority on such terms and conditions as may be determined by the Board;
4. Plan, develop, undertake, carry out, construct, equip, improve, rehabilitate, repair, furnish, maintain and operate projects;

5. Adopt bylaws for the management and regulation of its affairs;

6. Fix, alter, charge and collect rates, rentals, fees, and other charges for the use of projects of, the sale of products of, or services rendered by the Authority at rates to be determined by it for the purpose of providing for the payment of the expenses of the Authority; the planning, development, construction, improvement, rehabilitation, repair, furnishing, maintenance, and operation of its projects and properties; the payment of the costs accomplishing its purposes set forth in § 2.2-2202; the payment of the principal of and interest on its obligations; and the creation of reserves for such purposes, for other purposes of the Authority and to pay the cost of maintaining, repairing and operating any project and fulfilling the terms and provisions of any agreements made with the purchasers or holders of any such obligations;

7. Borrow money, make and issue bonds including bonds as the Authority may determine to issue for the purpose of accomplishing the purposes set forth in § 2.2-2202 or for refunding bonds previously issued by the Authority, whether such outstanding bonds have matured or are then subject to redemption, or any combination of such purposes; secure the payment of all bonds, or any part thereof, by pledge, assignment or deed of trust of all or any of its revenues, rentals, and receipts or of any project or property, real, personal or mixed, tangible or intangible, or any rights and interest therein; make such agreements with the purchasers or holders of such bonds or with others in connection with any such bonds, whether issued or to be issued, as the Authority shall deem advisable; and in general to provide for the security for said bonds and the rights of holders thereof;

8. Make and enter into all contracts and agreements necessary or incidental to the performance of its duties, the furtherance of its purposes and the execution of its powers under this article, including interstate compacts and agreements with any person or federal agency;

9. Employ, in its discretion, consultants, attorneys, architects, engineers, accountants, financial experts, investment bankers, superintendents, managers and such other employees and agents as may be necessary, and to fix their compensation to be payable from funds made available to the Authority;

10. Receive and accept from any federal or private agency, foundation, corporation, association or person grants, donations of money, real or personal property for the benefit of the Authority, and to receive and accept from the Commonwealth or any state, and any municipality, county or other political subdivision thereof and from any other source, aid or contributions of either money, property, or other things of value, to be held, used and applied for the purposes for which such grants and contributions may be made;

11. Render advice and assistance, and to provide services, to institutions of higher education including, but not limited to, Old Dominion University, and to other persons providing services or facilities for scientific and technological research or graduate education, provided that credit toward a degree, certificate or diploma shall be granted only if such education is provided in conjunction with an institution of higher education authorized to operate in Virginia;

12. Develop, undertake and provide programs, alone or in conjunction with any person or federal agency, for scientific and technological research, technology management, continuing education and in-service training; however, credit towards a degree, certificate or diploma shall be granted only if such education is provided in conjunction with an institution of higher education authorized to operate in Virginia; foster the utilization of scientific and technological research, information discoveries and data and obtain patents, copyrights and trademarks thereon; coordinate the scientific and technological research efforts of public institutions and private industry and collect and maintain data on the development and utilization of scientific and technological research capabilities;

13. Pledge or otherwise encumber all or any of the revenues or receipts of the Authority as security for all or any of the obligations of the Authority;

14. Appoint an industry advisory board to advise the Authority on issues related to the performance of its duties, the furtherance of its purposes and the execution of its powers under this article. The Authority shall have full discretion in determining the number and qualifications of members it appoints to the industry advisory board, and whether such members shall be compensated from the funds made available to the Authority; and

15. Do all acts and things necessary or convenient to carry out the powers granted to it by law. (1995, c. 758, § 9-266.5; 1996, c. 111; 2001, c. 844.)

§ 2.2-2205. Form, terms, execution and sale of bonds; use of proceeds; interim receipts or temporary bonds; lost or destroyed bonds; faith and credit of state and political subdivisions not pledged; expenses. — The bonds of each issue shall be dated, shall bear interest at such rates as are fixed by the Authority, or as may be determined in such manner as the Authority may provide, including the determination by agents designated by the Authority under guidelines established by the Authority, shall mature at such time not exceeding forty years from their date as may be determined by the Authority, and may be made redeemable before maturity, at the option of the Authority, at such price and under such terms and conditions as may be fixed by the Authority prior to the issuance of the bonds. The Authority shall determine the form of bonds and their manner of execution, and shall fix the denomination of the bonds and the place of payment of principal and interest, which may be at any bank or trust company within or without the Commonwealth. The bonds shall be signed by the chairman or vice-chairman of the Authority or, if so authorized by the Authority, shall bear his facsimile signature, and the official seal of the Authority, or, if so authorized by the Authority, a facsimile thereof shall be impressed or imprinted thereon and attested by the secretary or any assistant secretary of the Authority, or, if so authorized by the Authority, with the facsimile signature of such secretary or assistant secretary. Any coupons attached to bonds issued by the Authority shall bear the signature of the chairman or vice-chairman of the Authority or a facsimile thereof. In case any officer whose signature or a facsimile of whose signature appears on any bonds or coupons ceases to be an officer before the delivery of the bonds, his signature or facsimile shall nevertheless be valid and sufficient for all purposes the same as if he had remained in office until such delivery and any bonds may bear the facsimile signature of, or may be signed by, such persons as at the actual time of the execution of such bonds shall be the proper officers to sign such bonds although at the date of such bonds such persons may not have been such officers. The bonds may be issued in coupon or in registered form, or both, as the Authority may determine, and provision may be made for the registration of any coupon bonds as to principal alone and also as to both principal and interest, for the reconversion into coupon bonds of any bonds registered as to both principal and interest, and for the interchange of registered and coupon bonds. Bonds issued in registered form may be issued under a system of book-entry for recording the ownership and transfer of ownership of rights to receive payment of principal of, and premium on, if any, and interest on such bonds. The Authority may contract for the services of one or more banks, trust companies, financial institutions or other entities or persons, within or without the Commonwealth for the authentication, registration, transfer, exchange and payment of the bonds, or may provide such services itself. The Authority may sell such bonds in such manner, either at public or private sale, and for such price as it may determine will best effect the purposes of this article.

The proceeds of the bonds of each issue shall be used solely for the purposes, and in furtherance of the powers, of the Authority as may be provided in the resolution authorizing the issuance of such bonds or in a trust agreement authorized by § 2.2-2206 securing the bonds.

In addition to the above powers, the Authority may issue interim receipts or temporary bonds as provided in § 15.2-2616 and execute and deliver new bonds in place of bonds mutilated, lost or destroyed, as provided in § 15.2-2621.

No obligation of the Authority shall be deemed to constitute a debt, or pledge of the faith and credit, of the Commonwealth or of any political subdivision thereof, but shall be payable solely from the revenues and other funds of the Authority pledged thereto. All such obligations shall contain on the face thereof a statement to the effect that the Commonwealth, any political subdivision thereof and the Authority shall not be obligated to pay the same or the interest thereon except from revenues and other funds of the Authority pledged thereto, and that neither the faith and credit nor the taxing power of the Commonwealth or of any political subdivision thereof is pledged to the payment of the principal of or the interest on such obligations.

All expenses incurred in carrying out the provisions of the act shall be payable solely from funds provided under the provisions of this act, and no liability shall be incurred by the Authority beyond the extent to which moneys have been provided under the provisions of this article. (1995, c. 758, § 9-266.6; 2001, c. 844.)

§ 2.2-2206. Trust indenture or agreement securing bonds. — In the discretion of the Authority, any bonds issued under the provisions of this article may be secured by a trust indenture or agreement by and between the Authority and a corporate trustee, which may be any trust company or bank having the powers of a trust company within or without the Commonwealth. The trust indenture or agreement or the resolution providing for the issuance of the bonds may (i) pledge or assign the revenues to be received and provide for the mortgage of any project or property or any part thereof and (ii) contain provisions for protecting and enforcing the rights and remedies of the bondholders as may be reasonable and proper and not in violation of law, including covenants providing for the repossession and sale by the Authority or any trustees under any trust indenture or agreement of any project, or part thereof, upon any default under the lease or sale of such project, setting forth the duties of the Authority in relation to the acquisition of property and the planning, development, acquisition, construction, rehabilitation, establishment, improvement, extension, enlargement, maintenance, repair, operation and insurance of the project in connection with which the bonds shall have been authorized; the amounts of rates, rents, fees and other charges to be charged; the collection of such rates, rents, fees and other charges; the custody, safeguarding and application of all moneys; and conditions or limitations with respect to the issuance of additional bonds. It shall be lawful for any national bank with its main office in the Commonwealth or any other state or any bank or trust company incorporated under the laws of the Commonwealth or another state that may act as depository of the proceeds of bonds or of revenues to furnish the indemnifying bonds or to pledge the securities required by the Authority. Any trust indenture or agreement or resolution may set forth the rights of action by bondholders. In addition to the foregoing, any such trust indenture or agreement or resolution may contain such other provisions as the Authority may deem reasonable and proper for the security of the bondholders including, without limitation, provisions for the assignment to a corporate trustee or escrow agent of any rights of the Authority in any project owned by, or leases or sales of any projects made by, the Authority. All expenses incurred in carrying out the provisions of the trust indenture or agreement or resolution or other agreements relating to any project, including those to which the

Authority may not be a party, may be treated as a part of the cost of the operation of the project or projects. (1995, c. 758, § 9-266.7; 2001, c. 844.)

§ 2.2-2207. Moneys received deemed trust funds. — All moneys received pursuant to the authority of this article, whether as proceeds from the sale of bonds or as revenues, shall be deemed to be trust funds to be held and applied solely as provided in this article. The resolution authorizing the bonds of any issue or the trust indenture or agreement or resolution securing such bonds shall provide that any officer with whom, or any bank or trust company with which, such moneys shall be deposited shall act as a trustee of such moneys and shall hold and apply the same for the purposes hereof, subject to the regulations as this article and the trust indenture or agreement or resolution may provide. (1995, c. 758, § 9-266.8; 2001, c. 844.)

§ 2.2-2208. Proceedings by bondholder or trustee to enforce rights. — Any holder of bonds issued under the provisions of this article or any of the coupons appertaining thereto, and the trustee under any trust indenture or agreement or resolution, except to the extent the rights given may be restricted by the trust indenture or agreement or resolution authorizing the issuance of the bonds, may either at law or in equity, by suit, action, mandamus or other proceeding, protect and enforce any and all rights under the laws of the Commonwealth or granted hereunder or under the trust indenture or agreement or resolution, and may enforce and compel the performance of all duties required by this article or by the trust indenture or agreement or resolution to be performed by the Authority or by any officer thereof, including the fixing, charging, and collecting of rates, rentals, fees, and other charges. (1995, c. 758, § 9-266.9; 2001, c. 844.)

§ 2.2-2209. Bonds made securities for investment and deposit. — Bonds issued by the Authority under the provisions of this article are made securities in which all public officers and public bodies of the Commonwealth and its political subdivisions, all insurance companies, trust companies, banking associations, investment companies, executors, administrators, trustees, and other fiduciaries may properly and legally invest funds, including capital in their control or belonging to them. Such bonds shall be securities that may properly and legally be deposited with and received by any state or municipal officer or any agency or political subdivision of the Commonwealth for any purpose for which the deposit of bonds or obligations of the Commonwealth is now or may hereafter be authorized by law. (1995, c. 758, § 9-266.10; 2001, c. 844.)

§ 2.2-2210. Refunding bonds; bonds for refunding and for costs of additional projects. — The Authority may provide for the issuance of refunding bonds of the Authority for the purpose of refunding any bonds then outstanding that have been issued under the provisions of this article, including the payment of any redemption premium thereon and any interest accrued or to accrue to the date of redemption of bonds. The issuance of the bonds, the maturities and other details thereof, the rights of the holders thereof, and the rights, duties and obligations of the Authority in respect of the same shall be governed by the provisions of this article insofar as they may be applicable. (1995, c. 758, § 9-266.11; 2001, c. 844.)

§ 2.2-2211. Grants or loans of public or private funds. — The Authority may accept, receive, receipt for, disburse, and expend federal and state moneys and other moneys, public or private, made available by grant or loan or both or otherwise, to accomplish, in whole or in part, any of the purposes of this article. All federal moneys accepted under this section shall be accepted and expended by the Authority upon such terms and conditions as are prescribed by the United States and as are consistent with state law; and all state moneys accepted under this section shall be accepted and expended by the Authority upon such terms and conditions as are prescribed by the Commonwealth. (1995, c. 758, § 9-266.12; 2001, c. 844.)

§ **2.2-2212. Moneys of Authority.** — All moneys of the Authority, from whatever source derived, shall be paid to the treasurer of the Authority. Such moneys shall be deposited in the first instance by the treasurer in one or more banks or trust companies, in one or more special accounts. All banks and trust companies are authorized to give such security for such deposits, if required by the Authority. The moneys in such accounts shall be paid out on the warrant or other order of such persons as the Authority may authorize to execute such warrants or orders. (1995, c. 758, § 9-266.16; 2001, c. 844.)

§ **2.2-2213. Forms of accounts and records; audit; annual report.** — The accounts and records of the Authority showing the receipt and disbursement of funds from whatever source derived, shall be in a form prescribed by the Auditor of Public Accounts. The Auditor of Public Accounts or his legally authorized representatives, shall annually examine the accounts and books of the Authority. Such accounts shall correspond as nearly as possible to the accounts and records for such matters maintained by corporate enterprises.

The Authority shall submit an annual report to the Governor and General Assembly on or before November 1 of each year. Such report shall contain the audited annual financial statements of the Authority for the year ending the preceding June 30. (1995, c. 758, § 9-266.17; 2001, c. 844; 2004, c. 650.)

§ **2.2-2214. Exemption from taxes or assessments.** — The exercise of the powers granted by this article shall be in all respects for the benefit of the people of the Commonwealth, for the increase of their commerce and prosperity, and for the improvement of their health and living conditions, and as the operation and maintenance of the projects by the Authority and the undertaking of activities in the furtherance of the purposes of the Authority constitutes the performance of the essential governmental functions, the Authority shall not be required to pay any taxes or assessments upon any project or any property acquired or used by the Authority under the provisions of this article or upon the income therefrom, including sales and use taxes on the tangible personal property used in the operations of the Authority. The exemption granted in this section shall not be construed to extend to persons conducting on the premises of the facility businesses for which local or state taxes would otherwise be required.

Any bonds or refunding bonds issued under the provisions of this article and any transfer of such bonds shall at all times be free from state and local taxation. The interest on the bonds and any refunding bonds or bond anticipation notes shall at all times be exempt from taxation by the Commonwealth and by any of its political subdivisions. (1995, c. 758, § 9-266.18; 2001, c. 844.)

§ **2.2-2215. Exemption of Authority from personnel and procurement procedures.** — The provisions of the Virginia Personnel Act (§ 2.2-2900 et seq.) and the Virginia Public Procurement Act (§ 2.2-4300 et seq.) of this title shall not apply to the Authority in the exercise of any power conferred under this article. (1995, c. 758, § 9-266.15; 2001, c. 844.)

§ 2.2-2216. Appropriations by any government. — Any government may make appropriations for the acquisition, construction, improvement, maintenance or operation of any project acquired, constructed, improved, maintained or operated by the Authority. (1995, c. 758, § 9-266.13; 2001, c. 844.)

§ 2.2-2217. Conveyance, lease or transfer of property by a city or county to the Authority. — Any city or county within the Commonwealth in order to provide for the construction, reconstruction, improvement, repair or management of any project, or in order to accomplish any of the purposes of this article may, with or without consideration or for a nominal consideration, lease, sell, convey or otherwise transfer to the Authority any real, personal or mixed property located within such city or county. (1995, c. 758, § 9-266.14; 2001, c. 844.)

Article 3.

Innovative Technology Authority.

§ 2.2-2218. Short title; definitions. — A. This article may be cited as the "Innovative Technology Authority Act of 1984."

B. As used in this article, unless the context requires a different meaning:

"Project" shall mean the construction, improvement, furnishing, maintenance, acquisition or operation of any facility or the provision for or funding of any activity that will further the purposes described in § 2.2-2219. (1984, c. 782, §§ 9-250, 9-251; 2001, c. 844.)

§ 2.2-2219. Declaration of public purpose; Authority created. — A. It is found and determined by the General Assembly that there exists in the Commonwealth of Virginia a need to (i) promote the economic development of the Commonwealth by attracting and retaining high technology jobs and businesses in Virginia; (ii) increase industry competitiveness by supporting the application of innovative technologies that improve productivity and efficiency; (iii) mobilize support for high technology industries to commercialize new products and processes, including organizing assistance for small business and supporting select industry sectors and regional high technology efforts; (iv) enhance and expand the scientific and technological research and development capabilities of the institutions of higher education in the Commonwealth and coordinate such capabilities with the scientific and technological research and development activities and requirements of the public and private sectors, including transferring technological advances to the private sector; (v) expand knowledge pertaining to scientific and technological research and development among public and private entities; (vi) attract research and development (R&D) facilities and contracts from the federal government and private sector, including coordinating efforts to identify and compete for large federal and private sector R&D facilities, tracking federal technology initiatives and recommending state actions, and developing a statewide strategy to compete for large R&D contracts; and (vii) facilitate and coordinate the marketing, organization, utilization and development of scientific and technological research and development in the Commonwealth.

B. To achieve the objectives of subsection A, there is created and constituted a political subdivision of the Commonwealth to be known as "The Innovative Technology Authority." The Authority's exercise of powers conferred by this article shall be deemed to be the performance of an essential governmental function and matters of public necessity for which public moneys may be spent and private property acquired. (1984, c. 782, § 9-252; 1993, c. 967; 2001, c. 844.)

§ 2.2-2220. Board of directors; members; President. — The Authority shall be governed by a board of directors consisting of 13 members appointed by the Governor as follows: two members shall be the presidents of the major research universities, and one member shall represent the other public colleges or universities in Virginia. After the original appointments, all appointments of presidents shall be for terms of five years, except that appointments to fill vacancies shall be for the unexpired terms. No president shall be eligible to serve for more than two successive five-year terms; however, after the expiration of a term of four years or less, or after the expiration of the remainder of a term to which appointed to fill a vacancy, two additional terms may be served by such member if appointed thereto. The Secretary of Technology shall serve on the Board for a term coincident with his term of office. The Governor shall appoint the nine other members of the Board who shall be nominated by established industry groups and technology councils within the Commonwealth. These appointees shall include representatives of a variety of businesses, industries and corporations of different types, sizes, locations and stages of development. All members of the Board appointed by the Governor shall be confirmed by each house of the General Assembly. After the original appointments, the members of the Board shall be appointed for terms of four years. Vacancies in the membership of the Board shall be filled by appointment of the Governor for the unexpired portion of the term. No member of the Board shall be eligible to serve for more than two successive terms; however, after the expiration of a term of four years or less, or after the expiration of the remainder of a term to which appointed to fill a vacancy, two additional terms may be served by such member if appointed thereto. Members of the Board shall be subject to removal from office in like manner as are state, county, town and district officers under the provisions of §§ 24.2-230 through 24.2-238. Immediately after appointment, the members of the Board shall enter upon the performance of their duties.

The Board shall annually elect from among its members a chairman and a vice-chairman. The Board shall also elect annually a secretary, who need not be a member of the Board, and may also elect such other subordinate officers who need not be members of the Board, as it deems proper. The chairman, or in his absence, the vice-chairman, shall preside at all meetings of the Board. In the absence of both the chairman and vice-chairman, the Board shall appoint a chairman pro tempore, who shall preside at such meetings.

The Board shall employ a President of the Authority, who shall serve at the pleasure of the Board, to direct the day-to-day operations and activities of the Authority and carry out such of the powers and duties conferred upon him by the Board. The President and employees of the Authority shall be compensated in the manner provided by the Board and shall not be subject to the provisions of the Virginia Personnel Act (§ 2.2-2900 et seq.) of this title. (1984, c. 782, § 9-253; 1993, c. 967; 1999, cc. 412, 421, 433; 2001, c. 844; 2005, c. 439; 2008, cc. 299, 611.)

The 2008 amendments. — The 2008 amendments by cc. 299 and 611 are nearly identical, and in the first paragraph, substituted "13" for "sixteen," inserted "as follows," substituted "two members" for "two of whom," and substituted "one member" for "one of whom" in the first sentence; in the fourth sentence, deleted "Secretary of Education, the Secretary of Commerce and Trade, the" preceding "Secretary of Technology" and deleted "and the Director of the State Council of Higher Education" thereafter and substituted "a term" for "terms" and "his term of office" for "their terms of office" near the end.

§ **2.2-2221. Powers of the Authority.** — The Authority is granted all powers necessary or convenient for the carrying out of its statutory purposes, including, but not limited to, the following rights and powers to:

1. Sue and be sued, implead and be impleaded, complain and defend in all courts.
2. Adopt, use, and alter at will a corporate seal.
3. Acquire, purchase, hold, use, lease or otherwise dispose of any project and property, real, personal or mixed, tangible or intangible, or any interest therein necessary or desirable for carrying out the purposes of the Authority, and, without limitation of the foregoing, to lease as lessee, any project and any property, real, personal or mixed, or any interest therein, at such annual rental and on such terms and conditions as may be determined by the Board and to lease as lessor to any person, any project and any property, real, personal or mixed, tangible or intangible, or any interest therein, at any time acquired by the Authority, whether wholly or partially completed, at such annual rental and on such terms and conditions as may be determined by the Board, and to sell, transfer or convey any property, real, personal or mixed, tangible or intangible or any interest therein, at any time acquired or held by the Authority on such terms and conditions as may be determined by the board of the Authority.
4. Plan, develop, undertake, carry out, construct, improve, rehabilitate, repair, furnish, maintain, and operate projects.
5. Adopt bylaws for the management and regulation of its affairs.
6. Establish and maintain satellite offices within the Commonwealth.
7. Fix, alter, charge, and collect rates, rentals, and other charges for the use of projects of, or for the sale of products of or for the services rendered by, the Authority, at rates to be determined by it for the purpose of providing for the payment of the expenses of the Authority, the planning, development, construction, improvement, rehabilitation, repair, furnishing, maintenance, and operation of its projects and properties, the payment of the costs accomplishing its purposes set forth in § 2.2-2219, the payment of the principal of and interest on its obligations, and to fulfill the terms and provisions of any agreements made with the purchasers or holders of any such obligations.
8. Borrow money, make and issue bonds including bonds as the Authority may determine to issue for the purpose of accomplishing the purposes set forth in § 2.2-2219 or of refunding bonds previously issued by the Authority, and to secure the payment of all bonds, or any part thereof, by pledge or deed of trust of all or any of its revenues, rentals, and receipts or of any project or property, real, personal or mixed, tangible or intangible, or any interest therein, and to make agreements with the purchasers or holders of such bonds or with others in connection with any such bonds, whether issued or to be issued, as the Authority deems advisable, and in general to provide for the security for the bonds and the rights of holders thereof.
9. Make and enter into all contracts and agreements necessary or incidental to the performance of its duties, the furtherance of its purposes and the execution of its powers under this article, including agreements with any person or federal agency.
10. Employ, in its discretion, consultants, attorneys, architects, engineers, accountants, financial experts, investment bankers, superintendents, managers and such other employees and agents as may be necessary, and to fix their compensation to be payable from funds made available to the Authority.
11. Receive and accept from any federal or private agency, foundation, corporation, association or person grants to be expended in accomplishing the objectives of the Authority, and to receive and accept from the Commonwealth or any state, and any municipality, county or other political subdivision thereof and from any other source, aid or contributions of either money, property, or

other things of value, to be held, used and applied only for the purposes for which such grants and contributions may be made.

12. Render advice and assistance, and to provide services, to institutions of higher education and to other persons providing services or facilities for scientific and technological research or graduate education, provided that credit towards a degree, certificate or diploma shall be granted only if such education is provided in conjunction with an institution of higher education authorized to operate in Virginia.

13. Develop, undertake and provide programs, alone or in conjunction with any person or federal agency, for scientific and technological research, technology management, continuing education and in-service training, provided that credit towards a degree, certificate or diploma shall be granted only if such education is provided in conjunction with an institution of higher education authorized to operate in Virginia; to foster the utilization of scientific and technological research information, discoveries and data and to obtain patents, copyrights and trademarks thereon; to coordinate the scientific and technological research efforts of public institutions and private industry and to collect and maintain data on the development and utilization of scientific and technological research capabilities. The universities set forth in § 2.2-2220 shall be the principal leading universities in the research institutes.

14. Pledge or otherwise encumber all or any of the revenues or receipts of the Authority as security for all or any of the obligations of the Authority.

15. Receive, administer, and market any interest in patents, copyrights and materials that were potentially patentable or copyrightable developed by or for state agencies, public institutions of higher education and political subdivisions of the Commonwealth. The Authority shall return to the agency, institution or political subdivision any revenue in excess of its administrative and marketing costs. When general funds are used to develop the patent or copyright or material that was potentially patentable or copyrightable, any state agency, except a public institution of higher education in Virginia, shall return any revenues it receives from the Authority to the general fund unless the Governor authorizes a percentage of the net royalties to be shared with the developer of the patented, copyrighted, or potentially patentable or copyrightable property.

16. Do all acts and things necessary or convenient to carry out the powers granted to it by law. (1984, c. 782, § 9-254; 1985, c. 502; 2001, c. 844.)

Editor's note. — Acts 2008, c. 879, effective for the biennium ending June 30, 2010, in Item 430 F, provides: "The Center for Innovative Technology shall continue to support efforts of public and quasi-public bodies within the Commonwealth to enhance or facilitate the prompt availability of and access to advanced electronic communications services, commonly known as broadband, throughout the Commonwealth, monitoring trends and advances in advanced electronic communications technology to plan and forecast future needs for such technology, and identify funding options."

§ 2.2-2221.01. Designation of staff of Center for Innovative Technology. — The Board of the Authority may designate the President and staff of the Center for Innovative Technology to carry out the day-to-day operations and activities of the Authority and to perform such other duties as may be directed by the Board. (2008, cc. 70, 610.)

§ 2.2-2221.1. Reporting requirement for the Center for Innovative Technology. — The president of the Center for Innovative Technology shall report annually to the Joint Commission on Technology and Science, created pursuant to § 30-85, regarding a review of the Center's initiatives and projects, its work plan for the year and the expected results therefrom, and an overview of the results that it has achieved to date, to assist the Commission in its effort to stimulate, encourage, and promote the development of technology and science in the Commonwealth and sound public policies related thereto. (2001, c. 57, § 9-254.1.)

Editor's note. — Acts 2001, c. 57 enacted § 9-254.1, from which this section is derived. Pursuant to § 30-152, Acts 2001, c. 57 has been given effect in this section as set out above.

Acts 2008, c. 879, effective for the biennium ending June 30, 2010, in Item 430 D, provides: "Before the beginning of each fiscal year, the Innovative Technology Authority shall provide to the Chairmen of the House Appropriations and Senate Finance Committees and the Director, Department of Planning and Budget, a report of its operating plan. Within three months after the end of the fiscal year, the Center shall submit to the same entities a detailed expenditure report for the concluded fiscal year. Both reports shall be prepared in the formats as approved by the Director, Department of Planning and Budget."

§ 2.2-2222. Form, terms, execution and sale of bonds; use of proceeds; interim receipts or temporary bonds; lost or destroyed bonds; faith and credit of state and political subdivisions not pledged; expenses. — The bonds of each issue shall be dated, shall bear interest at such rates as shall be fixed by the Authority, shall mature at such time not exceeding forty years from their date as may be determined by the Authority, and may be made redeemable before maturity, at the option of the Authority, at such price or prices and under such terms and conditions as may be fixed by the Authority prior to the issuance of the bonds. The Authority shall determine the form of bonds and their manner of execution, and shall fix the denomination of the bonds and the place of payment of principal and interest, which may be at any bank or trust company within or without the Commonwealth. The bonds shall be signed by the chairman or vice-chairman of the Authority, or if so authorized by the Authority, shall bear his facsimile signature, and the official seal of the Authority, or, if so authorized by the Authority, a facsimile signature thereof shall be impressed or imprinted thereon and attested by the secretary or any assistant secretary of the Authority, or, if so authorized by the Authority, with the facsimile signature of such secretary or assistant secretary. Any coupons attached to bonds issued by the Authority shall bear the signature of the chairman or vice-chairman of the Authority or a facsimile thereof. In case any officer whose signature or a facsimile of whose signature shall appear on any bonds or coupons shall cease to be such officer before the delivery of such bonds, such signature or such facsimile shall nevertheless be valid and sufficient for all purposes the same as if he had remained in office until such delivery and any bonds may bear the facsimile signature of, or may be signed by, such persons as at the actual time of the execution of such bonds shall be the proper officers to sign such bonds although at the date of such bonds such persons may not have been such officers. The bonds may be issued in coupon or in registered form, or both, as the Authority may determine, and provision may be made for the registration of any coupon bonds as to principal alone and also as to both principal and interest, for the reconversion into coupon bonds of any bonds registered as to both principal and interest, and for the interchange of registered and coupon bonds. The Authority may sell such bonds in such manner, either at public or private sale, and for such price, as it may determine will best effect the purposes of this article.

The proceeds of the bonds of each issue shall be used solely for the purposes, and in furtherance of the powers, of the Authority as may be provided in the resolution authorizing the issuance of such bonds or in the trust agreement authorized by § 2.2-2223 securing the bonds.

In addition to the above powers, the Authority may issue interim receipts or temporary bonds as provided in § 15.2-2616 and to execute and deliver new bonds in place of bonds mutilated, lost or destroyed, as provided in § 15.2-2621.

No obligation of the Authority shall be deemed to constitute a debt, or pledge of the faith and credit, of the Commonwealth or of any political subdivision thereof, but shall be payable solely from the revenue and other funds of the Authority pledged thereto. All such obligations shall contain on the face thereof a statement to the effect that the Commonwealth, political subdivisions thereof and the Authority shall not be obligated to pay the same or the interest thereon except from revenues and other funds of the Authority pledged thereto, and that neither the faith and credit nor the taxing power of the Commonwealth or of any political subdivision thereof is pledged to the payment of the principal of or the interest on such obligations.

All expenses incurred in carrying out the provisions of this article shall be payable solely from funds provided under the provisions of this article and no liability shall be incurred by the Authority beyond the extent to which moneys have been provided under the provisions of this article. (1984, c. 782, § 9-255; 2001, c. 844.)

§ **2.2-2223. Trust agreement securing bonds.** — In the discretion of the Authority any bonds issued under the provisions of this article may be secured by a trust agreement by and between the Authority and a corporate trustee, which may be any trust company or bank having the powers of a trust company within or without the Commonwealth. The trust agreement or the resolution providing for the issuance of the bonds may (i) pledge or assign the revenues to be received and provide for the mortgage of any project or property or any part thereof and (ii) contain provisions for protecting and enforcing the rights and remedies of the bondholders as may be reasonable and proper and not in violation of law, including covenants setting forth the duties of the Authority in relation to the acquisition of property and the planning, development, acquisition, construction, rehabilitation, establishment, improvement, extension, enlargement, maintenance, repair, operation and insurance of the project in connection with which the bonds have been authorized, the rates and fees to be charged, the custody, safeguarding and application of all moneys, and conditions or limitations with respect to the issuance of additional bonds. It shall be lawful for any bank or trust company incorporated under the laws of the Commonwealth which may act as depository of the proceeds of bonds or of revenue to furnish the indemnifying bonds or to pledge the securities required by the Authority. Any trust agreement may set forth the rights of action by bondholders. In addition to the foregoing, any trust agreement or resolution may contain such other provisions as the Authority may deem reasonable and proper for the security of the bondholders. All expenses incurred in carrying out the provisions of the trust agreement or resolution may be treated as a part of the cost of the operation of the project or projects. (1984, c. 782, § 9-256; 2001, c. 844.)

§ **2.2-2224. Moneys received deemed trust funds.** — All moneys received pursuant to the authority of this article, whether as proceeds from the sale of bonds or as revenues, shall be deemed to be trust funds to be held and applied solely as provided in this article. The resolution authorizing the bonds of any issue or the trust agreement securing such bonds shall provide that any officer with whom, or any bank or trust company with which, such moneys shall be deposited shall act as a trustee of such moneys and shall hold and apply the same for the purposes hereof, subject to the regulations as this article and the resolution or trust agreement may provide. (1984, c. 782, § 9-257; 2001, c. 844.)

§ **2.2-2225. Proceedings by bondholder or trustee to enforce rights.** — Any holder of bonds issued under the provisions of this article or any of the coupons appertaining thereto, and the trustee under any trust agreement, except to the extent the rights herein given may be restricted by the trust agreement or the resolution authorizing the issuance of such bonds, may either at law or in equity, by suit, action, mandamus or other proceeding, protect and enforce any and all rights under the laws of the Commonwealth or granted hereunder or under the trust agreement or resolution, and may enforce and compel the performance of all duties required by this article or by the trust agreement or resolution to be performed by the Authority or by any officer thereof, including the fixing, charging, and collecting of rates, rentals, and other charges. (1984, c. 782, § 9-258; 2001, c. 844.)

§ 2.2-2226. Bonds made securities for investment and deposit. — Bonds issued by the Authority under the provisions of this article shall be securities in which all public officers and public bodies of the Commonwealth and its political subdivisions, all insurance companies, trust companies, banking associations, investment companies, executors, administrators, trustees, and other fiduciaries may properly and legally invest funds, including capital in their control or belonging to them. Such bonds shall be securities that may properly and legally be deposited with and received by any state or municipal officer or any agency or political subdivision of the Commonwealth for any purpose for which the deposit of bonds or obligations of the Commonwealth is now or may be authorized by law. (1984, c. 782, § 9-259; 2001, c. 844.)

§ 2.2-2227. Revenue refunding bonds; bonds for refunding and for cost of additional projects. — The Authority may provide for the issuance of revenue refunding bonds of the Authority for the purpose of refunding any bonds then outstanding that have been issued under the provisions of this article, including the payment of any redemption premium thereon and any interest accrued or to accrue to the date of redemption of the bonds, and, if deemed advisable by the Authority, for the additional purpose of constructing improvements, extensions, or enlargements of the project or projects in connection with which the bonds to be refunded shall have been issued. The Authority may provide by resolution for the issuance of its revenue bonds for the combined purpose of (i) refunding any bonds then outstanding which shall have been issued under the provisions of this article, including the payment of any redemption premium thereon and any interest accrued or to accrue to the date of redemption of the bonds, and (ii) paying all or any part of the cost of any additional project or any portion thereof. The issuance of the bonds, the maturities and other details thereof, the rights of the holders thereof, and the rights, duties and obligations of the Authority in respect of the same shall be governed by the provisions of this article insofar as they may be applicable. (1984, c. 782, § 9-260; 2001, c. 844.)

§ 2.2-2228. Grants or loans of public or private funds. — The Authority may accept, receive, receipt for, disburse, and expend federal and state moneys and other moneys, public or private, made available by grant or loan or both or otherwise, to accomplish, in whole or in part, any of the purposes of this article. All federal moneys accepted under this section shall be accepted and expended by the Authority upon such terms and conditions as are prescribed by the United States and as are consistent with state law; and all state moneys accepted under this section shall be accepted and expended by the Authority upon such terms and conditions as are prescribed by the Commonwealth. (1984, c. 782, § 9-261; 2001, c. 844.)

§ 2.2-2229. Moneys of Authority; examination of books by the Auditor of Public Accounts. — All moneys of the Authority, from whatever source derived, shall be paid to the treasurer of the Authority. Such moneys shall be deposited in the first instance by the treasurer in one or more banks or trust companies, in one or more special accounts. All banks and trust companies are authorized to give such security for such deposits, if required by the Authority. The moneys in such accounts shall be paid out on the warrant or other order of the treasurer of the Authority or of other persons as the Authority may authorize to execute such warrants or orders. The Auditor of Public Accounts or his legally authorized representatives, shall examine the accounts and books of the Authority. (1984, c. 782, § 9-265; 2001, c. 844.)

§ **2.2-2230. Exemption from taxes or assessments.** — The exercise of the powers granted by this article shall be in all respects for the benefit of the people of the Commonwealth, for the increase of their commerce and prosperity, and for the improvement of their health and living conditions, and as the operation and maintenance of projects by the Authority and the undertaking of activities in furtherance of the purpose of the Authority constitute the performance of essential governmental functions, the Authority shall not be required to pay any taxes or assessments upon any project or any property acquired or used by the Authority under the provisions of this article or upon the income therefrom, including sales and use taxes on tangible personal property used in the operations of the Authority, and any bonds issued under the provisions of this article, their transfer and the income therefrom (including any profit made on the sale thereof) shall at all times be free from state and local taxation. The exemption granted in this section shall not be construed to extend to persons conducting on the premises of a facility businesses for which local or state taxes would otherwise be required. (1984, c. 782, § 9-262; 2001, c. 844.)

§ **2.2-2231. Exemption of Authority from personnel and procurement procedures.** — The provisions of the Virginia Personnel Act (§ 2.2-2900 et seq.) of and the Virginia Public Procurement Act (§ 2.2-4300 et seq.) of this title shall not apply to the Authority in the exercise of any power conferred under this article. (1984, c. 782, § 9-264; 2001, c. 844.)

§ **2.2-2232. Auxiliaries.** — A. The Governor may provide for the formation of a nonstock corporation to carry out the purpose of this article. The board of directors of the nonstock corporation shall consist of the fifteen members of the Board of the Authority. The articles of incorporation of the nonstock corporation shall provide that upon dissolution the net assets of the corporation shall be transferred to the Commonwealth. The nonstock corporation shall ensure that the economic benefits attributable to the income and property rights arising from any transactions in which the nonstock corporation is involved are allocated on a basis that is equitable in the reasonable business judgment of the board of directors, with due account being given to the interest of the citizens of the Commonwealth and the needs of the nonstock corporation. Any such nonstock corporation shall not be deemed to be a state or governmental agency, advisory agency, public body or agency or instrumentality for purposes of Chapters 8 (§ 2.2-800 et seq.), 18 (§ 2.2-1800 et seq.), 24 (§ 2.2-2400 et seq.), 29 (§ 2.2-2900 et seq.), 31 (§ 2.2-3100 et seq.), 37 (§ 2.2-3700 et seq.), 38 (§ 2.2-3800 et seq.), 43 (§ 2.2-4300 et seq.), 44 (§ 2.2-4400 et seq.), 45 (§ 2.2-4500 et seq.), 46 (§ 2.2-4600 et seq.), and 47 (§ 2.2-4700 et seq.) of this title, Chapter 14 (§ 30-130 et seq.) of Title 30 or Chapter 1 (§ 51.1-124.1 et seq.) of Title 51.1. No director, officer or employee of any such nonstock corporation or entity be shall deemed to be an officer or employee for purposes of Chapter 31 (§ 2.2-3100 et seq.) of this title. Notwithstanding the foregoing, the Auditor of Public Accounts, or his legally authorized representatives, shall annually audit the financial accounts of the Authority and any such nonstock corporation entity, provided that the working papers and files of the Auditor of Public Accounts relating to such audits shall not be subject to the provisions of The Freedom of Information Act (§ 2.2-3700 et seq.).

B. Notwithstanding the provisions of subsection A, as an entity receiving state funds, any such nonstock corporation shall be subject to periodic external review either (i) under the provisions of the Legislative Program Review and Evaluation Act (§ 30-64 et seq.) or (ii) by an entity appointed for that purpose by the Governor. Any such nonstock corporation shall be deemed to be an institution of higher education within the meaning of §§ 23-3.1 and 23-9.2, but only for the limited purposes therein stated. (1984, c. 782, § 9-263; 1987, Sp. Sess., c. 1; 1993, c. 967; 2001, c. 844.)

§ 2.2-2233. Advanced Communications Assistance Fund created; purposes. — A. From such funds as may be appropriated by the General Assembly and any gifts, grants, or donations from public or private sources, there is created in the state treasury a special nonreverting, permanent fund, to be known as the Advanced Communications Assistance Fund ("the Fund"), to be administered by the Authority. The Fund shall be established on the books of the Comptroller. Interest earned on moneys in the Fund shall remain in the Fund and be credited to it. Any moneys remaining in the Fund at the end of each fiscal year, including interest thereon, shall not revert to the general fund but shall remain in the Fund. Expenditures and disbursements from the Fund, which may consist of grants or loans, shall be made by the State Treasurer on warrants issued by the Comptroller upon written request bearing the signature of the chairman or the vice-chairman of the Authority, or, if so authorized by the Authority, bearing his facsimile signature, and the official seal of the Authority.

B. Moneys in the Fund shall be used solely for the purpose of helping underserved localities in the Commonwealth take full advantage of advanced communications services. Loans or grants from the Fund shall be used in underserved localities for (i) the internal communication needs of such localities, which may include but are not limited to fiber-optic, satellite, and wireless communications networks, or (ii) help in financing the costs of planning, designing, purchasing, leasing, installing, or maintaining dark fiber to the extent permitted in § 15.2-1500.

C. For purposes of this section:

"Dark fiber" means fiber optic cable that is not lighted by lasers or other electronic equipment.

"Underserved locality" means a locality wherein advanced communication services are not readily and generally available from three or more nonaffiliated certificated local exchange companies. (1999, c. 924, § 9-265.1; 2001, c. 844.)

§ 2.2-2233.1. Commonwealth Technology Research Fund; continued; purposes; report. — A. From such funds as may be appropriated by the General Assembly and any gifts, grants, or donations from public or private sources, there is created in the state treasury a special nonreverting, permanent fund, to be known as the Commonwealth Technology Research Fund (the Fund), to be administered by the Authority. The Fund shall be established on the books of the Comptroller. Interest earned on moneys in the Fund shall remain in the Fund and be credited to it. Any moneys remaining in the Fund at the end of each fiscal year, including interest thereon, shall not revert to the general fund but shall remain in the Fund. Expenditures and disbursements from the Fund, which may consist of grants or loans, shall be made by the State Treasurer on warrants issued by the Comptroller upon written request bearing the signature of the chairman or the vice-chairman of the Authority, or, if so authorized by the Authority, bearing his facsimile signature, and the official seal of the Authority.

B. Moneys in the Fund shall be used for the sole purpose of attracting public and private research funding for institutions of higher education, in order to increase technological and economic development in Virginia. Awards from the Fund shall be made to Virginia public institutions of higher education or to their associated intellectual property foundations.

C. For purposes of awards, the Fund shall have four components: (i) a matching funds program to leverage federal and private research dollars; (ii) a strategic enhancement program to upgrade the research capacity of those academic departments that have demonstrated the ability to perform innovative research in technology fields that has strong potential to contribute to economic development in the Commonwealth; (iii) a program to upgrade research capacity in key departments of the institutions in order to attract specific companies to locate or expand in Virginia; and (iv) a program to enhance the capability of the institutions of higher education to commercialize technologies developed through their research.

Awards for the matching funds component shall be contingent upon the approval of the institution's grant proposal for federal or private funds.

Awards from the Fund shall be matched on at least a dollar-for-dollar basis by the respective institution of higher education, with private funds, or combinations thereof. However, for good cause, this requirement may be waived, in whole or in part, by the chairman of the Authority, provided that such action is reported to the Chairmen of the House Appropriations and Senate Finance Committees at least 10 days prior to the award or disbursement of such funds for such purpose.

D. Awards shall be based on scientific merit and economic development potential of research programs in the following fields: aerospace, biotechnology, energy, environmental and information technologies, high performance manufacturing, sensor sciences, telecommunications, and transportation. However, for good cause, awards supporting research in other relevant fields or disciplines may be made by the chairman of the Authority, provided that such action is reported to the Chairmen of the House Appropriations and Senate Finance Committees at least 10 days prior to the award or disbursement of such funds for such purpose.

Specific guidelines for the award of funds from this program shall be established and maintained by the Authority, in consultation with the Virginia Economic Development Partnership and the State Council of Higher Education. These guidelines shall address, at a minimum, the application process, and the composition and operation of proposal review panels, and give special emphasis to fostering collaboration between institutions of higher education and partnerships between institutions of higher education and business and industry.

The chairman of the Authority shall coordinate the evaluation of proposals, to be conducted by review panels with the appropriate science and technology expertise, drawn from federal agencies and academic and industrial research institutions across the country.

Recommendations on the grants shall be made by representatives from the Virginia Research and Technology Advisory Commission pursuant to § 2.2-2515, the Virginia Economic Development Partnership, and the State Council of Higher Education based on the recommendations of the review panels.

E. The chairman of the Authority shall provide the Governor and the General Assembly with an annual report to include a detailed list of awards committed, the amount of each approved award, a description of the approved proposals, and the amount of federal or private matching funds anticipated where applicable, and an assessment of the effectiveness of the Fund in attracting public and private research funding and increasing technological and economic development in Virginia. (2003, c. 362; 2008, cc. 63, 527.)

The 2008 amendments. — The 2008 amendments by cc. 63 and 527 are identical and inserted "sensor sciences" in the first sentence of subsection D.

§ 2.2-2233.2. Biotechnology Commercialization Loan Fund; created; purposes; report. — A. From such funds as may be appropriated by the General Assembly and any gifts, grants, or donations from public or private sources, there is created in the state treasury a special nonreverting, permanent fund, to be known as the Biotechnology Commercialization Loan Fund (the Fund), to be administered by the Authority. The Fund shall be established on the books of the Comptroller. Interest earned on moneys in the Fund shall remain in the Fund and be credited to it. Any moneys remaining in the Fund at the end of each fiscal year, including interest thereon, shall not revert to the general fund but shall remain in the Fund. Expenditures and disbursements from the Fund, which shall consist of loans, shall be made by the State Treasurer on warrants issued by the Comptroller upon written request bearing the signature of the chairman or the vice-chairman of the Authority, or, if so authorized by the Authority, bearing his facsimile signature, and the official seal of the Authority.

B. Moneys in the Fund shall be used for the sole purpose of financing technology transfer and commercialization activities related to biotechnology inventions made, solely or in cooperation with other organizations, at qualifying institutions. Such activities shall include, but not be limited to, legal and business consulting services and expenses, including employee compensation, relating to assessing the patentability of inventions, obtaining patent protection for such inventions in the United States and internationally, marketing for such inventions and patents thereon to potential licensees, and negotiating licensing or commercialization agreements with licensees, as well as development of new technology transfer and commercialization programs at qualifying institutions.

The maximum amount of any loans outstanding under the Fund shall be $3,000,000.

C. Qualifying institutions may apply to the Fund for loans to the extent that such institution's outstanding principal balance at any one time does not exceed $500,000. Loan applications shall include business plans that detail and explain the anticipated uses of funds received and the proposed repayment schedule.

Loans from the Fund shall take the form of a contractual commitment to the recipient qualifying institution for a line of credit for up to three years, along with an approved schedule of repayment. During the contractual period the recipient qualifying institution may draw upon the line of credit for any expense for which the loan was made, not to exceed the stated amount of the loan award. At the end of the contractual period, the line of credit shall terminate and the outstanding balance of the withdrawals on that line of credit shall become the established basis for that loan.

During the contractual period, deferred interest shall accumulate on the outstanding balance at a rate of three percent compounded annually. Borrowing institutions may prepay part or all of any loan received from the Fund without penalty, and, if repayment is completed within the contractual period of the line of credit, the accumulated interest obligation shall be forgiven.

Repayment of the established basis shall consist of a maximum of 84 equal monthly payments of principal and compounded interest at the determined rate beginning on the first day of the month following the end of the contractual period.

D. Decisions to make loans to applicants from the Fund shall be made by a panel, which shall consist of the President of the Center for Innovative Technology, the Director of the Department of Planning and Budget and the Executive Director of the Virginia Economic Development Partnership, or their designees. The President of the Center for Innovative Technology, or his designee, shall serve as chair. The panel may seek the advice of experts in technology, business, technology transfer or other relevant fields as appropriate in devising guidelines for the implementation of this loan program as well as in making loan decisions.

Specific guidelines for the award of funds from this program shall be established and maintained by the Authority, in consultation with the Virginia Economic Development Partnership and the State Council of Higher Education.

E. A recipient of a loan from the Fund shall report annually to the panel on the uses of loan proceeds during the previous year and on plans for the use of any additional funds it may plan to draw. Such reports shall be filed for so long as the recipient owes money to the Fund.

F. The chairman of the Authority shall report annually to the Governor and the General Assembly on activities of the Fund, including a detailed list of awards committed, the amount and description of each approved award, and an assessment of the effectiveness of the Fund in encouraging the commercialization of bioscience and biotechnology inventions made at Virginia institutions of higher education.

G. A record transmitted or delivered by a loan applicant or a loan recipient to a public body in the conduct of its duties under this section shall be excluded from disclosure under the Virginia Freedom of Information Act to the extent such record reveals information that (a) is the property of the submitting party, (b) has independent economic value to the owner that causes it to be maintained in secrecy by the owner, and (c) is clearly and specifically identified in writing as proprietary, confidential information at the time of its delivery or transmission to the public body. Nothing in this paragraph shall be construed to prevent the disclosure of information regarding the financial or administrative oversight of the Fund by the Authority.

H. For purposes of this section:

"Determined rate" means the rate of interest paid by the Commonwealth on the most recent sale of tax-exempt bonds backed by the full faith and credit of the Commonwealth.

"Qualifying institution" means an institution of higher education in the Commonwealth or its associated intellectual property foundation that adopts a policy regarding the ownership, protection, assignment, and use of intellectual property pursuant to § 23-4.3.

I. No loan shall be made to any entity which conducts human stem cell research from human embryos, or for any loan to conduct such research; however, research conducted using adult stem cells may be funded. (2004, c. 942; 2006, cc. 77, 899.)

ARTICLE 4.

Virginia Economic Development Partnership Authority.

§ 2.2-2234. Short title; declaration of public purpose; Authority created. — A. This article shall be known and may be cited as the "Virginia Economic Development Partnership Act."

B. The General Assembly has determined that there exists in the Commonwealth a need to encourage, stimulate and support the development and expansion of the economy of the Commonwealth through economic development.

C. To achieve the objective of subsection B, there is created a political subdivision of the Commonwealth to be known as the Virginia Economic Development Partnership Authority. The Authority's exercise of powers and duties conferred by this article shall be deemed the performance of an essential governmental function and matters of public necessity for which public moneys may be spent and private property acquired. (1995, c. 638, §§ 2.1-548.26, 2.1-548.28; 2001, c. 844.)

§ 2.2-2235. Board of directors; members and officers; Executive Director. — The Authority shall be governed by board of directors consisting of the Secretary of Commerce and Trade, the Secretary of Finance, and the Chancellor of the Virginia Community College System, all serving ex officio, and 18 members to be appointed as follows: (i) one from each congressional district in the Commonwealth and one citizen at large, appointed by the Governor, subject to confirmation by the General Assembly; (ii) four citizens at large appointed by the Speaker of the House; and (iii) two citizens at large appointed by the Senate Committee on Rules. The six citizens appointed by the General Assembly shall reside in regions of the Commonwealth that have a higher unemployment rate than that of the statewide average unemployment rate as reported by the Virginia Employment Commission for the preceding four years from the date of appointment. Ex officio members of the Board shall serve terms coincident with their terms of office. Four of the 12 directors initially appointed by the Governor shall be appointed for terms of two and one-half years, three for terms of four and one-half years, and five for terms of six and one-half years, from the effective date of their appointment; and thereafter the terms of members of the Board shall be six years. No member shall be eligible to serve more than two terms; however, after the expiration of the term of a member appointed to serve three years or less, two additional terms may be served if appointed thereto. Any appointment to fill a vacancy shall be for the unexpired term. A person appointed to fill a vacancy may be appointed to serve two additional terms. Members of the Board shall receive their expenses and shall be compensated at the rate provided in § 2.2-2104 for each day spent on the business of the Board.

The Board shall elect from its membership a chairman and a vice-chairman, and shall also elect a secretary and a treasurer, who need not be members of the Board, and may also elect other subordinate officers, who need not be members of the Board. The Board may also form committees and advisory councils, which may include representatives who are not members of the Board, to undertake more extensive study and discussion of the issues before the Board.

A majority of the Board shall constitute a quorum for the transaction of the Authority's business, and no vacancy in the membership shall impair the right of a quorum to exercise the rights and perform all duties of the Authority.

The Board shall appoint the chief executive officer of the Authority, who shall not be a member of the Board, who shall be known as the Executive Director and who shall serve at the pleasure of the Board and carry out such of the powers and duties conferred upon him by the Board. (1995, c. 638, § 2.1-548.31; 2001, c. 844; 2005, c. 900; 2008, c. 787.)

Editor's note. — Acts 2005, c. 900, cl. 2, provides: "That the initial terms of the members of the board of directors appointed pursuant to this act shall be staggered as follows: (i) one member appointed by the Speaker of the House of Delegates and one member appointed by the Senate Committee on Rules to a term of four years, (ii) one member appointed by the Speaker of the House of Delegates and one member appointed by the Senate Committee on Rules to a term of five years, and (iii) two members appointed by the Speaker of the House of Delegates for a term of six years. Thereafter the terms of members shall be six years."

Acts 2008, c. 787, cl. 2, provides: "That the

provisions of this act shall not be construed to affect existing appointments for which the terms have not expired as of July 1, 2008."

The 2008 amendments. — The 2008 amendment by c. 787, in the first paragraph, inserted "and the Chancellor of the Virginia Community College System, all serving ex officio" following "the Secretary of Finance"; substituted "18 members" for "19 members"; substituted "one citizen" for "two citizens" in clause (i); inserted the third sentence; and in the fourth sentence, substituted "12 directors" for "13 directors" and substituted "three for terms" for "four for terms" near the middle.

§ **2.2-2236. Powers and duties of the Executive Director.** — The Executive Director shall employ or retain such agents or employees subordinate to the Executive Director as may be necessary to fulfill the duties of the Authority conferred upon the Executive Director, subject to the Board's approval. Employees of the Authority shall be eligible for membership in the Virginia Retirement System and participation in all of the health and related insurance and other benefits, including premium conversion and flexible benefits, available to state employees as provided by law. The Executive Director shall also exercise such of the powers and duties relating to the direction of the Commonwealth's economic development efforts conferred upon the Authority as may be delegated to him by the Board, including powers and duties involving the exercise of discretion. The Executive Director shall also exercise and perform such other powers and duties as may be lawfully delegated to him or as may be conferred or imposed upon him by law. (1995, c. 638, § 2.1-548.32; 1996, cc. 590, 598; 1998, c. 359; 2001, c. 844.)

§ **2.2-2237. Powers of Authority.** — The Authority is granted all powers necessary or convenient for the carrying out of its statutory purposes, including, but not limited to, the power to:

1. Sue and be sued, implead and be impleaded, complain and defend in all courts;
2. Adopt, use, and alter at will a common seal;
3. Acquire, purchase, hold, use, lease or otherwise dispose of any property, real, personal or mixed, tangible or intangible, or any interest therein necessary or desirable for carrying out the purposes of the Authority, and to lease as lessee, any property, real, personal or mixed, tangible or intangible, or any interest therein, at such annual rental and on such terms and conditions as may be determined by the Board and to lease as lessor to any person, any property, real, personal or mixed, tangible or intangible, or any interest therein, at any time acquired by the Authority, whether wholly or partially completed, at such annual rental and on such terms and conditions as may be determined by the Board and to sell, transfer or convey any property, real, personal or mixed, tangible or intangible, or any interest therein, at any time acquired or held by the Authority on such terms and conditions as may be determined by the Board, provided that the terms of any conveyance or lease of real property shall be subject to the prior written approval of the Governor;
4. Fix, alter, charge and collect rates, rentals, fees, and other charges for the use of property of, the sale of products of, or services rendered by the Authority at rates to be determined by it for the purpose of providing for the payment of the expenses of the Authority;
5. Make and enter into all contracts and agreements necessary or incidental to the performance of its duties, the furtherance of its purposes, and the execution of its powers under this article, including agreements with any person or federal agency;
6. Employ, at its discretion, consultants, researchers, architects, engineers, accountants, financial experts, investment bankers, superintendents, managers and such other employees and agents as may be necessary, and to fix their compensation to be payable from funds made available to the Authority. The Authority may hire employees within and without the Commonwealth and the

United States without regard to whether such employees are citizens of the Commonwealth. Legal services for the Authority shall be provided by the Attorney General in accordance with Chapter 5 (§ 2.2-500 et seq.) of this title;

7. Receive and accept from any federal or private agency, foundation, corporation, association or person, grants or other aid to be expended in accomplishing the objectives of the Authority, and receive and accept from the Commonwealth or any state, and any municipality, county or other political subdivision thereof or from any other source, aid or contributions of either money, property, or other things of value, to be held, used, and applied only for the purposes for which such grants and contributions may be made. All federal moneys accepted under this section shall be accepted and expended by the Authority upon such terms and conditions as are prescribed by the United States and as are consistent with state law; and all state moneys accepted under this section shall be expended by the Authority upon such terms and conditions as are prescribed by the Commonwealth;

8. Render advice and assistance and to provide services to state agencies, local and regional economic development entities, private firms, and other persons providing services or facilities for economic development in Virginia;

9. Develop, undertake, and provide programs, alone or in conjunction with any person, for economic research, industrial development research, and all other research that might lead to improvements in economic development in Virginia;

10. Adopt, alter, and repeal bylaws, rules, and regulations governing the manner in which its business shall be transacted and the manner in which the powers of the Authority shall be exercised and its duties performed; and

11. Do all acts and things necessary or convenient to carry out the powers granted to it by law, and perform any act or carry out any function not inconsistent with state law that may be useful in carrying out the provisions of this article. (1995, c. 638, §§ 2.1-548.33, 2.1-548.34, 2.1-548.35; 2001, c. 844.)

§ **2.2-2238. Economic development services.** — A. It shall be the duty of the Authority to encourage, stimulate, and support the development and expansion of the economy of the Commonwealth. The Authority is charged with the following duties and responsibilities to:

1. See that there are prepared and carried out effective economic development marketing and promotional programs;

2. Make available, in conjunction and cooperation with localities, chambers of commerce, industrial authorities, and other public and private groups, to prospective new businesses basic information and pertinent factors of interest and concern to such businesses;

3. Formulate, promulgate, and advance programs throughout the Commonwealth for encouraging the location of new businesses in the Commonwealth and the retention and growth of existing businesses;

4. Encourage and solicit private sector involvement, support, and funding for economic development in the Commonwealth;

5. Encourage the coordination of the economic development efforts of public institutions, regions, communities, and private industry and collect and maintain data on the development and utilization of economic development capabilities;

6. Establish such offices within and without the Commonwealth that are necessary to the expansion and development of industries and trade;

7. Encourage the export of products and services from the Commonwealth to international markets; and

8. Advise, upon request, the State Board for Community Colleges in designating technical training programs in Virginia's comprehensive community colleges for the Community College Incentive Scholarship Program pursuant to § 23-220.4.

B. The Authority shall prepare a specific plan annually that shall serve as the basis for marketing high unemployment areas of Virginia. This plan shall be submitted to the Governor and General Assembly annually on or before November 1 of each year. The report shall contain the plan and activities conducted by the Authority to market these high unemployment areas. The annual report shall be part of the report required by § 2.2-2242. (1995, c. 638, § 2.1-548.29; 1996, cc. 590, 598; 1997, cc. 437, 448; 1999, c. 542; 2001, cc. 483, 557, 844; 2004, cc. 650, 872.)

Editor's note. — Acts 2001, cc. 483 and 557 amended § 2.1-548.29, from which this section is derived. Pursuant to § 30-152, Acts 2001, cc. 483 and 557 have been given effect in this section as set out above.

Acts 2004, c. 872, which deleted subdivision A 9, in cl. 9 provides: "That the amendments to § 2.2-2238 of the Code of Virginia of this act shall become effective if no specific appropriation has been made to the Virginia Undergraduate Career and Technical Incentive Scholarship Program for fiscal year 2004 or fiscal year 2005." No specific appropriation was made. Subdivision A 9 was repealed effective May 4, 2005.

§ 2.2-2238.1. Special economic development services in rural communities; strategic plan. — A. In order to assist the rural communities of the Commonwealth, the Authority shall develop a program for reviewing existing economic development programs of rural communities, upon request. The program shall include (i) a review and evaluation of existing industrial sites and infrastructure, including existing streets, water and sewer systems, electricity, natural gas and communications facilities that will provide high-speed or broadband Internet access to rural and underserved areas of the Commonwealth; (ii) an assessment of the existing workforce and the provision of information on state and federal programs such as tax incentives that may be available to local or prospective employers to assist in hiring and training in areas of high unemployment; (iii) assistance in identifying community resources and the type of industries that may benefit from locating in a community with such resources; and (iv) marketing assistance to help rural communities improve their visibility to expanding industries looking for new facilities.

B. The Authority, the Center for Rural Virginia, the Virginia Department of Housing and Community Development, the Virginia Resources Authority, the Virginia Department of Business Assistance, the Virginia Tobacco Indemnification and Community Revitalization Commission, the Virginia Employment Commission, the Virginia Tourism Corporation, the Virginia Community College System, institutions of higher education within rural regions of the Commonwealth, and the Department of Agriculture and Consumer Services shall jointly develop and implement a rural economic development strategic plan that at a minimum addresses: (i) education, including pre-kindergarten, primary, secondary and post-graduate resources, and comprehensive workforce development programs, as they may pertain to the Workforce Investment Act; (ii) infrastructure, including capital for water and sewer upgrading, waste management, law enforcement, housing, primary and secondary roads, and telecommunications; (iii) traditional industrial development and industry retention programs, including assistance in financing and in workforce training; (iv) recreational and cultural enhancement and related quality of life measures, including parks, civic centers, and theaters; (v) agribusiness incentives to promote the use of new technologies, and the exploration of new market opportunities; and (vi) a revolving loan fund or loan guarantee program to help start or expand entrepreneurial activities, especially small business activities in rural communities. (2001, c. 531, § 2.1-548.29:1; 2005, cc. 737, 797; 2006, c. 251.)

Editor's note. — Acts 2001, c. 531 enacted § 2.1-548.29:1, from which this section is derived. Pursuant to § 30-152, Acts 2001, c. 531 has been given effect in this section as set out above.

Acts 2005, cc. 737 and 797, in the preface provide: "Whereas, a number of organizations and agencies such as the Rural Economic Analysis Program of Virginia Tech, the Virginia Department of Agriculture and Consumer Services, and selected community colleges have identified rural economic development issues and have begun to address some of the problems facing Virginia's rural communities; and

"Whereas, these organizations should work together to develop a plan with the following goals: (i) create an environment that strengthens and diversifies the agriculture industry by (a) educating the public on the economic benefit of agriculture, manufacturing and advanced technology-based business, (b) developing the necessary infrastructure to support rural Virginia, (c) expanding the worldwide market opportunities for Virginia products and services, and (d) continuing to develop a skilled and productive workforce; and (ii) create rural and urban partnerships to increase the contributions of agriculture, manufactured products and service-based corporations to the state's economy; and

"Whereas, rural Virginia is in need of a comprehensive strategic plan incorporating the goals above and such plan does not currently exist; now, therefore,"

Acts 2005, cc. 737 and 797, cl. 2 provides: "That the Virginia Economic Development Partnership, the Virginia Department of Housing and Community Development, the Virginia Resources Authority, the Virginia Department of Business Assistance, the Virginia Tobacco Indemnification and Community Revitalization Commission, the Virginia Employment Commission, the Virginia Tourism Corporation, the Virginia Community College System, institutions of higher education within rural regions of the Commonwealth, and the Department of Agriculture and Consumer Services shall report their progress in establishing and implementing a rural economic development strategic plan to the House Committee on Agriculture, Chesapeake and Natural Resources and the Senate Committee on Agriculture, Conservation and Natural Resources by November 1 of each year until the strategic plan is fully implemented."

§ 2.2-2239. Planning and research. — It shall also be the duty of the Authority to:

1. Assist in the development of the comprehensive economic development strategy for the Commonwealth, starting the first year of each new gubernatorial administration, consistent with the provisions of Article 3 (§ 2.2-204 et seq.) of Chapter 2 of this title;

2. Report annually to the Governor on the status of the implementation of the comprehensive economic development strategy and recommend legislative and executive actions related to the implementation of the comprehensive economic development strategy; and

3. Conduct such studies and research, in collaboration with state agencies, universities, local and regional industrial authorities and organizations, and other persons within and without the Commonwealth, as the Board deems necessary, to assist in the development of the comprehensive economic strategy and the development of recommendations and advice on the improvement of economic development and related programs and strategies across the Commonwealth. (1995, c. 638, § 2.1-548.30; 2001, c. 844.)

§ 2.2-2240. Nonstock corporation to assist economic development. — The Board may establish nonprofit, nonstock corporations under Chapter 10 (§ 13.1-801 et seq.) of Title 13.1 as public instrumentalities exercising public and essential governmental functions, to assist the Board and the Authority in (i) promoting Virginia's economic development and tourism promotion efforts in the national and international corporate community; (ii) raising money in the corporate and nonprofit community to pay for advertising and promotion of the Commonwealth; (iii) raising nonstate dollars to complement state and local economic development activities; or (iv) conducting or undertaking other activities useful in carrying out the provisions of this article.

The board of directors of any such corporation shall be composed of the Executive Director of the Authority and eight members appointed by the Board of the Authority. However, any such corporation established to promote the tourism industry in the Commonwealth shall be composed of the Executive Director of the Authority, six members appointed by the Board of the Authority, and six members who represent the tourism industry appointed by the Governor. The terms of the members of any corporation established to promote the tourism industry in the Commonwealth appointed by the Governor shall be four years.

The Board shall require any such corporation to report to it at least annually on its activities. (1995, c. 638, § 2.1-548.43; 1996, cc. 590, 598; 2001, c. 844.)

§ 2.2-2240.1. Grants paid to the Authority to promote research, development, and commercialization of products. — A. The General Assembly may appropriate grants to the Authority for use by a nonprofit, public benefit research institute that (i) conducts research and development for government agencies, commercial businesses, foundations, and other organizations and (ii) commercializes technology.

B. The Authority is hereby authorized to create a nonprofit, nonstock corporation to receive such grants and to oversee the administration of the payment of the grants. As a condition to the payment of any grants to the Authority under this section, the General Assembly may require that such nonprofit, nonstock corporation be created.

C. Notwithstanding the provisions of § 2.2-2240, the Board of Directors of the nonprofit, nonstock corporation shall consist of nine voting members as follows: (i) the president of the University of Virginia, or his designee, (ii) the president of Virginia Polytechnic Institute and State University, or his designee, (iii) the president of James Madison University, or his designee, (iv) the president (or the designee of such president) of Virginia Commonwealth University, Christopher Newport University, the University of Mary Washington, Radford University, Virginia State University, Norfolk State University, Old Dominion University, George Mason University, or Longwood University, as appointed by the Governor, with appointments to this position rotated equally among such universities, (v) one citizen member who shall have substantial experience in research and development in the fields of pharmaceuticals, engineering, energy, or similar sciences, appointed by the Governor, (vi) a representative of a nonprofit, public benefit research institute that has entered into a Memorandum of Agreement with the Commonwealth, (vii) the Secretary of Commerce and Trade, or his designee, (viii) the Secretary of Technology, or his designee, and (ix) a representative of a local government that has concluded a Memorandum of Agreement with such research institute. Citizen members appointed by the Governor shall serve for four-year terms, but no citizen member shall serve for more than two full successive terms. A vacancy for a citizen member shall be filled by the Governor for the unexpired term.

D. The Board is authorized to make grant payments only to those nonprofit, public benefit research institutes described in subsection A that have entered into a Memorandum of Agreement (MOA) with the Commonwealth. The MOA shall, at a minimum, (i) require the research institute to perform research, development, and commercialization activities that improve society and facilitate economic growth; (ii) require research to be conducted collaboratively with Virginia public and private institutions and that such collaborative research benefit the capabilities, facilities, and staff of all organizations involved; (iii) require the research institute to develop protocols for the commercialization efforts of the institute, including protocols addressing intellectual property rights; (iv) require the Board to evaluate fulfillment of key milestones for the research institute, which shall include but not be limited to milestones relating to job creation, research institute reinvestment goals, research proposals submissions, and royalties, and to annually evaluate the Commonwealth's investment in the research institute by reporting on the institute's progress in meeting such milestones; and (v) establish relationships and expectations between the research institutes and Virginia colleges and universities, including opportunities for principal investigators to serve as adjunct faculty and the creation of internships for students and postdoctoral appointees.

E. The maximum amount of grants awarded by the Board shall not exceed a total of $22 million per recipient through June 30, 2013.

F. The Board of any nonprofit, nonstock corporation created under this section shall be established in the executive branch of state government. The records of the corporation, its Board members, and employees that are deemed confidential or proprietary shall be exempt from disclosure pursuant to subdivision 3 of § 2.2-3705.6 of the Virginia Freedom of Information Act (§ 2.2-3700 et seq.). (2007, c. 693.)

§ 2.2-2241. Moneys of Authority. — All moneys of the Authority, from whatever source derived, shall be paid to the treasurer of the Authority. Such moneys shall be deposited in the first instance by the treasurer in one or more banks or trust companies, in one or more special accounts. All banks and trust companies are authorized to give such security for such deposits, if required by the Authority. The moneys in such accounts shall be paid out on the warrant or other orders of such persons as the Authority may authorize to execute such warrants or orders. (1995, c. 638, § 2.1-548.39; 2001, c. 844.)

§ 2.2-2242. Forms of accounts and records; audit; annual report. — The accounts and records of the Authority showing the receipt and disbursement of funds from whatever source derived shall be in a form prescribed by the Auditor of Public Accounts. The Auditor of Public Accounts or his legally authorized representatives, shall annually examine the accounts and books of the Authority.

The Authority shall submit an annual report to the Governor and General Assembly on or before November 1 of each year. Such report shall contain the audited annual financial statements of the Authority for the year ending the previous June 30.

The Authority shall submit a detailed annual operational plan and budget to the Secretary of Commerce and Trade and the Director of the Department of Planning and Budget by November 1. Notwithstanding other provisions of this article, the form and content of the operating plan and budget shall be determined by the Director of the Department of Planning and Budget and shall include information on salaries, expenditures, indebtedness and other information as determined by the Director of the Department of Planning and Budget. (1995, c. 638, § 2.1-548.40; 2001, c. 844; 2004, c. 650.)

§ 2.2-2243. Exemptions from taxes or assessments. — The exercise of the powers granted by this article shall be in all respects for the benefit of the people of the Commonwealth, for the increase of their commerce and prosperity, and for the improvement of their living conditions, and as the undertaking of activities in the furtherance of the purposes of the Authority constitutes the performance of essential governmental functions, the Authority shall not be required to pay any taxes or assessments upon any property acquired or used by the Authority under the provisions of this article or upon the income therefrom, including sales and use taxes on the tangible personal property used in the operations of the Authority. The exemption granted in this section shall not be construed to extend to persons conducting on the premises of any property of the Authority businesses for which local or state taxes would otherwise be required. (1995, c. 638, § 2.1-548.41; 2001, c. 844.)

§ 2.2-2244. Exemption of Authority from personnel and procurement procedures. — The provisions of the Virginia Personnel Act (§ 2.2-2900 et seq.) of and the Virginia Public Procurement Act (§ 2.2-4300 et seq.) of this title shall not apply to the Authority in the exercise of any power conferred under this article. (1995, c. 638, § 2.1-548.38; 2001, c. 844.)

§ 2.2-2245. Appropriations by any government. — Any government may make appropriations for the acquisition, construction, improvement, maintenance or operation of any property acquired, constructed, improved, maintained or operated by the Authority. (1995, c. 638, § 2.1-548.36; 2001, c. 844.)

§ 2.2-2246. Conveyance, lease or transfer of property by a city or county to the Authority. — Any city or county within the Commonwealth in order to provide for the construction, reconstruction, improvement, repair or management of any property, or in order to accomplish any of the purposes of this article may, with or without consideration or for a nominal consideration, lease, sell, convey or otherwise transfer to the Authority any real, personal or mixed property located within such city or county. (1995, c. 638, § 2.1-548.37; 2001, c. 844.)

ARTICLE 5.

Virginia Information Providers Network Authority.

§§ 2.2-2247 through 2.2-2259: Repealed by Acts 2003, cc. 981 and 1021.

Editor's note. — For provisions of Acts 2003, cc. 981 and 1021, cls. 4 to 16, reflecting the intent of the General Assembly to provide for the consolidation of the procurement and operational functions of information technology for state agencies in a single agency, and related transitional and other provisions, see the Editor's note at § 2.2-2005.

ARTICLE 6.

Virginia Public Building Authority.

§ 2.2-2260. Short title; definition. — A. This article may be cited as Virginia Public Building Authority Act of 1981.

B. As used in this article, unless the context requires a different meaning:

"Construction" or *"to construct"* means acquisition and construction, all in such manner as may be deemed desirable.

"Cost" means as applied to a project financed under the provisions of this article, the sum total of all costs reasonable and necessary for carrying out all works and undertakings necessary or incident to accomplish a project, including, but not limited to the cost of all necessary developmental, planning and feasibility studies, surveys, plans and specifications, architectural, engineering, financial, legal or other special services, the cost of acquisition of land and any buildings and improvements thereon, including the discharge of any obligations of the vendor of such land, buildings or improvements, site preparation and development including demolition or removal of existing structures, construction, and reconstruction, furnishing of a project, the reasonable cost of financing incurred in the course of the development of a project, carrying charges during construction to the occupancy date, interest

on bonds issued to finance a project to a date subsequent to the estimated date of completion of a project, necessary expenses incurred in connection with the initial occupancy of a project, the cost of reimbursing the Central Capital Planning Fund, established under § 2.2-1520, for payments made for pre-planning or detailed planning of all projects that have been approved for construction by the General Assembly, the funding of such funds and accounts as the Authority determines to be reasonable and necessary and the cost of such other items as the Authority determines to be reasonable and necessary.

"Fixtures" and *"furnishings"* means any fixtures, leasehold improvements, equipment, office furniture and furnishings whatsoever necessary or desirable for the use and occupancy of such project, and the terms "to furnish" and "furnishing" means the acquisition and installation of such fixtures, equipment and furnishings.

"Improvement" or *"to improve"* means extension, enlargement, improvement, and renovation, all in such manner as may be deemed desirable.

"Personal property" means all items of equipment, fixtures, and furnishings, including items affixed to real property.

"Project" means any structure, facility, personal property or undertaking that the Authority is authorized to finance, refinance, construct, improve, furnish, equip, maintain, acquire, or operate under the provisions of this article. (1981, c. 569, §§ 2.1-234.10, 2.1-234.11; 1992, c. 878; 1994, c. 823; 1996, c. 835; 1998, cc. 498, 504; 2000, cc. 67, 279; 2001, c. 844; 2008, Sp. Sess. I, cc. 1, 2.)

Editor's note. — Acts 2008, Sp. Sess. I, cc. 1 and 2, in cl. 21 provide: "That an emergency exists and this act is in force from its passage [May 21, 2008]."

The 2008 amendments. — The 2008 amendments by Sp. Sess. I, cc. 1 and 2, effective May 21, 2008, in subsection B, inserted "the cost of reimbursing the Central Capital Planning Fund, established under § 2.2-1520, for payments made for pre-planning or detailed planning of all projects that have been approved for construction by the General Assembly" near the end of the paragraph defining "Cost."

§ 2.2-2261. Virginia Public Building Authority created; purpose; membership; terms; expenses; staff. — There is created a political subdivision of the Commonwealth to be known as the "Virginia Public Building Authority." The Authority is created for the purpose of constructing, improving, furnishing, maintaining, acquiring, financing, refinancing, and operating public buildings for the use of the Commonwealth (heretofore or hereafter constructed), state arsenals, armories, and military reserves, state institutions of every kind and character (heretofore and hereafter constructed), additions and improvements to land grant colleges, state colleges, universities and medical colleges, and the purchase of lands for rehabilitation purposes in connection with state institutions and for use of state colleges, and museum facilities for a trust instrumentality of the United States, and the purchase of lands for the development of public buildings that may be authorized by the General Assembly in the future, the acquisition of items of personal property for the use of the Commonwealth, the constructing, improving, maintaining, acquiring, financing, and refinancing of major information technology projects as defined in § 2.2-2006, the financing or refinancing of capital projects that benefit the Commonwealth and any of its agencies, authorities, boards, departments, instrumentalities, institutions, or regional or local authorities, and the financing or refinancing of reimbursements to localities or governmental entities of all or any portion of the Commonwealth's share of the costs for capital projects made pursuant to other applicable provisions of Virginia law, and the refinancing of (i) obligations issued by other state and local authorities or political subdivisions of the Commonwealth where such obligations are secured by a lease or other payment agreement with the Commonwealth or (ii) the Commonwealth's obligations under such leases or payment agreements, the purpose and intent of this article being to benefit the people of the Commonwealth by, among other things, increasing their commerce and prosperity.

The Authority shall be comprised of the State Treasurer or his designee, the State Comptroller, and five additional members appointed by the Governor, subject to confirmation by the General Assembly, who shall serve at the pleasure of the Governor. Unconfirmed appointments shall expire 30 days after the convening of the General Assembly. Members of the Authority shall be entitled to no compensation for their services as members, but shall be reimbursed for all reasonable and necessary expenses incurred in the discharge of their duties as provided in § 2.2-2825. The term of each member appointed by the Governor shall be five years.

Vacancies in the membership of the Authority shall be filled by appointment for the unexpired portion of the term. The Governor shall designate one member of the Authority as chairman. The Department of the Treasury shall serve as staff to the Authority. (1981, c. 569, § 2.1-234.12; 1995, c. 841; 1998, cc. 498, 504; 2001, c. 844; 2002, cc. 501, 542; 2003, cc. 981, 1021.)

Editor's note. — For provisions of Acts 2003, cc. 981 and 1021, cls. 4 to 16, reflecting the intent of the General Assembly to provide for the consolidation of the procurement and operational functions of information technology for state agencies in a single agency, and related transitional and other provisions, see the Editor's note at § 2.2-2005.

§ **2.2-2262. Board of directors.** — The powers of the Authority shall be exercised by a governing body consisting of the members of the Authority acting as a board. The Board shall elect from its membership a vice-chairman, treasurer and secretary. The offices of secretary and treasurer may be combined. The Board may elect such other officers who need not be a member of the Board.

Four members shall constitute a quorum of the Board for the purpose of organizing the Authority, conducting its business, and for all other purposes. All actions shall be taken by vote of a majority of the members of the Board, unless Authority bylaws require a larger number.

The Board shall have full authority to manage the properties and business of the Authority, and to prescribe, amend, and repeal bylaws, rules, and regulations governing the manner in which the business of the Authority may be conducted, and the powers granted to it may be exercised. The Board may assign to the Treasury Board or the State Treasurer such powers and duties as it deems proper. (1981, c. 569, § 2.1-234.25; 1993, Sp. Sess., c. 1; 1996, c. 835; 1998, cc. 498, 504; 2001, c. 844.)

§ **2.2-2263. Powers and duties of Authority; limitations.** — A. The Authority is granted all powers necessary or convenient for carrying out its purposes, including, but not limited to, the following powers to:

1. Have perpetual existence as a corporation.
2. Sue and be sued, implead and be impleaded, complain and defend in all courts.
3. Adopt, use, and alter at will a corporate seal.
4. Acquire, purchase, hold and use any property, real, personal or mixed, tangible or intangible, or any interest therein necessary or desirable for carrying out the purposes of the Authority; lease as lessee, with the approval of the Governor, any property, real, personal or mixed, or any interest therein for a term not exceeding 99 years at a nominal rental or at such annual rental as may be determined; with the approval of the Governor, lease as lessor to the Commonwealth and any city, county, town or other political subdivision, or any

agency, department, or public body of the Commonwealth, or land grant college, any project at any time constructed by the Authority and any property, real, personal or mixed, tangible or intangible, or any interest therein, at any time acquired by the Authority, whether wholly or partially completed; with the approval of the Governor, sell, transfer and convey to the Commonwealth, any project at any time constructed by the Authority; and, with the approval of the Governor, sell, transfer and convey any property, real, personal or mixed, tangible or intangible, or any interest therein, at any time acquired by the Authority.

5. Acquire by purchase, lease, or otherwise, and construct, improve, furnish, maintain, repair, and operate projects.

6. Adopt bylaws for the management and regulation of its affairs.

7. Fix, alter, charge, and collect rates, rentals, and other charges for the use of the facilities of, or for the services rendered by, the Authority, or projects thereof, at reasonable rates to be determined by it for the purpose of providing for the payment of the expenses of the Authority, the construction, improvement, repair, furnishing, maintenance, and operation of its facilities and properties, the payment of the principal of and interest on its bonds, and to fulfill the terms and provisions of any agreements made with the purchasers or holders of any such bonds.

8. Borrow money; make and issue bonds of the Authority and such bonds as the Authority may determine to issue for the purpose of refunding obligations previously issued by the Authority; secure the payment of all bonds, or any part thereof, by pledge or deed of trust of all or any of its revenues, rentals, and receipts; make such agreements with the purchasers or holders of such bonds or with others in connection with any such bonds, whether issued or to be issued, as the Authority deems advisable; and in general, provide for the security for the bonds and the rights of holders thereof.

The Authority shall submit an annual report to the Governor and General Assembly on or before November 1 of each year containing, at a minimum, the annual financial statements of the Authority for the year ending the preceding June 30.

9. Make contracts of every name and nature, and to execute all instruments necessary or convenient to carry out its business.

10. Borrow money and accept grants from, and enter into contracts, leases or other transactions with, any federal agency.

11. Have the power of eminent domain.

12. Pledge or otherwise encumber all or any of the revenues or receipts of the Authority as security for all or any of the bonds of the Authority.

13. Do all acts and things necessary or convenient to carry out the powers granted to it by law.

14. Acquire, by assignment from the Commonwealth or the Virginia Retirement System, all contracts, including those that are not completed, which involve constructing, improving, furnishing, maintaining, and operating the structures, facilities, or undertakings similar to those designated herein as projects.

15. Enter into contractual agreements with localities or governmental entities undertaking a capital project that benefits the Commonwealth for which the financing or refinancing of reimbursements of all or any portion of the Commonwealth's share of the costs of such project will be made pursuant to other applicable provisions of Virginia law.

B. The Authority shall not undertake or finance or refinance any projects that are not specifically included in a bill or resolution passed by a majority of those elected to each house of the General Assembly, authorizing such projects or the reimbursement of all or any portion of the Commonwealth's share of the costs of such projects and, as to any project relating to a public institution of higher education in Virginia, not specifically designated by the board of visitors of that institution as a project to be undertaken by the Authority.

C. Except as otherwise provided by law, when projects are to be constructed, improved, furnished, maintained, repaired or operated for the use of any department of the Commonwealth, no plans or specifications therefor shall be presented for quotations or bids until the plans and specifications have been submitted to and approved by the Department of General Services and any other department of the Commonwealth having any jurisdiction over the projects, so that the project will conform to standards established by such departments. (1981, c. 569, § 2.1-234.13; 1984, c. 734; 1985, c. 146; 1987, cc. 11, 616; 1988, cc. 23, 731, 761, 830; 1990, cc. 815, 876; 1991, c. 656; 1992, c. 878; 1993, Sp. Sess., c. 1; 1994, c. 823; 1995, c. 841; 1996, c. 835; 1998, cc. 498, 504; 2000, cc. 67, 279; 2001, c. 844; 2002, cc. 501, 542; 2004, c. 650.)

§ 2.2-2264. Revenue bonds generally. — The Authority may, with the consent of the Governor, provide for the issuance of revenue bonds of the Authority for the purpose of paying all or any part of the cost of any one or more projects or portions thereof. The principal of and the interest on such bonds shall be payable solely from the funds provided in this article for such payment. Any bonds of the Authority issued pursuant to this article shall not constitute a debt of the Commonwealth, or any political subdivision thereof other than the Authority, and shall so state on their face. Neither the members of the Authority nor any person executing the bonds shall be liable personally by reason of the issuance thereof. The bonds of each issue shall be dated, shall bear interest, shall mature at such time not exceeding forty years from their date as determined by the Authority, and may be made redeemable before maturity, at the option of the Authority, at such price and under such terms and conditions as determined by the Authority, prior to the issuance of the bonds. The Authority shall determine the form and the manner of execution of the bonds, including any interest coupons to be attached thereto, and shall fix the denominations of the bonds and the places of payment of principal and interest, which may be at any bank or trust company within or without the Commonwealth. In case any officer whose signature or a facsimile of whose signature appears on any bonds or coupons shall cease to be such officer before the delivery of the bonds, such signature or such facsimile shall nevertheless be valid and sufficient for all purposes as if he had remained in office until such delivery. The bonds may be issued in coupon or in registered form or both, as the Authority may determine, and provision may be made for the registration of any coupon bonds as to principal alone and also as to both principal and interest, for the reconversion into coupon bonds of any bonds registered as to both principal and interest, and for the interchange of registered and coupon bonds. The Authority may sell such bonds in a manner, either at public or private sale, and for such price as it determines will best effect the purposes of this article.

The proceeds of the bonds of each issue shall be used solely for the payment of the cost of the projects for which such bonds shall have been issued, and shall be disbursed in the manner and under the restrictions, if any, the Authority may provide in the resolution authorizing the issuance of such bonds or in the trust agreement securing the bonds. If the proceeds of the bonds of any issue, by error of estimates or otherwise, is less than the cost, additional bonds may be issued to provide the amount of such deficit, and, unless otherwise provided in the resolution authorizing the issuance of the bonds or in the trust agreement securing the bonds, shall be deemed to be entitled to payment from the same fund without preference or priority of the bonds first issued. If the proceeds of the bonds of any issue shall exceed such cost, the surplus shall be deposited to the credit of the sinking fund for such bonds, or may be applied to the payment of the cost of any additional projects.

Prior to the preparation of definitive bonds, the Authority may, under like restrictions issue interim receipts or temporary bonds, with or without coupons, exchangeable for definitive bonds when such bonds shall have been executed and are available for delivery. The Authority may also provide for the replacement of any bonds that shall become mutilated or shall be destroyed or lost. Bonds may be issued under the provisions of this article without obtaining the consent of any department, division, commission, board, bureau or agency of the Commonwealth, and without any other proceedings or the happening of any other conditions or things than those proceedings, conditions or things that are specifically required by this article. (1981, c. 569, § 2.1-234.14; 1998, cc. 498, 504; 2001, c. 844.)

CASE NOTES

Editor's note. — The case below was decided under former Title 2.1 or prior provisions.

Prior legislative authorization of projects does not value separation of powers. — This section, requiring prior authorization by the General Assembly of any project undertaken by the Authority, does not contravene the separation of powers as required by Va. Const., Art. I, § 5, and Art. III, § 1. Baliles v. Mazur, 224 Va. 462, 297 S.E.2d 695 (1982).

§ 2.2-2265. Trust agreement securing bonds. — In the discretion of the Authority any bonds issued under the provisions of this article may be secured by a trust agreement by and between the Authority and a corporate trustee, which may be any trust company or bank having the powers of a trust company within or without the Commonwealth. The trust agreement or the resolution providing for the issuance of the bonds may pledge or assign the revenues to be received, but shall not convey or mortgage any project or any part thereof. The trust agreement or resolution providing for the issuance of such bonds may contain such provisions for protecting and enforcing the rights and remedies of the bondholders as may be reasonable and proper and not in violation of law, including covenants setting forth the duties of the Authority in relation to the acquisition of property and the acquisition, construction, establishment, improvement, extension, enlargement, maintenance, repair, operation and insurance of the project in connection with which the bonds have been authorized, the rates and fees to be charged, the custody, safeguarding and application of all moneys, and conditions or limitations with respect to the issuance of additional bonds. It shall be lawful for any bank or trust company incorporated under the laws of the Commonwealth which may act as depository of the proceeds of bonds or of revenues to furnish the indemnifying bonds or to pledge the securities required by the Authority. Any such trust agreement may set forth the rights of action by bondholders. In addition to the foregoing, any such trust agreement or resolution may contain such other provisions as the Authority deems reasonable and proper for the security of the bondholders. All expenses incurred in carrying out the provisions of a trust agreement or resolution may be treated as a part of the cost of the operation of the project. (1981, c. 569, § 2.1-234.15; 2001, c. 844.)

CASE NOTES

Editor's note. — The case below was decided under former Title 2.1 or prior provisions.

Revenue bonds issued by the Authority are not state debts in violation of Va. Const., Art. X, § 9, because the full faith and credit of the Commonwealth is not pledged or committed to pay said bonds. Baliles v. Mazur, 224 Va. 462, 297 S.E.2d 695 (1982).

§ 2.2-2266. Rents, fees and charges for financing or refinancing, services or use of facilities; use and disposition of revenues. — The

Authority may fix, revise, charge, and collect rates, fees, and other charges for the financing or refinancing of, the use of or for the services and facilities furnished by each project and the different parts thereof, and to contract with any agency, commission, political subdivision or other entity desiring the use of any part thereof, and to fix the terms, conditions, rents, and rates of charges for such use or financing or refinancing. Such rates, fees, and other charges shall be fixed and adjusted so that revenues of the Authority, together with any other available funds, will be sufficient at all times to pay (i) the cost of maintaining, repairing and operating such project and (ii) the principal of and the interest on the related bonds as they become due and payable, and to create reserves for such purposes. Such rates, fees, and other charges shall not be subject to supervision or regulation by any other commission, board, bureau, or agency of the Commonwealth. The revenues derived from the project in connection with which the bonds have been issued, except such part thereof as may be necessary to pay the cost of maintenance, repair and operation and to provide such reserves therefor as may be provided for in the resolution authorizing the issuance of such bonds or in the trust agreement securing the bonds, shall be set aside at such regular intervals as may be provided in the resolution or trust agreement in a sinking fund which is pledged to, and charged with, the payment of the principal of and the interest on such bonds as they become due, and the redemption price or the purchase price of bonds retired by call or purchase as therein provided. Such pledge shall be valid and binding from the time when the pledge is made, the revenues or other moneys so pledged and thereafter received by the Authority shall immediately be subject to the lien of such pledge without any physical delivery thereof or further act, and the lien of any such pledge shall be valid and binding as against all parties having claims of any kind in tort, contract or otherwise against the Authority, irrespective of whether such parties have notice thereof. Neither the resolution nor any trust agreement by which a pledge is created need be filed or recorded except in the records of the Authority. The use and disposition of moneys to the credit of such sinking fund shall be subject to the provisions of the resolution authorizing the issuance of the bonds or of the trust agreement. Except as may otherwise be provided in the resolution or trust agreement, such sinking fund shall be a fund for all such bonds without distinction or priority of one over another. (1981, c. 569, § 2.1-234.16; 1998, cc. 498, 504; 2001, c. 844.)

§ 2.2-2267. Moneys received deemed trust funds. — All moneys received pursuant to the authority of this article, whether as proceeds from the sale of bonds or as revenues, shall be deemed to be trust funds to be held and applied solely as provided in this article. The resolution authorizing the bonds of any issue or the trust agreement securing the bonds shall provide that any officer with whom, or any bank or trust company with which, such moneys are deposited shall act as a trustee of the moneys and shall hold and apply the same for the purposes hereof, subject to the regulations as this article and the resolution or trust agreement may provide. (1981, c. 569, § 2.1-234.17; 2001, c. 844.)

§ 2.2-2268. Proceedings by bondholder or trustee to enforce rights. — Any holder of bonds issued under the provisions of this article or any of the coupons appertaining thereto, and the trustee under any trust agreement, except to the extent the rights herein given may be restricted by the trust agreement or the resolution authorizing the issuance of the bonds, may, either at law or in equity, by suit, action, mandamus or other proceeding, protect and enforce any and all rights under the laws of the Commonwealth or granted hereunder or under the trust agreement or resolution, and may enforce and compel the performance of all duties required by this article or by the trust agreement or resolution to be performed by the Authority or by any officer thereof, including the fixing, charging, and collecting of rates, fees, and other charges. (1981, c. 569, § 2.1-234.18; 2001, c. 844.)

§ **2.2-2269. Bonds made securities for investment and deposit.** — Bonds issued by the Authority under the provisions of this article shall be securities in which all public officers and public bodies of the Commonwealth and its political subdivisions, all insurance companies, trust companies, banking associations, investment companies, executors, administrators, trustees, and other fiduciaries may properly and legally invest funds, including capital in their control or belonging to them. Such bonds shall be securities that may properly and legally be deposited with and received by any state or municipal officer or any agency or political subdivision of the Commonwealth for any purpose for which the deposit of bonds or obligations of the Commonwealth is now or may be authorized by law. (1981, c. 569, § 2.1-234.19; 2001, c. 844.)

§ **2.2-2270. Revenue refunding bonds; bonds for refunding and for cost of additional projects.** — The Authority may provide for the issuance of revenue refunding bonds of the Authority for the purpose of refunding any obligations then outstanding which have been issued under the provisions of this article or by other state and local authorities or political subdivisions of the Commonwealth where such obligations are secured by a lease or other payment agreement with the Commonwealth, including the payment of any redemption premium thereon and any interest accrued or to accrue to the date of redemption of the obligations, and, if deemed advisable by the Authority, for the additional purpose of constructing improvements, extensions, or enlargements of the project in connection with which the obligations to be refunded have been issued. The Authority may provide by resolution for the issuance of its revenue obligations for the combined purpose of (i) refunding any obligations then outstanding that have been issued under the provisions of this article or by other state and local authorities or political subdivisions of the Commonwealth where such obligations are secured by a lease or other payment agreement with the Commonwealth, including the payment of any redemption premium thereon and any interest accrued or to accrue to the date of redemption of such obligations, and (ii) paying all or any part of the cost of any additional project or any portion thereof. The issuance of the bonds, the maturities and other details thereof, the rights of the holders thereof, and the rights, duties and obligations of the Authority shall be governed by the provisions of this article insofar as they may be applicable. (1981, c. 569, § 2.1-234.20; 1998, cc. 498, 504; 2001, c. 844; 2002, cc. 501, 542.)

§ **2.2-2271. Grants or loans of public or private funds.** — The Authority may accept, receive, receipt for, disburse, and expend federal and state moneys and other moneys, public or private, including proceeds of the Authority's bonds, made available by grant or loan or both, to accomplish, in whole or in part, any of the purposes of this article. All federal moneys accepted under this section shall be accepted and expended by the Authority upon such terms and conditions as are prescribed by the United States and as are consistent with state law; and all state moneys accepted under this section shall be accepted and expended by the Authority upon such terms and conditions as are prescribed by the Commonwealth. (1981, c. 569, § 2.1-234.23; 1998, cc. 498, 504; 2001, c. 844.)

§ **2.2-2272. Moneys of Authority; audit.** — All moneys of the Authority, from whatever source derived, shall be paid to the treasurer of the Authority.

Such moneys shall be deposited in the first instance by the treasurer in one or more banks or trust companies, in one or more special accounts, and each of such special accounts shall be continuously secured by a pledge of direct obligations of the United States or of the Commonwealth, having an aggregate market value, exclusive of accrued interest, at all times at least equal to the balance on deposit in such account. Such securities shall either be deposited with the treasurer or be held by a trustee or agent satisfactory to the Authority. All banks and trust companies are authorized to give such security for such deposits. The moneys in such accounts shall be paid out on the warrant or other order of the treasurer of the Authority, or of such other persons as the Authority may authorize to execute such warrants or orders.

The Auditor of Public Accounts or his legally authorized representatives may examine the accounts and books of the Authority, including its receipts, disbursements, contracts, leases, sinking funds, investments, and any other matters relating to its finances, operation and affairs. (1981, c. 569, § 2.1-234.26; 2001, c. 844.)

§ **2.2-2273. Contracts, leases and other arrangements.** — A. In connection with the operation of a facility owned or controlled by the Authority, the Authority may enter into contracts, leases, and other arrangements with any person (i) granting the privilege of using or improving the facility or any portion or facility thereof or space therein consistent with the purposes of this article; (ii) conferring the privilege of supplying goods, commodities, things, services, or facilities at the facility; (iii) making available services to be furnished by the Authority or its agents at the facility; and (iv) providing for the payment therefor.

In each case the Authority may establish the terms and conditions and fix the charges, rentals, or fee for the privilege or service, which shall be reasonable and uniform for the same class of privilege or service at each facility and shall be established with due regard to the property and improvements used and the expenses of operation to the Authority.

B. Except as may be limited by the terms and conditions of any grant, loan or agreement authorized by § 2.2-2271, the Authority may by contract, lease, or other arrangements, upon a consideration fixed by it, grant to any qualified person, for a term not to exceed thirty years, the privilege of operating, as agent of the Authority or otherwise, any facility owned or controlled by the Authority; provided that no person shall be granted any authority to operate a facility other than as a public facility or to enter into any contracts, leases, or other arrangements in connection with the operation of the facility that the Authority might not have undertaken under subsection A.

C. In connection with a project leased to or financed or refinanced for a trust instrumentality of the United States where payments or contributions by the Commonwealth and any political subdivision, together with amounts pursuant to an agreement with such trust instrumentality to pay rent or other amounts, are sufficient to pay the principal of and interest on the Authority's bonds issued to finance or refinance such project, the Authority may agree that such trust instrumentality shall assume all responsibility for the acquisition, construction, operation, maintenance, and repair of the project and may further agree that when the principal of all such bonds of the Authority and the interest thereon have been paid in full or provision made therefor satisfactory to the Authority, the trust instrumentality may acquire the Authority's interest in such project without payment of additional consideration. (1981, c. 569, § 2.1-234.21; 1990, c. 815; 1998, cc. 498, 504; 2001, c. 844.)

§ **2.2-2274. Resolutions, rules and regulations, etc.** — The Authority may adopt, amend, and repeal such reasonable resolutions, rules, regulations, and orders as it deems necessary for the management, government, and use of any facility owned by it or under its control. No rule, regulation, order, or standard prescribed by the Authority shall be inconsistent with, or contrary to, any law of the Commonwealth or act of the Congress of the United States or any regulation adopted or standard established pursuant thereto. The Authority shall keep on file at the principal office of the Authority for public inspection a copy of all its rules and regulations. (1981, c. 569, § 2.1-234.22; 2001, c. 844.)

§ **2.2-2275. Competition in award of contracts; contractors to give surety; terms of contracts.** — If any project or any portion thereof or any improvement thereof shall be constructed, or furnished pursuant to a contract and the estimated cost thereof exceeds $10,000, such contract with the Authority shall be awarded to the lowest responsible bidder after advertisement for bids. The Authority may make rules and regulations for the submission of bids and the construction, furnishing, or improvement of any project or portion thereof to be owned by the Authority, the Commonwealth or any agency, institution, or department thereof. No contract shall be entered into by the Authority for construction, furnishing, or improvement of any project, or portion thereof, or for the purchase of materials, unless the contractor gives an undertaking with a sufficient surety approved by the Authority, and in an amount fixed by the Authority in accordance with § 2.2-4337, for the faithful performance of the contract. Such contract shall be accompanied by an additional bond for the protection of those who furnish labor and material or rental equipment for such amount and subject to the same terms and conditions as established by the Authority in accordance with § 2.2-4337. All construction contracts shall provide, among other things, that the person or corporation entering into such contract with the Authority will pay for all materials furnished, rental equipment used and services rendered for the performance of the contract, and that any person or corporation furnishing such materials, rental equipment or rendering such services may maintain an action to recover for the same against the obligor in the undertaking as though such person or corporation was named therein, provided the action is brought within one year after the time the cause of action accrued. The additional bond shall be conditioned upon the prompt payment of actual equipment rentals and shall not be conditioned upon or guarantee payment of equipment rentals, all or any part of which, directly or indirectly, apply on the purchase price of such equipment under the terms of a bailment lease or conditional sales contract or by any other arrangement by which title to the equipment will be transferred to the contractor and the rentals form any part of the consideration.

Subject to the foregoing, the Authority may, but without intending by this provision to limit any powers of the Authority, enter into and carry out such contracts, or establish or comply with such rules and regulations concerning labor and materials to rental equipment and other related matters in connection with any project, or portion thereof, as the Authority deems desirable. (1981, c. 569, § 2.1-234.27; 1998, cc. 498, 504; 2001, c. 844.)

§ **2.2-2276. Eminent domain; right of entry.** — The Authority is vested with the power of eminent domain and may exercise it for the purposes set forth in this article. If the owner, lessee, or occupier of any property to be condemned or otherwise acquired refuses to remove his property therefrom or give up possession, the Authority may proceed to obtain possession in any manner provided by law. (1981, c. 569, § 2.1-234.28; 2001, c. 844.)

§ **2.2-2277. Jurisdiction of suits against Authority; service of process.** — The Circuit Court of the City of Richmond shall have exclusive jurisdiction of any suit brought in Virginia against the Authority, and process in any such suit shall be served either on the State Treasurer or the chairman of the Authority. (1993, Sp. Sess., c. 1, § 2.1-234.28:1; 2001, c. 844.)

§ 2.2-2278. Exemption from taxes or assessments. — The exercise of the powers granted by this article shall be in all respects for the benefit of the people of the Commonwealth, for the increase of their commerce and prosperity, and for the improvement of their health and living conditions, and as the operation and maintenance of projects by the Authority constitutes the performance of essential governmental functions, the Authority shall not be required to pay any taxes or assessments upon any project or any property acquired or used by the Authority under the provisions of this article or upon the income therefrom, and any bonds issued under the provisions of this article, their transfer and the income therefrom (including any profit made on the sale thereof), shall at all times be free from taxation within the Commonwealth. The exemption granted in this section shall not be construed to extend to persons conducting on the premises of a facility businesses for which local or state taxes would otherwise be required. (1981, c. 569, § 2.1-234.24; 2001, c. 844.)

Article 7.

Virginia Small Business Financing Authority.

§ 2.2-2279. Short title; definitions. — A. This article shall be known and may be cited as the "Virginia Small Business Financing Act."

B. As used in this article, unless the context requires a different meaning:

"Business enterprise" means (i) any industry for the manufacturing, processing, assembling, storing, warehousing, servicing, distributing, or selling of any products of agriculture, mining, or industry or professional services; (ii) commercial enterprises making sales or providing services to industries described in clause (i); (iii) enterprises for research and development, including but not limited to scientific laboratories; (iv) not-for-profit entity operating in the Commonwealth; or (v) such other businesses as will be in furtherance of the public purposes of this article.

"Cost," as applied to the eligible business, means the cost of construction; the cost of acquisition of all lands, structures, rights-of-way, franchises, easements and other property rights and interests; the cost of demolishing, removing, rehabilitating or relocating any buildings or structures on lands acquired, including the cost of acquiring any such lands to which such buildings or structures may be moved, rehabilitated or relocated; the cost of all labor, materials, machinery and equipment, financing charges, letter of credit or other credit enhancement fees, insurance premiums, interest on all bonds prior to and during construction or acquisition and, if deemed advisable by the Authority, for a period not exceeding one year after completion of such construction or acquisition, cost of engineering, financial and legal services, plans, specifications, studies, surveys, estimates of cost and of revenues, commissions, guaranty fees, other expenses necessary or incident to determining the feasibility or practicality of constructing, financing or operating a project of an eligible business; administrative expenses, provisions for working capital, reserves for interest and for extensions, enlargements, additions, improvements and replacements, and such other expenses as may be necessary or incidental to the construction or acquisition of a project of an eligible business or the financing of such construction, acquisition or expansion and the placing of a project of an eligible business in operation. Any obligation or expense incurred by the Commonwealth or any agency thereof, with the

approval of the Authority for studies, surveys, borings, preparation of plans and specifications or other work or materials in connection with the construction or acquisition of a project of an eligible business may be regarded as a part of the cost of a project of an eligible business and may be reimbursed to the Commonwealth or any agency thereof out of the proceeds of the bonds issued therefor.

"Eligible business" means any person engaged in one or more business enterprises in the Commonwealth that satisfies one or more of the following requirements for a for-profit enterprise: (i) has received $10 million or less in annual gross income under generally accepted accounting principles for each of its last three fiscal years or lesser time period if it has been in existence less than three years, (ii) has fewer than 250 employees, (iii) has a net worth of $2 million or less, or (iv) such other satisfactory requirements as the Board shall determine from time to time if it finds and determines such person is in need of its assistance or is a not-for-profit entity granted tax-exempt status under § 501 (c) (3) of the Internal Revenue Code and operating in the Commonwealth.

"Federal Act" means the Small Business Investment Act of 1958, 15 U.S.C. § 661 et seq., as amended from time to time.

"Indenture" means any trust agreement, deed of trust, mortgage or other security agreement under which bonds authorized pursuant to this article shall be issued or secured.

"Lender" means any federal- or state-chartered bank, federal land bank, production credit association, bank for cooperatives, federal- or state-chartered savings institution, building and loan association, small business investment company or any other financial institution qualified within the Commonwealth to originate and service loans, including but not limited to insurance companies, credit unions, investment banking or brokerage companies and mortgage loan companies.

"Loan" means any lease, loan agreement or sales contract as hereinafter defined:

(i) *"Lease"* means any lease containing an option to purchase the project or projects of the eligible business being financed for a nominal sum upon payment in full, or provision thereof, of all bonds issued in connection with the eligible business and all interest thereon and principal of and premium, if any, thereon and all other expenses in connection therewith.

(ii) *"Loan agreement"* means an agreement providing for a loan of proceeds from the sale and issuance of bonds by the Authority or by a lender with which the Authority has contracted to loan such proceeds to one or more contracting parties to be used to pay the cost of one or more projects of an eligible business and providing for the repayment of such loan including but not limited to all interest thereon, and principal of and premium, if any, thereon and all other expenses in connection therewith, by such contracting party or parties and which may provide for such loans to be secured or evidenced by one or more notes, debentures, bonds or other secured or unsecured debt obligations of such contracting party or parties, delivered to the Authority or to a trustee under an indenture pursuant to which the bonds were issued.

(iii) *"Sales contract"* means a contract providing for the sale of one or more projects of an eligible business to one or more contracting parties and includes but is not limited to a contract providing for payment of the purchase price including but not limited to all interest thereon, and principal of and premium, if any, thereon and all other expenses in connection therewith, in one or more installments. If the sales contract permits title to a project being sold to an eligible business to pass to such contracting party or parties prior to payment in full of the entire purchase price, it also shall provide for such contracting party or parties to deliver to the Authority or to the trustee under the indenture pursuant to which the bonds were issued, one or more notes, debentures, bonds or other secured or unsecured debt obligations of such contracting party or parties providing for timely payments of the purchase price thereof.

"Municipality" means any county or incorporated city or town in the Commonwealth.

"Preferred lender" means a bank that is subject to continuing supervision and examination by state or federal chartering, licensing, or similar regulatory authority satisfactory to the Authority and that meets the eligibility requirements established by the Authority.

"Revenue Code" means the Internal Revenue Code of 1954, as amended.

"Revenues" means any and all fees, rates, rentals, profits and receipts collected by, payable to, or otherwise derived by, the Authority, and all other moneys and income of whatsoever kind or character collected by, payable to, or otherwise derived by, the Authority in connection with loans to any eligible business in furtherance of the purposes of this article.

"Statewide Development Company" means the corporation chartered under this article for purposes of qualification as a state development company as such term is defined in the Federal Act. (1984, c. 749, §§ 9-197, 9-199; 1996, c. 77; 2001, c. 844; 2003, c. 339; 2008, c. 744.)

The 2008 amendments. — The 2008 amendment by c. 744 inserted the definition of "Preferred lender."

§ 2.2-2280. Declaration of public purpose; Authority created. — A. The General Assembly finds and determines that (i) there exists in the Commonwealth a need to assist small business in the Commonwealth in obtaining financing for new business or in the expansion of existing business in order to promote and develop industrial development and to further the long-term economic development of the Commonwealth through the improvement of its tax base and the promotion of employment and (ii) it is necessary to create a governmental body to provide financial assistance to small business in the Commonwealth by providing loans, guarantees, insurance and other assistance to small business, thereby encouraging the investment of private capital in small business in the Commonwealth. The creation of this governmental body to assist in such matters is essential to the industrial development of the Commonwealth. In making these determinations, the General Assembly has considered and affirmatively expresses its policy to assist small businesses in Virginia, acknowledging that this determination has and will affect competition.

It is further declared that all of the foregoing are public purposes and that the activities of the Authority will serve a public purpose in that they will promote industry, develop trade and increase employment opportunities for the benefit of the inhabitants of the Commonwealth, either through the increase of commerce or through the promotion of safety, health, welfare, convenience or prosperity; and that the necessity of enacting the provisions herein set forth is in the public interest and is so declared as a matter of express legislative determination.

B. The Virginia Small Business Financing Authority is created, with such powers and duties as are set forth in this article, as a public body corporate and as a political subdivision of the Commonwealth. All powers, rights and duties conferred by this article or other provisions of law upon the Authority shall be exercised by the Board. (1984, c. 749, § 9-201; 2001, c. 844.)

§ 2.2-2281. Construction of article. — Nothing contained in this article shall be construed as a restriction or limitation upon any powers that the

Authority might otherwise have under any other law of the Commonwealth, and this article supersedes all other laws in conflict herewith and is cumulative to such powers. Insofar as the provisions of this article are inconsistent with the provisions of any other law, the provisions of this article shall be controlling and the powers conferred by this article shall be regarded as supplemental and additional to powers conferred by any other laws. No proceedings, notice or approval shall be required for the issuance of any bonds or any instrument or the security therefor, except as provided in this article.

The provisions of this article shall be liberally construed to accomplish the purposes of this article. (1984, c. 749, § 9-200; 2001, c. 844.)

§ 2.2-2282. Board of directors; membership; terms, compensation and expenses; chairman, vice-chairman, secretary and treasurer; quorum; staff. — A. The Board shall consist of the State Treasurer or his designee, the Director of the Department of Business Assistance, and nine members who are not employees of the Commonwealth or of any political subdivision thereof who shall be appointed by the Governor and who shall have such small business experience as he deems necessary or desirable. The appointment of members of the Board by the Governor shall be subject to confirmation by the General Assembly. All members of the Board shall be residents of the Commonwealth and shall have full voting privileges. Appointments shall be for terms of four years, except that appointments to fill vacancies shall be made for the unexpired terms. No member appointed by the Governor shall serve more than two complete terms in succession. The members of the Board shall receive no salaries but shall be paid travel and other expenses incurred to attend meetings or while otherwise engaged in the discharge of their duties, all as may be deemed appropriate by the Board.

B. The Governor shall appoint one member as chairman. Five members of the Board shall constitute a quorum for the transaction of all business of the Authority. The Board shall elect one member from the group of nine members appointed by the Governor as vice-chairman who shall exercise the powers of the chairman in the absence of the chairman. The Board shall elect a secretary and a treasurer, or a secretary-treasurer, who need not be members of the Board and who shall continue to hold such office until their respective successors are elected. The Department of Business Assistance of the Commonwealth shall serve as staff to the Authority. (1984, c. 749, § 9-202; 1987, c. 688; 1991, c. 190; 1996, cc. 589, 599; 2001, c. 844; 2004, c. 239.)

§ 2.2-2283. Meetings of the Board. — Board meetings shall be held at the call of the chairman or whenever any four members so request. In any event, the Board shall meet as necessary to attend to the business of the Authority. (1984, c. 749, § 9-203; 1990, c. 387; 2001, c. 844.)

§ 2.2-2284. Executive Director; appointment; duties. — The Director of the Department of Business Assistance shall appoint the Executive Director of the Authority. The Executive Director shall administer, manage and direct the affairs and activities of the Authority in accordance with the policies and under the control and the direction of the Board and the Director of the Department of Business Assistance. Except as otherwise stated in this article, the Executive Director shall approve all accounts for allowable expenses for the Authority or of any employee or consultant or other person providing services to the Board, and for expenses incidental to the operation of the Authority subject to approval of the Director of the Department of Business Assistance. The Executive Director shall maintain and be custodian of all books, documents and papers of or filed with the Authority, including but not limited to the minute book or journal of the Authority, and of its official seal.

The Executive Director may cause copies to be made of all minutes and other records and documents of the Authority and may in the place and stead of the Secretary of the Authority give certificates under seal of the Authority to the effect that such copies are true copies, and all persons dealing with the Authority may rely on such certificates. The Executive Director also shall perform such other duties as prescribed by the Board in carrying out the purposes of this article. (1984, c. 749, § 9-204; 1990, c. 387; 1996, cc. 589, 599; 2001, c. 844.)

§ **2.2-2285. Powers of the Authority.** — The Authority is granted all powers necessary or appropriate to carry out and effectuate its purposes including, but not limited to, the following powers to:

1. Have perpetual existence as a public body corporate and as a political subdivision of the Commonwealth;
2. Adopt, amend, and repeal bylaws, rules and regulations not inconsistent with this article, to regulate its affairs and to carry into effect the powers and the purposes of the Authority and for the conduct of its business;
3. Sue and be sued in its name including but not limited to bringing actions pursuant to Article 6 (§ 15.2-2650 et seq.) of Chapter 26 of Title 15.2 to determine the validity of any issuance or proposed issuance of its bonds under this article and the legality and validity of all proceedings previously taken or proposed in a resolution of the Authority to be taken for the authorization, issuance, sale and delivery of such bonds and for the payment of the principal thereof and interest thereon;
4. Have an official seal and alter it at will;
5. Maintain an office at such place within the Commonwealth as it may designate;
6. Make and execute contracts and all other instruments necessary and convenient for the performance of its duties and the exercise of its powers under this article upon such terms and conditions it deems appropriate;
7. Employ office personnel, advisers, consultants, professionals and agents as may be necessary in its judgment, and to fix their compensation;
8. Procure insurance against any loss in connection with its property and other assets, including but not limited to loans in such amounts and from such insurers as it deems advisable;
9. Borrow money and issue bonds as provided by this article;
10. Procure insurance or guarantees from any public or private entities, including any department, agency or instrumentality of the United States of America, or, subject to the provisions of and to the extent moneys are available in the fund created by § 2.2-2290, insure or guarantee the payment of any bonds issued by the Authority, including the power to pay premiums on any such insurance or guarantees or other instruments of indebtedness;
11. Receive and accept from any source aid or contributions of money, property, labor or other things of value to be held, used and applied to carry out the purposes of this article (subject, however, to any conditions upon which grants or contributions are made) including, but not limited to gifts or grants from any department, agency or instrumentality of the United States;
12. Enter into agreements with any department, agency or instrumentality of the United States or of the Commonwealth and with lenders and enter into loans with contracting parties for the purpose of planning, regulating and providing for the financing or assisting in the financing of any eligible business or any project thereof;
13. Enter into contracts or agreements with lenders for the servicing and/or processing of loans;
14. Provide technical assistance to local industrial development authorities and to profit and nonprofit entities in the development or operation by, or

assistance to, persons engaged in small business enterprises and distribute data and information concerning the encouragement and improvement of small business enterprises in the Commonwealth;

15. To the extent permitted in the proceedings pursuant to which the bonds of the Authority are issued, consent to any modification with respect to the rate of interest, time for, and payment of, any installment of principal or interest, or any other term of any contract, loan, sales contract, lease, indenture or agreement of any kind to which the Authority is a party;

16. To the extent permitted in the proceedings pursuant to which the bonds of the Authority are issued, enter into contracts with any lender containing provisions authorizing the lender to reduce the charges or fees, exclusive of loan payments, to persons unable to pay the regular schedule thereof when, by reason of other income or payment by any department, agency or instrumentality of the United States or the Commonwealth, the reduction can be made without jeopardizing the economic stability of the eligible business being financed;

17. Allocate any of its property to the insurance or guarantee fund established by § 2.2-2290 or to any other fund of the Authority, such property consisting of:

a. Moneys appropriated by the Commonwealth;

b. Premiums, fees and any other amounts received by the Authority with respect to financial assistance provided by the Authority;

c. Proceeds as designated by the Authority from the loan or other disposition of property held or acquired by the Authority;

d. Income from investments that were made by the Authority or on the behalf of the Authority from moneys in one or more of its funds; or

e. Any other moneys made available to the Authority consistent with this article;

18. Use any fund of the Authority for any and all expenses to be paid by the Authority including, but not limited to: (i) any and all expenses for administrative, legal, actuarial, and other services; (ii) all costs, charges, fees and expenses of the Authority relating to the authorizing, preparing, printing, selling, issuing, and insuring of bonds and the funding of reserves; and (iii) all expenses and costs relating to the guaranteeing, insuring or procurement of guarantees, insurance or other instruments providing credit or the enhancement of credit for the bonds;

19. Collect fees and charges the Authority determines to be reasonable in connection with its loans, insurance, guarantees, commitments and servicing thereof;

20. Sell, at public or private sale, with or without public bidding, any obligation held by the Authority;

21. Invest any funds not needed for immediate disbursement, including any funds held in reserve, in any obligations or securities that may be legally purchased by political subdivisions in the Commonwealth or as may be otherwise permitted by § 2.2-2305;

22. Administer the Private Activity Bonds program in Chapter 50 (§ 15.2-5000 et seq.) of Title 15.2 jointly with the Director of the Department of Housing and Community Development and the Virginia Housing Development Authority;

23. Create and establish such funds and accounts as may be necessary or desirable for its purposes;

24. Enter into agreements the purpose of which is to authorize lenders that have been designated as preferred lenders to undertake loan decisioning and processing functions and responsibilities with respect to certain Authority guaranteed loans without obtaining prior Authority approval. Under such agreements, the Authority will provide each preferred lender credit authority

equal to an amount determined by the Authority, or an amount equal to the funds available for such guarantees, whichever is less, for the period designated in the allocation. The preferred lender's allocation of credit authority shall be increased only by written permission of the Authority and shall not be restored automatically by the receipt of payments on Authority loans; and

25. Take any action necessary or convenient for the exercise of the powers granted by this article or reasonably implied from them. (1984, c. 749, §§ 9-205, 9-228; 1995, c. 128; 2001, c. 844; 2003, c. 339; 2005, c. 624; 2008, cc. 445, 744.)

The 2008 amendments. — The 2008 amendment by c. 445 added "jointly with the Director of the Department of Housing and Community Development and the Virginia Housing Development Authority" to the end of subdivision 22.

The 2008 amendment by c. 744 inserted subdivision 24, redesignated former subdivision 24 as subdivision 25 and made a related change.

§ **2.2-2286. Power to condemn.** — The Authority may condemn property in furtherance of its purposes; provided, that any such condemnation shall be approved by the governing body of the municipality having jurisdiction over the property so condemned. Any property condemned by the Authority shall not be sold or leased by the Authority unless the Authority, preceding the consummation of any such sale or lease, finds and determines that such sale or lease is in furtherance of, or incidental to, the main purposes of the Authority under this article or that such property is no longer needed in furtherance of, or incidental to, such purposes. Any exercise of the power to condemn as authorized by this section shall be in accordance with the provisions of Chapter 2 (§ 25.1-200 et seq.) of Title 25.1. (1984, c. 749, § 9-206; 2001, c. 844; 2003, c. 940.)

§ **2.2-2287. Power to borrow money and issue bonds.** — The Authority may borrow money and issue bonds to pay the cost of the projects for which the bonds have been issued, including but not limited to the power to issue bonds to renew or to pay bonds, including the interest thereon. Whenever it deems refunding expedient it may refund any bonds by the issuance of new bonds, whether the bonds to be refunded have or have not matured, and to issue bonds partly to refund outstanding bonds. Refunding bonds may be sold and the proceeds applied to the purchase, redemption or payment of the bonds to be refunded, or exchanged for the bonds to be refunded. The Authority may undertake the financing of the cost of a project for an eligible business from the proceeds of its bonds by one or more of the following methods: (i) entering into a lease for the facilities of the eligible business being financed; (ii) selling such facilities to the eligible business under a sales contract; (iii) lending the proceeds of the sale of the bonds under a loan agreement with the eligible business; (iv) entering into a loans to lenders transaction in the manner described in § 2.2-2293; or (v) entering into such other transactions as the Board deems appropriate to accomplish the purposes of this article. (1984, c. 749, § 9-207; 2001, c. 844; 2003, c. 339.)

§ **2.2-2288. Power to issue bonds to purchase ninety percent guaranteed portion of loans.** — In addition to and not as a limitation upon the powers to issue bonds as elsewhere expressed in this article, the Authority may, with proceeds of an issue of its bonds, participate with lenders in making or purchasing small business loans, not exceeding as to any one such loan one million dollars in principal amount, to be serviced by such lenders, provided that:

1. The Authority's share shall not exceed ninety percent of the total principal amount of any such loan, and such participation shall be payable with interest at the same times, but not necessarily at the same interest rate, as the share of the lender, and both shares shall be equally and ratably secured by a valid mortgage on, or security interest in, real or personal property or by any other security satisfactory to the Authority to secure payment of the loan; however, the Authority's share of any such loan may equal 100 percent of the total principal amount of the small business loan if the lender participating in the making or purchasing of such small business loan by servicing the loan, purchases 100 percent of the total amount of the bonds issued by the Authority in connection with or allocable to such small business loan;

2. The total principal amount of the Authority's share shall not exceed ninety percent of the value of the property securing the small business loan, unless the amount in excess of ninety percent is:

a. Loaned from available funds that are not proceeds received directly from the sale of the Authority's bonds and are not restricted under the terms of the resolution authorizing, or the indenture securing such bonds, or

b. Insured or guaranteed by a federal agency or by a private insurer qualified to write such insurance in the Commonwealth, insuring a percentage of any claim for loss at least equal to that percentage of the value by which the small business loan exceeds ninety percent thereof;

3. The value of the property securing the small business loan is certified by the participating lender, on the basis of such appraisals, bids, purchase orders, and engineers' certificates as the Authority may require; provided that the value of items purchased and constructed from the proceeds of the small business loan shall not be deemed, for purposes of this section, to exceed the contract price in respect of purchase or construction;

4. The Authority shall not disburse funds under a commitment to participate in a small business loan for the construction or substantial improvement of property until the construction or improvement has been completed, unless a lender furnishes an irrevocable letter of credit or a qualified corporate surety furnishes payment and performance bonds, in either event satisfactory to the Authority and in an aggregate amount equal to the cost of such construction or improvement;

5. No other indebtedness may be secured by a mortgage on, or security interest in, property securing a small business loan made or purchased pursuant to this subdivision without the prior express written authorization of the Authority; and

6. The participating lender agrees to use the proceeds of the small business loan to lend to eligible small businesses in the Commonwealth. (1984, c. 749, § 9-209; 2001, c. 844.)

§ **2.2-2289. Power to issue umbrella bonds.** — In addition to the powers of the Authority to issue bonds, it may issue bonds, the proceeds of which, after payment of the costs of issuance thereof, shall be used to make loans, no single loan to be in excess of ten million dollars in aggregate principal amount, to finance or refinance the projects of eligible small businesses. The Authority shall adopt such rules and regulations as are necessary to carry out the purposes of this section and to provide procedures for the making of such loans and the repayment thereof. (1984, c. 749, § 9-210; 1986, c. 297; 2001, c. 844.)

§ **2.2-2290. Insurance or guarantee fund.** — There is created an insurance or guarantee fund of the Authority that may be used for any of the following purposes:

1. To insure the payment or repayment of all or any part of the principal of, redemption or prepayment premiums or penalties on, and interest on its bonds;

2. To insure the payment or repayment of all or any part of the principal of, redemption or prepayment premiums or penalties on, and interest on any instrument executed, obtained or delivered in connection with the issuance and sale of its bonds; and

3. To pay or insure the payment of any fees or premiums necessary to obtain insurance, guarantees, or other instruments or enhancement of credit for or support from any person in connection with financing assistance provided by the Authority under this article including but not limited to working capital loans made by a lender, a preferred lender, or both. (1984, c. 749, § 9-211; 2001, c. 844; 2008, c. 744.)

The 2008 amendments. — The 2008 amendment by c. 744 added "a preferred lender, or both" to the end of subdivision 3.

§ 2.2-2291. Security for bonds; fees and expenses; limitations. — A. The bonds or instruments with respect to which financial assistance is provided by the Authority shall be secured or unsecured in a manner approved by the Board in its sole discretion.

B. The Board may set the premiums and fees to be paid to it for providing financial assistance under this article. The premiums and fees and expenses set by the Board shall be payable in the amounts, at the time and in the manner that the Board, in its discretion, requires. The premiums and fees need not be uniform among transactions and may vary in amount among transactions and at different stages during the terms of the transactions.

C. No portion of the proceeds of an issue of the Authority's bonds that are exempt under federal taxation as industrial development bonds under Section 103 (b) of the Revenue Code shall be used to provide facilities prohibited in Section 103 (b) (6) (O) of such Revenue Code. (1984, c. 749, §§ 9-212, 9-213, 9-215; 2001, c. 844.)

Editor's note. — The reference to "Section 103 (b) (6) (O)" refers to 26 U.S.C. § 103. Later amendment to that section deleted former subdivision (b) (6) (O), however.

§ 2.2-2292. Public hearing and approval. — Whenever federal law requires public hearings and public approval as a prerequisite to obtaining federal tax exemption for the interest paid on industrial development bonds under Section 103 of the Revenue Code, unless otherwise specified by federal law or regulation, the public hearing for industrial development bonds of the Authority shall be conducted by the Authority and the procedure for the public hearing and public approvals shall be as follows:

1. For a public hearing by the Authority:

a. Notice of the hearing shall be published once a week for two successive weeks in a newspaper published or having general circulation in the municipality in which the facility to be financed is to be located of intention to provide financing for a named applicant. The applicant shall pay the cost of notification. The notice shall also be mailed or otherwise delivered to the clerk of the local governing body of the municipality. The notice shall specify the time and place of hearing at which persons may appear and present their views. The hearing shall be held not less than six days nor more than 21 days after the second notice shall appear in such newspaper. The hearing may be held at any place within the Commonwealth determined by the Board.

b. The notice shall contain (i) the name and address of the Authority; (ii) the name and address of the principal place of business, if any, of the applicant seeking financing; (iii) the maximum dollar amount of financing sought; and (iv) the type of business and purpose and specific location, if known, of the facility to be financed.

c. Every request for industrial development bond financing when submitted to the Authority shall be accompanied by a statement in the following form:

Name of Applicant: ....

Facility: ....

Date: ....

Maximum amount of financing sought: $ ....

Estimated taxable value of the facility's real property in the municipality in which it is located. $ ....

Estimated taxable value of the facility's real property once constructed or expanded. $ ....

Estimated real property tax per year using present tax rates on the facility's real property once constructed or expanded. $ ....

Estimated personal property tax per year from property to be located in expanded or constructed facility using present tax rate. $ ....

Estimated merchants' capital tax per year from property to be located in expanded or constructed facility using present tax rate. $ ....

Estimated dollar value per year of goods and services that will be purchased in the Commonwealth during construction or expansion of facility. $ ....

Estimated dollar value per year of goods and services that will be purchased in the Commonwealth for the operation of the facility. $ ....

Estimated dollar value per year of goods and services that will be produced and sold from the facility. $ ....

Estimated number of employees during construction or expansion ....

Estimated number of regular employees on a year round basis during operation of the facility ....

Average annual salary per regular employee during operation of the facility. $ ....

Estimated payroll for labor during construction or expansion of the facility. $ ....

If any of the above questions do not apply to the eligible business being financed, indicate by writing N/A (not applicable) on the appropriate line.

2. For public approval, the Governor is appointed by this article as the applicable elected representative within the meaning of Section 103 (k) of the Revenue Code. (1984, c. 749, § 9-216; 2001, c. 844; 2003, c. 339.)

§ **2.2-2293. Loans to lenders; conditions.** — The Authority may make, and undertake commitments to make, loans to lenders under terms and conditions requiring the proceeds thereof to be used by the lenders to make loans to eligible small businesses. Loan commitments or actual loans may be originated through and serviced by any such lender. As a condition to a lender's participating in the loan, the lender shall agree to use the proceeds of the loan within a reasonable period of time to make loans or purchase loans to provide to eligible small businesses, or finance the projects of eligible small businesses, in the Commonwealth or, if the lender has made a commitment to make loans to eligible small businesses on the basis of a commitment from the Authority to purchase the loans, the lender shall make the loans within a reasonable period of time. (1984, c. 749, § 9-217; 2001, c. 844.)

§ **2.2-2294. Investment in, purchase or assignment of loans; conditions.** — The Authority may invest in, purchase or make commitments to invest in or purchase, and take assignments or make commitments to take assignments, of loans made by lenders for the acquisition, construction, rehabilitation, expansion or purchase of a project for eligible business. (1984, c. 749, § 9-218; 2001, c. 844; 2003, c. 339.)

§ **2.2-2295. Regulations of the Authority.** — Prior to carrying out the powers granted under §§ 2.2-2293 and 2.2-2294, the Authority shall adopt rules and regulations governing its activities including but not limited to rules and regulations relating to the following:

1. Procedures for the submission of requests or invitations and proposals for making loans to lenders and the investment in, purchase, assignment and sale of loans;

2. The reinvestment by a lender of the proceeds, or an equivalent amount, from any loan to a lender in loans to provide financing for eligible business in the Commonwealth;

3. Assurances that the eligible business to be financed will improve employment conditions or otherwise improve industrial development in the Commonwealth;

4. Rates, fees, charges, and other terms and conditions for originating or servicing loans in order to protect against realization of an excessive financial return or benefit by the originator or servicer;

5. The type and amount of collateral or security to be provided to assure repayment of loans to lenders made by the Authority;

6. The type of collateral, payment bonds, performance bonds or other security to be provided for any loans made by a lender for construction loans;

7. The nature and amount of fees to be charged by the Authority to provide for expenses and reserves of the Authority;

8. Standards and requirements for the allocation of available money among lenders and the determination of the maturities, terms, conditions and interest rates for loans made, purchased, sold, assigned or committed pursuant hereto;

9. Commitment requirements for financing by lenders involving money provided, directly or indirectly, by the Authority; or

10. Any other appropriate matters related to the duties or exercise of the Authority's powers. (1984, c. 749, § 9-219; 2001, c. 844; 2003, c. 339.)

§ **2.2-2296. How bonds paid and secured.** — Except as may otherwise be expressly provided by the Authority in proceedings relating to a particular issue of bonds, every issue of its bonds shall be payable solely out of any revenues of the Authority. The bonds additionally may be secured by a pledge of any grant, contribution or guarantee from the federal government or any person or a pledge by the Authority of any revenues from any source. (1984, c. 749, § 9-220; 2001, c. 844.)

§ **2.2-2297. Liability of Commonwealth, political subdivisions and members of Board.** — No bonds issued or loans or loan guarantees made by the Authority under this article shall constitute a debt, liability or general obligation of the Commonwealth or any political subdivision thereof (other than the Authority), or a pledge of the faith and credit of the Commonwealth or any political subdivision thereof (other than the Authority), but shall be payable solely as provided by the Authority. No member or officer of the Board nor any person executing the bonds, loans, or loan guarantees shall be liable personally on the bonds, loans, or loan guarantees by reason of the issuance thereof. Each bond issued or loan or loan guarantee made under this article shall contain on the face thereof a statement that neither the Commonwealth, nor any other political subdivision thereof, shall be obligated to pay the same or the interest thereon or other costs incident thereto except from the revenue or money pledged by the Authority and that neither the faith and credit nor the taxing power of the Commonwealth or any political subdivision thereof is pledged to the payment of the principal of, or the interest on, such bond, loan, or loan guarantee. (1984, c. 749, § 9-221; 1997, c. 815; 2001, c. 844.)

§ **2.2-2298. Authorization of bonds by resolution; contents of bond sale; manner.** — The bonds shall be authorized by a resolution of the Board, shall bear such date or dates, and shall mature at such time as such resolution may provide, except that no bond shall mature more than fifty years from the date of issue. The bonds shall (i) bear interest at such rates, including variations of such rates; (ii) be in such denominations; (iii) be in such form; (iv) carry such registration privileges; (v) be executed in such manner; (vi) be payable in such medium of payment, at such place; and (vii) be subject to such terms of redemption, including redemption prior to maturity, as the resolution may provide. Except as expressly provided otherwise in this article, the provisions of other laws of the Commonwealth relating to the issuance of revenue bonds shall not apply to bonds issued by the Authority. Bonds of the Authority may be sold by the Authority at public or private sale and at such price as the Authority determines. (1984, c. 749, § 9-222; 2001, c. 844.)

§ **2.2-2299. Resolution authorizing issuance of bonds; provisions.** — Any resolution authorizing the issuance of bonds may contain provisions for:

1. Pledging all or any part of the revenues of the Authority to secure the payment of the bonds, subject to the terms of the proceedings relating to other bonds of the Authority as may then exist;
2. Pledging all or any part of the assets of the Authority, including loans and obligations securing the same, to secure the payment of the bonds, subject to the terms of the proceedings relating to other bonds of the Authority as may then exist;
3. The use and disposition of the gross income from loans owned by the Authority and payment of the principal of loans owned by the Authority;
4. The setting aside of reserves or sinking funds and the regulations and disposition thereof;
5. Limitations on the purposes to which the proceeds from the sale of bonds may be applied and pledging the proceeds to secure the payment of the bonds;
6. Limitations on the issuance of additional bonds, the terms upon which additional bonds may be issued and secured, and the refunding of outstanding or other bonds;
7. The procedure, if any, by which the terms of any of the proceedings under which the bonds are being issued may be amended or abrogated, the number or percentage of bondholders who or which must consent thereto, and the manner in which the consent may be given;
8. The vesting in a trustee of such property, rights, powers and duties in trust as the Authority may determine, and limiting or abrogating the right of bondholders to appoint a trustee or limiting the rights, powers and duties of the trustee;
9. Defining the act or omissions to act that shall constitute a default and the obligations or duties of the Authority to the holders of the bonds, and providing for the rights and remedies of the holders of the bonds in the event of default, which rights and remedies may include the general laws of the Commonwealth and other provisions of this article; or
10. Any other matter, of like or different character, which in any way affects the security or protection of the holders of the bonds. (1984, c. 749, § 9-223; 2001, c. 844.)

§ **2.2-2300. Pledge by Authority.** — Any pledge made by the Authority shall be valid and binding from the time when the pledge was made. The revenues or properties so pledged and thereafter received by the Authority shall immediately be subject to the lien of such pledge without any physical delivery thereof or further act, and the lien of any such pledge shall be valid and binding as against all parties having claims of any kind in tort, contract or otherwise against the Authority, irrespective of whether the parties have notice thereof. Neither the resolution nor any other instrument by which a pledge is created need be recorded. (1984, c. 749, § 9-224; 2001, c. 844.)

§ 2.2-2301. Purchase of bonds of Authority. — The Authority, subject to the provisions in proceedings relating to outstanding bonds as may then exist, may purchase bonds out of any funds available therefor, which shall thereupon be cancelled, at any reasonable price which, if the bonds are then redeemable, shall not exceed the redemption price (and premium, if any) then applicable plus accrued interest to the redemption date thereof. (1984, c. 749, § 9-225; 2001, c. 844.)

§ 2.2-2302. Bonds secured by indenture; contents; expenses; how treated. — The bonds may be secured by an indenture by and between the Authority and a corporate trustee that may be any bank or other corporation having the power of a trust company or any trust company within or without the Commonwealth. The indenture may contain such provisions for protecting and enforcing the rights and remedies of the bondholders as may be reasonable and proper and not in violation of law, including covenants setting forth the duties of the Authority in relation to the exercise of its powers and the custody, safekeeping and application of all money. The Authority may provide by the indenture for the payment of the proceeds of the bonds and revenues to the trustee under the indenture or other depository, and for the method of disbursement thereof, with such safeguards and restrictions as the Authority may determine. If the bonds are secured by an indenture, the bondholders shall have no authority to appoint a separate trustee to represent them. (1984, c. 749, § 9-226; 2001, c. 844.)

§ 2.2-2303. Signatures of prior members or officers; validity. — In the event that any of the members or officers of the Board cease to be members or officers of the Board prior to the delivery of any bonds signed by them, their signatures or facsimiles thereof shall nevertheless be valid and sufficient for all purposes as if they had remained in office until such delivery. (1984, c. 749, § 9-227; 2001, c. 844.)

§ 2.2-2304. Deposit of money; expenditures; security for deposits. — All money of the Authority, except as otherwise authorized in this article, shall be deposited as soon as practicable in a separate account in banks or trust companies organized under the laws of the Commonwealth or in national banking associations doing business in the Commonwealth. The money in such accounts shall be paid by checks signed by the Executive Director or other officer or employees of the Authority as the Authority shall authorize. All deposits of money shall, if required by the Authority, be secured in such manner as the Authority determines to be prudent, and all banks or trust companies are authorized to give security for the deposits. (1984, c. 749, § 9-229; 2001, c. 844.)

§ 2.2-2305. Contracts with holders of bonds; how money secured. — Notwithstanding the provisions of § 2.2-2304, the Authority may contract with the holders of any of its bonds as to the custody, collection, securing, investment and payment of any money of the Authority and of any money held in trust or otherwise for the payment of bonds, and to carry out such contract. Money held in trust or otherwise for the payment of bonds or in any way to secure bonds and deposits of money may be secured in the same manner as money of the Authority, and all banks and trust companies are authorized to give security for the deposits. (1984, c. 749, § 9-230; 2001, c. 844.)

Cross references. — As to the powers of the Virginia Small Business Financing Authority, see § 2.2-2285.

§ 2.2-2306. Bondholder protection. — Subsequent amendments to this article shall not limit the rights vested in the Authority with respect to any agreements made with, or remedies available to, the holders of bonds issued under this article prior to the enactment of the amendments until the bonds, together with all interest thereon, and all costs and expenses in connection with any proceeding by or on behalf of the holders, are fully met and discharged. (1984, c. 749, § 9-231; 2001, c. 844.)

§ 2.2-2307. Bonds as legal investments and securities. — The bonds issued by the Authority in accordance with this article shall be legal investments in which all public officers or public bodies of the Commonwealth, its political subdivisions, all municipalities and municipal subdivisions, all insurance companies and associations and other persons carrying on insurance business, all banks, bankers, banking associations, trust companies, savings institutions, building and loan associations, and investment companies, all administrators, guardians, executors, trustees and other fiduciaries, and all other persons who are now or may later be authorized to invest in bonds or in other obligations of the Commonwealth, may invest funds, including capital, in their control or belonging to them. The bonds shall also be securities that may be deposited with and received by all public officers and bodies of the Commonwealth or any agency or political subdivision of the Commonwealth and all municipalities and public corporations for any purpose for which the deposit of bonds or other obligations of the Commonwealth is now or may be later authorized by law. (1984, c. 749, § 9-234; 1996, c. 77; 2001, c. 844.)

§ 2.2-2308. Expenses of Authority; liability of Commonwealth or political subdivision prohibited. — All expenses incurred by the Authority in carrying out the provisions of this article shall be payable solely from funds provided under this article, and nothing in this article shall be construed to authorize the Authority to incur indebtedness or liability on behalf of or payable by the Commonwealth or any of its other political subdivisions. (1984, c. 749, § 9-232; 2001, c. 844.)

§ 2.2-2309. Creation, administration, and management of Virginia Export Fund. — A. In addition to any other fund or account the Authority may create pursuant to subdivision 23 of § 2.2-2285, there shall be a permanent fund known as the Virginia Export Fund (the Fund). The Fund shall be comprised of (i) sums appropriated to it by the General Assembly, (ii) receipts by the Fund from loans or loan guarantees made against it, (iii) all income from the investment of moneys held by the Fund, and (iv) any other sums designated for deposit to the Fund from any source, public or private. The Fund shall be administered and managed by the Authority, and all moneys in the Fund shall be used to provide loans or loan guarantees as provided in subsection D. Any balances remaining in the Fund shall not revert to the general fund but shall be retained in order to make additional loans or loan guarantees.

B. All moneys belonging to the Fund shall be deposited to the credit of the State Treasurer and recorded on the books of the State Comptroller. Earnings from investments and interest shall be returned to the Fund.

C. The Authority, or its designated agent, may collect moneys due to the Fund. Proceedings to recover moneys due to the Fund may be instituted by the Authority in the name of the Fund in any appropriate court.

D. The Fund shall be used to make loans or to provide a guarantee for up to ninety percent of the principal amount of any commercial loan or line of credit made by a lender for the purpose of facilitating the sale of goods, products, or services outside of the United States by persons, firms, or corporations utilizing a Virginia air, land, or sea port to ship such goods, products, or services. Such guarantee shall not exceed one million dollars.

E. The Authority shall determine the terms and conditions of any loans or loan guarantee made against the Fund and may allow for use of the Fund in single or multiple transactions. No loan shall exceed a term of twelve months, nor shall a loan guarantee exceed a term of eighteen months. In the case of loans, the Authority shall charge an annual interest rate. In the case of guarantees, the Authority shall charge an annual guarantee fee. However, the Authority may waive such guarantee fees in an economically distressed area as defined in § 58.1-439. In connection with applications for loans or loan guarantees made against the Fund, the Authority may require the production of any document, instrument, certificate, legal opinion, or other information it deems necessary or convenient.

F. All loans or loan guarantees made against the Fund shall be approved by the Board or an authorized committee or subcommittee thereof. (1997, c. 815, §§ 9-228.1, 9-228.2, 9-228.3, 9-228.4; 1999, c. 785; 2001, c. 844.)

§ 2.2-2310. Creation, administration, and management of Virginia Small Business Growth Fund. — A. In addition to any other fund or account the Authority may create pursuant to subdivision 23 of § 2.2-2285, there shall be a permanent fund known as the Virginia Small Business Growth Fund (the "Fund"). The Fund shall be comprised of (i) sums appropriated to it by the General Assembly, (ii) all income from the investment of moneys held by the Fund, and (iii) any other sums designated for deposit to the Fund from any source, public or private. The Fund shall be administered and managed by the Authority, and all moneys in the Fund shall be used to create special reserve funds to cover potential future losses from the loan portfolios of participating banks and lending institutions as provided in subsection D. Any remaining balances in the Fund shall not revert to the general fund but shall be retained in order to create additional special reserve funds.

B. All moneys belonging to the Fund shall be deposited to the credit of the State Treasurer and recorded on the books of the State Comptroller. Earnings from investments and interest shall be returned to the Fund.

C. The Authority, or its designated agent, may collect moneys owed to the Fund. Proceedings to recover moneys owed to the Fund may be instituted by the Authority in the name of the Fund in any appropriate court.

D. The Fund shall be used as a special reserve fund to cover potential future losses from the loan portfolios of participating banks and lending institutions. The Authority shall (i) work with banks and lending institutions to establish a separate account for the Virginia Small Business Growth Fund in each participating bank or lending institution and (ii) deposit into such accounts moneys from the Fund in an amount at least equal to the total of the sum of the bank or lending institution's and the individual borrower's deposits into such account. Such matching sum by the Authority shall not exceed fourteen percent of the principal amount of the loan.

E. The Authority shall determine the qualifications, terms, and conditions for the use of the Fund and the accounts thereof. In connection with applications for claims made against the Fund, the Authority may require the production of any document, instrument, certificate, legal opinion, or any other information it deems necessary or convenient. All claims made against the Fund shall be approved by the Board or an authorized committee or subcommittee thereof. All claims made against each account shall be reported to the Board or an authorized committee thereof. (1997, c. 870, §§ 9-228.5, 9-228.6, 9-228.7, 9-228.8; 2000, c. 40; 2001, c. 844.)

§ 2.2-2311. Creation, administration, and management of the Capital Access Fund for Disadvantaged Businesses. — A. For the purposes of this section:

"Disadvantaged business" means a for-profit small business concern that is majority-owned by one or more economically disadvantaged individuals. In the case of a corporation, a majority of the stock shall be owned by one or more such individuals and the management and daily business operations shall be controlled by one or more of the economically disadvantaged individuals who own it.

"Economically disadvantaged individual" means an individual whose ability to compete in the free market has been impaired due to diminished capital and credit opportunities as compared to others in the same or similar line of business and competitive market area.

B. There is created in the state treasury a permanent nonreverting fund to be known as the Capital Access Fund for Disadvantaged Businesses (the Fund). The Fund shall be comprised of (i) moneys appropriated to the Fund by the General Assembly, (ii) all income from the investment of moneys held by the Fund, and (iii) any other moneys designated for deposit to the Fund from any source, public or private. Interest earned on moneys in the Fund shall remain in the Fund and be credited to it. Any moneys remaining in the Fund, including interest thereon, at the end of each fiscal year shall not revert to the general fund but shall remain in the Fund. Moneys in the Fund shall be used to provide loan guarantees, loan loss reserves, and interest rate write downs. The Fund shall be managed by the Department of Minority Business Enterprise (the Department) and administered by the Virginia Small Business Financing Authority (the Authority).

C. The operation of the Fund shall be as follows:

1. The Fund may be used as a special reserve fund to cover potential future losses from the loan portfolios of participating banks and lending institutions. The Authority shall (i) establish with one or more banks and lending institutions one or more accounts or pools for the Capital Access Fund for Disadvantaged Businesses and (ii) deposit into such accounts or pools moneys from the Fund in an amount at least equal to the total of the sum of the bank or lending institutions and the individual borrower's deposits, cash equivalents or other acceptable securities, including but not limited to letters of credit, for each loan sought to be covered for future losses. Such matching sum by the Authority shall not exceed fourteen percent of the principal amount of the loan. The Authority may require up to a one hundred percent match by the individual borrowers pursuant to established guidelines.

2. The Fund may also be used to guarantee up to ninety percent of the principal amount of any loan to cover potential future losses from the loan portfolios of participating banks and lending institutions to cover specific loans on such terms and conditions as set forth in established guidelines. Such guarantees shall not exceed a term of five years.

3. The Fund may also be used to provide interest rate write downs or other payments to achieve a concessionary rate of interest that shall be limited to seven percent of the balance of the Fund that is unencumbered by any special reserves or guarantees or the income earned by the Fund from all sources including fees, interest, or other investment income. No interest rate write down or payment to achieve a concessionary rate shall extend for more than five years and such rates shall include provisions for an increase in such rates to a near market rate but not more than the prime rate.

4. Provisions may be made for a borrower to use a combination of subdivisions C. 1., C. 2., and C. 3. pursuant to established guidelines.

D. The determination of economic disadvantage shall be made by the Director of the Department of Minority Business Enterprise pursuant to the guidelines developed in accordance with subsections B and C.

E. The Department and the Authority, or their designated agents, shall determine the qualifications, terms, and conditions for the use of the Fund and the accounts thereof. In connection with applications for claims made against the Fund, the Department may require the production of any document, instrument, certificate, legal opinion, or any other information it deems necessary or convenient. All claims made against the Fund shall be approved by the Department and the Authority. (1999, cc. 765, 791, § 2.1-64.34:1; 2001, cc. 224, 844.)

Editor's note. — Acts 1999, cc. 765 and 791, cl. 2, provides: "That prior to executing any provisions of subsection C of § 2.1-64.34:1 [see now § 2.2-2311] of the Code of Virginia, the Department of Minority Business Enterprise and the Virginia Small Business Financing Authority shall submit for review the Access Fund for Disadvantaged Businesses guidelines to the Chairmen of the House Appropriations Committee and the Chairmen of the Senate Finance Committee."

Acts 2001, c. 224 amended § 2.1-64.34:1, from which this section is derived. Pursuant to § 30-152, Acts 2001, c. 224 has been given effect in this section as set out above. The 2001 amendment by c. 224, in subsection C, deleted "and shall not exceed fifty thousand dollars" at the end of subdivision 2, and substituted "seven" for "five" in the first sentence of subdivision 3.

§ **2.2-2312. Annual report; audit.** — The Authority shall, within 120 days of the close of each fiscal year, submit an annual report of its activities for the preceding fiscal year to the Governor and the chairmen of the House Committee on Appropriations and the Senate Committee on Finance. Each report shall set forth, for the preceding fiscal year, a complete operating and financial statement for the Authority and any loan fund or loan guarantee fund the Authority administers or manages. The Auditor of Public Accounts or his legally authorized representatives shall at least once in a year audit the books and accounts of the Authority and any loan fund or loan guarantee fund the Authority administers or manages. (1984, c. 749, § 9-235; 1997, c. 815; 2001, c. 844.)

§ **2.2-2313. Exemption from taxation.** — The Authority is declared to be performing a public function and to be a public body corporate and a political subdivision of the Commonwealth. Accordingly, the income, including any profit made on the sale thereof from all bonds issued by the Authority, shall at all times be exempt from all taxation by the Commonwealth or any public subdivision thereof. If, after all indebtedness and other obligations of the Authority are discharged, the Authority is dissolved, its remaining assets shall inure to the benefit of the Commonwealth. (1984, c. 749, § 9-233; 2001, c. 844.)

§ **2.2-2314. Administrative Process Act not applicable.** — The provisions of the Administrative Process Act (§ 2.2-4000 et seq.) shall not apply to this article. (1984, c. 749, § 9-208; 2001, c. 844.)

Article 8.

Virginia Tourism Authority.

§ **2.2-2315. Short title; declaration of public purpose; Authority created.** — A. This article shall be known and may be cited as the Virginia Tourism Authority Act.

B. The General Assembly finds and declares that:

1. There exists in all geographical regions of the Commonwealth a plethora of tourist attractions, including cultural, historical, commercial, educational, and recreational activities, locations, and sources of entertainment;

2. Such tourist attractions are of potential interest to millions of people who reside both in and outside the Commonwealth;

3. Promotion of tourism in the Commonwealth is necessary to increase the prosperity of the people of the Commonwealth;

4. A state tourism development authority is therefore necessary to stimulate the tourism segment of the economy by promoting, advertising, and marketing the Commonwealth's many tourist attractions and by coordinating other private and public efforts to do the same; and

5. The film industry is a legitimate and important part of economic development in the Commonwealth.

The General Assembly determines that the creation of an authority for this purpose is in the public interest, serves a public purpose and will promote the health, safety, welfare, convenience or prosperity of the people of the Commonwealth.

C. The Virginia Tourism Authority is created, with the duties and powers set forth in this article, as a public body corporate and as a political subdivision of the Commonwealth. The Authority is constituted a public instrumentality exercising public and essential governmental functions, and the exercise by the Authority of the duties and powers conferred by this article shall be deemed and held to be the performance of an essential governmental function of the Commonwealth. The exercise of the powers granted by this article shall be in all respects for the benefit of the inhabitants of the Commonwealth and the increase of their commerce and prosperity. The Authority may do business as the "Virginia Tourism Corporation," and any references in the Code of Virginia or in any regulations adopted thereunder that refer to the Virginia Tourism Corporation shall, whenever necessary, be deemed to refer to the Authority. (1999, cc. 852, 881, §§ 2.1-548.53, 2.1-548.54, 2.1-548.56; 2001, c. 844.)

§ **2.2-2316. Executive Director; Board of Directors; members and officers.** — A. Notwithstanding the provisions of § 2.2-2318, all powers, rights and duties conferred by this article or other provisions of law upon the Authority shall be exercised by an Executive Director with the advice and comment of a Board of Directors. The Board of Directors shall be an advisory board within the meaning of § 2.2-2100.

B. The Board of Directors shall consist of the Secretary of Commerce and Trade, the Secretary of Finance, the Secretary of Natural Resources, and twelve members appointed by the Governor, subject to confirmation by the General Assembly. The members of the Board appointed by the Governor shall serve terms of six years each, except that the original terms of four members appointed by the Governor shall end on June 30, 2000, the original term of four members appointed by the Governor shall end on June 30, 2001, and the original terms of three members appointed by the Governor shall end on June 30, 2002, all as designated by the Governor. Any appointment to fill a vacancy on the Board shall be made for the unexpired term of the member whose death, resignation or removal created the vacancy. All members of the Board shall be residents of the Commonwealth. Members may be appointed to successive terms on the Board of Directors. The Governor shall make appointments in such a manner as to ensure the widest possible geographical representation of all parts of the Commonwealth.

Each member of the Board shall be reimbursed for his or her reasonable expenses incurred in attendance at meetings or when otherwise engaged in the business of the Authority and shall be compensated at the rate provided in § 2.2-2104 for each day or portion thereof in which the member is engaged in the business of the Authority.

C. The Governor shall designate one member of the Board as chairman. The Board may elect one member as vice-chairman, who shall exercise the powers of chairman in the absence of the chairman or as directed by the chairman. The Secretary of Commerce and Trade, the Secretary of Finance, the Secretary of Natural Resources shall not be eligible to serve as chairman or vice-chairman.

D. Meetings of the Board shall be held at the call of the chairman or of any seven members. Eight members of the Board shall constitute a quorum for the transaction of the business of the Authority. An act of the majority of the members of the Board present at any regular or special meeting at which a quorum is present shall be an act of the Board of Directors.

E. Notwithstanding the provisions of any other law, no officer or employee of the Commonwealth shall be deemed to have forfeited or shall have forfeited his or her office or employment by reason of acceptance of membership on the Board or by providing service to the Authority. (1999, cc. 852, 881, § 2.1-548.57; 2000, c. 899; 2001, c. 844; 2007, c. 779.)

The 2007 amendments. — The 2007 amendment by c. 779 inserted subsection A; rewrote former subsection A as subsection B by substituting "The Board of Directors shall consist" for "All powers, rights, and duties conferred by this article or other provisions of law upon the Authority shall be exercised by a Board of Directors consisting," redesignated the remaining subsections accordingly; and deleted the last sentence of subsection D, pertaining to powers of a majority of a quorum in the event of Board vacancies.

§ 2.2-2317. Appointment and duties of Executive Director. — The Governor shall appoint an Executive Director of the Authority, who shall serve as President and chief executive officer of the Authority. The Executive Director shall not be a member of the Board. The Governor shall set the salary and other compensation of the Executive Director, and shall approve any changes in the Executive Director's salary or compensation. The Executive Director shall serve as the ex officio secretary of the Board and shall administer, manage and direct the affairs and activities of the Authority. He shall attend meetings of the Board, shall keep a record of the proceedings of the Board and shall maintain and be custodian of all books, documents and papers of the Authority, the minute book of the Authority and its official seal. He may cause copies to be made of all minutes and other records and documents of the Authority and may give certificates under seal of the Authority to the effect that the copies are true copies, and all persons dealing with the Authority may rely upon the certificates. He shall also perform other duties as is necessary to carry out the purposes of this article. The Executive Director shall employ or retain such agents or employees subordinate to him as may be necessary to fulfill the duties of the Authority as conferred upon the Executive Director. Employees of the Authority, including the Executive Director, shall be eligible for membership in the Virginia Retirement System and participation in all of the health and related insurance and other benefits, including premium conversion and flexible benefits, available to state employees as provided by law. (1999, cc. 852, 881, § 2.1-548.58; 2001, c. 844; 2007, c. 779.)

The 2007 amendments. — The 2007 amendment by c. 779 substituted "The Executive Director shall not be a member of the Board" for "The Executive Director shall report to, but not be a member of, the Board" in the first sentence, deleted "in accordance with the policies and under the control and direction of the Board" from the end of the fourth sentence, substituted "is necessary to carry" for "instructed by the Board in carrying" in the seventh sentence, and deleted "subject to the Board's approval" from the end of the eighth sentence.

§ 2.2-2318. Powers of Authority. — The Authority, acting through the Executive Director, shall be granted all powers necessary or appropriate to carry out and to effectuate its purposes, including the following to:

1. Have perpetual succession as a public body corporate and as a political subdivision of the Commonwealth;
2. Adopt, amend and repeal bylaws, rules and regulations, not inconsistent with this article for the administration and regulation of its affairs, to carry into effect the powers and purposes of the Authority and the conduct of its business;
3. Sue and be sued in its own name;
4. Have an official seal and alter it at will although the failure to affix this seal shall not affect the validity of any instrument executed on behalf of the Authority;
5. Maintain an office at any place within or without the Commonwealth that it designates;
6. Make and execute contracts and all other instruments and agreements necessary or convenient for the performance of its duties and the exercise of its powers and functions under this article;
7. Acquire real or personal property, or any interest therein, by purchase, exchange, gift, assignment, transfer, foreclosure, lease or otherwise, including rights or easements, and hold, manage, operate or improve such property;
8. Sell, convey, mortgage, pledge, lease, exchange, transfer and otherwise dispose of all or any part of its properties and assets;
9. Employ officers, employees, agents, advisers and consultants, including without limitation, financial advisers and other technical advisers and public accountants and, the provisions of any other law to the contrary notwithstanding, to determine their duties and compensation without the approval of any other agency or instrumentality;
10. Procure insurance, in amounts and from insurers of its choice, or provide self-insurance, against any loss, cost, or expense in connection with its property, assets or activities, including insurance or self-insurance against liability for its acts or the acts of its directors, employees or agents and for the indemnification of the members of its Board and its employees and agents;
11. Receive and accept from any source aid, grants and contributions of money, property, labor or other things of value to be held, used and applied to carry out the purposes of this article subject to the conditions upon which the aid, grants or contributions are made;
12. Enter into agreements with any department, agency or instrumentality of the United States, the Commonwealth, the District of Columbia or any state for purposes consistent with its mission;
13. Establish and revise, amend and repeal, and charge and collect, fees and charges in connection with any activities or services of the Authority;
14. Make grants to local governments with any funds of the Authority available for this purpose;
15. Develop policies and procedures generally applicable to the procurement of goods, services, and construction based on competitive principles;
16. Issue periodicals and carry and charge for advertising therein;
17. Raise money in the corporate, nonprofit, and nonstate communities to finance the Authority's activities;
18. Support and encourage each locality to foster its own tourism development programs;
19. Enter into agreements with public or private entities that provide participating funding to establish and operate tourism centers, funded jointly by the entity and the Authority, as shall be determined by the Executive Director, and as approved by the Authority;
20. Encourage, stimulate, and support tourism in the Commonwealth by promoting, marketing, and advertising the Commonwealth's many tourist attractions and locations;
21. Encourage, stimulate, and support the film industry in the Commonwealth;

22. Do all things necessary or proper to administer and manage the Cooperative Tourism Advertising Fund and the Governor's Motion Picture Opportunity Fund;

23. Update a travel guide for the disabled in the first year of every biennium beginning in fiscal year 2003;

24. Develop a comprehensive plan to promote destinations of historical and other significance located throughout the Commonwealth in anticipation of the 400th anniversary of the Jamestown settlement; and

25. Do any act necessary or convenient to the exercise of the powers granted or reasonably implied by this article and not otherwise inconsistent with state law. (1999, cc. 852, 881, § 2.1-548.59; 2001, cc. 67, 844; 2005, c. 360; 2007, c. 779.)

Editor's note. — Acts 2001, c. 67 amended § 2.1-548.59, from which this section is derived. Pursuant to § 30-152, Acts 2001, c. 67 has been given effect in this section as set out above. The 2001 amendment by c. 67 deleted "and" at the end of subdivision 22, added present subdivision 23, and redesignated former subdivision 23 as subdivision 24.

Acts 2008, c. 879, effective for the biennium ending June 30, 2010, in Item 130 C, provides: "Prior to July 1 of each fiscal year, the Virginia Tourism Authority shall provide to the Chairmen of the House Appropriations and Senate Finance Committees and the Director, Department of Planning and Budget a report of its operating plan. Prior to September 1 of each fiscal year, the Authority shall provide to the Chairmen of the House Appropriations and Senate Finance Committees and the Director, Department of Planning and Budget a detailed expenditure report and a listing of the salaries and bonuses for all Authority employees for the prior fiscal year. All three reports shall be prepared in the formats as previously approved by the Department of Planning and Budget."

The 2007 amendments. — The 2007 amendment by c. 779 inserted "acting through the Executive Director" in the introductory paragraph.

§ **2.2-2319. Cooperative Marketing Fund.** — A. There is established the Cooperative Marketing Fund (Marketing Fund) for the purpose of encouraging, stimulating, and supporting the tourism segment of the economy of the Commonwealth and the direct and indirect benefits that flow from the success of such industry. To create the public-private partnership envisioned by such Marketing Fund, the Marketing Fund shall be established out of the sums appropriated by the General Assembly for the purpose of matching private funds to be used for the promotion, marketing, and advertising of the Commonwealth's many tourist attractions and locations. Proposals shall be eligible for matching grant funds under this section only if they promote, benefit, market and advertise locations or destinations that are (i) solely within the territorial limits of the Commonwealth or (ii) in both the Commonwealth and any adjoining state, in which instance the matching grant funds should be used to promote locations and destinations located within the territorial limits of the Commonwealth. The funds made available in the appropriations act for the Marketing Fund shall be administered and managed by the Authority.

B. In the event more than one person seeks to take advantage of the benefits conferred by this section and the Marketing Fund is insufficient to accommodate all such requests, the matching formula shall be adjusted, to the extent practicable, to afford each request for which there is a valid public purpose an equitable share.

C. All persons seeking to receive or qualify for such matching funds shall apply to the Authority in January of the year preceding the fiscal year for which funds are sought, and to the extent the Governor concurs in such funding request, it shall be reflected in the Governor's Budget Bill filed pursuant to § 2.2-1509. The application shall set forth the applicant's proposals in detail. The Authority shall develop guidelines setting forth the criteria it will weigh in considering such applications; such guidelines may indicate a preference for proposals submitted by nonprofit organizations. (1999, cc. 852, 881, § 2.1-548.60; 2001, c. 844; 2002, c. 442.)

§ **2.2-2320. Governor's Motion Picture Opportunity Fund.** — There is created a Governor's Motion Picture Opportunity Fund (the Fund) to be used, in the sole discretion of the Governor, to support the film and video industries in Virginia by providing the means for attracting production companies and producers who make their projects in the Commonwealth using Virginia employees, goods and services. The Fund shall consist of any moneys appropriated to it in the general appropriation act or revenue from any other source. The Fund shall be established on the books of the Comptroller and any moneys remaining in the Fund at the end of a biennium shall not revert to the general fund but shall remain in the Fund. Interest earned on the Fund shall be credited to the Fund.

The Fund shall be used by the Governor to assist production companies or producers that meet the eligibility requirements set forth in the guidelines. The Authority shall assist the Governor in the development of guidelines for the use of the Fund. The guidelines should include provisions for geographic diversity and a cap on the amount of money available for a certain project. The types of projects eligible for consideration will be feature films, children's programs, documentaries, television series or other television programs designed to fit a thirty-minute or longer format slot. Projects not eligible are industrial, corporate or commercial projects, education programs not intended for rebroadcast, adult films, music videos and news shows or reports. (1999, cc. 852, 881, § 2.1-548.61; 2001, c. 844.)

§ **2.2-2321. Grants from Commonwealth.** — The Commonwealth may make grants of money or property to the Authority for the purpose of enabling it to carry out its corporate purposes and for the exercise of its powers. This section shall not be construed to limit any other power the Commonwealth may have to make grants to the Authority. (1999, cc. 852, 881, § 2.1-548.62; 2001, c. 844.)

§ **2.2-2322. Deposit of money; expenditures; security for deposits.** — A. All money of the Authority, except as otherwise authorized by law or this article, shall be deposited in accounts in banks or trust companies organized under the laws of the Commonwealth or in national banking associations located in Virginia or in savings institutions located in Virginia organized under the laws of the Commonwealth or the United States. The money in these accounts shall be paid by check signed by the Executive Director or any other officer or employee designated by the Authority. All deposits of money shall, if required by the Authority, be secured in a manner determined by the Authority to be prudent, and all banks, trust companies and savings institutions are authorized to give security for the deposits.

B. Funds of the Authority not needed for immediate use or disbursement, including any funds held in reserve, may be invested in (i) obligations or securities that are considered lawful investments for fiduciaries, both individual and corporate, as set forth in § 26-40, (ii) bankers' acceptances, or (iii) repurchase agreements, reverse repurchase agreements, rate guarantee or investment agreements or other similar banking arrangements. (1999, cc. 852, 881, § 2.1-548.65; 2001, c. 844.)

§ **2.2-2323. Forms of accounts and records; annual reports; audit.** — The Authority shall maintain accounts and records showing the receipt and disbursement of funds from whatever source derived in a form as prescribed by the Auditor of Public Accounts. Such accounts and records shall correspond as nearly as possible to accounts and records maintained by corporate enterprises.

The accounts of the Authority shall be audited annually by the Auditor of Public Accounts, or his legally authorized representatives, and the costs of such audits shall be borne by the Authority. The Authority shall, following the close of each fiscal year, submit an annual report of its activities for the preceding year to the Governor. Each report shall set forth a complete operating and financial statement for the Authority during the fiscal year it covers. (1999, cc. 852, 881, § 2.1-548.66; 2001, c. 844.)

§ **2.2-2324. Exemption from taxation.** — As set forth in subsection C of § 2.2-2315, the Authority shall be performing an essential governmental function in the exercise of the powers conferred upon it by this article. Accordingly, the Authority shall not be required to pay any taxes or assessments upon any project or any property or upon any operations of the Authority or the income therefrom. Agents, lessees, sublessees, or users of tangible personal property owned by or leased to the Authority also shall not be required to pay any sales or use tax upon such property or the revenue derived therefrom. (1999, cc. 852, 881, § 2.1-548.64; 2001, c. 844.)

§ **2.2-2325. Exemptions from personnel and procurement procedures.** — The provisions of the Virginia Public Procurement Act (§ 2.2-4300 et seq.) and the Virginia Personnel Act (§ 2.2-2900 et seq.) shall not apply to the Authority. (1999, cc. 852, 881, § 2.1-548.63; 2001, c. 844.)

§ **2.2-2326. Sovereign immunity.** — No provisions of this article nor act of the Authority, including the procurement of insurance or self-insurance, shall be deemed a waiver of any sovereign immunity to which the Authority or its directors, officers, employees, or agents are otherwise entitled. (1999, cc. 852, 881, § 2.1-548.67; 2001, c. 844.)

§ **2.2-2327. Liberal construction of article.** — The provisions of this article shall be liberally construed to the end that its beneficial purposes may be effectuated. (2002, c. 491.)

Article 9.

Virginia National Defense Industrial Authority.

§ **2.2-2328. Short title; declaration of public purpose; Authority created.** — A. This article shall be known and may be cited as the Virginia National Defense Industrial Authority Act.

B. The General Assembly finds and declares that:

1. There exists a need to foster and promote business, technology, transportation, education, economic development and other efforts in support of the mission, execution, and transformation of the United States government military and national defense activities located in the Commonwealth;

2. The industrial and economic development of localities included in or adjacent to United States government military and other national defense activities and those of the Commonwealth are greatly dependent on successful cooperation between the localities, the Commonwealth, and the United States military and national defense activities; and

3. There exists a need for the provision of technical assistance and coordination between the Commonwealth, its political subdivisions, and the United

States government military and national defense activities located within the Commonwealth.

The General Assembly determines that the creation of an authority for this purpose is in the public interest, serves a public purpose, and will promote the health, safety, welfare, convenience, and prosperity of the people of the Commonwealth.

C. The Virginia National Defense Industrial Authority is created, with the duties and powers set forth in this article, as a public body corporate and as a political subdivision of the Commonwealth. The Authority is constituted as a public instrumentality exercising public and essential governmental functions, and the exercise by the Authority of the duties and powers conferred by this article shall be deemed and held to be the performance of an essential governmental function of the Commonwealth. The exercise of the powers granted by this article and its public purpose shall be in all respects for the benefit of the inhabitants of the Commonwealth and the increase of their commerce and prosperity and in support of national defense. (2005, c. 858.)

Editor's note. — Acts 2005, c. 858, cl. 2, provides: "That the initial terms of the members of the board of directors appointed pursuant to this act shall be staggered as follows: (i) three members appointed by the Governor, one member appointed by the Speaker of the House of Delegates and one member appointed by the Senate Committee on Rules to a term of three years; (ii) four members appointed by the Governor, two members appointed by the Speaker of the House of Delegates and one member appointed by the Senate Committee on Rules to a term of five years, and (iii) three members appointed by the Governor and one member appointed by the Speaker of the House of Delegates for a term of six years. Thereafter the terms of members shall be six years."

§ 2.2-2329. Board of directors; members and officers; executive director. — A. The Authority shall be governed by a board of directors consisting of 17 nonlegislative members appointed as follows: four members to be appointed by the Speaker of the House of Delegates; two members to be appointed by the Senate Committee on Rules; and 11 members to be appointed by the Governor as follows: (i) three persons who are retired General Officers or Department of Defense Senior Executive Service members representing the United States Armed Forces or the Department of Defense, (ii) four persons representing civic interests in the regions of Central Virginia, Southwestern Virginia, Northern Virginia, and Hampton Roads, (iii) one person representing higher education, (iv) two persons with experience in commercial real estate and public financing, and (v) the Adjutant General of Virginia.

B. With the exception of initial staggered terms and the appointment of the Adjutant General of Virginia, who shall serve a term coincident with his term of office, all appointments shall be for six years. Any appointment to fill a vacancy on the Board shall be made for the unexpired term of the member whose death, resignation or removal created the vacancy.

C. The Board shall annually elect one of its members as chairman and another as vice-chairman. The chairman or, in his absence, the vice-chairman shall preside at all meetings of the Board. Meetings of the Board shall be held at the call of the chairman or of any seven members. Eight members shall constitute a quorum for the transaction of the Authority's business, and no vacancy in the membership shall impair the right of a quorum to exercise all the rights and perform all the duties of the Authority.

D. The members of the Board shall be entitled to reimbursement for their reasonable travel, meal, and lodging expenses incurred in attending the meetings of the Board or while otherwise engaged in the discharge of their duties. Such expenses shall be paid out of the treasury of the Authority upon vouchers signed by the chairman of the Board or by such other person designated by the Board for this purpose.

E. The Board may employ an Executive Director of the Authority, who shall serve at the pleasure of the Board, to direct the day-to-day operations and activities of the Authority and carry out the powers and duties conferred upon him by the Board. The Executive Director and employees of the Authority shall be compensated in the manner provided by the Board and shall not be subject to the provisions of the Virginia Personnel Act (§ 2.2-2900 et seq.). (2005, c. 858; 2007, c. 117.)

Editor's note. — Acts 2005, c. 858, cl. 2, provides: "That the initial terms of the members of the board of directors appointed pursuant to this act shall be staggered as follows: (i) three members appointed by the Governor, one member appointed by the Speaker of the House of Delegates and one member appointed by the Senate Committee on Rules to a term of three years; (ii) four members appointed by the Governor, two members appointed by the Speaker of the House of Delegates and one member appointed by the Senate Committee on Rules to a term of five years, and (iii) three members appointed by the Governor and one member appointed by the Speaker of the House of Delegates for a term of six years. Thereafter the terms of members shall be six years."

The 2007 amendments. — The 2007 amendment by c. 117, in subsection A, substituted "17 nonlegislative members" for "16 nonlegislative members" and "11 members" for "10 members," added clause (v) and made related changes; inserted "and the appointment of the Adjutant General of Virginia, who shall serve a term coincident with his term of office" in the first sentence of subsection B; and substituted "Eight members" for "Seven members" in the last sentence of subsection C.

§ 2.2-2330. Powers of Authority. — The Authority shall be granted all powers necessary or appropriate to carry out and to effectuate its purposes, including the power to:

1. Have perpetual succession as a public body corporate and as a political subdivision of the Commonwealth;
2. Adopt, amend, and repeal bylaws, rules, and regulations, consistent with this article for the administration and regulation of its affairs, to carry into effect the powers and purposes of the Authority and the conduct of its business;
3. Sue and be sued in its own name;
4. Have an official seal and alter it at will, although the failure to affix this seal shall not affect the validity of any instrument executed on behalf of the Authority;
5. Maintain an office at any place that it designates;
6. Make and execute contracts and all other instruments and agreements necessary or convenient for the performance of its duties and the exercise of its powers and functions under this article;
7. Make and enter into all contracts and agreements necessary or incidental to the performance of its duties, the furtherance of its purposes and the execution of its powers under this article, including interstate compacts and agreements with any person or federal agency;
8. Employ, in its discretion, consultants, attorneys, architects, engineers, accountants, financial experts, investment bankers, superintendents, managers, and such other employees and agents as may be necessary, and to fix their compensation to be payable from funds made available to the Authority;
9. Receive and accept from any federal or private agency, foundation, corporation, association, or person grants, donations of money, real property, or personal property for the benefit of the Authority, and to receive and accept from the Commonwealth or any state, any municipality, county or other political subdivision thereof, and from any other source, aid, or contributions of either money, property, or other things of value, to be held, used, and applied for the purposes for which such grants and contributions may be made;
10. Receive and accept from any source aid, grants, and contributions of money, property, labor, or other things of value to be held, used, and applied to carry out the purposes of this article subject to the conditions upon which the aid, grants, or contributions are made;

11. Enter into agreements with any department, agency or instrumentality of the United States, the Commonwealth, the District of Columbia, or any state for purposes consistent with the Authority's mission;

12. Make grants to local governments, state and federal agencies, and private entities with any funds of the Authority available for this purpose;

13. Raise money in the corporate, nonprofit, and nonstate communities to finance the Authority's activities; and

14. Do any act necessary or convenient to the exercise of the powers granted or reasonably implied by this article and not otherwise inconsistent with the law of this Commonwealth. (2005, c. 858.)

§ **2.2-2331. Grants from Commonwealth.** — The Commonwealth may make grants of money or real or personal property to the Authority for the purpose of enabling it to carry out its corporate purposes and for the exercise of its powers. This section shall not be construed to limit any other power the Commonwealth may have to make grants to the Authority. (2005, c. 858.)

§ **2.2-2332. Moneys received deemed trust funds.** — All moneys received pursuant to the authority of this article shall be deemed to be trust funds to be held and applied solely as provided in this article. (2005, c. 858.)

§ **2.2-2333. Acceptance of grants or loans of public or private funds.** — The Authority may accept, receive, receipt for, disburse, and expend federal and state moneys and other moneys, public or private, made available by grant or loan or both or otherwise, to accomplish, in whole or in part, any of the purposes of this article. All federal moneys accepted under this section shall be accepted and expended by the Authority upon such terms and conditions as are prescribed by the United States and as are consistent with state law; and all state moneys accepted under this section shall be accepted and expended by the Authority upon such terms and conditions as are prescribed by the Commonwealth. (2005, c. 858.)

§ **2.2-2334. Moneys of Authority; examination of books by the Auditor of Public Accounts.** — All moneys of the Authority, from whatever source derived, shall be paid to the treasurer of the Authority. Such moneys shall be deposited in the first instance by the treasurer in one or more banks or trust companies, in one or more special accounts. All banks and trust companies are authorized to give such security for such deposits, if required by the Authority. The moneys in such accounts shall be paid out on the warrant or other order of the treasurer of the Authority or of other persons as the Authority may authorize to execute such warrants or orders. The Auditor of Public Accounts or his legally authorized representatives shall examine the accounts and books of the Authority. (2005, c. 858.)

§ **2.2-2335. Exemption from taxes or assessments.** — The exercise of the powers granted by this article shall be in all respects for the benefit of the people of the Commonwealth, for the increase of their commerce and prosperity, and for the improvement of their health and living conditions, and as the operation and maintenance of projects by the Authority and the undertaking of activities in furtherance of the purpose of the Authority constitute the performance of essential governmental functions, the Authority shall not be required to pay any taxes or assessments upon any project or any property acquired or used by the Authority under the provisions of this article or upon the income therefrom, including sales and use taxes on tangible personal property used in the operations of the Authority, and any bonds issued under the provisions of this article, their transfer and the income therefrom (including any profit made on the sale thereof) shall at all times be free from state and local taxation. The exemption granted in this section shall not be construed to extend to persons conducting, on the premises of the facility, businesses for which local or state taxes would otherwise be required. (2005, c. 858.)

CHAPTER 23.

[Reserved.]

CHAPTER 24.

BOARDS.

Article 9.

Board on Veterans' Affairs.

Article 10.

Virginia Geographic Information Network Advisory Board.

Article 11.

Virginia-Israel Advisory Board.

Article 12.

Virginia Public Broadcasting Board.

Article 13.

Virginia Public Buildings Board.

Article 14.

Virginia Veterans Care Center Board of Trustees.

Article 15.

Virginia Veterans Cemetery Board.

Article 16.

Herbert H. Bateman Virginia Advanced Shipbuilding And Carrier Integration Center Board.

Article 17.

Virginia-Asian Advisory Board.

Article 18.

Board of Veterans Services.

Article 19.

Charitable Gaming Board.

Article 20.

Information Technology Investment Board.

Article 21.

Latino Advisory Board.

ARTICLE 1.

Art and Architectural Review Board.

§ 2.2-2400. Art and Architectural Review Board; members and officers; travel expenses; quorum; compensation; staff; report. — A. The Art and Architectural Review Board (the Board) is established as an advisory board, within the meaning of § 2.2-2100, in the executive branch of state government. The Board shall consist of six members as follows: the Director of the Department of Historic Resources, or his designee, serving as an ex officio member and five citizen members, appointed by the Governor. Of the citizen members, one shall be appointed from a list of architects nominated by the governing board of the Virginia Society of the American Institute of Architects; one shall be appointed from a list of persons nominated by the governing board of the University of Virginia; one shall be appointed from a list of persons nominated by the board of trustees of the Virginia Museum of Fine Arts; and two shall be appointed from the Commonwealth at large, one of whom shall be a painter or sculptor.

B. The members of the Board shall be appointed for terms of four years each, except appointments to fill vacancies, which shall be for the unexpired terms. No member shall serve for more than two consecutive four-year terms, except that any member appointed to the unexpired term of another shall be eligible to serve two consecutive four-year terms. Vacancies shall be filled in the manner of the original appointments. The Director of the Department of Historic Resources shall serve a term coincident with his term of office.

C. Annually, the Board shall elect a chairman and vice-chairman and may elect such other officers as the Board deems proper from among its membership. A majority of the members of the Board shall constitute a quorum.

D. The members of the Board shall serve without compensation, but shall be reimbursed for all reasonable and necessary expenses incurred in the discharge of their duties as provided in § 2.2-2825.

E. The Division of Engineering and Buildings of the Department of General Services shall provide assistance to the Board in the undertaking of its responsibilities.

F. The Board shall submit a biennial report to the Governor and General Assembly on or before October 1 of each even-numbered year. (Code 1919, § 581; 1922, p. 757; 1927, p. 106; 1932, p. 37; 1938, p. 724; Michie Code 1942, § 585(64); R.P. 1948, § 9-7; 1964, c. 234; 1975, c. 510; 1976, c. 484; 1978, c. 580, §§ 2.1-488.1, 2.1-488.6; 1979, c. 66; 1981, c. 221; 1984, c. 734, § 2.1-488.2:1; 1985, c. 448; 1989, c. 656; 2001, c. 844; 2004, c. 650.)

CASE NOTES

Editor's note. — The case below was decided under former § 9-7.

Former Art Commission not agency within purview of former General Administrative Agencies Act. — See Commonwealth ex rel. Art Comm'n v. Silvette, 215 Va. 596, 212 S.E.2d 261 (1975).

There was no requirement that former Art Commission conduct hearings. Commonwealth ex rel. Art Comm'n v. Silvette, 215 Va. 596, 212 S.E.2d 261 (1975).

§ 2.2-2401. Works of art accepted by Governor; approval by Board; meaning of "work of art". — A. The Governor may accept, in the name of the Commonwealth, gifts to the Commonwealth of works of art as defined in subsection B. But no work of art shall be so accepted until submitted to the Board or otherwise brought to its attention for its advice and counsel to the Governor.

B. As used in this article, *"work of art"* means all paintings, mural decorations, stained glass, statues, bas-reliefs, tablets, sculptures, monuments, fountains, arches or other structure of a permanent character intended for ornament or commemoration. (Code 1919, § 583; 1920, p. 51; Michie Code 1942, § 582a; R. P. 1948, §§ 9-10, 9-12; 1975, c. 514; 1978, c. 580, §§ 2.1-488.3, 2.1-488.5; 2001, c. 844.)

CASE NOTES

Editor's note. — The cases cited in the notes below were decided under former Title 9.

Former § 9-12 not unconstitutional. — See Silvette v. Art Comm'n, 413 F. Supp. 1342 (E.D. Va. 1976).

The duty to advise and counsel includes the right to state the reasons therefor, and suggesting changes in a portrait intended as a gift to the State did not violate an artist's First Amendment right of free artistic expression. Silvette v. Art Comm'n, 413 F. Supp. 1342 (E.D. Va. 1976).

Former §§ 9-11 and 9-12 delineated only the means by which the Commonwealth might acquire works of art by purchase or otherwise. Silvette v. Art Comm'n, 413 F. Supp. 1342 (E.D. Va. 1976).

Clear and exact acquisition procedures. — The procedures for acquiring works of art by the Commonwealth by purchase, gift or otherwise have been spelled out with exactitude and clarity. Silvette v. Art Comm'n, 413 F. Supp. 1342 (E.D. Va. 1976).

An artist cannot compel the acceptance of his painting any more than an author can force the publication of his article. Silvette v. Art Comm'n, 413 F. Supp. 1342 (E.D. Va. 1976).

Former Art Commission had right to reject finished portrait submitted to it. Commonwealth ex rel. Art Comm'n v. Silvette, 215 Va. 596, 212 S.E.2d 261 (1975).

The advisory function of the former Art Commission involved an assessment of judgment, an artistic judgment, a conclusion which delights the chosen and offends the rejected. Silvette v. Art Comm'n, 413 F. Supp. 1342 (E.D. Va. 1976).

No artist was required to submit preliminary work to former Art Commission for approval or revision. Commonwealth ex rel. Art Comm'n v. Silvette, 215 Va. 596, 212 S.E.2d 261 (1975).

§ 2.2-2402. Governor's approval of works of art; removal, etc.; structures, fixtures and works of art placed on or extending over state property. — A. No work of art shall become the property of the Commonwealth by purchase, gift or otherwise, unless the work of art or a design thereof, together with its proposed location, have been submitted to and approved by the Governor acting with the advice and counsel of the Board. Nor shall any work of art, until so submitted and approved, be contracted for, placed in or upon or allowed to extend over any property belonging to the Commonwealth. No existing work of art owned by the Commonwealth shall be removed, relocated or altered in any way without submission to the Governor.

This subsection shall not apply to any portrait, tablet or work of art portraying, or pertaining to, a present or former Governor and presented to, or acquired, by the Governor and displayed in that part of the building under the direct supervision of the Governor or a present or former presiding officer of the Senate or a member or former member of the Supreme Court, the Senate, or the House of Delegates, presented to, or acquired by, the member's or presiding officer's respective body and displayed in that part of any building under the direct supervision and jurisdiction of such body nor shall they apply to any portrait, tablet or work of art acquired by the Virginia Museum of Fine Arts or museums operated in conjunction with art or architectural departments at public colleges or universities in Virginia.

B. No construction or erection of any building or any appurtenant structure of any nature, which is to be placed on or allowed to extend over any property belonging to the Commonwealth, and no construction or erection of any bridge, arch, gate, fence, or other structure or fixture intended primarily for ornamental or memorial purposes, and which is to be paid for, either wholly or in part by appropriation from the state treasury, and, which is to be placed on or allowed to extend over any property belonging to the Commonwealth, shall be begun, unless the design and proposed location thereof have been submitted to the Governor and its artistic character approved in writing by him acting with the advice and counsel of the Board, unless the Governor has failed to disapprove in writing the design within thirty days after its submission. No existing structure of the kinds described in this subsection, owned by the Commonwealth, shall be removed, remodeled or added to, nor shall any appurtenant structure be attached without submission to the Governor and the artistic character of the proposed new structure approved in writing by him acting with the advice and counsel of the Board, unless the Governor has failed to disapprove in writing the design within thirty days after its submission.

C. No work of art not owned by the Commonwealth shall be placed in or upon or allowed to extend over any property belonging to the Commonwealth for a period of more than two years unless such work of art or a design thereof has been submitted to and approved by the Governor acting with the advice and counsel of the Board.

This subsection shall not apply to the Virginia Museum of Fine Arts or museums operated in conjunction with art or architectural departments at public colleges and universities in Virginia. (Code 1919, § 582; 1920, p. 393; 1942, p. 197; R. P. 1948, § 9-11; 1956, c. 223; 1970, c. 203; 1975, c. 514; 1978, c. 580, § 2.1-488.4; 2000, c. 551; 2001, c. 844.)

Editor's note. — Acts 2008, c. 879, effective for the biennium ending June 30, 2010, in Item 391 I, provides: "Notwithstanding any requirement to the contrary, any building, fixture, or structure to be placed, erected or constructed on, or removed or demolished from the property of the Commonwealth of Virginia under the control of the Department of Corrections shall not be subject to review and approval by the Art and Architectural Review Board as contemplated by § 2.2-2402, Code of Virginia. However, if the Department of Corrections seeks to construct a facility that is not a secure correctional facility or a structure located on the property of a secure correctional facility, then the Department of Corrections shall submit that structure to the Art and Architectural Review Board for review and approval by that board. Such other structures could include probation and parole district offices or regional offices."

CASE NOTES

Editor's note. — The case cited in the notes below was decided under former Title 9.

Former § 9-11 not unconstitutional. — See Silvette v. Art Comm'n, 413 F. Supp. 1342 (E.D. Va. 1976).

The duty to advise and counsel includes the right to state the reasons therefor, and suggesting changes in a portrait intended as a gift to the State did not violate an artist's First Amendment right of free artistic expression. Silvette v. Art Comm'n, 413 F. Supp. 1342 (E.D. Va. 1976).

Former §§ 9-11 and 9-12 delineated only the means by which the Commonwealth might acquire works of art by purchase or otherwise. Silvette v. Art Comm'n, 413 F. Supp. 1342 (E.D. Va. 1976).

Clear and exact acquisition procedures. — The procedures for acquiring works of art by the Commonwealth by purchase, gift or otherwise have been spelled out with exactitude and clarity. Silvette v. Art Comm'n, 413 F. Supp. 1342 (E.D. Va. 1976).

The advisory function of the former Art Commission involved an assessment of judgment, an artistic judgment, a conclusion which delights the chosen and offends the rejected. Silvette v. Art Comm'n, 413 F. Supp. 1342 (E.D. Va. 1976).

An artist cannot compel the acceptance of his painting any more than an author can force the publication of his article. Silvette v. Art Comm'n, 413 F. Supp. 1342 (E.D. Va. 1976).

ARTICLE 2.

Chief Information Officer Advisory Board.

§ 2.2-2403: Repealed by Acts 2003, cc. 981 and 1021.

Editor's note. — For provisions of Acts 2003, cc. 981 and 1021, cls. 4 to 16, reflecting the intent of the General Assembly to provide for the consolidation of the procurement and operational functions of information technology for state agencies in a single agency, and related transitional and other provisions, see the Editor's note at § 2.2-2005.

ARTICLE 3.

Design-Build/Construction Management Review Board.

§ 2.2-2404. Design-Build/Construction Management Review Board; membership; terms; compensation; staff; seal. — A. The Design-Build/Construction Management Review Board (the "Review Board") is established as an advisory board, within the meaning of § 2.2-2100, in the executive branch of state government.

B. The Board shall consist of nine members to be appointed by the Governor as follows: the Director of the Division of Engineering and Buildings of the Department of General Services, or his designee; two Class A general contractors selected from a list recommended by the Associated General Contractors; one architect and one engineer selected from a list recommended by the Consulting Engineers Council of Virginia, the Virginia Society of the American Institute of Architects, and the Virginia Society of Professional Engineers; and four representatives of public bodies other than the Commonwealth selected from a list recommended by the Virginia Municipal League and the Virginia Association of Counties. Each such list, other than those recommended as representatives of public bodies, shall include the names of at least four persons who are experienced and actively engaged in competitive sealed bidding or competitive negotiation and in design-build or construction management procedures. The list for representatives of public bodies shall include at least four persons who are experienced in competitive sealed bidding or competitive negotiation and in design-build or construction management procedures. The Director of the Division of Engineering and Buildings or his designee shall be a nonvoting member of the Review Board, except in the event of a tie vote of the Review Board.

C. After the original appointments, all appointments shall be for terms of four years, except that appointments to fill vacancies shall be for the unexpired terms. No person shall be eligible to serve for more than two successive full terms, except the Director of the Division of Engineering and Buildings, who shall serve until a successor qualifies.

D. The Review Board shall elect its chairman and vice-chairman from among its members. The Review Board shall meet monthly to conduct its business as required by § 2.2-2405. However, monthly meetings may be canceled by the chairman if there is no business before the Review Board. Five members shall constitute a quorum.

E. Members of the Review Board shall receive no compensation for their services, but shall be reimbursed for all reasonable and necessary expenses incurred in the discharge of their duties as provided in § 2.2-2825.

F. Such staff support as is necessary for the conduct of the Review Board's business shall be furnished by the Division of Engineering and Buildings of the Department of General Services pursuant to § 2.2-1134.

G. The Review Board shall adopt a seal by which it shall authenticate its proceedings. (1996, c. 962, § 11-41.2:3; 1998, c. 357; 1999, c. 127; 2001, c. 844.)

§ 2.2-2405. Powers and duties of the Design-Build/Construction Management Review Board. — A. The Review Board shall have the power and duty to:

1. Review submissions by public bodies other than the Commonwealth of draft or adopted ordinances or resolutions to determine if the process for the selection, evaluation and award of a design-build or construction management contract is in compliance with the provisions of subdivision A. 1. of § 2.2-4308;

2. Determine if the public body has complied with the provisions of § 2.2-4308 relating to the retention of a licensed architect or engineer;

3. Review the findings and the basis of such findings submitted by the public body to determine if the public body has complied with the requirements of § 2.2-4308 and that the findings made by the public body pursuant to § 2.2-4308 are not unreasonable;

4. Develop guidelines relating to the documents and information to be reviewed by the Review Board;

5. Make post-project evaluations of construction projects procured by design-build or construction management contracts entered into by public bodies other than the Commonwealth, including cost and time savings, effectiveness of the selection, evaluation and award of such contracts, and the benefit to the public body; and

6. Report to the General Assembly and the Governor on or before December 1, 1999, and again on or before December 31, 2002, concerning the Review Board's evaluation of and findings regarding all design-build and construction management construction undertaken by public bodies other than the Commonwealth within the reporting year, and any recommendations relating to future use of design-build or construction management contracts by such public bodies.

B. The Review Board shall adopt regulations, as it deems appropriate, based on the substantive requirements of Chapter IX of the Capital Outlay Manual of the Commonwealth, for a two-step competitive negotiation process which shall be applied to design-build and construction management projects undertaken by public bodies other than the Commonwealth. For construction management projects, such regulations shall also include applicable provisions of the Required Construction Management Contract Terms of the Capital Outlay Manual. Such regulations shall also allow the Review Board to approve deviations from provisions of the Capital Outlay Manual that it deems appropriate. Regulations of the Review Board shall be adopted in accordance with the Administrative Process Act (§ 2.2-4000 et seq.). (1996, c. 962, § 11-41.2:4; 2000, c. 29; 2001, c. 844.)

§ 2.2-2406. Review by the Review Board for design-build or construction management approval; effect of disapproval; review of Review Board decision. — The Review Board shall conduct such inquiry it deems appropriate and may require the submission of additional documents or information by the public body, in a form prescribed by the Review Board, to determine if the public body has complied with the provisions of § 2.2-4308.

Within sixty days of the receipt of the request for review, the Review Board shall render a decision, unless a different timetable is agreed to by the public body. If the Review Board determines that the public body has complied with the provisions of § 2.2-4308 and the findings made by the public body pursuant to subdivision A. 2. of § 2.2-4308 are not unreasonable, the Review Board shall approve such use. If the Review Board determines that (i) the public body has not complied with the provisions of § 2.2-4308 or (ii) the findings made by the public body pursuant to subdivision A. 2. of § 2.2-4308 are unreasonable, it shall disapprove such use, and the public body shall not use a design-build or construction management contract to procure construction for the proposed project. If no decision is made by the Review Board within the sixty-day period or as otherwise agreed to by the public body, the proposed use of a design-build or construction management contract shall be deemed approved.

Any public body other than the Commonwealth which has been aggrieved by any action of the Review Board shall be entitled to a review of such action. Appeals from such actions shall be in accordance with the provisions of the Administrative Process Act (§ 2.2-4000 et seq.). (1996, c. 962, § 11-41.2:5; 2001, c. 844.)

Article 4.

Migrant And Seasonal Farmworkers Board.

§ 2.2-2407. Migrant and Seasonal Farmworkers Board; purpose; membership; terms; quorum; compensation; staff; biennial report. — A. The Migrant and Seasonal Farmworkers Board (the Board) is established as an advisory board, within the meaning of § 2.2-2100, in the executive branch of state government. The purpose of the Board shall be to:

1. Provide for the coordination and evaluation of state and federal services and, to the degree feasible, other governmental, public and private agency services to migrant and seasonal farmworkers within the Commonwealth;

2. Identify and evaluate the needs of migrant and seasonal farmworkers and needs of employers of such workers;

3. Study problems of the target population, provide background information, and recommend options for solutions along with impact projections of such recommendations to the General Assembly, governmental, public and private agencies; and

4. Encourage and foster the development of area migrant and seasonal farmworkers councils for the purpose of seeking problem resolution and communication at the local level.

B. The Board shall consist of 15 members who shall be appointed by the Governor to serve at his pleasure. The Board shall include representatives of grower communities, migrant and seasonal farmworkers and crew leaders, if practical, and government, public and private agencies and interest groups or citizens concerned with migrant and seasonal farmworkers.

C. A majority of the members of the Board shall constitute a quorum.

D. Members of the Board shall receive no compensation for their services but shall be reimbursed for all reasonable and necessary expenses incurred in the discharge of their duties as provided in § 2.2-2825.

E. The Virginia Employment Commission shall provide staff support to the Board and serve as fiscal agent for any funds received.

F. The Virginia Employment Commission shall submit a biennial report to the Governor and General Assembly on or before October 1 of each even-numbered year on the activities of the Board. (1978, c. 270, §§ 9-149, 9-150, 9-152; 1983, c.163; 1984, c. 734; 1985, c. 448; 1987, c. 162; 2001, c. 844; 2004, cc. 592, 650.)

§ 2.2-2408. Powers and duties of Board. — The Board shall have the power and duty to:

1. Request and receive from any state department, division, board, bureau, commission or other agency, information, assistance and cooperation as will enable it to properly perform its duties;

2. Request, in the name of the Board, information for any governmental, public or private agency, or individual, information, assistance and cooperation as will enable it to carry out its specified functions;

3. Disperse information to public and private bodies;

4. Request and receive grants and funds from governmental, public and private agencies and foundations and, with those funds, to enter into agreements and contracts necessary or incidental to the purposes of the Board;

5. Establish citizen panels as may be requisite or expedient in fulfilling the objectives of the Board; and

6. Request and receive, in the name of the Board and for its benefit and that of the Interagency Migrant Worker Policy Committee, periodic reports from persons or entities receiving federal grants or other federal funding for the purpose of assisting the Commonwealth's migrant and seasonal farm worker population. (1978, c. 270, § 9-151; 1998, c. 97; 2001, c. 844.)

Article 5.

Personnel Advisory Board.

§§ **2.2-2409, 2.2-2410:** Repealed by Acts 2001, cc. 520 and 806.

Editor's note. — Acts 2001, cc. 520 and 806 repealed §§ 2.1-113.1 through 2.1-113.3, from which these sections are derived. Pursuant to § 30-152, Acts 2001, cc. 520 and 806 have been given effect in these sections as set out above.

Article 6.

Public Guardian And Conservator Advisory Board.

§ 2.2-2411. Public Guardian and Conservator Advisory Board; purpose; membership; terms. — A. The Public Guardian and Conservator Advisory Board (the "Board") is established as an advisory board, within the meaning of § 2.2-2100, in the executive branch of state government. The purpose of the Board shall be to report to and advise the Commissioner of the Department for the Aging on the means for effectuating the purposes of this article and shall assist in the coordination and management of the local and regional programs appointed to act as public guardians and conservators pursuant to Chapter 10 (§ 37.2-1000 et seq.) of Title 37.2.

B. The Board shall consist of no more than fifteen members who shall be appointed by the Governor as follows: one representative of the Virginia Guardianship Association, one representative of the Virginia Area Agencies on Aging, one representative of the Virginia State Bar, one active or retired circuit court judge upon recommendation of the Chief Justice of the Supreme Court, one representative of the Association of Retarded Citizens, one representative of the Virginia Alliance for the Mentally Ill, one representative of the Virginia League of Social Service Executives, one representative of the Association of Community Service Boards, the Commissioner of the Department of Social Services or his designee, the Commissioner of the Department of Mental Health, Mental Retardation and Substance Abuse Services or his designee, the Director of the Virginia Office for Protection and Advocacy or his designee, and one person who is a member of the Commonwealth Council on Aging and such other individuals who may be qualified to assist in the duties of the Board.

C. The Commissioners of the Departments of Social Services and Mental Health, Mental Retardation and Substance Abuse Services or their designees, the Director of the Virginia Office for Protection and Advocacy or his designee, and the representative of the Commonwealth Council on Aging, shall serve terms coincident with their terms of office or in the case of designees, the term of the Commissioner or Director. Of the other members of the Board, five of the appointees shall serve for four-year terms and the remainder shall serve for three-year terms. No member shall serve more than two successive terms. A vacancy occurring other than by expiration of term shall be filled for the unexpired term.

D. Each year, the Board shall elect a chairman and a vice-chairman from among its members. Five members of the Board shall constitute a quorum.

E. Members shall receive no compensation for their services but shall be reimbursed for all reasonable and necessary expenses incurred in the discharge of their duties as provided in § 2.2-2823. (1998, c. 787, § 2.1-373.13; 2001, c. 844; 2002, cc. 491, 572.)

§ 2.2-2412. Powers and duties of the Board. — The Board shall have the power and duty to:

1. Assist in the coordination and management of the local and regional programs appointed to act as public guardians and conservators pursuant to Chapter 10 (§ 37.2-1000 et seq.) of Title 37.2;
2. Provide advice and counsel on the provision of high quality guardianship service and avoidance of conflicts of interest;
3. Promote the mobilization of activities and resources of public and private sector entities to effectuate the purposes of this article; and
4. Make recommendations regarding appropriate legislative and executive actions, including, but not limited to, recommendations governing alternatives for local programs to follow upon repeal of the authority granted to the courts pursuant to § 37.2-1015 to appoint the sheriff as guardian or conservator when the maximum staff-to-client ratio of the local program is met or exceeded. (1998, c. 787, § 2.1-373.13; 2001, c. 844.)

Article 7.

Small Business Advisory Board.

§ 2.2-2413. Small Business Advisory Board; membership; terms; quorum; compensation. — A. The Small Business Advisory Board (the "Board") is established as an advisory board, within the meaning of § 2.2-2100, in the executive branch of state government. The Board shall consist of the following members: fourteen members appointed by the Governor and subject to confirmation by the General Assembly; the Chairman of the Small Business Financing Authority and the Director of the Department of Business Assistance and the District Director for Virginia of the U.S. Small Business Administration or their designees as nonvoting ex officio members. The appointed members of the Board shall represent small businesses as defined by the Small Business Financing Act (§ 2.2-2279 et seq.). There shall be at least one member appointed from each congressional district who does business in that district and three members appointed at large from within the Commonwealth.

B. Terms of the appointed members shall be for four years except that appointments to fill vacancies shall be for the unexpired terms. No member appointed by the Governor shall serve more than two complete terms in succession.

C. The Governor shall appoint one member of the Board to be chairman. The Board shall annually elect one of its members as vice-chairman, and shall also elect annually a secretary, who need not be a member of the Board. The chairman, or in his absence, the vice-chairman, shall preside at all meetings of the Board. In the absence of both the chairman and the vice-chairman at any meeting, the Board shall elect a chairman pro tempore, who shall preside at such meeting.

D. The Board shall meet at least semiannually, at the call of the chairman, Director of the Department of Business Assistance or Governor or at the request of a majority of the Board members. A majority of the members of the Board shall constitute a quorum.

E. Members of the Board shall serve without compensation but shall be reimbursed for all reasonable and necessary expenses incurred in the discharge of their duties as provided in § 2.2-2825. (1996, cc. 589, 599, §§ 2.1-548.49, 2.1-548.50; 2001, cc. 301, 310, 844.)

Editor's note. — Acts 2001, cc. 301 and 310 amended § 2.1-548.49, from which this section is derived. Pursuant to § 30-152, Acts 2001, cc. 301 and 310 have been given effect in this section as set out above. The 2001 amendments by cc. 301 and 310 are identical, and substituted "fourteen" for "thirteen" in the first sentence of subsection A.

§ **2.2-2414. Duties of the Board.** — The Board shall advise the Department of Business Assistance on the small business programs, including, but not limited to, locally based centers to assist and develop small businesses. It shall make recommendations to the Director, the Secretary of Commerce and Trade, and the Governor concerning the actions that the Department of Business Assistance and the state government might take to enhance the growth of small businesses. Additionally, the Board shall be a resource to the Department of Business Assistance, the Secretary of Commerce and Trade, the Executive Director of the Virginia Economic Development Partnership, and the Governor as they conduct the economic development efforts of the Commonwealth. (1996, cc. 589, 599, § 2.1-548.51; 2001, c. 844.)

Article 8.

Treasury Board.

§ **2.2-2415. Treasury Board membership; chairman; quorum; compensation.** — A. The Treasury Board (the "Board") is established as a policy board, within the meaning of § 2.2-2100, in the executive branch of state government. The Board shall consist of seven members to be appointed as follows: four members to be appointed by the Governor, subject to confirmation by the General Assembly, who shall serve at the pleasure of the Governor; the State Treasurer, the Comptroller, and the Tax Commissioner. The members appointed by the Governor should have a background and experience in financial management and investments. The State Treasurer, the Comptroller, and the Tax Commissioner shall serve terms coincident with their terms of office. Vacancies shall be filled in the manner of the original appointment.

B. The State Treasurer shall act as the chairman, and the Board shall elect a secretary who need not be a member of the Board. The Board shall have regularly scheduled meetings at least monthly, and shall keep a regular and sufficient set of books, which include a record of all of their proceedings and any action taken by them with respect to any funds which by any provision of law are required to be administered by the Treasury Board. Four members of the Board shall constitute a quorum.

C. Members of the Board appointed by the Governor shall receive compensation, including all reasonable and necessary expenses incurred in the discharge of their duties as provided in § 2.2-2813. (Code 1950, § 2-149.1; 1966, c. 677, § 2.1-178; 1979, c. 215; 1984, c. 720; 1987, c. 601; 2001, c. 844.)

§ **2.2-2416. Powers and duties of Treasury Board.** — The Board shall have the power and duty to:

1. Exercise general supervision over all investments of state funds;

2. Give advice and supervision in the financing of state buildings and to make recommendations, as requested, to the Governor on methods by which

capital outlay requirements of the Commonwealth, including its agencies and institutions, may be financed;

3. Control and manage all sinking funds and other funds in possession of the Commonwealth in a fiduciary capacity;

4. Administer the Virginia Security for Public Deposits Act (§ 2.2-4400 et seq.);

5. Make recommendations to the Governor, notwithstanding any provisions to the contrary, on proposed bond issues or other financing arrangements; approve the terms and structure of bonds or other financing arrangements executed by or for the benefit of educational institutions and state agencies other than independent state authorities, including bonds or other financing arrangements secured by leases, lease purchase agreements, financing leases, capital leases or other similar agreements; and agreements relating to the sale of bonds;

6. Take or cause to be taken and omit to take all actions, as to any tax exempt bonds for which it has issuing authority, either by statute or by act of the General Assembly, the taking or omission of which is necessary on behalf of the Commonwealth to prevent such bonds from being or becoming subject to federal income taxation or being considered to be "arbitrage bonds" within the meaning of federal tax laws, including compliance with the arbitrage rebate provisions thereof;

7. Approve, notwithstanding any provisions to the contrary, the terms and structure of bonds or other financing arrangements executed by or for the benefit of state agencies, boards and authorities where debt service payments on such bonds or other financing arrangements are expected by such agency, board or authority to be made, in whole or in part, directly or indirectly, from appropriations of the Commonwealth, including bonds or other financing arrangements secured by leases, lease purchase agreements, financing leases, capital leases or other similar agreements, and agreements relating to the sale of bonds;

8. Establish debt structuring guidelines for bonds or other financing arrangements executed by or for the benefit of all state agencies, institutions, boards, and authorities where the debt service payments on such bonds or other financing arrangements are expected to be made, in whole or in part, directly or indirectly, from appropriations of the Commonwealth, in which guidelines the Board may, in its sole discretion, include such items as it deems necessary and appropriate, including, but not limited to, defining terms such as "terms and structure" and "bonds and other financing arrangements" and exempting from its review and approval pursuant to subdivision 5 or 7 (a) specific bond issues and other financing arrangements, (b) certain types or classes of bond issues and other financing arrangements, and (c) bond issues and other financing arrangements that are below a stated dollar amount;

9. Do all acts and things necessary or convenient to efficiently carry out and enforce the powers granted to and duties imposed on it by law, including delegating to the State Treasurer or to a committee composed of not less than three members of the Board such powers and duties, as it deems proper, to the extent designated and permitted by the Board;

10. Exercise such other powers and perform such other duties conferred or imposed upon it by law, including the local government investment pool authorized by Chapter 46 (§ 2.2-4600 et seq.) of this title; and

11. Do all acts and things necessary or convenient to wind up the affairs of, and protect the Commonwealth's interests in such matters that may survive the termination of the State Education Assistance Authority, the Virginia Student Assistance Authorities, and the Virginia Education Loan Authority. Nothing herein shall be construed to amend, enhance or otherwise alter such commitments, security interests, guarantees or other pledges entered into by

the State Education Assistance Authority, the Virginia Student Assistance Authorities, and the Virginia Education Loan Authority, acting in their official capacity and effective on or before March 31, 1997. (Code 1950, § 2-149.2; 1966, c. 677, § 2.1-179; 1979, c. 215; 1984, c. 720; 1987, cc. 210, 211, 242; 1988, c. 258; 1990, c. 712; 1991, c. 578; 1996, cc. 636, 656; 1998, cc. 39, 784; 2001, c. 844.)

§ 2.2-2417. Approval of financial terms of certain contracts; using agencies to procure certain financial services through Treasury Board. — A. The Board, or its designee, shall review and approve the financial terms of all contracts for the purchase or financing of the purchase by agencies, institutions, boards and authorities which receive appropriations from the Commonwealth, i.e., the using agencies, of personal property, including personal property to be affixed to realty, whether by lease-purchase, installment purchase or otherwise, where payment of the purchase price is deferred through installment payments, includes the payment of interest, or is otherwise financed by the seller, lessor, or third parties.

B. The Board may specifically exempt from its review and approval specific purchases, and purchases below a stated amount, and may adopt regulations governing the financial terms of contracts, as described in subsection A, including but not limited to the authority to negotiate with a seller or lessor the public or private sale of securities, the security interest which may be granted to a seller or lessor, and the types and value of property which may be acquired under such contracts. Approval of the Board or its designee and compliance with regulations adopted pursuant to this section shall be required in addition to and notwithstanding any other provision of law pertaining to the review, approval or award of contracts by agencies and institutions of the Commonwealth.

C. Notwithstanding any of the foregoing and except as the Board shall direct and authorize otherwise, every using agency shall procure through the Board all contracts for the financing of the purchases described in subsection A or other financial services needed for the purpose of financing such purchases. The Board may acquire such financing services, including, but is not limited to employing financial advisors and private or public placement agents.

D. An agency, institution, board, or authority which receives appropriations from the Commonwealth shall procure state agency energy efficiency projects under this section. State agency energy efficiency projects may include personal property, the installation or modification of an installation in a building, and professional, management, and other special services which are primarily intended to reduce energy consumption and demand, or allow the use of an alternative energy source, and which may contain integral control and measurement devices. (1986, c. 280, § 2.1-179.2; 1987, c. 613; 1991, c. 578; 1994, c. 231; 2001, c. 844.)

§ 2.2-2418. Use of bond anticipation notes by the Treasury Board. — Whenever the General Assembly has enacted legislation pursuant to Article X, Section 9 (b), (c), or (d) of the Constitution of Virginia authorizing the issuance of bonds for capital projects of the Commonwealth or any state agency, institution, board, or authority (a "state instrumentality") where debt service payments on the bonds are expected to be made in whole or in part from appropriations of the Commonwealth, the Board, with the consent of the Governor, may borrow money in anticipation of the issuance of the bonds to provide funds, with any other available funds, to pay the costs of acquiring, constructing, renovating, enlarging, improving, and equipping any one or more of the capital projects for which such bonds have been authorized. Any such borrowing shall be evidenced by notes of the Commonwealth that shall be in such form, shall be executed in such manner, shall bear interest at such rates, either at fixed rates or at rates established by formula or other method, and may contain such other provisions, all as the Board, or the State Treasurer when authorized by the Board, may determine. Such notes may bear interest at a rate subject to inclusion in gross income for federal income tax purposes as determined by the Board, with the consent of the Governor. Such notes may be made payable from the proceeds of the bonds, other notes, or other sources of funds authorized by the General Assembly. The proceeds of the notes, to the extent not required to pay the principal or interest on maturing notes, or expenses associated therewith, shall be paid or otherwise made available to the Commonwealth or appropriate state instrumentality to pay the costs of such capital projects. However, the undertaking and obligation of (i) the Board to make such note proceeds available to the state instrumentality and (ii) the state instrumentality to pay or provide for the payment of the interest and principal coming due on the notes and to issue its own bonds or otherwise retire the notes within five years of the date of their initial issuance shall be set forth in a written agreement between the Board and the state instrumentality. No such notes shall be issued by the Board for or on behalf of a state instrumentality unless the Board first determines that such written agreement provides reasonable assurance of the full and timely payment of the debt service on the notes.

No law authorizing the issuance of bonds and notes for which bond anticipation notes have been issued by the Board shall be repealed or otherwise vitiated without first providing for the payment of the related bond anticipation notes of the Board. (1991, c. 554, § 2.1-179.3; 1996, cc. 636, 656; 2001, c. 844.)

§ 2.2-2419. Issuance of refunding bonds by the Treasury Board. — The Board may, with the consent of the Governor, sell and issue refunding bonds of the Commonwealth to refund any or all of the Commonwealth's bonds or other debt. The aggregate principal amount of such refunding bonds shall not exceed the amount required to redeem or otherwise provide for the payment of the unpaid principal of and interest on and any redemption premium payable on the bonds to be refunded to their date of redemption or payment, plus all expenses incurred in such refunding transaction. (1996, cc. 636, 656, § 2.1-179.4; 2001, c. 844.)

§ 2.2-2420. Combined issuance of general obligation debt by the Treasury Board. — Bonds and notes issued by the Board may be issued and sold at the same time with other bonds and notes issued by the Board either as separate issues, a combined issue, or a combination of both. (1996, cc. 636, 656, § 2.1-179.5; 2001, c. 844.)

Article 9.

Board on Veterans' Affairs.

§§ 2.2-2421 through 2.2-2422: Repealed by Acts 2003, cc. 657 and 670.

Cross references. — As to Department of Veterans Services, see § 2.2-2000 et seq. and Editor's notes thereunder.

ARTICLE 10.

Virginia Geographic Information Network Advisory Board.

§ 2.2-2423. Virginia Geographic Information Network Advisory Board; membership; terms; quorum; compensation and expenses. — A. The Virginia Geographic Information Network Advisory Board (the Board) is hereby established as an advisory board, within the meaning of § 2.2-2100, in the executive branch of state government. The Board shall advise the Geographic Information Network Division (the Division) of the Virginia Information Technologies Agency on issues related to the exercise of the Division's powers and duties.

B. The Board shall consist of 18 members appointed as follows: nine nonlegislative citizen members to be appointed by the Governor that consist of one agency director from one of the natural resources agencies, one official from a state university, one elected official representing a local government in the Commonwealth, one member of the Virginia Association of Surveyors, one elected official who serves on a planning district commission, two representatives of utilities or transportation industries utilizing geographic data, and two representatives of private businesses with expertise and experience in the establishment, operation, and maintenance of geographic information systems; four members of the House of Delegates to be appointed by the Speaker of the House of Delegates; two members of the Senate to be appointed by the Senate Committee on Rules; the Chief Information Officer, the Commonwealth Transportation Commissioner, and the Executive Director of the Economic Development Partnership Authority or their designees who shall serve as ex officio, voting members. Gubernatorial appointees may be nonresidents of the Commonwealth. All members of the Board appointed by the Governor shall be confirmed by each house of the General Assembly. The agency director and state university official appointed by the Governor may each designate a member of his organization as an alternate who may attend meetings in his place and be counted as a member of the Board for the purposes of a quorum.

Any members of the Board who are representatives of private businesses that provide geographic information services, and their companies, are precluded from contracting to provide goods or services to the Division.

C. Legislative members' terms shall be coincident with their terms of office. The gubernatorial appointees to the Board shall serve five-year terms, except for the initial appointees whose terms were staggered. Members appointed by the Governor shall serve no more than two consecutive five-year terms. Vacancies occurring other than by expiration of a term shall be filled for the unexpired term. Vacancies shall be filled in the same manner as the original appointments. The remainder of any term to which a member is appointed to fill a vacancy shall not constitute a term in determining the member's eligibility to serve.

D. The Board shall elect from its membership a chairman, vice-chairman, and any other officers deemed necessary. The duties and terms of the officers shall be prescribed by the members. A majority of the Board shall constitute a quorum. The Board shall meet at least quarterly or at the call of its chairman or the Chief Information Officer.

E. Legislative members of the Board shall receive such compensation as provided in § 30-19.12 and nonlegislative citizen members shall receive such compensation as provided in § 2.2-2813 for their services. All members shall be reimbursed for all reasonable and necessary expenses incurred in the performance of their duties as provided in §§ 2.2-2813 and 2.2-2825. Funding for the costs of compensation and expenses of the members shall be provided by the Virginia Geographic Information Network Division of the Virginia Information Technologies Agency.

F. The Geographic Information Network Division shall provide staff support to the Board. (1997, c. 817, § 2.1-563.41; 1999, cc. 412, 421, 433; 2001, c. 844; 2003, cc. 981, 1021; 2004, c. 1000.)

Editor's note. — For provisions of Acts 2003, cc. 981 and 1021, cls. 4 to 16, reflecting the intent of the General Assembly to provide for the consolidation of the procurement and operational functions of information technology for state agencies in a single agency, and related transitional and other provisions, see the Editor's note at § 2.2-2005.

Acts 2004, c. 1000, cl. 5, provides: "That this act shall not be construed to affect existing appointments for which the terms have not expired. However, any new appointments or appointments to fill vacancies made after the effective date of this act shall be made in accordance with the provisions of this act."

ARTICLE 11.

Virginia-Israel Advisory Board.

§ 2.2-2424. Virginia-Israel Advisory Board; purpose; membership; terms; compensation and expenses; staff; chairman's executive summary. — A. The Virginia-Israel Advisory Board (the Board) is established as an advisory board, within the meaning of § 2.2-2100, in the executive branch of state government. The purpose of the Board shall be to advise the Governor on ways to improve economic and cultural links between the Commonwealth and the State of Israel, with a focus on the areas of commerce and trade, art and education, and general government.

B. The Board shall consist of 31 members that include 29 citizen members and two ex officio members as follows: six citizen members appointed by the Speaker of the House of Delegates, who may be members of the House of Delegates or other state or local elected officials; six citizen members appointed by the Senate Committee on Rules, who may be members of the Senate or other state or local elected officials; 13 members appointed by the Governor who represent business, industry, education, the arts, and government; the president, or his designee, of each of the four Jewish Community Federations serving the Richmond, Northern Virginia, Tidewater and Peninsula regions; and the Secretary of Commerce and Trade and the Secretary of Education, or their designees, who shall serve as ex officio voting members of the Board.

C. Nonlegislative citizen members appointed by the Governor shall serve for terms of four years and nonlegislative citizen members appointed by the Senate Committee on Rules and the Speaker of the House of Delegates shall serve for terms of two years. Legislative members and the Secretaries of Commerce and Trade, and Education, or their designees, shall serve terms coincident with their terms of office. Vacancies occurring other than by expiration of a term shall be filled for the unexpired term. Vacancies shall be filled in the same manner as the original appointments. Any member may be reappointed for successive terms.

D. The members of the Board shall elect a chairman and vice-chairman annually from among its membership. The Board shall meet at such times as it deems appropriate or on call of the chairman. A majority of the members of the Board shall constitute a quorum.

E. Members shall receive no compensation for their services. However, all members shall be reimbursed for all reasonable and necessary expenses incurred in the performance of their duties as provided in §§ 2.2-2813 and 2.2-2825. Funding for the costs of the expenses of the members shall be provided by the Office of the Governor.

F. The Office of the Governor shall serve as staff to the Board.

G. The chairman of the Board shall submit to the Governor and the General Assembly an annual executive summary of the interim activity and work of the

Board no later than the first day of each regular session of the General Assembly. The executive summary shall be submitted as provided in the procedures of the Division of Legislative Automated Systems for the processing of legislative documents and reports and shall be posted on the General Assembly's website. (1996, c. 97, §§ 9-350, 9-351, 9-353; 1997, c. 181; 2001, c. 844; 2003, c. 885; 2004, c. 1000.)

Editor's note. — Acts 2003, c. 885, cl. 7, provides: "That all current members of the collegial bodies whose terms have been modified by this act shall be eligible, if reappointed, to the full number of terms provided by this act regardless of prior service."

Acts 2003, c. 885, cl. 8, provides: "That notwithstanding the provisions of § 2.2-2424 of the Code of Virginia, beginning July 1, 2004, the Governor shall stagger the terms of his appointments to the Virginia-Israel Advisory Board as follows: three members shall serve initial terms of one year; three members shall serve initial terms of two years; three members shall serve initial terms of three years; and four members shall serve initial terms of four years. Thereafter, all members appointed by the Governor shall serve terms of four years."

Acts 2004, c. 1000, cl. 5, provides: "That this act shall not be construed to affect existing appointments for which the terms have not expired. However, any new appointments or appointments to fill vacancies made after the effective date of this act shall be made in accordance with the provisions of this act."

§ **2.2-2425. Powers and duties of the Board.** — The Board shall have the power and duty to:

1. Undertake studies and gather information and data in order to accomplish its purposes as set forth in § 2.2-2424, and to formulate and present its recommendations to the Governor and the General Assembly.

2. Apply for, accept, and expend gifts, grants, or donations from public, quasi-public or private sources, including any matching funds as may be designated in the appropriation act, to enable it to better carry out its purposes.

3. Report annually its findings and recommendations to the Governor. The Board may make interim reports to the Governor as it deems advisable.

4. Account annually on its fiscal activities, including any matching funds received or expended by the Board. (1996, c. 97, § 9-352; 1997, c. 181; 2001, c. 844.)

Article 12.

Virginia Public Broadcasting Board.

§ **2.2-2426. Declaration of public purpose.** — It is found and determined by the General Assembly that there exists in the Commonwealth a need to support and capitalize on the universal access of public broadcasting to (i) enrich the lives of all citizens of the Commonwealth without regard to their geographic location or economic status by providing them with programs and services that educate, inform and enlighten; (ii) improve and enhance the educational opportunities available to children from pre-kindergarten through secondary schools, adults, home educators, and students and personnel at colleges and universities of the Commonwealth; (iii) provide the citizens of the Commonwealth with comprehensive information on the activities of state government; (iv) maintain and improve the public broadcasting stations' infrastructures for distribution of broadcast and related services; (v) promote economic development through the wider availability of worker-training and job-skills enhancements; (vi) promote tourism through the widespread distribution of programming that recognizes and displays Virginia's historical, educational, recreational and cultural resources; and (vii) improve efficiency in state government through the use of public broadcasting production and distribution systems. (1997, c. 858, § 2.1-563.27:1; 2001, c. 844.)

Cross references. — As to the creation of the Virginia Information Technologies Agency, see § 2.2-2005.

§ 2.2-2427. Definitions. — As used in this article, unless context requires a different meaning:

"Board" means the Virginia Public Broadcasting Board.

"Public broadcasting services" means the acquisition, production, and distribution by public broadcasting stations of noncommercial educational, instructional, informational, or cultural television and radio programs and information that may be transmitted by means of electronic communications, and any related materials and services provided by such stations.

"Public broadcasting station" means any noncommercial, educational television or radio station that (i) is licensed and regulated by the Federal Communications Commission as a noncommercial, educational broadcasting station; (ii) is operated by a public agency or a nonprofit private foundation, corporation, or association; (iii) has offices and studios located in Virginia; and (iv) on or before January 1, 1997, was qualified to receive or was the recipient of a Virginia community service grant or other instructional television service funds, or, after January 1, 1997, was qualified by the Board to receive state funds under standards and criteria established by the Board pursuant to § 2.2-2429, but shall not include any institution of higher education that produces or transmits distance education and other credit and noncredit television programs, unless such institution requests qualification as a public broadcasting station and the Board approves its request. (1997, c. 858, § 2.1-563.27:2; 2000, cc. 32, 281; 2001, c. 844.)

§ 2.2-2428. Virginia Public Broadcasting Board; membership; terms; chairman; compensation. — A. To achieve the public purposes set forth in § 2.2-2426, the Virginia Public Broadcasting Board (the Board) is established as a policy board, within the meaning of § 2.2-2100, in the executive branch of state government. The Board shall be under the direction and supervision of the Secretary of Administration. The exercise by the Board of the powers conferred by this article shall be deemed and held to be the performance of essential governmental functions.

B. The Board shall consist of 14 members. The Governor shall appoint 11 members, one from each congressional district of the Commonwealth, each of whom shall be confirmed by the affirmative vote of a majority of those voting in each house of the General Assembly. Three of the appointees shall have expertise in at least one of the areas of education, tourism, telecommunications, and economic development, and two shall be participating members of different public broadcasting stations in the Commonwealth. The president of the State Board of Education and the chairmen of the State Board of Community Colleges and the Board of Trustees of the Virginia Museum of Fine Arts, or their designees, shall serve as Board members concurrent with their terms in office. No Board member shall be the chief executive officer or head of any state agency, a member of the General Assembly, or an officer, director, employee, or member of the board of directors of any public broadcasting station.

C. After the original appointments, all other appointments shall be for four-year terms. A member appointed to an initial term may serve one additional four-year term.

D. Vacancies for unexpired terms shall be filled by the Governor in the same manner as the original appointment. If the General Assembly refuses or fails to confirm any appointment, such person shall not be eligible for reappointment.

E. The Governor shall designate a Board member to serve as chairman, who shall preside over meetings of the Board, communicate on behalf of the Board to the outside entities interested in public broadcasting, and perform additional duties as may be set by resolution of the Board. Board members may elect a vice-chairman from their membership and appoint a secretary who need not be a member of the Board. The Board shall meet at the call of its chairman. A majority of the Board members shall constitute a quorum.

F. Board members shall be reimbursed for the reasonable and necessary expenses incurred in discharge of their duties as provided in § 2.2-2823. Such reimbursements and other expenses of the Board shall be paid from funds that the Department of Planning and Budget shall annually withhold from appropriations to public broadcasting stations in an amount sufficient to defray the estimated reasonable and necessary expenses of the Board. (1997, c. 858, § 2.1-563.27:3; 2001, c. 844; 2007, cc. 114, 358.)

The 2007 amendments. — The 2007 amendments by cc. 114 and 358 are identical, and, in subsection B, substituted "14 members" for "fifteen members" in the first sentence and "11 members" for "eleven members" in the second sentence and in the fourth sentence, deleted "State Council of Higher Education, the" preceding "State Board of Community Colleges" and made a related change.

§ **2.2-2429. Powers and duties of the Board.** — The Board shall have the power and duty to:

1. Receive, allocate, and dispense funds appropriated by the General Assembly and any funds received by the Board from other sources, subject to the approval of the Director of the Department of Planning and Budget;
2. Develop reasonable and fair formulas for allocating and distributing state funds and other funds of the Board to Virginia's public broadcasting stations consistent with the intent of such appropriations;
3. Apply for, accept, and receive grants of federal funds and funds from other public and private sources;
4. Adopt, administer, and apply standards and criteria by which the Board may permit television and radio stations to qualify as public broadcasting stations if those stations did not qualify for or receive Virginia community service grants or other instructional television service funds as of January 1, 1997, but otherwise qualify as such under the definition of a public broadcasting station in § 2.2-2427. To avoid unnecessary duplication of public broadcasting services, the Board shall consider the: (i) adequacy of existing programming, coverage, and other public broadcasting services in the geographic area to be served and the extent to which those services would be duplicated by an additional public broadcasting station and (ii) sufficiency of funds administered by the Board to support existing or proposed public broadcasting stations;
5. Coordinate such strategic planning by the public broadcasting stations as the Board deems appropriate and identify and communicate to the Governor and the General Assembly the funding and other requirements of Virginia's public broadcasting stations; and
6. Enter into contracts with public broadcasting stations, state agencies and institutions, public schools and private entities for goods and services. (1997, c. 858, § 2.1-563.27:4; 2001, c. 844.)

§ **2.2-2430. Funds of the Board.** — The Director of the Department of Planning and Budget shall oversee and approve the disbursement of all funds appropriated to the Board. Upon approval, the funds of the Board shall be disbursed for the following general purposes:

1. Annual operating grant-funding to public broadcasting stations for developing, acquiring, producing, and distributing programs and related services

that support local needs of pre-school and adult education; disseminating information to the citizenry regarding the government and its affairs; promoting tourism and enhancing the Commonwealth's economic development; and supporting other programs that inform, educate, and entertain the citizenry with noncommercial programming.

2. Annual contract-funding to public broadcasting stations to regionally manage and provide programming and related services that directly support the instructional activities of local schools and home educators.

3. Matching capital-funding to public broadcasting stations for construction and equipment modernization to keep Virginia stations consistent with industry standards.

4. Funding for specific programs and projects to be provided by a public broadcasting station that may not be included in another funding category. (1997, c. 858, § 2.1-563.27:5; 2001, c. 844.)

§ 2.2-2431. Staff and employees prohibited. — The Board shall not hire, employ, or contract for its own staff or employees, but may request administrative support from the public broadcasting stations. The Virginia Information Technologies Agency shall, upon request, provide to the Board and public broadcasting stations the same scope of technical communications and related services that it provided on or before July 1, 1997, to the Virginia Public Telecommunications Board and to Virginia's public telecommunications entities and public broadcast stations. (1997, c. 858, § 2.1-563.27:7; 2001, c. 844; 2003, cc. 981, 1021.)

Editor's note. — For provisions of Acts 2003, cc. 981 and 1021, cls. 4 to 16, reflecting the intent of the General Assembly to provide for the consolidation of the procurement and operational functions of information technology for state agencies in a single agency, and related transitional and other provisions, see the Editor's note at § 2.2-2005.

§ 2.2-2432. Forms of accounts and records; audit; annual report. — The accounts and records of the Board showing the receipt and disbursement of funds from whatever source derived shall be in a form as prescribed by the Auditor of Public Accounts. The Auditor of Public Accounts, or his legally authorized representatives, shall annually examine the accounts and books of the Board.

The Board shall submit an annual report to the Governor and General Assembly on or before November 1 of each year. The report shall contain the audited annual financial statements of the Board for the year ending the preceding June 30. (1997, c. 858, § 2.1-563.27:8; 2001, c. 844; 2004, c. 650.)

§ 2.2-2433. Exemption from Virginia Public Procurement Act. — State agencies, institutions, and political subdivisions of the Commonwealth may enter into contracts with public broadcasting stations for program production, broadcasting, transmission, distribution, and related communications services without competitive sealed bidding or competitive negotiation as required by the Virginia Public Procurement Act (§ 2.2-4300 et seq.). (1997, c. 858, § 2.1-563.27:6; 2001, c. 844.)

Article 13.

Virginia Public Buildings Board.

§ 2.2-2434. Virginia Public Buildings Board; purpose; membership; terms; quorum; compensation and expenses. — A. The Virginia Public Buildings Board (the Board) is established as an advisory board, within the meaning of § 2.2-2100, in the executive branch of state government. The purpose of the Board shall be to assist and advise the Governor and the Department of General Services in the preparation and maintenance of a long-range site plan at the seat of government, and in the determination of the need for the acquisition of land, buildings and improvements, through purchases or construction.

B. The Board shall consist of 10 members to be appointed as follows: four members shall be appointed by the Speaker of the House of Delegates from the membership of the House of Delegates, two members shall be appointed by the Senate Committee on Rules from the membership of the Senate; three nonlegislative citizen members appointed by the Governor from the public at large; and the Director of the Department of General Services who shall serve as an ex officio member of the Board with voting privileges. Members of the Board shall be citizens of the Commonwealth.

C. Legislative members shall serve terms coincident with their terms of office. The nonlegislative citizen members shall serve for terms coincident with that of the Governor. The Director of the Department of General Services shall serve a term coincident with his term of office. Vacancies for unexpired terms shall be filled in the same manner as the original appointments. Members may be reappointed for successive terms.

D. The members of the Board shall elect a chairman and vice-chairman annually. A majority of the members of the Board shall constitute a quorum. The meetings of the Board shall be held at the call of the chairman or whenever the majority of the members so request.

E. The members of the Board shall not be entitled to compensation, but shall be reimbursed for all reasonable and necessary expenses incurred in the performance of their duties as provided in §§ 2.2-2813 and 2.2-2825, to be paid by the Department of General Services from any funds that may be appropriated or made available for such purposes. (Code 1950, §§ 2-77.1, 2-77.4, 2-77.8; 1966, cc. 55, 677, §§ 2.1-98, 2.1-101, 2.1-105; 1973, c. 524; 1977, c. 672, §§ 2.1-486, 2.1-487, 2.1-488; 1978, cc. 770, 811; 1984, c. 720; 1985, c. 448; 2001, c. 844; 2004, c. 1000.)

Editor's note. — Acts 2004, c. 1000, cl. 5, provides: "That this act shall not be construed to affect existing appointments for which the terms have not expired. However, any new appointments or appointments to fill vacancies made after the effective date of this act shall be made in accordance with the provisions of this act."

Article 14.

Virginia Veterans Care Center Board of Trustees.

§§ **2.2-2435 through 2.2-2437:** Repealed by Acts 2003, cc. 657 and 670.

Cross references. — As to Board of Veterans Services, see § 2.2-2452 et seq. and Editor's notes thereunder.

Article 15.

Virginia Veterans Cemetery Board.

§§ **2.2-2438 through 2.2-2439:** Repealed by Acts 2003, cc. 657 and 670.

Cross references. — As to Board of Veterans Services, see § 2.2-2452 et seq. and Editor's notes thereunder.

Article 16.

Herbert H. Bateman Virginia Advanced Shipbuilding And Carrier Integration Center Board.

§§ 2.2-2440 through 2.2-2447: Expired.

Editor's note. — Acts 1998, c. 790, cls. 2 and 3, enacted §§ 9-371 through 9-378, from which this Article was derived. Acts 1998, c. 790, cl. 4, as amended by Acts 2002, c. 877, cl. 2, and Acts 2003, c. 366, cl. 2, provides: "That the provisions of enactment 2 and enactment 3 of this act shall expire on July 1, 2008."

Article 17.

Virginia-Asian Advisory Board.

§ 2.2-2448. Virginia-Asian Advisory Board established; purpose. — The Virginia-Asian Advisory Board (the Board) is hereby established as an advisory board within the meaning of § 2.2-2100 in the executive branch of state government. The purpose of the Board shall be to advise the Governor on ways to improve economic and cultural links between the Commonwealth and Asian nations, with a focus on the areas of commerce and trade, art and education, and general government, and on issues affecting the Asian-American communities in the Commonwealth. (2001, c. 566, § 9-400; 2004, cc. 971, 1005.)

Editor's note. — Acts 2001, c. 566 enacted § 9-400, from which this section is derived. Pursuant to § 30-152, Acts 2001, c. 566 has been given effect in this section as set out above.

§ 2.2-2449. Membership; terms; vacancies; chairman. — The Board shall consist of twenty-one members to be appointed by the Governor as follows: eighteen citizen members who shall represent business, education, the arts, and government, at least eleven of whom shall be of Asian descent; and the Secretaries of Commerce and Trade, Health and Human Resources, and Education, or their designees to serve as ex officio members of the Board.

Citizen members shall serve for terms of four years. The Secretaries of Commerce and Trade, Health and Human Resources, and Education, or their designees, shall serve terms coincident with their terms of office. Vacancies occurring other than by expiration of term shall be filled for the unexpired term. Any member may be reappointed for successive terms.

The members of the Board shall elect a chairman and vice-chairman annually.

Members shall receive no compensation for their services, but shall be reimbursed for their actual and necessary expenses in accordance with § 2.2-2823. (2001, c. 566, § 9-401.)

Editor's note. — Acts 2001, c. 566 enacted § 9-401, from which this section is derived. Pursuant to § 30-152, Acts 2001, c. 566 has been given effect in this section as set out above.

§ 2.2-2450. Powers and duties of the Board. — The Board shall:

1. Undertake studies and gather information and data in order to accomplish its purposes as set forth in § 2.2-2448, and to formulate and present its recommendations to the Governor.

2. Apply for, accept, and expend gifts, grants, or donations from public, quasi-public or private sources, including any matching funds as may be

designated in the Appropriation Act, to enable it to better carry out its purposes.

3. Report annually its findings and recommendations to the Governor. The Board may make interim reports to the Governor as it deems advisable.

4. Account annually on its fiscal activities, including any matching funds received or expended by the Board. (2001, c. 566, § 9-402.)

Editor's note. — Acts 2001, c. 566 enacted § 9-402, from which this section is derived. Pursuant to § 30-152, Acts 2001, c. 566 has been given effect in this section as set out above.

§ **2.2-2451. Staff; cooperation from other state agencies.** — The Office of the Governor shall serve as staff to the Board. All agencies of the Commonwealth shall assist the Board upon request. (2001, c. 566, § 9-403.)

Editor's note. — Acts 2001, c. 566 enacted § 9-403, from which this section is derived. Pursuant to § 30-152, Acts 2001, c. 566 has been given effect in this section as set out above.

Article 18.

Board of Veterans Services.

§ **2.2-2452. Board of Veterans Services; membership; terms; quorum; compensation; staff.** — A. The Board of Veterans Services (the Board) is established as a policy board, within the meaning of § 2.2-2100, in the executive branch of state government. The Board shall have a total membership of 19 members that shall consist of five legislative members, 11 nonlegislative citizen members, and three ex officio members. Members shall be appointed as follows: three members of the House of Delegates to be appointed by the Speaker of the House of Delegates in accordance with the principles of proportional representation contained in the Rules of the House of Delegates; two members of the Senate to be appointed by the Senate Committee on Rules; and 11 nonlegislative citizen members to be appointed by the Governor. The Commissioner of the Department of Veterans Services shall serve ex officio with full voting privileges; and the Chairman of the Board of Trustees of the Veterans Services Foundation and the Chairman of the Joint Leadership Council of Veterans Service Organizations shall serve ex officio without voting privileges. Nonlegislative citizen members of the Board shall be citizens of the Commonwealth.

In making appointments, the Governor shall endeavor to ensure a balanced geographical representation on the Board while at the same time selecting appointees of such qualifications and experience as will allow them to provide expertise and insight into:

1. Best practices in benefits claims services, medical and health care management, or cemetery operations;
2. Performance measurements and general management principles; and
3. Nonprofit volunteer operations and management.

Each of the three areas of expertise shall be represented on the Board by at least two different appointees per area of expertise in order to allow for the Board to be capable of developing reasonable and effective policy recommendations related to the services provided to veterans of the armed forces of the United States and their eligible spouses, orphans, and dependents by the Department of Veterans Services.

Legislative members and the Commissioner of the Department of Veterans Services shall serve terms coincident with their terms of office. After the initial staggering of terms, nonlegislative citizen members shall be appointed for a term of four years. Appointments to fill vacancies, other than by expiration of a term, shall be for the unexpired terms. All members may be reappointed. However, no House member shall serve more than four consecutive two-year terms, no Senate member shall serve more than two consecutive four-year terms, and no nonlegislative citizen member shall serve more than two consecutive four-year terms.

The remainder of any term to which a member is appointed to fill a vacancy shall not constitute a term in determining the member's eligibility for reappointment. Vacancies shall be filled in the same manner as the original appointments.

B. The Board shall select a chairman from its membership and, pursuant to rules adopted by it, may elect one of its members as vice-chairman. The Commissioner of the Department of Veterans Services shall not be eligible to serve as chairman. The Board shall also elect one of its members as secretary. The Board shall meet at least three times a year at such times as it deems appropriate or on call of the chairman. A majority of the members of the Board shall constitute a quorum.

C. The Board shall be organized with at least three standing committees that shall be responsible for (i) veterans benefits, (ii) veterans care services, and (iii) veterans cemeteries.

D. The Department of Veterans Services shall provide staff to the Board. (2003, cc. 657, 670; 2004, c. 697; 2005, c. 758; 2008, cc. 467, 768.)

Editor's note. — Acts 2003, cc. 657 and 670, cl. 3, provide: "That as of the effective date of this act [July 1, 2003], the Department of Veterans Services shall be deemed the successor in interest to the Department of Veterans' Affairs. All right, title, and interest in and to any real or tangible personal property vested in the Department of Veterans' Affairs as of the effective date of this act shall be transferred to and taken as standing in the name of the Department of Veterans Services."

Acts 2003, cc. 657 and 670, cl. 4, provide: "That all rules and regulations adopted by the Department of Veterans' Affairs that are in effect as of the effective date of this act and that pertain to the subject of this act shall remain in full force and effect until altered, amended or rescinded by the Department of Veterans Services."

Acts 2005, c. 758, cl. 2, provides: "That this act shall not be construed to affect existing appointments, made by the Senate Committee on Privileges and Elections, for which the terms have not expired. However, any new appointments made after July 1, 2005 shall be made in accordance with the provisions of this act."

The 2008 amendments. — The 2008 amendments by cc. 467 and 768 are identical, and substituted "eligible spouses" for "Virginia domiciled surviving spouses" in the paragraph following subdivision A 3; and substituted "standing committees" for "subcommittees" in subsection C.

§ 2.2-2453. Compensation; expenses. — Legislative members of the Board shall receive such compensation as provided in § 30-19.12, and nonlegislative citizen members shall receive such compensation as provided in § 2.2-2813 for the performance of their duties. All members shall be reimbursed for all reasonable and necessary expenses incurred in the performance of their duties as provided in §§ 2.2-2813 and 2.2-2825. Funding for the costs of compensation and expenses of the members shall be provided by the Department of Veterans Services. (2003, cc. 657, 670; 2004, c. 1000.)

§ 2.2-2454. Powers and duties of Board. — The Board shall have the power and duty to:

1. Advise and make recommendations to the Commissioner of Veterans Services upon such matters as may arise in the performance of his duties;

2. Investigate issues related to the provision of care and services to veterans, upon request of the Commissioner of Veterans Services or the Governor;

3. Study all matters affecting the welfare of Virginia citizens who are veterans or dependents or survivors of such veterans, and make recommendations to the Commissioner of the Department of Veterans Services;

4. Develop recommendations for policies and procedures related to the efficient and effective delivery of the services provided by the Department of Veterans Services;

5. Establish policies related to the coordinated delivery of veterans services, in consultation with those agencies, entities, and organizations, including counties, cities, towns or other political subdivisions of the Commonwealth capable of providing such services;

6. Monitor the administration of all laws concerning veterans and their dependents;

7. Review and advise the Commissioner of the Department of Veterans Services on the Department's strategic plan;

8. Based on rigorous cost-benefit-value analysis, provide recommendations to the Department of Veterans Services regarding future projects and the acquisition of facilities that may benefit the State's veterans, including but not limited to veterans cemeteries and veterans care centers; and

9. Provide recommendations to the Department of Veterans Services and the Veterans Services Foundation created in § 2.2-2715 regarding gifts, grants, and other resources from public and private entities and organizations to support veterans services. (2003, cc. 657, 670.)

Article 19.

Charitable Gaming Board.

The number of this article was assigned by the Virginia Code Commission, the article having been enacted as Article 18.

§ **2.2-2455. Charitable Gaming Board; membership; terms; quorum; compensation; staff.** — A. The Charitable Gaming Board (the Board) is hereby established as a policy board within the meaning of § 2.2-2100 in the executive branch of state government. The purpose of the Board shall be to advise the Department of Agriculture and Consumer Services on all aspects of the conduct of charitable gaming in Virginia.

B. The Board shall consist of nine members appointed by the Governor subject to confirmation by the General Assembly as follows: one member who is a member of a charitable organization subject to Article 1.1:1 (§ 18.2-340.15 et seq.) of Chapter 8 of Title 18.2 in good standing with the Department; one member who is a charitable gaming supplier registered and in good standing with the Department; one member who is an owner, lessor, or lessee of premises where charitable gaming is conducted; at least one member who is or has been a law-enforcement officer in Virginia but who is not (i) a charitable gaming supplier registered with the Department, (ii) a lessor of premises where charitable gaming is conducted, or (iii) a member of a charitable organization, or who has an interest in such supplier or charitable organization or owner, lessor, or lessee of premises where charitable gaming is conducted; and five citizens who are not affiliated with a charitable organization, charitable gaming supplier, or owner, lessor, or lessee of premises where charitable gaming is conducted. To the extent practicable, the Board shall consist of individuals from different geographic regions of the Commonwealth. Each member of the Board shall have been a resident of the Commonwealth for a period of at least three years next preceding his appointment, and his continued residency shall be a condition of his tenure in office. Upon initial appointment, three members shall be appointed for four-year terms, three for three-year terms, and three for two-year terms. Thereafter, all members shall be appointed for four-year terms. Vacancies shall be filled by the Governor in the same manner as the original appointment for the unexpired portion of the term. Each Board member shall be eligible for reappointment for a second consecutive term at the discretion of the Governor. Persons who are first appointed to initial terms of less than four years shall thereafter be eligible for reappointment to two consecutive terms of four years each. No sitting member of the General Assembly shall be eligible for appointment to the Board. The members of the Board shall serve at the pleasure of the Governor.

C. The Board shall elect a chairman from among its members.

D. A quorum shall consist of five members. The decision of a majority of those members present and voting shall constitute a decision of the Board.

E. For each day or part thereof spent in the performance of his duties, each member of the Board shall receive such compensation and reimbursement for his reasonable expenses as provided in § 2.2-2104.

F. The Board shall adopt rules and procedures for the conduct of its business, including a provision that Board members shall abstain or otherwise recuse themselves from voting on any matter in which they or a member of their immediate family have a personal interest in a transaction as defined in § 2.2-3101. The Board shall meet at least four times a year, and other meetings may be held at any time or place determined by the Board or upon call of the chairman or upon a written request to the chairman by any two members. Except for emergency meetings and meetings governed by § 2.2-3708 requiring a longer notice, all members shall be duly notified of the time and place of any regular or other meeting at least 10 days in advance of such meeting.

G. Staff to the Board shall be provided by the Department of Agriculture and Consumer Services. (2003, c. 884; 2008, cc. 387, 689.)

The number of this section was assigned by the Virginia Code Commission, the number in the 2003 act having been 2.2-2452.

Cross references. — As to the Department of Charitable Gaming, see § 2.2-905 et seq.

Editor's note. — Acts 2003, c. 884, cl. 3 provides: "That all rules and regulations of the Virginia Charitable Gaming Commission that are in effect as of the effective date of this act shall remain in full force and effect until altered, amended, or rescinded by the Charitable Gaming Board created in accordance with this act."

Acts 2008, cc. 387 and 689, cl. 3 provides: "That as of July 1, 2008, the Department of Agriculture and Consumer Services shall be deemed successor in interest to the Department of Charitable Gaming to the extent that this act transfers powers and duties. All right, title, and interest in and to any real or tangible personal property vested in the Department of Charitable Gaming shall be transferred to and taken as standing in the name of the Department of Agriculture and Consumer Services."

Acts 2008, cc. 387 and 689, cl. 4 provides: "That the Governor may transfer an appropriation or any portion thereof within a state agency established, abolished, or otherwise affected by the provisions of this act, or from one such agency to another, to support the changes in organization or responsibility resulting from or required by the provisions of this act."

Acts 2008, cc. 387 and 689, cl. 5 provides: "That all rules and regulations adopted by the Department of Charitable Gaming or the Charitable Gaming Board that are in effect as of July 1, 2008, and that pertain to the subject of this act, shall remain in full force and effect until altered, amended, or rescinded by the Department of Agriculture and Consumer Services or the Charitable Gaming Board."

The 2008 amendments. — The 2008 amendments by cc. 387 and 689 are identical, and substituted "Department of Agriculture and Consumer Services" for "Department of Charitable Gaming" in the second sentence of subsection A and in subsection G.

§ 2.2-2456. Duties of the Charitable Gaming Board. — The Board shall:

1. Promulgate regulations in accordance with the Administrative Process Act (§ 2.2-4000 et seq.) not inconsistent with the laws of Virginia necessary to carry out the provisions of this chapter and the provisions of Article 1.1:1

(§ 18.2-340.15 et seq.) of Chapter 8 of Title 18.2. Such regulations may include penalties for violations;

2. Advise the Department of Agriculture and Consumer Services on the conduct of charitable gaming in Virginia and recommend changes to Article 1.1:1 (§ 18.2-340.15 et seq.) of Chapter 8 of Title 18.2; and

3. Keep a complete and accurate record of its proceedings. A copy of such record and any other public records not exempt from disclosure under the Freedom of Information Act (§ 2.2-3700 et seq.) shall be available for public inspection and copying during regular office hours at the Department of Agriculture and Consumer Services. (2003, c. 884; 2008, cc. 387, 689.)

The number of this section was assigned by the Virginia Code Commission, the number in the 2003 act having been 2.2-2453.

Editor's note. — Acts 2008, cc. 387 and 689, cl. 3 provides: "That as of July 1, 2008, the Department of Agriculture and Consumer Services shall be deemed successor in interest to the Department of Charitable Gaming to the extent that this act transfers powers and duties. All right, title, and interest in and to any real or tangible personal property vested in the Department of Charitable Gaming shall be transferred to and taken as standing in the name of the Department of Agriculture and Consumer Services."

Acts 2008, cc. 387 and 689, cl. 4 provides: "That the Governor may transfer an appropriation or any portion thereof within a state agency established, abolished, or otherwise affected by the provisions of this act, or from one such agency to another, to support the changes in organization or responsibility resulting from or required by the provisions of this act."

Acts 2008, cc. 387 and 689, cl. 5 provides: "That all rules and regulations adopted by the Department of Charitable Gaming or the Charitable Gaming Board that are in effect as of July 1, 2008, and that pertain to the subject of this act, shall remain in full force and effect until altered, amended, or rescinded by the Department of Agriculture and Consumer Services or the Charitable Gaming Board."

The 2008 amendments. — The 2008 amendments by cc. 387 and 689 are identical, and substituted "Department of Argriculture and Consumer Services" for "Department of Charitable Gaming" in subdivisions 2 and 3.

Article 20.

Information Technology Investment Board.

The number of this article was assigned by the Virginia Code Commission, the article having been enacted as Article 18.

§ 2.2-2457. Information Technology Investment Board; membership; terms; quorum; compensation; staff. — A. The Information Technology Investment Board (the Board) is established as a supervisory board, within the meaning of § 2.2-2100, in the executive branch of state government. The Board shall be responsible for the planning, budgeting, acquiring, using, disposing, managing, and administering of information technology in the Commonwealth.

B. The Board shall consist of 10 members that include eight nonlegislative citizen members and two ex officio members as follows: (i) four nonlegislative citizen members appointed by the Governor, of whom one shall be appointed from a list of not less than seven individuals nominated jointly by the Chairs of the Senate Committee on General Laws and the House Committee on Science and Technology in consultation with their respective committee memberships; (ii) four nonlegislative citizen members appointed by the Joint Rules Committee from a list recommended by the Joint Commission on Technology and Science; (iii) the Secretary of Technology who shall serve ex officio with full voting privileges; and (iv) the Auditor of Public Accounts shall serve ex officio without voting privileges. The individuals jointly nominated by the Chairs of the Senate Committee on General Laws and the House Committee on Science and Technology shall, at a minimum, have experience as senior information technology management personnel for a company with annual gross revenues in excess of $50 million. The other nonlegislative citizen members shall have experience in information technology systems or other technology systems including but not limited to human resources, environment, transportation, or finance.

The ex officio members of the Board shall serve terms coincident with their respective terms of office. After the initial staggering of terms, nonlegislative citizen members shall be appointed for terms of four years. Appointments to fill vacancies, other than by expiration of a term, shall be for the unexpired terms. All members may be reappointed. However, no nonlegislative citizen member shall serve more than two consecutive four-year terms. The remainder of any term to which a member is appointed to fill a vacancy shall not constitute a term in determining the member's eligibility for reappointment. Vacancies shall be filled in the same manner as the original appointments.

C. The Board shall elect its chairman and vice-chairman from among its members for two-year terms. A majority of the members shall constitute a quorum. The Board shall meet at least quarterly each year. The meetings of the Board shall be held at the call of the chairman or whenever the majority of the members so request.

D. Nonlegislative citizen members shall receive compensation and shall be reimbursed for all reasonable and necessary expenses incurred in the performance of their duties, as provided in §§ 2.2-2813 and 2.2-2825. Funding for the costs of compensation and expenses of the members shall be provided by the Virginia Information Technologies Agency.

E. The disclosure requirements of subsection B of § 2.2-3114 of the State and Local Government Conflict of Interest Act shall apply to citizen members of the Board.

F. The Virginia Information Technologies Agency shall serve as staff to the Board. (2003, cc. 981, 1021; 2004, c. 1000.)

The number of this section was assigned by the Virginia Code Commission, the number in the 2003 act having been 2.2-2452.

Cross references. — For the Council on Technology Services, and its purpose of advising the Chief Information Officer, see § 2.2-2651.

Editor's note. — For provisions of Acts 2003, cc. 981 and 1021, cls. 4 to 16, reflecting the intent of the General Assembly to provide for the consolidation of the procurement and operational functions of information technology for state agencies in a single agency, and related transitional and other provisions, see the Editor's note at § 2.2-2005.

Acts 2004, c. 1000, cl. 5, provides: "That this act shall not be construed to affect existing appointments for which the terms have not expired. However, any new appointments or appointments to fill vacancies made after the effective date of this act shall be made in accordance with the provisions of this act."

Acts 2008, c. 879, effective for the biennium ending June 30, 2010, in Item 434 E, provides: "The Board shall not delegate any duties or responsibilities to the chairman other than to preside over meetings or act as the Board's spokesperson in public meetings. The chairman shall have no powers or duties greater than those given to any other Board member. The Board shall use the Chief Information Officer to arrange Board and committee meetings and agendas and solicit the Chief Information Officer's advice on Information Technology Investment Board meeting topics and the frequency of meetings."

§ **2.2-2458. Powers and duties of the Board.** — The Board shall have the power and duty to:

1. Appoint the Chief Information Officer as the chief administrative officer of the Board to oversee the operation of VITA pursuant to § 2.2-2005;
2. Adopt rules and procedures for the conduct of its business;
3. Approve or disapprove the development of all major information technology projects as defined in § 2.2-2006. The Board may terminate any major information technology project recommended for termination by the Chief Information Officer pursuant to § 2.2-2015;

4. Approve strategies, standards, and priorities recommended by the Chief Information Officer for the use of information technology for state agencies in the executive branch of state government;

5. Approve the four-year plan for information technology projects;

6. Approve statewide technical and data standards for information technology and related systems;

7. Approve statewide information technology architecture and related set of system standards;

8. Approve criteria for the review and approval of the planning, scheduling and tracking of major information technology projects as defined in § 2.2-2006;

9. Adopt resolutions or regulations conferring upon the Chief Information Officer all such powers, authorities and duties as the Board deems necessary or proper to carry out the purposes of Chapter 20.1 of Title 2.2; and

10. Submit by September 1 of each year a list of recommended technology investment projects and priorities for funding such projects to the Governor and the General Assembly. (2003, cc. 981, 1021.)

The number of this section was assigned by the Virginia Code Commission, the number in the 2003 act having been 2.2-2453.

Editor's note. — Acts 2008, c. 879, effective for the biennium ending June 30, 2010, in Item 63 A 3 b, provides: "In addition to the processes and data standards used to support work performed for the Department of Transportation's system modernization effort, the VEAP Office Director shall identify major Commonwealth financial and information collection processes and establish data standards for each process. On December 1, 2008, and every six months thereafter, the VEAP Office Director shall report and recommend to the Chief Information Officer and the Information Technology Investment Board, the processes reviewed and the data standards established which merit adoption as part of § 2.2-2458, Code of Virginia. The VEAP Office Director shall also develop, along with the Chief Information Officer, a migration strategy to implement the data standards and provide such strategy to the Governor and the Information Technology Investment Board for their review beginning December 1, 2008. As part of the migration strategy and its implementation, the VEAP Office Director shall identify agencies and institutions which have sufficiently modern accounting systems that can adopt and implement these data standards. All agencies and institutions shall cooperate with the VEAP Office Director in implementing the data standards at those agencies and institutions with sufficiently modern accounting systems and the VEAP Office Director shall report, every six months after submitting the Plan to the Governor and the Information Technology Investment Board, those agencies and institutions having adopted the data standards and any agencies or institutions that have not cooperated with the implementation."

Article 21.

Latino Advisory Board.

§ 2.2-2459. Latino Advisory Board; membership; terms; compensation and expenses. — A. The Latino Advisory Board (the Board) is established as an advisory board, within the meaning of § 2.2-2100, in the executive branch of state government. The Board shall consist of 21 nonlegislative citizen members, at least 15 of whom shall be of Latino descent, who shall be appointed by the Governor and serve at his pleasure. In addition, the Secretaries of the Commonwealth, Commerce and Trade, Education, Health and Human Resources, Public Safety, and Transportation, or their designees shall serve as ex officio members without voting privileges. All members shall be residents of the Commonwealth.

B. After the initial staggering of terms, nonlegislative citizen members shall be appointed for a term of four years. Appointments to fill vacancies shall be for the unexpired terms. No member shall be eligible to serve more than two successive four-year terms; however, after the expiration of the remainder of a term to which a member was appointed to fill a vacancy, two additional terms may be served by such member if appointed thereto.

C. The Board shall elect from its membership a chairman and vice-chairman. A majority of the members of the Board shall constitute a quorum. Meetings of the Board shall be limited to four per year and shall be held upon the call of the chairman or whenever the majority of the members so request.

D. Members of the Board shall receive no compensation for their services, but shall be reimbursed for all reasonable and necessary expenses incurred in the performance of their duties as provided in §§ 2.2-2813 and 2.2-2825. (2005, c. 636.)

Editor's note. — Acts 2005, c. 636, cl. 2, provides: "That the intent of this act is to codify the Latino Advisory Commission, which exists pursuant to an executive order of the Governor, as the Latino Advisory Board, a permanent advisory board in the executive branch."

Acts 2005, c. 636, cl. 3, provides: "That the initial appointments of nonlegislative citizen members in accordance with this act shall be staggered as follows: seven members for a one-year term, six members for a two-year term, five members for a three-year term, and three members for a four-year term."

Acts 2005, c. 636, cl. 4, provides: "That the provisions of this act shall become effective on October 15, 2005."

§ 2.2-2460. Powers and duties; acceptance of gifts and grants. — A. The Board shall have the power and duty to:

1. Advise the Governor regarding the development of economic, professional, cultural, educational, and governmental links between the Commonwealth of Virginia, the Latino community in Virginia, and Latin America;
2. Undertake studies, symposiums, research, and factual reports to gather information to formulate and present recommendations to the Governor relative to issues of concern and importance to the Latino community in the Commonwealth; and
3. Advise the Governor as needed regarding any statutory, regulatory, or other issues of importance to the Latino community in the Commonwealth.

B. The Board may apply for, accept, and expend gifts, grants, or donations from public or private sources to enable it to carry out its objectives. (2005, c. 636.)

§ 2.2-2461. Staff; cooperation from other state agencies. — The Office of the Governor shall serve as staff to the Board. All agencies of the Commonwealth shall assist the Board upon request. (2005, c. 636.)

CHAPTER 25.

Commissions.

ARTICLE 1.

Southside Virginia Business and Education Commission.

§§ 2.2-2500 through 2.2-2502: Repealed by Acts 2003, c. 349.

ARTICLE 2.

Special Advisory Commission on Mandated Health Insurance Benefits.

§ 2.2-2503. Special Advisory Commission on Mandated Health Insurance Benefits; membership; terms; meetings; compensation and expenses; staff; chairman's executive summary. — A. The Special Advisory Commission on Mandated Health Insurance Benefits (the Commission) is established as an advisory commission within the meaning of § 2.2-2100, in the executive branch of state government. The purpose of the Commission shall be to advise the Governor and the General Assembly on the social and financial impact of current and proposed mandated benefits and providers, in the manner set forth in this article.

B. The Commission shall consist of 18 members that include six legislative members, 10 nonlegislative citizen members, and two ex officio members as follows: one member of the Senate Committee on Education and Health and one member of the Senate Committee on Commerce and Labor appointed by the Senate Committee on Rules; two members of the House Committee on Health, Welfare and Institutions and two members of the House Committee on Commerce and Labor appointed by the Speaker of the House of Delegates in accordance with the principles of proportional representation contained in the Rules of the House of Delegates; 10 nonlegislative citizen members appointed by the Governor that include one physician, one chief executive officer of a general acute care hospital, one allied health professional, one representative of small business, one representative of a major industry, one expert in the field of medical ethics, two representatives of the accident and health insurance industry, and two nonlegislative citizen members; and the State Commissioner of Health and the State Commissioner of Insurance, or their designees, who shall serve as ex officio nonvoting members.

C. All nonlegislative citizen members shall be appointed for terms of four years. Legislative and ex officio members shall serve terms coincident with their terms of office. All members may be reappointed. However, no House member shall serve more than four consecutive two-year terms, no Senate member shall serve more than two consecutive four-year terms, and no nonlegislative citizen member shall serve more than two consecutive four-year terms. Vacancies occurring other than by expiration of a term shall be filled for the unexpired term. Vacancies shall be filled in the manner as the original appointments. The remainder of any term to which a member is appointed to fill a vacancy shall not constitute a term in determining the member's eligibility for reappointment.

D. The Commission shall meet at the request of the chairman, the majority of the voting members or the Governor. The Commission shall elect a chairman and a vice-chairman, as determined by the membership. A majority of the members of the Commission shall constitute a quorum.

E. Legislative members of the Commission shall receive such compensation as provided in § 30-19.12, and nonlegislative citizen members shall receive such compensation for the performance of their duties as provided in § 2.2-2813. All members shall be reimbursed for all reasonable and necessary expenses incurred in the performance of their duties as provided in §§ 2.2-2813 and 2.2-2825. Funding for the compensation and costs of expenses of the members shall be provided by the State Corporation Commission.

F. The Bureau of Insurance, the State Health Department, and the Joint Legislative Audit and Review Commission and such other state agencies as may be considered appropriate by the Commission shall provide staff assistance to the Commission. The Joint Legislative Audit and Review Commission shall conduct assessments, analyses, and evaluations of proposed mandated health insurance benefits and mandated providers as provided in subsection D of § 30-58.1, and report its findings with respect to the proposed mandates to the Commission.

G. The chairman of the Commission shall submit to the Governor and the General Assembly an annual executive summary of the interim activity and work of the Commission no later than the first day of each regular session of the General Assembly. The executive summary shall be submitted as provided in the procedures of the Division of Legislative Automated Systems for the processing of legislative documents and reports and shall be posted on the General Assembly's website. (1990, cc. 618, 634, §§ 9-297, 9-298, 9-300; 1997, c. 415; 2001, c. 844; 2003, c. 885; 2005, c. 758; 2006, c. 413.)

Editor's note. — Acts 2003, c. 885, cl. 7, provides: "That all current members of the collegial bodies whose terms have been modified by this act shall be eligible, if reappointed, to the full number of terms provided by this act regardless of prior service."

Acts 2005, c. 758, cl. 2, provides: "That this act shall not be construed to affect existing appointments, made by the Senate Committee on Privileges and Elections, for which the terms have not expired. However, any new appointments made after July 1, 2005 shall be made in accordance with the provisions of this act."

§ **2.2-2504. Duties of the Commission.** — The Special Advisory Commission shall:

1. Develop and maintain, with the Bureau of Insurance, a system and program of data collection to assess the impact of mandated benefits and providers, including costs to employers and insurers, impact of treatment, cost savings in the health care system, number of providers and other data as may be appropriate.

2. Advise and assist the Bureau of Insurance on matters relating to mandated insurance benefits and provider regulations.

3. Prescribe the format, content, and timing of information to be submitted to it in its assessment of proposed and existing mandated benefits and providers. Such format, content, and timing requirements shall be binding upon all parties submitting information to the Commission in its assessment of proposed and existing mandated benefits and providers.

4. Provide assessments of proposed and existing mandated benefits and providers and other studies of mandated benefits and provider issues as requested by the General Assembly.

5. Provide additional information and recommendations, relating to any system of mandated health insurance benefits and providers, to the Governor and the General Assembly upon request.

6. Report annually on its activities to the joint standing committees of the General Assembly having jurisdiction over insurance by December 1 of each year.

7. Review and evaluate as necessary the benefits and other provisions of the essential and standard health benefits plans established pursuant to § 38.2-3431, and submit to the State Corporation Commission, for adoption in the State Corporation Commission's applicable regulations pursuant to § 38.2-3431, any modifications needed to maintain or enhance the affordability and marketability of the plans. (1990, cc. 618, 634, § 9-298; 1997, c. 415; 2001, c. 844.)

§ **2.2-2505. Assessment of proposed mandated benefits and providers.** — A. Except as may be otherwise provided in this section, whenever a legislative measure containing a mandated health insurance benefit or provider is proposed, the standing committee of the General Assembly having jurisdiction over the proposal shall request that the Commission prepare and forward to the Governor and the General Assembly a study that assesses the social and financial impact and the medical efficacy of the proposed mandate. The Commission shall be given a period of twenty-four months to complete and submit its assessment.

B. Whenever a legislative measure, as described in subsection A, is identical or substantially similar to a legislative measure previously reviewed by the Special Advisory Commission within the three-year period immediately preceding the then current session of the General Assembly, the standing committee may request a Commission study as provided in subsection A.

C. The standing committees of the General Assembly having jurisdiction over health insurance matters shall request that the Commission assess the social and financial impact and the medical efficacy of existing mandated benefits and providers. The committees shall submit a schedule of evaluations to the Commission setting forth the dates by which particular mandates shall be evaluated by the Commission. (1990, cc. 618, 634, § 9-299; 1992, c. 626; 2001, c. 844.)

Article 3.

Virginia Advisory Commission on Intergovernmental Relations.

§§ **2.2-2506, 2.2-2507:** Repealed by Acts 2004, cc. 34, 155.

Editor's note. — Repealed § 2.2-2506 was amended by Acts 2004, c. 650.

Article 4.

Virginia Commission for the Arts.

§ **2.2-2508. Virginia Commission for the Arts; official agency to receive and disburse funds from National Foundation on the Arts; membership; terms; compensation.** — A. The Virginia Commission for the Arts (the "Commission") is established as an advisory commission within the meaning of § 2.2-2100, in the executive branch of state government.

B. The Commission is designated the official agency of the Commonwealth to receive and disburse any funds made available to the Commonwealth by the National Foundation on the Arts.

C. The Commission shall consist of thirteen members appointed by the Governor subject to confirmation by the General Assembly. No employee of the Commonwealth or member of the General Assembly shall be eligible for appointment as a member of the Commission. At least one member, but no more than two members, shall be appointed from each Congressional district in the Commonwealth.

D. Except for initial appointments, each member shall serve a five-years term; provided that no member of the Commission who serves a full five-year term shall be eligible for appointment during the five-year period following the expiration of his term. All vacancies shall be filled for the balance of the unexpired term in the same manner as original appointments.

E. The Commission shall designate one of its members as chairman. A majority of the members of the Commission shall constitute a quorum.

F. The members of the Commission shall not receive any compensation for their services, but shall be reimbursed for the reasonable and necessary expenses incurred in the discharge of their duties as provided in § 2.2-2825. (1968, c. 567, §§ 9-84.01:1, 9-84.02, 9-84.03; 1979, c. 314; 2001, c. 844.)

§ **2.2-2509. Duties of the Commission.** — A. The Commission shall perform among others the following duties:

1. Stimulate and encourage throughout the Commonwealth growth in artistic quality and excellence, public interest and participation in the arts, and access to high quality and affordable art for all Virginians;

2. Make recommendations concerning appropriate methods to encourage economic viability, an intellectually stimulating environment for artists, and participation in and appreciation of the arts to meet the legitimate needs and aspirations of persons in all parts of the Commonwealth;

3. Promote the development and implementation of a planned, sequential, and comprehensive program of arts education, taught by licensed teachers endorsed in arts education, in the public elementary and secondary schools of the Commonwealth;

4. Provide supplemental learning opportunities to the public school arts education curriculum;

5. Encourage the development of a network of professional arts organizations, the media, and arts promoters, including, but not limited to, the literary, visual, and performing arts for the production of classical and new works of art, and diversity in artistic expressions;

6. Provide funding for and technical assistance to artists, recognized nonprofit arts organizations, and arts organizations and activities which celebrate and preserve the various cultures represented among the citizens of the Commonwealth;

7. Encourage and support the creation of new works of art, arts organizations whose primary objective is to increase public access to the arts, particularly in underserved areas, and performing arts tours to increase the availability of this form of artistic expression throughout the Commonwealth;

8. Establish a program of financial assistance to provide scholarships, grants, and other awards to artists who demonstrate exceptional ability and talent;

9. Establish an advisory panel composed of artists, art administrators, and citizens to advise the Commission concerning fiscal matters;

10. Encourage arts organizations to dedicate to endowment at least one dollar of the price of each adult admission to performances or exhibitions or at least one percent of moneys collected in fund campaigns;

11. Encourage arts organizations to develop and implement endowment enlargement plans which yield enough income to underwrite one-third of the organizations' annual operating costs;

12. Apply to any appropriate agency or officer of the United States for participation in or receipt of aid from any federal program respecting the arts, and, in respect thereto, enter into contracts and agreements with the United States or any appropriate agency thereof;

13. Provide incentives to local governments to encourage public support and funding of the arts;

14. Accept gifts, contributions and bequests of money or any other thing to be used for carrying out the purposes of this article;

15. Develop specific procedures for the administration and implementation of a program, so long as any such program is for the benefit of a nonprofit organization, qualifying as a § 501 (c) (3) organization under the Internal Revenue Code, whereby interest earned on endowment funds donated to stimulate and encourage public interest and enjoyment of music and the performing arts may be matched by state funds appropriated for this program, and prepare written guidelines to govern such program; and

16. Administer any funds available to the Commission and disburse such funds in accordance with the purposes of this article. In allocating funds to be disbursed to arts organizations, the Commission shall give preferential consideration to arts organizations actively implementing an endowment enlargement plan, either individually or as members of a regional consortium of arts organizations.

B. Nothing in this article shall be construed to affect the statutory purposes of the Virginia Museum of Fine Arts. (1968, c. 567, §§ 9-84.03, 9-84.06; 1979, c. 314; 1989, c. 331; 1992, cc. 218, 432; 1996, c. 161; 2001, c. 844.)

§ 2.2-2510. Agency supervision; employment of personnel; budget preparation. — The Governor may appoint a Director who shall serve at his pleasure. The Director may employ the personnel required to assist the Commission in the exercise and performance of its powers and duties. The Director shall supervise and manage such personnel and shall prepare, approve and submit all requests for appropriations, and be responsible for all expenditures pursuant to appropriations. (1970, c. 334, § 9-84.07; 1984, c. 444; 1985, c. 397; 2001, c. 844.)

Article 5.

Commissioners for Promotion of Uniformity of Legislation.

§§ **2.2-2511, 2.2-2512:** Repealed by Acts 2002, c. 491, effective April 5, 2002.

Cross references. — As to the Commissioners for Promotion of Uniformity of Legislation, see § 30-196 et seq.

Article 6.

Virginia Research and Technology Advisory Commission.

§ 2.2-2513. Commission established; purpose. — The Virginia Research and Technology Advisory Commission (Commission) is established as an advisory commission within the meaning of § 2.2-2100, in the executive branch of state government. The purpose of the Commission shall be to advise the Governor on appropriate research and technology strategies for the Commonwealth with emphasis on policy recommendations that will enhance the global competitive advantage of both research institutions and technology-based commercial endeavors within the Commonwealth. (2001, c. 788, § 9-396.)

Editor's note. — Acts 2001, c. 788 enacted § 9-396, from which this section is derived. Pursuant to § 30-152, Acts 2001, c. 788 has been given effect in this article as set out above.

§ 2.2-2514. Membership; terms; vacancies; chairmen. — A. Persons appointed to the Board shall be selected for their knowledge of, background in, or experience with basic and applied research, emerging technologies, commercialization of the results and outputs of research activities, and the development and financing of technology intensive enterprises.

B. The Commission shall consist of 31 members as follows: two members of the House Committee on Science and Technology appointed by the Speaker of the House of Delegates; the chairman of the Senate Committee on General Laws or his designee; and 13 citizen members representing research- and technology-intensive industries, four of whom shall be appointed by the Speaker of the House of Delegates, two of whom shall be appointed by the Senate Committee on Rules, and seven of whom shall be appointed by the Governor; the Secretaries of Commerce and Trade, Education, and Technology, or their designees; and the President of the Center for Innovative Technology or his designee. The following members shall serve as ex officio members with voting privileges: the Vice-Provosts of Research, or their designees, at The College of William and Mary, Eastern Virginia Medical School, George Mason University, James Madison University, Old Dominion University, University of Virginia, Virginia Commonwealth University, and Virginia Polytechnic Institute and State University; the Director of the Thomas Jefferson National Accelerator Facility (Jefferson Lab) or his designee, and the senior technology executive of the Naval Surface Warfare Center, Dahlgren Division or his designee. The Director of the NASA Langley Research Center or his designee shall also serve as an ex officio member, but without voting privileges. Legislative members shall be appointed to serve terms coincident with their terms of office. The citizen members shall be appointed for terms of four years, except that appointments to fill vacancies shall be for the unexpired term. Vacancies shall be filled in the manner of the original appointments.

C. The Governor shall designate one member representing Virginia's research universities and one member representing the private sector as cochairs.

D. A majority of the members of the Commission shall constitute a quorum. Commission meetings shall be upon the call of the cochairs.

E. Members of the Commission shall receive compensation and be entitled to be reimbursed for all reasonable and necessary expenses incurred in the performance of their duties as provided in §§ 2.2-2104, 2.2-2813, 2.2-2823, 2.2-2825 and 30-19.12. (2001, c. 788, § 9-397; 2002, c. 381; 2005, cc. 611, 687, 758.)

Editor's note. — Acts 2001, c. 788 enacted § 9-397, from which this section is derived. Pursuant to § 30-152, Acts 2001, c. 788 has been given effect in this section as set out above.

Acts 2005, c. 758, cl. 2, provides: "That this act shall not be construed to affect existing appointments, made by the Senate Committee on Privileges and Elections, for which the terms have not expired. However, any new appointments made after July 1, 2005 shall be made in accordance with the provisions of this act."

§ 2.2-2515. Powers and duties of the Commission. — The Commission shall:

1. Undertake studies and gather information and data in order to accomplish its purposes as set forth in § 2.2-2513, and to formulate and present its recommendations to the Governor and the General Assembly;

2. Make recommendations upon all proposals submitted to the Grant Allocation Committee, as described in paragraph 4 of subsection D of § 2.2-2233.1, for grant allocations to be disbursed from the Commonwealth Technology Research Fund created by § 2.2-2233.1;

3. Apply for, accept, and expend gifts, grants, or donations from public, quasi-public or private sources and state funds that may be appropriated by the General Assembly to carry out its purpose; and

4. Report annually its findings and recommendations to the Governor. The Commission may make interim reports to the Governor as it deems advisable. (2001, c. 788, § 9-398; 2003, c. 362.)

Editor's note. — Acts 2001, c. 788 enacted § 9-398, from which this section is derived. Pursuant to § 30-152, Acts 2001, c. 788 has been given effect in this section as set out above.

§ 2.2-2516. Funding for Commission's activities. — Funding necessary to support the Commission's work, including but not limited to the compensation and reimbursement pursuant to subsection E of § 2.2-2514, shall be provided by the Innovative Technology Authority and other sources pursuant to subdivision 2 of § 2.2-2515. (2001, c. 788, § 9-399.)

Editor's note. — Acts 2001, c. 788 enacted § 9-399, from which this section is derived. Pursuant to § 30-152, Acts 2001, c. 788 has been given effect in this section as set out above.

§ 2.2-2517. Staff; cooperation from other state agencies. — The Innovative Technology Authority shall provide staff support to the Commission. All agencies of the Commonwealth shall assist the Commission upon request. (2001, c. 788, § 9-400.)

Editor's note. — Acts 2001, c. 788 enacted § 9-400, from which this section is derived. Pursuant to § 30-152, Acts 2001, c. 788 has been given effect in this section as set out above.

Article 7.

Virginia Commission on Higher Education Board Appointments.

§ **2.2-2518. The Virginia Commission on Higher Education Board Appointments; purpose.** — The Virginia Commission on Higher Education Board Appointments, (the Commission) is established as an advisory commission in the executive branch of state government.

The purpose of the Commission shall be to review and evaluate potential appointees to the governing bodies of Virginia's public institutions of higher education, the Virginia Community College Board, and the State Council of Higher Education for Virginia, and to make recommendations to the Governor. (2005, cc. 933, 945.)

§ **2.2-2519. Membership; terms; quorum; meetings.** — The Commission shall have a total membership of seven members that shall consist of five nonlegislative citizen members and two ex officio members. Nonlegislative citizen members shall be appointed as follows: two nonlegislative citizen members who shall be former members of either the board of visitors of a public institution of higher education or the State Board for Community Colleges; one nonlegislative citizen member who shall be either a former president, provost, or executive vice-president of a public institution of higher education; and two nonlegislative citizen members who shall be citizens-at-large to be appointed by the Governor. The Secretary of Education or his designee and the Secretary of the Commonwealth or his designee shall serve ex officio with nonvoting privileges. Nonlegislative citizen members of the Commission shall be citizens of the Commonwealth.

Nonlegislative citizen members shall serve at the pleasure of the Governor, and ex officio members of the Commission shall serve terms coincident with their terms of office. (2005, cc. 933, 945.)

§ **2.2-2520. Compensation; expenses.** — Members of the Commission shall serve without compensation. All members shall be reimbursed for all reasonable and necessary expenses incurred in the performance of their duties as provided in §§ 2.2-2813 and 2.2-2825. Funding for the expenses of the members shall be provided by the Office of the Secretary of the Commonwealth. (2005, cc. 933, 945.)

§ **2.2-2521. Powers and duties of the Commission.** — The Commission shall have the following powers and duties:

1. Develop and implement a process for evaluating potential appointees to higher education governing boards, based on substantive qualifications, including merit and experience.

2. Make recommendations to the Governor at least 30 days prior to the expiration of terms for which recommendations have been requested to fill vacancies on higher education governing boards. (2005, cc. 933, 945.)

§ **2.2-2522. Staffing.** — The Office of the Secretary of the Commonwealth shall serve as staff to the Commission, and shall provide to the members copies of resumes and correspondence it receives related to appointments to higher education governing boards. All agencies of the Commonwealth shall provide assistance to the Commission, upon request. (2005, cc. 933, 945.)

§ **2.2-2523:** Repealed by Acts 2008, cc. 50 and 710, cl. 1.

Editor's note. — This section had provided for a July 1, 2008, sunset for this article.

ARTICLE 7.1.

Community Integration Advisory Commission.

(Expires July 1, 2009.)

§ **2.2-2524. (Expires July 1, 2009) The Community Integration Advisory Commission; purpose.** — The Community Integration Advisory Commission (the Commission) is established as an advisory commission in the executive branch of state government. The purpose of the Commission shall be to monitor the progress of all executive branch state agencies toward community integration of Virginians with disabilities in accordance with all applicable state and federal laws in order that persons with disabilities may enjoy the benefits of society and the freedoms of daily living. (2006, c. 894.)

Cross references. — For July 1, 2009, sunset provision for this article, see § 2.2-2529.

§ **2.2-2525. (Expires July 1, 2009) Membership; terms; quorum; meetings.** — The Commission shall have a total membership of 21 nonlegislative citizen members to be appointed as follows: four nonlegislative citizen members, of whom two shall be persons with disabilities, one shall be the relative of a citizen of the Commonwealth with a disability, and one shall be a provider of services to citizens of the Commonwealth with disabilities or an advocate for persons with disabilities or for services to such persons to be appointed by the Senate Committee on Rules; six nonlegislative citizen members, of whom three shall be persons with disabilities, one shall be the relative of a citizen of the Commonwealth with a disability, and two shall be providers of services to citizens of the Commonwealth with disabilities or an advocate for persons with disabilities or for services to such persons to be appointed by the Speaker of the House of Delegates; and 11 nonlegislative citizen members, of whom three shall be persons with disabilities, one shall be a resident of a state mental health facility, one shall be a resident of a state mental retardation training facility, one shall be a resident of a nursing facility, two shall be the relatives of citizens of the Commonwealth with disabilities, and three shall be providers of services to citizens of the Commonwealth with disabilities or an advocate for persons with disabilities or for services to such persons to be appointed by the Governor. Nonlegislative citizen members of the Commission shall be citizens of the Commonwealth.

Nonlegislative citizen members shall serve a term of four years; however, no nonlegislative citizen member shall serve more than two consecutive four-year terms. Appointments to fill vacancies, other than by expiration of a term, shall be for the unexpired terms. Vacancies shall be filled in the same manner as the original appointments. All members may be reappointed. The remainder of any term to which a member is appointed to fill a vacancy shall not constitute a term in determining the member's eligibility for reappointment.

The Commission shall elect a chairman and vice-chairman from among its membership. A majority of the members shall constitute a quorum. The Commission shall meet not less than four times each year. The meetings of the Commission shall be held at the call of the chairman or whenever the majority of the members so request. (2006, c. 894.)

Cross references. — For July 1, 2009, sunset provision for this article, see § 2.2-2529.

§ **2.2-2526. (Expires July 1, 2009) Compensation; expenses.** — Members shall serve without compensation. However, all members shall be reimbursed for all reasonable and necessary expenses incurred in the performance of their duties as provided in §§ 2.2-2813 and 2.2-2825. Funding for the costs of expenses of the members shall be provided by such executive branch agencies as the Governor designates. (2006, c. 894.)

Cross references. — For July 1, 2009, sunset provision for this article, see § 2.2-2529.

§ **2.2-2527. (Expires July 1, 2009) Powers and duties of the Commission.** — The Commission shall have the following powers and duties:

1. To monitor the implementation of state and federal laws pertaining to community integration of Virginians with disabilities; and
2. To make appropriate recommendations to the Governor concerning community integration of Virginians with disabilities. (2006, c. 894.)

Cross references. — For July 1, 2009, sunset provision for this article, see § 2.2-2529.

§ **2.2-2528. (Expires July 1, 2009) Staffing.** — The Virginia Board for People with Disabilities, to the extent permitted by federal law, and such other executive branch agencies as the Governor may designate, shall provide staff support to the Commission. All agencies of the Commonwealth shall provide assistance to the Commission, upon request. (2006, c. 894.)

Cross references. — For July 1, 2009, sunset provision for this article, see § 2.2-2529.

§ **2.2-2529. (Expires July 1, 2009) Sunset.** — This article shall expire on July 1, 2009. (2006, c. 894.)

Article 8.

Virginia Commission on Immigration.

§§ **2.2-2530, 2.2-2531:** Expired.

Editor's note. — Acts 2007, c. 849, which enacted this article, in cl. 2, provides: "For its first year of existence, if the Commission is not funded by a separate appropriation in the Appropriation Act, compensation and reimbursement of expenses for legislative members of the Commission may be funded from the operating budgets of the Clerk of the House of Delegates and the Clerk of the Senate upon the approval of the Joint Rules Committee. If the Commission is not funded by a separate appropriation in the Appropriation Act for any year thereafter, this chapter shall expire on July 1 of the fiscal year that the Commission fails to receive such funding." Funding was not provided in the 2008 appropriation bill, effective July 1, 2008.

Acts 2007, c. 849, cl. 3, provides: "That the provisions of this act shall expire on August 1, 2009."

Article 9.

Southwest Virginia Cultural Heritage Commission.

(Expires July 1, 2011.)

§ 2.2-2532. (Expires July 1, 2011) Southwest Virginia Cultural Heritage Commission; purpose. — The Southwest Virginia Cultural Heritage Commission (the Commission) is established as an advisory commission in the executive branch of state government. The purpose of the Commission is to encourage the economic development of Southwest Virginia through the expansion of cultural heritage ventures and initiatives related to tourism and other asset-based enterprises, including the Southwest Virginia Artisan Center, the Crooked Road, Round The Mountain, and related cultural heritage organizations, and venues that promote entrepreneurial and employment opportunities. (2008, cc. 654, 659.)

Cross references. — As to July 1, 2011, sunset provision, see § 2.2-2536.

Editor's note. — Acts 2008, cc. 654 and 659, cl. 2 provides: "That an emergency exists and this act is in foce from its passage [March 27, 2008].

§ 2.2-2533. (Expires July 1, 2011) Membership; qualifications; terms; vacancies; officers; compensation. — A. The Commission shall have a total membership of 23 members that shall consist of five legislative members, 11 nonlegislative citizen members and seven ex officio members. Members shall be appointed as follows: two members of the Senate to be appointed by the Senate Committee on Rules; three members of the House of Delegates to be appointed by the Speaker of the House of Delegates in accordance with the principles of proportional representation contained in the Rules of the House of Delegates; two nonlegislative citizen members who shall be residents of Southwest Virginia, and two nonlegislative citizen members who shall be executive directors of either Planning District Commissions 1, 2, 3, 4, or 12 or their designees, to be appointed by the Governor; one nonlegislative citizen member who shall be an elected or appointed official of the Town of Abingdon to be appointed by the Governor upon the recommendation of the Abingdon Town Council, if any; one nonlegislative citizen member who shall be an elected or appointed official of Washington County to be appointed by the Governor upon the recommendation of the Washington County Board of Supervisors, if any; four nonlegislative citizen members who shall be artisans and members of Round the Mountain, who shall be appointed by the Governor upon the recommendation of the executive committee of Round the Mountain; and one nonlegislative citizen member who shall represent the Ninth Congressional District and serve as a member of the Virginia Commission for the Arts, to be appointed by the Governor upon the recommendation of the Executive Director of the Virginia Commission for the Arts, if any. The Chancellor of the Virginia Community College System, the President of Virginia Highlands Community College, the Chairman of The Crooked Road, the Chairman of Round the Mountain; the Director of the Virginia Department of Housing and Community Development, the Director of the Virginia Tourism Corporation, and the Executive Director of the Southwest Virginia Higher Education Center or their designees shall serve ex officio with nonvoting privileges.

B. Legislative members and ex officio members of the Commission shall serve terms coincident with their terms of office. Appointments to fill vacancies, other than by expiration of a term, shall be for the unexpired term. Vacancies shall be filled in the same manner as the original appointments. All members may be reappointed.

No House member shall serve more than four consecutive two-year terms, no Senate member shall serve more than two consecutive four-year terms, and no nonlegislative citizen member shall serve more than two consecutive four-year terms. The remainder of any term to which a member is appointed to fill a vacancy shall not constitute a term in determining the member's eligibility for reappointment.

C. Legislative members shall receive such compensation as provided in § 30-19.12. All members of the Commission shall be reimbursed for all reasonable and necessary expenses incurred in the performance of their duties as provided in §§ 2.2-2813 and 2.2-2825. Funding for the costs of compensation and expenses of the members shall be provided by the Department of Housing and Community Development.

D. The Commission shall elect a chairman and a vice-chairman from among its members and may appoint such other officers as it deems necessary. The Commission shall appoint an executive committee and such other committees as it deems necessary to oversee personnel and other areas related to operations and the achievement of the goals of the Commission. (2008, cc. 654, 659.)

Cross references. — As to July 1, 2011, sunset provision, see § 2.2-2536.

§ 2.2-2534. (Expires July 1, 2011) Powers and duties of the Commission. — A. The Commission shall have the following powers and duties:

1. Accept, execute, and administer any trust in which it may have an interest under the terms of the instrument creating the trust;
2. Establish and administer agreements with public or private agencies in order to achieve its goals;
3. Rent, lease, including the execution of leases with option to purchase, buy, own, acquire, and dispose of such property, real and personal, as the Commission deems proper to carry out any of the purposes and provisions of this article;
4. Finance, fund, plan, establish, construct, enlarge, extend, equip, update, and maintain buildings, structures, and facilities that are necessary or desirable to achieve its goals;
5. Operate, manage, and oversee the retail sales, demonstration, performance, and interpretation of artisan, musical, or other cultural activities, food and visitor services, and other functions as may be necessary or desirable to achieve its goals;
6. Employ and compensate such employees and agents as the Commission deems necessary. The Commission may appoint an executive director who shall be authorized to employ such staff as necessary to enable the Commission to achieve its goals. The Commission shall determine the duties of such staff and fix salaries and compensation from such funds as may be received;
7. Borrow and seek, accept, and expend gifts, grants, or donations from public or private sources;
8. Manage the operations of any existing or new facility in accordance with the provisions of this section;
9. Facilitate the sustainability of economic development initiatives relating to the cultural heritage of Southwest Virginia by providing financial resources and technical assistance to organizations and venues that contribute to achieving the goals of the Commission;
10. Serve as a resource and referral center by maintaining and disseminating information about Southwest Virginia cultural heritage efforts and venues;
11. Develop specific goals and initiatives intended to improve the quality of life and entrepreneurial opportunities in Southwest Virginia, in coordination

with the Virginia Tourism Corporation, the Virginia Department of Housing and Community Development, Southwest Virginia tourism, and economic development organizations, local governments, and other entities; and

12. Submit to the Governor and the General Assembly an annual report for publication as a report document as provided in the procedures of the Division of Legislative Automated Systems for the processing of legislative documents and reports. The chairman shall submit to the Governor and the General Assembly an annual executive summary of the interim activity and work of the Commission no later than the first day of each regular session of the General Assembly. The executive summary shall be submitted for publication as a report document as provided in the procedures of the Division of Legislative Automated Systems for the processing of legislative documents and reports and shall be posted on the General Assembly's website.

B. The Commission may establish nonprofit, nonstock corporations under Chapter 10 (§ 13.1-801 et seq.) of Title 13.1 as public instrumentalities exercising public and essential governmental functions to assist the Commission in (i) encouraging the economic development of Southwest Virginia through the expansion of cultural heritage ventures and initiatives related to tourism and other asset-based enterprises, including the Southwest Virginia Artisan Center, the Crooked Road, Round The Mountain, and related cultural heritage organizations and venues that promote entrepreneurial and employment opportunities, and (ii) conducting other activities useful in carrying out the provisions of this article.

The board of directors of any such corporation shall be composed of the chairman of the Commission and eight persons appointed by the Commission. The terms of the members of any corporation established shall be four years.

The Commission shall require any such corporation to report to it at least annually on its activities. (2008, cc. 654, 659.)

Cross references. — As to July 1, 2011, sunset provision, see § 2.2-2536.

§ **2.2-2535. (Expires July 1, 2011) Staffing.** — The Department of Housing and Community Development shall provide staff support to the Commission. All agencies of the Commonwealth shall provide assistance to the Commission, upon request. (2008, cc. 654, 659.)

Cross references. — As to July 1, 2011, sunset provision, see § 2.2-2536.

§ **2.2-2536. (Expires July 1, 2011) Sunset.** — This article shall expire on July 1, 2011. (2008, cc. 654, 659.)

CHAPTER 26.

Councils.

Article 1.

Advisory Council on the Virginia Business-Education Program.

Article 2.

Blue Ridge Economic Development Advisory Council.

Article 16.

State Executive Council For Comprehensive Services For At-Risk Youth And Families.

Article 17.

State Health Benefits Advisory Council.

Article 18.

Technology Services, Council On.

Article 19.

Virginia Advisory Council For Adult Education.

Article 20.

Virginia Equal Employment Opportunity Council.

Article 21.

Virginia Council On Coordinating Prevention.

Article 22.

Virginia Interagency Coordinating Council.

Article 23.

Virginia Military Advisory Council.

Article 23.1.

Virginia Military Advisory Council.

Article 24.

Virginia Recycling Markets Development Council.

Article 25.

Virginia Workforce Council.

Article 26.

Virginia Council on Human Resources.

Article 27.

The Advisory Council on the Future of Nursing in Virginia.

Article 28.

Joint Leadership Council of Veterans Service Organizations.

Article 1.

Advisory Council on the Virginia Business-Education Program.

§§ **2.2-2600 through 2.2-2602:** Repealed by 2004, c. 37.

Article 2.

Blue Ridge Economic Development Advisory Council.

§§ **2.2-2603, 2.2-2604:** Repealed by Acts 2003, c. 348.

Article 3.

Blue Ridge Regional Education And Training Council.

§§ **2.2-2605 through 2.2-2608:** Repealed by Acts 2003, c. 210, cl. 1, effective July 1, 2004.

Article 4.

Blue Ridge Regional Tourism Council.

§ 2.2-2609. Blue Ridge Regional Tourism Council; membership; meetings; Blue Ridge defined. — A. The Blue Ridge Regional Tourism Council (the Council) is established as an advisory council, within the meaning of § 2.2-2100, in the executive branch of state government. The Council shall be composed of one representative of each of the destination marketing organizations (DMOs) located in the Blue Ridge region and the President of the Virginia Tourism Authority.

B. The Council shall elect a chairman and a vice-chairman from among its members. The Council shall meet at least four times a year at such dates and times as they determine.

C. For the purposes of this article, the "Blue Ridge" region shall include the Counties of Alleghany, Amherst, Appomattox, Augusta, Bath, Bedford, Bland, Botetourt, Campbell, Craig, Floyd, Franklin, Giles, Highland, Montgomery, Nelson, Pulaski, Roanoke, Rockbridge, and Wythe and the Cities of Bedford, Buena Vista, Covington, Lexington, Lynchburg, Radford, Roanoke, Salem, Staunton, and Waynesboro. (1993, c. 330, §§ 9-145.39:1, 9-145.39:2; 1996, cc. 590, 598; 2001, c. 844; 2006, c. 861.)

§ 2.2-2610. Duties of the Council; acceptance of gifts and grants. — A. The Council shall perform the following functions:

1. Assist localities in the region, as well as the General Assembly, with the problems, concerns and issues of the tourism industry in the Blue Ridge region;
2. Encourage a cooperative attitude among the localities of the region and assist in the establishment of successful tourism partnerships between private and public organizations;
3. Develop and assist in the implementation of a plan to increase tourism revenue within the Blue Ridge region;
4. Review and disseminate information to the localities in this region concerning statewide and national tourism associations;
5. Encourage localities in the region to participate in the Virginia Local Tourism Accreditation Program; and
6. Encourage localities to invest in tourism development as an integral part of their overall economic development.

B. The Council may apply for, accept, and expend gifts, grants, or donations from public or private sources to enable it to carry out its objectives. (1993, c. 330, §§ 9-145.39:3, 9-145.39:4; 2001, c. 844.)

ARTICLE 5.

Capitol Square Preservation Council.

§§ 2.2-2611 through 2.2-2613: Repealed by Acts 2002, c. 491, effective April 5, 2002.

Cross references. — As to the Capitol Square Preservation Council, see § 30-193 et seq.

ARTICLE 6.

Citizens' Advisory Council on Furnishing and Interpreting the Executive Mansion.

§ 2.2-2614. Citizens' Advisory Council on Furnishing and Interpreting the Executive Mansion; purpose as a nonprofit charitable organization; membership; terms; officers and executive groups; compensation. — A. The Citizens' Advisory Council on Furnishing and Interpreting the Executive Mansion (the "Council") is established as an advisory council in the executive branch of state government to operate as a nonprofit charitable organization. No part of the Council's net earnings shall inure to the benefit of any private individual nor shall it carry on propaganda or otherwise attempt to influence legislation or participate in any political campaign on behalf of any candidate for public office.

B. The Council shall not exceed thirty members, who shall be appointed by the Governor. No employee of the Commonwealth or member of the General Assembly shall be eligible for appointment as a member of the Council. All members shall be deemed members-at-large charged with the responsibility of serving the best interests of the whole Commonwealth and no member shall act as representative of any particular region or of any particular agency or activity.

C. Of the members first appointed, nine shall be appointed for terms of one year, nine for terms of three years, and the remaining number for terms of five years. After the original appointments, all appointments shall be for five-year terms. No member of the Council who serves a full five-year term shall be eligible for reappointment; provided, that one year after the termination of his or her appointment, a member shall be eligible for reappointment. All vacancies shall be filled for the unexpired term in the same manner as the original appointments.

D. The spouse of the Governor, if any, shall be the honorary chairperson of the Council. The Governor shall designate one member of the Council to serve as chairman of an executive group, such executive group to be determined by the Council, and to be composed of members of the Council. Other advisory and cooperative groups may be appointed by the chairman. After the chairman has served three years, the Council thereafter shall elect its chairman.

E. Members of the Council shall not receive any compensation or reimbursement of expenses for their services. (1973, c. 431, §§ 9-84.5, 9-84.6; 1985, c. 448; 2001, c. 844.)

§ 2.2-2615. Powers and duties of Council; compensation for consultants. — A. The Council shall have the following powers and duties:

1. Promote a greater understanding and awareness of the history and significance of the Executive Mansion;
2. Take the leadership in guiding the development of research and publications on the history of the Executive Mansion, thus establishing a continuity of effort in this area;
3. Encourage, approve, and accept contributions and bequests and gifts or loans of furniture, works of art, memorabilia, and other property for its use in carrying out the purposes of this article;
4. Purchase appropriate period furnishings and works of art for the Executive Mansion, and exchange or sell property, tangible or intangible, which has been acquired by the Council through gifts or otherwise from the Commonwealth or other public or private organizations, associations, or individuals;
5. Acquire or provide for accession and replacement of objects for the Executive Mansion, either directly or through the Virginia Museum of Fine Arts;
6. Administer all funds, public and private, made available to the Council and to disburse such funds in accordance with the purposes of this article.

B. The Council may employ and fix the compensation of researchers, writers, curators, and other such consultants and professional personnel as it may deem necessary to assist in the exercise and performance of its duties and powers.

C. Purchases, exchanges, gifts and sales by the Council shall be exempt from the requirements of the Virginia Public Procurement Act. The Mansion Director and/or the Department of General Services shall assist the Council in keeping record of all such transactions. (1973, c. 431, §§ 9-84.7, 9-45.8; 2001, cc. 392, 409, 844.)

Cross references. — For the Virginia Public Procurement Act, see § 2.2-4300 et seq.

Editor's note. — Acts 2001, cc. 392 and 409 amended § 9-84.7, from which this section is derived. Pursuant to § 30-152, Acts 2001, cc. 392 and 409 have been given effect in this section as set out above. The 2001 amendments by cc. 392 and 409 are identical, and added present subsection C.

§ **2.2-2616. Disposition of moneys and property received.** — All moneys received by the Council shall be paid into the state treasury and segregated as a special fund to be used by the Council to carry out the purposes of this article. All other property, tangible or intangible, which is acquired by the Council shall become the property of the Commonwealth upon such acquisition. Such other intangible property may be held in the name of a nominee to facilitate its sale or exchange by the Council, and such other tangible property may be sold or exchanged by the Council as agent for the Commonwealth notwithstanding any other provision of law concerning the sale or exchange of property of the Commonwealth. (1973, c. 431, § 9-84.10; 2001, c. 844.)

Article 7.

Commonwealth Attorneys Services Council.

§ **2.2-2617. Commonwealth Attorneys Services Council; purpose; membership terms; compensation.** — A. The Commonwealth Attorneys Services Council is established as a supervisory council, within the meaning of § 2.2-2100, in the executive branch of state government. The purpose of the Council shall be to ensure the upgrading of criminal justice administration by providing and coordinating training, education and services for attorneys for the Commonwealth, there is created in the executive branch the Commonwealth's Attorneys' Services Council that shall be under the direction and control of the Governor.

B. The Council shall consist of not more than sixteen members, as follows: one attorney for the Commonwealth for each congressional district in the Commonwealth to be elected as provided in subsection C; the president, the president-elect, the vice-president and the secretary-treasurer of the Virginia Association of Commonwealth's Attorneys, and the immediate past president of the Virginia Association of Commonwealth's Attorneys. The president of the Association shall be the chairman of the Council; the president-elect and vice-president shall be first and second vice-chairmen, respectively, and the secretary-treasurer shall serve as secretary of the Council.

C. The initial terms of the members elected from congressional districts shall be as follows: for the members from the odd-numbered districts, until July 1 of the next following even-numbered year after their election; for the members from the even-numbered districts, until July 1 of the next following odd-numbered year after the election; thereafter, all terms shall be for two years.

The election for members shall be held annually at the annual meeting of the Virginia Association of Commonwealth's Attorneys. One member shall be elected initially, and every two years thereafter, from each of the several congressional districts by the membership of the Association at large. Each such member shall be an attorney for the Commonwealth holding office within his congressional district.

D. Upon the termination of the office of any member as attorney for the Commonwealth, his membership on the Council shall be terminated. Vacancies shall be filled for the congressional district in which the former member resided for the unexpired term by a majority vote of the Council. Members shall be eligible for more than one term.

E. The Council shall establish its own bylaws, procedures and requirements with respect to quorum, place and conduct of its meetings and its other business matters, provided, that such bylaws shall include a provision that the Council hold no less than ten meetings a year, and that other meetings be held when called by the chairman, or, in the absence of the chairman, the first vice-chairman, or upon the written request of four members.

F. Members of the Council shall receive no salaries but shall be reimbursed their reasonable and necessary expenses incurred in the discharge of their duties as provided in § 2.2-2825. (1978, c. 455, §§ 2.1-64.28:1, 2.1-64.28:2; 1984, c. 720; 1992, c. 81; 2001, c. 844.)

§ **2.2-2618. Powers and duties of Council.** — The Council, in order to (i) strengthen the criminal justice system in the Commonwealth; (ii) provide a professional organization for the education, training, service and coordination of technical efforts of state prosecutors; and (iii) maintain and improve prosecutor efficiency and effectiveness in enforcing the law of the Commonwealth, shall have, but are not limited to, the following powers and duties:

1. Organize, supervise and perform functions consistent with this article;
2. Coordinate training and continuing legal education activities for attorneys for the Commonwealth;
3. Contract or enter into agreements with state or federal agencies or education institutions;
4. Gather and disseminate information to attorneys for the Commonwealth relative to their official duties, including changes in the law affecting their office and information on individuals identified as criminal gang members, as transmitted by the Department of Corrections and the Department of Juvenile Justice;
5. Coordinate with the Department of Criminal Justice Services and the Judicial Conference in reference to training and interdisciplinary criminal justice matters;
6. Obtain statistical reports from attorneys for the Commonwealth relating to their performance, function and work-load;
7. Receive and establish an equitable distribution plan for the allocation of any funds from public or private sources;
8. Maintain close contact with the office of the Attorney General and with all attorneys for the Commonwealth and assistant attorneys for the Commonwealth in the discussion of problems or recommendations concerning necessary research, minimum standards, educational needs and other matters relative to upgrading the professional status of attorneys for the Commonwealth; and
9. Perform such other acts as may be necessary for the effective performance of its duties. (1978, c. 455, § 2.1-64.28:4; 1984, c. 779; 2001, c. 844; 2006, cc. 431, 500.)

Editor's note. — Acts 2006, cc. 431 and 500, in cl. 2 provide: "That the information forwarded by the Department of Corrections and the Department of Juvenile Justice to the Commonwealth's Attorneys' Services Council shall be in a form mutually agreeable to all parties."

§ **2.2-2619. Administrator.** — The Council, with the concurrence of the Governor, shall appoint an administrator, who shall serve under the supervision and at the pleasure of the Council. He shall perform the duties and exercise the functions the Council assigns to him. He shall receive a salary for his services to be paid by the Council subject to the approval of the Governor. (1978, c. 455, § 2.1-64.28:3; 1984, c. 720; 1992, c. 81; 2001, c. 844.)

ARTICLE 8.

Commonwealth Competition Council.

§ 2.2-2620. Definitions. — As used in this article, unless the context requires a different meaning:

"Commercial activity" means performing services or providing goods that can normally be obtained from private enterprise.

"Commercial source" means any business or other concern that is eligible for a contract award in accordance with the Virginia Public Procurement Act (§ 2.2-4300 et seq.).

"Competitive process" means the process approved by the Council to determine the most cost-effective privatization technique.

"Council" means the Commonwealth Competition Council.

"Fully allocated cost" means a cost that includes all direct personnel costs, materials and supplies, equipment, capital and equipment depreciation costs, rent, maintenance and repairs, utilities, insurance, travel, operations overhead, and general administrative overhead as these terms are defined in the Council's "Compete" cost comparison program.

"Managed competition" means a competitive process between a state agency and the private sector in which (i) the state agency submits its own proposal after completing the fully allocated cost of the commercial activity and (ii) the proposal is based on its most efficient proposed organization to compete with a private sector bid or proposal for the provision of the commercial activity.

"Privatization" means a variety of techniques and activities that promote more involvement of the private sector in providing services that have traditionally been provided by government. It also includes methods of providing a portion or all of select government-provided or government-produced programs and services through the private sector.

"State agency" means any board, council, authority, department, agency, or institution of the Commonwealth that employs state or nonstate personnel. (1995, c. 815, § 9-341; 1998, c. 881; 2001, c. 844.)

§ 2.2-2621. Commonwealth Competition Council; membership; terms; chairman; quorum; compensation; staff. — A. The Commonwealth Competition Council (the Council) is established as an advisory council, within the meaning of § 2.2-2100, in the executive branch of state government. The Council shall be composed of 15 members to be appointed as follows: four employees of executive branch agencies to be appointed by the Governor; two members of the House of Delegates to be appointed by the Speaker of the House of Delegates; two members of the Senate to be appointed by the Senate Committee on Rules; three members of the private sector to be appointed by the Governor; two members of the private sector to be appointed by the Speaker of the House of Delegates; and two members of the private sector, who shall be private sector members of the Small Business Commission, to be appointed by the Senate Committee on Rules.

B. Legislative members shall serve on the Council until the expiration of their terms of office or until their successors shall qualify. Executive branch agency members shall serve only as long as they retain their positions. After the initial staggering of terms, all nonlegislative members of the Council shall be appointed for terms of three years.

C. Appointments to fill vacancies shall be for the unexpired terms. No nonlegislative citizen member shall be eligible to serve more than two successive three-year terms. The remainder of any term to which a member is appointed to fill a vacancy shall not constitute a term in determining the member's eligibility for reappointment.

D. The Council shall annually elect its chairman and vice-chairman from among its members. A majority of the members of the Council shall constitute a quorum.

E. Legislative members shall be compensated as specified in § 30-19.12, and members, who are private sector members of the Small Business Commission, shall be compensated as specified in § 30-182. All members of the Council shall be reimbursed for their reasonable and necessary expenses incurred in the performance of their duties as provided in §§ 2.2-2813 and 2.2-2825.

F. The Council shall employ such staff as necessary to enable it to perform its duties as directed in the appropriation act. (1995, c. 815, §§ 9-343, 9-345; 1998, c. 881; 2001, c. 844; 2005, c. 758.)

Editor's note. — Acts 2005, c. 758, cl. 2, provides: "That this act shall not be construed to affect existing appointments, made by the Senate Committee on Privileges and Elections, for which the terms have not expired. However, any new appointments made after July 1, 2005 shall be made in accordance with the provisions of this act."

§ 2.2-2622. Duties of Council; acceptance of gifts and grants; annual report. — A. The Council shall:

1. Examine and promote methods of providing a portion or all of select government-provided or government-produced programs and services through the private sector by a competitive contracting program, and advise the Governor, the General Assembly, and executive branch agencies of the Council's findings and recommendations.

2. Develop an institutional framework for a statewide competitive program to encourage innovation and competition within state government.

3. Establish a system to encourage the use of feasibility studies and innovation to determine where competition could reduce government costs without harming the public.

4. Monitor the products and services of state agencies to bring an element of competition and to ensure a spirit of innovation and entrepreneurship to compete with the private sector.

5. Advocate, develop and accelerate implementation of a competitive program for state entities to ensure competition for the provision or production of government services, or both, from both public and private sector entities.

6. Establish approval, planning, and reporting processes required to carry out the functions of the Council.

7. Determine the privatization potential of a program or activity; perform cost/benefit analyses; and conduct public and private performance analyses. The Secretary of Finance shall independently certify the results of the comparison.

8. Devise, in consultation with the Secretary of Finance, evaluation criteria to be used in conducting performance reviews of any program or activity that is subject to a privatization recommendation.

9. To the extent practicable and to the extent that resources are available, make its services available for a fair compensation to any political subdivision of the Commonwealth.

10. Review the practices of government agencies and nonprofit organizations that may constitute inappropriate competition with private enterprise. The Council shall develop proposals for (i) preserving the traditional role of private enterprise; (ii) encouraging the expansion of existing, and the creation of new, private enterprise; and (iii) monitoring inappropriate competition by nonprofit organizations.

11. Review the procurement process under the Public-Private Transportation Act of 1995 (§ 56-556 et seq.) and the Public-Private Education Facilities

and Infrastructure Act of 2002 (§ 56-575.1 et seq.) and make recommendations for (i) improving the use and efficiency of process, (ii) releasing information to the public during all stages of the process, and (iii) ensuring accountability on the part of public officials and employees involved in projects under the Acts.

B. The commercial activities list developed by the Council in accordance with this section shall be updated every two years.

C. The Council may apply for, accept, and expend gifts, grants, or donations from public or private sources to enable it to better carry out its objectives. No entity that provides a gift, donation or grant shall be eligible for a contract award that results from action of a Council recommendation.

D. The Council shall not impose unreasonable burdens or costs in connection with requests of agencies.

E. The Council shall annually by December 1 report its findings and recommendations to the Governor, the General Assembly and the Small Business Commission created pursuant to § 30-182. The Council may make interim reports to the Governor, the General Assembly and the Small Business Commission as it deems advisable. (1995, c. 815, §§ 9-342, 9-344, 9-345, 9-949; 1997, c. 223; 1998, c. 881; 2001, c. 844; 2007, cc. 584, 630.)

The 2007 amendments. — The 2007 amendment by c. 584 inserted subdivision A 11.

The 2007 amendment by c. 630 added present subsection B; redesignated former subsections B through D as present subsections C through E.

§ 2.2-2623. Unsolicited proposals. — The Governor or the General Assembly may direct any state agency to perform a public/private performance analysis covering any commercial activity for which the Council has received a qualifying unsolicited proposal from a private entity that is consistent with the Council's purposes and duties as provided in § 2.2-2622.

The provisions of this section shall not apply to transportation-related projects initiated pursuant to Chapter 22 (§ 56-556 et seq.) of Title 56. (1995, c. 815, § 9-346; 1998, c. 881; 2001, c. 844.)

§ 2.2-2624. Public/private performance analysis. — A. The Council shall use the procurement methods cited in the Virginia Public Procurement Act (§ 2.2-4300 et seq.) to solicit proposals and bids from private entities in order to make cost comparison decisions. However, the Council shall not execute contracts.

B. The Council shall explore methods to encourage state agencies to compete for contracts. (1995, c. 815, § 9-347; 2001, c. 844.)

§ 2.2-2625. Duties of the Department of Planning and Budget. — The Department of Planning and Budget shall determine the amount of the existing appropriation no longer needed by a state agency or institution where all or a portion of such agency's function has been privatized in accordance with the recommendations of the Council, and shall unallot such funding. The Department shall also ensure that all appropriate reporting requirements to the Governor and the General Assembly are met. Nothing in this section shall preclude the Governor from recommending in future budget submissions the restoration of a portion of the original appropriation to the state agency or institution. (1995, c. 815, § 9-348; 2001, c. 844.)

Article 9.

Commonwealth Council On Aging.

§ 2.2-2626. Commonwealth Council on Aging; purpose; membership; terms. — A. The Commonwealth Council on Aging (the Council) is established as an advisory council, within the meaning of § 2.2-2100, in the executive branch of state government. The purpose of the Council shall be to promote an efficient, coordinated approach by state government to meeting the needs of older Virginians.

B. The Council shall consist of 23 members as follows: one member from each of the 11 congressional districts of the Commonwealth appointed by the Governor subject to confirmation by the General Assembly; four at-large nonlegislative citizen members appointed by the Speaker of the House of Delegates; four at-large nonlegislative citizen members appointed by the Senate Committee on Rules; and the Commissioner of the Department for the Aging, the Director of the Department of Medical Assistance Services, the Commissioner of Social Services and the Secretary of Health and Human Resources, or their designees, who shall serve as nonvoting ex officio members. Members of the Council shall be citizens of the Commonwealth appointed at large without regard to political affiliation but with due consideration of geographical representation. Appointees shall be selected for their ability, and all appointments shall be of such nature as to aid the work of the Council and to inspire the highest degree of cooperation and confidence.

C. After the initial staggering of terms, all appointments shall be for four-year terms.

Appointments to fill vacancies shall be for the unexpired term. No person having served on the Council for two consecutive terms shall be eligible for reappointment to the Council for two years thereafter. The remainder of any term to which a member is appointed to fill a vacancy shall not constitute a term in determining the member's eligibility to serve.

D. The Council shall elect a chairman and a vice-chairman from among its members and shall appoint a secretary and such other officers as it deems necessary and prescribe their duties and terms of office. The Council may adopt bylaws to govern its operations.

E. Members shall receive compensation for the performance of their duties as provided in § 2.2-2813. All members shall be reimbursed for all reasonable and necessary expenses incurred in the performance of their duties as provided in §§ 2.2-2813 and 2.2-2825. Funding for the costs of compensation and expenses of the members shall be provided by the Department for the Aging.

F. The Department for the Aging shall provide staff support to the Council. (1998, c. 665, § 2.1-373.02; 2000, cc. 877, 896; 2001, c. 844; 2004, c. 1000.)

Editor's note. — Acts 2000, c. 877, cl. 2, provided: "That the provisions of this act shall not become effective unless an appropriation effectuating the purposes of this act is included in the 2000 Appropriation Act, passed during the 2000 Session of the General Assembly and signed into law by the Governor." Acts 2000, c. 896 does not contain a contingency clause. An appropriation for Individual Care Services was made in the 2000 Appropriation Act, c. 1073. See Item 295.

Acts 2004, c. 1000, cl. 5, provides: "That this act shall not be construed to affect existing appointments for which the terms have not expired. However, any new appointments or appointments to fill vacancies made after the effective date of this act shall be made in accordance with the provisions of this act."

§ **2.2-2627. Duties of the Council.** — A. The Council shall have the following duties:

1. Examine the needs of older Virginians and ways in which state government can most effectively and efficiently assist in meeting those needs;

2. Advise the Governor and General Assembly on aging issues and aging policy for the Commonwealth;

3. Advise the Governor on any proposed regulations deemed by the Director of the Department of Planning and Budget to have a substantial and distinct impact on older Virginians. Such advice shall be provided in addition to other

regulatory reviews required by the Administrative Process Act (§ 2.2-4000 et seq.);

4. Advocate and develop the Commonwealth's planning for meeting the needs of the growing number of older Virginians;

5. Advise the Governor and General Assembly regarding the activities of the Department for the Aging; and

6. Assist and advise the Department with the development and ongoing review of the Virginia Respite Care Grant Program pursuant to Article 3 (§ 2.2-714 et seq.) of Chapter 7 of this title.

B. The Council may apply for and expend such grants, gifts, or bequests from any source as may become available in connection with its duties under this section, and may comply with such conditions and requirements as may be imposed in connection therewith.

C. For the purposes of this section, *"older Virginians"* means persons aged sixty years and older. (1998, c. 665, § 2.1-373.02; 2000, cc. 877, 896; 2001, c. 844.)

Article 10.

Council On Indians.

§ 2.2-2628. Council on Indians; membership; terms; chairman; compensation and expenses; chairman's executive summary. — A. The Council on Indians (the Council) is established as an advisory council, within the meaning of § 2.2-2100, in the executive branch of state government. The Council shall be composed of (i) the chiefs of the Virginia tribes officially recognized by the Commonwealth, (ii) two members appointed at large by the Governor from the Indian population residing in Virginia, and (iii) one nonvoting member appointed by the Governor who is a senior member of his staff. Each at-large member from the Indian population residing in the Commonwealth shall be required, as a condition of his appointment to the Council, to provide verification of his status as an enrolled member of a tribe recognized by either the Commonwealth, another state, or territory. Such verification shall consist of a valid tribal identification card, confirmation of membership through a central tribal registry, a written statement of a tribal chief or council confirming membership, or certification of the enrolled member status from a tribal office.

B. Each chief shall serve a term coincident with his term of office as chief and may appoint one designee who may serve as his representative at Council meetings and other Council activities. The senior member of the Governor's staff shall serve a term coincident with the member's term of office. After the original appointments, the appointments of the at large members shall be for terms of two years except appointments to fill vacancies, which shall be for the unexpired terms. At large members may be reappointed. However, no at large member shall be eligible to serve more than three successive two-year terms.

C. The Council shall annually elect a chair and vice-chair from among its membership. The meetings of the Council shall be held at the call of the chairman or whenever the majority of the voting members so request. A majority of members shall constitute a quorum.

D. Members of the Council shall receive no compensation for their services, but shall be reimbursed for all reasonable and necessary expenses incurred in the performance of their duties as provided in §§ 2.2-2813 and 2.2-2825. Funding for the costs of expenses of the members shall be provided by the Office of the Governor.

E. The chairman of the Council shall submit to the Governor and the General Assembly an annual executive summary of the interim activity and work of the Council no later than the first day of each regular session of the General Assembly. The executive summary shall be submitted as provided in the procedures of the Division of Legislative Automated Systems for the processing of legislative documents and reports and shall be posted on the General Assembly's website. (1983, c. 20, § 9-138.1; 1985, c. 448; 1989, c. 406; 1991, c. 563; 1994, c. 755; 2001, c. 844; 2003, c. 885; 2004, c. 142; 2005, cc. 61, 758; 2007, c. 915.)

Editor's note. — Acts 2003, c. 885, cl. 7, provides: "That all current members of the collegial bodies whose terms have been modified by this act shall be eligible, if reappointed, to the full number of terms provided by this act regardless of prior service."

Acts 2004, c. 142, cl. 2, provides: "That the provisions of this act shall not be construed to affect existing members of the Council on Indians whose terms have not expired as of July 1, 2004. However, any new appointments made after July 1, 2004, shall be made in accordance with the provisions of this act."

Acts 2005, c. 758, cl. 2, provides: "That this act shall not be construed to affect existing appointments, made by the Senate Committee on Privileges and Elections, for which the terms have not expired. However, any new appointments made after July 1, 2005 shall be made in accordance with the provisions of this act."

Acts 2007, c. 915, cl. 2, provides: "That the initial appointments of the at large members appointed by the Governor shall be staggered as follows: one member appointed for an initial term of one year; and one member appointed for a term of three years."

The 2007 amendments. — The 2007 amendment by c. 915 rewrote subsections A, B, and C.

§ 2.2-2629. Powers and duties of Council; acceptance of gifts and grants; reporting requirement. — A. The Council shall gather information on and make studies and conduct research concerning the Indians in the Commonwealth and advise the Governor on issues affecting the Virginia Indian communities. The Council shall be an advocate for education of the general public regarding the past and present Indians of Virginia.

B. The Council may apply for, accept and expend gifts, grants or donations from public or private sources to enable it to better carry out its objectives.

C. The Council shall establish criteria for tribal recognition and shall recommend to the General Assembly and the Governor in its biennial report those tribes meeting the criteria that should be given official state recognition.

D. The Council shall report its findings and recommendations to the Governor and the General Assembly not less than 60 days prior to the convening of the session of the General Assembly held in each even-numbered year. (1983, c. 20, §§ 9-138.2, 9-138.3, 9-138.4; 1991, c. 563; 2001, c. 844; 2002, c. 562; 2005, c. 61.)

CASE NOTES

Applied in Alliance to Save the Mattaponi v. Commonwealth Dep't of Envtl. Quality ex rel. State Water Control Bd., 270 Va. 423, 621 S.E.2d 78, 2005 Va. LEXIS 100 (2005).

§ 2.2-2629.1. Advisory Committee. — The Council shall establish a non voting advisory committee consisting of representatives of Virginia tribes officially recognized by the Commonwealth and non-recognized Indian descendant communities. The advisory committee shall perform duties which may be assigned by the Council. (2007, c. 915.)

§ 2.2-2629.2. Recognition of Tribal Relations. — The Commonwealth of Virginia recognizes the continuous contributions of the Indian tribal nations to the Commonwealth's history and culture and hereby reaffirms the spirit and intent of the original treaties between the Tribes and the British Crown in 1646 and 1677 and shall operate, to the extent permitted by the United States

Constitution, in accordance with that spirit and intent when dealing with such Virginia tribes as may be officially recognized by the Commonwealth. (2007, c. 915.)

ARTICLE 11.

Council On The Status Of Women.

§ **2.2-2630. Council on the Status of Women; purpose; membership; terms; chairman.** — A. The Council on the Status of Women (the "Council") is established as an advisory council, within the meaning of § 2.2-2100, in the executive branch of state government. The purpose of the Council shall be to identify ways in which women can reach their potential and make their full contribution to society and this Commonwealth as wage earners and citizens.

B. The Council shall consist of nineteen members, to be appointed by the Governor from the Commonwealth at large. Appointments shall be for terms of three years, except appointments to fill vacancies, which shall be for the unexpired terms. A majority of the membership of the Council shall constitute a quorum.

C. The Governor shall appoint the chairman of the Council. (1970, c. 685, § 9-116; 1972, c. 632; 1985, cc. 448, 497; 1991, c. 563; 2001, c. 844.)

§ **2.2-2631. Powers and duties of Council.** — The Council shall have the following powers and duties to:

1. Determine the studies and research to be conducted by the Council;
2. Collect and disseminate information regarding the status of women in the Commonwealth and the nation;
3. Advise the Governor, General Assembly and Secretary of Health and Human Resources on matters pertaining to women in the Commonwealth and the nation;
4. Establish and award scholarships pursuant to regulations and conditions prescribed by the Council; and
5. Review and comment on all budgets, appropriation requests and grant applications concerning the Council, prior to their submission to the Secretary of Health and Human Resources or the Governor. (1985, c. 497, § 9-116.1; 2001, c. 844.)

ARTICLE 12.

Human Rights Council.

§ **2.2-2632. Human Rights Council; membership; terms; quorum; compensation.** — A. The Human Rights Council (the "Council") is established as a policy council, within the meaning of § 2.2-2100, in the executive branch of state government. The Council shall consist of nine members, who shall be appointed by the Governor, subject to confirmation by the General Assembly. The members appointed by the Governor shall, insofar as possible, be diverse with respect to economic status, race, sex, color, ethnicity, age, disabilities, political affiliation and marital status.

B. Of the members first appointed, four shall be appointed to two-year terms, and five shall be appointed to four-year terms. Thereafter members shall be appointed to four-year terms, except members appointed to fill vacancies shall be appointed for the remainder of the unexpired term.

In the case of vacancies on the Council during a recess of the General Assembly, the Governor shall make an appointment to fill the vacancy, and the appointee shall hold office until thirty days after the commencement of the next session of the General Assembly and, if confirmed by the General Assembly, for the remainder of the unexpired term.

C. The Governor shall designate one of the members of the Council to be chairperson. The chairperson shall preside at all the meetings of the Council. The Council by majority vote shall elect one of its members as vice-chairperson who, in the absence of the chairperson, shall perform all the duties and functions of the chairperson.

D. A simple majority of the members serving on the Council shall constitute a quorum. No power pursuant to § 2.2-2634 may be exercised by the Council unless agreed to by a majority of the nine members of the Council appointed. Vacancies in the Council shall not impair the authority of remaining members to exercise all the powers of the Council.

E. Members of the Council shall receive compensation for the discharge of their duties as provided in § 2.2-2813. (1987, c. 581, § 2.1-718; 2001, c. 844.)

§ **2.2-2633. Human Rights Director.** — A. There is established under the Council the position of Human Rights Director (the "Director"). The Director shall be appointed by and serve at the pleasure of the Governor.

B. The Director may, within guidelines established by the Council:

1. Accept and investigate complaints of alleged unlawful discriminatory practices or alleged unfounded charges of unlawful discrimination filed in writing within 180 days of the alleged discriminatory events;

2. Attempt to conciliate any complaint of unlawful discrimination under this article;

3. In the event conciliation fails, recommend to the Council that a hearing be held or other appropriate action be taken;

4. Carry out the policies of the Council and any other duty assigned by this article. (1987, c. 581, § 2.1-719; 2001, c. 844.)

§ **2.2-2634. Powers and duties of Council.** — In addition to the other powers and duties prescribed in this article, the Council shall have the following powers to:

1. Meet and function at any place in the Commonwealth;

2. Establish and maintain an office;

3. Select, and fix the compensation of, such technical advisors and employees as it deems necessary, or to authorize such action by the Director. The Attorney General shall represent the Council in all litigation to which the Council is a party;

4. Appoint and compensate qualified hearing officers from the list of hearing officers maintained by the Executive Secretary of the Supreme Court of Virginia;

5. Promote creation of local commissions to aid in effectuating the policies of this article and to enter into cooperative worksharing or other agreements with federal agencies or local commissions, including the deferral of complaints of discrimination to federal agencies or local commissions;

6. Adopt, promulgate, amend and rescind regulations consistent with this article pursuant to the Virginia Administrative Process Act (§ 2.2-4000 et seq.). No such regulation shall be inconsistent with any state or federal law or regulation. However, the Council shall not have the authority to adopt regulations on a substantive matter when another state agency is authorized to adopt such regulations;

7. Receive, investigate, seek to conciliate, refer to another agency, hold hearings pursuant to the Virginia Administrative Process Act (§ 2.2-4000 et seq.), and make findings and recommendations upon complaints alleging unlawful discriminatory practices;

8. Make studies and appoint advisory councils to effectuate the purposes and policies of the article and to make the results thereof available to the public;

9. Accept public grants or private gifts, bequests, or other payments, as appropriate;

10. Furnish technical assistance upon request of persons subject to this article to further comply with the article or an order issued thereunder;

11. Inquire into incidents that may constitute unlawful acts of discrimination or unfounded charges of unlawful discrimination under state or federal law, and to take such action within the Council's authority designed to prevent such acts;

12. Create an official seal that shall be judicially noticed; and

13. Seek, with the approval of the Attorney General, through appropriate enforcement authorities, prevention of or relief from an alleged unlawful discriminatory practice; however, the Council itself shall have no power to issue subpoenas, award damages, or grant injunctive relief. (1987, c. 581, § 2.1-720; 2001, c. 844; 2004, c. 58.)

CASE NOTES

Editor's note. — The cases below were decided under former Title 2.1 or prior provisions.

The Virginia Council on Human Rights is a qualifying "deferral agency" for purposes of Title VII because it has the authority to seek relief from unlawful employment practices, and therefore, discrimination claims filed with the EEOC in Virginia are subject to a longer limitations period than would apply if Virginia had no deferral agency. Tinsley v. First Union Nat'l Bank, 155 F.3d 435 (4th Cir. 1998).

Notice not required. — While the council is given the authority to investigate and make findings and recommendations regarding complaints of discrimination, it does not have the power to "grant or seek relief from such practice" as required by 42 U.S.C. § 2000a-3(c). Therefore, because no local or state law of the type contemplated by § 2000a-3(c) exists in Virginia, plaintiff was not required to provide notice as a prerequisite to filing suit under the federal statute. Dorsey v. Duff's Motel, Inc., 878 F. Supp. 869 (W.D. Va. 1995).

§ 2.2-2635. Procedure for issuance of subpoena duces tecum. — Whenever the Council has reasonable cause to believe that any person has engaged in or is engaging in any unlawful discriminatory practice, and the Council, after a good faith effort to obtain the date and information necessary to determine whether a violation has occurred, has been unable to obtain such information, it may request the Attorney General to apply to the judge of the circuit court of the jurisdiction in which the respondent resides or is doing business for a subpoena duces tecum against any person refusing to produce such data and information. The judge of the court, upon good cause shown, may cause the subpoena to be issued. Any person failing to comply with such subpoena shall be subject to punishment for contempt by the court issuing the subpoena. For purposes of this section *"person"* includes any individual, partnership, corporation, association, legal representative, mutual company, joint stock company, trust, unincorporated organization, employee, employer, employment agency, labor organization, joint labor-management committee, or an agent thereof. (1987, c. 581, § 2.1-721; 2000, c. 64; 2001, c. 844.)

§ 2.2-2636. Filing with Council deemed filing with other state agencies. — Filing of a written complaint with the Council shall be deemed filing with any state agency for the purpose of complying with any time limitation on the filing of a complaint, provided the time limit for filing with the other agency has not expired. The time limit for filing with other agencies shall be tolled while the Council is either investigating the complaint or making a decision to refer it. Complaints under this article shall be filed with the Council within 180 days of the alleged discriminatory event. (1987, c. 581, § 2.1-722; 2001, c. 844.)

§ 2.2-2637. Confidentiality of information; penalty. — A. It shall be unlawful for any officer, employee or member of the Council to make public, prior to a public hearing pursuant to § 2.2-2634, investigative notes and other correspondence and information furnished to the Council in confidence with respect to an investigation or conciliation process involving an alleged unlawful discriminatory practice.

B. Nothing in this section, however, shall prohibit the distribution of information taken from inactive reports in a form that does not reveal the identity of the parties involved or other persons supplying information.

C. Any person convicted of a violation of this section shall be guilty of a Class 3 misdemeanor. (1987, c. 581, § 2.1-723; 2001, c. 844.)

Cross references. — As to punishment for Class 3 misdemeanors, see § 18.2-11.

§ 2.2-2638. Powers of local commissions. — A local human rights or human relations commission established prior to the effective date of this article, in addition to the powers granted under this article, may exercise any such additional powers as may have been granted heretofore to that commission pursuant to applicable provisions of §§ 15.2-725, 15.2-853, and 15.2-854 or municipal charter provisions. (1987, c. 581, § 2.1-724; 2000, c. 933; 2001, c. 844.)

§ 2.2-2639. Causes of action not created. — A. Nothing in this article creates, nor shall it be construed to create, an independent or private cause of action to enforce its provisions, except as specifically provided in subsections B and C.

B. No employer employing more than five but less than 15 persons shall discharge any such employee on the basis of race, color, religion, national origin, sex, pregnancy, childbirth or related medical conditions, including lactation, or of age if the employee is 40 years old or older. For the purposes of this section, "lactation" means a condition that may result in the feeding of a child directly from the breast or the expressing of milk from the breast.

C. The employee may bring an action in a general district or circuit court having jurisdiction over the employer who allegedly discharged the employee in violation of this section. Any such action shall be brought within 300 days from the date of the discharge or, if the employee has filed a complaint with the Council or a local human rights or human relations agency or commission within 300 days of the discharge, such action shall be brought within 90 days from the date that the Council or a local human rights or human relations agency or commission has rendered a final disposition on the complaint. The court may award up to 12 months' back pay with interest at the judgment rate as provided in § 6.1-330.54. However, if the court finds that either party engaged in tactics to delay resolution of the complaint, it may (i) diminish the award or (ii) award back pay to the date of judgment without regard to the 12-month limitation.

In any case where the employee prevails, the court shall award attorneys' fees from the amount recovered, not to exceed 25 percent of the back pay awarded. The court shall not award other damages, compensatory or punitive, nor shall it order reinstatement of the employee.

D. Causes of action based upon the public policies reflected in this article shall be exclusively limited to those actions, procedures and remedies, if any, afforded by applicable federal or state civil rights statutes or local ordinances. Nothing in this section or § 2.2-3900 shall be deemed to alter, supersede, or otherwise modify the authority of the Council or of any local human rights or human relations commissions established pursuant to § 15.2-853 or 15.2-965 or subject to the provisions of § 2.2-2638. (1987, c. 581, § 2.1-725; 1995, c. 838; 1997, c. 404; 2000, c. 933; 2001, c. 844; 2002, c. 561; 2005, cc. 756, 770, 857.)

Editor's note. — Acts 1997, c. 404, cl. 2, provides: "That the provisions of this act are declarative of existing law."

Law Review. — For 1995 survey of employment law, see 29 U. Rich. L. Rev. 1027 (1995). For an article relating to a variety of developments in employment law, see 32 U. Rich. L. Rev. 1199 (1998). For a note, "Hanging in the Balance: Confidentiality Clauses and Postjudgment Settlements of Employment Discrimination Disputes," see 86 Va. L. Rev. 1537 (2000). For 2000 survey of Virginia labor and employment law, see 34 U. Rich. L. Rev. 907 (2000). For article reviewing recent developments and changes in legislation, case law, and Virginia Supreme Court Rules affecting civil litigation, "Civil Practice and Procedure," see 40 U. Rich. L. Rev. 95 (2005). For annual survey of Virginia labor and employment law, see 40 U. Rich. L. Rev. 241 (2005).

Michie's Jurisprudence. — For related discussion, see 12B M.J. Master and Servant, § 11.

CASE NOTES

Editor's note. — Some of the cases below were decided under former Title 2.1 or prior provisions.

Applicability. — Former employee, who worked as a shipfitter, but who was unable to return to work after an accident because her permanent medical restrictions made her unable to perform the essential functions of her job and who did not show that the employer failed to make any reasonable accommodations, was unable to state a claim against her former employer under the Virginia Human Rights Act, § 2.2-2639, because this law only applied where an independent violation of existing laws was found. Wells v. BAE Sys. Norfolk Ship Repair, 483 F. Supp. 2d 497, 2007 U.S. Dist. LEXIS 26107 (E.D. Va. 2007).

Effect of 1995 amendment. — In the 1995 amendments to the Human Rights Act, the legislature eliminated the availability of common law wrongful termination actions based on any public policy that is contained in this Act. McCarthy v. Texas Instruments, Inc., 999 F. Supp. 823 (E.D. Va. 1998).

Common law cause of action based on Human Rights Act policies. — Subsection D prohibits a common law cause of action based upon the public policies reflected in the Virginia Human Rights Act. Doss v. Jamco, Inc., 254 Va. 362, 492 S.E.2d 441 (1997).

The Virginia legislature, in enacting the 1995 amendments to this section, eliminated a common law cause of action for wrongful termination based on any public policy which is reflected in the Virginia Human Rights Act, regardless of whether the policy is articulated elsewhere. Conner v. National Pest Control Ass'n, 257 Va. 286, 513 S.E.2d 398 (1999).

The Virginia Human Rights Act, as amended, no longer provides an exception to the at-will employment doctrine or the public policy basis for a cause of action for wrongful discharge. Oakley v. May Dep't Stores Co., 17 F. Supp. 2d 533 (E.D. Va. 1998).

Subsection D does not prohibit a common law cause of action for wrongful termination based on public policies against fornication and lewd and lascivious behavior, because those policies are not reflected in the Virginia Human Rights Act. Mitchem v. Counts, 259 Va. 179, 523 S.E.2d 246 (2000).

Claim based on reduction in job responsibilities failed. — As the employment action alleged by the former president was not a discharge, but rather a reduction in job responsibilities, the president's Virginia Human Rights Act claim failed. Huizenga v. Am. Int'l Auto. Dealers Ass'n, — F. Supp. 2d —, 2005 U.S. Dist. LEXIS 30972 (E.D. Va. Nov. 22, 2005).

Number of employees. — Employee failed to state a claim under the Virginia Human Rights Act, § 2.2-3900 et seq., because the Act limited private rights of action to employees seeking redress against employers of more than five but less than 15 employees, under § 2.2-2639, and her employer had more than 15 employees. Reiterman v. Costco Wholesale Mgmt. # 238, — F. Supp. 2d —, 2005 U.S. Dist. LEXIS 15219 (W.D. Va. July 28, 2005).

Employer not covered. — Employer with more than 500 employees was not included within the coverage of the Virginia Human Rights Act, § 2.2-2639. Oglesby v. Ford Motor Co., — F. Supp. 2d —, 2005 U.S. Dist. LEXIS 41472 (E.D. Va. Aug. 16, 2005).

Former employee, who worked as a shipfitter, but who was unable to return to work after an accident because her permanent medical restrictions made her unable to perform the essential functions of her job and who did not show that the employer failed to make any reasonable accommodations, was unable to state a claim against her former employer under the Virginia Human Rights Act, subsection B of § 2.2-2639, because the employer had 15 or more employees. Wells v. BAE Sys. Norfolk Ship Repair, 483 F. Supp. 2d 497, 2007 U.S.

Dist. LEXIS 26107 (E.D. Va. 2007).

Amendments inapplicable to claim arising before effective date. — The 1995 amendments to the Virginia Human Rights Act place certain limits upon an employee's right to recover punitive damages for wrongful termination of employment but these provisions do not apply if the employee was terminated and the motion for judgment was filed before those amendments became effective. Smith v. Litten, 256 Va. 573, 507 S.E.2d 77 (1998).

Age discrimination claim disallowed. — Sixty three-year-old former auxiliary deputy sheriff, did not state a viable age discrimination claim under the Virginia Human Rights Act, because his claim against the sheriff, who attested to having hundreds of employees, did not fall under the special provisions of this section, and so it was disallowed. Blankenship v. City of Portsmouth, 372 F. Supp. 2d 496, 2005 U.S. Dist. LEXIS 11124 (E.D. Va. 2005).

Applied in Bullard v. Panasonic Corp., 418 F. Supp. 2d 802, 2006 U.S. Dist. LEXIS 6649 (E.D. Va. 2006).

CIRCUIT COURT OPINIONS

Common-law cause of action based on Human Rights Act policies. — Defendant officers' demurrer to count V of plaintiff's complaint, which alleged racial bias and prejudice, was sustained because former § 2.1-725(D) (now § 2.2-2639 D) prohibited a common-law cause of action based upon the public policies reflected in the Virginia Human Rights Act. Chandler v. Routin, 63 Va. Cir. 139, 2003 Va. Cir. LEXIS 347 (Norfolk 2003).

ARTICLE 13.

Interagency Coordinating Council On Housing For The Disabled.

§§ 2.2-2640, 2.2-2641: Repealed by Acts 2004, cc. 16, 153.

ARTICLE 14.

Maternal And Child Health Council.

§§ 2.2-2642, 2.2-2643: Repealed by Acts 2003, c. 451.

ARTICLE 15.

Specialized Transportation Council.

§§ 2.2-2644 through 2.2-2647: Repealed by Acts 2003, c. 454.

Cross references. — For provisions transferring the former specialized transportation council's duties to the Disabilities Commission, see § 15.2-4217.1.

ARTICLE 16.

State Executive Council For Comprehensive Services For At-Risk Youth And Families.

§ 2.2-2648. State Executive Council for Comprehensive Services for At-Risk Youth and Families; membership; meetings; powers and duties. — A. The State Executive Council for Comprehensive Services for At-Risk Youth and Families (the Council) is established as a supervisory council, within the meaning of § 2.2-2100, in the executive branch of state government.

B. The Council shall consist of one member of the House of Delegates to be appointed by the Speaker of the House and one member of the Senate to be appointed by the Senate Committee on Rules; the Commissioners of Health, of Mental Health, Mental Retardation and Substance Abuse Services, and of Social Services; the Superintendent of Public Instruction; the Executive

Secretary of the Virginia Supreme Court; the Director of the Department of Juvenile Justice; the Director of the Department of Medical Assistance Services; the chairman of the state and local advisory team established pursuant to § 2.2-5202; two local government representatives to include a member of a county board of supervisors or a city council and a county administrator or city manager, to be appointed by the Governor; a private provider representative from a facility that maintains membership in an association of providers for children's or family services and receives funding as authorized by the Comprehensive Services Act (§ 2.2-5200 et seq.), to be appointed by the Governor, who may appoint from nominees recommended by the Virginia Coalition of Private Provider Associations; and a parent representative. The parent representative shall be appointed by the Governor for a term not to exceed three years and shall not be an employee of any public or private program that serves children and families. Appointments of legislative members shall be for terms coincident with their terms of office. Legislative members shall not be included for the purposes of constituting a quorum.

C. The Council shall be chaired by the Secretary of Health and Human Resources or a designated deputy who shall be responsible for convening the council. The Council shall meet, at a minimum, quarterly, to oversee the administration of this article and make such decisions as may be necessary to carry out its purposes. Legislative members shall receive compensation as provided in § 30-19.12 and nonlegislative citizen members shall receive compensation for their services as provided in §§ 2.2-2813 and 2.2-2825.

D. The Council shall have the following powers and duties:

1. Hire and supervise a director of the Office of Comprehensive Services for At-Risk Youth and Families;

2. Appoint the members of the state and local advisory team in accordance with the requirements of § 2.2-5201;

3. Provide for the establishment of interagency programmatic and fiscal policies developed by the Office of Comprehensive Services for At-Risk Youth and Families, which support the purposes of the Comprehensive Services Act (§ 2.2-5200 et seq.), through the promulgation of regulations by the participating state boards or by administrative action, as appropriate;

4. Provide for a public participation process for programmatic and fiscal guidelines and dispute resolution procedures developed for administrative actions that support the purposes of the Comprehensive Services Act (§ 2.2-5200 et seq.). The public participation process shall include, at a minimum, 60 days of public comment and the distribution of these guidelines and procedures to all interested parties;

5. Oversee the administration of and consult with the Virginia Municipal League and the Virginia Association of Counties about state policies governing the use, distribution and monitoring of moneys in the state pool of funds and the state trust fund;

6. Provide for the administration of necessary functions that support the work of the Office of Comprehensive Services for At-Risk Youth and Families;

7. Review and take appropriate action on issues brought before it by the Office of Comprehensive Services for At-Risk Youth and Families, Community Policy and Management Teams (CPMTs), local governments, providers and parents;

8. Advise the Governor and appropriate Cabinet Secretaries on proposed policy and operational changes that facilitate interagency service development and implementation, communication and cooperation;

9. Provide administrative support and fiscal incentives for the establishment and operation of local comprehensive service systems;

10. Oversee coordination of early intervention programs to promote comprehensive, coordinated service delivery, local interagency program manage-

ment, and co-location of programs and services in communities. Early intervention programs include state programs under the administrative control of the state executive council member agencies;

11. Oversee the development and implementation of a mandatory uniform assessment instrument and process to be used by all localities to identify levels of risk of Comprehensive Services Act (CSA) youth;

12. Oversee the development and implementation of uniform guidelines to include initial intake and screening assessment, development and implementation of a plan of care, service monitoring and periodic follow-up, and the formal review of the status of the youth and the family;

13. Oversee the development and implementation of uniform guidelines for documentation for CSA-funded services;

14. Review and approve a request by a CPMT to establish a collaborative, multidisciplinary team process for referral and reviews of children and families pursuant to § 2.2-5209;

15. Oversee the development and implementation of mandatory uniform guidelines for utilization management; each locality receiving funds for activities under the Comprehensive Services Act shall have a locally determined utilization management plan following the guidelines or use of a process approved by the Council for utilization management, covering all CSA-funded services;

16. Oversee the development and implementation of uniform data collection standards and the collection of data, utilizing a secure electronic client-specific database for CSA-funded services, which shall include, but not be limited to, the following client specific information: (i) children served, including those placed out of state; (ii) individual characteristics of youths and families being served; (iii) types of services provided; (iv) service utilization including length of stay; (v) service expenditures; (vi) provider identification number for specific facilities and programs identified by the state in which the child receives services; (vii) a data field indicating the circumstances under which the child ends each service; and (viii) a data field indicating the circumstances under which the child exits the Comprehensive Services Act program. All client-specific information shall remain confidential and only non-identifying aggregate demographic, service, and expenditure information shall be made available to the public;

17. Oversee the development and implementation of a uniform set of performance measures for evaluating the Comprehensive Services Act program, including, but not limited to, the number of youths served in their homes, schools and communities. Performance measures shall be based on information: (i) collected in the client-specific database referenced in subdivision 16, (ii) from the mandatory uniform assessment instrument referenced in subdivision 11, and (iii) from available and appropriate client outcome data that is not prohibited from being shared under federal law and is routinely collected by the state child-serving agencies that serve on the Council. If provided client-specific information, state child serving agencies shall report available and appropriate outcome data in clause (iii) to the Office of Comprehensive Services for At-Risk Youth and Families. Outcome data submitted to the Office of Comprehensive Services for At-Risk Youth and Families shall be used solely for the administration of the Comprehensive Services Act program. Applicable client outcome data shall include, but not be limited to: (a) permanency outcomes by the Virginia Department of Social Services, (b) recidivism outcomes by the Virginia Department of Juvenile Justice, and (c) educational outcomes by the Virginia Department of Education. All client-specific information shall remain confidential and only non-identifying aggregate outcome information shall be made available to the public;

18. The Council shall oversee the development and distribution of management reports that provide information to the public and CPMTs to help

evaluate child and family outcomes and public and private provider performance in the provision of services to children and families through the Comprehensive Services Act program. Management reports shall include total expenditures on children served through the Comprehensive Services Act program as reported to the Office of Comprehensive Services for At-Risk Youth and Families by state child-serving agencies on the Council and shall include, but not be limited to: (i) client-specific payments for inpatient and outpatient mental health services, treatment foster care services and residential services made through the Medicaid program and reported by the Virginia Department of Medical Assistance Services and (ii) client-specific payments made through the Title IV-E foster care program reported by the Virginia Department of Social Services. The Office of Comprehensive Services shall provide client-specific information to the state agencies for the sole purpose of the administration of the Comprehensive Services Act program. All client-specific information shall remain confidential and only non-identifying aggregate demographic, service, expenditure, and outcome information shall be made available to the public;

19. Establish and oversee the operation of an informal review and negotiation process with the Director of the Office of Comprehensive Services and a formal dispute resolution procedure before the State Executive Council, which include formal notice and an appeals process, should the Director or Council find, upon a formal written finding, that a CPMT failed to comply with any provision of this Act. "Formal notice" means the Director or Council provides a letter of notification, which communicates the Director's or the Council's finding, explains the effect of the finding, and describes the appeal process, to the chief administrative officer of the local government with a copy to the chair of the CPMT. The dispute resolution procedure shall also include provisions for remediation by the CPMT that shall include a plan of correction recommended by the Council and submitted to the CPMT. If the Council denies reimbursement from the state pool of funds, the Council and the locality shall develop a plan of repayment;

20. Deny state funding to a locality where the CPMT fails to provide services that comply with the Comprehensive Services Act (§ 2.2-5200 et seq.), in accordance with subdivision 19;

21. Biennially publish and disseminate to members of the General Assembly and community policy and management teams a state progress report on comprehensive services to children, youth and families and a plan for such services for the next succeeding biennium. The state plan shall:

a. Provide a fiscal profile of current and previous years' federal and state expenditures for a comprehensive service system for children, youth and families;

b. Incorporate information and recommendations from local comprehensive service systems with responsibility for planning and delivering services to children, youth and families;

c. Identify and establish goals for comprehensive services and the estimated costs of implementing these goals, report progress toward previously identified goals and establish priorities for the coming biennium; and

d. Include such other information or recommendations as may be necessary and appropriate for the improvement and coordinated development of the state's comprehensive services system; and

22. Oversee the development and implementation of mandatory uniform guidelines for intensive care coordination services for children who are at risk of entering, or are placed in, residential care through the Comprehensive Services Act program. The guidelines shall: (i) take into account differences among localities, (ii) specify children and circumstances appropriate for intensive care coordination services, (iii) define intensive care coordination

services, and (iv) distinguish intensive care coordination services from the regular case management services provided within the normal scope of responsibility for the child-serving agencies, including the community services board, the local school division, local social services agency, court service unit, and Department of Juvenile Justice. Such guidelines shall address: (a) identifying the strengths and needs of the child and his family through conducting or reviewing comprehensive assessments including, but not limited to, information gathered through the mandatory uniform assessment instrument; (b) identifying specific services and supports necessary to meet the identified needs of the child and his family, building upon the identified strengths; (c) implementing a plan for returning the youth to his home, relative's home, family-like setting, or community at the earliest appropriate time that addresses his needs, including identification of public or private community-based services to support the youth and his family during transition to community-based care; and (d) implementing a plan for regular monitoring and utilization review of the services and residential placement for the child to determine whether the services and placement continue to provide the most appropriate and effective services for the child and his family. (1992, cc. 837, 880, § 2.1-746; 1995, c. 800; 1996, c. 1024; 1998, c. 622; 1999, c. 669; 2000, cc. 900, 937; 2001, c. 844; 2002, c. 410; 2003, cc. 483, 498; 2004, c. 836; 2005, c. 930; 2008, cc. 39, 170, 277.)

Cross references. — As to the Comprehensive Services Act for At-Risk Youth and Families, see § 2.2-5200. As to the powers and duties of the family assessment and planning team, see § 2.2-5208.

The 2008 amendments. — The 2008 amendments by cc. 39 and 170 are nearly identical, and added subdivision D 20 [now D 22], and made related changes.

The 2008 amendment by c. 277 rewrote subdivision D 16; inserted subdivisions D 17 and D 18 and made related changes; and substituted "19" for "17" in subdivision D 20.

Law Review. — For an article, "Legal Issues Involving Children," see 32 U. Rich. L. Rev. 1345 (1998). For 2000 survey of Virginia law regarding children, see 34 U. Rich. L. Rev. 939 (2000). For 2003/2004 survey of family and juvenile law, see 39 U. Rich. L. Rev. 241 (2004).

§ 2.2-2649. Office of Comprehensive Services for At-Risk Youth and Families established; powers and duties. — A. The Office of Comprehensive Services for At-Risk Youth and Families is hereby established to serve as the administrative entity of the Council and to ensure that the decisions of the council are implemented. The director shall be hired by and subject to the direction and supervision of the Council pursuant to § 2.2-2648.

B. The director of the Office of Comprehensive Services for At-Risk Youth and Families shall:

1. Develop and recommend to the state executive council programs and fiscal policies that promote and support cooperation and collaboration in the provision of services to troubled and at-risk youths and their families at the state and local levels;

2. Develop and recommend to the Council state interagency policies governing the use, distribution and monitoring of moneys in the state pool of funds and the state trust fund;

3. Develop and provide for the consistent oversight for program administration and compliance with state policies and procedures;

4. Provide for training and technical assistance to localities in the provision of efficient and effective services that are responsive to the strengths and needs of troubled and at-risk youths and their families;

5. Serve as liaison to the participating state agencies that administratively support the Office and that provide other necessary services;

6. Provide an informal review and negotiation process pursuant to subdivision D 19 of § 2.2-2648;

7. Implement, in collaboration with participating state agencies, policies, guidelines and procedures adopted by the State Executive Council;

8. Consult regularly with the Virginia Municipal League, the Virginia Coalition of Private Provider Associations, and the Virginia Association of Counties about implementation and operation of the Comprehensive Services Act (§ 2.2-5200 et seq.);

9. Hire appropriate staff as approved by the Council;

10. Identify, disseminate, and provide annual training for CSA staff and other interested parties on best practices and evidence-based practices related to the Comprehensive Services Program;

11. Perform such other duties as may be assigned by the State Executive Council;

12. Develop and implement uniform data collection standards and collect data, utilizing a secure electronic database for CSA-funded services, in accordance with subdivision D 16 of § 2.2-2648;

13. Develop and implement a uniform set of performance measures for the Comprehensive Services Act program in accordance with subdivision D 17 of § 2.2-2648; and

14. Develop, implement, and distribute management reports in accordance with subdivision D 18 of § 2.2-2648.

C. The director of the Office of Comprehensive Services, in order to provide support and assistance to the Comprehensive Policy and Management Teams (CPMTs) and Family Assessment and Planning Teams (FAPTs) established pursuant to the Comprehensive Services Act for At-Risk Youth and Families (§ 2.2-5200 et seq.), shall:

1. Develop and maintain a web-based statewide automated database, with support from the Department of Information Technology or its successor agency, of the authorized vendors of the Comprehensive Services Act (CSA) services to include verification of a vendor's licensure status, a listing of each discrete CSA service offered by the vendor, and the discrete CSA service's rate determined in accordance with § 2.2-5214; and

2. Develop, in consultation with the Department of General Services, CPMTs, and vendors, a standardized purchase of services contract, which in addition to general contract provisions when utilizing state pool funds will enable localities to specify the discrete service or services they are purchasing for the specified client, the required reporting of the client's service data, including types and numbers of disabilities, mental health and mental retardation diagnoses, or delinquent behaviors for which the purchased services are intended to address, the expected outcomes resulting from these services and the performance timeframes mutually agreed to when the services are purchased. (2000, c. 937, § 2.1-746.1; 2001, c. 844; 2002, c. 410; 2003, c. 485; 2008, cc. 38, 277.)

The 2008 amendments. — The 2008 amendment by c. 38 inserted subdivision B 10 and made related changes.

The 2008 amendment by c. 277 substituted "19" for "17" in subdivision B 6; inserted "the Virginia Coalition of Private Provider Associations" in subdivision B 8; added subdivisions B 11 through B 13 [B 12 through B 14].

Law Review. — For annual survey article on legal issues involving children, see 38 U. Rich. L. Rev. 161 (2003).

Article 17.

State Health Benefits Advisory Council.

§ **2.2-2650:** Repealed by Acts 2001, cc. 520 and 806.

Cross references. — For the Virginia Council on Human Resources, see § 2.2-2675 et seq.

Editor's note. — Acts 2001, cc. 520 and 806 repealed § 2.1-20.1:01, from which this section is derived. Pursuant to § 30-152, Acts 2001, cc. 520 and 806 have been given effect in this section as set out above.

Article 18.

Technology Services, Council On.

§ **2.2-2651. Council on Technology Services; purpose; membership; chairman.** — A. The Council on Technology Services (the COTS) is established as an advisory council, within the meaning of § 2.2-2100, in the executive branch of state government. The purpose of the Council shall be to advise the Chief Information Officer on the services provided by the Virginia Information Technologies Agency and the development and use of applications in state agencies and public institutions of higher education.

B. The COTS shall consist of 19 members that include 16 members to be appointed by the Chief Information Officer and three ex officio members as follows: one designated information technology resource of an executive branch agency from each of the Secretariats of Administration, Commerce and Trade, Education, Finance, Health and Human Resources, Natural Resources, Public Safety, and Transportation; four designated information technology resources from public institutions of higher education; one representative from an independent agency of state government; three representatives from public bodies other than the Commonwealth selected from a list of names submitted by the Virginia Local Government Information Technology Executives; and the Secretary of Technology, the Director of Information Systems of the Supreme Court of Virginia, and the Director of the Division of Legislative Automated Systems who shall serve as ex officio, voting members.

Ex officio members shall serve terms coincident with their terms of office. Other members shall be appointed for a term of two years and shall be eligible for reappointment.

C. The Chief Information Officer shall be the chairman of the COTS. The COTS shall meet quarterly and at such other times as may be called by the chairman. (1999, cc. 412, 421, 433, § 2.1-51.48; 2001, c. 844; 2002, c. 425; 2003, cc. 981, 1021; 2004, c. 989.)

Cross references. — As to the duties of the Chief Information Officer appointed by the Information Technology Investment Board relating to the security of government databases, see § 2.2-2009.

Editor's note. — For provisions of Acts 2003, cc. 981 and 1021, cls. 4 to 16, reflecting the intent of the General Assembly to provide for the consolidation of the procurement and operational functions of information technology for state agencies in a single agency, and related transitional and other provisions, see the Editor's note at § 2.2-2005.

Article 19.

Virginia Advisory Council For Adult Education.

§§ **2.2-2652 through 2.2-2654:** Repealed by Acts 2003, c. 452.

Article 20.

Virginia Equal Employment Opportunity Council.

§§ 2.2-2655, 2.2-2656: Repealed by Acts 2001, cc. 520 and 806.

Editor's note. — Acts 2001, cc. 520 and 806 repealed former §§ 2.1-116.10 through 2.1-116.14, from which these sections are derived. Pursuant to § 30-152, Acts 2001, cc. 520 and 806 have been given effect in these sections as set out above.

Article 21.

Virginia Council On Coordinating Prevention.

§§ 2.2-2657 through 2.2-2663: Repealed by Acts 2001, c. 577.

Editor's note. — Acts 2001, c. 577 repealed §§ 9-267 through 9-273, from which these sections are derived. Pursuant to § 30-152, Acts 2001, c. 577 has been given effect in these sections as set out above.

Article 22.

Virginia Interagency Coordinating Council.

§ 2.2-2664. Virginia Interagency Coordinating Council; purpose; membership; duties. — A. The Virginia Interagency Coordinating Council (the Council) is established as an advisory council, within the meaning of § 2.2-2100, in the executive branch of state government. The purpose of the Council shall be to promote and coordinate early intervention services in the Commonwealth.

B. The membership and operation of the Council shall be as required by Part C of the Individuals with Disabilities Education Act (20 U.S.C. § 1431 et seq.). The Commissioner of the Department of Health, the Director of the Department for the Deaf and Hard-of-Hearing, the Superintendent of Public Instruction, the Director of the Department of Medical Assistance Services, the Commissioner of the Department of Mental Health, Mental Retardation and Substance Abuse Services, the Commissioner of the Department of Social Services, the Commissioner of the Department for the Blind and Vision Impaired, the Director of the Virginia Office for Protection and Advocacy, and the Commissioner of the Bureau of Insurance within the State Corporation Commission shall each appoint one person from his agency to serve as the agency's representative on the Council.

Agency representatives shall regularly inform their agency head of the Council's activities and the status of the implementation of an early intervention services system in the Commonwealth.

C. The Council's duties shall include advising and assisting the state lead agency in the following:

1. Performing its responsibilities for the early intervention services system;

2. Identifying sources of fiscal and other support for early intervention services, recommending financial responsibility arrangements among agencies, and promoting interagency agreements;

3. Developing strategies to encourage full participation, coordination, and cooperation of all appropriate agencies;

4. Resolving interagency disputes;

5. Gathering information about problems that impede timely and effective service delivery and taking steps to ensure that any identified policy problems are resolved;

6. Preparing federal grant applications; and
7. Preparing and submitting an annual report to the Governor and the U.S. Secretary of Education on the status of early intervention services within the Commonwealth. (1992, c. 771, § 2.1-765; 2001, c. 844; 2004, c. 38; 2005, c. 695.)

Cross references. — As to the coordination of the council established under this section with the early intervention services system, see § 2.2-5300.

ARTICLE 23.

Virginia Military Advisory Council.

§§ **2.2-2665, 2.2-2666:** Repealed by Acts 2001, c. 577.

Editor's note. — Acts 2001, c. 577 repealed §§ 9-95.5 and 9-95.6, from which these sections are derived. Pursuant to § 30-152, Acts 2001, c. 577 has been given effect in these sections as set out above.

ARTICLE 23.1.

Virginia Military Advisory Council.

§ **2.2-2666.1. Council created; composition; compensation and expenses; meetings; chairman's executive summary.** — A. The Virginia Military Advisory Council (the Council) is hereby created as an advisory council, within the meaning of § 2.2-2100, in the executive branch of state government, to maintain a cooperative and constructive relationship between the Commonwealth and the leadership of the several Armed Forces of the United States and the military commanders of such Armed Forces stationed in the Commonwealth, and to encourage regular communication on continued military facility viability, the exploration of privatization opportunities and issues affecting preparedness, public safety and security.

B. The Council shall be composed of 27 members as follows: the Lieutenant Governor, the Attorney General, the Secretary of Public Safety, the Adjutant General, the Chairman of the House Committee on Militia, Police and Public Safety and the Chairman of the Senate Committee on General Laws, or their designees; four members, one of whom shall be a representative of the Virginia State Defense Force, to be appointed by and serve at the pleasure of the Governor; and 17 members, including representatives of major military commands and installations located in the Commonwealth or in jurisdictions adjacent thereto, who shall be appointed by the Governor after consideration of the persons nominated by the Secretaries of the Armed Forces of the United States and who shall serve at the pleasure of the Governor. However, any legislative member who is appointed by the Governor shall serve a term coincident with his term of office. The provisions of § 49-1 shall not apply to federal civilian officials and military personnel appointed to the Council.

C. Legislative members of the Council shall receive such compensation as provided in § 30-19.12, and nonlegislative members shall receive such compensation as provided in § 2.2-2813 for the performance of their duties. All members shall be reimbursed for all reasonable and necessary expenses incurred in the performance of their duties as provided in §§ 2.2-2813 and 2.2-2825. Funding for the costs of compensation and expenses of the members shall be provided by the Department of Military Affairs.

D. The Council shall elect a chairman from among its membership. The vice-chairman of the Council shall be the Assistant to the Governor for Commonwealth Preparedness. The meetings of the Council shall be held at the call of the chairman or whenever the majority of members so request. A majority of the members shall constitute a quorum.

E. The chairman of the Council shall submit to the Governor and the General Assembly an annual executive summary of the interim activity and work of the Council no later than the first day of each regular session of the General Assembly. The executive summary shall be submitted as provided in the procedures of the Division of Legislative Automated Systems for the processing of legislative documents and reports and shall be posted on the General Assembly's website. (2002, c. 676; 2003, c. 885; 2004, c. 1000; 2005, c. 248; 2006, cc. 860, 901; 2007, c. 415.)

Editor's note. — Acts 2003, c. 885, cl. 7, provides: "That all current members of the collegial bodies whose terms have been modified by this act shall be eligible, if reappointed, to the full number of terms provided by this act regardless of prior service."

Acts 2004, c. 1000, cl. 5, provides: "That this act shall not be construed to affect existing appointments for which the terms have not expired. However, any new appointments or appointments to fill vacancies made after the effective date of this act shall be made in accordance with the provisions of this act."

The 2007 amendments. — The 2007 amendment by c. 415, in subsection B, substituted "27 members" for "25 members," inserted "the Secretary of Public Safety," and substituted "17 members" for "16 members" in the first sentence.

§ 2.2-2666.2. Duties of Council; staff support. — The Council shall identify and study and provide advice and comments to the Governor on issues of mutual concern to the Commonwealth and the Armed Forces of the United States, including exclusive and concurrent jurisdiction over military installations, educational quality and the future of federal impact aid, preparedness, public safety and security concerns, transportation needs, alcoholic beverage law enforcement, substance abuse, social service needs, possible expansion and growth of military facilities in the Commonwealth and such other issues as the Governor or the Council may determine to be appropriate subjects of joint consideration.

Such staff support as is necessary for the conduct of the Council's business shall be furnished by the Office of the Governor, the Office of the Secretary of Public Safety, the Department of Military Affairs, and such other executive agencies as the Governor may designate. The Governor shall designate the chairman from among the members. (2002, c. 676.)

§ 2.2-2666.3. (For contingent expiration — see Editor's note) Oceana/Fentress Military Advisory Council created; composition; duties; staff support. — A. The Oceana/Fentress Military Advisory Council (the Oceana/Fentress Council) is hereby created as a subunit of the Virginia Military Advisory Council. The Oceana/Fentress Council shall be composed of two members of the Chesapeake City Council, two members of the Virginia Beach City Council, those members of the Virginia General Assembly whose districts encompass Naval Air Station Oceana and Naval Auxiliary Landing Field Fentress, the Commander, Navy Mid-Atlantic Region or his representative, and the Commanding Officer of Naval Air Station Oceana or his representative.

B. The Oceana/Fentress Council shall identify and study and provide advice and comments to the Virginia Military Advisory Council on issues of mutual concern to the Commonwealth and the Navy concerning Naval Air Station Oceana and Naval Auxiliary Landing Field Fentress and address such other issues as the Governor or the Virginia Military Advisory Council may determine to be appropriate subjects of consideration.

C. Such staff support as is necessary for the conduct of the Oceana/Fentress Council's business shall be furnished by the Office of Commonwealth Preparedness. (2006, cc. 266, 328.)

Editor's note. — Acts 2006, c. 266, cl. 1, § 1, as amended by Acts 2008, c. 653, cl. 1, provides: "§ 1. Land use adjacent to certain jet bases.

"A. The governing body of any locality in which a United States Navy Master Jet Base, or an auxiliary landing field used in connection with flight operations arising from such Master Jet Base, is located shall:

"1. Adopt zoning ordinances that require the governing body to follow Navy Air Installation Compatible Use Zone (AICUZ) guidelines in deciding discretionary applications for property in noise levels 70 dB DNL or greater;

"2. Undertake an evaluation of undeveloped properties located in noise zones 70 dB DNL or greater to determine the suitability of such properties for rezoning classifications that would prohibit uses incompatible under AICUZ guidelines;

"3. Adopt such ordinances or take such other actions as may be recommended in any Joint Land Use Study that has been officially approved by the governing body of the locality; and

"4. Establish programs to purchase land or development rights in the corridor of land underneath the flight path between the Master Jet Base and the auxiliary landing field known as an interfacility traffic area.

"B. For the purpose of preventing further encroachment, the governing body of any locality in which a United States Navy Master Jet Base is located shall adopt ordinances to establish a program to purchase or condemn pursuant to § 2, incompatible use property or otherwise seek to convert such property to an appropriate compatible use and to prohibit new uses or development deemed incompatible with air operations in the Accident Potential Zone 1 (APZ-1) and Clear Zone areas, as depicted in the Navy's 1999 AICUZ Pamphlet. Such ordinances may include provisions for interfacility traffic areas, or any other area designated by the military as an area of special concern by reason of the potential for adverse affects on military operations caused by the encroachment of incompatible land uses. A locality may fund and expend no less than $15 million annually in state and local funds in furtherance of the program, to the extent that properties or development rights are reasonably available for acquisition or their use reasonably may be converted. Such funding and expenditures shall be subject to annual appropriations from the state and locality, and shall continue until such time as all reasonably available properties or development rights have been acquired in the designated areas."

Acts 2006, c. 328, cl. 1, § 1, provides: "§ 1. Land use adjacent to certain jet bases.

"A. The governing body of any locality in which a United States Navy Master Jet Base, or an auxiliary landing field used in connection with flight operations arising from such Master Jet Base, is located shall:

"1. Adopt zoning ordinances that require the governing body to follow Navy Air Installation Compatible Use Zone (AICUZ) guidelines in deciding discretionary applications for property in noise levels 70 dB DNL or greater;

"2. Undertake an evaluation of undeveloped properties located in noise zones 70 dB DNL or greater to determine the suitability of such properties for rezoning classifications that would prohibit uses incompatible under AICUZ guidelines;

"3. Adopt such ordinances or take such other actions as may be recommended in any Joint Land Use Study that has been officially approved by the governing body of the locality; and

"4. Establish programs to purchase land or development rights in the corridor of land underneath the flight path between the Master Jet Base and the auxiliary landing field known as an interfacility traffic area.

"B. For the purpose of preventing further encroachment, the governing body of any locality in which a United States Navy Master Jet Base is located shall adopt ordinances to establish a program to purchase or condemn pursuant to § 2, incompatible use property or otherwise seek to convert such property to an appropriate compatible use and to prohibit new uses or development deemed incompatible with air operations in the Accident Potential Zone 1 (APZ-1) and Clear Zone areas, as depicted in the Navy's 1999 AICUZ Pamphlet, and fund and expend no less than $15 million annually in state and local funds in furtherance of the program, to the extent that properties or development rights are reasonably available for acquisition or their use reasonably may be converted. Such funding and expenditures shall be subject to annual appropriations from the state and locality, and shall continue until such time as all reasonably available properties or development rights have been acquired in the designated areas."

Acts 2006, cc. 266 and 328, cl. 1, § 2, provides: "§ 2. Acquisition of property to prevent further encroachment in Accident Potential Zone 1 and Clear Zone areas of United States Master Jet Bases; limited power to exercise right of eminent domain.

"A. For the purpose of preventing further encroachment, all localities in which a United States Navy Master Jet Base is located are hereby granted the power to exercise the limited right of eminent domain in acquisition of any lands, easements, and privileges for the purpose of protecting public safety by providing unobstructed airspace for the landing and take-off of aircraft utilizing such Master Jet Base and preventing incompatible development within APZ-1 and Clear Zone areas surrounding such Master Jet Base. The power to exercise the limited right of eminent domain may only be exercised where:

"1. The property is located wholly or partially within an APZ-1 or Clear Zone area as described in the United States Navy's 1999 AICUZ Pamphlet;

"2. The property is zoned for residential use, but is undeveloped, and use restrictions imposed by the locality to protect the APZ-1 or Clear Zone areas have left the property without a reasonable use;

"3. The locality has made a bona fide offer to purchase the property from the owner and the owner and the locality have not been able to agree on the terms thereof; and

"4. The owner of the property has made a written request to the locality that the property be acquired by the locality by eminent domain.

"B. Condemnation proceedings authorized by subsection A shall be conducted under the provisions of Chapter 2 (§ 25.1-200 et seq.) of Title 25.1 of the Code of Virginia, mutatis mutandis.

"C. Any property acquired by any locality pursuant to this section shall be valued as if any use restriction enacted by such locality prohibiting incompatible development in APZ-1 or Clear Zone areas surrounding the United States Master Jet Base does not apply.

"D. With respect to any property acquired pursuant to this section, the locality (i) may use, lease, dispose, or convey the property to adjoining land owners where such disposition does not result in any incompatible use under AICUZ guidelines or increased density or intensity of use within the APZ-1 or Clear Zone areas; or (ii) may convert the use of any property to a compatible use as under the United States Navy's OPNAV Instruction 11010.36B (or any superseding Navy AICUZ program regulation) and use, lease, dispose, or convey the property for a use consistent with the AICUZ Pamphlet."

Acts 2006, cc. 266 and 328, cl. 3 provides: "That the provisions of this act and all authority contained herein shall terminate in the event that the aircraft and activities necessary to support the operations of a Master Jet Base are designated for realignment outside of the locality."

Article 24.

Virginia Recycling Markets Development Council.

§ 2.2-2667. The Virginia Recycling Markets Development Council; membership; meetings; staff. — A. The Virginia Recycling Markets Development Council (the Council) is established as an advisory council, within the meaning of § 2.2-2100, in the executive branch of state government. The Council shall be composed of 20 members as follows: the Directors, or a policy-making designee, of the Departments of Business Assistance, Environmental Quality, General Services and Transportation, who shall serve ex officio with voting privileges; and 16 nonlegislative citizen members appointed by the Governor. The nonlegislative citizen members shall be appointed from among residents of the Commonwealth who are knowledgeable about recycling and the development of markets for recyclable materials and shall be comprised of: one member representing county governments appointed following the consideration of nominations, if any, submitted by the Virginia Association of Counties; one member representing municipal governments appointed following the consideration of nominations, if any, submitted by the Virginia Municipal League; one member representing urban Planning District Commissions and one member representing rural Planning District Commissions appointed following the consideration of nominations, if any, submitted by the Association of Planning Districts; one member from the general public; and one representative each, appointed following the consideration of nominations, if any, submitted by recognized industry associations representing solid waste collection and disposal, recycling, glass, paper, aluminum, plastic, tire, oil, scrap metal, electronics, and organic waste.

B. Citizen members of the Council shall serve four-year terms. Directors and their policy designees shall serve terms coincident with the terms of office of the director. Appointments to fill vacancies shall be for the unexpired terms. All members may be reappointed. However, no citizen member of the Council shall be eligible to serve more than two consecutive four-year terms. The remainder of any term to which a citizen member is appointed to fill a vacancy shall not constitute a term in determining the member's eligibility for reappointment. Vacancies shall be filled in the same manner as the original appointments.

Notwithstanding any provision to the contrary, citizen members of the Council shall not receive expenses as defined in § 2.2-2813 and shall serve without compensation.

C. The Council shall elect a chairman and vice-chairman annually from among its members. The Council shall meet at least quarterly on such dates and at such times as they determine. A majority of the appointed members of the Council shall constitute a quorum.

D. Staff support shall be provided by the members of the Council. (1993, c. 162, §§ 9-145.47, 9-145.48; 1997, cc. 240, 269; 1998, c. 7; 2001, cc. 844, 847; 2004, c. 385.)

Editor's note. — Acts 2001, c. 847 amended § 9-145.48, from which this section is derived. Pursuant to § 30-152, Acts 2001, c. 847 has been given effect in this section as set out above. The 2001 amendment by c. 847, in subsection B, added "However, for the terms of the fifteen citizen members to be appointed July 1, 2001, eight shall be appointed for four-year terms and seven shall be appointed for two-year terms. Thereafter, all appointments shall be for terms of four years, except that appointments to fill vacancies shall be for the unexpired terms," and rewrote the last sentence which formerly read: "They shall not receive a per diem, compensation for their service, or travel expenses"; and inserted "appointed" preceding "members" in subsection C.

Acts 2004, c. 385, cl. 2, provides: "That all current members of the Virginia Recycling Markets Development Council shall complete their current terms and shall be eligible, if reappointed, to the full number of terms provided by this act regardless of prior service."

Law Review. — For an article reviewing key environmental developments at the federal and state levels during the period from June 1996 to June 1998, see 32 U. Rich. L. Rev. 1217 (1998).

§ 2.2-2668. Powers and duties of Council. — The Council shall have the power and duty to:

1. Upon request, assist local governments, regional authorities and agencies of the Commonwealth in meeting recycling mandates established under state law and identify markets for recycled or recovered materials collected or generated by local governments, regional authorities or agencies of the Commonwealth;

2. Identify and evaluate existing or proposed state statutes, policies, regulations, and procedures that may attract or deter new businesses or the expansion or retention of existing businesses that can use recycled or recovered materials generated in the Commonwealth or that may create barriers to the development of markets for or the reuse of recycled materials collected by or on behalf of local governments and regional authorities;

3. Facilitate access to markets for recycled or recovered materials collected by local governments, authorities, businesses, and residents of the Commonwealth;

4. Develop, update annually, and implement a plan to fulfill its powers and duties; and

5. Upon request of the Governor, resolution of the General Assembly, a standing or joint study committee, the Secretary of Natural Resources, or the Department of Environmental Quality, report its findings and recommenda-

tions as directed. (1993, c. 162, § 9-145.47; 1997, cc. 240, 269; 2001, c. 844; 2004, c. 385.)

ARTICLE 25.

Virginia Workforce Council.

§ 2.2-2669. Virginia Workforce Council; purpose; membership; terms; compensation and expenses; staff. — A. The Virginia Workforce Council (the Council) is established as a policy council, within the meaning of § 2.2-2100, in the executive branch of state government. The purpose of the Council shall be to assist the Governor in meeting workforce training needs in the Commonwealth.

B. The Council shall consist of 29 members as follows:

1. The Council shall include two members of the House of Delegates to be appointed by the Speaker of the House of Delegates; and two members of the Senate to be appointed by the Senate Committee on Rules. Legislative members shall serve terms coincident with their terms of office and may be reappointed for successive terms.

2. The Governor or his designee; the Secretaries of Commerce and Trade, Education, and Health and Human Resources; the Chancellor of the Virginia Community College System; the Commissioner of the Virginia Employment Commission; and the president of the Virginia AFL-CIO shall serve as members.

3. The Governor shall appoint members as follows: one mayor and one chairperson of a county board of supervisors; one representative of labor in addition to the president of the Virginia AFL-CIO; and 15 nonlegislative citizen members representing the business community, to include the presidents of the Virginia Chamber of Commerce and the Virginia Manufacturer's Association, one representative of proprietary employment training schools, one representative of health care employers, and the remaining members who are business owners, chief executive officers, chief operating officers, chief financial officers, senior managers or other business executives or employers with optimum policy-making or hiring authority and who shall represent diverse regions of the state, to include urban, suburban, and rural areas, at least two of whom shall be members of local workforce investment boards. Nonlegislative citizen members may be nonresidents of the Commonwealth.

Members appointed in accordance with this subdivision shall serve four-year terms, subject to the pleasure of the Governor, and may be reappointed.

C. If one person appointed to fill one of the enumerated positions in subsection B also qualifies to fill any other of the enumerated positions, such person may, at the discretion of the Governor, be deemed to fill any or all of the enumerated positions for which such person qualifies.

D. The Governor shall select a chairman and vice-chairman from among the 15 members representing the business community appointed in accordance with subdivision 3 of subsection B. The Council shall meet upon the call of the chair or the Governor.

E. Compensation and reimbursement of expenses of the members shall be as follows:

1. Legislative members appointed in accordance with subdivision B 1 shall receive such compensation and reimbursement of expenses incurred in the performance of their duties as provided in §§ 2.2-2813, 2.2-2825, and 30-19.12.

2. Members of the Council appointed in accordance with subdivision B 2 shall not receive compensation but shall be reimbursed for all reasonable and necessary expenses incurred in the performance of their duties as provided in §§ 2.2-2813 and 2.2-2825.

3. Members of the Council appointed in accordance with subdivision B 3 shall not receive compensation but shall be reimbursed for all reasonable and necessary expenses incurred in the performance of their duties as provided in §§ 2.2-2813 and 2.2-2825.

Funding for the costs of compensation and expenses of the members shall be provided from federal funds received under the Workforce Investment Act of 1998 (P.L. 105-220, as amended).

F. The Office of the Chancellor of the Virginia Community College System shall provide strategic guidance and staff support to the Council. (1998, cc. 701, 899, § 9-329.1; 1999, cc. 840, 855; 2001, cc. 336, 844; 2003, c. 642; 2004, c. 1000; 2006, cc. 696, 751; 2008, cc. 269, 388.)

Editor's note. — Acts 2001, c. 336 amended § 9-329.1, from which this section is derived. Pursuant to § 30-152, Acts 2001, c. 336 has been given effect in this section as set out above. The 2001 amendment by c. 336 in subsection B, deleted "the Director of the Governor's Employment and Training Department" following "Development Partnership" in the first paragraph; in the second paragraph, substituted "twenty-three" for "twenty-two" and inserted "one representative of health care employers"; and substituted "twenty-three" for "twenty-one" in subsections C and D.

Acts 2003, c. 642, cl. 2, provides: "That members of the Virginia Workforce Council appointed prior to July 1, 2003 shall continue to serve out their existing terms, subject to the pleasure of the Governor."

For Governor's statewide strategic plan addressing needed reforms in workforce policy and the role of the Virginia Community College System in workforce development, see Acts 2006, cc. 696 and 751, cls. 2 and 3, noted in full under § 2.2-435.6.

The 2008 amendments. — The 2008 amendments by cc. 269 and 388 are nearly identical, and inserted "or his designee" in subdivision B 2; rewrote subsection F, which read: "The Governor, or a senior staff member within his immediate office to whom the Governor has delegated such function, shall serve as lead staff to the Council. The Council's lead staff shall supervise the subordinate staff of the Council. The subordinate staff of the Council shall be independent of any other state agency that provides workforce services."

§ 2.2-2670. Powers and duties of the Council; Virginia Workforce Network created. — A. The Council shall undertake the following actions to implement and foster workforce training, exclusive of the career and technical education programs provided through and administered by the public school system:

1. Provide policy advice to the Governor on workforce and workforce development issues;

2. Provide policy direction to local workforce investment boards;

3. Identify current and emerging statewide workforce needs of the business community;

4. Forecast and identify training requirements for the new workforce;

5. Create strategies that will match trained workers with available jobs;

6. Provide an annual report to the Governor concerning its actions and determinations under subdivisions 1 through 5;

7. Create procedures, guidelines, and directives applicable to local workforce investment boards and the operation of one-stops, as necessary and appropriate to carry out the purposes of this article; and

8. Perform any act or function in accordance with the purposes of this article.

B. The Council shall establish at least two committees as follows: one committee to accomplish the aims of the WIA and one committee to focus on high-technology workforce training needs.

C. The Council and the Governor's cabinet secretaries shall assist the Governor in complying with the provisions of the WIA and ensuring the coordination and effectiveness of programs and providers comprising elements of the Virginia Workforce Network.

D. The Council shall assist the Governor in the following areas with respect to workforce development: development of the WIA State Plan; development and continuous improvement of a statewide workforce development system; development of linkages to ensure coordination and nonduplication among programs and activities; review of local plans; designation of local areas; development of local discretionary allocation formulas; development and continuous improvement of comprehensive state performance measures including, without limitation, performance measures reflecting the degree to which one-stop centers provide comprehensive services with all mandatory partners and the degree to which local workforce investment boards have obtained funding from sources other than the WIA; preparation of the annual report to the U.S. Secretary of Labor; development of a statewide employment statistics system; development of incentive grant applications; and development of a statewide system of one-stop centers that provide comprehensive workforce services to employers, employees, and job seekers.

The Council shall share information regarding its meetings and activities with the public.

E. Each local workforce investment board shall develop and submit to the Governor and the Virginia Workforce Council an annual workforce demand plan for its workforce investment board area based on a survey of local and regional businesses that reflects the local employers' needs and requirements and the availability of trained workers to meet those needs and requirements; designate or certify one-stop operators; identify eligible providers of youth activities; identify eligible providers of intensive services if unavailable at one-stop; develop a budget; conduct local oversight of one-stop operators and training providers in partnership with its local chief elected official; negotiate local performance measures, including incentives for good performance and penalties for inadequate performance; assist in developing statewide employment statistics; coordinate workforce investment activities with economic development strategies and the annual demand plan, and develop linkages among them; develop and enter into memoranda of understanding with one-stop partners and implement the terms of such memoranda; promote participation by the private sector; actively seek sources of financing in addition to WIA funds; report performance statistics to the Virginia Workforce Council; and certify local training providers in accordance with criteria provided by the Virginia Workforce Council.

Each local workforce investment board shall share information regarding its meetings and activities with the public.

F. Each chief local elected official shall consult with the Governor regarding designation of local workforce investment areas; appoint members to the local board in accordance with state criteria; serve as the local grant recipient unless another entity is designated in the local plan; negotiate local performance measures with the Governor; ensure that all mandated partners are active participants in the local workforce investment board and one-stop center and collaborate with the local workforce investment board on local plans and program oversight.

G. Each local workforce investment board shall develop and enter into a memorandum of understanding concerning the operation of the one-stop delivery system in the local area with each entity that carries out any of the following programs or activities:

1. Programs authorized under Title I of the WIA;
2. Programs authorized under the Wagner-Peyser Act (29 U.S.C. § 49 et seq.);
3. Adult education and literacy activities authorized under Title II of the WIA;
4. Programs authorized under Title I of the Rehabilitation Act of 1973 (29 U.S.C. § 720 et seq.);

5. Welfare-to-work programs authorized under § 403 (a) (5) of the Social Security Act (42 U.S.C. § 603 (a) (5));

6. Activities authorized under title V of the Older Americans Act of 1965 (42 U.S.C. § 3056 et seq.);

7. Postsecondary vocational education activities authorized under the Carl D. Perkins Vocational and Applied Technology Education Act (20 U.S.C. § 2301 et seq.);

8. Activities authorized under chapter 2 of Title II of the Trade Act of 1974 (19 U.S.C. § 2271 et seq.);

9. Activities pertaining to employment and training programs for veterans authorized under chapter 41 of title 38, United States Code;

10. Employment and training activities carried out under the Community Services Block Grant Act (42 U.S.C. § 9901 et seq.);

11. Employment and training activities carried out by the United States Department of Housing and Urban Development;

12. Programs authorized under Title 60.2, in accordance with applicable federal law;

13. Workforce development activities or work requirements of the Temporary Assistance to Needy Families (TANF) program known in Virginia as the Virginia Initiative for Employment, not Welfare (VIEW) program established pursuant to § 63.2-608; and

14. The workforce development activities or work programs authorized under the Food Stamp Act of 1977 (7 U.S.C. § 2011 et seq.).

H. The Governor shall be responsible for the coordination of the Virginia Workforce Network and the implementation of the WIA. (1998, cc. 701, 899, §§ 9-329.1, 9-329.2; 1999, cc. 840, 855; 2000, cc. 566, 608; 2001, cc. 483, 844; 2003, c. 642; 2004, cc. 686, 872; 2006, cc. 696, 751.)

Editor's note. — Acts 2001, c. 483 amended § 9-329.2, from which this section is derived. Pursuant to § 30-152, Acts 2001, c. 483 has been given effect in this section as set out above. The 2001 amendment by c. 483 substituted "career" for "vocational" in the introductory paragraph of subsection A.

For Governor's statewide strategic plan addressing needed reforms in workforce policy and the role of the Virginia Community College System in workforce development, see Acts 2006, cc. 696 and 751, cls. 2 and 3, noted in full under § 2.2-435.6.

Acts 2008, c. 879, effective for the biennium ending June 30, 2010, in Item 213 L, provides: "L.1. As recommended by House Joint Resolution No. 622 (1997), the Joint Subcommittee to Study Noncredit Education for Workforce Training in the Commonwealth, the Virginia Community College System is directed to establish one or more Institutes of Excellence responsible for development of statewide training programs to meet current, high demand workforce needs of the Commonwealth. Out of this appropriation, at least $846,900 the first year and $846,900 the second year from the general fund is available to support the Institutes of Excellence.

"2. Under the guidance of the Virginia Workforce Council, authorized in Title 2.2, Chapter 26, Article 25, Code of Virginia, the Virginia Community College System shall submit to the Chairmen of the Senate Finance and House Appropriations Committees by November 4 of each year a report detailing the financing, activities, accomplishments and plans for the Institutes of Excellence and the four workforce development centers, and outcomes of the appropriations for 23 workforce coordinators and for non-credit training. The report shall include, but not be limited to:

"a. performance measures to be used to evaluate the effectiveness of the workforce coordinators at all 23 colleges;

"b. detailed information on number of students trained, employers served and courses offered; the types of certifications awarded; and the participation by local governments and the public or private sector, and other data relevant to the activities of the four regional workforce development centers;

"c. the number of students trained, employers served and courses offered through non-credit instruction, and the amounts of local government, public or private sector funding used to match this appropriation; and

"d. the amount or percentage of private and public funding contributed for the institutes' programming and operating needs; the number of private and public partnerships involved in the institutes' programming; the number of faculty and colleges affected by the institutes' programming; and performance measures to be used to evaluate the sharing or broadcasting of information and new/improved/updated curricula to other Virginia Community College campuses."

§ 2.2-2671. Regional workforce training centers. — A. Regional workforce training centers shall be established at institutions within the Virginia Community College System in the Peninsula, Southside, Central Virginia, and Western Tidewater regions to assist the Council in (i) coordinating specific high-skill training, (ii) developing industry standards and related curricula, and (iii) providing skills assessments.

B. The Virginia Community College System shall evaluate other regional workforce center locations and recommend to the Council their establishment as such needs are identified. The Virginia Community College System shall support regional workforce training centers created by the Regional Competitiveness Act (§ 15.2-1306 et seq.) in which community colleges participate.

C. Approved noncredit workforce training programs offered by community colleges may receive general fund support as provided in the appropriation act. (1998, cc. 701, 899, §§ 9-329.1, 9-329.5; 1999, cc. 840, 855; 2001, c. 844.)

§ 2.2-2672. Authorization of facilities use and equipment rental; fees. — Workforce training students at local community college boards and public institutions of higher education may be required to pay facility use and equipment rental fees beyond regular tuition charges for workforce training programs requiring specialized facilities or equipment. Such fees shall either be paid by such students directly to the provider of the facility or equipment or to the college for reimbursement to such provider. The fees shall be no more than the normal fees charged to the general public for the same or similar facilities or equipment. The nature of each fee authorized by this section shall be described in course schedules. All fees authorized by this section shall be reported annually to the Virginia Community College System and public institutions' boards. (1998, c. 899, § 9-329.3; 2001, c. 844.)

§ 2.2-2673. Trade secrets. — Trade secrets that a nonpublic body submits as an offeror in connection with a proposed workforce training program shall not be subject to disclosure under the Virginia Freedom of Information Act (§ 2.2-3700 et seq.). However, such offeror shall (i) invoke the protections of this section prior to or upon submission of the data or other materials, (ii) identify the data or other materials to be protected, and (iii) state the reasons why protection is necessary. (1998, c. 899, § 9-329.4; 2001, c. 844.)

§ 2.2-2674. Workforce Training Access Program and Fund. — A. To facilitate the employment of residents of this Commonwealth, to provide a qualified and competent workforce for Virginia's employers, and to promote the industrial and economic development of the Commonwealth, which purposes are declared and determined to be public purposes, there is created the Workforce Training Access Program, to be administered by the Secretary of Finance as provided in this section.

B. From such funds as are appropriated for this purpose and from such gifts, donations, grants, bequests, and other funds as may be received on its behalf, there is created in the state treasury a special nonreverting fund to be known as the Workforce Training Access Fund, hereafter referred to as "the Fund." The Fund shall be established on the books of the Comptroller. Interest earned on moneys in the Fund shall remain in the Fund and be credited to it. Any moneys remaining in the Fund, including interest thereon, at the end of each fiscal year shall not revert to the general fund but shall remain in the Fund.

The assets of the Fund shall be reserved, invested, and expended solely pursuant to and for the purposes of this section and shall not be expended or otherwise transferred or used by the Commonwealth for any other purpose. Expenditures and disbursements from the Fund shall be made by the State Treasurer on warrants issued by the Comptroller upon written request signed by the Secretary of Finance only as a guaranty of payment of workforce training loans made by a national student loan marketing association pursuant to the provisions of this section.

C. The Secretary of Finance is authorized to enter into an agreement with a national student loan marketing association that shall originate, fund and service workforce training loans in accordance with the provisions of this section, to persons enrolled in workforce training courses and programs that the Statewide Workforce Training Council has certified to be responding to the technology needs of business and industry in the Commonwealth pursuant to § 2.2-2670.

The terms and conditions of such workforce training loans shall be consistent with market conditions, and shall provide a repayment sufficient to amortize the cost of the training over its expected useful life, not to exceed sixty months. No person may receive a workforce training loan or loans that would result in that person owing an outstanding amount in excess of the tuition and required fees for the certified workforce training course or program in which such person participates.

Only persons (i) who have established domicile in Virginia, as provided in § 23-7.4 or (ii) who are employed in Virginia and whose employers make loan repayments directly by payroll deduction or tuition assistance, before providing for the training needs of other students in such certified courses, shall be eligible to receive workforce training loans. Nothing herein shall be construed to impose an obligation upon an employer to make loan payments or to continue tuition assistance after termination of the student's employment.

Consistent with Sections 10 and 11 of Article VIII of the Constitution of Virginia, the assets of the Fund shall be pledged as a guaranty of payment of workforce training loans made by such national student loan marketing association and may be expended in satisfaction of the guaranty obligations incurred thereby. Neither the Commonwealth, nor any of its agencies, political subdivisions, nor employees shall have any other or further liability in connection with such workforce training loans.

The agreement shall provide for annual evaluation by such national student loan marketing association and the Secretary of Finance, or his designee, of the aggregate unpaid amount of workforce training loans that such national student loan marketing association shall make available hereunder. Such association shall agree to make available workforce training loans in an aggregate unpaid amount of not less than five times the amount of all cash, cash equivalents, investments, and other assets that would then be available in the Fund.

D. If such association ceases to make workforce training loans available as provided under the agreement, the Fund will revert to the general fund of the Commonwealth, free of the restrictions imposed by this section, after payment of or provision for any outstanding obligations that the Fund guarantees. (1999, c. 794, § 9-329.6; 2001, c. 844.)

§ 2.2-2674.01. Virginia Career Readiness Certificate Program. — A. There is created the Virginia Career Readiness Certificate Program (the Program) to certify the workplace and college readiness skills of Virginians, in order to better prepare them for continued education and workforce training, successful employment, and career advancement.

B. The Program may be offered through public high schools, community colleges, one-stop centers, technical centers, vocation rehabilitation centers, the Department of Correctional Education, institutions of higher education, and any other appropriate institutions as determined by the Virginia Workforce Council.

C. The Program shall include, but not be limited to, the following:

1. A nationally recognized multilevel Career Readiness Certificate and related pre-instructional assessment tool to quantify an individual's level of proficiency in the following measurable work-ready skills: (i) reading, (ii) applied math, (iii) locating information, and (iv) any additional skills necessary to meet business and industry skill demand;

2. Targeted instruction and remediation skills training to address those work-ready skills in which the individual is not proficient as measured by the pre-instructional assessment tool designed to meet identified specific skill needs of local employers;

3. A Career Readiness Certificate awarded to individuals upon successful attainment of work-ready skills as documented by the assessment tool; and

4. A statewide online data system to serve as the repository for Career Readiness Certificate attainment data. The system shall (i) serve as the administrative tool to administer and help promote the Program; (ii) incorporate online services that enable employers to search individual Career Readiness Certificate data to determine skill levels and locate certified individuals in the state or a region; and (iii) incorporate online services that offer individuals tools for career exploration, continued education opportunities, job-readiness practice, and job search capabilities. The Virginia Workforce Council shall seek to ensure the confidentiality of individual Career Readiness Certificate recipients. This shall include provisions for individuals, except for employer-sponsored individuals, to opt-in and opt-out of the statewide online data system at any test occurrence. Additionally, the provisions of §§ 2.2-3800 through 2.2-3803 shall be considered in individual confidentiality protections adopted by the Virginia Workforce Council.

D. The Council, in consultation with the Secretary of Education, shall develop policies and guidelines necessary to implement and administer the Program.

E. The Council shall report Program outcomes to the Governor, the Senate Commerce and Labor Committee, Senate Education and Health Committee, House Commerce and Labor Committee, and House Education Committee of the General Assembly by December 1 of each year. The report shall make recommendations for improving the program, including funding recommendations. (2008, cc. 243, 679.)

Editor's note. — Acts 2008, cc. 243 and 679, cl. 2 provides: "That the Council shall investigate the creation of a Work-Ready Community Certification Program and report its findings to the Governor, the House Commerce and Labor Committee, House Education Committee, Senate Commerce and Labor Committee, and Senate Education and Health Committee of the General Assembly by December 1, 2008."

Acts 2008, cc. 243 and 679, cl. 3 provides: "That funding for the provisions of this act shall be based on a budget approved by the Virginia Workforce Council and shall come from funds made available under the Workforce Investment Act, or from other sources as shall be made available, in an amount not to exceed $1 million."

§ **2.2-2674.1. Definitions.** — As used in this article:

"Local workforce investment board" means a local workforce investment board established under § 117 of the WIA.

"One stop" means a conceptual approach to service delivery intended to provide a single point of access for receiving a wide range of workforce development and employment services, either on-site or electronically, through a single system.

"One-stop center" means a physical site where core services are provided, either on-site or electronically, and access to intensive services, training

services, and other partner program services are available for employers, employees, and job seekers.

"One-stop operator" means a single entity or consortium of entities that operate a one-stop center or centers. Operators may be public or private entities competitively selected or designated through an agreement with a local workforce board.

"Virginia Workforce Network" includes the programs and activities enumerated in subsection G of § 2.2-2670.

"WIA" means the federal Workforce Investment Act of 1998 (P.L. 105-220). (2003, c. 642; 2006, cc. 696, 751.)

Editor's note. — Section 117 of the WIA can be found at 29 U.S.C.S. § 2832.

For Governor's statewide strategic plan addressing needed reforms in workforce policy and the role of the Virginia Community College System in workforce development, see Acts 2006, cc. 696 and 751, cls. 2 and 3, noted in full under § 2.2-435.6.

Article 26.

Virginia Council on Human Resources.

§ 2.2-2675. Purpose of chapter. — This chapter merges the Virginia Equal Employment Opportunity Council, the Personnel Advisory Board, Local Health Benefits Advisory Committee, the State Health Benefits Advisory Council, and consolidates their functions under the Virginia Council on Human Resources. (2001, cc. 520, 806, § 9-396.)

Editor's note. — Acts 2001, cc. 520 and 806 enacted §§ 9-396 to 9-399, from which this article is derived. Pursuant to § 30-152, Acts 2001, cc. 520 and 806 have been given effect in this article as set out above.

Acts 2008, c. 879, effective for the biennium ending June 30, 2010, in Item 85 A, provides: "Administration of any health benefit plan or plans provided for state employees pursuant to § 2.2-2818, Code of Virginia, shall be subject to the review of the Virginia Council on Human Resources, which is provided for in § 2.2-2675, Code of Virginia. Additionally, the department shall report any proposed changes in premiums, benefits, carriers, or provider networks to the Governor and the Chairmen of the House Appropriations and Senate Finance Committees at least sixty days prior to implementation."

Law Review. — For article, "The Law of Wrongful Discharge in Virginia," see 10 G.M.U. L. Rev. 133 (1988). For a note, "Hanging in the Balance: Confidentiality Clauses and Postjudgment Settlements of Employment Discrimination Disputes," see 86 Va. L. Rev. 1537 (2000).

Research References. — Janice Goodman, Employee Rights Litigation: Pleading and Practice (Matthew Bender).

Lex K. Larson, Employment Discrimination (Matthew Bender).

§ 2.2-2676. Virginia Council on Human Resources; membership; terms; compensation and expenses. — A. The Virginia Council on Human Resources (the Council) is established as an advisory council, within the meaning of § 2.2-2100, in the executive branch of state government. The Council shall consist of 17 members. Eight nonlegislative citizen members shall be appointed by the Governor, subject to confirmation by the General Assembly, as follows: two state employees in management positions, two state employees in nonmanagement positions, one retired state employee, one citizen member at large, one member that is either a teacher or a member of a local school board and one member from local government as defined in § 2.2-1204. Four nonlegislative citizen members shall be appointed by the Speaker of the House of Delegates as follows: one state employee, one retired state employee, and two citizens at large. Three members shall be appointed by the Senate Committee on Rules as follows: one state employee, one retired employee, and one citizen at large. In addition, the Director of the Department of Human Resource Management and the Director of the Department of Employment Dispute Resolution, or their designees, shall serve as ex officio members without voting privileges. All members shall be citizens of the Commonwealth.

B. After the initial staggering of terms, all appointments shall be for a term of four years. Vacancies shall be filled for the unexpired terms. No member shall be eligible to serve more than two successive four-year terms; however, after the expiration of the remainder of a term to which he was appointed to fill a vacancy, two additional terms may be served by such member if appointed thereto.

C. The Council shall elect a chairman and a vice-chairman annually from among its membership. A majority of the members of the Council shall constitute a quorum. Meetings of the Council shall be held upon the call of the chairman or whenever the majority of the members so request.

D. Members of the Council shall receive no compensation for their services but shall be reimbursed for all reasonable and necessary expenses incurred in the performance of their duties as provided in §§ 2.2-2813 and 2.2-2825. Funding for the costs of expenses shall be provided by the Department of Human Resources. (2001, cc. 520, 806, § 9-397; 2004, c. 1000.)

Editor's note. — Acts 2001, cc. 520 and 806 enacted § 9-397, from which this section is derived. Pursuant to § 30-152, Acts 2001, cc. 520 and 806 have been given effect in this section as set out above.

Acts 2004, c. 1000, cl. 5, provides: "That this act shall not be construed to affect existing appointments for which the terms have not expired. However, any new appointments or appointments to fill vacancies made after the effective date of this act shall be made in accordance with the provisions of this act."

§ **2.2-2677. Powers and duties.** — A. The Council shall have the power and duty to:

1. Advise the Governor, the Director of the Department of Human Resource Management and the Director of the Department of Employment Dispute Resolution on all matters relating to personnel administration;
2. Review all public employer-employee relations throughout the Commonwealth;
3. Review the Department of Employment Dispute Resolution's program of employee management relations and make recommendations to improve communications between employees and agencies and instrumentalities of the Commonwealth;
4. Carry out such other functions as the Governor deems appropriate;
5. Review the Department of Human Resource Management's training and management programs, compensation and classification practices, benefit programs, and recruitment practices;
6. Advise the Governor on issues and concerns of state retirees and active employees regarding health insurance coverage and other health related benefits; and
7. Advise the Department of Human Resource Management on any plan or plans, subject to approval by the Governor, for providing health insurance coverage for employees of local governments, local officers, teachers, and retirees, and the dependents of such employees, officers, teachers and retirees.

The Council shall be charged with the responsibility of monitoring the Commonwealth's equal employment opportunity practices so as to assure that such practices fulfill the Commonwealth's obligations of providing equal opportunity to all employees and applicants. The Council may (i) call upon the Director of Human Resource Management and other state officials for information and reports to assist them in their work; (ii) act as a communications channel for groups both inside and outside of state government that wish to have their views on equal employment opportunity expressed to state government; and (iii) make recommendations to state agencies concerning the implementation of their affirmative action plans and programs.

B. The Council members shall refer employees who have work-related discrimination complaints to the Director of Equal Opportunity and Employee Programs. Once the discrimination complaint is referred to the Director, the matter shall be reviewed in accordance with the Equal Employment Opportunity Complaint Procedure of the Department of Human Resource Management, or at the employee's option, the State Grievance Procedure. The Committee shall audit and review the Commonwealth's equal opportunity posture at least once a year and recommend improvements to the Governor.

The Council shall review the progress of state agency affirmative action plans and programs, and make recommendations for changes as warranted. (2001, cc. 520, 806, § 9-398.)

Editor's note. — Acts 2001, cc. 520 and 806 enacted § 9-398, from which this section is derived. Pursuant to § 30-152, Acts 2001, cc. 520 and 806 have been given effect in this section as set out above.

§ **2.2-2678. Staff.** — Staff assistance to the Council shall be provided by the Department of Human Resource Management and shall include, but not be limited to, the establishment of the Council's schedule of meetings and providing notice of the meeting to members of the Council and the public. (2001, cc. 520, 806, § 9-399.)

Editor's note. — Acts 2001, cc. 520 and 806 enacted § 9-399, from which this section is derived. Pursuant to § 30-152, Acts 2001, cc. 520 and 806 have been given effect in this section as set out above.

Article 27.

The Advisory Council on the Future of Nursing in Virginia.

§§ **2.2-2679, 2.2-2680:** Expired.

Editor's note. — Acts 2001, c. 777, which enacted §§ 9-404, 9-405, from which this article was derived, provides in cl. 2: "That this act shall expire on July 1, 2006. "

Article 28.

Joint Leadership Council of Veterans Service Organizations.

§ **2.2-2681. Joint Leadership Council of Veterans Service Organizations; membership; terms; chairman; quorum; compensation.** — A. The Joint Leadership Council of Veterans Service Organizations (the Council) is established as an advisory council, within the meaning of § 2.2-2100, in the executive branch of state government. The Council shall be composed of one representative from each qualifying veterans service organization to be appointed by the Governor, the Commissioner of the Department of Veterans Services, and the Chairmen of the Board of Veterans Services and the Veterans Services Foundation, who shall serve as nonvoting ex officio members. Each veterans service organization representative may designate an alternate to attend meetings of the Council in the absence of such representative.

Qualifying veterans service organizations shall be (i) composed principally of and controlled by veterans of the United States Armed Forces, (ii) a registered nonprofit organization in good standing, incorporated for the purpose of promoting programs designed to assist veterans of the armed forces of the United States and their eligible spouses, orphans, and dependents, and (iii) active and in good standing with its parent national organization, if such a parent organization exists.

B. Voting members shall be appointed for terms of three years. Appointments to fill vacancies shall be for the unexpired terms. No person shall be eligible to serve for or during more than two successive three-year terms. Each qualifying veterans service organization shall be responsible for recommending a member for appointment to the Council by the Governor.

C. The Council shall annually elect its chairman and vice-chairman from among its members. The Council shall develop and adopt its own charter, and shall develop and adopt a mission and vision statement in consultation with the Department of Veterans Services. A majority of the voting members of the Council shall constitute a quorum.

D. The Council shall meet at least four times per year. Additional meetings shall be subject to majority approval by the members of the Council.

E. Members of the Council shall not receive any compensation, but shall be reimbursed for reasonable and necessary expenses incurred in the performance of their duties as provided in § 2.2-2825. (2003, cc. 657, 670; 2004, c. 697; 2006, c. 150; 2008, cc. 467, 768.)

Editor's note. — For transition of property and powers of the Department of Veterans' Affairs to the Department of Veterans Services, see Acts 2003, cc. 657 and 670, cl. 3 and 4, noted under § 2.2-2000.

Acts 2008, cc. 467 and 768, cl. 2 provides: "That any three-year term being served by a Governor-appointed member of the Virginia Veterans Services Foundation on July 1, 2008, may in the discretion of the Governor, be extended to a four-year term in accordance with the provisions of this act. However, nothing in this act shall allow any such member to serve more than two consecutive terms."

The 2008 amendments. — The 2008 amendments by cc. 467 and 768 are identical, and in subsection A, substituted "Chairmen" for "Chairman" and inserted "and the Veterans Services Foundation" in the second sentence; and substituted "eligible spouses" for "Virginia domiciled surviving spouses" in clause (ii) in the second paragraph of subsection A.

§ 2.2-2682. Powers and duties. — A. The Council shall have the following powers and duties:

1. Advise the Department of Veterans Services regarding (i) methods of providing support for ongoing veterans services and programs, and (ii) addressing veterans issues on an ongoing basis;

2. Recommend issues that may potentially impact veterans of the armed forces of the United States and their eligible spouses, orphans, and dependents;

3. Advise the Department of Veterans Services and the Board of Veterans Services on matters of concern to Virginia-domiciled veterans and their eligible spouses, orphans, and dependents;

4. Promote and support existing veterans services and programs;

5. Recommend and promote implementation of new efficient and effective administrative initiatives that enhance existing veterans services and programs or provide for necessary veterans services and programs not currently provided; and

6. Maintain a nonpartisan approach to maintaining and improving veterans services and programs in the Commonwealth.

B. The chairman shall report to the Commissioner and the Board of Veterans Services the results of its meetings and submit an annual report on or before November 30 of each year.

C. The Council may apply for funds from the Veterans Services Foundation to enable it to better carry out its objectives. The Council shall not impose unreasonable burdens or costs in connection with requests of agencies. (2003, cc. 657, 670; 2008, cc. 467, 768.)

The 2008 amendments. — The 2008 amendments by cc. 467 and 768 are identical, and substituted "eligible spouses" for "Virginia domiciled surviving spouses" in subdivision A 2; and in subdivision A 3, inserted "Virginia-domiciled" preceding "veterans and their" and substituted "eligile spouses" for "Virginia-domiciled surviving spouses."

Article 29.

Council on Virginia's Future.

(Effective until July 1, 2013)

The number of this article was assigned by the Virginia Code Commission, the article having been enacted as Article 28.

§ 2.2-2683. (Effective until July 1, 2013) Definitions. — As used in this article:

"Long-term objective" means a measurable standard of desired performance achievement extending at least five years into the future.

"Performance budgeting" means a systematic incorporation of planning, strategic performance and productivity measurement, and program evaluation information into the budgetary process.

"Performance management" means a management system consisting of strategic planning, strategic performance and productivity measurement, program evaluation, and performance budgeting.

"Program evaluation" means an evaluation of the progress made toward the achievement of long-term objectives, current initiatives, and increased productivity.

"Roadmap" or *"Roadmap for Virginia's Future"* means a planning process that may include some or all of the following sequential steps: (i) developing a set of guiding principles that are reflective of public sentiment and relevant to critical decision-making; (ii) establishing a long-term vision for the Commonwealth; (iii) conducting a situation analyses of core state service categories; (iv) setting long-term objectives for state services; (v) aligning state services to the long-term objectives; (vi) instituting a planning and performance management system consisting of strategic planning, performance measurement, program evaluation, and performance budgeting; and (vii) performing plan adjustments based on public input and evaluation of the results of the Roadmap.

"Situational analyses" means the assessment of state agency performance in core service areas.

"Strategic planning" means the systematic clarification and documentation of what a state agency wishes to achieve and how to achieve it. The objective of strategic planning is a set of goals, action steps, and measurements constructed to guide performance.

"Strategic performance and productivity measures" means the use of data to review the current performance, improvement in productivity, and progress against the long-term objectives.

"Vision" means an aspirational expression of a future condition for the Commonwealth that is both essential and desirable and extends at least 10 years into the future. (2003, c. 900.)

The number of this section was assigned by the Virginia Code Commission, the number in the 2003 act having been 2.2-2681.

Editor's note. — Acts 2003, c. 900, cl. 3, as amended by Acts 2008, c. 240, provides: "That the provisions of this act shall expire on July 1, 2013."

§ 2.2-2684. (Effective until July 1, 2013) Council on Virginia's Future; purpose. — The Council on Virginia's Future (the Council) is established as an advisory council, within the meaning of § 2.2-2100, in the executive branch of state government. The purpose of the Council is to advise the Governor and the General Assembly on the implementation of the Roadmap for Virginia's Future process. (2003, c. 900.)

The number of this section was assigned by the Virginia Code Commission, the number in the 2003 act having been 2.2-2682.

Editor's note. — Acts 2003, c. 900, cl. 3, as amended by Acts 2008, c. 240, provides: "That the provisions of this act shall expire on July 1, 2013."

§ 2.2-2685. (Effective until July 1, 2013) Membership; terms; quorum; meetings; compensation and expenses. — A. The Council shall be composed of 18 members that include eight legislative members and 10 nonlegislative members as follows:

1. The Governor;
2. The Speaker of the House;
3. The majority and minority leaders of the House of Delegates;
4. The Chairman of the House Committee on Appropriations;
5. The President Pro Tempore of the Senate;
6. The majority and minority leaders of the Senate;
7. The Chairman of the Senate Finance Committee;
8. One nonlegislative citizen member appointed by the Speaker of the House;
9. One nonlegislative citizen member appointed by the Senate Committee on Rules;
10. Two Cabinet Secretaries appointed by the Governor; and
11. Five nonlegislative citizen members appointed by the Governor.

B. Legislative members and the two Cabinet Secretaries appointed by the Governor shall serve terms coincident with their terms of office. In the event that a legislative member holds more than one of the positions listed in subsection A, such legislative member shall designate another legislative member or members, as applicable, to serve as the representative for the other position or positions. After the initial staggering of terms, nonlegislative citizen members appointed by the Speaker of the House of Delegates or the Senate Committee on Rules shall be appointed for a term of two years, and nonlegislative citizen members appointed by the Governor shall be appointed for a term of four years. Appointments to fill vacancies, other than by expiration of a term, shall be for the unexpired terms. All members may be reappointed. No nonlegislative citizen member appointed by the legislative appointing authorities shall serve more than four consecutive two-year terms and no nonlegislative citizen member appointed by the Governor shall serve more than two consecutive four-year terms. The remainder of any term to which a member is appointed to fill a vacancy shall not constitute a term in determining the member's eligibility for reappointment. Vacancies shall be filled in the same manner as the original appointments.

The Governor shall serve as the chairman of the Council. The Council shall elect a vice-chairman from its membership. A majority of members of the Council shall constitute a quorum. The Council shall meet at least four times each year. The meetings of the Council shall be held at the call of the chairman or whenever four or more members so request.

C. Legislative members of the Council shall receive such compensation as provided in § 30-19.12 and nonlegislative citizen members shall receive compensation as provided in § 2.2-2813 for the performance of their duties. All members shall be reimbursed for all reasonable and necessary expenses incurred in the performance of their duties as provided in §§ 2.2-2813 and 2.2-2825. Funding for the costs of compensation and expenses of the members shall be provided by the Department of Planning and Budget. (2003, c. 900; 2004, c. 1000.)

The number of this section was assigned by the Virginia Code Commission, the number in the 2003 act having been 2.2-2683.

Editor's note. — Acts 2003, c. 900, cl. 3, as amended by Acts 2008, c. 240, provides: "That the provisions of this act shall expire on July 1, 2013."

Acts 2004, c. 1000, cl. 5, provides: "That this act shall not be construed to affect existing appointments for which the terms have not expired. However, any new appointments or appointments to fill vacancies made after the effective date of this act shall be made in accordance with the provisions of this act."

§ 2.2-2686. (Effective until July 1, 2013) Duties of the Council. — A. The Council shall have the following duties:

1. Recommend a timetable for phasing in and establishing guiding principles for the Roadmap;
2. Recommend long-term objectives for the Commonwealth and monitor and advise the Governor and the General Assembly regarding the progress toward the objectives;
3. Provide advice on the implementation of the performance-management system across state government;
4. Disseminate information to the public on the Commonwealth's performance-management system;
5. Recommend a systematic process for the periodic evaluation of the Roadmap and adherence to the long-term goals and recommend improvements to the Governor and the General Assembly. The periodic evaluation process shall provide for enhanced opportunities for public participation and input;
6. Beginning November 1, 2004, develop and submit annually to the General Assembly and the Governor and publish to the public a balanced accountability scorecard containing an assessment of (i) current service performance, (ii) productivity improvement, and (iii) progress against long-term objectives. The balanced scorecard shall also contain other evaluative recommendations that will enhance the provision of state services and suggested measures to evaluate progress against long-term objectives; and
7. Solicit public input on appropriate aspects of the Roadmap as determined by the Council.

B. By January 1, 2004, the Council shall recommend to the Governor and the General Assembly legislation defining the vision, long-term objectives, and appropriate performance measures for state government. The Council shall review the long-term objectives for state government every two years. (2003, c. 900.)

The number of this section was assigned by the Virginia Code Commission, the number in the 2003 act having been 2.2-2684.

Editor's note. — Acts 2003, c. 900, cl. 3, as amended by Acts 2008, c. 240, provides: "That the provisions of this act shall expire on July 1, 2013."

§ 2.2-2687. (Effective until July 1, 2013) Advisory committees. — The Council may form such advisory committees as it deems necessary, convenient, or desirable to advise and assist in performing the duties conferred by this article. The disclosure requirements of subsection B of § 2.2-3114 of the State and Local Government Conflict of Interests Act shall apply to members of the advisory committees. (2003, c. 900.)

The number of this section was assigned by the Virginia Code Commission, the number in the 2003 act having been 2.2-2685.

Editor's note. — Acts 2003, c. 900, cl. 3, as

amended by Acts 2008, c. 240, provides: "That the provisions of this act shall expire on July 1, 2013."

§ 2.2-2688. (Effective until July 1, 2013) Staff; cooperation and assistance. — A. The Department of Planning and Budget shall provide staff assistance to the Council. Additional assistance as needed shall be provided by the Joint Legislative Audit and Review Commission, the Auditor of Public Accounts, and the staffs of the House Committee on Appropriations and the Senate Finance Committee. All agencies, authorities, and institutions of the Commonwealth shall cooperate and provide such assistance to the Commission as the Commission may request.

B. The Chairman, in consultation with the Council, may hire or appoint an Executive Director for the Council if deemed appropriate. (2003, c. 900.)

The number of this section was assigned by the Virginia Code Commission, the number in the 2003 act having been 2.2-2686.

Editor's note. — Acts 2003, c. 900, cl. 3, as amended by Acts 2008, c. 240, provides: "That the provisions of this act shall expire on July 1, 2013."

§ 2.2-2689. (Effective until July 1, 2013) Chairman's executive summary of activity and work of the Council. — The chairman shall submit to the Governor and the General Assembly an annual executive summary of the interim activity and work of the Council no later than the first day of each regular session of the General Assembly. The executive summary shall be submitted as provided in the procedures of the Division of Legislative Automated Systems for the processing of legislative documents and reports and shall be posted on the General Assembly's website. (2003, c. 900.)

The number of this section was assigned by the Virginia Code Commission, the number in the 2003 act having been 2.2-2687.

Editor's note. — Acts 2003, c. 900, cl. 3, as amended by Acts 2008, c. 240, provides: "That the provisions of this act shall expire on July 1, 2013."

Article 30.

The Interagency Civil Admissions Advisory Council.

§ 2.2-2690. The Interagency Civil Admissions Advisory Council; purpose. — The Interagency Civil Admissions Advisory Council (the Council) is established as an advisory council, within the meaning of § 2.2-2100, in the executive branch of state government. The purpose of the Council is to study issues related to the provisions of Virginia law regarding the emergency custody, temporary detention, admission, and involuntary inpatient and outpatient treatment of persons with mental illness, to propose recommendations and provide advice addressing those issues, and to improve the coordination and effectiveness of the implementation of those recommendations. (2005, c. 81.)

Editor's note. — Acts 2005, c. 81, cl. 2, provides: "That the initial appointments of nonlegislative citizen members appointed by the Governor shall be staggered as follows: six of the members for three-year terms and six of the members for two-year terms. The initial appointments by the Commissioner of the Department of Mental Health, Mental Retardation and Substance Abuse Services and the Director of the Department of Medical Assistance Services shall be for three years, and the initial appointments by the Director of the

Department of Criminal Justice Services and the Executive Secretary of the Supreme Court of Virginia shall be for two years."

§ 2.2-2691. Membership; terms; quorum; meetings. — The Council shall be composed of 17 members and two ex officio members as follows: one appointee of the Commissioner of the Department of Mental Health, Mental Retardation and Substance Abuse Services; one appointee of the Director of the Department of Medical Assistance Services; one appointee of the Director of the Department of Criminal Justice Services; one appointee of the Executive Secretary of the Supreme Court of Virginia; and 13 nonlegislative citizen members to be appointed by the Governor.

The 13 nonlegislative citizen members shall be citizens of the Commonwealth with appropriate and relevant knowledge and experience, representative of the various geographic regions of the Commonwealth, and comprised of: (i) two representatives of community services boards, one of whom shall be an emergency services director of a community services board and one of whom shall represent the Virginia Association of Community Services Boards; (ii) one representative each from the Virginia Hospital and Healthcare Association, the Virginia College of Emergency Physicians, the Psychiatric Society of Virginia, the Virginia Sheriff's Association, the Virginia Association of Chiefs of Police, the Virginia Municipal League, and the Virginia Association of Counties, upon consideration by the Governor of the nominations, if any, submitted by each organization; (iii) one consumer of mental health services and one family member of a consumer of mental health services; (iv) one attorney licensed to practice law in Virginia; and (v) one individual licensed by a board within the purview of the Department of Health Professions to provide mental health or substance abuse services.

The Secretary of Health and Human Resources and the Secretary of Public Safety shall serve ex officio on the Council with voting privileges. Ex officio members of the Council shall serve terms coincident with their terms of office. The Office of the Attorney General shall receive notice of each Council meeting.

After the initial staggering of terms, each non ex officio member shall be appointed for a term of three years. Appointments to fill vacancies, other than by expiration of a term, shall be for the unexpired terms. Vacancies shall be filled in the same manner as the original appointments. All members may be reappointed.

The Secretary of Health and Human Resources shall chair the Council and the Council shall elect a vice-chairman from among its membership. A majority of the members shall constitute a quorum. The meetings of the Council shall be held regularly at the call of the chairman or his designee. (2005, c. 81.)

§ 2.2-2692. Compensation; expenses. — Members may receive no compensation for the performance of their duties, however, members shall be reimbursed for all reasonable and necessary expenses incurred in the performance of their duties as provided in §§ 2.2-2813 and 2.2-2825. Funding for the costs of expenses of the consumer and family members shall be provided by the Department of Mental Health, Mental Retardation and Substance Abuse Services. (2005, c. 81.)

§ 2.2-2693. Powers and duties of the Council. — The Council shall have the following powers and duties:

1. Identify and discuss issues related to emergency custody, temporary detention, admission, and involuntary inpatient and outpatient treatment in order to improve services, foster increased coordination among all involved state and local public and private agencies and organizations in the imple-

mentation of relevant Virginia laws, and promote a more effective and cost-efficient approach to meeting the needs of individuals requiring these mental health services.

2. Address issues, including transportation; medical screening, evaluation, and treatment; and detention in ways that (i) recognize the varying conditions and needs of individuals who are subject to emergency and temporary detention orders and involuntary inpatient and outpatient treatment; (ii) protect the safety of patients in and staff and employees of facilities providing emergency medical evaluation or treatment, detention, or involuntary inpatient and outpatient treatment services; and (iii) are consistent with the requirements of the Emergency Medical Treatment and Active Labor Act, 42 USC 1395dd and implementing regulations.

3. Develop and revise recommendations, including statutory, regulatory, and policy changes and administrative actions, to address and resolve those issues and communicate those recommendations to and advise all state and local public and private agencies and organizations that are involved in the emergency custody, temporary detention, admission, and involuntary inpatient and outpatient treatment of persons with mental illness on their implementation when uniform procedures or actions are feasible and desirable.

4. Describe a process through which community services boards may convene all public and private agencies and organizations involved in these mental health services at local or regional levels, to (i) review recommendations issued by the Council, (ii) meet regularly as appropriate to discuss issues and the implementation of Council recommendations, and (iii) develop and implement additional state, local, or regional policies and procedures, as needed, including a process for resolving problems that arise in implementation of this article.

5. Consult as needed with individuals, agencies, and organizations other than those serving on the Council in order to access relevant expertise.

6. Report whenever appropriate, as determined by the Council, any recommendations or guidance to the Governor and the General Assembly committees with jurisdiction over mental health issues. (2005, c. 81.)

§ **2.2-2694. Staffing.** — Staff support shall be provided to the Council by the Department of Mental Health, Mental Retardation and Substance Abuse Services, and the Office of the Secretary of Public Safety. All agencies of the Commonwealth shall provide assistance to the Council, upon request. (2005, c. 81.)

§ **2.2-2695:** Repealed by Acts 2008, c. 293, cl. 1.

Editor's note. — This section contained a July 1, 2008, sunset provision for this article.

ARTICLE 31.

Substance Abuse Services Council.

The number of this article was assigned by the Virginia Code Commission, the article having been enacted as Article 30.

§ **2.2-2696. Substance Abuse Services Council.** — A. The Substance Abuse Services Council (the Council) is established as an advisory council, within the meaning of § 2.2-2100, in the executive branch of state government.

The purpose of the Council is to advise and make recommendations to the Governor, the General Assembly, and the State Mental Health, Mental Retardation and Substance Abuse Services Board on broad policies and goals and on the coordination of the Commonwealth's public and private efforts to control substance abuse, as defined in § 37.2-100.

B. The Council shall consist of 30 members. Four members of the House of Delegates shall be appointed by the Speaker of the House of Delegates, in accordance with the principles of proportional representation contained in the Rules of the House of Delegates, and two members of the Senate shall be appointed by the Senate Committee on Rules. The Governor shall appoint one member representing the Virginia Sheriffs' Association, one member representing the Virginia Drug Courts Association, one member representing the Substance Abuse Certification Alliance of Virginia, two members representing the Virginia Association of Community Services Boards, and two members representing statewide consumer and advocacy organizations. The Council shall also include the Commissioner of the Department of Mental Health, Mental Retardation and Substance Abuse Services; the Commissioner of Health; the Commissioner of the Department of Motor Vehicles; the Superintendent of Public Instruction; the Directors of the Departments of Juvenile Justice, Corrections, Criminal Justice Services, Medical Assistance Services, and Social Services; the Chief Operating Officer of the Department of Alcoholic Beverage Control; the Executive Director of the Governor's Office for Substance Abuse Prevention or his designee; the Executive Director of the Virginia Tobacco Settlement Foundation or his designee; the Executive Director of the Commission on the Virginia Alcohol Safety Action Program or his designee; and the chairs or their designees of the Virginia Association of Drug and Alcohol Programs, the Virginia Association of Alcoholism and Drug Abuse Counselors, and the Substance Abuse Council and the Prevention Task Force of the Virginia Association of Community Services Boards.

C. Appointments of legislative members and heads of agencies or representatives of organizations shall be for terms consistent with their terms of office. All other appointments of nonlegislative members shall be for terms of three years, except an appointment to fill a vacancy, which shall be for the unexpired term. The Governor shall appoint a chairman from among the members.

No person shall be eligible to serve more than two successive terms, provided that a person appointed to fill a vacancy may serve two full successive terms.

D. The Council shall meet at least four times annually and more often if deemed necessary or advisable by the chairman.

E. Members of the Council shall receive no compensation for their services but shall be reimbursed for all reasonable and necessary expenses incurred in the performance of their duties as provided in §§ 2.2-2813 and 2.2-2825. Funding for the cost of expenses shall be provided by the Department of Mental Health, Mental Retardation and Substance Abuse Services.

F. The duties of the Council shall be:

1. To recommend policies and goals to the Governor, the General Assembly, and the State Mental Health, Mental Retardation and Substance Abuse Services Board;

2. To coordinate agency programs and activities, to prevent duplication of functions, and to combine all agency plans into a comprehensive interagency state plan for substance abuse services;

3. To review and comment on annual state agency budget requests regarding substance abuse and on all applications for state or federal funds or services to be used in substance abuse programs;

4. To define responsibilities among state agencies for various programs for persons with substance abuse and to encourage cooperation among agencies; and

5. To make investigations, issue annual reports to the Governor and the General Assembly, and make recommendations relevant to substance abuse upon the request of the Governor.

G. Staff assistance shall be provided to the Council by the Office of Substance Abuse Services of the Department of Mental Health, Mental Retardation and Substance Abuse Services. (1976, c. 767, § 37.1-207; 1977, c. 18; 1978, c. 171; 1979, c. 678; 1980, c. 582; 1984, c. 589; 1990, cc. 1, 288, 317; 1998, c. 724; 1999, c. 614; 2005, cc. 713, 716.)

The number of this section was assigned by the Virginia Code Commission, the number in the 2005 act having been § 2.2-2690.

Cross references. — For provisions as to the recodification of Title 37.1, see Editor's notes under § 37.2-100.

Editor's note. — Acts 2005, c. 713, amended § 37.1-207, from which this section is derived. Pursuant to § 30-152, Acts 2005, c. 713 has been given effect in this section as set out above. The 2005 amendment by c. 713, in subsection B, substituted "30 members" for "24 members" in the first sentence, inserted "one member representing the Virginia Drug Courts Association" in the third sentence, and inserted "the commissioner of the Department of Motor Vehicles," "Medical Assistance Services" and "the Chief Operating Officer of the Department of Alcoholic Beverage Control; the Executive Director of the Governor's Office for Substance Abuse Prevention or his designee; the Executive Director of the Virginia Tobacco Settlement Foundation or his designee" in the fourth sentence; and in subsection C, substituted "heads of agencies or representatives of organizations" for "agency heads" in the first sentence.

§ 2.2-2697. Review of state agency substance abuse treatment programs. — A. On or before December 1, 2005, the Council shall forward to the Governor and the General Assembly a Comprehensive Interagency State Plan identifying for each agency in state government (i) the substance abuse treatment program the agency administers; (ii) the program's objectives, including outcome measures for each program objective; (iii) program actions to achieve the objectives; (iv) the costs necessary to implement the program actions; and (v) an estimate of the extent these programs have met demand for substance abuse treatment services in the Commonwealth. The Council shall develop specific criteria for outcome data collection for all affected agencies, including a comparison of the extent to which the existing outcome measures address applicable federally mandated outcome measures and an identification of common outcome measures across agencies and programs. The plan shall also include an assessment of each agency's capacity to collect, analyze, and report the information required by subsection B.

B. Beginning in 2006, the Comprehensive Interagency State Plan shall include the following analysis for each agency-administered substance abuse treatment program: (i) the amount of funding expended under the program for the prior fiscal year; (ii) the number of individuals served by the program using that funding; (iii) the extent to which program objectives have been accomplished as reflected by an evaluation of outcome measures; (iv) identifying the most effective substance abuse treatment, based on a combination of per person costs and success in meeting program objectives; (v) how effectiveness could be improved; (vi) an estimate of the cost effectiveness of these programs; and (vii) recommendations on the funding of programs based on these analyses.

C. All agencies identified in the Comprehensive Interagency State Plan as administering a substance abuse treatment program shall provide the information and staff support necessary for the Council to complete the Plan. In addition, any agency that captures outcome-related information concerning substance abuse programs identified in subsection B shall make this information available for analysis upon request. (2004, c. 686, § 37.1-207.1; 2005, c. 716.)

The number of this section was assigned by the Virginia Code Commission, the number in the 2005 act having been § 2.2-2691.

Cross references. — For provisions as to the recodification of Title 37.1, see Editor's notes under § 37.2-100.

ARTICLE 32.

Modeling and Simulation Advisory Council.

§ 2.2-2698. Modeling and Simulation Advisory Council; purpose; membership; chairman. — A. The Modeling and Simulation Advisory Council (the Council) is established as an advisory council, within the meaning of § 2.2-2100, in the executive branch of state government. The purpose of the Council shall be to advise the Governor on policy and funding priorities to promote the modeling and simulation industry in the Commonwealth.

B. The Council shall consist of 13 members as follows: three legislative members of the House of Delegates to be appointed by the Speaker of the House of Delegates; one legislative member of the Senate to be appointed by the Senate Committee on Rules; six citizen representatives of the modeling and simulation industry to be appointed by the Governor; the Secretary of Technology and the Secretary of Commerce and Trade or their designees; and the Executive Director of the Virginia Modeling, Analysis and Simulation Center.

Ex officio members shall serve terms coincident with their terms of office. Other members shall be appointed for a term of two years and shall be eligible for reappointment.

C. The Council shall elect a chairman and a vice-chairman annually from among its membership. A majority of the members shall constitute a quorum. The Council shall meet biannually and at such other times as may be called by the chairman or a majority of the Council. Staff to the Council shall be provided by the office of the Secretary of Technology. (2007, c. 857.)

§ 2.2-2699. Powers and duties of the Council. — The Council shall have the power and duty to:

1. Advise the Governor on funding priorities for modeling and simulation programs at the Commonwealth's institutions of higher education.
2. Develop policy initiatives and advise the Governor on strategies to promote the modeling and simulation industry in the Commonwealth.
3. Advise the Virginia Economic Development Partnership regarding (i) attracting new modeling and simulation businesses to the Commonwealth and (ii) assisting the development of the Commonwealth's existing modeling and simulation industry.
4. Develop recommendations in conjunction with the Virginia Economic Development Partnership on how to market the Commonwealth's modeling and simulation capabilities to all businesses and industries, especially those not fully utilizing modeling and simulation applications.
5. Develop recommendations that will assist in making Virginia a national leader in the modeling and simulation industry. (2007, c. 857.)

ARTICLE 33.

Aerospace Advisory Council.

(Expires July 1, 2010.)

§ 2.2-2699.1. (Expires July 1, 2010) Aerospace Advisory Council; purpose; membership; compensation; chairman. — A. The Aerospace

Advisory Council (the Council) is established as an advisory council, within the meaning of § 2.2-2100, in the executive branch of state government. The purpose of the Council shall be to advise the Governor on policy and funding priorities to promote the aerospace and space exploration industry in the Commonwealth.

B. The Council shall have a total membership of 13 members that shall consist of four legislative members and 9 nonlegislative citizen members. Members shall be appointed as follows: three members of the House of Delegates to be appointed by the Speaker of the House of Delegates in accordance with the principles of proportional representation contained in the Rules of the House of Delegates; one member of the Senate, to be appointed by the Senate Committee on Rules and nine nonlegislative citizen members, of whom one shall represent the Mid-Atlantic Regional Spaceport, one shall represent Old Dominion University, and one shall represent Virginia Tech, to be appointed by the Governor. A representative of NASA Wallops Flight Facility, a representative of NASA's Langley Research Center, and a representative of the National Institute of Aerospace, all to be appointed by the Governor, shall serve as ex-officio liaisons to the Council with nonvoting privileges. Legislative members shall serve terms coincident with their terms of office. Other members shall be appointed for terms of two years. Appointments to fill vacancies, other than by expiration of a term, shall be for the unexpired terms. Vacancies shall be filled in the same manner as the original appointments. All members may be reappointed.

C. Legislative members of the Council shall receive such compensation as provided in § 30-19.12. Nonlegislative citizen members shall serve without compensation. All members shall be reimbursed for all reasonable and necessary expenses incurred in the performance of their duties as provided in §§ 2.2-2813 and 2.2-2825. Funding for compensation and expenses of legislative members shall be provided by the operating budgets of the Clerk of the House of Delegates and the Clerk of the Senate upon approval of the Joint Rules Committee. Funding for the costs of expenses of the nonlegislative citizen members and all other expenses of the Council shall be provided by the Office of the Secretary of Technology.

D. The Council shall elect a chairman and a vice-chairman annually from among its membership. A majority of the members shall constitute a quorum. The Council shall meet at such times as may be called by the chairman or a majority of the Council.

E. Staff to the Council shall be provided by the Office of the Secretary of Technology. (2007, c. 891; 2008, c. 745.)

The number of this article and sections were assigned by the Virginia Code Commission, the numbers in the 2007 act having been Article 32, §§ 2.2-2698 and 2.2-2699.

Editor's note. — Acts 2007, c. 891, cl. 2, provides: "That the provisions of this act shall expire on July 1, 2010."

The 2008 amendments. — The 2008 amendment by c. 745, in subsection B, substituted "13 members" for "15 members" and "9 nonlegislative" for "11 nonlegislative" in the first sentence; in the second sentence, substituted "nine nonlegislative" for "eleven nonlegislative" and deleted "one shall represent NASA Wallops Flight Facility, one shall represent NASA's Langley Research Center" preceding "one shall represent the Mid-Atlantic"; inserted the present third sentence; and made minor stylistic changes.

§ 2.2-2699.2. (Expires July 1, 2010) Powers and duties of the Council. — The Council shall have the power and duty to:

1. Identify any federal or state regulatory impediments, including taxation, to the development of the Mid-Atlantic Regional Spaceport;

2. Identify threats to the spaceport's viability, such as encroachment, zoning, mineral exploration and exploitation, and noncompatible uses of the spaceport;
3. Advise the Governor on potential economic development opportunities and marketing strategies to attract launch companies to Virginia;
4. Identify and recommend policy and legislative solutions to potential state legal barriers to human spaceflight, including liability and assumption of risk issues;
5. Advise the Governor on infrastructure and marketing investments needed to achieve the spaceport's full potential and that of Virginia's aerospace sector as a whole;
6. Develop a long-term strategic plan to make the Mid-Atlantic Regional Spaceport the premiere commercial hub for space travel in the United States;
7. Identify and recommend actions to position Virginia's aerospace sector to take advantage of newly emerging opportunities as part of NASA's Vision for Space Exploration; and
8. Identify and recommend policies to support the critical role of Virginia's universities in providing human capital and research contributions that significantly impact aerospace-related economic development in the Commonwealth. (2007, c. 891.)

Editor's note. — Acts 2007, c. 891, cl. 2, provides: "That the provisions of this act shall expire on July 1, 2010."

CHAPTER 27.

Foundations and Other Collegial Bodies.

Article 1.

Virginia Arts Foundation.

Article 2.

Virginia War Memorial Foundation.

Article 3.

World Trade Alliance Of The Blue Ridge.

Article 4.

Boating Advisory Committee.

Article 5.

Debt Capacity Advisory Committee.

Article 6.

Veterans Services Foundation.

ARTICLE 1.

Virginia Arts Foundation.

§ 2.2-2700. Virginia Arts Foundation; board of trustees; compensation; staff. — A. The Virginia Arts Foundation (the "Foundation"), is established to serve as an advisory foundation, within the meaning of § 2.2-2100, in the executive branch of state government and shall be deemed a body politic and corporate to be organized and to have such powers and duties as provided in this article.

B. The Foundation shall be governed by a board of trustees, consisting of the members of the Virginia Commission for the Arts.

C. Any person designated by the board of trustees to handle the funds of the Foundation shall give bond, with corporate surety, in a penalty fixed by the Governor, conditioned upon the faithful discharge of his duties. Any premium on the bond shall be paid from funds available to the Foundation.

D. The board of trustees, acting as members of the Virginia Commission for the Arts, shall be entitled to reimbursement for all actual and necessary expenses, as provided by § 2.2-2509.

E. The Director of the Virginia Commission for the Arts shall serve as the chairman, and the staff of such Commission shall serve as staff for the Foundation. (1997, c. 878, §§ 9-84.08, 9-84.09; 2001, c. 844.)

§ 2.2-2701. Powers of Foundation. — The Foundation may:

1. Make expenditures from the Fund's interest and income to assist the Virginia Commission for the Arts in promoting the arts in the Commonwealth in accordance with § 2.2-2704 and to assist not-for-profit arts and cultural institutions and organizations within the Commonwealth to assess, enhance, and plan for enhancement of their fiscal stability, financial management and control capabilities, and capacity to raise funds for the furtherance of their respective missions from nongovernmental sources.

2. Accept, hold and administer gifts and bequests of money, securities, or other property, absolutely or in trust, for the purposes for which the Foundation is created.

3. Enter into contracts and execute all instruments necessary and appropriate to carry out the Foundation's purposes.

4. Explore and make recommendations concerning other possible dedicated revenue sources for the Fund.

5. Perform any lawful acts necessary or appropriate to carry out the purposes of the Foundation. (1997, c. 878, § 9-84.09:2; 2001, c. 844; 2002, c. 260.)

§ 2.2-2702. Virginia Arts Foundation Fund. — A. There is created the Virginia Arts Foundation Fund, a special nonreverting trust fund on the books of the Comptroller, to be administered by the Foundation.

B. The Fund shall include such funds as may be appropriated by the General Assembly; revenues transferred to the Fund from the special license plates for Virginians for the Arts program pursuant to § 46.2-749.2:2; voluntary contributions collected through the income tax checkoff for the arts pursuant to subdivision B 8 of § 58.1-344.3; and designated gifts, contributions and bequests of money, securities, or other property of whatsoever character.

C. All money, securities, or other property designated for the Fund and any interest or income therefrom shall remain in the Fund and shall not revert to the general fund. The Fund's principal shall not be subject to expenditure by the Foundation. (1997, c. 878, § 9-84.09:1; 2001, c. 844; 2005, cc. 860, 889.)

§ 2.2-2703: Expired.

Editor's note. — This section was derived from former § 9-84.09:4, as enacted by Acts 1997, c. 878, and amended by Acts 2000, c. 27, and expired by its own terms on June 30, 2001.

§ 2.2-2704. Gifts and bequests; exemption from taxation. — Gifts and bequests of money, securities, or other property to the Fund, and the interest or income therefrom, shall be deemed gifts to the Commonwealth, and the Fund shall be exempt from all state and local taxes. Unless otherwise restricted by the terms of the gift or bequest, the Foundation may sell, exchange, or otherwise dispose of such gifts and bequests. The proceeds from such transactions shall be deposited to the credit of the Fund. The Foundation shall not actively solicit private donations for the Fund; however, this limitation shall not prevent the Foundation from actively encouraging financial support for the Foundation through the special license plate and income tax checkoff programs. Notwithstanding any other provision of this section, the Foundation may accept and solicit public and private contributions for the limited purpose of assisting Virginia not-for-profit arts and cultural institutions and organizations, to enhance the fiscal stability, financial management, and fundraising abilities of such organizations. (1997, c. 878, § 9-84.09:3; 2001, c. 844; 2002, c. 260.)

Article 2.

Virginia War Memorial Foundation.

§ 2.2-2705. Virginia War Memorial Foundation; purpose; membership; terms; compensation and expenses; staff; chairman's executive summary. — A. The Virginia War Memorial Foundation (the Foundation) is established to serve as a policy foundation, within the meaning of § 2.2-2100, in the executive branch of state government. The Foundation shall be governed and administered by a board of trustees for the purpose of honoring patriotic Virginians who rendered faithful service and sacrifice in the cause of freedom and liberty for the Commonwealth and the nation in time of war.

B. The board of trustees shall have a total membership of 22 members that shall consist of 10 legislative members, 10 nonlegislative citizen members, and two ex officio members as follows: six members of the House of Delegates to be appointed by the Speaker of the House of Delegates in accordance with the principles of proportional representation contained in the Rules of the House of Delegates; four members of the Senate to be appointed by the Senate Committee on Rules; 10 nonlegislative citizen members appointed by the Governor, subject to confirmation by the General Assembly; and the Secretary of Public Safety and the Commissioner of Veterans Services, who shall serve ex officio with voting privileges. A majority of the trustees shall be members or veterans of the armed forces of the United States or the Virginia National Guard. Members appointed should include representatives of some or all of the various veterans organizations active in Virginia, as the Governor deems appropriate.

C. Except for initial appointments, all nonlegislative citizen member appointments shall be for terms of three years. Legislative members, the Secretary of Public Safety and the Commissioner of Veterans Services shall serve terms coincident with their terms of office. All members may be reappointed. However, no nonlegislative citizen member shall be eligible to serve for more than four successive three-year terms. No Senate member shall be eligible to serve more than three successive four-year terms and no member of the House of Delegates shall be eligible to serve more than six successive two-year terms. The remainder of any term to which a member is appointed to fill a vacancy shall not constitute a term in determining the member's eligibility for reappointment. Appointments to fill vacancies, other than by expiration of a term, shall be made for the unexpired terms. Vacancies shall be filled in the same manner as the original appointments. Trustees appointed by the Governor shall serve at his pleasure.

D. Legislative members of the Foundation shall receive such compensation as is set forth in § 30-19.12. All members shall be reimbursed for all reasonable and necessary expenses incurred in the performance of their duties as provided in §§ 2.2-2813 and 2.2-2825. Funding for the costs of compensation of legislative members shall be provided by the Office of the Clerk of the Senate or the Office of the Clerk of the House of Delegates, as appropriate. Funding for the costs of expenses of all members shall be provided by the Foundation.

E. The Department of Veterans Services shall provide the Foundation with administrative and other services.

F. The trustees shall adopt bylaws governing their organization and procedures and may amend the same. The trustees shall elect from their number a chairman, vice-chairman, and such other officers as their bylaws may provide. They shall also appoint an executive committee, composed of not less than five trustees, which committee shall exercise the powers and duties imposed on the Foundation by this section to the extent permitted by the trustees in their bylaws. Meetings of the board of trustees shall be held at the call of the chairman or whenever a majority of the members so request. A majority of members shall constitute a quorum.

G. The chairman of the board of trustees shall submit to the Governor and the General Assembly an annual executive summary of the interim activity and work of the board no later than the first day of each regular session of the General Assembly. The executive summary shall be submitted as provided in the procedures of the Division of Legislative Automated Systems for the processing of legislative documents and reports and shall be posted on the General Assembly's website. (1992, c. 592, § 2.1-51.27:1; 1996, c. 300; 2000, c. 156; 2001, c. 844; 2002, c. 416; 2003, cc. 239, 885; 2005, c. 758; 2008, c. 625.)

Editor's note. — Acts 2003, c. 885, cl. 7, provides: "That all current members of the collegial bodies whose terms have been modified by this act shall be eligible, if reappointed, to the full number of terms provided by this act regardless of prior service."

Acts 2005, c. 758, cl. 2, provides: "That this act shall not be construed to affect existing appointments, made by the Senate Committee on Privileges and Elections, for which the terms have not expired. However, any new appointments made after July 1, 2005 shall be made in accordance with the provisions of this act."

Acts 2008, c. 625, cl. 2, provides: "That it is the intent of the General Assembly to align the missions, functions, and goals of the Virginia War Memorial Foundation with those of other state agencies located within the Public Safety Secretariat of state government that have similar missions, functions, and goals while ensuring continued support for the board of trustees and staff of the Foundation. The appropriate staff of the Virginia War Memorial Foundation, the Department of Veterans Services and the Department of General Services shall work to ensure the proper transfer of authority."

Acts 2008, c. 625, cl. 3 provides: "That the Department of General Services shall continue to provide for the maintenance of the building and grounds of the Virginia War Memorial."

Acts 2008, c. 625, cl. 4 provides: "That the provisions of this act shall not be construed to infringe upon any bond indenture, trust agreement, resolution, treasury loan, or contract associated with any fiduciary obligations entered into by the Virginia War Memorial Foundation."

The 2008 amendments. — The 2008 amendment by c. 625, in subsection B, substituted "membership of 22 members" for "membership of 19 members," "10 legislative members" for "eight legislative members," "two ex officio members as follows: six members" for "one ex officio member as follows: five members," "four members of the senate" for "three members of the senate," "Secretary of Public Safety and the Commissioner of Veterans Services" for "Secretary of Administration"; in subsection C, substituted "the Secretary of Public Safety and the Commissioner of Veterans Services" for "and the Secretary of Administration"; and in subsection E, substituted "Veterans Services" for "General Services."

§ **2.2-2706. Authority of Foundation.** — The Foundation is vested with full authority to:

1. Manage, control, maintain, and operate the Virginia War Memorial, including the contents, furnishings, grounds, funds, property and endowments thereof;

2. Set fees for the use of the Memorial;

3. Adopt regulations for the use and visitation to the Memorial, which regulations shall be exempt from the provisions of the Administrative Process Act (§ 2.2-4000 et seq.);

4. Participate with the military forces of the United States and the Commonwealth and with veterans organizations in the planning, development and execution of appropriate programs and events that further the purposes of the Memorial;

5. Employ and discharge from employment such persons as may be necessary to manage, control, maintain, operate and raise funds for the Memorial;

6. Determine what programs and activities may and should be carried out at the Memorial;

7. Enter into contracts with respect to the duties and responsibilities imposed upon the Foundation herein; all such contracts shall be approved by the Attorney General;

8. Establish a nonprofit corporation as an instrumentality to assist in the details of administering the affairs of the Foundation;

9. Create, invest and use an endowment fund for the purposes set forth in this section;

10. Take such actions as may be reasonably necessary to seek, promote and stimulate contributions for the endowment, maintenance, and improvement of the Memorial and activities therein;

11. Receive, expend and administer on behalf of the Commonwealth donations, gifts, grants, bequests and devises of real and personal property for the endowment of the Memorial or for any special purpose designated by the donor that is consistent with the purposes of the Memorial set forth in this article; and

12. Change the form of any funds, securities, or other property, real or personal, provided that such change is consistent with the terms of the instrument under which the same was acquired. (1992, c. 592, § 2.1-51.27:2; 2001, c. 844.)

§ 2.2-2707. Form of accounts and records; annual audit. — The accounts and records of the Foundation showing the receipt and disbursement of funds from whatever source derived shall be established by the Auditor of Public Accounts in a manner similar to other organizations. The Auditor of Public Accounts or his legally authorized representative shall annually audit the accounts of the Foundation, and the cost of such audit services shall be borne by the Foundation. (1992, c. 592, § 2.1-51.27:3; 2001, c. 844.)

§ 2.2-2708. Names of Virginians "Missing in Action"; ownership of War Memorial. — A. The names and homes of record designation of all Virginians "Missing In Action" as a result of the Vietnam War and all Virginians "Killed in Action" as a result of the Persian Gulf Conflict shall be placed in the Virginia War Memorial.

B. The Virginia War Memorial, its grounds, all its contents, furnishings, funds, endowments, and other property, now owned or hereafter acquired, are and shall remain property of the Commonwealth. (1992, c. 592, §§ 2.1-51.27:1, 2.1-51.27:4; 1996, c. 300; 2000, c. 156; 2001, c. 844.)

§ 2.2-2708.1. Possession of certain military medals. — To preserve the dignity of military medals authorized to be worn by the United States Department of Defense and the memory of those who have rendered faithful service and sacrifice in the cause of freedom and liberty, the Foundation shall be vested with the full authority to take possession of any military medals, ribbons or certificates that come into the possession of the Commonwealth for which the ownership is unknown until such time as the true owner is able to take possession. The Foundation shall take reasonable efforts, based on available resources, to determine the true owner and return any military medal, ribbon or certificate that comes into its possession pursuant to this section. (2002, c. 838.)

ARTICLE 3.

World Trade Alliance Of The Blue Ridge.

§§ 2.2-2709, 2.2-2710: Repealed by Acts 2003, c. 885.

ARTICLE 4.

Boating Advisory Committee.

§ 2.2-2711. Boating Advisory Committee; purpose; membership; meetings; compensation. — A. The Boating Advisory Committee (the "Committee") is established as an advisory committee, within the meaning of § 2.2-2100, in the executive branch of state government. The purpose of the Board shall be to advise and make recommendations to the Board of Game and Inland Fisheries, the Marine Resources Commission and other state agencies concerning any proposed regulations, policies or other issues that would directly affect the recreational boating public.

B. The Committee shall consist of eleven members to be appointed by the Secretary of Natural Resources, as follows: members shall represent the United States Power Squadrons; the United States Coast Guard Auxiliary; the Chesapeake Bay Yacht Clubs Association; and the general boating public of this Commonwealth.

C. Members of the Boating Advisory Committee shall meet at least once a year and serve without compensation but shall be reimbursed for their reasonable and necessary expenses incurred in the discharge of their duties as provided in § 2.2-2825. (1978, c. 88, § 2.1-51.9:1; 1984, c. 720; 1985, c. 448; 1991, c. 211; 2001, c. 844.)

Article 5.

Debt Capacity Advisory Committee.

§ 2.2-2712. Debt Capacity Advisory Committee; membership; terms; chairman; compensation; staff. — A. The Debt Capacity Advisory Committee (the "Committee") is established as an advisory committee, within the meaning of § 2.2-2100, in the executive branch of state government.

B. The Committee shall consist of the Secretary of Finance; the State Treasurer; the Director of the Department of Planning and Budget; the Auditor of Public Accounts; the Director of the Joint Legislative Audit and Review Commission; and two citizen members who have expertise in financial matters to be appointed by the Governor.

C. Of the citizen members appointed for terms beginning July 1, 1994, one shall be appointed for an initial term of three years and the other for an initial term of five years. Successors shall be appointed to serve for terms of four years each. Vacancies occurring other than by expiration of term shall be filled by appointment of the Governor for the remainder of the unexpired term. All appointments shall be subject to confirmation by the General Assembly. Members shall continue to hold office until their successors have been appointed and qualified.

D. The Secretary of Finance shall be the chairperson of the Committee.

E. All members of the Committee shall serve without compensation but shall receive reasonable and necessary expenses incurred in the discharge of their duties as provided in § 2.2-2825.

F. The Department of the Treasury shall serve as staff to the Committee. (1994, c. 43, § 2.1-304.2; 2001, c. 844.)

Cross references. — As to the Governor's obligation to consider the recommendations of the Debt Capacity Advisory Committee prior to recommending any new tax-supported debt, see § 2.2-4903.

§ 2.2-2713. Powers and duties of the Committee. — The Committee shall have the power and duty to:

1. Annually review the size and condition of the Commonwealth's tax-supported debt and submit to the Governor and to the General Assembly an estimate of the maximum amount of new tax-supported debt that prudently may be authorized for the next biennium. The estimate shall be advisory and in no way bind the Governor or the General Assembly;

2. Annually review the amount and condition of bonds, notes, and other security obligations of the Commonwealth's agencies, institutions, boards, and authorities, for which the (i) Commonwealth has a contingent or limited liability or (ii) General Assembly is permitted to replenish reserve funds if deficiencies occur, and submit to the Governor and the General Assembly an annual report with the Committee's recommendation to ensure the prudent use of such obligations. Such review shall be submitted on or before January 1 of each year; and

3. Conduct ongoing reviews of the amount and condition of bonds, notes, and other security obligations of the Commonwealth's agencies, institutions, boards, and authorities not secured by the full faith and credit of the Commonwealth or for which the General Assembly is not permitted to replenish reserve funds, and when appropriate, shall recommend limits on such additional obligations to the Governor and to the General Assembly. (1994, c. 43, § 2.1-304.3; 1997, c. 187; 2001, c. 844.)

§ 2.2-2714. Estimated amount of prudent tax-supported debt; affordability considerations. — Before January 1 of each year, the Committee shall submit to the Governor and to the General Assembly the Committee's estimate of tax-supported debt that prudently may be authorized for the next fiscal year, together with a report explaining the basis for the estimate. In developing its annual estimate and in preparing its annual report, the Committee shall, at a minimum, consider:

1. The amount of tax-supported debt that, during the next fiscal year and annually for the following nine fiscal years (i) will be outstanding and (ii) has been authorized but not yet issued;
2. A projected schedule of affordable, state tax-supported debt authorizations for the next biennium. The assessment of the affordability of the projected authorizations shall include but not be limited to the considerations specified in this section;
3. Projected debt-service requirements during the next fiscal year and annually for the following nine fiscal years based upon (i) existing outstanding debt, (ii) previously authorized but unissued debt, and (iii) projected bond authorizations;
4. The criteria that recognized bond rating agencies use to judge the quality of issues of Commonwealth bonds;
5. Any other factor that is relevant to (i) the ability of the Commonwealth to meet its projected debt service requirements for the next two fiscal years; (ii) the ability of the Commonwealth to support additional debt service in the upcoming biennium; (iii) the requirements of the statewide capital plan; and (iv) the interest rate to be borne by, the credit rating on, or any other factor affecting the marketability of such bonds; and
6. The effect of authorizations of new tax-supported debt on each of the considerations of this section. (1994, c. 43, § 2.1-304.4; 1997, c. 187; 2001, c. 844.)

ARTICLE 6.

Veterans Services Foundation.

§ 2.2-2715. Veterans Services Foundation; purpose; membership; terms; compensation; staff. — A. The Veterans Services Foundation (the Foundation) is established as a body politic and corporate supporting the Department of Veterans Services in the executive branch of state government. The Foundation shall be governed and administered by a board of trustees. The Foundation shall (i) administer the Veterans Services Fund (the Fund), (ii) provide funding for veterans services and programs in the Commonwealth through the Fund, and (iii) raise revenue from all sources including private source fundraising to support the Fund. The Foundation shall submit a quarterly report to the Commissioner of Veterans Services on the Foundation's funding levels and services.

B. The board of trustees of the Foundation shall consist of the Commissioner of Veterans Services and the Chairmen of the Board of Veterans Services and the Joint Leadership Council of Veterans Services Organizations, who shall serve as ex officio voting members, and 16 members to be appointed as follows: (i) eight nonlegislative citizens appointed by the Governor; five nonlegislative citizens appointed by the Speaker of the House of Delegates; and three nonlegislative citizens appointed by the Senate Committee on Rules. A majority of the trustees shall be active or retired chairmen, chief executive officers, or chief financial officers for large private corporations or nonprofit organizations or individuals who have extensive fundraising experience in the private sector. Trustees appointed shall, insofar as possible, be veterans. Each appointing authority shall endeavor to ensure a balanced geographical representation on the Board to facilitate fundraising efforts across the state.

Initial appointments by the Governor shall be staggered as follows: two members for a term of one year, three members for a term of two years, and three members for a term of four years. After initial appointments, members shall be appointed for a term of four years. Appointments to fill vacancies, other than by expiration of a term, shall be for the unexpired terms. All members may be reappointed. However, no member shall serve more than two consecutive four-year terms. The remainder of any term to which a member is appointed to fill a vacancy shall not constitute a term in determining the member's eligibility for reappointment. Vacancies shall be filled in the same manner as the original appointments. Any member of the Board of Trustees may be removed by the Governor at his pleasure.

C. Trustees shall be reimbursed for their actual expenses incurred while attending meetings of the trustees or performing other duties. However, such reimbursement shall not exceed the per diem rate established for members of the General Assembly pursuant to § 30-19.12.

D. The Secretary of Public Safety shall designate a state agency to provide the Foundation with administrative and other services.

E. The trustees shall adopt bylaws governing their organization and procedures and may amend the same. The trustees shall elect from their number a chairman and such other officers as their bylaws may provide.

F. Any person designated by the board of trustees to handle the funds of the Foundation or the Fund shall give bond, with corporate surety, in a penalty fixed by the Governor, conditioned upon the faithful discharge of his duties. Any premium on the bond shall be paid from funds available to the Foundation. (2003, cc. 657, 670; 2004, c. 697; 2006, c. 150; 2008, cc. 467, 486, 768, 872.)

Editor's note. — Acts 2003, cc. 657 and 670, cl. 3, provide: "That as of the effective date of this act [July 1, 2003], the Department of Veterans Services shall be deemed the successor in interest to the Department of Veterans' Affairs. All right, title, and interest in and to any real or tangible personal property vested in the Department of Veterans' Affairs as of the effective date of this act shall be transferred to and taken as standing in the name of the Department of Veterans Services."

Acts 2003, cc. 657 and 670, cl. 4, provide: "That all rules and regulations adopted by the Department of Veterans' Affairs that are in effect as of the effective date of this act and that pertain to the subject of this act shall remain in full force and effect until altered, amended or rescinded by the Department of Veterans Services."

Acts 2008, cc. 467 and 768, cl. 2 provides: "That any three-year term being served by a Governor-appointed member of the Virginia Veterans Services Foundation on July 1, 2008, may in the discretion of the Governor, be extended to a four-year term in accordance with the provisions of this act. However, nothing in this act shall allow any such member to serve more than two consecutive terms."

Acts 2008, cc. 486 and 872, cl. 2 provides: "That the initial terms of the members of the board of trustees appointed pursuant to this act shall be staggered as follows: (i) two members appointed by the Speaker of the House of Delegates and one member appointed by the Senate Committee on Rules to a term of four years, (ii) two members appointed by the Speaker of the House of Delegates and one member appointed by the Senate Committee on Rules to a term of three years, and (iii) one member appointed by the Speaker of the House of Delegates and one member appointed by the Senate Committee on Rules to a term of two years. Thereafter, the terms of members shall be four years."

The 2008 amendments. — The 2008 amendments by cc. 467 and 768 are nearly identical, and in subsection A, substituted "as a body politic and corporate supporting the Department of Veterans Services" for "to serve as an advisory foundation, within the meaning of § 2.2-2100" in the first sentence and substituted "to provide funding" for "for the purpose of providing funding" in the second sentence; in subsection B, inserted "board of trustees of the" preceding "Foundation shall consist," substituted "Chairmen" for "Chairman," and inserted "and the Joint Leadership Council of Veterans Services Organizations" in the first sentence; and in the undesignated paragraph under subsection B, substituted "four years" for "three years" at the end of the second sentence and substituted "four-year terms" for "three-year terms" at the end of the fourth sentence.

The 2008 amendments by cc. 486 and 872 are nearly identical, and in subsection A, substituted "a body politic and corporate supporting the Department of Veterans Services" for "an advisory foundation, within the meaning of § 2.2-2100" in the first sentence, deleted "for the purpose of providing funding for veteran services and programs in the Commonwealth through the Veterans Services Fund (the Fund)" in the second sentence, and inserted the third sentence; in subsection B, substituted "Chairmen" for "Chairman" preceding "of the Board of Veteran Services," inserted "16 members to be appointed as follows" and inserted the clause (i) designation following that same language, deleted "subject to confirmation by the General Assembly" and inserted "five nonlegislative citizens appointed by the Speaker of the House of Delegates; and three nonlegislative citizens appointed by the Senate Committee on Rules" in the first sentence, inserted "and individuals who have extensive fundraising experience in the private sector" at the end of the second sentence, deleted "by the Governor" from the third sentence, and added the last sentence; and in the undesignated paragraph of subsection B, substituted "After initial appointments" for "Thereafter," and substituted "four years" for "three years" in the second sentence, and substituted "four-year terms" for "three-year terms" in the third sentence.

§ **2.2-2716. Authority of Foundation.** — The Foundation has the authority to:

1. Administer the Veterans Services Fund and make expenditures from the Fund to the Department of Veterans Services to provide supplemental funding for the Department's services and programs;
2. Accept, hold, and administer gifts and bequests of money, securities, or other property, absolutely or in trust, for the purposes for which the Foundation is created;
3. Enter into contracts and execute all instruments necessary and appropriate to carry out the Foundation's purposes;
4. Take such actions as may be reasonably necessary to seek, promote, and stimulate contributions for the Fund;
5. Develop other possible dedicated revenue sources for the Fund; and
6. Perform any lawful acts necessary or appropriate to carry out the purposes of the Foundation. (2003, cc. 657, 670; 2008, cc. 467, 486, 768, 872.)

The 2008 amendments. — The 2008 amendments by cc. 467, 486, 768 and 872 are identical, and substituted "Develop" for "Make recommendations concerning" at the beginning of subdivision 5.

§ **2.2-2717. Form of accounts and records; annual audit.** — The accounts and records of the Foundation showing the receipt and disbursement of funds from whatever source derived shall be established by the Auditor of Public Accounts in a manner similar to other organizations. The Auditor of Public Accounts or his legally authorized representative shall annually audit the accounts of the Foundation, and the cost of such audit services shall be borne by the Foundation. (2003, cc. 657, 670.)

§ **2.2-2718. Veterans Services Fund.** — A. There is created the Veterans Services Fund, a special nonreverting trust fund on the books of the Comptroller, to be administered by the Foundation.

B. The Fund shall include such funds as may be appropriated by the General Assembly; revenues transferred to the Fund from other state programs established for the Fund's benefit; and designated gifts, contributions and bequests of money, securities, or other property of whatsoever character.

C. Any moneys remaining in the Virginia Veterans Care Center Endowment Fund as of June 30, 2003, shall be transferred to the Veterans Services Fund on July 1, 2003. Based on an audited accounting of the June 30, 2003, balance, those transferred moneys from the Virginia Veterans Care Center Endowment Fund shall be used to support (i) capital repair and replacement projects and activities undertaken by the Department of Veterans Services, (ii) programs, activities, and services for residents of veterans care centers, or (iii) other programs, activities, and services provided by the Department of Veterans Services identified by such audit. It is the intent of the General Assembly that the transferred moneys from the Virginia Veterans Care Center Endowment Fund shall not be used as operating revenue for the veterans care centers, but shall be used according to the purposes identified by the audit of its accounts.

D. All money, securities, or other property designated for the Fund and any interest or income therefrom shall remain in the Fund and shall not revert to the general fund. (2003, cc. 657, 670.)

§ **2.2-2719. Gifts and bequests; exemption from taxation.** — Gifts and bequests of money, securities, or other property to the Fund, and the interest or income therefrom, shall be deemed gifts to the Commonwealth, and the Fund shall be exempt from all state and local taxes. Unless otherwise restricted by the terms of the gift or bequest, the Foundation may sell, exchange, or otherwise dispose of such gifts and bequests. The proceeds from such transactions shall be deposited to the credit of the Fund. The Foundation may actively solicit private donations for the Fund. (2003, cc. 657, 670.)

Article 7.

The Center for Rural Virginia.

§ **2.2-2720. The Center for Rural Virginia; purpose.** — The Center for Rural Virginia, hereinafter referred to as "the Center," is hereby created as an independent nonprofit local entity without political subdivision status, for the purpose of sustaining economic growth in the rural areas of the Commonwealth and lessening the burdens of government through the activities prescribed in subsection B of § 2.2-2723. (2004, cc. 938, 964; 2005, c. 703.)

§ **2.2-2721. Center for Rural Virginia Board of Trustees established; membership; terms; vacancies; chairman, vice-chairman, secretary and other officers as necessary; quorum; meetings.** — A. The Center shall be governed by a board of trustees consisting of 18 members that include six legislative members and 12 nonlegislative citizen members to be appointed as follows: four members of the House of Delegates, to be appointed by the Speaker of the House of Delegates in accordance with the principles of proportional representation contained in the Rules of the House of Delegates; two members of the Senate, to be appointed by the Senate Committee on Rules; six nonlegislative citizen members to be appointed by the Speaker of the House of Delegates; four nonlegislative citizen members to be appointed by the Senate Committee on Rules; and two nonlegislative citizen members to be appointed by the Governor, subject to confirmation by the General Assembly. Nonlegislative citizen members of the Board shall be citizens of the Commonwealth of Virginia.

B. Legislative members shall serve terms coincident with their terms of office. Initial appointments of nonlegislative citizen members shall be staggered as follows: four members for a term of three years appointed by the Speaker of the House of Delegates; two members for a term of two years appointed by the Senate Committee on Rules; and one member for a term of two years appointed by the Governor. Thereafter, nonlegislative citizen members appointed by the Speaker of the House of Delegates or the Senate Committee on Rules shall be appointed for a term of two years, and nonlegislative citizen members appointed by the Governor shall be appointed for a term of four years. Appointments to fill vacancies, other than by expiration of a term, shall be for the unexpired terms. All members may be reappointed. However, no nonlegislative citizen member appointed by the Speaker of the House of Delegates or the Senate Committee on Rules shall serve more than four consecutive two-year terms, and no nonlegislative citizen member appointed by the Governor shall serve more than two consecutive four-year terms. The remainder of any term to which a member is appointed to fill a vacancy shall not constitute a term in determining the member's eligibility for reappointment. Vacancies shall be filled in the same manner as the original appointments.

C. The Board of Trustees shall elect a chairman, vice-chairman, secretary, and such other officers as may be necessary from among its membership. A majority of the members shall constitute a quorum. The meetings of the Board shall be held at the call of the chairman or whenever the majority of the members so request. (2004, cc. 938, 964.)

§ **2.2-2722. Compensation; expenses.** — Legislative members of the Board shall receive such compensation as provided in § 30-19.12, and nonlegislative citizen members shall receive such compensation for the performance of their duties as provided in § 2.2-2813. All members shall be reimbursed for reasonable and necessary expenses incurred in the performance of their duties as provided in §§ 2.2-2813 and 2.2-2825. Funding for the costs of compensation and expenses of the members shall be provided from such funds as may be available to the Center. (2004, cc. 938, 964.)

§ **2.2-2723. Powers and duties of the Board of Trustees and the Center.** — A. The Board of Trustees shall have the following powers and duties:

1. Manage, control, maintain, and operate the Center;
2. Take all actions necessary to qualify the Center as exempt from taxation pursuant to § 501 (c) (3) of the Internal Revenue Code and operate the Center in accordance with the provisions governing nonstock corporations as set out in Chapter 10 of Title 13.1, provided that, in the event of the dissolution of the Center, assets shall be distributed for one or more exempt purposes within the meaning of § 501 (c) (3) of the Internal Revenue Code, or corresponding section of any future federal tax code, or shall be distributed to the Commonwealth or a local government for a public purpose;
3. Establish bylaws as may be necessary for the governance and conduct of business of the Board;
4. Employ and establish the qualifications and duties, and fix salaries and compensation of staff of the Center from such funds as may be available to the Center;
5. Seek federal funds available to state rural development councils, pursuant to the Farm Security and Rural Investment Act of 2002, P.L. 107-171;
6. Seek, accept, administer, and expend gifts, grants, donations, bequests, and any other funds on behalf of the Center to support and facilitate its work;
7. Accept, administer, and expend donations, bequests, or devises of real and personal property for the endowment of the Center or for any special purpose designated by the donor that is consistent with the purposes of the Center set forth in this article;
8. Have, in addition to its other powers, all the corporate powers given to nonstock corporations by the provisions of Title 13.1. The Board shall also have the power to accept, execute, and administer any trust in which it may have an interest under the terms of the instrument creating the trust;
9. Enter into contracts with respect to the duties and responsibilities imposed upon the Center herein;
10. Report annually concerning the status, needs, and accomplishments of the Center to the Governor and the General Assembly; and

11. Perform any lawful acts necessary or appropriate to carry out the purposes of this article.

B. The Center shall have the following powers and duties:

1. Develop a broad-based constituency to advocate for the interests of rural Virginia in the formulation of the Commonwealth's public policies;

2. Coordinate and facilitate research on rural issues and analyze the effect of public policies and private sector interests on rural communities;

3. Prepare a detailed analysis of rural Virginia economies annually for submission to the Board, together with feasible and appropriate alternatives designed to sustain economic growth in rural areas of the Commonwealth;

4. Facilitate public-private investments in the infrastructure of rural Virginia;

5. Develop programs designed to train local elected officials and community leaders for effective leadership in rural communities;

6. Foster innovative strategies that promote the development and prosperity of rural communities in the Commonwealth;

7. Provide for the collection, organization, storage, and dissemination of documents, data, and other information concerning issues relevant to the needs and continuous development of Virginia's rural areas, including technical and research assistance to rural localities in the development and implementation of their strategic plans;

8. Identify potential public and private resources for the Board's consideration and review that may be used to generate additional funds to support and facilitate the Center's work and foster the development of rural communities;

9. Submit to the Board of Trustees such reports regarding the Center's work, including, but not limited to, programs, activities, policy analyses, and financial statements, as may be requested by the Board; and

10. Perform such other acts as may be necessary to accomplish the objectives of this article. (2004, cc. 938, 964; 2005, c. 703.)

Editor's note. — Acts 2008, c. 879, effective for the biennium ending June 30, 2010, in Item 110 F 3, provides: "As part of its mission, the Center for Rural Virginia shall monitor the implementation of the budget initiatives approved by the 2005 Session of the General Assembly for rural Virginia and shall report periodically to the Chairmen of the Senate Finance and House Appropriations Committees on the effectiveness of these various programs in addressing rural economic development problems. Any unexpended balance for the Center for Rural Virginia at the close of business on June 30, 2009, and June 30, 2010, shall not revert to the general fund but shall be carried forward and reappropriated."

§ 2.2-2724. Staffing. — The Board shall employ an executive director and such other persons as it deems necessary to assist it in performing its duties as set forth in this article, and, at its pleasure, remove such employees. The Board shall determine the duties of all staff and fix the salaries and compensation of such persons within the amounts allocated therefor from such funds as may be available to the Board. (2004, cc. 938, 964.)

Article 8.

Martin Luther King, Jr. Living History and Public Policy Center.

§§ 2.2-2725 through 2.2-2731: Expired.

Editor's note. — This article expired by the terms of Acts 2005, c. 731, cl. 3 on July 1, 2007.

Section 2.2-2731 was repealed by Acts 2006, c. 165, cl. 3, effective July 1, 2006.

ARTICLE 9.

State Interoperability Executive Committee.

§ 2.2-2732. State Interoperability Executive Committee; membership; responsibilities; terms; compensation. — A. The State Interoperability Executive Committee (Committee) is established as an advisory committee within the meaning of § 2.2-2100 in the executive branch of state government. The purpose of the Committee is to make recommendations via the Office of Commonwealth Preparedness' Commonwealth Interoperability Coordinator to the Commonwealth Preparedness Working Group, Secure Commonwealth Panel, and the Office of the Governor concerning communications interoperability.

B. The Committee shall consist of 30 members and alternates as follows: the Commonwealth Interoperability Coordinator appointed by the Assistant to the Governor for Commonwealth Preparedness and the following 29 members to be appointed by the Governor: one member representing the Virginia Association of Chiefs of Police; one member representing the Virginia Association of Governmental Emergency Medical Services Administrators; one member representing the Virginia Fire Chiefs Association; one member representing the Office of Commonwealth Preparedness; one member representing the Virginia Sheriffs' Association; one member representing the Virginia Association of Counties; one member representing the Virginia Chapter of the Association of Public-Safety Communications Officials; one member representing the Statewide Agencies Radio System; one member representing the Virginia Information Technologies Agency; one member representing the Virginia Municipal League; one member representing the Secretary of Public Safety; one member representing the Secretary of Technology; one member representing the Virginia Military Advisory Council; one member representing the Virginia Department of State Police; one member representing the Virginia Department of Military Affairs; one member representing the Virginia Department of Emergency Management; one member representing the Virginia Department of Transportation; one member representing the Virginia Emergency Managers Association; one member representing Virginia Professional Fire Fighters; one member representing the Virginia State Firefighter's Association; one member representing the Virginia Department of Criminal Justice Services; one member representing the Virginia Office of Emergency Medical Services; and one member from each of the seven Regional Preparedness Advisory Committees.

C. Each member shall serve a four-year term; provided that no member, other than the Commonwealth Interoperability Coordinator, shall serve more than two consecutive terms. All vacancies shall be filled for the balance of the unexpired term in the same manner as original appointments.

D. The Committee shall elect a chair and may elect a vice-chair from its membership for two-year terms. The Committee shall meet at least six times per year as is deemed appropriate or on the call of the Committee chair. A majority of the members of the Committee shall constitute a quorum.

E. Members of the Committee shall not receive compensation but shall be reimbursed for all reasonable and necessary expenses incurred in the performance of their duties as provided in §§ 2.2-2813 and 2.2-2825 and as approved by the Commonwealth Interoperability Coordinator. Funding for the costs of expenses of the members shall be provided by the Office of Commonwealth Preparedness. (2008, cc. 306, 531.)

§ 2.2-2733. Powers and duties of the Committee; staffing. — A. The Committee shall plan, promote, and offer assistance to the Commonwealth Interoperability Coordinator in the:

1. Annual review and update of the Statewide Interoperability Strategic Plan (Statewide Plan) required by § 9.1-1200;

2. Implementation of initiatives contained in the Statewide Plan;

3. Developing formal recommendations to the Commonwealth Preparedness Working Group, the Secure Commonwealth Panel, and the Governor on the use of interoperability grants to support local, regional, and state projects for the statewide development, deployment, and maintenance of voice and data communications technologies;

4. Reviewing all communications-related grant requests from state agencies and localities as required by § 2.2-305; and

5. Development of the annual report on the status of the Statewide Plan to the Governor required by November 1 of each year.

B. The Commonwealth Interoperability Coordinator's Office within the Governor's Office of Commonwealth Preparedness shall provide staff support to the Committee. (2008, cc. 306, 531.)

PART E.

STATE OFFICERS AND EMPLOYEES.

CHAPTER 28.

GENERAL PROVISIONS.

§ 2.2-2800. Disability to hold state office. — No person shall be capable of holding any office of honor, profit or trust under the Constitution of Virginia, who (i) holds any office or post of profit, trust, or emolument, civil or military, legislative, executive, or judicial, under the government of the United States; (ii) is in the employment of such government; or (iii) receives from it in any way any emolument whatever. The acceptance of any office, post, trust, or emolument, or the acceptance of any emolument whatever under the government of the United States, shall, ipso facto, vacate any office, or post of profit, trust or emolument under the government of the Commonwealth or under any county, city, or town thereof. (Code 1950, § 2-27; 1966, c. 677, § 2.1-30; 2001, c. 844.)

Cross references. — See Va. Const., Art. II, § 5 and Art. IV, § 4. See also § 2.2-2801.

Michie's Jurisprudence. — For related discussion, see 4A M.J. Commonwealth's and State's Attorney, § 3.

CASE NOTES

Editor's note. — Some of the cases below were decided under former Title 2.1 or prior provisions.

Legislative history. — For a full discussion of the legislative history of this section, see Dean v. Paolicelli, 194 Va. 219, 72 S.E.2d 506 (1952).

Constitutionality. — This section is not special and private legislation violative of Va. Const., Art. II, § 5 and Art. IV, § 15. It is legislation, general in character, and upon a subject well within the field of general legislation. It applies alike to all officeholders. Dean v. Paolicelli, 194 Va. 219, 72 S.E.2d 506 (1952).

The long continued sanction of this section by its repeated reenactment from time to time by the General Assembly, the positive application and enforcement of its mandate by the court, and the continued acquiescence in and adherence to its restrictions by the departments of the state government, impel the belief and confirm the conclusion that it does not infringe upon Va. Const., Art. II, § 5 and Art. IV, § 15, declaring the eligibility to any public office of every qualified voter. Dean v. Paolicelli, 194 Va. 219, 72 S.E.2d 506 (1952).

Purpose. — The purpose of this section is to prevent a conflict of interest in those who would serve both the federal and state governments. Joy v. Green, 194 Va. 1003, 76 S.E.2d 178 (1953).

The object sought to be accomplished by this section was, and is, to safeguard and protect the state's independent sovereignty by requiring strict and undivided allegiance to the duties and obligations of a public office by its incumbent. Dean v. Paolicelli, 194 Va. 219, 72 S.E.2d 506 (1952).

The rule forbidding the holding of two offices at the same time, whether at common law or under constitutions and statutes, never contemplated a disability to be elected to the second office, but, on the contrary, conclusively affirms the legality and efficiency of such election. It is only the holding, that is, the occupation, of two offices at the same time that offends public policy, and is therefore forbidden by law. Dean v. Paolicelli, 194 Va. 219, 72 S.E.2d 506 (1952).

Charter provisions as exception to section. — The General Assembly may grant new charters, or amendments to existing charters, which contain provisions permitting certain federal employees to hold specified offices from which they might otherwise be barred by this section under the authority of Art. VII, § 2, of the Constitution of Virginia. Pierce v. Dennis, 205 Va. 478, 138 S.E.2d 6 (1964).

Resignation from federal office accepted after commencement of state office. — Where a federal official was elected to the office of sheriff, which commenced on July 1, and resigned his federal office before his state office began, but performed certain federal duties on the morning of July 1, and his resignation was not formally accepted until July 2, his office as sheriff was thereby vacated and he was not entitled to qualify as such. Bunting v. Willis, 68 Va. (27 Gratt.) 144 (1876).

Service in state and in military. — Trial court was authorized, pursuant to § 19.2-156, to appoint an attorney-at-law to fulfill the duties of the duly-elected Commonwealth's attorney while he was serving with his military unit in Iraq and, thus, petitioner's application for writ of mandamus and/or prohibition was denied; although this section would prohibit petitioner from serving both the federal government and the state government at the same time, § 2.2-2802 contained an exception for Virginia office holders who were called into active military service and prevented him from vacating or forfeiting his title as the Commonwealth's attorney. In re Hannett, 270 Va. 223, 619 S.E.2d 465, 2005 Va. LEXIS 82 (2005).

A district attorney for the Home Owners' Loan Corporation, an instrumentality of the United States, receiving, besides his salary as such district attorney, other emoluments under the government of the United States, vacates his office as attorney for the Commonwealth under this section. Commonwealth ex rel. Kelly v. Rouse, 163 Va. 841, 178 S.E. 37 (1935).

Where county board member was employed by the United States when he first assumed his duties on the board and his claimed exemption from the provisions of this section appearing in former § 2.1-33 (see now § 2.2-2801) was held unconstitutional, board member was from the first incapable of holding office because of the provisions of this section. Though duly elected, he never became a de jure officer and the trial court should have declared office vacated and restrained treasurer from paying his salary. Dean v. Paolicelli, 194 Va. 219, 72 S.E.2d 506 (1952).

§ 2.2-2801. Disability to hold state office; exceptions. — A. Section 2.2-2800 shall not be construed to prevent:

1. Members of Congress from acting as visitors of the University of Virginia or the Virginia Military Institute, or from holding offices in the militia;

2. United States commissioners or United States census enumerators, supervisors, or the clerks under the supervisor of the United States census, or fourth-class or third-class postmasters, or United States caretakers of the Virginia National Guard, from acting as notaries, school board selection commission members, or supervisors, or from holding any district office under the government of any county, or the office of councilman of any town or city in the Commonwealth;

3. Any United States rural mail carrier, or star route mail carrier from being appointed and acting as notary public or holding any county or district office;

4. Any civilian employee of the United States government from being appointed and acting as notary public;

5. Any United States commissioners or United States park commissioners from holding the office of commissioner in chancery, bail commissioner, jury commissioner, commissioner of accounts, assistant commissioner of accounts, substitute or assistant civil justice, or assistant judge of a municipal court of any city or assistant judge of a juvenile and domestic relations district court of any city, or judge of any county court or juvenile and domestic relations district court of any county, or the municipal court or court of limited jurisdiction, by whatever name designated, of any incorporated town;

6. Any person employed by, or holding office or a post of profit, trust or emolument, civil, legislative, executive or judicial, under the government of the United States, from being a member of the militia or holding office therein, or from being a member or director of any board, council, commission or institution of the Commonwealth who serves without compensation except one who serves on a per diem compensation basis;

7. Foremen, quartermen, leading men, artisans, clerks or laborers, employed in any navy yard or naval reservation in Virginia from holding any office under the government of any city, town or county in the Commonwealth;

8. Any United States government clerk from holding any office under the government of any town or city; or from being appointed as special policeman for a county by the circuit court or judge thereof as provided for in § 15.2-1737;

9. Any person holding an office under the United States government from holding a position under the management and control of the State Board of Health;

10. Any state federal director of the Commonwealth in the employment service of the United States Department of Labor from holding the office of Commissioner of Labor of the Commonwealth;

11. Clerks and employees of the federal government engaged in the departmental service in Washington from acting as school trustees;

12. Any person, who is otherwise eligible, from serving as a member of the governing body or school board of any county, city or town, or as a member of any public body who is appointed by such governing body or school board, or as an appointive officer or employee of any county, city or town or the school board thereof;

13. Game management agents of the United States Fish and Wildlife Service or United States deputy game wardens from acting as special conservation police officers;

14. Any appointive state or local official or employee from serving, with compensation, on an advisory board of the federal government;

15. Any state or local law-enforcement officer from serving as a United States law-enforcement officer; however, this subdivision shall not be construed to authorize any law-enforcement officer to receive double compensation;

16. Any United States law-enforcement officer from serving as a state or local law-enforcement officer when requested by the chief law-enforcement officer of the subject jurisdiction; however, this subdivision shall not be construed to authorize any law-enforcement officer to receive double compensation;

17. Any attorney for the Commonwealth or assistant attorney for the Commonwealth from serving as or performing the duties of a special assistant United States attorney or assistant United States attorney; however, this subdivision shall not be construed to authorize any attorney for the Commonwealth or assistant attorney for the Commonwealth to receive double compensation;

18. Any assistant United States attorney from serving as or performing the duties of an assistant attorney for the Commonwealth when requested by the attorney for the Commonwealth of the subject jurisdiction; however, this subdivision shall not be construed to authorize any assistant United States attorney to receive double compensation;

19. Any elected state or local official from serving, without compensation, on an advisory board of the federal government; however, this subdivision shall not be construed to prohibit reimbursement for actual expenses;

20. Sheriffs' deputies from patrolling federal lands pursuant to contracts between federal agencies and local sheriffs;

21. State judicial officers from performing acts or functions with respect to United States criminal proceedings when such acts or functions are authorized by federal law to be performed by state judicial officers; or

22. Any member of the Armed Forces of the United States from serving on the Virginia Military Advisory Council.

B. Nor shall § 2.2-2800 be construed to exclude:

1. A person to whom a pension has been granted by the United States or who receives retirement compensation in any manner from the United States, or any person receiving or entitled to receive benefits under the Federal Old-Age and Survivors' Insurance System or under the Federal Railroad Retirement Act.

2. Officers or soldiers on account of the recompense they may receive from the United States when called out in actual duty. (Code 1950, § 2-29; 1950, p. 101; 1952, c. 120; 1958, c. 414; 1960, c. 39; 1962, c. 247; 1966, c. 677, § 2.1-33; 1968, c. 788; 1970, c. 745; 1971, Ex. Sess., cc. 137, 143; 1972, cc. 356, 405; 1975, c. 575; 1978, cc. 83, 420; 1983, c. 539; 1984, c. 110; 1985, c. 77; 1988, cc. 361, 901; 2001, cc. 577, 844; 2002, c. 676.)

Editor's note. — Acts 2001, c. 577 amended § 2.1-33, from which this section is derived. Pursuant to § 30-152, Acts 2001, c. 577 has been given effect in this section as set out above. The 2001 amendment by c. 577 inserted "or" at the end of subdivision 20, deleted "or" at the end of subdivision 21, and deleted subdivision 22, which formerly read: "To prevent any member of the Armed Forces of the United States from serving on the Virginia Military Advisory Council."

CASE NOTES

Editor's note. — The cases below were decided under former Title 2.1 or prior provisions.

Legislative history. — For a full discussion of the legislative history of this section, see Dean v. Paolicelli, 194 Va. 219, 72 S.E.2d 506 (1952).

Exception for federal clerk. — Subdivision 10 of former § 2.1-33 (see now subdivision A 10 of this section) is constitutional and is not invalid as special legislation. Hanes v. Fox, 196 Va. 51, 82 S.E.2d 495 (1954).

Hence, federal clerk may hold office of police justice. — A federal clerk is not disqualified because of his occupation to hold the office of police justice of a Virginia town. Hanes v. Fox, 196 Va. 51, 82 S.E.2d 495 (1954).

Federal employee on school board. — Subdivision 14 of former § 2.1-33 (see now subdivision A 11 of this section) meets the requirements for a general act and is not violative of Art. IV, § 15, of the Virginia Constitution. Joy v. Green, 194 Va. 1003, 76 S.E.2d 178 (1953).

And is not suspended by § 22.1-30. — Section 22.1-30 does not prescribe the exclusive qualifications for members of county school boards and does not supersede the provisions of subdivision 14 of former § 2.1-33 (see now subdivision A 11 of this section) with respect to the qualification of federal employees to sit on county school boards. These two statutory provisions are complementary and should be read together. Joy v. Green, 194 Va. 1003, 76 S.E.2d 178 (1953).

The history of § 22.1-30 and subdivision 14 of former § 2.1-33 (see now subdivision A 11 of this section) shows that the General Assembly has determined that there is no conflict of interest in the service by "clerks and employees of the federal government engaged in the departmental service in Washington" and their service on county school boards. Joy v. Green, 194 Va. 1003, 76 S.E.2d 178 (1953).

As to unconstitutionality of former subdivision 11 of former § 2.1-33, preventing United States government employees from holding any office under the government of counties with a certain population or of cities or counties adjoining counties with a certain population, see Dean v. Paolicelli, 194 Va. 219, 72 S.E.2d 506 (1952).

Members of regular army or national guard. — The provision of subdivision 3 of former § 2.1-33 (see now subdivision B 2 of this section) applies to any "actual duty" in the service of the United States to which "officers and soldiers" of the National Guard may be "called out" under the acts of Congress, passed pursuant to the authority granted it in the federal Constitution. City of Lynchburg v. Suttenfield, 177 Va. 212, 13 S.E.2d 323 (1941).

Reading this section and former § 2.1-30 (see now § 2.2-2800) together, the manifest purpose of the General Assembly is to disqualify as officeholders members of the regular army of the United States who are permanently in the service without being "called," and to except from such disqualification "officers and soldiers" of the state militia or National Guard who may be called into the service of the United States for a temporary period, even though it may be for as long as "twelve consecutive months." City of Lynchburg v. Suttenfield, 177 Va. 212, 13 S.E.2d 323 (1941).

§ 2.2-2802. Exception as to public officer or employee engaging in war service or called to active duty with the armed forces. — No state, county or municipal officer or employee shall forfeit his title to office or position or vacate the same by reason of either engaging in the war service of the United States when called forth by the Governor pursuant to the provisions of § 44-75.1, or when called to active duty in the armed forces of the United

States. Any such officer or employee who, voluntarily or otherwise, enters upon such war service or is called to service may notify the officer or body authorized by law to fill vacancies in his office, of such fact, and thereupon be relieved from the duties of his office or position during the period of such service. The officer or body authorized to fill vacancies shall designate some suitable person to perform the duties of such office as acting officer during the period the regular officer is engaged in such service, and during such period the acting officer shall be vested with all the powers, authority, rights and duties of the regular officer for whom he is acting. (Code 1950, § 2-28; 1950, p. 242, § 2-27.1; 1964, c. 227; 1966, c. 677, § 2.1-31; 2001, c. 844.)

Law Review. — For 2006 survey article, "Election Law," see 41 U. Rich. L. Rev. 121 (2006).

CASE NOTES

Position not forfeited or vacated. — Trial court was authorized, pursuant to § 19.2-156, to appoint an attorney-at-law to fulfill the duties of the duly-elected Commonwealth's attorney while he was serving with his military unit in Iraq and, thus, petitioner's application for writ of mandamus and/or prohibition was denied; although § 2.2-2800 would prohibit petitioner from serving both the federal government and the state government at the same time, this section contained an exception for Virginia office holders who were called into active military service and prevented from vacating or forfeiting title as the Commonwealth's attorney and § 15.2-1627 provided that the attorney appointed to act in his absence had the power to carry out the duties of the office. In re Hannett, 270 Va. 223, 619 S.E.2d 465, 2005 Va. LEXIS 82 (2005).

OPINIONS OF THE ATTORNEY GENERAL

County treasurer is not required to relinquish office when involuntarily recalled to active military duty. — A county treasurer, who is a constitutional officer and also a member of the organized reserves of the United States, is not required to relinquish his office when involuntarily recalled to active military duty. See opinion of Attorney General to Ms. Phyllis C. Katz, County Attorney for New Kent County, 02-003 (1/31/02).

Notice requirement. — The notice specified in this section is a prerequisite to the appointment by the county board of supervisors of a temporary replacement member and, in the event the notice given does not request the appointment of a temporary replacement member, the board is not authorized to make such an appointment. See opinion of Attorney General to Mr. Darvin E. Satterwhite, County Attorney for Cumberland County, 04-016 (3/22/04).

The position of the affected member on the county board of supervisors is not vacant unless or until he provides the notice; consequently, neither the board nor the circuit court is authorized to make an appointment of a temporary replacement member. See opinion of Attorney General to Mr. Darvin E. Satterwhite, County Attorney for Cumberland County, 04-016 (3/22/04).

§ 2.2-2803. Exception as to public officer or employee serving in the Selective Service System of the United States. — No state, county or municipal officer or employee shall forfeit or vacate his office or position, by reason of serving or of having served as an officer, member, agent or employee, or in any other position or capacity, in the Selective Service System of the United States.

No person shall be ineligible to hold any state, county or municipal office or position by reason of being engaged in service in Virginia in the Selective Service System of the United States. (1952, Ex. Sess., c. 21, § 2-27.2; 1966, c. 677, § 2.1-32; 2001, c. 844.)

§ **2.2-2804. Selective Service compliance.** — Any person who has failed to meet the federal requirement to register for the Selective Service shall be ineligible for employment by or service for the Commonwealth, or a political subdivision of the Commonwealth, including all boards and commissions, departments, agencies, institutions, and instrumentalities. A person shall not be denied employment under this section by reason of failure to present himself for and submit to the federal registration requirement if: (i) the requirement for the person to so register has terminated or become inapplicable to the person and (ii) the person shows by a preponderance of the evidence that the failure of the person to register was not a knowing and willful failure to register. (1999, c. 434, § 2.1-32.1; 2001, c. 844.)

§ **2.2-2805. Members of armed forces; reserve forces.** — No person shall, by reason of being a member of the armed forces of the United States, whether active or reserved, or by reason of being a retired officer of the armed forces of the United States and receiving pay therefor, be disqualified from holding any office under the government of the Commonwealth, or under any county, city, town, magisterial district or school district thereof. (Code 1950, § 2-30; 1966, c. 677, § 2.1-34; 2001, c. 844.)

§ **2.2-2806. Holding other office by officers of state institutions.** — No person serving as a member of the governing board of any institution, supported in whole or in part by funds paid out of the state treasury, or as rector of such institution, or as president or chairman of the governing board thereof, shall hold, during his term of office, any other office or position with the institution on the board of which he is serving. If any such person accepts any such office or position, the acceptance shall ipso facto vacate his office as a member of such board. Nothing in this section shall be construed to prevent members of boards of agricultural colleges from doing field or extension work. (Code 1950, § 2-31; 1966, c. 677, § 2.1-35; 2001, c. 844.)

§ **2.2-2807. Prohibition against holding two elected offices simultaneously; exceptions.** — No person shall hold more than one elected office at the same time. This section shall apply to every office elected by the qualified voters of the Commonwealth or any political subdivision or part thereof.

The qualification for and taking of the oath for a second elected office by any person shall operate to vacate any other elected office held by him.

This section shall not be construed to repeal or affect provisions of law authorizing the sharing of elected offices by two or more jurisdictions. Any person serving in more than one elected office on July 1, 1993, shall be entitled to complete the terms for which he was elected.

A person may serve as a Presidential elector while holding any other elective office of the Commonwealth or any political subdivision or part thereof, and this section shall not be construed to prohibit such dual officeholding. (1993, cc. 621, 781, § 2.1-37.01; 2001, c. 844.)

CASE NOTES

Two-office restriction a valid end. — In an action by a candidate against the Secretary of the State Board of Elections alleging that his constitutional rights were violated by the two-office ballot restriction under §§ 24.2-504 and 24.2-525, summary judgment was granted for the Secretary where (1) the burden on the candidate's U.S. Const., amend. I and XIV, rights from the two-office restriction was reasonable, nondiscriminatory, and relatively minimal as the restriction only required him to focus his efforts on two races, (2) the state had a regulatory interest in limiting the size of the ballot, (3) the two-office restriction was rationally related to measuring the seriousness of the candidate's desire and motivation for seeking public office, (4) the two-office restriction was intended to avoid voter confusion, and (5) the state's prohibition under § 2.2-2807 of a candidate holding two offices was a legitimate end. Levy v. Jensen, 285 F. Supp. 2d 710, 2003 U.S. Dist. LEXIS 17542 (E.D. Va. 2003).

§ 2.2-2808. Acts under color of office; contracts in violation of chapter. — All judgments given, and all acts executed or done by any person by authority or color of any office or post, or the deputation thereof, before his removal therefrom, shall be as valid as they would be if this chapter had not been enacted; but every contract or security made or obtained in violation of this chapter shall be void. (Code 1950, § 2-33; 1966, c. 677, § 2.1-37; 2001, c. 844.)

CASE NOTES

Editor's note. — The cases below were decided under former Title 2.1 or prior provisions.

The acts of a public officer de facto are valid and binding just as if he were an officer de jure. Monteith v. Commonwealth, 56 Va. (15 Gratt.) 172 (1859); Griffin's Ex'r v. Cunningham, 61 Va. (20 Gratt.) 31 (1870); Bolling v. Lersner, 67 Va. (26 Gratt.) 36, appeal dismissed, 91 U.S. 594, 23 L. Ed. 366 (1875); Roche v. Jones, 87 Va. 484, 12 S.E. 965 (1891).

Upon grounds of public policy. — The rule which declares that the acts of an officer de facto are as valid and binding as if he were an officer de jure, is founded on the soundest principles of public policy, and is absolutely essential to the protection of the best interests of society. McCraw v. Williams, 74 Va. (33 Gratt.) 510 (1880).

A duly elected judge who held court before his term of office began was a judge de facto, and his judgments were as valid and binding as if he had been judge de jure. McCraw v. Williams, 74 Va. (33 Gratt.) 510 (1880).

Where a clerk of court before being duly qualified administered the oath to the grand jury, it was held that his act in administering such oath was as valid as though he were a clerk de jure. Hord v. Commonwealth, 31 Va. (4 Leigh) 674 (1833).

Where a justice of the peace accepts the office of coroner, such acceptance does not vacate his subsequent acts as justice done before his disqualification was established by some proper judicial proceeding for that purpose instituted. Maddox v. Ewell, 4 Va. (2 Va. Cas.) 59 (1817).

§ 2.2-2809. Bonds of certain officers required; condition; form; effect of failure to give bond; additional bonds. — Certain officers designated by the Governor shall each give bond with sufficient surety to the Commonwealth. The bond shall be conditioned upon the faithful discharge of the duties of his office in such penalty as fixed by the Governor.

The form of bond shall be prescribed by the Attorney General and when given by such officer shall bear the certification of the Attorney General and the approval of the Governor.

If the bond required of such officer is not given or not deemed to be proper within thirty days after his appointment, the appointment of such officer shall be deemed void and his office shall be deemed vacant.

Whenever in the opinion of the Governor it is necessary for the protection of the public interest, that a new bond or a bond in addition to the one already given by such officer, it shall be given within a reasonable time as prescribed by the Governor after the officer has been notified of the requirement. If the officer fails or refuses to give the new or additional bond required, his office shall be deemed vacant. (1980, c. 119, § 2.1-11.1; 2001, c. 844.)

§ 2.2-2810. Premiums on such bonds. — The Comptroller may pay out of the state treasury the premiums on the surety bonds of all state officials who are required to be bonded, for a period of more than one year when a discount for advanced payment of the premiums may be obtained under the rates, and regulations adopted by the State Corporation Commission according to law.

If any such surety bond is cancelled prior to its expiration, the portion of the premium to be returned shall be calculated on the basis of the regular annual rate of premiums for the duration of the bond as such refunds are prescribed by the rates, and regulations adopted by the State Corporation Commission according to law. (Code 1950, § 2-8; 1966, c. 677, § 2.1-12; 2001, c. 844.)

§ **2.2-2811. Where bonds filed.** — The bonds of all officers and employees of all the departments, institutions, agencies, boards, commissions and authorities of the Commonwealth, except the Department of Accounts, shall, after being recorded by the Secretary of the Commonwealth, as required by § 49-12, be transmitted to the Comptroller and be filed in the office of the Comptroller.

The bonds of all officers and employees in the Department of Accounts shall be filed in the office of the Secretary of the Commonwealth. Nothing in this section shall be construed to apply to notaries public, nor to commissioners of the revenue, attorneys for the Commonwealth, clerks of courts and treasurers of the counties and cities who are covered by other sections of the Code; nor to other similar officers of a purely local character. (Code 1950, § 2-11; 1966, cc. 249, 677, § 2.1-15; 2001, c. 844.)

§ **2.2-2812. Employment of personnel.** — A. Notwithstanding any other provision of law to the contrary, the agency administrator of each executive branch agency, except those that by law are appointed by their respective boards, shall employ the personnel necessary for the proper performance of all responsibilities of their agency subject to the Virginia Personnel Act (§ 2.2-2900 et seq.) of this title and within the limits of appropriations made therefor by law.

B. Notwithstanding any other provision of law to the contrary, any employee of an agency in the executive branch of state government, who is promoted within the same agency to a higher position classification shall serve a period of time in a probationary status incident to such promotion, and shall be offered to be returned to such employee's previous classified position or an equivalent position for which a vacancy exists if, for any reason other than misconduct, the probationary period of employment is not satisfied or completed. (1984, c. 744, § 2.1-20.01; 1997, c. 31; 2001, c. 844.)

§ **2.2-2813. Definitions; compensation and expense payments from state funds for service on collegial bodies.** — A. As used in this chapter:

"Compensation" means any amount paid in addition to reimbursement for expenses.

"Expenses" means all reasonable and necessary expenses incurred in the performance of duties.

"Salary" means a fixed compensation for services, paid to part-time and full-time employees on a regular basis.

B. Subject to the provisions of subsections C and D, members of boards, commissions, committees, councils and other collegial bodies, who are appointed at the state level, shall be compensated at the rate of $50 per day, unless a different rate of compensation is specified by statute for such members, plus expenses for each day or portion thereof in which the member is engaged in the business of that body. The funding for the compensation and reimbursement of expenses of members shall be provided by the collegial body or, if funds are not appropriated to the collegial body for such purpose, by the entity that supports the work of the collegial body. The collegial body or supporting agency shall reimburse the Clerk of the Senate and the Clerk of the House of Delegates for expenditures incurred in providing compensation and expenses of their respective members for service on the collegial body.

C. Full-time employees of the Commonwealth or any of its local political subdivisions, including full-time faculty members of public institutions of higher education, shall be limited to reimbursement for such employee's expenses.

D. No member shall receive total compensation for a single day of more than one payment of the highest per diem amount specified in subsection B for attending meetings and for services performed that day for all boards, commissions, or other similar bodies, of which such person is a member, including all committees, subcommittees, or other related entities of such boards, commissions, or other similar bodies. Whenever a member performs services or attends two or more meetings in a single day for two or more boards, commissions, etc., compensation and expenses shall be prorated among the bodies served. (1980, c. 728, §§ 2.1-20.2, 2.1-20.3; 1981, c. 181; 1998, cc. 790, 872; 2001, cc. 227, 844; 2003, cc. 814, 821.)

Cross references. — As to compensation for members of Joint Commission on Health Care, see § 30-168.2. As to compensation for members of Out-of-Family Investigations Advisory Committee, see § 63.2-1527. For limit on travel reimbursement for members of the Child Day-Care Council, see § 63.2-1735.

Editor's note. — Acts 2001, c. 227 amended § 2.1-20.3, from which this section is derived. Pursuant to § 30-152, Acts 2001, c. 227 has been given effect in this section as set out above. The 2001 amendment by c. 227 inserted "by statute" in present subsection B, and in present subsection D, rewrote the first sentence, which formerly read: "No person shall receive total compensation of more than fifty dollars per day for services performed on any one day," and in the last sentence, inserted "performs services or," and inserted "for two or more boards, commissions, etc."

OPINIONS OF THE ATTORNEY GENERAL

"[M]embers of ________ collegial bodies, who are appointed at the state level" are those persons who are appointed by an authorized state official or entity, or as set forth in the collegial bodies' enabling legislation and the phrase "state level" refers only to those collegial bodies established or authorized by the General Assembly to function at the state level and does not include such bodies that operate at a local government level. See opinion of Attorney General to The Honorable Stephen H. Martin, Member, Senate of Virginia, 03-032 (9/11/03).

Construction with other law. — Members of the Litter Control and Recycling Fund Advisory Board are not entitled to compensation or reimbursement of expenses under this section. See opinion of Attorney General to The Honorable Stephen H. Martin, Member, Senate of Virginia, 03-032 (9/11/03).

Because § 23-9.3 is silent as to compensation and expense reimbursement for members of the State Council of Higher Education for Virginia, there is no conflict with this section; the two statutes may be read together in harmony, with the provisions of this section providing the method and amount of compensation and expense reimbursement. See opinion of Attorney General to The Honorable Stephen H. Martin, Member, Senate of Virginia, 03-032 (9/11/03).

Because § 46.2-1503 pertaining to reimbursement of actual and necessary expenses of members of the Motor Vehicle Dealer Board is silent as to compensation, the compensation provisions of this section apply; as to expenses, to the extent the two statutes are in conflict or it is unclear which of the two statutes applies, the specific provisions of subsection E of § 46.2-1503 dictate the method and amount of such reimbursement. See opinion of Attorney General to The Honorable Stephen H. Martin, Member, Senate of Virginia, 03-032 (9/11/03).

It does not matter whether this section or specific enabling legislation of a collegial body is the later enacted statute; only in those instances where the provisions of this section and the statute in question are so irreconcilably repugnant or inconsistent would the timing of enactment be implicated. See opinion of Attorney General to The Honorable Stephen H. Martin, Member, Senate of Virginia, 03-032 (9/11/03).

Entitlement to compensation. — Only members of collegial bodies that are established or authorized to be established by the General Assembly are entitled to compensation or reimbursement for expenses under this section. See opinion of Attorney General to The Honorable Stephen H. Martin, Member, Senate of Virginia, 03-032 (9/11/03).

Ad hoc collegial bodies established only on the authority of a state-level official or entity are not entitled to receive compensation and reimbursement for expenses. See opinion of Attorney General to The Honorable Stephen H. Martin, Member, Senate of Virginia, 03-032 (9/11/03).

§ 2.2-2814. How salaries, expenses and other allowances paid; time of payment. — The salaries, expenses and other allowances, including mileage, mentioned in this chapter, Chapter 1 (§ 2.2-100 et seq.) of this title and Chapter 1.1 (§ 30-19.11 et seq.) of Title 30 shall, except where otherwise specifically provided, be paid out of the state treasury after being duly audited, and the Comptroller shall draw his warrants on the State Treasurer for the payment thereof. Salaries shall be paid every two weeks, semimonthly or monthly, at the discretion of the Comptroller, upon such dates as the Comptroller may prescribe. Expenses shall be paid when they have been incurred, and the other allowances shall be paid when the services have been rendered or the travel has been performed however, members of the General Assembly and others traveling to the seat of government who would be entitled to mileage for traveling home may receive such mileage before going home. (Code 1950, §§ 14-1, 14-27; 1962, c. 547; 1964, c. 386, § 14.1-1; 1998, c. 872, § 2.1-20.5; 2001, c. 844.)

Cross references. — As to payment by the Department of Social Services of assistant attorney for the Commonwealth for prosecution of public assistance fraud cases, see § 63.2-525. As to payment by the Department of Social Services for legal services, notwithstanding any provision of §§ 2.2-2814, 2.2-2815, 2.2-2816, 2.2-2823, 2.2-2824, 2.2-2825, or 2.2-2826, see § 63.2-1948.

§ 2.2-2815. Increase in salaries. — The salary of no state officer or employee payable by the Commonwealth and not specifically fixed by law shall be increased, or authorized to be increased, without the written consent of the Governor.

The salary of no officer or employee of any state institution, board, commission or agency payable by the Commonwealth and not specifically fixed by law, shall be increased, or authorized to be increased, without prior written authorization of such board or commission and the written consent of the Governor.

Any violation of this section shall constitute misfeasance in office. Nothing herein shall apply to teachers in the elementary or secondary schools of the Commonwealth or to employees receiving compensation not in excess of $100 per month. (Code 1950, § 14-2; 1964, c. 386, § 14.1-2; 1998, c. 872, § 2.1-20.6; 2001, c. 844.)

Cross references. — As to establishment or change of rate of pay under the Virginia Personnel Act, see §§ 2.2-2900 et seq. As to payment by the Department of Social Services of assistant attorney for the Commonwealth for prosecution of public assistance fraud cases, see § 63.2-525. As to payment by the Department of Social Services for legal services, notwithstanding any provision of §§ 2.2-2814, 2.2-2815, 2.2-2816, 2.2-2823, 2.2-2824, 2.2-2825, or 2.2-2826, see § 63.2-1948.

§ 2.2-2816. Liability of salary of officer for debt he owes Commonwealth; how enforced; when officer's right to file petition barred. — A. Whenever any officer, other than one whose office is created by the Constitution of Virginia, is indebted to the Commonwealth for money collected by him or improperly drawn by him or upon his order from the state treasury during his term of office and, after payment of such indebtedness is demanded by the Comptroller, such officer continues in default, the Comptroller shall not issue his warrant for, nor shall the State Treasurer pay, any part of the salary due, or to become due, to such officer until he has made good his default. He may, however, file his petition in the Circuit Court of the City of Richmond against the Comptroller, asserting his claim to his salary, and asking for payment thereof. The Comptroller shall answer the petition, and the proceedings shall be held according to the provisions of Article 18 (§ 8.01-192 et seq.)

of Chapter 3 of Title 8.01 and § 8.01-255. If it is found that the petitioner is indebted, the Commonwealth shall be credited on his salary then due with the amount of such indebtedness and if, after such credit is given, there is a balance in his favor, judgment shall be rendered on his behalf. If the indebtedness exceeds his salary then due, judgment for the excess shall be rendered against him and the amount thereof, unless sooner paid, shall be credited to the Commonwealth on his salary thereafter becoming due. The Comptroller shall issue his warrant on the State Treasurer for the payment of any judgment rendered on behalf of the petitioner. In the proceeding by petition the Attorney General shall represent the Commonwealth, unless he is interested, in which case the Comptroller shall employ other counsel to represent the Commonwealth.

B. If the officer fails to file a petition under this section within twelve months after payment of any installment of his salary is withheld, his right to file the petition shall be barred. In such case the Comptroller shall credit the Commonwealth on the officer's salary with the amount of his indebtedness, and make that fact appear on the books of his office. (Code 1950, §§ 14-3, 14-4; 1964, cc. 386, §§ 14.1-3, 14.1-4; 1998, c. 872, § 2.1-20.7; 2001, c. 844.)

Cross references. — As to payment by the Department of Social Services of assistant attorney for the Commonwealth for prosecution of public assistance fraud cases, see § 63.2-525. As to payment by the Department of Social Services for legal services, notwithstanding any provision of §§ 2.2-2814, 2.2-2815, 2.2-2816, 2.2-2823, 2.2-2824, 2.2-2825, or 2.2-2826, see § 63.2-1948.

§ 2.2-2817. Defense of employees. — Notwithstanding any other law, if any state employee, as defined in this chapter, is investigated for a crime, arrested or indicted, or otherwise prosecuted on any charge, arising out of any act committed in the discharge of his official duties, the state agency, board, or other employer of such state employee, upon a preliminary finding by such agency, board or employer that (i) the employee did not violate any law, ordinance or regulation as a result of the act in question and (ii) the employee will not be terminated from employment as a result of such act, may employ special counsel approved by the Attorney General to defend such person. The reasonable compensation for special counsel employed, pursuant to this section, shall, subject to the approval of the Attorney General, be paid out of the funds appropriated for the state agency, board, or other employer of such state employee. (2000, c. 1030, § 2.1-20.1:8; 2001, c. 844.)

§ 2.2-2817.1. State agencies to establish alternative work schedules; reporting requirement. — A. In accordance with the statewide telecommuting and alternative work schedule policy, to be developed by the Secretary of Administration pursuant to § 2.2-203.1, the head of each state agency shall establish a telecommuting and alternative work policy under which eligible employees of such agency may telecommute, participate in alternative work schedules, or both, to the maximum extent possible without diminished employee performance or service delivery. The policy shall identify types of employees eligible for telecommuting and alternative work schedules, the broad categories of positions determined to be ineligible for telecommuting and the justification therefor, any benefits of telecommuting including the use of alternate work locations that are separate from the agency's central workplace, and any benefits of using alternative work schedules. The policy shall promote use of Commonwealth information technology assets where feasible but may allow for eligible employees to use computers, computing devices, or related electronic equipment not owned or leased by the Commonwealth to telecommute, if such use is technically and economically practical, and so long as such use meets information security standards as established by the Virginia Information Technologies Agency, or receives an exception from such standards approved by the CIO of the Commonwealth or his designee. The policy shall be updated periodically as necessary.

B. The head of each agency shall set annual percentage targets for the number of positions eligible for alternative work schedules. By July 1, 2009, each state agency shall have a goal of not less than 25 percent of its eligible workforce participating in alternative work schedules. By January 1, 2010, each state agency, except the Department of State Police, shall have a goal of not less than 20 percent of its eligible workforce telecommuting.

C. The head of each state agency shall annually report to the Secretary of Administration or his designee on the status and efficiency of telecommuting and participation in alternative work schedules, including specific budget requests for information technology, software, telecommunications connectivity (i.e., broadband Internet access, additional telephone lines, and online collaborative tools), or other equipment or services needed to increase opportunities for telecommuting and participation in alternate work locations.

D. As used in this section:

"Alternate work locations" means approved locations other than the employee's central workplace where official state business is performed. Such locations may include, but not be limited to the home of an employee and satellite offices.

"Alternative work schedule" means schedules that differ from the standard workweek, 40-hour workweek schedule, if such schedules are deemed to promote efficient agency operations. Alternative work schedules may include, but not be limited to, four 10-hour days, rotational shifts, and large-scale job sharing.

"Central workplace" means an employer's place of work where employees normally are located.

"Telecommuting" means a work arrangement in which supervisors direct or permit employees to perform their usual job duties away from their central workplace at least one day per week and in accordance with work agreements.

"Work agreement" means a written agreement between the employer and employee that details the terms and conditions of an employee's work away from his central workplace. (2001, c. 405, § 2.1-20.1:9; 2004, cc. 701, 755; 2005, c. 421; 2006, c. 137; 2007, c. 716; 2008, cc. 374, 375.)

Editor's note. — Acts 2001, c. 405 enacted § 2.1-20.1:9, from which this section is derived. Pursuant to § 30-152, Acts 2001, c. 405 has been given effect in this section as set out above.

The 2007 amendments. — The 2007 amendment by c. 716 inserted the next-to-last sentence in subsection A.

The 2008 amendments. — The 2008 amendment by c. 374 inserted "at least one day per week and" and made a minor stylistic change in the definition of "Telecommuting" in subsection D.

The 2008 amendment by c. 375 added the last sentence in subsection B.

§ 2.2-2817.2. Employees of the University of Virginia Medical Center. — The University of Virginia Medical Center, hereafter referred to as the Medical Center, may purchase basic group life, accidental death and dismemberment, and disability insurance policies covering in whole or in part any of its employees. In addition, the Medical Center may establish, administer and make available to employees a program of optional insurance, including life, accidental death and dismemberment, and disability insurance. Employees of the Medical Center covered under the aforesaid basic insurance policies purchased by the Medical Center shall not be covered by the insurance program established pursuant to § 51.1-501 or be considered "eligible employees" under § 51.1-1100, unless the University of Virginia Board of Visitors, or a duly authorized agent or representative of the Board, purchases such insurance policies from the Virginia Retirement System. Nor shall they be required to present at their own expense evidence of insurability satisfactory to an insurance company upon changing from one form of coverage to another form of coverage provided pursuant to this section. Chapter 5 of Title 51.1 (§ 51.1-500 et seq.) shall not apply to any insurance coverage offered by the Medical Center except that the provisions of §§ 51.1-510 and 51.1-511 shall apply to such insurance coverage; provided that any administrative or ministerial functions performed by or on behalf of the Board of the Virginia Retirement System under §§ 51.1-510 and 51.1-511 shall be performed by the Medical Center.

Notwithstanding the definition of "state employee" contained in § 51.1-124.3, all employees of the Medical Center may be enrolled in a health care plan other than that provided for in § 2.2-2818 at the election of the Medical Center and subject to the review and approval of the Board of Visitors of the University of Virginia; however, any Medical Center employee who was first employed by the Medical Center prior to July 1, 1996, and who had not been classified as a health care provider under the provisions of § 51.1-502.1 prior to July 1, 1996, shall be provided the option of enrolling in a health care plan elected by the Medical Center or enrolling in the health care plan established pursuant to § 2.2-2818 until such time as the University of Virginia Board of Visitors may determine that it is not in the best interest of the University to continue to provide that option to any employees of the Medical Center. If the Board of Visitors determines that such health plan option will not continue to be provided, any Medical Center employees who must reenroll in a different health plan shall be allowed to do so with a waiver of preexisting medical conditions for the employees and, if applicable, their spouses and dependents.

Subject to such eligibility criteria as it may establish, the Medical Center may make available to any of its employees the insurance programs established pursuant to this section, including health plan coverage, notwithstanding the fact that such employees may not be eligible for participation in any retirement plan established pursuant to § 51.1-126.3 or the retirement system established pursuant to Chapter 1 (§ 51.1-124.1 et seq.) of this title.

The eligibility of any employee of the Medical Center for participation in any insurance program established pursuant to this section shall not of itself render such employees eligible for participation in the Virginia Retirement System or any optional retirement program. (2001, c. 694, § 2.1-20.1:9.1.)

Editor's note. — Acts 2001, c. 694 enacted § 2.1-20.1:9.1, from which this section is derived. Pursuant to § 30-152, Acts 2001, c. 694 has been given effect in this section as set out above.

§ 2.2-2818. Health and related insurance for state employees. — A. The Department of Human Resource Management shall establish a plan, subject to the approval of the Governor, for providing health insurance coverage, including chiropractic treatment, hospitalization, medical, surgical and major medical coverage, for state employees and retired state employees with the Commonwealth paying the cost thereof to the extent of the coverage included in such plan. The same plan shall be offered to all part-time state employees, but the total cost shall be paid by such part-time employees. The Department of Human Resource Management shall administer this section. The plan chosen shall provide means whereby coverage for the families or dependents of state employees may be purchased. Except for part-time employees, the Commonwealth may pay all or a portion of the cost thereof, and for such portion as the Commonwealth does not pay, the employee, including a part-time employee, may purchase the coverage by paying the additional cost over the cost of coverage for an employee.

Such contribution shall be financed through appropriations provided by law.

B. The plan shall:

1. Include coverage for low-dose screening mammograms for determining the presence of occult breast cancer. Such coverage shall make available one screening mammogram to persons age 35 through 39, one such mammogram biennially to persons age 40 through 49, and one such mammogram annually to persons age 50 and over and may be limited to a benefit of $50 per mammogram subject to such dollar limits, deductibles, and coinsurance factors as are no less favorable than for physical illness generally.

The term *"mammogram"* shall mean an X-ray examination of the breast using equipment dedicated specifically for mammography, including but not limited to the X-ray tube, filter, compression device, screens, film, and cassettes, with an average radiation exposure of less than one rad mid-breast, two views of each breast.

In order to be considered a screening mammogram for which coverage shall be made available under this section:

a. The mammogram shall be (i) ordered by a health care practitioner acting within the scope of his licensure and, in the case of an enrollee of a health maintenance organization, by the health maintenance organization provider; (ii) performed by a registered technologist; (iii) interpreted by a qualified radiologist; and (iv) performed under the direction of a person licensed to practice medicine and surgery and certified by the American Board of Radiology or an equivalent examining body. A copy of the mammogram report shall be sent or delivered to the health care practitioner who ordered it;

b. The equipment used to perform the mammogram shall meet the standards set forth by the Virginia Department of Health in its radiation protection regulations; and

c. The mammography film shall be retained by the radiologic facility performing the examination in accordance with the American College of Radiology guidelines or state law.

2. Include coverage for postpartum services providing inpatient care and a home visit or visits that shall be in accordance with the medical criteria, outlined in the most current version of or an official update to the "Guidelines for Perinatal Care" prepared by the American Academy of Pediatrics and the American College of Obstetricians and Gynecologists or the "Standards for Obstetric-Gynecologic Services" prepared by the American College of Obstetricians and Gynecologists. Such coverage shall be provided incorporating any changes in such Guidelines or Standards within six months of the publication of such Guidelines or Standards or any official amendment thereto.

3. Include an appeals process for resolution of written complaints concerning denials or partial denials of claims that shall provide reasonable procedures for resolution of such written complaints and shall be published and disseminated to all covered state employees. The appeals process shall include a separate expedited emergency appeals procedure that shall provide resolution within one business day of receipt of a complaint concerning situations requiring immediate medical care. For appeals involving adverse decisions as defined in § 32.1-137.7, the Department shall contract with one or more impartial health entities to review such decisions. Impartial health entities may include medical peer review organizations and independent utilization review companies. The Department shall adopt regulations to assure that the impartial health entity conducting the reviews has adequate standards, credentials and experience for such review. The impartial health entity shall examine the final denial of claims to determine whether the decision is objective, clinically valid, and compatible with established principles of health

care. The decision of the impartial health entity shall (i) be in writing, (ii) contain findings of fact as to the material issues in the case and the basis for those findings, and (iii) be final and binding if consistent with law and policy.

Prior to assigning an appeal to an impartial health entity, the Department shall verify that the impartial health entity conducting the review of a denial of claims has no relationship or association with (i) the covered employee; (ii) the treating health care provider, or any of its employees or affiliates; (iii) the medical care facility at which the covered service would be provided, or any of its employees or affiliates; or (iv) the development or manufacture of the drug, device, procedure or other therapy that is the subject of the final denial of a claim. The impartial health entity shall not be a subsidiary of, nor owned or controlled by, a health plan, a trade association of health plans, or a professional association of health care providers. There shall be no liability on the part of and no cause of action shall arise against any officer or employee of an impartial health entity for any actions taken or not taken or statements made by such officer or employee in good faith in the performance of his powers and duties.

4. Include coverage for early intervention services. For purposes of this section, "early intervention services" means medically necessary speech and language therapy, occupational therapy, physical therapy and assistive technology services and devices for dependents from birth to age three who are certified by the Department of Mental Health, Mental Retardation and Substance Abuse Services as eligible for services under Part H of the Individuals with Disabilities Education Act (20 U.S.C. § 1471 et seq.). Medically necessary early intervention services for the population certified by the Department of Mental Health, Mental Retardation and Substance Abuse Services shall mean those services designed to help an individual attain or retain the capability to function age-appropriately within his environment, and shall include services that enhance functional ability without effecting a cure.

For persons previously covered under the plan, there shall be no denial of coverage due to the existence of a preexisting condition. The cost of early intervention services shall not be applied to any contractual provision limiting the total amount of coverage paid by the insurer to or on behalf of the insured during the insured's lifetime.

5. Include coverage for prescription drugs and devices approved by the United States Food and Drug Administration for use as contraceptives.

6. Not deny coverage for any drug approved by the United States Food and Drug Administration for use in the treatment of cancer on the basis that the drug has not been approved by the United States Food and Drug Administration for the treatment of the specific type of cancer for which the drug has been prescribed, if the drug has been recognized as safe and effective for treatment of that specific type of cancer in one of the standard reference compendia.

7. Not deny coverage for any drug prescribed to treat a covered indication so long as the drug has been approved by the United States Food and Drug Administration for at least one indication and the drug is recognized for treatment of the covered indication in one of the standard reference compendia or in substantially accepted peer-reviewed medical literature.

8. Include coverage for equipment, supplies and outpatient self-management training and education, including medical nutrition therapy, for the treatment of insulin-dependent diabetes, insulin-using diabetes, gestational diabetes and noninsulin-using diabetes if prescribed by a healthcare professional legally authorized to prescribe such items under law. To qualify for coverage under this subdivision, diabetes outpatient self-management training and education shall be provided by a certified, registered or licensed health care professional.

9. Include coverage for reconstructive breast surgery. For purposes of this section, "reconstructive breast surgery" means surgery performed on and after July 1, 1998, (i) coincident with a mastectomy performed for breast cancer or (ii) following a mastectomy performed for breast cancer to reestablish symmetry between the two breasts. For persons previously covered under the plan, there shall be no denial of coverage due to preexisting conditions.

10. Include coverage for annual pap smears, including coverage, on and after July 1, 1999, for annual testing performed by any FDA-approved gynecologic cytology screening technologies.

11. Include coverage providing a minimum stay in the hospital of not less than 48 hours for a patient following a radical or modified radical mastectomy and 24 hours of inpatient care following a total mastectomy or a partial mastectomy with lymph node dissection for treatment of breast cancer. Nothing in this subdivision shall be construed as requiring the provision of inpatient coverage where the attending physician in consultation with the patient determines that a shorter period of hospital stay is appropriate.

12. Include coverage (i) to persons age 50 and over and (ii) to persons age 40 and over who are at high risk for prostate cancer, according to the most recent published guidelines of the American Cancer Society, for one PSA test in a 12-month period and digital rectal examinations, all in accordance with American Cancer Society guidelines. For the purpose of this subdivision, "PSA testing" means the analysis of a blood sample to determine the level of prostate specific antigen.

13. Permit any individual covered under the plan direct access to the health care services of a participating specialist (i) authorized to provide services under the plan and (ii) selected by the covered individual. The plan shall have a procedure by which an individual who has an ongoing special condition may, after consultation with the primary care physician, receive a referral to a specialist for such condition who shall be responsible for and capable of providing and coordinating the individual's primary and specialty care related to the initial specialty care referral. If such an individual's care would most appropriately be coordinated by such a specialist, the plan shall refer the individual to a specialist. For the purposes of this subdivision, "special condition" means a condition or disease that is (i) life-threatening, degenerative, or disabling and (ii) requires specialized medical care over a prolonged period of time. Within the treatment period authorized by the referral, such specialist shall be permitted to treat the individual without a further referral from the individual's primary care provider and may authorize such referrals, procedures, tests, and other medical services related to the initial referral as the individual's primary care provider would otherwise be permitted to provide or authorize. The plan shall have a procedure by which an individual who has an ongoing special condition that requires ongoing care from a specialist may receive a standing referral to such specialist for the treatment of the special condition. If the primary care provider, in consultation with the plan and the specialist, if any, determines that such a standing referral is appropriate, the plan or issuer shall make such a referral to a specialist. Nothing contained herein shall prohibit the plan from requiring a participating specialist to provide written notification to the covered individual's primary care physician of any visit to such specialist. Such notification may include a description of the health care services rendered at the time of the visit.

14. Include provisions allowing employees to continue receiving health care services for a period of up to 90 days from the date of the primary care physician's notice of termination from any of the plan's provider panels. The plan shall notify any provider at least 90 days prior to the date of termination of the provider, except when the provider is terminated for cause.

For a period of at least 90 days from the date of the notice of a provider's termination from any of the plan's provider panels, except when a provider is terminated for cause, a provider shall be permitted by the plan to render health care services to any of the covered employees who (i) were in an active course of treatment from the provider prior to the notice of termination and (ii) request to continue receiving health care services from the provider.

Notwithstanding the provisions of this subdivision, any provider shall be permitted by the plan to continue rendering health services to any covered employee who has entered the second trimester of pregnancy at the time of the provider's termination of participation, except when a provider is terminated for cause. Such treatment shall, at the covered employee's option, continue through the provision of postpartum care directly related to the delivery.

Notwithstanding the provisions of this subdivision, any provider shall be permitted to continue rendering health services to any covered employee who is determined to be terminally ill (as defined under § 1861(dd)(3)(A) of the Social Security Act) at the time of a provider's termination of participation, except when a provider is terminated for cause. Such treatment shall, at the covered employee's option, continue for the remainder of the employee's life for care directly related to the treatment of the terminal illness.

A provider who continues to render health care services pursuant to this subdivision shall be reimbursed in accordance with the carrier's agreement with such provider existing immediately before the provider's termination of participation.

15. Include coverage for patient costs incurred during participation in clinical trials for treatment studies on cancer, including ovarian cancer trials.

The reimbursement for patient costs incurred during participation in clinical trials for treatment studies on cancer shall be determined in the same manner as reimbursement is determined for other medical and surgical procedures. Such coverage shall have durational limits, dollar limits, deductibles, copayments and coinsurance factors that are no less favorable than for physical illness generally.

For purposes of this subdivision:

"Cooperative group" means a formal network of facilities that collaborate on research projects and have an established NIH-approved peer review program operating within the group. "Cooperative group" includes (i) the National Cancer Institute Clinical Cooperative Group and (ii) the National Cancer Institute Community Clinical Oncology Program.

"FDA" means the Federal Food and Drug Administration.

"Multiple project assurance contract" means a contract between an institution and the federal Department of Health and Human Services that defines the relationship of the institution to the federal Department of Health and Human Services and sets out the responsibilities of the institution and the procedures that will be used by the institution to protect human subjects.

"NCI" means the National Cancer Institute.

"NIH" means the National Institutes of Health.

"Patient" means a person covered under the plan established pursuant to this section.

"Patient cost" means the cost of a medically necessary health care service that is incurred as a result of the treatment being provided to a patient for purposes of a clinical trial. "Patient cost" does not include (i) the cost of nonhealth care services that a patient may be required to receive as a result of the treatment being provided for purposes of a clinical trial, (ii) costs associated with managing the research associated with the clinical trial, or (iii) the cost of the investigational drug or device.

Coverage for patient costs incurred during clinical trials for treatment studies on cancer shall be provided if the treatment is being conducted in a Phase II, Phase III, or Phase IV clinical trial. Such treatment may, however, be provided on a case-by-case basis if the treatment is being provided in a Phase I clinical trial.

The treatment described in the previous paragraph shall be provided by a clinical trial approved by:

a. The National Cancer Institute;

b. An NCI cooperative group or an NCI center;

c. The FDA in the form of an investigational new drug application;

d. The federal Department of Veterans Affairs; or

e. An institutional review board of an institution in the Commonwealth that has a multiple project assurance contract approved by the Office of Protection from Research Risks of the NCI.

The facility and personnel providing the treatment shall be capable of doing so by virtue of their experience, training, and expertise.

Coverage under this subdivision shall apply only if:

(1) There is no clearly superior, noninvestigational treatment alternative;

(2) The available clinical or preclinical data provide a reasonable expectation that the treatment will be at least as effective as the noninvestigational alternative; and

(3) The patient and the physician or health care provider who provides services to the patient under the plan conclude that the patient's participation in the clinical trial would be appropriate, pursuant to procedures established by the plan.

16. Include coverage providing a minimum stay in the hospital of not less than 23 hours for a covered employee following a laparoscopy-assisted vaginal hysterectomy and 48 hours for a covered employee following a vaginal hysterectomy, as outlined in Milliman & Robertson's nationally recognized guidelines. Nothing in this subdivision shall be construed as requiring the provision of the total hours referenced when the attending physician, in consultation with the covered employee, determines that a shorter hospital stay is appropriate.

17. Include coverage for biologically based mental illness.

For purposes of this subdivision, a "biologically based mental illness" is any mental or nervous condition caused by a biological disorder of the brain that results in a clinically significant syndrome that substantially limits the person's functioning; specifically, the following diagnoses are defined as biologically based mental illness as they apply to adults and children: schizophrenia, schizoaffective disorder, bipolar disorder, major depressive disorder, panic disorder, obsessive-compulsive disorder, attention deficit hyperactivity disorder, autism, and drug and alcoholism addiction.

Coverage for biologically based mental illnesses shall neither be different nor separate from coverage for any other illness, condition or disorder for purposes of determining deductibles, benefit year or lifetime durational limits, benefit year or lifetime dollar limits, lifetime episodes or treatment limits, copayment and coinsurance factors, and benefit year maximum for deductibles and copayment and coinsurance factors.

Nothing shall preclude the undertaking of usual and customary procedures to determine the appropriateness of, and medical necessity for, treatment of biologically based mental illnesses under this option, provided that all such appropriateness and medical necessity determinations are made in the same manner as those determinations made for the treatment of any other illness, condition or disorder covered by such policy or contract.

In no case, however, shall coverage for mental disorders provided pursuant to this section be diminished or reduced below the coverage in effect for such disorders on January 1, 1999.

18. Offer and make available coverage for the treatment of morbid obesity through gastric bypass surgery or such other methods as may be recognized by the National Institutes of Health as effective for the long-term reversal of morbid obesity. Such coverage shall have durational limits, dollar limits,

deductibles, copayments and coinsurance factors that are no less favorable than for physical illness generally. Access to surgery for morbid obesity shall not be restricted based upon dietary or any other criteria not approved by the National Institutes of Health. For purposes of this subdivision, "morbid obesity" means (i) a weight that is at least 100 pounds over or twice the ideal weight for frame, age, height, and gender as specified in the 1983 Metropolitan Life Insurance tables, (ii) a body mass index (BMI) equal to or greater than 35 kilograms per meter squared with comorbidity or coexisting medical conditions such as hypertension, cardiopulmonary conditions, sleep apnea, or diabetes, or (iii) a BMI of 40 kilograms per meter squared without such comorbidity. As used herein, "BMI" equals weight in kilograms divided by height in meters squared.

19. Include coverage for colorectal cancer screening, specifically screening with an annual fecal occult blood test, flexible sigmoidoscopy or colonoscopy, or in appropriate circumstances radiologic imaging, in accordance with the most recently published recommendations established by the American College of Gastroenterology, in consultation with the American Cancer Society, for the ages, family histories, and frequencies referenced in such recommendations. The coverage for colorectal cancer screening shall not be more restrictive than or separate from coverage provided for any other illness, condition or disorder for purposes of determining deductibles, benefit year or lifetime durational limits, benefit year or lifetime dollar limits, lifetime episodes or treatment limits, copayment and coinsurance factors, and benefit year maximum for deductibles and copayments and coinsurance factors.

20. On and after July 1, 2002, require that a prescription benefit card, health insurance benefit card, or other technology that complies with the requirements set forth in § 38.2-3407.4:2 be issued to each employee provided coverage pursuant to this section, and shall upon any changes in the required data elements set forth in subsection A of § 38.2-3407.4:2, either reissue the card or provide employees covered under the plan such corrective information as may be required to electronically process a prescription claim.

21. Include coverage for infant hearing screenings and all necessary audiological examinations provided pursuant to § 32.1-64.1 using any technology approved by the United States Food and Drug Administration, and as recommended by the national Joint Committee on Infant Hearing in its most current position statement addressing early hearing detection and intervention programs. Such coverage shall include follow-up audiological examinations as recommended by a physician, physician assistant, nurse practitioner or audiologist and performed by a licensed audiologist to confirm the existence or absence of hearing loss.

C. Claims incurred during a fiscal year but not reported during that fiscal year shall be paid from such funds as shall be appropriated by law. Appropriations, premiums and other payments shall be deposited in the employee health insurance fund, from which payments for claims, premiums, cost containment programs and administrative expenses shall be withdrawn from time to time. The funds of the health insurance fund shall be deemed separate and independent trust funds, shall be segregated from all other funds of the Commonwealth, and shall be invested and administered solely in the interests of the employees and their beneficiaries. Neither the General Assembly nor any public officer, employee, or agency shall use or authorize the use of such trust funds for any purpose other than as provided in law for benefits, refunds, and administrative expenses, including but not limited to legislative oversight of the health insurance fund.

D. For the purposes of this section:

"Peer-reviewed medical literature" means a scientific study published only after having been critically reviewed for scientific accuracy, validity, and

reliability by unbiased independent experts in a journal that has been determined by the International Committee of Medical Journal Editors to have met the Uniform Requirements for Manuscripts submitted to biomedical journals. Peer-reviewed medical literature does not include publications or supplements to publications that are sponsored to a significant extent by a pharmaceutical manufacturing company or health carrier.

"Standard reference compendia" means the American Medical Association Drug Evaluations, the American Hospital Formulary Service Drug Information, or the United States Pharmacopoeia Dispensing Information.

"State employee" means state employee as defined in § 51.1-124.3; employee as defined in § 51.1-201; the Governor, Lieutenant Governor and Attorney General; judge as defined in § 51.1-301 and judges, clerks and deputy clerks of regional juvenile and domestic relations, county juvenile and domestic relations, and district courts of the Commonwealth; and interns and residents employed by the School of Medicine and Hospital of the University of Virginia, and interns, residents, and employees of the Virginia Commonwealth University Health System Authority as provided in § 23-50.16:24.

"Part-time state employees" means classified or similarly situated employees in legislative, executive, judicial or independent agencies who are compensated on a salaried basis and work at least 20 hours, but less than 32 hours, per week.

E. Provisions shall be made for retired employees to obtain coverage under the above plan, including, as an option, coverage for vision and dental care. The Commonwealth may, but shall not be obligated to, pay all or any portion of the cost thereof.

F. Any self-insured group health insurance plan established by the Department of Human Resource Management that utilizes a network of preferred providers shall not exclude any physician solely on the basis of a reprimand or censure from the Board of Medicine, so long as the physician otherwise meets the plan criteria established by the Department.

G. The plan shall include, in each planning district, at least two health coverage options, each sponsored by unrelated entities. No later than July 1, 2006, one of the health coverage options to be available in each planning district shall be a high deductible health plan that would qualify for a health savings account pursuant to § 223 of the Internal Revenue Code of 1986, as amended.

In each planning district that does not have an available health coverage alternative, the Department shall voluntarily enter into negotiations at any time with any health coverage provider who seeks to provide coverage under the plan.

This subsection shall not apply to any state agency authorized by the Department to establish and administer its own health insurance coverage plan separate from the plan established by the Department.

H. Any self-insured group health insurance plan established by the Department of Human Resource Management that includes coverage for prescription drugs on an outpatient basis may apply a formulary to the prescription drug benefits provided by the plan if the formulary is developed, reviewed at least annually, and updated as necessary in consultation with and with the approval of a pharmacy and therapeutics committee, a majority of whose members are actively practicing licensed (i) pharmacists, (ii) physicians, and (iii) other health care providers.

If the plan maintains one or more drug formularies, the plan shall establish a process to allow a person to obtain, without additional cost-sharing beyond that provided for formulary prescription drugs in the plan, a specific, medically necessary nonformulary prescription drug if, after reasonable investigation and consultation with the prescriber, the formulary drug is determined to be an inappropriate therapy for the medical condition of the person. The plan shall act on such requests within one business day of receipt of the request.

I. Any plan established in accordance with this section requiring preauthorization prior to rendering medical treatment shall have personnel available to provide authorization at all times when such preauthorization is required.

J. Any plan established in accordance with this section shall provide to all covered employees written notice of any benefit reductions during the contract period at least 30 days before such reductions become effective.

K. No contract between a provider and any plan established in accordance with this section shall include provisions that require a health care provider or health care provider group to deny covered services that such provider or group knows to be medically necessary and appropriate that are provided with respect to a covered employee with similar medical conditions.

L. The Department of Human Resource Management shall appoint an Ombudsman to promote and protect the interests of covered employees under any state employee's health plan.

The Ombudsman shall:

1. Assist covered employees in understanding their rights and the processes available to them according to their state health plan.

2. Answer inquiries from covered employees by telephone and electronic mail.

3. Provide to covered employees information concerning the state health plans.

4. Develop information on the types of health plans available, including benefits and complaint procedures and appeals.

5. Make available, either separately or through an existing Internet web site utilized by the Department of Human Resource Management, information as set forth in subdivision 4 and such additional information as he deems appropriate.

6. Maintain data on inquiries received, the types of assistance requested, any actions taken and the disposition of each such matter.

7. Upon request, assist covered employees in using the procedures and processes available to them from their health plan, including all appeal procedures. Such assistance may require the review of health care records of a covered employee, which shall be done only with that employee's express written consent. The confidentiality of any such medical records shall be maintained in accordance with the confidentiality and disclosure laws of the Commonwealth.

8. Ensure that covered employees have access to the services provided by the Ombudsman and that the covered employees receive timely responses from the Ombudsman or his representatives to the inquiries.

9. Report annually on his activities to the standing committees of the General Assembly having jurisdiction over insurance and over health and the Joint Commission on Health Care by December 1 of each year.

M. The plan established in accordance with this section shall not refuse to accept or make reimbursement pursuant to an assignment of benefits made to a dentist or oral surgeon by a covered employee.

For purposes of this subsection, "assignment of benefits" means the transfer of dental care coverage reimbursement benefits or other rights under the plan. The assignment of benefits shall not be effective until the covered employee notifies the plan in writing of the assignment.

N. Beginning July 1, 2006, any plan established pursuant to this section shall provide for an identification number, which shall be assigned to the covered employee and shall not be the same as the employee's social security number.

O. Any group health insurance plan established by the Department of Human Resource Management that contains a coordination of benefits provision shall provide written notification to any eligible employee as a prominent part of its enrollment materials that if such eligible employee is covered under another group accident and sickness insurance policy, group accident and sickness subscription contract, or group health care plan for health care services, that insurance policy, subscription contract or health care plan may have primary responsibility for the covered expenses of other family members enrolled with the eligible employee. Such written notification shall describe generally the conditions upon which the other coverage would be primary for dependent children enrolled under the eligible employee's coverage and the method by which the eligible enrollee may verify from the plan that coverage would have primary responsibility for the covered expenses of each family member.

P. Any plan established by the Department of Human Resource Management pursuant to this section shall provide that coverage under such plan for family members enrolled under a participating state employee's coverage shall continue for a period of at least 30 days following the death of such state employee.

Q. The plan established in accordance with this section that follows a policy of sending its payment to the covered employee or covered family member for a claim for services received from a nonparticipating physician or osteopath shall (i) include language in the member handbook that notifies the covered employee of the responsibility to apply the plan payment to the claim from such nonparticipating provider, (ii) include this language with any such payment sent to the covered employee or covered family member, and (iii) include the name and any last known address of the nonparticipating provider on the explanation of benefits statement. (1970, c. 557, § 2.1-20.1; 1972, c. 803; 1973, cc. 69, 297; 1978, c. 70; 1984, c. 430; 1988, c. 634; 1989, cc. 559, 664; 1990, c. 607; 1993, c. 138; 1995, c. 353; 1996, cc. 155, 201, 905, 1046; 1997, cc. 43, 468, 521, 656; 1998, cc. 35, 56, 257, 386, 631, 709, 851, 858, 875; 1999, cc. 643, 649, 921, 941; 2000, cc. 66, 149, 465, 534, 657, 720, 888; 2001, cc. 334, 558, 663, 844; 2004, cc. 156, 279, 855; 2005, cc. 503, 572, 640, 739; 2006, c. 396; 2008, c. 420.)

Editor's note. — Acts 2001, cc. 334, 558 and 663 amended § 2.1-20.1, from which this section is derived. Pursuant to § 30-152, Acts 2001, cc. 334, 558 and 663 have been given effect in this section as set out above.

For the definition of "terminally ill," defined under § 1861(dd)(3)(A) of the Social Security Act, referred to in subdivision B 15 above, see 42 U.S.C.S. § 1395x(dd)(3)(A).

Acts 2004, c. 156 repealed Acts 1999, c. 941, cl. 5, which had provided that the provisions of c. 941 would expire on July 1, 2004. Therefore, the 1999 amendments will not expire.

Acts 2004, c. 855, cl. 2, provides: "That this act shall take effect 60 days following the effective date of the regulations promulgated by the Board of Medicine and Board of Nursing required by the third enactment clause of this act." Emergency regulations took effect July 15, 2004.

Acts 2004, c. 855, cl. 3, provides: "That the Board of Medicine and Board of Nursing shall amend regulations governing the licensure of nurse practitioners to be effective within 280 days of enactment of this act. Such amendments shall require inclusion of the nurse practitioner's authority for signatures, certifications, stamps, verifications, affidavits and endorsements in the written protocol between the supervising physician and the nurse practitioner."

Acts 2008, c. 879, effective for the biennium ending June 30, 2010, in Item 85 A, provides: "Administration of any health benefit plan or plans provided for state employees pursuant to § 2.2-2818, Code of Virginia, shall be subject to the review of the Virginia Council on Human Resources, which is provided for in § 2.2-2675, Code of Virginia. Additionally, the department shall report any proposed changes in premiums, benefits, carriers, or provider networks to the Governor and the Chairmen of the House Appropriations and Senate Finance Committees at least sixty days prior to implementation."

The 2008 amendments. — The 2008 amendment by c. 420 deleted subdivision B 2, which read: "Include coverage for the treatment of breast cancer by dose-intensive chemotherapy with autologous bone marrow transplants or stem cell support when performed at a clinical program authorized to provide such therapies as a part of clinical trials sponsored by the National Cancer Institute. For persons previously covered under the plan, there shall be no denial of coverage due to the existence of a preexisting condition" and renumbered remaining subdivisions accordingly.

Michie's Jurisprudence. — For related discussion, see 17 M.J. State, § 9.

OPINIONS OF THE ATTORNEY GENERAL

Certain individuals entitled to health benefits under the Line of Duty Act may receive those benefits through the state health benefits program. See opinion of Attorney General to Ms. Sara Redding Wilson, Director, Department of Human Resource Management, 03-090 (12/18/03).

§ 2.2-2818.1. Supplemental health insurance coverage; state employees eligible for military health insurance coverage. — A. The Department of Human Resource Management may offer a voluntary supplemental health coverage program for state employees under this section.

B. Under the supplemental health coverage program, a state employee who is eligible to participate in the health insurance program pursuant to § 2.2-2818 and who is also eligible for benefits under the TRICARE Military Health System may elect to receive primary coverage under the TRICARE Military Health System, and receive supplemental health coverage under the state program. An individual participating in the supplemental health coverage program does not receive primary coverage through the group benefits program, but receives supplemental health coverage under this section.

C. The cost of supplemental health coverage provided under this section shall be paid in the same manner that the cost of basic coverage is paid under § 2.2-2818.

D. The Department of Human Resource Management may not implement a supplemental health coverage program under this section if the Department finds that the program would not be cost-effective or would otherwise not be advantageous to the state or program participants.

E. Notwithstanding any other provision of this section, if the Department of Human Resource Management establishes a supplemental health coverage program, the amount of the contribution made for an individual who elects to receive supplemental health coverage under the program may be reduced, as provided in the general appropriations act, to reflect the reduced cost of the supplemental health coverage. (2006, c. 93.)

§ 2.2-2819. Purchase of continued health insurance coverage by the surviving spouse and any dependents of an active or retired state employee. — A. The surviving spouse and any dependents of an active state employee or a retired state employee may, upon proper application to the Department of Human Resource Management, purchase continued health insurance coverage on the following conditions: (i) on the date of death, the state employee participated in a health insurance plan administered by the Department of Human Resource Management pursuant to § 2.2-2818 or § 2.2-1204 and (ii) on the date of the deceased's death, the applicants were included in the health insurance plan in condition (i) of this subsection. The health insurance plans administered by the Department of Human Resource Management pursuant to § 2.2-2818 or § 2.2-1204 shall provide means whereby coverage for the spouse and dependents of active or retired state employees may be purchased.

B. Any application to purchase continued health insurance coverage hereunder shall be made in writing to the Department of Human Resource Management within sixty days of the date of the deceased's death. The time for making application may be extended by the Department for good cause shown.

C. In addition to any necessary information requested by the Department of Human Resource Management, the application shall state whether conditions

(i) and (ii) set forth in subsection A have been met. If the Department states that such conditions have not been met, the Department shall conduct an informal fact-finding conference or consultation with the applicant pursuant to § 2.2-4019 of the Administrative Process Act (§ 2.2-4000 et seq.). Upon scheduling the conference or consultation, the provisions of the Administrative Process Act shall apply thereafter.

D. Upon payment of any required premiums, coverage shall automatically be extended during the period for making application and shall be effective retroactive to the date of the deceased's death.

E. The terms, conditions, and costs of continued health insurance coverage purchased hereunder shall be subject to administration by the Department of Human Resource Management. The Department may increase the cost of coverage consistent with its administration of health insurance plans under § 2.2-2818 or § 2.2-1204.

F. For the surviving spouse, continued health insurance coverage purchased hereunder shall automatically terminate upon occurrence of any of the following: (i) death, (ii) remarriage, (iii) alternate health insurance coverage being obtained, or (iv) any applicable condition outlined in the policies and procedures of the Department of Human Resource Management governing health insurance plans administered pursuant to § 2.2-2818 or § 2.2-1204.

G. For any surviving dependents, continued health insurance coverage purchased hereunder shall automatically terminate upon occurrence of any of the following: (i) death; (ii) marriage; (iii) alternate health insurance coverage being obtained; (iv) attaining the age of twenty-one, unless the dependent is (a) a full-time college student, in which event coverage shall not terminate until such dependent has either attained the age of twenty-five or until such time as the dependent ceases to be a full-time college student, whichever occurs first, or (b) under a mental or physical disability, in which event coverage shall not terminate until three months following cessation of the disability; or (v) any applicable condition outlined in the policies and procedures of the Department of Human Resource Management governing health insurance plans administered pursuant to § 2.2-2818 or § 2.2-1204. (1995, c. 179, § 2.1-20.1:03; 1997, c. 886; 2000, cc. 66, 657; 2001, c. 844.)

§ 2.2-2820. Purchase of health insurance coverage by part-time state employees. — A. Any part-time state employee employed by the Commonwealth and working twenty or more hours per week for a period of at least six months may, upon proper application to the Department of Human Resource Management (the Department), to purchase health insurance coverage for himself through a health insurance plan administered by the Department. This plan for part-time employees may differ from the other plans sponsored by the Department for state employees and shall be exempt from all mandates contained in § 2.2-2818.

B. Applications to purchase health insurance coverage under this section shall be made on an application form prescribed by the Department. In addition to his application, the applicant shall provide any necessary supporting documents requested by the Department.

C. Upon payment of the required premiums, coverage shall be effective retroactive to the date of the application.

D. The terms, conditions, and costs of health insurance coverage purchased under this section shall be subject to administration by the Department. The Department may increase the cost of coverage consistent with its administration of the health insurance plans under § 2.2-2818.

E. Health insurance coverage purchased under this section shall automatically terminate upon the occurrence of any of the following: (i) the applicant's death, (ii) alternate health insurance coverage being obtained by the applicant,

(iii) the applicant's separation from state service, or (iv) any applicable condition outlined in the policies and procedures of the Department governing its administration of health insurance plans pursuant to § 2.2-2818. (1999, c. 758, § 2.1-20.1:06; 2000, cc. 66, 657; 2001, c. 844.)

§ **2.2-2820.1:** Repealed by Acts 2004, c. 58.

§ **2.2-2821. Workers' compensation insurance plan for state employees trust fund for payment of claims.** — A. The Workers' Compensation Insurance Program (the Program) established under former § 2.1-526.10 and administered by the Department of General Services through its Division of Risk Management is hereby continued and transferred to the Department of Human Resource Management.

B. The Program shall be established through a program of self-insurance, purchased insurance or a combination of self-insurance and purchased insurance that is determined to be the most cost effective on a statewide basis and will be of less cost to the Commonwealth than the aggregate of individual agency policies. If the Department of Human Resource Management is informed by the Office of the Attorney General that it will not provide a defense due to a conflict or other appropriate reason, the Department shall provide for payment of attorneys' fees and expenses incurred in defending workers' compensation claims against the Commonwealth, its agencies and institutions.

C. The Program shall provide for the establishment of a trust fund for the payment of claims covered under the Program. The funds shall be invested as provided in § 2.2-1806, and interest shall be added to the fund as earned. The trust fund shall also provide for payment of administrative costs, contractual costs, and other necessary expenses related to the administration of the Program.

D. The Program shall be submitted to the Governor for approval prior to implementation.

E. The Department of Human Resource Management may confer with the proper officials or employees of all agencies and institutions of the Commonwealth for the purpose of providing loss prevention programs. The Department may seek the assistance of state agencies, risk management consulting companies, loss prevention engineering companies, and their representatives in devising means by which causes of loss may be reduced or eliminated.

F. Information contained in investigative reports of any state or local police department, sheriff's office, fire department or fire marshal relevant to the Program established pursuant to this section shall be made available upon request by the Department. Information so requested shall be furnished within a reasonable time, not to exceed thirty days. (2000, cc. 633, 697, § 2.1-114.5:02; 2001, c. 844.)

Cross references. — As to the duties of the Department of Human Resource Management, see § 2.2-1201.

Editor's note. — Section 2.1-526.10, referred to in subsection A, was repealed by Acts 2001, c. 844.

Acts 2000, cc. 633 and 697, cl. 3, provide: "That the Governor may transfer an appropriation, or any portion thereof, or any employees, within an agency established, abolished or otherwise affected by the provisions of this act or from one such agency to another, to support the changes in organization or responsibility resulting from or required by the provisions of this act."

Acts 2000, cc. 633 and 697, cl. 4, provide: "That, as of the effective date of this act, the Department of Personnel and Training shall be deemed successor in interest to the Department of General Services to the extent that this act transfers powers and duties. All right, title and interest in and to any real or tangible personal property vested in the Department of General Services to the extent that this act transfers powers and duties as of the effective date of this act shall be transferred to and taken as standing in the name of the Department of Personnel and Training."

§ 2.2-2821.1. Leave for bone marrow or organ donation. — State employees shall be allowed up to thirty days of paid leave in any calendar year, in addition to other paid leave, to serve as bone marrow or organ donors. The Department shall develop personnel policies providing for the use of such leave. For the purposes of this section, *"state employee"* means any person who is regularly employed full time on a salaried basis, whose tenure is not restricted as to temporary or provisional appointment, in the service of, and whose compensation is payable, no more often than biweekly, in whole or in part, by the Commonwealth or any department, institution, or agency thereof. (2001, c. 714, § 2.1-114.5:03.)

Editor's note. — Acts 2001, c. 714 enacted § 2.1-114.5:03, from which this section is derived. Pursuant to § 30-152, Acts 2001, c. 714 has been given effect in this section as set out above.

§ 2.2-2821.2. Leave for volunteer fire and rescue service. — State employees shall be allowed up to sixteen hours of paid leave in any calendar year, in addition to other paid leave, to serve with a volunteer fire department and rescue squad or auxiliary unit thereof that has been recognized in accordance with § 15.2-955 by an ordinance or resolution of the political subdivision where the volunteer fire department or rescue squad is located as being a part of the safety program of such political subdivision. The Department shall develop personnel policies providing for the use of such leave. For the purposes of this section, "state employee" means any person who is regularly employed full time on a salaried basis, whose tenure is not restricted as to temporary or provisional appointment, in the service of, and whose compensation is payable, no more often than biweekly, in whole or in part, by the Commonwealth or any department, institution, or agency thereof. (2001, c. 760, § 2.1-114.5:04.)

Editor's note. — Acts 2001, c. 760 enacted § 2.1-114.5:04, from which this section is derived. Pursuant to § 30-152, Acts 2001, c. 760 has been given effect in this section as set out above.

§ 2.2-2822. Ownership of patents and copyrights developed by state employees. — Patents, copyrights or materials that were potentially patentable or copyrightable developed by a state employee during working hours or within the scope of his employment or when using state-owned or state-controlled facilities shall be the property of the Commonwealth. The Governor shall set such policies as he deems necessary to implement this section.

This section shall not apply to employees of public institutions of higher education who shall be subject to the patent and copyright policies of the institution employing them. (1985, c. 502, § 2.1-20.1:1; 2001, c. 844.)

§ 2.2-2823. Traveling expenses on state business; public or private transportation. — A. Pursuant to § 2.2-2825, any person traveling on state business shall be entitled to reimbursement for certain actual expenses as are necessary and ordinarily incidental to travel. If transportation is by public means, reimbursement shall be at the actual cost thereof. If transportation is by private means, reimbursement shall be at the rate as specified in the current general appropriation act.

B. Mileage allowed under subsection A or § 30-19.15 shall be construed to include all costs incident to the maintenance and operation of private transportation except storage and parking fees, turnpike, tunnel, ferry and bridge tolls. (Code 1950, §§ 14-5, 14-5.4; 1954, c. 709; 1964, c. 386, §§ 14.1-5, 14.1-9; 1968, c. 711; 1969, Ex. Sess., c. 4; 1972, cc. 69, 719; 1975, c. 132; 1976, c. 385;

1977, c. 493; 1980, c. 224; 1984, c. 161; 1995, c. 358; 1998, c. 872, §§ 2.1-20.8, 2.1-20.12; 2001, c. 844.)

Cross references. — As to payment by the Department of Social Services of assistant attorney for the Commonwealth for prosecution of public assistance fraud cases, see § 63.2-525. As to payment by the Department of Social Services for legal services, notwithstanding any provision of §§ 2.2-2814, 2.2-2815, 2.2-2816, 2.2-2823, 2.2-2824, 2.2-2825, or 2.2-2826, see § 63.2-1948.

§ 2.2-2824. Monitoring travel expenses while on state business. — It shall be the duty of the head of each state agency, commission, or board, or his designee, or any other official granted supervisory control for the expending of state funds to examine all applications for the reimbursement of personal funds expended by any employee of such agency, commission, or board for travel while conducting official business for state government. All such expenditures shall be necessary and reasonable for the efficient and effective operation of the agency, commission or board. (1977, c. 493, § 14.1-5.1; 1998, c. 872, § 2.1-20.9; 2001, c. 844.)

Cross references. — As to payment by the Department of Social Services of assistant attorney for the Commonwealth for prosecution of public assistance fraud cases, see § 63.2-525. As to payment by the Department of Social Services for legal services, notwithstanding any provision of §§ 2.2-2814, 2.2-2815, 2.2-2816, 2.2-2823, 2.2-2824, 2.2-2825, or 2.2-2826, see § 63.2-1948.

§ 2.2-2825. Reimbursement for certain travel expenditures; restrictions on reimbursement. — Persons conducting official business of the Commonwealth shall be reimbursed for their reasonable and necessary travel expenditures that shall include transportation as provided in § 2.2-2823, parking, and lodging. Receipts for lodging and transportation, if by other than privately owned automobile or state-owned vehicle, shall be submitted with any travel expense account presented to the Comptroller for payment. Transportation by common carrier shall be limited to the cost for travel by the most direct and practical route, and in amounts not exceeding those for tourist or coach class accommodations, if such accommodations are available. Travel shall be over the most direct and practical route. Reimbursement for the cost of transportation shall not be certified to the Comptroller for payment by state agencies in excess of the reimbursement allowed in § 2.2-2823 except in an emergency or, when in the interest of the Commonwealth, a greater expense is justified, the facts in each such instance to be stated in the expense account.

Persons conducting official business of the Commonwealth shall be reimbursed for the reasonable and necessary actual costs of meals, gratuities, and other incidental expenses. At the discretion of the governing authority, a per diem payment may be made in lieu of this reimbursement for meals, gratuities, and other incidental expenses.

The Comptroller shall establish policies on travel expenses for all agencies in the executive branch of state government. Policies on travel expenses for the legislative branch, judicial branch, and independent agencies shall be established by the appropriate governing authority. (1954, c. 709, § 14-5.1; 1964, c. 386, § 14.1-6; 1977, c. 493, § 14.1-5.2; 1995, c. 358; 1998, c. 872, § 2.1-20.10; 2001, c. 844.)

Cross references. — As to compensation for members of Joint Commission on Health Care, see § 30-168.2. As to payment by the Department of Social Services of assistant attorney for the Commonwealth for prosecution of public assistance fraud cases, see § 63.2-525. As to reimbursement of travel expenses for members of the Out-of-Family Investigations Advisory Committee, see § 63.2-1527. As to payment by the Department of Social Services for legal services, notwithstanding any provision of §§ 2.2-2814, 2.2-2815, 2.2-2816, 2.2-2823, 2.2-2824, 2.2-2825, or 2.2-2826, see § 63.2-1948.

Editor's note. — Acts 2003, c. 601, cl. 1, provides: "§ 1. The governing bodies of the Virginia Economic Development Partnership, the Virginia Tourism Authority, and the Virginia Port Authority shall establish policies on travel expenses that are substantially consistent with the policies on travel expenses established by the State Comptroller pursuant to § 2.2-2825. If a particular travel situation is not covered by the policies established pursuant to this act or the amount of expense or reimbursement is greater than 10 percent of what is allowed by such policies, then the traveler must get the approval of the cabinet secretary to which his agency reports as indicated in Chapter 2 (§ 2.2-200 et seq.) of Title 2.2."

§ 2.2-2826. Travel expense accounts; review by Comptroller. — All travel expense accounts shall be submitted on forms prescribed or approved by the Comptroller. Review shall be made by the Comptroller of such accounts subject to the provisions of § 2.2-1822. If accounts do not conform to the provisions of § 2.2-2825, the Comptroller shall return those accounts to the agency or commission with an explanation of why they do not conform. The agency or commission may correct the accounts and resubmit them to the Comptroller. (1954, c. 709, § 14-5.5; 1964, c. 386, § 14.1-10; 1977, c. 493, § 14.1-5.3; 1998, c. 872, § 2.1-20.11; 2001, c. 844.)

Cross references. — As to payment by the Department of Social Services of assistant attorney for the Commonwealth for prosecution of public assistance fraud cases, see § 63.2-525. As to payment by the Department of Social Services for legal services, notwithstanding any provision of §§ 2.2-2814, 2.2-2815, 2.2-2816, 2.2-2823, 2.2-2824, 2.2-2825, or 2.2-2826, see § 63.2-1948.

§ 2.2-2827. Restrictions on state employee access to information infrastructure. — A. For the purpose of this section:

"Agency" means any agency, authority, board, department, division, commission, institution, public institution of higher education, bureau, or like governmental entity of the Commonwealth, except the Department of State Police.

"Information infrastructure" means telecommunications, cable, and computer networks and includes the Internet, the World Wide Web, Usenet, bulletin board systems, on-line systems, and telephone networks.

"Sexually explicit content" means (i) any description of or (ii) any picture, photograph, drawing, motion picture film, digital image or similar visual representation depicting sexual bestiality, a lewd exhibition of nudity, as nudity is defined in § 18.2-390, sexual excitement, sexual conduct or sadomasochistic abuse, as also defined in § 18.2-390, coprophilia, urophilia, or fetishism.

B. Except to the extent required in conjunction with a bona fide, agency-approved research project or other agency-approved undertaking, no agency employee shall utilize agency-owned or agency-leased computer equipment to access, download, print or store any information infrastructure files or services having sexually explicit content. Agency approvals shall be given in writing by agency heads, and any such approvals shall be available to the public under the provisions of the Virginia Freedom of Information Act (§ 2.2-3700).

C. All agencies shall immediately furnish their current employees copies of this section's provisions, and shall furnish all new employees copies of this section concurrent with authorizing them to use agency computers. (1996, c. 382, §§ 2.1-804, 2.1-805, 2.1-806; 1999, c. 384; 2001, c. 844.)

Law Review. — For note, "Who Owns Academic Freedom?: The Standard for Academic Free Speech at Public Universities," see 59 Wash. & Lee L. Rev. 299 (2002). For note,

"Academic Freedom in Urofsky's Wake: Post September 11 Remarks on 'Who Owns Academic Freedom?,'" see 59 Wash. & Lee L. Rev. 361 (2002).

CASE NOTES

Editor's note. — The cases below were decided under former Title 2.1 or prior provisions.

Law upheld. — Although Virginia public university professors claimed they were entitled to access sexually explicit material in their capacity as state employees by using equipment owned or leased by the state, they acknowledged that the challenged aspect of this section did not affect speech by them in their capacity as private citizens speaking on matters of public concern; thus, the Act did not infringe the First Amendment rights of state employees. Urofsky v. Gilmore, 216 F.3d 401, 2000 U.S. App. LEXIS 14484 (4th Cir. 2000), cert. denied, 531 U.S. 1070, 121 S. Ct. 759, 148 L. Ed. 2d 662 (2001).

Since declaring that public employees, including teachers, do not forfeit First Amendment rights upon accepting public employment, the Supreme Court has focused its discussions of academic freedom solely on issues of institutional autonomy; because this section did not infringe the constitutional rights of public employees in general, it also did not violate the rights of professors. Urofsky v. Gilmore, 216 F.3d 401, 2000 U.S. App. LEXIS 14484 (4th Cir. 2000), cert. denied, 531 U.S. 1070, 121 S. Ct. 759, 148 L. Ed. 2d 662 (2001).

This section does not infringe upon First Amendment rights of state employees. Urofsky v. Gilmore, 167 F.3d 191 (4th. Cir. 1999), rehearing en banc, 216 F.3d 401 (4th Cir. 2000).

The act regulates the speech of individuals speaking in their capacity as Commonwealth employees, not as citizens, and thus the act does not touch upon a matter of public concern. Consequently, the speech may be restricted consistent with the First Amendment. Urofsky v. Gilmore, 167 F.3d 191 (4th. Cir. 1999), rehearing en banc, 216 F.3d 401 (4th Cir. 2000).

Plaintiffs' claim that this act violates their First Amendment right to academic freedom is foreclosed by this court's en banc decision in Boring. See Boring v. Buncombe County Bd. of Educ., 136 F.3d 364 (4th Cir.) (en banc), cert. denied, 142 L. Ed. 2d 36, 119 S. Ct. 47 (1998). Urofsky v. Gilmore, 167 F.3d 191 (4th. Cir. 1999), rehearing en banc, 216 F.3d 401 (4th Cir. 2000).

This act is not unconstitutionally vague because it gives a person of ordinary intelligence a reasonable opportunity to know what is prohibited. Urofsky v. Gilmore, 167 F.3d 191 (4th. Cir. 1999), rehearing en banc, 216 F.3d 401 (4th Cir. 2000).

§ 2.2-2828. How certain officers removed from office. — The Secretary of the Commonwealth, the State Treasurer, the Comptroller, the Superintendent of Public Instruction or the Commissioner of Agriculture and Consumer Services may be removed from office by joint vote of the two houses of the General Assembly, or, during the recess thereof, may be suspended by the Governor. This power shall not be exercised by the Governor except for misbehavior, incapacity, neglect of official duty, or acts performed without due authority of law. In any case in which this power is so exercised by the Governor, he shall fill the office by a temporary appointment, and report to the General Assembly, at the beginning of the next session thereof, the fact of such suspension and the cause therefor, whereupon the General Assembly shall determine whether such officer shall be restored or finally removed. (Code 1950, § 2-13; 1966, c. 677, § 2.1-17; 2001, c. 844.)

Cross references. — As to impeachment, see Va. Const., Art. IV, § 17. As to Governor's power to remove officers, see Va. Const., Art. V, § 10. As to removal of public officers, see § 24.2-230 et seq.

§ 2.2-2829. Disappearance of public officer; when office presumed vacant. — Notwithstanding any other provision of law relating to the length of time after which the continued absence of a person shall create a presumption of death, when a petition alleging that a person who is a public officer elected by the people or by the General Assembly or appointed by the Governor has disappeared and after diligent search cannot be found is presented to a court of record in the city or county in which the last known residence of the person is located, and when it appears to the satisfaction of the court that the circumstances surrounding the disappearance afford reasonable grounds for the belief that the person is dead, then the office held by such person shall be presumed to be vacant and the court shall enter an order to that effect. (1973, c. 168, § 2.1-17.1; 2001, c. 844.)

§ 2.2-2830. Governor to fill vacancy in any state office where no other provision is made by law; term of appointment; benefits. — A. When a vacancy occurs in any state office, whether the officer is elected by the people or the General Assembly, or is appointed by the Governor, and no other provision is made for filling the same, it shall be filled by the Governor.

B. If the office is one filled by election by the people, the appointee shall hold such office until the next general election, and thereafter until his successor qualifies, according to law. If the office is filled by an election by the General Assembly or appointment by the Governor, and such appointment requires confirmation of the Senate or the General Assembly, the appointee shall temporarily hold such office until thirty days after the commencement of the next session of the General Assembly. Notwithstanding any provision of law to the contrary, any individual temporarily appointed under this section shall be eligible for, receive, and accrue all benefits, retirement, health and life insurance, personnel and otherwise, due such appointee by virtue of his holding such office. (Code 1950, §§ 2-14, 2-15; 1966, c. 677, §§ 2.1-18, 2.1-19; 1981, c. 511; 2001, c. 844.)

CASE NOTES

Editor's note. — The case below was decided under former Title 2.1 or prior provisions.

Former corresponding section undertook to supplement Va. Const., Art. V, § 7, as to the power of the Governor to fill vacancies. Insofar as it accorded with Va. Const., Art. V, § 7, it was valid, but it could not be construed to make mandatory that which the Constitution has made discretionary, for this would be an invalid exercise of the legislative power. Allen v. Byrd, 151 Va. 21, 144 S.E. 469 (1928).

§ 2.2-2831. Payment of severance benefits; exceptions. — No severance benefit shall be provided to any state officer or employee except as specifically provided by law. The provisions of this section shall not apply to any severance benefit provided to (i) any officers or faculty of a public institution of higher education as defined in § 23-38.89 or (ii) a state officer or employee who is not eligible for a transitional severance benefit pursuant to Chapter 32 (§ 2.2-3200 et seq.) of this title. Nothing in this section shall be construed to prohibit payments in settlement of an employment dispute approved pursuant to § 2.2-514 or payments in satisfaction of a judgment. (2006, cc. 813, 902.)

CHAPTER 29.

Virginia Personnel Act.

§ 2.2-2900. Short title; purpose. — This chapter shall be known and may be cited as the "Virginia Personnel Act."

The purpose of this chapter is to ensure for the Commonwealth a system of personnel administration based on merit principles and objective methods of appointment, promotion, transfer, layoff, removal, discipline, and other incidents of state employment. (Code 1950, § 2-78; 1966, c. 677, § 2.1-110; 1970, c. 546; 2001, c. 844.)

Cross references. — As to the authority of the Governor to execute the provisions of this chapter, see § 2.2-103. As to the duties of agencies and their appointing authorities for the proper and efficient enforcement of this act, see § 2.2-602. As to the recovery of certain improper payments to state employees, see § 2.2-804. As procurement of information technology and telecommunications goods and services, see § 2.2-2012. As to the board of directors, its members, officers, and the Executive Director of the Virginia Commercial Space Flight Authority, see § 2.2-2203. As to exemption of the Virginia Commercial Space Flight Authority from personnel and procurement procedures, see § 2.2-2215. As to the members and President of the board of directors of the Innovative Technology Authority, see § 2.2-2220. As to the exemption of the Virginia Economic Development Partnership Authority from personnel and procurement procedures, see § 2.2-2244. As to the exemption of the Virginia Tourism Authority from personnel and procurement procedures, see § 2.2-2325. As to eligibility for transitional severance benefits, see § 2.2-3202. As to appointment of division heads by the Commissioner of Social Services, subject to the provisions of this chapter, see § 63.2-210.

Editor's note. — Acts 1995, c. 152 and Acts 1995, c. 811 provided for incentives for voluntary terminations of certain state employees in 1995, and outlined applicable terms and conditions.

Law Review. — For article, "Job Security for Public Employees," see 31 Wash. & Lee L. Rev. 545 (1974).

CASE NOTES

Legislative intent to preclude judicial review. — The "final authority" language in former § 2.1-114.5:6 (7) supported and was consistent with a legislative intent shown throughout the act to preclude judicial review in certain areas. Murray v. Stokes, 237 Va. 653, 378 S.E.2d 834 (1989) (decided under prior law).

Judicial review of the interpretation of a personnel policy regarding employee compensation by the Director of the Department of Personnel and Training (now Department of Human Resource Management) is precluded under the Virginia Personnel Act, and therefore, the trial court had no jurisdiction to entertain a bill of complaint seeking review of the interpretation of Rule 8.3(d) of the Department's rules by the director of that department. Murray v. Stokes, 237 Va. 653, 378 S.E.2d 834 (1989) (decided under prior law).

Applied in Boynton v. Kilgore, 271 Va. 220, 623 S.E.2d 922, 2006 Va. LEXIS 2 (2006).

CIRCUIT COURT OPINIONS

Attorney General employees were not covered by the Virginia Personnel Act. — Attorney General employees were not covered by the Virginia Personnel Act, § 2.2-2900 et seq., so former employees of Attorney General's office were not eligible for severance benefits under the Work Force Transition Act, § 2.2-3203 et seq., because that eligibility was dependent on coverage under the Virginia Personnel Act. Boynton v. Kilgore, 66 Va. Cir. 37, 2004 Va. Cir. LEXIS 339 (Richmond Aug. 27, 2004), aff'd, 271 Va. 220, 623 S.E.2d 922 (2006).

§ 2.2-2901. Appointments, promotions and tenure based upon merit and fitness. — A. In accordance with the provisions of this chapter all appointments and promotions to and tenure in positions in the service of the Commonwealth shall be based upon merit and fitness, to be ascertained, as far as possible, by the competitive rating of qualifications by the respective appointing authorities.

Persons holding positions in the service of the Commonwealth on July 1, 1952, shall be deemed to be holding their positions as though they had received appointment under the terms of this chapter.

B. Persons who leave the service of the Commonwealth for service in any of the armed forces of the United States shall be entitled to be restored to such positions upon the termination of their service with the armed forces, provided such persons, except for good cause shown, have filed an application for restoration to such positions within 90 calendar days following such termination of military service, accompanied by a certificate attesting that the military duty was satisfactorily performed. Such persons shall thereafter hold such positions as though they had received appointment under the terms of this chapter, except as to any such position which, in the meantime, may have been abolished. Any such former employee returning to, or applying for, employment in the state service, as provided by this section, shall be considered as having at least as favorable a status with reference to this chapter as he would have occupied if his service had been continuous.

C. No establishment of a position or rate of pay, and no change in rate of pay shall become effective except on order of the appointing authority and approval by the Governor. This subsection shall not apply to any position the compensation of which is at a rate of $1,200 per annum or less.

D. In order to attract and retain professional auditors, accountants and staff members in the service of the Auditor of Public Accounts, the Joint Legislative Audit and Review Commission may establish scales of pay for such positions notwithstanding the provisions of this chapter. Such scales when established and certified to the Department of Human Resource Management and the Comptroller shall be applicable in the stead of the scales established under the personnel plan.

E. The Board of Visitors of public institutions of higher education shall establish policies for the designation of administrative and professional faculty positions at institutions of higher education. Those designations shall be reserved for positions that require a high level of administrative independence, responsibility, and oversight within the organization or specialized expertise within a given field as defined by the Board of Visitors. The authority under this subsection to establish policies for the designation of administrative and professional faculty positions shall be granted only to those institutions that meet the conditions prescribed in subsection B of § 23-38.88. (Code 1950, § 2-79; 1956, c. 380; 1966, c. 677, § 2.1-111; 1968, c. 784; 1972, c. 582; 1973, c. 507; 2000, cc. 66, 657; 2001, c. 844; 2005, cc. 933, 945.)

Cross references. — As to liberal construction of legislation of this type, see note to § 51.1-812.

CASE NOTES

Employees of the Office of the Attorney General were ineligible for Workforce Transition Act benefits. — Circuit court properly sustained a demurrer filed by defendant, the Office of the Attorney General who employed a group of former employees, which was filed in response to the employees' amended motion for judgment, as the employees were not covered by the Virginia Personnel Act, because they were exempt under § 2.2-2905; hence, the employees were ineligible to receive Workforce Transition Act benefits under clause (i) of subsection A of § 2.2-3202. Boynton v. Kilgore, 271 Va. 220, 623 S.E.2d 922, 2006 Va. LEXIS 2 (2006).

§ 2.2-2902. Use of tobacco products by state employees. — No employee of or applicant for employment with the Commonwealth shall be required, as a condition of employment, to smoke or use tobacco products on the job, or to abstain from smoking or using tobacco products outside the course of his employment, provided that this section shall not apply to those classes of employees to which § 27-40.1 or § 51.1-813 is applicable. (1989, c. 511, § 15.1-29.18; 1997, c. 587, § 2.1-111.1; 2001, c. 844.)

§ 2.2-2902.1. Rights of state employees to contact elected officials. — Nothing in this chapter or Chapter 12 (§ 2.2-1200 et seq.) of this title shall be construed to prohibit or otherwise restrict the right of any state employee to express opinions to state or local elected officials on matters of public concern, nor shall a state employee be subject to acts of retaliation because the employee has expressed such opinions.

For the purposes of this section *"matters of public concern"* means those matters of interest to the community as a whole, whether for social, political, or other reasons and shall include discussions that disclose any (i) evidence of corruption, impropriety, or other malfeasance on the part of government officials; (ii) violations of law; or (iii) incidence of fraud, abuse, or gross mismanagement. (2005, c. 483.)

§ 2.2-2903. Grade or rating increase and other preferences for veterans. — A. In a manner consistent with federal and state law, if any veteran applies for employment with the Commonwealth that is based on the passing of any written examination, the veteran's grade or rating on such examination shall be increased by five percent. However, if the veteran has a service-connected disability rating fixed by the United States Veterans Administration, his grade or rating shall be increased by 10 percent on such written examination. Such increases shall apply only if the veteran passes such examination.

B. In a manner consistent with federal and state law, if any veteran applies for employment with the Commonwealth that is not based on the passing of any examination, such veteran shall be given preference by the Commonwealth during the selection process, provided that such veteran meets all of the knowledge, skill, and ability requirements for the available position. Additional consideration shall also be given to veterans who have a service-connected disability rating fixed by the United States Veterans Administration. The Department of Human Resource Management shall develop and distribute guidelines as an addendum to the Hiring Policy for Executive Branch agencies to provide guidance to agencies to comply with the veterans' preference requirement.

C. If any veteran is denied employment with the Commonwealth, he shall be entitled, to the extent permitted by law, to request and inspect information regarding the reasons for such denial.

D. For purposes of this section, *"veteran"* means any person who has received an honorable discharge and has (i) provided more than 180 consecutive days of full-time, active-duty service in the armed forces of the United States or reserve components thereof, including the National Guard, or (ii) has a service-connected disability rating fixed by the United States Veterans Affairs. (Code 1950, § 2-80; 1952, c. 119; 1966, c. 677, § 2.1-112; 1985, c. 115; 1997, c. 309; 2001, c. 844; 2005, c. 413; 2007, cc. 336, 605.)

The 2007 amendments. — The 2007 amendments by cc. 336 and 605 are identical, and substituted "veteran" for "veteran's military service" and "given preference" for "taken into consideration" in the first sentence and added the third sentence of subsection B.

Law Review. — For comment on veterans' preference, see 26 Wash. & Lee L. Rev. 160 (1969).

CIRCUIT COURT OPINIONS

Preference not properly applied. — Virginia Employment Commission did not properly apply subsection B of § 2.2-2903 where the hiring authority declined to consider the applicant's military service and service-connected disability because the applicant was not otherwise equal to the successful candidate; § 2.2-2903 required that a veteran's military service be taken into account during the selection process. Hudson v. Va. Empl. Comm'n, 69 Va. Cir. 318, 2005 Va. Cir. LEXIS 365 (Richmond 2005).

Executive order reaffirmed statute. — Executive order was merely a reaffirmation of § 2.2-2903, not an expansion of it, where the executive order directed state agency heads to renew their commitment to veterans' preference in hiring; subsection B of § 2.2-2903, indeed, granted veterans a preference, as non-veterans had no military service for an agency to consider. Hudson v. Va. Empl. Comm'n, 69 Va. Cir. 318, 2005 Va. Cir. LEXIS 365 (Richmond 2005).

§ 2.2-2903.1. State employees ordered to active military service. — A. As used in this section, unless the context requires a different meaning:

"Active military duty" means federally funded military duty as (i) a member of the armed forces of the United States on active duty pursuant to Title 10 U.S.C. or (ii) a member of the Virginia National Guard on active duty pursuant to either Title 10 or Title 32 U.S.C.

"State employee" means any person who is regularly employed full time on either a salaried or wage basis, whose tenure is not restricted as to temporary or provisional appointment, in the service of, and whose compensation is payable, no more often than biweekly, in whole or in part, by the Commonwealth or any department, institution or agency thereof.

B. For any state employee who has been ordered to active military service in the armed forces of the United States or in the organized reserve forces of any of the armed services of the United States or of the Virginia National Guard, the Commonwealth shall allow the use of accrued annual leave for active military duty according to personnel policies developed by the Department of Human Resource Management. (2003, c. 789.)

§ 2.2-2904. Classification of persons who have passed certified professional secretary examination. — Clerical personnel who have passed all parts of the certified professional secretary examination, evidenced by certification by the Institute for Certifying Secretaries, a department of the National Secretaries Association (International), or the professional legal secretary examination, evidenced by certification by the Certifying Board of the National Association of Legal Secretaries (International), shall be assured that this certification will be taken into consideration when opportunity for promotion becomes available. (1975, c. 393, § 2.1-114.1; 1977, c. 104; 2001, c. 844.)

§ 2.2-2905. Certain officers and employees exempt from chapter. — The provisions of this chapter shall not apply to:

1. Officers and employees for whom the Constitution specifically directs the manner of selection;
2. Officers and employees of the Supreme Court and the Court of Appeals;
3. Officers appointed by the Governor, whether confirmation by the General Assembly or by either house thereof is required or not;
4. Officers elected by popular vote or by the General Assembly or either house thereof;
5. Members of boards and commissions however selected;

6. Judges, referees, receivers, arbiters, masters and commissioners in chancery, commissioners of accounts, and any other persons appointed by any court to exercise judicial functions, and jurors and notaries public;

7. Officers and employees of the General Assembly and persons employed to conduct temporary or special inquiries, investigations, or examinations on its behalf;

8. The presidents, and teaching and research staffs of state educational institutions;

9. Commissioned officers and enlisted personnel of the National Guard and the naval militia;

10. Student employees in institutions of learning, and patient or inmate help in other state institutions;

11. Upon general or special authorization of the Governor, laborers, temporary employees and employees compensated on an hourly or daily basis;

12. County, city, town and district officers, deputies, assistants and employees;

13. The employees of the Virginia Workers' Compensation Commission;

14. The officers and employees of the Virginia Retirement System;

15. Employees whose positions are identified by the State Council of Higher Education and the boards of the Virginia Museum of Fine Arts, The Science Museum of Virginia, the Jamestown-Yorktown Foundation, the Frontier Culture Museum of Virginia, the Virginia Museum of Natural History and The Library of Virginia, and approved by the Director of the Department of Human Resource Management as requiring specialized and professional training;

16. Employees of the State Lottery Department;

17. Production workers for the Virginia Industries for the Blind Sheltered Workshop programs;

18. Employees of the Virginia Commonwealth University Health System Authority;

19. Employees of the University of Virginia Medical Center. Any changes in compensation plans for such employees shall be subject to the review and approval of the Board of Visitors of the University of Virginia. The University of Virginia shall ensure that its procedures for hiring University of Virginia Medical Center personnel are based on merit and fitness. Such employees shall remain subject to the provisions of the State Grievance Procedure (§ 2.2-3000 et seq.);

20. In executive branch agencies the employee who has accepted serving in the capacity of chief deputy, or equivalent, and the employee who has accepted serving in the capacity of a confidential assistant for policy or administration. An employee serving in either one of these two positions shall be deemed to serve on an employment-at-will basis. An agency may not exceed two employees who serve in this exempt capacity;

21. Employees of Virginia Correctional Enterprises. Such employees shall remain subject to the provisions of the State Grievance Procedure (§ 2.2-3000 et seq.);

22. Officers and employees of the Virginia Port Authority;

23. Employees of the Virginia College Savings Plan;

24. Directors of state facilities operated by the Department of Mental Health, Mental Retardation and Substance Abuse Services employed or reemployed by the Commissioner after July 1, 1999, under a contract pursuant to § 37.2-707. Such employees shall remain subject to the provisions of the State Grievance Procedure (§ 2.2-3000 et seq.);

25. The Director of the Virginia Office for Protection and Advocacy;

26. Employees of the Virginia Tobacco Settlement Foundation. Such employees shall be treated as state employees for purposes of participation in the Virginia Retirement System, health insurance, and all other employee benefits offered by the Commonwealth to its classified employees; and

27. Employees of the Virginia Indigent Defense Commission. (Code 1950, § 2-84; 1966, c. 677, § 2.1-116; 1973, c. 401; 1981, c. 8; 1982, c. 582; 1984, cc. 290, 703; 1985, c. 596; 1987, c. 531; 1989, c. 560; 1990, c. 937; 1992, Sp. Sess., c. 5; 1993, c. 510; 1994, cc. 48, 64, 653; 1995, c. 757; 1996, cc. 53, 905, 933, 995, 1046; 1997, cc. 232, 711, 785, 861; 1999, c. 576; 2000, cc. 66, 382, 400, 657, 720; 2001, c. 844; 2002, cc. 271, 572; 2003, c. 652; 2005, c. 716; 2007, c. 192.)

Editor's note. — Acts 1995, c. 152 and Acts 1995, c. 811 provided for incentives for voluntary terminations of certain state employees in 1995, and outlined applicable terms and conditions.

The 2007 amendments. — The 2007 amendment by c. 192 added subdivision 27 and made related changes.

CASE NOTES

Editor's note. — Most of the cases below were decided under former Title 2.1 or prior provisions.

Virginia's layoff-rights scheme and rules on exemptions circumscribe property interest in continued employment. — Although a nonprobationary employee has a property interest in continued employment that is created by the state, the scope of this interest is circumscribed by Virginia's rules on exemptions from the classified employment scheme and from access to the grievance procedure and by Virginia's layoff-rights scheme. Mandel v. Allen, 889 F. Supp. 857 (E.D. Va. 1995), aff'd, 81 F.3d 478 (4th Cir. 1996).

No property interest when statute makes exercise of classification power non-grievable. — Where, as in the relevant Virginia statutes, the state statute vests the power to classify solely in management and then makes the exercise of that power non-grievable, there can be no property interest in the classification. Mandel v. Allen, 889 F. Supp. 857 (E.D. Va. 1995), aff'd, 81 F.3d 478 (4th Cir. 1996).

This section specifically grants state officials the power to take actions that directly or indirectly cause changes in the classification status of state employees. Accordingly, plaintiffs possessed no entitlement and thus no property right to a continued classification. Mandel v. Allen, 81 F.3d 478 (4th Cir. 1996).

Appropriate to presume change in reporting line is for legitimate reasons. — The appropriate course is to presume that a change in an employee's reporting line occurs for legitimate systemic reasons absent a showing of pretext by the employee. Mandel v. Allen, 889 F. Supp. 857 (E.D. Va. 1995), aff'd, 81 F.3d 478 (4th Cir. 1996).

Plaintiff has burden to show state avoiding procedural due process. — To present sufficient evidence that the state in justifying elimination of positions is seeking to use administrative efficiency as a pretext for avoiding procedural due process is the plaintiff's burden. The burden is not onerous, nor does it necessarily require a "smoking gun" memorandum or the like. It may not be satisfied by conjecture or surmise. Mandel v. Allen, 889 F. Supp. 857 (E.D. Va. 1995), aff'd, 81 F.3d 478 (4th Cir. 1996).

Retroactive application of 1985 amendment. — Of course, a state official who simply enforces a presumptively valid state statute will rarely lose his immunity from suit. However, two defendants in instant case did not simply enforce a presumptively valid state statute. Rather, totally disregarding long-standing Virginia law prohibiting new legislation from being construed to eliminate pre-existing substantive rights, they attempted to apply the 1985 amendment to former § 2.1-116 (see now this section) retroactively to do precisely this. Moreover, they did this in the face of several holdings of this court that the act established a property interest in continued public employment, and a holding of the Virginia Supreme Court that the right to continued public employment is substantive and cannot be retroactively eliminated. Garraghty v. Virginia, Dep't of Cors., 52 F.3d 1274 (4th Cir. 1995).

Attorney General employees not covered. — Circuit court properly sustained a demurrer filed by defendant, the Office of the Attorney General who employed a group of former employees, which was filed in response to the employees' amended motion for judgment, as the employees were not covered by the Virginia Personnel Act, because they were exempt under subdivision 1; hence, the employees were ineligible to receive Workforce Transition Act benefits under § 2.2-3202. Boynton v. Kilgore, 271 Va. 220, 623 S.E.2d 922, 2006 Va. LEXIS 2 (2006).

CIRCUIT COURT OPINIONS

Attorney General employees not covered. — Attorney General employees were not covered by the Virginia Personnel Act, § 2.2-2900 et seq., so former employees of Attorney General's office were not eligible for severance benefits under the Work Force Transition Act, § 2.2-3203 et seq., because that eligibility was dependent on coverage under the Virginia Personnel Act. Boynton v. Kilgore, 66 Va. Cir. 37, 2004 Va. Cir. LEXIS 339 (Richmond Aug. 27, 2004), aff'd, 271 Va. 220, 623 S.E.2d 922 (2006).

Virginia Personnel Act, § 2.2-2400 et seq., exempted from coverage officers and employees for whom the constitution directed the manner of selection; this included the attorney general and, derivatively, any of his appointed employees, and, thus, those employees were ineligible for severance benefits under the Worker Transition Act, § 2.2-3203 et seq. Boynton v. Kilgore, 69 Va. Cir. 5, 2005 Va. Cir. LEXIS 354 (Richmond 2005).

CHAPTER 30.

State Grievance Procedure.

§ 2.2-3000. Policy of the Commonwealth; responsibilities of state agencies under this chapter. — A. It shall be the policy of the Commonwealth, as an employer, to encourage the resolution of employee problems and complaints. To that end, employees shall be able to discuss freely, and without retaliation, their concerns with their immediate supervisors and management. To the extent that such concerns cannot be resolved informally, the grievance procedure shall afford an immediate and fair method for the resolution of employment disputes that may arise between state agencies and those employees who have access to the procedure under § 2.2-3001.

B. To fully achieve the objectives of this chapter and to create uniformity, each agency in the executive branch of state government shall:

1. Require supervisory personnel to be trained in the grievance procedure, personnel policies, and conflict resolution;

2. Familiarize employees with their grievance rights and promote the services of the Department of Employment Dispute Resolution;

3. Cooperate with investigations conducted pursuant to the authority granted by clause (iii) of subdivision 4 of § 2.2-1001;

4. Participate in the mediation program;

5. Evaluate supervisors on the effectiveness of employee relations management, including, but not limited to, their handling of grievances; and

6. Recognize the right of employees to fully participate in the grievance process without retaliation.

C. The Department of Employment Dispute Resolution shall monitor agencies' activities under this section. (1995, cc. 770, 818, §§ 2.1-116.04, 2.1-116.05; 1996, cc. 164, 869; 1999, cc. 703, 726; 2000, cc. 947, 1006; 2001, c. 844; 2004, c. 674.)

Cross references. — As to the Virginia Council on Human Resources, see § 2.2-2675. As to the effect of the Virginia Administrative Dispute Resolution Act, § 2.2-4115 et seq., on mediation programs administered by the Department of Employment Dispute Resolution, see § 2.2-4117.

CASE NOTES

Federal court jurisdiction. — Employee's action, which alleged disciplinary action by the employer was retaliation for engaging in protected communications, was dismissed because the Rooker-Feldman doctrine applied to Virginia's grievance procedure under § 2.2-3000 et seq. and dictated a conclusion that the court was without subject matter jurisdiction to entertain the employee's claims; the factual basis for the constitutional claims under 42 U.S.C.S. § 1983 did not differ, in any substantial part, from those essential facts presented in the state proceedings. Horner v. Dep't of Mental Health, — F. Supp. 2d —, 2003 U.S. Dist. LEXIS 10094 (W.D. Va. June 17, 2003).

State grievance process subject to *Rooker-Feldman* doctrine. — In an action by a former state employee against his former state employer and former supervisors, a magistrate correctly found that the court lacked subject matter jurisdiction over the employee's complaint based on the *Rooker-Feldman* doctrine because, although 28 U.S.C.S. § 1257 did not explicitly mention decisions by lower state courts or administrative agencies, the state grievance process under § 2.2-3000 et seq., which the employee had invoked, was an adjudicatory process subject to the *Rooker-Feldman* doctrine. Horner v. Dep't of Mental Health, — F. Supp. 2d —, 2003 U.S. Dist. LEXIS 26935 (W.D. Va. May 1, 2003).

Remedy by immediate supervisor precludes further review. — The language "Each level of management review shall have the authority to provide the employee with a remedy," meant that the decision of the employee's immediate supervisor that the employee should be reinstated, after the employee had committed offenses while working for the state employer that called for immediate dismissal, was not a mere recommendation, and precluded subsequent review by the state employer's higher-level management. Horner v. Dep't of Mental Health, Mental Retardation, & Substance Abuse Servs., 268 Va. 187, 597 S.E.2d 202, 2004 Va. LEXIS 83 (2004), reversing 40 Va. App. 338, 579 S.E.2d 372, 2003 Va. App. LEXIS 229 (2003), which held that the legislature did not intend that the low-level supervisor could make a final, conclusive determination on the grievance and thereby thwart review by more senior management. See also, 59 Va. Cir. 250 (2002).

CIRCUIT COURT OPINIONS

Local government employees are exempt. — Charlottesville Redevelopment and Housing Authority is not subject to the state grievance procedure. Although grievance-hearing decisions are grievable under the state grievance procedure, § 2.2-3002 and the Virginia Personnel Act, § 2.2-2905, expressly exempt local government employees. Crawley-Evans v. Charlottesville Redevelopment & Hous. Auth., 73 Va. Cir. 494, 2007 Va. Cir. LEXIS 209 (Charlottesville Aug. 7, 2007).

Discipline requiring grievance hearing. — State employment resolution department erred in determining that e-mail that an office director sent to petitioner was not disciplinary action that qualified for a hearing on petitioner's grievance regarding an altercation with a fellow employee over what material could be posted at work; the trial court determined that petitioner was entitled to a grievance hearing because the e-mail outlined a course of conduct that was to be followed and how future conduct regarding the issue would be handled, and, thus, qualified as a formal disciplinary action that entitled petitioner to a grievance hearing. Gillispie v. Va. Dep't of Envtl. Quality, 67 Va. Cir. 580, 2004 Va. Cir. LEXIS 356 (Richmond Dec. 16, 2004).

§ 2.2-3001. State employees. — A. Unless exempted by law, all nonprobationary state employees shall be covered by the grievance procedure established pursuant to this chapter and any regulations adopted pursuant thereto. Employees not covered by the grievance procedure may be covered by an alternative grievance procedure.

B. The Office of the Attorney General and every legislative, judicial, and independent agency that is not subject to the state grievance procedure shall establish and administer a grievance procedure. (1995, cc. 770, 818, § 2.1-

116.09; 1996, cc. 164, 869; 1997, c. 711; 1998, c. 245; 2000, cc. 947, 1006; 2001, c. 844.)

§ **2.2-3002. Exemptions from chapter.** — The provisions of this chapter shall not apply to:

1. Appointees of elected groups or individuals except as provided in subsection B of § 2.2-3001;
2. Agency heads or chief executive officers of government agencies and public institutions of higher education appointed by boards and commissions;
3. Law-enforcement officers as defined in § 9.1-500 whose grievances are subject to Chapter 5 (§ 9.1-500 et seq.) and who have elected to resolve such grievances under those provisions; and
4. Employees in positions designated in § 2.2-2905 as exempt from the Virginia Personnel Act (§ 2.2-2900 et seq.). (1995, cc. 770, 818, § 2.1-116.013; 2001, c. 844.)

§ **2.2-3003. Grievance procedure generally.** — A. As part of the Commonwealth's program of employee relations management, the Department of Employment Dispute Resolution shall develop a grievance procedure that includes not more than three successively higher grievance resolution steps and a formal hearing as provided in this chapter.

B. Prior to initiating a written grievance, the employee shall be encouraged to pursue an informal complaint with his immediate supervisor. The supervisor shall have authority to resolve the complaint if it involves actions within his control.

C. An employee may pursue a formal written grievance through the grievance resolution steps if the complaint has been presented to management within 30 calendar days of the employee's knowledge of the event that gave rise to the complaint. Employees' rights to pursue grievances shall not be used to harass or otherwise impede the efficient operations of government.

D. Upon receipt of a timely written complaint, management shall review the grievance and respond to the merits thereof. Each level of management review shall have the authority to provide the employee with a remedy, subject to the agency head's approval. At least one face-to-face meeting between the employee and management shall be required. The persons who may be present at this meeting are the employee, the appropriate manager, an individual selected by the employee, and an individual selected by the manager. Witnesses may be called by either party.

E. Absent just cause, all documents, as defined in the Rules of the Supreme Court of Virginia, relating to the actions grieved shall be made available, upon request from a party to the grievance, by the opposing party, in a timely fashion. Upon such request a party shall have a duty to search its records to ensure that all such relevant documents are provided. Documents pertaining to nonparties that are relevant to the grievance shall be produced in such a manner as to preserve the privacy of the individuals not personally involved in the grievance. A party shall not be required to create a document if the document does not exist.

F. All time limitations prescribed in the grievance procedure, including, but not limited to, submission of an initial complaint and employee appeal of management decisions, shall be reasonable, specific, and equally applicable to the agency and the employee. Expedited grievance procedures shall be established for terminations, demotions, suspensions, and lost wages or salaries.

G. Within five workdays of the receipt of a written notice of noncompliance, failure of the employee or the agency to comply with a substantial procedural requirement of the grievance procedure without just cause may result in a decision against the noncomplying party on any qualified issue. Written notice of noncompliance by the agency shall be made to the agency head. The Director of the Department of Employment Dispute Resolution shall render all decisions related to procedural compliance, and such decisions shall contain the reasons for such decision and shall be final.

H. Grievances qualified pursuant to § 2.2-3004 that have not been resolved through the grievance resolution steps shall advance to a hearing that shall be the final step in the grievance procedure. (1995, cc. 770, 818, § 2.1-116.05; 1996, cc. 164, 869; 1999, cc. 703, 726; 2000, cc. 947, 1006; 2001, c. 844; 2003, c. 252; 2004, c. 674.)

Law Review. — For survey of Virginia law on municipal corporations for the year 1977-1978, see 64 Va. L. Rev. 1487 (1978). For survey of Virginia law on governmental services and social welfare for the year 1978-1979, see 66 Va. L. Rev. 301 (1980). For survey of administrative procedure in Virginia for 1989, see 23 U. Rich. L. Rev. 431 (1989).

CASE NOTES

Editor's note. — Many of the cases below were decided under former Title 2.1 or prior provisions.

Remedy by immediate supervisor precludes further review. — The language "Each level of management review shall have the authority to provide the employee with a remedy," meant that the decision of the employee's immediate supervisor that the employee should be reinstated, after the employee had committed offenses while working for the state employer that called for immediate dismissal, was not a mere recommendation, and precluded subsequent review by the state employer's higher-level management. Horner v. Dep't of Mental Health, Mental Retardation, & Substance Abuse Servs., 268 Va. 187, 597 S.E.2d 202, 2004 Va. LEXIS 83 (2004), reversing 40 Va. App. 338, 579 S.E.2d 372, 2003 Va. App. LEXIS 229 (2003), which held that the legislature did not intend that the low-level supervisor could make a final, conclusive determination on the grievance and thereby thwart review by more senior management. See also, 59 Va. Cir. 250 (2002).

Application of issue preclusion to hearing officer's findings of fact. — Issue preclusion applied to a former hospital employee's action that alleged retaliation in violation of the Rehabilitation Act, 29 U.S.C.S. § 794(a), and the First Amendment because the employee had previously litigated all of the issues presented in the instant case surrounding his termination in an impartial forum, the Virginia Department of Employment Dispute Resolution. There was no basis to find that the decisions of the hearing officer on the factual issues surrounding the discharge were contradictory to law or policy; thus, the hearing officer's findings that the employee was terminated for failing to follow a supervisor's instructions and failing to comply with written policy, not because of retaliation, were final and binding under Virginia law. Horner v. Va. Dep't of Mental Health, — F. Supp. 2d —, 2004 U.S. Dist. LEXIS 29022 (W.D. Va. Apr. 26, 2004).

Court deference to administrative decision. — Where an agency failed to show that a hearing officer's decision contradicted any law, the circuit court's ruling, unduly limiting the officer's authority and overturning the officer's decision, was reversed to reinstate the officer's decision. Tatum v. Va. Dep't of Agric. & Consumer Servs., 41 Va. App. 110, 582 S.E.2d 452, 2003 Va. App. LEXIS 356 (2003), reversing 59 Va. Cir. 262 (2002).

Virginia's layoff-rights scheme and rules on exemptions circumscribe property interest in continued employment. — Although a nonprobationary employee has a property interest in continued employment that is created by the state the scope of this interest, is circumscribed by Virginia's rules on exemptions from the classified employment scheme and from access to the grievance procedure and by Virginia's layoff-rights scheme. Mandel v. Allen, 889 F. Supp. 857 (E.D. Va. 1995), aff'd, 81 F.3d 478 (4th Cir. 1996).

No property interest when statute makes exercise of classification power non-grievable. — Where, as in the relevant Virginia statutes, the state statute vests the power to classify solely in management and then makes the exercise of that power non-grievable, there can be no property interest in the classification. Mandel v. Allen, 889 F. Supp. 857 (E.D. Va. 1995), aff'd, 81 F.3d 478 (4th Cir. 1996).

A nonprobationary employee does not serve at the will of the agency that employs him. Detweiler v. Virginia Dep't of Rehabilitative Servs., 705 F.2d 557 (4th Cir. 1983).

Nonprobationary employees of state have property interest in continued employment. — Former § 2.1-114.5:1's distinction between probationary employees and nonprobationary employees, its distinction between disciplinary discharges and discharges for reduction in work force, the specifications in the "Policy Standards of Conduct" for state employees concerning breaches of discipline for which an employee could be discharged, and the authority conferred on an impartial panel to reverse the agency's decision and to order reinstatement with back pay (pursuant to "The Rules for the Conduct of Panel Hearings"), established that a nonprobationary employee had a property interest in continued employment that was created by the State. Detweiler v. Virginia Dep't of Rehabilitative Servs., 705 F.2d 557 (4th Cir. 1983).

Probationary employee had no right to grievance procedures and no property interest in her job, and thus the protections of due process were not triggered by her firing. Assa'ad-Faltas v. Virginia, 738 F. Supp. 982 (E.D. Va. 1989), aff'd, 902 F.2d 1564 (4th Cir. 1990).

Former § 2.1-114.5:1 did not necessarily create a property interest in promotion, as promotions are not awarded as a matter of right or entitlement under Virginia law, but are based on merit and fitness. James v. Powell, 765 F. Supp. 314 (E.D. Va. 1991).

The protections in former § 2.1-114.5:1 were inapplicable to an at-will employee of the general district court who was not subject to the provisions of the Virginia Personnel Act. James v. Powell, 765 F. Supp. 314 (E.D. Va. 1991).

Virginia law required four basic elements in a post-termination grievance hearing. These requirements included: (1) Written notice of the termination with reasons therefor; (2) a hearing before an impartial three-member panel; (3) an opportunity to present, examine, and cross-examine witnesses; and (4) a panel discussion that adheres to "law and written policies." Leftwich v. Bevilacqua, 635 F. Supp. 238 (W.D. Va. 1986).

For discussion of the procedures required by the due process clause when an employee, who has established a property interest in continued employment, is discharged. Detweiler v. Virginia Dep't of Rehabilitative Servs., 705 F.2d 557 (4th Cir. 1983).

Retroactive application of 1985 amendment to former § 2.1-116. — A state official who simply enforces a presumptively valid state statute will rarely lose his immunity from suit. However, two defendants in instant case did not simply enforce a presumptively valid state statute. Rather, totally disregarding longstanding Virginia law prohibiting new legislation from being construed to eliminate preexisting substantive rights, they attempted to apply the 1985 amendment to former § 2.1-116 retroactively to do precisely this. Moreover, they did this in the face of several holdings of this court that the act established a property interest in continued public employment, and a holding of the Virginia Supreme Court that the right to continued public employment is substantive and cannot be retroactively eliminated. Garraghty v. Virginia, Dep't of Cors., 52 F.3d 1274 (4th Cir. 1995).

Failure to apprise employee of rights. — Director of county board of public welfare (now local board of social services), charged with counseling employees on the rights and procedures available with regard to adverse personnel actions, was not denied due process where the board, after forcing her to resign, did not affirmatively apprise her of her grievance rights, due to director's actual knowledge of both their existence as well as the mechanics of the procedure, and the fact that she consulted with an attorney regarding this matter well within the time frame prescribed for filing a grievance. Crocker v. Fluvanna County Bd. of Pub. Welfare, 859 F.2d 14 (4th Cir. 1988).

Petition to implement panel action does not initiate or toll a grievance. — The filing of a petition in circuit court pursuant to subdivision F of former § 2.1-114.5:1, the purpose of which is to require a party to implement a grievance panel's decision, should not have been treated as the initiation of a grievance over a separate disciplinary action; the petition to implement a panel action did not serve to initiate a grievance or toll the limitation for doing so. Commonwealth, Dep't of Taxation v. Hogan, 11 Va. App. 306, 397 S.E.2d 902 (1990).

Where the trial court correctly determined that the employee's demotion upon reinstatement was an issue that had to be grieved separately and was not enforceable as part of the panel's reinstatement decision without exhausting the administrative grievance procedure, the trial court lacked authority to treat the petition filed pursuant to subdivision F of former § 2.1-114.5:1 as filing notice of a grievance with an agency. Commonwealth, Dep't of Taxation v. Hogan, 11 Va. App. 306, 397 S.E.2d 902 (1990).

Local committee at mental hospital not authorized to hear grievances. — The Local Human Rights Committee at the Western State Mental Hospital was created under proper Commonwealth regulations to investigate solely charges of patient abuse; it had no other authority. Any investigation of employee grievances is by state law differently provided for under a procedure laid out precisely under the law. For the Committee to have intruded into the area of employee grievances would have been an improper and illegal encroachment on the grievance procedure created by statute for investigating such complaints. Buschi v. Kirven, 775 F.2d 1240 (4th Cir. 1985).

Authority of grievance panel to promote should be left to General Assembly. — The determination whether a grievance panel has the authority to promote clearly is best left to the wisdom of the General Assembly and the state officials charged with the administration of the grievance procedure. Therefore, the board was without authority to award a policeman, denied promotion, a retroactive promotion and compensation for back pay. Jones v. Carter, 234 Va. 621, 363 S.E.2d 921 (1988).

Procedural due process where job abolition is cited as reason to terminate employee. — When the state chooses to terminate an employee for cause, it may not avoid the requirements of procedural due process by merely citing job abolition as a pretextual justification. It is the employee's burden, however, to present evidence that the job abolition was a pretext for action intended to target the individual rather than the abolished position. Only then can there be a claim for deprivation of procedural due process. Mandel v. Allen, 889 F. Supp. 857 (E.D. Va. 1995), aff'd, 81 F.3d 478 (4th Cir. 1996).

Plaintiff has burden to show state avoiding procedural due process. — To present sufficient evidence that the state in justifying elimination of positions is seeking to use administrative efficiency as a pretext for avoiding procedural due process is the plaintiff's burden. The burden is not onerous, nor does it necessarily require a "smoking gun" memorandum or the like. It may not be satisfied by conjecture or surmise. Mandel v. Allen, 889 F. Supp. 857 (E.D. Va. 1995), aff'd, 81 F.3d 478 (4th Cir. 1996).

Plaintiff has burden of showing that admission of evidence denied due process. — Even if evidence of prior similar acts by an employee was inadmissible in federal court, its admission in a grievance hearing does not violate due process unless notions of fundamental fairness were violated. Plaintiff has the burden of showing that the admission of the extraneous evidence denied him minimal due process. Leftwich v. Bevilacqua, 635 F. Supp. 238 (W.D. Va. 1986).

Preclusive effect of local administrative findings. — Findings of local administrative body are given preclusive effect in a federal Americans with Disabilities Act, 42 U.S.C. § 12101 et seq., suit, particularly where the body acted pursuant to a grievance procedure mandated by state law. Roberts v. County of Fairfax, 937 F. Supp. 541 (E.D. Va. 1996).

Grievance panel decision binding on sheriff. — Grievance panel decision against demoting police lieutenant for violation of sheriff's orders was not recommendation but under former § 2.1-114.5:1 was binding, since if the sheriff was free to reject panel's decisions the grievance procedure mandated by the General Assembly would be rendered impotent. Angle v. Overton, 235 Va. 103, 365 S.E.2d 758 (1988).

Trial court decision final and nonappealable. — Decision of the trial court, which reversed city manager's decision that complaint was not "grievable," concluded that the complaint was grievable, and ordered a full hearing, was final and nonappealable. City of Danville v. Franklin, 234 Va. 275, 361 S.E.2d 634 (1987).

Jurisdiction on appeal. — The Court of Appeals does not have jurisdiction to review the judgment of a circuit court entered pursuant to subsection F of former § 2.1-114.5:1. Therefore, appeal should be transferred to the Supreme Court of Virginia. Virginia Dep't of Cors. v. Dillon, No. 1871-93-2 (Ct. of Appeals Nov. 15, 1994).

Where the grievance panel's decision was "final and binding", only its implementation could be granted or denied by the circuit court. Therefore, proceeding before the circuit court was not an appeal of the grievance panel's decision, thus, the Court of Appeals lacked jurisdiction and properly ordered the appeal transferred to the Supreme Court. Virginia Dep't of Taxation v. Daughtry, 19 Va. App. 135, 449 S.E.2d 57 (1994).

Agency decision not subject to review. — In a case involving Virginia's State Grievance Procedure, specifically §§ 2.2-3003, 2.2-3004, and 2.2-3006, the Department of Employment Dispute Resolution's decision was not subject to review by the circuit court because it involved an interpretation of agency procedures created pursuant to subdivision 2 of § 2.2-1001 rather than an issue of law; also, the delay by the Department of Human Resource Management (DHRM) in rendering its decision on the request for review did not nullify its ruling because subsection A of § 2.2-3006 contained no prohibitory or limiting language preventing the DHRM from ruling after the expiration of 60 days. Va. Dep't of Taxation v. Brailey, — Va. App. —, — S.E.2d —, 2008 Va. App. LEXIS 19 (Jan. 15, 2008).

Dismissal of federal claim. — Due process claim which was in fact a mere pretext and simply a claim that the Virginia Employment Commission violated its own standards of conduct in handling plaintiff's grievance was a case of a Virginia resident suing Virginia employees, over an interpretation of Virginia law, and as such, would be dismissed from the district court for lack of jurisdiction. Davis v. Pak, 856 F.2d 648 (4th Cir. 1988).

City ordered to implement panel's decision. — Although a city employee does not have a vested right to remain in a personnel classification indefinitely, where the employee sought to be reinstated to his former position in accordance with the decision of the grievance panel, the court reversed the judgment of the trial court and remanded the case with directions that the trial court enter an order which required that the employee be reinstated to the position of golf course superintendent in accordance with the panel's decision. Zicca v. City of Hampton, 240 Va. 468, 397 S.E.2d 882 (1990).

Deputy sheriff served at the will of the sheriff under state law, and therefore had no property interest in his continued employment as deputy even though sheriff's department adopted regulations concerning dismissal and grievance procedures patterned on that outlined in former § 2.1-114.5:1. Jenkins v. Weatherholtz, 719 F. Supp. 468 (W.D. Va. 1989), aff'd, 909 F.2d 105 (4th Cir. 1990).

Adoption of handbook patterned after section did not compromise statutory authority. — Sheriff's adoption of employees handbook patterned after the procedures in this section could not compromise his statutory authority under former § 15.1-48 (see now § 15.2-1603) to remove deputies at his discretion. Jenkins v. Weatherholtz, 909 F.2d 105 (4th Cir. 1990).

District court erred to the extent that it held that defendants were not entitled to qualified immunity on plaintiff's claim that they had deprived him of a property right in the state grievance procedure without due process. Even if such a right is possible, there is nothing that suggests it is vested or substantive and so nothing to suggest that any property right to participation in the state grievance procedure survived the 1985 amendment to former § 2.1-116 (see now § 2.2-2905), let alone that this was clearly established. Garraghty v. Virginia, Dep't of Cors., 52 F.3d 1274 (4th Cir. 1995).

Threats to supervisor. — Where plaintiff made death threat to her supervisor, the department's transfer of plaintiff to another office and its requirement of a mental health evaluation before she resumed work were within management's prerogative under former section and consistent with its duty to provide a safe working environment for all employees. Virginia Dep't of Taxation v. Daughtry, 250 Va. 542, 463 S.E.2d 847 (1995).

Missing work and signing inaccurate reports. — The former section gave the department the right to transfer plaintiff to another job for which he was well-qualified at the same pay, where he had missed work although denied leave time and had signed grossly inaccurate sales reports for his department. Virginia Dep't of Taxation v. Daughtry, 250 Va. 542, 463 S.E.2d 847 (1995).

§ 2.2-3004. Grievances qualifying for a grievance hearing; grievance hearing generally. — A. A grievance qualifying for a hearing shall involve a complaint or dispute by an employee relating to the following adverse employment actions in which the employee is personally involved, including but not limited to (i) formal disciplinary actions, including suspensions, demotions, transfers and assignments, and dismissals resulting from formal discipline or unsatisfactory job performance; (ii) the application of all written personnel policies, procedures, rules and regulations where it can be shown that policy was misapplied or unfairly applied; (iii) discrimination on the basis of race, color, religion, political affiliation, age, disability, national origin or sex; (iv) arbitrary or capricious performance evaluations; (v) acts of retaliation as the result of the use of or participation in the grievance procedure or because the employee has complied with any law of the United States or of the Commonwealth, has reported any violation of such law to a governmental authority, has sought any change in law before the Congress of the United States or the General Assembly, or has reported an incidence of fraud, abuse, or gross mismanagement; and (vi) retaliation for exercising any right otherwise protected by law.

B. Management reserves the exclusive right to manage the affairs and operations of state government. Management shall exercise its powers with the highest degree of trust. In any employment matter that management precludes from proceeding to a grievance hearing, management's response, including any appropriate remedial actions, shall be prompt, complete, and fair.

C. Complaints relating solely to the following issues shall not proceed to a hearing: (i) establishment and revision of wages, salaries, position classifications, or general benefits; (ii) work activity accepted by the employee as a condition of employment or which may reasonably be expected to be a part of the job content; (iii) contents of ordinances, statutes or established personnel policies, procedures, and rules and regulations; (iv) methods, means, and personnel by which work activities are to be carried on; (v) termination, layoff, demotion, or suspension from duties because of lack of work, reduction in work force, or job abolition; (vi) hiring, promotion, transfer, assignment, and retention of employees within the agency; and (vii) relief of employees from duties of the agency in emergencies.

D. Decisions regarding whether a grievance qualifies for a hearing shall be made in writing by the agency head or his designee within five workdays of the employee's request for a hearing. A copy of the decision shall be sent to the employee. The employee may appeal the denial of a hearing by the agency head to the Director of the Department of Employment Dispute Resolution (the "Director"). Upon receipt of an appeal, the agency shall transmit the entire grievance record to the Department of Employment Dispute Resolution within five workdays. The Director shall render a decision on whether the employee is entitled to a hearing upon the grievance record and other probative evidence.

E. Proceedings for review of the decision of the Director may be made by an employee filing a notice of appeal within five workdays of receipt of the decision. Within five workdays thereafter, the agency shall transmit to the clerk of the circuit court in the jurisdiction in which the grievance arose a copy of the grievance record. The court, on motion of the grievant, may issue a writ of certiorari requiring the Director to transmit the record on or before a certain date. Within thirty days of receipt of such records, the court, sitting without a jury, shall hear the appeal on the record and such additional evidence as may be necessary to resolve any controversy as to the correctness of the record. The court, in its discretion, may receive such other evidence as the ends of justice require. The court may affirm the decision of the Director or may reverse or modify the decision. The decision of the court shall be rendered no later than the fifteenth day from the date of the conclusion of the hearing. The decision of the court shall be final and shall not be appealable. The circuit court hearing shall be at no cost to the Commonwealth or the grievant.

F. The hearing pursuant to § 2.2-3005 shall be held in the locality in which the employee is employed or in any other locality agreed to by the employee, employer, and hearing officer. The employee and the agency may be represented by legal counsel or a lay advocate, the provisions of § 54.1-3904 notwithstanding. The employee and the agency may call witnesses to present testimony and be cross-examined. (1995, cc. 770, 818, § 2.1-116.06; 1996, cc. 164, 869; 2001, c. 844.)

CASE NOTES

The judgment of the city court had no preclusive effect because, under Virginia law, subsequent actions are not barred by res judicata if the court in the first action did not have subject matter jurisdiction over the proceedings; the city court dismissed plaintiff's first action without reaching the merits because plaintiff had not exhausted his administrative remedies. Pignato v. Virginia Dep't of Envtl. Quality, 948 F. Supp. 532 (E.D. Va 1996) (decided under former Title 2.1).

Court deference to administrative decision. — Where an agency failed to show that a hearing officer's decision contradicted any law, the circuit court's ruling, unduly limiting the officer's authority and overturning the officer's decision, was reversed to reinstate the officer's decision. Tatum v. Va. Dep't of Agric. & Consumer Servs., 41 Va. App. 110, 582 S.E.2d 452, 2003 Va. App. LEXIS 356 (2003), reversing 59 Va. Cir. 262 (2002).

Letters not a "case decision." — Two letters, one written by an employee's attorney, and another written by the Department of Corrections, did not meet the definition of a "case decision," as defined in § 2.2-4001, as neither letter involved the application of law to the facts in an agency proceeding, the first amounted to merely a request for clarification of the Department's position concerning a grievance matter, and the Department's response to the same acknowledged that it had responded to the merits during the grievance process and that denial of a grievance hearing was affirmed; further, the letter written by the employee's attorney did not have the effect of filing a claim for retirement benefits. Garraghty v. Va. Ret. Sys., 45 Va. App. 1, 608 S.E.2d 477, 2005 Va. App. LEXIS 44 (2005).

Agency decision not subject to review. — In a case involving Virginia's State Grievance Procedure, specifically §§ 2.2-3003, 2.2-3004, and 2.2-3006, the Department of Employment Dispute Resolution's decision was not subject to review by the circuit court because it involved an interpretation of agency procedures created pursuant to subdivision 2 of § 2.2-1001 rather than an issue of law; also, the delay by the Department of Human Resource Management (DHRM) in rendering its decision on the request for review did not nullify its ruling because subsection A of § 2.2-3006 contained no prohibitory or limiting language preventing the DHRM from ruling after the expiration of 60 days. Va. Dep't of Taxation v. Brailey, — Va. App. —, — S.E.2d —, 2008 Va. App. LEXIS 19 (Jan. 15, 2008).

Applied in Va. Dep't of State Police v. Barton, 39 Va. App. 439, 573 S.E.2d 319, 2002 Va. App. LEXIS 756 (2002).

CIRCUIT COURT OPINIONS

Severity of discipline. — University was in its rights when it imposed a discipline upon a campus police officer following an auto accident that was more severe than the discipline it had imposed upon other police officers for similar conduct, but conduct that caused less damage; therefore, a hearing officer's decision in a grievance proceeding that the university could not impose a more severe discipline on the officer than what other officers had received for similar conduct was contradictory to law. Siewert v. Virginia Commonwealth Univ., 58 Va. Cir. 212, 2002 Va. Cir. LEXIS 143 (Richmond 2002).

Hearing officer misapplied subdivision C 6 of § 2.2-3005 in mitigating the termination of a grievant for patient abuse as mitigation was reserved by policy to a training center's management and subsection B of § 2.2-3004 reserved to the management of the center the right to manage the center's affairs and operations. Woodson v. Cent. Va. Training Ctr., 66 Va. Cir. 480, 2002 Va. Cir. LEXIS 457 (Amherst County 2002).

"Discipline" requiring a hearing. — State employment resolution department erred in determining that e-mail that an office director sent to petitioner, was not discipline that qualified for a hearing on petitioner's grievance regarding an altercation with a fellow employee over what material could be posted at work; the trial court determined that petitioner was entitled to a grievance hearing because the e-mail outlined a course of conduct that was to be followed and how future conduct regarding the issue would be handled, and, thus, qualified as a formal disciplinary action that entitled petitioner to a grievance hearing. Gillispie v. Va. Dep't of Envtl. Quality, 67 Va. Cir. 580, 2004 Va. Cir. LEXIS 356 (Richmond Dec. 16, 2004).

Failure to provide reasonable accommodation. — City's failure to provide a policeman with a "reasonable accommodation" given his medical condition was grievable under clause (ii) of subsection A of § 2.2-3004 where the duty to provide the policeman with sedentary employment in the light of his medical condition was a duty imposed on the city by its personnel rules and regulations. November v. City of Richmond, 66 Va. Cir. 326, 2005 Va. Cir. LEXIS 42 (Richmond Jan. 13, 2005).

§ 2.2-3005. Hearing officers; duties. — A. Nothing in this chapter shall create, nor shall be construed to create, a property interest in selection or assignment to serve as a hearing officer for grievance hearings.

B. The Director of the Department of Employment Dispute Resolution shall assign a hearing officer to conduct the grievance hearing. All hearing officers shall be selected, on a rotating basis, (i) from the list of administrative hearing officers maintained by the Supreme Court of Virginia pursuant to § 2.2-4024 or (ii) from attorneys hired as classified employees by the Department through a competitive selection process. Hearing officer fees shall be reasonable, in accordance with compensation guidelines developed by the Department of Employment Dispute Resolution. In addition to the training requirements imposed by the Supreme Court, each hearing officer shall meet the criteria established by the Director pursuant to subdivision 6 of § 2.2-1001 and attend annually at least one day of training in employment law or state personnel policies and organizations. The training shall be conducted by the Department of Employment Dispute Resolution or an organization approved by the Virginia State Bar for continuing legal education.

C. Hearing officers shall have the following powers and duties:

1. Hold conferences for the settlement or simplification of issues;
2. Dispose of procedural requests;
3. Issue orders requiring testimony or the production of evidence;
4. Administer oaths and affirmations;

5. Receive probative evidence; exclude irrelevant, immaterial, insubstantial, privileged, or repetitive proofs, rebuttals, or cross-examinations; rule upon offers of proof; and oversee a verbatim recording of the evidence;

6. Receive and consider evidence in mitigation or aggravation of any offense charged by an agency in accordance with rules established by the Department of Employment Dispute Resolution pursuant to § 2.2-1001; and

7. Take other actions as necessary or specified in the grievance procedure. (1995, cc. 770, 818, § 2.1-116.07; 1998, cc. 263, 438; 1999, c. 713; 2000, cc. 66, 657, 947, 1006; 2001, c. 844; 2004, c. 674.)

Cross references. — As to the jurisdiction of the Court of Appeals to hear appeals from any final decision of a circuit court on appeal from a grievance hearing decision issued pursuant to this section, see § 17.1-405.

Michie's Jurisprudence. — For related discussion, see 15 M.J. Public Officers, § 46.

CASE NOTES

Locality procedure decisions. — Decision rendered under a locality procedure is not a decision issued pursuant to § 2.2-3005 or a final grievance hearing decision issued pursuant to subsection B of § 2.2-3007; thus, a city manager's decision refusing to abide by a personnel board decision that a police officer should be reinstated to his job could not be considered by a Virginia appellate court. Styles v. City of Colonial Heights, 43 Va. App. 588, 600 S.E.2d 174, 2004 Va. App. LEXIS 378 (2004).

Reversal of hearing officer's decision in error. — Upon judicial review of a hearing officer's decision to amend a disciplinary notice against two penitentiary employees, the trial court erred by concluding that the hearing officer had no authority to amend the disciplinary notice and, therefore, dismissed the Group II disciplinary notice. Because the hearing officer's amendment of the disciplinary notice did not violate any statute, judicial precedent, or accepted legal principal, it was proper and should have been upheld. Commonwealth v. Doyle, — Va. App. —, — S.E.2d —, 2005 Va. App. LEXIS 255 (July 5, 2005).

Hearing officer did not exceed his authority. — Hearing officer acted within the scope of the authority conferred when he held that a corrections officer's conduct, though apparently insufficient to sustain a conviction for assault, was enough to mandate termination for cause. Va. Dep't of Corr. v. Compton, 47 Va. App. 202, 623 S.E.2d 397, 2005 Va. App. LEXIS 517 (2005).

CIRCUIT COURT OPINIONS

Hearing officer exceeded his authority. — Hearing officer misapplied subdivision C 6 in mitigating the termination of a grievant for patient abuse as mitigation was reserved by policy to a training center's management and subsection B of § 2.2-3004 reserved to the management of the center the right to manage the center's affairs and operations. Woodson v. Cent. Va. Training Ctr., 66 Va. Cir. 480, 2002 Va. Cir. LEXIS 457 (Amherst County 2002).

§ 2.2-3005.1. Scope of hearing officer's decision; agency cooperation; cost of hearing; decision of hearing officer. — A. For those issues qualified for a hearing, the hearing officer may order appropriate remedies. Relief may include (i) reinstatement, (ii) back pay, (iii) full reinstatement of fringe benefits and seniority rights, (iv) mitigation or reduction of the agency disciplinary action, or (v) any combination of these remedies. In grievances challenging discharge, if the hearing officer finds that the employee has substantially prevailed on the merits of the grievance, the employee shall be entitled to recover reasonable attorneys' fees, unless special circumstances would make an award unjust. All awards of relief, including attorneys' fees, by a hearing officer must be in accordance with rules established by the Department of Employment Dispute Resolution.

B. The agency from which the grievance arises shall bear the costs for the hearing officer and other associated hearing expenses including the grievant's attorneys' fees that the hearing officer may award.

C. The decision of the hearing officer shall (i) be in writing, (ii) contain findings of fact as to the material issues in the case and the basis for those findings, including any award of reasonable attorneys' fees pursuant to this section, and (iii) be final and binding if consistent with law and policy.

D. The provisions of this section relating to the award of attorneys' fees shall not apply to any local government or agency thereof that is otherwise subject to the grievance procedure set forth in this chapter. (2004, c. 674.)

CASE NOTES

Application of issue preclusion to hearing officer's findings of fact. — Issue preclusion applied to a former hospital employee's action that alleged retaliation in violation of the Rehabilitation Act, 29 U.S.C.S. § 794(a), and the First Amendment because the employee had previously litigated all of the issues presented in the instant case surrounding his termination in an impartial forum, the Virginia Department of Employment Dispute Resolution. There was no basis to find that the decisions of the hearing officer on the factual issues surrounding the discharge were contradictory to law or policy; thus, the hearing officer's findings that the employee was terminated for failing to follow a supervisor's instructions and failing to comply with written policy, not because of retaliation, were final and binding under Virginia law. Horner v. Va. Dep't of Mental Health, — F. Supp. 2d —, 2004 U.S. Dist. LEXIS 29022 (W.D. Va. Apr. 26, 2004).

Circuit court's authority limited to implementing decision. — Under this section, the circuit court's authority with respect to a petition for enforcement of a hearing officer's decision is limited to the act of implementing or refusing to implement the hearing officer's ruling; the court lacks the authority to consider the grievance de novo, to modify the hearing officer's decision, to substitute the court's view of the facts for those of the hearing officer or to invoke its broad equitable powers to arrive at a decision that the court may think is fair. Commonwealth, Dep't of Envtl. Quality v. Wright, 256 Va. 236, 504 S.E.2d 862 (1998) (decided under former Title 2.1).

Where an agency failed to show that a hearing officer's decision contradicted any law, the circuit court's ruling, unduly limiting the officer's authority and overturning the officer's decision, was reversed to reinstate the officer's decision. Tatum v. Va. Dep't of Agric. & Consumer Servs., 41 Va. App. 110, 582 S.E.2d 452, 2003 Va. App. LEXIS 356 (2003), reversing 59 Va. Cir. 262 (2002).

Reversal of hearing officer's decision in error. — Upon judicial review of a hearing officer's decision to amend a disciplinary notice against two penitentiary employees, the trial court erred by concluding that the hearing officer had no authority to amend the disciplinary notice and, therefore, dismissed the Group II disciplinary notice. Because the hearing officer's amendment of the disciplinary notice did not violate any statute, judicial precedent, or accepted legal principal, it was proper and should have been upheld. Commonwealth v. Doyle, — Va. App. —, — S.E.2d —, 2005 Va. App. LEXIS 255 (July 5, 2005).

Applied in Va. Dep't of Corr. v. Compton, 47 Va. App. 202, 623 S.E.2d 397, 2005 Va. App. LEXIS 517 (2005).

CIRCUIT COURT OPINIONS

Circuit court's authority limited to implementing decision. — Where an amendment to former § 2.1-116.07(1) (now § 2.2-3005) was substantive because it afforded a right of review that previously did not exist, the court lacked authority to implement a hearing officer's determination because it was not a "decision" subject to implementation under § 2.1-116.07(D); therefore, the matter had to be dismissed. Bala v. Dep't of Conservation & Rec., 57 Va. Cir. 132, 2001 Va. Cir. LEXIS 519 (Richmond 2001) (decided under former Title 2.1).

Attorney's fees. — University police officer who was terminated from an employment position and who was reinstated by a hearing officer was properly awarded substantial attorney's fees pursuant to § 2.2-3005.1, as the employee substantially prevailed on the merits of his grievance; arguments by the university regarding lack of timeliness were disregarded pursuant to authority under subdivision 5 of § 2.2-1001. Old Dominion Univ. v. Birkmeyer, 73 Va. Cir. 341, 2007 Va. Cir. LEXIS 131 (Norfolk 2007).

§ 2.2-3006. Review of hearing decisions; costs. — A. Upon the request of a party to a grievance hearing for an administrative review of the hearing decision, the Director of the Department of Human Resource Management shall determine, within 60 days of receipt of such request, whether the hearing decision is consistent with policy.

B. Within 30 days of a final decision, a party may appeal on the grounds that the determination is contradictory to law by filing a notice of appeal with the clerk of the circuit court in the jurisdiction in which the grievance arose. The agency shall request and receive prior approval of the Director before filing a notice of appeal. After a notice of appeal has been filed by either party, the agency shall then transmit a copy of the grievance record to the clerk of the court. The court, on motion of a party, shall issue a writ of certiorari requiring transmission of the record on or before a certain date. Within 30 days of receipt of the grievance record, the court, sitting without a jury, shall hear the appeal on the record. The court may affirm the decision or may reverse or modify the decision. The decision of the court shall be rendered no later than the fifteenth day from the date of the conclusion of the hearing. The circuit court hearing shall be at no cost to the Commonwealth or the grievant.

C. The hearing officer's final decision shall be effective from the latter of the date issued or the date of the conclusion of any administrative review and judicial appeal, and shall be implemented immediately thereafter, unless circumstances beyond the control of the agency delay such implementation.

D. Either party may petition the circuit court having jurisdiction in the locality in which the grievance arose for an order requiring implementation of the final decision or recommendation of a hearing officer.

E. The court shall award reasonable attorneys' fees and costs to the employee if the employee substantially prevails on the merits of a case brought under subsection B or D. (2000, cc. 947, 1006, § 2.1-116.07:1; 2001, cc. 393, 420, 844; 2003, c. 252; 2004, c. 229.)

Editor's note. — Acts 2001, cc. 393 and 420 amended § 2.1-116.07:1, from which this section is derived. Pursuant to § 30-152, Acts 2001, cc. 393 and 420 have been given effect in this section as set out above. The 2001 amendments by cc. 393 and 420 are identical, and deleted the former second sentence of subsection A, which read: "In grievances arising out of the Department of Mental Health, Mental Retardation and Substance Abuse Services that challenge allegations of patient abuse, the Director of the Department of Employment Dispute Resolution shall determine within sixty days of the decision whether the decision is consistent with law."

Michie's Jurisprudence. — For related discussion, see 15 M.J. Public Officers, § 46.

CASE NOTES

The decision must be contradictory to law. — State trooper failed to identify a specific statute, constitutional provision, regulation, or judicial decision that was violated by a hearing officer's suspension of the trooper for three days, and under § 2.2-3006 the trial court had no jurisdiction over the trooper's appeal of the hearing officer's decision. Va. Dep't of State Police v. Barton, 39 Va. App. 439, 573 S.E.2d 319, 2002 Va. App. LEXIS 756 (2002).

Where an agency failed to show that a hearing officer's decision contradicted any law, the circuit court's ruling, unduly limiting the officer's authority and overturning the officer's decision, was reversed to reinstate the officer's decision. Tatum v. Va. Dep't of Agric. & Consumer Servs., 41 Va. App. 110, 582 S.E.2d 452, 2003 Va. App. LEXIS 356 (2003), reversing 59 Va. Cir. 262 (2002).

Interpretation of agency procedures not subject to review. — In a case involving Virginia's State Grievance Procedure, specifically §§ 2.2-3003, 2.2-3004, and 2.2-3006, the Department of Employment Dispute Resolution's decision was not subject to review by the circuit court because it involved an interpretation of agency procedures created pursuant to subdivision 2 of § 2.2-1001 rather than an issue of law; also, the delay by the Department of Human Resource Management (DHRM) in rendering its decision on the request for review did not nullify its ruling because subsection A of § 2.2-3006 contained no prohibitory or limiting language preventing the DHRM from ruling after the expiration of 60 days. Va. Dep't of Taxation v. Brailey, — Va. App. —, — S.E.2d —, 2008 Va. App. LEXIS 19 (Jan. 15, 2008).

University employee afforded due process prior to termination. — University employee was afforded due process rights prior to her termination where: (1) she received notice of the reasons for the termination in two letters and a Group III Written Notice; (2) she was provided an opportunity to respond to the charges and did so in conjunction with the investigation conducted by the university's human resources department; and (3) she was afforded further opportunity to respond to the allegations through the grievance process of which she availed herself. Porter v. Dep't of Human Res. Mgmt., No. 3093-03-1, 2004 Va. App. LEXIS 225 (Ct. of Appeals May 18, 2004).

Probation officer afforded due process prior to termination. — Circuit court did not err in affirming a hearing officer's decision that despite the employer's failure to strictly comply with its own termination policy, that noncompliance was harmless error, as only the circuit court was authorized to rescind the employee's appointment as a probation officer serving that court; further, the action of the court could not have been challenged to the employer, even if the employee had been provided an opportunity to respond to the charges before her termination, as the employer could neither authorize nor rescind authorization for the employee to serve as a court-appointed probation officer under § 53.1-143. Barker v. Va. Dep't of Corr., — Va. App. —, — S.E.2d —, 2005 Va. App. LEXIS 327 (Aug. 30, 2005).

Reversal of hearing officer's decision in error. — Upon judicial review of a hearing officer's decision to amend a disciplinary notice against two penitentiary employees, the trial court erred by concluding that the hearing officer had no authority to amend the disciplinary notice and, therefore, dismissed the Group II disciplinary notice. Because the hearing officer's amendment of the disciplinary notice did not violate any statute, judicial precedent, or accepted legal principal, it was proper and should have been upheld. Commonwealth v. Doyle, — Va. App. —, — S.E.2d —, 2005 Va. App. LEXIS 255 (July 5, 2005).

Circuit court erred in reversing a hearing officer's decision sustaining disciplinary action against a state trooper for failing to follow a supervisor's instructions because the circuit court, in contravention of its standard of review under § 2.2-3006, improperly disregarded the hearing officer's factual finding that the trooper understood the supervisor's instructions. Va. Dep't of State Police v. Thompson, — Va. App. —, — S.E.2d —, 2007 Va. App. LEXIS 476 (Dec. 27, 2007).

Jurisdictional issue waived. — State employer waived the issue of whether the trial court had jurisdiction to hear the employee's grievance appeal from the hearing officer's denial of relief to the employee, based on the state employer's claim that the grievance appeal was not timely filed, as the state employer did not properly assign that alleged cross-error for review by the state supreme court. Horner v. Dep't of Mental Health, Mental Retardation, & Substance Abuse Servs., 268 Va. 187, 597 S.E.2d 202, 2004 Va. LEXIS 83 (2004).

Procedures for making transcript part of record. — By sending the circuit court cassette tapes of an administrative hearing and a transcript of those tapes, both of which were part of the grievance record, the Virginia Department of Corrections (VDOC) complied with this section and, therefore, properly made the transcript part of the circuit court record. Once the transcript was part of the record, VDOC did not need to take any further steps to "file" the transcript for purposes of its appeal of the circuit court's decision. Va. Dep't of Corr. v. Compton, 47 Va. App. 202, 623 S.E.2d 397, 2005 Va. App. LEXIS 517 (2005).

Applied in Pound v. Dep't of Game & Inland Fisheries, 40 Va. App. 59, 577 S.E.2d 533, 2003 Va. App. LEXIS 119 (2003).

CIRCUIT COURT OPINIONS

Severity of discipline. — University was in its rights when it imposed a discipline upon a campus police officer following an auto accident that was more severe than the discipline it had imposed upon other police officers for similar conduct, but conduct that caused less damage; therefore, a hearing officer's decision in a grievance proceeding that the university could not impose a more severe discipline on the officer than what other officers had received for similar conduct was contradictory to law. Siewert v. Virginia Commonwealth Univ., 58 Va. Cir. 212, 2002 Va. Cir. LEXIS 143 (Richmond 2002).

The decision must be contradictory to law. — Hearing officer's decision that affirmed the state employer's decision to issue two separate "Group II" written violations and subsequently terminate the state employee based on those violations was affirmed as the only ground of appeal of the hearing officer's decision was that the decision was contradictory to law; since that ground was not apparent in the state employee's case, the hearing officer's decision was affirmed. Green v. Mary Washington College, 63 Va. Cir. 47, 2003 Va. Cir. LEXIS 196 (Fredericksburg 2003).

Because an employee failed to show that a decision by the Department of Employment Dispute Resolution terminating his employment, and the hearing officer's final decision upholding the same, were contradictory to law, the circuit court lacked jurisdiction to review the hearing officer's final decision. Thus, an appeal therefrom was dismissed. Shulz v. Univ.

of Va., 73 Va. Cir. 482, 2007 Va. Cir. LEXIS 234 (Charlottesville Aug. 2, 2007).

Termination not contradictory to law. — Agency's termination of an employee was not contradictory to law, because the termination was supported by sufficient evidence showing, inter alia, that the employee was terminated for improper use of agency resources and equipment and causing agency expenses for things other than agency business. Jacobs v. Va. Empl. Comm'n, 69 Va. Cir. 66, 2005 Va. Cir. LEXIS 343 (Richmond 2005).

Scope of review. — Court had no authority to review decisions of a hearing officer that involved the sufficiency of the evidence pursuant to subsection B of § 2.2-3006, based on the plain wording therein and the explicit references to evidentiary support contained in §§ 8.01-680, 2.2-4027, and 60.2-625, with respect to the hearing officer's reversal of a university's termination of a university police officer and the hearing officer's award of attorney's fees to the officer. Old Dominion Univ. v. Birkmeyer, 73 Va. Cir. 341, 2007 Va. Cir. LEXIS 131 (Norfolk 2007).

Contents of notice of appeal. — University's appeal of a final decision of a hearing officer, which reversed its termination of a university police officer and awarded the officer substantial attorney's fees, was not subject to the officer's motion to dismiss, as the court's jurisdiction was granted by subsection B of § 2.2-3006 and accordingly, was not determined by a grievance procedure rule that required that a copy of the notice of appeal be served on the Employment Dispute Resolution Director at the university; there were no requirements imposed on the content of the notice of appeal. Old Dominion Univ. v. Birkmeyer, 73 Va. Cir. 341, 2007 Va. Cir. LEXIS 131 (Norfolk 2007).

§ 2.2-3007. Certain employees of the Departments of Corrections and Juvenile Justice. — A. Employees of the Departments of Corrections and Juvenile Justice who work in institutions or juvenile correctional centers or have client, inmate, or resident contact and who are terminated on the grounds of client, inmate, or resident abuse, criminal conviction, or as a result of being placed on probation under the provisions of § 18.2-251, may appeal their termination only through the grievance resolution steps.

B. If no resolution is reached by the conclusion of the last grievance step, the employee may advance the grievance to the circuit court of the jurisdiction in which the grievance occurred for a de novo hearing on the merits. In its discretion, the court may refer the matter to a commissioner in chancery to take such evidence as may be proper and to make a report to the court. Both the grievant and the respondent may call upon witnesses and be represented by legal counsel or other representatives before the court or the commissioner in chancery. Such representatives may examine, cross-examine, question and present evidence on behalf of the grievant or respondent before the court or commissioner in chancery without being in violation of the provisions of § 54.1-3904.

C. A termination shall be upheld unless shown to have been unwarranted by the facts or contrary to law or policy. (1995, cc. 770, 818, § 2.1-116.08; 1996, cc. 755, 914; 2001, cc. 393, 420, 844.)

Editor's note. — Acts 2001, cc. 393 and 420 amended § 2.1-116.08, from which this section is derived. Pursuant to § 30-152, Acts 2001, cc. 393 and 420 have been given effect in this section as set out above.

CASE NOTES

Locality procedure decisions. — Decision rendered under a locality procedure is not a decision issued pursuant to § 2.2-3005 or a final grievance hearing decision issued pursuant to subsection B of § 2.2-3007; thus, a city manager's decision refusing to abide by a personnel board decision that a police officer should be reinstated to his job could not be considered by a Virginia appellate court. Styles v. City of Colonial Heights, 43 Va. App. 588, 600 S.E.2d 174, 2004 Va. App. LEXIS 378 (2004).

§ 2.2-3008. Employees of local constitutional officers. — Constitutional officers shall not be required to provide a grievance procedure for their employees; however, such employees may be accepted in a local governing body's grievance procedure or personnel system if agreed to by the constitutional officer and the local governing body. (1995, cc. 770, 818, § 2.1-116.012; 1996, cc. 164, 869; 2001, c. 844.)

CHAPTER 31.

State and Local Government Conflict of Interests Act.

ARTICLE 1.

General Provisions.

§ 2.2-3100. Policy; application; construction. — The General Assembly, recognizing that our system of representative government is dependent in part upon (i) citizen legislative members representing fully the public in the legislative process and (ii) its citizens maintaining the highest trust in their public officers and employees, finds and declares that the citizens are entitled to be assured that the judgment of public officers and employees will be guided by a law that defines and prohibits inappropriate conflicts and requires disclosure of economic interests. To that end and for the purpose of establishing a single body of law applicable to all state and local government officers and employees on the subject of conflict of interests, the General Assembly enacts this State and Local Government Conflict of Interests Act so that the standards of conduct for such officers and employees may be uniform throughout the Commonwealth.

This chapter shall supersede all general and special acts and charter provisions which purport to deal with matters covered by this chapter except that the provisions of §§ 15.2-852, 15.2-2287, 15.2-2287.1, and 15.2-2289 and ordinances adopted pursuant thereto shall remain in force and effect. The provisions of this chapter shall be supplemented but not superseded by the provisions on ethics in public contracting in Article 6 (§ 2.2-4367 et seq.) of Chapter 43 of this title and ordinances adopted pursuant to § 2.2-3104.2 regulating receipt of gifts.

This chapter shall be liberally construed to accomplish its purpose. (1987, Sp. Sess., c. 1, § 2.1-639.1; 1990, c. 672; 2001, c. 844; 2003, c. 694; 2008, c. 532.)

Cross references. — As to the disposition of surplus materials by the Department of General Services, see § 2.2-1124. As to the membership of the Tobacco Indemnification and Community Revitalization Commission, see § 3.1-1108.

The 2008 amendments. — The 2008 amendment by c. 532 inserted "15.2-2287.1" following "15.2-2287," in the second paragraph.

Law Review. — For note on conflict of interests and State government employees, see 47 Va. L. Rev. 1034 (1961). For survey of legislation on administration of government — conflict of interest, see 5 U. Rich. L. Rev. 182 (1970).

Michie's Jurisprudence. — For related discussion, see 5A M.J. Counties, §§ 2, 19, 34; 13B M.J. Municipal Corporations, § 20; 17 M.J. State, §§ 4, 7, 11.

CASE NOTES

Editor's note. — Some of the cases below were decided under former Title 2.1 or prior provisions.

Applicability. — Since a majority of council members did not vote on the retailer's applications for rezoning and special use permits, the town council's vote, by less than a majority of council members, meant that a quorum had not voted on the applications, and, thus, the three council members vote to approve the applications was invalid; too, it did not matter that some of the missing council members had absented themselves pursuant to the State and Local Government Conflict of Interests Act (COIA), § 2.2-3100 et seq., since COIA did not apply the laws involving "Meetings of Governing Bodies" since those laws had nothing to do with conflicts of interests. Jakabcin v. Town of Front Royal, 271 Va. 660, 628 S.E.2d 319, 2006 Va. LEXIS 49 (2006).

Conflicts of interest are proscribed precisely because they may compromise or affect judgment of public servants at the expense of private citizens. If, at the time the transaction is pending, it is reasonably foreseeable that the public servant's personal interest could benefit or suffer from his participation in that transaction, the conflict and the danger it poses to the public interest arise at the moment the transaction occurs. West v. Jones, 228 Va. 409, 323 S.E.2d 96 (1984).

Public servant's interest may not exceed that as member of public at large. — A public servant whose interest is "involved" in a transaction may participate in that transaction only when his interest is one limited to that which he shares in common with other members of the public at large. West v. Jones, 228 Va. 409, 323 S.E.2d 96 (1984).

High school principal may not nominate or appoint school board members. — The former Comprehensive Conflict of Interests Act of 1984 prohibited school principal from participating in the nomination and appointment of members of the school board so long as he was employed by the board. West v. Jones, 228 Va. 409, 323 S.E.2d 96 (1984).

§ **2.2-3100.1. Copy of chapter; review by officers and employees.** — Any person required to file a disclosure statement of personal interests pursuant to subsections A or B of § 2.2-3114, subsections A or B of § 2.2-3115 or § 2.2-3116 shall be furnished by the public body's administrator a copy of this chapter within two weeks following the person's election, reelection, employment, appointment or reappointment.

All officers and employees shall read and familiarize themselves with the provisions of this chapter. (2004, cc. 134, 392.)

§ **2.2-3101. Definitions.** — As used in this chapter:

"Advisory agency" means any board, commission, committee or post which does not exercise any sovereign power or duty, but is appointed by a governmental agency or officer or is created by law for the purpose of making studies or recommendations, or advising or consulting with a governmental agency.

"Affiliated business entity relationship" means a relationship, other than a parent-subsidiary relationship, that exists when (i) one business entity has a controlling ownership interest in the other business entity, (ii) a controlling owner in one entity is also a controlling owner in the other entity, or (iii) there is shared management or control between the business entities. Factors that may be considered in determining the existence of an affiliated business entity relationship include that the same person or substantially the same person owns or manages the two entities, there are common or commingled funds or assets, the business entities share the use of the same offices or employees, or otherwise share activities, resources or personnel on a regular basis, or there is otherwise a close working relationship between the entities.

"Business" means a corporation, partnership, sole proprietorship, firm, enterprise, franchise, association, trust or foundation, or any other individual or entity carrying on a business or profession, whether or not for profit.

"Contract" means any agreement to which a governmental agency is a party, or any agreement on behalf of a governmental agency that involves the payment of money appropriated by the General Assembly or political subdivision, whether or not such agreement is executed in the name of the Commonwealth, or some political subdivision thereof. "Contract" includes a subcontract only when the contract of which it is a part is with the officer's or employee's own governmental agency.

"Dependent" means a son, daughter, father, mother, brother, sister or other person, whether or not related by blood or marriage, if such person receives from the officer or employee, or provides to the officer or employee, more than one-half of his financial support.

"Employee" means all persons employed by a governmental or advisory agency, unless otherwise limited by the context of its use.

"Financial institution" means any bank, trust company, savings institution, industrial loan association, consumer finance company, credit union, broker-dealer as defined in § 13.1-501, or investment company or advisor registered under the federal Investment Advisors Act or Investment Company Act of 1940.

"Gift" means any gratuity, favor, discount, entertainment, hospitality, loan, forbearance, or other item having monetary value. It includes services as well as gifts of transportation, local travel, lodgings and meals, whether provided in-kind, by purchase of a ticket, payment in advance or reimbursement after the expense has been incurred. "Gift" shall not include any offer of a ticket or other admission or pass unless the ticket, admission, or pass is used. "Gift" shall not include honorary degrees and presents from relatives. For the purpose of this definition, "relative" means the donee's spouse, child, uncle, aunt, niece, or nephew; a person to whom the donee is engaged to be married; the donee's or his spouse's parent, grandparent, grandchild, brother, or sister; or the donee's brother's or sister's spouse.

"Governmental agency" means each component part of the legislative, executive or judicial branches of state and local government, including each office, department, authority, post, commission, committee, and each institution or board created by law to exercise some regulatory or sovereign power or duty as distinguished from purely advisory powers or duties. Corporations organized or controlled by the Virginia Retirement System are "governmental agencies" for purposes of this chapter.

"Immediate family" means (i) a spouse and (ii) any other person residing in the same household as the officer or employee, who is a dependent of the officer or employee or of whom the officer or employee is a dependent.

"Officer" means any person appointed or elected to any governmental or advisory agency including local school boards, whether or not he receives compensation or other emolument of office. Unless the context requires otherwise, "officer" includes members of the judiciary.

"Parent-subsidiary relationship" means a relationship that exists when one corporation directly or indirectly owns shares possessing more than 50 percent of the voting power of another corporation.

"Personal interest" means a financial benefit or liability accruing to an officer or employee or to a member of his immediate family. Such interest shall exist by reason of (i) ownership in a business if the ownership interest exceeds three percent of the total equity of the business; (ii) annual income that exceeds, or may reasonably be anticipated to exceed, $10,000 from ownership in real or personal property or a business; (iii) salary, other compensation, fringe benefits, or benefits from the use of property, or any combination thereof, paid or provided by a business or governmental agency that exceeds, or may reasonably be anticipated to exceed, $10,000 annually; (iv) ownership of real or personal property if the interest exceeds $10,000 in value and excluding ownership in a business, income, or salary, other compensation, fringe benefits or benefits from the use of property; (v) personal liability incurred or assumed on behalf of a business if the liability exceeds three percent of the asset value of the business; or (vi) an option for ownership of a business or real or personal property if the ownership interest will consist of (i) or (iv) above.

"Personal interest in a contract" means a personal interest that an officer or employee has in a contract with a governmental agency, whether due to his being a party to the contract or due to a personal interest in a business that is a party to the contract.

"Personal interest in a transaction" means a personal interest of an officer or employee in any matter considered by his agency. Such personal interest exists when an officer or employee or a member of his immediate family has a personal interest in property or a business or governmental agency, or represents or provides services to any individual or business and such property, business or represented or served individual or business (i) is the subject of the transaction or (ii) may realize a reasonably foreseeable direct or indirect benefit or detriment as a result of the action of the agency considering the transaction. Notwithstanding the above, such personal interest in a

transaction shall not be deemed to exist where an elected member of a local governing body serves without remuneration as a member of the board of trustees of a not-for-profit entity and such elected member or member of his immediate family has no personal interest related to the not-for-profit entity.

"State and local government officers and employees" shall not include members of the General Assembly.

"State filer" means those officers and employees required to file a disclosure statement of their personal interests pursuant to subsection A or B of § 2.2-3114.

"Transaction" means any matter considered by any governmental or advisory agency, whether in a committee, subcommittee, or other entity of that agency or before the agency itself, on which official action is taken or contemplated. (1987, Sp. Sess., c. 1, § 2.1-639.2; 1988, c. 536; 1992, c. 865; 1993, c. 303; 1994, cc. 74, 724; 1995, c. 495; 1996, c. 77; 1997, c. 641; 2001, c. 844; 2003, c. 694; 2004, cc. 134, 392.)

Article 2.

Generally Prohibited and Unlawful Conduct.

§ **2.2-3102. Application.** — This article applies to generally prohibited conduct that shall be unlawful and to state and local government officers and employees. (1987, Sp. Sess., c. 1, § 2.1-639.3; 2001, c. 844.)

§ **2.2-3103. Prohibited conduct.** — No officer or employee of a state or local governmental or advisory agency shall:

1. Solicit or accept money or other thing of value for services performed within the scope of his official duties, except the compensation, expenses or other remuneration paid by the agency of which he is an officer or employee. This prohibition shall not apply to the acceptance of special benefits that may be authorized by law;

2. Offer or accept any money or other thing of value for or in consideration of obtaining employment, appointment, or promotion of any person with any governmental or advisory agency;

3. Offer or accept any money or other thing of value for or in consideration of the use of his public position to obtain a contract for any person or business with any governmental or advisory agency;

4. Use for his own economic benefit or that of another party confidential information that he has acquired by reason of his public position and which is not available to the public;

5. Accept any money, loan, gift, favor, service, or business or professional opportunity that reasonably tends to influence him in the performance of his official duties. This subdivision shall not apply to any political contribution actually used for political campaign or constituent service purposes and reported as required by Chapter 9.3 (§ 24.2-945 et seq.) of Title 24.2;

6. Accept any business or professional opportunity when he knows that there is a reasonable likelihood that the opportunity is being afforded him to influence him in the performance of his official duties;

7. Accept any honoraria for any appearance, speech, or article in which the officer or employee provides expertise or opinions related to the performance of his official duties. The term "honoraria" shall not include any payment for or reimbursement to such person for his actual travel, lodging, or subsistence expenses incurred in connection with such appearance, speech, or article or in the alternative a payment of money or anything of value not in excess of the per diem deduction allowable under § 162 of the Internal Revenue Code, as amended from time to time. The prohibition in this subdivision shall apply only

to the Governor, Lieutenant Governor, Attorney General, Governor's Secretaries, and heads of departments of state government;

8. Accept a gift from a person who has interests that may be substantially affected by the performance of the officer's or employee's official duties under circumstances where the timing and nature of the gift would cause a reasonable person to question the officer's or employee's impartiality in the matter affecting the donor. Violations of this subdivision shall not be subject to criminal law penalties; or

9. Accept gifts from sources on a basis so frequent as to raise an appearance of the use of his public office for private gain. Violations of this subdivision shall not be subject to criminal law penalties. (1987, Sp. Sess., c. 1, § 2.1-639.4; 1994, cc. 663, 815, 851; 2001, c. 844; 2006, cc. 787, 892.)

OPINIONS OF THE ATTORNEY GENERAL

Health regulatory board members. — It is not a violation of the State and Local Government Conflict of Interests Act or the Virginia Public Procurement Act for a member of a health regulatory board to vote to authorize the board to contract with or join an organization in the business of administering licensure examinations, where the Department of Health Professions reimburses the board member for per diem and expenses as allowable under state law and travel regulations. See opinion of Attorney General to Mr. Robert A. Nebiker, Director, Department of Health Professions, 05-029 (6/21/05).

It would be a violation of the State and Local Government Conflict of Interests Act or the Virginia Public Procurement Act for a board member to vote to approve a contract or to join an organization where, at the time of the vote, there is an existing arrangement concerning prospective employment of such board member after departure from the board or the board member accepts the payment of monies in excess of allowable per diem payments and travel reimbursement allowances. See opinion of Attorney General to Mr. Robert A. Nebiker, Director, Department of Health Professions, 05-029 (6/21/05).

§ 2.2-3104. Prohibited conduct for certain officers and employees of state government. — In addition to the prohibitions contained in § 2.2-3103, no state officer or employee shall, during the one year after the termination of his public employment or service, represent a client or act in a representative capacity on behalf of any person or group, for compensation, on any matter before the agency of which he was an officer or employee.

For the purposes of this section, *"state officer or employee"* shall mean (i) the Governor, Lieutenant Governor, Attorney General, and officers appointed by the Governor, whether confirmation by the General Assembly or by either house thereof is required or not, who are regularly employed on a full-time salaried basis; those officers and employees of executive branch agencies who report directly to the agency head; and those at the level immediately below those who report directly to the agency head and are at a payband 6 or higher and (ii) the officers and professional employees of the legislative branch designated by the joint rules committee of the General Assembly. For the purposes of this section, the General Assembly and the legislative branch agencies shall be deemed one agency.

The prohibitions of this section shall apply only to persons engaged in activities that would require registration as a lobbyist under § 2.2-422.

Any person subject to the provisions of this section may apply to the Attorney General, as provided in § 2.2-3126, for an advisory opinion as to the application of the restriction imposed by this section on any post-public employment position or opportunity. (1994, cc. 727, 776, § 2.1-639.4:1; 2001, c. 844.)

§ 2.2-3104.1. Exclusion of certain awards from scope of chapter. — The provisions of this chapter shall not be construed to prohibit or apply to the acceptance by (i) any employee of a local government, or (ii) a teacher or other employee of a local school board of an award or payment in honor of meritorious or exceptional services performed by the teacher or employee and made by an organization exempt from federal income taxation pursuant to the provisions of Section 501(c)(3) of the Internal Revenue Code. (2001, c. 48, § 2.1-639.4:2; 2008, cc. 478, 497.)

Editor's note. — Acts 2001, c. 48 enacted § 2.1-639.4:2, from which this section is derived. Pursuant to § 30-152, Acts 2001, c. 48 has been given effect in this section as set out above.

The 2008 amendments. — The 2008 amendments by cc. 478 and 497 are identical, and inserted "(i) any employee of a local government, or (ii)" and added "and made by an organization exempt from federal income taxation pursuant to the provisions of Section 501(c)(3) of the Internal Revenue Code" at the end.

§ 2.2-3104.2. Ordinance regulating receipt of gifts. — The governing body of any county, city, or town may adopt an ordinance setting a monetary limit on the acceptance of any gift by the officers, appointees or employees of the county, city or town and requiring the disclosure by such officers, appointees or employees of the receipt of any gift. (2003, c. 694.)

Article 3.

Prohibited Conduct Relating to Contracts.

§ 2.2-3105. Application. — This article proscribes certain conduct relating to contracts by state and local government officers and employees. The provisions of this article shall be supplemented but not superseded by the provisions on ethics in public contracting in Article 6 (§ 2.2-4367 et seq.) of Chapter 43 of this title. (1987, Sp. Sess., c. 1, § 2.1-639.5; 2001, c. 844; 2003, c. 694.)

§ 2.2-3106. Prohibited contracts by officers and employees of state government and Eastern Virginia Medical School. — A. No officer or employee of any governmental agency of state government or Eastern Virginia Medical School shall have a personal interest in a contract with the governmental agency of which he is an officer or employee, other than his own contract of employment.

B. No officer or employee of any governmental agency of state government or Eastern Virginia Medical School shall have a personal interest in a contract with any other governmental agency of state government unless such contract is (i) awarded as a result of competitive sealed bidding or competitive negotiation as defined in § 2.2-4301 or (ii) is awarded after a finding, in writing, by the administrative head of the governmental agency that competitive bidding or negotiation is contrary to the best interest of the public.

C. The provisions of this section shall not apply to:

1. An employee's personal interest in additional contracts of employment with his own governmental agency that accrue to him because of a member of his immediate family, provided the employee does not exercise any control over the employment or the employment activities of the member of his immediate family and the employee is not in a position to influence those activities;

2. The personal interest of an officer or employee of a state institution of higher education or the Eastern Virginia Medical School in additional contracts of employment with his own governmental agency that accrue to him because of a member of his immediate family, provided (i) the officer or employee and the immediate family member are engaged in teaching, research or administrative support positions at the educational institution or the

Eastern Virginia Medical School, (ii) the governing board of the educational institution finds that it is in the best interests of the institution or the Eastern Virginia Medical School and the Commonwealth for such dual employment to exist, and (iii) after such finding, the governing board of the educational institution or the Eastern Virginia Medical School ensures that the officer or employee, or the immediate family member, does not have sole authority to supervise, evaluate or make personnel decisions regarding the other;

3. An officer's or employee's personal interest in a contract of employment with any other governmental agency of state government;

4. Contracts for the sale by a governmental agency or the Eastern Virginia Medical School of services or goods at uniform prices available to the general public;

5. An employee's personal interest in a contract between a public institution of higher education in Virginia or the Eastern Virginia Medical School and a publisher or wholesaler of textbooks or other educational materials for students, which accrues to him solely because he has authored or otherwise created such textbooks or materials;

6. An employee's personal interest in a contract with his or her employing public institution of higher education to acquire the collections or scholarly works owned by the employee, including manuscripts, musical scores, poetry, paintings, books or other materials, writings, or papers of an academic, research, or cultural value to the institution, provided the president of the institution approves the acquisition of such collections or scholarly works as being in the best interests of the institution's public mission of service, research, or education;

7. Subject to approval by the board of visitors, an employee's personal interest in a contract between the Eastern Virginia Medical School or a public institution of higher education in Virginia that operates a school of medicine or dentistry and a not-for-profit nonstock corporation that operates a clinical practice within such public institution of higher education or the Eastern Virginia Medical School and of which such employee is a member or employee;

8. Subject to approval by the relevant board of visitors, an employee's personal interest in a contract for research and development or commercialization of intellectual property between a public institution of higher education in Virginia or the Eastern Virginia Medical School and a business in which the employee has a personal interest, if (i) the employee's personal interest has been disclosed to and approved by such public institution of higher education or the Eastern Virginia Medical School prior to the time at which the contract is entered into; (ii) the employee promptly files a disclosure statement pursuant to § 2.2-3117 and thereafter files such statement annually on or before January 15; (iii) the institution has established a formal policy regarding such contracts, approved by the State Council of Higher Education or, in the case of the Eastern Virginia Medical School, a formal policy regarding such contracts in conformity with any applicable federal regulations that has been approved by its board of visitors; and (iv) no later than December 31 of each year, the institution or the Eastern Virginia Medical School files an annual report with the Secretary of the Commonwealth disclosing each open contract entered into subject to this provision, the names of the parties to each contract, the date each contract was executed and its term, the subject of each contractual arrangement, the nature of the conflict of interest, the institution's or the Eastern Virginia Medical School's employee responsible for administering each contract, the details of the institution's or the Eastern Virginia Medical School's commitment or investment of resources or finances for each contract, and any other information requested by the Secretary of the Commonwealth; or

9. Subject to approval by the relevant board of visitors, an employee's personal interest in a contract between a public institution of higher education

in Virginia or the Eastern Virginia Medical School and a business in which the employee has a personal interest, if (i) the personal interest has been disclosed to the institution or the Eastern Virginia Medical School prior to the time the contract is entered into; (ii) the employee files a disclosure statement pursuant to § 2.2-3117 and thereafter annually on or before January 15; (iii) the employee does not participate in the institution's or the Eastern Virginia Medical School's decision to contract; (iv) the president of the institution or the Eastern Virginia Medical School finds and certifies in writing that the contract is for goods and services needed for quality patient care, including related medical education or research, by the institution's medical center or the Eastern Virginia Medical School, its affiliated teaching hospitals and other organizations necessary for the fulfillment of its mission, including the acquisition of drugs, therapies and medical technologies; and (v) no later than December 31 of each year, the institution or the Eastern Virginia Medical School files an annual report with the Secretary of the Commonwealth disclosing each open contract entered subject to this provision, the names of the parties to each contract, the date each contract was executed and its term, the subject of each contractual arrangement, the nature of the conflict of interest, the institution's or the Eastern Virginia Medical School's employee responsible for administering each contract, the details of the institution's or the Eastern Virginia Medical School's commitment or investment of resources or finances for each contract, and any other information requested by the Secretary of the Commonwealth.

D. Notwithstanding the provisions of subdivisions C 8 and C 9, if the research and development or commercialization of intellectual property or the employee's personal interest in a contract with a business is subject to policies and regulations governing conflicts of interest promulgated by any agency of the United States government, including the adoption of policies requiring the disclosure and management of such conflicts of interests, the policies established by the Eastern Virginia Medical School pursuant to such federal requirements shall constitute compliance with subdivisions C 8 and C 9, upon notification by the Eastern Virginia Medical School to the Secretary of the Commonwealth by January 31 of each year of evidence of their compliance with such federal policies and regulations.

E. The board of visitors may delegate the authority granted under subdivision C 8 to the president of the institution. If the board elects to delegate such authority, the board shall include this delegation of authority in the formal policy required by clause (iii) of subdivision C 8. In those instances where the board has delegated such authority, on or before December 1 of each year, the president of the relevant institution shall file a report with the relevant board of visitors disclosing each open contract entered into subject to this provision, the names of the parties to each contract, the date each contract was executed and its term, the subject of each contractual arrangement, the nature of the conflict of interest, the institution's or the Eastern Virginia Medical School's employee responsible for administering each contract, the details of the institution's or the Eastern Virginia Medical School's commitment or investment of resources or finances for each contract, the details of how revenues are to be dispersed, and any other information requested by the board of visitors. (1987, Sp. Sess., c. 1, § 2.1-639.6; 1989, c. 74; 1991, c. 470; 1993, c. 876; 1995, c. 403; 1998, c. 838; 2001, c. 844; 2002, cc. 87, 478; 2003, c. 646; 2006, c. 839.)

§ 2.2-3107. Prohibited contracts by members of county boards of supervisors, city councils and town councils. — A. No person elected or appointed as a member of the governing body of a county, city or town shall have a personal interest in (i) any contract with his governing body, or (ii) any contract with any governmental agency that is a component part of his local government and which is subject to the ultimate control of the governing body of which he is a member, or (iii) any contract other than a contract of employment with any other governmental agency if such person's governing body appoints a majority of the members of the governing body of the second governmental agency.

B. The provisions of this section shall not apply to:

1. A member's personal interest in a contract of employment provided (i) the officer or employee was employed by the governmental agency prior to July 1, 1983, in accordance with the provisions of the former Conflict of Interests Act, Chapter 22 (§ 2.1-347 et seq.) of Title 2.1 as it existed on June 30, 1983, or (ii) the employment first began prior to the member becoming a member of the governing body;

2. Contracts for the sale by a governmental agency of services or goods at uniform prices available to the public; or

3. A contract awarded to a member of a governing body as a result of competitive sealed bidding where the governing body has established a need for the same or substantially similar goods through purchases prior to the election or appointment of the member to serve on the governing body. However, the member shall have no involvement in the preparation of the specifications for such contract, and the remaining members of the governing body, by written resolution, shall state that it is in the public interest for the member to bid on such contract. (1987, Sp. Sess., c. 1, § 2.1-639.7; 2001, c. 844.)

Michie's Jurisprudence. — For related discussion, see 5A M.J. Counties, §§ 36, 60.

CASE NOTES

Editor's note. — The cases below were decided under former Title 2.1 or prior provisions.

Appointment of agency officers by agency employee not authorized by this section. — Former § 2.1-606 (see now this section) has two effects. It forbids a member of a local governing body to have a personal interest in certain contracts with a governmental agency if the majority of the officers of that agency are appointed by the local governing body. And, by way of exception, it permits a member of a local governing body to hold a job with such an agency. Nothing in the section authorizes such a person who works for such an agency to participate in the appointment of the officers of that agency. West v. Jones, 228 Va. 409, 323 S.E.2d 96 (1984).

No requirement that resolution be approved by unanimous vote. — Subdivision B 3 of this section does not state that the resolution must be approved by a unanimous vote of the remaining members of the governing body. It simply provides that only those members who do not have a personal interest in the contract may vote on the resolution. Harris v. Ingram, 240 Va. 46, 392 S.E.2d 816 (1990).

§ 2.2-3108. Prohibited contracts by members of school boards. — A. No person elected or appointed as a member of a local school board shall have a personal interest in (i) any contract with his school board or (ii) any contract with any governmental agency that is subject to the ultimate control of the school board of which he is a member.

B. The provisions of this section shall not apply to:

1. A member's personal interest in a contract of employment provided the employment first began prior to the member becoming a member of the school board;

2. Contracts for the sale by a governmental agency of services or goods at uniform prices available to the public; or

3. A contract awarded to a member of a school board as a result of competitive sealed bidding where the school board has established a need for the same or substantially similar goods through purchases prior to the election

or appointment of the member to serve on the school board. However, the member shall have no involvement in the preparation of the specifications for such contract, and the remaining members of the school board, by written resolution, shall state that it is in the public interest for the member to bid on such contract. (1996, c. 548, § 2.1-639.7:1; 2001, c. 844.)

§ 2.2-3109. Prohibited contracts by other officers and employees of local governmental agencies. — A. No other officer or employee of any governmental agency of local government shall have a personal interest in a contract with the agency of which he is an officer or employee other than his own contract of employment.

B. No officer or employee of any governmental agency of local government shall have a personal interest in a contract with any other governmental agency that is a component of the government of his county, city or town unless such contract is (i) awarded as a result of competitive sealed bidding or competitive negotiation as defined in § 2.2-4301 or is awarded as a result of a procedure embodying competitive principles as authorized by subdivisions 10 or 11 of § 2.2-4343 or (ii) is awarded after a finding, in writing, by the administrative head of the governmental agency that competitive bidding or negotiation is contrary to the best interest of the public.

C. The provisions of this section shall not apply to:

1. An employee's personal interest in additional contracts of employment with his own governmental agency that accrue to him because of a member of his immediate family, provided the employee does not exercise any control over the employment or the employment activities of the member of his immediate family and the employee is not in a position to influence those activities;

2. An officer's or employee's personal interest in a contract of employment with any other governmental agency that is a component part of the government of his county, city or town;

3. Contracts for the sale by a governmental agency of services or goods at uniform prices available to the general public;

4. Members of local governing bodies who are subject to § 2.2-3107;

5. Members of local school boards who are subject to § 2.2-3108; or

6. **(Effective until July 1, 2009)** Any ownership or financial interest of members of the governing body, administrators, and other personnel serving in a public charter school in renovating, lending, granting, or leasing public charter school facilities, as the case may be, provided such interest has been disclosed in the public charter school application as required by § 22.1-212.8. (1987, Sp. Sess., c. 1, § 2.1-639.8; 1996, c. 548; 2001, c. 844; 2004, c. 530.)

Editor's note. — Acts 2004, c. 530, cl. 2, provides: "That the provisions of this act shall expire on July 1, 2009."

The 2004 amendments. — The 2004 amendment by c. 530 added subdivision C 6 and made a stylistic change. For expiration provision, see Editor's note.

Law Review. — For 2003/2004 survey of education law, see 39 U. Rich. L. Rev. 183 (2004).

Michie's Jurisprudence. — For related discussion, see 5A M.J. Counties, § 60.

§ 2.2-3110. Further exceptions. — A. The provisions of Article 3 (§ 2.2-3106 et seq.) of this chapter shall not apply to:

1. The sale, lease or exchange of real property between an officer or employee and a governmental agency, provided the officer or employee does not participate in any way as such officer or employee in such sale, lease or exchange, and this fact is set forth as a matter of public record by the governing body of the governmental agency or by the administrative head thereof;

2. The publication of official notices;

3. Contracts between the government or school board of a town or city with a population of less than 10,000 and an officer or employee of that town or city government or school board when the total of such contracts between the town or city government or school board and the officer or employee of that town or city government or school board or a business controlled by him does not exceed $10,000 per year or such amount exceeds $10,000 and is less than $25,000 but results from contracts arising from awards made on a sealed bid basis, and such officer or employee has made disclosure as provided for in § 2.2-3115;

4. An officer or employee whose sole personal interest in a contract with the governmental agency is by reason of income from the contracting firm or governmental agency in excess of $10,000 per year, provided the officer or employee or a member of his immediate family does not participate and has no authority to participate in the procurement or letting of such contract on behalf of the contracting firm and the officer or employee either does not have authority to participate in the procurement or letting of the contract on behalf of his governmental agency or he disqualifies himself as a matter of public record and does not participate on behalf of his governmental agency in negotiating the contract or in approving the contract;

5. When the governmental agency is a public institution of higher education, an officer or employee whose personal interest in a contract with the institution is by reason of an ownership in the contracting firm in excess of 3% of the contracting firm's equity, provided that (i) the officer or employee's ownership or other equity interest and that of any immediate family member in the contracting firm is disclosed in writing to the president of the institution, which writing certifies that the officer or employee has not and will not participate in the contract negotiations on behalf of the contracting firm or the institution, (ii) the president of the institution makes a written finding as a matter of public record that the contract is in the best interests of the institution, (iii) the officer or employee either does not have authority to participate in the procurement or letting of the contract on behalf of the institution or disqualifies himself as a matter of public record, and (iv) does not participate on behalf of the institution in negotiating the contract or approving the contract;

6. Except when the governmental agency is the Virginia Retirement System, contracts between an officer's or employee's governmental agency and a public service corporation, financial institution, or company furnishing public utilities in which the officer or employee has a personal interest, provided the officer or employee disqualifies himself as a matter of public record and does not participate on behalf of his governmental agency in negotiating the contract or in approving the contract;

7. Contracts for the purchase of goods or services when the contract does not exceed $500;

8. Grants or other payment under any program wherein uniform rates for, or the amounts paid to, all qualified applicants are established solely by the administering governmental agency; or

9. An officer or employee whose sole personal interest in a contract with his own governmental agency is by reason of his marriage to his spouse who is employed by the same agency, if the spouse was employed by such agency for five or more years prior to marrying such officer or employee.

B. Neither the provisions of this chapter nor, unless expressly provided otherwise, any amendments thereto shall apply to those employment contracts or renewals thereof or to any other contracts entered into prior to August 1, 1987, which were in compliance with either the former Virginia Conflict of Interests Act, Chapter 22 (§ 2.1-347 et seq.) or the former Comprehensive Conflict of Interests Act, Chapter 40 (§ 2.1-599 et seq.) of Title 2.1 at the time of their formation and thereafter. Those contracts shall continue to be governed by the provisions of the appropriate prior Act. Notwithstanding the provisions of subdivision (f) (4) of § 2.1-348 Title 2.1 in effect prior to July 1, 1983, the employment by the same governmental agency of an officer or employee and spouse or any other relative residing in the same household shall not be deemed to create a material financial interest except when one of such persons is employed in a direct supervisory or administrative position, or both, with respect to such spouse or other relative residing in his household and the annual salary of such subordinate is $22,500 or more. (1987, Sp. Sess., c. 1, § 2.1-639.9; 1990, c. 51; 1993, c. 303; 1994, cc. 450, 713; 1997, c. 641; 2001, c. 844; 2006, c. 839.)

Michie's Jurisprudence. — For related discussion, see 5A M.J. Counties, § 36.

ARTICLE 4.

Prohibited Conduct Relating to Transactions.

§ **2.2-3111. Application.** — This article proscribes certain conduct by state and local government officers and employees having a personal interest in a transaction. (1987, Sp. Sess., c. 1, § 2.1-639.10; 2001, c. 844.)

§ **2.2-3112. Prohibited conduct concerning personal interest in a transaction; exceptions.** — A. Each officer and employee of any state or local governmental or advisory agency who has a personal interest in a transaction:

1. Shall disqualify himself from participating in the transaction if (i) the transaction has application solely to property or a business or governmental agency in which he has a personal interest or a business that has a parent-subsidiary or affiliated business entity relationship with the business in which he has a personal interest or (ii) he is unable to participate pursuant to subdivision 2, 3 or 4. Any disqualification under the provisions of this subdivision shall be recorded in the public records of the officer's or employee's governmental or advisory agency. The officer or employee shall disclose his personal interest as required by § 2.2-3114 E or 2.2-3115 E and shall not vote or in any manner act on behalf of his agency in the transaction. The officer or employee shall be prohibited from (i) attending any portion of a closed meeting authorized by the Virginia Freedom of Information Act (§ 2.2-3700 et seq.) when the matter in which he has a personal interest is discussed and (ii) discussing the matter in which he has a personal interest with other governmental officers or employees at any time;

2. May participate in the transaction if he is a member of a business, profession, occupation, or group of three or more persons the members of which are affected by the transaction, and he complies with the declaration requirements of § 2.2-3114 F or 2.2-3115 G;

3. May participate in the transaction when a party to the transaction is a client of his firm if he does not personally represent or provide services to such client and he complies with the declaration requirements of § 2.2-3114 G or 2.2-3115 H; or

4. May participate in the transaction if it affects the public generally, even though his personal interest, as a member of the public, may also be affected by that transaction.

B. Disqualification under the provisions of this section shall not prevent any employee having a personal interest in a transaction in which his agency is involved from representing himself or a member of his immediate family in such transaction provided he does not receive compensation for such representation and provided he complies with the disqualification and relevant disclosure requirements of this chapter.

C. Notwithstanding any other provision of law, if disqualifications of officers or employees in accordance with this section leave less than the number required by law to act, the remaining member or members shall constitute a quorum for the conduct of business and have authority to act for the agency by majority vote, unless a unanimous vote of all members is required by law, in which case authority to act shall require a unanimous vote of remaining members. Notwithstanding any provisions of this chapter to the contrary, members of a local governing body whose sole interest in any proposed sale, contract of sale, exchange, lease or conveyance is by virtue of their employment by a business involved in a proposed sale, contract of sale, exchange, lease or conveyance, and where such member's or members' vote is essential to a constitutional majority required pursuant to Article VII, Section 9 of the Constitution of Virginia and § 15.2-2100, such member or members of the local governing body may vote and participate in the deliberations of the governing body concerning whether to approve, enter into or execute such sale, contract of sale, exchange, lease or conveyance. Official action taken under circumstances that violate this section may be rescinded by the agency on such terms as the interests of the agency and innocent third parties require.

D. The provisions of subsection A shall not prevent an officer or employee from participating in a transaction merely because such officer or employee is a party in a legal proceeding of a civil nature concerning such transaction.

E. The provisions of subsection A shall not prevent an employee from participating in a transaction regarding textbooks or other educational material for students at state institutions of higher education, when those textbooks or materials have been authored or otherwise created by the employee. (1987, Sp. Sess., c. 1, § 2.1-639.11; 2001, c. 844; 2003, c. 694; 2007, c. 613.)

The 2007 amendments. — The 2007 amendment by c. 613 inserted "Notwithstanding any other provision of law" and "constitute a quorum for the conduct of business and" in the first sentence of subsection C.

CASE NOTES

Applicability. — Since a majority of council members did not vote on the retailer's applications for rezoning and special use permits, the town council's vote, by less than a majority of council members, meant that a quorum had not voted on the applications, and, thus, the three council members vote to approve the applications was invalid; too, it did not matter that some of the missing council members had absented themselves pursuant to the State and Local Government Conflict of Interests Act (COIA), § 2.2-3100 et seq., since COIA did not apply the laws involving "Meetings of Governing Bodies" since those laws had nothing to do with conflicts of interests. Jakabcin v. Town of Front Royal, 271 Va. 660, 628 S.E.2d 319, 2006 Va. LEXIS 49 (2006).

Public servant's interest may not exceed that as member of public at large. — A public servant whose interest is "involved" in a transaction may participate in that transaction only when his interest is one limited to that which he shares in common with other members of the public at large. West v. Jones, 228 Va. 409, 323 S.E.2d 96 (1984) (decided under prior law).

Article 5.

Disclosure Statements Required to Be Filed.

§ 2.2-3113. Application. — This article requires disclosure of certain personal and financial interests by state and local government officers and employees. (1987, Sp. Sess., c. 1, § 2.1-639.12; 2001, c. 844.)

§ 2.2-3114. Disclosure by state officers and employees. — A. The Governor, Lieutenant Governor, Attorney General, Justices of the Supreme Court, judges of the Court of Appeals, judges of any circuit court, judges and substitute judges of any district court, members of the State Corporation Commission, members of the Virginia Workers' Compensation Commission, members of the Commonwealth Transportation Board, members of the Board of Trustees of the Virginia Retirement System, and members of the State Lottery Board and other persons occupying such offices or positions of trust or employment in state government, including members of the governing bodies of authorities, as may be designated by the Governor or, in the case of officers or employees of the legislative branch, by the Joint Rules Committee of the General Assembly, shall file, as a condition to assuming office or employment, a disclosure statement of their personal interests and such other information as is specified on the form set forth in § 2.2-3117 and thereafter shall file such a statement annually on or before January 15. When the filing deadline falls on a Saturday, Sunday, or legal holiday, the disclosure statement shall be filed on the next day that is not a Saturday, Sunday, or legal holiday.

B. Nonsalaried citizen members of all policy and supervisory boards, commissions and councils in the executive branch of state government, other than the Commonwealth Transportation Board, members of the Board of Trustees of the Virginia Retirement System, and the State Lottery Board, shall file, as a condition to assuming office, a disclosure form of their personal interests and such other information as is specified on the form set forth in § 2.2-3118 and thereafter shall file such form annually on or before January 15. When the filing deadline falls on a Saturday, Sunday, or legal holiday, the disclosure statement shall be filed on the next day that is not a Saturday, Sunday, or legal holiday. Nonsalaried citizen members of other boards, commissions and councils, including advisory boards and authorities, may be required to file a disclosure form if so designated by the Governor, in which case the form shall be that set forth in § 2.2-3118.

C. The disclosure forms required by subsections A and B shall be provided by the Secretary of the Commonwealth to each officer and employee so designated, including officers appointed by legislative authorities, not later than November 30 of each year. Disclosure forms shall be filed and maintained as public records for five years in the Office of the Secretary of the Commonwealth.

D. Candidates for the offices of Governor, Lieutenant Governor or Attorney General shall file a disclosure statement of their personal interests as required by § 24.2-502.

E. Any officer or employee of state government who has a personal interest in any transaction before the governmental or advisory agency of which he is an officer or employee and who is disqualified from participating in that transaction pursuant to subdivision A 1 of § 2.2-3112, or otherwise elects to disqualify himself, shall forthwith make disclosure of the existence of his interest, including the full name and address of the business and the address or parcel number for the real estate if the interest involves a business or real estate, and his disclosure shall also be reflected in the public records of the agency for five years in the office of the administrative head of the officer's or employee's governmental agency or advisory agency or, if the agency has a clerk, in the clerk's office.

F. An officer or employee of state government who is required to declare his interest pursuant to subdivision A 2 of § 2.2-3112, shall declare his interest by stating (i) the transaction involved, (ii) the nature of the officer's or employee's personal interest affected by the transaction, (iii) that he is a member of a business, profession, occupation, or group the members of which are affected by the transaction, and (iv) that he is able to participate in the transaction fairly, objectively, and in the public interest. The officer or employee shall either make his declaration orally to be recorded in written minutes for his agency or file a signed written declaration with the clerk or administrative head of his governmental or advisory agency, as appropriate, who shall, in either case, retain and make available for public inspection such declaration for a period of five years from the date of recording or receipt. If reasonable time is not available to comply with the provisions of this subsection prior to participation in the transaction, the officer or employee shall prepare and file the required declaration by the end of the next business day.

G. An officer or employee of state government who is required to declare his interest pursuant to subdivision A 3 of § 2.2-3112, shall declare his interest by stating (i) the transaction involved, (ii) that a party to the transaction is a client of his firm, (iii) that he does not personally represent or provide services to the client, and (iv) that he is able to participate in the transaction fairly, objectively, and in the public interest. The officer or employee shall either make his declaration orally to be recorded in written minutes for his agency or file a signed written declaration with the clerk or administrative head of his governmental or advisory agency, as appropriate, who shall, in either case, retain and make available for public inspection such declaration for a period of five years from the date of recording or receipt. If reasonable time is not available to comply with the provisions of this subsection prior to participation in the transaction, the officer or employee shall prepare and file the required declaration by the end of the next business day. (1987, Sp. Sess., c. 1, § 2.1-639.13; 1988, cc. 767, 849; 1992, c. 710; 1993, c. 303; 1997, c. 641; 2001, cc. 217, 844; 2003, c. 694; 2005, c. 169; 2006, c. 779.)

Editor's note. — Acts 2001, c. 217 amended § 2.1-639.13, from which this section is derived. Pursuant to § 30-152, Acts 2001, c. 217 has been given effect in this section as set out above. The 2001 amendment by c. 217 inserted "including members of the governing bodies of authorities" in subsection A; inserted "and authorities" in subsection B, in the last sentence; substituted "subdivision A 1 of § 2.2-3112" for "§ 2.2-3112 A 1" in subsection E; and substituted "subdivision A 2 of § 2.2-3112" for "§ 2.2-3112 A 2" in subsection F.

§ 2.2-3114.1. Filings of statements of economic interests by General Assembly members. — The filing of a current statement of economic interests by a General Assembly member, member-elect, or candidate for the General Assembly pursuant to §§ 30-110 and 30-111 of the General Assembly Conflict of Interests Act (§ 30-100 et seq.) shall suffice for the purposes of this chapter (§ 2.2-3100 et seq.). The Secretary of the Commonwealth may obtain from the Clerk of the House of Delegates or the Senate, as appropriate, a copy of the statement of a General Assembly member who is appointed to a position for which a statement is required pursuant to § 2.2-3114. No General Assembly member, member-elect, or candidate shall be required to file a separate statement of economic interests for the purposes of § 2.2-3114. (2002, c. 36.)

§ 2.2-3115. Disclosure by local government officers and employees. — A. The members of every governing body and school board of each county and city and of towns with populations in excess of 3,500 shall file, as a condition to assuming office or employment, a disclosure statement of their personal interests and other information as is specified on the form set forth in § 2.2-3117 and thereafter shall file such a statement annually on or before January 15.

The members of the governing body of any authority established in any county or city, or part or combination thereof, and having the power to issue bonds or expend funds in excess of $10,000 in any fiscal year, shall file, as a condition to assuming office, a disclosure statement of their personal interests and other information as is specified on the form set forth in § 2.2-3118 and thereafter shall file such a statement annually on or before January 15, unless the governing body of the jurisdiction that appoints the members requires that the members file the form set forth in § 2.2-3117.

Persons occupying such positions of trust appointed by governing bodies and persons occupying such positions of employment with governing bodies as may be designated to file by ordinance of the governing body shall file, as a condition to assuming office or employment, a disclosure statement of their personal interests and other information as is specified on the form set forth in § 2.2-3117 and thereafter shall file such a statement annually on or before January 15.

Persons occupying such positions of trust appointed by school boards and persons occupying such positions of employment with school boards as may be designated to file by an adopted policy of the school board shall file, as a condition to assuming office or employment, a disclosure statement of their personal interests and other information as is specified on the form set forth in § 2.2-3117 and thereafter shall file such a statement annually on or before January 15.

B. Nonsalaried citizen members of local boards, commissions and councils as may be designated by the governing body shall file, as a condition to assuming office, a disclosure form of their personal interests and such other information as is specified on the form set forth in § 2.2-3118 and thereafter shall file such form annually on or before January 15.

C. The disclosure forms required by subsections A and B shall be provided by the Secretary of the Commonwealth to the clerks of the governing bodies and school boards not later than November 30 of each year, and the clerks of the governing body and school board shall distribute the forms to designated individuals no later than December 10 of each year. Forms shall be filed and maintained as public records for five years in the office of the clerk of the respective governing body or school board. Forms filed by members of governing bodies of authorities shall be filed and maintained as public records for five years in the office of the clerk of the governing body of the county or city.

D. Candidates for membership in the governing body or school board of any county, city or town with a population of more than 3,500 persons shall file a disclosure statement of their personal interests as required by § 24.2-502.

E. Any officer or employee of local government who has a personal interest in any transaction before the governmental or advisory agency of which he is an officer or employee and who is disqualified from participating in that transaction pursuant to subdivision A 1 of § 2.2-3112 or otherwise elects to disqualify himself, shall forthwith make disclosure of the existence of his interest, including the full name and address of the business and the address or parcel number for the real estate if the interest involves a business or real estate, and his disclosure shall be reflected in the public records of the agency for five years in the office of the administrative head of the officer's or employee's governmental or advisory agency.

F. In addition to any disclosure required by subsections A and B, in each county and city and in towns with populations in excess of 3,500, members of planning commissions, boards of zoning appeals, real estate assessors, and all county, city and town managers or executive officers shall make annual disclosures of all their interests in real estate located in the county, city or town in which they are elected, appointed, or employed. Such disclosure shall include any business in which such persons own an interest, or from which income is received, if the primary purpose of the business is to own, develop or derive compensation through the sale, exchange or development of real estate in the county, city or town. Such disclosure shall be filed as a condition to assuming office or employment, and thereafter shall be filed annually with the clerk of the governing body of such county, city or town on or before January 15. Such disclosures shall be filed and maintained as public records for five years. Forms for the filing of such reports shall be prepared and distributed by the Secretary of the Commonwealth to the clerk of each governing body.

G. An officer or employee of local government who is required to declare his interest pursuant to subdivision A 2 of § 2.2-3112 shall declare his interest by stating (i) the transaction involved, (ii) the nature of the officer's or employee's personal interest affected by the transaction, (iii) that he is a member of a business, profession, occupation, or group the members of which are affected by the transaction, and (iv) that he is able to participate in the transaction fairly, objectively, and in the public interest. The officer or employee shall either make his declaration orally to be recorded in written minutes of his agency or file a signed written declaration with the clerk or administrative head of his governmental or advisory agency, as appropriate, who shall, in either case, retain and make available for public inspection such declaration for a period of five years from the date of recording or receipt. If reasonable time is not available to comply with the provisions of this subsection prior to participation in the transaction, the officer or employee shall prepare and file the required declaration by the end of the next business day. The officer or employee shall also orally disclose the existence of the interest during each meeting of the governmental or advisory agency at which the transaction is discussed and such disclosure shall be recorded in the minutes of the meeting.

H. An officer or employee of local government who is required to declare his interest pursuant to subdivision A 3 of § 2.2-3112, shall declare his interest by stating (i) the transaction involved, (ii) that a party to the transaction is a client of his firm, (iii) that he does not personally represent or provide services to the client, and (iv) that he is able to participate in the transaction fairly, objectively, and in the public interest. The officer or employee shall either make his declaration orally to be recorded in written minutes for his agency or file a signed written declaration with the clerk or administrative head of his governmental or advisory agency, as appropriate, who shall, in either case, retain and make available for public inspection such declaration for a period of five years from the date of recording or receipt. If reasonable time is not available to comply with the provisions of this subsection prior to participation in the transaction, the officer or employee shall prepare and file the required declaration by the end of the next business day. (1987, Sp. Sess., c. 1, § 2.1-639.14; 1988, c. 849; 1995, c. 495; 1996, c. 526; 2000, c. 317; 2001, cc. 217, 844; 2003, c. 694.)

Editor's note. — Acts 2001, c. 217 amended § 2.1-639.14, from which this section is derived. Pursuant to § 30-152, Acts 2001, c. 217 has been given effect in this section as set out above. The 2001 amendment by c. 217 added the second paragraph in subsection A; added the last sentence in subsection C; substituted "subdivision A 1 of § 2.2-3112" for " § 2.2-3112 A 1" in subsection E; and substituted "subdivision A 2 of § 2.2-3112" for " § 2.2-3112 A 2" in subsection G.

§ 2.2-3116. Disclosure by certain constitutional officers. — For the purposes of this chapter, holders of the constitutional offices of treasurer, sheriff, attorney for the Commonwealth, clerk of the circuit court and commissioner of the revenue of each county and city, shall be deemed to be local officers and shall be required to file the Statement of Economic Interests set forth in § 2.2-3117. These officers shall file statements pursuant to § 2.2-3115 and candidates shall file statements as required by § 24.2-502. (1988, c. 469, § 2.1-639.14:1; 2001, c. 844.)

§ 2.2-3117. Disclosure form. — The disclosure form to be used for filings required by § 2.2-3114 A and D, and § 2.2-3115 A and D shall be substantially as follows:

STATEMENT OF ECONOMIC INTERESTS.

Name ....
Office or position held or sought ....
Address ....
Names of members of immediate family ....

DEFINITIONS AND EXPLANATORY MATERIAL.

"Business" means a corporation, partnership, sole proprietorship, firm, enterprise, franchise, association, trust or foundation, or any other individual or entity carrying on a business or profession, whether or not for profit.

"Close financial association" means an association in which the person filing shares significant financial involvement with an individual and the filer would reasonably be expected to be aware of the individual's business activities and would have access to the necessary records either directly or through the individual. "Close financial association" does not mean an association based on (i) the receipt of retirement benefits or deferred compensation from a business by which the person filing this statement is no longer employed, or (ii) the receipt of compensation for work performed by the person filing as an independent contractor of a business that represents an entity before any state governmental agency when the person filing has had no communications with the state governmental agency.

"Contingent liability" means a liability that is not presently fixed or determined, but may become fixed or determined in the future with the occurrence of some certain event.

"Dependent" means any person, whether or not related by blood or marriage, who receives from the officer or employee, or provides to the officer or employee, more than one-half of his financial support.

"Gift" means any gratuity, favor, discount, entertainment, hospitality, loan, forbearance, or other item having monetary value. It includes services as well as gifts of transportation, local travel, lodgings and meals, whether provided in-kind, by purchase of a ticket, payment in advance or reimbursement after the expense has been incurred. "Gift" shall not include any offer of a ticket or other admission or pass unless the ticket, admission, or pass is used. "Gift" shall not include honorary degrees and presents from relatives. "Relative" means the donee's spouse, child, uncle, aunt, niece, or nephew; a person to whom the donee is engaged to be married; the donee's or his spouse's parent, grandparent, grandchild, brother, or sister; or the donee's brother's or sister's spouse.

"Immediate family" means (i) a spouse and (ii) any other person residing in the same household as the officer or employee, who is a dependent of the officer or employee or of whom the officer or employee is a dependent.

TRUST. If you or your immediate family, separately or together, are the only beneficiaries of a trust, treat the trust's assets as if you own them directly. If you or your immediate family has a proportional interest in a trust, treat that proportion of the trust's assets as if you own them directly. For example, if you and your immediate family have a one-third interest in a trust, complete your Statement as if you own one-third of each of the trust's assets. If you or a member of your immediate family created a trust and can revoke it without the beneficiaries' consent, treat its assets as if you own them directly.

REPORT TO THE BEST OF INFORMATION AND BELIEF. Information required on this Statement must be provided on the basis of the best knowledge, information and belief of the individual filing the Statement as of the date of this report unless otherwise stated.

COMPLETE ITEMS 1 THROUGH 10. REFER TO SCHEDULES ONLY IF DIRECTED.

You may attach additional explanatory information.

1. Offices and Directorships.
   Are you or a member of your immediate family a paid officer or paid director of a business?
   EITHER check NO / / OR check YES / / and complete Schedule A.
2. Personal Liabilities.
   Do you or a member of your immediate family owe more than $10,000 to any one creditor including contingent liabilities? (Exclude debts to any government and loans secured by recorded liens on property at least equal in value to the loan.)
   EITHER check NO / / OR check YES / / and complete Schedule B.
3. Securities.
   Do you or a member of your immediate family, directly or indirectly, separately or together, own securities valued in excess of $10,000 invested in one business? Account for mutual funds, limited partnerships and trusts.
   EITHER check NO / / OR check YES / / and complete Schedule C.
4. Payments for Talks, Meetings, and Publications.
   During the past 12 months did you receive lodging, transportation, money, or anything else of value with a combined value exceeding $200 for a single talk, meeting, or published work in your capacity as an officer or employee of your agency?
   EITHER check NO / / OR check YES / / and complete Schedule D.
5. Gifts.
   During the past 12 months did a business, government, or individual other than a relative or personal friend (i) furnish you with any gift or entertainment at a single event, and the value received by you exceeded $50 in value or (ii) furnish you with gifts or entertainment in any combination and the value received by you exceeded $100 in total value; and for which you neither paid nor rendered services in exchange? Account for entertainment events only if the average value per person attending the event exceeded $50 in value. Account for all business entertainment (except if related to your private profession or occupation) even if unrelated to your official duties.
   EITHER check NO / / OR check YES / / and complete Schedule E.
6. Salary and Wages.
   List each employer that pays you or a member of your immediate family salary or wages in excess of $10,000 annually. (Exclude state or local government or advisory agencies.)
   If no reportable salary or wages, check here / /.
   ....
   ....
   ....
7. Business Interests.
   Do you or a member of your immediate family, separately or together, operate your own business, or own or control an interest in excess of $10,000 in a business?

EITHER check NO / / OR check YES / / and complete Schedule F.

8. Payments for Representation and Other Services.

8A. Did you represent, excluding activity defined as lobbying in § 2.2-419, any businesses before any state governmental agencies, excluding courts or judges, for which you received total compensation during the past 12 months in excess of $1,000, excluding compensation for other services to such businesses and representation consisting solely of the filing of mandatory papers and subsequent representation regarding the mandatory papers? (Officers and employees of local governmental and advisory agencies do NOT need to answer this question or complete Schedule G-1.)

EITHER check NO / / OR check YES / / and complete Schedule G-1.

8B. Subject to the same exceptions as in 8A, did persons with whom you have a close financial association (partners, associates or others) represent, excluding activity defined as lobbying in § 2.2-419, any businesses before any state governmental agency for which total compensation was received during the past 12 months in excess of $1,000? (Officers and employees of local governmental and advisory agencies do NOT need to answer this question or complete Schedule G-2.)

EITHER check NO / / OR check YES / / and complete Schedule G-2.

8C. Did you or persons with whom you have a close financial association furnish services to businesses operating in Virginia pursuant to an agreement between you and such businesses, or between persons with whom you have a close financial association and such businesses for which total compensation in excess of $1,000 was received during the past 12 months?

EITHER check NO / / OR check YES / / and complete Schedule G-3.

9. Real Estate.

9A. State Officers and Employees.

Do you or a member of your immediate family hold an interest, including a partnership interest, valued at $10,000 or more in real property (other than your principal residence) for which you have not already listed the full address on Schedule F? Account for real estate held in trust.

EITHER check NO / / OR check YES / / and complete Schedule H-1.

9B. Local Officers and Employees.

Do you or a member of your immediate family hold an interest, including a partnership interest, or option, easement, or land contract, valued at $10,000 or more in real property (other than your principal residence) for which you have not already listed the full address on Schedule F? Account for real estate held in trust.

EITHER check NO / / OR check YES / / and complete Schedule H-2.

10. Real Estate Contracts with Governmental Agencies.

Do you or a member of your immediate family hold an interest valued at more than $10,000 in real estate, including a corporate, partnership, or trust interest, option, easement, or land contract, which real estate is the subject of a contract, whether pending or completed within the past 12 months, with a governmental agency? If the real estate contract provides for the leasing of the property to a governmental agency, do you or a member of your immediate family hold an interest in the real estate valued at more than $1,000? Account for all such contracts whether or not your interest is reported in Schedule F, H-1, or H-2. This requirement to disclose an interest in a lease does not apply to an interest derived through an ownership interest in a business unless the ownership interest exceeds three percent of the total equity of the business.

EITHER check NO / / OR check YES / / and complete Schedule I.

Statements of Economic Interests are open for public inspection.

AFFIRMATION BY ALL FILERS.

I swear or affirm that the foregoing information is full, true and correct to the best of my knowledge.

Signature ....
Commonwealth of Virginia
.... of .... to wit:
The foregoing disclosure form was acknowledged before me
This .... day of ...., 20... , by ....
Notary Public
My commission expires ....
(Return only if needed to complete Statement.)

SCHEDULES
to
STATEMENT OF ECONOMIC INTERESTS.

NAME ....

SCHEDULE A — OFFICES AND DIRECTORSHIPS.

Identify each business of which you or a member of your immediate family is a paid officer or paid director.

Name of Business	Address of Business	Position Held
______	______	______
______	______	______
______	______	______
______	______	______

RETURN TO ITEM 2

SCHEDULE B — PERSONAL LIABILITIES.

Report personal liability by checking each category. Report only debts in excess of $10,000. Do not report debts to any government. Do not report loans secured by recorded liens on property at least equal in value to the loan.
Report contingent liabilities below and indicate which debts are contingent.

1. My personal debts are as follows:

Check appropriate categories	Check one: $10,001 to $50,000	More than $50,000
Banks	______	______
Savings institutions	______	______
Other loan or finance companies	______	______
Insurance companies	______	______
Stock, commodity or other brokerage companies	______	______

Check appropriate categories	Check one $10,001 to $50,000	More than $50,000
Other businesses: (State principal business activity for each creditor.)	______	______
______	______	______
______	______	______
Individual creditors: (State principal business or occupation of each creditor.)	______	______
______	______	______
______	______	______

2. The personal debts of the members of my immediate family are as follows:

Check appropriate categories	Check one $10,001 to $50,000	More than $50,000
Banks	______	______
Savings institutions	______	______
Other loan or finance companies	______	______
Insurance companies	______	______
Stock, commodity or other brokerage companies	______	______
Other businesses: (State principal business activity for each creditor.)	______	______
______	______	______
______	______	______
Individual creditors: (State principal business or occupation of each creditor.)	______	______
______	______	______
______	______	______

RETURN TO ITEM 3

SCHEDULE C — SECURITIES.

"Securities" INCLUDES stocks, bonds, mutual funds, limited partnerships, and commodity futures contracts.

"Securities" EXCLUDES certificates of deposit, money market funds, annuity contracts, and insurance policies.

Identify each business or Virginia governmental entity in which you or a member of your immediate family, directly or indirectly, separately or together, own securities valued in excess of $10,000.

Name each entity and type of security individually.

Do not list U.S. Bonds or other government securities not issued by the Commonwealth of Virginia or its authorities, agencies, or local governments. Do not list organizations that do not do business in this Commonwealth, but most major businesses conduct business in Virginia. Account for securities held in trust.

If no reportable securities, check here / /.

Name of Issuer	Type of Entity	Type of Security (stocks, bonds, mutual funds, etc.)	Check one $10,001 to $50,000	$50,001 to $250,000	More than $250,000

RETURN TO ITEM 4

SCHEDULE D — PAYMENTS FOR TALKS, MEETINGS, AND PUBLICATIONS.

List each source from which you received during the past 12 months lodging, transportation, money, or any other thing of value (excluding meals or drinks coincident with a meeting) with combined value exceeding $200 for your presentation of a single talk, participation in one meeting, or publication of a work in your capacity as an officer or employee of your agency.

List payments or reimbursements by an advisory or governmental agency only for meetings or travel outside the Commonwealth.

List a payment even if you donated it to charity.

Do not list information about a payment if you returned it within 60 days or if you received it from an employer already listed under Item 6 or from a source of income listed on Schedule F.

If no payment must be listed, check here / /.

Payer	Approximate Value	Circumstances	Type of payment (e.g. Honoraria, travel reimbursement, etc.)

RETURN TO ITEM 5

SCHEDULE E — GIFTS.

List each business, governmental entity, or individual that, during the past 12 months, (i) furnished you with any gift or entertainment at a single event and the value received by you exceeded $50 in value, or (ii) furnished you with gifts or entertainment in any combination and the value received by you exceeded $100 in total value; and for which you neither paid nor rendered services in exchange. List each such gift or event. Do not list entertainment events unless the average value per person attending the event exceeded $50 in value. Do not list business entertainment related to your private profession or occupation. Do not list gifts or other things of value given by a relative or personal friend for reasons clearly unrelated to your public position. Do not list campaign contributions publicly reported as required by Chapter 9.3 (§ 24.2-945 et seq.) of Title 24.2 of the Code of Virginia.

Name of Business, Organization, or Individual	City or County and State	Gift or Event	Approximate Value

RETURN TO ITEM 6

SCHEDULE F — BUSINESS INTERESTS.

Complete this Schedule for each self-owned or family-owned business (including rental property, a farm, or consulting work), partnership, or corporation in which you or a member of your immediate family, separately or together, own an interest having a value in excess of $10,000.

If the enterprise is owned or operated under a trade, partnership, or corporate name, list that name; otherwise, merely explain the nature of the enterprise. If rental property is owned or operated under a trade, partnership, or corporate name, list the name only; otherwise, give the address of each property. Account for business interests held in trust.

Name of Business, Corporation, Partnership, Farm; Address of Rental Property	City or County and State	Nature of Enterprise (farming, law, rental property, etc.)	Gross Income		
			$50,000 or less	$50,001 to $250,000	More than $250,000

RETURN TO ITEM 8

SCHEDULE G-1 — PAYMENTS FOR REPRESENTATION BY YOU.

List the businesses you represented, excluding activity defined as lobbying in § 2.2-419, before any state governmental agency, excluding any court or judge, for which you received total compensation during the past 12 months in excess of $1,000, excluding compensation for other services to such businesses and representation consisting solely of the filing of mandatory papers and subsequent representation regarding the mandatory papers filed by you.

Identify each business, the nature of the representation and the amount received by dollar category from each such business. You may state the type, rather than name, of the business if you are required by law not to reveal the name of the business represented by you.

Only STATE officers and employees should complete this Schedule.

				Amount Received				
Name of Business	Type of Business	Purpose of Representation	Name of Agency	$1,001 to $10,000	$10,001 to $50,000	$50,001 to $100,000	$100,001 to $250,000	$250,001 and over
______	______	______	______	______	______	______	______	______
______	______	______	______	______	______	______	______	______
______	______	______	______	______	______	______	______	______
______	______	______	______	______	______	______	______	______

If you have received $250,001 or more from a single business within the reporting period, indicate the amount received, rounded to the nearest $10,000. Amount Received:__________.

SCHEDULE G-2 — PAYMENTS FOR REPRESENTATION BY ASSOCIATES.

List the businesses that have been represented, excluding activity defined as lobbying in § 2.2-419, before any state governmental agency, excluding any court or judge, by persons who are your partners, associates or others with whom you have a close financial association and who received total compensation in excess of $1,000 for such representation during the past 12 months, excluding representation consisting solely of the filing of mandatory papers and subsequent representation regarding the mandatory papers filed by your partners, associates or others with whom you have a close financial association.

Identify such businesses by type and also name the state governmental agencies before which such person appeared on behalf of such businesses.

Only STATE officers and employees should complete this Schedule.

Type of business	Name of state governmental agency
______________	______________
______________	______________
______________	______________
______________	______________

SCHEDULE G-3 — PAYMENTS FOR SERVICES GENERALLY.

Indicate below types of businesses that operate in Virginia to which services were furnished by you or persons with whom you have a close financial association pursuant to an agreement between you and such businesses, or between persons with whom you have a close financial association and such businesses and for which total compensation in excess of $1,000 was received during the past 12 months.

Identify opposite each category of businesses listed below (i) the type of business, (ii) the type of service rendered and (iii) the value by dollar category of the compensation received for all businesses falling within each category.

			Value of Compensation				
	Check if services were rendered	Type of service rendered	$1,001 to $10,000	$10,001 to $50,000	$50,001 to $100,000	$100,001 to $250,000	$250,001 and over
Electric utilities	______	______	______	______	______	______	______
Gas utilities	______	______	______	______	______	______	______
Telephone utilities	______	______	______	______	______	______	______
Water utilities	______	______	______	______	______	______	______
Cable television companies	______	______	______	______	______	______	______
Interstate transportation companies	______	______	______	______	______	______	______
Intrastate transportation companies	______	______	______	______	______	______	______
Oil or gas retail companies	______	______	______	______	______	______	______
Banks	______	______	______	______	______	______	______
Savings institutions	______	______	______	______	______	______	______
Loan or finance companies	______	______	______	______	______	______	______
Manufacturing companies (state type of product, e.g., textile, furniture, etc.)	______	______	______	______	______	______	______
Mining companies	______	______	______	______	______	______	______
Life insurance companies	______	______	______	______	______	______	______
Casualty insurance companies	______	______	______	______	______	______	______
Other insurance companies	______	______	______	______	______	______	______
Retail companies	______	______	______	______	______	______	______
Beer, wine or liquor companies or distributors	______	______	______	______	______	______	______
Trade associations	______	______	______	______	______	______	______
Professional associations	______	______	______	______	______	______	______
Associations of public employees or officials	______	______	______	______	______	______	______
Counties, cities or towns	______	______	______	______	______	______	______
Labor organizations	______	______	______	______	______	______	______
Other	______	______	______	______	______	______	______

RETURN TO ITEM 9

SCHEDULE H-1 — REAL ESTATE — STATE OFFICERS AND EMPLOYEES.

List real estate other than your principal residence in which you or a member of your immediate family holds an interest, including a partnership interest, option, easement, or land contract, valued at $10,000 or more. You may list each parcel of real estate individually if you wish.

List each location (state, and county or city) where you own real estate.	Describe the type of real estate you own in each location (business, recreational, apartment, commercial, open land, etc.).	If the real estate is owned or recorded in a name other than your own, list that name.

SCHEDULE H-2 — REAL ESTATE — LOCAL OFFICERS AND EMPLOYEES.

List real estate other than your principal residence in which you or a member of your immediate family holds an interest, including a partnership interest or option, easement, or land contract, valued at $10,000 or more. You may list each parcel of real estate individually if you wish. Also list the names of any co-owners of such property, if applicable.

List each location (state, and county or city) where you own real estate.	Describe the type of real estate you own in each location (business, recreational, apartment, commercial, open land, etc.).	If the real estate is owned or recorded in a name other than your own, list that name.	List the names of any co-owners, if applicable.

SCHEDULE I — REAL ESTATE CONTRACTS WITH GOVERNMENTAL AGENCIES.

List all contracts, whether pending or completed within the past 12 months, with a governmental agency for the sale or exchange of real estate in which you or a member of your immediate family holds an interest, including a corporate, partnership or trust interest, option, easement, or land contract, valued at $10,000 or more. List all contracts with a governmental agency for the lease of real estate in which you or a member of your immediate family holds such an interest valued at $1,000 or more. This requirement to disclose an interest in a lease does not apply to an interest derived through an ownership interest in a business unless the ownership interest exceeds three percent of the total equity of the business.

State officers and employees report contracts with state agencies.

Local officers and employees report contracts with local agencies.

List your real estate interest and the person or entity, including the type of entity, which is party to the contract. Describe any management role and the percentage ownership interest you or your immediate family member has in the real estate or entity.	List each governmental agency which is a party to the contract and indicate the county or city where the real estate is located.	State the annual income from the contract, and the amount, if any, of income you or any immediate family member derives annually from the contract.
________________	________________	________________
________________	________________	________________
________________	________________	________________
________________	________________	________________
________________	________________	________________

(1987, Sp. Sess., c. 1, § 2.1-639.15; 1988, c. 849; 1994, cc. 724, 733, 777, 793; 1995, c. 763; 1996, c. 77; 1997, cc. 577, 844; 1998, c. 732; 2001, c. 844; 2006, cc. 310, 779, 787, 892; 2008, c. 239.)

The 2008 amendments. — The 2008 amendment by c. 239 rewrote paragraph 9B under the DEFINITIONS AND EXPLANATORY MATERIAL heading; and under Schedule H-2, rewrote the introductory paragraph and added the fourth column "List the names of any co-owners, if applicable."

§ 2.2-3118. Disclosure form; certain citizen members. — A. The financial disclosure form to be used for filings required pursuant to subsection B of § 2.2-3114 and subsection B of § 2.2-3115 shall be substantially as follows:

DEFINITIONS AND EXPLANATORY MATERIAL.

"Business" means a corporation, partnership, sole proprietorship, firm, enterprise, franchise, association, trust or foundation, or any other individual or entity carrying on a business or profession, whether or not for profit.

"Close financial association" means an association in which the person filing shares significant financial involvement with an individual and the filer would reasonably be expected to be aware of the individual's business activities and would have access to the necessary records either directly or through the individual. "Close financial association" does not mean an association based on (i) the receipt of retirement benefits or deferred compensation from a business by which the person filing this statement is no longer employed, or (ii) the receipt of compensation for work performed by the person filing as an independent contractor of a business that represents an entity before any state governmental agency when the person filing has no communications with the state governmental agency.

"Contingent liability" means a liability that is not presently fixed or determined, but may become fixed or determined in the future with the occurrence of some certain event.

"Immediate family" means (i) a spouse and (ii) any other person residing in the same household as the filer, who is a dependent of the filer or of whom the filer is a dependent.

"Dependent" means any person, whether or not related by blood or marriage, who receives from the filer, or provides to the filer, more than one-half of his financial support.

"Personal interest" means, for the purposes of this form only, a personal and financial benefit or liability accruing to a filer or a member of his immediate family. Such interest shall exist by reason of (i) ownership in real or personal property, tangible or intangible; (ii) ownership in a business; (iii) income from a business; or (iv) personal liability on behalf of a business; however, unless the ownership interest in a business exceeds three percent of the total equity of the business, or the liability on behalf of a business exceeds three percent of the total assets of the business, or the annual income, and/or property or use of such property, from the business exceeds $10,000 or may reasonably be anticipated to exceed $10,000, such interest shall not constitute a "personal interest."

Name ....

Office or position held or to be held

....

Address ....

I. FINANCIAL INTERESTS

My personal interests and those of my immediate family are as follows:

Include all forms of personal interests held at the time of filing: real estate, stocks, bonds, equity interests in proprietorships and partnerships. You may exclude:

1. Deposits and interest bearing accounts in banks, savings institutions and other institutions accepting such deposits or accounts;
2. Interests in any business, other than a news medium, representing less than three percent of the total equity value of the business;
3. Liability on behalf of any business representing less than three percent of the total assets of such business; and
4. Income (other than from salary) less than $10,000 annually from any business. You need not state the value of any interest. You must state the name or principal business activity of each business in which you have a personal interest.

A. My personal interests are:

1. Residence, address, or, if no address, location ....
2. Other real estate, address, or, if no address, location ....
3. Name or principal business activity of each business in which stock, bond or equity interest is held ....

B. The personal interests of my immediate family are:

1. Real estate, address or, if no address, location ....
2. Name or principal business activity of each business in which stock, bond or equity interest is held ....

II. OFFICES, DIRECTORSHIPS AND SALARIED EMPLOYMENTS

The paid offices, paid directorships and salaried employments which I hold or which members of my immediate family hold and the businesses from which I or members of my immediate family receive retirement benefits are as follows:

(You need not state any dollar amounts.)

A. My paid offices, paid directorships and salaried employments are:

Position held	Name of business
______________	______________
______________	______________
______________	______________

B. The paid offices, paid directorships and salaried employments of members of my immediate family are:

Position held	Name of business
______________	______________
______________	______________
______________	______________

III. BUSINESSES TO WHICH SERVICES WERE FURNISHED

A. The businesses I have represented, excluding activity defined as lobbying in § 2.2-419, before any state governmental agency, excluding any court or judge, for which I have received total compensation in excess of $1,000 during the preceding year, excluding compensation for other services to such businesses and representation consisting solely of the filing of mandatory papers, are as follows:

Identify businesses by name and name the state governmental agencies before which you appeared on behalf of such businesses.

Name of business	Name of governmental agency
______________	______________
______________	______________
______________	______________

B. The businesses that, to my knowledge, have been represented, excluding activity defined as lobbying in § 2.2-419, before any state governmental agency, excluding any court or judge, by persons with whom I have a close financial association and who received total compensation in excess of $1,000 during the preceding year, excluding compensation for other services to such businesses and representation consisting solely of the filing of mandatory papers, are as follows:

Identify businesses by type and name the state governmental agencies before which such person appeared on behalf of such businesses.

Type of business	Name of state governmental agency
______________	______________
______________	______________

C. All other businesses listed below that operate in Virginia to which services were furnished pursuant to an agreement between you and such businesses and for which total compensation in excess of $1000 was received during the preceding year:

Check each category of business to which services were furnished.

Electric utilities	______
Gas utilities	______
Telephone utilities	______
Water utilities	______
Cable television companies	______
Intrastate transportation companies	______
Interstate transportation companies	______
Oil or gas retail companies	______
Banks	______
Savings institutions	______
Loan or finance companies	______
Manufacturing companies (state type of product, e.g., textile, furniture, etc.)	______
Mining companies	______
Life insurance companies	______
Casualty insurance companies	______
Other insurance companies	______
Retail companies	______
Beer, wine or liquor companies or distributors	______
Trade associations	______
Professional associations	______
Associations of public employees or officials	______
Counties, cities or towns	______
Labor organizations	______

IV. COMPENSATION FOR EXPENSES

The persons, associations, or other sources other than my governmental agency from which I or a member of my immediate family received remuneration in excess of $200 during the preceding year, in cash or otherwise, as honorariums or payment of expenses in connection with my attendance at any meeting or other function to which I was invited in my official capacity are as follows:

Name of source	Description of occasion	Amount of remuneration for each occasion
______	______	______
______	______	______

B. The provisions of Part III A and B of the disclosure form prescribed by this section shall not be applicable to officers and employees of local governmental and local advisory agencies.

C. Except for real estate located within the county, city or town in which the officer or employee serves or a county, city or town contiguous to the county, city or town in which the officer or employee serves, officers and employees of local governmental or advisory agencies shall not be required to disclose under Part I of the form any other interests in real estate. (1988, c. 849, § 2.1-639.15:1; 1996, c. 77; 2001, c. 844; 2006, c. 779.)

§ 2.2-3118.1. Special provisions for individuals serving in or seeking multiple positions or offices; reappointees. — A. The filing of a single current statement of economic interests by a state officer or employee required to file the form prescribed in § 2.2-3117 shall suffice for the purposes of this chapter as filing for all state positions or offices held or sought by such individual during a single reporting period. The filing of a single current financial disclosure statement by a state officer or employee required to file the form prescribed in § 2.2-3118 shall suffice for the purposes of this chapter as filing for all state positions or offices held or sought by such individual and requiring the filing of the § 2.2-3118 form during a single reporting period.

B. Any individual who has met the requirement for annually filing a statement provided in § 2.2-3117 or 2.2-3118 shall not be required to file an additional statement upon such individual's reappointment to the same office or position for which he is required to file, provided such reappointment occurs within 12 months after the annual filing. (2005, c. 397.)

Article 6.

School Boards and Employees of School Boards.

§ 2.2-3119. Additional provisions applicable to school boards, and employees of school boards. — A. Notwithstanding any other provision of this chapter, it shall be unlawful for the school board of any county or city or of any town constituting a separate school division to employ or pay any teacher or other school board employee from the public funds, federal, state or local, or for a division superintendent to recommend to the school board the employment of any teacher or other employee, if the teacher or other employee is the father, mother, brother, sister, spouse, son, daughter, son-in-law, daughter-in-law, sister-in-law or brother-in-law of the superintendent, or of any member of the school board.

This section shall apply to any person employed by any school board in the operation of the public free school system, adult education programs or any other program maintained and operated by a local county, city or town school board.

B. This section shall not be construed to prohibit the employment, promotion, or transfer within a school division of any person within a relationship described in subsection A when such person:

1. Has been employed pursuant to a written contract with a school board or employed as a substitute teacher or teacher's aide by a school board prior to the taking of office of any member of such board or division superintendent of schools; or

2. Has been employed pursuant to a written contract with a school board or employed as a substitute teacher or teacher's aide by a school board prior to the inception of such relationship; or

3. Was employed by a school board at any time prior to June 10, 1994, and had been employed at any time as a teacher or other employee of any Virginia school board prior to the taking of office of any member of such school board or division superintendent of schools.

C. A person employed as a substitute teacher may not be employed to any greater extent than he was employed by the school board in the last full school year prior to the taking of office of such board member or division superintendent or to the inception of such relationship. The exceptions in subdivisions B. 1., B. 2., and B. 3. shall apply only if the prior employment has been in the same school division where the employee and the superintendent or school board member now seek to serve simultaneously.

D. If any member of the school board or any division superintendent knowingly violates these provisions, he shall be personally liable to refund to the local treasury any amounts paid in violation of this law, and the funds shall be recovered from the individual by action or suit in the name of the Commonwealth on the petition of the attorney for the Commonwealth. Recovered funds shall be paid into the local treasury for the use of the public schools. (1987, Sp. Sess., c. 1, § 2.1-639.16; 1994, c. 758; 1995, c. 186; 1997, c. 84; 2001, c. 844.)

CASE NOTES

Editor's note. — The case below was decided under former Title 2.1 or prior provisions.

Exemption not applicable. — Where the exemption applies to one who "has been employed" prior to a relative becoming a member of the school board, since the verb form used is the present perfect tense, which denotes an action beginning in the past and continuing to the present, and teacher's interpretation of the exemption, namely, employment at any time before the conflict arose, would require use of a verb form in the past perfect tense, that is, "had been employed," i.e., an event beginning and ending in the past, the exemption contained in this section was not applicable to teacher because she was not regularly employed by the board at the time her brother-in-law was appointed to the board. Williams v. Augusta County Sch. Bd., 248 Va. 124, 445 S.E.2d 118 (1994).

Article 7.

Penalties and Remedies.

§ 2.2-3120. Knowing violation of chapter a misdemeanor. — Any person who knowingly violates any of the provisions of Articles 2 through 6 (§§ 2.2-3102 through 2.2-3119) of this chapter shall be guilty of a Class 1 misdemeanor, except that any member of a local governing body who knowingly violates § 2.2-3112 A or § 2.2-3115 C or E shall be guilty of a Class 3 misdemeanor. A knowing violation under this section is one in which the person engages in conduct, performs an act or refuses to perform an act when he knows that the conduct is prohibited or required by this chapter. (1987, Sp. Sess., c. 1, § 2.1-639.17; 2001, c. 844.)

Cross references. — As to punishment for Class 1 and Class 3 misdemeanors, see § 18.2-11.

§ 2.2-3121. Advisory opinions. — A. A state officer or employee shall not be prosecuted for a knowing violation of this chapter if the alleged violation resulted from his good faith reliance on a written opinion of the Attorney General made in response to his written request for such opinion and the opinion was made after a full disclosure of the facts.

B. A local officer or employee shall not be prosecuted for a knowing violation of this chapter if the alleged violation resulted from his good faith reliance on a written opinion of the attorney for the Commonwealth made in response to his written request for such opinion and the opinion was made after a full disclosure of the facts. The written opinion shall be a public record and shall be released upon request.

C. If any officer or employee serving at the local level of government is charged with a knowing violation of this chapter, and the alleged violation resulted from his reliance upon a written opinion of his city, county or town attorney, made after a full disclosure of the facts, that such action was not in violation of this chapter, then the officer or employee shall have the right to introduce a copy of the opinion at his trial as evidence that he did not knowingly violate this chapter. (1987, Sp. Sess., c. 1, § 2.1-639.18; 2001, c. 844; 2003, c. 694.)

§ **2.2-3122. Knowing violation of chapter constitutes malfeasance in office or employment.** — Any person who knowingly violates any of the provisions of this chapter shall be guilty of malfeasance in office or employment. Upon conviction thereof, the judge or jury trying the case, in addition to any other fine or penalty provided by law, may order the forfeiture of such office or employment. (1987, Sp. Sess., c. 1, § 2.1-639.19; 2001, c. 844.)

§ **2.2-3123. Invalidation of contract; recision of sales.** — A. Any contract made in violation of § 2.2-3103 or §§ 2.2-3106 through 2.2-3109 may be declared void and may be rescinded by the governing body of the contracting or selling governmental agency within five years of the date of such contract. In cases in which the contract is invalidated, the contractor shall retain or receive only the reasonable value, with no increment for profit or commission, of the property or services furnished prior to the date of receiving notice that the contract has been voided. In cases of recision of a contract of sale, any refund or restitution shall be made to the contracting or selling governmental agency.

B. Any purchase by an officer or employee made in violation of § 2.2-3103 or §§ 2.2-3106 through 2.2-3109 may be rescinded by the governing body of the contracting or selling governmental agency within five years of the date of such purchase. (1987, Sp. Sess., c. 1, § 2.1-639.20; 2001, c. 844.)

Michie's Jurisprudence. — For related discussion, see 5A M.J. Counties, § 60.

§ **2.2-3124. Forfeiture of money, etc., derived from violation of this chapter.** — In addition to any other fine or penalty provided by law, any money or other thing of value derived by an officer or employee from a violation of §§ 2.2-3103 through 2.2-3112 shall be forfeited and, in the event of a knowing violation, there may also be imposed a civil penalty in an amount equal to the amount of money or thing of value forfeited to the Commonwealth or the local government as the case may be. If the thing of value received by the officer or employee in violation of this chapter should enhance in value between the time of the violation and the time of discovery of the violation, the greater value shall determine the amount of forfeiture. (1987, Sp. Sess., c. 1, § 2.1-639.21; 1994, cc. 727, 776; 2001, c. 844.)

§ **2.2-3125. Limitation of actions.** — The statute of limitations for the criminal prosecution of a person for violation of any provision of this chapter shall be one year from the time the Attorney General, if the violation is by a state officer or employee, or the attorney for the Commonwealth, if the violation is by a local officer or employee, has actual knowledge of the violation or five years from the date of the violation, whichever event occurs first. Any prosecution for malfeasance in office shall be governed by the statute of limitations provided by law. (1987, Sp. Sess., c. 1, § 2.1-639.22; 2001, c. 844.)

§ **2.2-3126. Enforcement.** — A. The provisions of this chapter relating to an officer or employee serving at the state level of government shall be enforced by the Attorney General.

In addition to any other powers and duties prescribed by law, the Attorney General shall have the following powers and duties within the area for which he is responsible under this section:

1. He shall advise the agencies of state government and officers and employees serving at the state level of government on appropriate procedures for complying with the requirements of this chapter. He may review any disclosure statements, without notice to the affected person, for the purpose of determining satisfactory compliance, and shall investigate matters that come to his attention reflecting possible violations of the provisions of this chapter by officers and employees serving at the state level of government;

2. If he determines that there is a reasonable basis to conclude that any officer or employee serving at the state level of government has knowingly violated any provision of this chapter, he shall designate an attorney for the Commonwealth who shall have complete and independent discretion in the prosecution of such officer or employee;

3. He shall render advisory opinions to any state officer or employee who seeks advice as to whether the facts in a particular case would constitute a violation of the provisions of this chapter. He shall determine which opinions or portions thereof are of general interest to the public and may, from time to time, be published.

Irrespective of whether an opinion of the Attorney General has been requested and rendered, any person has the right to seek a declaratory judgment or other judicial relief as provided by law.

B. The provisions of this chapter relating to an officer or employee serving at the local level of government shall be enforced by the attorney for the Commonwealth within the political subdivision for which he is elected.

Each attorney for the Commonwealth shall be responsible for prosecuting violations by an officer or employee serving at the local level of government and, if the Attorney General designates such attorney for the Commonwealth, violations by an officer or employee serving at the state level of government. In the event the violation by an officer or employee serving at the local level of government involves more than one local jurisdiction, the Attorney General shall designate which of the attorneys for the Commonwealth of the involved local jurisdictions shall enforce the provisions of this chapter with regard to such violation.

Each attorney for the Commonwealth shall establish an appropriate written procedure for implementing the disclosure requirements of local officers and employees of his county, city or town, and for other political subdivisions, whose principal offices are located within the jurisdiction served by such attorney for the Commonwealth. The attorney for the Commonwealth shall provide a copy of this act to all local officers and employees in the jurisdiction served by such attorney who are required to file a disclosure statement pursuant to Article 5 (§ 2.2-3113 et seq.) of this chapter. Failure to receive a copy of the act shall not be a defense to such officers and employees if they are prosecuted for violations of the act.

Each attorney for the Commonwealth shall render advisory opinions as to whether the facts in a particular case would constitute a violation of the provisions of this chapter to the governing body and any local officer or employee in his jurisdiction and to political subdivisions other than a county, city or town, including regional political subdivisions whose principal offices are located within the jurisdiction served by such attorney for the Commonwealth. If the advisory opinion is written, then such written opinion shall be a public record and shall be released upon request. In case the opinion given by the attorney for the Commonwealth indicates that the facts would constitute a violation, the officer or employee affected thereby may request that the Attorney General review the opinion. A conflicting opinion by the Attorney

General shall act to revoke the opinion of the attorney for the Commonwealth. The Attorney General shall determine which of his reviewing opinions or portions thereof are of general interest to the public and may, from time to time, be published.

Irrespective of whether an opinion of the attorney for the Commonwealth or the Attorney General has been requested and rendered, any person has the right to seek a declaratory judgment or other judicial relief as provided by law. (1987, Sp. Sess., c. 1, § 2.1-639.23; 2001, c. 844; 2003, c. 694.)

Michie's Jurisprudence. — For related discussion, see 4A M.J. Commonwealth's and State's Attorney, § 7.

CASE NOTES

Editor's note. — The case below was decided under former Title 2.1 or prior provisions.

The Commonwealth's attorneys have exclusive authority to enforce the provisions of this chapter as to violations by those serving at the local level of government. Commonwealth v. Holland, 211 Va. 530, 178 S.E.2d 506 (1971).

§ **2.2-3127. Venue.** — Any prosecution for a violation involving an officer serving at the state level of government shall be brought in the Circuit Court of the City of Richmond. Any prosecution for a violation involving an employee serving at the state level of government shall be within the jurisdiction in which the employee has his principal place of state employment.

Any proceeding provided in this chapter shall be brought in a court of competent jurisdiction within the county or city in which the violation occurs if the violation involves an officer or employee serving at the local level of government. (1987, Sp. Sess., c. 1, § 2.1-639.24; 2001, c. 844.)

Article 8.

Orientation for State Filers.

§ **2.2-3128. Semiannual orientation course.** — Each state agency shall offer at least semiannually to each of its state filers an orientation course on this chapter, on ethics in public contracting pursuant to Article 6 (§ 2.2-4367 et seq.) of Chapter 43 of this title, if applicable to the filer, and on any other applicable regulations that govern the official conduct of state officers and employees. (2004, cc. 134, 392.)

Editor's note. — Acts 2004, cc. 134 and 392, cl. 2, provides: "On or before August 1, 2004, the Office of the Attorney General shall make available to all state agencies appropriate course content for the training requirements of § 2.2-3128 of the Code of Virginia. Such course content shall be updated periodically to conform with changes in applicable law. Completion of such course offered by the Office of the Attorney General by state filers shall satisfy the training requirements Article 8 (§ 2.2-3128 et seq.) of Chapter 31 of Title 2.2 of the Code of Virginia."

Acts 2004, cc. 134 and 392, cl. 3, provides: "The Virginia Information Technologies Agency shall provide any technical assistance required by the Office of the Attorney General in order to post all course content, including the ability to post course content as an interactive program, on the Internet."

§ **2.2-3129. Records of attendance.** — Each state agency shall maintain records indicating the specific attendees, each attendee's job title, and dates of their attendance for each orientation course offered pursuant to § 2.2-3128 for a period of not less than five years after each course is given. These records shall be public records subject to inspection and copying consistent with § 2.2-3704. (2004, cc. 134, 392.)

§ **2.2-3130. Attendance requirements.** — Except as set forth in § 2.2-3131, each state filer shall attend the orientation course required in § 2.2-3128, as follows:

1. For a state filer who holds a position with the agency on January 1, 2004, not later than December 31, 2004 and, thereafter, at least once during each consecutive period of two calendar years commencing on January 1, 2006.

2. For a person who becomes a state filer with the agency after January 1, 2004, within two months after he or she becomes a state filer and at least once during each consecutive period of two calendar years commencing on the first odd-numbered year thereafter. (2004, cc. 134, 392.)

§ **2.2-3131. Exemptions.** — A. The requirements of § 2.2-3130 shall not apply to state filers with a state agency who have taken an equivalent ethics orientation course through another state agency within the time periods set forth in subdivision 1 or 2 of § 2.2-3130, as applicable.

B. State agencies may jointly conduct and state filers from more than one state agency may jointly attend an orientation course required by § 2.2-3128, as long as the course content is relevant to the official duties of the attending state filers.

C. Before conducting each orientation course required by § 2.2-3128, state agencies shall consult with the Attorney General regarding appropriate course content. (2004, cc. 134, 392.)

CHAPTER 32.

WORKFORCE TRANSITION ACT OF 1995.

§ **2.2-3200. Short title; purpose.** — A. This chapter shall be known as the Workforce Transition Act of 1995.

B. The purpose of this chapter is to provide a transitional severance benefit, under the conditions specified, to eligible state employees who are involuntarily separated from their employment with the Commonwealth. *"Involuntary separation"* includes, but is not limited to, terminations and layoffs from employment with the Commonwealth, or being placed on leave without pay-layoff or equivalent status, due to budget reductions, agency reorganizations, workforce down-sizings, or other causes not related to the job performance or misconduct of the employee, but shall not include voluntary resignations. As used in this chapter, a *"terminated employee"* shall mean an employee who is involuntarily separated from employment with the Commonwealth. (1995, cc. 152, 811, § 2.1-116.20; 2001, c. 844.)

Editor's note. — Acts 1995, c. 152, cl. 11, effective March 10, 1995, and Acts 1995, c. 811, cl. 11, effective April 6, 1995, provide: "That any employee of the Commonwealth who applied for retirement under the Virginia Retirement System (§ 51.1-124.1 et seq. of the Code of Virginia) or the State Police Officers' Retirement System (§ 51.1-200 et seq. of the Code of Virginia) on or before December 1, 1994, shall not be eligible for the incentive programs established in the second or third enactments of this act, or for the benefits provided by Chapter 10.5 (§ 2.1-116.20 et seq.) [see now Chapter 32 (§ 2.2-3200 et seq.) of Title 2.2] of the Code of Virginia."

CASE NOTES

Editor's note. — The case below was decided under former Title 2.1 or prior provisions.

Obligation to pay benefits found. — Payments made pursuant to agreement with the claimant were not for work performed or services rendered to the employer in anticipation of compensation, but were to induce claimant not to perform work for the employer; thus under the Workforce Transition Act, employer was obligated to pay claimant workers' compensation benefits. Commonwealth/DOT v. Swiney, 23 Va. App. 467, 477 S.E.2d 777 (1996).

§ 2.2-3201. Duties of Department of Human Resource Management and executive branch agencies to involuntarily separated employees. — A. Prior to terminating or placing on leave without pay-layoff or equivalent status any employee of an agency or institution in the executive branch of state government, the management of the agency or institution shall make every effort to place the employee in any vacant position within the agency for which the employee is qualified. If reemployment within the agency or institution is not possible because there is no available position for which the employee is qualified or the position offered to the employee requires relocation or a reduction in salary, the name of the employee shall be forwarded to the Department of Human Resource Management (the "Department").

B. Any preferential employment rights vested in the employee under the Commonwealth's layoff policy shall not be denied, abridged, or modified in any way by the Department. The Department shall coordinate the preferential hiring of the employee, at the same salary classification, in any agency or institution of the executive branch of state government. The Department shall also establish a program to assist employees in finding employment outside of state government.

C. If, as of the date the employee is terminated from employment or placed on leave without pay-layoff or equivalent status, reemployment within his agency or institution or any other agency or institution of the executive branch of state government is not possible because there is no available position for which the employee is qualified or the position offered to the employee requires relocation or a reduction in salary, then the employee shall be deemed to be involuntarily separated. If such employee is otherwise eligible, he shall be entitled, under the conditions specified, to receive the transitional severance benefit conferred by this chapter.

D. The Department shall report all involuntary separations in the executive branch of state government to the Department of Planning and Budget, which shall make an appropriate reduction, pursuant to § 2.2-1501, in the terminating agency's maximum employment level in preparing its executive budget for the next session of the General Assembly. (1995, cc. 152, 811, § 2.1-116.21; 2000, cc. 66, 657; 2001, c. 844.)

CASE NOTES

Applied in Boynton v. Kilgore, 271 Va. 220, 623 S.E.2d 922, 2006 Va. LEXIS 2 (2006).

§ 2.2-3202. Eligibility for transitional severance benefit. — A. Any full-time employee of the Commonwealth (i) whose position is covered by the

Virginia Personnel Act (§ 2.2-2900 et seq.), (ii) whose position is exempt from the Virginia Personnel Act pursuant to subdivisions 2, 4 (except those persons specified in subsection C of this section), 7, 15 or 16 of § 2.2-2905, (iii) who is employed by the State Corporation Commission, (iv) who is employed by the Virginia Workers' Compensation Commission, (v) who is employed by the Virginia Retirement System, (vi) who is employed by the State Lottery Department, (vii) who is employed by the Medical College of Virginia Hospitals or the University of Virginia Medical Center, (viii) who is employed at a state educational institution as faculty (including, but not limited to, presidents and teaching and research faculty) as defined in the Consolidated Salary Authorization for Faculty Positions in Institutions of Higher Education, 1994-95, or (ix) whose position is exempt from the Virginia Personnel Act pursuant to subdivision 3 or 20 of § 2.2-2905; and (a) for whom reemployment with the Commonwealth is not possible because there is no available position for which the employee is qualified or the position offered to the employee requires relocation or a reduction in salary and (b) whose involuntary separation was due to causes other than job performance or misconduct, shall be eligible, under the conditions specified, for the transitional severance benefit conferred by this chapter. The date of involuntary separation shall mean the date an employee was terminated from employment or placed on leave without pay-layoff or equivalent status.

B. An otherwise eligible employee whose position is contingent upon project grants as defined in the Catalogue of Federal Domestic Assistance, shall not be eligible for the transitional severance benefit conferred by this chapter unless the funding source had agreed to assume all financial responsibility therefor in its written contract with the Commonwealth.

C. Members of the Judicial Retirement System (§ 51.1-300 et seq.) and officers elected by popular vote shall not be eligible for the transitional severance benefit conferred by this chapter.

D. Eligibility shall commence on the date of involuntary separation.

E. Persons authorized by § 2.2-106 or 51.1-124.22 to appoint a chief administrative officer or the administrative head of an agency shall adhere to the same criteria for eligibility for transitional severance benefits as is required for gubernatorial appointees pursuant to subsection A. (1995, cc. 152, 811, § 2.1-116.22; 2001, c. 844; 2002, c. 491; 2003, c. 782; 2006, cc. 813, 902.)

Editor's note. — Acts 1995, c. 152 and Acts 1995, c. 811 provided for incentives for voluntary terminations of certain state employees in 1995, and outlined applicable terms and conditions.

Acts 2003, c. 782, cl. 2, provides: "That the provisions of this act shall apply to appointments made on and after the effective date of this act [July 1, 2003]."

Acts 2006, cc. 813 and 902, in cl. 2 provide: "That the provisions of § 2.2-3202 of this act shall be applicable to involuntary separations occurring on or after July 1, 2006."

CASE NOTES

Employees of the Office of the Attorney General were ineligible for Workforce Transition Act benefits. — Circuit court properly sustained a demurrer filed by defendant, the Office of the Attorney General, who employed a group of former employees, which was filed in response to the employees' amended motion for judgment, as the employees were not covered by the Virginia Personnel Act, § 2.2-2900 et seq., because they were exempt under § 2.2-2905; hence, the employees were ineligible to receive Workforce Transition Act benefits. Boynton v. Kilgore, 271 Va. 220, 623 S.E.2d 922, 2006 Va. LEXIS 2 (2006).

§ 2.2-3203. Transitional severance benefit conferred. — A. On his date of involuntary separation, an eligible employee with (i) two years' service or less to the Commonwealth shall be entitled to receive a transitional severance benefit equivalent to four weeks of salary; (ii) three years through and including nine years of consecutive service to the Commonwealth shall be entitled to receive a transitional severance benefit equivalent to four weeks of salary plus one additional week of salary for every year of service over two years; (iii) ten years through and including fourteen years of consecutive service to the Commonwealth shall be entitled to receive a transitional severance benefit equivalent to twelve weeks of salary plus two additional weeks of salary for every year of service over nine years; or (iv) fifteen years or more of consecutive service to the Commonwealth shall be entitled to receive a transitional severance benefit equivalent to two weeks of salary for every year of service, not to exceed thirty-six weeks of salary.

B. Transitional severance benefits shall be computed by the terminating agency's payroll department. Partial years of service shall be rounded up to the next highest year of service.

C. Transitional severance benefits shall be paid in the same manner as normal salary. In accordance with § 60.2-229, transitional severance benefits shall be allocated to the date of involuntary separation. The right of any employee who receives a transitional severance benefit to also receive unemployment compensation pursuant to § 60.2-100 et seq. shall not be denied, abridged, or modified in any way due to receipt of the transitional severance benefit; however, any employee who is entitled to unemployment compensation shall have his transitional severance benefit reduced by the amount of such unemployment compensation. Any offset to a terminated employee's transitional severance benefit due to reductions for unemployment compensation shall be paid in one lump sum at the time the last transitional severance benefit payment is made.

D. For twelve months after the employee's date of involuntary separation, the employee shall continue to be covered under the (i) health insurance plan created in § 2.2-2818 for the Commonwealth's employees, if he participated in such plan prior to his date of involuntary separation, and (ii) group life insurance plan administered by the Virginia Retirement System pursuant to Chapter 5 (§ 51.1-500 et seq.) of Title 51.1. During such twelve months, the terminating agency shall continue to pay its share of the terminated employee's premiums. Upon expiration of such twelve month period, the terminated employee shall be eligible to purchase continuing health insurance coverage under COBRA.

E. Transitional severance benefit payments shall cease if a terminated employee is reemployed or hired in an individual capacity as an independent contractor or consultant by any agency or institution of the Commonwealth during the time he is receiving such payments.

F. All transitional severance benefits payable pursuant to this section shall be subject to applicable federal laws and regulations. (1995, cc. 152, 811, § 2.1-116.23; 2001, c. 844.)

CIRCUIT COURT OPINIONS

Attorney General employees not covered. — Attorney General employees were not covered by the Virginia Personnel Act, § 2.2-2900 et seq., so former employees of Attorney General's office were not eligible for severance benefits under the Work Force Transition Act, § 2.2-3203 et seq., because that eligibility was dependent on coverage under the Virginia Personnel Act. Boynton v. Kilgore, 66 Va. Cir. 37, 2004 Va. Cir. LEXIS 339 (Richmond Aug. 27, 2004), aff'd, 271 Va. 220, 623 S.E.2d 922 (2006).

Virginia Personnel Act, § 2.2-2400 et seq., exempted from coverage officers and employees for whom the constitution directed the manner of selection; this included the attorney general and, derivatively, any of his appointed employees, and, thus, those employees were ineligible for severance benefits under the Worker Transition Act, § 2.2-3203 et seq. Boynton v. Kilgore, 69 Va. Cir. 5, 2005 Va. Cir. LEXIS 354 (Richmond 2005).

§ **2.2-3204. Retirement program.** — A. In lieu of the transitional severance benefit provided in § 2.2-3203, any otherwise eligible employee who, on the date of involuntary separation, is also (i) a vested member of the Virginia Retirement System, the State Police Officers' Retirement System, or the Virginia Law Officers' Retirement System and (ii) at least fifty years of age, may elect to have the Commonwealth purchase on his behalf years to be credited to either his age or creditable service or a combination of age and creditable service, except that any years of credit purchased on behalf of a member of the Virginia Retirement System, the State Police Officers' Retirement System, or the Virginia Law Officers' Retirement System who is eligible for unreduced retirement shall be added to his creditable service and not his age. The cost of each year of age or creditable service purchased by the Commonwealth shall be equal to fifteen percent of the employee's present annual compensation. The number of years of age or creditable service to be purchased by the Commonwealth shall be equal to the quotient obtained by dividing (i) the cash value of the benefits to which the employee would be entitled under subsections A and D of § 2.2-3203 by (ii) the cost of each year of age or creditable service. Partial years shall be rounded up to the next highest year. Deferred retirement under the provisions of subsection C of §§ 51.1-153, 51.1-205, and 51.1-216, and disability retirement under the provisions of § 51.1-156 et seq. and § 51.1-209, shall not be available under this section.

B. In lieu of the (i) transitional severance benefit provided in § 2.2-3203 and (ii) the retirement program provided in subsection A, any employee who is otherwise eligible may take immediate retirement pursuant to § 51.1-155.1.

C. The retirement allowance for any employee electing to retire under this section who, by adding years to his age, is between ages fifty-five and sixty-five, shall be reduced on the actuarial basis provided in subdivision A. 2. of § 51.1-155. (1995, cc. 152, 811, § 2.1-116.24; 2000, c. 911; 2001, c. 844.)

§ **2.2-3205. Costs associated with this chapter; payment.** — A. The terminating agency shall pay all costs associated with the provisions of this chapter within the twelve months following the date of an employee's involuntary separation, or within such shorter period as may be required. The costs shall be paid first from appropriations available to the terminating agency. If such sums are insufficient, then, if the agency's governing authority certifies that the agency is unable to pay the costs when due from appropriations available to the terminating agency without affecting the agency's ability to deliver essential services, aid to localities, or aid to individuals, the State Treasurer shall make a treasury loan to the agency to be used to finance the unsatisfied balance of the agency's obligations.

B. As used in this section, the *"governing authority"* shall mean (i) for an agency in the executive branch, the Governor or his designee; (ii) for an agency in the judicial branch, the Supreme Court of Virginia; (iii) and for an agency in the legislative branch or an independent agency, the appropriate collegial body.

C. Any treasury loan made pursuant to subsection A shall be repaid by the agency in the following order: (i) first, from unexpended fund balances available to the agency; (ii) next, from the unexpended year-end balances, less mandated uses as set out in the appropriation act, of all other state agencies and institutions in the terminating agency's branch of government (i.e., judicial, legislative, or executive); and (iii) finally, from such appropriations as the General Assembly may provide for such purpose. In budgeting for the payment of these costs, the general fund shall bear its actual share of such costs. (1995, cc. 152, 811, § 2.1-116.25; 2001, c. 844.)

§ 2.2-3206. Review of program. — The Senate Committee on Finance and the House Committee on Appropriations shall periodically review the transitional severance program established by this chapter and report their findings to the Governor and the members of the General Assembly every three years beginning on July 1, 1998. (1995, cc. 152, 811, § 2.1-116.26; 2001, c. 844.)

SUBTITLE II.

ADMINISTRATION OF STATE GOVERNMENT.

PART A.

GENERAL PROVISIONS.

CHAPTER 33.

STATE HOLIDAYS AND OTHER SPECIAL DAYS.

§ 2.2-3300. Legal holidays. — It is the policy of the Commonwealth to fix and set aside certain days in the calendar year as legal holidays for the people of Virginia. In each year, the following days are designated as legal holidays:

January 1 — New Year's Day.

The Friday preceding the third Monday in January — Lee-Jackson Day to honor Robert Edward Lee (1807-1870) and Thomas Jonathan (Stonewall) Jackson (1824-1863), defenders of causes.

The third Monday in January — Martin Luther King, Jr., Day to honor Martin Luther King, Jr., (1929-1968), defender of causes.

The third Monday in February — George Washington Day to honor George Washington (1732-1799), the first President of the United States.

The last Monday in May — Memorial Day to honor all persons who made the supreme sacrifice in giving their lives in defense of Virginia and the United States in the following wars and engagements and otherwise: Indian Uprising (1622), French and Indian Wars (1754-1763), Revolutionary War (1775-1783), War of 1812 (1812-1815), Mexican War (1846-1848), War Between the States (1861-1865), Spanish-American War (1898), World War I (1917-1918), World War II (1941-1945), Korean War (1950-1953), Vietnam War (1965-1973), and Operation Desert Shield-Desert Storm (1990-1991). On this day all flags, national, state, and local, shall be flown at half staff or mast to honor and acknowledge respect for those who made the supreme sacrifice.

July 4 — Independence Day to honor the signing of the Declaration of Independence.

The first Monday in September — Labor Day to honor all people who work in Virginia.

The second Monday in October — Columbus Day and Yorktown Victory Day to honor Christopher Columbus (1451-1506), a discoverer of the Americas, and the final victory at Yorktown on October 19, 1781, in the Revolutionary War.

November 11 — Veterans Day to honor all persons who served in the Armed Forces of Virginia and the United States in the following wars and engagements and otherwise: Indian Uprising (1622), French and Indian Wars (1754-1763), Revolutionary War (1775-1783), War of 1812 (1812-1815), Mexican War (1846-1848), War Between the States (1861-1865), Spanish American War (1898), World War I (1917-1918), World War II (1941-1945), Korean War (1950-1953), Vietnam War (1965-1973), and Operation Desert Shield-Desert Storm (1990-1991).

The fourth Thursday in November and the Friday next following — Thanksgiving Day to honor and give thanks in each person's own manner for the blessings bestowed upon the people of Virginia and honoring the first Thanksgiving in 1619.

December 25 — Christmas Day.

Whenever any of such days falls on Saturday, the Friday next preceding such day, or whenever any of such days falls on Sunday, the Monday next following such day, and any day so appointed by the Governor of the Commonwealth or the President of the United States, shall be a legal holiday as to the transaction of all business. (Code 1950, § 2-19; 1954, c. 328; 1958, c. 167; 1966, c. 677, § 2.1-21; 1970, c. 682; 1972, c. 114; 1973, c. 421; 1978, c. 7; 1982, c. 325; 1984, c. 671; 1989, c. 190; 1992, c. 622; 1993, cc. 177, 872; 2000, cc. 392, 454; 2001, c. 844.)

Editor's note. — Acts 2007, c. 124, cl. 1, provides: "That the Department of Education shall make available to local school divisions information regarding the commemoration of Veterans Day in the public schools. Such information shall include, but need not be limited to (i) history of the holiday, (ii) discussion topics, (iii) activities, and (iv) appropriate instructional materials."

Acts 2007, c. 132, cl. 1, provides: "That the Department of Education shall make available to local school divisions information regarding the commemoration of George Washington's birthday on or around February 22 in the public schools. Such information shall include, but need not be limited to, (i) discussion topics, (ii) activities, and (iii) appropriate instructional materials about George Washington."

Michie's Jurisprudence. — For related discussion, see 18 M.J. Sundays and Holidays, § 1.

§ 2.2-3301. Acts, business transactions, legal proceedings, etc., on holidays valid. — No contract made, instrument executed, or act done on any of the legal holidays named in § 2.2-3300 or on any Saturday shall be thereby rendered invalid. Nothing in § 2.2-3300 shall be construed to prevent or invalidate the entry, issuance, service or execution of any writ, summons, confession, judgment, order or decree, or other legal process whatever, or the session of the proceedings of any court or judge on any of the legal holidays or Saturdays nor to prevent any bank, banker, banking corporation, firm or association from keeping their doors open and transacting any lawful business on any of the legal holidays or Saturdays. (Code 1950, § 2-20; 1966, c. 677, § 2.1-22; 2001, c. 844.)

Michie's Jurisprudence. — For related discussion, see 4A M.J. Contracts, § 39.

§ **2.2-3302. Observance of Yorktown Day.** — The nineteenth day of October of each year shall be recognized and celebrated as Yorktown Day throughout the Commonwealth. The observance of Yorktown Day shall not be considered a paid state holiday. (1983, c. 540, § 2.1-21.1; 2001, c. 844.)

Editor's note. — Acts 1986, c. 68, cl. 1 provides: "All public schools should set aside time during the school day on October 19 of each year to commemorate Yorktown Day — the Revolutionary War victory."

§ **2.2-3303. Observance of Motherhood and Apple Pie Day in recognition of the need to prevent infant mortality.** — A. The twenty-sixth day of January of each year shall be recognized and celebrated as Motherhood and Apple Pie Day throughout the Commonwealth. Upon this date, all citizens of the Commonwealth are urged to reflect upon the need to continue efforts to reduce the state's infant mortality rate to preserve our heritage and to ensure the health and well-being of future generations.

B. On the third Thursday of every session of the Virginia General Assembly, the General Assembly shall give proper recognition to Motherhood and Apple Pie Day in the Commonwealth. (1989, c. 114, § 2.1-21.2; 2001, c. 844.)

Michie's Jurisprudence. — For related discussion, see 9B M.J. Infants, § 2.

§ **2.2-3304. Display of flags on Mother's Day.** — The Governor may issue annually a proclamation calling upon state officials to display the flag of the United States and of the Commonwealth on all public buildings, and the people of the Commonwealth to display such flags at their homes and other suitable places on the second Sunday in May, known as "Mother's Day," as a public expression of love and reverence for the mothers of the Commonwealth. (Code 1950, § 2-21; 1966, c. 677, § 2.1-24; 2001, c. 844.)

§ **2.2-3304.1. Little League Challenger Week in Virginia.** — The first full week of May preceding Mother's Day of each year shall be designated as Little League Baseball Challenger Week in Virginia. (2006, c. 109.)

§ **2.2-3305. Commonwealth Day of Prayer.** — The first Thursday in May of each year shall be designated the "Commonwealth Day of Prayer" and shall be a day on which the people of the Commonwealth may turn to God in prayer and meditation and may celebrate the religious freedom secured for them by the laws of the Commonwealth and nation. (1997, c. 388, § 2.1-24.2; 2001, c. 844.)

§ **2.2-3306. Arbor Day.** — The last Friday in April of each year shall be designated and known as "Arbor Day." (Code 1950, § 2-22; 1966, c. 677, § 2.1-25; 1993, c. 222; 2001, c. 844; 2005, c. 242.)

§ 2.2-3307. Dogwood Day. — The third Saturday in April of each year shall be known and designated as "Dogwood Day." (1952, c. 111, § 2-22.1; 1966, c. 677, § 2.1-26; 2001, c. 844.)

§ 2.2-3308. First Lady's Day in Virginia. — Martha Washington's birthday, the second day of June of each year, shall be designated as First Lady's Day in Virginia in special tribute to Martha Washington as America's first First Lady and to each of her successors as First Ladies of this Nation. Upon this date, in perpetuity, all citizens, groups and appropriate agencies in and of the Commonwealth and of the nation are urged to reflect upon and give appropriate recognition to the magnificent contribution of this Nation's First Ladies to the heritage of the United States. (1960, c. 245, § 2-22.3; 1966, c. 677, § 2.1-27; 2001, c. 844.)

§ 2.2-3309. Pearl Harbor Remembrance Day. — The seventh day of December of each year shall be designated as Pearl Harbor Remembrance Day in the Commonwealth in special tribute to those members of our armed forces who lost their lives, and also to those who survived, the attack on Pearl Harbor, Territory of Hawaii, December 7, 1941. Upon this date, in perpetuity, all citizens of the Commonwealth and the nation are urged to pay homage to the members of our armed forces for the manner in which they bore the attack. (1983, c. 247, § 2.1-27.2; 2001, c. 844.)

§ 2.2-3309.1. Virginia World War II Veterans Appreciation Week; Virginia Korean War Veterans Appreciation Week; honorary diplomas to be awarded under certain circumstances during such weeks. — A. In recognition of the sacrifice of the members of the United States Armed Forces who served in World War II, the first full week in September, i.e., the week that was the first full official week of peace in 1945, shall hereby be designated the Virginia World War II Veterans Appreciation Week, beginning in September 2001.

In accordance with the Board of Education's guidelines as authorized by § 22.1-17.4, any veteran of World War II may apply for a Commonwealth of Virginia World War II Veteran Honorary High School Diploma by filing with the Virginia Board of Education a statement declaring that:

1. During the years between 1939 and 1945, he served in any branch of the United States Armed Forces;
2. He was drafted or did enlist in the United States Armed Forces while still enrolled as a secondary school student in any school in any state or territory of the United States or any school located on or associated with a United States military base or embassy; and
3. He was unable to resume his secondary education upon returning to civilian life.

B. In recognition of the sacrifice of the members of the United States Armed Forces who served during the Korean War, the first full week in November shall hereby be designated the Virginia Korean War Veterans Appreciation Week, beginning in November 2002.

In accordance with the Board of Education's guidelines as authorized by § 22.1-17.4, any veteran of the Korean War may apply for a Commonwealth of Virginia Korean War Veteran Honorary High School Diploma by filing with the Virginia Board of Education a statement declaring that:

1. During the years between 1950 and 1953, he served in any branch of the United States Armed Forces;
2. He enlisted in or was drafted into the United States Armed Forces while still enrolled as a secondary school student in any school in any state or

territory of the United States or any school located on or associated with a United States military base or embassy; and

3. He was unable to resume his secondary education upon returning to civilian life.

C. Upon receiving a statement in compliance with this section and § 22.1-17.4 that has been filed in accordance with its guidelines, the Board of Education shall award the veteran described in subsections A or B, a Commonwealth of Virginia World War II Veteran Honorary High School Diploma or a Commonwealth of Virginia Korean War Veteran Honorary High School Diploma, as appropriate. Such diploma shall also be delivered during Virginia World War II Veterans Appreciation Week or Virginia Korean War Veterans Appreciation Week, as appropriate. (2001, c. 263, § 2.1-27.2:01; 2002, c. 162.)

Editor's note. — Acts 2001, c. 263 enacted § 2.1-27.2:01, from which this section is derived. Pursuant to § 30-152, Acts 2001, c. 263 has been given effect in this section as set out above.

§ **2.2-3310. Vietnam War Memorial Dedication and Veterans' Recognition Week.** — The first full week of November of each year shall be designated as Vietnam War Memorial Dedication Week and Veterans' Recognition Week in the Commonwealth, to honor in perpetuity the men and women who have served their country as members of the armed forces during the Vietnam Conflict. (1984, c. 691, § 2.1-27.3; 2001, c. 844; 2003, c. 684.)

§ **2.2-3310.1. Display of the POW/MIA flag.** — It is the sense of the General Assembly that members of the armed forces of the United States who are or were prisoners of war or reported missing in action should be honored and remembered for their service and sacrifice. In observance of that service and sacrifice, all agencies and institutions of the Commonwealth shall display the POW/MIA flag on public buildings on the following days each year:

Armed Forces Day — the third Saturday in May.
Memorial Day — the last Monday in May.
Flag Day — June 14.
Independence Day — July 4.
National POW/MIA Recognition Day — the third Friday in September.
Veterans Day — November 11. (2001, c. 835, § 2.1-27.3:1.)

Editor's note. — Acts 2001, c. 835 enacted § 2.1-27.3:1, from which this section is derived. Pursuant to § 30-152, Acts 2001, c. 835 has been given effect in this section as set out above.

§ **2.2-3310.2. Vietnamese-American Heritage Flag.** — The flag of the former Republic of Vietnam, with three horizontal red stripes on a field of golden-yellow, which symbolizes freedom and democracy and represents the cultural heritage of Vietnamese-Americans, is recognized by the Commonwealth as the Vietnamese-American Heritage Flag. (2004, c. 970.)

§ **2.2-3311. Day of recognition for early childhood and day-care providers and professionals.** — The Friday before Mother's Day of each year shall be designated as a day of recognition for early childhood and day-care providers and professionals to acknowledge the contributions of and pay tribute to early childhood and day-care providers and professionals who serve the children of the Commonwealth. (1989, c. 132, § 2.1-27.6; 2001, c. 844; 2006, c. 156.)

§ 2.2-3311.1. Day of recognition for direct care staffs and other long-term care professionals. — The second Wednesday of every June shall be designated as a day of recognition to acknowledge the contributions of and pay tribute to direct care staffs and members of other professions that provide dedicated assistance and health care services to enhance the quality of life of persons receiving long-term care in the Commonwealth. (2005, c. 454.)

§ 2.2-3312. Day of recognition for bone marrow donor programs. — The eighth day of April of each year shall be designated as a day of recognition for bone marrow donor programs to acknowledge the critical value of these initiatives in facilitating bone marrow transplant therapy and to increase awareness among the citizens of the Commonwealth regarding opportunities to participate in these programs as donors and volunteers. (1992, c. 605, § 2.1-27.7; 2001, c. 844.)

§ 2.2-3313. Virginia Drug Free Day. — The Saturday of the last week in October of each year shall be designated and known as "Virginia Drug Free Day" to recognize and support education about the dangers of drug abuse, the penalties for drug crimes, the availability of substance abuse programs, and the need to eradicate drug abuse in Virginia's communities. (1994, c. 480, § 2.1-27.8; 2001, c. 844.)

§ 2.2-3314. Bill of Rights Day. — The fifteenth day of December of each year shall be designated and known as the "Bill of Rights Day" in recognition of the ratification of the first ten amendments to the United States Constitution. (1998, c. 383, § 2.1-27.10; 2001, c. 844.)

§ 2.2-3315. Citizenship Day and Constitution Week. — The Governor shall annually issue a proclamation setting the seventeenth day of September as Citizenship Day and September seventeen through twenty-three as Constitution Week and recommending that they be observed by the Commonwealth with appropriate exercises in the schools and otherwise so that the eventful day on which the Constitution of the United States was formally adopted may forever remain enshrined in the hearts and minds of all citizens and so that they may be reminded on that date annually of the blessings of liberty that they enjoy by the adoption of the United States Constitution, the Bill of Rights and all other amendments thereto. (1974, c. 531, § 2.1-24.1; 2001, c. 844.)

§ 2.2-3315.1. White Cane Safety Day. — Each year, the Governor may take suitable public notice of October 15 as White Cane Safety Day. He may issue a proclamation in which:

1. He comments upon the significance of the white cane;
2. He calls upon the citizens of the Commonwealth to observe the provisions of the White Cane Law and to take precautions necessary to the safety of the disabled;
3. He reminds the citizens of the Commonwealth of the policies with respect to the disabled herein declared and urges the citizens to cooperate in giving effect to them; and
4. He emphasizes the need of the citizens to be aware of the presence of disabled persons in the community and to keep safe and functional for the disabled the streets, highways, sidewalks, walkways, public buildings, public facilities, other public places, places of public accommodation, amusement and resort, and other places to which the public is invited, and to offer assistance to disabled persons upon appropriate occasions. (1972, c. 156, § 63.1-171.5; 2002, c. 747.)

§ 2.2-3316. Landscape Architecture Week in Virginia. — The second full week of April of each year shall be designated as Landscape Architecture Week in Virginia in recognition of the value and importance of the profession of landscape architecture, which encourages environmental stewardship, promotes energy conservation, enhances the preservation of the Commonwealth's historical heritage, and ensures that the place known as Virginia is preserved through wise design, management, and maintenance of its landscape. (1999, c. 164, § 2.1-27.11; 2001, c. 844.)

§ 2.2-3317. Virginia Championship Applebutter Making Contest. — The Virginia Championship Applebutter Making Contest, held in Winchester in conjunction with the Rotary Club's Apple Harvest Festival, shall be the third week in September of each year. (1983, c. 95, § 2.1-27.1; 2001, c. 844.)

§ 2.2-3318. Virginia and American History Month. — January nineteenth through February twenty-second, both inclusive of each year, shall be designated as Virginia and American History Month in special tribute to the founders, builders, and preservers of the Commonwealth and Nation. (1960, c. 354, § 2-22.4; 1966, c. 677, § 2.1-28; 2001, c. 844.)

§ 2.2-3319. American Indian Month and Day of Appreciation. — The month of November shall be designated as "American Indian Month" in Virginia, to honor the culture and heritage of the American Indian, to recognize the historic and continuing contribution of that heritage to American society, and in particular to commemorate the special place of the tribes native to Virginia in the life and history of the Commonwealth. Further, the Wednesday immediately preceding Thanksgiving of each year is designated a special Day of Appreciation for American Indians residing in the Commonwealth. (1987, c. 292, § 2.1-27.4; 1988, c. 685; 1996, c. 1020; 1997, c. 451; 2001, c. 844.)

§ 2.2-3320. Month for Children in Virginia. — The month of May shall be designated as the "Month for Children" in Virginia to focus on children's special contributions to family, school, and community; to counter the manifold ills that afflict children in the Commonwealth, the nation, and the world; and to encourage the citizens of Virginia to rededicate themselves and to redouble their efforts to improve the lives and ensure the futures of children everywhere. (1997, cc. 432, 442, § 2.1-27.9; 2001, c. 844.)

§ 2.2-3321. Virginia Mushroom Festival. — The Annual Front Royal and Warren County Mushroom Festival, in conjunction with the Appalachian Mushroom Growers Association's annual meeting, is designated as the Virginia Mushroom Festival, and shall be designated as the official state mushroom festival within the Commonwealth. (1987, c. 593, § 2.1-27.5; 2001, c. 844.)

§ 2.2-3322. Office hours to be in accordance with executive orders of Governor. — The offices of all state officers, departments, boards, bureaus, commissions, divisions and institutions in the executive branch of state government required by law to maintain regular business quarters at the seat of government shall be kept open for the transaction of public business in accordance with executive orders issued by the Governor.

This section shall not apply to the offices of the legislative and judicial departments of the state government. (Code 1950, § 2-23; 1966, c. 677, § 2.1-29; 2001, c. 844.)

CHAPTER 34.

INTERPRETERS FOR THE DEAF IN AGENCY PROCEEDINGS.

§ 2.2-3400. Definitions. — As used in this chapter, unless the context requires a different meaning:

"Agency" means any state board, department, commission, agency or other unit of state government except a county, city, town or any agency thereof.

"Deaf person" means any person whose hearing is so seriously impaired as to prohibit the person from understanding oral communications spoken in a normal conversational tone. (1978, c. 602, § 2.1-570; 2001, c. 844.)

§ 2.2-3401. Agency proceedings and determinations; application for licenses and services. — A. In the case of any agency proceeding or determination as to whether there is a violation of law or regulation by a deaf person or whether such person may obtain or retain a license or other right or benefit, and when the agency or deaf person requests an interpreter for the deaf, the agency shall request the Virginia Department for the Deaf and Hard-of-Hearing to appoint a qualified interpreter or shall appoint such an interpreter from a list of qualified interpreters supplied by the Department to interpret the proceedings to the deaf person and to interpret any testimony the deaf person may give.

B. Whenever a deaf person applies for or receives any license, service, assistance or other right or benefit provided by an agency, the agency shall either request the Virginia Department for the Deaf and Hard-of-Hearing to appoint a qualified interpreter for the deaf or appoint such an interpreter from the list of qualified interpreters maintained by the Department to assist the deaf person in communicating with agency personnel. (1978, c. 602, §§ 2.1-571, 2.1-572; 2001, c. 844.)

§ 2.2-3402. How interpreters paid. — An interpreter for the deaf appointed pursuant to § 2.2-3401 shall be paid by the agency out of such state and federal funds as may be available for the purpose or, if the agency has insufficient funds to pay an interpreter, the Virginia Department for the Deaf and Hard-of-Hearing may appoint and pay an interpreter from the funds it may have available for the purpose. (1978, c. 602, § 2.1-573; 2001, c. 844.)

CHAPTER 35.

INFORMATION TECHNOLOGY ACCESS ACT.

§ 2.2-3500. Findings; policy. — A. The General Assembly finds that (i) the advent of the information age throughout the United States and around the world has resulted in lasting changes in information technology; (ii) use of interactive visual display terminals by state and state-assisted organizations is becoming a widespread means of access for employees and the public to obtain information available electronically, but nonvisual access, whether by speech, Braille, or other appropriate means has been overlooked in purchasing and deploying the latest information technology; (iii) presentation of electronic data solely in a visual format is a barrier to access by individuals who are blind or visually impaired, preventing them from participating on equal terms in crucial areas of life, such as education and employment; (iv) alternatives, including both software and hardware adaptations, have been created so that interactive control of computers and use of the information presented is possible by both visual and nonvisual means; and (v) the goals of the state in obtaining and deploying the most advanced forms of information technology properly include universal access so that the segments of society with particular needs (including individuals unable to use visual displays) will not be left out of the information age.

B. It is the policy of the Commonwealth that all covered entities shall conduct themselves in accordance with the following principles: (i) individuals who are blind or visually impaired have the right to full participation in the life of the Commonwealth, including the use of advanced technology that is provided by such covered entities for use by employees, program participants, and members of the general public, and (ii) technology purchased in whole or in part with funds provided by the Commonwealth to be used for the creation, storage, retrieval, or dissemination of information and intended for use by employees, program participants, and members of the general public shall be adaptable for access by individuals who are blind or visually impaired. The implementation of nonvisual access technology under this chapter shall be determined on a case-by-case basis as the need arises. (1999, cc. 769, 773, § 2.1-807; 2001, c. 844.)

§ **2.2-3501. Definitions.** — As used in this chapter, unless the context requires a different meaning:

"Access" means the ability to receive, use, and manipulate data and operate controls included in information technology.

"Blind" or *"visually impaired"* individual means an individual who has: (i) a visual acuity of 20/200 or less in the better eye with correcting lenses or has a limited field of vision so that the widest diameter of the visual field subtends an angle no greater than 20 degrees; (ii) a medically indicated expectation of visual deterioration; or (iii) a medically diagnosed limitation in visual functioning that restricts the individual's ability to read and write standard print at levels expected of individuals of comparable ability.

"Covered entity" means all state agencies, public institutions of higher education, and political subdivisions of the Commonwealth.

"Information technology" means all electronic information processing hardware and software, including telecommunications.

"Nonvisual" means synthesized speech, Braille, and other output methods not requiring sight.

"Telecommunications" means the transmission of information, images, pictures, voice or data by radio, video, or other electronic or impulse means, but shall not include public broadcasting services as defined in § 2.2-2427. (1999, cc. 769, 773, § 2.1-808; 2001, c. 844.)

Law Review. — For a symposium, "Convergence: The Future of Technology & Competition Policy," see 8 Geo. Mason L. Rev. 619 (2000). For an article, "The Impact of Convergence and the Gramm-Leach-Bliley Act on the Insurance Industry," see 8 Geo. Mason L. Rev. 623 (2000). For an article, "The Cable Open Access Debate: The Case for a Wholesale Market," see 8 Geo. Mason L. Rev. 653 (2000). For an article, "Nonregulation of Advanced Internet Services," see 8

Geo. Mason L. Rev. 681 (2000). For an article, "Technology and Bank Competition Policy," see 8 Geo. Mason L. Rev. 721 (2000).

§ 2.2-3502. Assurance of nonvisual access. — In general, the head of each covered entity shall ensure that information technology equipment and software used by blind or visually impaired employees, program participants, or members of the general public (i) provide access (including interactive use of the equipment and services) that is equivalent to that provided to individuals who are not blind or visually impaired; (ii) are designed to present information (including prompts used for interactive communications) in formats adaptable to both visual and nonvisual use; and (iii) have been purchased under a contract that includes the technology access clause required pursuant to § 2.2-3503. (1999, cc. 769, 773, § 2.1-809; 2001, c. 844.)

§ 2.2-3503. Procurement requirements. — A. The technology access clause specified in clause (iii) of § 2.2-3502 shall be developed by the Secretary of Technology and shall require compliance with the nonvisual access standards established in subsection B of this section. The clause shall be included in all future contracts for the procurement of information technology by, or for the use of, entities covered by this chapter on or after the effective date of this chapter.

B. At a minimum, the nonvisual access standards shall include the following: (i) the effective, interactive control and use of the technology (including the operating system), applications programs, and format of the data presented, shall be readily achievable by nonvisual means; (ii) the technology equipped for nonvisual access shall be compatible with information technology used by other individuals with whom the blind or visually impaired individual interacts; (iii) nonvisual access technology shall be integrated into networks used to share communications among employees, program participants, and the public; and (iv) the technology for nonvisual access shall have the capability of providing equivalent access by nonvisual means to telecommunications or other interconnected network services used by persons who are not blind or visually impaired. A covered entity may stipulate additional specifications in any procurement.

Compliance with the nonvisual access standards shall not be required if the head of a covered entity determines that (i) the information technology is not available with nonvisual access because the essential elements of the information technology are visual and (ii) nonvisual equivalence is not available. (1999, cc. 769, 773, § 2.1-810; 2001, c. 844.)

§ 2.2-3504. Implementation. — A. The head of any covered entity may, with respect to nonvisual access software or peripheral devices, approve the exclusion of the technology access clause only to the extent that the cost of the software or devices for the covered entity would increase the total cost of the procurement by more than five percent. All exclusions of the technology access clause from any contract shall be reported annually to the Secretary of Technology.

B. The acquisition and installation of hardware, software, or peripheral devices used for nonvisual access when the information technology is being used exclusively by individuals who are not blind or visually impaired shall not be required.

C. Notwithstanding the provisions of subsection B, the applications programs and underlying operating systems (including the format of the data) used for the manipulation and presentation of information shall permit the installation and effective use of nonvisual access software and peripheral devices. (1999, cc. 769, 773, § 2.1-811; 2001, c. 844.)

CHAPTER 36.

State Government Volunteers Act.

§ 2.2-3600. Short title; declaration of legislative intent. — A. This chapter may be cited as the Virginia State Government Volunteers Act.

B. Since the spirit of volunteerism has long animated generations of Americans to give of their time and abilities to help others, the Commonwealth would be wise to make use of volunteers in state service wherever practically possible. Effective use of volunteers in state service, however, requires that state agencies be provided guidelines for the development of volunteer programs and the utilization of volunteers. The General Assembly intends by this chapter to assure that people of Virginia may derive optimal benefit from volunteers, and that the time and talents of volunteers in state service may be put to their best use. (1977, c. 347, § 2.1-554; 2001, c. 844.)

§ 2.2-3601. Definitions. — As used in this chapter, unless the context requires a different meaning:

"Department" includes all departments established in the executive branch of state government and local agencies under the jurisdiction or supervision thereof, and for the purposes of §§ 2.2-3602, 2.2-3604 and 2.2-3605, shall include political subdivisions of the Commonwealth.

"Material donor" means any person who, without financial gain, provides funds, materials, employment, or opportunities for clients of agencies, instrumentalities, or political subdivisions of the Commonwealth;

"Occasional-service volunteer" means any person who provides a one-time or occasional voluntary service;

"Regular-service volunteer" means any person engaged in specific voluntary service activities on an ongoing or continuous basis;

"Volunteer" means any person who, of his own free will, provides goods or services, without any financial gain, to any agency, instrumentality or political subdivision of the Commonwealth;

"Volunteer in state and local services" shall include, but shall not be limited to, any person who serves in a Medical Reserve Corps (MRC) unit or on a Community Emergency Response Team (CERT) while engaged in emergency services and preparedness activities as defined in § 44-146.16. (1977, c. 347, § 2.1-555; 1979, c. 131; 2001, c. 844; 2005, c. 474.)

§ 2.2-3602. Scope of chapter; status of volunteers; reimbursements. — A. Every department, through its executive head, may develop volunteer programs and accept the services of volunteers, including regular-service volunteers, occasional-service volunteers, or material donors, to assist in programs carried out or administered by that department.

B. Volunteers recruited, trained, or accepted by any department shall, to the extent of their voluntary service, be exempt from all provisions of law relating to state employment, hours of work, rate of compensation, leave time, and employee benefits except those enumerated in or consistent with § 2.2-3605. Volunteers shall, however, at all times comply with applicable work rules.

C. Every department utilizing the services of volunteers may provide volunteers with such incidental reimbursements as are consistent with the provisions of § 2.2-3605, including transportation costs, lodging, and subsistence, as the department deems appropriate to assist volunteers in performing their duties.

D. For the purposes of this chapter, individuals involved in emergency services and preparedness activities pursuant to the definition of "emergency services" in § 44-146.16 shall be considered volunteers in state and local services and shall be accordingly entitled to the benefits conferred in this chapter. As volunteers in state and local services, such individuals shall be deemed to be regular-service volunteers. (1977, c. 347, § 2.1-556; 2001, c. 844; 2005, c. 474.)

§ 2.2-3603. Responsibilities of departments. — Each department utilizing the services of volunteers shall:

1. Take actions necessary and appropriate to develop meaningful opportunities for volunteers involved in its programs and to improve public services;
2. Develop written rules governing the recruitment, screening, training, responsibility, utilization and supervision of volunteers;
3. Take actions necessary to ensure that volunteers and paid staff understand their respective duties and responsibilities, their relationship to each other, and their respective roles in fulfilling the objectives of their department;
4. Take actions necessary and appropriate to ensure a receptive climate for citizen volunteers;
5. Provide for the recognition of volunteers who have offered exceptional service to the Commonwealth; and
6. Recognize prior volunteer service as partial fulfillment of state employment requirements for training and experience established by the Department of Human Resource Management. (1977, c. 347, § 2.1-557; 1979, c. 107; 1991, c. 563; 2000, cc. 66, 657; 2001, c. 844.)

Editor's note. — Acts 1984, c. 194, cl. 2, repealed cl. 2 of Acts 1979, c. 107, which had provided: "That the provisions of this act shall expire on June 30, 1984, unless extended by an act of the General Assembly."

§ 2.2-3604. Solicitation of aid from community. — Each department may, through the officer, agent, or employee primarily responsible for the utilization of volunteers in that department, solicit volunteers and voluntary assistance for that department from the community. (1978, c. 121, § 2.1-557.1; 2001, c. 844.)

§ 2.2-3605. Volunteer benefits. — A. Meals may be furnished without charge to regular-service volunteers if scheduled work assignments extend over an established meal period. Meals may be furnished without charge to occasional-service volunteers at the discretion of the department's executive head.

B. Lodging, if available, may be furnished temporarily, at no charge, to regular-service volunteers.

C. Transportation reimbursement may be furnished those volunteers whose presence is determined to be necessary to the department. Rates or amounts of such reimbursement shall not exceed those provided in § 2.2-2823. Volunteers may utilize state vehicles in the performance of their duties, subject to those regulations governing use of state vehicles by paid staff.

D. Liability insurance may be provided by the department utilizing their services both to regular-service and occasional-service volunteers to the same extent as may be provided by the department to its paid staff. Volunteers in state and local service, including, but not limited to, any person who serves in a Medical Reserve Corps (MRC) unit or on a Community Emergency Response

Team (CERT), shall enjoy the protection of the Commonwealth's sovereign immunity to the same extent as paid staff. (1977, c. 347, § 2.1-558; 1979, c. 131; 2001, c. 844; 2005, c. 474.)

PART B.

TRANSACTION OF PUBLIC BUSINESS.

CHAPTER 37.

VIRGINIA FREEDOM OF INFORMATION ACT.

§ **2.2-3700. Short title; policy.** — A. This chapter may be cited as "The Virginia Freedom of Information Act."

B. By enacting this chapter, the General Assembly ensures the people of the Commonwealth ready access to public records in the custody of a public body or its officers and employees, and free entry to meetings of public bodies wherein the business of the people is being conducted. The affairs of government are not intended to be conducted in an atmosphere of secrecy since at all times the public is to be the beneficiary of any action taken at any level of government. Unless a public body or its officers or employees specifically elect to exercise an exemption provided by this chapter or any other statute, every meeting shall be open to the public and all public records shall be available for inspection and copying upon request. All public records and meetings shall be presumed open, unless an exemption is properly invoked.

The provisions of this chapter shall be liberally construed to promote an increased awareness by all persons of governmental activities and afford every opportunity to citizens to witness the operations of government. Any exemption from public access to records or meetings shall be narrowly construed and no record shall be withheld or meeting closed to the public unless specifically made exempt pursuant to this chapter or other specific provision of law. This chapter shall not be construed to discourage the free discussion by government officials or employees of public matters with the citizens of the Commonwealth.

All public bodies and their officers and employees shall make reasonable efforts to reach an agreement with a requester concerning the production of the records requested.

Any ordinance adopted by a local governing body that conflicts with the provisions of this chapter shall be void. (1968, c. 479, § 2.1-340; 1976, c. 467, § 2.1-340.1; 1989, c. 358; 1990, c. 538; 1999, cc. 703, 726; 2001, c. 844; 2002, c. 393.)

Cross references. — As to the duty of the Secretary of the Commonwealth to report on gubernatorial appointments to certain committee chairmen and to the General Assembly, see § 2.2-406. As to the authority of agency directors to prohibit agency employees from discussing the functions and policies of the agency beyond the limitations of this act, see § 2.2-603. As to the confidentiality of certain records of the Office of the State Long-Term Care Ombudsman, see § 2.2-706. As to restrictions on the release of Department of Human Resource Management employee information, see § 2.2-1203. As to restrictions on the release of certain Virginia Economic Development Partnership corporate information, see § 2.2-2445. As to certain restrictions on the release of trade secrets submitted as part of a proposed workforce training program, see § 2.2-2673. As to the rights of data subjects to refuse to provide personal information, see § 2.2-3806. As to the publication of the Virginia Register of Regulations, see § 2.2-4031. As to exemption of confidential information under the Virginia Administrative Dispute Resolution Act, § 2.2-4115 et seq., from the Virginia Freedom of Information Act, see § 2.2-4119. As to the availability of public records pertaining to procurement transactions, see § 2.2-4342. As to members of the board and employees of the Tobacco Indemnification and Community Revitalization Commission being subject to this chapter, see § 3.1-1108. As to exemption of confidential records of and reports on adult persons under investigation by or placed on probation supervision with a local community-based probation services agency, see § 9.1-177.1 As to exemption of confidential records of and reports on adult persons under investigation by or in the custody or supervision of a local pretrial service agency, see § 19.2-152.4:2. As to exemption from disclosure of trade secrets or proprietary information submitted to the Virginia Code Commission, see § 30-147. As to the powers and duties of the Virginia Freedom of Information Advisory Council, see § 30-179. As to restrictions on the release of information by the Disease Prevention and Control regarding the use of biological weapons, see § 32.1-39. As to confidentiality of certain information and records collected and maintained by the Office of the Chief Medical Examiner, see § 32.1-283.4. As to confidentiality of documents submitted to Advance Health Care Directive Registry, see § 54.1-2995.

Editor's note. — Acts 2002, c. 393, cl. 2, provides: "That it is the intent of the General Assembly to address the recent Virginia Supreme Court holding in the case styled Connell v. Kersey [262 Va. 154, 547 S.E.2d 228 (2001)], which held that attorneys for the Commonwealth are not 'public bodies' as defined in the Freedom of Information Act (§ 2.2-3700 et seq.), by clarifying that the Freedom of Information Act (FOIA) applies to constitutional officers and providing an exemption for attorneys for the Commonwealth."

Law Review. — For comment on court interpretations of the Virginia Freedom of Information Act, see 17 U. Rich. L. Rev. 153 (1982). For article on legislative changes to Virginia administrative rulemaking, see 19 U. Rich. L. Rev. 107 (1984). For note discussing inadequate enforcement of the Virginia Freedom of Information Act, see 25 Wm. & Mary L. Rev. 487 (1984). For a review of administrative procedure in Virginia for year 1999, see 33 U. Rich. L. Rev. 727 (1999). For a review of 1999 technology legislation in Virginia, see 33 U. Rich. L. Rev. 1037 (1999). For 2002 survey of Virginia technology law, see 37 U. Rich. L. Rev. 341 (2002). For article, "Some Assembly Required: The Application of State Open Meeting Laws to Email Correspondence," 12 Geo. Mason L. Rev. 719 (2004).

Michie's Jurisprudence. — For related discussion, see 5A M.J. Counties, § 2; 13B M.J. Municipal Corporations, § 22.

CASE NOTES

Editor's note. — Most of the cases below were decided under former Title 2.1 or prior provisions.

The policy expressly stated in this section is that this chapter shall be liberally construed to enable citizens to observe the operations of government and that the exemptions shall be narrowly construed in order that nothing which should be public may be hidden from any person. City of Danville v. Laird, 223 Va. 271, 288 S.E.2d 429 (1982).

Purpose of this chapter is to remove any necessity for a reporter seeking access to a report or document in an agency's file to resort to subornation on the part of public employees, by providing him with a prompt and easy remedy to secure access to such document. If the agency refused access improperly, the reporter would have his remedy and would be awarded in addition attorney's fees and costs against the agency. There is accordingly no need for the reporter to engage in protracted pressure to induce a public employee to engage in subornation in violation of his duty under the regulations governing his employment. Jurgensen v. Fairfax County, 745 F.2d 868 (4th Cir. 1984).

There is no common-law right of the public or press to attend the meetings of governmental bodies. Roanoke City School Bd. v. Times-World Corp., 226 Va. 185, 307 S.E.2d 256 (1983).

An administrative request is a condition precedent to judicial remedies. — An administrative request for minutes or other records is a condition precedent to judicial remedies under the act. Hale v. Washington County School Bd., 241 Va. 76, 400 S.E.2d 175 (1991).

When prior request for records not required. — Where records exist, the legislative purpose was to require a request addressed to the public body, followed by a refusal, as a condition precedent to judicial proceedings for the production of those records. However, the act cannot be read to require either a request for records when the relief requested does not involve production of records, or a fruitless request for records which the requester knows to be nonexistent. Hale v. Washington County School Bd., 241 Va. 76, 400 S.E.2d 175 (1991).

Where school board superintendent alleged the nonexistence of any minutes of a closed meeting, the superintendent obviated any need to allege a prior request for, and denial of, those records. Hale v. Washington County School Bd., 241 Va. 76, 400 S.E.2d 175 (1991).

The purpose or motivation behind a request is irrelevant to a citizen's entitlement to requested information under the Freedom of Information Act. Associated Tax Serv., Inc. v. Fitzpatrick, 236 Va. 181, 372 S.E.2d 625 (1988).

Real estate assessment information. — City treasurer's reliance on the Privacy Protection Act (see now § 2.2-3900 et seq.) in denying a request for certain real estate tax information was totally misplaced, because the Act specifically excludes real estate assessment information. Associated Tax Serv., Inc. v. Fitzpatrick, 236 Va. 181, 372 S.E.2d 625 (1988).

Telephone conference call. — It was not the intent of the General Assembly that a telephone conference call between members of a public body be construed as a "meeting" of such members. Roanoke City School Bd. v. Times-World Corp., 226 Va. 185, 307 S.E.2d 256 (1983).

Mandamus erroneously denied. — Landowner, who alleged a violation of the rights and privileges afforded by the Virginia Freedom of Information Act, § 2.2-3700 et seq., and seeking relief by mandamus pursuant to § 2.2-3713, was not required to prove a lack of an adequate remedy at law, nor could his mandamus proceeding be barred on the ground that there might have been some other remedy at law available; moreover, because the circuit court did not reach the issue whether a sales brochure in connection with a highway construction project was subject to disclosure under the Act, the matter was remanded for further consideration of that issue and a determination as to whether the landowner was entitled to reasonable costs and attorneys' fees. Cartwright v. Commonwealth Transp. Comm'r, 270 Va. 58, 613 S.E.2d 449, 2005 Va. LEXIS 62 (2005).

Applied in Beck v. Shelton, 267 Va. 482, 593 S.E.2d 195, 2004 Va. LEXIS 40 (2004); White Dog Publ., Inc. v. Culpeper County Bd. of Supervisors, 272 Va. 377, 634 S.E.2d 334, 2006 Va. LEXIS 81 (2006); Fenter v. Norfolk Airport Auth., 274 Va. 524, 649 S.E.2d 704, 2007 Va. LEXIS 102 (2007).

CIRCUIT COURT OPINIONS

Construction. — In order to discuss the performance of its city manager as it related to the rising crime in the city, the circuit court ordered the depositions transcribed be opened to allow public access, as the focus of the meeting was on the city's plans and programs to meet the soaring crime issue, and not on the city manager personally; thus, said discussion did not meet the requirements of subdivision A 1 of § 2.2-3711 to justify closure. Media Gen. Operations, Inc. v. City Council of Richmond, 64 Va. Cir. 406, 2004 Va. Cir. LEXIS 191 (Richmond 2004).

Inmate's request for records. — Inmate was not denied rights and privileges conferred by the Virginia Freedom of Information Act (FOIA), § 2.2-3700 et seq., when his request for the release of certain police investigative reports was denied; the records sought were not subject to disclosure under express exemptions within FOIA. Chavez v. Manger, 62 Va. Cir. 146, 2003 Va. Cir. LEXIS 98 (Fairfax County 2003).

Proceedings before judicial inquiry and review commission. — Where a judge's request for an opinion regarding future conduct was not a proceeding or "papers filed" before the Virginia Judicial Inquiry and Review Commission, it was not confidential under § 17.1-913 and was subject to disclosure under the Virginia Freedom of Information Act, § 2.2-3700 et seq. Zaleski v. Judicial Inquiry & Review Comm'n, 64 Va. Cir. 495, 2004 Va. Cir. LEXIS 186 (Richmond 2004).

OPINIONS OF THE ATTORNEY GENERAL

Access to digital copies of court records. — The Virginia Freedom of Information Act and § 17.1-208 impose a duty on circuit court clerks to furnish copies of records requested by a citizen, without distinction between paper and digital formats, provided the records are not sealed by court order or otherwise exempt from disclosure by law. See opinion of Attorney General to The Honorable J. Jack Kennedy, Jr., Clerk, Circuit Court for Wise County and City of Norton, 02-095 (12/19/02).

§ **2.2-3701. Definitions.** — As used in this chapter, unless the context requires a different meaning:

"Closed meeting" means a meeting from which the public is excluded.

"Electronic communication" means any audio or combined audio and visual communication method.

"Emergency" means an unforeseen circumstance rendering the notice required by this chapter impossible or impracticable and which circumstance requires immediate action.

"Meeting" or *"meetings"* means the meetings including work sessions, when sitting physically, or through telephonic or video equipment pursuant to § 2.2-3708 or 2.2-3708.1, as a body or entity, or as an informal assemblage of (i) as many as three members or (ii) a quorum, if less than three, of the constituent membership, wherever held, with or without minutes being taken, whether or not votes are cast, of any public body. The gathering of employees of a public body shall not be deemed a "meeting" subject to the provisions of this chapter.

"Open meeting" or *"public meeting"* means a meeting at which the public may be present.

"Public body" means any legislative body, authority, board, bureau, commission, district or agency of the Commonwealth or of any political subdivision of the Commonwealth, including cities, towns and counties, municipal councils, governing bodies of counties, school boards and planning commissions; boards of visitors of public institutions of higher education; and other organizations, corporations or agencies in the Commonwealth supported wholly or principally by public funds. It shall include (i) the Virginia Birth-Related Neurological Injury Compensation Program and its board of directors established pursuant to Chapter 50 (§ 38.2-5000 et seq.) of Title 38.2 and (ii) any committee, subcommittee, or other entity however designated, of the public body created to perform delegated functions of the public body or to advise the public body. It shall not exclude any such committee, subcommittee or entity because it has

private sector or citizen members. Corporations organized by the Virginia Retirement System are "public bodies" for purposes of this chapter.

For the purposes of the provisions of this chapter applicable to access to public records, constitutional officers shall be considered public bodies and, except as otherwise expressly provided by law, shall have the same obligations to disclose public records as other custodians of public records.

"Public records" means all writings and recordings that consist of letters, words or numbers, or their equivalent, set down by handwriting, typewriting, printing, photostatting, photography, magnetic impulse, optical or magneto-optical form, mechanical or electronic recording or other form of data compilation, however stored, and regardless of physical form or characteristics, prepared or owned by, or in the possession of a public body or its officers, employees or agents in the transaction of public business.

"Regional public body" means a unit of government organized as provided by law within defined boundaries, as determined by the General Assembly, whose members are appointed by the participating local governing bodies, and such unit includes two or more counties or cities.

"Scholastic records" means those records containing information directly related to a student and maintained by a public body that is an educational agency or institution or by a person acting for such agency or institution. (1968, c. 479, § 2.1-341; 1970, c. 456; 1974, c. 332; 1975, c. 307; 1977, c. 677; 1978, cc. 573, 826; 1979, cc. 369, 687; 1980, c. 754; 1984, c. 252; 1989, c. 358; 1990, c. 538; 1993, cc. 270, 720; 1994, cc. 845, 931; 1996, c. 609; 1997, c. 641; 1999, cc. 703, 726; 2001, c. 844; 2002, c. 393; 2003, c. 897; 2007, c. 945; 2008, cc. 233, 789.)

Editor's note. — Acts 2002, c. 393, cl. 2, provides: "That it is the intent of the General Assembly to address the recent Virginia Supreme Court holding in the case styled Connell v. Kersey [262 Va. 154, 547 S.E.2d 228 (2001)], which held that attorneys for the Commonwealth are not 'public bodies' as defined in the Freedom of Information Act (§ 2.2-3700 et seq.), by clarifying that the Freedom of Information Act (FOIA) applies to constitutional officers and providing an exemption for attorneys for the Commonwealth."

The 2007 amendments. — The 2007 amendment by c. 945 added the definitions of "Electronic communication" and "Regional public body."

The 2008 amendments. — The 2008 amendments by cc. 233 and 789 are identical, and inserted "or 2.2-3708.1" in the definition of "Meeting."

Law Review. — For a review of administrative procedure in Virginia for year 1999, see 33 U. Rich. L. Rev. 727 (1999).

CIRCUIT COURT OPINIONS

Information gathering session not a "meeting." — A "meeting," as defined by this section, did not include a conference where board of supervisors, without giving notice or keeping minutes, met with the Attorney General for the purpose of gathering information, where the board conducted no public business and did not exclude the public. Nageotte v. Board of Supvrs., 223 Va. 259, 288 S.E.2d 423 (1982) (decided under former Title 2.1).

Telephone conference call not a "meeting." — It was not the intent of the General Assembly that a telephone conference call between members of a public body be construed as a "meeting" of such members. Roanoke City School Bd. v. Times-World Corp., 226 Va. 185, 307 S.E.2d 256 (1983) (decided under former Title 2.1).

City council members-elect not "members" under FOIA. — Judgment was properly awarded to a mayor and city council members in plaintiff's action alleging that they e-mailed each other in a knowing, willful, and deliberate attempt to hold secret meetings, avoid public scrutiny, discuss city business, and decide city issues without the input of all of the council members and the public because the Virginia Freedom of Information Act did not apply to conduct of members-elect of the city council. Beck v. Shelton, 267 Va. 482, 593 S.E.2d 195, 2004 Va. LEXIS 40 (2004).

E-mail communications not "meeting." — Judgment was properly awarded to a mayor and city council members in an action alleging that they deliberately e-mailed each other in an attempt to hold secret meetings because e-mail communications did not constitute a "meeting" under the Virginia Freedom of Information Act. Beck v. Shelton, 267 Va. 482, 593 S.E.2d 195, 2004 Va. LEXIS 40 (2004).

Commonwealth's attorney. — A Commonwealth's attorney is not a "public body" within the meaning of the Virginia Freedom of Information Act (FOIA), and a request for information pursuant to § 2.1-342.2 [see now § 2.2-3706] is not subject to the procedures and time limits prescribed by § 2.1-342 [see now § 2.2-3704], which by its express terms relates only to requests made under the FOIA to "public bodies." Connell v. Kersey, 262 Va. 154, 547 S.E.2d 228, 2001 Va. LEXIS 67 (2001) (decided prior to the amendment by Acts 2002, c. 393.)

Distinction between "public bodies" and "public officials" under FOIA. — As used in the Virginia Freedom of Information Act (FOIA), the terms "authority" and "agency" clearly refer to entities to which responsibility to conduct the business of the people is delegated by legislative or executive action, whereas, by contrast, a Commonwealth's attorney derives his authority from the Constitution; while a Commonwealth's attorney, like a sheriff or other constitutional officer, is undoubtedly a public official, the FOIA distinguishes between "public officials" and "public bodies." Connell v. Kersey, 262 Va. 154, 547 S.E.2d 228, 2001 Va. LEXIS 67 (2001) (decided prior to the amendment by Acts 2002, c. 393.)

County's tape of calls to its 911 system is an official record where the system was created with public funds and created to provide for public safety. Tull v. Brown, 255 Va. 177, 494 S.E.2d 855 (1998) (decided under former Title 2.1).

Biological material not "public record." — Biological material recovered on swabs from the vagina of the victim did not meet the test of a "public record," and even if it did, the Virginia Freedom of Information Act (FOIA) allowed for inspection and copying, not testing. Globe Newspaper Co. v. Commonwealth, 264 Va. 622, 570 S.E.2d 809, 2002 Va. LEXIS 156 (2002).

CIRCUIT COURT OPINIONS

Corporation not supported wholly by public funds. — Although the public broadcasting corporation had to be covered under the Freedom of Information Act, §§ 2.2-3700 through 2.2-3714, as a corporation that was supported wholly or principally by public funds; less than 25% of its funding came from government support and it did not perform a delegated governmental function. Wigand v. Wilkes, 65 Va. Cir. 437, 2004 Va. Cir. LEXIS 290 (Norfolk 2004).

Municipal liability pool is public body. — City's police officer, who was injured in a collision with an uninsured/underinsured motorist, could not recover under an insurance policy issued by a municipal liability pool where the pool was a § 2.2-3701 public body that had to keep minutes reflecting actions taken by resolution, and there was no resolution showing that the city elected UM/UIM insurance coverage. Johnson v. Va. Mun. Liab. Pool, 73 Va. Cir. 138, 2007 Va. Cir. LEXIS 231 (Richmond Mar. 23, 2007).

OPINIONS OF THE ATTORNEY GENERAL

An institutional review board of a public institution of higher learning in the Commonwealth engaged in human research projects is not a "public body" as defined by the statute as such a board is not an independent entity charged by law with the governance of, or responsibility for, some discrete public agency. See opinion of Attorney General to The Honorable Thomas C. Wright Jr., Member, House of Delegates, 01-101 (10/22/01).

Records generated by an institutional review board of a public institution of higher learning in the Commonwealth engaged in human research projects are not "public records" prepared or owned by, or in the possession of, a public body. See opinion of Attorney General to The Honorable Thomas C. Wright Jr., Member, House of Delegates, 01-101 (10/22/01).

Application to nonprofit organizations. — The fact that a nonprofit organization receives public funds from a locality does not result in the documents of the charitable organization being subject to the disclosure requirements of The Virginia Freedom of Information Act. See opinion of Attorney General to Mr. David W. Rowan, Town Attorney for the Town of Onancock, 01-094 (3/27/02).

A legislative caucus is not a "public body" as that term is defined in The Virginia Freedom of Information Act; therefore, the notice and open meeting requirements of the Act do not apply to such organizations. See opinion of Attorney General to The Honorable Clifton A. Woodrum, Member, House of Delegates, 03-063 (1/6/04).

An informal assemblage of three or more legislators at a meeting prearranged or called for the purpose of discussing expected votes on matters pending before the General Assembly constitutes a meeting under The Virginia Freedom of Information Act, requiring that such a meeting be open to the public. See opinion of Attorney General to The Honorable Clifton A. Woodrum, Member, House of Delegates, 03-063 (1/6/04).

§ 2.2-3702. Notice of chapter. — Any person elected, reelected, appointed or reappointed to any body not excepted from this chapter shall (i) be furnished by the public body's administrator or legal counsel with a copy of this chapter within two weeks following election, reelection, appointment or reappointment and (ii) read and become familiar with the provisions of this chapter. (1976, c. 467, § 2.1-341.1; 1999, cc. 703, 726; 2001, c. 844; 2002, c. 393.)

Editor's note. — Acts 2002, c. 393, cl. 2, provides: "That it is the intent of the General Assembly to address the recent Virginia Supreme Court holding in the case styled Connell v. Kersey [262 Va. 154, 547 S.E.2d 228 (2001)], which held that attorneys for the Commonwealth are not 'public bodies' as defined in the Freedom of Information Act (§ 2.2-3700 et seq.), by clarifying that the Freedom of Information Act (FOIA) applies to constitutional officers and providing an exemption for attorneys for the Commonwealth."

CASE NOTES

Applied in Beck v. Shelton, 267 Va. 482, 593 S.E.2d 195, 2004 Va. LEXIS 40 (2004).

§ 2.2-3703. Public bodies and records to which chapter inapplicable; voter registration and election records; access by persons incarcerated in a state, local, or federal correctional facility. — A. The provisions of this chapter shall not apply to:

1. The Virginia Parole Board, except that (i) information from the Virginia Parole Board providing the number of inmates considered by such Board for discretionary parole, the number of inmates granted or denied parole, and the number of parolees returned to the custody of the Department of Corrections solely as a result of a determination by such Board of a violation of parole shall be open to inspection and available for release, on a monthly basis, as provided by § 2.2-3704 and (ii) all records concerning the finances of the Virginia Parole Board shall be public records and subject to the provisions of this chapter. The information required by clause (i) shall be furnished by offense, sex, race, age of the inmate, and the locality in which the conviction was obtained, upon the request of the party seeking the information;
2. Petit juries and grand juries;
3. Family assessment and planning teams established pursuant to § 2.2-5207;
4. The Virginia State Crime Commission; and
5. The records required by law to be maintained by the clerks of the courts of record, as defined in § 1-212, and courts not of record, as defined in § 16.1-69.5. However, other records maintained by the clerks of such courts shall be public records and subject to the provisions of this chapter.

B. Public access to voter registration and election records shall be governed by the provisions of Title 24.2 and this chapter. The provisions of Title 24.2 shall be controlling in the event of any conflict.

C. No provision of this chapter or Chapter 21 (§ 30-178 et seq.) of Title 30 shall be construed to afford any rights to any person (i) incarcerated in a state, local or federal correctional facility, whether or not such facility is (a) located in the Commonwealth or (b) operated pursuant to the Corrections Private Management Act (§ 53.1-261 et seq.) or (ii) civilly committed pursuant to the Sexually Violent Predators Act (§ 37.2-900 et seq.). However, this subsection shall not be construed to prevent such persons from exercising their constitutionally protected rights, including, but not limited to, their right to call for evidence in their favor in a criminal prosecution. (1999, cc. 703, 726, § 2.1-341.2; 2001, c. 844; 2003, cc. 989, 1018; 2004, cc. 398, 690; 2007, cc. 438, 548, 626.)

The 2007 amendments. — The 2007 amendment by c. 438 rewrote subsection C, by redesignating former clauses (i) and (ii) as (a) and (b), inserting a new clause (i) designator, inserting clause (ii), and making minor stylistic changes.

The 2007 amendments by cc. 548 and 626 are identical, and added subdivision A 5 and made related changes.

CASE NOTES

Constitutionality. — The prisoner exclusion provision in subsection C is not subject to a facial overbreadth challenge because it does not carry the threat of prosecution for violating the statute and it does not restrict expressive speech but simply regulates access to information in the possession of Virginia state agencies. Fisher v. King, 232 F.3d 391, 2000 U.S. App. LEXIS 28962 (4th Cir. 2000) (decided under prior provisions).

The First Amendment did not provide a prisoner, as a member of the general public, a right of physical access to an audio tape that was played in open court in a criminal trial, admitted into evidence, and for which he possessed a complete verbatim transcript. Fisher v. King, 232 F.3d 391, 2000 U.S. App. LEXIS 28962 (4th Cir. 2000) (decided under prior provisions).

Prisoner exclusion provision of the Virginia Freedom of Information Act, subsection C of § 2.2-3703, was not facially unconstitutional as there were numerous rational reasons for it, such as preventing frivolous requests that would unduly burden state resources, and it was not unconstitutional as applied to an inmate, who sought records regarding his medical condition to determine if he had a viable claim against various state department of correction officials, because even if the inmate's request was not frivolous, he was not thereby denied equal protection, and the exclusion did not deny the inmate's access to the courts as it did not obstruct his ability to file suit challenging his medical treatment. Giarratano v. Johnson, 456 F. Supp. 2d 747, 2006 U.S. Dist. LEXIS 74882 (W.D. Va. 2006).

Prisoner exclusion from the Virginia Freedom of Information Act, subsection C of § 2.2-3703, did not violate equal protection, due process, or the right of access to the courts because an inmate's conclusory allegation that this provision was not rationally related to a legitimate state interest was insufficient to overcome the presumption of rationality of the law; while the inmate did not file frivolous complaints, his conclusory allegation also failed to show an as-applied equal protection violation; and denial of the inmate's information request under subsection C did not obstruct his capability to file suit. Giarratano v. Johnson, 521 F.3d 298, 2008 U.S. App. LEXIS 6144 (4th Cir. 2008).

Standing. — District court dismissed an action which a state inmate filed under 42 U.S.C.S. § 1983, alleging that Virginia officials violated his rights under the U.S. Constitution when they denied his request under the Virginia Freedom of Information Act for police reports and other information that pertained to his conviction on charges of abduction and spousal rape. The court found that the inmate did not have standing to challenge § 2.2-3703(C), the statute that allowed Commonwealth officials to deny requests for information they received from prisoners. Patterson v. Mundy, — F. Supp. 2d —, 2005 U.S. Dist. LEXIS 38216 (W.D. Va. Dec. 16, 2005).

CIRCUIT COURT OPINIONS

Inmate's request for records. — None of an inmate's constitutionally protected rights were denied as a result of a police official's exercise of an exemption pursuant to the Virginia Freedom of Information Act (FOIA) nor did the inmate point to any such rights; in addition, the FOIA did not clearly establish any right on the part of the inmate to access the criminal investigative reports in the custody of the police department. Chavez v. Manger, 62 Va. Cir. 146, 2003 Va. Cir. LEXIS 98 (Fairfax County 2003).

§ 2.2-3704. Public records to be open to inspection; procedure for requesting records and responding to request; charges. — A. Except as otherwise specifically provided by law, all public records shall be open to inspection and copying by any citizens of the Commonwealth during the regular office hours of the custodian of such records. Access to such records shall not be denied to citizens of the Commonwealth, representatives of newspapers and magazines with circulation in the Commonwealth, and representatives of radio and television stations broadcasting in or into the Commonwealth. The custodian may require the requester to provide his name and legal address. The custodian of such records shall take all necessary precautions for their preservation and safekeeping.

B. A request for public records shall identify the requested records with reasonable specificity. The request need not make reference to this chapter in order to invoke the provisions of this chapter or to impose the time limits for response by a public body. Any public body that is subject to this chapter and that is the custodian of the requested records shall promptly, but in all cases within five working days of receiving a request, provide the requested records to the requester or make one of the following responses in writing:

1. The requested records are being entirely withheld because their release is prohibited by law or the custodian has exercised his discretion to withhold the records in accordance with this chapter. Such response shall identify with reasonable particularity the volume and subject matter of withheld records, and cite, as to each category of withheld records, the specific Code section that authorizes the withholding of the records.

2. The requested records are being provided in part and are being withheld in part because the release of part of the records is prohibited by law or the custodian has exercised his discretion to withhold a portion of the records in accordance with this chapter. Such response shall identify with reasonable particularity the subject matter of withheld portions, and cite, as to each category of withheld records, the specific Code section that authorizes the withholding of the records. When a portion of a requested record is withheld, the public body may delete or excise only that portion of the record to which an exemption applies and shall release the remainder of the record.

3. The requested records could not be found or do not exist. However, if the public body that received the request knows that another public body has the requested records, the response shall include contact information for the other public body.

4. It is not practically possible to provide the requested records or to determine whether they are available within the five-work-day period. Such response shall specify the conditions that make a response impossible. If the response is made within five working days, the public body shall have an additional seven work days in which to provide one of the four preceding responses.

C. Any public body may petition the appropriate court for additional time to respond to a request for records when the request is for an extraordinary volume of records or requires an extraordinarily lengthy search, and a response by the public body within the time required by this chapter will prevent the public body from meeting its operational responsibilities. Before proceeding with the petition, however, the public body shall make reasonable efforts to reach an agreement with the requester concerning the production of the records requested.

D. Subject to the provisions of subsections G and J, no public body shall be required to create a new record if the record does not already exist. However, a public body may abstract or summarize information under such terms and conditions as agreed between the requester and the public body.

E. Failure to respond to a request for records shall be deemed a denial of the request and shall constitute a violation of this chapter.

F. A public body may make reasonable charges not to exceed its actual cost incurred in accessing, duplicating, supplying, or searching for the requested records. No public body shall impose any extraneous, intermediary or surplus fees or expenses to recoup the general costs associated with creating or maintaining records or transacting the general business of the public body. Any duplicating fee charged by a public body shall not exceed the actual cost of duplication. The public body may also make a reasonable charge for the cost incurred in supplying records produced from a geographic information system at the request of anyone other than the owner of the land that is the subject of the request. However, such charges shall not exceed the actual cost to the public body in supplying such records, except that the public body may charge, on a pro rata per acre basis, for the cost of creating topographical maps developed by the public body, for such maps or portions thereof, which encompass a contiguous area greater than 50 acres. All charges for the supplying of requested records shall be estimated in advance at the request of the citizen.

G. Public records maintained by a public body in an electronic data processing system, computer database, or any other structured collection of data shall be made available to a requester at a reasonable cost, not to exceed the actual cost in accordance with subsection F. When electronic or other databases are combined or contain exempt and nonexempt records, the public body may provide access to the exempt records if not otherwise prohibited by law, but shall provide access to the nonexempt records as provided by this chapter.

Public bodies shall produce nonexempt records maintained in an electronic database in any tangible medium identified by the requester, including, where the public body has the capability, the option of posting the records on a website or delivering the records through an electronic mail address provided by the requester, if that medium is used by the public body in the regular course of business. No public body shall be required to produce records from an electronic database in a format not regularly used by the public body. However, the public body shall make reasonable efforts to provide records in any format under such terms and conditions as agreed between the requester and public body, including the payment of reasonable costs. The excision of exempt fields of information from a database or the conversion of data from one available format to another shall not be deemed the creation, preparation or compilation of a new public record.

H. In any case where a public body determines in advance that charges for producing the requested records are likely to exceed $200, the public body may, before continuing to process the request, require the requester to agree to payment of a deposit not to exceed the amount of the advance determination. The deposit shall be credited toward the final cost of supplying the requested records. The period within which the public body shall respond under this section shall be tolled for the amount of time that elapses between notice of the advance determination and the response of the requester.

I. Before processing a request for records, a public body may require the requester to pay any amounts owed to the public body for previous requests for records that remain unpaid 30 days or more after billing.

J. Every public body of state government shall compile, and annually update, an index of computer databases that contains at a minimum those databases created by them on or after July 1, 1997. "Computer database" means a structured collection of data or records residing in a computer. Such index shall be a public record and shall include, at a minimum, the following information with respect to each database listed therein: a list of data fields, a description of the format or record layout, the date last updated, a list of any data fields to which public access is restricted, a description of each format in which the database can be copied or reproduced using the public body's computer facilities, and a schedule of fees for the production of copies in each available form. The form, context, language, and guidelines for the indices and the databases to be indexed shall be developed by the Virginia Information Technologies Agency in consultation with the Librarian of Virginia and the State Archivist. The public body shall not be required to disclose its software security, including passwords. (1968, c. 479, § 2.1-342; 1973, c. 461; 1974, c. 332; 1975, cc. 307, 312; 1976, cc. 640, 709; 1977, c. 677; 1978, c. 810; 1979, cc. 682, 684, 686, 689; 1980, cc. 678, 754; 1981, cc. 456, 464, 466, 589; 1982, cc. 225, 449, 452, 560, 635; 1983, cc. 372, 462, 607; 1984, cc. 85, 395, 433, 513, 532; 1985, cc. 81, 155, 502, 618; 1986, cc. 273, 291, 383, 469, 592; 1987, cc. 401, 491, 581; 1988, cc. 39, 151, 395, 411, 891, 902; 1989, cc. 56, 358, 478; 1990, cc. 217, 538, 721, 819, 968; 1991, cc. 213, 561; 1992, cc. 40, 150, 167, 200, 203, 207, 593, 612; 1993, cc. 205, 270, 296, 537, 552, 638, 750, 883; 1994, cc. 485, 532, 606, 839, 853, 918; 1995, cc. 299, 362, 499, 562, 638, 722, 812, 837; 1996, cc. 168, 469, 589, 599, 783, 786, 794, 855, 862, 902, 905, 1001, 1046; 1997, cc. 198, 295, 439, 567, 636, 641, 777, 782, 785, 838, 861; 1998, cc. 427, 891; 1999, cc. 438, 703, 726; 2001, c. 844; 2002, cc. 715, 830; 2003, cc. 275, 981, 1021; 2007, c. 439.)

Cross references. — For provisions as to confidentiality of records of the Office of the State Long-Term Care Ombudsman, see § 2.2-706. As to the powers and duties of the Virginia Information Technologies Agency and Chief Information Officer, see §§ 2.2-2007 et seq. For provision that the Freedom of Information Act shall not apply to certified abstracts of votes or any other documents used by the State Board of Elections in ascertaining the results of an election until such results have been finally determined by the Board, see § 24.2-677.

Editor's note. — For provisions of Acts 2003, cc. 981 and 1021, cls. 4 to 16, reflecting the intent of the General Assembly to provide for the consolidation of the procurement and operational functions of information technology for state agencies in a single agency, and related transitional and other provisions, see the Editor's note at § 2.2-2005.

The 2007 amendments. — The 2007 amendment by c. 439 inserted "provide the requested records to the requestor or" in the introductory paragraph of subsection B; deleted subdivision B 1, which read: "The requested records will be provided to the requestor"; redesignated former subdivisions B 2 and B 3 as present subdivisions B 1 and B 2; in present subdivision B 1, substituted "are being" for "will be" near the beginning, deleted clause (i), which read: "be in writing," deleted the clause designations (ii) and (iii); in present subdivision B 2, substituted "are being" for "will be" and inserted "are being" near the beginning, deleted clause (i), which read: "be in writing," and deleted the clause designations (ii) and (iii); added present subdivision B 3; in subdivision B 4, deleted "be in writing and" following "Such response shall" near the beginning of the second sentence and substituted "four" for "three" in the last sentence; and inserted "or requires an extraordinarily lengthy search" in the first sentence in subsection C.

Law Review. — For a review of administrative procedure in Virginia for year 1999, see 33 U. Rich. L. Rev. 727 (1999).

CASE NOTES

Editor's note. — Most of the cases below were decided under former Title 2.1 or prior provisions.

Policy of openness does not override need for confidentiality in every circumstance. — Although the General Assembly sought to ensure public access to governmental records and meetings, to avoid an "atmosphere of secrecy" in the conduct of government affairs, and to encourage resolution of disputes in these areas through agreement rather than litigation, the General Assembly does not consider the policy absolute, however, and currently has identified 44 instances in which certain information is exempt from mandatory disclosure; taken together, these exemptions reflect the General Assembly's determination that the policy of openness does not override the need for confidentiality in every circumstance, that the best interests of the Commonwealth may require that certain governmental records and activities not be subject to compelled disclosure. Taylor v. Worrell Enters., Inc., 242 Va. 219, 409 S.E.2d 136 (1991).

An administrative request is a condition precedent to judicial remedies. — An administrative request for minutes or other records is a condition precedent to judicial remedies under the act. Hale v. Washington County School Bd., 241 Va. 76, 400 S.E.2d 175 (1991).

When prior request for records not required. — Where records exist, the legislative purpose was to require a request addressed to the public body, followed by a refusal, as a condition precedent to judicial proceedings for the production of those records. However, the act cannot be read to require either a request for records when the relief requested does not involve production of records, or a fruitless request for records which the requester knows to be nonexistent. Hale v. Washington County School Bd., 241 Va. 76, 400 S.E.2d 175 (1991).

Where school board superintendent alleged the nonexistence of any minutes of a closed meeting, the superintendent obviated any need to allege a prior request for, and denial of, those records. Hale v. Washington County School Bd., 241 Va. 76, 400 S.E.2d 175 (1991).

The jury list is not an "official record" within the intent and meaning of the provisions of this chapter. Archer v. Mayes, 213 Va. 633, 194 S.E.2d 707 (1973).

Failure to cite Freedom of Information Act section. — Property owner was not entitled to the names of complainants redacted from documents disclosed to him pursuant to his Freedom of Information Act (FOIA) request to zoning administrator. The requester received all the information he was entitled to receive under FOIA and the administrator's failure to cite the FOIA section that established the exception did not deny any of the requester's rights and privileges under the Act. Lawrence v. Jenkins, 258 Va. 598, 521 S.E.2d 523 (1999).

Agency employee not authorized to remove and publish agency document. — This section gives no agency employee the right to remove a report or document from the files and records of the agency and to publish it. Jurgensen v. Fairfax County, 745 F.2d 868 (4th Cir. 1984).

Section does not authorize removal of documents in violation of departmental regulation. — This section relates only to the right to inspect and copy "during regular office hours" in the office of the "custodian" of "official records." It plainly did not clothe a police department employee with the right to remove files, reports or documents from the police department in knowing violation of his obligation as an employee under the regulations of the department. Jurgensen v. Fairfax County, 745 F.2d 868 (4th Cir. 1984).

Regulation granting certain officers exclusive authority to make reports public was not unreasonable. — A police department regulation which prescribed a formula for processing applications for the exercise of the right to inspect and copy reports by identifying the specific officers in the department with the exclusive authority to make a report public was not invalid for repugnancy to this chapter. There is nothing either illegal or unreasonable in such a regulation. Jurgensen v. Fairfax County, 745 F.2d 868 (4th Cir. 1984).

List of telephone calls by Governor does not need to be disclosed. — Itemized list of long distance telephone calls placed by the Governor's office does not need to be disclosed when requested pursuant to the Freedom of Information Act; a legislatively imposed disclosure requirement would constitute a violation of the separation of powers doctrine because disclosure of the information in question would unduly interfere with the chief executive officer's ability to perform his duties, and is not warranted by an overriding need to promote a policy of open government in this instance; therefore, the information at issue fell within exemption and was not subject to compelled disclosure under the act. Taylor v. Worrell Enters., Inc., 242 Va. 219, 409 S.E.2d 136 (1991).

High school election vote count does not need to be disclosed. — The Virginia Freedom of Information Act does not require the disclosure of the total number of votes received by each candidate in a public high school student election. Wall v. Fairfax County Sch. Bd., 252 Va. 156, 475 S.E.2d 803 (1996).

Failure to timely make statutorily required response. — City airport authority's response to appellant's request for information under the Freedom of Information Act (FOIA), § 2.2-3700 et seq., did not comply with the FOIA as it did not timely make one of the four statutorily required responses under § 2.2-3704 but merely stated that the matter had been referred to its legal counsel or to the transportation security administration; appellant was entitled to attorney's fees under § 2.2-3713(D) as the trial court's judgment was reversed on appeal. Fenter v. Norfolk Airport Auth., 274 Va. 524, 649 S.E.2d 704, 2007 Va. LEXIS 102 (2007).

CIRCUIT COURT OPINIONS

Costs of redaction not reimbursable. — Labor costs, including travel and lodging expenses, related to redacting records to remove protected information, were not costs for which a department was allowed to charge for reimbursement under the Virginia Freedom of Information Act. Albright v. Woodfin, 68 Va. Cir. 115, 2005 Va. Cir. LEXIS 104 (Nelson County 2005).

OPINIONS OF THE ATTORNEY GENERAL

Records generated by an institutional review board of a public institution of higher learning in the Commonwealth engaged in human research projects are not required to be open for public inspection. See opinion of Attorney General to The Honorable Thomas C. Wright Jr., Member, House of Delegates, 01-101 (10/22/01).

Clerk of the circuit court is not required to produce records from an electronic database in a tangible medium that is not used in the regular course of business. See opinion of Attorney General to The Honorable Charles V. Mason, Clerk, Circuit Court of King George County, 03-101 (2/2/04).

Clerk's charge for reproduction of records from an electronic database must be reasonable and should not exceed the actual costs. See opinion of Attorney General to The Honorable Charles V. Mason, Clerk, Circuit Court of King George County, 03-101 (2/2/04).

§ 2.2-3704.1. Posting of notice of rights and responsibilities by state public bodies; assistance by the Freedom of Information Advisory Council. — A. All state public bodies created in the executive branch of state government and subject to the provisions of this chapter shall make available the following information to the public upon request and shall post such information on the Internet:

1. A plain English explanation of the rights of a requester under this chapter, the procedures to obtain public records from the public body, and the responsibilities of the public body in complying with this chapter. For purposes of this subdivision *"plain English"* means written in nontechnical, readily understandable language using words of common everyday usage and avoiding legal terms and phrases or other terms and words of art whose usage or special meaning primarily is limited to a particular field or profession;

2. Contact information for the person designated by the public body to (i) assist a requester in making a request for records or (ii) respond to requests for public records; and

3. Any policy the public body has concerning the type of public records it routinely withholds from release as permitted by this chapter.

B. The Freedom of Information Advisory Council, created pursuant to § 30-178, shall assist in the development and implementation of the provisions of subsection A, upon request. (2004, c. 730.)

§ 2.2-3705: Repealed by Acts 2004, c. 690.

Cross references. — For present provisions as to exclusions to application of chapter, see §§ 2.2-3705.1 through 2.2-3705.8.

§ 2.2-3705.1. Exclusions to application of chapter; exclusions of general application to public bodies. — The following records are excluded from the provisions of this chapter but may be disclosed by the custodian in his discretion, except where such disclosure is prohibited by law:

1. Personnel records containing information concerning identifiable individuals, except that access shall not be denied to the person who is the subject thereof. Any person who is the subject of any personnel record and who is 18 years of age or older may waive, in writing, the protections afforded by this subdivision. If the protections are so waived, the public body shall open such records for inspection and copying.

2. Written advice of legal counsel to state, regional or local public bodies or the officers or employees of such public bodies, and any other records protected by the attorney-client privilege.

3. Legal memoranda and other work product compiled specifically for use in litigation or for use in an active administrative investigation concerning a matter that is properly the subject of a closed meeting under § 2.2-3711.

4. Any test or examination used, administered or prepared by any public body for purposes of evaluation of (i) any student or any student's performance, (ii) any employee or employment seeker's qualifications or aptitude for employment, retention, or promotion, or (iii) qualifications for any license or certificate issued by a public body.

As used in this subdivision, "test or examination" shall include (a) any scoring key for any such test or examination and (b) any other document that would jeopardize the security of the test or examination. Nothing contained in this subdivision shall prohibit the release of test scores or results as provided by law, or limit access to individual records as provided by law. However, the subject of such employment tests shall be entitled to review and inspect all records relative to his performance on such employment tests.

When, in the reasonable opinion of such public body, any such test or examination no longer has any potential for future use, and the security of future tests or examinations will not be jeopardized, the test or examination shall be made available to the public. However, minimum competency tests administered to public school children shall be made available to the public contemporaneously with statewide release of the scores of those taking such tests, but in no event shall such tests be made available to the public later than six months after the administration of such tests.

5. Records recorded in or compiled exclusively for use in closed meetings lawfully held pursuant to § 2.2-3711. However, no record that is otherwise open to inspection under this chapter shall be deemed exempt by virtue of the fact that it has been reviewed or discussed in a closed meeting.

6. Vendor proprietary information software that may be in the official records of a public body. For the purpose of this subdivision, *"vendor proprietary software"* means computer programs acquired from a vendor for purposes of processing data for agencies or political subdivisions of the Commonwealth.

7. Computer software developed by or for a state agency, state-supported institution of higher education or political subdivision of the Commonwealth.

8. Appraisals and cost estimates of real property subject to a proposed purchase, sale or lease, prior to the completion of such purchase, sale or lease.

9. Records concerning reserves established in specific claims administered by the Department of the Treasury through its Division of Risk Management as provided in Article 5 (§ 2.2-1832 et seq.) of Chapter 18 of this title, or by any county, city, or town; and investigative notes, correspondence and information furnished in confidence with respect to an investigation of a claim or a potential claim against a public body's insurance policy or self-insurance plan. However, nothing in this subdivision shall prohibit the disclosure of information taken from inactive reports upon expiration of the period of limitations for the filing of a civil suit.

10. Personal information, as defined in § 2.2-3801, including electronic mail addresses, furnished to a public body for the purpose of receiving electronic mail from the public body, provided that the electronic mail recipient has requested that the public body not disclose such information. However, access shall not be denied to the person who is the subject of the record.

11. Communications and materials required to be kept confidential pursuant to § 2.2-4119 of the Virginia Administrative Dispute Resolution Act (§ 2.2-4115 et seq.).

12. Records relating to the negotiation and award of a specific contract where competition or bargaining is involved and where the release of such records would adversely affect the bargaining position or negotiating strategy of the public body. Such records shall not be withheld after the public body has

made a decision to award or not to award the contract. In the case of procurement transactions conducted pursuant to the Virginia Public Procurement Act (§ 2.2-4300 et seq.), the provisions of this subdivision shall not apply, and any release of records relating to such transactions shall be governed by the Virginia Public Procurement Act. (1999, cc. 485, 518, 703, 726, 793, 849, 852, 867, 868, 881, § 2.1-342.01; 2000, cc. 66, 237, 382, 400, 430, 583, 589, 592, 594, 618, 632, 657, 720, 932, 933, 947, 1006, 1064; 2001, cc. 288, 518, 844, § 2.2-3705; 2002, cc. 87, 155, 242, 393, 478, 481, 499, 522, 571, 572, 633, 655, 715, 798, 830; 2003, cc. 274, 307, 327, 332, 358, 704, 801, 884, 891, 893, 897, 968; 2004, c. 690.)

CASE NOTES

Documents to be made part of record on appeal. — Trial court erred in refusing to require a university to produce reports sought under the Freedom of Information Act so they could be made part of the record under Va. Sup. Ct. R. 5:10(a)(3), as the refusal prevented review by the appellate court of a professor's request for reports made by the university to an accrediting agency, and confidential personnel information under § 2.2-3705.1 could have been shielded by a protective order. Bland v. Va. State Univ., 272 Va. 198, 630 S.E.2d 525, 2006 Va. LEXIS 55 (2006).

Mandamus erroneously denied. — Landowner, who alleged a violation of the rights and privileges afforded by the Virginia Freedom of Information Act, § 2.2-3700 et seq., and seeking relief by mandamus pursuant to § 2.2-3713, was not required to prove a lack of an adequate remedy at law, nor could his mandamus proceeding be barred on the ground that there might have been some other remedy at law available; moreover, because the circuit court did not reach the issue whether a sales brochure in connection with a highway construction project was subject to disclosure under the Act, the matter was remanded for further consideration of that issue and a determination as to whether the landowner was entitled to reasonable costs and attorneys' fees. Cartwright v. Commonwealth Transp. Comm'r, 270 Va. 58, 613 S.E.2d 449, 2005 Va. LEXIS 62 (2005).

CIRCUIT COURT OPINIONS

Employment discrimination. — Because a county failed to prove that it advised the sources of information that information gathered would be treated confidentially, which was a necessary element in order to invoke the exception found in § 2.2-3705.3.3, a former employee was entitled to all information related to an employment discrimination complaint, investigation, and reprimand, pursuant to § 2.2-3705.1.1. McChrystal v. Fairfax County Bd. of Supervisors, 67 Va. Cir. 171, 2005 Va. Cir. LEXIS 26 (Fairfax County 2005).

Confidential information. — Even if a county could have shown that it advised the sources of information that information gathered would be treated confidentially, which was a necessary element in order to invoke the exception to the Virginia Freedom of Information Act found in § 2.2-3705.3, a former employee would have been entitled to all information in a report of a county's office of equity program but not the investigatory materials giving rise to it, pursuant to § 2.2-3705.1. McChrystal v. Fairfax County Bd. of Supervisors, 67 Va. Cir. 171, 2005 Va. Cir. LEXIS 26 (Fairfax County 2005).

§ 2.2-3705.2. Exclusions to application of chapter; records relating to public safety. — The following records are excluded from the provisions of this chapter but may be disclosed by the custodian in his discretion, except where such disclosure is prohibited by law:

1. Confidential records, including victim identity, provided to or obtained by staff in a rape crisis center or a program for battered spouses.

2. Those portions of engineering and construction drawings and plans submitted for the sole purpose of complying with the Building Code in obtaining a building permit that would identify specific trade secrets or other information, the disclosure of which would be harmful to the competitive position of the owner or lessee. However, such information shall be exempt only

until the building is completed. Information relating to the safety or environmental soundness of any building shall not be exempt from disclosure.

Those portions of engineering and construction drawings and plans that reveal critical structural components, security equipment and systems, ventilation systems, fire protection equipment, mandatory building emergency equipment or systems, elevators, electrical systems, telecommunications equipment and systems, and other utility equipment and systems submitted for the purpose of complying with the Uniform Statewide Building Code (§ 36-97 et seq.) or the Statewide Fire Prevention Code (§ 27-94 et seq.), the disclosure of which would jeopardize the safety or security of any public or private commercial office, multifamily residential or retail building or its occupants in the event of terrorism or other threat to public safety, to the extent that the owner or lessee of such property, equipment or system in writing (i) invokes the protections of this paragraph; (ii) identifies the drawings, plans, or other materials to be protected; and (iii) states the reasons why protection is necessary.

Nothing in this subdivision shall prevent the disclosure of information relating to any building in connection with an inquiry into the performance of that building after it has been subjected to fire, explosion, natural disaster or other catastrophic event.

3. Documentation or other information that describes the design, function, operation or access control features of any security system, whether manual or automated, which is used to control access to or use of any automated data processing or telecommunications system.

4. Plans and information to prevent or respond to terrorist activity, the disclosure of which would jeopardize the safety of any person, including (i) critical infrastructure sector or structural components; (ii) vulnerability assessments, operational, procedural, transportation, and tactical planning or training manuals, and staff meeting minutes or other records; and (iii) engineering or architectural records, or records containing information derived from such records, to the extent such records reveal the location or operation of security equipment and systems, elevators, ventilation, fire protection, emergency, electrical, telecommunications or utility equipment and systems of any public building, structure or information storage facility, or telecommunications or utility equipment or systems. The same categories of records of any governmental or nongovernmental person or entity submitted to a public body for the purpose of antiterrorism response planning may be withheld from disclosure if such person or entity in writing (a) invokes the protections of this subdivision, (b) identifies with specificity the records or portions thereof for which protection is sought, and (c) states with reasonable particularity why the protection of such records from public disclosure is necessary to meet the objective of antiterrorism planning or protection. Such statement shall be a public record and shall be disclosed upon request. Nothing in this subdivision shall be construed to prohibit the disclosure of records relating to the structural or environmental soundness of any building, nor shall it prevent the disclosure of information relating to any building in connection with an inquiry into the performance of that building after it has been subjected to fire, explosion, natural disaster or other catastrophic event.

5. Information that would disclose the security aspects of a system safety program plan adopted pursuant to 49 C.F.R. Part 659 by the Commonwealth's designated Rail Fixed Guideway Systems Safety Oversight agency; and information in the possession of such agency, the release of which would jeopardize the success of an ongoing investigation of a rail accident or other incident threatening railway safety.

6. Engineering and architectural drawings, operational, procedural, tactical planning or training manuals, or staff meeting minutes or other records, the

disclosure of which would reveal surveillance techniques, personnel deployments, alarm or security systems or technologies, or operational and transportation plans or protocols, to the extent such disclosure would jeopardize the security of any governmental facility, building or structure or the safety of persons using such facility, building or structure.

7. Security plans and specific assessment components of school safety audits, as provided in § 22.1-279.8.

Nothing in this subdivision shall be construed to prohibit the disclosure of records relating to the effectiveness of security plans after (i) any school building or property has been subjected to fire, explosion, natural disaster or other catastrophic event, or (ii) any person on school property has suffered or been threatened with any personal injury.

8. [Expired.]

9. Records of the Commitment Review Committee concerning the mental health assessment of an individual subject to commitment as a sexually violent predator under Chapter 9 (§ 37.2-900 et seq.) of Title 37.2; except that in no case shall records identifying the victims of a sexually violent predator be disclosed.

10. Subscriber data, which for the purposes of this subdivision, means the name, address, telephone number, and any other information identifying a subscriber of a telecommunications carrier, provided directly or indirectly by a telecommunications carrier to a public body that operates a 911 or E-911 emergency dispatch system or an emergency notification or reverse 911 system, if the data is in a form not made available by the telecommunications carrier to the public generally. Nothing in this subdivision shall prevent the release of subscriber data generated in connection with specific calls to a 911 emergency system, where the requester is seeking to obtain public records about the use of the system in response to a specific crime, emergency or other event as to which a citizen has initiated a 911 call.

11. Subscriber data, which for the purposes of this subdivision, means the name, address, telephone number, and any other information identifying a subscriber of a telecommunications carrier, collected by a local governing body in accordance with the Enhanced Public Safety Telephone Services Act (§ 56-484.12 et seq.), and other identifying information of a personal, medical, or financial nature provided to a local governing body in connection with a 911 or E-911 emergency dispatch system or an emergency notification or reverse 911 system, if such records are not otherwise publicly available. Nothing in this subdivision shall prevent the release of subscriber data generated in connection with specific calls to a 911 emergency system, where the requester is seeking to obtain public records about the use of the system in response to a specific crime, emergency or other event as to which a citizen has initiated a 911 call.

12. Records of the Virginia Military Advisory Council, the Virginia National Defense Industrial Authority, or a local or regional military affairs organization appointed by a local governing body, to the extent such records (i) contain information relating to strategies under consideration or development by the Council, the Authority, or such organizations to prevent the closure or realignment of federal military installations located in Virginia, to limit the adverse economic effect of such realignment or closure, or to seek additional tenant activity growth from the Department of Defense or (ii) disclose trade secrets, as defined in the Uniform Trade Secrets Act (§ 59.1-336 et seq.), provided to the Council, the Authority, or such organizations in connection with their work. In order to invoke the trade secret protection provided by clause (ii), the submitting entity shall, in writing and at the time of submission (a) invoke this exclusion, (b) identify with specificity the information for which such protection is sought, and (c) state the reason why such protection is

necessary. Nothing in this subdivision shall be construed to authorize the withholding of all or part of any record, other than a trade secret that has been specifically identified as required by this subdivision, after the Department of Defense has issued a final, unappealable decision, or in the event of litigation, a court of competent jurisdiction has entered a final, unappealable order concerning the closure, realignment, or expansion of the military installation or tenant activities for which records are sought. (1999, cc. 485, 518, 703, 726, 793, 849, 852, 867, 868, 881, § 2.1-342.01; 2000, cc. 66, 237, 382, 400, 430, 583, 589, 592, 594, 618, 632, 657, 720, 932, 933, 947, 1006, 1064; 2001, cc. 288, 518, 844, § 2.2-3705; 2002, cc. 87, 155, 242, 393, 478, 481, 499, 522, 571, 572, 633, 655, 715, 798, 830; 2003, cc. 274, 307, 327, 332, 358, 704, 801, 884, 891, 893, 897, 968; 2004, cc. 398, 482, 690, 770; 2005, c. 410; 2008, c. 721.)

Editor's note. — Acts 2004, c. 398 amended former § 2.2-3705, from which this section is derived. Pursuant to § 30-152, Acts 2004, c. 398 has been given effect in this section as set out above. The 2004 amendment by c. 398 added subdivision 9.

Acts 2004, c. 482 amended former § 2.2-3705, from which this section is derived. Pursuant to § 30-152, Acts 2004, c. 482 has been given effect in this section as set out above. The 2004 amendment by c. 482 inserted "or telecommunications or utility equipment or systems" following "structure or information storage facility" in clause (iii) of subdivision 4, and added subdivision 10.

Acts 2004, c. 770 amended former § 2.2-3705, from which this section is derived. Pursuant to § 30-152, Acts 2004, c. 770 has been given effect in this section as set out above. The 2004 amendment by c. 770, effective April 12, 2004, added subdivision 8.

Acts 2004, c. 770, which added subdivision 8, in cl. 2 provides: "That the provisions of this act shall expire on July 1, 2006."

The 2008 amendments. — The 2008 amendment by c. 721 added subdivision 12.

§ 2.2-3705.3. Exclusions to application of chapter; records relating to administrative investigations. — The following records are excluded from the provisions of this chapter but may be disclosed by the custodian in his discretion, except where such disclosure is prohibited by law:

1. Confidential records of all investigations of applications for licenses and permits, and of all licensees and permittees, made by or submitted to the Alcoholic Beverage Control Board, the State Lottery Department, the Virginia Racing Commission, the Department of Agriculture and Consumer Services relating to investigations and applications pursuant to Article 1.1:1 (§ 18.2-340.15 et seq.) of Chapter 8 of Title 18.2, or the Private Security Services Unit of the Department of Criminal Justice Services.

2. Records of active investigations being conducted by the Department of Health Professions or by any health regulatory board in the Commonwealth.

3. Investigator notes, and other correspondence and information, furnished in confidence with respect to an active investigation of individual employment discrimination complaints made to the Department of Human Resource Management or to such personnel of any local public body, including local school boards as are responsible for conducting such investigations in confidence. However, nothing in this section shall prohibit the disclosure of information taken from inactive reports in a form that does not reveal the identity of charging parties, persons supplying the information or other individuals involved in the investigation.

4. Records of active investigations being conducted by the Department of Medical Assistance Services pursuant to Chapter 10 (§ 32.1-323 et seq.) of Title 32.1.

5. Investigative notes and other correspondence and information furnished in confidence with respect to an investigation or conciliation process involving an alleged unlawful discriminatory practice under the Virginia Human Rights Act (§ 2.2-3900 et seq.) or under any local ordinance adopted in accordance with the authority specified in § 2.2-2638, or adopted pursuant to § 15.2-965,

or adopted prior to July 1, 1987, in accordance with applicable law, relating to local human rights or human relations commissions. However, nothing in this section shall prohibit the distribution of information taken from inactive reports in a form that does not reveal the identity of the parties involved or other persons supplying information.

6. Records of studies and investigations by the State Lottery Department of (i) lottery agents, (ii) lottery vendors, (iii) lottery crimes under §§ 58.1-4014 through 58.1-4018, (iv) defects in the law or regulations that cause abuses in the administration and operation of the lottery and any evasions of such provisions, or (v) the use of the lottery as a subterfuge for organized crime and illegal gambling where such official records have not been publicly released, published or copyrighted. All studies and investigations referred to under clauses (iii), (iv) and (v) shall be open to inspection and copying upon completion of the study or investigation.

7. Investigative notes, correspondence and information furnished in confidence, and records otherwise exempted by this chapter or any Virginia statute, provided to or produced by or for the (i) Auditor of Public Accounts; (ii) Joint Legislative Audit and Review Commission; (iii) Department of the State Internal Auditor with respect to an investigation initiated through the State Employee Fraud, Waste and Abuse Hotline; (iv) committee or the auditor with respect to an investigation or audit conducted pursuant to § 15.2-825; or (v) auditors, appointed by the local governing body of any county, city or town or a school board, who by charter, ordinance, or statute have responsibility for conducting an investigation of any officer, department or program of such body. Records of completed investigations shall be disclosed in a form that does not reveal the identity of the complainants or persons supplying information to investigators. Unless disclosure is prohibited by this section, the records disclosed shall include, but not be limited to, the agency involved, the identity of the person who is the subject of the complaint, the nature of the complaint, and the actions taken to resolve the complaint. If an investigation does not lead to corrective action, the identity of the person who is the subject of the complaint may be released only with the consent of the subject person. Local governing bodies shall adopt guidelines to govern the disclosure required by this subdivision.

8. Records of the Virginia Office for Protection and Advocacy consisting of documentary evidence received or maintained by the Office or its agents in connection with specific complaints or investigations, and records of communications between employees and agents of the Office and its clients or prospective clients concerning specific complaints, investigations or cases. Upon the conclusion of an investigation of a complaint, this exclusion shall no longer apply, but the Office may not at any time release the identity of any complainant or person with mental illness, mental retardation, developmental disabilities or other disability, unless (i) such complainant or person or his legal representative consents in writing to such identification or (ii) such identification is required by court order.

9. Information furnished in confidence to the Department of Employment Dispute Resolution with respect to an investigation, consultation, or mediation under Chapter 10 (§ 2.2-1000 et seq.) of this title, and memoranda, correspondence and other records resulting from any such investigation, consultation or mediation. However, nothing in this section shall prohibit the distribution of information taken from inactive reports in a form that does not reveal the identity of the parties involved or other persons supplying information.

10. The names, addresses and telephone numbers of complainants furnished in confidence with respect to an investigation of individual zoning enforcement complaints made to a local governing body.

11. Records of active investigations being conducted by the Department of Criminal Justice Services pursuant to Article 4 (§ 9.1-138 et seq.), Article 4.1

(§ 9.1-150.1 et seq.), Article 11 (§ 9.1-185 et seq.), and Article 12 (§ 9.1-186 et seq.) of Chapter 1 of Title 9.1.

12. Records furnished to or prepared by the Board of Education pursuant to subsection D of § 22.1-253.13:3 in connection with the review or investigation of any alleged breach in security, unauthorized alteration, or improper administration of tests by local school board employees responsible for the distribution or administration of the tests. However, this section shall not prohibit the disclosure of records to (i) a local school board or division superintendent for the purpose of permitting such board or superintendent to consider or to take personnel action with regard to an employee or (ii) any requester, after the conclusion of a review or investigation, in a form that (a) does not reveal the identity of any person making a complaint or supplying information to the Board on a confidential basis and (b) does not compromise the security of any test mandated by the Board.

13. Investigator notes, and other correspondence and information, furnished in confidence with respect to an active investigation conducted by or for the Board of Education related to the denial, suspension, or revocation of teacher licenses. However, this subdivision shall not prohibit the disclosure of records to a local school board or division superintendent for the purpose of permitting such board or superintendent to consider or to take personnel action with regard to an employee. Records of completed investigations shall be disclosed in a form that does not reveal the identity of any complainant or person supplying information to investigators. The records disclosed shall include information regarding the school or facility involved, the identity of the person who was the subject of the complaint, the nature of the complaint, and the actions taken to resolve the complaint. If an investigation fails to support a complaint or does not lead to corrective action, the identity of the person who was the subject of the complaint may be released only with the consent of the subject person. No personally identifiable information in the records regarding a current or former student shall be released except as permitted by state or federal law.

14. Records, notes and information provided in confidence and related to an investigation by the Attorney General under Article 5 (§ 3.1-336.1 et seq.) or Article 6 (§ 3.1-336.3 et seq.) of Chapter 18 of Title 3.1, Article 10 (§ 18.2-246.6 et seq.) of Chapter 6 or Chapter 13 (§ 18.2-512 et seq.) of Title 18.2, or Article 1 (§ 58.1-1000) of Chapter 10 of Title 58.1. However, records related to an investigation that has been inactive for more than six months shall, upon request, be disclosed provided such disclosure is not otherwise prohibited by law and does not reveal the identity of charging parties, complainants, persons supplying information, witnesses or other individuals involved in the investigation. (1999, cc. 485, 518, 703, 726, 793, 849, 852, 867, 868, 881, § 2.1-342.01; 2000, cc. 66, 237, 382, 400, 430, 583, 589, 592, 594, 618, 632, 657, 720, 932, 933, 947, 1006, 1064; 2001, cc. 288, 518, 844, § 2.2-3705; 2002, cc. 87, 155, 242, 393, 478, 481, 499, 522, 571, 572, 633, 655, 715, 798, 830; 2003, cc. 274, 307, 327, 332, 358, 704, 801, 884, 891, 893, 897, 968; 2004, cc. 605, 690, 766; 2005, c. 601; 2006, cc. 25, 95; 2008, cc. 387, 668, 689, 758.)

Editor's note. — Effective October 1, 2008, the reference in subdivision 14 to "Article 5 (§ 3.1-336.1 et seq.) or Article 6 (§ 3.1-336.3 et seq.) of Chapter 18 of Title 3.1" should read "Article 1 (§ 3.2-4200 et seq.) or Article 3 (§ 3.2-4204 et seq.) of Chapter 42 of Title 3.2".

Acts 2004, c. 605 amended former § 2.2-3705, from which this section is derived. Pursuant to § 30-152, Acts 2004, c. 605 has been given effect in this section as set out above. The 2004 amendment by c. 605, in subdivision 7, added clause (v) and added the last sentence.

Acts 2004, c. 766 amended former § 2.2-3705, from which this section is derived. Pursuant to § 30-152, Acts 2004, c. 766 has been given effect in this section as set out above. The 2004 amendment by c. 766 added "or the Private Security Services Unit of the Department of Criminal Justice Services" at the end of subdivision 1.

The 2008 amendments. — The 2008 amendments by cc. 387 and 689 are nearly identical, and substituted "Agriculture and Consumer Services relating to investigations and applications pursuant to Article 1.1:1 (§ 18.2-340.15 et seq.) of Chapter 8 of Title 18.2" for "Charitable Gaming" in subdivision 1. Additionally, c. 689 inserted a comma following "Article 11 (§ 9.1-185 et seq.)" in subdivision 11.

The 2008 amendment by c. 668 added subdivision 13.

The 2008 amendment by c. 758 added subdivision 13 [now 14].

CIRCUIT COURT OPINIONS

Employment discrimination complaints. — Because a county failed to prove that it advised the sources of information that information gathered would be treated confidentially, which was a necessary element in order to invoke the exception found in § 2.2-3705.3, a former employee was entitled to all information related to an employment discrimination complaint, investigation, and reprimand, pursuant to § 2.2-3705.1. McChrystal v. Fairfax County Bd. of Supervisors, 67 Va. Cir. 171, 2005 Va. Cir. LEXIS 26 (Fairfax County 2005).

Investigatory materials. — Even if a county could have shown that it advised the sources of information that information gathered would be treated confidentially, which was a necessary element in order to invoke the exception to the Virginia Freedom of Information Act found in § 2.2-3705.3, a former employee would have been entitled to all information in a report of a county's office of equity program but not the investigatory materials giving rise to it, pursuant to § 2.2-3705.1. McChrystal v. Fairfax County Bd. of Supervisors, 67 Va. Cir. 171, 2005 Va. Cir. LEXIS 26 (Fairfax County 2005).

§ 2.2-3705.4. Exclusions to application of chapter; educational records and certain records of educational institutions. — The following records are excluded from the provisions of this chapter but may be disclosed by the custodian in his discretion, except where such disclosure is prohibited by law:

1. Scholastic records containing information concerning identifiable individuals, except that such access shall not be denied to the person who is the subject thereof, or the parent or legal guardian of the student. However, no student shall have access to (i) financial records of a parent or guardian or (ii) records of instructional, supervisory, and administrative personnel and educational personnel ancillary thereto, that are in the sole possession of the maker thereof and that are not accessible or revealed to any other person except a substitute.

The parent or legal guardian of a student may prohibit, by written request, the release of any individual information regarding that student until the student reaches the age of 18 years. For scholastic records of students under the age of 18 years, the right of access may be asserted only by his legal guardian or parent, including a noncustodial parent, unless such parent's parental rights have been terminated or a court of competent jurisdiction has restricted or denied such access. For scholastic records of students who are emancipated or attending a state-supported institution of higher education, the right of access may be asserted by the student.

Any person who is the subject of any scholastic record and who is 18 years of age or older may waive, in writing, the protections afforded by this subdivision. If the protections are so waived, the public body shall open such records for inspection and copying.

2. Confidential letters and statements of recommendation placed in the records of educational agencies or institutions respecting (i) admission to any educational agency or institution, (ii) an application for employment, or (iii) receipt of an honor or honorary recognition.

3. Records of the Brown v. Board of Education Scholarship Awards Committee relating to personally identifiable information, including scholarship applications, personal financial information, and confidential correspondence and letters of recommendation.

4. Data, records or information of a proprietary nature produced or collected by or for faculty or staff of public institutions of higher education, other than the institutions' financial or administrative records, in the conduct of or as a result of study or research on medical, scientific, technical or scholarly issues, whether sponsored by the institution alone or in conjunction with a governmental body or a private concern, where such data, records or information has not been publicly released, published, copyrighted or patented.

5. All records of the University of Virginia or the University of Virginia Medical Center or Eastern Virginia Medical School, as the case may be, that contain proprietary, business-related information pertaining to the operations of the University of Virginia Medical Center or Eastern Virginia Medical School, as the case may be, including business development or marketing strategies and activities with existing or future joint venturers, partners, or other parties with whom the University of Virginia Medical Center or Eastern Virginia Medical School, as the case may be, has formed, or forms, any arrangement for the delivery of health care, if disclosure of such information would be harmful to the competitive position of the Medical Center or Eastern Virginia Medical School, as the case may be.

6. Personal information, as defined in § 2.2-3801, provided to the Board of the Virginia College Savings Plan or its employees by or on behalf of individuals who have requested information about, applied for, or entered into prepaid tuition contracts or savings trust account agreements pursuant to Chapter 4.9 (§ 23-38.75 et seq.) of Title 23. Nothing in this subdivision shall be construed to prohibit disclosure or publication of information in a statistical or other form that does not identify individuals or provide personal information. Individuals shall be provided access to their own personal information.

7. Records maintained in connection with fundraising activities by or for a public institution of higher education to the extent that such records reveal (i) personal fundraising strategies relating to identifiable donors or prospective donors or (ii) wealth assessments; estate, financial, or tax planning information; health-related information; employment, familial, or marital status information; electronic mail addresses, facsimile or telephone numbers; birth dates or social security numbers of identifiable donors or prospective donors. Nothing in this subdivision, however, shall be construed to authorize the withholding of records relating to the amount, date, purpose, and terms of the pledge or donation, or the identity of the donor unless the donor has requested anonymity in connection with or as a condition of making a pledge or donation. The exclusion provided by this subdivision shall not apply to protect from disclosure (i) the identities of sponsors providing grants to or contracting with the institution for the performance of research services or other work or (ii) the terms and conditions of such grants or contracts. (1999, cc. 485, 518, 703, 726, 793, 849, 852, 867, 868, 881, § 2.1-342.01; 2000, cc. 66, 237, 382, 400, 430, 583, 589, 592, 594, 618, 632, 657, 720, 932, 933, 947, 1006, 1064; 2001, cc. 288, 518, 844, § 2.2-3705; 2002, cc. 87, 155, 242, 393, 478, 481, 499, 522, 571, 572, 633, 655, 715, 798, 830; 2003, cc. 274, 307, 327, 332, 358, 704, 801, 884, 891, 893, 897, 968; 2004, c. 690; 2006, c. 518; 2008, cc. 561, 665.)

The 2008 amendments. — The 2008 amendments by cc. 561 and 665 are identical and added subdivision 7.

§ 2.2-3705.5. Exclusions to application of chapter; health and social services records. — The following records are excluded from the provisions of this chapter but may be disclosed by the custodian in his discretion, except where such disclosure is prohibited by law:

1. Health records, except that such records may be personally reviewed by the individual who is the subject of such records, as provided in subsection F of § 32.1-127.1:03.

Where the person who is the subject of health records is confined in a state or local correctional facility, the administrator or chief medical officer of such facility may assert such confined person's right of access to the health records if the administrator or chief medical officer has reasonable cause to believe that such confined person has an infectious disease or other medical condition from which other persons so confined need to be protected. Health records shall only be reviewed and shall not be copied by such administrator or chief medical officer. The information in the health records of a person so confined shall continue to be confidential and shall not be disclosed by the administrator or chief medical officer of the facility to any person except the subject or except as provided by law.

Where the person who is the subject of health records is under the age of 18, his right of access may be asserted only by his guardian or his parent, including a noncustodial parent, unless such parent's parental rights have been terminated, a court of competent jurisdiction has restricted or denied such access, or a parent has been denied access to the health record in accordance with § 20-124.6. In instances where the person who is the subject thereof is an emancipated minor, a student in a public institution of higher education, or is a minor who has consented to his own treatment as authorized by § 16.1-338 or 54.1-2969, the right of access may be asserted by the subject person.

For the purposes of this chapter, statistical summaries of incidents and statistical data concerning patient abuse as may be compiled by the Commissioner of the Department of Mental Health, Mental Retardation and Substance Abuse Services shall be open to inspection and copying as provided in § 2.2-3704. No such summaries or data shall include any patient-identifying information.

2. Applications for admission to examinations or for licensure and scoring records maintained by the Department of Health Professions or any board in that department on individual licensees or applicants. However, such material may be made available during normal working hours for copying, at the requester's expense, by the individual who is the subject thereof, in the offices of the Department of Health Professions or in the offices of any health regulatory board, whichever may possess the material.

3. Reports, documentary evidence and other information as specified in §§ 2.2-706 and 63.2-104.

4. Investigative notes; proprietary information not published, copyrighted or patented; information obtained from employee personnel records; personally identifiable information regarding residents, clients or other recipients of services; and other correspondence and information furnished in confidence to the Department of Social Services in connection with an active investigation of an applicant or licensee pursuant to Chapters 17 (§ 63.2-1700 et seq.) and 18 (§ 63.2-1800 et seq.) of Title 63.2. However, nothing in this section shall prohibit disclosure of information from the records of completed investigations in a form that does not reveal the identity of complainants, persons supplying information, or other individuals involved in the investigation.

5. Information and records collected for the designation and verification of trauma centers and other specialty care centers within the Statewide Emergency Medical Services System and Services pursuant to Article 2.1 (§ 32.1-111.1 et seq.) of Chapter 4 of Title 32.1.

6. Reports and court documents relating to involuntary admission required to be kept confidential pursuant to § 37.2-818.

7. Data formerly required to be submitted to the Commissioner of Health relating to the establishment of new or the expansion of existing clinical health

services, acquisition of major medical equipment, or certain projects requiring capital expenditures pursuant to former § 32.1-102.3:4.

8. Information required to be provided to the Department of Health Professions by certain licensees pursuant to § 54.1-2506.1.

9. Information and records acquired (i) during a review of any child death conducted by the State Child Fatality Review team established pursuant to § 32.1-283.1 or by a local or regional child fatality review team to the extent made confidential by § 32.1-283.2; (ii) during a review of any death conducted by a family violence fatality review team to the extent made confidential by § 32.1-283.3; or (iii) during a review of any adult death conducted by the Adult Fatality Review Team to the extent made confidential by § 32.1-283.5.

10. Patient level data collected by the Board of Health and not yet processed, verified, and released, pursuant to § 32.1-276.9, to the Board by the nonprofit organization with which the Commissioner of Health has contracted pursuant to § 32.1-276.4.

11. Records of the Intervention Program Committee within the Department of Health Professions, to the extent such records may identify any practitioner who may be, or who is actually, impaired to the extent disclosure is prohibited by § 54.1-2517.

12. Records submitted as a grant application, or accompanying a grant application, to the Commonwealth Neurotrauma Initiative Advisory Board pursuant to Chapter 3.1 (§ 51.5-12.1 et seq.) of Title 51.5, to the extent such records contain (i) medical or mental records, or other data identifying individual patients or (ii) proprietary business or research-related information produced or collected by the applicant in the conduct of or as a result of study or research on medical, rehabilitative, scientific, technical or scholarly issues, when such information has not been publicly released, published, copyrighted or patented, if the disclosure of such information would be harmful to the competitive position of the applicant.

13. Any record copied, recorded or received by the Commissioner of Health in the course of an examination, investigation or review of a managed care health insurance plan licensee pursuant to §§ 32.1-137.4 and 32.1-137.5, including books, records, files, accounts, papers, documents, and any or all computer or other recordings.

14. Records, information and statistical registries required to be kept confidential pursuant to §§ 63.2-102 and 63.2-104.

15. All data, records, and reports relating to the prescribing and dispensing of covered substances to recipients and any abstracts from such data, records, and reports that are in the possession of the Prescription Monitoring Program pursuant to Chapter 25.2 (§ 54.1-2519 et seq.) of Title 54.1 and any material relating to the operation or security of the Program.

16. Records of the Virginia Birth-Related Neurological Injury Compensation Program required to be kept confidential pursuant to § 38.2-5002.2.

17. Records of the State Health Commissioner relating to the health of any person or persons subject to an order of quarantine or an order of isolation pursuant to Article 3.02 (§ 32.1-48.05 et seq.) of Chapter 2 of Title 32.1; this provision shall not, however, be construed to prohibit the disclosure of statistical summaries, abstracts or other information in aggregate form.

18. Records containing the names and addresses or other contact information of persons receiving transportation services from a state or local public body or its designee under Title II of the Americans with Disabilities Act, (42 U.S.C. § 12131 et seq.) or funded by Temporary Assistance for Needy Families (TANF) created under § 63.2-600. (1999, cc. 485, 518, 703, 726, 793, 849, 852, 867, 868, 881, § 2.1-342.01; 2000, cc. 66, 237, 382, 400, 430, 583, 589, 592, 594, 618, 632, 657, 720, 932, 933, 947, 1006, 1064; 2001, cc. 288, 518, 844, § 2.2-3705; 2002, cc. 87, 155, 242, 393, 478, 481, 499, 522, 571, 572, 633, 655,

715, 798, 830; 2003, cc. 274, 307, 327, 332, 358, 704, 801, 884, 891, 893, 897, 968; 2004, cc. 65, 666, 690, 773, 1014, 1021; 2005, cc. 181, 227, 716; 2008, c. 539.)

Editor's note. — Acts 2004, cc. 65 and 1014 amended former § 2.2-3705, from which this section is derived. Pursuant to § 30-152, Acts 2004, cc. 65 and 1014 have been given effect in this section as set out above. The 2004 amendments by cc. 65 and 1014 are identical, and rewrote the first paragraph of subdivision 1, which formerly read: "Medical and mental records, except that such records may be personally reviewed by the subject person or a physician of the subject person's choice. However, the subject person's mental records may not be personally reviewed by such person when the subject person's treating physician has made a part of such person's records a written statement that in his opinion a review of such records by the subject person would be injurious to the subject person's physical or mental health or well-being."

Acts 2004, c. 666 amended former § 2.2-3705, from which this section is derived. Pursuant to § 30-152, Acts 2004, c. 666 has been given effect in this section as set out above. The 2004 amendment by c. 666 added subdivision 18.

Acts 2004, cc. 773 and 1021 amended former § 2.2-3705, from which this section is derived. Pursuant to § 30-152, Acts 2004, cc. 773 and 1021 have been given effect in this section as set out above. The 2004 amendments by cc. 773 and 1021, effective April 12, 2004, are identical, and added subdivision 17.

Acts 2004, cc. 773 and 1021, cl. 2, provide: "That the Board of Health shall promulgate regulations to implement the provisions of this act to be effective within 280 days of its enactment."

Acts 2002, c. 481, amended former § 2.2-3705 by adding subdivision 78, now subdivision 15 of this section. Amendments to former § 2.2-3705 by Acts 2002, c. 481, were limited to State Health Planning Region III and contingent on funding pursuant to Acts 2002, c. 481, cls. 4 and 5. Acts 2005, cc. 637 and 678, cl. 2, repealed the fourth and fifth enactment clauses of Acts 2002, c. 481.

The 2008 amendments. — The 2008 amendment by c. 539 rewrote subdivision 9, which read: "All information and records acquired during a review of any child death by the State Child Fatality Review team established pursuant to § 32.1-283.1, during a review of any child death by a local or regional child fatality review team established pursuant to § 32.1-283.2, and all information and records acquired during a review of any death by a family violence fatality review team established pursuant to § 32.1-283.3."

§ 2.2-3705.6. Exclusions to application of chapter; proprietary records and trade secrets. — The following records are excluded from the provisions of this chapter but may be disclosed by the custodian in his discretion, except where such disclosure is prohibited by law:

1. Proprietary information gathered by or for the Virginia Port Authority as provided in § 62.1-132.4 or 62.1-134.1.

2. Financial statements not publicly available filed with applications for industrial development financings in accordance with Chapter 49 (§ 15.2-4900 et seq.) of Title 15.2.

3. Confidential proprietary records, voluntarily provided by private business pursuant to a promise of confidentiality from the Department of Business Assistance, the Virginia Economic Development Partnership, the Virginia Tourism Authority, the Tobacco Indemnification and Community Revitalization Commission, a nonprofit, nonstock corporation created pursuant to § 2.2-2240.1, or local or regional industrial or economic development authorities or organizations, used by the Department, the Partnership, the Authority, or such entities for business, trade and tourism development; and memoranda, working papers or other records related to businesses that are considering locating or expanding in Virginia, prepared by such entities, where competition or bargaining is involved and where, if such records are made public, the financial interest of the governmental unit would be adversely affected.

4. Information that was filed as confidential under the Toxic Substances Information Act (§ 32.1-239 et seq.), as such Act existed prior to July 1, 1992.

5. Fisheries data that would permit identification of any person or vessel, except when required by court order as specified in § 28.2-204.

6. Confidential financial statements, balance sheets, trade secrets, and revenue and cost projections provided to the Department of Rail and Public Transportation, provided such information is exempt under the federal Freedom of Information Act or the federal Interstate Commerce Act or other laws administered by the Surface Transportation Board or the Federal Railroad Administration with respect to data provided in confidence to the Surface Transportation Board and the Federal Railroad Administration.

7. Confidential proprietary records related to inventory and sales, voluntarily provided by private energy suppliers to the Department of Mines, Minerals and Energy, used by that Department for energy contingency planning purposes or for developing consolidated statistical information on energy supplies.

8. Confidential proprietary information furnished to the Board of Medical Assistance Services or the Medicaid Prior Authorization Advisory Committee pursuant to Article 4 (§ 32.1-331.12 et seq.) of Chapter 10 of Title 32.1.

9. Proprietary, commercial or financial information, balance sheets, trade secrets, and revenue and cost projections provided by a private transportation business to the Virginia Department of Transportation and the Department of Rail and Public Transportation for the purpose of conducting transportation studies needed to obtain grants or other financial assistance under the Transportation Equity Act for the 21st Century (P.L. 105-178) for transportation projects, provided such information is exempt under the federal Freedom of Information Act or the federal Interstate Commerce Act or other laws administered by the Surface Transportation Board or the Federal Railroad Administration with respect to data provided in confidence to the Surface Transportation Board and the Federal Railroad Administration. However, the exemption provided by this subdivision shall not apply to any wholly owned subsidiary of a public body.

10. Confidential information designated as provided in subsection F of § 2.2-4342 as trade secrets or proprietary information by any person who has submitted to a public body an application for prequalification to bid on public construction projects in accordance with subsection B of § 2.2-4317.

11. a. Memoranda, staff evaluations, or other records prepared by the responsible public entity, its staff, outside advisors, or consultants exclusively for the evaluation and negotiation of proposals filed under the Public-Private Transportation Act of 1995 (§ 56-556 et seq.) or the Public Private Education Facilities and Infrastructure Act of 2002 (§ 56-575.1 et seq.), where (i) if such records were made public prior to or after the execution of an interim or a comprehensive agreement, § 56-573.1:1 or 56-575.17 notwithstanding, the financial interest or bargaining position of the public entity would be adversely affected, and (ii) the basis for the determination required in clause (i) is documented in writing by the responsible public entity; and

b. Records provided by a private entity to a responsible public entity, affected jurisdiction, or affected local jurisdiction pursuant to the provisions of the Public-Private Transportation Act of 1995 or the Public-Private Education Facilities and Infrastructure Act of 2002, to the extent that such records contain (i) trade secrets of the private entity as defined in the Uniform Trade Secrets Act (§ 59.1-336 et seq.); (ii) financial records of the private entity, including balance sheets and financial statements, that are not generally available to the public through regulatory disclosure or otherwise; or (iii) other information submitted by the private entity, where, if the records were made public prior to the execution of an interim agreement or a comprehensive agreement, the financial interest or bargaining position of the public or private entity would be adversely affected. In order for the records specified in clauses (i), (ii) and (iii) to be excluded from the provisions of this chapter, the private entity shall make a written request to the responsible public entity:

1. Invoking such exclusion upon submission of the data or other materials for which protection from disclosure is sought;

2. Identifying with specificity the data or other materials for which protection is sought; and

3. Stating the reasons why protection is necessary.

The responsible public entity shall determine whether the requested exclusion from disclosure is necessary to protect the trade secrets or financial records of the private entity. To protect other records submitted by the private entity from disclosure, the responsible public entity shall determine whether public disclosure prior to the execution of an interim agreement or a comprehensive agreement would adversely affect the financial interest or bargaining position of the public or private entity. The responsible public entity shall make a written determination of the nature and scope of the protection to be afforded by the responsible public entity under this subdivision. Once a written determination is made by the responsible public entity, the records afforded protection under this subdivision shall continue to be protected from disclosure when in the possession of any affected jurisdiction or affected local jurisdiction.

Except as specifically provided in subdivision 11 a, nothing in this subdivision shall be construed to authorize the withholding of (a) procurement records as required by § 56-573.1:1 or 56-575.17; (b) information concerning the terms and conditions of any interim or comprehensive agreement, service contract, lease, partnership, or any agreement of any kind entered into by the responsible public entity and the private entity; (c) information concerning the terms and conditions of any financing arrangement that involves the use of any public funds; or (d) information concerning the performance of any private entity developing or operating a qualifying transportation facility or a qualifying project.

For the purposes of this subdivision, the terms "affected jurisdiction," "affected local jurisdiction," "comprehensive agreement," "interim agreement," "qualifying project," "qualifying transportation facility," "responsible public entity," and "private entity" shall mean the same as those terms are defined in the Public-Private Transportation Act of 1995 or in the Public-Private Education Facilities and Infrastructure Act of 2002.

12. Confidential proprietary information or trade secrets, not publicly available, provided by a private person or entity to the Virginia Resources Authority or to a fund administered in connection with financial assistance rendered or to be rendered by the Virginia Resources Authority where, if such information were made public, the financial interest of the private person or entity would be adversely affected, and, after June 30, 1997, where such information was provided pursuant to a promise of confidentiality.

13. Trade secrets, as defined in the Uniform Trade Secrets Act (§ 59.1-336 et seq.), or confidential proprietary records that are not generally available to the public through regulatory disclosure or otherwise, provided by a (a) bidder or applicant for a franchise or (b) franchisee under Chapter 21 (§ 15.2-2100 et seq.) of Title 15.2 to the applicable franchising authority pursuant to a promise of confidentiality from the franchising authority, to the extent the records relate to the bidder's, applicant's, or franchisee's financial capacity or provision of new services, adoption of new technologies or implementation of improvements, where such new services, technologies or improvements have not been implemented by the franchisee on a nonexperimental scale in the franchise area, and where, if such records were made public, the competitive advantage or financial interests of the franchisee would be adversely affected.

In order for trade secrets or confidential proprietary information to be excluded from the provisions of this chapter, the bidder, applicant, or franchisee shall (i) invoke such exclusion upon submission of the data or other materials for which protection from disclosure is sought, (ii) identify the data or other materials for which protection is sought, and (iii) state the reason why protection is necessary.

No bidder, applicant, or franchisee may invoke the exclusion provided by this subdivision if the bidder, applicant, or franchisee is owned or controlled by a public body or if any representative of the applicable franchising authority serves on the management board or as an officer of the bidder, applicant, or franchisee.

14. Documents and other information of a proprietary nature furnished by a supplier of charitable gaming supplies to the Department of Agriculture and Consumer Services pursuant to subsection E of § 18.2-340.34.

15. Records and reports related to Virginia apple producer sales provided to the Virginia State Apple Board pursuant to §§ 3.1-622 and 3.1-624.

16. Trade secrets, as defined in the Uniform Trade Secrets Act (§ 59.1-336 et seq.) of Title 59.1, submitted by CMRS providers as defined in § 56-484.12 to the Wireless Carrier E-911 Cost Recovery Subcommittee created pursuant to § 56-484.15, relating to the provision of wireless E-911 service.

17. Records submitted as a grant application, or accompanying a grant application, to the Innovative Technology Authority pursuant to Article 3 (§ 2.2-2233.1 et seq.) of Chapter 22 of Title 2.2 or to the Commonwealth Health Research Board pursuant to Chapter 22 (§ 23-277 et seq.) of Title 23 to the extent such records contain proprietary business or research-related information produced or collected by the applicant in the conduct of or as a result of study or research on medical, rehabilitative, scientific, technical, technological, or scholarly issues, when such information has not been publicly released, published, copyrighted, or patented, if the disclosure of such information would be harmful to the competitive position of the applicant.

18. Confidential proprietary records and trade secrets developed and held by a local public body (i) providing telecommunication services pursuant to § 56-265.4:4 and (ii) providing cable television services pursuant to Article 1.1 (§ 15.2-2108.2 et seq.) of Chapter 21 of Title 15.2, to the extent that disclosure of such records would be harmful to the competitive position of the locality. In order for confidential proprietary information or trade secrets to be excluded from the provisions of this chapter, the locality in writing shall (i) invoke the protections of this subdivision, (ii) identify with specificity the records or portions thereof for which protection is sought, and (iii) state the reasons why protection is necessary.

19. Confidential proprietary records and trade secrets developed by or for a local authority created in accordance with the Virginia Wireless Service Authorities Act (§ 15.2-5431.1 et seq.) to provide qualifying communications services as authorized by Article 5.1 (§ 56-484.7:1 et seq.) of Chapter 15 of Title 56, where disclosure of such information would be harmful to the competitive position of the authority, except that records required to be maintained in accordance with § 15.2-2160 shall be released.

20. Trade secrets as defined in the Uniform Trade Secrets Act (§ 59.1-336 et seq.) or financial records of a business, including balance sheets and financial statements, that are not generally available to the public through regulatory disclosure or otherwise, provided to the Department of Minority Business Enterprise as part of an application for (i) certification as a small, women- or minority-owned business in accordance with Chapter 14 (§ 2.2-1400 et seq.) of this title or (ii) a claim made by a disadvantaged business or an economically disadvantaged individual against the Capital Access Fund for Disadvantaged Businesses created pursuant to § 2.2-2311. In order for such trade secrets or financial records to be excluded from the provisions of this chapter, the business shall (a) invoke such exclusion upon submission of the data or other materials for which protection from disclosure is sought, (b) identify the data or other materials for which protection is sought, and (c) state the reasons why protection is necessary.

21. Documents and other information of a proprietary or confidential nature disclosed by a carrier to the State Health Commissioner pursuant to § 32.1-276.5:1.

22. Trade secrets, as defined in the Uniform Trade Secrets Act (§ 59.1-336 et seq.), including, but not limited to, financial records, including balance sheets and financial statements, that are not generally available to the public through regulatory disclosure or otherwise, and revenue and cost projections supplied by a private or nongovernmental entity to the Inspector General of the Virginia Department of Transportation for the purpose of an audit, special investigation, or any study requested by the Inspector General's Office in accordance with law.

In order for the records specified in this subdivision to be excluded from the provisions of this chapter, the private or nongovernmental entity shall make a written request to the Department:

1. Invoking such exclusion upon submission of the data or other materials for which protection from disclosure is sought;
2. Identifying with specificity the data or other materials for which protection is sought; and
3. Stating the reasons why protection is necessary.

The Inspector General of the Virginia Department of Transportation shall determine whether the requested exclusion from disclosure is necessary to protect the trade secrets or financial records of the private entity. The Virginia Department of Transportation shall make a written determination of the nature and scope of the protection to be afforded by it under this subdivision. (1999, cc. 485, 518, 703, 726, 793, 849, 852, 867, 868, 881, § 2.1-342.01; 2000, cc. 66, 237, 382, 400, 430, 583, 589, 592, 594, 618, 632, 657, 720, 932, 933, 947, 1006, 1064; 2001, cc. 288, 518, 844, § 2.2-3705; 2002, cc. 87, 155, 242, 393, 478, 481, 499, 522, 571, 572, 633, 655, 715, 798, 830; 2003, cc. 274, 307, 327, 332, 358, 704, 801, 884, 891, 893, 897, 968; 2004, cc. 593, 690; 2005, cc. 258, 411; 2006, cc. 73, 76, 467, 831, 921, 936; 2006, Sp. Sess. I, c. 1; 2007, cc. 374, 693; 2008, cc. 71, 102, 266, 387, 633, 689, 736, 743.)

Editor's note. — Sections 3.1-622 and 3.1-624, referenced in subdivision 15 above were repealed effective February 12, 2003, by Acts 2001, c. 609.

Acts 2004, c. 593 amended former § 2.2-3705, from which this section is derived. Pursuant to § 30-152, Acts 2004, c. 593 has been given effect in this section as set out above. The 2004 amendment by c. 593 substituted "such entities" for "the Partnership" near the end in subdivision 3.

Acts 2006, c. 936, cl. 3, which amended subdivision 11, provides: "That the provisions of this act shall apply only to proposals for qualifying transportation facilities and qualifying projects filed on or after July 1, 2006."

Acts 2006, Sp. Sess. I, c. 1, which amended subdivision 11, in cl. 2 provides: "That the provisions of this act shall expire on July 1, 2007." The section is set out above without the amendments by Acts 2006, Sp. Sess. I, c. 1.

The 2006 amendments. — The 2006 amendment by Special Session I, c. 1, effective July 1, 2006, and which expires July 1, 2007, inserted "Memoranda staff evaluations ... the responsible public agency" at the beginning of subdivision 11.

The 2007 amendments. — The 2007 amendment by c. 374, designated the provisions of subdivision 11 as subdivision 11 b; added subdivision 11 a; in subdivision 11 b, deleted "(§ 56-556 et seq.)" following "the Public-Private Transportation Act of 1995" and "(§ 56-575.1 et seq.)" following "Public-Private Education Facilities and Infrastructure Act of 2002"; in the first undesignated paragraph of subdivision 11, substituted "entity" for "body" following "by the responsible public" and deleted "to which such records are provided by the responsible public entity"; and substituted "Except as specifically provided in subdivision 11 a, nothing" for "Nothing" at the beginning of the second undesignated paragraph of subdivision 11.

The 2007 amendment by c. 693 inserted "a nonprofit, nonstock corporation created pursuant to § 2.2-2240.1" in subdivision 3.

The 2008 amendments. — The 2008 amendments by cc. 71 and 102 are identical and added subdivision 21.

The 2008 amendment by c. 266 added subdivision 21 [now subdivision 22].

The 2008 amendments by cc. 387 and 689 are identical, and substituted "Department of Agriculture and Consumer Services" for "Department of Charitable Gaming" in subdivision 14.

The 2008 amendments by cc. 633 and 743 are identical and, in subsection 17, inserted "the Innovative Technology Authority pursuant to Article 3 (§ 2.2-2233.1 et seq.) of Chapter 22 of Title 2.2 or" and substituted "technological, or scholarly issues" for "or scholarly issues."

The 2008 amendment by c. 736 rewrote subdivision 13.

§ 2.2-3705.7. Exclusions to application of chapter; records of specific public bodies and certain other limited exemptions. — The following records are excluded from the provisions of this chapter but may be disclosed by the custodian in his discretion, except where such disclosure is prohibited by law:

1. State income, business, and estate tax returns, personal property tax returns, scholastic and confidential records held pursuant to § 58.1-3.

2. Working papers and correspondence of the Office of the Governor; Lieutenant Governor; the Attorney General; the members of the General Assembly or the Division of Legislative Services; the mayor or chief executive officer of any political subdivision of the Commonwealth; or the president or other chief executive officer of any public institution of higher education in Virginia. However, no record, which is otherwise open to inspection under this chapter, shall be deemed exempt by virtue of the fact that it has been attached to or incorporated within any working paper or correspondence.

As used in this subdivision:

"Office of the Governor" means the Governor; his chief of staff, counsel, director of policy, Cabinet Secretaries, and the Director of the Virginia Liaison Office; and those individuals to whom the Governor has delegated his authority pursuant to § 2.2-104.

"Working papers" means those records prepared by or for an above-named public official for his personal or deliberative use.

3. Library records that can be used to identify both (i) any library patron who has borrowed material from a library and (ii) the material such patron borrowed.

4. Contract cost estimates prepared for the confidential use of the Department of Transportation in awarding contracts for construction or the purchase of goods or services, and records and automated systems prepared for the Department's Bid Analysis and Monitoring Program.

5. Lists of registered owners of bonds issued by a political subdivision of the Commonwealth, whether the lists are maintained by the political subdivision itself or by a single fiduciary designated by the political subdivision.

6. Records and writings furnished by a member of the General Assembly to a meeting of a standing committee, special committee or subcommittee of his house established solely for the purpose of reviewing members' annual disclosure statements and supporting materials filed under § 30-110 or of formulating advisory opinions to members on standards of conduct, or both.

7. Customer account information of a public utility affiliated with a political subdivision of the Commonwealth, including the customer's name and service address, but excluding the amount of utility service provided and the amount of money paid for such utility service.

8. Personal information, as defined in § 2.2-3801, (i) filed with the Virginia Housing Development Authority concerning individuals who have applied for or received loans or other housing assistance or who have applied for occupancy of or have occupied housing financed, owned or otherwise assisted by the Virginia Housing Development Authority; (ii) concerning persons participating in or persons on the waiting list for federally funded rent-assistance programs; (iii) filed with any local redevelopment and housing authority created pursuant to § 36-4 concerning persons participating in or persons on the waiting list for housing assistance programs funded by local governments or by any such authority; or (iv) filed with any local redevelop-

ment and housing authority created pursuant to § 36-4 or any other local government agency concerning persons who have applied for occupancy or who have occupied affordable dwelling units established pursuant to § 15.2-2304 or 15.2-2305. However, access to one's own information shall not be denied.

9. Records regarding the siting of hazardous waste facilities, except as provided in § 10.1-1441, if disclosure of them would have a detrimental effect upon the negotiating position of a governing body or on the establishment of the terms, conditions and provisions of the siting agreement.

10. Records containing information on the site specific location of rare, threatened, endangered or otherwise imperiled plant and animal species, natural communities, caves, and significant historic and archaeological sites if, in the opinion of the public body that has the responsibility for such information, disclosure of the information would jeopardize the continued existence or the integrity of the resource. This exemption shall not apply to requests from the owner of the land upon which the resource is located.

11. Records, memoranda, working papers, graphics, video or audio tapes, production models, data and information of a proprietary nature produced by or for or collected by or for the State Lottery Department relating to matters of a specific lottery game design, development, production, operation, ticket price, prize structure, manner of selecting the winning ticket, manner of payment of prizes to holders of winning tickets, frequency of drawings or selections of winning tickets, odds of winning, advertising, or marketing, where such official records have not been publicly released, published, copyrighted or patented. Whether released, published or copyrighted, all game-related information shall be subject to public disclosure under this chapter upon the first day of sales for the specific lottery game to which it pertains.

12. Records of the Virginia Retirement System, acting pursuant to § 51.1-124.30, or of a local retirement system, acting pursuant to § 51.1-803, or of the Rector and Visitors of the University of Virginia, acting pursuant to § 23-76.1, relating to the acquisition, holding or disposition of a security or other ownership interest in an entity, where such security or ownership interest is not traded on a governmentally regulated securities exchange, to the extent that: (i) such records contain confidential analyses prepared for the Rector and Visitors of the University of Virginia, prepared by the retirement system or provided to the retirement system under a promise of confidentiality, of the future value of such ownership interest or the future financial performance of the entity; and (ii) disclosure of such confidential analyses would have an adverse effect on the value of the investment to be acquired, held or disposed of by the retirement system or the Rector and Visitors of the University of Virginia. Nothing in this subdivision shall be construed to prevent the disclosure of records relating to the identity of any investment held, the amount invested, or the present value of such investment.

13. Names and addresses of subscribers to Virginia Wildlife magazine, published by the Department of Game and Inland Fisheries, provided the individual subscriber has requested in writing that the Department not release such information.

14. Financial, medical, rehabilitative and other personal information concerning applicants for or recipients of loan funds submitted to or maintained by the Assistive Technology Loan Fund Authority under Chapter 11 (§ 51.5-53 et seq.) of Title 51.5.

15. Records of the Virginia Commonwealth University Health System Authority pertaining to any of the following: an individual's qualifications for or continued membership on its medical or teaching staffs; proprietary information gathered by or in the possession of the Authority from third parties pursuant to a promise of confidentiality; contract cost estimates prepared for confidential use in awarding contracts for construction or the

purchase of goods or services; data, records or information of a proprietary nature produced or collected by or for the Authority or members of its medical or teaching staffs; financial statements not publicly available that may be filed with the Authority from third parties; the identity, accounts or account status of any customer of the Authority; consulting or other reports paid for by the Authority to assist the Authority in connection with its strategic planning and goals; the determination of marketing and operational strategies where disclosure of such strategies would be harmful to the competitive position of the Authority; and data, records or information of a proprietary nature produced or collected by or for employees of the Authority, other than the Authority's financial or administrative records, in the conduct of or as a result of study or research on medical, scientific, technical or scholarly issues, whether sponsored by the Authority alone or in conjunction with a governmental body or a private concern, when such data, records or information have not been publicly released, published, copyrighted or patented.

16. Records of the Department of Environmental Quality, the State Water Control Board, State Air Pollution Control Board or the Virginia Waste Management Board relating to (i) active federal environmental enforcement actions that are considered confidential under federal law and (ii) enforcement strategies, including proposed sanctions for enforcement actions. Upon request, such records shall be disclosed after a proposed sanction resulting from the investigation has been proposed to the director of the agency. This subdivision shall not be construed to prohibit the disclosure of records related to inspection reports, notices of violation, and documents detailing the nature of any environmental contamination that may have occurred or similar documents.

17. As it pertains to any person, records related to the operation of toll facilities that identify an individual, vehicle, or travel itinerary including, but not limited to, vehicle identification data, vehicle enforcement system information; video or photographic images; Social Security or other identification numbers appearing on driver's licenses; credit card or bank account data; home addresses; phone numbers; or records of the date or time of toll facility use.

18. Records of the State Lottery Department pertaining to (i) the social security number, tax identification number, state sales tax number, home address and telephone number, personal and lottery banking account and transit numbers of a retailer, and financial information regarding the nonlottery operations of specific retail locations; and (ii) individual lottery winners, except that a winner's name, hometown, and amount won shall be disclosed.

19. Records of the Board for Branch Pilots relating to the chemical or drug testing of a person regulated by the Board, where such person has tested negative or has not been the subject of a disciplinary action by the Board for a positive test result.

20. Records, investigative notes, correspondence, and information pertaining to the planning, scheduling and performance of examinations of holder records pursuant to the Uniform Disposition of Unclaimed Property Act (§ 55-210.1 et seq.) prepared by or for the State Treasurer, his agents, employees or persons employed to perform an audit or examination of holder records.

21. Records of the Virginia Department of Emergency Management or a local governing body relating to citizen emergency response teams established pursuant to an ordinance of a local governing body, to the extent that such records reveal the name, address, including e-mail address, telephone or pager numbers, or operating schedule of an individual participant in the program.

22. Records of state or local park and recreation departments and local and regional park authorities to the extent such records contain information

identifying a person under the age of 18 years, where the parent or legal guardian of such person has requested in writing that such information not be disclosed. However, nothing in this subdivision shall operate to prohibit the disclosure of information defined as directory information under regulations implementing the Family Educational Rights and Privacy Act, 20 U.S.C. § 1232g, unless the public body has undertaken the parental notification and opt-out requirements provided by such regulations. Access shall not be denied to the parent, including a noncustodial parent, or guardian of such person, unless the parent's parental rights have been terminated or a court of competent jurisdiction has restricted or denied such access. For records of such persons who are emancipated, the right of access may be asserted by the subject thereof.

23. Records submitted for inclusion in the Statewide Alert Network administered by the Department of Emergency Management, to the extent that they reveal names, physical addresses, email addresses, computer or internet protocol information, telephone numbers, pager numbers, other wireless or portable communications device information, or operating schedules of individuals or agencies, where the release of such information would compromise the security of the Statewide Alert Network or individuals participating in the Statewide Alert Network.

24. Records of the Judicial Inquiry and Review Commission made confidential by § 17.1-913.

25. Records of the Virginia Retirement System acting pursuant to § 51.1-124.30 or of a local retirement system acting pursuant to § 51.1-803 (hereinafter collectively referred to as the retirement system) relating to:

a. Internal deliberations of or decisions by the retirement system on the pursuit of particular investment strategies, or the selection or termination of investment managers, prior to the execution of such investment strategies or the selection or termination of such managers, to the extent that disclosure of such records would have an adverse impact on the financial interest of the retirement system; and

b. Trade secrets, as defined in the Uniform Trade Secrets Act (§ 59.1-336 et seq.), provided by a private entity to the retirement system, to the extent disclosure of such records would have an adverse impact on the financial interest of the retirement system.

For the records specified in subdivision b to be excluded from the provisions of this chapter, the entity shall make a written request to the retirement system:

(1) Invoking such exclusion prior to or upon submission of the data or other materials for which protection from disclosure is sought;

(2) Identifying with specificity the data or other materials for which protection is sought; and

(3) Stating the reasons why protection is necessary.

The retirement system shall determine whether the requested exclusion from disclosure meets the requirements set forth in subdivision b.

Nothing in this subdivision shall be construed to authorize the withholding of the identity or amount of any investment held or the present value and performance of all asset classes and subclasses.

26. Records of the Department of Corrections made confidential by § 53.1-233.

27. Records maintained by the Department of the Treasury or participants in the Local Government Investment Pool (§ 2.2-4600 et seq.), to the extent such records relate to information required to be provided by such participants to the Department to establish accounts in accordance with § 2.2-4602. (1999, cc. 485, 518, 703, 726, 793, 849, 852, 867, 868, 881, § 2.1-342.01; 2000, cc. 66, 237, 382, 400, 430, 583, 589, 592, 594, 618, 632, 657, 720, 932, 933, 947, 1006,

1064; 2001, cc. 288, 518, 844, § 2.2-3705; 2002, cc. 87, 155, 242, 393, 478, 481, 499, 522, 571, 572, 633, 655, 715, 798, 830; 2003, cc. 274, 307, 327, 332, 358, 704, 801, 884, 891, 893, 897, 968; 2004, cc. 426, 690, 832; 2005, cc. 165, 508; 2007, cc. 406, 652, 660, 737, 739; 2008, cc. 16, 739.)

Editor's note. — Acts 2004, c. 426 amended former § 2.2-3705, from which this section is derived. Pursuant to § 30-152, Acts 2004, c. 426 has been given effect in this section as set out above. The 2004 amendment by c. 426 added subdivision 21.

Acts 2004, c. 832 amended former § 2.2-3705, from which this section is derived. Pursuant to § 30-152, Acts 2004, c. 832 has been given effect in this section as set out above. The 2004 amendment by c. 832 added subdivision 22.

Acts 2005, c. 508, cl. 2, provides: "That the provisions of this act are declaratory of existing law."

Acts 2007, c. 660, which added subdivision 27, in cl. 2 provides: "That the provisions of this act shall expire on July 1, 2008."

The 2007 amendments. — The 2007 amendment by c. 406 inserted "and local and regional park authorities" in subdivision 22.

The 2007 amendments by cc. 652 and 737 are identical, and added subsection 25 [now 26].

The 2007 amendment by c. 660 added subdivision 25 [now 27]. See Editor's note for expiration date.

The 2007 amendment by c. 739, effective March 21, 2007, added subdivision 25.

The 2008 amendments. — The 2008 amendment by c. 16 deleted former subdivision 27, which related to information on dog breed or personal identifying information of the owner contained in rabies vaccination certificates.

The 2008 amendment by c. 739 added subdivision 28 [now 27].

OPINIONS OF THE ATTORNEY GENERAL

Release of library records to parent of minor. — It is within the discretion of the records' custodian whether to release library records to the parent of a minor for the purpose of identifying and locating books checked out by the minor that are overdue. See opinion of Attorney General to The Honorable Robert G. Marshall, Member, House of Delegates, 02-002 (2/25/02) (decided under prior provisions).

Information provided to the Virginia Retirement System. — Confidential information provided to the Virginia Retirement System by limited partnerships in the private equity market may be exempt from disclosure under The Virginia Freedom of Information Act, provided such information meets the requirements of this section. See opinion of Attorney General to W. Forrest Matthews, Jr., Director, Virginia Retirement System, 02-149 (1/27/03) (decided under prior provisions).

Even though the Virginia Retirement System may deny public access to confidential information provided by limited partnerships, it is required to provide to a valid requester under the Act the identity of any private equity limited partnership in which it invests and the amount and present value of such investments. See opinion of Attorney General to W. Forrest Matthews, Jr., Director, Virginia Retirement System, 02-149 (1/27/03) (decided under prior provisions).

§ 2.2-3705.8. Limitation on record exclusions. — A. Neither any provision of this chapter nor any provision of Chapter 38 (§ 2.2-3800 et seq.) of this title shall be construed as denying public access to (i) contracts between a public body and its officers or employees, other than contracts settling public employee employment disputes held confidential as personnel records under § 2.2-3705.1; (ii) records of the position, job classification, official salary or rate of pay of, and records of the allowances or reimbursements for expenses paid to any officer, official or employee of a public body; or (iii) the compensation or benefits paid by any corporation organized by the Virginia Retirement System or its officers or employees.

The provisions of this subsection, however, shall not require public access to records of the official salaries or rates of pay of public employees whose annual rate of pay is $10,000 or less.

B. Nothing in this chapter shall be construed as denying public access to the nonexempt portions of a report of a consultant hired by or at the request of a local public body or the mayor or chief executive or administrative officer of such public body if (i) the contents of such report have been distributed or disclosed to members of the local public body or (ii) the local public body has scheduled any action on a matter that is the subject of the consultant's report. (1999, cc. 485, 518, 703, 726, 793, 849, 852, 867, 868, 881, § 2.1-342.01; 2000, cc. 66, 237, 382, 400, 430, 583, 589, 592, 594, 618, 632, 657, 720, 932, 933, 947, 1006, 1064; 2001, cc. 288, 518, 844, § 2.2-3705; 2002, cc. 87, 155, 242, 393, 478, 481, 499, 522, 571, 572, 633, 655, 715, 798, 830; 2003, cc. 274, 307, 327, 332, 358, 704, 801, 884, 891, 893, 897, 968; 2004, c. 690.)

§ **2.2-3706. Disclosure of criminal records; limitations.** — A. As used in this section:

"Criminal incident information" means a general description of the criminal activity reported, the date and general location the alleged crime was committed, the identity of the investigating officer, and a general description of any injuries suffered or property damaged or stolen.

B. Law-enforcement agencies shall make available upon request criminal incident information relating to felony offenses. However, where the release of criminal incident information is likely to jeopardize an ongoing investigation or prosecution, or the safety of an individual; cause a suspect to flee or evade detection; or result in the destruction of evidence, such information may be withheld until the above-referenced damage is no longer likely to occur from release of the information. Nothing in this subsection shall be construed to prohibit the release of those portions of such information that are not likely to cause the above-referenced damage.

C. Information in the custody of law-enforcement agencies relative to the identity of any individual, other than a juvenile, who is arrested and charged, and the status of the charge or arrest shall be released.

D. The identity of any victim, witness or undercover officer, or investigative techniques or procedures need not but may be disclosed unless disclosure is prohibited or restricted under § 19.2-11.2.

E. The identity of any individual providing information about a crime or criminal activity under a promise of anonymity shall not be disclosed.

F. The following records are excluded from the provisions of this chapter, but may be disclosed by the custodian, in his discretion, except where such disclosure is prohibited by law:

1. Complaints, memoranda, correspondence, case files or reports, witness statements, and evidence relating to a criminal investigation or prosecution, other than criminal incident information as defined in subsection A;

2. Adult arrestee photographs when necessary to avoid jeopardizing an investigation in felony cases until such time as the release of the photograph will no longer jeopardize the investigation;

3. Reports submitted in confidence to (i) state and local law-enforcement agencies, (ii) investigators authorized pursuant to § 53.1-16 or § 66-3.1, and (iii) campus police departments of public institutions of higher education established pursuant to Chapter 17 (§ 23-232 et seq.) of Title 23;

4. Portions of records of local government crime commissions that would identify individuals providing information about crimes or criminal activities under a promise of anonymity;

5. Records of local law-enforcement agencies relating to neighborhood watch programs that include the names, addresses, and operating schedules of individual participants in the program that are provided to such agencies under a promise of anonymity;

6. All records of persons imprisoned in penal institutions in the Commonwealth provided such records relate to the imprisonment;

7. Records of law-enforcement agencies, to the extent that such records contain specific tactical plans, the disclosure of which would jeopardize the safety or security of law-enforcement personnel or the general public;

8. All records of adult persons under (i) investigation or supervision by a local pretrial services agency in accordance with Article 5 (§ 19.2-152.2 et seq.) of Chapter 9 of Title 19.2; (ii) investigation, probation supervision or monitoring by a local community-based probation services agency in accordance with Article 9 (§ 9.1-173 et seq.) of Chapter 1 of Title 9.1; or (iii) investigation or supervision by state probation and parole services in accordance with Article 2 (§ 53.1-141 et seq.) of Chapter 4 of Title 53.1; and

9. Records of a law-enforcement agency to the extent that they disclose the telephone numbers for cellular telephones, pagers, or comparable portable communication devices provided to its personnel for use in the performance of their official duties.

G. Records kept by law-enforcement agencies as required by § 15.2-1722 shall be subject to the provisions of this chapter except:

1. Those portions of noncriminal incident or other investigative reports or materials containing identifying information of a personal, medical or financial nature provided to a law-enforcement agency where the release of such information would jeopardize the safety or privacy of any person;

2. Those portions of any records containing information related to plans for or resources dedicated to undercover operations; or

3. Records of background investigations of applicants for law-enforcement agency employment or other confidential administrative investigations conducted pursuant to law.

H. Records of the Sex Offender and Crimes Against Minors Registry maintained by the Department of State Police pursuant to Chapter 9 (§ 9.1-900 et seq.) of Title 9.1 are excluded from the provisions of this chapter, including information obtained from state, local and regional officials, except to the extent that information is required to be posted on the Internet pursuant to § 9.1-913.

I. In the event of conflict between this section as it relates to requests made under this section and other provisions of law, this section shall control. (1999, cc. 703, 726, § 2.1-342.2; 2000, c. 227; 2001, c. 844; 2002, cc. 393, 715, 769, 830; 2004, cc. 685, 735; 2006, cc. 857, 914; 2007, c. 133.)

Editor's note. — Acts 2002, c. 393, cl. 2, provides: "That it is the intent of the General Assembly to address the recent Virginia Supreme Court holding in the case styled Connell v. Kersey [262 Va. 154, 547 S.E.2d 228 (2001)], which held that attorneys for the Commonwealth are not 'public bodies' as defined in the Freedom of Information Act (§ 2.2-3700 et seq.), by clarifying that the Freedom of Information Act (FOIA) applies to constitutional officers and providing an exemption for attorneys for the Commonwealth."

The 2007 amendments. — The 2007 amendment by c. 133 substituted "services agency" for "program" in clause (ii) of subdivision F 8.

CASE NOTES

Commonwealth's attorney not required to release actual records. — This section does not require a Commonwealth's attorney's office or other law enforcement official to release actual records relating to a criminal incident, but only to provide a summary of the information available from the specified records, subject to any mandatory or discretionary exemptions provided for in the statute. Connell v. Kersey, 262 Va. 154, 547 S.E.2d 228, 2001 Va. LEXIS 67 (2001) (decided under prior law).

CIRCUIT COURT OPINIONS

Undercover operations. — Certain portions of the records were properly redacted because they related to plans or resources dedicated to undercover operations, or contained credit card or account numbers, but other pages improperly redacted information concerning equipment and supplies which could have been used for many purposes, including general police work and surveillance. Albright v. Woodfin, 68 Va. Cir. 115, 2005 Va. Cir. LEXIS 104 (Nelson County 2005).

§ 2.2-3707. Meetings to be public; notice of meetings; recordings; minutes. — A. All meetings of public bodies shall be open, except as provided in §§ 2.2-3707.01 and 2.2-3711.

B. No meeting shall be conducted through telephonic, video, electronic or other communication means where the members are not physically assembled to discuss or transact public business, except as provided in § 2.2-3708, 2.2-3709 or as may be specifically provided in Title 54.1 for the summary suspension of professional licenses.

C. Every public body shall give notice of the date, time, and location of its meetings by placing the notice in a prominent public location at which notices are regularly posted and in the office of the clerk of the public body, or in the case of a public body that has no clerk, in the office of the chief administrator. All state public bodies subject to the provisions of this chapter shall also post notice of their meetings on their websites and on the electronic calendar maintained by the Virginia Information Technologies Agency commonly known as the Commonwealth Calendar. Publication of meeting notices by electronic means by other public bodies shall be encouraged. The notice shall be posted at least three working days prior to the meeting. Notices for meetings of state public bodies on which there is at least one member appointed by the Governor shall state whether or not public comment will be received at the meeting and, if so, the approximate point during the meeting when public comment will be received.

D. Notice, reasonable under the circumstance, of special or emergency meetings shall be given contemporaneously with the notice provided members of the public body conducting the meeting.

E. Any person may annually file a written request for notification with a public body. The request shall include the requester's name, address, zip code, daytime telephone number, electronic mail address, if available, and organization, if any. The public body receiving such request shall provide notice of all meetings directly to each such person. Without objection by the person, the public body may provide electronic notice of all meetings in response to such requests.

F. At least one copy of all agenda packets and, unless exempt, all materials furnished to members of a public body for a meeting shall be made available for public inspection at the same time such documents are furnished to the members of the public body.

G. Nothing in this chapter shall be construed to prohibit the gathering or attendance of two or more members of a public body (i) at any place or function where no part of the purpose of such gathering or attendance is the discussion or transaction of any public business, and such gathering or attendance was not called or prearranged with any purpose of discussing or transacting any business of the public body or (ii) at a public forum, candidate appearance, or debate, the purpose of which is to inform the electorate and not to transact public business or to hold discussions relating to the transaction of public business, even though the performance of the members individually or collectively in the conduct of public business may be a topic of discussion or debate at such public meeting. The notice provisions of this chapter shall not apply to informal meetings or gatherings of the members of the General Assembly.

H. Any person may photograph, film, record or otherwise reproduce any portion of a meeting required to be open. The public body conducting the meeting may adopt rules governing the placement and use of equipment necessary for broadcasting, photographing, filming or recording a meeting to prevent interference with the proceedings.

I. Minutes shall be recorded at all open meetings. However, minutes shall not be required to be taken at deliberations of (i) standing and other committees of the General Assembly; (ii) legislative interim study commissions and committees, including the Virginia Code Commission; (iii) study committees or commissions appointed by the Governor; or (iv) study commissions or study committees, or any other committees or subcommittees appointed by the governing bodies or school boards of counties, cities and towns, except where the membership of any such commission, committee or subcommittee includes a majority of the governing body of the county, city or town or school board.

Minutes, including draft minutes, and all other records of open meetings, including audio or audio/visual records shall be deemed public records and subject to the provisions of this chapter.

Minutes shall include, but are not limited to, (i) the date, time, and location of the meeting; (ii) the members of the public body recorded as present and absent; and (iii) a summary of the discussion on matters proposed, deliberated or decided, and a record of any votes taken. In addition, for electronic communication meetings conducted in accordance with § 2.2-3708, minutes of state public bodies shall include (a) the identity of the members of the public body at each remote location identified in the notice who participated in the meeting through electronic communications means, (b) the identity of the members of the public body who were physically assembled at the primary or central meeting location, and (c) the identity of the members of the public body who were not present at the locations identified in clauses (a) and (b), but who monitored such meeting through electronic communications means. (1968, c. 479, § 2.1-343; 1973, c. 461; 1976, c. 467; 1977, c. 677; 1982, c. 333; 1989, c. 358; 1990, c. 538; 1993, c. 720; 1995, c. 562; 1999, cc. 696, 703, 726; 2000, c. 227; 2001, c. 844; 2004, cc. 730, 768; 2005, c. 352; 2007, c. 300.)

Editor's note. — Acts 2004, c. 768, cl. 2, provides: "That technical assistance to the Joint Rules Committee for the implementation of the provisions of this act shall be provided by the Virginia Freedom of Information Advisory Council, upon request."

The 2007 amendments. — The 2007 amendment by c. 300, in subsection C, substituted "their websites and on the electronic calendar maintained by the Virginia Information Technologies Agency commonly known as the Commonwealth Calendar" for "the Internet" at the end of the second sentence.

Michie's Jurisprudence. — For related discussion, see 5A M.J. Counties, § 32.

CASE NOTES

Street gathering not "meeting." — Judgment was properly awarded to a mayor and city officials in an action alleging that a particular street gathering of citizens and city council members was a "meeting" under the Virginia Freedom of Information Act because the street gathering was a citizen-organized "informational forum;" no part of the purpose of the gathering or attendance was the discussion or transaction of any public business. Beck v. Shelton, 267 Va. 482, 593 S.E.2d 195, 2004 Va. LEXIS 40 (2004).

OPINIONS OF THE ATTORNEY GENERAL

An institutional review board of a public institution of higher learning in the Commonwealth engaged in human research projects is not subject to the open meeting requirements set forth in the statute. See opinion of Attorney General to The Honorable Thomas C. Wright Jr., Member, House of Delegates, 01-101 (10/22/01).

A legislative caucus is not a "public body" as that term is defined in The Virginia Freedom of Information Act; therefore, the notice and open meeting requirements of the Act do not apply to such organizations. See opinion of Attorney General to The Honorable Clifton A. Woodrum, Member, House of Delegates, 03-063 (1/6/04).

An informal assemblage of three or more legislators at a meeting prearranged or called for the purpose of discussing expected votes on matters pending before the General Assembly constitutes a meeting under The Virginia Freedom of Information Act, requiring that such a meeting be open to the public. See opinion of Attorney General to The Honorable Clifton A. Woodrum, Member, House of Delegates, 03-063 (1/6/04).

§ **2.2-3707.01. Meetings of the General Assembly.** — A. Except as provided in subsection B, public access to any meeting of the General Assembly or a portion thereof shall be governed by rules established by the Joint Rules Committee and approved by a majority vote of each house at the next regular session of the General Assembly. At least 60 days before the adoption of such rules, the Joint Rules Committee shall (i) hold regional public hearings on such proposed rules and (ii) provide a copy of such proposed rules to the Virginia Freedom of Information Advisory Council.

B. Floor sessions of either house of the General Assembly; meetings, including work sessions, of any standing or interim study committee of the General Assembly; meetings, including work sessions, of any subcommittee of such standing or interim study committee; and joint committees of conference of the General Assembly; or a quorum of any such committees or subcommittees, shall be open and governed by this chapter.

C. Meetings of the respective political party caucuses of either house of the General Assembly, including meetings conducted by telephonic or other electronic communication means, without regard to (i) whether the General Assembly is in or out of regular or special session or (ii) whether such caucuses invite staff or guests to participate in their deliberations, shall not be deemed meetings for the purposes of this chapter.

D. No regular, special, or reconvened session of the General Assembly held pursuant to Article IV, Section 6 of the Constitution of Virginia shall be conducted using electronic communication means pursuant § 2.2-3708. (2004, c. 768; 2005, c. 352.)

Editor's note. — Acts 2004, c. 768, cl. 2, provides: "That technical assistance to the Joint Rules Committee for the implementation of the provisions of this act shall be provided by the Virginia Freedom of Information Advisory Council, upon request."

§ **2.2-3707.1. Posting of minutes for state boards and commissions.** — All boards, commissions, councils, and other public bodies created in the executive branch of state government and subject to the provisions of this chapter shall post minutes of their meetings on such body's website, if any, and on the electronic calendar maintained by the Virginia Information Technologies Agency commonly known as the Commonwealth Calendar. Draft minutes of meetings shall be posted as soon as possible but no later than ten working days after the conclusion of the meeting. Final approved meeting minutes shall be posted within three working days of final approval of the minutes. (2002, cc. 580, 618; 2006, cc. 474, 595; 2007, c. 300.)

The 2007 amendments. — The 2007 amendment by c. 300 substituted "electronic calendar maintained by the Virginia Information Technologies Agency commonly known as the Commonwealth Calendar" for "Virginia Regulatory Town Hall."

§ **2.2-3708. Electronic communication meetings; applicability; physical quorum required; notice; report.** — A. Except as expressly provided in subsection G of this section or § 2.2-3708.1, no local governing body, school board, or any authority, board, bureau, commission, district or agency of local government, any committee thereof, or any entity created by a local governing body, school board, or any local authority, board, or commission shall conduct a meeting wherein the public business is discussed or transacted through telephonic, video, electronic or other communication means where the members are not physically assembled. Nothing in this section shall be construed to prohibit the use of interactive audio or video means to expand public participation.

B. Except as provided in subsection D of § 2.2-3707.01, state public bodies may conduct any meeting wherein the public business is discussed or transacted through electronic communication means, provided (i) a quorum of the public body is physically assembled at one primary or central meeting location, (ii) notice of the meeting has been given in accordance with subsection C, and (iii) the remote locations, from which additional members of the public body participate through electronic communication means, are open to the public. All persons attending the meeting at any of the meeting locations shall be afforded the same opportunity to address the public body as persons attending the primary or central location. State public bodies, however, may meet by electronic communication means without a quorum of the public body physically assembled at one location when (a) the Governor has declared a state of emergency in accordance with § 44-146.17, (b) the meeting is necessary to take action to address the emergency, and (c) the public body otherwise complies with the provisions of this section.

If an authorized public body holds an electronic meeting pursuant to this section, it shall also hold at least one meeting annually where members in attendance at the meeting are physically assembled at one location and where no members participate by electronic communication means.

C. Notice of any meetings held pursuant to this section shall be provided at least three working days in advance of the date scheduled for the meeting. The notice shall include the date, time, place, and purpose for the meeting; shall identify the locations for the meeting; and shall include a telephone number that may be used at remote locations to notify the primary or central meeting location of any interruption in the telephonic or video broadcast of the meeting to the remote locations. Any interruption in the telephonic or video broadcast of the meeting shall result in the suspension of action at the meeting until repairs are made and public access restored.

D. Agenda packets and, unless exempt, all materials that will be distributed to members of the public body and that have been made available to the staff of the public body in sufficient time for duplication and forwarding to all locations where public access will be provided shall be made available to the public at the time of the meeting. Minutes of all meetings held by electronic communication means shall be recorded as required by § 2.2-3707. Votes taken during any meeting conducted through electronic communication means shall be recorded by name in roll-call fashion and included in the minutes.

E. Three working days' notice shall not be required for meetings authorized under this section held in accordance with subsection G or that are continued to address an emergency or to conclude the agenda of the meeting for which proper notice has been given, when the date, time, place, and purpose of the continued meeting are set during the meeting prior to adjournment. Public bodies conducting emergency meetings through electronic communication means shall comply with the provisions of subsection D requiring minutes of the meeting. The nature of the emergency shall be stated in the minutes.

F. Any authorized public body that meets by electronic communication means shall make a written report of the following to the Virginia Freedom of Information Advisory Council and the Joint Commission on Technology and Science by December 15 of each year:

1. The total number of electronic communication meetings held that year;
2. The dates and purposes of the meetings;
3. The number of sites for each meeting;
4. The types of electronic communication means by which the meetings were held;

5. The number of participants, including members of the public, at each meeting location;

6. The identity of the members of the public body recorded as absent and those recorded as present at each meeting location;

7. A summary of any public comment received about the electronic communication meetings; and

8. A written summary of the public body's experience using electronic communication meetings, including its logistical and technical experience.

G. Any local governing body, school board, or any authority, board, bureau, commission, district, or agency of local government may meet by electronic communication means without a quorum of the public body physically assembled at one location when the Governor has declared a state of emergency in accordance with § 44-146.17, provided (i) the catastrophic nature of the declared emergency makes it impracticable or unsafe to assemble a quorum in a single location and (ii) the purpose of the meeting is to address the emergency. The local public body convening a meeting in accordance with this subsection shall (a) give public notice using the best available method given the nature of the emergency, which notice shall be given contemporaneously with the notice provided members of the local public body conducting the meeting; (b) make arrangements for public access to such meeting; and (c) otherwise comply with the provisions of this section. The nature of the emergency and the fact that the meeting was held by electronic communication means shall be stated in the minutes. (1984, c. 252, § 2.1-343.1; 1989, c. 358; 1991, c. 473; 1992, c. 153; 1993, c. 270; 1995, c. 278; 1996, c. 289; 1999, cc. 703, 726; 2001, c. 844; 2003, cc. 981, 1021; 2005, c. 352; 2007, cc. 512, 945; 2008, cc. 233, 789.)

Editor's note. — For provisions of Acts 2003, cc. 981 and 1021, cls. 4 to 16, reflecting the intent of the General Assembly to provide for the consolidation of the procurement and operational functions of information technology for state agencies in a single agency, and related transitional and other provisions, see the Editor's note at § 2.2-2005.

The 2007 amendments. — The 2007 amendment by c. 512 added the last sentence in the second paragraph (now the first paragraph) of subsection B.

The 2007 amendment by c. 945 rewrote the section.

The 2008 amendments. — The 2008 amendments by cc. 233 and 789 are identical, and inserted "subsection G of this section or" near the beginning of subsection A; in the third sentence of the first paragraph of subsection B, added "State" at the beginning, and substituted clause (a) through (c) designators for clause (i) through (iii) designators; inserted "held in accordance with subsection G or" in the first sentence of subsection E; and added subsection G.

CASE NOTES

Applied in Beck v. Shelton, 267 Va. 482, 593 S.E.2d 195, 2004 Va. LEXIS 40 (2004).

§ 2.2-3708.1. Participation in meetings in event of emergency; certain disabilities; distance from meeting location for certain public bodies. — A. A member of a public body may participate in a meeting governed by this chapter through electronic communication means from a remote location that is not open to the public only as follows and subject to the requirements of subsection B:

1. If, on the day of a meeting, a member of the public body holding the meeting notifies the chair of the public body that such member is unable to attend the meeting due to an emergency and identifies with specificity the nature of the emergency, and the public body holding the meeting (a) approves

such member's participation by a majority vote of the members present and (b) records in its minutes the specific nature of the emergency and the remote location from which the member participated.

Such participation by the member shall be limited each calendar year to two meetings or 25 percent of the meetings of the public body, whichever is fewer;

2. If a member of a public body notifies the chair of the public body that such member is unable to attend a meeting due to a temporary or permanent disability or other medical condition that prevents the member's physical attendance and the public body records this fact and the remote location from which the member participated in its minutes; or

3. If, on the day of a meeting, a member of a regional public body notifies the chair of the public body that such member's principal residence is more than 60 miles from the meeting location identified in the required notice for such meeting and the public body holding the meeting (a) approves such member's participation by a majority vote of the members present and (b) records in its minutes the remote location from which the member participated.

B. Participation by a member of a public body as authorized under subsection A shall be only under the following conditions:

1. A quorum of the public body is physically assembled at the primary or central meeting location; and

2. The public body makes arrangements for the voice of the remote participant to be heard by all persons at the primary or central meeting location. (2007, c. 945.)

§ **2.2-3709:** Expired.

Editor's note. — Acts 1998, cc. 777 and 839, cl. 2, as amended by Acts 2000, c. 909, cl. 1, Acts 2002, c. 297, Acts 2003, c. 475, cl. 2, and Acts 2005, c. 17, cl. 1, provide: "That the provisions of this act shall expire on July 1, 2007. From July 1, 1998, to July 1, 2007, the Board of Visitors of the University of Virginia shall record the date and name of each board or committee meeting held pursuant to this chapter and, for each meeting, record the name of each board member who participates by video or telephone. The Board of Visitors also shall record any complaints about telephonic or video participation at meetings expressed by board members, members of the public, or members of the media. No later than January 1, 2007, the Board shall provide the Secretary of Education, the Virginia Freedom of Information Advisory Council, and the General Assembly a written report containing the information required to be recorded as well as a narrative summary of the positive and negative experiences of employing telephonic and video meetings."

§ **2.2-3710. Transaction of public business other than by votes at meetings prohibited.** — A. Unless otherwise specifically provided by law, no vote of any kind of the membership, or any part thereof, of any public body shall be taken to authorize the transaction of any public business, other than a vote taken at a meeting conducted in accordance with the provisions of this chapter. No public body shall vote by secret or written ballot, and unless expressly provided by this chapter, no public body shall vote by telephone or other electronic communication means.

B. Notwithstanding the foregoing, nothing contained herein shall be construed to prohibit (i) separately contacting the membership, or any part thereof, of any public body for the purpose of ascertaining a member's position with respect to the transaction of public business, whether such contact is done in person, by telephone or by electronic communication, provided the contact is done on a basis that does not constitute a meeting as defined in this chapter or (ii) the House of Delegates or the Senate of Virginia from adopting rules relating to the casting of votes by members of standing committees. Nothing in this subsection shall operate to exclude any public record from the provisions of this chapter. (1987, c. 71, § 2.1-343.2; 1999, cc. 703, 726; 2000, c. 932; 2001, cc. 710, 844; 2002, c. 491.)

Editor's note. — Acts 2001, c. 710 amended § 2.1-343.2, from which this section is derived. Pursuant to § 30-152, Acts 2001, c. 710 has been given effect in this section as set out above. The 2001 amendment by c. 710, in the second paragraph, inserted "whether such contact is done in person, by telephone or by electronic communication, provided the contact is done on a basis that does not constitute a meeting as defined in this chapter" at the end of the first sentence, and added the second sentence.

CASE NOTES

Applied in Beck v. Shelton, 267 Va. 482, 593 S.E.2d 195, 2004 Va. LEXIS 40 (2004).

§ 2.2-3711. Closed meetings authorized for certain limited purposes. — A. Public bodies may hold closed meetings only for the following purposes:

1. Discussion, consideration, or interviews of prospective candidates for employment; assignment, appointment, promotion, performance, demotion, salaries, disciplining, or resignation of specific public officers, appointees, or employees of any public body; and evaluation of performance of departments or schools of public institutions of higher education where such evaluation will necessarily involve discussion of the performance of specific individuals. Any teacher shall be permitted to be present during a closed meeting in which there is a discussion or consideration of a disciplinary matter that involves the teacher and some student and the student involved in the matter is present, provided the teacher makes a written request to be present to the presiding officer of the appropriate board.

2. Discussion or consideration of admission or disciplinary matters or any other matters that would involve the disclosure of information contained in a scholastic record concerning any student of any Virginia public institution of higher education or any state school system. However, any such student, legal counsel and, if the student is a minor, the student's parents or legal guardians shall be permitted to be present during the taking of testimony or presentation of evidence at a closed meeting, if such student, parents, or guardians so request in writing and such request is submitted to the presiding officer of the appropriate board.

3. Discussion or consideration of the acquisition of real property for a public purpose, or of the disposition of publicly held real property, where discussion in an open meeting would adversely affect the bargaining position or negotiating strategy of the public body.

4. The protection of the privacy of individuals in personal matters not related to public business.

5. Discussion concerning a prospective business or industry or the expansion of an existing business or industry where no previous announcement has been made of the business' or industry's interest in locating or expanding its facilities in the community.

6. Discussion or consideration of the investment of public funds where competition or bargaining is involved, where, if made public initially, the financial interest of the governmental unit would be adversely affected.

7. Consultation with legal counsel and briefings by staff members or consultants pertaining to actual or probable litigation, where such consultation or briefing in open meeting would adversely affect the negotiating or litigating posture of the public body; and consultation with legal counsel employed or retained by a public body regarding specific legal matters requiring the provision of legal advice by such counsel. For the purposes of this subdivision, "probable litigation" means litigation that has been specifically threatened or on which the public body or its legal counsel has a reasonable basis to believe will be commenced by or against a known party. Nothing in this subdivision shall be construed to permit the closure of a meeting merely

because an attorney representing the public body is in attendance or is consulted on a matter.

8. In the case of boards of visitors of public institutions of higher education, discussion or consideration of matters relating to gifts, bequests and fund-raising activities, and grants and contracts for services or work to be performed by such institution. However, the terms and conditions of any such gifts, bequests, grants, and contracts made by a foreign government, a foreign legal entity, or a foreign person and accepted by a public institution of higher education in Virginia shall be subject to public disclosure upon written request to the appropriate board of visitors. For the purpose of this subdivision, (i) "foreign government" means any government other than the United States government or the government of a state or a political subdivision thereof; (ii) "foreign legal entity" means any legal entity created under the laws of the United States or of any state thereof if a majority of the ownership of the stock of such legal entity is owned by foreign governments or foreign persons or if a majority of the membership of any such entity is composed of foreign persons or foreign legal entities, or any legal entity created under the laws of a foreign government; and (iii) "foreign person" means any individual who is not a citizen or national of the United States or a trust territory or protectorate thereof.

9. In the case of the boards of trustees of the Virginia Museum of Fine Arts, the Virginia Museum of Natural History, and The Science Museum of Virginia, discussion or consideration of matters relating to specific gifts, bequests, and grants.

10. Discussion or consideration of honorary degrees or special awards.

11. Discussion or consideration of tests, examinations, or other records excluded from this chapter pursuant to subdivision 4 of § 2.2-3705.1.

12. Discussion, consideration, or review by the appropriate House or Senate committees of possible disciplinary action against a member arising out of the possible inadequacy of the disclosure statement filed by the member, provided the member may request in writing that the committee meeting not be conducted in a closed meeting.

13. Discussion of strategy with respect to the negotiation of a hazardous waste siting agreement or to consider the terms, conditions, and provisions of a hazardous waste siting agreement if the governing body in open meeting finds that an open meeting will have an adverse effect upon the negotiating position of the governing body or the establishment of the terms, conditions and provisions of the siting agreement, or both. All discussions with the applicant or its representatives may be conducted in a closed meeting.

14. Discussion by the Governor and any economic advisory board reviewing forecasts of economic activity and estimating general and nongeneral fund revenues.

15. Discussion or consideration of medical and mental records excluded from this chapter pursuant to subdivision 1 of § 2.2-3705.5.

16. Deliberations of the State Lottery Board in a licensing appeal action conducted pursuant to subsection D of § 58.1-4007 regarding the denial or revocation of a license of a lottery sales agent; and discussion, consideration or review of State Lottery Department matters related to proprietary lottery game information and studies or investigations exempted from disclosure under subdivision 6 of § 2.2-3705.3 and subdivision 11 of § 2.2-3705.7.

17. Those portions of meetings by local government crime commissions where the identity of, or information tending to identify, individuals providing information about crimes or criminal activities under a promise of anonymity is discussed or disclosed.

18. Those portions of meetings in which the Board of Corrections discusses or discloses the identity of, or information tending to identify, any prisoner who

(i) provides information about crimes or criminal activities, (ii) renders assistance in preventing the escape of another prisoner or in the apprehension of an escaped prisoner, or (iii) voluntarily or at the instance of a prison official renders other extraordinary services, the disclosure of which is likely to jeopardize the prisoner's life or safety.

19. Discussion of plans to protect public safety as it relates to terrorist activity and briefings by staff members, legal counsel, or law-enforcement or emergency service officials concerning actions taken to respond to such activity or a related threat to public safety; or discussion of reports or plans related to the security of any governmental facility, building or structure, or the safety of persons using such facility, building or structure.

20. Discussion by the Board of the Virginia Retirement System, acting pursuant to § 51.1-124.30, or of any local retirement system, acting pursuant to § 51.1-803, or of the Rector and Visitors of the University of Virginia, acting pursuant to § 23-76.1, regarding the acquisition, holding or disposition of a security or other ownership interest in an entity, where such security or ownership interest is not traded on a governmentally regulated securities exchange, to the extent that such discussion (i) concerns confidential analyses prepared for the Rector and Visitors of the University of Virginia, prepared by the retirement system or provided to the retirement system under a promise of confidentiality, of the future value of such ownership interest or the future financial performance of the entity, and (ii) would have an adverse effect on the value of the investment to be acquired, held or disposed of by the retirement system or the Rector and Visitors of the University of Virginia. Nothing in this subdivision shall be construed to prevent the disclosure of information relating to the identity of any investment held, the amount invested or the present value of such investment.

21. Those portions of meetings in which individual child death cases are discussed by the State Child Fatality Review team established pursuant to § 32.1-283.1, and those portions of meetings in which individual child death cases are discussed by a regional or local child fatality review team established pursuant to § 32.1-283.2, and those portions of meetings in which individual death cases are discussed by family violence fatality review teams established pursuant to § 32.1-283.3.

22. Those portions of meetings of the University of Virginia Board of Visitors or the Eastern Virginia Medical School Board of Visitors, as the case may be, and those portions of meetings of any persons to whom management responsibilities for the University of Virginia Medical Center or Eastern Virginia Medical School, as the case may be, have been delegated, in which there is discussed proprietary, business-related information pertaining to the operations of the University of Virginia Medical Center or Eastern Virginia Medical School, as the case may be, including business development or marketing strategies and activities with existing or future joint venturers, partners, or other parties with whom the University of Virginia Medical Center or Eastern Virginia Medical School, as the case may be, has formed, or forms, any arrangement for the delivery of health care, if disclosure of such information would adversely affect the competitive position of the Medical Center or Eastern Virginia Medical School, as the case may be.

23. In the case of the Virginia Commonwealth University Health System Authority, discussion or consideration of any of the following: the acquisition or disposition of real or personal property where disclosure would adversely affect the bargaining position or negotiating strategy of the Authority; operational plans that could affect the value of such property, real or personal, owned or desirable for ownership by the Authority; matters relating to gifts, bequests and fund-raising activities; grants and contracts for services or work to be performed by the Authority; marketing or operational strategies where disclo-

sure of such strategies would adversely affect the competitive position of the Authority; members of its medical and teaching staffs and qualifications for appointments thereto; and qualifications or evaluations of other employees.

24. Those portions of the meetings of the Intervention Program Committee within the Department of Health Professions to the extent such discussions identify any practitioner who may be, or who actually is, impaired pursuant to Chapter 25.1 (§ 54.1-2515 et seq.) of Title 54.1.

25. Meetings or portions of meetings of the Board of the Virginia College Savings Plan wherein personal information, as defined in § 2.2-3801, which has been provided to the Board or its employees by or on behalf of individuals who have requested information about, applied for, or entered into prepaid tuition contracts or savings trust account agreements pursuant to Chapter 4.9 (§ 23-38.75 et seq.) of Title 23 is discussed.

26. Discussion or consideration, by the Wireless Carrier E-911 Cost Recovery Subcommittee created pursuant to § 56-484.15, of trade secrets, as defined in the Uniform Trade Secrets Act (§ 59.1-336 et seq.), submitted by CMRS providers as defined in § 56-484.12, related to the provision of wireless E-911 service.

27. Those portions of disciplinary proceedings by any regulatory board within the Department of Professional and Occupational Regulation, Department of Health Professions, or the Board of Accountancy conducted pursuant to § 2.2-4019 or 2.2-4020 during which the board deliberates to reach a decision or meetings of health regulatory boards or conference committees of such boards to consider settlement proposals in pending disciplinary actions or modifications to previously issued board orders as requested by either of the parties.

28. Discussion or consideration of records excluded from this chapter pursuant to subdivision 11 of § 2.2-3705.6 by a responsible public entity or an affected local jurisdiction, as those terms are defined in § 56-557, or any independent review panel appointed to review information and advise the responsible public entity concerning such records.

29. Discussion of the award of a public contract involving the expenditure of public funds, including interviews of bidders or offerors, and discussion of the terms or scope of such contract, where discussion in an open session would adversely affect the bargaining position or negotiating strategy of the public body.

30. Discussion or consideration of grant application records excluded from this chapter pursuant to subdivision 17 of § 2.2-3705.6 by (i) the Commonwealth Health Research Board or (ii) the Innovative Technology Authority or a grant allocation committee appointed to advise the Innovative Technology Authority on the grant applications.

31. Discussion or consideration by the Commitment Review Committee of records excluded from this chapter pursuant to subdivision 9 of § 2.2-3705.2 relating to individuals subject to commitment as sexually violent predators under Chapter 9 (§ 37.2-900 et seq.) of Title 37.2.

32. [Expired.]

33. Discussion or consideration of confidential proprietary records and trade secrets excluded from this chapter pursuant to subdivision 18 of § 2.2-3705.6.

34. Discussion or consideration by a local authority created in accordance with the Virginia Wireless Service Authorities Act (§ 15.2-5431.1 et seq.) of confidential proprietary records and trade secrets excluded from this chapter pursuant to subdivision 19 of § 2.2-3705.6.

35. Discussion or consideration by the State Board of Elections or local electoral boards of voting security matters made confidential pursuant to § 24.2-625.1.

36. Discussion or consideration by the Forensic Science Board or the Scientific Advisory Committee created pursuant to Article 2 (§ 9.1-1109 et

seq.) of Chapter 11 of Title 9.1 of records excluded from this chapter pursuant to subdivision F 1 of § 2.2-3706.

37. Discussion or consideration by the Brown v. Board of Education Scholarship Program Awards Committee of records or confidential matters excluded from this chapter pursuant to subdivision 3 of § 2.2-3705.4, and meetings of the Committee to deliberate concerning the annual maximum scholarship award, review and consider scholarship applications and requests for scholarship award renewal, and cancel, rescind, or recover scholarship awards.

38. Discussion or consideration by the Virginia Port Authority of records excluded from this chapter pursuant to subdivision 1 of § 2.2-3705.6.

39. Discussion or consideration by the Board of Trustees of the Virginia Retirement System acting pursuant to § 51.1-124.30, or the Investment Advisory Committee appointed pursuant to § 51.1-124.26, or by any local retirement system, acting pursuant to § 51.1-803 of records excluded from this chapter pursuant to subdivision 25 of § 2.2-3705.7.

40. Discussion or consideration by the Department of Business Assistance, the Virginia Economic Development Partnership, the Virginia Tourism Authority, the Tobacco Indemnification and Community Revitalization Commission, a nonprofit, nonstock corporation created pursuant to § 2.2-2240.1, or local or regional industrial or economic development authorities or organizations of records excluded from this chapter pursuant to subdivision 3 of § 2.2-3705.6.

41. Discussion or consideration by the Board of Education of records relating to the denial, suspension, or revocation of teacher licenses excluded from this chapter pursuant to subdivision 13 of § 2.2-3705.3.

42. Those portions of meetings of the Virginia Military Advisory Council, the Virginia National Defense Industrial Authority, or a local or regional military affairs organization appointed by a local governing body, during which there is discussion of records excluded from this chapter pursuant to subdivision 12 of § 2.2-3705.2.

B. No resolution, ordinance, rule, contract, regulation or motion adopted, passed or agreed to in a closed meeting shall become effective unless the public body, following the meeting, reconvenes in open meeting and takes a vote of the membership on such resolution, ordinance, rule, contract, regulation, or motion that shall have its substance reasonably identified in the open meeting.

C. Public officers improperly selected due to the failure of the public body to comply with the other provisions of this section shall be de facto officers and, as such, their official actions are valid until they obtain notice of the legal defect in their election.

D. Nothing in this section shall be construed to prevent the holding of conferences between two or more public bodies, or their representatives, but these conferences shall be subject to the same procedures for holding closed meetings as are applicable to any other public body.

E. This section shall not be construed to (i) require the disclosure of any contract between the Intervention Program Committee within the Department of Health Professions and an impaired practitioner entered into pursuant to Chapter 25.1 (§ 54.1-2515 et seq.) of Title 54.1 or (ii) require the board of directors of any authority created pursuant to the Industrial Development and Revenue Bond Act (§ 15.2-4900 et seq.), or any public body empowered to issue industrial revenue bonds by general or special law, to identify a business or industry to which subdivision A 5 applies. However, such business or industry shall be identified as a matter of public record at least 30 days prior to the actual date of the board's authorization of the sale or issuance of such bonds. (1968, c. 479, § 2.1-344; 1970, c. 456; 1973, c. 461; 1974, c. 332; 1976, cc. 467, 709; 1979, cc. 369, 684; 1980, cc. 221, 475, 476, 754; 1981, cc. 35, 471; 1982, cc. 497, 516; 1984, cc. 473, 513; 1985, c. 277; 1988, c. 891; 1989, cc. 56, 358, 478; 1990, cc. 435, 538; 1991, c. 708; 1992, c. 444; 1993, cc. 270, 499; 1995, c. 499;

1996, cc. 855, 862, 902, 905, 1046; 1997, cc. 439, 641, 785, 861; 1999, cc. 485, 518, 703, 726, 849, 867, 868; 2000, cc. 382, 400, 720, 1064; 2001, cc. 231, 844; 2002, cc. 87, 393, 455, 478, 499, 655, 715, 830; 2003, cc. 274, 291, 332, 618, 703; 2004, cc. 398, 690, 770; 2005, cc. 258, 411, 568; 2006, cc. 430, 499, 518, 560; 2007, cc. 133, 374, 566, 739; 2008, cc. 626, 633, 668, 721, 743.)

Editor's note. — Acts 2001, c. 231 amended § 2.1-344, from which this section is derived. Pursuant to § 30-152, Acts 2001, c. 231 has been given effect in this section as set out above. The 2001 amendment by c. 231 inserted "or any other matters that would involve the disclosure of information contained in a scholastic record" in the first sentence in subdivision A 2.

Acts 2002, c. 393, cl. 2, provides: "That it is the intent of the General Assembly to address the recent Virginia Supreme Court holding in the case styled Connell v. Kersey [262 Va. 154, 547 S.E.2d 228 (2002)], which held that attorneys for the Commonwealth are not 'public bodies' as defined in the Freedom of Information Act (§ 2.2-3700 et seq.), by clarifying that the Freedom of Information Act (FOIA) applies to constitutional officers and providing an exemption for attorneys for the Commonwealth."

Acts 2003, c. 291, cl. 2, provides: "That the Board of Accountancy shall promulgate regulations to implement the provisions of this act to be effective within 280 days of its enactment."

Acts 2004, c. 770, which added subdivision A 33 [now subdivision A 32], in cl. 2 provides: "That the provisions of this act shall expire on July 1, 2006."

The 2007 amendments. — The 2007 amendment by c. 133 deleted former subdivision A 18, which read: "Discussion, consideration, review, and deliberations by local community corrections resources boards regarding the placement in community diversion programs of individuals previously sentenced to state correctional facilities" and redesignated former subdivisions A 19 through A 39 as present subdivisions A 18 through A 38.

The 2007 amendment by c. 374, rewrote subdivision A 29 [now A 28].

The 2007 amendment by c. 566 added the language beginning "or discussion of reports or plans" at the end of subdivision A 20 [now A 19].

The 2007 amendment by c. 739, effective March 21, 2007, added subdivision A 40 [now A 39].

The 2008 amendments. — The 2008 amendment by c. 626 added subdivision A 40.

The 2008 amendments by cc. 633 and 743 are identical and, in subdivision A 30, deleted "by the Commonwealth Health Research Board" following "Discussion or consideration" and added clauses (i) and (ii).

The 2008 amendment by c. 668 added subdivision A 40, which was subsequently renumbered as subdivision A 41 at the direction of the Virginia Code Commission.

The 2008 amendment by c. 721 added subdivision A 40, which was subsequently renumbered as subdivision A 42 at the direction of the Virginia Code Commission.

Michie's Jurisprudence. — For related discussion, see 5A M.J. Counties, § 22.

CASE NOTES

Closed meeting to discuss previously awarded public contract improper. — Subdivision A 30 [now A 29] of § 2.2-3711 does not allow a public body to close a meeting in order to discuss the application or enforcement of the scope or terms of a previously awarded public contract. White Dog Publ., Inc. v. Culpeper County Bd. of Supervisors, 272 Va. 377, 634 S.E.2d 334, 2006 Va. LEXIS 81 (2006) (decided prior to 2007 amendments to subdivision A 29 of this section and subdivision 11 of § 2.2-3705.6).

CIRCUIT COURT OPINIONS

Requirements for holding closure. Where a city council previously voted to go into closed session in order to discuss the performance of its city manager as it related to the rising crime in the city, the circuit court ordered the depositions transcribed be opened to allow public access, as the focus of the meeting was on the city's plans and programs to meet the soaring crime issue, and not on the city manager personally; thus, said discussion did not meet the requirements for holding closed meetings. Media Gen. Operations, Inc. v. City Council of Richmond, 64 Va. Cir. 406, 2004 Va. Cir. LEXIS 191 (Richmond 2004).

Discussion of zoning application improper in executive session — Written demurrer of defendants was overruled because the complaint set forth sufficient allegations that matters not lawfully exempted under the Freedom of Information Act were discussed at a county board of supervisors' executive session. While it is proper for a county board of supervisors to go into executive session for the purpose of consultation with legal counsel on specific legal matters requiring provision of legal advice under subdivision A 7 of § 2.2-3711, this does not authorize a general discussion of the merits of a zoning application or a decision to approve the application while in executive session. Robinson v. Brugiere, 72 Va. Cir. 109, 2006 Va. Cir. LEXIS 191 (Amherst County 2006).

§ 2.2-3712. Closed meetings procedures; certification of proceedings. — A. No closed meeting shall be held unless the public body proposing to convene such meeting has taken an affirmative recorded vote in an open meeting approving a motion that (i) identifies the subject matter, (ii) states the purpose of the meeting and (iii) makes specific reference to the applicable exemption from open meeting requirements provided in § 2.2-3707 or subsection A of § 2.2-3711. The matters contained in such motion shall be set forth in detail in the minutes of the open meeting. A general reference to the provisions of this chapter, the authorized exemptions from open meeting requirements, or the subject matter of the closed meeting shall not be sufficient to satisfy the requirements for holding a closed meeting.

B. The notice provisions of this chapter shall not apply to closed meetings of any public body held solely for the purpose of interviewing candidates for the position of chief administrative officer. Prior to any such closed meeting for the purpose of interviewing candidates, the public body shall announce in an open meeting that such closed meeting shall be held at a disclosed or undisclosed location within fifteen days thereafter.

C. The public body holding a closed meeting shall restrict its discussion during the closed meeting only to those matters specifically exempted from the provisions of this chapter and identified in the motion required by subsection A.

D. At the conclusion of any closed meeting, the public body holding such meeting shall immediately reconvene in an open meeting and shall take a roll call or other recorded vote to be included in the minutes of that body, certifying that to the best of each member's knowledge (i) only public business matters lawfully exempted from open meeting requirements under this chapter and (ii) only such public business matters as were identified in the motion by which the closed meeting was convened were heard, discussed or considered in the meeting by the public body. Any member of the public body who believes that there was a departure from the requirements of clauses (i) and (ii), shall so state prior to the vote, indicating the substance of the departure that, in his judgment, has taken place. The statement shall be recorded in the minutes of the public body.

E. Failure of the certification required by subsection D to receive the affirmative vote of a majority of the members of the public body present during a meeting shall not affect the validity or confidentiality of such meeting with respect to matters considered therein in compliance with the provisions of this chapter. The recorded vote and any statement made in connection therewith, shall upon proper authentication, constitute evidence in any proceeding brought to enforce the provisions of this chapter.

F. A public body may permit nonmembers to attend a closed meeting if such persons are deemed necessary or if their presence will reasonably aid the public body in its consideration of a topic that is a subject of the meeting.

G. Except as specifically authorized by law, in no event may any public body take action on matters discussed in any closed meeting, except at an open meeting for which notice was given as required by § 2.2-3707.

H. Minutes may be taken during closed meetings of a public body, but shall not be required. Such minutes shall not be subject to mandatory public disclosure. (1989, c. 358, § 2.1-344.1; 1999, cc. 703, 726; 2001, c. 844.)

CASE NOTES

Nonmember attendance. — Doctor involved in medical license revocation proceeding did not have the doctor's due process rights violated when the board allowed people who were not members of the state board of medicine to attend the board's closed session. The board, pursuant to subsection F of § 2.2-3712, was specifically authorized to permit nonmembers to attend a closed meeting if such persons were deemed necessary or if their presence would reasonably aid the public body in its consideration of a topic, and the doctor did not show prejudice from that decision. Vuyyuru v. Va. Bd. of Med., — Va. App. —, — S.E.2d —, 2008 Va. App. LEXIS 30 (Jan. 15, 2008).

Closed meeting to discuss previously awarded public contract improper. — Subdivision A 30 [now A 29] of § 2.2-3711 does not allow a public body to close a meeting in order to discuss the application or enforcement of the scope or terms of a previously awarded public contract. White Dog Publ., Inc. v. Culpeper County Bd. of Supervisors, 272 Va. 377, 634 S.E.2d 334, 2006 Va. LEXIS 81 (2006).

Attorney's fees and costs. — As newspaper publishers "substantially prevailed" in their suit against a county board of supervisors for violating the Virginia Freedom of Information Act, § 2.2-3700 et seq., by holding a closed meeting, they were entitled to an award of attorney's fees and reasonable costs under subsection D of § 2.2-3713. The fact that the board's violation was not willful and knowing was not a "special circumstance" that would make such an award unjust. White Dog Publ., Inc. v. Culpeper County Bd. of Supervisors, 272 Va. 377, 634 S.E.2d 334, 2006 Va. LEXIS 81 (2006).

§ 2.2-3713. Proceedings for enforcement of chapter. — A. Any person, including the attorney for the Commonwealth acting in his official or individual capacity, denied the rights and privileges conferred by this chapter may proceed to enforce such rights and privileges by filing a petition for mandamus or injunction, supported by an affidavit showing good cause. Venue for the petition shall be addressed as follows:

1. In a case involving a local public body, to the general district court or circuit court of the county or city from which the public body has been elected or appointed to serve and in which such rights and privileges were so denied;

2. In a case involving a regional public body, to the general district or circuit court of the county or city where the principal business office of such body is located; and

3. In a case involving a board, bureau, commission, authority, district, institution, or agency of the state government, including a public institution of higher education, or a standing or other committee of the General Assembly, to the general district court or the circuit court of the residence of the aggrieved party or of the City of Richmond.

B. In any action brought before a general district court, a corporate petitioner may appear through its officer, director or managing agent without the assistance of counsel, notwithstanding any provision of law or Rule of the Supreme Court of Virginia to the contrary.

C. The petition for mandamus or injunction shall be heard within seven days of the date when the same is made. However, any petition made outside of the regular terms of the circuit court of a county that is included in a judicial circuit with another county or counties, the hearing on the petition shall be given precedence on the docket of such court over all cases that are not otherwise given precedence by law.

D. The petition shall allege with reasonable specificity the circumstances of the denial of the rights and privileges conferred by this chapter. A single instance of denial of the rights and privileges conferred by this chapter shall be sufficient to invoke the remedies granted herein. If the court finds the denial to be in violation of the provisions of this chapter, the petitioner shall be entitled to recover reasonable costs and attorneys' fees from the public body if the petitioner substantially prevails on the merits of the case, unless special circumstances would make an award unjust. In making this determination, a court may consider, among other things, the reliance of a public body on an opinion of the Attorney General or a decision of a court that substantially supports the public body's position.

E. In any action to enforce the provisions of this chapter, the public body shall bear the burden of proof to establish an exemption by a preponderance of the evidence. Any failure by a public body to follow the procedures established by this chapter shall be presumed to be a violation of this chapter.

F. Failure by any person to request and receive notice of the time and place of meetings as provided in § 2.2-3707 shall not preclude any person from enforcing his rights and privileges conferred by this chapter. (1968, c. 479, § 2.1-346; 1976, c. 709; 1978, c. 826; 1989, c. 358; 1990, c. 217; 1996, c. 578; 1999, cc. 703, 726; 2001, c. 844; 2007, c. 560.)

The 2007 amendments. — The 2007 amendment by c. 560 rewrote subsections A and B; and added subsection F.

Law Review. — For a review of administrative procedure in Virginia for year 1999, see 33 U. Rich. L. Rev. 727 (1999).

CASE NOTES

Editor's note. — Most of the cases below were decided under former Title 2.1 or prior provisions.

This section is unconstitutional as applied to State Corporation Commission. — Where petitioner invoked jurisdiction of circuit court, and filed petition for writ of mandamus against State Corporation Commission (SCC), trial court correctly ruled that this section was not constitutional as applied to the SCC because of jurisdictional limitations of Va. Const., Art. IX, § 4. Framers of Va. Const., Art. IX, § 4, intended that Supreme Court have exclusive jurisdiction over all challenges to all actions of the SCC, both judgmental and ministerial, and issuance of writ of mandamus directing SCC to reverse its action in refusing petitioner's demand for access to official records was equivalent to entry of injunction restraining SCC in the performance of its official duties. Atlas Underwriters, Ltd. v. SCC, 237 Va. 45, 375 S.E.2d 733 (1989).

Extraordinary relief not to be casually or perfunctorily ordered. — Under this section, a single violation is sufficient to permit the grant of relief based on the inference that future violations will occur, but such an extraordinary and drastic remedy is not to be casually or perfunctorily ordered. Nageotte v. Board of Supvrs., 223 Va. 259, 288 S.E.2d 423 (1982).

The petition need not contain an allegation of "irreparable injury." WTAR Radio-TV Corp. v. City Council, 216 Va. 892, 223 S.E.2d 895 (1976).

Inference insufficient to justify sanction. — A previous course of conduct might raise an inference that such conduct would be repeated but a mere inference did not support an apprehension with reasonable probability such as would have justified imposition of a judicial sanction against a legislative body. WTAR Radio-TV Corp. v. City Council, 216 Va. 892, 223 S.E.2d 895 (1976).

When injunctive relief, etc., not justified. — The 1976 amendment to this section in effect permits a trial court to infer from a single violation that future violations will follow. However, where the court expresses the view that there will be no future violations, there is no justification for injunctive relief. Marsh v. Richmond Newspapers, Inc., 223 Va. 245, 288 S.E.2d 415 (1982).

Where violations occur under this chapter, but are not willful and knowing violations or violations that would invalidate board actions with which concerned citizens who brought suit were concerned, such violations do not justify injunctive relief or the award of attorneys' fees and costs. Nageotte v. Board of Supvrs., 223 Va. 259, 288 S.E.2d 423 (1982).

Injunctive relief discretionary and not granted unless violation willful, knowing, and substantial. — Although this section permits injunctive relief upon proof of a single violation of the act, based upon the inference that future violations will occur, such relief remains discretionary with the court and it will not be granted unless the court finds that the violation was willful, knowing, and substantial. Hale v. Washington County School Bd., 241 Va. 76, 400 S.E.2d 175 (1991).

Attorney's fees and costs awarded. — City airport authority's response to appellant's request for information under the Freedom of Information Act, § 2.2-3700 et seq., did not comply with the FOIA as it did not timely make one of the four statutorily required responses under § 2.2-3704 but merely stated that the matter had been referred to its legal counsel or to the transportation security administration; appellant was entitled to attorney's fees under subsection D of § 2.2-3713 as the trial court's judgment was reversed on appeal. Fenter v.

Norfolk Airport Auth., 274 Va. 524, 649 S.E.2d 704, 2007 Va. LEXIS 102 (2007).

Attorney's fees and costs erroneously denied. — As newspaper publishers "substantially prevailed" in their suit against a county board of supervisors for violating the Virginia Freedom of Information Act, they were entitled to an award of attorney's fees and reasonable costs under subsection D of § 2.2-3713. The fact that the board's violation was not willful and knowing was not a "special circumstance" that would make such an award unjust. White Dog Publ., Inc. v. Culpeper County Bd. of Supervisors, 272 Va. 377, 634 S.E.2d 334, 2006 Va. LEXIS 81 (2006).

Mandamus erroneously denied. — Landowner, who alleged a violation of the rights and privileges afforded by the Virginia Freedom of Information Act, and seeking relief by mandamus pursuant to subsection A, was not required to prove a lack of an adequate remedy at law, nor could his mandamus proceeding be barred on the ground that there might have been some other remedy at law available; moreover, because the circuit court did not reach the issue whether a sales brochure in connection with a highway construction project was subject to disclosure under the Act, the matter was remanded for further consideration of that issue and a determination as to whether the landowner was entitled to reasonable costs and attorneys' fees. Cartwright v. Commonwealth Transp. Comm'r, 270 Va. 58, 613 S.E.2d 449, 2005 Va. LEXIS 62 (2005).

Newspaper publishers that sued a county board of supervisors for holding a closed meeting in violation of subsection A of § 2.2-3712 had been entitled to a writ of mandamus, as subdivision A 30 [now A 29] of § 2.2-3711 did not allow the board to close the meeting in order to discuss the application or enforcement of a previously awarded public contract. White Dog Publ., Inc. v. Culpeper County Bd. of Supervisors, 272 Va. 377, 634 S.E.2d 334, 2006 Va. LEXIS 81 (2006).

§ 2.2-3714. Violations and penalties. — In a proceeding commenced against members of public bodies under § 2.2-3713 for a violation of § 2.2-3704, 2.2-3705.1 through 2.2-3705.8, 2.2-3706, 2.2-3707, 2.2-3708, 2.2-3708.1, 2.2-3710, 2.2-3711 or 2.2-3712, the court, if it finds that a violation was willfully and knowingly made, shall impose upon such member in his individual capacity, whether a writ of mandamus or injunctive relief is awarded or not, a civil penalty of not less than $250 nor more than $1,000, which amount shall be paid into the State Literary Fund. For a second or subsequent violation, such civil penalty shall be not less than $1,000 nor more than $2,500. (1976, c. 467, § 2.1-346.1; 1978, c. 826; 1984, c. 252; 1989, c. 358; 1996, c. 578; 1999, cc. 703, 726; 2001, c. 844; 2003, c. 319; 2004, c. 690; 2008, cc. 233, 789.)

The 2008 amendments. — The 2008 amendments by cc. 233 and 789 are identical, and deleted a section symbol preceding "2.2-3704" and "2.2-3712"; and inserted "2.2-3708.1" in the first sentence.

Michie's Jurisprudence. — For related discussion, see 5A M.J. Counties, § 22.

CASE NOTES

Editor's note. — The case below was decided under former Title 2.1 or prior provisions.

The evidentiary burden of a preponderance of the evidence is applicable to the proof of violations of this section. RF & P Corp. v. Little, 247 Va. 309, 440 S.E.2d 908 (1994).

The evidence was sufficient to support the trial court's finding that the chairman of the Virginia Retirement System Board willfully and knowingly violated Virginia Freedom of Information Act. RF & P Corp. v. Little, 247 Va. 309, 440 S.E.2d 908 (1994).

CHAPTER 38.

Government Data Collection and Dissemination Practices Act.

§ 2.2-3800. Short title; findings; principles of information practice. — A. This chapter may be cited as the "Government Data Collection and Dissemination Practices Act."

B. The General Assembly finds that:

1. An individual's privacy is directly affected by the extensive collection, maintenance, use and dissemination of personal information;

2. The increasing use of computers and sophisticated information technology has greatly magnified the harm that can occur from these practices;

3. An individual's opportunities to secure employment, insurance, credit, and his right to due process, and other legal protections are endangered by the misuse of certain of these personal information systems; and

4. In order to preserve the rights guaranteed a citizen in a free society, legislation is necessary to establish procedures to govern information systems containing records on individuals.

C. Recordkeeping agencies of the Commonwealth and political subdivisions shall adhere to the following principles of information practice to ensure safeguards for personal privacy:

1. There shall be no personal information system whose existence is secret.

2. Information shall not be collected unless the need for it has been clearly established in advance.

3. Information shall be appropriate and relevant to the purpose for which it has been collected.

4. Information shall not be obtained by fraudulent or unfair means.

5. Information shall not be used unless it is accurate and current.

6. There shall be a prescribed procedure for an individual to learn the purpose for which information has been recorded and particulars about its use and dissemination.

7. There shall be a clearly prescribed and uncomplicated procedure for an individual to correct, erase or amend inaccurate, obsolete or irrelevant information.

8. Any agency holding personal information shall assure its reliability and take precautions to prevent its misuse. On and after July 1, 2004, no agency shall display the social security number of a data subject on a student or employee identification card, except that for universities and colleges that have such a prevention plan for misuse of personal information in place on or before July 1, 2004, in compliance with this section, the date shall be January 1, 2005. On and after July 1, 2006, no agency shall display an individual's entire social security number on any student or employee identification card.

9. There shall be a clearly prescribed procedure to prevent personal information collected for one purpose from being used for another purpose.

10. The Commonwealth or any agency or political subdivision thereof shall not collect personal information except as explicitly or implicitly authorized by law.

D. After July 1, 2004, no agency, as defined in § 42.1-77, shall send or deliver or cause to be sent or delivered, any letter, envelope or package that displays a social security number on the face of the mailing envelope or package or from which a social security number is visible, whether on the outside or inside of the mailing envelope or package. (1976, c. 597, §§ 2.1-377, 2.1-378; 1987, c. 506; 2001, c. 844; 2003, cc. 791, 914, 918, 927.)

Cross references. — As to records that are excluded from the provisions of the Virginia Freedom of Information Act, see §§ 2.2-3705.1 through 2.2-3705.8. As to the requirement to furnish a copy of this section to every patient included in the statewide cancer registry, see § 32.1-71.01. As to releases of information to parties involved in administrative proceedings pursuant to § 63.2-1900 et seq., relating to child support enforcement, notwithstanding the provisions of § 2.2-3800 et seq., see § 63.2-103.

Editor's note. — Acts 2001, c. 844, cl. 10, effective October 1, 2001, provides: "That any reference in the Code of Virginia or the Acts of Assembly to the Privacy Protection Act of 1976 shall be construed to mean the Government Data Collection and Dissemination Practices Act."

Law Review. — For 2000 survey of Virginia technology law, see 34 U. Rich. L. Rev. 1051 (2000).

CASE NOTES

Government Data Collection and Dissemination Practices Act does not apply to constitutional officers. — Court held that constitutional officer does not come within the definition of "agency" in § 2.2-3801 of the Government Data Collection and Dissemination Practices Act, §§ 2.2-3800 to 2.2-3809, therefore, the act did not apply to a city treasurer who allegedly gave a newspaper reporter information from a former city employee's employment file. The case was decided before the 2003 amendment to § 2.2-3801 specifically included constitutional officers in the definition of agency. Carraway v. Hill, 265 Va. 20, 574 S.E.2d 274, 2003 Va. LEXIS 7 (2003).

Chapter does not render personal information confidential. Indeed, the act does not generally prohibit the dissemination of information. Instead, it requires certain procedural steps to be taken in the collection, maintenance, use, and dissemination of such data. Hinderliter v. Humphries, 224 Va. 439, 297 S.E.2d 684 (1982) (decided under former Title 2.1 provisions).

Real estate assessment information. — City treasurer's reliance on this act in denying a request under the Freedom of Information Act (see now § 2.2-3700 et seq.) for certain real estate tax information was totally misplaced, because the act specifically excludes real estate assessment information. Associated Tax Serv., Inc. v. Fitzpatrick, 236 Va. 181, 372 S.E.2d 625 (1988) (decided under former Title 2.1 provisions).

OPINIONS OF THE ATTORNEY GENERAL

Town may install surveillance cameras and audio monitoring equipment at town recreation center. — The Government Data Collection and Dissemination Practices Act permits the installation of surveillance cameras and audio monitoring equipment in and on the premises of a town recreation center, along with the clearly visible notices advising of such surveillance. See opinion of Attorney General to Mr. William J. McGhee, Town Attorney for the Town of Christiansburg, 00-044 (1/7/02).

§ 2.2-3801. (Effective until July 1, 2009) Definitions. — As used in this chapter, unless the context requires a different meaning:

1. *"Information system"* means the total components and operations of a record-keeping process, including information collected or managed by means of computer networks and the Internet, whether automated or manual, containing personal information and the name, personal number, or other identifying particulars of a data subject.

2. *"Personal information"* means all information that describes, locates or indexes anything about an individual including his real or personal property holdings derived from tax returns, and his education, financial transactions,

medical history, ancestry, religion, political ideology, criminal or employment record, or that affords a basis for inferring personal characteristics, such as finger and voice prints, photographs, or things done by or to such individual; and the record of his presence, registration, or membership in an organization or activity, or admission to an institution. "Personal information" shall not include routine information maintained for the purpose of internal office administration whose use could not be such as to affect adversely any data subject nor does the term include real estate assessment information.

3. *"Data subject"* means an individual about whom personal information is indexed or may be located under his name, personal number, or other identifiable particulars, in an information system.

4. *"Disseminate"* means to release, transfer, or otherwise communicate information orally, in writing, or by electronic means.

5. *"Purge"* means to obliterate information completely from the transient, permanent, or archival records of an organization.

6. *"Agency"* means any agency, authority, board, department, division, commission, institution, bureau, or like governmental entity of the Commonwealth or of any unit of local government including counties, cities, towns, regional governments, and the departments thereof, and includes constitutional officers, except as otherwise expressly provided by law. "Agency" shall also include any entity, whether public or private, with which any of the foregoing has entered into a contractual relationship for the operation of a system of personal information to accomplish an agency function. Any such entity included in this definition by reason of a contractual relationship shall only be deemed an agency as relates to services performed pursuant to that contractual relationship, provided that if any such entity is a consumer reporting agency, it shall be deemed to have satisfied all of the requirements of this chapter if it fully complies with the requirements of the Federal Fair Credit Reporting Act as applicable to services performed pursuant to such contractual relationship. (1976, c. 597, § 2.1-379; 1983, c. 372; 1999, c. 41; 2001, c. 844; 2003, c. 272; 2006, c. 474.)

Section set out twice. — The section above is effective until July 1, 2009. For the version of this section effective July 1, 2009, see the following section, also numbered 2.2-3801.

CASE NOTES

Real estate assessment information. — City treasurer's reliance on this act in denying a request under the Freedom of Information Act (see now § 2.2-3700 et seq.) for certain real estate tax information was totally misplaced, because the act specifically excludes real estate assessment information. Associated Tax Serv., Inc. v. Fitzpatrick, 236 Va. 181, 372 S.E.2d 625 (1988) (decided under former provisions).

"Agency" defined. — The court held that constitutional officer does not come within the definition of "agency" for purposes of the Government Data Collection and Dissemination Practices Act; therefore, the act did not apply to a city treasurer who allegedly gave a newspaper reporter information from a former city employee's employment file. The case was decided before the 2003 amendment to § 2.2-3801 specifically included constitutional officers in the definition of agency. Carraway v. Hill, 265 Va. 20, 574 S.E.2d 274, 2003 Va. LEXIS 7 (2003).

Individuals may be sued as representatives of agencies. — The term "agency" under this statute also includes representatives, or agents, of those agencies and a plaintiff may, therefore, bring suit against individual public employees who are subject to the act in their official capacities, as representatives of their respective agencies. Mansoor v. County of Albemarle, 124 F. Supp. 2d 367, 2000 U.S. Dist. LEXIS 18612 (W.D. Va. 2000) (decided under former Title 2.1).

OPINIONS OF THE ATTORNEY GENERAL

The definition of the term "agency" includes a local constitutional officer. See opinion of Attorney General to The Honorable Barbara O. Carraway, Treasurer for the City of Chesapeake, 01-121 (4/4/02).

Disclosure to police of identity and presence of residents at a spouse abuse shelter. — Citizens Against Family Violence (CAFV) may provide law enforcement officials with information regarding the identity and presence of residents at a spouse abuse shelter operated by CAFV where (1) the police possess and wish to serve a criminal warrant, a civil warrant, or a subpoena or (2) the police do not have a warrant but nevertheless wish to question the resident in connection with an ongoing criminal investigation. See opinion of Attorney General to The Honorable Ward L. Armstrong, Member, House of Delegates, 02-005 (5/29/02).

§ **2.2-3801. (Effective July 1, 2009) Definitions.** — As used in this chapter, unless the context requires a different meaning:

"Agency" means any agency, authority, board, department, division, commission, institution, bureau, or like governmental entity of the Commonwealth or of any unit of local government including counties, cities, towns, regional governments, and the departments thereof, and includes constitutional officers, except as otherwise expressly provided by law. "Agency" shall also include any entity, whether public or private, with which any of the foregoing has entered into a contractual relationship for the operation of a system of personal information to accomplish an agency function. Any such entity included in this definition by reason of a contractual relationship shall only be deemed an agency as relates to services performed pursuant to that contractual relationship, provided that if any such entity is a consumer reporting agency, it shall be deemed to have satisfied all of the requirements of this chapter if it fully complies with the requirements of the Federal Fair Credit Reporting Act as applicable to services performed pursuant to such contractual relationship.

"Data subject" means an individual about whom personal information is indexed or may be located under his name, personal number, or other identifiable particulars, in an information system.

"Disseminate" means to release, transfer, or otherwise communicate information orally, in writing, or by electronic means.

"Information system" means the total components and operations of a record-keeping process, including information collected or managed by means of computer networks and the Internet, whether automated or manual, containing personal information and the name, personal number, or other identifying particulars of a data subject.

"Personal information" means all information that (i) describes, locates or indexes anything about an individual including, but not limited to, his social security number, driver's license number, agency-issued identification number, student identification number, real or personal property holdings derived from tax returns, and his education, financial transactions, medical history, ancestry, religion, political ideology, criminal or employment record, or (ii) affords a basis for inferring personal characteristics, such as finger and voice prints, photographs, or things done by or to such individual; and the record of his presence, registration, or membership in an organization or activity, or admission to an institution. "Personal information" shall not include routine information maintained for the purpose of internal office administration whose use could not be such as to affect adversely any data subject nor does the term include real estate assessment information.

"Purge" means to obliterate information completely from the transient, permanent, or archival records of an organization. (1976, c. 597, § 2.1-379; 1983, c. 372; 1999, c. 41; 2001, c. 844; 2003, c. 272; 2006, c. 474; 2008, cc. 840, 843.)

Section set out twice. — The section above is effective July 1, 2009. For the version of this section effective until July 1, 2009, see the preceding section, also numbered 2.2-3801.

Editor's note. — Acts 2008, cc. 840 and 843, cl. 2 provides: "That the provisions of this act shall become effective on July 1, 2009, except that the third and fourth enactments of this act shall become effective on July 1, 2008."

Acts 2008, cc. 840 and 843, cl. 3 provides: "That every state agency subject to the provisions of the Government Data Collection and Dissemination Practices Act (§ 2.2-3800 et seq.) shall conduct an analysis and review of its collection and use of social security numbers, to be completed by October 1, 2008. Each such agency shall submit, no later than October 1, 2008, to the chairmen of the Freedom of Information Advisory Council and the Joint Commission on Technology and Science, on forms developed by the Council and the Commission, (i) a list of (a) all state or federal statutes authorizing or requiring the collection of social security numbers by such agency and (b) instances where social security numbers are voluntarily collected or (ii) in the absence of statutory authority to collect social security numbers, written justification explaining why continued collection is essential to its transaction of public business. In conducting such a review, each agency shall be encouraged to consider whether such collection and use is essential for its transaction of public business and to find alternative means of identifying individuals. The chairmen of the Council and the Commission may withhold from public disclosure any such lists or portions of lists as legislative working papers, if it deems that the public dissemination of such lists or portions of lists would cause a potential invasion of privacy."

Acts 2008, cc. 840 and 843, cl. 4 provides: "That every county and city, and any town with a population in excess of 15,000 shall, no later than September 10, 2008, provide the Virginia Municipal League or the Virginia Association of Counties, as appropriate, information on a form agreed upon by the Virginia Municipal League, the Virginia Association of Counties and staff of the Freedom of Information Advisory Council and the Joint Commission on Technology and Science identifying (i) all state or federal statutes authorizing or requiring the collection of social security numbers by such county, city or town and (ii) instances where social security numbers are voluntarily collected or (iii) in the absence of statutory authority to collect social security numbers, written justification explaining why continued collection is essential to its transaction of public business. In conducting such a review, each such county, city or town shall be encouraged to consider whether such collection and use is essential for its transaction of public business and to find alternative means of identifying individuals. The information required by this enactment shall be submitted no later than October 1, 2008 to the chairmen of the Freedom of Information Advisory Council and the Joint Commission on Technology and Science, on forms developed by the Council and the Commission."

The 2008 amendments. — The 2008 amendments by cc. 840 and 843, effective July 1, 2009, are identical, and deleted subdivision designators, arranged definitions in alphabetical order, and in the definition for "Personal information" inserted clause (i) and (ii) designators and made a related change, inserted "but not limited to" and "social security number, driver's license number, agency-issued identification number, student identification number" in clause (i).

§ 2.2-3802. Systems to which chapter inapplicable. — The provisions of this chapter shall not apply to personal information systems:

1. Maintained by any court of the Commonwealth;
2. Which may exist in publications of general circulation;
3. Contained in the Criminal Justice Information System as defined in §§ 9.1-126 through 9.1-137 or in the Sex Offender and Crimes Against Minors Registry maintained by the Department of State Police pursuant to Chapter 9 (§ 9.1-900 et seq.) of Title 9.1, except to the extent that information is required to be posted on the Internet pursuant to § 9.1-913;
4. Contained in the Virginia Juvenile Justice Information System as defined in §§ 16.1-222 through 16.1-225;
5. Maintained by agencies concerning persons required by law to be licensed in the Commonwealth to engage in the practice of any profession, in which case the names and addresses of persons applying for or possessing the license may be disseminated upon written request to a person engaged in the profession or business of offering professional educational materials or courses for the sole purpose of providing the licensees or applicants for licenses with informational materials relating solely to available professional educational materials or

courses, provided the disseminating agency is reasonably assured that the use of the information will be so limited;

6. Maintained by the Parole Board, the Crime Commission, the Judicial Inquiry and Review Commission, the Virginia Racing Commission, and the Department of Alcoholic Beverage Control;

7. Maintained by the Department of State Police; the police department of the Chesapeake Bay Bridge and Tunnel Commission; police departments of cities, counties, and towns; and the campus police departments of public institutions of higher education as established by Chapter 17 (§ 23-232 et seq.) of Title 23, and that deal with investigations and intelligence gathering relating to criminal activity; and maintained by local departments of social services regarding alleged cases of child abuse or neglect while such cases are also subject to an ongoing criminal prosecution;

8. Maintained by the Virginia Port Authority as provided in § 62.1-134.1 or 62.1-132.4;

9. Maintained by the Virginia Tourism Authority in connection with or as a result of the promotion of travel or tourism in the Commonwealth, in which case names and addresses of persons requesting information on those subjects may be disseminated upon written request to a person engaged in the business of providing travel services or distributing travel information, provided the Virginia Tourism Authority is reasonably assured that the use of the information will be so limited;

10. Maintained by the Division of Consolidated Laboratory Services of the Department of General Services and the Department of Forensic Science, which deal with scientific investigations relating to criminal activity or suspected criminal activity, except to the extent that § 9.1-1104 may apply;

11. Maintained by the Department of Corrections that deal with investigations and intelligence gathering by persons acting under the provisions of § 53.1-16; and

12. Maintained by the Department of the State Internal Auditor or internal audit departments of state agencies or institutions that deal with communications and investigations relating to the State Employee Fraud, Waste and Abuse Hotline. (1976, c. 597, § 2.1-384; 1979, c. 685; 1980, c. 752; 1981, cc. 461, 464, 504, 589; 1982, c. 225; 1983, c. 289; 1984, c. 750; 1986, c. 62; 1990, c. 825; 1992, c. 620; 1993, cc. 205, 963; 1996, cc. 154, 590, 598, 952; 2001, c. 844; 2003, c. 406; 2005, cc. 868, 881; 2006, cc. 196, 857, 914.)

Law Review. — For article discussing decisions of Virginia courts dealing with state administrative procedures between June 1, 2002 and June 1, 2003, see U. Rich. L. Rev. 39 (2003).

§ 2.2-3803. Administration of systems including personal information; Internet privacy policy; exceptions. — A. Any agency maintaining an information system that includes personal information shall:

1. Collect, maintain, use, and disseminate only that personal information permitted or required by law to be so collected, maintained, used, or disseminated, or necessary to accomplish a proper purpose of the agency;

2. Collect information to the greatest extent feasible from the data subject directly;

3. Establish categories for maintaining personal information to operate in conjunction with confidentiality requirements and access controls;

4. Maintain information in the system with accuracy, completeness, timeliness, and pertinence as necessary to ensure fairness in determinations relating to a data subject;

5. Make no dissemination to another system without (i) specifying requirements for security and usage including limitations on access thereto, and (ii) receiving reasonable assurances that those requirements and limitations will

be observed. This subdivision shall not apply, however, to a dissemination made by an agency to an agency in another state, district or territory of the United States where the personal information is requested by the agency of such other state, district or territory in connection with the application of the data subject therein for a service, privilege or right under the laws thereof, nor shall this apply to information transmitted to family advocacy representatives of the United States Armed Forces in accordance with subsection N of § 63.2-1503;

6. Maintain a list of all persons or organizations having regular access to personal information in the information system;

7. Maintain for a period of three years or until such time as the personal information is purged, whichever is shorter, a complete and accurate record, including identity and purpose, of every access to any personal information in a system, including the identity of any persons or organizations not having regular access authority but excluding access by the personnel of the agency wherein data is put to service for the purpose for which it is obtained;

8. Take affirmative action to establish rules of conduct and inform each person involved in the design, development, operation, or maintenance of the system, or the collection or use of any personal information contained therein, about all the requirements of this chapter, the rules and procedures, including penalties for noncompliance, of the agency designed to assure compliance with such requirements;

9. Establish appropriate safeguards to secure the system from any reasonably foreseeable threat to its security; and

10. Collect no personal information concerning the political or religious beliefs, affiliations, and activities of data subjects that is maintained, used or disseminated in or by any information system operated by any agency unless authorized explicitly by statute or ordinance.

B. Every public body, as defined in § 2.2-3701, that has an Internet website associated with that public body shall develop an Internet privacy policy and an Internet privacy policy statement that explains the policy to the public. The policy shall be consistent with the requirements of this chapter. The statement shall be made available on the public body's website in a conspicuous manner. The Secretary of Technology or his designee shall provide guidelines for developing the policy and the statement, and each public body shall tailor the policy and the statement to reflect the information practices of the individual public body. At minimum, the policy and the statement shall address (i) what information, including personally identifiable information, will be collected, if any; (ii) whether any information will be automatically collected simply by accessing the website and, if so, what information; (iii) whether the website automatically places a computer file, commonly referred to as a "cookie," on the Internet user's computer and, if so, for what purpose; and (iv) how the collected information is being used or will be used.

C. Notwithstanding the provisions of subsection A, the Virginia Retirement System may disseminate information as to the retirement status or benefit eligibility of any employee covered by the Virginia Retirement System, the Judicial Retirement System, the State Police Officers' Retirement System, or the Virginia Law Officers' Retirement System, to the chief executive officer or personnel officers of the state or local agency by which he is employed.

D. Notwithstanding the provisions of subsection A, the Department of Social Services may disseminate client information to the Department of Taxation for the purposes of providing specified tax information as set forth in clause (ii) of subsection C of § 58.1-3. (1976, c. 597, § 2.1-380; 1978, c. 409, § 2.1-384.1; 1989, c. 547; 2000, cc. 405, 500; 911; 2001, c. 844; 2002, c. 747; 2006, cc. 159, 590.)

Editor's note. — Acts 2006, cc. 159 and 590, cl. 2, provide: "That in the implementation of the provisions of this act the Department of Social Services shall only provide information on customers on file with the Department to the Department of Taxation and the Department of Taxation shall only provide information on taxpayers who have claimed the federal earned income tax credit for the taxable year to the Department of Social Services."

Law Review. — For survey on legal issues involving children in Virginia for 1989, see 23 U. Rich. L. Rev. 705 (1989).

CASE NOTES

Chapter does not render personal information confidential. Indeed, the act does not generally prohibit the dissemination of information. Instead, it requires certain procedural steps to be taken in the collection, maintenance, use, and dissemination of such data. Hinderliter v. Humphries, 224 Va. 439, 297 S.E.2d 684 (1982) (decided under former Title 2.1).

Burden is on plaintiff to establish lack of necessity or improper purpose for dissemination. Hinderliter v. Humphries, 224 Va. 439, 297 S.E.2d 684 (1982) (decided under former Title 2.1).

Since public officials presumed to obey the law. — There is a presumption that public officials will obey the law, and there is nothing in this act that reverses such presumption or imposes the ultimate burden of proof on defendants sued under it. Consequently, the presumption stands until rebutted by contrary evidence. Hinderliter v. Humphries, 224 Va. 439, 297 S.E.2d 684 (1982) (decided under former Title 2.1).

The Government Data Collection and Dissemination Practices Act, does not apply to constitutional officers. — Constitutional officer does not come within the definition of "agency" in § 2.2-3801, therefore, the act did not apply to a city treasurer who allegedly gave a newspaper reporter information from a former city employee's employment file, and the city treasurer did not violate subdivision A 1 of § 2.2-3803. Carraway v. Hill, 265 Va. 20, 574 S.E.2d 274, 2003 Va. LEXIS 7 (2003) (decided prior to 2003 amendment to § 2.2-3801).

CIRCUIT COURT OPINIONS

Employment record. — Because a report and investigatory materials were related to an employee's employment record and because the report plainly involved an employment discrimination complaint about things done by the employee that adversely affected him, § 2.2-3803 of the Virginia Government Data Collection and Dissemination Act, required disclosure by the county to the employee of that personal information, including the identity of the complainants, informants, and others involved in the investigation. McChrystal v. Fairfax County Bd. of Supervisors, 67 Va. Cir. 171, 2005 Va. Cir. LEXIS 26 (Fairfax County 2005).

§ 2.2-3804. Military recruiters to have access to student information, school buildings, etc. — If a public school board or public institution of higher education provides access to its buildings and grounds and the student information directory to persons or groups that make students aware of occupational or educational options, the board or institution shall provide access on the same basis to official recruiting representatives of the armed forces of the Commonwealth and the United States for the purpose of informing students of educational and career opportunities available in the armed forces. (1981, c. 377, § 2.1-380.1; 2001, c. 844.)

§ 2.2-3805. Dissemination of reports. — Any agency maintaining an information system that disseminates statistical reports or research findings based on personal information drawn from its system, or from other systems shall:

1. Make available to any data subject or group, without revealing trade secrets, methodology and materials necessary to validate statistical analysis, and

2. Make no materials available for independent analysis without guarantees that no personal information will be used in any way that might prejudice judgments about any data subject. (1976, c. 597, § 2.1-381; 2001, c. 844.)

CASE NOTES

Editor's note. — The case below was decided under former Title 2.1 or prior provisions.

Burden is on plaintiff to establish lack of necessity or improper purpose for dissemination. Hinderliter v. Humphries, 224 Va. 439, 297 S.E.2d 684 (1982).

Since public officials presumed to obey the law. — There is a presumption that public officials will obey the law, and there is nothing in this act that reverses such presumption or imposes the ultimate burden of proof on defendants sued under it. Consequently, the presumption stands until rebutted by contrary evidence. Hinderliter v. Humphries, 224 Va. 439, 297 S.E.2d 684 (1982).

§ 2.2-3806. Rights of data subjects. — A. Any agency maintaining personal information shall:

1. Inform an individual who is asked to supply personal information about himself whether he is legally required, or may refuse, to supply the information requested, and also of any specific consequences that are known to the agency of providing or not providing the information.

2. Give notice to a data subject of the possible dissemination of part or all of this information to another agency, nongovernmental organization or system not having regular access authority, and indicate the use for which it is intended, and the specific consequences for the individual, which are known to the agency, of providing or not providing the information. However documented permission for dissemination in the hands of the other agency or organization shall satisfy the requirement of this subdivision. The notice may be given on applications or other data collection forms prepared by data subjects.

3. Upon request and proper identification of any data subject, or of his authorized agent, grant the data subject or agent the right to inspect, in a form comprehensible to him:

a. All personal information about that data subject except as provided in subdivision 1 of § 2.2-3705.1, subdivision 1 of § 2.2-3705.4, and subdivision 1 of § 2.2-3705.5.

b. The nature of the sources of the information.

c. The names of recipients, other than those with regular access authority, of personal information about the data subject including the identity of all persons and organizations involved and their relationship to the system when not having regular access authority, except that if the recipient has obtained the information as part of an ongoing criminal investigation such that disclosure of the investigation would jeopardize law-enforcement action, then no disclosure of such access shall be made to the data subject.

4. Comply with the following minimum conditions of disclosure to data subjects:

a. An agency shall make disclosures to data subjects required under this chapter, during normal business hours, in accordance with the procedures set forth in subsections B and C of § 2.2-3704 for responding to requests under the Virginia Freedom of Information Act (§ 2.2-3700 et seq.) or within a time period as may be mutually agreed upon by the agency and the data subject.

b. The disclosures to data subjects required under this chapter shall be made (i) in person, if he appears in person and furnishes proper identification, or (ii) by mail, if he has made a written request, with proper identification. Copies of the documents containing the personal information sought by a data subject shall be furnished to him or his representative at reasonable charges for document search and duplication in accordance with subsection F of § 2.2-3704.

c. The data subject shall be permitted to be accompanied by a person of his choosing, who shall furnish reasonable identification. An agency may require the data subject to furnish a written statement granting the agency permission to discuss the individual's file in such person's presence.

5. If the data subject gives notice that he wishes to challenge, correct, or explain information about him in the information system, the following minimum procedures shall be followed:

a. The agency maintaining the information system shall investigate, and record the current status of that personal information.

b. If, after such investigation, the information is found to be incomplete, inaccurate, not pertinent, not timely, or not necessary to be retained, it shall be promptly corrected or purged.

c. If the investigation does not resolve the dispute, the data subject may file a statement of not more than 200 words setting forth his position.

d. Whenever a statement of dispute is filed, the agency maintaining the information system shall supply any previous recipient with a copy of the statement and, in any subsequent dissemination or use of the information in question, clearly note that it is disputed and supply the statement of the data subject along with the information.

e. The agency maintaining the information system shall clearly and conspicuously disclose to the data subject his rights to make such a request.

f. Following any correction or purging of personal information the agency shall furnish to past recipients notification that the item has been purged or corrected whose receipt shall be acknowledged.

B. Nothing in this chapter shall be construed to require an agency to disseminate any recommendation or letter of reference from or to a third party that is a part of the personnel file of any data subject nor to disseminate any test or examination used, administered or prepared by any public body for purposes of evaluation of (i) any student or any student's performance, (ii) any seeker's qualifications or aptitude for employment, retention, or promotion, or (iii) qualifications for any license or certificate issued by any public body.

As used in this subsection, "test or examination" includes (i) any scoring key for any such test or examination and (ii) any other document that would jeopardize the security of the test or examination. Nothing contained in this subsection shall prohibit the release of test scores or results as provided by law, or to limit access to individual records as provided by law; however, the subject of the employment tests shall be entitled to review and inspect all documents relative to his performance on those employment tests.

When, in the reasonable opinion of the public body, any such test or examination no longer has any potential for future use, and the security of future tests or examinations will not be jeopardized, the test or examination shall be made available to the public. Minimum competency tests administered to public school children shall be made available to the public contemporaneously with statewide release of the scores of those taking such tests, but in no event shall such tests be made available to the public later than six months after the administration of such tests.

C. Neither any provision of this chapter nor any provision of the Freedom of Information Act (§ 2.2-3700 et seq.) shall be construed to deny public access to records of the position, job classification, official salary or rate of pay of, and to records of the allowances or reimbursements for expenses paid to any public officer, official or employee at any level of state, local or regional government in the Commonwealth. The provisions of this subsection shall not apply to records of the official salaries or rates of pay of public employees whose annual rate of pay is $10,000 or less.

D. Nothing in this section or in this chapter shall be construed to require an agency to disseminate information derived from tax returns in violation of §§ 2.2-3705.7 and 58.1-3. (1976, c. 597, § 2.1-382; 1978, c. 810; 1979, cc. 683, 688, 689; 1983, c. 372; 1995, c. 400; 2001, c. 844; 2004, c. 690; 2007, c. 232.)

The 2007 amendments. — The 2007 amendment by c. 232 inserted "in accordance with the procedures ... agreed upon by the agency and the data subject" at the end of subdivision A 4 a, and deleted "standard" preceding "charges" and added "in accordance with subsection F of § 2.2-3704" in the second sentence of subdivision A 4 b.

§ 2.2-3807. Agencies to report concerning systems operated or developed; publication of information. — Every agency shall make report of the existence of any information system that it operates or develops that shall include a description of the nature of the data in the system and purpose for which it is used. An inventory listing or similar display of the information shall be made available for inspection by the general public in the office of the head of each agency. Copies of the information shall be provided upon request and a fee shall be charged for them sufficient to cover the reasonable costs of reproduction. (1976, c. 597, § 2.1-383; 1977, c. 279; 1979, c. 683; 2001, c. 844.)

§ 2.2-3808. (Effective until July 1, 2009) Disclosure or display of social security number. — A. It shall be unlawful for any agency to require an individual to disclose or furnish his social security account number not previously disclosed or furnished, for any purpose in connection with any activity, or to refuse any service, privilege or right to an individual wholly or partly because the individual does not disclose or furnish such number, unless the disclosure or furnishing of such number is specifically required by federal or state law.

B. Agency-issued identification cards, student identification cards, or license certificates issued or replaced on or after July 1, 2003, shall not display an individual's entire social security number except as provided in § 46.2-703.

C. Any agency-issued identification card, student identification card, or license certificate that was issued prior to July 1, 2003, and that displays an individual's entire social security number shall be replaced no later than July 1, 2006, except that voter registration cards issued with a social security number and not previously replaced shall be replaced no later than the December 31st following the completion by the state and all localities of the decennial redistricting following the 2010 census. This subsection shall not apply to (i) driver's licenses and special identification cards issued by the Department of Motor Vehicles pursuant to Chapter 3 (§ 46.2-300 et seq.) of Title 46.2 and (ii) road tax registrations issued pursuant to § 46.2-703.

D. The provisions of subsections A and C of this section shall not be applicable to licenses issued by the State Corporation Commission's Bureau of Insurance until such time as a national insurance producer identification number has been created and implemented in all states. Commencing with the date of such implementation, the licenses issued by the State Corporation Commission's Bureau of Insurance shall be issued in compliance with subsection A of this section. Further, all licenses issued prior to the date of such implementation shall be replaced no later than 12 months following the date of such implementation. (1976, c. 597, § 2.1-385; 2001, c. 844; 2003, c. 974.)

Section set out twice. — The section above is effective until July 1, 2009. For the version of this section effective July 1, 2009, see the following section, also numbered 2.2-3808.

CASE NOTES

Editor's note. — The case below was decided under former Title 2.1 or prior provisions.

Federal court could not hear claim under this section against local registrar and state election officials for conditioning voting on disclosure of social security number where none of the exceptions to the Eleventh Amendment's bar against federal jurisdiction were present. The state did not waive its immunity and consent to suit, nor could defendants' actions be classified as beyond the scope of their statutory authority. Greidinger v. Davis, 782 F. Supp.

1106 (E.D. Va. 1992), rev'd on other grounds, 988 F.2d 1344 (4th Cir. 1993).

§ 2.2-3808. (Effective July 1, 2009) Collection, disclosure, or display of social security number. — A. No agency shall require an individual to furnish or disclose his social security number or driver's license number unless the furnishing or disclosure of such number is (i) authorized or required by state or federal law and (ii) essential for the performance of that agency's duties. Nor shall any agency require an individual to disclose or furnish his social security account number not previously disclosed or furnished, for any purpose in connection with any activity, or to refuse any service, privilege or right to an individual wholly or partly because the individual does not disclose or furnish such number, unless the disclosure or furnishing of such number is specifically required by federal or state law.

B. Agency-issued identification cards, student identification cards, or license certificates issued or replaced on or after July 1, 2003, shall not display an individual's entire social security number except as provided in § 46.2-703.

C. Any agency-issued identification card, student identification card, or license certificate that was issued prior to July 1, 2003, and that displays an individual's entire social security number shall be replaced no later than July 1, 2006, except that voter registration cards issued with a social security number and not previously replaced shall be replaced no later than the December 31st following the completion by the state and all localities of the decennial redistricting following the 2010 census. This subsection shall not apply to (i) driver's licenses and special identification cards issued by the Department of Motor Vehicles pursuant to Chapter 3 (§ 46.2-300 et seq.) of Title 46.2 and (ii) road tax registrations issued pursuant to § 46.2-703.

D. The provisions of subsections A and C shall not be applicable to licenses issued by the State Corporation Commission's Bureau of Insurance until such time as a national insurance producer identification number has been created and implemented in all states. Commencing with the date of such implementation, the licenses issued by the State Corporation Commission's Bureau of Insurance shall be issued in compliance with subsection A of this section. Further, all licenses issued prior to the date of such implementation shall be replaced no later than 12 months following the date of such implementation. (1976, c. 597, § 2.1-385; 2001, c. 844; 2003, c. 974; 2008, cc. 840, 843.)

Section set out twice. — The section above is effective July 1, 2009. For the version of this section effective until July 1, 2009, see the preceding section, also numbered 2.2-3808.

Editor's note. — Acts 2008, cc. 840 and 843, cl. 2 provides: "That the provisions of this act shall become effective on July 1, 2009, except that the third and fourth enactments of this act shall become effective on July 1, 2008."

Acts 2008, cc. 840 and 843, cl. 3 provides: "That every state agency subject to the provisions of the Government Data Collection and Dissemination Practices Act (§ 2.2-3800 et seq.) shall conduct an analysis and review of its collection and use of social security numbers, to be completed by October 1, 2008. Each such agency shall submit, no later than October 1, 2008, to the chairmen of the Freedom of Information Advisory Council and the Joint Commission on Technology and Science, on forms developed by the Council and the Commission, (i) a list of (a) all state or federal statutes authorizing or requiring the collection of social security numbers by such agency and (b) instances where social security numbers are voluntarily collected or (ii) in the absence of statutory authority to collect social security numbers, written justification explaining why continued collection is essential to its transaction of public business. In conducting such a review, each agency shall be encouraged to consider whether such collection and use is essential for its transaction of public business and to find alternative means of identifying individuals. The chairmen of the Council and the Commission may withhold from public disclosure any such lists or portions of lists as legislative working papers, if it deems that the public dissemination of such lists or portions of lists would cause a potential invasion of privacy."

Acts 2008, cc. 840 and 843, cl. 4 provides: "That every county and city, and any town with a population in excess of 15,000 shall, no later than September 10, 2008, provide the Virginia Municipal League or the Virginia Association of Counties, as appropriate, information on a form agreed upon by the Virginia Municipal League, the Virginia Association of Counties and staff of the Freedom of Information Advisory Council and the Joint Commission on Technology and Science identifying (i) all state or federal statutes authorizing or requiring the collection of social security numbers by such county, city or town and (ii) instances where social security numbers are voluntarily collected or (iii) in the absence of statutory authority to collect social security numbers, written justification explaining why continued collection is essential to its transaction of public business. In conducting such a review, each such county, city or town shall be encouraged to consider whether such collection and use is essential for its transaction of public business and to find alternative means of identifying individuals. The information required by this enactment shall be submitted no later than October 1, 2008 to the chairmen of the Freedom of Information Advisory Council and the Joint Commission on Technology and Science, on forms developed by the Council and the Commission."

The 2008 amendments. — The 2008 amendments by cc. 840 and 843, effective July 1, 2009, are identical, and in subsection A, inserted the first sentence and substituted "Nor shall any agency" for "It shall be unlawful for any agency to" at the beginning of the second sentence; and in subsection D, deleted "of this section" following "subsections A and C".

§ 2.2-3808.1. Agencies' disclosure of certain account information prohibited. — Notwithstanding Chapter 37 (§ 2.2-3700 et seq.) of this title, it shall be unlawful for any agency to disclose the social security number or other identification numbers appearing on driver's licenses or information on credit cards, debit cards, bank accounts, or other electronic billing and payment systems that was supplied to an agency for the purpose of paying fees, fines, taxes, or other charges collected by such agency. The prohibition shall not apply where disclosure of such information is required (i) to conduct or complete the transaction for which such information was submitted or (ii) by other law or court order. (2001, c. 415, § 2.1-385.1; 2007, cc. 548, 626.)

Cross references. — For prohibition under the Virginia Voter Registration System on disclosure of social security numbers, see § 24.2-407.1.

Editor's note. — Acts 2001, c. 415 enacted § 2.1-385.1, from which this section is derived. Pursuant to § 30-152, Acts 2001, c. 415 has been given effect in this section as set out above.

The 2007 amendments. — The 2007 amendments by cc. 548 and 626 are identical, and deleted "or § 2.2-3802" following "this title" and deleted "or court clerk" following "agency" three times in the first sentence.

§ 2.2-3808.2: Repealed by Acts 2007, cc. 548 and 626, cl. 5.

Cross references. — For current provisions as to posting and availability of certain information on the Internet, see § 17.1-293.

§ 2.2-3809. (Effective until July 1, 2009) Injunctive relief; attorneys' fees. — Any aggrieved person may institute a proceeding for injunction or mandamus against any person or agency that has engaged, is engaged, or is about to engage in any acts or practices in violation of the provisions of this chapter. The proceeding shall be brought in the circuit court of any county or city wherein the person or agency made defendant resides or has a place of business.

In the case of any successful proceeding by an aggrieved party, the person or agency enjoined or made subject to a writ of mandamus by the court shall be liable for the costs of the action together with reasonable attorneys' fees as determined by the court. (1976, c. 597, § 2.1-386; 2001, c. 844.)

Section set out twice. — The section above is effective until July 1, 2009. For the version of this section effective July 1, 2009, see the following section, also numbered 2.2-3809.

CASE NOTES

Only remedy for violation of this chapter is set forth in this section. Hinderliter v. Humphries, 224 Va. 439, 297 S.E.2d 684 (1982) (decided under former Title 2.1).

Plaintiff relieved of normal burden of proof. — This section relieves plaintiff of the normal burden of proving that an adequate remedy at law does not exist and that irreparable injury will occur. Hinderliter v. Humphries, 224 Va. 439, 297 S.E.2d 684 (1982) (decided under former Title 2.1).

Damages not recoverable under act. — Only injunctive relief and mandamus are available under this act, and a claim for damages is, accordingly, subject to being stricken. Mansoor v. County of Albemarle, 124 F. Supp. 2d 367, 2000 U.S. Dist. LEXIS 18612 (W.D. Va. 2000) (decided under former Title 2.1).

"Any person" refers to persons through whom covered agencies conduct their business. — Phrase "any person" in § 2.2-3809 refers to those persons through whom covered agencies conduct their business; a city treasurer, who was a constitutional officer, did not come within that phrase. Carraway v. Hill, 265 Va. 20, 574 S.E.2d 274, 2003 Va. LEXIS 7 (2003) (decided prior to 2003 amendment to § 2.2-3801).

§ 2.2-3809. (Effective July 1, 2009) Injunctive relief; civil penalty; attorneys' fees. — Any aggrieved person may institute a proceeding for injunction or mandamus against any person or agency that has engaged, is engaged, or is about to engage in any acts or practices in violation of the provisions of this chapter. The proceeding shall be brought in the district or circuit court of any county or city where the aggrieved person resides or where the agency made defendant has a place of business.

In the case of any successful proceeding by an aggrieved party, the agency enjoined or made subject to a writ of mandamus by the court shall be liable for the costs of the action together with reasonable attorneys' fees as determined by the court.

In addition, if the court finds that a violation of subsection A of § 2.2-3808 was willfully and knowingly made by a specific public officer, appointee, or employee of any agency, the court may impose upon such individual a civil penalty of not less than $250 nor more than $1,000, which amount shall be paid into the State Literary Fund. For a second or subsequent violation, such civil penalty shall be not less than $1,000 nor more than $2,500. For a violation of subsection A of § 2.2-3808 by any agency, the court may impose a civil penalty of not less than $250 nor more than $1,000, which amount shall be paid into the State Literary Fund. For a second or subsequent violation, such civil penalty shall be not less than $1,000 nor more than $2,500. (1976, c. 597, § 2.1-386; 2001, c. 844; 2008, cc. 840, 843.)

Section set out twice. — The section above is effective July 1, 2009. For the version of this section effective until July 1, 2009, see the preceding section, also numbered 2.2-3809.

Editor's note. — Acts 2008, cc. 840 and 843, cl. 2 provides: "That the provisions of this act shall become effective on July 1, 2009, except that the third and fourth enactments of this act shall become effective on July 1, 2008."

Acts 2008, cc. 840 and 843, cl. 3 provides: "That every state agency subject to the provisions of the Government Data Collection and Dissemination Practices Act (§ 2.2-3800 et seq.) shall conduct an analysis and review of its collection and use of social security numbers, to be completed by October 1, 2008. Each such agency shall submit, no later than October 1, 2008, to the chairmen of the Freedom of Information Advisory Council and the Joint Commission on Technology and Science, on forms developed by the Council and the Commission, (i) a list of (a) all state or federal statutes authorizing or requiring the collection of social security numbers by such agency and (b) instances where social security numbers are voluntarily collected or (ii) in the absence of statutory authority to collect social security numbers, written justification explaining why continued collection is essential to its transaction of public business. In conducting such a review, each agency shall be encouraged to consider whether such collection and use is essential for its transaction of public business and to find alternative means of identifying individuals. The chairmen of the Council and the Commission may withhold from public disclosure any such lists or portions of lists as legislative working papers, if it deems that the public dissemination of such lists or portions of lists would cause a potential invasion of privacy."

Acts 2008, cc. 840 and 843, cl. 4 provides: "That every county and city, and any town with a population in excess of 15,000 shall, no later than September 10, 2008, provide the Virginia Municipal League or the Virginia Association of Counties, as appropriate, information on a form agreed upon by the Virginia Municipal League, the Virginia Association of Counties and staff of the Freedom of Information Advisory Council and the Joint Commission on Technology and Science identifying (i) all state or federal statutes authorizing or requiring the collection of social security numbers by such county, city or town and (ii) instances where social security numbers are voluntarily collected or (iii) in the absence of statutory authority to collect social security numbers, written justification explaining why continued collection is essential to its transaction of public business. In conducting such a review, each such county, city or town shall be encouraged to consider whether such collection and use is essential for its transaction of public business and to find alternative means of identifying individuals. The information required by this enactment shall be submitted no later than October 1, 2008 to the chairmen of the Freedom of Information Advisory Council and the Joint Commission on Technology and Science, on forms developed by the Council and the Commission."

The 2008 amendments. — The 2008 amendments by cc. 840 and 843, effective July 1, 2009, are identical, and in the first paragraph, inserted "district or" and substituted "where the aggrieved person resides or where the agency made defendant has a place of business" for "wherein the person or agency made defendant resides or has a place of business" at the end of the second sentence; in the second paragraph, deleted "person or" preceding "agency enjoined"; and added the last paragraph.

CHAPTER 39.

VIRGINIA HUMAN RIGHTS ACT.

§ 2.2-3900. Short title; declaration of policy. — A. This chapter shall be known and cited as the Virginia Human Rights Act.

B. It is the policy of the Commonwealth to:

1. Safeguard all individuals within the Commonwealth from unlawful discrimination because of race, color, religion, national origin, sex, pregnancy, childbirth or related medical conditions, age, marital status, or disability, in places of public accommodation, including educational institutions and in real estate transactions; in employment; preserve the public safety, health and general welfare; and further the interests, rights and privileges of individuals within the Commonwealth; and

2. Protect citizens of the Commonwealth against unfounded charges of unlawful discrimination. (1987, c. 581, §§ 2.1-714, 2.1-715; 1997, c. 404; 2001, c. 844.)

Cross references. — As to causes of action under the article creating the Human Rights Council, see § 2.2-2639. As to records which are excluded from the provisions of the Virginia Freedom of Information Act, see § 2.2-3705.1 et seq.

Editor's note. — Acts 1997, c. 404, cl. 2, provides: "That the provisions of this act are declarative of existing law."

Law Review. — For article, "The Law of Wrongful Discharge in Virginia," see 10 G.M.U. Mason L. Rev. 133 (1988). For an article relating to a variety of developments in employment law, see 32 U. Rich. L. Rev. 1199 (1998). For an article, "A Uniform Standard for Exemplary Damages in Employment Discrimination Cases," see 33 U. Rich. L. Rev. 41 (1999). For a casenote, "Holding the Same-Sex Sexual Harassment Claim at Arm's Length: The Supreme Court's Strict (and Correct) Interpretation of Title VII In Oncale v. Sundowner Offshore Services, Inc.," see 33 U. Rich. L. Rev. 257

(1999). For a casenote, "The Duty To Treat Asymptomatic HIV-Positive Patients or Face Disability Discrimination Under Abbott v. Bragdon: The Scylla and Charybdis Facing Today's Dental and Health Care Providers," see 33 U. Rich. L. Rev. 665 (1999). For a review of employment law in Virginia for year 1999, see 33 U. Rich. L. Rev. 965 (1999). For a review of civil practice and procedure in Virginia for year 1999, see 33 U. Rich. L. Rev. 801 (1999). For a note, "Eradicating Discrimination Among Individuals with Disabilities: Parity in Employer-Provided, Long-Term Disability Benefit Plans," see 56 Wash. & Lee L. Rev. 1341 (1999). For a note, "Hanging in the Balance: Confidentiality Clauses and Postjudgment Settlements of Employment Discrimination Disputes," see 86 Va. L. Rev. 1537 (2000). For 2000 survey of Virginia labor and employment law, see 34 U. Rich. L. Rev. 907 (2000). For article, "Labor and Employment Law," see 35 U. Rich. L. Rev. 725 (2001).

Research References. — Cook and Sobieski, Civil Rights Actions (Matthew Bender).

Janice Goodman, Employee Rights Litigation: Pleading and Practice (Matthew Bender).

Lex K. Larson, Employment Discrimination (Matthew Bender).

Michie's Jurisprudence. — For related discussion, see 3B M.J. Civil Rights, § 2; 12B M.J. Master and Servant, § 11.

CASE NOTES

Editor's note. — Most of the cases below were decided under former Title 2.1 or prior provisions.

The Virginia Human Rights Act does not create any new causes of action, applying only where a violation of existing laws is found. Ennis v. National Ass'n of Bus. & Educ. Radio, 53 F.3d 55 (4th Cir. 1995).

Former § 2.1-725 D (now § 2.2-2639 D) prohibited a common law cause of action based upon the public policies reflected in the Virginia Human Rights Act. Doss v. Jamco, Inc., 254 Va. 362, 492 S.E.2d 441 (1997).

A common-law wrongful discharge claim cannot be based on the public polices of the Virginia Human Rights Act. Williamson v. Virginia First Sav. Bank, 26 F. Supp. 2d 798 (E.D. Va. 1998).

The Virginia legislature, in enacting the 1995 amendments to former § 2.1-725 (see now § 2.2-2639), eliminated a common law cause of action for wrongful termination based on any public policy which is reflected in the Virginia Human Rights Act, regardless of whether the policy is articulated elsewhere. Conner v. National Pest Control Ass'n, 257 Va. 286, 513 S.E.2d 398 (1999).

Employment-at-will doctrine. — The Virginia Human Rights Act, as amended, no longer provides an exception to the at-will employment doctrine or the public policy basis for a cause of action for wrongful discharge. Oakley v. May Dep't Stores Co., 17 F. Supp. 2d 533 (E.D. Va. 1998).

Construction with other law. — The policy against discrimination because of disability expressed in this act is also expressed in the Virginians with Disabilities Act (VWDA), § 51.5-1 et seq., and the provisions of former § 2.1-725 (now § 2.2-2639) exclusively limiting causes of action to those afforded by other federal or state civil rights statutes or local ordinances bars any claim for wrongful termination in violation of the public policy embodied in both this act and the VWDA. Lamb v. Qualex, Inc., 28 F. Supp. 2d 374 (E.D. Va. 1998).

Plaintiff's request for a declaratory judgment under the Virginia Human Rights Act, subdivision B 2 of § 2.2-3900 was properly dismissed under Fed. R. Civ. P. 12(b)(6), because plaintiff was not seeking to determine "legal rights" or "legal relationships," and plaintiff's request for a declaratory judgment only duplicated his attempt to seek relief under the Age Discrimination in Employment Act (ADEA), 29 U.S.C.S. § 621, and various common law theories. Carpenter v. County Sch. Bd., — F.3d —, 2004 U.S. App. LEXIS 17577 (4th Cir. Aug. 19, 2004).

Failure to state a claim. — Employee failed to state a claim under the Virginia Human Rights Act, § 2.2-3900 et seq., because the Act limited private rights of action to employees seeking redress against employers of more than five but less than 15 employees, under § 2.2-2639, and her employer had more than 15 employees. Reiterman v. Costco Wholesale Mgmt. # 238, — F. Supp. 2d —, 2005 U.S. Dist. LEXIS 15219 (W.D. Va. July 28, 2005).

Statute of limitations. — Counts were claims for wrongful discharge, not for breach of contract, personal injury, or violation of any federal statute. Thus, the statute of limitations exception for claims dependent upon "federally created rights" did not help plaintiffs in the instant case. Michael v. Sentara Health Sys., 939 F. Supp. 1220 (E.D. Va. 1996).

CIRCUIT COURT OPINIONS

Virginia Human Rights Act barred claims for wrongful termination that alleged violations of the Act's public policy provisions. — Virginia Human Rights Act, § 2.2-3900 et seq. (VHRA), limited claims to those afforded under the Act, and barred any claim for wrongful termination in violation of the public policy embodied in either the VHRA or the Virginians with Disabilities Act, § 51.5-1 et seq., and, thus, the terminated worker did not state a sufficient claim for wrongful termination due to a disability as there was no common law wrongful discharge claim. Wright v. St. Charles Water Auth., 59 Va. Cir. 244, 2002 Va. Cir. LEXIS 350 (Lee County July 11, 2002).

§ 2.2-3901. Unlawful discriminatory practice and gender discrimination defined. — Conduct that violates any Virginia or federal statute or regulation governing discrimination on the basis of race, color, religion, national origin, sex, pregnancy, childbirth or related medical conditions, age, marital status, or disability shall be an "unlawful discriminatory practice" for the purposes of this chapter.

The terms "because of sex or gender" or "on the basis of sex or gender" or terms of similar import when used in reference to discrimination in the Code and acts of the General Assembly include because of or on the basis of pregnancy, childbirth or related medical conditions. Women affected by pregnancy, childbirth or related medical conditions shall be treated the same for all purposes as persons not so affected but similar in their abilities or disabilities. (1987, c. 581, § 2.1-716; 1991, c. 457; 1997, c. 404; 2001, c. 844; 2005, c. 839.)

Cross references. — For application of the definition of "unlawful discriminatory practice" in this section to prohibition of discrimination in awarding contracts, see § 2.2-4200.

Editor's note. — Acts 1997, c. 404, cl. 2, provides: "That the provisions of this act are declarative of existing law."

CASE NOTES

Editor's note. — Some of the cases below were decided under former Title 2.1 or prior provisions.

Coterminous with federal antidiscrimination law. — The Virginia Human Rights Act essentially makes any federal violation a violation of Virginia law as well. Grimes v. Canadian Am. Transp., C.A.T. (U.S.), Inc., 72 F. Supp. 2d 629 (W.D. Va. 1999).

As the court determined that the association and the subsidiary were not "employers" under the Age Discrimination in Employment Act (ADEA), summary judgment against the Virginia Human Rights Act (VHRA) claim was appropriate to the extent that the former president's VHRA claim rested on an alleged violation of the ADEA. Huizenga v. Am. Int'l Auto. Dealers Ass'n, — F. Supp. 2d —, 2005 U.S. Dist. LEXIS 30972 (E.D. Va. Nov. 22, 2005).

Sex discrimination prohibited. — Virginia law does not allow and, therefore, prohibits, discrimination on the basis of sex. Walker v. Electrolux Corp., 55 F. Supp. 2d 501 (W.D. Va. 1999).

§ 2.2-3902. Construction of chapter; other programs to aid persons with disabilities, minors and the elderly. — The provisions of this chapter shall be construed liberally for the accomplishment of its policies. Nothing contained in this chapter shall be deemed to repeal, supersede or expand upon any of the provisions of any other state or federal law relating to discrimination because of race, color, religion, national origin, sex, pregnancy, childbirth or related medical conditions, age, marital status, or disability.

Nothing in this chapter shall prohibit or alter any program, service, facility, school, or privilege that is afforded, oriented or restricted to a person because of disability or age from continuing to habilitate, rehabilitate, or accommodate that person.

In addition, nothing in this chapter shall be construed to affect any governmental program, law or activity differentiating between persons on the basis of age over the age of eighteen years (i) where the differentiation is reasonably necessary to normal operation or the activity is based upon reasonable factors other than age or (ii) where the program, law or activity constitutes a legitimate exercise of powers of the Commonwealth for the general health, safety and welfare of the population at large.

Complaints filed with the Human Rights Council (the "Council") in accordance with § 2.2-2634 alleging unlawful discriminatory practice under a Virginia statute that is enforced by a Virginia agency shall be referred to that agency. The Council may investigate complaints alleging an unlawful discriminatory practice under a federal statute or regulation and attempt to resolve it through conciliation. Unsolved complaints shall thereafter be referred to the federal agency with jurisdiction over the complaint. Upon such referral, the Council shall have no further jurisdiction over the complaint. The Council shall have no jurisdiction over any complaint filed under a local ordinance adopted pursuant to § 15.2-965. (1987, c. 581, § 2.1-717; 1991, c. 457; 1997, c. 404; 2000, c. 933; 2001, c. 844.)

Editor's note. — Acts 1997, c. 404, cl. 2, provides: "That the provisions of this act are declarative of existing law."

CHAPTER 40.

Administrative Process Act.

Article 1.

General Provisions.

Article 2.

Regulations.

Article 3.

Case Decisions.

Michie's Jurisprudence. — For related discussion, see 1A M.J. Administrative Law, §§ 1, 2, 5, 9 — 13, 20 — 22.

Article 1.

General Provisions.

Michie's Jurisprudence. — For related discussion, see 1A M.J. Administrative Law, §§ 1, 2, 5, 10, 11.

§ 2.2-4000. Short title; purpose. — A. This chapter may be cited as the "Administrative Process Act."

B. The purpose of this chapter is to supplement present and future basic laws conferring authority on agencies either to make regulations or decide cases as well as to standardize court review thereof save as laws hereafter enacted may otherwise expressly provide. This chapter shall not supersede or repeal additional procedural requirements in such basic laws. (1975, c. 503, §§ 9-6.14:1. 9-6.14:3; 1977, c. 647; 1984, c. 5; 2001, c. 844.)

Cross references. — As to standards for the inspection of buildings for asbestos, see § 2.2-1164. As to establishing regulations for preplanning of capital outlay projects, see § 2.2-1502. As to the exclusion of the Virginia Small Business Financing Act from the provisions of the Administrative Process Act, see § 2.2-2314. As to the authority of the Virginia War Memorial Foundation, see § 2.2-2706. As to exception of the Virginia Administrative Code from the provisions of the Administrative Process Act, see § 2.2-4104. As to the effect of the Virginia Administrative Dispute Resolution Act on the Administrative Process Act, see § 2.2-4116. As to exemption of the Treasury Board regulations from Administrative Process Act, see § 2.2-4605. As to the authority of the Treasury Board under the Government Non-Arbitrage Investment Act to adopt regulations without complying with the Administrative Process Act, see § 2.2-4702. As to exemption of operations of the Virginia Dangerous Dog Registry from Administrative Process Act, see § 3.1-796.93:3. As to the duty of the Virginia Code Commission to monitor the operation of the Administrative Process Act, see § 30-155. As to participation of advisory boards in disciplinary proceedings for professions and occupations regulated by the Department of Health Professions, see § 54.1-2409.3. As to applicability of § 2.2-4000 et seq. to appeals from refusal, denial of renewal or revocation of licenses for assisted living facilities, adult day care centers, or child welfare agencies, see § 63.2-1710. As to appeal of the revocation or denial of the certification of a preschool program, see § 63.2-1717 I. For Rules of Court governing appeals under the

Administrative Process Act, see Sup. Ct. Rules, Part 2A.

Editor's note. — Acts 2008, c. 879, effective for the biennium ending June 30, 2010, in Item 275 F, provides: "F.1. The State Treasurer is authorized to charge qualified public depositories holding public deposits, as defined in §2.2-4401, Code of Virginia, an annual administrative fee of not more that one-half of one basis point of their average public deposit balances over a twelve month period. The State Treasurer shall issue guidelines to effect the implementation of this fee. However, the total fees collected from all qualified depositories shall not exceed $100,000 in any one year.

"2. Any regulations or guidelines necessary to implement or change the amount of the fee may be adopted without complying with the Administrative Process Act (§2.2-4000 et seq.) provided that input is solicited from qualified public depositories. Such input requires only that notice and an opportunity to submit written comments be given."

Acts 2008, c. 879, effective for the biennium ending June 30, 2010, in Item 295 F, provides: "Out of this appropriation, $200,000 the first year and $200,000 the second year from the general fund shall be provided to the department's sickle cell program to address rising pediatric caseloads in the current program. Any remaining funds shall be used to develop transition services for youth who will require adult services to ensure appropriate medical services are available and provided for youth who age out of the current program."

Law Review. — For survey of Virginia administrative law for the year 1974-1975, see 61 Va. L. Rev. 1632 (1975). For survey of Virginia administrative law for the year 1976-77, see 63 Va. L. Rev. 1366 (1977). For survey of Virginia law on governmental services and social welfare for the year 1978-1979, see 66 Va. L. Rev. 301 (1980). For article on Virginia tax procedures, see 38 Wash. & Lee L. Rev. 1115 (1981). For article, "Legislative and Executive Veto of Rules of Administrative Agencies: Models and Alternatives," see 24 Wm. & Mary L. Rev. 79 (1982). For article on legislative changes to Virginia administrative rulemaking, see 19 U. Rich. L. Rev. 107 (1984). For article on opening Virginia courthouse doors to review of administrative decisions involving public assistance, see 21 U. Rich. L. Rev. 161 (1986). For article, "The Federal APA and State Administrative Law," see 72 Va. L. Rev. 297 (1986). For 1987 survey of Virginia administrative procedure, see 21 U. Rich. L. Rev. 611 (1987). For survey of administrative procedure in Virginia for 1989, see 23 U. Rich. L. Rev. 431 (1989). For survey on environmental law in Virginia for 1989, see 23 U. Rich. L. Rev. 625 (1989). For article covering changes made to the Administrative Process Act during the 1992 session of the General Assembly as well as recent Virginia cases dealing with state administrative procedure decided between August 30, 1990 and September 17, 1992, see 26 U. Rich. L. Rev. 561 (1992). For note, "Standards of Judicial Review in the Virginia Administrative Process Act", see 30 U. Rich. L. Rev. 905 (1996). For an article, "Administrative Procedure," see 31 U. Rich. L. Rev. 907 (1997). For an article, "Shattering the Fragile Case for Judicial Review of Rulemaking," see 85 Va. L. Rev. 1243 (1999). For a review of administrative procedure in Virginia for year 1999, see 33 U. Rich. L. Rev. 727 (1999). For an article, "Agency Adjudication, the Importance of Facts, and the Limitation of Labels," see 57 Wash. & Lee L. Rev. 351 (2000). For 2000 survey of Virginia health law, see 34 U. Rich. L. Rev. 853 (2000). For article discussing decisions of Virginia courts dealing with state administrative procedures between June 1, 2002 and June 1, 2003, see 38 U. Rich. L. Rev. 39 (2003).

CASE NOTES

Editor's note. — Some of the cases below were decided under former corresponding provisions.

Applicability. — Where an agency's basic law provides expressly for Virginia Administrative Process Act coverage of certain proceedings under specified conditions and makes no provision for judicial review of other proceedings, the unmentioned proceedings are subject to the Act unless otherwise expressly excluded. May Dep't Stores Co. v. Commonwealth, Dep't of Envtl. Quality, 29 Va. App. 589, 513 S.E.2d 880 (1999).

Article 6 of this Act (former § 9-6.14:21, see now § 2.2-4030), providing for awards of attorney fees, does not apply to judicial review of determinations of claims for unemployment compensation. Shuler v. VEC, 14 Va. App. 1013, 420 S.E.2d 257 (1992).

Agency may be exempted from promulgation process under certain conditions. — The General Assembly clearly evinced its intent that regulations must be promulgated since it specifically provided that an agency may be exempted from the entire promulgation process under certain circumstances. Johnston-Willis, Ltd. v. Kenley, 6 Va. App. 231, 369 S.E.2d 1 (1988).

Right to intervene. — In a case dealing with an application seeking permission to install a raw water intake on state-owned bottomlands, nothing in former Va. Sup. Ct. R. 2:15 [see now R. 3.14], the Virginia Administrative Process Act, or the enabling statutes for the Virginia Marine Resources Commission

(VMRC) gave the tribe the right to intervene; additionally, no settlement between the city and the VMRC could prejudice any rights the tribe had under its treaty. Thus, the settlement between the city and the VMRC, consummated by the entry of a consent dismissal order, mooted the tribe's appeal of the circuit court's decision to deny the tribe's motion to intervene. Mattaponi Indian Tribe v. Va. Marine Res. Comm'n, 45 Va. App. 208, 609 S.E.2d 619, 2005 Va. App. LEXIS 85 (2005).

The hearing determination chart is not a substantive rule of the Industrial (now Workers' Compensation) Commission subject to the Virginia Administrative Process Act or the Virginia Register Act. Bader v. Norfolk Redevelopment & Hous. Auth., 10 Va. App. 697, 396 S.E.2d 141 (1990).

Review of decisions concerning special education programs for handicapped children not subject to this chapter. — Special education programs for handicapped children are subject to the provisions of subsection D of § 22.1-214, which subsection allows the court to hear additional evidence and requires it to weigh the evidence and base its decision on the preponderance of the evidence, instead of simply finding substantial evidence in the record to support the hearing officer's decision. Thus, the proper standard for the circuit court is to determine, based on a preponderance of the evidence, whether the substance of the proposed individualized educational program is reasonably calculated to enable the child to receive educational benefits. Beasley v. School Bd., 6 Va. App. 206, 367 S.E.2d 738 (1988), rev'd on other grounds, 238 Va. 44, 380 S.E.2d 884 (1989).

Appeals from decisions of agencies which are not covered by this chapter. — The legislative purpose set forth in this section does not restrict appeals of all decisions of administrative agencies not encompassed by the Administrative Process Act to the Court of Appeals rather than the Virginia Supreme Court. County of Roanoke v. Friendship Manor Apt. Village Corp., No. 0394-85 (Ct. of Appeals Sept. 4, 1985).

Decisions of board upheld. — The Building Code Technical Review Board correctly decided that it had jurisdiction to review the inspection decision, it did not err in ruling on the merits of the appeal, and correctly reversed the inspection decision under this statute. Strawbridge v. County of Chesterfield, 23 Va. App. 493, 477 S.E.2d 789 (1996).

Applied in Citland, Ltd. v. Commonwealth ex rel. Kilgore, 45 Va. App. 268, 610 S.E.2d 321, 2005 Va. App. LEXIS 113 (2005); Christian v. Va. Dep't of Soc. Servs., 45 Va. App. 310, 610 S.E.2d 870, 2005 Va. App. LEXIS 123 (2005); Campbell v. Dep't of Forestry, 46 Va. App. 91, 616 S.E.2d 33, 2005 Va. App. LEXIS 283 (2005); Jones v. West, 46 Va. App. 309, 616 S.E.2d 790, 2005 Va. App. LEXIS 307 (2005).

CIRCUIT COURT OPINIONS

Standing to challenge agency decision. — River association did not have standing to challenge, in its representative capacity, Virginia Waste Management Board's decision to charge a fee to transport waste on Virginia's waters because the plain language of Virginia's Administrative Process Act, § 2.2-4000 et seq., clearly provided that standing to seek judicial review of a decision of the board was not conferred on persons in a representative capacity; however, the association stated sufficient facts to show that it was a "person aggrieved" under § 10.1-1457; thus it did have standing to appeal the Board's decision. James River Ass'n v. Commonwealth ex rel. Waste Mgmt. Bd., 63 Va. Cir. 602, 2004 Va. Cir. LEXIS 88 (Richmond 2004).

Court lacked jurisdiction. — Because the Virginia Administrative Procedures Act (VAPA) was the exclusive avenue to challenge an administrative action involving the denial of a hospital's certificate of public need application, because § 32.1-102.1 et seq., and the VAPA provided sufficient procedural due process, and because the hospital had an adequate remedy at law, the court lacked jurisdiction to hear the appeal; therefore, the competitors' demurrers were sustained. Loudoun Hosp. Ctr. v. Stroube, 68 Va. Cir. 271, 2005 Va. Cir. LEXIS 229 (Loudoun County July 19, 2005).

§ 2.2-4001. Definitions. — As used in this chapter, unless the context requires a different meaning:

"Agency" means any authority, instrumentality, officer, board or other unit of the state government empowered by the basic laws to make regulations or decide cases.

"Agency action" means either an agency's regulation or case decision or both, any violation, compliance, or noncompliance with which could be a basis for the imposition of injunctive orders, penal or civil sanctions of any kind, or the grant or denial of relief or of a license, right, or benefit by any agency or court.

"Basic law" or *"basic laws"* means provisions of the Constitution and statutes of the Commonwealth authorizing an agency to make regulations or decide cases or containing procedural requirements therefor.

"Case" or *"case decision"* means any agency proceeding or determination that, under laws or regulations at the time, a named party as a matter of past or present fact, or of threatened or contemplated private action, either is, is not, or may or may not be (i) in violation of such law or regulation or (ii) in compliance with any existing requirement for obtaining or retaining a license or other right or benefit.

"Guidance document" means any document developed by a state agency or staff that provides information or guidance of general applicability to the staff or public to interpret or implement statutes or the agency's rules or regulations, excluding agency minutes or documents that pertain only to the internal management of agencies. Nothing in this definition shall be construed or interpreted to expand the identification or release of any document otherwise protected by law.

"Hearing" means agency processes other than those informational or factual inquiries of an informal nature provided in §§ 2.2-4007.01 and 2.2-4019 and includes only (i) opportunity for private parties to submit factual proofs in formal proceedings as provided in § 2.2-4009 in connection with the making of regulations or (ii) a similar right of private parties or requirement of public agencies as provided in § 2.2-4020 in connection with case decisions.

"Hearing officer" means an attorney selected from a list maintained by the Executive Secretary of the Supreme Court in accordance with § 2.2-4024.

"Public assistance and social services programs" means those programs specified in § 63.2-100.

"Rule" or *"regulation"* means any statement of general application, having the force of law, affecting the rights or conduct of any person, adopted by an agency in accordance with the authority conferred on it by applicable basic laws.

"Subordinate" means (i) one or more but less than a quorum of the members of a board constituting an agency, (ii) one or more of its staff members or employees, or (iii) any other person or persons designated by the agency to act in its behalf. (1975, c. 503, § 9-6.14:4; 1977, cc. 377, 381; 1979, c. 613; 1984, c. 187; 1985, cc. 67, 602; 1997, c. 11; 2001, c. 844; 2002, c. 747; 2007, cc. 873, 916.)

Cross references. — As to exemptions, see now § 2.2-4002.

The 2007 amendments. — The 2007 amendments by cc. 873 and 916 are identical, and substituted "2.2-4007.01" for "2.2-4007" in the definition of "Hearing."

Law Review. — For survey of Virginia administrative law for the year 1974-1975, see 61 Va. L. Rev. 1632 (1975). For survey of Virginia administrative law for the year 1976-77, see 63 Va. L. Rev. 1366 (1977). For 1985 survey of Virginia administrative procedure, see 19 U. Rich. L. Rev. 657 (1985). For a review of administrative procedure in Virginia for year 1999, see 33 U. Rich. L. Rev. 727 (1999).

Michie's Jurisprudence. — For related discussion, see 1A M.J. Administrative Law, §§ 1, 5, 10, 11.

CASE NOTES

Editor's note. — Most of the cases below were decided under former corresponding provisions.

Counties excluded from definition of "agency." — Under the definition of "agency," an administrative agency must be a unit of state government; counties are expressly excluded. County of Roanoke v. Friendship Manor Apt. Village Corp., No. 0394-85 (Ct. of Appeals Sept. 4, 1985).

A local school board is not a board or unit of the state government, but rather is an entity of a municipality or a county. As such, it is not an administrative agency as contemplated by the Administrative Process Act. Schwartz v. Highland County School Bd., 2 Va. App. 554, 346 S.E.2d 544 (1986).

The Virginia Historic Landmarks Board under former § 10-135 et seq. was not an agency as defined by former § 9-6.2 because the General Assembly did not authorize the Board to make rules or to adjudicate contested cases in Louisa County. Virginia Historic Landmarks Comm'n v. Board of Supvrs., 217 Va. 468, 230 S.E.2d 449 (1976) (decided under former § 9-6.2 and prior to enactment of former § 10-138.2).

Where there is a specific provision for standing in the basic law, such provision is controlling over the standardized court review in former § 9-6.14:16 (see now §§ 2.2-4025 B, 2.2-4026). Citizens for Clean Air v. Commonwealth ex rel. State Air Pollution Control Bd., 13 Va. App. 430, 412 S.E.2d 715 (1991).

"Basic law" to make regulations or decide cases. — Former § 9-6.14:16 (see now §§ 2.2-4025 B, 2.2-4026) does not supplement § 62.1-44.29 because the latter is not a "basic law conferring authority on agencies either to make regulations or decide cases." Environmental Defense Fund v. Virginia State Water Control Bd., 12 Va. App. 456, 404 S.E.2d 728 (1991).

Former § 9-6.14:16 (see now §§ 2.2-4025 B, 2.2-4026) gives deference to provisions of the basic law, such as § 62.1-44.29, which make express provisions for standing. This construction is supported by the concluding sentence of former § 9-6.14:3 (see now § 2.2-4000 B). Environmental Defense Fund v. Virginia State Water Control Bd., 12 Va. App. 456, 404 S.E.2d 728 (1991).

Reach of administrative, ministerial duties. — The granting and renewal of professional licenses are part of the administrative, ministerial duties of the real estate board. Such duties do not involve the quasi-judicial process of determining whether a person subject to regulation by the board is in violation of applicable statutes and regulations. Carpenter v. Virginia Real Estate Bd., 20 Va. App. 100, 455 S.E.2d 287 (1995).

A de facto rule may be challenged by bringing a suit claiming the unlawfulness of a case decision, as defined by the Virginia Administrative Process Act. Virginia Bd. of Medicine v. Virginia Physical Therapy Ass'n, 13 Va. App. 458, 413 S.E.2d 59 (1991), aff'd, Virginia Physical Therapy Ass'n v. Virginia Bd. of Medicine, 245 Va. 125, 427 S.E.2d 183 (1993).

The Alcoholic Beverage Control Board's refusal to permit a licensee's use of a 22-foot counter surfaced with five wood-inlaid backgammon boards for the service of alcoholic beverages constituted a "case decision." Virginia ABC Comm'n v. York St. Inn, Inc., 220 Va. 310, 257 S.E.2d 851 (1979).

The resolution of the Virginia Historic Landmarks Board identifying the Green Springs Historic District cannot be construed as a "rule" of general application, and the proceedings conducted by the Board incident to the adoption of the resolution was not "a contested case" involving such rights, duties or privileges of a person that are required by law to be determined after a hearing. Virginia Historic Landmarks Comm'n v. Board of Supvrs., 217 Va. 468, 230 S.E.2d 449 (1976) (decided under former § 9-6.2 and prior to enactment of former § 10-138.2).

The Virginia Board of Medicine has consented to and may be sued only for its promulgation of a rule or its decision of a case, as both are defined in the Virginia Administrative Process Act. Virginia Bd. of Medicine v. Virginia Physical Therapy Ass'n, 13 Va. App. 458, 413 S.E.2d 59 (1991), aff'd, Virginia Physical Therapy Ass'n v. Virginia Bd. of Medicine, 245 Va. 125, 427 S.E.2d 183 (1993).

The General Assembly has waived sovereign immunity only to allow a party to obtain judicial review of the Virginia Board of Medicine's adoption of rules of the Board's case decisions, as such are defined in the Virginia Administrative Process Act, in the manner provided in the Act. Virginia Bd. of Medicine v. Virginia Physical Therapy Ass'n, 13 Va. App. 458, 413 S.E.2d 59 (1991), aff'd, Virginia Physical Therapy Ass'n v. Virginia Bd. of Medicine, 245 Va. 125, 427 S.E.2d 183 (1993).

Actions of the State Water Control Board in effect requiring privately owned utilities to abandon the treatment of sewage and connect their lines to those of publicly owned utility by a certain date were "case decisions" as defined by this section, and the "basic law under which the agency acted" was the State Water Control Law, § 62.1-44.2 et seq., which contains a detailed procedural scheme for judicial review of board actions; thus the appeal procedures of the State Water Control Law applied and those of Part 2A of the Supreme Court Rules did not. Commonwealth ex rel. State Water Control Bd. v. County Utils. Corp., 223 Va. 534, 290 S.E.2d 867 (1982).

Denial of request for formal hearing not "case decision." — Appeal was unavailable under the Virginia Administrative Process Act. Former § 9-6.14:16 (see now §§ 2.2-4025 B, 2.2-4026) provides for appeal by a "party aggrieved by and claiming unlawfulness of a case decision." The denial of Environmental Defense Fund's request for a formal hearing was not a "case decision." Environmental Defense Fund was not a "named party" in the proceedings before the State Water Control Board. Environmental Defense Fund v. Virginia State Water Control Bd., 12 Va. App. 456, 404 S.E.2d 728 (1991).

Denial of application for a septic tank permit after formal hearing and informal rejection of post-hearing applications constituted agency "case decision," but only the formal denial disposed of a litigated issue within the meaning of former § 9-6.14:12 (see now §§ 2.2-4020, 2.2-4021). State Bd. of Health v. Godfrey,

223 Va. 423, 290 S.E.2d 875 (1982).

Letter applying rules and regulations to facts constituted case decision. — A letter from the State Health Commissioner to a hospital regarding its program of open heart surgery constituted a case decision, where it was addressed to the hospital, applied rules and regulations to the facts, and ruled that the hospital required a certificate of public need before performing open heart surgery. Kenley v. Newport News Gen. & Non-Sectarian Hosp. Ass'n, 227 Va. 39, 314 S.E.2d 52 (1984).

Letter not containing application of law nor findings was not a case decision. — In a proceeding as to whether a hospital required a certificate of need for its program of open heart surgery, a letter from the State Health Commissioner which contained no more than a general statement of position regarding certificates of public need, which letter was not addressed to the hospital owned and operated by one of the parties but to the health systems agency, with a copy to the hospital, and which merely stated that any hospital service that is reactivated after an absence of 12 months is considered to be a new service, with neither an application of law to hospital's program of open heart surgery nor any finding of facts as to the kind of program it was providing was not a case decision under this chapter. Kenley v. Newport News Gen. & Non-Sectarian Hosp. Ass'n, 227 Va. 39, 314 S.E.2d 52 (1984).

Two letters, one written by an employee's attorney, and another written by the Department of Corrections, did not meet the definition of a "case decision," as defined in § 2.2-4001, as neither letter involved the application of law to the facts in an agency proceeding; the first amounted to merely a request for clarification of the Department's position concerning a grievance matter, and the Department's response to the same acknowledged that it had responded to the merits during the grievance process and that denial of a grievance hearing was affirmed; further, the letter written by the employee's attorney did not have the effect of filing a claim for retirement benefits. Garraghty v. Va. Ret. Sys., 45 Va. App. 1, 608 S.E.2d 477, 2005 Va. App. LEXIS 44 (2005).

Letter from Medical Board not "case decision." — Medical board's letter advising that a consent order finding that a doctor violated Virginia law by failing to submit a professional profile describing her qualifications and practice would be reported to the federal Healthcare Integrity and Protection Data Bank did not constitute a "case decision" and, thus, was not appealable to the circuit court, because the letter could not be characterized as an independent determination that the doctor violated state regulations by failing to file her profile with the licensing authority; rather, such a determination had already been made under the consent order. Giannoukos v. Va. Bd. of Med. & Dep't of Health Professions, 44 Va. App. 694, 607 S.E.2d 136, 2005 Va. App. LEXIS 7 (2005).

Board's action held not appealable. — Where the action taken by a board did not amount to a case decision or the promulgation of a rule within the meaning of the Virginia Administrative Process Act, the board's action was not appealable or subject to judicial review and, therefore, the trial court lacked subject matter jurisdiction. Virginia Physical Therapy Ass'n v. Virginia Bd. of Medicine, 245 Va. 125, 427 S.E.2d 183 (1993).

The landfill permit holder was not any other affected person or aggrieved person who appeared in person or by counsel at a hearing because it was undisputed that no "hearing" as defined by former § 2.2-4001 (see now this section) was held concerning the permit holder's permit request. Residents Involved in Saving Env't, Inc. v. Commonwealth, Dep't of Envtl. Quality, 22 Va. App. 532, 471 S.E.2d 796 (1996).

Applied in Campbell v. Dep't of Forestry, 46 Va. App. 91, 616 S.E.2d 33, 2005 Va. App. LEXIS 283 (2005); George Mason Univ. v. Floyd, 275 Va. 32, 654 S.E.2d 556, 2008 Va. LEXIS 11 (2008).

CIRCUIT COURT OPINIONS

Violation letter was a case decision. — Demurrer to a petition for an appeal was denied in a dispute regarding the disposal of solid waste because a notice of violation sent to a county by the Virginia Department of Environmental Quality constituted a "case decision" since it was a determination of a violation of existing law; therefore, a county was entitled to judicial review of the matter. Rockbridge County v. Burnley, 66 Va. Cir. 308, 2004 Va. Cir. LEXIS 321 (Rockbridge County Dec. 21, 2004).

Letter applying rules and regulations to facts constituted case decision. — Letter from the Virginia Department of Environmental Quality to a county in which it refused to terminate a consent order and claimed that further study of the county's compliance with the consent order was necessary was an appealable case decision under § 2.2-4001 because the county had alleged facts in a letter to the agency that could be proved or disproved and would entitle the county to termination. The department's failure to articulate facts justifying denial of termination, and its contention that further study was needed, was agency inaction that could continue indefinitely and constituted a final agency decision; since the consent order could be considered "laws or regulations" and termination could be considered a "right or benefit" for purposes of ripeness, the department's demurrer alleging that the letter was not an appealable case decision was denied and the county's petition for termination of the consent order was allowed to proceed. Accomack County v. Burnley, 66 Va. Cir. 83, 2004 Va. Cir. LEXIS 328 (Accomack County Oct. 5, 2004).

§ 2.2-4002. Exemptions from chapter generally. — A. Although required to comply with § 2.2-4103 of the Virginia Register Act (§ 2.2-4100 et seq.), the following agencies shall be exempted from the provisions of this chapter, except to the extent that they are specifically made subject to §§ 2.2-4024, 2.2-4030 and 2.2-4031:

1. The General Assembly.

2. Courts, any agency of the Supreme Court, and any agency that by the Constitution is expressly granted any of the powers of a court of record.

3. The Department of Game and Inland Fisheries in promulgating regulations regarding the management of wildlife and for all case decisions rendered pursuant to any provisions of Chapters 2 (§ 29.1-200 et seq.), 3 (§ 29.1-300 et seq.), 4 (§ 29.1-400 et seq.), 5 (§ 29.1-500 et seq.), and 7 (§ 29.1-700 et seq.) of Title 29.1.

4. The Virginia Housing Development Authority.

5. Municipal corporations, counties, and all local, regional or multijurisdictional authorities created under this Code, including those with federal authorities.

6. Educational institutions operated by the Commonwealth, provided that, with respect to § 2.2-4031, such educational institutions shall be exempt from the publication requirements only with respect to regulations that pertain to (i) their academic affairs, (ii) the selection, tenure, promotion and disciplining of faculty and employees, (iii) the selection of students, and (iv) rules of conduct and disciplining of students.

7. The Milk Commission in promulgating regulations regarding (i) producers' licenses and bases, (ii) classification and allocation of milk, computation of sales and shrinkage, and (iii) class prices for producers' milk, time and method of payment, butterfat testing and differential.

8. The Virginia Resources Authority.

9. Agencies expressly exempted by any other provision of this Code.

10. The Department of General Services in promulgating standards for the inspection of buildings for asbestos pursuant to § 2.2-1164.

11. The State Council of Higher Education for Virginia, in developing, issuing, and revising guidelines pursuant to § 23-9.6:2.

12. The Commissioner of Agriculture and Consumer Services in adopting regulations pursuant to subsection B of § 3.1-726 and in adopting regulations pursuant to § 3.1-741.6.

13. The Commissioner of Agriculture and Consumer Services and the Board of Agriculture and Consumer Services in promulgating regulations pursuant to subsections B and C of § 3.1-106.4, subsection B of § 3.1-126.12:1, §§ 3.1-271.1, 3.1-530.1, and 3.1-398, subsections B and C of § 3.1-828.4, and subsection A of § 3.1-884.21:1.

14. The Board of Optometry when specifying therapeutic pharmaceutical agents, treatment guidelines, and diseases and abnormal conditions of the human eye and its adnexa for TPA-certification of optometrists pursuant to Article 5 (§ 54.1-3222 et seq.) of Chapter 32 of Title 54.1.

15. The Virginia War Memorial Foundation.

16. The Virginia Medicaid Prior Authorization Advisory Committee in making recommendations to the Board of Medical Assistance Services regarding prior authorization for prescription drug coverage pursuant to Article 4 (§ 32.1-331.12 et seq.) of Chapter 10 of Title 32.1.

17. The State Board of Education, in developing, issuing, and revising guidelines pursuant to § 22.1-203.2.

18. The Virginia Racing Commission, (i) when acting by and through its duly appointed stewards or in matters related to any specific race meeting or (ii) in promulgating technical rules regulating actual live horse racing at race meetings licensed by the Commission.

19. The Virginia Small Business Financing Authority.

20. The Virginia Economic Development Partnership Authority.

21. The Board of Agriculture and Consumer Services in adopting, amending or repealing regulations pursuant to subsection A (ii) of § 59.1-156.

22. The Insurance Continuing Education Board pursuant to § 38.2-1867.

23. The Board of Health in promulgating the list of diseases that shall be reported to the Department of Health pursuant to § 32.1-35 and in adopting, amending or repealing regulations pursuant to subsection C of § 35.1-14 that incorporate the Food and Drug Administration's Food Code pertaining to restaurants or food service.

24. The nonprofit, nonstock corporation established by the Commissioner of Agriculture and Consumer Services pursuant to § 3.1-14.01.

25. **(Expires December 31, 2010)** The Secretary of Natural Resources in setting a date of closure for the Chesapeake Bay purse seine fishery for Atlantic menhaden for reduction purposes pursuant to § 28.2-1000.2.

26. The Board of Pharmacy when specifying special subject requirements for continuing education for pharmacists pursuant to § 54.1-3314.1.

B. Agency action relating to the following subjects shall be exempted from the provisions of this chapter:

1. Money or damage claims against the Commonwealth or agencies thereof.

2. The award or denial of state contracts, as well as decisions regarding compliance therewith.

3. The location, design, specifications or construction of public buildings or other facilities.

4. Grants of state or federal funds or property.

5. The chartering of corporations.

6. Customary military, naval or police functions.

7. The selection, tenure, dismissal, direction or control of any officer or employee of an agency of the Commonwealth.

8. The conduct of elections or eligibility to vote.

9. Inmates of prisons or other such facilities or parolees therefrom.

10. The custody of persons in, or sought to be placed in, mental, penal or other state institutions as well as the treatment, supervision, or discharge of such persons.

11. Traffic signs, markers or control devices.

12. Instructions for application or renewal of a license, certificate, or registration required by law.

13. Content of, or rules for the conduct of, any examination required by law.

14. The administration of pools authorized by Chapter 47 (§ 2.2-4700 et seq.) of this title.

15. Any rules for the conduct of specific lottery games, so long as such rules are not inconsistent with duly adopted regulations of the State Lottery Board, and provided that such regulations are published and posted.

16. Orders condemning or closing any shellfish, finfish, or crustacea growing area and the shellfish, finfish or crustacea located thereon pursuant to Article 2 (§ 28.2-803 et seq.) of Chapter 8 of Title 28.2.

17. Any operating procedures for review of child deaths developed by the State Child Fatality Review Team pursuant to § 32.1-283.1.

18. The regulations for the implementation of the Health Practitioners' Intervention Program and the activities of the Intervention Program Committee pursuant to Chapter 25.1 (§ 54.1-2515 et seq.) of Title 54.1.

19. The process of reviewing and ranking grant applications submitted to the Commonwealth Neurotrauma Initiative Advisory Board pursuant to Chapter 3.1 (§ 51.5-12.1 et seq.) of Title 51.5.

20. Loans from the Small Business Environmental Compliance Assistance Fund pursuant to Article 4 (§ 10.1-1197.1 et seq.) of Chapter 11.1 of Title 10.1.

21. The Virginia Breeders Fund created pursuant to § 59.1-372.

22. The types of pari-mutuel wagering pools available for live or simulcast horse racing.

23. The administration of medication or other substances foreign to the natural horse.

C. Minor changes to regulations published in the Virginia Administrative Code under the Virginia Register Act, Chapter 41 (§ 2.2-4100 et seq.) of this title, made by the Virginia Code Commission pursuant to § 30-150, shall be exempt from the provisions of this chapter. (1985, c. 602, § 9-6.14:4.1; 1986, c. 615; 1987, cc. 375, 652; 1988, cc. 364, 424, 498, 723, 765, 820; 1989, cc. 54, 299, 478; 1990, cc. 721, 968; 1991, cc. 80, 294, 344; 1992, cc. 200, 409, 488, 592, 793; 1993, cc. 537, 669, 898; 1994, cc. 237, 577, 649, 740, 743, 801; 1995, cc. 103, 499, 516; 1996, cc. 51, 152, 158, 189, 205, 279, 320, 345, 573, 590, 598, 638, 705, 735, 818, 1012; 1997, cc. 87, 88, 109, 212, 390, 439, 567, 624, 785, 806, 845, 850, 861, 868; 1998, cc. 39, 619, 784; 1999, cc. 412, 421, 433, 603; 2000, cc. 382, 400, 924, 1011; 2001, cc. 465, 523, 688, 820, 844; 2003, cc. 639, 695; 2004, c. 802; 2006, c. 442; 2007, cc. 41, 870, 932; 2008, c. 672.)

Cross references. — As to the purchase of continued health insurance coverage by the surviving spouse and any dependents of an active local law-enforcement officer, firefighter, etc., through a plan sponsor, see § 2.2-1206.

Editor's note. — Effective October 1, 2008, in subdivision A 12, the reference to "subsection B of § 3.1-726" should read "subsection B of § 3.2-6002" and the reference to "§ 3.1-741.6" should read "§ 3.2-6023." In subdivision A 13, the reference to "subsections B and C of § 3.1-106.4, subsection B of § 3.1-126.12:1, §§ 3.1-271.1, 3.1-530.1, and 3.1-398, subsections B and C of § 3.1-828.4, and subsection A of § 3.1-884.21:1" should read "subsections B and D of § 3.2-3601, subsection B of § 3.2-3701, § 3.2-4002, subsections B and D of § 3.2-4801, §§ 3.2-5121 and 3.2-5206, and subsection A of § 3.2-5406." The reference in subdivision A 24 to "§ 3.1-14.01" should read "subdivision B 5 of § 3.2-102."

Acts 2001, cc. 465, 523, 688, and 820 amended § 9-6.14:4.1, from which this section is derived. Pursuant to § 30-152, Acts 2001, cc. 465, 523, 688 and 820 have been given effect in this section as set out above.

Acts 2004, c. 802, cl. 2, provides: "That the Rules and Regulations Pertaining to the Sanitary and Operating Procedures in Retail Food Stores adopted by the Board of Agriculture and Consumer Services in effect as of July 1, 2004, shall remain in effect until the effective date of new regulations that have been adopted by the Board of Agriculture and Consumer Services pursuant to subsection B of § 3.1-398."

Acts 2007, c. 41, which added subdivision A 25, in cl. 2 provides: "The provisions of this act shall expire on December 31, 2010."

Acts 2007, cc. 870 and 932, cl. 3, provides: "That the Commissioner of Agriculture and Consumer Services shall implement the provisions of this act consistent with an opinion of the Attorney General dated April 18, 2006, within 90 days of the effective date of this act."

The 2007 amendments. — The 2007 amendment by c. 41, which expires December 31, 2010, added subdivision A 24 [now 25].

The 2007 amendments by cc. 870 and 932, effective April 4, 2007, are identical, and added subdivision A 24.

The 2008 amendments. — The 2008 amendment by c. 672, added subdivision A 26.

Law Review. — For 1985 survey of Virginia administrative procedure, see 19 U. Rich. L. Rev. 657 (1985). For article on opening Virginia courthouse doors to review of administrative decisions involving public assistance, see 21 U. Rich. L. Rev. 161 (1986). For 1987 survey of Virginia administrative procedure, see 21 U. Rich. L. Rev. 611 (1987). For survey of administrative procedure in Virginia for 1989, see 23 U. Rich. L. Rev. 431 (1989). For an article, "Administrative Procedure," see 31 U. Rich. L. Rev. 907 (1997).

Michie's Jurisprudence. — For related discussion, see 1A M.J. Administrative Law, § 2.

CASE NOTES

Editor's note. — Some of the cases below were decided under former corresponding provisions.

A local school board is not a board or unit of the state government, but rather is an entity of a municipality or a county. As such, it is not an administrative agency as contemplated by the Administrative Process Act. Schwartz v. Highland County School Bd., 2 Va. App. 554, 346 S.E.2d 544 (1986).

Where the Workers' Compensation Commission merely implemented an expedited procedure to determine the continuing award or denial of claimant's benefits, the Commission was acting in a quasi-judicial function and, therefore, was not subject to the Virginia Administrative Process Act. Williams v. VEPCO, 18 Va. App. 569, 445 S.E.2d 693 (1994).

State Water Control Law. — Any agency action rendered under the State Water Control Law must be subject to appeal under the Virginia Administrative Process Act if the action otherwise meets the Act's criteria for judicial review and is not subject to any other statutory exclusion. May Dep't Stores Co. v. Commonwealth, Dep't of Envtl. Quality, 29 Va. App. 589, 513 S.E.2d 880 (1999).

Because state emergency regulations are statutorily short-lived, there is no need for a "good cause" requirement, as defined in the federal cases that deal with emergency regulations of undefined duration; instead, the Governor's prior approval is the appropriate safeguard. Committee of Concerned Citizens for Property Rights v. Chesapeake Bay Local Assistance Bd., 15 Va. App. 664, 426 S.E.2d 499 (1993).

A committee of concerned citizens did not meet its burden of proof in claiming that the Chesapeake Local Assistance Board acted unlawfully in determining an "emergency" to exist to warrant dispensing with the public notice comment requirements of former § 9-6.14:7.1 (see now § 2.2-4007), in repromulgating, on an emergency basis, regulations which had been invalidated by a circuit court on procedural grounds. Committee of Concerned Citizens for Property Rights v. Chesapeake Bay Local Assistance Bd., 15 Va. App. 664, 426 S.E.2d 499 (1993).

Applied in Garraghty v. Va. Ret. Sys., 45 Va. App. 1, 608 S.E.2d 477, 2005 Va. App. LEXIS 44 (2005); Alliance to Save the Mattaponi v. Commonwealth Dep't of Envtl. Quality ex rel. State Water Control Bd., 270 Va. 423, 621 S.E.2d 78, 2005 Va. LEXIS 100 (2005).

§ 2.2-4003. Venue. — In all proceedings under § 2.2-4019 or 2.2-4020 venue shall be in the city or county where the administrative agency maintains its principal office or as the parties may otherwise agree. In all proceedings under § 2.2-4026, venue shall be as specified in subdivision 1 of § 8.01-261. (1975, c. 503, § 9-6.14:5; 1977, c. 624; 2001, c. 844; 2007, cc. 873, 916.)

The 2007 amendments. — The 2007 amendments by cc. 873 and 916 are identical, and rewrote this section.

§ 2.2-4004. Severability. — The provisions of regulations adopted under this chapter or the application thereof to any person or circumstances that are held invalid shall not affect the validity of other regulations, provisions or applications that can be given effect without the invalid provisions or applications. The provisions of all regulations are severable unless (i) the regulation specifically provides that its provisions are not severable or (ii) it is apparent that two or more regulations or provisions must operate in accord with one another. (1987, c. 55, § 9-6.14:5.1; 2001, c. 844.)

§ 2.2-4005. Review of exemptions by Joint Legislative Audit and Review Commission. — The Joint Legislative Audit and Review Commission shall conduct a review periodically of the exemptions authorized by this chapter. The purpose of this review shall be to assess whether there are any exemptions that should be discontinued or modified. (1985, c. 602, § 9-6.14:4.1; 1986, c. 615; 1987, cc. 375, 652; 1988, cc. 364, 424, 498, 723, 765, 820; 1989, cc. 54, 299, 478; 1990, cc. 721, 968; 1991, cc. 80, 294, 344; 1992, cc. 200, 409, 488, 592, 793; 1993, cc. 537, 669, 898; 1994, cc. 237, 577, 649, 740, 743, 801; 1995, cc. 103, 499, 516; 1996, cc. 51, 152, 158, 189, 205, 279, 320, 345, 573, 590, 598,

638, 705, 735, 818, 1012; 1997, cc. 87, 88, 109, 212, 390, 439, 567, 624, 785, 806, 845, 850, 861, 868; 1998, cc. 39, 619, 784; 1999, cc. 412, 421, 433, 603; 2000, cc. 382, 400, 924, 1011; 2001, c. 844.)

Article 2.

Regulations.

Michie's Jurisprudence. — For related discussion, see 1A M.J. Administrative Law, §§ 9 — 12.

§ **2.2-4006. Exemptions from requirements of this article.** — A. The following agency actions otherwise subject to this chapter and § 2.2-4103 of the Virginia Register Act shall be exempted from the operation of this article:

1. Agency orders or regulations fixing rates or prices.

2. Regulations that establish or prescribe agency organization, internal practice or procedures, including delegations of authority.

3. Regulations that consist only of changes in style or form or corrections of technical errors. Each promulgating agency shall review all references to sections of the Code of Virginia within their regulations each time a new supplement or replacement volume to the Code of Virginia is published to ensure the accuracy of each section or section subdivision identification listed.

4. Regulations that are:

a. Necessary to conform to changes in Virginia statutory law or the appropriation act where no agency discretion is involved;

b. Required by order of any state or federal court of competent jurisdiction where no agency discretion is involved; or

c. Necessary to meet the requirements of federal law or regulations, provided such regulations do not differ materially from those required by federal law or regulation, and the Registrar has so determined in writing. Notice of the proposed adoption of these regulations and the Registrar's determination shall be published in the Virginia Register not less than 30 days prior to the effective date of the regulation.

5. Preliminary program permit fees of the Department of Environmental Quality assessed pursuant to subsection C of § 10.1-1322.2.

6. Regulations of the Pesticide Control Board adopted pursuant to subsection B of § 3.1-249.51 or clause (v) or (vi) of subsection C of § 3.1-249.53 after having been considered at two or more Board meetings and one public hearing.

7. Regulations of the regulatory boards served by (i) the Department of Labor and Industry pursuant to Title 40.1 and (ii) the Department of Professional and Occupational Regulation or the Department of Health Professions pursuant to Title 54.1 that are limited to reducing fees charged to regulants and applicants.

8. The development and issuance of procedural policy relating to risk-based mine inspections by the Department of Mines, Minerals and Energy authorized pursuant to §§ 45.1-161.82 and 45.1-161.292:55.

9. General permits issued by the (a) State Air Pollution Control Board pursuant to Chapter 13 (§ 10.1-1300 et seq.) of Title 10.1 or (b) State Water Control Board pursuant to the State Water Control Law (§ 62.1-44.2 et seq.), Chapter 24 (§ 62.1-242 et seq.) of Title 62.1 and Chapter 25 (§ 62.1-254 et seq.) of Title 62.1, (c) Virginia Soil and Water Conservation Board pursuant to the Virginia Stormwater Management Act (§ 10.1-603.1 et seq.) of Title 10.1, and (d) the development and issuance of general wetlands permits by the Marine Resources Commission pursuant to subsection B of § 28.2-1307, if the respective Board or Commission (i) provides a Notice of Intended Regulatory

Action in conformance with the provisions of § 2.2-4007.01, (ii) following the passage of 30 days from the publication of the Notice of Intended Regulatory Action forms a technical advisory committee composed of relevant stakeholders, including potentially affected citizens groups, to assist in the development of the general permit, (iii) provides notice and receives oral and written comment as provided in § 2.2-4007.03, and (iv) conducts at least one public hearing on the proposed general permit.

10. The development and issuance by the Board of Education of guidelines on constitutional rights and restrictions relating to the recitation of the pledge of allegiance to the American flag in public schools pursuant to § 22.1-202.

11. Regulations of the Board of the Virginia College Savings Plan adopted pursuant to § 23-38.77.

12. Regulations of the Marine Resources Commission.

13. Regulations adopted by the Board of Housing and Community Development pursuant to (i) Statewide Fire Prevention Code (§ 27-94 et seq.), (ii) the Industrialized Building Safety Law (§ 36-70 et seq.), (iii) the Uniform Statewide Building Code (§ 36-97 et seq.), and (iv) § 36-98.3, provided the Board (a) provides a Notice of Intended Regulatory Action in conformance with the provisions of § 2.2-4007.01, (b) publishes the proposed regulation and provides an opportunity for oral and written comments as provided in § 2.2-4007.03, and (c) conducts at least one public hearing as provided in §§ 2.2-4009 and 36-100 prior to the publishing of the proposed regulations. Notwithstanding the provisions of this subdivision, any regulations promulgated by the Board shall remain subject to the provisions of § 2.2-4007.06 concerning public petitions, and §§ 2.2-4013 and 2.2-4014 concerning review by the Governor and General Assembly.

14. Amendments to the list of drugs susceptible to counterfeiting adopted by the Board of Pharmacy pursuant to subsection B of § 54.1-3307.

B. Whenever regulations are adopted under this section, the agency shall state as part thereof that it will receive, consider and respond to petitions by any interested person at any time with respect to reconsideration or revision. The effective date of regulations adopted under this subsection shall be in accordance with the provisions of § 2.2-4015, except in the case of emergency regulations, which shall become effective as provided in subsection B of § 2.2-4012.

C. A regulation for which an exemption is claimed under this section or § 2.2-4002, or 2.2-4011 and that is placed before a board or commission for consideration shall be provided at least two days in advance of the board or commission meeting to members of the public that request a copy of that regulation. A copy of that regulation shall be made available to the public attending such meeting. (1985, c. 602, § 9-6.14:4.1; 1986, c. 615; 1987, cc. 375, 652; 1988, cc. 364, 424, 498, 723, 765, 820; 1989, cc. 54, 299, 478; 1990, cc. 721, 968; 1991, cc. 80, 294, 344; 1992, cc. 200, 409, 488, 592, 793; 1993, cc. 537, 669, 898; 1994, cc. 237, 577, 649, 740, 743, 801; 1995, cc. 103, 499, 516; 1996, cc. 51, 152, 158, 189, 205, 279, 320, 345, 573, 590, 598, 638, 705, 735, 818, 1012; 1997, cc. 87, 88, 109, 212, 390, 439, 567, 624, 785, 806, 845, 850, 861, 868; 1998, cc. 39, 619, 784; 1999, cc. 412, 421, 433, 603; 2000, cc. 382, 400, 924, 1011; 2001, c. 844; 2003, c. 436; 2005, c. 102; 2006, cc. 632, 719; 2007, cc. 873, 916.)

Cross references. — As to the Virginia Respite Care Grant Fund being exempt from the Administrative Process Act, see § 2.2-717. As to the purchase of continued health insurance coverage by the surviving spouse and any dependents of an active local law-enforcement officer, firefighter, etc., through a plan sponsor, see § 2.2-1206. As to guidelines for the award of Virginia Investment Performance Grants, see § 2.2-5101. As to the allocation and awarding of grants under the Virginia Investment Partnership Grant Fund, see § 2.2-5104. As to streamlined permitting process for qualified energy generators, see § 10.1-1308.1.

Editor's note. — Effective October 1, 2008, in subdivision A 6, the reference to "subsection

B of § 3.1-249.51 or clause (v) or (vi) of subsection C of § 3.1-249.53" should read "subsection B of § 3.2-3929 or clause (v) or (vi) of subsection C of § 3.2-3931."

Acts 2005, c. 102, cl. 2, provides: "That the Governor shall make new appointments for each of the three at-large members of the Board in accordance with the provisions of this act on July 1, 2005. The new appointments of the at-large members of the Board shall go into effect upon the expiration of the current members' terms in January 2006, and the terms shall be staggered as follows: one member for a term of two years; one member for a term of three years; and one member for a term of four years. The Governor shall designate the term to be served by each appointee at the time of appointment and may reappoint the existing at-large members of the Board."

Acts 2005, c. 102, cl. 3, provides: "That the Director of the Department of Conservation and Recreation shall amend the Stormwater Management Regulations by removing the out-of-date Best Management Practices (BMP) nutrient removal efficiency information and adding it into the Virginia Stormwater Management Handbook guidance document where it shall be more effectively updated for public use."

The 2007 amendments. — The 2007 amendments by cc. 873 and 916 are identical, and substituted "§ 2.2-4007.01" for "subsection B of § 2.2-4007" and "§ 2.2-4007.03" for "subsection F of § 2.2-4007" in subdivisions A 9 and 13; and substituted "§ 2.2-4007.06" for "subsection K of § 2.2-4007" in subdivision A 13.

§ 2.2-4007. Petitions for new or amended regulations; opportunity for public comment. — A. Any person may petition an agency to request the agency to develop a new regulation or amend an existing regulation. The petition shall state (i) the substance and purpose of the rulemaking that is requested, including reference to any applicable Virginia Administrative Code sections, and (ii) reference to the legal authority of the agency to take the action requested.

B. Within 14 days of receiving a petition, the agency shall send a notice identifying the petitioner, the nature of the petitioner's request and the agency's plan for disposition of the petition to the Registrar for publication in the Virginia Register of Regulations in accordance with the provisions of subsection B of § 2.2-4031.

C. A 21-day period for acceptance of written public comment on the petition shall be provided after publication in the Virginia Register. The agency shall issue a written decision to grant or deny the petitioner's request within 90 days following the close of the comment period. However, if the rulemaking authority is vested in an entity that has not met within that 90-day period, the entity shall issue a written decision no later than 14 days after it next meets. The written decision issued by the agency shall include a statement of its reasons and shall be submitted to the Registrar for publication in the Virginia Register of Regulations. Agency decisions to initiate or not initiate rulemaking in response to petitions shall not be subject to judicial review. (1984, c. 5, § 9-6.14:7.1; 1985, c. 602; 1989, c. 71; 1991, c. 488; 1993, cc. 898, 944; 1994, c. 938; 1995, cc. 25, 677, 717, 790; 1997, c. 87; 2001, c. 844; 2002, cc. 241, 391, 747; 2003, c. 224; 2005, cc. 619, 682; 2007, cc. 873, 916.)

Editor's note. — Acts 2007, cc. 316 and 561, amended former subsection H, which was deleted by Acts 2007, cc. 873 and 916. At the direction of the Virginia Code Commission, amendments by Acts 2007, cc. 316 and 561, have been given effect in § 2.2-4007.04.

The 2007 amendments. — The 2007 amendments by cc. 873 and 916 are identical, and deleted subsections B through M, pertaining to notice of intended regulatory actions, informational proceedings, effect of noncompliance, and economic impact analysis and made related changes.

Law Review. — For survey of Virginia administrative law for the year 1974-1975, see 61 Va. L. Rev. 1632 (1975). For survey of Virginia administrative law for the year 1976-77, see 63 Va. L. Rev. 1366 (1977). For article on legislative changes to Virginia administrative rulemaking, see 19 U. Rich. L. Rev. 107 (1984). For survey of administrative procedure in Virginia for 1989, see 23 U. Rich. L. Rev. 431 (1989). For survey on environmental law in Virginia for 1989, see 23 U. Rich. L. Rev. 625 (1989).

CASE NOTES

Burden of proof on challenger to "emergency" regulations. — A committee of concerned citizens did not meet its burden of proof in claiming that the Chesapeake Local Assistance Board acted unlawfully in determining an "emergency" to exist to warrant dispensing with the public notice comment requirements of this section, in repromulgating, on an emergency basis, regulations which had been invalidated by a circuit court on procedural grounds. Committee of Concerned Citizens for Property Rights v. Chesapeake Bay Local Assistance Bd., 15 Va. App. 664, 426 S.E.2d 499 (1993) (decided under former corresponding provisions).

CIRCUIT COURT OPINIONS

Adoption of regulations. — Trial court concluded that the Virginia Waste Management Board did not violate the Administrative Process Act in adopting two regulations that the association challenged, as it allowed interested parties to submit data, views, and arguments, it allowed the proposed regulations and notice of opportunity to submit material, and it was shown not to have been required to deliver to the Registrar of Regulations a statement of the purpose of the regulation. James River Ass'n v. Commonwealth ex rel. Waste Mgmt. Bd., 67 Va. Cir. 44, 2005 Va. Cir. LEXIS 148 (Richmond Feb. 4, 2005).

§ 2.2-4007.01. Notice of intended regulatory action; public hearing. — A. In the case of all regulations, except those regulations exempted by § 2.2-4002, 2.2-4006, 2.2-4011, or 2.2-4012.1, an agency shall provide the Registrar of Regulations with a Notice of Intended Regulatory Action that describes the subject matter and intent of the planned regulation. At least 30 days shall be provided for public comment, to include an on-line public comment forum on the Virginia Regulatory Town Hall, after publication of the Notice of Intended Regulatory Action. An agency shall not file proposed regulations with the Registrar until the public comment period on the Notice of Intended Regulatory Action has closed.

B. Agencies shall state in the Notice of Intended Regulatory Action whether they plan to hold a public hearing on the proposed regulation after it is published. Agencies shall hold such public hearings if required by basic law. If the agency states an intent to hold a public hearing on the proposed regulation in the Notice of Intended Regulatory Action, then it shall hold the public hearing. If the agency states in its Notice of Intended Regulatory Action that it does not plan to hold a hearing on the proposed regulation, then no public hearing is required unless, prior to completion of the comment period specified in the Notice of Intended Regulatory Action, (i) the Governor directs the agency to hold a public hearing or (ii) the agency receives requests for a public hearing from at least 25 persons. (2007, cc. 873, 916.)

§ 2.2-4007.02. Public participation guidelines. — A. Public participation guidelines for soliciting the input of interested parties in the formation and development of its regulations shall be developed, adopted, and used by each agency pursuant to the provisions of this chapter. The guidelines shall set out any methods for the identification and notification of interested parties and any specific means of seeking input from interested persons or groups that the agency intends to use in addition to the Notice of Intended Regulatory Action. The guidelines shall set out a general policy for the use of standing or ad hoc advisory panels and consultation with groups and individuals registering interest in working with the agency. Such policy shall address the circumstances in which the agency considers the panels or consultation appropriate and intends to make use of the panels or consultation.

B. In formulating any regulation, including but not limited to those in public assistance and social services programs, the agency pursuant to its public participation guidelines shall afford interested persons an opportunity to submit data, views, and arguments, either orally or in writing, to the agency, to include an on-line public comment forum on the Virginia Regulatory Town Hall, or other specially designated subordinate. However, the agency may begin drafting the proposed regulation prior to or during any opportunities it provides to the public to submit comments. (2007, cc. 873, 916.)

Editor's note. — Acts 2008, cc. 321 and 575, cl. 1 provides: "§ 1. That on or before July 1, 2008, the Department of Planning and Budget, in consultation with the Office of the Attorney General, shall (i) develop model public participation guidelines meeting the requirements of § 2.2-4007.02 of the Code of Virginia and (ii) provide these model public participation guidelines to each agency that has the authority to promulgate regulations. By December 1, 2008, each agency shall either (a) adopt the model public participation guidelines or (b) if significant additions or changes are proposed, promulgate the model public participation guidelines with the proposed changes as fast-track regulations pursuant to § 2.2-4012.1 of the Code of Virginia. Agency action in adopting the model public participation guidelines in accordance with clause (a) shall be exempt from the operation of Article 2 (§ 2.2-4006 et seq.) of Chapter 40 of Title 2.2 of the Code of Virginia. The repeal of any existing public participation guidelines shall occur in the same regulatory action as the promulgation of the model public participation guidelines required by this section.

"§ 2. The model public participation guidelines adopted pursuant to this act shall apply to the promulgation and adoption of regulations for which a notice of intended regulatory action is filed in accordance with § 2.2-4007.01 of the Code of Virginia on or after January 1, 2009.

"§ 3. However, any amendments made after January 1, 2009, to an agency's public participation guidelines adopted as required by this act shall be subject to the requirements of the Administrative Process Act (§ 2.2-4000 et seq.) of the Code of Virginia.

"§ 4. For the purposes of this act, the terms 'agency' and 'regulations' mean the same as those terms are defined in § 2.2-4001 of the Code of Virginia."

§ 2.2-4007.03. Informational proceedings; effect of noncompliance. — A. In the case of all regulations, except those regulations exempted by § 2.2-4002, 2.2-4006, or 2.2-4011, the proposed regulation and general notice of opportunity for oral or written submittals as to that regulation shall be posted on the Virginia Regulatory Town Hall and published in the Virginia Register of Regulations in accordance with the provisions of subsection B of § 2.2-4031. In addition, the agency may, in its discretion, (i) publish the notice in any newspaper and (ii) publicize the notice through press releases and such other media as will best serve the purpose and subject involved. The Register and any newspaper publication shall be made at least 60 days in advance of the last date prescribed in the notice for such submittals. All notices, written submittals, and transcripts and summaries or notations of oral presentations, as well as any agency action thereon, shall be matters of public record in the custody of the agency.

B. If an agency wishes to change a proposed regulation before adopting it as a final regulation, it may choose to publish a revised proposed regulation, provided the latter is subject to a public comment period of at least 30 additional days and the agency complies in all other respects with this section.

C. In no event shall the failure to comply with the requirements of this section be deemed mere harmless error for the purposes of § 2.2-4027. (2007, cc. 873, 916.)

§ 2.2-4007.04. Economic impact analysis. — A. Before delivering any proposed regulation under consideration to the Registrar as required in § 2.2-4007.05, the agency shall submit on the Virginia Regulatory Town Hall a copy of that regulation to the Department of Planning and Budget. In addition to determining the public benefit, the Department of Planning and Budget in coordination with the agency shall, within 45 days, prepare an economic impact analysis of the proposed regulation, as follows:

1. The economic impact analysis shall include but need not be limited to the projected number of businesses or other entities to whom the regulation would apply; the identity of any localities and types of businesses or other entities particularly affected by the regulation; the projected number of persons and employment positions to be affected; the impact of the regulation on the use and value of private property, including additional costs related to the development of real estate for commercial or residential purposes; and the projected costs to affected businesses, localities, or entities of implementing or complying with the regulations, including the estimated fiscal impact on such localities and sources of potential funds to implement and comply with such regulation. A copy of the economic impact analysis shall be provided to the Joint Commission on Administrative Rules;

2. If the regulation may have an adverse effect on small businesses, the economic impact analysis shall also include (i) an identification and estimate of the number of small businesses subject to the regulation; (ii) the projected reporting, recordkeeping, and other administrative costs required for small businesses to comply with the regulation, including the type of professional skills necessary for preparing required reports and other documents; (iii) a statement of the probable effect of the regulation on affected small businesses; and (iv) a description of any less intrusive or less costly alternative methods of achieving the purpose of the regulation. As used in this subdivision, "small business" has the same meaning as provided in subsection A of § 2.2-4007.1; and

3. In the event the Department cannot complete an economic impact statement within the 45-day period, it shall advise the agency and the Joint Commission on Administrative Rules as to the reasons for the delay. In no event shall the delay exceed 30 days beyond the original 45-day period.

B. Agencies shall provide the Department with such estimated fiscal impacts on localities and sources of potential funds. The Department may request the assistance of any other agency in preparing the analysis. The Department shall deliver a copy of the analysis to the agency drafting the regulation, which shall comment thereon as provided in § 2.2-4007.05, a copy to the Registrar for publication with the proposed regulation, and an electronic copy to each member of the General Assembly. No regulation shall be promulgated for consideration pursuant to § 2.2-4007.05 until the impact analysis has been received by the Registrar. For purposes of this section, the term "locality, business, or entity particularly affected" means any locality, business, or entity that bears any identified disproportionate material impact that would not be experienced by other localities, businesses, or entities. The analysis shall represent the Department's best estimate for the purposes of public review and comment on the proposed regulation. The accuracy of the estimate shall in no way affect the validity of the regulation, nor shall any failure to comply with or otherwise follow the procedures set forth in this subsection create any cause of action or provide standing for any person under Article 5 (§ 2.2-4025 et seq.) or otherwise to challenge the actions of the Department hereunder or the action of the agency in adopting the proposed regulation. (2007, cc. 316, 561, 873, 916.)

Editor's note. — Acts 2007, c. 316, amended former subsection H of § 2.2-4007. The language from subsection H was rewritten as this section as enacted by Acts 2007, cc. 873 and 916. At the direction of the Virginia Code Commission, the amendment by Acts 2007, c. 316, was given effect in this section by deleting "and" preceding "a copy" and inserting "and an electronic copy to each member of the General Assembly" following "regulation" in the third sentence of subsection B.

Acts 2007, c. 561, amended former subsection H of § 2.2-4007. The language from subsection H was rewritten as this section as enacted by Acts 2007, cc. 873 and 916. At the direction of the Virginia Code Commission the amendments by Acts 2007, c. 561, were given effect in this section by inserting "including additional costs related to the development of real estate for commercial or residential purposes" following "private property" in the first sentence and adding the last sentence of subdivision A 1.

§ 2.2-4007.05. Submission of proposed regulations to the Registrar. — Before promulgating any regulation under consideration, the agency shall deliver a copy of that regulation to the Registrar together with a summary of the regulation and a separate and concise statement of (i) the basis of the regulation, defined as the statutory authority for promulgating the regulation, including an identification of the section number and a brief statement relating the content of the statutory authority to the specific regulation proposed; (ii) the purpose of the regulation, defined as the rationale or justification for the new provisions of the regulation, from the standpoint of the public's health, safety, or welfare; (iii) the substance of the regulation, defined as the identification and explanation of the key provisions of the regulation that make changes to the current status of the law; (iv) the issues of the regulation, defined as the primary advantages and disadvantages for the public, and as applicable for the agency or the state, of implementing the new regulatory provisions; and (v) the agency's response to the economic impact analysis submitted by the Department of Planning and Budget pursuant to § 2.2-4007.04. Any economic impact estimate included in the agency's response shall represent the agency's best estimate for the purposes of public review and comment, but the accuracy of the estimate shall in no way affect the validity of the regulation. Staff as designated by the Code Commission shall review proposed regulation submission packages to ensure that the requirements of this subsection are met prior to publication of the proposed regulation in the Register. The summary; the statement of the basis, purpose, substance, and issues; the economic impact analysis; and the agency's response shall be published in the Virginia Register of Regulations and be available on the Virginia Regulatory Town Hall, together with the notice of opportunity for oral or written submittals on the proposed regulation. (2007, cc. 873, 916.)

§ 2.2-4007.06. Changes between proposed and final regulations. — If one or more changes with substantial impact are made to a proposed regulation from the time that it is published as a proposed regulation to the time it is published as a final regulation, any person may petition the agency within 30 days from the publication of the final regulation to request an opportunity for oral and written submittals on the changes to the regulation. If the agency receives requests from at least 25 persons for an opportunity to submit oral and written comments on the changes to the regulation, the agency shall (i) suspend the regulatory process for 30 days to solicit additional public comment and (ii) file notice of the additional 30-day public comment period with the Registrar of Regulations, unless the agency determines that the changes made are minor or inconsequential in their impact. The comment period, if any, shall begin on the date of publication of the notice in the Register. Agency denial of petitions for a comment period on changes to the regulation shall be subject to judicial review. (2007, cc. 873, 916.)

§ 2.2-4007.07. State Air Pollution Control Board; variances. — The provisions of §§ 2.2-4007 through 2.2-4007.06 shall not apply to the issuance by the State Air Pollution Control Board of variances to its regulations. (2007, cc. 873, 916.)

§ 2.2-4007.1. Regulatory flexibility for small businesses; periodic review of regulations. — A. As used in this section, *"small business"* means a business entity, including its affiliates, that (i) is independently owned and operated and (ii) employs fewer than 500 full-time employees or has gross annual sales of less than $6 million.

B. In addition to the requirements of §§ 2.2-4007 through 2.2-4007.06, prior to the adoption of any proposed regulation, the agency proposing a regulation shall prepare a regulatory flexibility analysis in which the agency shall consider utilizing alternative regulatory methods, consistent with health, safety, environmental, and economic welfare, that will accomplish the objectives of applicable law while minimizing the adverse impact on small businesses. The agency shall consider, at a minimum, each of the following methods of reducing the effects of the proposed regulation on small businesses:

1. The establishment of less stringent compliance or reporting requirements;

2. The establishment of less stringent schedules or deadlines for compliance or reporting requirements;

3. The consolidation or simplification of compliance or reporting requirements;

4. The establishment of performance standards for small businesses to replace design or operational standards required in the proposed regulation; and

5. The exemption of small businesses from all or any part of the requirements contained in the proposed regulation.

C. Prior to the adoption of any proposed regulation that may have an adverse effect on small businesses, each agency shall notify the Joint Commission on Administrative Rules, through the Virginia Regulatory Town Hall, of its intent to adopt the proposed regulation. The Joint Commission on Administrative Rules shall advise and assist agencies in complying with the provisions of this section.

D. In addition to the requirements of § 2.2-4017, on or before July 1, 2009, an agency shall review its existing regulations to determine whether they should be continued without change or be amended or repealed, consistent with the stated objectives of applicable law, to minimize the economic impact of regulations on small businesses. If an agency head determines that completion of the review of existing regulations is not feasible by July 1, 2009, that agency shall publish a statement certifying that determination. An agency may extend the date required by this subsection in increments of one year, not to exceed a total of five years.

E. In addition to other requirements of § 2.2-4017, all final regulations adopted after July 1, 2005, shall be reviewed every five years to ensure that they minimize the economic impact on small businesses in a manner consistent with the stated objectives of applicable law.

F. The regulatory review required by this section shall include consideration of:

1. The continued need for the rule;

2. The nature of complaints or comments received concerning the regulation from the public;

3. The complexity of the regulation;

4. The extent to which the regulation overlaps, duplicates, or conflicts with federal or state law or regulation; and

5. The length of time since the regulation has been evaluated or the degree to which technology, economic conditions, or other factors have changed in the area affected by the regulation. (2005, cc. 619, 682; 2007, cc. 873, 916.)

The 2007 amendments. — The 2007 amendments by cc. 873 and 916 are nearly identical, and inserted "2.2-4007.06" in the introductory language of subsection B and made related changes; and inserted "through the Virginia Regulatory Town Hall" in subsection C.

Subsection C is set out in the form above at the direction of the Virginia Code Commission.

§ **2.2-4008. Availability of guidance documents.** — It shall be the duty of every agency to annually file with the Registrar for publication in the Virginia Register of Regulations a list of any guidance documents upon which the agency currently relies. The filing shall be made on or before January 1 of each year in a format to be developed by the Registrar. Each agency shall also (i) maintain a complete list of all of its currently operative guidance documents and make the list available for public inspection, (ii) make available for public inspection the full texts of all guidance documents to the extent inspection is permitted by law, and (iii) upon request, make copies of such lists or guidance documents available without charge, at cost, or on payment of a reasonable fee. (1997, c. 11, § 9-6.14:7.2; 2001, c. 844.)

§ **2.2-4009. Evidentiary hearings on regulations.** — Where an agency proposes to consider the exercise of authority to promulgate a regulation, it may conduct or give interested persons an opportunity to participate in a public evidentiary proceeding; and the agency shall always do so where the basic law requires a hearing. Evidentiary hearings may be limited to the trial of factual issues directly related to the legal validity of the proposed regulation in any of the relevant respects outlined in § 2.2-4027 of this chapter.

General notice of the proceedings shall be published as prescribed in § 2.2-4007.01. In addition, where the proposed regulation is to be addressed to named persons, the latter shall also be given the same notice individually by mail or otherwise if acknowledged in writing. The proceedings may be conducted separately from, and in any event the record thereof shall be separate from, any other or additional proceedings the agency may choose or be required to conduct for the reception of general data, views, and argument pursuant to § 2.2-4007.02 or otherwise. Any probative evidence may be received except that the agency shall as a matter of efficiency exclude irrelevant, immaterial, insubstantial, privileged, or repetitive proofs, and may deny rebuttal, or cross-examination. Testimony may be admitted in written form provided those who have prepared it are made available for examination in person.

The agency or one or more of its subordinates specially designated for the purpose shall preside at the taking of evidence and may administer oaths and affirmations. The proceedings shall be recorded verbatim and the record thereof shall be made available to interested persons for transcription at their expense or, if transcribed by or for the agency, for inspection or purchase at cost.

Where subordinates preside at the taking of the evidence, they shall report their recommendations and proposed findings and conclusions that shall be made available upon request to the participants in the taking of evidence as well as other interested persons and serve as a basis for exceptions, briefs, or oral argument to the agency itself. Whether or not subordinates take the evidence, after opportunity for the submittal of briefs on request and such oral argument as may be scheduled, the agency may settle the terms of the regulation and shall promulgate it only upon (i) its findings of fact based upon the record of evidence made pursuant to this section and facts of which judicial notice may be taken, (ii) statements of basis and purpose as well as comment upon data received in any informational proceedings held under § 2.2-4007.01 and (iii) the conclusions required by the terms of the basic law under which the agency is operating. (1975, c. 503, § 9-6.14:8; 1985, c. 602; 2001, c. 844; 2007, cc. 873, 916.)

The 2007 amendments. — The 2007 amendments by cc. 873 and 916 are identical, and substituted "2.2-4007.01" for "2.2-4007" in the second and fourth paragraphs; and substituted "2.2-4007.02" for "2.2-4007" in the second paragraph.

Law Review. — For survey of Virginia administrative law for the year 1974-1975, see 61 Va. L. Rev. 1632 (1975).

CASE NOTES

Editor's note. — The cases below were decided under former corresponding provisions.

When an agency fails to conform to required statutory authority when enacting its regulations, an affected party may successfully challenge the regulations without the necessity of showing that it was harmed by the agency's failure to comply with the law. Commonwealth ex rel. State Water Control Bd. v. APCO, 9 Va. App. 254, 386 S.E.2d 633 (1989), aff'd, 12 Va. App. 73, 402 S.E.2d 703 (1991).

State Water Control Board required to hold formal evidential hearing. — Under its basic law, the State Water Control Board is required to hold a formal evidential hearing to receive any probative evidence on any relevant fact pursuant to this section before it could exercise its authority in setting state water quality standards. Commonwealth ex rel. State Water Control Bd. v. APCO, 9 Va. App. 254, 386 S.E.2d 633 (1989), aff'd, 12 Va. App. 73, 402 S.E.2d 703 (1991).

State Water Control Board failed to comply with this section. — The State Water Control Board failed to comply with the requirements of former § 9-6.14:8 (see now this section) and § 62.1-44.15(3a) by failing to hold an evidential hearing in order to promulgate its regulations. Commonwealth ex rel. State Water Control Bd. v. APCO, 9 Va. App. 254, 386 S.E.2d 633 (1989), aff'd, 12 Va. App. 73, 402 S.E.2d 703 (1991).

§ 2.2-4010. Pilot programs for regulations imposing local government mandates. — Where an agency proposes to consider the exercise of authority to promulgate a regulation that will impose a statewide mandate on the Commonwealth's localities, the agency shall consider, where appropriate, implementing the regulation on a limited basis with a representative number of localities. An agency may use such a pilot program to determine the effectiveness or impact of proposed regulations prior to statewide adoption. (1993, c. 168, § 9-6.14:8.1; 2001, c. 844.)

§ 2.2-4011. Emergency regulations; publication; exceptions. — A. Regulations that an agency finds are necessitated by an emergency situation may be adopted by an agency upon consultation with the Attorney General, which approval shall be granted only after the agency has submitted a request stating in writing the nature of the emergency, and the necessity for such action shall be at the sole discretion of the Governor.

B. Agencies may also adopt emergency regulations in situations in which Virginia statutory law or the appropriation act or federal law or federal regulation requires that a regulation be effective in 280 days or less from its enactment, and the regulation is not exempt under the provisions of subdivision A. 4. of § 2.2-4006. In such cases, the agency shall state in writing the nature of the emergency and of the necessity for such action and may adopt the regulations. Pursuant to § 2.2-4012, such regulations shall become effective upon approval by the Governor and filing with the Registrar of Regulations.

C. All emergency regulations shall be limited to no more than twelve months in duration. During the twelve-month period, an agency may issue additional emergency regulations as needed addressing the subject matter of the initial emergency regulation, but any such additional emergency regulations shall not be effective beyond the twelve-month period from the effective date of the initial emergency regulation. If the agency wishes to continue regulating the subject matter governed by the emergency regulation beyond the twelve-month limitation, a regulation to replace the emergency regulation shall be promulgated in accordance with this article. The Notice of Intended Regulatory Action to promulgate a replacement regulation shall be filed with the Registrar within sixty days of the effective date of the emergency regulation and published as soon as practicable, and the proposed replacement regulation shall be filed with the Registrar within 180 days after the effective date of the emergency regulation and published as soon as practicable.

D. In the event that an agency concludes that despite its best efforts, a replacement regulation cannot be adopted before expiration of the 12-month period described in subsection C, it may seek the prior written approval of the Governor to extend the duration of the emergency regulation for a period of not more than six additional months. Any such request must be submitted to the Governor at least 30 days prior to the scheduled expiration of the emergency regulation and shall include a description of the agency's efforts to adopt a replacement regulation together with the reasons that a replacement regulation cannot be adopted before the expiration of the emergency regulation. Upon approval of the Governor, the duration of the emergency regulation shall be extended for a period of no more than six months. Such approval shall be in the sole discretion of the Governor and shall not be subject to judicial review. Agencies shall notify the Registrar of Regulations of the new expiration date of the emergency regulation as soon as practicable.

E. Emergency regulations shall be published as soon as practicable in the Register.

F. The Regulations of the Marine Resources Commission shall be excluded from the provisions of this section. (1975, c. 503, § 9-6.14:9; 1977, cc. 450, 459; 1981, c. 387; 1982, c. 425; 1983, c. 295; 1984, c. 5; 1985, c. 602, § 9-6.14:4.1; 1986, c. 615; 1987, cc. 375, 652; 1988, cc. 364, 424, 498, 723, 765, 820; 1989, cc. 54, 71, 299, 478; 1990, cc. 721, 968; 1991, cc. 80, 294, 344; 1992, cc. 200, 409, 488, 592, 793, 829; 1993, cc. 537, 669, 898; 1994, cc. 237, 577, 649, 740, 743, 801, 938; 1995, cc. 103, 499, 516; 1996, cc. 51, 152, 158, 189, 205, 279, 320, 345, 573, 590, 598, 638, 705, 735, 818, 1012; 1997, cc. 87, 88, 109, 212, 390, 439, 567, 624, 785, 806, 845, 850, 861, 868; 1998, cc. 39, 619, 784; 1999, cc. 412, 421, 433, 603; 2000, cc. 382, 400, 924, 1011; 2001, c. 844; 2007, cc. 873, 916.)

Editor's note. — Acts 2008, c. 879, effective for the biennium ending June 30, 2010, in Item 306 M, provides: "M.1. The Department of Medical Assistance Services shall have the authority to seek federal approval of changes to its MEDALLION waiver and its Medallion II waiver.

"2. In order to conform the state regulations to the federally approved changes and to implement the provisions of this act, the department shall promulgate emergency regulations to become effective within 280 days or less from the enactment of this act. The department shall implement these necessary regulatory changes to be consistent with federal approval of the waiver changes."

The 2007 amendments. — The 2007 amendments by cc. 873 and 916 are identical, and redesignated former subsection A as A through C; added the language beginning "may be adopted" to the end of subsection A; substituted "Agencies may also adopt emergency regulations in situations in" for "For the purposes of this subsection, 'emergency situation' means a situation (i) involving an imminent threat to public health or safety or (ii) in" in subsection B; substituted "All emergency" for "The" in subsection C; and inserted subsection D and redesignated the remaining subsections accordingly.

Law Review. — For survey of Virginia administrative law for the year 1974-1975, see 61 Va. L. Rev. 1632 (1975). For survey of Virginia administrative law for the year 1976-77, see 63 Va. L. Rev. 1366 (1977). For article, "Legislative and Executive Veto of Rules of Administrative Agencies: Models and Alternatives," see 24 Wm. & Mary L. Rev. 79 (1982).

CASE NOTES

Editor's note. — The case below was decided under former corresponding provisions.

Even those regulations exempted from promulgation process must go through adoption procedure. Johnston-Willis, Ltd. v. Kenley, 6 Va. App. 231, 369 S.E.2d 1 (1988).

OPINIONS OF THE ATTORNEY GENERAL

Suspension of requirements for licensure of health professionals. — Health boards may promulgate emergency regulations suspending licensure requirements for health professionals in the event of a public health disaster. See opinion of Attorney General to The Honorable John M. O'Bannon, III, Member, House of Delegates, 02-069 (11/13/02).

§ 2.2-4012. Purpose; adoption; effective date; filing; duties of Registrar of Regulations. — A. The purpose of the regulatory procedures shall be to provide a regulatory plan that is predictable, based on measurable and anticipated outcomes, and is inclined toward conflict resolution.

B. Subject to the provisions of §§ 2.2-4013 and 2.2-4014, all regulations, including those that agencies, pursuant to § 2.2-4002, 2.2-4006, or 2.2-4011, may elect to dispense with the public procedures provided by §§ 2.2-4007.01 and 2.2-4009, may be formally and finally adopted by the signed order of the agency so stating. No regulation except an emergency regulation or a noncontroversial regulation promulgated pursuant to § 2.2-4012.1 shall be effective until the expiration of the applicable period as provided in § 2.2-4015. In the case of an emergency regulation filed in accordance with § 2.2-4011, the regulation shall become effective upon its adoption and filing with the Registrar of Regulations, unless a later date is specified. The originals of all regulations shall remain in the custody of the agency as public records subject to judicial notice by all courts and agencies. They, or facsimiles thereof, shall be made available for public inspection or copying. Full and true copies shall also be additionally filed, registered, published, or otherwise made publicly available as required by other laws.

C. Prior to the publication for hearing of a proposed regulation, copies of the regulation and copies of the summary and statement as to the basis, purpose, substance, issues, and the economic impact estimate of the regulation submitted by the Department of Planning and Budget and the agency's response thereto as required by § 2.2-4007.04 shall be transmitted to the Registrar of Regulations, who shall retain these documents.

D. All regulations adopted pursuant to this chapter shall contain a citation to the section of the Code of Virginia that authorizes or requires the regulations and, where the regulations are required to conform to federal law or regulation in order to be valid, a citation to the specific federal law or regulation to which conformity is required.

E. Immediately upon the adoption by any agency of any regulation in final form, a copy of (i) the regulation, (ii) a then current summary and statement as to the basis, purpose, substance, issues, and the economic impact estimate of the regulation submitted by the Department of Planning and Budget, and (iii) the agency's summary description of the nature of the oral and written data, views, or arguments presented during the public proceedings and the agency's comments thereon shall be transmitted to the Registrar of Regulations, who shall retain these documents as permanent records and make them available for public inspection. A draft of the agency's summary description of public comment shall be sent by the agency to all public commenters on the proposed regulation at least five days before final adoption of the regulation. (1975, c. 503, § 9-6.14:9; 1977, cc. 450, 459; 1981, c. 387; 1982, c. 425; 1983, c. 295; 1984, c. 5; 1989, c. 71; 1992, c. 829; 1993, c. 898; 1994, c. 938; 2001, c. 844; 2003, c. 224; 2007, cc. 873, 916.)

The 2007 amendments. — The 2007 amendments by cc. 873 and 916 are identical, and substituted "2.2-4007.01" for "2.2-4007" in subsection B; and substituted "2.2-4007.04" for "2.2-4007" in subsection C.

Law Review. — For article discussing decisions of Virginia courts dealing with state administrative procedures between June 1, 2002 and June 1, 2003, see 38 U. Rich. L. Rev. 39 (2003).

§ **2.2-4012.1. Fast-track rulemaking process.** — Notwithstanding any other provision, rules that are expected to be noncontroversial may be promulgated or repealed in accordance with the process set out in this section. Upon the concurrence of the Governor, and after written notice to the applicable standing committees of the Senate of Virginia and the House of Delegates, and to the Joint Commission on Administrative Rules, the agency may submit a fast-track regulation without having previously published a Notice of Intended Regulatory Action. The fast-track regulation shall be published in the Virginia Register of Regulations and posted on the Virginia Regulatory Town Hall, along with an agency statement setting out the reasons for using the fast-track rulemaking process. Such regulations shall be subject to the requirements set out in §§ 2.2-4007.03, 2.2-4007.04, and 2.2-4007.05, except that the time for receiving public comment need not exceed 30 days after (i) publication of the regulation in the Virginia Register of Regulations and (ii) a public comment forum opens on the Virginia Regulatory Town Hall. The time for preparation of the economic impact analysis shall not exceed 30 days. If an objection to the use of the fast-track process is received within the public comment period from 10 or more persons, any member of the applicable standing committee of either house of the General Assembly or of the Joint Commission on Administrative Rules, the agency shall (i) file notice of the objection with the Registrar of Regulations for publication in the Virginia Register, and (ii) proceed with the normal promulgation process set out in this article with the initial publication of the fast-track regulation serving as the Notice of Intended Regulatory Action. Otherwise, the regulation will become effective or shall be repealed as appropriate, 15 days after the close of the comment period, unless the regulation or repeal is withdrawn or a later effective date is specified by the agency. (2003, c. 224; 2007, cc. 873, 916.)

The 2007 amendments. — The 2007 amendments by cc. 873 and 916 are nearly identical, and inserted "or repealed," the language beginning "be published in" and ending "Such regulations shall," "or shall be repealed as appropriate," and "or repeal," and substituted the language beginning "§§ 2.2-4007.03" and ending "not exceed 30 days" for "subsections F, H, and I of § 2.2-4007 and shall be published in the Virginia Register of Regulations along with an agency statement setting out the reasons for using the fast-track rulemaking process."

§ **2.2-4013. Executive review of proposed and final regulations; changes with substantial impact.** — A. The Governor shall adopt and publish procedures by executive order for review of all proposed regulations governed by this chapter by June 30 of the year in which the Governor takes office. The procedures shall include (i) review by the Attorney General to ensure statutory authority for the proposed regulations; and (ii) examination by the Governor to determine if the proposed regulations are (a) necessary to protect the public health, safety and welfare and (b) clearly written and easily understandable. The procedures may also include review of the proposed regulation by the appropriate Cabinet Secretary.

The Governor shall transmit his comments, if any, on a proposed regulation to the Registrar and the agency no later than fifteen days following the completion of the public comment period provided for in § 2.2-4007.01. The Governor may recommend amendments or modifications to any regulation that would bring that regulation into conformity with statutory authority or state or federal laws, regulations or judicial decisions.

Not less than fifteen days following the completion of the public comment period provided for in § 2.2-4007.01, the agency may (i) adopt the proposed regulation if the Governor has no objection to the regulation; (ii) modify and adopt the proposed regulation after considering and incorporating the Governor's objections or suggestions, if any; or (iii) adopt the regulation without changes despite the Governor's recommendations for change.

B. Upon final adoption of the regulation, the agency shall forward a copy of the regulation to the Registrar of Regulations for publication as soon as practicable in the Register. All changes to the proposed regulation shall be highlighted in the final regulation, and substantial changes to the proposed regulation shall be explained in the final regulation.

C. If the Governor finds that one or more changes with substantial impact have been made to the proposed regulation, he may require the agency to provide an additional thirty days to solicit additional public comment on the changes by transmitting notice of the additional public comment period to the agency and to the Registrar within the thirty-day adoption period described in subsection D, and publishing the notice in the Register. The additional public comment period required by the Governor shall begin upon publication of the notice in the Register.

D. A thirty-day final adoption period for regulations shall commence upon the publication of the final regulation in the Register. The Governor may review the final regulation during this thirty-day final adoption period and if he objects to any portion or all of a regulation, the Governor may file a formal objection to the regulation, suspend the effective date of the regulation in accordance with subsection B of § 2.2-4014, or both.

If the Governor files a formal objection to the regulation, he shall forward his objections to the Registrar and agency prior to the conclusion of the thirty-day final adoption period. The Governor shall be deemed to have acquiesced to a promulgated regulation if he fails to object to it or if he fails to suspend the effective date of the regulation in accordance with subsection B of § 2.2-4014 during the thirty-day final adoption period. The Governor's objection, or the suspension of the regulation, or both if applicable, shall be published in the Register.

A regulation shall become effective as provided in § 2.2-4015.

E. This section shall not apply to the issuance by the State Air Pollution Control Board of variances to its regulations. (1984, c. 5, § 9-6.14:9.1; 1993, cc. 551, 772, 898; 1995, cc. 25, 736; 2001, c. 844; 2007, cc. 873, 916.)

The 2007 amendments. — The 2007 amendments by cc. 873 and 916 are identical, and substituted "2.2-4007.01" for "2.2-4007" in the second and third paragraphs of subsection A.

Michie's Jurisprudence. — For related discussion, see 1A M.J. Administrative Law, § 10.

§ 2.2-4014. Legislative review of proposed and final regulations. — A. After publication of the Register pursuant to § 2.2-4031, the standing committee of each house of the General Assembly to which matters relating to the content of the regulation are most properly referable or the Joint Commission on Administrative Rules may meet and, during the promulgation or final adoption process, file with the Registrar and the promulgating agency an objection to a proposed or final adopted regulation. The Registrar shall publish any such objection received by him as soon as practicable in the Register. Within 21 days after the receipt by the promulgating agency of a legislative objection, that agency shall file a response with the Registrar, the objecting legislative committee or the Joint Commission on Administrative Rules, and the Governor. If a legislative objection is filed within the final adoption period, subdivision A 1 of § 2.2-4015 shall govern.

B. In addition or as an alternative to the provisions of subsection A, the standing committee of both houses of the General Assembly to which matters relating to the content are most properly referable or the Joint Commission on Administrative Rules may suspend the effective date of any portion or all of a final regulation with the Governor's concurrence. The Governor and (i) the applicable standing committee of each house or (ii) the Joint Commission on Administrative Rules may direct, through a statement signed by a majority of their respective members and by the Governor, that the effective date of a portion or all of the final regulation is suspended and shall not take effect until the end of the next regular legislative session. This statement shall be transmitted to the promulgating agency and the Registrar within the 30-day adoption period, and shall be published in the Register.

If a bill is passed at the next regular legislative session to nullify a portion but not all of the regulation, then the promulgating agency (i) may promulgate the regulation under the provision of subdivision A 4 a of § 2.2-4006, if it makes no changes to the regulation other than those required by statutory law or (ii) shall follow the provisions of §§ 2.2-4007.01 through 2.2-4007.06, if it wishes to also make discretionary changes to the regulation. If a bill to nullify all or a portion of the suspended regulation, or to modify the statutory authority for the regulation, is not passed at the next regular legislative session, then the suspended regulation shall become effective at the conclusion of the session, unless the suspended regulation is withdrawn by the agency.

C. A regulation shall become effective as provided in § 2.2-4015.

D. This section shall not apply to the issuance by the State Air Pollution Control Board of variances to its regulations. (1984, c. 5, § 9-6.14:9.2; 1993, cc. 551, 772; 2001, c. 844; 2002, c. 677; 2003, c. 212; 2004, c. 777; 2007, cc. 873, 916.)

Cross references. — As to powers of the Joint Commission on Administrative Rules to suspend the effective date of any portion or all of a final resolution, see § 30-73.3.

Editor's note. — Acts 2004, c. 777, cl. 2 repealed Acts 2002, c. 677, cl. 2, which had provided that the provisions of c. 677 would expire on June 30, 2004. Therefore, the 2002 amendment will not expire.

Acts 2007, c. 732, cl. 2, provides: "That the Board of Game and Inland Fisheries shall submit the proposed and final regulations authorized under the provisions of this act to the Senate Committee on Agriculture, Conservation and Natural Resources and the House Committee on Agriculture, Chesapeake and Natural Resources at the same time such regulations are submitted to the Virginia Register, so that the Committees may exercise their oversight responsibilities pursuant to § 2.2-4014 of the Code of Virginia."

The 2007 amendments. — The 2007 amendments by cc. 873 and 916 are identical, and substituted "§§ 2.2-4007.01 through 2.2-4007.06" for "§ 2.2-4007" in the second paragraph of subsection B.

§ 2.2-4015. Effective date of regulation; exception. — A. A regulation adopted in accordance with this chapter and the Virginia Register Act (§ 2.2-4100 et seq.) shall become effective at the conclusion of the thirty-day final adoption period provided for in subsection D of § 2.2-4013, or any other later date specified by the agency, unless:

1. A legislative objection has been filed in accordance with § 2.2-4014, in which event the regulation, unless withdrawn by the agency, shall become effective on a date specified by the agency that shall be after the expiration of the applicable twenty-one-day extension period provided in § 2.2-4014;

2. The Governor has exercised his authority in accordance with § 2.2-4013 to require the agency to provide for additional public comment, in which event the regulation, unless withdrawn by the agency, shall become effective on a date specified by the agency that shall be after the period for which the Governor has provided for additional public comment;

3. The Governor and (i) the appropriate standing committees of each house of the General Assembly or (ii) the Joint Commission on Administrative Rules have exercised their authority in accordance with subsection B of § 2.2-4014 to suspend the effective date of a regulation until the end of the next regular legislative session; or

4. The agency has suspended the regulatory process in accordance with § 2.2-4007.06, or for any reason it deems necessary or appropriate, in which event the regulation, unless withdrawn by the agency, shall become effective in accordance with subsection B.

B. Whenever the regulatory process has been suspended for any reason, any action by the agency that either amends the regulation or does not amend the regulation but specifies a new effective date shall be considered a readoption of the regulation for the purposes of appeal. If the regulation is suspended under § 2.2-4007.06, such readoption shall take place after the thirty-day public comment period required by that subsection. Suspension of the regulatory process by the agency may occur simultaneously with the filing of final regulations as provided in subsection B of § 2.2-4013.

When a regulation has been suspended, the agency must set the effective date no earlier than fifteen days from publication of the readoption action and any changes made to the regulation. During that fifteen-day period, if the agency receives requests from at least twenty-five persons for the opportunity to comment on new substantial changes, it shall again suspend the regulation pursuant to § 2.2-4007.06.

C. This section shall not apply to the issuance by the State Air Pollution Control Board of variances to its regulations. (1984, c. 5, § 9-6.14:9.3; 1993, cc. 551, 772, 898; 1995, c. 25; 2001, c. 844; 2002, cc. 391, 677; 2004, c. 777; 2007, cc. 873, 916.)

Cross references. — As to powers of the Joint Commission on Administrative Rules to suspend the effective date of any portion or all of a final resolution, see § 30-73.3.

Editor's note. — Acts 2004, c. 777, cl. 2 repealed Acts 2002, c. 677, cl. 2, which had provided that the provisions of c. 677 would expire on June 30, 2004. Therefore, the 2002 amendment will not expire.

The 2007 amendments. — The 2007 amendments by cc. 873 and 916 are identical, and substituted "§ 2.2-4007.06" for "subsection K of § 2.2-4007" in subdivision A 4 and twice throughout subsection B.

§ 2.2-4016. Withdrawal of regulation. — Nothing in this chapter shall prevent any agency from withdrawing any regulation at any time prior to the effective date of that regulation. A regulation may be repealed after its effective date only in accordance with the provisions of this chapter that govern the adoption of regulations. (1984, c. 5, § 9-6.14:9.4; 1985, c. 602; 2001, c. 844.)

§ 2.2-4017. Periodic review of regulations. — Each Governor shall mandate through executive order a procedure for periodic review during that Governor's administration of regulations of agencies within the executive branch of state government. The procedure shall include (i) a review by the Attorney General to ensure statutory authority for regulations and (ii) a determination by the Governor whether the regulations are (a) necessary for the protection of public health, safety and welfare and (b) clearly written and easily understandable.

The Governor may require each agency (i) to review all regulations promulgated by that agency to determine whether new regulations should be adopted and old regulations amended or repealed, and (ii) to prepare a written report summarizing the agency's findings about its regulations, its reasons for its findings and any proposed course of action. (1984, c. 5, § 9-6.14:25; 2001, c. 844.)

Law Review. — For article on legislative changes to Virginia administrative rulemaking, see 19 U. Rich. L. Rev. 107 (1984).

Article 3.

Case Decisions.

Michie's Jurisprudence. — For related discussion, see 1A M.J. Administrative Law, §§ 10, 11, 13.

§ 2.2-4018. Exemptions from operation of Article 3. — The following agency actions otherwise subject to this chapter shall be exempted from the operation of this article.

1. The assessment of taxes or penalties and other rulings in individual cases in connection with the administration of the tax laws.
2. The award or denial of claims for workers' compensation.
3. The grant or denial of public assistance or social services.
4. Temporary injunctive or summary orders authorized by law.
5. The determination of claims for unemployment compensation or special unemployment.
6. The suspension of any license, certificate, registration or authority granted any person by the Department of Health Professions or the Department of Professional and Occupational Regulation for the dishonor, by a bank or financial institution named, of any check, money draft or similar instrument used in payment of a fee required by statute or regulation.
7. The determination of accreditation or academic review status of a public school or public school division or approval by the Board of Education of a school division corrective action plan required by § 22.1-253.13:3. (1985, c. 602, § 9-6.14:4.1; 1986, c. 615; 1987, cc. 375, 652; 1988, cc. 364, 424, 498, 723, 765, 820; 1989, cc. 54, 299, 478; 1990, cc. 721, 968; 1991, cc. 80, 294, 344; 1992, cc. 200, 409, 488, 592, 793; 1993, cc. 537, 669, 898; 1994, cc. 237, 577, 649, 740, 743, 801; 1995, cc. 103, 499, 516; 1996, cc. 51, 152, 158, 189, 205, 279, 320, 345, 573, 590, 598, 638, 705, 735, 818, 1012; 1997, cc. 87, 88, 109, 212, 390, 439, 567, 624, 785, 806, 845, 850, 861, 868; 1998, cc. 39, 619, 784; 1999, cc. 412, 421, 433, 603; 2000, cc. 382, 400, 924, 1011; 2001, c. 844; 2002, c. 747; 2004, c. 965.)

Editor's note. — Acts 2004, c. 965, which added subdivision 7, in cl. 2 provides: "That the Board of Education shall promulgate regulations to implement the provisions of this act to be effective within 280 days of its enactment."

Law Review. — For 2003/2004 survey of education law, see 39 U. Rich. L. Rev. 183 (2004).

§ 2.2-4019. Informal fact finding proceedings. — A. Agencies shall ascertain the fact basis for their decisions of cases through informal conference or consultation proceedings unless the named party and the agency consent to waive such a conference or proceeding to go directly to a formal hearing. Such conference-consultation procedures shall include rights of parties to the case to (i) have reasonable notice thereof, (ii) appear in person or by counsel or other qualified representative before the agency or its subordinates, or before a hearing officer for the informal presentation of factual data, argument, or proof in connection with any case, (iii) have notice of any contrary fact basis or information in the possession of the agency that can be relied upon in making an adverse decision, (iv) receive a prompt decision of any application for a license, benefit, or renewal thereof, and (v) be informed, briefly and generally in writing, of the factual or procedural basis for an adverse decision in any case.

B. Agencies may, in their case decisions, rely upon public data, documents or information only when the agencies have provided all parties with advance notice of an intent to consider such public data, documents or information. This requirement shall not apply to an agency's reliance on case law and administrative precedent. (1975, c. 503, § 9-6.14:11; 1986, c. 615; 1989, c. 601; 1993, c. 898; 1994, c. 748; 1995, c. 398; 2001, c. 844.)

Cross references. — As to issuance of a special order by the Commissioner of Social Services, following a proceeding as provided in § 2.2-4019, for violations of the provisions of § 63.2-1700 et seq., § 54.1-3408, or regulations adopted under § 63.2-1700 et seq., see § 63.2-1709.2.

Law Review. — For survey of Virginia administrative law for the year 1974-1975, see 61 Va. L. Rev. 1632 (1975). For article, "The Federal APA and State Administrative Law," see 72 Va. L. Rev. 297 (1986). For survey of administrative procedure in Virginia for 1989, see 23 U. Rich. L. Rev. 431 (1989). For a review of administrative procedure in Virginia for year 1999, see 33 U. Rich. L. Rev. 727 (1999).

CASE NOTES

Editor's note. — Some of the cases below were decided under former corresponding provisions.

Former 9-6.14:11 (see now this section and § 2.2-4021) and former § 9-6.14:12 (see now §§ 2.2-4020, 2.2-4021) are designed to bring cases to final decision at the agency level. State Bd. of Health v. Virginia Hosp. Ass'n, 1 Va. App. 5, 332 S.E.2d 793 (1985).

Nothing in the Virginia Administrative Process Act limits number of fact-finding conferences to one. Surprenant v. Board for Contractors, 30 Va. App. 165, 516 S.E.2d 220 (1999).

"Initial determination" defined. — Date on which the Virginia Department of Medical Assistance Services held its first informal fact-finding conference (IFFC) with a corporation that was allegedly overpaid under the Medicaid program, governed the issue of whether the Department was barred by § 32.1-325.1:1 from recovering overpayments; the trial court's judgment finding that the Department could not recover payments made more than four years before it held its first IFFC was upheld, even though a cost analyst sent a Notice of Program Reimbursement to the corporation within four years after each overpayment was made. Finnerty v. Thornton Hall, Inc., 42 Va. App. 628, 593 S.E.2d 568, 2004 Va. App. LEXIS 100 (2004).

No right to cross-examination in informal hearings. — That a real estate appraiser was not able to cross examine witnesses at her license revocation hearing did not deprive her of due process. Section 2.2-4020, providing for cross-examination of witnesses, was inapplicable, because she had an informal hearing under § 2.2-4019, which did not entitle her to cross-examine witnesses or force them to testify under oath. Haley v. Commonwealth, — Va. App. —, — S.E.2d —, 2006 Va. App. LEXIS 441 (Oct. 3, 2006).

Standard of review. — Whether reviewing the Commissioner's decision as if a formal proceeding had been conducted pursuant to former § 9-6.14:12 (see now §§ 2.2-4020, 2.2-4021) or an informal proceeding conducted pursuant to this section, the circuit court was required to determine whether the Commissioner had complied with statutory or legal authority in reaching his decision. Roanoke Mem. Hosps. v. Kenley, 3 Va. App. 599, 352 S.E.2d 525 (1987).

Ninety-day period commenced when fact-finding conference held by Virginia Retirement System. — Ninety-day period for review of disability retirement benefits commenced when Virginia Retirement System (VRS) representative held informal fact-finding conference, not when VRS received medical board report on claimant's condition; agency's failure to render decision meant that decision was deemed to be in claimant's favor 30 days after agency received notice from claimant that a decision was due. Rizzo v. Virginia Retirement Sys., 255 Va. 375, 497 S.E.2d 852 (1998).

Consideration of consent order proper. — Virginia Auctioneers Board's consideration of a prior consent order complied with § 2.2-4019 and did not prejudice an auctioneer where the auctioneer knew for three months that the Board had considered the consent order in its previous meeting and thus he had advance notice that the board might consider the consent order in its reconsideration of the decision made at the prior meeting. Khan v. Auctioneers Bd., 42 Va. App. 469, 592 S.E.2d 755, 2004 Va. App. LEXIS 78 (2004).

Remand to correct alleged taint by ex parte communications. — Remand ordered by the trial court to include ex parte communications that were made during the administrative adjudication was sufficient to cleanse the decisionmaking process regarding applications for a certificate of public need filed by two competing hospitals of any alleged taint as to the ex parte communications. Loudoun Hosp. Ctr. v. Stroube, 50 Va. App. 478, 650 S.E.2d 879, 2007 Va. App. LEXIS 371 (2007).

Award of certificate of public need was appropriate. — Virginia State Health Commissioner's award of a certificate of public need to a hospital was affirmed upon judicial review because: (1) a remand ordered by the trial court to include ex parte communications that were made during the administrative adjudication was sufficient to cleanse the decisionmaking process of any alleged taint as to the ex parte communications; and (2) the Commissioner's decision was not arbitrary and capricious under § 2.2-4019 as the Commissioner, by way of the hearing officer, identified several factual differences between the application of the hospital that was denied and the subsequent amended application of the hospital that was accepted. Loudoun Hosp. Ctr. v. Stroube, 50 Va. App. 478, 650 S.E.2d 879, 2007 Va. App. LEXIS 371 (2007).

Any error in consideration of challenged evidence was harmless. — Any consideration of evidence challenged by two landfill operators admitted at an informal fact finding conference was harmless as the presiding officer did not refer to the challenged evidence, but referenced certain evidence of the operators; even if the Director of the Virginia Department of Environmental Quality considered the challenged materials, the Director's conclusions were based on some information that was provided by the operators that part of the Columbia aquifer remained at the site. Elbow Farm, Inc. v. Paylor, — Va. App. —, — S.E.2d —, 2007 Va. App. LEXIS 48 (Feb. 13, 2007).

CIRCUIT COURT OPINIONS

Reliance on public data, documents, information. — Pursuant to subsection B of § 2.2-4019, the Board was permitted to rely upon public information or documents as the Board informed the license applicant of its intent to rely upon such information in a letter. Dick's Inn, L.L.C. v. Va. Alcoholic Bev. Control Bd., 60 Va. Cir. 407, 2002 Va. Cir. LEXIS 411 (Richmond 2002).

"Initial determination" defined. — By defining "initial determination" in terms of §§ 32.1-325.1, 2.2-4019, and 2.2-4020, the legislature has made it clear that it intends for "initial determination" to mean the decision of the agency after an informal fact finding conference and before the formal agency hearing. Thornton Hall, Inc. v. Finnerty, 61 Va. Cir. 346, 2003 Va. Cir. LEXIS 140 (Norfolk 2003), aff'd, 42 Va. App. 628, 593 S.E.2d 568 (2004).

§ 2.2-4020. Formal hearings; litigated issues. — A. The agency shall afford opportunity for the formal taking of evidence upon relevant fact issues in any case in which the basic laws provide expressly for decisions upon or after hearing and may do so in any case to the extent that informal procedures under § 2.2-4019 have not been had or have failed to dispose of a case by consent.

B. Parties to formal proceedings shall be given reasonable notice of the (i) time, place, and nature thereof, (ii) basic law under which the agency contemplates its possible exercise of authority, and (iii) matters of fact and law asserted or questioned by the agency. Applicants for licenses, rights, benefits, or renewals thereof have the burden of approaching the agency concerned without such prior notice but they shall be similarly informed thereafter in the further course of the proceedings whether pursuant to this section or to § 2.2-4019.

C. In all such formal proceedings the parties shall be entitled to be accompanied by and represented by counsel, to submit oral and documentary evidence and rebuttal proofs, to conduct such cross-examination as may elicit a full and fair disclosure of the facts, and to have the proceedings completed and a decision made with dispatch. The burden of proof shall be upon the proponent or applicant. The presiding officers at the proceedings may (i) administer oaths and affirmations, (ii) receive probative evidence, exclude irrelevant, immaterial, insubstantial, privileged, or repetitive proofs, rebuttal, or cross-examination, rule upon offers of proof, and oversee a verbatim recording of the evidence, (iii) hold conferences for the settlement or simplification of issues by consent, (iv) dispose of procedural requests, and (v) regulate and expedite the course of the hearing. Where a hearing officer presides, or where a subordinate designated for that purpose presides in hearings specified in subsection F of § 2.2-4024, he shall recommend findings and a decision unless the agency shall by its procedural regulations provide for the making of findings and an initial decision by the presiding officers subject to review and reconsideration by the agency on appeal to it as of right or on its own motion. The agency shall give deference to findings by the presiding officer explicitly based on the demeanor of witnesses.

D. Prior to the recommendations or decisions of subordinates, the parties concerned shall be given opportunity, on request, to submit in writing for the record (i) proposed findings and conclusions and (ii) statements of reasons therefor. In all cases, on request, opportunity shall be afforded for oral argument (i) to hearing officers or subordinate presiding officers, as the case may be, in all cases in which they make such recommendations or decisions or (ii) to the agency in cases in which it makes the original decision without such prior recommendation and otherwise as it may permit in its discretion or provide by general rule. Where hearing officers or subordinate presiding officers, as the case may be, make recommendations or decisions, the agency shall receive and act on exceptions thereto.

E. All decisions or recommended decisions shall be served upon the parties, become a part of the record, and briefly state or recommend the findings, conclusions, reasons, or basis therefor upon the evidence presented by the record and relevant to the basic law under which the agency is operating together with the appropriate order, license, grant of benefits, sanction, relief, or denial thereof. (1975, c. 503, § 9-6.14:12; 1986, c. 615; 1991, c. 584; 1993, c. 898; 1995, c. 398; 2001, c. 844.)

Cross references. — As to interpreters for the deaf in agency proceedings, see § 2.2-3400 et seq.

Law Review. — For a review of administrative procedure in Virginia for year 1999, see 33 U. Rich. L. Rev. 727 (1999).

CASE NOTES

Editor's note. — Some of the cases below were decided under former corresponding provisions.

Former §§ 9-6.14:11 and 9-6.14:12 (see now §§ 2.2-4019 to 2.2-4021) are designed to bring cases to final decision at the agency level. State Bd. of Health v. Virginia Hosp. Ass'n, 1 Va. App. 5, 332 S.E.2d 793 (1985).

Right to a formal hearing is governed by the Virginia Administrative Process Act and the basic law (§ 62.1-44.2 et seq.). Environmental Defense Fund v. Virginia State Water Control Bd., 12 Va. App. 456, 404 S.E.2d 728 (1991).

Former § 9-6.14:12 (see now this section and § 2.2-4021) does not mandate formal hearings where basic law does not. — Where basic law (§ 62.1-44.2 et seq.) does not expressly provide for issuance of Virginia Pollutant Discharge Elimination System (VPDES) permits only upon or after formal hearings, formal hearings are not mandatory under former § 9-6.14:12 (see now this section and § 2.2-4021). Environmental Defense Fund v. Virginia State Water Control Bd., 12 Va. App. 456, 404 S.E.2d 728 (1991).

"Initial determination" defined. — Date on which the Virginia Department of Medical Assistance Services held its first informal fact-finding conference (IFFC) with a corporation that was allegedly overpaid under the Medicaid program, governed the issue of whether the Department was barred by § 32.1-325.1:1 from recovering overpayments; the trial court's judgment finding that the Department could not recover payments made more than four years before it held its first IFFC was upheld, even though a cost analyst sent a Notice of Program Reimbursement to the corporation within four years after each overpayment was made. Finnerty v. Thornton Hall, Inc., 42 Va. App. 628, 593 S.E.2d 568, 2004 Va. App. LEXIS 100 (2004).

Procedural due process. — Where the board: (1) afforded the doctor a formal hearing; (2) considered evidence from both the Attorney General and the doctor; (3) found that the doctor's misconduct led to the performance of unnecessary medical procedures, physical harm to patients, and death in one case; (4) and determined that the doctor violated several regulations, the board was authorized to conclude that the doctor posed a continuing threat to public health. The board had afforded the doctor the required procedural due process of notice and an opportunity to be heard regarding the charges against the doctor. Vuyyuru v. Va. Bd. of Med., — Va. App. —, — S.E.2d —, 2008 Va. App. LEXIS 30 (Jan. 15, 2008).

Procedural objection not waived. — The mere failure to mention issue during oral argument of the facts of the matter does not amount to a waiver of the procedural objection. This statute does not require the party who is the target of the proceeding to present oral argument before the board, or even to appear at the full board hearing. Virginia Bd. of Medicine v. Fetta, 244 Va. 276, 421 S.E.2d 410 (1992).

Denial of application for a septic tank permit after formal hearing and informal rejection of post-hearing applications constituted agency "case decision," but only the formal denial disposed of the litigated issue within the meaning of former § 9-6.14:12 (see now this section and § 2.2-4021). State Bd. of Health v. Godfrey, 223 Va. 423, 290 S.E.2d 875 (1982).

Standard of review. — Whether reviewing the Commissioner's decision as if a formal proceeding had been conducted pursuant to this section or an informal proceeding conducted pursuant to former § 9-6.14:11 (see now §§ 2.2-4019, 2.2-4021), the circuit court was required to determine whether the Commissioner had complied with statutory or legal authority in reaching his decision. Roanoke Mem. Hosps. v. Kenley, 3 Va. App. 599, 352 S.E.2d 525 (1987).

Determination of fact issues on review. — Under former § 9-6.14:17 (see now § 2.2-4027) the burden is upon the party complaining of agency action to designate and demonstrate an error of law subject to review, and the determination of an issue of fact is to be made upon the agency record if the proceeding was required to be conducted under this section. State Bd. of Health v. Godfrey, 223 Va. 423, 290 S.E.2d 875 (1982).

Failure to provide sufficient statement of particulars. — As in the criminal context, the Virginia Board of Dentistry should be required to fairly particularize the charge or charges it intends to prosecute and not be permitted to go on a fishing expedition with a drag net; the bill should be directed at those charges as to which the board expects to introduce supporting testimony. Doe v. Virginia Bd. of Dentistry, No. 0298-00-1, 2000 Va. App. LEXIS 705 (Ct. of Appeals Oct. 31, 2000).

Failure to make findings required remand. — Because the Virginia Alcoholic Beverage Control Board granted an applicant licenses allowing liquor sales only until 12:00 a.m., without making findings of fact or conclusions of law to support these time restrictions, as required by § 2.2-4020, the case was remanded to Board pursuant to § 2.2-4029 so it could make such findings. Harrison v. Ocean View Fishing Pier, LLC, 50 Va. App. 556, 651 S.E.2d 421, 2007 Va. App. LEXIS 397 (2007).

Virginia Supplemental Retirement System was not required to give formal hearing. — Circuit court was correct in finding that Virginia Supplemental Retirement System (VSRS) had not violated appellant's due process rights when it did not provide him opportunity for cross examination, conference, and consultation before denying prior service credits of retirement since basic laws establishing VSRS, set forth in former Title 51, do not require formal hearing process and appellant was given opportunity, pursuant to former § 9-6.14:11 (see now §§ 2.2-4019, 2.2-4021), to appear before hearing officer to present any additional evidence in support of his claim; therefore VSRS was required only to provide informal fact finding hearing pursuant to former § 9-6.14:11 (see now §§ 2.2-4019, 2.2-4021). Greenlee v. Virginia Supplemental Retirement Sys., No. 0765-88-2 (Ct. of Appeals Mar. 28, 1989).

Informal hearings. — That a real estate appraiser was not able to cross examine witnesses at her license revocation hearing did not deprive her of due process. This section, providing for cross-examination of witnesses, was inapplicable, because she had an informal hearing under § 2.2-4019, and under § 2.2-4019, she was not entitled to cross-examine witnesses or force them to testify under oath. Haley v. Commonwealth, — Va. App. —, — S.E.2d —, 2006 Va. App. LEXIS 441 (Oct. 3, 2006).

Case to be reheard de novo by new hearing officer after death of original officer. — Death of a hearing officer during recess of a formal administrative hearing required that case be reheard de novo by new hearing officer in disciplinary action against real estate broker, for new hearing officer had not an opportunity to observe and examine all the witnesses and especially where broker's intentions and credibility were at issue. Virginia Real Estate Bd. v. Kline, 17 Va. App. 173, 435 S.E.2d 596 (1993).

Admission of evidence and cross-examination. — At an administrative hearing at which a retailer was charged with selling alcohol to a minor, the admission of a photocopy of the minor's identification card, showing that he was 17 years of age, was not error under Va. Alcoholic Bev. Cont. Bd. R. Prac. § 1.9 as there was testimony that the photocopy was a true copy of the original, nor was the board required to call the minor, where neither the minor nor the original were available. Mirabile Corp. v. Va. Alcoholic Bev. Control Bd., No. 2126-02-4, 2003 Va. App. LEXIS 493 (Ct. of Appeals Sept. 30, 2003).

Evidence sufficient to establish violation. — Where a store relied to its detriment on subpoenas issued to witnesses (who failed to appear) by the Board and conceded that the Board had sufficient evidence to find an alcoholic beverage license violation, the store was not denied due process. 7-11, Inc. v. Va. Alcoholic Bev. Control Bd., No. 2740-02-4, 2003 Va.

App. LEXIS 324 (Ct. of Appeals June 3, 2003).

At an administrative hearing at which a retailer was charged with selling alcohol to a minor, the evidence was sufficient to establish the retailer's violation of § 4.1-304 and 3 VAC § 5-50-10 as the only identification card the minor had when he entered the retailer's store indicated he was 17, he gave the card to the retailer's employee, and the employee, after looking at it, sold the minor beer, and the clerk admitted looking at the card and miscalculating the minor's age due to blurred vision and anxiety about a long line of waiting customers. Mirabile Corp. v. Va. Alcoholic Bev. Control Bd., No. 2126-02-4, 2003 Va. App. LEXIS 493 (Ct. of Appeals Sept. 30, 2003).

CIRCUIT COURT OPINIONS

"Initial determination" defined. — By defining "initial determination" in terms of §§ 32.1-325.1, 2.2-4019, and 2.2-4020, the legislature has made it clear that it intends for "initial determination" to mean the decision of the agency after an informal fact finding conference and before the formal agency hearing. Thornton Hall, Inc. v. Finnerty, 61 Va. Cir. 346, 2003 Va. Cir. LEXIS 140 (Norfolk 2003), aff'd, 42 Va. App. 628, 593 S.E.2d 568 (2004).

Authority of director. — Director of the Virginia Department of Medical Assistance Services was free to accept all, part, or none of a hearing officer's decision without exceeding his statutory authority. Convalescent Care, Inc. v. Dep't of Med. Assistance Servs., 58 Va. Cir. 133, 2002 Va. Cir. LEXIS 136 (Richmond 2002).

Hearing officer's recommendations. — Where a Medicaid provider sought to require a state Medicaid reimbursement agency to accept corrected data from the provider, used to determine the provider's reimbursement, the agency's director, under subsection D of § 2.2-4020, did not exceed his statutory authority by refusing to accept a hearing officer's recommendation that the agency be required to accept the corrected data. Convalescent Care, Inc. v. Dep't of Med. Assistance Servs., 58 Va. Cir. 133, 2002 Va. Cir. LEXIS 136 (Richmond 2002).

Resolution without formal hearing. — After a restaurant initially requested a full unrestricted license, but when informed of the objections from a neighborhood association to the full license voluntarily agreed to a restricted license, the Board appropriately granted the restaurant a restricted license without a formal hearing. After voluntarily agreeing to a restricted license, the restaurant could not claim that the Board denied it a formal hearing. Dick's Inn, L.L.C. v. Va. Alcoholic Bev. Control Bd., 60 Va. Cir. 407, 2002 Va. Cir. LEXIS 411 (Richmond 2002).

§ **2.2-4020.1. Summary case decisions.** — A. Any person who has (i) applied for a permit, certificate, or license from an agency or (ii) received written notice of a potential violation from an agency may request a summary case decision from the agency. The request for a summary case decision shall be in writing, signed by or on behalf of the requestor, and be submitted to the agency secretary as defined by the Rules of the Supreme Court of Virginia. The request shall include:

1. A statement that no material facts are in dispute;
2. A proposed stipulation of all such undisputed material facts concerning the application or notice;
3. A clear and concise statement of the questions of law to be decided by summary case decision; and
4. A statement that the requestor waives his right to any other administrative proceeding provided in this article by the agency on the questions of law to be decided by summary case decision.

B. Within 21 days of receipt of a complete request for summary case decision, the agency shall determine whether the matter in dispute properly may be decided by summary case decision and shall promptly notify the requestor of its determination in writing. If a request for summary case decision is not complete, the agency may request additional specific information from the requestor. The agency shall decide the matter by summary case decision if it determines that there are no disputed issues of material fact. However, if (i) an informal fact-finding proceeding as provided in § 2.2-4019, a formal hearing as provided in § 2.2-4020, or other proceeding authorized by the agency's basic law concerning the application or notice has been scheduled, the requestor has been notified, and the issues that are the subject of such proceeding or hearing include questions that are the subject of the request for summary case decision or (ii) the matter must be decided through any public participation requirements under this chapter or the agency's basic law, the agency shall not be required to decide the matter by summary case decision.

C. Denial of a request for summary case decision shall not be subject to judicial review in accordance with this chapter and the Rules of the Supreme Court of Virginia, and shall not prejudice any rights the requestor has or may have under this chapter or the agency's basic law. Nothing in this article shall prevent an agency from consolidating the summary case decision proceeding into, or proceeding with, a separate informal fact-finding proceeding, formal hearing, or other proceeding authorized by the agency's basic law concerning the matter in question.

D. Upon granting a request for summary case decision, the agency shall establish a schedule for the parties to submit briefs on the questions of law in dispute and may, by agreement of the parties, provide for oral argument.

E. All decisions or recommended decisions shall be served on the requestor, become a part of the record, and briefly state or recommend the findings, conclusions, reasons, or basis therefor upon the evidence contained in the record and relevant to the basic law under which the agency is operating, together with the appropriate order, license, grant of benefits, sanction, relief, or denial thereof. (2006, c. 702.)

§ 2.2-4021. Timetable for decision; exemptions. — A. In cases where a board or commission meets to render (i) an informal fact-finding decision or (ii) a decision on a litigated issue, and information from a prior proceeding is being considered, persons who participated in the prior proceeding shall be provided an opportunity to respond at the board or commission meeting to any summaries of the prior proceeding prepared by or for the board or commission.

B. In any informal fact-finding, formal proceeding, or summary case decision proceeding in which a hearing officer is not used or is not empowered to recommend a finding, the board, commission, or agency personnel responsible for rendering a decision shall render that decision within 90 days from the date of the informal fact-finding, formal proceeding, or completion of a summary case decision proceeding, or from a later date agreed to by the named party and the agency. If the agency does not render a decision within 90 days, the named party to the case decision may provide written notice to the agency that a decision is due. If no decision is made within 30 days from agency receipt of the notice, the decision shall be deemed to be in favor of the named party. The preceding sentence shall not apply to case decisions before (i) the State Water Control Board or the Department of Environmental Quality to the extent necessary to comply with the federal Clean Water Act, (ii) the State Air Pollution Control Board or the Department of Environmental Quality to the extent necessary to comply with the federal Clean Air Act, or (iii) the Virginia Soil and Water Conservation Board or the Department of Conservation and Recreation to the extent necessary to comply with the federal Clean Water Act. An agency shall provide notification to the named party of its decision within five days of the decision.

C. In any informal fact-finding, formal proceeding, or summary case decision proceeding in which a hearing officer is empowered to recommend a finding, the board, commission, or agency personnel responsible for rendering a decision shall render that decision within 30 days from the date that the agency receives the hearing officer's recommendation. If the agency does not render a decision within 30 days, the named party to the case decision may provide written notice to the agency that a decision is due. If no decision is made within 30 days from agency receipt of the notice, the decision is deemed to be in favor of the named party. The preceding sentence shall not apply to case decisions before (i) the State Water Control Board or the Department of Environmental Quality to the extent necessary to comply with the federal Clean Water Act, (ii) the State Air Pollution Control Board or the Department of Environmental Quality to the extent necessary to comply with the federal Clean Air Act, or (iii) the Virginia Soil and Water Conservation Board or the Department of Conservation and Recreation to the extent necessary to comply with the federal Clean Water Act. An agency shall provide notice to the named party of its decision within five days of the decision.

D. The provisions of subsection B notwithstanding, if the board members or agency personnel who conducted the informal fact-finding, formal proceeding, or summary case decision proceeding are unable to attend to official duties due to sickness, disability, or termination of their official capacity with the agency, then the timeframe provisions of subsection B shall be reset and commence from the date that either new board members or agency personnel are assigned to the matter or a new proceeding is conducted if needed, whichever is later. An agency shall provide notice within five days to the named party of any incapacity of the board members or agency personnel that necessitates a replacement or a new proceeding. (1975, c. 503, §§ 9-6.14:11, 9-6.14:12; 1986, c. 615; 1989, c. 601; 1991, c. 584; 1993, c. 898; 1994, c. 748; 1995, c. 398; 2001, c. 844; 2005, c. 102; 2006, c. 702.)

Cross references. — As to interpreters for the deaf in agency proceedings, see § 2.2-3400 et seq.

Editor's note. — Acts 2005, c. 102, cl. 2, provides: "That the Governor shall make new appointments for each of the three at-large members of the Board in accordance with the provisions of this act on July 1, 2005. The new appointments of the at-large members of the Board shall go into effect upon the expiration of the current members' terms in January 2006, and the terms shall be staggered as follows: one member for a term of two years; one member for a term of three years; and one member for a term of four years. The Governor shall designate the term to be served by each appointee at the time of appointment and may reappoint the existing at-large members of the Board."

Acts 2005, c. 102, cl. 3, provides: "That the Director of the Department of Conservation and Recreation shall amend the Stormwater Management Regulations by removing the out-of-date Best Management Practices (BMP) nutrient removal efficiency information and adding it into the Virginia Stormwater Management Handbook guidance document where it shall be more effectively updated for public use."

Law Review. — For survey of Virginia administrative law for the year 1974-1975, see 61 Va. L. Rev. 1632 (1975). For article, "The Federal APA and State Administrative Law," see 72 Va. L. Rev. 297 (1986). For survey of administrative procedure in Virginia for 1989, see 23 U. Rich. L. Rev. 431 (1989). For a review of administrative procedure in Virginia for year 1999, see 33 U. Rich. L. Rev. 727 (1999).

CASE NOTES

Editor's note. — The cases below were decided under former corresponding provisions.

Former §§ 9-6.14:11 and 9-6.14:12 (see now § 2.2-4020) are designed to bring cases to final decision at the agency level. State Bd. of Health v. Virginia Hosp. Ass'n, 1 Va. App. 5, 332 S.E.2d 793 (1985).

Nothing in the Virginia Administrative Process Act limits number of fact-finding conferences to one. Surprenant v. Board for Contractors, 30 Va. App. 165, 516 S.E.2d 220 (1999).

Standard of review. — Whether reviewing the Commissioner's decision as if a formal proceeding had been conducted pursuant to former § 9-6.14:12 (see now this section and § 2.2-4020) or an informal proceeding conducted pursuant to this section, the circuit court was required to determine whether the Commissioner had complied with statutory or legal authority in reaching his decision. Roanoke Mem. Hosps. v. Kenley, 3 Va. App. 599, 352 S.E.2d 525 (1987).

Ninety-day period commenced when fact-finding conference held by Virginia Retirement System. — Ninety-day period for review of disability retirement benefits commenced when Virginia Retirement System (VRS) representative held informal fact-finding conference, not when VRS received medical board report on claimant's condition; agency's failure to render decision meant that decision was deemed to be in claimant's favor 30 days after agency received notice from claimant that a decision was due. Rizzo v. Virginia Retirement Sys., 255 Va. 375, 497 S.E.2d 852 (1998).

Right to a formal hearing is governed by the Virginia Administrative Process Act and the basic law (§ 62.1-44.2 et seq.). Environmental Defense Fund v. Virginia State Water Control Bd., 12 Va. App. 456, 404 S.E.2d 728 (1991).

Former § 9-6.14:12 (see now this section and § 2.2-4020) does not mandate formal hearings where basic law does not. — Where basic law (§ 62.1-44.2 et seq.) does not expressly provide for issuance of Virginia Pollutant Discharge Elimination System (VPDES) permits only upon or after formal hearings, formal hearings are not mandatory under former § 9-6.14:12 (see now this section and § 2.2-4020). Environmental Defense Fund v. Virginia State Water Control Bd., 12 Va. App. 456, 404 S.E.2d 728 (1991).

Procedural objection not waived. — The mere failure to mention issue during oral argument of the facts of the matter does not amount to a waiver of the procedural objection. This statute does not require the party who is the target of the proceeding to present oral argument before the board, or even to appear at the full board hearing. Virginia Bd. of Medicine v. Fetta, 244 Va. 276, 421 S.E.2d 410 (1992).

Denial of application for a septic tank permit after formal hearing and informal rejection of post-hearing applications constituted agency "case decision", but only the formal denial disposed of the litigated issue within the meaning of former § 9-6.14:12 (see now this section and § 2.2-4020). State Bd. of Health v. Godfrey, 223 Va. 423, 290 S.E.2d 875 (1982).

Determination of fact issues on review. — Under former § 9-6.14:17 (see now § 2.2-4027) the burden is upon the party complaining of agency action to designate and demonstrate an error of law subject to review, and the determination of an issue of fact is to be made upon the agency record if the proceeding was required to be conducted under this section. State Bd. of Health v. Godfrey, 223 Va. 423, 290 S.E.2d 875 (1982).

Failure to provide sufficient statement of particulars. — As in the criminal context, the Virginia Board of Dentistry should be required to fairly particularize the charge or charges it intends to prosecute and not be permitted to go on a fishing expedition with a drag net; the bill should be directed at those charges as to which the board expects to introduce supporting testimony. Doe v. Virginia Bd. of Dentistry, No. 0298-00-1, 2000 Va. App. LEXIS 705 (Ct. of Appeals Oct. 31, 2000).

Virginia Supplemental Retirement System was not required to give formal hearing. — Circuit court was correct in finding that Virginia Supplemental Retirement System (VSRS) had not violated appellant's due process rights when it did not provide him opportunity for cross examination, conference, and consultation before denying prior service credits of retirement since basic laws establishing VSRS, set forth in former Title 51, do not require formal hearing process and appellant was given opportunity, pursuant to former § 9-6.14:11 (see now this section and § 2.2-4019), to appear before hearing officer to present any additional evidence in support of his claim; therefore VSRS was required only to provide informal fact finding hearing pursuant to § 9-6.14:11 (see now this section and § 2.2-4019). Greenlee v. Virginia Supplemental Retirement Sys., No. 0765-88-2 (Ct. of Appeals Mar. 28, 1989).

Case to be reheard de novo by new hearing officer after death of original officer. — Death of a hearing officer during recess of a formal administrative hearing required that case be reheard de novo by new hearing officer in disciplinary action against real estate broker, for new hearing officer had not an opportunity to observe and examine all the witnesses and especially where broker's intentions and credibility were at issue. Virginia Real Estate Bd. v. Kline, 17 Va. App. 173, 435 S.E.2d 596 (1993).

§ 2.2-4022. Subpoenas, depositions and requests for admissions. — The agency or its designated subordinates may, and on request of any party to a case shall, issue subpoenas requiring testimony or the production of books, papers, and physical or other evidence. Any person so subpoenaed who objects may, if the agency does not quash or modify the subpoena at his timely request as illegally or improvidently granted, immediately procure by petition a decision on the validity thereof in the circuit court as provided in § 2.2-4003; and otherwise in any case of refusal or neglect to comply with an agency subpoena, unless the basic law under which the agency is operating provides some other recourse, enforcement, or penalty, the agency may procure an order of enforcement from such court. Depositions de bene esse and requests for admissions may be directed, issued, and taken on order of the agency for good cause shown; and orders or authorizations therefor may be challenged or enforced in the same manner as subpoenas. Nothing in this section shall be taken to authorize discovery proceedings. (1975, c. 503, § 9-6.14:13; 2001, c. 844.)

Law Review. — For survey of Virginia administrative law for the year 1974-1975, see 61 Va. L. Rev. 1632 (1975). For survey of Virginia administrative law and utility regulation for the year 1978-1979, see 66 Va. L. Rev. 193 (1980).

CASE NOTES

Editor's note. — The case below was decided under former corresponding provisions.

Right to subpoena. — Former § 9-6.14:13 (see now this section) creates a statutory right, under certain conditions, to a subpoena in an administrative proceeding for parties thereto. State Health Dep't Sewage Handling & Disposal v. Britton, 15 Va. App. 68, 421 S.E.2d 37 (1992).

Standard for quashing subpoena duces tecum. — While the State Health Department Sewage Handling and Disposal Appeal Review Board may quash a subpoena as "illegally or improvidently granted," it may not do so merely because it deems as too burdensome the requirement that it identify and produce relevant evidence. State Health Dep't Sewage Handling & Disposal v. Britton, 15 Va. App. 68, 421 S.E.2d 37 (1992).

Appeal review board erred in quashing appellee's subpoena duces tecum although the board argued that the other permits appellee sought to subpoena had been illegally issued in violation of the regulations, and therefore, the evidence would not establish a legal basis for his entitlement to a permit. The statute does not deny a party access to relevant evidence when, in the board's judgment, the otherwise relevant evidence might not convince it to act. While the evidence ultimately may not be sufficient to prove appellee's entitlement, he has the right of access to relevant evidence in the board's possession and control and has the right to have it considered. State Health Dep't Sewage Handling & Disposal v. Britton, 15 Va. App. 68, 421 S.E.2d 37 (1992).

§ **2.2-4023. Final orders.** — The terms of any final agency case decision, as signed by it, shall be served upon the named parties by mail unless service otherwise made is duly acknowledged by them in writing. The signed originals shall remain in the custody of the agency as public records subject to judicial notice by all courts and agencies; and they, or facsimiles thereof, together with the full record or file in every case shall be made available for public inspection or copying except (i) so far as the agency may withhold the same in whole or part for the purpose of protecting individuals mentioned from personal embarrassment, obloquy, or disclosures of a private nature including statements respecting the physical, mental, moral, or financial condition of such individuals or (ii) for trade secrets or, so far as protected by other laws, other commercial or industrial information imparted in confidence. (1975, c. 503, § 9-6.14:14; 2001, c. 844.)

CASE NOTES

Section deals only with duties of agencies. — Former § 9-6.14:14 (see now this section) does not deal with appeals but only with the duties of the various agencies. Occoquan Land Dev. Corp. v. Cooper, 239 Va. 363, 389 S.E.2d 464 (1990) (decided under corresponding former provisions).

Applied in Giannoukos v. Va. Bd. of Med. & Dep't of Health Professions, 44 Va. App. 694, 607 S.E.2d 136, 2005 Va. App. LEXIS 7 (2005).

ARTICLE 4.

Hearing Officers.

§ **2.2-4024. Hearing officers.** — A. In all formal hearings conducted in accordance with § 2.2-4020, the hearing shall be presided over by a hearing officer selected from a list prepared by the Executive Secretary of the Supreme

Court and maintained in the Office of the Executive Secretary of the Supreme Court. Parties to informal fact-finding proceedings conducted pursuant to § 2.2-4019 may agree at the outset of the proceeding to have a hearing officer preside at the proceeding, such agreement to be revoked only by mutual consent. The Executive Secretary may promulgate rules necessary for the administration of the hearing officer system and shall have the authority to establish the number of hearing officers necessary to preside over administrative hearings in the Commonwealth.

Prior to being included on the list, all hearing officers shall meet the following minimum standards:

1. Active membership in good standing in the Virginia State Bar;
2. Active practice of law for at least five years; and
3. Completion of a course of training approved by the Executive Secretary of the Supreme Court. In order to comply with the demonstrated requirements of the agency requesting a hearing officer, the Executive Secretary may require additional training before a hearing officer shall be assigned to a proceeding before that agency.

B. On request from the head of an agency, the Executive Secretary shall name a hearing officer from the list, selected on a rotation system administered by the Executive Secretary. Lists reflecting geographic preference and specialized training or knowledge shall be maintained by the Executive Secretary if an agency demonstrates the need.

C. A hearing officer shall voluntarily disqualify himself and withdraw from any case in which he cannot accord a fair and impartial hearing or consideration, or when required by the applicable rules governing the practice of law in the Commonwealth. Any party may request the disqualification of a hearing officer by filing an affidavit, prior to the taking of evidence at a hearing, stating with particularity the grounds upon which it is claimed that a fair and impartial hearing cannot be accorded, or the applicable rule of practice requiring disqualification.

The issue shall be determined not less than ten days prior to the hearing by the Executive Secretary of the Supreme Court.

D. Any hearing officer empowered by the agency to provide a recommendation or conclusion in a case decision matter shall render that recommendation or conclusion within ninety days from the date of the case decision proceeding or from a later date agreed to by the named party and the agency. If the hearing officer does not render a decision within ninety days, then the named party to the case decision may provide written notice to the hearing officer and the Executive Secretary of the Supreme Court that a decision is due. If no decision is made within thirty days from receipt by the hearing officer of the notice, then the Executive Secretary of the Supreme Court shall remove the hearing officer from the hearing officer list and report the hearing officer to the Virginia State Bar for possible disciplinary action, unless good cause is shown for the delay.

E. The Executive Secretary shall remove hearing officers from the list, upon a showing of cause after written notice and an opportunity for a hearing. When there is a failure by a hearing officer to render a decision as required by subsection D, the burden shall be on the hearing officer to show good cause for the delay. Decisions to remove a hearing officer may be reviewed by a request to the Executive Secretary for reconsideration, followed by judicial review in accordance with this chapter.

F. This section shall not apply to hearings conducted by (i) any commission or board where all of the members, or a quorum, are present; (ii) the Alcoholic Beverage Control Board, the Virginia Workers' Compensation Commission, the State Corporation Commission, the Virginia Employment Commission, the Department of Motor Vehicles under Title 46.2 (§ 46.2-100 et seq.), § 58.1-

2409, or Chapter 27 (§ 58.1-2700 et seq.) of Title 58.1, or the Motor Vehicle Dealer Board under Chapter 15 (§ 46.2-1500 et seq.) of Title 46.2; or (iii) any panel of a health regulatory board convened pursuant to § 54.1-2400, including any panel having members of a relevant advisory board to the Board of Medicine. All employees hired after July 1, 1986, pursuant to §§ 65.2-201 and 65.2-203 by the Virginia Workers' Compensation Commission to conduct hearings pursuant to its basic laws shall meet the minimum qualifications set forth in subsection A. Agency employees who are not licensed to practice law in the Commonwealth, and are presiding as hearing officers in proceedings pursuant to clause (ii) shall participate in periodic training courses.

G. Notwithstanding the exemptions of subsection A of § 2.2-4002, this article shall apply to hearing officers conducting hearings of the kind described in § 2.2-4020 for the Department of Game and Inland Fisheries, the Virginia Housing Development Authority, the Milk Commission and the Virginia Resources Authority pursuant to their basic laws. (1986, c. 615, § 9-6.14:14.1; 1988, c. 865; 1990, c. 219; 1991, c. 214; 1992, c. 659; 1993, c. 898; 1995, cc. 744, 776, 803, 805; 1996, cc. 189, 205, 639, 658; 2001, c. 844; 2002, cc. 448, 698.)

Cross references. — As to policies and procedures for the conduct of a grievance hearing, see § 2.2-3005.

Law Review. — For 1987 survey of Virginia administrative procedure, see 21 U. Rich. L. Rev. 611 (1987). For article on changes made to the VAPA during the 1990 session of the General Assembly, see 24 U. Rich. L. Rev. 431 (1990).

Article 5.

Court Review.

Michie's Jurisprudence. — For related discussion, see 1A M.J. Administrative Law, §§ 20 — 22.

§ 2.2-4025. Exemptions operation of this article; limitations. — A. This article shall not apply to any agency action that (i) is placed beyond the control of the courts by constitutional or statutory provisions expressly precluding court review, (ii) involves solely the internal management or routine of an agency, (iii) is a decision resting entirely upon an inspection, test, or election save as to want of authority therefor or claim of arbitrariness or fraud therein, (iv) is a case in which the agency is acting as an agent for a court, or (v) encompasses matters subject by law to a trial de novo in any court.

B. The provisions of this article, however, shall apply to case decisions regarding the grant or denial of Temporary Assistance for Needy Families, Medicaid, food stamps, general relief, auxiliary grants, or state-local hospitalization. However, no appeal may be brought regarding the adequacy of standards of need and payment levels for public assistance and social services programs. Notwithstanding the provisions of § 2.2-4027, the review shall be based solely upon the agency record, and the court shall be limited to ascertaining whether there was evidence in the agency record to support the case decision of the agency acting as the trier of fact. If the court finds in favor of the party complaining of agency action, the court shall remand the case to the agency for further proceedings. The validity of any statute, regulation, standard or policy, federal or state, upon which the action of the agency was based shall not be subject to review by the court. No intermediate relief shall be granted under § 2.2-4028. (1975, c. 503, §§ 9-6.14:4.1, 9-6.14:15, 9-6.14:16; 1986, c. 615; 1989, cc. 677, 734; 2001, c. 844; 2002, c. 747.)

Cross references. — As to appeals of certain actions of local departments of social services in civil proceedings involving alleged abuse or neglect of a child, see § 63.2-1526.

Law Review. — For survey of Virginia administrative law and utility regulation for the year 1978-1979, see 66 Va. L. Rev. 193 (1980). For comment, "'Working to the Contract' in Virginia: Legal Consequences of Teachers' Attempts to Limit Their Contractual Duties," see 16 U. Rich. L. Rev. 449 (1982).

CASE NOTES

Editor's note. — Some of the cases below were decided under former Title 2.1 or prior provisions.

Review only at insistence of "owner aggrieved." — Former § 9-6.14:15 (see now this section) prohibits judicial review of a board's decision at the insistence of any one other than an "owner aggrieved." Town of Fries v. State Water Control Bd., 13 Va. App. 213, 409 S.E.2d 634 (1991).

Legislative intent. — When the legislature created the trial de novo exclusion under former § 9-6.14:15 (see now this section), it contemplated agency actions whose subject matters were not subject to the standard of review set forth in former § 9-6.14:17 (see now § 2.2-4027). School Bd. v. Nicely, 12 Va. App. 1051, 408 S.E.2d 545 (1991).

Failure to name proper party on appeal to circuit court. — Both former § 9-6.14:16 (see now this section and § 2.2-4026) and Supreme Court Rule 2A:1(b) require that the agency rendering a case decision be made a party to the judicial review proceeding; where such agency is not named, the appellant's petition may be dismissed. Somers v. Accomack County Dep't of Soc. Servs., No. 2899-00-1, 2001 Va. App. LEXIS 291 (Ct. of Appeals May 29, 2001).

An action brought pursuant to subsection D of § 22.1-214 (pertaining to provision of special education programs for handicapped children) amounts to a trial de novo for the purposes of clause (v) of former § 9-6.14:15 (see now this section), which excludes matters subject to trial de novo from the Virginia Administrative Process Act's provisions governing court review of agency decisions. School Bd. v. Nicely, 12 Va. App. 1051, 408 S.E.2d 545 (1991).

Agency's action arbitrary and capricious. — Excavation company was entitled to recover reasonable costs and fees under this section where all issues in dispute were decided in its favor, the Department of Mines, Minerals & Energy's actions were arbitrary and capricious (Department sought determination that removal of dirt was "mining" within meaning of § 45.1-180), and there were no special circumstances to render the award unjust. Commonwealth Dep't of Mines, Minerals & Energy v. May Bros., 11 Va. App. 115, 396 S.E.2d 695 (1990).

CIRCUIT COURT OPINIONS

No appeal intervention. — Neighbor of landowner who appealed administrative decision concerning landowner's land could not intervene in the appeal because she did not challenge the unlawfulness of the agency decision, but rather sought to preserve her interests, which had been obtained in the administrative procedure, and she was not an aggrieved person nor a necessary party. City of Norfolk Wetlands Bd. v. Va. Marine Resources Comm'n, 54 Va. Cir. 294, 2000 Va. Cir. LEXIS 599 (Norfolk 2000) (decided under prior law).

Reviewability of claim. — Spouse's claim that a Medicaid eligibility worker failed to advise her that she should set funds aside for burial was not reviewed, as it was not submitted to the agency for consideration. Sherline v. Finnerty, 65 Va. Cir. 154, 2004 Va. Cir. LEXIS 143 (Fairfax County 2004).

Failure to exhaust administrative remedies. — Owner's suit seeking to enjoin a city from demolishing improvements on the owner's property was barred because the owner's failure to seek review provided for by § 36-105 was a failure to exhaust administrative remedies; § 2.2-4025 et seq. provided for review by the circuit courts, which was due process of law. Family Home Servs., Inc. v. City of Norfolk, 72 Va. Cir. 320, 2006 Va. Cir. LEXIS 311 (Norfolk 2006).

Medicaid benefits denial affirmed. — Substantial evidence supported a hearing officer's conclusion that there was no real agreement to transfer property in exchange for care as alleged by Medicaid applicants, and a decision denying Medicaid benefits to the applicants based on the transfer of their home to their daughter was affirmed. Moss v. Lemoine, 65 Va. Cir. 263, 2004 Va. Cir. LEXIS 135 (Spotsylvania County 2004).

§ 2.2-4026. Right, forms, venue. — Any person affected by and claiming the unlawfulness of any regulation, or party aggrieved by and claiming unlawfulness of a case decision and whether exempted from the procedural requirements of Article 2 (§ 2.2-4006 et seq.) or 3 (§ 2.2-4018 et seq.) of this chapter, shall have a right to the direct review thereof by an appropriate and timely court action against the agency or its officers or agents in the manner provided by the rules of the Supreme Court of Virginia. Actions may be instituted in any court of competent jurisdiction as provided in § 2.2-4003, and the judgments of the courts of original jurisdiction shall be subject to appeal to or review by higher courts as in other cases unless otherwise provided by law. In addition, when any regulation or case decision is the subject of an enforcement action in court, it shall also be reviewable by the court as a defense to the action, and the judgment or decree therein shall be appealable as in other cases. (1975, c. 503, § 9-6.14:16; 1986, c. 615; 1989, cc. 677, 734; 2001, c. 844.)

Law Review. — For survey of Virginia administrative law for the year 1974-1975, see 61 Va. L. Rev. 1632 (1975). For 1985 survey of Virginia administrative procedure, see 19 U. Rich. L. Rev. 657 (1985). For survey of administrative procedure in Virginia for 1989, see 23 U. Rich. L. Rev. 431 (1989). For note, "Protecting the Environment: Creating a Citizen Standing-to-Sue Statute in Virginia," see 26 U. Rich. L. Rev. 235 (1991).

CASE NOTES

Editor's note. — Some of the cases below were decided under former corresponding provisions.

Purpose of section. — Section 62.1-44.29 is a statute providing for judicial review. The purpose of this section is to "standardize court review ... save as laws hereafter enacted may otherwise expressly provide." Environmental Defense Fund v. Virginia State Water Control Bd., 12 Va. App. 456, 404 S.E.2d 728 (1991).

This section does not supplement § 62.1-44.29 because the latter is not a "basic law conferring authority on agencies either to make regulations or decide cases." Environmental Defense Fund v. Virginia State Water Control Bd., 12 Va. App. 456, 404 S.E.2d 728 (1991).

Applicability. — Where an agency's basic law provides expressly for Virginia Administrative Process Act coverage of certain proceedings under specified conditions and makes no provision for judicial review of other proceedings, the unmentioned proceedings are subject to the Act unless otherwise expressly excluded. May Dep't Stores Co. v. Commonwealth, Dep't of Envtl. Quality, 29 Va. App. 589, 513 S.E.2d 880 (1999).

Prerequisites to judicial review. — A party must pursue administrative avenues that result in agency regulations and final case decisions before seeking judicial review. Fauquier County Dep't of Social Servs. v. Robinson, 20 Va. App. 142, 455 S.E.2d 734 (1995).

Section 32.1-164.1 provides special statutory form for review. — The procedure provided in § 32.1-164.1 is adequate to avoid the preclusive provisions of clause (ii) of the first sentence of former § 9-6.14:16 (see now this section). Forbes v. Kenley, 227 Va. 55, 314 S.E.2d 49 (1984).

This section does not create an additional basis for jurisdiction, but instead "gives deference to provisions of the basic law, such as § 62.1-44.29, which makes express provisions for standing." Town of Fries v. State Water Control Bd., 13 Va. App. 213, 409 S.E.2d 634 (1991).

Jurisdiction of circuit court. — The Administrative Process Act confers upon the circuit court the power to review agency case decisions. Avery v. Virginia Retirement Sys., 33 Va. App. 210, 532 S.E.2d 348, 2000 Va. App. LEXIS 589 (2000).

A determination addressing only an agency's legal duties does not qualify for review under the Virginia Administrative Process Act. Giannoukos v. Va. Bd. of Med. & Dep't of Health Professions, 44 Va. App. 694, 607 S.E.2d 136, 2005 Va. App. LEXIS 7 (2005).

Basic law standing requirement controls over this section. — Where the basic law contains a specific standing requirement, such as that contained in § 62.1-44.29, this requirement is controlling over the standardized court review in this section. Environmental Defense Fund v. Virginia State Water Control Bd., 12 Va. App. 456, 404 S.E.2d 728 (1991).

This section gives deference to provisions of the basic law, such as § 62.1-44.29, which make express provisions for standing. This construction is supported by the concluding sentence of former § 9-6.14:3 (see now § 2.2-4000 B). Environmental Defense Fund v. Virginia State Water Control Bd., 12 Va. App. 456, 404 S.E.2d 728 (1991).

Where there is a specific provision for standing in the basic law, such provision is controlling over the standardized court review in this section. Citizens for Clean Air v. Commonwealth ex rel. State Air Pollution Control Bd., 13 Va. App. 430, 412 S.E.2d 715 (1991).

The State Air Pollution Control Law, §§ 10.1-1300 et seq., contains a specific provision with respect to standing to appeal and, thus, precludes recourse through the Administrative Process Act, unless the party seeking review is an owner aggrieved by a final decision of the board. Citizens for Clean Air v. Commonwealth ex rel. State Air Pollution Control Bd., 13 Va. App. 430, 412 S.E.2d 715 (1991).

Neighbor had standing in appeal of liquor license restrictions. — Neighbor objected to the Virginia Alcoholic Beverage Control Board's granting of liquor licenses to an applicant. Her failure to timely appeal the Board's decision to grant such licenses was a waiver only of her challenge to the issuance of the licenses, not of her right to defend the Board's decision to impose a 12:00 a.m. restriction on alcohol sales. Harrison v. Ocean View Fishing Pier, LLC, 50 Va. App. 556, 651 S.E.2d 421, 2007 Va. App. LEXIS 397 (2007).

Appeal must be brought in manner provided by Rules of Supreme Court of Virginia. — Section 2.2-4026 of the Virginia Administrative Process Act, § 2.2-4000 et seq., provides that an appeal of a decision by the Virginia State Water Control Board must be brought in the manner provided by the rules of the Supreme Court of Virginia; under Va. Sup. Ct. R. 2A:1, appeals brought under the Act are governed by Part 2A of the Rules of the Supreme Court of Virginia. State Water Control Bd. v. Crutchfield, 265 Va. 416, 578 S.E.2d 762, 2003 Va. LEXIS 42 (2003).

A de facto rule may be challenged by bringing a suit claiming the unlawfulness of a case decision, as defined by the Virginia Administrative Process Act. Virginia Bd. of Medicine v. Virginia Physical Therapy Ass'n, 13 Va. App. 458, 413 S.E.2d 59 (1991), aff'd, Virginia Physical Therapy Ass'n v. Virginia Bd. of Medicine, 245 Va. 125, 427 S.E.2d 183 (1993).

Failure to name proper party on appeal to circuit court. — Both former § 9-6.14:16 (see now this section and § 2.2-4025) and Supreme Court Rule 2A:1(b) require that the agency rendering a case decision be made a party to the judicial review proceeding; where such agency is not named, the appellant's petition may be dismissed. Somers v. Accomack County Dep't of Soc. Servs., No. 2899-00-1, 2001 Va. App. LEXIS 291 (Ct. of Appeals May 29, 2001).

Standing to appeal expungement of name of suspected child abuser. — Father of an allegedly sexually abused child did not have standing under the Administrative Process Act to appeal the ruling of the Commissioner of Social Services that expunged the name of the suspected abuser from the central registry for child abuse and neglect. D'Alessio v. Lukhard, 5 Va. App. 404, 363 S.E.2d 715 (1988).

Denial of request for formal hearing not case decision. — Appeal was unavailable under the Virginia Administrative Process Act. This section provides for appeal by a "party aggrieved by and claiming unlawfulness of a case decision." The denial of Environmental Defense Fund's request for a formal hearing was not a "case decision" as that term is defined. Environmental Defense Fund was not a "named party" in the proceedings before the State Water Control Board. Environmental Defense Fund v. Virginia State Water Control Bd., 12 Va. App. 456, 404 S.E.2d 728 (1991).

The Virginia Board of Medicine has consented to and may be sued only for its promulgation of a rule or its decision of a case, as both are defined in the Virginia Administrative Process Act. Virginia Bd. of Medicine v. Virginia Physical Therapy Ass'n, 13 Va. App. 458, 413 S.E.2d 59 (1991), aff'd, Virginia Physical Therapy Ass'n v. Virginia Bd. of Medicine, 245 Va. 125, 427 S.E.2d 183 (1993).

The General Assembly has waived sovereign immunity only to allow a party to obtain judicial review of the Virginia Board of Medicine's adoption of rules of the Board's case decisions, as such are defined in the Virginia Administrative Process Act, in the manner provided in the Act. Virginia Bd. of Medicine v. Virginia Physical Therapy Ass'n, 13 Va. App. 458, 413 S.E.2d 59 (1991), aff'd, Virginia Physical Therapy Ass'n v. Virginia Bd. of Medicine, 245 Va. 125, 427 S.E.2d 183 (1993).

A final decision on the part of the State Air Pollution Control Board to deny a formal petition for a hearing would, under § 10.1-1318, entitle any "owner aggrieved" by that decision a right to judicial review. Citizens for Clean Air v. Commonwealth ex rel. State Air Pollution Control Bd., 13 Va. App. 430, 412 S.E.2d 715 (1991).

Unincorporated association composed of owners of real property adversely affected by poultry processing facility did not have standing to appeal the State Air Pollution Control Board's denial of the association's petition for a formal hearing regarding issuance of an air permit to the poultry processing facility, because the association was not an "owner" under § 10.1-1318, and the association was not a "party aggrieved" under this section. Citizens for Clean Air v. Commonwealth ex rel. State Air Pollution Control Bd., 13 Va. App. 430, 412 S.E.2d 715 (1991).

Transcript from circuit court hearing found not essential for review. — While Court of Appeals' consideration of issues in instant case might have been aided by review of transcript from circuit court hearing which reversed commissioner's ruling, the written record, encompassing the parties' pre-hearing briefs, the trial court's letter opinion, and the agency record, along with transcripts of the Department's informal fact-finding conference and argument before the trial court to reconsider its decision, provided a sufficient record of consideration of appeal. Therefore, the transcript was not indispensable to a determination of the issues. Gordon v. Allen, 24 Va. App. 272, 482 S.E.2d 66 (1997).

Applied in 7-Eleven, Inc. v. Dep't of Envtl. Quality, 42 Va. App. 65, 590 S.E.2d 84 (2003).

CIRCUIT COURT OPINIONS

Substantial evidence. — When there was some evidence supporting an administrative determination by the Virginia Department of Social Services that a complaint of child sexual abuse lodged against a father was founded, the court, applying a substantial evidence standard of review, was constrained to affirm the Department's decision. Twyman v. Comm'r, Va. Dep't of Soc. Servs., — Va. Cir. —, 2007 Va. Cir. LEXIS 108 (Richmond Aug. 7, 2007).

Violation letter was a case decision. — Demurrer to a petition for an appeal was denied in a dispute regarding the disposal of solid waste because a notice of violation sent to a county by the Virginia Department of Environmental Quality constituted a "case decision" since it was a determination of a violation of existing law; therefore, a county was entitled to judicial review of the matter. Rockbridge County v. Burnley, 66 Va. Cir. 308, 2004 Va. Cir. LEXIS 321 (Rockbridge County Dec. 21, 2004).

§ **2.2-4027. Issues on review.** — The burden shall be upon the party complaining of agency action to designate and demonstrate an error of law subject to review by the court. Such issues of law include: (i) accordance with constitutional right, power, privilege, or immunity, (ii) compliance with statutory authority, jurisdiction limitations, or right as provided in the basic laws as to subject matter, the stated objectives for which regulations may be made, and the factual showing respecting violations or entitlement in connection with case decisions, (iii) observance of required procedure where any failure therein is not mere harmless error, and (iv) the substantiality of the evidentiary support for findings of fact. The determination of such fact issue shall be made upon the whole evidentiary record provided by the agency if its proceeding was required to be conducted as provided in § 2.2-4009 or 2.2-4020 or, as to subjects exempted from those sections, pursuant to constitutional requirement or statutory provisions for opportunity for an agency record of and decision upon the evidence therein.

In addition to any other judicial review provided by law, a small business, as defined in subsection A of § 2.2-4007.1, that is adversely affected or aggrieved by final agency action shall be entitled to judicial review of compliance with the requirements of subdivision A 2 of § 2.2-4007.04 and § 2.2-4007.1 within one year following the date of final agency action.

When the decision on review is to be made on the agency record, the duty of the court with respect to issues of fact shall be limited to ascertaining whether there was substantial evidence in the agency record upon which the agency as the trier of the facts could reasonably find them to be as it did.

Where there is no agency record so required and made, any necessary facts in controversy shall be determined by the court upon the basis of the agency file, minutes, and records of its proceedings under § 2.2-4007.01 or 2.2-4019 as augmented, if need be, by the agency pursuant to order of the court or supplemented by any allowable and necessary proofs adduced in court except that the function of the court shall be to determine only whether the result reached by the agency could reasonably be said, on all such proofs, to be within the scope of the legal authority of the agency.

Whether the fact issues are reviewed on the agency record or one made in the review action, the court shall take due account of the presumption of official regularity, the experience and specialized competence of the agency, and the purposes of the basic law under which the agency has acted. (1975, c. 503, § 9-6.14:17; 1989, c. 601; 2001, c. 844; 2005, cc. 619, 682; 2007, cc. 873, 916.)

The 2007 amendments. — The 2007 amendments by cc. 873 and 916 are identical, and substituted "subdivision A 2 of § 2.2-4007.04" for "subdivision H 2 of § 2.2-4007" in the second paragraph; and substituted "2.2-4007.01" for "2.2-4007" in the fourth paragraph.

Law Review. — For survey of Virginia administrative law for the year 1974-1975, see 61 Va. L. Rev. 1632 (1975). For comment, "'Working to the Contract' in Virginia: Legal Consequences of Teachers' Attempts to Limit Their Contractual Duties," see 16 U. Rich. L. Rev. 449 (1982). For article on opening Virginia courthouse doors to review of administrative decisions involving public assistance, see 21 U. Rich. L. Rev. 161 (1986). For a review of administrative procedure in Virginia for year 1999, see 33 U. Rich. L. Rev. 727 (1999).

CASE NOTES

I. IN GENERAL.

Editor's note. — Some of the cases below were decided under former corresponding provisions.

Cases subject to the standard of review outlined in this section cannot be considered a trial de novo since the factual issues on appeal are controlled solely by the agency record. The reviewing court is not free to take additional evidence, even at the request of one of the parties. School Bd. v. Nicely, 12 Va. App. 1051, 408 S.E.2d 545 (1991).

When the legislature created the trial de novo exclusion under former § 9-6.14:15 (see now § 2.2-4025), it contemplated agency actions whose subject matters were not subject to the standard of review set forth in this section. School Bd. v. Nicely, 12 Va. App. 1051, 408 S.E.2d 545 (1991).

The scope of court review of a litigated issue under this chapter is limited to a determination of whether there was substantial evidence in the agency record to support the decision. State Bd. of Health v. Godfrey, 223 Va. 423, 290 S.E.2d 875 (1982).

Proper judicial review of board's action must not be restricted to legal issues, but must encompass "all ... proofs" found within the entire record. Interrelated factual and legal issues must be considered together in the context of the entire record, with each examined under the appropriate standard of review. Environmental Defense Fund, Inc. v. Virginia State Water Control Bd., 15 Va. App. 271, 422 S.E.2d 608 (1992).

Limitation on evidence. — In an agency appeal, the circuit court is not free to take additional evidence at the request of one of the parties, but is obliged to defer to the trier of fact. J.P. v. Carter, 24 Va. App. 707, 485 S.E.2d 162 (1997).

Burden to establish insufficiency of evidence. — The burden of proof rests upon the party challenging the agency determination to show that there was not substantial evidence in the record to support it. Baumann v. Virginia Retirement Sys., No. 1194-99-4, 2000 Va. App. LEXIS 632 (Ct. of Appeals Aug. 29, 2000).

The circuit court's role. — Under the Virginia Administrative Process Act, the circuit court's role in an appeal from an agency decision is equivalent to an appellate court's role in an appeal from a trial court. School Bd. v. Nicely, 12 Va. App. 1051, 408 S.E.2d 545 (1991).

Scope of federal review compared. — The scope of court review under the Virginia Administrative Process Act is virtually identical to that in the Federal Administrative Procedure Act. State Bd. of Health v. Godfrey, 223 Va. 423, 290 S.E.2d 875 (1982).

Factors to be considered on review. — A reviewing court must review the facts in the light most favorable to sustaining the agency's action and take due account of the presumption of official regularity, the experience and specialized competence of the agency and the purposes of the basic law under which the agency has acted. Baumann v. Virginia Retirement Sys., No. 1194-99-4, 2000 Va. App. LEXIS 632 (Ct. of Appeals Aug. 29, 2000).

Facts taken in the light most favorable to sustaining the administrative agency's action, giving due account of the presumption of official regularity, the experience and specialized competence of the agency, and the purposes of the basic law under which the agency has acted, showed that substantial evidence supported the trial court's ruling that affirmed the administrative agency's decision to grant the county's permit request allowing the county to discharge treated wastewater into the river. Crutchfield v. State Water Control Bd., Dep't of Envtl. Quality, 45 Va. App. 546, 612 S.E.2d 249, 2005 Va. App. LEXIS 170 (2005).

Degree of deference afforded an agency decision depends upon not only the nature of the issue, legal or factual, but also upon whether the issue falls within the area of experience and specialized competence of the agency. Johnston-Willis, Ltd. v. Kenley, 6 Va. App. 231, 369 S.E.2d 1 (1988).

The degree of deference afforded an agency decision depends upon several considerations to be weighed by the reviewing court: whether the issues are legal or factual; whether the issues involve a denial of constitutional rights or failure to follow required procedures; and whether the issues fall within the area of experience and specialized competence of the agency. Turner v. Jackson, 14 Va. App. 423, 417 S.E.2d 881 (1992).

The fact that the case may involve questions of constitutional or procedural rights does not, standing alone, require the reviewing court to apply a less deferential standard of review to the agency's decision. Turner v. Jackson, 14 Va. App. 423, 417 S.E.2d 881 (1992).

Challenging repromulgation of regulations on emergency basis. — A committee of concerned citizens did not meet its burden of proof in claiming that the Chesapeake Local Assistance Board acted unlawfully in determining an "emergency" to exist to warrant dispensing with the public notice comment requirements of former § 9-6.14:7.1 (see now § 2.2-4007.01 et seq.), in repromulgating, on an emergency basis, regulations which had been invalidated by a circuit court on procedural grounds. Committee of Concerned Citizens for Property Rights v. Chesapeake Bay Local Assistance Bd., 15 Va. App. 664, 426 S.E.2d 499 (1993).

Reviewing decision affecting handicapped children. — This section permits the third court to hear additional evidence when reviewing administrative decision by officers appointed under authority of the Board of Education concerning a special education program for handicapped children, to weigh the evidence as a whole, and to base its decision on a preponderance of the evidence and the trial court is not limited to determining, as under the Administrative Process Act, whether there is "substantial evidence in the agency record" to support the administrative findings of fact. School Bd. v. Beasley, 238 Va. 44, 380 S.E.2d 884 (1989).

The proper standard to be employed by the circuit court is to determine, based on a preponderance of the evidence, whether the substance of the proposed individualized educational program is reasonably calculated to enable the child to receive educational benefits, however, due weight must be given by the trial court to the administrative proceedings. School Bd. v. Beasley, 238 Va. 44, 380 S.E.2d 884 (1989).

Proper standard of review applied. — Trial court did not require appellant to bear an erroneous burden of proof in his appeal from agency determination that he had abused his daughter. Schultz v. Carter, No. 0031-99-4 (Ct. of Appeals Dec. 7, 1999).

Failure to make findings required remand. — Because the Virginia Alcoholic Beverage Control Board granted an applicant licenses allowing liquor sales only until 12:00 a.m., without making findings of fact or conclusions of law to support these time restrictions, as required by § 2.2-4020, the case was remanded to Board pursuant to § 2.2-4029 so it could make such findings. Harrison v. Ocean View Fishing Pier, LLC, 50 Va. App. 556, 651 S.E.2d 421, 2007 Va. App. LEXIS 397 (2007).

Transcript from circuit court hearing found not essential for review. — While court of appeals consideration of issues in instant case might have been aided by review of transcript from circuit court hearing which reversed commissioner's ruling, the written record, encompassing the parties' pre-hearing briefs, the trial court's letter opinion, and the agency record, along with transcripts of the Department's informal fact-finding conference and argument before the trial court to reconsider its decision, provides a sufficient record of consideration of appeal. Therefore, the transcript was not indispensable to a determination of the issues. Gordon v. Allen, 24 Va. App. 272, 482 S.E.2d 66 (1997).

Applied in Aegis Waste Solutions, Inc. v. Concerned Taxpayers of Brunswick County, 261 Va. 395, 544 S.E.2d 660, 2001 Va. LEXIS 46 (2001); Alliance to Save the Mattaponi v. Commonwealth Dep't of Envtl. Quality ex rel. State Water Control Bd., 270 Va. 423, 621 S.E.2d 78, 2005 Va. LEXIS 100 (2005); Reynolds v. Conyers, — Va. App. —, — S.E.2d —, 2007 Va. App. LEXIS 302 (Aug. 14, 2007).

II. QUESTIONS OF LAW.

The question whether an agency decision making body acted within the scope of the authority conferred upon it by statute is a question of law. Muse v. Virginia ABC Bd., 9 Va. App. 74, 384 S.E.2d 110 (1989).

Judicial interference. — The commissioner's decision on whether the State Health Plan or State Medical Facilities Plan is inaccurate, outdated, inadequate or otherwise inapplicable, is a decision within the specialized competence of the commissioner and is entitled to special weight in the courts. For that reason judicial interference is permissible only for relief against the arbitrary and capricious action that constitutes a clear abuse of the delegated discretion. Johnston-Willis, Ltd. v. Kenley, 6 Va. App. 231, 369 S.E.2d 1 (1988).

Errors of law fall into two categories: First, whether the agency decisionmaker acted within the scope of his authority, and second, whether the decision itself was supported by the evidence. Where the agency has the statutory authorization to make the kind of decision it did and it did so within the statutory limits of its discretion and with the intent of the statute in mind, it has not committed an error of law in the first category. The second category of error is limited to a determination whether there is substantial evidence in the agency record to support the decision. Johnston-Willis, Ltd. v. Kenley, 6 Va. App. 231, 369 S.E.2d 1 (1988).

It has become the common practice to catalogue and define the limited judicial review of agency decisions pursuant to this section in the following manner: 1) Whether the agency acted in accordance with law; 2) whether the agency made a procedural error which was not harmless error; and 3) whether the agency had sufficient evidential support for its findings of fact. Johnston-Willis, Ltd. v. Kenley, 6 Va. App. 231, 369 S.E.2d 1 (1988).

Considerations not applicable to issues of law. — Since the issue before the court was purely one of law, containing no underlying factual issues, the court did not apply a presumption of official regularity or take account of the experience and specialized competence of the administrative agency. These considerations apply to the review of mixed questions of law and fact, and to the review of purely factual issues. Browning-Ferris Indus. of S. Atl., Inc. v. Residents Involved in Saving the Env't, Inc., 254 Va. 278, 492 S.E.2d 431 (1997).

General Assembly transferred decision-making power to Department of Motor Vehicles, and nothing in the record disclosed that it did so without first determining that the DMV was fully competent to render judgments concerning the issuance of certificates of public convenience and necessity. Groome Transp., Inc. v. DMV, 27 Va. App. 682, 500 S.E.2d 852 (1998).

Under this section the burden is upon the party complaining of agency action to designate and demonstrate an error of law subject to review, and the determination of an issue of fact is to be made upon the agency record if the proceeding was required to be conducted under former § 9-6.14:12 (see now §§ 2.2-4020, 2.2-4021). State Bd. of Health v. Godfrey, 223 Va. 423, 290 S.E.2d 875 (1982).

The burden is upon the party complaining of the agency action to demonstrate an error of law subject to review. Johnston-Willis, Ltd. v. Kenley, 6 Va. App. 231, 369 S.E.2d 1 (1988).

Error of law made. — Trial court erred in upholding the state environmental quality department's decision that found the corporation was entitled to reimbursement from the Petroleum Storage Tank Fund limited to the reduction in market value of the property that the corporation's spill damaged, and, thus, that it need not consider the amount of the settlement the corporation paid to the other company for the damage to its property. The settlement amount was a relevant indicator of the reasonable and necessary cost the corporation incurred in cleaning up the spill, and, thus, the record demonstrated that an error of law had occurred in calculating the proper amount of reimbursement; as a result, the trial court's affirmance of the state environmental quality department's decision had to be reversed and the case had to be remanded for further proceedings. 7-Eleven, Inc. v. Dep't of Envtl. Quality, 42 Va. App. 65, 590 S.E.2d 84, 2003 Va. App. LEXIS 703 (2003), reversing 7-Eleven, Inc. v. Va. Dept. of Envtl. Quality, 56 Va. Cir. 276, 2001 Va. Cir. LEXIS 458 (Richmond 2001).

No error of law made. — Where the evidence presented by the Department of Social Services that a father mentally abused his son, despite a late filing by DSS that said abuse was brought on by a prior act of physical assault and verbal derision, the son's condition was properly found to be directly related to said altercation. John S. v. Dep't of Soc. Servs., No. 2285-03-4, 2004 Va. App. LEXIS 502 (Ct. of Appeals Oct. 26, 2004).

When a question involves a statutory interpretation issue, little deference is required to be accorded an agency decision because the issue falls outside the agency's specialized competence; pure statutory interpretation is the prerogative of the judiciary. Sims Whsle. Co. v. Brown-Forman Corp., 251 Va. 398, 468 S.E.2d 905 (1996).

Although decisions by administrative agencies regarding matters within their specialized competence are entitled to special weight in the courts, when the question involves an issue of statutory interpretation, little deference is required to be accorded the agency decision because the issue falls outside the agency's specialized competence; in sum, pure statutory interpretation is the prerogative of the judiciary. Va. Imps., Ltd. v. Kirin Brewery of Am., LLC, 41 Va. App. 806, 589 S.E.2d 470, 2003 Va. App. LEXIS 650 (2003).

Setting aside agency action where failure to comply with statutory directive. — The reviewing court may set the agency action aside, even if it is supported by substantial evidence, if the court's review discloses that the agency failed to comply with a substantive statutory directive. Browning-Ferris Indus. of S. Atl., Inc. v. Residents Involved in Saving the Env't, Inc., 254 Va. 278, 492 S.E.2d 431 (1997).

Where the Alcoholic Beverage Control Board (ABC Board) found that a brewery's termination of its franchise agreement with a distributor was without good cause under subsection E of § 4.1-506 based solely on the continuing presence of stale beer in retail stores as identified in the brewery's letter, and where the circuit court, on review, deferred to the ABC Board's findings regarding the issue of stale beer but then went on to hold that the record lacked substantial evidence to support the ABC Board's finding because the Board failed to address and rule upon all of the issues raised by the brewery with respect to its grounds for termination, the court held that, although the circuit court correctly found that the ABC Board erroneously failed to consider all of the brewery's grounds for termination, it misapplied the substantial evidence standard of review because after determining that the ABC Board failed to comply with the mandatory directive of subsection D of § 4.1-506, the circuit court, rather than imposing its own judgment on the matter, should have suspended the ABC Board's decision and remanded the matter back to the ABC Board with instructions to make the additional required factual determination. Va. Imps., Ltd. v. Kirin Brewery of Am., LLC, 41 Va. App. 806, 589 S.E.2d 470, 2003 Va. App. LEXIS 650 (2003).

Circuit court's decision was upheld on appeal, because the Department of Social Service's (DSS's) failure to tape record its interview with the alleged victim constituted a procedural violation, which was not mere harmless error as 22 VAC § 40-705-80 mandated recording and the DSS's reasoning that the team leader deemed recording inappropriate was insufficient. Plus, because the victim and the accused had a close granddaughter/grandfather relationship, the tape recording was critical since slight nuances in the inflection or context of the words spoken by the victim could have substantially changed the meaning of her statements and would have impacted the issue of the accused's intent. Jones v. West, 46 Va. App. 309, 616 S.E.2d 790, 2005 Va. App. LEXIS 307 (2005).

Director's failure to comply with statutory directive not harmless error. — Director's failure to make an explicit determination pursuant to § 10.1-1408.1(D) was not harmless error under item (iii). That provision subjects the failure to comply with required procedures to a harmless error analysis. Here, however, the statutory compliance issue involved a substantive provision which was a prerequisite to the issuance of a permit. Thus, the Director's action was not subject to harmless error review. Browning-Ferris Indus. of S. Atl., Inc. v. Residents Involved in Saving the Env't, Inc., 254 Va. 278, 492 S.E.2d 431 (1997).

Assessment of purposes of basic law. — On review of a decision of the Alcoholic Beverage Control Board, the "basic law" under which the Board acted and the purposes thereof are crucial to the function of the reviewing court. Those purposes must be gleaned from an analysis of the overall statutory and regulatory scheme for the control of alcoholic beverages. Virginia ABC Comm'n v. York St. Inn, Inc., 220 Va. 310, 257 S.E.2d 851 (1979).

Ruling Alcoholic Beverage Control Board within scope of authority. — A ruling of the Alcoholic Beverage Control Board that a 22-foot counter surfaced with five wood-inlaid backgammon boards did not satisfy the regulatory standard governing mixed beverage restaurant licenses did not go beyond the scope of Board's legal authority. Virginia ABC Comm'n v. York St. Inn, Inc., 220 Va. 310, 257 S.E.2d 851 (1979).

Harmless error held where disqualification of one member of board. — Where, under former § 46.1-550.2 as to requirement that no two members of board may be dealers of same manufacturer, disqualification of one member of advisory board to commissioner of motor vehicles was harmless error and did not nullify statutorily required recommendations of remaining board members since there was no evidence indicating that competing dealer's rights were affected by disqualification of one board member, since board did not act as body and each member made his or her recommendations to commissioner, and since excluding disqualified members from consideration, majority of board recommended granting second franchise. Ford Motor Co. v. Courtesy Motors, Inc., 237 Va. 187, 375 S.E.2d 362 (1989).

Presence of board members not harmless error. — The presence of the four Virginia Board of Medicine members at the evidentiary hearing, and their subsequent participation in the full Virginia Board of Medicine deliberations, could have had a significant impact on the ultimate decision so as to undermine the "substantiality of the evidential support" for the factual findings, and thus was not harmless error. Virginia Bd. of Medicine v. Fetta, 244 Va. 276, 421 S.E.2d 410 (1992).

Seventy-five percent minimum occupancy standard not arbitrary and capricious. — The commissioner's adoption of a 75% minimum occupancy standard under the State Health Plan was not arbitrary and capricious, since the national guidelines are, at a minimum, suggestive, and the commissioner may properly consider the guidelines when exercising discretion given to him by the General Assembly. Johnston-Willis, Ltd. v. Kenley, 6 Va. App. 231, 369 S.E.2d 1 (1988).

Trial court incorrectly reversed agency's construction of regulation. — Where real estate board construed Regulation 8.2(36) to mean that an inadvertent failure to list in the contract of sale every element affecting title would constitute a violation and where trial court ruled that to prove a violation of the regulation the board had to show a "willful" or "wrongful effort" to withhold information by the licensee, trial court incorrectly reversed the administrative agency's interpretation since the agency's construction of its regulation was not arbitrary or capricious and the board applied the regulation in a manner promoting the board's mandate to maintain the integrity and competency of licensees. Virginia Real Estate Bd. v. Clay, 9 Va. App. 152, 384 S.E.2d 622 (1989).

III. SUFFICIENCY OF EVIDENCE.

Review limited to agency record. — The determination of an issue of fact is to be made solely on the basis of the whole evidentiary record provided by the agency and the reviewing court is limited to that agency record. Baumann v. Virginia Retirement Sys., No. 1194-99-4, 2000 Va. App. LEXIS 632 (Ct. of Appeals Aug. 29, 2000).

Evidence of arbitrary action or bad faith. — It is within the trial court's discretion to take evidence to resolve claims of arbitrary action or bad faith but such evidence should be limited to that purporting to show that the agency denied the applicant a fair and impartial review of his application in accordance with proper procedures. Baumann v. Virginia Retirement Sys., No. 1194-99-4, 2000 Va. App. LEXIS 632 (Ct. of Appeals Aug. 29, 2000).

Agency action not arbitrary and capricious. — Special condition to appellant's Virginia Pollutant Discharge Elimination System discharge permit required it to allow photography by the Virginia Department of Environmental Quality (VDEQ) as long as it was reasonably related to the purpose of the site visit and the particular inspection being carried out. That this condition might have been unique among all other permittees did not render the requirement ipso facto arbitrary and capricious, as appellant's continued refusal to permit photography by VDEQ was, apparently, unique among other permittees in Virginia. Bowman Apple Prods. Co. v. State Water Control Bd., 50 Va. App. 383, 650 S.E.2d 548, 2007 Va. App. LEXIS 345 (2007).

Virginia State Health Commissioner's decision to award a certificate of public need to a hospital, after having previously denied an application by the hospital, was not arbitrary and capricious under § 2.2-4019 because the Commissioner, by way of the hearing officer, identified several factual differences between the application of the hospital that was denied and the subsequent amended application of the hospital that was accepted. Loudoun Hosp. Ctr. v. Stroube, 50 Va. App. 478, 650 S.E.2d 879, 2007 Va. App. LEXIS 371 (2007).

The "substantial evidence" standard, adopted by the General Assembly, is designed to give great stability and finality to the fact-findings of an administrative agency. Virginia Real Estate Comm'n v. Bias, 226 Va. 264, 308 S.E.2d 123 (1983); Atkinson v. Virginia ABC Comm'n, 1 Va. App. 172, 336 S.E.2d 527 (1985); Roanoke Mem. Hosps. v. Kenley, 3 Va. App. 599, 352 S.E.2d 525 (1987); Ables v. Rivero, No. 0873-02-1, 2003 Va. App. LEXIS 83 (Ct. of Appeals Feb. 19, 2003).

Review of agency factual decisions is governed by the "substantial evidence" test. Under this standard, the scope of review is limited to ascertaining whether there was substantial evidence in the agency record to support the decision. Turner v. Jackson, 14 Va. App. 423, 417 S.E.2d 881 (1992).

The sole determination as to factual issues is whether substantial evidence exists in the agency record to support the agency's decision. The reviewing court may reject the agency's findings of fact only if, considering the record as a whole, a reasonable mind would necessarily come to a different conclusion. Johnston-Willis, Ltd. v. Kenley, 6 Va. App. 231, 369 S.E.2d 1 (1988).

It is helpful to define the appropriate standard of review in terms of the degree of deference to be given to agency decisions. Johnston-Willis, Ltd. v. Kenley, 6 Va. App. 231, 369 S.E.2d 1 (1988).

County welfare agency's finding that injury teacher inflicted on student was not accidental and constituted physical abuse was supported by "substantial evidence" in the agency's record, and, thus, that finding was properly upheld because the agency record contained such relevant evidence as a reasonable mind might accept as adequate to support a conclusion. Mulvey v. Jones, 41 Va. App. 600, 587 S.E.2d 728, 2003 Va. App. LEXIS 545 (2003).

Penalties imposed by the Department of Forestry against logging contractors were upheld, upon their violation of administrative emergency orders issued under § 10.1-1181.2, an environmental statute governing silvicultural activities affecting water quality, as except for one of the fines assessed, substantial evidence showed that the agency properly followed its statutory mandate in calculating the penalties; moreover, given the clarity of the emergency order, there was no basis to question that said decision implied that logging work could resume on a trial basis to see if the corrective actions would "hold up." Campbell v. Dep't of Forestry, 46 Va. App. 91, 616 S.E.2d 33, 2005 Va. App. LEXIS 283 (2005).

"Substantial evidence" defined. — The phrase "substantial evidence" refers to such relevant evidence as a reasonable mind might accept as adequate to support a conclusion. Virginia Real Estate Comm'n v. Bias, 226 Va. 264, 308 S.E.2d 123 (1983); Atkinson v. Virginia ABC Comm'n, 1 Va. App. 172, 336 S.E.2d 527 (1985); Roanoke Mem. Hosps. v. Kenley, 3 Va. App. 599, 352 S.E.2d 525 (1987); Ables v. Rivero, No. 0873-02-1, 2003 Va. App. LEXIS 83 (Ct. of Appeals Feb. 19, 2003).

Substantial evidence supported decision. — Virginia State Health Commissioner's award of a certificate of public need to a hospital was affirmed because substantial evidence regarding deficiencies and circumstances that failed to comport with modern health care needs and expectations supported the Commissioner's decision that on-site replacement of the hospital's physical plants was not feasible, and the Commissioner's decision was consistent with the Virginia State Medical Facilities Plan. Loudoun Hosp. Ctr. v. Stroube, 50 Va. App. 478, 650 S.E.2d 879, 2007 Va. App. LEXIS 371 (2007).

Substantial evidence under § 2.2-4027 supported the decision of a hearing officer who, based on a county tax assessment, determined the fair market value of a Medicaid applicant's residential property, as the officer was not required to accept an assessment performed by a private appraiser hired by the applicant. Further, the outstanding balance of a lien and the amount of real estate commission were not relevant to a determination of fair market value. Finnerty v. Robinson, — Va. App. —, — S.E.2d —, 2007 Va. App. LEXIS 425 (Dec. 4, 2007).

Findings of fact made by the Board of Dentistry in revoking the dentist's license to practice were supported by substantial evidence, including evidence that the dentist did not comply with the continuing education requirements, that the dentist failed to find a licensed practitioner to serve as the dentist's mentor, that the dentist filled a patient's tooth without consent of the patient's guardian or the use of an anesthetic, and that the dentist used unnecessary force on another minor patient. Lennon v. Va. Bd. of Dentistry, — Va. App. —, — S.E.2d —, 2007 Va. App. LEXIS 475 (Dec. 27, 2007).

Substantial evidence, as required by § 2.2-4027, existed in a record compiled after the board conducted a formal hearing and listened to the testimony of numerous witnesses, including expert testimony, supporting the revocation of the doctor's medical license. The evidence was enough to support a rational factfinder's conclusion that the doctor's continued practice of medicine could be a substantial danger to the public health and safety, pursuant to § 54.1-2408.1. Vuyyuru v. Va. Bd. of Med., — Va. App. —, — S.E.2d —, 2008 Va. App. LEXIS 30 (Jan. 15, 2008).

Substitution of court's judgment for agency's precluded on factual issues. — Where proffered evidence tends to show that fact-finding procedure was tainted by unfair prejudice or animosity, an agency may be said to have decided a case on factors irrelevant to the issues of fact before it. A reviewing court may not, however, use its review of an agency's procedures as a pretext for substituting its judgment for the agency's on the factual issues decided by the agency. State Bd. of Health v. Godfrey, 223 Va. 423, 290 S.E.2d 875 (1982).

A reviewing court may not use its review of an agency's procedures as a pretext for substituting its judgment for the agency on factual issues decided by the agency. Baumann v. Virginia Retirement Sys., No. 1194-99-4, 2000 Va. App. LEXIS 632 (Ct. of Appeals Aug. 29, 2000).

This section clearly mandates that agency findings of fact are to be accorded great deference under the substantial evidence standard of review. However, when deciding whether an agency has followed proper procedures or complied with statutory authority, an inquiry into whether there is substantial evidence in the record to support findings of fact of an agency is wholly inappropriate. Johnston-Willis, Ltd. v. Kenley, 6 Va. App. 231, 369 S.E.2d 1 (1988).

The interpretation and enforcement of water quality standards and stream designation by the State Water Control Board are presumed; however, where the issue falls outside the specialized competence of the agency, such as constitutional and statutory interpretation issues, little deference is required to be accorded the agency's decision. Thus, even though an agency's finding of fact may be supported by substantial evidence in the record, it may be subject to reversal because the agency failed to observe required procedures or to comply with statutory authority. Commonwealth ex rel. State Water Control Bd. v. APCO, 9 Va. App. 254, 386 S.E.2d 633 (1989), aff'd, 12 Va. App. 73, 402 S.E.2d 703 (1991).

On appeal, the Court of Appeals cannot seize upon questions, comments or incidences of an orderly administrative process to discredit agency action that is supported by the record, viewed in context and as a whole. Environmental Defense Fund, Inc. v. Virginia State Water Control Bd., 15 Va. App. 271, 422 S.E.2d 608 (1992).

When agency's findings may be rejected. — Under the substantial evidence standard the court may reject the agency's findings of fact only if, considering the record as a whole, a reasonable mind would necessarily come to a different conclusion. Virginia Real Estate Comm'n v. Bias, 226 Va. 264, 308 S.E.2d 123 (1983); Atkinson v. Virginia ABC Comm'n, 1 Va. App. 172, 336 S.E.2d 527 (1985); Roanoke Mem. Hosps. v. Kenley, 3 Va. App. 599, 352 S.E.2d 525 (1987); Environmental Defense Fund, Inc. v. Virginia State Water Control Bd., 15 Va. App. 271, 422 S.E.2d 608 (1992); Ables v. Rivero, No. 0873-02-1, 2003 Va. App. LEXIS 83 (Ct. of Appeals Feb. 19, 2003).

Under this section, the scope of review is limited to whether there was "substantial evidence in the record" to support the decision; the court may reject the agency's findings only if, considering the record as a whole, a reasonable mind would necessarily come to a different conclusion. Fever's Inc. v. Virginia ABC Bd., 24 Va. App. 213, 481 S.E.2d 476 (1997).

Interpretation of regulations by Board entitled to special weight. — On review of the Alcoholic Beverage Control Board's decision finding that a 22-foot counter surfaced with five wood-inlaid backgammon boards was not a "table" or "counter" as defined in the Board's regulations governing mixed beverage restaurant licenses, the definitions of "table" and "counter" must necessarily be construed and applied to support the purposes of the basic law, and the interpretation made by the Board vested with the authority to administer the law is entitled to special weight in the courts. Virginia ABC Comm'n v. York St. Inn, Inc., 220 Va. 310, 257 S.E.2d 851 (1979).

Court limited to agency record on review of facts. — Where a public hearing was conducted in accordance with former § 9-6.14:12 (see now §§ 2.2-4020, 2.2-4021) as to issues of fact that were or reasonably could have been determined by the agency, the reviewing court is limited to the agency record. State Bd. of Health v. Godfrey, 223 Va. 423, 290 S.E.2d 875 (1982).

Trial court was not authorized to consider evidence that the property owners did not place before the administrative agency in their attempt to prevent the administrative agency from granting the county's permit application to allow the county to discharge treated wastewater into a river, as the record on appeal could only be supplemented where there was no agency record, which was not true in the instant case. Crutchfield v. State Water Control Bd., Dep't of Envtl. Quality, 45 Va. App. 546, 612 S.E.2d 249, 2005 Va. App. LEXIS 170 (2005).

When admission of evidence constitutes reversible error. — The rules of evidence are considerably relaxed in administrative proceedings, and the findings of administrative agencies will not be reversed solely because evidence was received which would have been inadmissible in court. No reversible error will be found in such cases unless there is a clear showing of prejudice arising from the admission of such evidence, or unless it is plain that the agency's conclusions were determined by the improper evidence, and that a contrary result would have been reached in its absence. Virginia Real Estate Comm'n v. Bias, 226 Va. 264, 308 S.E.2d 123 (1983).

Evidence sufficient to support board's findings. — Fact that a dentist felt it necessary to explain his records before the Virginaia Board of Dentistry strengthened the Board's finding that they were inadequate. Also, in the case of several patients, the dentist did not record a diagnosis at all; thus, the evidence was sufficient to prove that the dentist violated 18 VAC 60-20-15(3). Doe v. Va. Bd. of Dentistry, 50 Va. App. 626, 652 S.E.2d 794, 2007 Va. App. LEXIS 418 (2007).

Contrary to the Alcohol and Beverage Control Board's finding, the record lacked substantial evidence to support the finding that defendant restaurant owner had "allowed noisy, lewd, or disorderly conduct upon the licensed premises" such that his license was properly revoked, where defendant took reasonable precautions as well as steps to regain control of the crowd on the night in question and was generally cooperative with law enforcement. Fever's Inc. v. Virginia ABC Bd., 24 Va. App. 213, 481 S.E.2d 476 (1997).

Any error in consideration of challenged evidence was harmless. — Any consideration of evidence challenged by two landfill operators admitted at an informal fact finding conference was harmless as the presiding officer did not refer to the challenged evidence, but referenced certain evidence of the operators; even if the Director of the Virginia Department of Environmental Quality considered the challenged materials, the Director's conclusions were based on some information that was provided by the operators that part of the Columbia aquifer remained at the site. Elbow Farm, Inc. v. Paylor, — Va. App. —, — S.E.2d —, 2007 Va. App. LEXIS 48 (Feb. 13, 2007).

CIRCUIT COURT OPINIONS

Burden is on party complaining of agency action to demonstrate error of law. — River association's petition challenging the decision of the Virginia Waste Management Board to charge a fee for transporting waste on Virginia's waters did not fail to allege cognizable grounds for relief; the association set out four assignments of error seeking to designate and demonstrate an error of law subject to review by the court in accordance with § 2.2-4027. First, the association alleged that the board failed to follow the Virginia Waste Management Act's mandate that its regulations require containers used to transport waste be tested and certified as watertight; second, the association stated that the board's decision to adopt the standing water test for such containers was not supported by substantial evidence that the test will ensure that containers are watertight and will prevent the spillage of leachate in the event of an accident; third, the association contended that the board's decision to adopt a $1 fee per ton of waste transported on Virginia's waters was not supported by substantial evidence that the fee was sufficient to fund the administration and enforcement of the Act; and fourth, the association alleged that the board violated the Act by concealing from the public its rationale for its adoption of the regulations at issue. James River Ass'n v. Commonwealth ex rel. Waste Mgmt. Bd., 63 Va. Cir. 602, 2004 Va. Cir. LEXIS 88 (Richmond 2004).

Error of law established. — Regulations cited by the board in entering final order against a surveyor, Regulation § 4.12(A) and Regulation § 4.13(A), did not require disclosure of information not on the plat, so the complaint, filed more than three years after completion of the survey was untimely; the surveyor carried his burden to demonstrate an error of law, and the board's order was reversed. May v. Bd. for Architects, — Va. Cir. —, 2002 Va. Cir. LEXIS 456 (Amherst County Nov. 22, 2002).

Deference accorded hearing officer's determination regarding testimony. — The trial court, as required under § 2.2-4027, gave deference to the hearing officer's determination that the mother's earlier accounts of the altercation with the victim were more accurate than the mother's later testimony, as the hearing officer was entitled to find that the mother's first and freshest account of the incident, which corroborated that of the victim, was the most reliable. Berryman v. Spotsylvania County Dep't of Soc. Servs., 62 Va. Cir. 443, 2003 Va. Cir. LEXIS 161 (Spotsylvania County 2003).

Deference not accorded to agency on procedural matter. — Virginia Marine Resources Commission's reversal, on procedural grounds, of a city wetlands board's approval of a landowner's application to install replacement bulkhead and backfill, was not accorded great deference, and was reversed by the court, as procedural matters were not within the Commission's specialized competence, and were in an area in which the court had special competence. Stearns v. Va. Marine Res. Comm'n, 57 Va. Cir. 213, 2001 Va. Cir. LEXIS 434 (Norfolk 2001).

When agency's findings may be rejected. — Virginia Marine Resources Commission (VMRC) failed to comply with its statutory authority within the meaning of § 2.2-4027 when: (1) the VMRC failed to observe its procedures when it accepted, but did not review, documentary evidence offered by an owner before making its decision; (2) a VMRC commissioner demonstrated bias in favor of an applicant for an after-the-fact permit; and (3) the VMRC failed to independently consider the effects that an unauthorized bar atop an authorized structure had on adjacent property owners and nearby properties. Harrison v. Va. Marine Res. Comm'n, 73 Va. Cir. 111, 2007 Va. Cir. LEXIS 222 (Norfolk Mar. 22, 2007).

Regulation adopted by Waste Management Board invalidated. — Evidence in the record did not support the Virginia Waste Management Board's adoption of the regulation that prescribed a 24-inch standing water test to determine whether containers handling certain types of waste were watertight; by definition, that test did not determine whether a container, which was nine-feet high, was watertight, and a court was authorized to invalidate agency action where such action was neither supported by the record nor justified by statutory authority, as was true of the 24-inch standing water test. James River Ass'n v. Commonwealth ex rel. Waste Mgmt. Bd., 67 Va. Cir. 44, 2005 Va. Cir. LEXIS 148 (Richmond Feb. 4, 2005).

Proper standard of review applied. — Giving due regard to the expertise of the findings rendered by a hearing officer, who affirmed a decision of the Fairfax Department of Family Services, an applicant's request for Medicaid Long Term Care coverage on account of an uncompensated transfer of her assets was upheld, where she failed to: (1) support her allegation that the Department erroneously based the value of her life estate interest on the equity in the property rather than upon the unencumbered value of the property; (2) provide any proof of an alternative motive for her asset transfer; and (3) demonstrate that there were other assets necessary to meet her current and expected medical needs. Groven v. Finnerty, 66 Va. Cir. 292, 2004 Va. Cir. LEXIS 304 (Fairfax County 2004).

The "substantial evidence" standard. — Substantial evidence in the record supported the decision of the Commonwealth motor vehicle department's commissioner that found the car manufacturer violated the Virginia Motor Vehicle Dealer Franchise Act, subdivision 7 of § 46.2-1569, as the evidence showed that despite the car dealer ordering two different models of cars during certain months, the car manufacturer's allocation of those cars to the car dealer was not equitably related to the number of vehicles that the car manufacturer imported given that no vehicles were shipped to the dealer even though the car manufacturer imported thousands of those two models each month. Volkswagen of Am., Inc. v. Smit, — Va. Cir. —, 2007 Va. Cir. LEXIS 168 (Richmond Oct. 3, 2007).

Substitution of court's judgment for agency's precluded on factual issues. — Court had no authority to review decisions of a hearing officer that involved the sufficiency of the evidence pursuant to subsection B of § 2.2-3006, based on the plain wording therein and the explicit references to evidentiary support contained in §§ 8.01-680, 2.2-4027, and 60.2-625, with respect to the hearing officer's reversal of a university's termination of a university police officer and the hearing officer's award of attorney's fees to the officer. Old Dominion Univ. v. Birkmeyer, 73 Va. Cir. 341, 2007 Va. Cir. LEXIS 131 (Norfolk 2007).

Pleadings sufficiently specific. — Although a pro se property owner did not articulate her complaints with legal precision at an after-the-fact permit hearing conducted by the Virginia Marine Resources Commission

(VMRC), the content of her testimony and that of her called witness, as well as the content of the exhibits she introduced, adequately stated concerns with the situs of a bar on a pier, the activities associated with a second-story bar structure, and how that structure and those activities allegedly would negatively affect her and her fellow neighbors' enjoyment of their residential properties; the VMRC record and the petition for appeal adequately met the specificity standards of § 2.2-4027 and Va. Sup. Ct. R.1:4(d), 2A:2, and 2A:4, as well as established Virginia precedent on the subject. Harrison v. Va. Marine Res. Comm'n, 73 Va. Cir. 111, 2007 Va. Cir. LEXIS 222 (Norfolk Mar. 22, 2007).

Decision of Virginia Department of Medical Assistance Services. — Decision of the Director of the Virginia Department of Medical Assistance Services (DMAS) was affirmed under § 2.2-4027 on the issue of collecting overpayments made to the prior operator of a nursing home, a lessee; in the absence of a DMAS reimbursement regulation on the assignment of provider numbers, 42 C.F.R. § 489.18(a)(4), the federal Medicare regulation that defined a change of ownership to include changes in a lease, applied and DMAS was entitled to assign the prior operator's provider number to the nursing home when it took over operations at the nursing facility. Thornton Hall, Inc. v. Finnerty, 61 Va. Cir. 346, 2003 Va. Cir. LEXIS 140 (Norfolk 2003), aff'd, 42 Va. App. 628, 593 S.E.2d 568 (2004).

Decision of the Director of the Virginia Department of Medical Assistance Services was reversed under § 2.2-4027 on the issue of overpayments of Medicaid funds made to a nursing home more than four years before an initial determination under subsection B of § 32.1-325.1:1, notwithstanding that the nursing home was responsible for the delays; an initial determination is the decision of the agency after an informal fact finding conference, and it must be made within four years of the overpayment or DMAS may not seek reimbursement for those amounts. Thornton Hall, Inc. v. Finnerty, 61 Va. Cir. 346, 2003 Va. Cir. LEXIS 140 (Norfolk 2003), aff'd, 42 Va. App. 628, 593 S.E.2d 568 (2004).

Denial of application. — Substantial and relevant evidence in the record concerning utilization of linear accelerators in medical facilities supported the administrative commissioner's decision to deny an application for certificate of public need to install new state-of-the-art medical treatment equipment at a medical facility. Georgetown Univ. v. Peterson, 54 Va. Cir. 383, 2001 Va. Cir. LEXIS 190 (Fairfax County 2001).

The Board's decision to deny a restaurant's application for removal of restrictions on the sale of alcohol was affirmed as: (1) the Board appropriately relied on a letter from the neighborhood association and its agent for its decision; (2) the Board's decision to deny a hearing was based upon substantial evidence; (3) limiting the time within which the restaurant was permitted to re-apply for a license was an acceptable standard developed by the Board; (4) the Board's decision to deny the claim was not arbitrary and capricious; and (5) subdivision B 4 of § 4.1-224 did not violate the restaurant's substantive and procedural due process rights, was not too broad in scope, and was not unconstitutional. Dick's Inn, L.L.C. v. Va. Alcoholic Bev. Control Bd., 60 Va. Cir. 407, 2002 Va. Cir. LEXIS 411 (Richmond 2002).

Substantial evidence supported a hearing officer's conclusion that there was no real agreement to transfer property in exchange for care as alleged by Medicaid applicants, and a decision denying Medicaid benefits to the applicants based on the transfer of their home to their daughter was affirmed. Moss v. Lemoine, 65 Va. Cir. 263, 2004 Va. Cir. LEXIS 135 (Spotsylvania County 2004).

Department of Medical Assistance Services properly upheld denial of Medicaid benefits to a surviving spouse for her deceased husband, as neither the spouse nor her husband had ever elected to set aside burial expenses, and thus they could not take advantage of the burial funds exclusion. Sherline v. Finnerty, 65 Va. Cir. 154, 2004 Va. Cir. LEXIS 143 (Fairfax County 2004).

Appeal of the denial of a claim for benefits by the Virginia Retirement System was denied because there was substantial evidence in the record on appeal, including the testimony of two physicians who examined the claimant and determined that the claimant was not disabled, to support the agency's decision. Thus, the claimant did not meet her burden of demonstrating an error regarding the substantiality of the evidentiary support for findings of fact. Mooney v. Va. Ret. Sys., — Va. Cir. —, 2005 Va. Cir. LEXIS 256 (Greene County Dec. 20, 2005).

Substantial evidence supported the Virginia Retirement System's denial of an instructional assistant's request for disability retirement pursuant to subsection E of § 51.1-156, because no medical evidence existed that identified the substance or environmental factor that was bothering the assistant at the school where she worked, the Virginia Retirement System could have found that further testing was necessary to identify the caustic substance or factor, thereby making way for effective medical treatment of the assistant's problem. Cronise v. Va. Ret. Sys., — Va. Cir. —, 2007 Va. Cir. LEXIS 181 (Roanoke County Nov. 15, 2007).

§ **2.2-4028. Intermediate relief.** — When judicial review is instituted or is about to be, the agency concerned may, on request of any party or its own motion, postpone the effective date of the regulation or decision involved where it deems that justice so requires. Otherwise the court may, on proper application and with or without bond, deposits in court, or other safeguards or assurances as may be suitable, issue all necessary and appropriate process to postpone the effective dates or preserve existing status or rights pending conclusion of the review proceedings if the court finds the same to be required to prevent immediate, unavoidable, and irreparable injury and that the issues of law or fact presented are not only substantial but that there is probable cause for it to anticipate a likelihood of reversible error in accordance with § 2.2-4027. Actions by the court may include (i) the stay of operation of agency decisions of an injunctive nature or those requiring the payment of money or suspending or revoking a license or other benefit and (ii) continuation of previous licenses in effect until timely applications for renewal are duly determined by the agency. (1975, c. 503, § 9-6.14:18; 2001, c. 844.)

Law Review. — For survey of Virginia administrative law for the year 1974-1975, see 61 Va. L. Rev. 1632 (1975).

CIRCUIT COURT OPINIONS

Illustrative cases. — Automobile dealer who sought judicial review of a decision by the Virginia Motor Vehicle Dealer Board, revoking his licenses and imposing a $1,500 fine, did not show he was likely to prevail in the courts, and the circuit court denied the dealer's motion for intermediate relief. Bryden v. Motor Vehicle Dealer Bd., 60 Va. Cir. 279, 2002 Va. Cir. LEXIS 393 (Arlington County 2002).

Although the trial court had the authority to act if it found that doing so was required to prevent immediate, unavoidable, and irreparable injury, such was not necessary in the instant case involving a dispute over whether the resident was entitled to a permit to fix a damaged bulkhead that was causing erosion to his waterfront property, as the resident had already been issued the permit and had completed the new bulkhead; accordingly, there was no basis that would permit the trial court to stay the action. Stearns v. Va. Marine Res. Comm'n, 60 Va. Cir. 296, 2002 Va. Cir. LEXIS 395 (Norfolk 2002).

§ **2.2-4029. Court judgments.** — Unless an error of law as defined in § 2.2-4027 appears, the court shall dismiss the review action or affirm the agency regulation or decision. Otherwise, it may compel agency action unlawfully and arbitrarily withheld or unreasonably delayed except that the court shall not itself undertake to supply agency action committed by the basic law to the agency. Where a regulation or case decision is found by the court not to be in accordance with law under § 2.2-4027, the court shall suspend or set it aside and remand the matter to the agency for further proceedings, if any, as the court may permit or direct in accordance with law. (1975, c. 503, § 9-6.14:19; 2001, c. 844.)

Law Review. — For survey of Virginia administrative law for the year 1974-1975, see 61 Va. L. Rev. 1632 (1975).

CASE NOTES

Court may not undertake agency action. — Where a circuit court has made a determination of invalidity, the court shall suspend or set the decision aside and remand the matter to the agency. The court itself may not undertake the agency action directly. Virginia Bd. of Medicine v. Fetta, 244 Va. 276, 421 S.E.2d 410 (1992) (decided under former corresponding provisions).

Action by the court. — The clear statutory

language contemplates that the circuit court may order a new hearing upon remand or may order dismissal of the charges, resulting in no further hearing at all. Virginia Bd. of Medicine v. Fetta, 244 Va. 276, 421 S.E.2d 410 (1992) (decided under former corresponding provisions).

Trial court erred in upholding the state environmental quality department's decision that found the corporation was entitled to reimbursement from the Petroleum Storage Tank Fund limited to the reduction in market value of the property that the corporation's spill damaged, and, thus, that it need not consider the amount of the settlement the corporation paid to the other company for the damage to its property. The settlement amount was a relevant indicator of the reasonable and necessary cost the corporation incurred in cleaning up the spill, and, thus, the record demonstrated that an error of law had occurred in calculating the proper amount of reimbursement; as a result, the trial court's affirmance of the state environmental quality department's decision had to be reversed and the case had to be remanded for further proceedings. 7-Eleven, Inc. v. Dep't of Envtl. Quality, 42 Va. App. 65, 590 S.E.2d 84, 2003 Va. App. LEXIS 703 (2003), reversing 7-Eleven, Inc. v. Va. Dept. of Envtl. Quality, 56 Va. Cir. 276, 2001 Va. Cir. LEXIS 458 (Richmond 2001).

Virginia Department of Environmental Quality (VDEQ) added a special requirement to a permittee's Virginia Pollutant Discharge Elimination System discharge permit obliging it to allow photography by VDEQ inspectors. Pursuant to § 2.2-4029, the trial court properly directed VDEQ to amend the special requirement to state that the permittee could not prevent photography "reasonably related" to the purpose of the site visit and the particular inspection being carried out under the permit. Bowman Apple Prods. Co. v. State Water Control Bd., 50 Va. App. 383, 650 S.E.2d 548, 2007 Va. App. LEXIS 345 (2007).

Failure to make findings required remand. — Because the Virginia Alcoholic Beverage Control Board granted an applicant licenses allowing liquor sales only until 12:00 a.m., without making findings of fact or conclusions of law to support these time restrictions, as required by § 2.2-4020, the case was remanded to Board pursuant to § 2.2-4029 so it could make such findings. Harrison v. Ocean View Fishing Pier, LLC, 50 Va. App. 556, 651 S.E.2d 421, 2007 Va. App. LEXIS 397 (2007).

Agency "final decision" not found. — Because a trial court's order did not address the merits of a sanction imposed on real estate agents by the Virginia Department of Professional and Occupational Regulation, Real Estate Board, but remanded the matter for or further consideration, its order was not a "final decision" within the meaning of § 17.1-405, and the court of appeals lacked jurisdiction to consider the Board's appeal. Commonwealth v. Lancaster, 45 Va. App. 723, 613 S.E.2d 828, 2005 Va. App. LEXIS 226 (2005).

Applied in Citland, Ltd. v. Commonwealth ex rel. Kilgore, 45 Va. App. 268, 610 S.E.2d 321, 2005 Va. App. LEXIS 113 (2005); Jones v. West, 46 Va. App. 309, 616 S.E.2d 790, 2005 Va. App. LEXIS 307 (2005); Rice v. Va. Dep't of Soc. Servs., — Va. App. —, — S.E.2d —, 2007 Va. App. LEXIS 123 (Mar. 27, 2007).

§ 2.2-4030. Recovery of costs and attorneys' fees from agency. — A. In any civil case brought under Article 5 (§ 2.2-4025 et seq.) of this chapter or §§ 2.2-4002, 2.2-4006, 2.2-4011, or § 2.2-4018, in which any person contests any agency action, such person shall be entitled to recover from that agency, including the Department of Game and Inland Fisheries, reasonable costs and attorneys' fees if such person substantially prevails on the merits of the case and the agency's position is not substantially justified, unless special circumstances would make an award unjust. The award of attorneys' fees shall not exceed $25,000.

B. Nothing in this section shall be deemed to grant permission to bring an action against an agency if the agency would otherwise be immune from suit, or to grant a right to bring an action by a person who would otherwise lack standing to bring the action.

C. Any costs and attorneys' fees assessed against an agency under this section shall be charged against the operating expenses of the agency for the fiscal year in which the assessment is made, and shall not be reimbursed from any other source. (1981, c. 446, § 9-6.14:21; 1997, c. 692; 2001, c. 844.)

CASE NOTES

Editor's note. — Some of the cases below were decided under former corresponding provisions.

Applicability. — Upon the trial court's dismissal of a protective order when it found that the Department of Family Services had failed to establish that the father's child was abused and/or neglected, the father was not entitled to an award of attorneys fees; the department was not an agency as defined under former § 9-6.14:4 (see now § 2.2-4501) and former § 9-6.14:15 et seq. (see now § 2.2-4025 et seq.) did not apply to matters subject by law to a trial de novo in any court. Simonds v. Fairfax County Dep't of Family Servs., 36 Va. App. 243, 549 S.E.2d 607, 2001 Va. App. LEXIS 434 (2001).

When nursing facilities were entitled to recover their attorney's fees and costs under subsection A of § 2.2-4030, the statute's $25,000 cap only applied to attorney's fees, and not to the facilities' costs. Dep't of Med. Assistance Servs. v. Beverly Healthcare, 41 Va. App. 468, 585 S.E.2d 858, 2003 Va. App. LEXIS 474 (2003), aff'd, remanded, 268 Va. 278, 601 S.E.2d 604 (2004).

Claimant who applied for but was denied retirement benefits based on the retiree's Commonwealth employment could not recover attorney fees, as such an award was available only to a prevailing party, which she was not. Shropshire v. Va. Ret. Sys., 48 Va. App. 436, 632 S.E.2d 601, 2006 Va. App. LEXIS 336 (2006).

Inapplicability to claims for unemployment compensation. — Former § 9-6.14:21 (see now this section), providing for awards of attorney fees, does not apply to judicial review of determinations of claims for unemployment compensation. Shuler v. VEC, 14 Va. App. 1013, 420 S.E.2d 257 (1992).

"Substantially prevails." — Retiree who appealed the revocation of her disability retirement benefits substantially prevailed on the merits of the litigation and was entitled to attorney fees where the court remanded the denial of her benefits to the Virginia Retirement System to reinstate her benefits and to conduct a statutorily permitted review of her disability. Avery v. Virginia Retirement Sys., 31 Va. App. 1, 520 S.E.2d 831 (1999), aff'd in part, 33 Va. App. 210, 532 S.E.2d 348 (2000).

Statutory limit applies to each defendant. — When eight nursing facilities were entitled to recover their attorney's fees and costs under subsection A of § 2.2-4030, the statutory limit of $25,000 applied to each facility, rather than to all of the facilities as a group, because, in permitting "any person" in "any civil case" to recover fees up to the stated limit, the legislature intended, where each facility independently filed its own notice of appeal, which was then consolidated with the other facilities' appeals into a single proceeding, in accordance with Va. Sup. Ct. R. 2A:3(b) and 2A:4(a), each notice represented the commencement of a separate civil case, presenting its own issues with regard to the jurisdiction and fiscal years involved and the timeliness of filings in each case. Dep't of Med. Assistance Servs. v. Beverly Healthcare, 41 Va. App. 468, 585 S.E.2d 858, 2003 Va. App. LEXIS 474 (2003), aff'd, remanded, 268 Va. 278, 601 S.E.2d 604 (2004).

Where several providers' appeals of the Virginia Department of Medical Assistance Services' denial of their claims for increased Medicaid reimbursement were consolidated into one case under Va. Sup. Ct. Rule 2A:3, and they substantially prevailed, the $25,000 cap on attorneys' fees awards had to be applied on a per party basis, rather than a per case basis. Dep't of Med. Assistance Servs. v. Beverly Healthcare, 268 Va. 278, 601 S.E.2d 604, 2004 Va. LEXIS 136 (2004).

Award upheld. — Trial court's award of attorney fees to corporation was proper pursuant to former § 9-6.14:21 (see now this section), as corporation substantially prevailed on the merits of its case that it had not received Medicaid payments in excess of what it was entitled to for two different years, state government agency was found to have acted unreasonably in trying to recover the alleged overpayments, and no special circumstances made the attorney fee award to the corporation unjust. Smith v. Liberty Nursing Home, Inc., No. 2942-00-3, 2001 Va. App. LEXIS 543 (Ct. of Appeals Oct. 2, 2001).

Denial upheld. — Denial of an accused's request for attorney's fees and costs with regard to a circuit court reversing a founded disposition of sexual abuse against the accused was upheld on appeal as substantially justified since the Department of Social Service's (DSS's) disposition was justified and it was reversed due to procedural violations, not substantive, in that the DSS's failure to record the victim's interview caused the reversal of the disposition. Jones v. West, 46 Va. App. 309, 616 S.E.2d 790, 2005 Va. App. LEXIS 307 (2005).

Two landfill operators did not substantially prevail on the merits of their appeals of the decisions of the Director of the Virginia Department of Environmental Quality denying their requests for variances from ground water monitoring requirements and requiring ground water monitoring at a closed portion of a landfill, and the Director's decisions were substantially justified; the trial court did not err by refusing to award the operators attorneys' fees and costs. Elbow Farm, Inc. v. Paylor, — Va. App. —,

— S.E.2d —, 2007 Va. App. LEXIS 48 (Feb. 13, 2007).

Award vacated. — Circuit court lacked jurisdiction to award attorneys' fees and costs more than 21 days after order that disposed of the whole subject of the litigation, and granted all contemplated relief, by affirming department's issuance of permit. Commonwealth v. Residents Involved in Saving Env't, Inc., No. 0769-99-2 (Ct. of Appeals Mar. 28, 2000).

Eight percent of requested fee award upheld. — Review of the record did not indicate convincingly that the circuit court was clearly wrong in awarding 8% of the attorney fee request or in its supporting conclusion that much of the effort spent by appellant's counsel was duplicative and overreaching. Greenwald Cassell Assocs. v. Guffey, 19 Va. App. 179, 450 S.E.2d 181 (1994).

CIRCUIT COURT OPINIONS

"Substantially prevails." — Where property owner substantially prevailed on the merits of her appeal of the Virginia Marine Resources Commission's (VMRC) grant of an after-the-fact permit, the property owner was entitled to an award of attorney's fees and costs. The VMRC's position was not substantially justified and no circumstances existed that would make such an award unjust. Harrison v. Va. Marine Res. Comm'n, 73 Va. Cir. 111, 2007 Va. Cir. LEXIS 222 (Norfolk Mar. 22, 2007).

Attorney's fees. — A retired officer was entitled to attorney's fees under the Virginia Administrative Process Act where the position that the commissioner of the Department of Social Services took was not substantially justified within the meaning of former § 9-6.14:21 (now this section), where the commissioner upheld a finding of abuse after court had twice ruled in the officer's favor. Neidig v. Carter, 55 Va. Cir. 476, 2000 Va. Cir. LEXIS 615 (Fairfax County 2000) (decided under prior law).

Attorney's fees denied. — Trial court declined to award fees or costs, as it would not be appropriate in a case where the association challenged two administrative regulations adopted by the Virginia Waste Management Board, as the association did not substantially prevail on the merits of the case and the Virginia Waste Management Board was in a precarious position with regard to federal litigation and constitutional issues. James River Ass'n v. Commonwealth ex rel. Waste Mgmt. Bd., 67 Va. Cir. 44, 2005 Va. Cir. LEXIS 148 (Richmond Feb. 4, 2005).

ARTICLE 6.

Virginia Register of Regulations.

§ 2.2-4031. Publication of Virginia Register of Regulations; exceptions; notice of public hearings of proposed regulations. — A. The Registrar shall publish every two weeks a Virginia Register of Regulations that shall include (i) proposed and final regulations; (ii) emergency regulations; (iii) executive orders; (iv) notices of all public hearings on regulations; (v) petitions for rulemaking made in accordance with § 2.2-4007; and (vi) tax bulletins. The entire proposed regulation shall be published in the Register; however, if an existing regulation has been previously published in the Virginia Administrative Code, then only those sections of regulations to be amended need to be published in the Register. If the length of the regulation falls within the guidelines established by the Registrar for the publication of a summary in lieu of the full text of the regulation, then, after consultation with the promulgating agency, the Registrar may publish only the summary of the regulation. In this event, the full text of the regulation shall be available for public inspection at the office of the Registrar and the promulgating agency.

If a proposed regulation is adopted as published or, in the sole discretion of the Registrar of Regulations, the only changes that have been made are those that can be clearly and concisely explained, the adopted regulation need not be published at length. Instead, the Register shall contain a notation that the proposed regulation has been adopted as published as a proposed regulation without change or stating the changes made. The proposed regulation shall be clearly identified with a citation to the issue and page numbers where published.

A copy of all reporting forms the promulgating agency anticipates will be incorporated into or be used in administering the regulation shall be published with the proposed and final regulation in the Register.

B. Each regulation shall be prefaced with a summary explaining that regulation in plain and clear language. Summaries shall be prepared by the promulgating agency and approved by the Registrar prior to their publication in the Register. The notice required by § 2.2-4007.03 shall include (i) a statement of the date, time and place of the hearing at which the regulation is to be considered; (ii) a brief statement as to the regulation under consideration; (iii) reference to the legal authority of the agency to act; and (iv) the name, address and telephone number of an individual to contact for further information about that regulation. Agencies shall present their proposed regulations in a standardized format developed by the Virginia Code Commission in accordance with subdivision 1 of § 2.2-4104 of the Virginia Register Act (§ 2.2-4100 et seq.). Notwithstanding the exemptions allowed under § 2.2-4002, 2.2-4006 or 2.2-4011, the proposed and final regulations of all agencies shall be published in the Register. However, proposed regulations of the Marine Resources Commission and regulations exempted by subject from the provisions of this chapter by subsection B of § 2.2-4002 shall be exempt from this section.

C. The Virginia Register of Regulations shall be published by posting the Register on the Virginia Code Commission's website. The Virginia Code Commission may arrange for the printing of the Virginia Register as provided in § 30-146. (1984, c. 5, § 9-6.14:22; 1985, cc. 67, 602; 1986, c. 615; 1988, c. 364; 1989, c. 71; 1992, c. 216; 2001, c. 844; 2002, c. 241; 2003, c. 212; 2007, cc. 300, 873, 916.)

The 2007 amendments. — The 2007 amendment by c. 300 deleted "meetings and public" preceding "hearings" and substituted "on regulations" for "of state agencies, legislative committees and study subcommittes" in subsection A; deleted former subsection C regarding requirements for publication of notice of meetings, and redesignated former subsection D as present subsection C.

The 2007 amendments by cc. 873 and 916 are identical, and deleted "subsection A of" preceding "§ 2.2-4007" in the first paragraph of subsection A; substituted "2.2-4007.01" for "2.2-4007" in subsection B; and made minor stylistic changes.

Law Review. — For article on legislative changes to Virginia administrative rulemaking, see 19 U. Rich. L. Rev. 107 (1984).

§§ 2.2-4032, 2.2-4033: Repealed by Acts 2003, c. 212, cl. 2, effective March 16, 2003.

Cross references. — As to current provisions regarding access to and distribution and sale of Virginia Register of Regulations, see §§ 30-34.10:2 and 30-146.

CHAPTER 41.

Virginia Register Act.

§ 2.2-4100. Short title; purpose of chapter; declaration of policy. — A. This chapter shall be known and may be cited as the "Virginia Register Act."

B. It is the purpose of this chapter to satisfy the need for public availability of information respecting the regulations of state agencies. Nothing in this chapter contemplates or is designed to limit or impede the present or future making, amendment, or repeal of regulations by administrative agencies. It is declared to be the policy of the Commonwealth to encourage, facilitate, and assist agencies in developing regulations that will inform the public of the requirements, policies, and procedures of the administrative authorities of the State. (1973, c. 535, §§ 9-6.15, 9-6.22; 1975, c. 502; 2001, c. 844.)

Cross references. — As to this Act in construction with the Virginia Administrative Process Act, see § 2.2-4002. As to the effective date of regulations adopted in accordance with this chapter and the Administrative Process Act, see § 2.2-4015. As to the duty of the Virginia Code Commission to monitor the operation of the Virginia Register Act, see § 30-155.

Law Review. — For survey of Virginia administrative law for the year 1972-1973, see 59 Va. L. Rev. 1401 (1973). For survey of Virginia administrative law for the year 1974-1975, see 61 Va. L. Rev. 1632 (1975). For article on legislative changes to Virginia administrative rulemaking, see 19 U. Rich. L. Rev. 107 (1984).

Michie's Jurisprudence. — For related discussion, see 1A M.J. Administrative Law, § 2.

CASE NOTES

Editor's note. — The cases below were decided under former corresponding provisions.

The hearing determination chart is not a substantive rule of the Industrial (now Workers' Compensation) Commission subject to the Virginia Administrative Process Act or the Virginia Register Act. Bader v. Norfolk Redevelopment & Hous. Auth., 10 Va. App. 697, 396 S.E.2d 141 (1990).

Failure to incorporate manual not dispositive. — Department of Medical Assistance Services' failure to incorporate the provider reimbursement manual was not dispositive where the language of its own manual indicated that the agency intended to utilize the federal policy manual to calculate reimbursements for reasonable costs; the record established that the appellants were aware of and possessed copies of the manual; one appellant agreed to participate in the program and was fully aware that the manual was to be utilized; and both parties relied on the manual as a definitive source of information regarding reasonable costs reimbursement questions. Fralin v. Kozlowski, 18 Va. App. 697, 447 S.E.2d 238 (1994).

§ 2.2-4101. Definitions. — As used in this chapter, unless the context requires a different meaning:

"Agency" means any authority, instrumentality, officer, board, or other unit of the government of the Commonwealth with express or implied authority to issue regulations other than the General Assembly, courts, municipal corporations, counties, other local or regional governmental authorities including sanitary or other districts and joint state-federal, interstate or intermunicipal authorities, the Virginia Resources Authority, the Virginia Code Commission with respect to minor changes made under the provisions of § 30-150, and educational institutions operated by the Commonwealth with respect to regulations that pertain to (i) their academic affairs; (ii) the selection, tenure, promotion and disciplining of faculty and employees; (iii) the selection of students; and (iv) rules of conduct and disciplining of students.

"Virginia Administrative Code" means the codified publication of regulations under the provisions of Chapter 15 (§ 30-145 et seq.) of Title 30.

"Commission" means the Virginia Code Commission.

"Guidance document" means any document developed by a state agency or staff that provides information or guidance of general applicability to the staff or public to interpret or implement statutes or the agency's rules or regulations, excluding agency minutes or documents that pertain only to the internal

management of agencies. Nothing in this definition shall be construed or interpreted to expand the identification or release of any document otherwise protected by law.

"Registrar" means the Registrar of Regulations appointed as provided in § 2.2-4102.

"Rule" or *"regulation"* means any statement of general application, having the force of law, affecting the rights or conduct of any person, promulgated by an agency in accordance with the authority conferred on it by applicable basic laws.

"Virginia Register of Regulations" means the publication issued under the provisions of Article 6 (§ 2.2-4031 et seq.) of the Administrative Process Act (§ 2.2-4000 et seq.). (1973, c. 535, § 9-6.16; 1975, c. 502; 1982, c. 489; 1984, c. 5; 1985, cc. 67, 602; 1993, c. 669; 1997, cc. 11, 87; 2001, c. 844.)

Law Review. — For survey of Virginia administrative law for the year 1974-1975, see 61 Va. L. Rev. 1632 (1975).

§ 2.2-4102. Registrar of Regulations; personnel, facilities and services; publications. — The Commission shall engage or appoint on a contract, part-time, or annual basis a professionally experienced or trained Registrar of Regulations. Under the direction of the Commission, the Registrar shall, at a suitable place to be designated by the Commission, perform the duties required by this chapter or assigned by the Commission in accordance with this chapter or Chapter 15 (§ 30-145 et seq.) of Title 30. The Commission shall as necessary also (i) appoint clerical or other personnel if any, (ii) arrange by contract or otherwise for the necessary facilities and services, and (iii) provide for the compilation and publication of the Virginia Register of Regulations and the Virginia Administrative Code pursuant to §§ 2.2-4031 and 30-146. (1973, c. 535, § 9-6.17; 1975, c. 502; 1982, c. 489; 1984, c. 5; 1992, c. 216; 1993, c. 669; 1997, c. 87; 2001, c. 844; 2003, c. 212.)

§ 2.2-4103. (Effective until December 31, 2010) Agencies to file regulations with Registrar; other duties; failure to file. — It shall be the duty of every agency to have on file with the Registrar the full text of all of its currently operative regulations, together with the dates of adoption, revision, publication, or amendment thereof and such additional information requested by the Commission or the Registrar for the purpose of publishing the Virginia Register of Regulations and the Virginia Administrative Code. Thereafter, coincidentally with the issuance thereof, each agency shall from day to day so file, date, and supplement all new regulations and amendments, repeals, or additions to its previously filed regulations. The filed regulations shall (i) indicate the laws they implement or carry out, (ii) designate any prior regulations repealed, modified, or supplemented, (iii) state any special effective or terminal dates, and (iv) be accompanied by a signed statement or certification that they are full, true, and correctly dated. No regulation or amendment or repeal thereof shall be effective until filed with the Registrar.

Orders condemning or closing any shellfish, finfish or crustacea growing area and the shellfish, finfish or crustacea located thereon pursuant to Article 2 (§ 28.2-803 et seq.) of Chapter 8, of Title 28.2, which are exempt from the requirements of the Administrative Process Act (§ 2.2-4000 et seq.) as provided in subsection B of § 2.2-4002, shall be effective on the date specified by the promulgating agency. Such orders shall continue to be filed with the Registrar either before or after their effective dates in order to satisfy the need for public availability of information respecting the regulations of state agencies. An order setting a date of closure for the Chesapeake Bay purse seine fishery for Atlantic menhaden for reduction purposes pursuant to § 28.2-1000.2, which is exempt from the requirements of the Administrative Process Act as provided by subsection A of § 2.2-4002, shall be effective on the date specified. Such orders shall be filed with the Registrar for prompt publication.

In addition, each agency shall itself (i) maintain a complete list of all of its currently operative regulations for public consultation, (ii) make available to public inspection a complete file of the full texts of all such regulations, and (iii) allow public copying thereof or make copies available either without charge, at cost, or on payment of a reasonable fee. Each agency shall also maintain as a public record a complete file of its regulations that have been superseded on and after June 1, 1975.

It shall be the duty of every agency to annually file with the Registrar for publication in the Virginia Register of Regulations a list of any guidance documents upon which the agency currently relies. The filing shall be made on or before January 1 of each year in a format to be developed by the Registrar. Each agency shall also (i) maintain a complete list of all of its currently operative guidance documents and make such list available for public inspection, (ii) make available for public inspection the full texts of all such guidance documents to the extent such inspection is permitted by law, and (iii) upon request, make copies of such lists or guidance documents available without charge, at cost, or on payment of a reasonable fee.

Where regulations adopt textual matter by reference to publications other than the Federal Register or Code of Federal Regulations, the agency shall (i) file with the Registrar copies of the referenced publications, (ii) state on the face of or as notations to regulations making such adoptions by reference the places where copies of the referred publications may be procured, and (iii) make copies of such referred publications available for public inspection and copying along with its other regulations.

Unless he finds that there are special circumstances requiring otherwise, the Governor, in addition to the exercise of his authority to see that the laws are faithfully executed, may, until compliance with this chapter is achieved, withhold the payment of compensation or expenses of any officer or employee of any agency in whole or part whenever the Commission certifies to him that the agency has failed to comply with this section or this chapter in stated respects, to respond promptly to the requests of the Registrar, or to comply with the regulations of the Commission. (1973, c. 535, § 9-6.18; 1975, c. 502; 1982, c. 489; 1989, c. 299; 1997, cc. 11, 87; 2001, c. 844; 2007, c. 41.)

Section set out twice. — The section above is effective until December 31, 2010. For this section as in effect December 31, 2010, see the following section, also numbered 2.2-4103.

Editor's note. — Acts 2007, c. 41, cl. 2, provides: "The provisions of this act shall expire on December 31, 2010."

The 2007 amendments. — The 2007 amendment by c. 41, which expires December 31, 2010, added the last two sentences to the second paragraph.

Law Review. — For survey of Virginia administrative law for the year 1974-1975, see 61 Va. L. Rev. 1632 (1975). For survey of administrative procedure in Virginia for 1989, see 23 U. Rich. L. Rev. 431 (1989).

Michie's Jurisprudence. — For related discussion, see 1A M.J. Administrative Law, § 9.

CASE NOTES

Failure to incorporate manual not dispositive. — Department of Medical Assistance Services' failure to incorporate the provider reimbursement manual was not dispositive where the language of its own manual indicated that the agency intended to utilize the federal policy manual to calculate reimbursements for reasonable costs; the record established that the appellants were aware of and possessed copies of the manual; one appellant agreed to participate in the program and was fully aware that the manual was to be utilized;

and both parties relied on the manual as a definitive source of information regarding reasonable costs reimbursement questions. Fralin v. Kozlowski, 18 Va. App. 697, 447 S.E.2d 238 (1994) (decided under former corresponding provisions).

§ 2.2-4103. (Effective December 31, 2010) Agencies to file regulations with Registrar; other duties; failure to file. — It shall be the duty of every agency to have on file with the Registrar the full text of all of its currently operative regulations, together with the dates of adoption, revision, publication, or amendment thereof and such additional information requested by the Commission or the Registrar for the purpose of publishing the Virginia Register of Regulations and the Virginia Administrative Code. Thereafter, coincidentally with the issuance thereof, each agency shall from day to day so file, date, and supplement all new regulations and amendments, repeals, or additions to its previously filed regulations. The filed regulations shall (i) indicate the laws they implement or carry out, (ii) designate any prior regulations repealed, modified, or supplemented, (iii) state any special effective or terminal dates, and (iv) be accompanied by a signed statement or certification that they are full, true, and correctly dated. No regulation or amendment or repeal thereof shall be effective until filed with the Registrar.

Orders condemning or closing any shellfish, finfish or crustacea growing area and the shellfish, finfish or crustacea located thereon pursuant to Article 2 (§ 28.2-803 et seq.) of Chapter 8, of Title 28.2, which are exempt from the requirements of the Administrative Process Act (§ 2.2-4000 et seq.) as provided in subsection B of § 2.2-4002, shall be effective on the date specified by the promulgating agency. Such orders shall continue to be filed with the Registrar either before or after their effective dates in order to satisfy the need for public availability of information respecting the regulations of state agencies.

In addition, each agency shall itself (i) maintain a complete list of all of its currently operative regulations for public consultation, (ii) make available to public inspection a complete file of the full texts of all such regulations, and (iii) allow public copying thereof or make copies available either without charge, at cost, or on payment of a reasonable fee. Each agency shall also maintain as a public record a complete file of its regulations that have been superseded on and after June 1, 1975.

It shall be the duty of every agency to annually file with the Registrar for publication in the Virginia Register of Regulations a list of any guidance documents upon which the agency currently relies. The filing shall be made on or before January 1 of each year in a format to be developed by the Registrar. Each agency shall also (i) maintain a complete list of all of its currently operative guidance documents and make such list available for public inspection, (ii) make available for public inspection the full texts of all such guidance documents to the extent such inspection is permitted by law, and (iii) upon request, make copies of such lists or guidance documents available without charge, at cost, or on payment of a reasonable fee.

Where regulations adopt textual matter by reference to publications other than the Federal Register or Code of Federal Regulations, the agency shall (i) file with the Registrar copies of the referenced publications, (ii) state on the face of or as notations to regulations making such adoptions by reference the places where copies of the referred publications may be procured, and (iii) make copies of such referred publications available for public inspection and copying along with its other regulations.

Unless he finds that there are special circumstances requiring otherwise, the Governor, in addition to the exercise of his authority to see that the laws are faithfully executed, may, until compliance with this chapter is achieved, withhold the payment of compensation or expenses of any officer or employee of any agency in whole or part whenever the Commission certifies to him that the agency has failed to comply with this section or this chapter in stated respects, to respond promptly to the requests of the Registrar, or to comply with the regulations of the Commission. (1973, c. 535, § 9-6.18; 1975, c. 502; 1982, c. 489; 1989, c. 299; 1997, cc. 11, 87; 2001, c. 844; 2007, c.0 41.)

Section set out twice. — The section above is effective December 31, 2010. For this section as in effect until December 31, 2010, see the preceding section, also numbered 2.2-4103.

Editor's note. — Acts 2007, c. 41, cl. 2, provides: "The provisions of this act shall expire on December 31, 2010." The section is set out above without the amendments by Acts 2007, c. 41.

The 2007 amendments. — The 2007 amendment by c. 41, which expires December 31, 2010, added the last two sentences to the second undesignated paragraph.

Law Review. — For survey of Virginia administrative law for the year 1974-1975, see 61 Va. L. Rev. 1632 (1975). For survey of administrative procedure in Virginia for 1989, see 23 U. Rich. L. Rev. 431 (1989).

Michie's Jurisprudence. — For related discussion, see 1A M.J. Administrative Law, § 9.

CASE NOTES

Failure to incorporate manual not dispositive. — Department of Medical Assistance Services' failure to incorporate the provider reimbursement manual was not dispositive where the language of its own manual indicated that the agency intended to utilize the federal policy manual to calculate reimbursements for reasonable costs; the record established that the appellants were aware of and possessed copies of the manual; one appellant agreed to participate in the program and was fully aware that the manual was to be utilized; and both parties relied on the manual as a definitive source of information regarding reasonable costs reimbursement questions. Fralin v. Kozlowski, 18 Va. App. 697, 447 S.E.2d 238 (1994) (decided under former corresponding provisions).

§ 2.2-4104. Duties of Commission in compiling Virginia Administrative Code and Register. — The Commission, through the Registrar and otherwise as it directs, may in the course of the work of compiling and maintaining the Virginia Administrative Code and the Register:

1. In writing at any time call upon all agencies to submit to the Registrar one or more copies of all existing regulations as well as all subsequent amendments, repeals, additions, or new regulations. However, this subdivision shall not affect the duty of agencies to comply with § 2.2-4103 without calls or reminders;
2. Advise agencies as to the form and style of their regulations as well as the codification thereof; and
3. Formulate and issue, without reference to or limitation by the requirements of the Administrative Process Act (§ 2.2-4000 et seq.), general or special regulations respecting the nature and content of the Virginia Administrative Code, making exceptions thereto, supplementing or limiting the duties of agencies hereunder, and otherwise carrying out the purposes of this chapter. (1973, c. 535, § 9-6.20; 1975, c. 502; 1982, c. 489; 1984, c. 5; 1993, c. 669; 2001, c. 844.)

CHAPTER 41.1.

VIRGINIA ADMINISTRATIVE DISPUTE RESOLUTION ACT.

§ 2.2-4115. Definitions. — As used in this chapter, unless the context requires otherwise:

"Dispute resolution proceeding" means any structured process in which a neutral assists parties to a dispute in reaching a voluntary settlement by means of dispute resolution processes such as mediation, conciliation, facilitation, partnering, fact-finding, neutral evaluation, use of ombudsmen or any other proceeding leading to a voluntary settlement. For the purposes of this chapter, the term "dispute resolution proceeding" does not include arbitration.

"Mediation" means a process in which a neutral facilitates communication between the parties and without deciding the issues or imposing a solution on the parties enables them to understand and resolve their dispute.

"Mediation program" means a program of a public body through which mediators or mediation is made available and includes the director, agents and employees of the program.

"Mediator" means a neutral who is an impartial third party selected by agreement of the parties to a dispute to assist them in mediation.

"Neutral" means an individual who is trained or experienced in conducting dispute resolution proceedings and in providing dispute resolution services.

"Public body" means any legislative body; any authority, board, bureau, commission, district or agency of the Commonwealth or any political subdivision of the Commonwealth, including counties, cities and towns, city councils, boards of supervisors, school boards, planning commissions, boards of visitors of institutions of higher education; and other organizations, corporations or agencies in the Commonwealth supported wholly or principally by public funds. "Public body" includes any committee, subcommittee, or other entity however designated, of the public body or formed to advise the public body, including those with private sector or citizen members and corporations organized by the Virginia Retirement System. For the purposes of this chapter the term "public body" does not include courts of the Commonwealth.

"State agency" or *"agency"* means any authority, instrumentality, officer, board or other unit of state government empowered by the basic laws to adopt regulations or decide cases. For the purposes of this chapter, the term "state agency" does not include the courts of the Commonwealth. (2002, c. 633.)

Editor's note. — Acts 2005, c. 577, cl. 1, expiring July 1, 2008, provides: "Notwithstanding the provisions of the Virginia Public Procurement Act (§ 2.2-4300 et seq.), the Virginia Information Technologies Agency is authorized to promulgate administrative rules allowing the use of alternative dispute resolution in procurement protests involving its procurement of information technology and telecommunications goods and services pursuant to § 2.2-2012. Such rules shall provide that deadlines specified in the Virginia Public Procurement Act for filing procurement protests are tolled during the use of alternative dispute resolution."

§ 2.2-4116. Authority to use dispute resolution proceedings. — A. Except as specifically prohibited by law, if the parties to the dispute agree, any public body may use dispute resolution proceedings to narrow or resolve any issue in controversy. Nothing in this chapter shall be construed to prohibit or limit other public body dispute resolution authority. Nothing in this chapter shall create or alter any right, action, cause of action, or be interpreted or applied in a manner inconsistent with the Administrative Process Act (§ 2.2-4000 et seq.), applicable federal or state law or any provision that requires the Commonwealth to obtain or maintain federal delegation or approval of any regulatory program. Nothing in this chapter shall prevent the use of the Virginia Freedom of Information Act to obtain the disclosure of information concerning expenses incurred in connection with a dispute resolution proceeding or the amount of money paid by a public body or agency to settle a dispute.

B. A decision by a public body to participate in or not to participate in a specific dispute resolution proceeding shall be within the discretion of the public body and is not subject to judicial review. This subsection does not affect or supersede any law mandating the use of a dispute resolution proceeding.

C. An agreement arising out of any dispute resolution proceeding shall not be binding upon a public body unless the agreement is affirmed by the public body. (2002, c. 633.)

§ **2.2-4117. State agency promotion of dispute resolution proceedings.** — A. Each state agency shall adopt a written policy that addresses the use of dispute resolution proceedings within the agency and for the agency's program and operations. The policy shall include, among other things, training for employees involved in implementing the agency's policy and the qualifications of a neutral to be used by the agency.

B. The head of each state agency shall designate an existing or new employee to be the dispute resolution coordinator of the agency. The duties of a dispute resolution coordinator may be collateral to those of an existing official.

C. Each state agency shall review its policies, procedures and regulations and shall determine whether and how to amend such policies, procedures and regulations to authorize and encourage the use of dispute resolution proceedings.

D. Any state agency may use the services of other agencies' employees as neutrals and an agency may allow its employees to serve as neutrals for other agencies as part of a neutral-sharing program.

E. This chapter does not supersede the provisions of subdivision 2 of § 2.2-1001 and subdivision B 4 of § 2.2-3000, which require certain agencies to participate in the mediation program administered by the Department of Employment Dispute Resolution. (2002, c. 633.)

§ **2.2-4118. Interagency Dispute Resolution Advisory Council.** — A. The Interagency Dispute Resolution Advisory Council is hereby created as an advisory council to the Secretary of Administration.

B. The Council shall consist of two dispute resolution coordinators from each Secretariat appointed by each Secretary, the Director of the Department of Employment Dispute Resolution, and three persons who are not employees of the Commonwealth, at least two of whom have experience in mediation, appointed by the Governor. The appointees who are not employees of the Commonwealth may be selected from nominations submitted by the Virginia Mediation Network and the Virginia State Bar and the Virginia Bar Association Joint Committee on Alternative Dispute Resolution, who shall each nominate two persons for each such vacancy. In no case shall the Governor be bound to make any appointment from such nominations. The Secretary of Administration or his designee shall serve as chairman of the Council.

C. The Council shall have the power and duty to:

1. Conduct training seminars and educational programs for the members and staff of agencies and public bodies and other interested persons on the use of dispute resolution proceedings.

2. Publish educational materials as it deems appropriate on the use of dispute resolution proceedings.

3. Report on its activities as may be appropriate and on the use of dispute resolution proceedings, including recommendations for changes in the law to the Governor and General Assembly.

D. Every state agency shall cooperate with and provide such assistance to the Council as the Council may request. (2002, c. 633.)

§ 2.2-4119. Confidentiality between parties; exemption to Freedom of Information Act. — A. Except for the materials described in subsection B, all dispute resolution proceedings conducted pursuant to this chapter are subject to the Virginia Freedom of Information Act (§ 2.2-3700 et seq.).

B. All memoranda, work products, or other materials contained in the case file of a mediator are confidential and all materials in the case file of a mediation program pertaining to a specific mediation are confidential. Any communication made in or in connection with a mediation that relates to the dispute, including communications to schedule a mediation, whether made to a mediator, a mediation program, a party or any other person is confidential. A written settlement agreement is not confidential unless the parties agree in writing. Confidential materials and communications are not subject to disclosure or discovery in any judicial or administrative proceeding except (i) when all parties to the mediation agree, in writing, to waive the confidentiality; (ii) to the extent necessary in a subsequent action between the mediator and a party for damages arising out of the mediation; (iii) statements, memoranda, materials and other tangible evidence, otherwise subject to discovery, which were not prepared specifically for use in and actually used in the mediation; (iv) where communications are sought or offered to prove or disprove a claim or complaint of professional misconduct or malpractice filed against the mediator; (v) where a threat to inflict bodily injury is made; (vi) where communications are intentionally used to plan, attempt to commit or commit a crime or conceal an ongoing crime; (vii) where communications are sought or offered to prove or disprove a claim or complaint of misconduct or malpractice filed against a party, nonparty, participant or representative of a party based on conduct occurring during a mediation; (viii) where communications are sought or offered to prove or disprove any of the reasons listed in § 8.01-576.12 that would enable a court to vacate a mediated agreement; or (ix) as provided by law or rule other than the Virginia Freedom of Information Act (§ 2.2-3700 et seq.). The use of attorney work product in a mediation shall not result in a waiver of the attorney work product privilege. Unless otherwise specified by the parties, no mediation proceeding shall be electronically or stenographically recorded. (2002, c. 633.)

Cross references. — As to records that are excluded from the provisions of the Virginia Freedom of Information Act, see § 2.2-3705.1 through 2.2-3705.8.

CHAPTER 42.

Fair Employment Contracting Act.

§ 2.2-4200. Declaration of policy; discrimination prohibited in awarding contracts; definitions. — A. It is declared to be the policy of the Commonwealth to eliminate all discrimination on account of race, color, religion, sex, or national origin from the employment practices of the Commonwealth, its agencies, and government contractors.

B. In the awarding of contracts, contracting agencies shall not engage in an unlawful discriminatory practice as defined in § 2.2-3901.

C. As used in this chapter, unless the context requires a different meaning:

"Agency" means any agency or instrumentality, corporate or otherwise, of the government of the Commonwealth.

"Contractor" means any individual, partnership, corporation or association that performs services for or supplies goods, materials, or equipment to the Commonwealth or any agency thereof. (1975, c. 626, §§ 2.1-374, 2.1-375, 2.1-376.1; 2001, cc. 45, 844.)

Editor's note. — Acts 2001, c. 45 amended § 2.1-376.1, from which this section is derived. Pursuant to § 30-152, Acts 2001, c. 45 has been given effect in this section as set out above. The 2001 amendment by c. 45 rewrote subsection B, which formerly read: "In the awarding of contracts, no contracting agencies shall discriminate because of race, religion, color, sex, or national origin."

Law Review. — For an article relating to a variety of developments in employment law, see 32 U. Rich. L. Rev. 1199 (1998). For an article, "A Uniform Standard for Exemplary Damages in Employment Discrimination Cases," see 33 U. Rich. L. Rev. 41 (1999). For a casenote, "Holding the Same-Sex Sexual Harassment Claim at Arm's Length: The Supreme Court's Strict (and Correct) Interpretation of Title VII In Oncale v. Sundowner Offshore Services, Inc.," see 33 U. Rich. L. Rev. 257 (1999). For a note, "Hanging in the Balance: Confidentiality Clauses and Postjudgment Settlements of Employment Discrimination Disputes," see 86 Va. L. Rev. 1537 (2000).

CASE NOTES

Construction with other law. — Because the provisions of the Virginia Fair Employment Contracting Act (VFECA) regarding gender discrimination embody the same public policy as is embodied in the Virginia Human Rights Act (VHRA) (see now § 2.2-3900 et seq.), and because the legislature has barred any cause of action based on the policies reflected in the VHRA, an action for wrongful discharge based on the VFECA is similarly barred. Williamson v. Virginia First Sav. Bank, 26 F. Supp. 2d 798 (E.D. Va. 1998) (decided under former Title 2.1).

§ 2.2-4201. Required contract provisions. — All contracting agencies shall include in every government contract of over $10,000 the following provisions:

During the performance of this contract, the contractor agrees as follows:

1. The contractor will not discriminate against any employee or applicant for employment because of race, religion, color, sex, or national origin, except where religion, sex, or national origin is a bona fide occupational qualification reasonably necessary to the normal operation of the contractor. The contractor agrees to post in conspicuous places, available to employees and applicants for employment, notices setting forth the provisions of this nondiscrimination

clause, including the names of all contracting agencies with which the contractor has contracts of over $10,000.

2. The contractor will, in all solicitations or advertisements for employees placed by or on behalf of the contractor, state that such contractor is an equal opportunity employer. However, notices, advertisements and solicitations placed in accordance with federal law, rule or regulation shall be deemed sufficient for the purpose of meeting the requirements of this chapter.

The contractor shall include the provisions of the subdivisions 1 and 2 in every subcontract or purchase order of over $10,000, so that such provisions shall be binding upon each subcontractor or vendor.

Nothing contained in this chapter shall be deemed to empower any agency to require any contractor to grant preferential treatment to, or discriminate against, any individual or any group because of race, color, religion, sex or national origin on account of an imbalance that may exist with respect to the total number or percentage of persons of any race, color, religion, sex or national origin employed by such contractor in comparison with the total number or percentage of persons of such race, color, religion, sex or national origin in any community or in the Commonwealth. (1975, c. 626, § 2.1-376; 2001, c. 844.)

Law Review. — For article, "Benign Racial Classifications: A Guide for Transportation Attorneys," see 19 U. Rich. L. Rev. 29 (1984).

CHAPTER 43.

Virginia Public Procurement Act.

Article 1.

General Provisions.

Article 2.

Contract Formation and Administration.

Article 3.

Exemptions and Limitations.

Article 4.

Prompt Payment.

Article 5.

Remedies.

Article 6.

Ethics in Public Contracting.

Article 1.

General Provisions.

§ 2.2-4300. Short title; purpose; declaration of intent. — A. This chapter may be cited as the Virginia Public Procurement Act.

B. The purpose of this chapter is to enunciate the public policies pertaining to governmental procurement from nongovernmental sources, to include governmental procurement that may or may not result in monetary consideration for either party. This chapter shall apply whether the consideration is monetary or nonmonetary and regardless of whether the public body, the contractor, or some third party is providing the consideration.

C. To the end that public bodies in the Commonwealth obtain high quality goods and services at reasonable cost, that all procurement procedures be conducted in a fair and impartial manner with avoidance of any impropriety or appearance of impropriety, that all qualified vendors have access to public business and that no offeror be arbitrarily or capriciously excluded, it is the intent of the General Assembly that competition be sought to the maximum feasible degree, that procurement procedures involve openness and administrative efficiency, that individual public bodies enjoy broad flexibility in fashioning details of such competition, that the rules governing contract awards be made clear in advance of the competition, that specifications reflect the procurement needs of the purchasing body rather than being drawn to favor a particular vendor, and that the purchaser and vendor freely exchange information concerning what is sought to be procured and what is offered. Public bodies may consider best value concepts when procuring goods and nonprofessional services, but not construction or professional services. The criteria, factors, and basis for consideration of best value and the process for the consideration of best value shall be as stated in the procurement solicitation. (1982, c. 647, § 11-35; 1983, c. 593; 1984, c. 764; 1986, cc. 149, 212, 559; 1994, cc. 661, 918; 1995, c. 18; 1996, cc. 683, 1019; 1997, cc. 85, 488, 785, 861, 863; 1998, cc. 121, 132; 1999, cc. 230, 248, 735; 2000, cc. 29, 382, 400, 642, 644, 666, 703; 2001, cc. 392, 409, 736, 753, 774, 844.)

Cross references. — For requirement of open negotiation for employment of special counsel by state agencies and state agents under certain circumstances, see § 2.2-510.1. As to the powers and duties of the Department with respect to the public guardian and conservator program, see § 2.2-712. As to the establishment of the Division of Purchases and Supply see, § 2.2-1109. As to any public body or public broadcasting station seeking the aid and cooperation of the Division of Purchases and Supply, see § 2.2-1122. As to recovery audits for state contracts, see § 2.2-1822.1. As to exemption of the Virginia Commercial Space Flight Authority from personnel and procurement procedures, see § 2.2-2215. As to exemption of the Innovative Technology Authority from personnel and procurement procedures, see § 2.2-2231. As to exemption of the Virginia Economic Development Partnership Authority from personnel and procurement procedures, see § 2.2-2244. As to exemption of the Virginia Public Broadcasting Board from the provisions of the Virginia Public Procurement Act, see § 2.2-2433. As to inapplicability of provisions of this article to contracts for advertising or publishing entered into by the Virginia Wine Board, see § 3.1-1064.7. As to appointment of counsel for parent or guardian of minor child, see § 16.1-266. For provision that this article shall not apply to contracts for the printing of ballots, statements of results, or other material essential to the conduct of an election, see § 24.2-602. As to exceptions for certain motor carriers under the Virginia Public Procurement Act to hearings on applications for a license or certificate, see § 46.2-2005. As to presumptions for certain motor carriers under the Virginia Public Procurement Act in granting of irregular route passenger certificates, see § 46.2-2080. As to procurement under the Public-Private Transportation Act of 1995, see § 56-556 et seq.

For the Public-Private Education Facilities and Infrastructure Act of 2002, see § 56-575.1 et seq. As to exemption of certain motor vehicles acquired from the centralized fleet of motor vehicles controlled by the Commonwealth Transportation Commissioner and sold or transferred to TANF recipients or former recipients from the provisions of §§ 2.2-4300 et seq., 2.2-1124, 2.2-1153, 2.2-1156, and 2.2-1177, see § 63.2-611 D.

Editor's note. — Acts 2008, c. 879, effective for the biennium ending June 30, 2010, in Item 472 E, provides: "E. The Governor is hereby authorized to transfer funds from agency appropriations to the accounts of participating state employees in such amounts as may be necessary to match the contributions of the qualified participating employees, consistent with the requirements of the Code of Virginia governing the deferred compensation cash match program. Such transfers shall be made consistent with the following:

"1. The maximum cash match provided to eligible employees shall not be less than $20.00 per pay period, or $40.00 per month. The Governor may direct the agencies of the Commonwealth to utilize funds contained within their existing appropriations to meet these requirements.

"2. The Governor may direct agencies supported in whole or in part with nongeneral funds to utilize existing agency appropriations to meet these requirements. Such nongeneral revenues and balances are hereby appropriated for this purpose, subject to the provisions of § 4-2.01 b of this act. The use of such nongeneral funds shall be consistent with any existing conditions and restrictions otherwise placed upon such nongeneral funds.

"3. Employees who are otherwise eligible but whose 403 (b) provider does not participate in the cash match program by establishing a 401 (a) account are ineligible to receive a cash match.

"4. The procurement of services related to the implementation of this program shall be governed by standards set forth in § 51.1-124.30 C, Code of Virginia, and shall not be subject to the provisions of Chapter 7 (§ 11-35 et seq.), Title 11, Code of Virginia."

Law Review. — For survey on construction law in Virginia for 1989, see 23 U. Rich. L. Rev. 541 (1989). For 2000 survey of Virginia construction law, see 34 U. Rich. L. Rev. 683 (2000). For 2000 survey of Virginia technology law, see 34 U. Rich. L. Rev. 1051. (2000). For article reviewing case law and changes in legislation affecting Virginia construction law, see 40 U. Rich. L. Rev. 143 (2005).

Research References. — Lane K. Anderson, Accounting for Government Contracts: Federal Acquisition Regulation (Matthew Bender).

Thomas J. Touhey, Government Contracts: Law, Administration and Procedure (Matthew Bender).

Michie's Jurisprudence. — For related discussion, see 5A M.J. Counties, § 63; 17 M.J. Streets and Highways, §§ 22, 42.

CASE NOTES

Application of chapter. — This chapter applies only to the purchase and sale of goods and services and not to real property, and applies only to "bidders" and "offerors" in the context of competitive bidding and negotiation. R.I.S.E., Inc. v. Kay, 768 F. Supp. 1141 (E.D. Va. 1991), aff'd, 977 F.2d 573 (4th Cir. 1992) (decided under former § 11-35 et seq.)

Disappointed bidder not allowed unjust enrichment action against successful bidder. — Virginia courts would not allow a disappointed bidder to maintain an unjust enrichment cause of action against a successful bidder. John C. Holland Enters., Inc. v. J.P. Mascaro & Sons, 653 F. Supp. 1242 (E.D. Va.), aff'd, 829 F.2d 1120 (4th Cir. 1987) (decided under former § 11-35 et seq.)

Applied in Mid-Atlantic Bus. Communs., Inc. v. Va. DMV, 269 Va. 51, 606 S.E.2d 835, 2005 Va. LEXIS 6 (2005).

CIRCUIT COURT OPINIONS

Appeal before announcement of award not allowed. — Virginia Public Procurement Act, § 2.2-4300 et seq., did not permit an appeal before the public body's announcement of its decision; a contractor's protest, submitted in response to information that it would not be awarded a contract, was not capable of being appealed as it was filed before announcement of the award. John T. Moore & Assocs., P.C. v. Va. Commonwealth Univ., 69 Va. Cir. 200, 2005 Va. Cir. LEXIS 356 (Richmond 2005).

Purchase of goods by agents of state agencies. — Virginia Public Procurement Act, § 2.2-4300 et seq., extends, arguably, to the purchase of goods by agents of state agencies; thus, where plaintiff complained that the procurement of simulated teeth for use by the Virginia Board of Dentistry in connection with a governmental activity, to wit licensing dentists for the benefit and welfare of the public, had been thwarted by an end run around the procurement competitive scheme without notice or opportunity to participate because the corporation, which developed and administered a dental examination under contract with the Board, decided to engage a manufacturer, for the use of the manufacturer's product line in the examination, a preliminary injunction order was issued because plaintiff was without an adequate remedy at law and could have suffered irreparable harm. Columbia Dentoform Corp. v. Va. Bd. of Dentistry, 64 Va. Cir. 222, 2004 Va. Cir. LEXIS 199 (Richmond 2004).

Construction contract. — Pursuant to the Virginia Procurement statute, a contractor could not recover sums allegedly due and owing under the theory of quantum meruit or unjust enrichment. Nothing in that statute expressly waived the Commonwealth's sovereign immunity defense for quasi-contractual recoveries. Turner Constr. Co. v. Va. Polytechnic Inst. & State Univ., 73 Va. Cir. 351, 2007 Va. Cir. LEXIS 207 (Montgomery County June 1, 2007).

OPINIONS OF THE ATTORNEY GENERAL

Application of competitive procurement procedures to economic development authority. — An economic development authority was exempt from the competitive procurement procedures of the Public Procurement Act with respect to the acquisition of property, but not with regard to the procurement of any contract for services. See opinion of Attorney General to The Honorable Jay K. Katzen, Member, House of Delegates, 00-105 (3/30/01).

Locality does not have the authority to require contractors to provide a "living wage" to their employees as a condition to the award of a public contract. See opinion of Attorney General to The Honorable Samuel A. Nixon, Jr., Member, House of Delegates, 02-107 (12/10/02).

§ **2.2-4301. Definitions.** — As used in this chapter:

"Affiliate" means an individual or business that controls, is controlled by, or is under common control with another individual or business. A person controls an entity if the person owns, directly or indirectly, more than 10 percent of the voting securities of the entity. For the purposes of this definition "voting security" means a security that (i) confers upon the holder the right to vote for the election of members of the board of directors or similar governing body of the business or (ii) is convertible into, or entitles the holder to receive, upon its exercise, a security that confers such a right to vote. A general partnership interest shall be deemed to be a voting security.

"Best value," as predetermined in the solicitation, means the overall combination of quality, price, and various elements of required services that in total are optimal relative to a public body's needs.

"Business" means any type of corporation, partnership, limited liability company, association, or sole proprietorship operated for profit.

"Competitive negotiation" is a method of contractor selection that includes the following elements:

1. Issuance of a written Request for Proposal indicating in general terms that which is sought to be procured, specifying the factors that will be used in evaluating the proposal and containing or incorporating by reference the other applicable contractual terms and conditions, including any unique capabilities or qualifications that will be required of the contractor.

2. Public notice of the Request for Proposal at least 10 days prior to the date set for receipt of proposals by posting in a public area normally used for posting of public notices and by publication in a newspaper or newspapers of general circulation in the area in which the contract is to be performed so as to provide reasonable notice to the maximum number of offerors that can be reasonably anticipated to submit proposals in response to the particular request. Public notice may also be published on the Department of General Services' central electronic procurement website and other appropriate websites. Effective July 1, 2002, publishing by state agencies, departments and institutions on the public Internet procurement website designated by the Department of General Services shall be required. In addition, proposals may be solicited directly from potential contractors.

3. a. Procurement of professional services. The public body shall engage in individual discussions with two or more offerors deemed fully qualified, responsible and suitable on the basis of initial responses and with emphasis on professional competence, to provide the required services. Repetitive informal interviews shall be permissible. The offerors shall be encouraged to elaborate on their qualifications and performance data or staff expertise pertinent to the proposed project, as well as alternative concepts. The Request for Proposal shall not, however, request that offerors furnish estimates of man-hours or cost for services. At the discussion stage, the public body may discuss nonbinding estimates of total project costs, including, but not limited to, life-cycle costing, and where appropriate, nonbinding estimates of price for services. Proprietary information from competing offerors shall not be disclosed to the public or to competitors. At the conclusion of discussion, outlined in this subdivision, on the basis of evaluation factors published in the Request for Proposal and all information developed in the selection process to this point, the public body shall select in the order of preference two or more offerors whose professional qualifications and proposed services are deemed most meritorious. Negotiations shall then be conducted, beginning with the offeror ranked first. If a contract satisfactory and advantageous to the public body can be negotiated at a price considered fair and reasonable, the award shall be made to that offeror. Otherwise, negotiations with the offeror ranked first shall be formally terminated and negotiations conducted with the offeror ranked second, and so on until such a contract can be negotiated at a fair and reasonable price. Notwithstanding the foregoing, if the terms and conditions for multiple awards are included in the Request for Proposal, a public body may award contracts to more than one offeror.

Should the public body determine in writing and in its sole discretion that only one offeror is fully qualified, or that one offeror is clearly more highly qualified and suitable than the others under consideration, a contract may be negotiated and awarded to that offeror.

A contract for architectural or professional engineering services relating to construction projects may be negotiated by a public body, for multiple projects provided (i) the projects require similar experience and expertise, (ii) the nature of the projects is clearly identified in the Request for Proposal, and (iii) the contract term is limited to one year or when the cumulative total project fees reach the maximum cost authorized in this paragraph, whichever occurs first. For state public bodies, such contract, except those awarded for environmental, location, design and inspection work regarding highways and bridges by the Commonwealth Transportation Commissioner may be renewable for four additional one-year terms at the option of the public body. For local public bodies, such contract may be renewable for two additional one-year terms at the option of the public body. Under such contract, (a) the fair and reasonable prices, as negotiated, shall be used in determining the cost of each project performed, (b) except those awarded for environmental, location, design and inspection work regarding highways and bridges by the Commonwealth Transportation Commissioner, the sum of all projects performed in one contract term shall not exceed $500,000 or, in the case of a state agency, as defined in § 2.2-4347, such greater amount as may be determined by the Director of the Department of General Services, not to exceed $1 million, except that in any locality or any authority or sanitation district with a population in excess of 80,000, the sum of all such projects shall not exceed $5 million; and (c) except those awarded for environmental, location, design and inspection work regarding highways and bridges by the Commonwealth Transportation Commissioner, the project fee of any single project shall not exceed $100,000 or, in the case of a state agency, such greater amount as may be determined by the Director of the Department of General Services not to exceed $200,000, except that in any locality or any authority or sanitation district with a population in excess of 80,000, such fee shall not exceed $1 million. Any unused amounts from the first contract term shall not be carried forward to the additional term. Competitive negotiations for such contracts may result in awards to more than one offeror provided (1) the Request for Proposal so states and (2) the public body has established procedures for distributing multiple projects among the selected contractors during the contract term. For contracts for environmental location, design and inspection work regarding highways and bridges by the Commonwealth Transportation Commissioner, the sum of all projects in one contract term shall not exceed $2 million and such contract may be renewable for two additional one-year terms at the option of the Commissioner.

Multiphase professional services contracts satisfactory and advantageous to the Department of Transportation for environmental, location, design and inspection work regarding highways and bridges may be negotiated and awarded based on a fair and reasonable price for the first phase only, when completion of the earlier phases is necessary to provide information critical to the negotiation of a fair and reasonable price for succeeding phases.

Multiphase professional services contracts satisfactory and advantageous to a local public body for environmental, location, design and inspection work regarding construction of infrastructure projects may be negotiated and awarded based on qualifications at a fair and reasonable price for the first phase only, when completion of the earlier phases is necessary to provide information critical to the negotiation of a fair and reasonable price for succeeding phases. Prior to the procurement of any such contract, the local public body shall state the anticipated intended total scope of the project and determine in writing that the nature of the work is such that the best interests of such public body require awarding the contract.

b. Procurement of other than professional services. Selection shall be made of two or more offerors deemed to be fully qualified and best suited among those submitting proposals, on the basis of the factors involved in the Request for Proposal, including price if so stated in the Request for Proposal. Negotiations shall then be conducted with each of the offerors so selected. Price shall be considered, but need not be the sole determining factor. After negotiations have been conducted with each offeror so selected, the public body shall select the offeror which, in its opinion, has made the best proposal, and shall award the contract to that offeror. When the terms and conditions of multiple awards are so provided in the Request for Proposal, awards may be made to more than one offeror. Should the public body determine in writing and in its sole discretion that only one offeror is fully qualified, or that one offeror is clearly more highly qualified than the others under consideration, a contract may be negotiated and awarded to that offeror.

"Competitive sealed bidding" is a method of contractor selection, other than for professional services, which includes the following elements:

1. Issuance of a written Invitation to Bid containing or incorporating by reference the specifications and contractual terms and conditions applicable to the procurement. Unless the public body has provided for prequalification of bidders, the Invitation to Bid shall include a statement of any requisite qualifications of potential contractors. When it is impractical to prepare initially a purchase description to support an award based on prices, an Invitation to Bid may be issued requesting the submission of unpriced offers to be followed by an Invitation to Bid limited to those bidders whose offers have been qualified under the criteria set forth in the first solicitation.

2. Public notice of the Invitation to Bid at least 10 days prior to the date set for receipt of bids by posting in a designated public area, or publication in a newspaper of general circulation, or both. Public notice may also be published

on the Department of General Services' central electronic procurement website and other appropriate websites. Effective July 1, 2002, posting by state agencies, departments and institutions on the public Internet procurement website designated by the Department of General Services shall be required. In addition, bids may be solicited directly from potential contractors. Any additional solicitations shall include businesses selected from a list made available by the Department of Minority Business Enterprise.

3. Public opening and announcement of all bids received.

4. Evaluation of bids based upon the requirements set forth in the invitation, which may include special qualifications of potential contractors, life-cycle costing, value analysis, and any other criteria such as inspection, testing, quality, workmanship, delivery, and suitability for a particular purpose, which are helpful in determining acceptability.

5. Award to the lowest responsive and responsible bidder. When the terms and conditions of multiple awards are so provided in the Invitation to Bid, awards may be made to more than one bidder.

"Construction" means building, altering, repairing, improving or demolishing any structure, building or highway, and any draining, dredging, excavation, grading or similar work upon real property.

"Construction management contract" means a contract in which a party is retained by the owner to coordinate and administer contracts for construction services for the benefit of the owner, and may also include, if provided in the contract, the furnishing of construction services to the owner.

"Design-build contract" means a contract between a public body and another party in which the party contracting with the public body agrees to both design and build the structure, roadway or other item specified in the contract.

"Goods" means all material, equipment, supplies, printing, and automated data processing hardware and software.

"Informality" means a minor defect or variation of a bid or proposal from the exact requirements of the Invitation to Bid, or the Request for Proposal, which does not affect the price, quality, quantity or delivery schedule for the goods, services or construction being procured.

"Multiphase professional services contract" means a contract for the providing of professional services where the total scope of work of the second or subsequent phase of the contract cannot be specified without the results of the first or prior phase of the contract.

"Nonprofessional services" means any services not specifically identified as professional services in the definition of professional services.

"Potential bidder or offeror" for the purposes of §§ 2.2-4360 and 2.2-4364 means a person who, at the time a public body negotiates and awards or proposes to award a contract, is engaged in the sale or lease of goods, or the sale of services, insurance or construction, of the type to be procured under the contract, and who at such time is eligible and qualified in all respects to perform that contract, and who would have been eligible and qualified to submit a bid or proposal had the contract been procured through competitive sealed bidding or competitive negotiation.

"Professional services" means work performed by an independent contractor within the scope of the practice of accounting, actuarial services, architecture, land surveying, landscape architecture, law, dentistry, medicine, optometry, pharmacy or professional engineering. "Professional services" shall also include the services of an economist procured by the State Corporation Commission.

"Public body" means any legislative, executive or judicial body, agency, office, department, authority, post, commission, committee, institution, board or political subdivision created by law to exercise some sovereign power or to perform some governmental duty, and empowered by law to undertake the activities described in this chapter.

"Public contract" means an agreement between a public body and a nongovernmental source that is enforceable in a court of law.

"Responsible bidder" or *"offeror"* means a person who has the capability, in all respects, to perform fully the contract requirements and the moral and business integrity and reliability that will assure good faith performance, and who has been prequalified, if required.

"Responsive bidder" means a person who has submitted a bid that conforms in all material respects to the Invitation to Bid.

"Reverse auctioning" means a procurement method wherein bidders are invited to bid on specified goods or nonprofessional services through real-time electronic bidding, with the award being made to the lowest responsive and responsible bidder. During the bidding process, bidders' prices are revealed and bidders shall have the opportunity to modify their bid prices for the duration of the time period established for bid opening.

"Services" means any work performed by an independent contractor wherein the service rendered does not consist primarily of acquisition of equipment or materials, or the rental of equipment, materials and supplies.

"Sheltered workshop" means a work-oriented rehabilitative facility with a controlled working environment and individual goals that utilizes work experience and related services for assisting the handicapped person to progress toward normal living and a productive vocational status. (1982, c. 647, § 11-37; 1984, cc. 279, 764; 1985, c. 164; 1987, cc. 176, 218, 474; 1989, cc. 309, 323; 1991, c. 559; 1996, cc. 460, 683; 2000, cc. 621, 638, 643, 644, 647, 665, 692, 703; 2001, cc. 395, 675, 844; 2003, cc. 185, 644, 895, 994, 1006; 2004, c. 458; 2006, c. 206; 2008, c. 371.)

Cross references. — As to powers and duties of the Virginia Information Technologies Agency and the Chief Information Officer, see, see § 2.2-2007 et seq. As to officers and employees of state government having a personal interest in state contracts, see § 2.2-3106. As to employees of a governmental agency of local government having a personal interest in a contract with that agency, see § 2.2-3109. As to prohibited conduct by legislators regarding contracts, see § 30-105. As to procurement of information technology and telecommunications goods and services, see § 2.2-2012.

Editor's note. — Acts 2001, c. 395 and 675 amended § 11-37, from which this section is derived. Pursuant to § 30-152, Acts 2001, cc. 395 and 675 have been given effect in this section as set out above.

Acts 2008, c. 879, effective for the biennium ending June 30, 2010, in § 4-5.06 f., provides: "Institutions that have executed memoranda of understanding with the Secretary of Administration for nongeneral fund capital outlay decentralization programs are hereby granted a waiver from the provisions of § 2.2-4301, Competitive Negotiation, subdivision 3a, Code of Virginia, regarding the not to exceed amount of $100,000 for a single project, the not to exceed sum of $500,000 for all projects performed, and the option to renew for two additional one-year terms."

The 2008 amendments. — The 2008 amendment by c. 371, in the third paragraph of subparagraph 3 a in the definition of "Competitive negotiation," substituted "$5 million" for "$1 million" at the end of clause (b) and substituted "$1 million" for "$200,000" at the end of clause (c) in the fourth sentence.

Michie's Jurisprudence. — For related discussion, see 17 M.J. Streets and Highways, § 22.

CASE NOTES

Small business development center not a "public body." — A small business development center was not an entity "created by law" to "perform [a] governmental duty" so as to qualify as a "public body" as defined in this section where the center was formed by an industrial development authority, the directors of the authority comprised the initial board of directors of the center, and, in the event of the dissolution of the center, all remaining assets were to be distributed to the authority or to political subdivisions that contributed funds to the center during the year of dissolution. Dr. William E.S. Flory Small Bus. Dev. Ctr., Inc. v. Commonwealth, 261 Va. 230, 541 S.E.2d 915, 2001 Va. LEXIS 39 (2001) (decided under former § 11-35 et seq.)

CIRCUIT COURT OPINIONS

"Informality." — Therapy provider's response to a corrections department's invitation for bids was not responsive because it differed in material respects from the invitation for bids and those material differences could not be considered to be allowable informalities because they were variations of the exact requirements of the invitation, which affected the price, quality, quantity, or delivery schedule for the services being procured. Peninsula Therapy Ctr., PLC v. Dep't of Corr., — Va. Cir. —, 2002 Va. Cir. LEXIS 271 (Newport News Aug. 1, 2002).

It was within a corrections department's discretion to waive a requirement that bidders responding to an invitation for bids to provide therapy services to inmates supply references or sign for an addendum and to permit the bidders to supply insurance certificates or licenses at a later time. Peninsula Therapy Ctr., PLC v. Dep't of Corr., — Va. Cir. —, 2002 Va. Cir. LEXIS 271 (Newport News Aug. 1, 2002).

"Responsive bidder." — Therapy provider's response to a corrections department's invitation for bids was not responsive because it differed in material respects from the invitation for bids by addressing issues not raised in the invitation and by following language that had been deleted from the invitation concerning decisions about the termination of services. Peninsula Therapy Ctr., PLC v. Dep't of Corr., — Va. Cir. —, 2002 Va. Cir. LEXIS 271 (Newport News Aug. 1, 2002).

OPINIONS OF THE ATTORNEY GENERAL

Locality does not have the authority to require contractors to provide a "living wage" to their employees as a condition to the award of a public contract. See opinion of Attorney General to The Honorable Samuel A. Nixon, Jr., Member, House of Delegates, 02-107 (12/10/02).

§ 2.2-4302. Implementation. — This chapter may be implemented by ordinances, resolutions or regulations consistent with this chapter and with the provisions of other applicable law promulgated by any public body empowered by law to undertake the activities described in this chapter. Any such public body may act by and through its duly designated or authorized officers or employees. (1982, c. 647, § 11-36; 2001, c. 844.)

ARTICLE 2.

Contract Formation and Administration.

§ 2.2-4303. Methods of procurement. — A. All public contracts with nongovernmental contractors for the purchase or lease of goods, or for the purchase of services, insurance, or construction, shall be awarded after competitive sealed bidding, or competitive negotiation as provided in this section, unless otherwise authorized by law.

B. Professional services shall be procured by competitive negotiation.

C. Upon a determination made in advance by the public body and set forth in writing that competitive sealed bidding is either not practicable or not fiscally advantageous to the public, goods, services, or insurance may be procured by competitive negotiation. The writing shall document the basis for this determination.

Upon a written determination made in advance by (i) the Governor or his designee in the case of a procurement by the Commonwealth or by a department, agency or institution thereof or (ii) the local governing body in the case of a procurement by a political subdivision of the Commonwealth, that competitive negotiation is either not practicable or not fiscally advantageous, insurance may be procured through a licensed agent or broker selected in the manner provided for the procurement of things other than professional services in subdivision 3 b of the definition of "competitive negotiation" in § 2.2-4301. The basis for this determination shall be documented in writing.

D. Construction may be procured only by competitive sealed bidding, except that competitive negotiation may be used in the following instances upon a determination made in advance by the public body and set forth in writing that competitive sealed bidding is either not practicable or not fiscally advantageous to the public, which writing shall document the basis for this determination:

1. By the Commonwealth, its departments, agencies and institutions on a fixed price design-build basis or construction management basis under § 2.2-4306;

2. By any (a) public body for the construction, alteration, repair, renovation or demolition of buildings or structures when the contract is not expected to cost more than $1 million and (b) local governing body on a fixed price design-build basis or construction management basis under § 2.2-4308 when the contract is not expected to cost more than $1 million;

3. By any public body for the construction of highways and any draining, dredging, excavation, grading or similar work upon real property;

4. By any governing body of a locality with a population in excess of 100,000 that the Design-Build/Construction Management Review Board has made a one-time determination that the locality has the personnel, procedures, and expertise to enter into a contract for construction on a fixed price or not-to-exceed price design-build or construction management basis, provided that projects undertaken by the local governing body shall be exempt only from approval of the Design-Build/Construction Management Review Board and shall otherwise be in compliance with the provisions of this section, § 2.2-4308, and other applicable law governing design-build or construction management contracts for public bodies other than the Commonwealth. The procedures of the local governing body shall be consistent with the two-step competitive negotiation process established in § 2.2-4301; or

5. As otherwise provided in § 2.2-4308.

E. Upon a determination in writing that there is only one source practicably available for that which is to be procured, a contract may be negotiated and awarded to that source without competitive sealed bidding or competitive negotiation. The writing shall document the basis for this determination. The public body shall issue a written notice stating that only one source was determined to be practicably available, and identifying that which is being procured, the contractor selected, and the date on which the contract was or will be awarded. This notice shall be posted in a designated public area or published in a newspaper of general circulation on the day the public body awards or announces its decision to award the contract, whichever occurs first. Public notice may also be published on the Department of General Services' central electronic procurement website and other appropriate websites.

F. In case of emergency, a contract may be awarded without competitive sealed bidding or competitive negotiation; however, such procurement shall be made with such competition as is practicable under the circumstances. A written determination of the basis for the emergency and for the selection of the particular contractor shall be included in the contract file. The public body shall issue a written notice stating that the contract is being awarded on an emergency basis, and identifying that which is being procured, the contractor selected, and the date on which the contract was or will be awarded. This notice shall be posted in a designated public area or published in a newspaper of general circulation on the day the public body awards or announces its decision to award the contract, whichever occurs first, or as soon thereafter as is practicable. Public notice may also be published on the Department of General Services' central electronic procurement website and other appropriate websites.

G. A public body may establish purchase procedures, if adopted in writing, not requiring competitive sealed bids or competitive negotiation for single or term contracts for goods and services other than professional services if the aggregate or the sum of all phases is not expected to exceed $50,000; however, such small purchase procedures shall provide for competition wherever practicable. Purchases under this subsection that are expected to exceed $30,000 shall require the written informal solicitation of a minimum of four bidders or offerors.

H. A public body may establish purchase procedures, if adopted in writing, not requiring competitive negotiation for single or term contracts for professional services if the aggregate or the sum of all phases is not expected to exceed $30,000; however such small purchase procedures shall provide for competition wherever practicable.

I. Upon a determination made in advance by a public body and set forth in writing that the purchase of goods, products or commodities from a public auction sale is in the best interests of the public, such items may be purchased at the auction, including online public auctions. Purchase of information technology and telecommunications goods and nonprofessional services from a public auction sale shall be permitted by any authority, department, agency, or institution of the Commonwealth if approved by the Chief Information Officer of the Commonwealth. The writing shall document the basis for this determination. However, bulk purchases of commodities used in road and highway construction and maintenance, and aggregates shall not be made by online public auctions.

J. The purchase of goods or nonprofessional services, but not construction or professional services, may be made by reverse auctioning. However, bulk purchases of commodities used in road and highway construction and maintenance, and aggregates shall not be made by reverse auctioning. (1982, c. 647, § 11-41; 1985, c. 164; 1986, cc. 332, 559; 1987, c. 456; 1988, cc. 40, 640; 1989, c. 296; 1991, c. 73; 1993, c. 242; 1996, cc. 827, 965, 1019; 1999, c. 178; 2000, cc. 637, 647, 664, 692; 2001, cc. 395, 844; 2003, cc. 644, 895; 2004, cc. 706, 874, 906; 2005, c. 394; 2006, cc. 464, 510; 2008, c. 78.)

Cross references. — As to inapplicability of provisions of this article to contracts for advertising or publishing entered into by the Virginia Wine Board, see § 3.1-1064.7. For provision that this article shall not apply to contracts for the printing of ballots, statements of results, or other material essential to the conduct of an election, see § 24.2-602. As to supersession of provisions of subdivision 2 of subsection C of § 11-41 (see now subsection D of this section), see § 33.1-12.

Editor's note. — Acts 2001, c. 395 amended § 11-41, from which this section is derived. Pursuant to § 30-152, Acts 2001, c. 395 has been given effect in this section as set out above. The 2001 amendment by c. 395 added subsection J. Acts 2003, c. 644, cl. 2 and c. 895, cl. 4, repealed cl. 2 of Acts 2001, c. 395, which had provided that the provisions of the 2001 act would expire on July 1, 2003.

Acts 2005, c. 394, cl. 2, provides: "That the provisions of this act shall not in any way amend or affect the Commonwealth's institutions of higher education as such institutions may be delegated the authority for the purchase of information technology facilities and services pursuant to any appropriation act adopted by the General Assembly."

Acts 2005, c. 394, cl. 3, provides: "That the provisions of this act shall not in any way amend or affect the existing delegations of telecommunications procurement granted by the Department of Information Technology or the Virginia Information Technologies Agency, as its successor in interest, to public bodies or inhibit the ability of the Department of Information Technology or the Virginia Information Technologies Agency as its successor in interest, to grant future delegations of such authority."

The 2008 amendments. — The 2008 amendment by c. 78 inserted "or structures" in clause (a) of subdivision D 2.

Michie's Jurisprudence. — For related discussion, see 17 M.J. Streets and Highways, § 22.

OPINIONS OF THE ATTORNEY GENERAL

A library board established pursuant to §§ 42.1-33 and 42.1-35 is a "public body" for purposes of the Virginia Public Procurement Act. See opinion of Attorney General to The Honorable Jackie T. Stump, Member, House of Delegates, 03-076 (9/22/03).

§ **2.2-4304. Cooperative procurement.** — A. Any public body may participate in, sponsor, conduct, or administer a cooperative procurement agreement on behalf of or in conjunction with one or more other public bodies, or public agencies or institutions or localities of the several states, of the United States or its territories, the District of Columbia, or the U.S. General Services Administration, for the purpose of combining requirements to increase efficiency or reduce administrative expenses in any acquisition of goods and services. Except for contracts for architectural and engineering services, a public body may purchase from another public body's contract even if it did not participate in the request for proposal or invitation to bid, if the request for proposal or invitation to bid specified that the procurement was being conducted on behalf of other public bodies. In instances where any authority, department, agency, or institution of the Commonwealth desires to purchase information technology and telecommunications goods and services from another public body's contract and the procurement was conducted on behalf of other public bodies, such purchase shall be permitted if approved by the Chief Information Officer of the Commonwealth. Any public body that enters into a cooperative procurement agreement with a county, city, or town whose governing body has adopted alternative policies and procedures pursuant to subdivisions 9 and 10 of § 2.2-4343 shall comply with the alternative policies and procedures adopted by the governing body of such county, city, or town.

B. Subject to the provisions of §§ 2.2-1110, 2.2-1111, 2.2-1120 and 2.2-2012, any authority, department, agency, or institution of the Commonwealth may participate in, sponsor, conduct, or administer a cooperative procurement arrangement on behalf of or in conjunction with public bodies, private health or educational institutions or with public agencies or institutions of the several states, territories of the United States, or the District of Columbia, for the purpose of combining requirements to effect cost savings or reduce administrative expense in any acquisition of goods and services, other than professional services. A public body may purchase from any authority, department, agency or institution of the Commonwealth's contract even if it did not participate in the request for proposal or invitation to bid, if the request for proposal or invitation to bid specified that the procurement was being conducted on behalf of other public bodies. In such instances, deviation from the procurement procedures set forth in this chapter and the administrative policies and procedures established to implement this chapter shall be permitted, if approved by the Director of the Division of Purchases and Supply.

Pursuant to § 2.2-2012, such approval is not required if the procurement arrangement is for telecommunications and information technology goods and services of every description. In instances where the procurement arrangement is for telecommunications and information technology goods and services, such arrangement shall be permitted if approved by the Chief Information Officer of the Commonwealth. However, such acquisitions shall be procured competitively.

Nothing herein shall prohibit the payment by direct or indirect means of any administrative fee that will allow for participation in any such arrangement.

C. As authorized by the United States Congress and consistent with applicable federal regulations, and provided the terms of the contract permit such purchases:

1. Any authority, department, agency, or institution of the Commonwealth may purchase goods and nonprofessional services, other than telecommunica-

tions and information technology, from a U.S. General Services Administration contract or a contract awarded by any other agency of the U.S. government, upon approval of the director of the Division of Purchases and Supply of the Department of General Services;

2. Any authority, department, agency, or institution of the Commonwealth may purchase telecommunications and information technology goods and nonprofessional services from a U.S. General Services Administration contract or a contract awarded by any other agency of the U.S. government, upon approval of the Chief Information Officer of the Commonwealth; and

3. Any county, city, town, or school board may purchase goods and nonprofessional services from a U.S. General Services Administration contract or a contract awarded by any other agency of the U.S. government. (1982, c. 647, § 11-40; 1984, c. 330; 1987, c. 583; 1991, c. 645; 1996, cc. 261, 280, 1019; 2001, c. 844; 2003, cc. 651, 895, 981, 1021; 2004, cc. 874, 906, 911, 936; 2005, c. 394; 2006, c. 100.)

Editor's note. — For provisions of Acts 2003, cc. 981 and 1021, cls. 4 to 16, reflecting the intent of the General Assembly to provide for the consolidation of the procurement and operational functions of information technology for state agencies in a single agency, and related transitional and other provisions, see the Editor's note at § 2.2-2005.

Acts 2003, c. 895, cl. 3, provides: "That the provisions of this act shall not in any way amend or affect existing delegations of telecommunications procurement authority granted by the Department of Information Technology to public bodies or inhibit the ability of the Department to grant future delegations of such authority."

Acts 2005, c. 394, cl. 2, provides: "That the provisions of this act shall not in any way amend or affect the Commonwealth's institutions of higher education as such institutions may be delegated the authority for the purchase of information technology facilities and services pursuant to any appropriation act adopted by the General Assembly."

Acts 2005, c. 394, cl. 3, provides: "That the provisions of this act shall not in any way amend or affect the existing delegations of telecommunications procurement granted by the Department of Information Technology or the Virginia Information Technologies Agency, as its successor in interest, to public bodies or inhibit the ability of the Department of Information Technology or the Virginia Information Technologies Agency as its successor in interest, to grant future delegations of such authority."

§ 2.2-4305. Competitive procurement by localities on state-aid projects. — No contract for the construction of any building or for an addition to or improvement of an existing building by any local governing body or subdivision thereof for which state funds of not more than $30,000 in the aggregate or for the sum of all phases of a contract or project either by appropriation, grant-in-aid or loan, are used or are to be used for all or part of the cost of construction shall be let except after competitive sealed bidding or after competitive negotiation as provided under subsection D of § 2.2-4303. The procedure for the advertising for bids or for proposals and for letting of the contract shall conform, mutatis mutandis, to this chapter. (1982, c. 647, § 11-41.1; 1983, c. 436; 1987, c. 456; 1989, c. 296; 1997, c. 163; 2001, c. 844.)

§ 2.2-4306. Design-build or construction management contracts for Commonwealth authorized. — A. Notwithstanding any other provisions of law, the Commonwealth may enter into contracts on a fixed price design-build basis or construction management basis in accordance with the provisions of this section and § 2.2-1502. Procedures to implement this section and any changes to such procedures shall be adopted by the Secretary of Administration after a public hearing and reviewed by the House Committee on Appropriations and the Senate Committee on Finance.

B. Procurement of construction by the design-build method shall be a two-step competitive negotiation process. In the first step, offerors shall be requested to submit their qualifications. Based upon the information submitted and any other relevant information which the Commonwealth may obtain, no more than five offerors deemed most suitable for the project shall be selected by the Commonwealth and requested to submit proposals.

C. Design-build contracts may be used by the Commonwealth only for those types of construction projects designated in the procedures adopted by the Secretary of Administration to implement this section. (1983, c. 615, § 11-41.2; 1987, cc. 218, 474; 1988, c. 829; 2001, c. 844.)

§ 2.2-4307. Fixed-price or not-to-exceed-price design-build and construction management contracts for juvenile correctional facilities authorized. — Notwithstanding the provisions of § 2.2-4306, but subject to the procedures adopted by the Secretary of Administration to implement the provisions of that section, the Commonwealth may enter into contracts for juvenile correctional facilities on a fixed-price or not-to-exceed-price design-build basis or construction management basis, including related leases, lease/purchase contracts, agreements relating to the sale of securities to finance such facilities, and similar financing agreements. (1996, cc. 795, 942, § 11-41.2:02; 2001, c. 844.)

§ 2.2-4308. Design-build or construction management contracts for public bodies other than the Commonwealth; eligibility requirements; award of contract; records to be kept. — A. While the competitive sealed bid process remains the preferred method of construction procurement for public bodies in the Commonwealth, any public body other than the Commonwealth may enter into a contract for construction on a fixed price or not-to-exceed price design-build or construction management basis provided the public body complies with the requirements of this section and has obtained the approval of the Design-Build/Construction Management Review Board (the Review Board) pursuant to § 2.2-2406. Provided, however, that projects undertaken pursuant to subdivision D 2 or D 4 of § 2.2-4303 shall be exempt from approval of the Review Board.

Prior to making a determination as to the use of design-build or construction management for a specific construction project, the public body shall have in its employ or under contract a licensed architect or engineer with professional competence appropriate to the project who shall advise the public body regarding the use of design-build or construction management for that project and who shall assist the public body with the preparation of the Request for Proposal and the evaluation of such proposals.

Prior to issuing a Request for Proposal for any design-build or construction management contract for a specific construction project, the public body shall:

1. Have adopted, by ordinance or resolution, written procedures governing the selection, evaluation and award of design-build and construction management contracts. Such procedures shall be consistent with those described in this chapter for the procurement of nonprofessional services through competitive negotiation. Such procedures shall also require Requests for Proposals to include and define the criteria of such construction project in areas such as site plans; floor plans; exterior elevations; basic building envelope materials; fire protection information plans; structural, mechanical (HVAC), and electrical systems; and special telecommunications; and may define such other requirements as the public body determines appropriate for that particular construction project. Except as may otherwise be approved by the Review Board, such procedures for:

a. Design-build construction projects shall include a two-step competitive negotiation process consistent with the Review Board's regulations.

b. Construction management projects shall include selection procedures and required construction management contract terms consistent with the Review Board's regulations.

2. Have documented in writing that for a specific construction project (i) a design-build or construction management contract is more advantageous than a competitive sealed bid construction contract; (ii) there is a benefit to the public body by using a design-build or construction management contract; and (iii) competitive sealed bidding is not practical or fiscally advantageous.

B. Once approved by the Review Board in accordance with § 2.2-2406, the public body may procure a design-build or construction management contract for the specific construction project presented to the Review Board. Unless otherwise specified in the Request for Proposal, the contract shall be awarded to the fully qualified offeror who submits an acceptable proposal determined to be the best value in response to the Request for Proposal.

C. The public body shall provide information as requested by the Review Board to allow post-project evaluation by the Review Board. (1996, c. 962, § 11-41.2:2; 2000, c. 29; 2001, c. 844; 2004, c. 706; 2006, c. 510.)

§ **2.2-4308.1. Purchase of owner-controlled insurance in construction projects.** — A. Notwithstanding any other provision of law to the contrary, a public body may purchase at its expense an owner-controlled insurance program in connection with any public construction contract where the amount of the contract or combination of contracts is more than $100 million, provided that no single contract valued at less than $50 million shall be combined pursuant to this section. The public body shall provide notice if it intends to use an owner-controlled insurance program, including the specific coverages of such program, in any request for proposal, invitation to bid, or other applicable procurement documents.

B. A public body shall not require a provider of architecture or professional engineering services to participate in the owner-controlled insurance program, except to the extent that the public body may elect to secure excess coverage. No contractor or subcontractor shall be required to provide insurance coverage for a construction project if that specified coverage is included in an owner-controlled insurance program in which the contractor or subcontractor is enrolled.

C. For the purposes of this section, *"owner-controlled insurance program"* means a consolidated insurance program or series of insurance policies issued to a public body that may provide for some or all of the following types of insurance coverage for any contractor or subcontractor working on or at a public construction contract or combination of such contracts: general liability, property damage, workers' compensation, employer's liability, pollution or environmental liability, excess or umbrella liability, builder's risk, and excess or contingent professional liability. (2006, cc. 569, 605.)

§ **2.2-4309. Modification of the contract.** — A. A public contract may include provisions for modification of the contract during performance, but no fixed-price contract may be increased by more than twenty-five percent of the amount of the contract or $50,000, whichever is greater, without the advance written approval of the Governor or his designee, in the case of state agencies, or the governing body, in the case of political subdivisions. In no event may the amount of any contract, without adequate consideration, be increased for any purpose, including, but not limited to, relief of an offeror from the consequences of an error in its bid or offer.

B. Any public body may extend the term of an existing contract for services to allow completion of any work undertaken but not completed during the original term of the contract.

C. Nothing in this section shall prevent any public body from placing greater restrictions on contract modifications. (1982, c. 647, §§ 11-45, 11-55; 1984, c. 764; 1985, c. 286; 1987, cc. 194, 248; 1989, c. 235; 1990, c. 395; 1991,

c. 175; 1993, cc. 110, 505, 638, 971; 1996, cc. 145, 897, 902, 950, 1038; 1998, cc. 222, 619, 666, 697, 791; 1999, cc. 160, 194, 1021, 1024; 2000, cc. 242, 637, 664, 696, 927; 2001, c. 844.)

§ 2.2-4310. Discrimination prohibited; participation of small, women-, minority- and service disabled veteran-owned business. — A. In the solicitation or awarding of contracts, no public body shall discriminate against a bidder or offeror because of race, religion, color, sex, national origin, age, disability, status as a service disabled veteran, or any other basis prohibited by state law relating to discrimination in employment. Whenever solicitations are made, each public body shall include businesses selected from a list made available by the Department of Minority Business Enterprise.

B. All public bodies shall establish programs consistent with this chapter to facilitate the participation of small businesses and businesses owned by women, minorities, and service disabled veterans in procurement transactions. The programs established shall be in writing and shall comply with the provisions of any enhancement or remedial measures authorized by the Governor pursuant to subsection C or, where applicable, by the chief executive of a local governing body pursuant to § 15.2-965.1, and shall include specific plans to achieve any goals established therein. State agencies shall submit annual progress reports on small, women- and minority-owned business procurement and on service disabled veteran-owned business procurement to the Department of Minority Business Enterprise in a form specified by the Department of Minority Business Enterprise. The Department of Minority Business Enterprise shall make information on service disabled veteran-owned procurement available to the Department of Veterans Services upon request.

C. Whenever there exists (i) a rational basis for small business enhancement or (ii) a persuasive analysis that documents a statistically significant disparity between the availability and utilization of women- and minority-owned businesses, the Governor is authorized and encouraged to require state agencies to implement appropriate enhancement or remedial measures consistent with prevailing law.

D. In the solicitation or awarding of contracts, no state agency, department or institution shall discriminate against a bidder or offeror because the bidder or offeror employs ex-offenders unless the state agency, department or institution has made a written determination that employing ex-offenders on the specific contract is not in its best interest.

E. As used in this section:

"Minority individual" means an individual who is a citizen of the United States or a non-citizen who is in full compliance with United States immigration law and who satisfies one or more of the following definitions:

1. *"African American"* means a person having origins in any of the original peoples of Africa and who is regarded as such by the community of which this person claims to be a part.

2. *"Asian American"* means a person having origins in any of the original peoples of the Far East, Southeast Asia, the Indian subcontinent, or the Pacific Islands, including but not limited to Japan, China, Vietnam, Samoa, Laos, Cambodia, Taiwan, Northern Mariana, the Philippines, a U.S. territory of the Pacific, India, Pakistan, Bangladesh, or Sri Lanka and who is regarded as such by the community of which this person claims to be a part.

3. *"Hispanic American"* means a person having origins in any of the Spanish-speaking peoples of Mexico, South or Central America, or the Caribbean Islands or other Spanish or Portuguese cultures and who is regarded as such by the community of which this person claims to be a part.

4. *"Native American"* means a person having origins in any of the original peoples of North America and who is regarded as such by the community of

which this person claims to be a part or who is recognized by a tribal organization.

"Minority-owned business" means a business concern that is at least 51% owned by one or more minority individuals or in the case of a corporation, partnership, or limited liability company or other entity, at least 51% of the equity ownership interest in the corporation, partnership, or limited liability company or other entity is owned by one or more minority individuals and both the management and daily business operations are controlled by one or more minority individuals.

"Service disabled veteran" means a veteran who (i) served on active duty in the United States military ground, naval, or air service, (ii) was discharged or released under conditions other than dishonorable, and (iii) has a service-connected disability rating fixed by the United States Department of Veterans Affairs.

"Service disabled veteran business" means a business concern that is at least 51% owned by one or more service disabled veterans or, in the case of a corporation, partnership, or limited liability company or other entity, at least 51% of the equity ownership interest in the corporation, partnership, or limited liability company or other entity is owned by one or more individuals who are service disabled veterans and both the management and daily business operations are controlled by one or more individuals who are service disabled veterans.

"Small business" means a business, independently owned or operated by one or more persons who are citizens of the United States or non-citizens who are in full compliance with United States immigration law, which, together with affiliates, has 250 or fewer employees, or average annual gross receipts of $10 million or less averaged over the previous three years.

"State agency" means any authority, board, department, instrumentality, institution, agency, or other unit of state government. *"State agency"* shall not include any county, city, or town.

"Women-owned business" means a business concern that is at least 51% owned by one or more women who are citizens of the United States or non-citizens who are in full compliance with United States immigration law, or in the case of a corporation, partnership, or limited liability company or other entity, at least 51% of the equity ownership interest is owned by one or more women who are citizens of the United States or non-citizens who are in full compliance with United States immigration law, and both the management and daily business operations are controlled by one or more women who are citizens of the United States or non-citizens who are in full compliance with United States immigration law. (1982, c. 647, §§ 11-44, 11-48; 1984, c. 279; 2000, c. 628; 2001, c. 844; 2003, c. 226; 2004, cc. 865, 891; 2006, cc. 831, 921; 2007, c. 787; 2008, cc. 521, 767.)

Editor's note. — Acts 2004, cc. 865 and 891, cl. 2, provide: "That any analysis that is used by the Governor or a locality as a basis for determining the existence of discrimination based on race or gender in the awarding of contracting opportunities shall use the standards established by the United States Supreme Court in *The City of Richmond v. J. A. Croson Company*, 488 U.S. 469, (1985) and any subsequent decisions of the United States Supreme Court or other binding authority concerning such standards."

The 2007 amendments. — The 2007 amendment by c. 787, inserted "status as a service disabled veteran" in subsection A; in subsection B, inserted "and service disabled veterans" and "and on service disabled veteran-owned business procurement" and made related changes; and in subsection E, added definitions of "Service disabled veteran" and "Service disabled veteran business."

The 2008 amendments. — The 2008 amendments by cc. 521 and 767 substituted "United States Department of Veterans Affairs" for "United States Veterans Administration of (a) 50% or greater or (b) 10% or greater if the service-connected disability is combat related" in the definition of "Service disabled veteran." In addition, c. 521 substituted "a business, independently owned or operated by one or more persons who are citizens of the United States or non-citizens who are in full compliance with United States immigration law" for "an independently owned and operated business" in the definition of "Small business."

Law Review. — For article, "Benign Racial Classifications: A Guide for Transportation Attorneys," see 19 U. Rich. L. Rev. 29 (1984).

CASE NOTES

City must first produce evidence of discrimination. — Appellant city council adopted a plan that required prime contractors to whom the city awarded construction contracts to subcontract at least 30 percent of the dollar amount of the contract to one or more Minority Business Enterprises to promote wider participation by minority business enterprises in the construction of public projects. However, because appellant city failed to provide evidence identifying discrimination in the construction industry, failed to demonstrate a compelling governmental interest in apportioning public contracting opportunities on the basis of race, or failed to show that its remedy had been narrowly tailored to the achievement of that interest, its treatment of its citizens on a racial basis violated the Equal Protection Clause. Richmond v. J. A. Croson Co., 488 U.S. 469, 102 L. Ed. 2d 854, 1989 LEXIS 579, 109 S. Ct. 706 (1989).

§ 2.2-4311. Employment discrimination by contractor prohibited; required contract provisions. — All public bodies shall include in every contract of more than $10,000 the following provisions:

1. During the performance of this contract, the contractor agrees as follows:

a. The contractor will not discriminate against any employee or applicant for employment because of race, religion, color, sex, national origin, age, disability, or other basis prohibited by state law relating to discrimination in employment, except where there is a bona fide occupational qualification reasonably necessary to the normal operation of the contractor. The contractor agrees to post in conspicuous places, available to employees and applicants for employment, notices setting forth the provisions of this nondiscrimination clause.

b. The contractor, in all solicitations or advertisements for employees placed by or on behalf of the contractor, will state that such contractor is an equal opportunity employer.

c. Notices, advertisements and solicitations placed in accordance with federal law, rule or regulation shall be deemed sufficient for the purpose of meeting the requirements of this section.

2. The contractor will include the provisions of the foregoing paragraphs a, b and c in every subcontract or purchase order of over $10,000, so that the provisions will be binding upon each subcontractor or vendor. (1982, c. 647, § 11-51; 2000, c. 628; 2001, c. 844.)

Law Review. — For article, "Benign Racial Classifications: A Guide for Transportation Attorneys," see 19 U. Rich. L. Rev. 29 (1984). For a note, "Hanging in the Balance: Confidentiality Clauses and Postjudgment Settlements of Employment Discrimination Disputes," see 86 Va. L. Rev. 1537 (2000).

§ 2.2-4311.1. Compliance with federal, state, and local laws and federal immigration law; required contract provisions. — All public bodies shall provide in every written contract that the contractor does not, and shall not during the performance of the contract for goods and services in the Commonwealth, knowingly employ an unauthorized alien as defined in the federal Immigration Reform and Control Act of 1986. (2008, cc. 598, 702.)

§ 2.2-4312. Drug-free workplace to be maintained by contractor; required contract provisions. — All public bodies shall include in every contract over $10,000 the following provisions:

During the performance of this contract, the contractor agrees to (i) provide a drug-free workplace for the contractor's employees; (ii) post in conspicuous places, available to employees and applicants for employment, a statement notifying employees that the unlawful manufacture, sale, distribution, dispensation, possession, or use of a controlled substance or marijuana is prohibited in the contractor's workplace and specifying the actions that will be taken against employees for violations of such prohibition; (iii) state in all solicitations or advertisements for employees placed by or on behalf of the contractor that the contractor maintains a drug-free workplace; and (iv) include the provisions of the foregoing clauses in every subcontract or purchase order of over $10,000, so that the provisions will be binding upon each subcontractor or vendor.

For the purposes of this section, *"drug-free workplace"* means a site for the performance of work done in connection with a specific contract awarded to a contractor in accordance with this chapter, the employees of whom are prohibited from engaging in the unlawful manufacture, sale, distribution, dispensation, possession or use of any controlled substance or marijuana during the performance of the contract. (2000, c. 417, § 11-51.1; 2001, c. 844.)

§ 2.2-4313. Petition for recycled goods and products; periodic review of procurement standards. — A. Any person who believes that particular goods or products with recycled content are functionally equivalent to the same goods or products produced from virgin materials may petition the Department of General Services or other appropriate agency of the Commonwealth to include the recycled goods or products in its procurement process. The petitioner shall submit, prior to or during the procurement process, documentation that establishes that the goods or products (i) contain recycled content and (ii) can meet the performance standards set forth in the applicable specifications. If the Department of General Services or other agency of the Commonwealth that receives the petition determines that the documentation demonstrates that the goods or products with recycled content will meet the performance standards set forth in the applicable specifications, it shall incorporate the goods or products into its procurement process.

B. The Department of General Services and all agencies of the Commonwealth shall review and revise their procurement procedures and specifications on a continuing basis to encourage the use of goods and products with recycled content and shall, in developing new procedures and specifications, encourage the use of goods and products with recycled content. (1993, c. 223, § 11-41.01; 2001, c. 844.)

§ 2.2-4314. Petition for procurement of less toxic goods and products; periodic review of procurement standards. — A. As used in this section:

"Goods and products" means goods and products that are used or consumed by an agency of the Commonwealth in the performance of its statutory functions. The term shall include, but not be limited to (i) cleaning materials, (ii) paints and coatings, (iii) solvents, (iv) adhesives, (v) inks, and (vi) pesticides and herbicides. The term shall not include: (i) fuels, (ii) food and beverages, (iii) furniture and fixtures, (iv) tobacco products, and (v) packaging and containers.

"Less toxic goods and products" means goods and products that (i) are functionally equivalent to and (ii) contain, emit, produce, or generate, less toxic or hazardous substances, or other toxic or hazardous substances that pose less of a hazard to public health and safety, or both, than goods and products procured by the Department of General Services or other agency of the Commonwealth.

"Toxic or hazardous substance" means (i) a chemical identified on the Toxic Chemical List established pursuant to § 313 of the Emergency Planning and

Community Right-to-Know Act, 42 U.S.C. § 11001 et seq. (P.L. 99-499) or (ii) a chemical listed pursuant to §§ 101 (14) or 102 of the Comprehensive Environmental Response, Compensation and Liability Act, 42 U.S.C. § 9601 et seq. (P.L. 92-500).

B. Any person who manufactures, sells, or supplies goods or products may petition the Department of General Services or other appropriate agency of the Commonwealth for the inclusion of the less toxic goods and products in its procurement process. The petitioner shall submit, prior to or during the procurement process, documentation that establishes that the goods or products meet the performance standards set forth in the applicable specifications. If the Department of General Services or other agency of the Commonwealth that receives the petition determines that the documentation establishes that the less toxic goods or products meet the performance standards set forth in the applicable specifications, it shall incorporate such goods or products into its procurement process.

C. The Department of General Services and all agencies of the Commonwealth shall review and revise their procurement procedures and specifications on a continuing basis to encourage the use of less toxic goods and products. However, nothing in this section shall require the Department or other agencies to purchase, test or evaluate any particular goods or products. Nor shall this section require the Department to purchase goods or products other than those that would be purchased under regular procurement procedures. (1994, c. 946, § 11-41.02; 2001, c. 844.)

§ **2.2-4315. Use of brand names.** — Unless otherwise provided in the Invitation to Bid, the name of a certain brand, make or manufacturer shall not restrict bidders to the specific brand, make or manufacturer named and shall be deemed to convey the general style, type, character, and quality of the article desired. Any article that the public body in its sole discretion determines to be the equal of that specified, considering quality, workmanship, economy of operation, and suitability for the purpose intended, shall be accepted. (1982, c. 647, § 11-49; 2001, c. 844.)

§ **2.2-4316. Comments concerning specifications.** — Every public body awarding public contracts shall establish procedures whereby comments concerning specifications or other provisions in Invitations to Bid or Requests for Proposal can be received and considered prior to the time set for receipt of bids or proposals or award of the contract. (1982, c. 647, § 11-50; 2001, c. 844.)

§ **2.2-4317. Prequalification generally; prequalification for construction.** — A. Prospective contractors may be prequalified for particular types of supplies, services, insurance or construction, and consideration of bids or proposals limited to prequalified contractors. Any prequalification procedure shall be established in writing and sufficiently in advance of its implementation to allow potential contractors a fair opportunity to complete the process.

B. Any prequalification of prospective contractors for construction by a public body shall be pursuant to a prequalification process for construction projects adopted by the public body. The process shall be consistent with the provisions of this section.

The application form used in such process shall set forth the criteria upon which the qualifications of prospective contractors will be evaluated. The application form shall request of prospective contractors only such information as is appropriate for an objective evaluation of all prospective contractors pursuant to such criteria. The form shall allow the prospective contractor seeking prequalification to request, by checking the appropriate box, that all information voluntarily submitted by the contractor pursuant to this subsection shall be considered a trade secret or proprietary information subject to the provisions of subsection D of § 2.2-4342.

In all instances in which the public body requires prequalification of potential contractors for construction projects, advance notice shall be given of the deadline for the submission of prequalification applications. The deadline for submission shall be sufficiently in advance of the date set for the submission of bids for such construction so as to allow the procedures set forth in this subsection to be accomplished.

At least thirty days prior to the date established for submission of bids or proposals under the procurement of the contract for which the prequalification applies, the public body shall advise in writing each contractor who submitted an application whether that contractor has been prequalified. In the event that a contractor is denied prequalification, the written notification to the contractor shall state the reasons for the denial of prequalification and the factual basis of such reasons.

A decision by a public body denying prequalification under the provisions of this subsection shall be final and conclusive unless the contractor appeals the decision as provided in § 2.2-4357.

C. A public body may deny prequalification to any contractor only if the public body finds one of the following:

1. The contractor does not have sufficient financial ability to perform the contract that would result from such procurement. If a bond is required to ensure performance of a contract, evidence that the contractor can acquire a surety bond from a corporation included on the United States Treasury list of acceptable surety corporations in the amount and type required by the public body shall be sufficient to establish the financial ability of the contractor to perform the contract resulting from such procurement;

2. The contractor does not have appropriate experience to perform the construction project in question;

3. The contractor or any officer, director or owner thereof has had judgments entered against him within the past ten years for the breach of contracts for governmental or nongovernmental construction, including, but not limited to, design-build or construction management;

4. The contractor has been in substantial noncompliance with the terms and conditions of prior construction contracts with a public body without good cause. If the public body has not contracted with a contractor in any prior construction contracts, the public body may deny prequalification if the contractor has been in substantial noncompliance with the terms and conditions of comparable construction contracts with another public body without good cause. A public body may not utilize this provision to deny prequalification unless the facts underlying such substantial noncompliance were documented in writing in the prior construction project file and such information relating thereto given to the contractor at that time, with the opportunity to respond;

5. The contractor or any officer, director, owner, project manager, procurement manager or chief financial official thereof has been convicted within the past ten years of a crime related to governmental or nongovernmental construction or contracting, including, but not limited to, a violation of (i) Article 6 (§ 2.2-4367 et seq.) of this chapter, (ii) the Virginia Governmental Frauds Act (§ 18.2-498.1 et seq.), (iii) Chapter 4.2 (§ 59.1-68.6 et seq.) of Title 59.1, or (iv) any substantially similar law of the United States or another state;

6. The contractor or any officer, director or owner thereof is currently debarred pursuant to an established debarment procedure from bidding or contracting by any public body, agency of another state or agency of the federal government; and

7. The contractor failed to provide to the public body in a timely manner any information requested by the public body relevant to subdivisions 1 through 6 of this subsection.

D. If a public body has a prequalification ordinance that provides for minority participation in municipal construction contracts, that public body may also deny prequalification based on minority participation criteria. However, nothing herein shall authorize the adoption or enforcement of minority participation criteria except to the extent that such criteria, and the adoption and enforcement thereof, are in accordance with the Constitution and laws of the United States and the Commonwealth.

E. The provisions of subsections B, C, and D shall not apply to prequalification for contracts let under § 33.1-12. (1982, c. 647, § 11-46; 1994, c. 918; 1995, c. 527; 2001, c. 844; 2007, c. 154.)

The 2007 amendments. — The 2007 amendment by c. 154 deleted "by the Commonwealth Transportation Board" following "contracts let" in subsection E.

§ 2.2-4318. Negotiation with lowest responsible bidder. — Unless canceled or rejected, a responsive bid from the lowest responsible bidder shall be accepted as submitted, except that if the bid from the lowest responsible bidder exceeds available funds, the public body may negotiate with the apparent low bidder to obtain a contract price within available funds. However, the negotiation may be undertaken only under conditions and procedures described in writing and approved by the public body prior to issuance of the Invitation to Bid and summarized therein. (1982, c. 647, § 11-53; 2001, c. 844.)

§ 2.2-4319. Cancellation, rejection of bids; waiver of informalities. — A. An Invitation to Bid, a Request for Proposal, any other solicitation, or any and all bids or proposals, may be canceled or rejected. The reasons for cancellation or rejection shall be made part of the contract file. A public body shall not cancel or reject an Invitation to Bid, a Request for Proposal, any other solicitation, bid or proposal pursuant to this section solely to avoid awarding a contract to a particular responsive and responsible bidder or offeror.

B. A public body may waive informalities in bids. (1982, c. 647, § 11-42; 1998, c. 753; 2001, c. 844.)

CASE NOTES

Editor's note. — The case below was decided under former § 11-35 et seq.

A requirement in an invitation to bid that fixes the time within which bids must be received is not a minor defect or an informality that may be waived but, rather, a material and formal requirement that, under the circumstances present in the instant case, must be fulfilled to the letter of the law. Holly's, Inc. v. County of Greensville, 250 Va. 12, 458 S.E.2d 454 (1995).

§ 2.2-4320. Exclusion of insurance bids prohibited. — Notwithstanding any other provision of law, no insurer licensed to transact the business of insurance in the Commonwealth or approved to issue surplus lines insurance in the Commonwealth shall be excluded from presenting an insurance bid proposal to a public body in response to a request for proposal or an invitation to bid. Nothing in this section shall preclude a public body from debarring a prospective insurer pursuant to § 2.2-4321. (1996, c. 989, § 11-44.1; 2001, c. 844.)

§ 2.2-4321. Debarment. — Prospective contractors may be debarred from contracting for particular types of supplies, services, insurance or construction, for specified periods of time. Any debarment procedure shall be established in writing for state agencies and institutions by the agency designated by the Governor and for political subdivisions by their governing bodies. Any debarment procedure may provide for debarment on the basis of a contractor's unsatisfactory performance for a public body. (1982, c. 647, § 11-46.1; 2001, c. 844.)

§ 2.2-4321.1. Prohibited contracts; exceptions; determination by Department of Taxation; appeal; remedies. — A. No state agency shall contract for goods or services with a nongovernmental source if the source, or any affiliate of the source, is subject to the provisions of (i) § 58.1-612 and fails or refuses to collect and remit the tax on its sales delivered by any means to locations within the Commonwealth or (ii) Article 2 (§ 58.1-320 et seq.) or Article 10 (§ 58.1-400 et seq.) of Chapter 3 of Title 58.1 and fails or refuses to remit any tax due thereunder. The provisions of clause (ii) shall not apply to any person that has (a) entered into a payment agreement with the Department of Taxation to pay the tax and is not delinquent under the terms of the agreement or (b) appealed the assessment of the tax in accordance with law and such appeal is pending.

B. A state agency may contract for goods or services with a source prohibited under subsection A in the event of an emergency or where the nongovernmental source is the sole source of such goods or services.

C. The determination of whether a source is a prohibited source shall be made by the Department of Taxation after providing the prohibited source with notice and an opportunity to respond to the proposed determination. The Department of Taxation shall notify the Department of General Services of its determination.

D. The Department of General Services shall post public notice of all prohibited sources on its public internet procurement website and on other appropriate websites.

E. The remedies provided in Article 5 (§ 2.2-4357 et seq.) of this chapter shall not apply to any determination made pursuant to this section and the sole remedy for any adverse determination shall be as provided in subsection F.

F. Any source aggrieved by a determination of the Department of Taxation made under this section may apply to the Tax Commissioner for correction of the determination. The Tax Commissioner shall respond within 30 days of receipt of the application for corrective action. Within 10 days after receipt of the Tax Commissioner's response, the aggrieved source may appeal to the Circuit Court for the City of Richmond. If it is determined that the determination of the Department of Taxation was arbitrary, capricious, or not in accordance with law, the sole relief shall be restoration of the source's eligibility to contract with state agencies. No claim for damages or attorney's fees shall be awarded.

G. Any action of the Department of Taxation, the Department of General Services, or of any state agency under this section shall be exempt from the provisions of the Administrative Process Act (§ 2.2-4000 et seq.).

H. For the purposes of this section, *"state agency"* means any authority, board, department, instrumentality, institution, agency or other unit of state government. State agency shall not include any public institution of higher education or any county, city or town or any local or regional governmental authority. (2003, cc. 994, 1006; 2006, c. 408.)

§ 2.2-4322. Acceptance of bids submitted to the Department of Transportation. — In a procurement by the Department of Transportation by competitive sealed bidding for highway construction and maintenance contracts, the Department may accept bids in response to an Invitation to Bid at the Department's central office or at district offices or other satellite locations designated in the Invitation to Bid, in accordance with specifications adopted by the Department. An Invitation to Bid may authorize agents of the Department to accept from bidders on a voluntary basis a supplemental submission referencing the total bid amount on a form prescribed by the Department. Information contained in any supplemental submission may be made available to the public by the Department after the time for receiving bids has expired and before the public opening and announcement of all sealed bids. (1997, c. 164, § 11-45.1; 2001, c. 844.)

§ 2.2-4323. Purchase programs for recycled goods; agency responsibilities. — A. All state agencies shall implement a purchase program for recycled goods and shall coordinate their efforts so as to achieve the goals and objectives established in subsection C as well as those set forth in §§ 10.1-1425.6, 10.1-1425.7, 10.1-1425.8, 2.2-4313, 2.2-4324, and 2.2-4326.

B. The Department of Environmental Quality, with advice from the Virginia Recycling Markets Development Council, shall advise the Department of General Services concerning the designation of recycled goods. In cooperation with the Department of General Services, the Department of Environmental Quality shall increase the awareness of state agencies as to the benefits of using such products.

C. The Department of General Services shall:

1. Ensure that the Commonwealth's procurement guidelines for state agencies promote the use of recycled goods.

2. Promote the Commonwealth's interest in the use of recycled products to vendors.

3. Make agencies aware of the availability of recycled goods, including those that use post-consumer and other recovered materials processed by Virginia-based companies.

D. All state agencies shall, to the greatest extent possible, adhere to the procurement program guidelines for recycled products to be established by the Department of General Services. (1994, c. 553, § 11-47.01; 2001, c. 844.)

§ 2.2-4324. Preference for Virginia products with recycled content and for Virginia firms. — A. In the case of a tie bid, preference shall be given to goods produced in Virginia, goods or services or construction provided by Virginia persons, firms or corporations; otherwise the tie shall be decided by lot.

B. Whenever the lowest responsive and responsible bidder is a resident of any other state and such state under its laws allows a resident contractor of that state a percentage preference, a like preference shall be allowed to the lowest responsive and responsible bidder who is a resident of Virginia and is the next lowest bidder. If the lowest bidder is a resident contractor of a state with an absolute preference, the bid shall not be considered. The Department of General Services shall post and maintain an updated list on its website of all states with an absolute preference for their resident contractors and those states that allow their resident contractors a percentage preference, including the respective percentage amounts. For purposes of compliance with this section, all public bodies may rely upon the accuracy of the information posted on this website.

C. Notwithstanding the provisions of subsections A and B, in the case of a tie bid in instances where goods are being offered, and existing price preferences have already been taken into account, preference shall be given to the bidder whose goods contain the greatest amount of recycled content. (1982, c. 647, § 11-47; 1993, c. 109; 2001, cc. 323, 844; 2005, c. 894.)

Editor's note. — Acts 2001, c. 323 amended § 11-47, from which this section is derived. Pursuant to § 30-152, Acts 2001, c. 323 has been given effect in this section as set out above. The 2001 amendment by c. 323, in subsection A, substituted "produced in Virginia, goods or services or construction" for "services and construction produced in Virginia or," and deleted "if such a choice is available" following "or corporations."

§ 2.2-4325. Preference for Virginia coal used in state facilities. — In determining the award of any contract for coal to be purchased for use in state facilities with state funds, the Department of General Services shall procure using competitive sealed bidding and shall award to the lowest responsive and responsible bidder offering coal mined in Virginia so long as its bid price is not more than four percent greater than the bid price of the low responsive and responsible bidder offering coal mined elsewhere. (1987, cc. 81, 91, § 11-47.1; 2001, c. 844.)

§ 2.2-4326. Preference for recycled paper and paper products used by state agencies. — A. In determining the award of any contract for paper and paper products to be purchased for use by agencies of the Commonwealth, the Department of General Services shall procure using competitive sealed bidding and shall award to the lowest responsible bidder offering recycled paper and paper products of a quality suitable for the purpose intended, so long as the bid price is not more than ten percent greater than the bid price of the low responsive and responsible bidder offering a product that does not qualify under subsection B.

B. For purposes of this section, recycled paper and paper products means any paper or paper products meeting the EPA Recommended Content Standards as defined in 40 C.F.R. Part 247. (1989, c. 442, § 11-47.2; 1990, cc. 449, 857; 2001, c. 844.)

§ 2.2-4327. Preference for community reinvestment activities in contracts for investment of funds. — Notwithstanding any other provision of law, any county, town, or city that is authorized to and has established affordable housing programs may provide by resolution that in determining the award of any contract for time deposits or investment of its funds, the treasurer or director of finance of such county, town, or city may consider, in addition to the typical criteria, the investment activities of qualifying institutions that enhance the supply of, or accessibility to, affordable housing within the jurisdiction, including the accessibility of such housing to employees of the county, town, or city or employees of the local school board. No more than 50 percent of the funds of the county, town, or city, calculated on the basis of the average daily balance of the general fund during the previous fiscal year, may be deposited or invested by considering such investment activities as a factor in the award of a contract. A qualifying institution shall meet the provisions of the Virginia Security for Public Deposits Act (§ 2.2-4400 et seq.) and all local terms and conditions for security, liquidity and rate of return.

For the purposes of this section, affordable housing means the same as that term is defined in § 15.2-2201. (1993, c. 937, § 11-47.3; 1995, c. 206; 1997, c. 176; 1999, c. 708; 2001, c. 844; 2007, c. 681.)

Editor's note. — Acts 1999, c. 708, which designated the first paragraph as subsection A, substituted "§ 15.2-2304 or § 15.2-2305" for "§ 15.1-491.8 or § 15.1-491.9" in the first sentence of subsection A, and added subsection B, provides in cl. 2: "That the provisions of this act shall expire on July 1, 2003." The section is set out above without the changes by Acts 1999, c. 708.

The 2007 amendments. — The 2007 amendment by c. 681 inserted "town" three times throughout; deleted "pursuant to (i) § 15.2-2304 or § 15.2-2305 or (ii) a local ordinance adopted prior to December 31, 1988" preceding "may provide"; added the language beginning "including the accessibility" to the end of the first sentence; added the final paragraph; and made minor stylistic changes.

§ 2.2-4328. Preference for local products and firms; applicability. — A. The governing body of a county, city or town may, in the case of a tie bid, give preference to goods, services and construction produced in such locality or provided by persons, firms or corporations having principal places of business in the locality, if such a choice is available; otherwise the tie shall be decided by lot, unless § 2.2-4324 applies.

B. The provisions of this section shall apply only to bids submitted pursuant to a written Invitation to Bid. (1994, c. 882, § 11-47.4; 2001, c. 844.)

§ 2.2-4329: Expired.

Editor's note. — Acts 2000, c. 696, cl. 2 provided: "That the provisions of § 11-47.5 [now § 2.2-4329] of this act shall expire on July 1, 2002."

§ 2.2-4330. Withdrawal of bid due to error. — A. A bidder for a public construction contract, other than a contract for construction or maintenance of public highways, may withdraw his bid from consideration if the price bid was substantially lower than the other bids due solely to a mistake in the bid, provided the bid was submitted in good faith, and the mistake was a clerical mistake as opposed to a judgment mistake, and was actually due to an unintentional arithmetic error or an unintentional omission of a quantity of work, labor or material made directly in the compilation of a bid, which unintentional arithmetic error or unintentional omission can be clearly shown by objective evidence drawn from inspection of original work papers, documents and materials used in the preparation of the bid sought to be withdrawn.

If a bid contains both clerical and judgment mistakes, a bidder may withdraw his bid from consideration if the price bid would have been substantially lower than the other bids due solely to the clerical mistake, that was an unintentional arithmetic error or an unintentional omission of a quantity of work, labor or material made directly in the compilation of a bid that shall be clearly shown by objective evidence drawn from inspection of original work papers, documents and materials used in the preparation of the bid sought to be withdrawn.

One of the following procedures for withdrawal of a bid shall be selected by the public body and stated in the advertisement for bids (i) the bidder shall give notice in writing of his claim of right to withdraw his bid within two business days after the conclusion of the bid opening procedure and shall submit original work papers with such notice; or (ii) the bidder shall submit to the public body or designated official his original work papers, documents and materials used in the preparation of the bid within one day after the date fixed for submission of bids. The work papers shall be delivered by the bidder in person or by registered mail at or prior to the time fixed for the opening of bids. In either instance, the work papers, documents and materials may be considered as trade secrets or proprietary information subject to the conditions of subsection F of § 2.2-4342. The bids shall be opened one day following the time fixed by the public body for the submission of bids. Thereafter, the bidder shall have two hours after the opening of bids within which to claim in writing any mistake as defined herein and withdraw his bid. The contract shall not be awarded by the public body until the two-hour period has elapsed. The mistake shall be proved only from the original work papers, documents and materials delivered as required herein.

B. A public body may establish procedures for the withdrawal of bids for other than construction contracts.

C. No bid shall be withdrawn under this section when the result would be the awarding of the contract on another bid of the same bidder or of another bidder in which the ownership of the withdrawing bidder is more than five percent.

D. If a bid is withdrawn in accordance with this section, the lowest remaining bid shall be deemed to be the low bid.

E. No bidder who is permitted to withdraw a bid shall, for compensation, supply any material or labor to or perform any subcontract or other work agreement for the person or firm to whom the contract is awarded or otherwise benefit, directly or indirectly, from the performance of the project for which the withdrawn bid was submitted.

F. If the public body denies the withdrawal of a bid under the provisions of this section, it shall notify the bidder in writing stating the reasons for its decision and award the contract to such bidder at the bid price, provided such bidder is a responsible and responsive bidder. (1982, c. 647, § 11-54; 1985, c. 286; 1994, c. 897; 1999, c. 344; 2001, c. 844.)

§ **2.2-4331. Contract pricing arrangements.** — A. Except as prohibited in this section, public contracts may be awarded on a fixed price or cost reimbursement basis, or on any other basis that is not prohibited.

B. Except in case of emergency affecting the public health, safety or welfare, no public contract shall be awarded on the basis of cost plus a percentage of cost.

C. A policy or contract of insurance or prepaid coverage having a premium computed on the basis of claims paid or incurred, plus the insurance carrier's administrative costs and retention stated in whole or part as a percentage of such claims, shall not be prohibited by this section. (1982, c. 647, § 11-43; 2001, c. 844.)

§ **2.2-4332. Workers' compensation requirements for construction contractors and subcontractors.** — A. No contractor shall perform any work on a construction project of a department, agency or institution of the Commonwealth or any of its political subdivisions unless he (i) has obtained, and continues to maintain for the duration of the work, workers' compensation coverage required pursuant to the provisions of Chapter 8 (§ 65.2-800 et seq.) of Title 65.2 and (ii) provides prior to the award of contract, on a form furnished by the department, agency, or institution of the Commonwealth or political subdivision thereof, evidence of such coverage.

B. The Department of General Services shall provide the form to such departments, agencies, institutions, and political subdivisions. Failure of a department, agency, institution or political subdivision to provide the form prior to the award of contract shall waive the requirements of clause (ii) of subsection A.

C. No subcontractor shall perform any work on a construction project of a department, agency or institution of the Commonwealth unless he has obtained, and continues to maintain for the duration of such work, workers' compensation coverage required pursuant to the provisions of Chapter 8 (§ 65.2-800 et seq.) of Title 65.2. (1993, c. 642, § 11-46.3; 2001, c. 844.)

§ **2.2-4333. Retainage on construction contracts.** — A. In any public contract for construction that provides for progress payments in installments based upon an estimated percentage of completion, the contractor shall be paid at least ninety-five percent of the earned sum when payment is due, with no more than five percent being retained to ensure faithful performance of the contract. All amounts withheld may be included in the final payment.

B. Any subcontract for a public project that provides for similar progress payments shall be subject to the provisions of this section. (1982, c. 647, § 11-56; 2001, c. 844.)

§ 2.2-4334. Deposit of certain retained funds on certain contracts with local governments; penalty for failure to timely complete. — A. Any county, city, town or agency thereof or other political subdivision of the Commonwealth when contracting directly with contractors for public contracts of $200,000 or more for construction of highways, roads, streets, bridges, parking lots, demolition, clearing, grading, excavating, paving, pile driving, miscellaneous drainage structures, and the installation of water, gas, sewer lines and pumping stations where portions of the contract price are to be retained, shall include in the Bid Proposal an option for the contractor to use an escrow account procedure for utilization of the political subdivision's retainage funds by so indicating in the space provided in the proposal documents. In the event the contractor elects to use the escrow account procedure, the escrow agreement form included in the Bid Proposal and Contract shall be executed and submitted to the political subdivision within fifteen calendar days after notification. If the escrow agreement form is not submitted within the fifteen-day period, the contractor shall forfeit his rights to the use of the escrow account procedure.

B. In order to have retained funds paid to an escrow agent, the contractor, the escrow agent, and the surety shall execute an escrow agreement form. The contractor's escrow agent shall be a trust company, bank or savings institution with its principal office located in the Commonwealth. The escrow agreement and all regulations adopted by the political subdivision entering into the contract shall be substantially the same as that used by the Virginia Department of Transportation.

C. This section shall not apply to public contracts for construction for railroads, public transit systems, runways, dams, foundations, installation or maintenance of power systems for the generation and primary and secondary distribution of electric current ahead of the customer's meter, the installation or maintenance of telephone, telegraph or signal systems for public utilities and the construction or maintenance of solid waste or recycling facilities and treatment plants.

D. Any such public contract for construction with a county, city, town or agency thereof or other political subdivision of the Commonwealth, which includes payment of interest on retained funds, may require a provision whereby the contractor, exclusive of reasonable circumstances beyond the control of the contractor stated in the contract, shall pay a specified penalty for each day exceeding the completion date stated in the contract.

E. Any subcontract for such public project that provides for similar progress payments shall be subject to the provisions of this section. (1989, c. 1, § 11-56.1; 2001, c. 844.)

§ 2.2-4335. Public construction contract provisions barring damages for unreasonable delays declared void. — A. Any provision contained in any public construction contract that purports to waive, release, or extinguish the rights of a contractor to recover costs or damages for unreasonable delay in performing such contract, either on his behalf or on behalf of his subcontractor if and to the extent the delay is caused by acts or omissions of the public body, its agents or employees and due to causes within their control shall be void and unenforceable as against public policy.

B. Subsection A shall not be construed to render void any provision of a public construction contract that:

1. Allows a public body to recover that portion of delay costs caused by the acts or omissions of the contractor, or its subcontractors, agents or employees;
2. Requires notice of any delay by the party claiming the delay;
3. Provides for liquidated damages for delay; or
4. Provides for arbitration or any other procedure designed to settle contract disputes.

C. A contractor making a claim against a public body for costs or damages due to the alleged delaying of the contractor in the performance of its work under any public construction contract shall be liable to the public body and shall pay it for a percentage of all costs incurred by the public body in investigating, analyzing, negotiating, litigating and arbitrating the claim, which percentage shall be equal to the percentage of the contractor's total delay claim that is determined through litigation or arbitration to be false or to have no basis in law or in fact.

D. A public body denying a contractor's claim for costs or damages due to the alleged delaying of the contractor in the performance of work under any public construction contract shall be liable to and shall pay such contractor a percentage of all costs incurred by the contractor to investigate, analyze, negotiate, litigate and arbitrate the claim. The percentage paid by the public body shall be equal to the percentage of the contractor's total delay claim for which the public body's denial is determined through litigation or arbitration to have been made in bad faith. (1991, c. 701, § 11-56.2; 2001, cc. 324, 844.)

Editor's note. — Acts 2001, c. 324 amended § 11-56.2, from which this section is derived. Pursuant to § 30-152, Acts 2001, c. 324 has been given effect in this section as set out above. The 2001 amendment by c. 324 added subsection D.

Law Review. — For article reviewing case law and changes in legislation affecting Virginia construction law, see 40 U. Rich. L. Rev. 143 (2005).

Michie's Jurisprudence. — For related discussion, see 3A M.J. Building Contracts, § 30; 17 M.J. State, § 11.

CASE NOTES

Unreasonable delay damages waiver void. — Provisions in a joint venture's (JV) contract with a waste water treatment facility, whereby the JV was to construct the facility, were held to be void as violative of subsection A of § 2.2-4335, as the contract provided that the JV waived, released, and extinguished all unreasonable delay damages unless the unreasonable delay was coupled with the facility's bad faith, malice, gross negligence, or abandonment of the contract; the contract provisions directly contradicted the specific statutory prohibition of subsection A of § 2.2-4335 and accordingly, the appellate court found that the trial court's judgment sustaining the validity of the contract provisions was erroneous under § 8.01-680. Blake Constr. Co./Poole & Kent v. Upper Occoquan Sewage Auth., 266 Va. 564, 587 S.E.2d 711, 2003 Va. LEXIS 108 (2003).

Provisions in a public construction contract that purport to bar certain delay damages recoverable by a contractor, and which define what constitutes "unreasonable delay damages" violates the statutory prohibition of subsection A of § 2.2-4335 and are therefore void as against public policy. Blake Constr. Co./Poole & Kent v. Upper Occoquan Sewage Auth., 266 Va. 564, 587 S.E.2d 711, 2003 Va. LEXIS 108 (2003).

No basis for cost application. — Trial court's denial of a waste water treatment facility's motion for costs, pursuant to subsection C of § 2.2-4335, was properly denied where the prior law of the case indicated that material breach damages were still in the consolidated cases between the parties, arising from contract disputes on a public project that were appealed to the circuit court pursuant to the Virginia Public Procurement Act, § 2.2-4300 et seq.; accordingly, there was no evidence of a false or statutorily baseless delay damages claim upon which the facility could anchor its application for statutory costs. Upper Occoquan Sewage Auth. v. Blake Constr. Co., 266 Va. 582, 587 S.E.2d 721, 2003 Va. LEXIS 110 (2003).

§ 2.2-4336. Bid bonds. — A. Except in cases of emergency, all bids or proposals for nontransportation-related construction contracts in excess of $100,000 or transportation-related projects authorized under § 33.1-12 that are in excess of $250,000 and partially or wholly funded by the Commonwealth shall be accompanied by a bid bond from a surety company selected by the bidder that is authorized to do business in Virginia, as a guarantee that if the contract is awarded to the bidder, he will enter into the contract for the work mentioned in the bid. The amount of the bid bond shall not exceed five percent of the amount bid.

B. No forfeiture under a bid bond shall exceed the lesser of (i) the difference between the bid for which the bond was written and the next low bid, or (ii) the face amount of the bid bond.

C. Nothing in this section shall preclude a public body from requiring bid bonds to accompany bids or proposals for construction contracts anticipated to be less than $100,000 for nontransportation-related projects or $250,000 for transportation-related projects authorized under § 33.1-12 and partially or wholly funded by the Commonwealth. (1982, c. 647, § 11-57; 1984, c. 160; 2001, c. 844; 2006, c. 925.)

§ 2.2-4337. Performance and payment bonds. — A. Upon the award of any (i) public construction contract exceeding $100,000 awarded to any prime contractor; (ii) construction contract exceeding $100,000 awarded to any prime contractor requiring the performance of labor or the furnishing of materials for buildings, structures or other improvements to real property owned or leased by a public body; (iii) construction contract exceeding $100,000 in which the performance of labor or the furnishing of materials will be paid with public funds; or (iv) transportation-related projects exceeding $250,000 that are partially or wholly funded by the Commonwealth, the contractor shall furnish to the public body the following bonds:

1. A performance bond in the sum of the contract amount conditioned upon the faithful performance of the contract in strict conformity with the plans, specifications and conditions of the contract. For transportation-related projects authorized under § 33.1-12, such bond shall be in a form and amount satisfactory to the public body.

2. A payment bond in the sum of the contract amount. The bond shall be for the protection of claimants who have and fulfill contracts to supply labor or materials to the prime contractor to whom the contract was awarded, or to any subcontractors, in furtherance of the work provided for in the contract, and shall be conditioned upon the prompt payment for all materials furnished or labor supplied or performed in the furtherance of the work. For transportation-related projects authorized under § 33.1-12 and partially or wholly funded by the Commonwealth, such bond shall be in a form and amount satisfactory to the public body.

"Labor or materials" shall include public utility services and reasonable rentals of equipment, but only for periods when the equipment rented is actually used at the site.

B. Each of the bonds shall be executed by one or more surety companies selected by the contractor that are authorized to do business in Virginia.

C. If the public body is the Commonwealth, or any agency or institution thereof, the bonds shall be payable to the Commonwealth of Virginia, naming also the agency or institution thereof. Bonds required for the contracts of other public bodies shall be payable to such public body.

D. Each of the bonds shall be filed with the public body that awarded the contract, or a designated office or official thereof.

E. Nothing in this section shall preclude a public body from requiring payment or performance bonds for construction contracts below $100,000 for nontransportation-related projects or $250,000 for transportation-related projects authorized under § 33.1-12 and partially or wholly funded by the Commonwealth.

F. Nothing in this section shall preclude the contractor from requiring each subcontractor to furnish a payment bond with surety thereon in the sum of the full amount of the contract with such subcontractor conditioned upon the payment to all persons who have and fulfill contracts that are directly with the subcontractor for performing labor and furnishing materials in the prosecution of the work provided for in the subcontract. (1982, c. 647, § 11-58; 1984, c. 160; 2001, c. 844; 2002, cc. 556, 643, 682; 2006, cc. 694, 925.)

Michie's Jurisprudence. — For related discussion, see 3A M.J. Building Contracts, § 22.

CASE NOTES

Editor's note. — The cases cited below were decided under former § 11-35.

This section is remedial in character, its language broad and inclusive, and obviously it was enacted to afford protection to materialmen and subcontractors, who cannot avail themselves of the mechanic's lien statutes, since liens cannot be perfected against public buildings. It must be liberally construed in their favor. Thomas Somerville Co. v. Broyhill, 200 Va. 358, 105 S.E.2d 824 (1958); R.C. Stanhope, Inc. v. Roanoke Constr. Co., 539 F.2d 992 (4th Cir. 1976); Solite Masonry Units Corp. v. Piland Constr. Co., 217 Va. 727, 232 S.E.2d 759 (1977).

It applies whether labor and materials are furnished to principal contractor or subcontractor. — The intent of this section is to protect those who furnish supplies, material and labor in and about the construction of the public buildings and improvements mentioned in the section, whether they be furnished to the principal contractor or to a subcontractor; of this a general contractor and his surety must take cognizance. They may readily protect themselves against the shortcomings of subcontractors by requiring bonds of the latter. Thomas Somerville Co. v. Broyhill, 200 Va. 358, 105 S.E.2d 824 (1958); R.C. Stanhope, Inc. v. Roanoke Constr. Co., 539 F.2d 992 (4th Cir. 1976).

This section and the bond are to be read together, for together they constitute the measure of the contractor's undertaking and the extent of his and the surety's liability. Thomas Somerville Co. v. Broyhill, 200 Va. 358, 105 S.E.2d 824 (1958).

The phrase "furnishing materials in the prosecution of the work" parallels the language used in the Miller Act, 40 USC § 270b. Solite Masonry Units Corp. v. Piland Constr. Co., 217 Va. 727, 232 S.E.2d 759 (1977).

"Materials furnished." — Rental charges and the value of missing rental equipment constitute "materials furnished" within the meaning of this section. R.C. Stanhope, Inc. v. Roanoke Constr. Co., 539 F.2d 992 (4th Cir. 1976).

When subcontractor's cause of action accrues. — A subcontractor's cause of action does not accrue or arise at the time the contract was executed. It accrues when the work is completed and contractor fails to pay the agreed amount for labor and materials. It is at that time that the subcontractor looks to the statute to determine its rights and the time in which it has to assert them. Johnson Serv. Co. v. Glaubke Constr. Co., 213 Va. 466, 193 S.E.2d 655 (1973).

Broader coverage not prohibited. — There is nothing in the language of this section which prohibits a bond executed by the prime contractor and his surety from providing broader coverage than that required by the provisions of this section. Reliance Ins. Co. v. Trane Co., 212 Va. 394, 184 S.E.2d 817 (1971).

There is no requirement under this section that a subcontractor obtain a performance bond for the protection of laborers and materialmen, and the reading in of such a provision would clearly go beyond the purpose of this section. Gallimore, Inc. v. Home Indem. Co., 432 F. Supp. 434 (W.D. Va. 1977).

This section does not require proof that a subcontractor's bond was not given before a materialman can recover on the prime contractor's bond. Reliance Ins. Co. v. Trane Co., 212 Va. 394, 184 S.E.2d 817 (1971).

A materialman was entitled to recovery from a general contractor for all the material it supplied a subcontractor and was not limited to recovery only for material actually used in the construction of a public building, where the materialman acted in good faith in supplying the material, and the general contractor had not required the subcontractor to give security by bond or otherwise for payment of those who contracted directly with the subcontractor. Solite Masonry Units Corp. v. Piland Constr. Co., 217 Va. 727, 232 S.E.2d 759 (1977).

§ 2.2-4338. Alternative forms of security. — A. In lieu of a bid, payment, or performance bond, a bidder may furnish a certified check or cash escrow in the face amount required for the bond.

B. If approved by the Attorney General in the case of state agencies, or the attorney for the political subdivision in the case of political subdivisions, a bidder may furnish a personal bond, property bond, or bank or savings institution's letter of credit on certain designated funds in the face amount required for the bid, payment or performance bond. Approval shall be granted only upon a determination that the alternative form of security proffered affords protection to the public body equivalent to a corporate surety's bond.

C. The provisions of this section shall not apply to the Department of Transportation. (1982, c. 647, § 11-61; 1989, c. 260; 1991, c. 574; 1992, c. 765; 1996, cc. 77, 827; 2001, c. 844.)

§ 2.2-4339. Bonds on other than construction contracts. — A public body may require bid, payment, or performance bonds for contracts for goods or services if provided in the Invitation to Bid or Request for Proposal. (1982, c. 647, § 11-62; 2001, c. 844.)

§ 2.2-4340. Action on performance bond. — No action against the surety on a performance bond shall be brought unless within five years after completion of the work on the project to the satisfaction of the Department of Transportation, in cases where the public body is the Department of Transportation, or, in all other cases, within one year after (i) completion of the contract, including the expiration of all warranties and guarantees, or (ii) discovery of the defect or breach of warranty that gave rise to the action. (1982, c. 647, § 11-59; 1996, c. 827; 2001, c. 844.)

§ 2.2-4341. Actions on payment bonds; waiver of right to sue. — A. Subject to the provisions of subsection B, any claimant who has performed labor or furnished material in accordance with the contract documents in furtherance of the work provided in any contract for which a payment bond has been given, and who has not been paid in full before the expiration of 90 days after the day on which the claimant performed the last of the labor or furnished the last of the materials for which he claims payment, may bring an action on the payment bond to recover any amount due him for the labor or material. The obligee named in the bond need not be named a party to the action.

B. Any claimant who has a direct contractual relationship with any subcontractor but who has no contractual relationship, express or implied, with the contractor, may bring an action on the contractor's payment bond only if he has given written notice to the contractor within 180 days from the day on which the claimant performed the last of the labor or furnished the last of the materials for which he claims payment, stating with substantial accuracy the amount claimed and the name of the person for whom the work was performed or to whom the material was furnished. Notice to the contractor shall be served by registered or certified mail, postage prepaid, in an envelope addressed to such contractor at any place where his office is regularly maintained for the transaction of business. Claims for sums withheld as retainages with respect to labor performed or materials furnished, shall not be subject to the time limitations stated in this subsection.

C. Any action on a payment bond shall be brought within one year after the day on which the person bringing such action last performed labor or last furnished or supplied materials.

D. Any waiver of the right to sue on the payment bond required by this section shall be void unless it is in writing, signed by the person whose right is waived, and executed after such person has performed labor or furnished material in accordance with the contract documents. (1982, c. 647, § 11-60; 2001, cc. 412, 844; 2003, c. 255.)

Editor's note. — Acts 2001, c. 412 amended § 11-60, from which this section is derived. Pursuant to § 30-152, Acts 2001, c. 412 has been given effect in this section as set out above. The 2001 amendment by c. 412 added subsection D.

Law Review. — For article reviewing case law and changes in legislation affecting Virginia construction law, see 40 U. Rich. L. Rev. 143 (2005).

CASE NOTES

Relationship with § 8.01-246. — In a case in which the underlying contracts for which the payment bonds were issued fell under the Virginia Public Procurement Act (VPPA), a paving company's contention that the five-year limitations period under subdivision 2 of § 8.01-246, which was applicable to written agreements, would apply rather than subsection C of § 2.2-4341, failed since under the VPPA, subsection C of this section was specifically applicable to VPPA-derived actions. APAC-Atlantic, Inc. v. General Ins. Co., 273 Va. 682, 643 S.E.2d 483, 2007 Va. LEXIS 49 (2007).

Contractual reduction of notice period held invalid. — A subcontractor on a public construction project, who was not a party to payment bonds, could not be bound by a provision in the bonds which required written notice of a claim within a 90-day period, as the parties to the bond could not reduce the 180-day notice period prescribed by this section without subcontractor's consent. Commercial Constr. Specialties, Inc. v. ACM Constr. Mgt. Corp., 242 Va. 102, 405 S.E.2d 852 (1991) (decided under prior law).

CIRCUIT COURT OPINIONS

Subcontractor for subcontractor could recover on general contractor's payment bond. — Sheet metal company, hired by a subcontractor, fell within the criteria for a claimant, and thus, the sheet metal company could recover against the general contractor's payment bond. Even if the surety was correct that the language of payment bond was more general than Virginia law required, there was no conflict with Virginia Public Procurement Act, § 2.2-4300 et seq., and the broader provisions of the bond took precedence. Stromberg Sheet Metal Works, Inc. v. United States Fid. & Guar. Co., 71 Va. Cir. 122, 2006 Va. Cir. LEXIS 102 (Fairfax County 2006).

§ 2.2-4342. Public inspection of certain records. — A. Except as provided in this section, all proceedings, records, contracts and other public records relating to procurement transactions shall be open to the inspection of any citizen, or any interested person, firm or corporation, in accordance with the Virginia Freedom of Information Act (§ 2.2-3700 et seq.).

B. Cost estimates relating to a proposed procurement transaction prepared by or for a public body shall not be open to public inspection.

C. Any competitive sealed bidding bidder, upon request, shall be afforded the opportunity to inspect bid records within a reasonable time after the opening of all bids but prior to award, except in the event that the public body decides not to accept any of the bids and to reopen the contract. Otherwise, bid records shall be open to public inspection only after award of the contract.

D. Any competitive negotiation offeror, upon request, shall be afforded the opportunity to inspect proposal records within a reasonable time after the evaluation and negotiations of proposals are completed but prior to award, except in the event that the public body decides not to accept any of the proposals and to reopen the contract. Otherwise, proposal records shall be open to public inspection only after award of the contract.

E. Any inspection of procurement transaction records under this section shall be subject to reasonable restrictions to ensure the security and integrity of the records.

F. Trade secrets or proprietary information submitted by a bidder, offeror or contractor in connection with a procurement transaction or prequalification application submitted pursuant to subsection B of § 2.2-4317 shall not be subject to the Virginia Freedom of Information Act (§ 2.2-3700 et seq.); however, the bidder, offeror or contractor shall (i) invoke the protections of this section prior to or upon submission of the data or other materials, (ii) identify the data or other materials to be protected, and (iii) state the reasons why protection is necessary. (1982, c. 647, § 11-52; 1984, c. 705; 1994, c. 918; 2001, c. 844.)

ARTICLE 3.

Exemptions and Limitations.

§ 2.2-4343. Exemption from operation of chapter for certain transactions. — A. The provisions of this chapter shall not apply to:

1. The Virginia Port Authority in the exercise of any of its powers in accordance with Chapter 10 (§ 62.1-128 et seq.) of Title 62.1, provided the Authority implements, by policy or regulation adopted by the Board of Commissioners and approved by the Department of General Services, procedures to ensure fairness and competitiveness in the procurement of goods and services and in the administration of its capital outlay program. This exemption shall be applicable only so long as such policies and procedures meeting the requirements remain in effect.

2. The Virginia Retirement System for selection of services related to the management, purchase or sale of authorized investments, actuarial services, and disability determination services. Selection of these services shall be governed by the standard set forth in § 51.1-124.30.

3. The State Treasurer in the selection of investment management services related to the external management of funds shall be governed by the standard set forth in § 2.2-4514, and shall be subject to competitive guidelines and policies that are set by the Commonwealth Treasury Board and approved by the Department of General Services.

4. The Department of Social Services or local departments of social services for the acquisition of motor vehicles for sale or transfer to Temporary Assistance to Needy Families (TANF) recipients.

5. The University of Virginia in the selection of services related to the management and investment of its endowment funds, endowment income, gifts, all other nongeneral fund reserves and balances, or local funds of or held by the University pursuant to § 23-76.1. However, selection of these services shall be governed by the Uniform Prudent Management of Institutional Funds Act (§ 55-268.11 et seq.) as required by § 23-76.1.

6. The Board of the Virginia College Savings Plan for the selection of services related to the operation and administration of the Plan, including, but not limited to, contracts or agreements for the management, purchase, or sale of authorized investments or actuarial, record keeping, or consulting services. However, such selection shall be governed by the standard set forth in § 23-38.80.

7. Public institutions of higher education for the purchase of items for resale at retail bookstores and similar retail outlets operated by such institutions. However, such purchase procedures shall provide for competition where practicable.

8. The purchase of goods and services by agencies of the legislative branch that may be specifically exempted therefrom by the Chairman of the Committee on Rules of either the House of Delegates or the Senate. Nor shall the contract review provisions of § 2.2-2011 apply to such procurements. The exemption shall be in writing and kept on file with the agency's disbursement records.

9. Any town with a population of less than 3,500, except as stipulated in the provisions of §§ 2.2-4305, 2.2-4308, 2.2-4311, 2.2-4315, 2.2-4330, 2.2-4333 through 2.2-4338, 2.2-4343.1, and 2.2-4367 through 2.2-4377.

10. Any county, city or town whose governing body has adopted, by ordinance or resolution, alternative policies and procedures which are (i) based on

competitive principles and (ii) generally applicable to procurement of goods and services by such governing body and its agencies, except as stipulated in subdivision 12.

This exemption shall be applicable only so long as such policies and procedures, or other policies and procedures meeting the requirements of § 2.2-4300, remain in effect in such county, city or town. Such policies and standards may provide for incentive contracting that offers a contractor whose bid is accepted the opportunity to share in any cost savings realized by the locality when project costs are reduced by such contractor, without affecting project quality, during construction of the project. The fee, if any, charged by the project engineer or architect for determining such cost savings shall be paid as a separate cost and shall not be calculated as part of any cost savings.

11. Any school division whose school board has adopted, by policy or regulation, alternative policies and procedures that are (i) based on competitive principles and (ii) generally applicable to procurement of goods and services by the school board, except as stipulated in subdivision 12.

This exemption shall be applicable only so long as such policies and procedures, or other policies or procedures meeting the requirements of § 2.2-4300, remain in effect in such school division. This provision shall not exempt any school division from any centralized purchasing ordinance duly adopted by a local governing body.

12. Notwithstanding the exemptions set forth in subdivisions 9 through 11, the provisions of subsections C and D of § 2.2-4303, and §§ 2.2-4305, 2.2-4308, 2.2-4311, 2.2-4315, 2.2-4317, 2.2-4330, 2.2-4333 through 2.2-4338, 2.2-4343.1, and 2.2-4367 through 2.2-4377 shall apply to all counties, cities and school divisions, and to all towns having a population greater than 3,500 in the Commonwealth.

The method for procurement of professional services set forth in subdivision 3 a of § 2.2-4301 in the definition of competitive negotiation shall also apply to all counties, cities and school divisions, and to all towns having a population greater than 3,500, where the cost of the professional service is expected to exceed $30,000 in the aggregate or for the sum of all phases of a contract or project. A school board that makes purchases through its public school foundation or purchases educational technology through its educational technology foundation, either as may be established pursuant to § 22.1-212.2:2 shall be exempt from the provisions of this chapter, except, relative to such purchases, the school board shall comply with the provisions of §§ 2.2-4311 and 2.2-4367 through 2.2-4377.

13. A public body that is also a utility operator may purchase services through or participate in contracts awarded by one or more utility operators that are not public bodies for utility marking services as required by the Underground Utility Damage Prevention Act (§ 56-265.14 et seq.). A purchase of services under this subdivision may deviate from the procurement procedures set forth in this chapter upon a determination made in advance by the public body and set forth in writing that competitive sealed bidding is either not practicable or not fiscally advantageous to the public, and the contract is awarded based on competitive principles.

14. Procurement of any construction or planning and design services for construction by a Virginia nonprofit corporation or organization not otherwise specifically exempted when (i) the planning, design or construction is funded by state appropriations of $10,000 or less or (ii) the Virginia nonprofit corporation or organization is obligated to conform to procurement procedures that are established by federal statutes or regulations, whether those federal procedures are in conformance with the provisions of this chapter.

15. Purchases, exchanges, gifts or sales by the Citizens' Advisory Council on Furnishing and Interpreting the Executive Mansion.

16. The Eastern Virginia Medical School in the selection of services related to the management and investment of its endowment and other institutional funds. The selection of these services shall, however, be governed by the Uniform Prudent Management of Institutional Funds Act (§ 55-268.11 et seq.).

17. The Department of Corrections in the selection of pre-release and post-incarceration services.

18. The Board of the Chippokes Plantation Farm Foundation in entering into agreements with persons for the construction, operation, and maintenance of projects consistent with the Chippokes Plantation State Park Master Plan approved by the Director of the Department of Conservation and Recreation pursuant to the requirements of § 10.1-200.1 and designed to further an appreciation for rural living and the contributions of the agricultural, forestry, and natural resource based industries of the Commonwealth, provided such projects are supported solely by private or nonstate funding.

19. The University of Virginia Medical Center to the extent provided by subdivision B 3 of § 23-77.4.

20. The purchase of goods and services by a local governing body or any authority, board, department, instrumentality, institution, agency or other unit of state government when such purchases are made under a remedial plan established by the Governor pursuant to subsection C of § 2.2-4310 or by a chief administrative officer of a county, city or town pursuant to § 15.2-965.1.

21. The contract by community services boards or behavioral health authorities with an administrator or management body pursuant to a joint agreement authorized by § 37.2-512 or 37.2-615.

B. Where a procurement transaction involves the expenditure of federal assistance or contract funds, the receipt of which is conditioned upon compliance with mandatory requirements in federal laws or regulations not in conformance with the provisions of this chapter, a public body may comply with such federal requirements, notwithstanding the provisions of this chapter, only upon the written determination of the Governor, in the case of state agencies, or the governing body, in the case of political subdivisions, that acceptance of the grant or contract funds under the applicable conditions is in the public interest. Such determination shall state the specific provision of this chapter in conflict with the conditions of the grant or contract. (1982, c. 647, §§ 11-35, 11-39, 11-40; 1983, c. 593; 1984, cc. 159, 330, 764, § 11-40.2; 1985, c. 74; 1986, cc. 149, 212, 559; 1987, c. 583; 1991, c. 645; 1994, cc. 661, 918; 1995, c. 18; 1996, cc. 261, 280, 683, 1019; 1997, cc. 85, 488, 785, 861, 863; 1998, cc. 121, 132; 1999, cc. 230, 248, 735, 910, § 11-40.4; 2000, cc. 29, 382, 400, 642, 644, 666, 703; 2001, cc. 392, 409, 736, 753, 774, 844; 2002, cc. 87, 478, 491, 582, 595; 2003, cc. 226, 1008; 2004, cc. 145, 865, 891; 2006, c. 656; 2007, cc. 434, 697; 2008, c. 184.)

Cross references. — As to employees of a governmental agency of local government having a personal interest in a contract with that agency, see § 2.2-3109. As to inapplicability of provisions of this article to contracts for advertising or publishing entered into by the Virginia Wine Board, see § 3.1-1064.7. As to the 1980, 1990 and 2000 United States Census population figures for counties and cities of the Commonwealth of Virginia, see the Appendix to Title 15.2. For provision that this article shall apply to contracts for the printing of ballots, statements of results, or other material essential to the conduct of an election, see § 24.2-602. As to prohibited conduct by legislators regarding contracts, see § 30-105.

Editor's note. — Acts 2001, cc. 392, 409, 736, 753 and 774 amended § 11-35, from which this section is derived. Pursuant to § 30-152, Acts 2001, cc. 392, 409, and 774 have been given effect in this section as set out above.

Acts 2004, cc. 865 and 891, cl. 2, provide: "That any analysis that is used by the Governor or a locality as a basis for determining the existence of discrimination based on race or gender in the awarding of contracting opportunities shall use the standards established by the United States Supreme Court in *The City of Richmond v. J. A. Croson Company,* 488 U.S. 469, (1985) and any subsequent decisions of the United States Supreme Court or other binding authority concerning such standards."

Acts 2007, c. 434, cl. 2, provides: "That the provisions of this act shall not be construed or interpreted to permit or allow the University of Virginia to invest revenues from tuition and educational fees that are used or required for the day-to-day operations of the University in other than cash accounts and fixed income securities."

The 2007 amendments. — The 2007 amendment by c. 434 in subdivision A 5, deleted "or" following "endowment income," and inserted "all other nongeneral fund reserves and balances, or local funds of or held by the University."

The 2007 amendment by c. 697, in subsection A 2, deleted "including but not limited to" preceding "actuarial services," and added "and disability determination services" to the end of the first sentence.

The 2008 amendments. — The 2008 amendment by c. 184 substituted "Uniform Prudent Management of Institutional Funds Act (§ 55-268.11 et seq.)" for "Uniform Management of Institutional Funds Act (§ 55-268.1 et seq.)" in subdivisions A 5 and A 16.

Michie's Jurisprudence. — For related discussion, see 5A M.J. Counties, § 63.

CASE NOTES

City plan to promote minority business enterprises. — Appellant city council adopted a plan that required prime contractors to whom the city awarded construction contracts to subcontract at least 30 percent of the dollar amount of the contract to one or more minority business enterprises to promote wider participation by minority business enterprises in the construction of public projects. However, because appellant city failed to provide evidence identifying discrimination in the construction industry, failed to demonstrate a compelling governmental interest in apportioning public contracting opportunities on the basis of race, or failed to show that its remedy had been narrowly tailored to the achievement of that interest, its treatment of its citizens on a racial basis violated the Equal Protection Clause. Richmond v. J. A. Croson Co., 488 U.S. 469, 102 L. Ed. 2d 854, 1989 LEXIS 579, 109 S. Ct. 706 (1989).

CIRCUIT COURT OPINIONS

Spotsylvania County has opted out. — Spotsylvania County has opted out of the Virginia Public Procurement Act, § 2.2-4343, and has adopted its own procurement policy, which is consistent with State law, specifically § 2.2-4363, except the county extends a 10-day grace period for giving notice of intention to submit a claim. MCI Constructors v. Spotsylvania County, 62 Va. Cir. 375, 2003 Va. Cir. LEXIS 115 (Spotsylvania County 2003).

§ 2.2-4343.1. Permitted contracts with certain religious organizations; purpose; limitations. — A. It is the intent of the General Assembly, in accordance with the Personal Responsibility and Work Opportunity Reconciliation Act of 1996, P.L. 104-193, to authorize public bodies to enter into contracts with faith-based organizations for the purposes described in this section on the same basis as any other nongovernmental source without impairing the religious character of such organization, and without diminishing the religious freedom of the beneficiaries of assistance provided under this section.

B. For the purposes of this section, *"faith-based organization"* means a religious organization that is or applies to be a contractor to provide goods or services for programs funded by the block grant provided pursuant to the Personal Responsibility and Work Opportunity Reconciliation Act of 1996, P.L. 104-193.

C. Public bodies, in procuring goods or services, or in making disbursements pursuant to this section, shall not (i) discriminate against a faith-based organization on the basis of the organization's religious character or (ii) impose conditions that (a) restrict the religious character of the faith-based organization, except as provided in subsection F, or (b) impair, diminish, or discourage the exercise of religious freedom by the recipients of such goods, services, or disbursements.

D. Public bodies shall ensure that all invitations to bid, requests for proposals, contracts, and purchase orders prominently display a nondiscrimination statement indicating that the public body does not discriminate against faith-based organizations.

E. A faith-based organization contracting with a public body (i) shall not discriminate against any recipient of goods, services, or disbursements made pursuant to a contract authorized by this section on the basis of the recipient's religion, religious belief, refusal to participate in a religious practice, or on the basis of race, age, color, gender or national origin and (ii) shall be subject to the same rules as other organizations that contract with public bodies to account for the use of the funds provided; however, if the faith-based organization segregates public funds into separate accounts, only the accounts and programs funded with public funds shall be subject to audit by the public body. Nothing in clause (ii) shall be construed to supersede or otherwise override any other applicable state law.

F. Consistent with the Personal Responsibility and Work Opportunity Reconciliation Act of 1996, P.L. 104-193, funds provided for expenditure pursuant to contracts with public bodies shall not be spent for religious worship, instruction, or proselytizing; however, this prohibition shall not apply to expenditures pursuant to contracts, if any, for the services of chaplains.

G. Nothing in this section shall be construed as barring or prohibiting a faith-based organization from any opportunity to make a bid or proposal or contract on the grounds that the faith-based organization has exercised the right, as expressed in 42 U.S.C. (§ 2000 e-1 et seq.), to employ persons of a particular religion.

H. If an individual, who applies for or receives goods, services, or disbursements provided pursuant to a contract between a public body and a faith-based organization, objects to the religious character of the faith-based organization from which the individual receives or would receive the goods, services, or disbursements, the public body shall offer the individual, within a reasonable period of time after the date of his objection, access to equivalent goods, services, or disbursements from an alternative provider.

The public body shall provide to each individual who applies for or receives goods, services, or disbursements provided pursuant to a contract between a public body and a faith-based organization a notice in bold face type that states: "Neither the public body's selection of a charitable or faith-based provider of services nor the expenditure of funds under this contract is an endorsement of the provider's charitable or religious character, practices, or expression. No provider of services may discriminate against you on the basis of religion, a religious belief, or your refusal to actively participate in a religious practice. If you object to a particular provider because of its religious character, you may request assignment to a different provider. If you believe that your rights have been violated, please discuss the complaint with your provider or notify the appropriate person as indicated in this form." (2001, c. 774, § 11-35.1; 2005, c. 928.)

Editor's note. — Acts 2001, c. 774 enacted § 11-35.1, from which this section is derived. Pursuant to § 30-152, Acts 2001, c. 774 has been given effect in this section as set out above.

§ 2.2-4344. Exemptions from competition for certain transactions. — A. Any public body may enter into contracts without competition for:

1. The purchase of goods or services that are produced or performed by:

a. Persons, or in schools or workshops, under the supervision of the Virginia Department for the Blind and Vision Impaired; or

b. Nonprofit sheltered workshops or other nonprofit organizations that offer transitional or supported employment services serving the handicapped.

2. The purchase of legal services, provided that the pertinent provisions of Chapter 5 (§ 2.2-500 et seq.) of this title remain applicable, or expert witnesses or other services associated with litigation or regulatory proceedings.

B. An industrial development authority or regional industrial facility authority may enter into contracts without competition with respect to any item of cost of "authority facilities" or "facilities" as defined in § 15.2-4902 or "facility" as defined in § 15.2-6400.

C. A community development authority formed pursuant to Article 6 (§ 15.2-5152 et seq.) of Chapter 51 of Title 15.2, with members selected pursuant to such article, may enter into contracts without competition with respect to the exercise of any of its powers permitted by § 15.2-5158. However, this exception shall not apply in cases where any public funds other than special assessments and incremental real property taxes levied pursuant to § 15.2-5158 are used as payment for such contract.

D. The Inspector General for Mental Health, Mental Retardation and Substance Abuse Services may enter into contracts without competition to obtain the services of licensed health care professionals or other experts to assist in carrying out the duties of the Office of the Inspector General for Mental Health, Mental Retardation and Substance Abuse Services. (1982, c. 647, § 11-45; 1984, c. 764; 1987, cc. 194, 248; 1989, c. 235; 1990, c. 395; 1991, c. 175; 1993, cc. 110, 505, 638, 971; 1996, cc. 145, 897, 902, 950, 1038; 1998, cc. 222, 619, 666, 697, 791; 1999, cc. 160, 194, 1021, 1024; 2000, cc. 242, 696, 927; 2001, c. 844; 2008, c. 52.)

The 2008 amendments. — The 2008 amendment by c. 52 inserted "or regional industrial facility authority" and "or 'facility' as defined in § 15.2-6400" in subsection B.

OPINIONS OF THE ATTORNEY GENERAL

Design-build contracts for construction of "authority facilities" or "facilities." — Industrial development authorities may use design-build contracts for the construction of "authority facilities" or "facilities," as those terms are defined in the statute, without engaging in competitive bidding or involving the Design-Build/Construction Management Review Board. See opinion of Attorney General to The Honorable Clarence E. Phillips, Member, House of Delegates, 01-105 (4/2/02).

§ 2.2-4345. Exemptions from competitive sealed bidding and competitive negotiation for certain transactions; limitations. — A. The following public bodies may enter into contracts without competitive sealed bidding or competitive negotiation:

1. The Director of the Department of Medical Assistance Services for special services provided for eligible recipients pursuant to subsection H of § 32.1-325, provided that the Director has made a determination in advance after reasonable notice to the public and set forth in writing that competitive sealed bidding or competitive negotiation for such services is not fiscally advantageous to the public, or would constitute an imminent threat to the health or welfare of such recipients. The writing shall document the basis for this determination.

2. The State Health Commissioner for the compilation, storage, analysis, evaluation, and publication of certain data submitted by health care providers and for the development of a methodology to measure the efficiency and productivity of health care providers pursuant to Chapter 7.2 (§ 32.1-276.2 et seq.) of Title 32.1, if the Commissioner has made a determination in advance, after reasonable notice to the public and set forth in writing, that competitive sealed bidding or competitive negotiation for such services is not fiscally advantageous to the public. The writing shall document the basis for this

determination. Such agreements and contracts shall be based on competitive principles.

3. The Virginia Code Commission when procuring the services of a publisher, pursuant to §§ 30-146 and 30-148, to publish the Code of Virginia or the Virginia Administrative Code.

4. The Department of Alcoholic Beverage Control for the purchase of alcoholic beverages.

5. The Department for the Aging, for the administration of elder rights programs, with (i) nonprofit Virginia corporations granted tax-exempt status under § 501(c)(3) of the Internal Revenue Code with statewide experience in Virginia in conducting a state long-term care ombudsman program or (ii) designated area agencies on aging.

6. The Department of Health for (a) child restraint devices, pursuant to § 46.2-1097; (b) health care services with Virginia corporations granted tax-exempt status under § 501(c)(3) of the Internal Revenue Code and operating as clinics for the indigent and uninsured that are organized for the delivery of primary health care services in a community (i) as federally qualified health centers designated by the Health Care Financing Administration or (ii) at a reduced or sliding fee scale or without charge; or (c) contracts with laboratories providing cytology and related services if competitive sealed bidding and competitive negotiations are not fiscally advantageous to the public to provide quality control as prescribed in writing by the Commissioner of Health.

7. Virginia Correctional Enterprises, when procuring materials, supplies, or services for use in and support of its production facilities, provided the procurement is accomplished using procedures that ensure as efficient use of funds as practicable and, at a minimum, includes obtaining telephone quotations. Such procedures shall require documentation of the basis for awarding contracts under this section.

8. The Virginia Baseball Stadium Authority for the operation of any facilities developed under the provisions of Chapter 58 (§ 15.2-5800 et seq.) of Title 15.2, including contracts or agreements with respect to the sale of food, beverages and souvenirs at such facilities.

9. With the consent of the Governor, the Jamestown-Yorktown Foundation for the promotion of tourism through marketing with private entities provided a demonstrable cost savings, as reviewed by the Secretary of Education, can be realized by the Foundation and such agreements or contracts are based on competitive principles.

10. The Chesapeake Hospital Authority in the exercise of any power conferred under Chapter 271, as amended, of the Acts of Assembly of 1966; provided that it does not discriminate against any person on the basis of race, color, religion, national origin, sex, pregnancy, childbirth or related medical conditions, age, marital status, or disability in the procurement of goods and services.

11. Richmond Eye and Ear Hospital Authority, any authorities created under Chapter 53 (§ 15.2-5300 et seq.) of Title 15.2 and any hospital or health center commission created under Chapter 52 (§ 15.2-5200 et seq.) of Title 15.2 in the exercise of any power conferred under their respective authorizing legislation; provided that these entities shall not discriminate against any person on the basis of race, color, religion, national origin, sex, pregnancy, childbirth or related medical conditions, age, marital status, or disability in the procurement of goods and services.

12. The Patrick Hospital Authority sealed in the exercise of any power conferred under the Acts of Assembly of 2000; provided that it does not discriminate against any person on the basis of race, color, religion, national origin, sex, pregnancy, childbirth or related medical conditions, age, marital status, or disability in the procurement of goods and services.

13. Public bodies for insurance or electric utility services if purchased through an association of which it is a member if the association was formed and is maintained for the purpose of promoting the interest and welfare of and developing close relationships with similar public bodies, provided such association has procured the insurance or electric utility services by use of competitive principles and provided that the public body has made a determination in advance after reasonable notice to the public and set forth in writing that competitive sealed bidding and competitive negotiation are not fiscally advantageous to the public. The writing shall document the basis for this determination.

14. Public bodies administering public assistance and social services programs as defined in § 63.2-100, community services boards as defined in § 37.2-100, or any public body purchasing services under the Comprehensive Services Act for At-Risk Youth and Families (§ 2.2-5200 et seq.) or the Virginia Juvenile Community Crime Control Act (§ 16.1-309.2 et seq.) for goods or personal services for direct use by the recipients of such programs if the procurement is made for an individual recipient. Contracts for the bulk procurement of goods or services for the use of recipients shall not be exempted from the requirements of § 2.2-4303.

15. The Eastern Virginia Medical School in the exercise of any power conferred pursuant to Chapter 471, as amended, of the Acts of Assembly of 1964.

B. No contract for the construction of any building or for an addition to or improvement of an existing building by any local government or subdivision of local government for which state funds of not more than $30,000 in the aggregate or for the sum of all phases of a contract or project either by appropriation, grant-in-aid or loan, are used or are to be used for all or part of the cost of construction shall be let except after competitive sealed bidding or after competitive negotiation as provided under of subsection D of § 2.2-4303. The procedure for the advertising for bids or for proposals and for letting of the contract shall conform, mutatis mutandis, to this chapter. (1982, c. 647, § 11-45; 1984, c. 764; 1987, cc. 194, 248; 1989, c. 235; 1990, c. 395; 1991, c. 175; 1993, cc. 110, 505, 638, 971; 1996, cc. 145, 897, 902, 950, 1038; 1998, cc. 222, 619, 666, 697, 791; 1999, cc. 160, 194, 1021, 1024; 2000, cc. 242, 696, 927; 2001, c. 844; 2002, cc. 87, 478, 747; 2006, c. 658.)

Editor's note. — Acts 1996, c. 902, cl. 5, as amended by Acts 1999, c. 691, cl. 1, by Acts 1999, c. 764, cl. 2, and by Acts 2002, c. 331, cl. 1, which provided that subdivision A 2 of § 2.2-4345 would expire on July 1, 2008, was repealed by Acts 2007, cc. 6 and 21, cl. 1. Subdivision A 2 will not expire.

Acts 1999, c. 1024, cl. 2, provides: "That the provisions of this act [which amended subsection I of § 11-45, now subdivision A 1 of § 2.2-4345 by substituting "H" for "E" following "special services provided for eligible recipients pursuant to § 32.1-325"] shall not become effective until receipt of a Section 1115 waiver from the Health Care Financing Administration in the United States Department of Health and Human Services. The Department of Medical Assistance Services shall apply for such waiver as soon as possible, but not later than December 31, 1999. If waiver approval is granted, implementation shall occur no later than three months following the date of the approval." Federal waivers were granted August 2002.

§ **2.2-4346. Other exemptions for certain transactions.** — The following public bodies may enter into contracts as provided in this section.

A. Contracts for certain essential election materials and services are exempted from the requirements of Articles 1 (§ 2.2-4300 et seq.), 2 (§ 2.2-4303 et seq.), and 5 (§ 2.2-4357 et seq.) of this chapter pursuant to § 24.2-602.

B. Any local school board may authorize any of its public schools or its school division to enter into contracts providing that caps and gowns, photographs, class rings, yearbooks and graduation announcements will be available for purchase or rental by students, parents, faculty or other persons using nonpublic money through the use of competitive negotiation as provided in this chapter; competitive sealed bidding is not necessarily required for such contracts. The Superintendent of Public Instruction may provide assistance to public school systems regarding this chapter and other related laws.

C. The Virginia Racing Commission may designate an entity to administer and promote the Virginia Breeders Fund created pursuant to § 59.1-372 without competitive procurement. (1982, c. 647, §§ 11-41, 11-45; 1984, c. 764; 1985, c. 164; 1986, cc. 332, 559; 1987, cc. 194, 248, 456; 1988, cc. 40, 640; 1989, cc. 235, 296; 1990, c. 395; 1991, cc. 73, 175; 1992, c. 105, § 11-40.3; 1993, cc. 110, 242, 505, 638, 971; 1996, cc. 145, 827, 897, 902, 950, 965, 1019, 1038; 1998, c. 222, 619, 666, 697, 791; 1999, cc. 160, 178, 194, 1021, 1024; 2000, cc. 242, 637, 647, 664, 692, 696, 927; 2001, c. 844.)

CASE NOTES

Former subsection G of § 11-41 (now subsection B of this section) did not support allegation school was purchasing agent. — Payment of profits from portrait sales by photographer to the schools did not constitute commercial bribery in violation of section 2(c) of the Robinson-Putman Act; because the words "will be available" implied that the students would not be obligated to purchase the photographs, former subsection G (now subsection B) did not support an allegation that the schools acted as purchasing agents. Stephen Jay Photography, Ltd. v. Olan Mills, Inc., 903 F.2d 988 (4th Cir. 1990) (decided under former corresponding provisions).

ARTICLE 4.

Prompt Payment.

§ **2.2-4347. Definitions.** — As used in this article, unless the context requires a different meaning:

"Contractor" means the entity that has a direct contract with any "state agency" as defined herein, or any agency of local government as discussed in § 2.2-4352.

"Debtor" means any individual, business, or group having a delinquent debt or account with any state agency that obligation has not been satisfied or set aside by court order or discharged in bankruptcy.

"Payment date" means either (i) the date on which payment is due under the terms of a contract for provision of goods or services; or (ii) if such date has not been established by contract, (a) thirty days after receipt of a proper invoice by the state agency or its agent or forty-five days after receipt by the local government or its agent responsible under the contract for approval of such invoices for the amount of payment due, or (b) thirty days after receipt of the goods or services by the state agency or forty-five days after receipt by the local government, whichever is later.

"State agency" means any authority, board, department, instrumentality, institution, agency or other unit of state government. The term shall not include any county, city or town or any local or regional governmental authority.

"Subcontractor" means any entity that has a contract to supply labor or materials to the contractor to whom the contract was awarded or to any subcontractor in the performance of the work provided for in such contract. (1984, c. 736, § 11-62.1; 1990, c. 824; 1992, c. 75; 2001, c. 844.)

§ **2.2-4348. Exemptions.** — The provisions of this article shall not apply to the late payment provisions contained in any public utility tariffs prescribed by the State Corporation Commission. (1984, c. 736, § 11-62.9; 2001, c. 844.)

CIRCUIT COURT OPINIONS

Breach of contract payment clause. — Under Virginia's Prompt Payment Act, the contractor was required to pay the subcontractor within the time the parties specified in the subcontract and the contractor was in breach of that requirement as the evidence showed that the contractor paid the subcontractor outside of the time specified in the contract, which meant the contractor was not entitled to any postjudgment relief on that issue. Shen Valley Masonry, Inc. v. S.P. Cahill & Assocs., 58 Va. Cir. 396, 2002 Va. Cir. LEXIS 156 (Charlottesville 2002).

Failure to make timely progress payments was material breach of contract. — In a trial involving claims between a general contractor and a masonry subcontractor, in which both parties breached the contract, damages were awarded to the subcontractor and denied the general contractor because the general contractor was found to have committed the first material breach of the contract by failing to make progress payments to the subcontractor as due. Shen Valley Masonary, Inc. v. S.P. Cahill & Assocs., 57 Va. Cir. 189, 2001 Va. Cir. LEXIS 431 (Charlottesville 2001).

§ **2.2-4349. Retainage to remain valid.** — Notwithstanding the provisions of this article, the provisions of § 2.2-4333 relating to retainage shall remain valid. (1984, c. 736, § 11-62.8; 2001, c. 844.)

§ **2.2-4350. Prompt payment of bills by state agencies.** — A. Every state agency that acquires goods or services, or conducts any other type of contractual business with nongovernmental, privately owned enterprises shall promptly pay for the completely delivered goods or services by the required payment date.

Payment shall be deemed to have been made when offset proceedings have been instituted, as authorized under the Virginia Debt Collection Act (§ 2.2-4800 et seq.).

B. Separate payment dates may be specified for contracts under which goods or services are provided in a series of partial deliveries or executions to the extent that such contract provides for separate payment for such partial delivery or execution. (1984, c. 736, §§ 11-62.2, 11-62.3; 1992, c. 75; 2001, c. 844.)

§ **2.2-4351. Defect or impropriety in the invoice or goods and/or services received.** — In instances where there is a defect or impropriety in an invoice or in the goods or services received, the state agency shall notify the supplier of the defect or impropriety, if the defect or impropriety would prevent payment by the payment date. The notice shall be sent within fifteen days after receipt of the invoice or the goods or services. (1984, c. 736, § 11-62.4; 2001, c. 844.)

§ **2.2-4352. Prompt payment of bills by localities.** — Every agency of local government that acquires goods or services, or conducts any other type of contractual business with a nongovernmental, privately owned enterprise, shall promptly pay for the completed delivered goods or services by the required payment date. The required payment date shall be either: (i) the date on which payment is due under the terms of the contract for the provision of the goods or services; or (ii) if a date is not established by contract, not more than forty-five days after goods or services are received or not more than forty-five days after the invoice is rendered, whichever is later.

Separate payment dates may be specified for contracts under which goods or services are provided in a series of partial executions or deliveries to the extent that the contract provides for separate payment for partial execution or delivery.

Within twenty days after the receipt of the invoice or goods or services, the agency shall notify the supplier of any defect or impropriety that would prevent payment by the payment date.

Unless otherwise provided under the terms of the contract for the provision of goods or services, every agency that fails to pay by the payment date shall pay any finance charges assessed by the supplier that shall not exceed one percent per month.

The provisions of this section shall not apply to the late payment provisions in any public utility tariffs or public utility negotiated contracts. (1985, c. 454, § 11-62.10; 2001, c. 844.)

CASE NOTES

Interest rate implied in contract. — Trial court erred in not applying the one percent interest rate applied by the jury to the compensatory damages awarded in the first trial where the joint venture sued the public authority for breach of contract. The one percent interest rate was implied in the parties contract pursuant to the Prompt Payment Act, § 2.2-4352, and, thus, the trial court erred in applying a nine percent rate for a certain time period pursuant to § 6.1-330.54. Upper Occoquan Sewage Auth. v. Blake Constr. Co., 275 Va. 41, 655 S.E.2d 10, 2008 Va. LEXIS 17 (2008).

§ 2.2-4353. Date of postmark deemed to be date payment is made. — In those cases where payment is made by mail, the date of postmark shall be deemed to be the date payment is made for purposes of this chapter. (1984, c. 736, § 11-62.6; 2001, c. 844.)

CIRCUIT COURT OPINIONS

Prompt payment evidence. — Evidence regarding postmark being made on a certain date that indicated contractor was paid by third party 20 days before the contractor paid the subcontractor was sufficient to show that the contractor breached the subcontract calling for payment within seven days of the date the third party paid the contractor, and, thus, neither the contractor nor the contractor's insurance company was entitled to relief after the trial court entered a judgment for the subcontractor. Shen Valley Masonry, Inc. v. S.P. Cahill & Assocs., 58 Va. Cir. 396, 2002 Va. Cir. LEXIS 156 (Charlottesville 2002).

Postmark evidence. — Under former § 11-62.6 (see now § 2.2-4353), the date of the postmark was the date a payment under a contract was made, and where the evidence relating to the postmark showed that the contractor's payment to the subcontractor was not made within the seven days specified in the subcontract, the subcontractor was entitled to relief and the contractor was not entitled to postjudgment relief. Shen Valley Masonry, Inc. v. S.P. Cahill & Assocs., 58 Va. Cir. 396, 2002 Va. Cir. LEXIS 156 (Charlottesville 2002).

§ 2.2-4354. Payment clauses to be included in contracts. — Any contract awarded by any state agency, or any contract awarded by any agency of local government in accordance with § 2.2-4352, shall include:

1. A payment clause that obligates the contractor to take one of the two following actions within seven days after receipt of amounts paid to the contractor by the state agency or local government for work performed by the subcontractor under that contract:

a. Pay the subcontractor for the proportionate share of the total payment received from the agency attributable to the work performed by the subcontractor under that contract; or

b. Notify the agency and subcontractor, in writing, of his intention to withhold all or a part of the subcontractor's payment with the reason for nonpayment.

2. A payment clause that requires (i) individual contractors to provide their social security numbers and (ii) proprietorships, partnerships, and corporations to provide their federal employer identification numbers.

3. An interest clause that obligates the contractor to pay interest to the subcontractor on all amounts owed by the contractor that remain unpaid after seven days following receipt by the contractor of payment from the state

agency or agency of local government for work performed by the subcontractor under that contract, except for amounts withheld as allowed in subdivision 1.

4. An interest rate clause stating, "Unless otherwise provided under the terms of this contract, interest shall accrue at the rate of one percent per month."

Any such contract awarded shall further require the contractor to include in each of its subcontracts a provision requiring each subcontractor to include or otherwise be subject to the same payment and interest requirements with respect to each lower-tier subcontractor.

A contractor's obligation to pay an interest charge to a subcontractor pursuant to the payment clause in this section shall not be construed to be an obligation of the state agency or agency of local government. A contract modification shall not be made for the purpose of providing reimbursement for the interest charge. A cost reimbursement claim shall not include any amount for reimbursement for the interest charge. (1990, c. 824, § 11-62.11; 1992, c. 110; 2001, c. 844.)

CASE NOTES

Applied in In re Jones Constr. & Renovation, Inc., 337 B.R. 579, 2006 Bankr. LEXIS 852 (Bankr. E.D. Va. 2006).

§ **2.2-4355. Interest penalty; exceptions.** — A. Interest shall accrue, at the rate determined pursuant to subsection B, on all amounts owed by a state agency to a vendor that remain unpaid after seven days following the payment date. However, nothing in this section shall affect any contract providing for a different rate of interest, or for the payment of interest in a different manner.

B. The rate of interest charged a state agency pursuant to subsection A shall be the base rate on corporate loans (prime rate) at large United States money center commercial banks as reported daily in the publication entitled The Wall Street Journal. Whenever a split prime rate is published, the lower of the two rates shall be used. However, in no event shall the rate of interest charged exceed the rate of interest established pursuant to § 58.1-1812.

C. Notwithstanding subsection A, no interest penalty shall be charged when payment is delayed because of disagreement between a state agency and a vendor regarding the quantity, quality or time of delivery of goods or services or the accuracy of any invoice received for the goods or services. The exception from the interest penalty provided by this subsection shall apply only to that portion of a delayed payment that is actually the subject of the disagreement and shall apply only for the duration of the disagreement.

D. This section shall not apply to § 2.2-4333 pertaining to retainage on construction contracts, during the period of time prior to the date the final payment is due. Nothing contained herein shall prevent a contractor from receiving interest on such funds under an approved escrow agreement.

E. Notwithstanding subsection A, no interest penalty shall be paid to any debtor on any payment, or portion thereof, withheld pursuant to the Comptroller's Debt Setoff Program, as authorized by the Virginia Debt Collection Act (§ 2.2-4800 et seq.), commencing with the date the payment is withheld. If, as a result of an error, a payment or portion thereof is withheld, and it is determined that at the time of setoff no debt was owed to the Commonwealth, then interest shall accrue at the rate determined pursuant to subsection B on amounts withheld that remain unpaid after seven days following the payment date. (1984, c. 736, § 11-62.5; 1985, c. 101; 1992, c. 75; 2001, c. 844.)

§ **2.2-4356. Comptroller to file annual report.** — The Comptroller shall file an annual report with the Governor, the Senate Committee on Finance, the

House Committees on Finance and Appropriations on November 1 for the preceding fiscal year including (i) the number and dollar amounts of late payments by departments, institutions and agencies, (ii) the total amount of interest paid and (iii) specific steps being taken to reduce the incidence of late payments. (1984, c. 736, § 11-62.7; 1985, c. 101; 1997, c. 165; 2001, c. 844.)

ARTICLE 5.

Remedies.

§ **2.2-4357. Ineligibility.** — A. Any bidder, offeror or contractor refused permission to participate, or disqualified from participation, in public contracts shall be notified in writing. Prior to the issuance of a written determination of disqualification or ineligibility, the public body shall (i) notify the bidder in writing of the results of the evaluation, (ii) disclose the factual support for the determination, and (iii) allow the bidder an opportunity to inspect any documents that relate to the determination, if so requested by the bidder within five business days after receipt of the notice.

Within ten business days after receipt of the notice, the bidder may submit rebuttal information challenging the evaluation. The public body shall issue its written determination of disqualification or ineligibility based on all information in the possession of the public body, including any rebuttal information, within five business days of the date the public body received such rebuttal information.

If the evaluation reveals that the bidder, offeror or contractor should be allowed permission to participate in the public contract, the public body shall cancel the proposed disqualification action. If the evaluation reveals that the bidder should be refused permission to participate, or disqualified from participation, in the public contract, the public body shall so notify the bidder, offeror or contractor. The notice shall state the basis for the determination, which shall be final unless the bidder appeals the decision within ten days after receipt of the notice by invoking administrative procedures meeting the standards of § 2.2-4365, if available, or in the alternative by instituting legal action as provided in § 2.2-4364.

B. If, upon appeal, it is determined that the action taken was arbitrary or capricious, or not in accordance with the Constitution of Virginia, applicable state law or regulations, the sole relief shall be restoration of eligibility. (1982, c. 647, § 11-63; 1998, c. 753; 2001, c. 844.)

Cross references. — As to inapplicability of provisions of this article to contracts for advertising or publishing entered into by the Virginia Wine Board, see § 3.1-1064.7. For provision that this article shall not apply to contracts for the printing of ballots, statements of results, or other material essential to the conduct of an election, see § 24.2-602.

CASE NOTES

The Procurement Act does not provide a right of action to those not involved in the bidding and procurement process. Concerned Taxpayers v. County of Brunswick, 249 Va. 320, 455 S.E.2d 712 (1995) (decided under former corresponding provisions).

CIRCUIT COURT OPINIONS

Application. — Ten-day limitation period of § 2.2-4357, of the Virginia Public Procurement Act, § 2.2-4300 et seq., applies to an appeal of an agency decision, whether invoked by the administrative process or by legal action; thus, where university notified contractor that it was disqualified from the bidding process, and the contractor filed its declaratory judgment action more than 10 days after receipt of the disqualification letter, the contractor's appeal was time barred. Specialty Mech., L.L.C v. Va. Commonwealth Univ., 61 Va. Cir. 121, 2003 Va. Cir. LEXIS 241 (Richmond 2003).

§ **2.2-4358. Appeal of denial of withdrawal of bid.** — A. A decision denying withdrawal of bid under the provisions of § 2.2-4330 shall be final and conclusive unless the bidder appeals the decision within ten days after receipt of the decision by invoking administrative procedures meeting the standards of § 2.2-4365, if available, or in the alternative by instituting legal action as provided in § 2.2-4364.

B. If no bid bond was posted, a bidder refused withdrawal of a bid under the provisions of § 2.2-4330, prior to appealing, shall deliver to the public body a certified check or cash bond in the amount of the difference between the bid sought to be withdrawn and the next low bid. Such security shall be released only upon a final determination that the bidder was entitled to withdraw the bid.

C. If, upon appeal, it is determined that the decision refusing withdrawal of the bid was not (i) an honest exercise of discretion, but rather was arbitrary or capricious or (ii) in accordance with the Constitution of Virginia, applicable state law or regulation, or the terms or conditions of the Invitation to Bid, the sole relief shall be withdrawal of the bid. (1982, c. 647, § 11-64; 1985, c. 164; 1999, c. 1008; 2001, c. 844.)

§ **2.2-4359. Determination of nonresponsibility.** — A. Following public opening and announcement of bids received on an Invitation to Bid, the public body shall evaluate the bids in accordance with element 4 of the definition of "Competitive sealed bidding" in § 2.2-4301. At the same time, the public body shall determine whether the apparent low bidder is responsible. If the public body so determines, then it may proceed with an award in accordance with element 5 of the definition of "Competitive sealed bidding" in § 2.2-4301. If the public body determines that the apparent low bidder is not responsible, it shall proceed as follows:

1. Prior to the issuance of a written determination of nonresponsibility, the public body shall (i) notify the apparent low bidder in writing of the results of the evaluation, (ii) disclose the factual support for the determination, and (iii) allow the apparent low bidder an opportunity to inspect any documents that relate to the determination, if so requested by the bidder within five business days after receipt of the notice.

2. Within ten business days after receipt of the notice, the bidder may submit rebuttal information challenging the evaluation. The public body shall issue its written determination of responsibility based on all information in the possession of the public body, including any rebuttal information, within five business days of the date the public body received the rebuttal information. At the same time, the public body shall notify, with return receipt requested, the bidder in writing of its determination.

3. Such notice shall state the basis for the determination, which shall be final unless the bidder appeals the decision within ten days after receipt of the notice by invoking administrative procedures meeting the standards of § 2.2-4365, if available, or in the alternative by instituting legal action as provided in § 2.2-4364.

The provisions of this subsection shall not apply to procurements involving the prequalification of bidders and the rights of any potential bidders under such prequalification to appeal a decision that such bidders are not responsible.

B. If, upon appeal pursuant to § 2.2-4364 or § 2.2-4365, it is determined that the decision of the public body was not (i) an honest exercise of discretion, but rather was arbitrary or capricious or (ii) in accordance with the Constitution of Virginia, applicable state law or regulation, or the terms or conditions of the Invitation to Bid, and the award of the contract in question has not been made, the sole relief shall be a finding that the bidder is a responsible bidder for the contract in question or directed award as provided in subsection A of § 2.2-4364 or both.

If it is determined that the decision of the public body was not an honest exercise of discretion, but rather was arbitrary or capricious or not in accordance with the Constitution of Virginia, applicable state law or regulation, or the terms or conditions of the Invitation to Bid, and an award of the contract has been made, the relief shall be as set forth in subsection B of § 2.2-4360.

C. A bidder contesting a determination that he is not a responsible bidder for a particular contract shall proceed under this section, and may not protest the award or proposed award under the provisions of § 2.2-4360.

D. Nothing contained in this section shall be construed to require a public body, when procuring by competitive negotiation, to furnish a statement of the reasons why a particular proposal was not deemed to be the most advantageous. (1982, c. 647, § 11-65; 1997, c. 864; 1998, c. 753; 1999, c. 1008; 2001, c. 844.)

§ **2.2-4360. Protest of award or decision to award.** — A. Any bidder or offeror, who desires to protest the award or decision to award a contract shall submit the protest in writing to the public body, or an official designated by the public body, no later than ten days after the award or the announcement of the decision to award, whichever occurs first. Public notice of the award or the announcement of the decision to award shall be given by the public body in the manner prescribed in the terms or conditions of the Invitation to Bid or Request for Proposal. Any potential bidder or offeror on a contract negotiated on a sole source or emergency basis who desires to protest the award or decision to award such contract shall submit the protest in the same manner no later than ten days after posting or publication of the notice of such contract as provided in § 2.2-4303. However, if the protest of any actual or potential bidder or offeror depends in whole or in part upon information contained in public records pertaining to the procurement transaction that are subject to inspection under § 2.2-4342, then the time within which the protest shall be submitted shall expire ten days after those records are available for inspection by such bidder or offeror under § 2.2-4342, or at such later time as provided in this section. No protest shall lie for a claim that the selected bidder or offeror is not a responsible bidder or offeror. The written protest shall include the basis for the protest and the relief sought. The public body or designated official shall issue a decision in writing within ten days stating the reasons for the action taken. This decision shall be final unless the bidder or offeror appeals within ten days of receipt of the written decision by invoking administrative procedures meeting the standards of § 2.2-4365, if available, or in the alternative by instituting legal action as provided in § 2.2-4364. Nothing in this subsection shall be construed to permit a bidder to challenge the validity of the terms or conditions of the Invitation to Bid or Request for Proposal.

B. If prior to an award it is determined that the decision to award is arbitrary or capricious, then the sole relief shall be a finding to that effect. The public body shall cancel the proposed award or revise it to comply with the law. If, after an award, it is determined that an award of a contract was arbitrary or capricious, then the sole relief shall be as hereinafter provided.

Where the award has been made but performance has not begun, the performance of the contract may be enjoined. Where the award has been made and performance has begun, the public body may declare the contract void upon a finding that this action is in the best interest of the public. Where a contract is declared void, the performing contractor shall be compensated for the cost of performance up to the time of such declaration. In no event shall the performing contractor be entitled to lost profits.

C. Where a public body, an official designated by that public body, or an appeals board determines, after a hearing held following reasonable notice to all bidders, that there is probable cause to believe that a decision to award was based on fraud or corruption or on an act in violation of Article 6 (§ 2.2-4367 et seq.) of this chapter, the public body, designated official or appeals board may enjoin the award of the contract to a particular bidder. (1982, c. 647, § 11-66; 1985, c. 164; 1997, c. 864; 2000, c. 641; 2001, c. 844.)

CASE NOTES

Purpose of protest. — This section authorizes the filing of protests based upon matters relating to alleged deficiencies in the contract award, not for the purpose of mitigating damages. Lockheed Info. Mgt. Sys. v. Maximus Inc., 259 Va. 92, 524 S.E.2d 420 (2000) (decided under former corresponding provisions).

Privileged statements. — The protest procedure provided in this statute contains none of the safeguards identified as prerequisites for the application of the absolute privilege defense to statements made during a protest proceedings. Lockheed Info. Mgt. Sys. v. Maximus Inc., 259 Va. 92, 524 S.E.2d 420 (2000) (decided under former corresponding provisions).

By describing alternatives available to protesting bidder as "appeals," the General Assembly made it clear that the purpose of the action is to review the public body's written decision regarding the bidder's protest. Sabre Constr. Corp. v. County of Fairfax, 256 Va. 68, 501 S.E.2d 144 (1998) (decided under former corresponding provisions).

Phrase "within ten days" doesn't allow "appeal" to be filed prior to the public body's release of its written decision. Sabre Constr. Corp. v. County of Fairfax, 256 Va. 68, 501 S.E.2d 144 (1998) (decided under former corresponding provisions).

CIRCUIT COURT OPINIONS

Appeal before announcement of award not allowed. — Virginia Public Procurement Act, § 2.2-4300 et seq., did not permit an appeal before the public body's announcement of its decision; a contractor's protest, submitted in response to information that it would not be awarded a contract, was not capable of being appealed as it was filed before announcement of the award. John T. Moore & Assocs., P.C. v. Va. Commonwealth Univ., 69 Va. Cir. 200, 2005 Va. Cir. LEXIS 356 (Richmond 2005).

§ **2.2-4361. Effect of appeal upon contract.** — Pending final determination of a protest or appeal, the validity of a contract awarded and accepted in good faith in accordance with this chapter shall not be affected by the fact that a protest or appeal has been filed. (1982, c. 647, § 11-67; 2001, c. 844.)

§ **2.2-4362. Stay of award during protest.** — An award need not be delayed for the period allowed a bidder or offeror to protest, but in the event of a timely protest as provided in § 2.2-4360, or the filing of a timely legal action as provided in § 2.2-4364, no further action to award the contract shall be taken unless there is a written determination that proceeding without delay is necessary to protect the public interest or unless the bid or offer would expire. (1982, c. 647, § 11-68; 1997, c. 864; 2001, c. 844.)

§ **2.2-4363. Contractual disputes.** — A. Contractual claims, whether for money or other relief, shall be submitted in writing no later than 60 days after final payment. However, written notice of the contractor's intention to file a claim shall be given at the time of the occurrence or beginning of the work upon which the claim is based. Nothing herein shall preclude a contract from requiring submission of an invoice for final payment within a certain time after completion and acceptance of the work or acceptance of the goods. Pendency of claims shall not delay payment of amounts agreed due in the final payment.

B. Each public body shall include in its contracts a procedure for consideration of contractual claims. Such procedure, which may be contained in the contract or may be specifically incorporated into the contract by reference and made available to the contractor, shall establish a time limit for a final decision in writing by the public body. If the public body has established administrative procedures meeting the standards of § 2.2-4365, such procedures shall be contained in the contract or specifically incorporated in the contract by reference and made available to the contractor.

C. If, however, the public body fails to include in its contracts a procedure for consideration of contractual claims, the following procedure shall apply:

1. Contractual claims, whether for money or other relief, shall be submitted in writing no later than 60 days after receipt of final payment; however, written notice of the contractor's intention to file a claim shall be given at the time of the occurrence or at the beginning of the work upon which the claim is based.

2. No written decision denying a claim or addressing issues related to the claim shall be considered a denial of the claim unless the written decision is signed by the public body's chief administrative officer or his designee. The contractor may not institute legal action prior to receipt of the final written decision on the claim unless the public body fails to render a decision within 90 days of submission of the claim. Failure of the public body to render a decision within 90 days shall not result in the contractor being awarded the relief claimed or in any other relief or penalty. The sole remedy for the public body's failure to render a decision within 90 days shall be the contractor's right to institute immediate legal action.

D. A contractor may not invoke administrative procedures meeting the standards of § 2.2-4365, if available, or institute legal action as provided in § 2.2-4364, prior to receipt of the public body's decision on the claim, unless the public body fails to render such decision within the time specified in the contract or, if no time is specified, then within the time provided by subsection C. A failure of the public body to render a final decision within the time provided in subsection C shall be deemed a final decision denying the claim by the public body.

E. The decision of the public body shall be final and conclusive unless the contractor appeals within six months of the date of the final decision on the claim by the public body by invoking administrative procedures meeting the standards of § 2.2-4365, if available, or in the alternative by instituting legal action as provided in § 2.2-4364. (1982, c. 647, § 11-69; 2001, cc. 106, 844; 2005, c. 815.)

Editor's note. — Acts 2001, c. 106 amended § 11-69, from which this section is derived. Pursuant to § 30-152, Acts 2001, c. 106 has been given effect in this section as set out above. The 2001 amendment by c. 106, in subsection B, inserted "may be contained in the contract or," inserted "specifically," inserted "and made available to the contractor," and added the last sentence.

CASE NOTES

Editor's note. — Some of the cases below were decided under former § 11-35 et seq.

Time and form of notice dependent on circumstances. — This section does not specifically require that the notice of intent be separate and distinct from the claim itself in time or in form. The statute acknowledges that not all claims will arise under the same circumstances and, thus, the timing and form of an alleged notice of intent pursuant to this section requires an examination of the circumstances of each case. Dr. William E.S. Flory Small Bus.

Dev. Ctr., Inc. v. Commonwealth, 261 Va. 230, 541 S.E.2d 915, 2001 Va. LEXIS 39 (2001).

Extension of time to sue under tolling statute. — There is no conflict between this section and subdivision E 1 of § 8.01-229, because this section does not address the tolling of actions, which is the subject of subdivision E 1 of § 8.01-229. The time limit for filing suit established by this section thus does not preclude the extension of such limit due to application of the statutory tolling provision. Welding, Inc. v. Bland County Serv. Auth., 261 Va. 218, 541 S.E.2d 909, 2001 Va. LEXIS 36 (2001).

The submission of invoices did not qualify as compliance with the requirement in subsection A that a notice of intention to file a claim be filed with the commonwealth within a specified time. Dr. William E.S. Flory Small Bus. Dev. Ctr., Inc. v. Commonwealth, 261 Va. 230, 541 S.E.2d 915, 2001 Va. LEXIS 39 (2001).

Trial court review of public agency decision. — Appellate court upheld trial court's determination on issues of whether a joint venturer, which had contracted with a waste water treatment facility owner to construct such a facility, had filed its claims in a timely manner, whether it had waived certain claims, submitted time impact analyses for certain claims, and timely submitted a notice of claim for other claims pursuant to the venturer's appeal under § 2.2-4363; pursuant to the applicable review standard under § 8.01-680, the trial court's determinations were not plainly wrong in all but one instance, as there was evidentiary support in the record. Upper Occoquan Sewage Auth. v. Blake Constr. Co., 266 Va. 582, 587 S.E.2d 721, 2003 Va. LEXIS 110 (2003).

Applied in Blake Constr. Co./Poole & Kent v. Upper Occoquan Sewage Auth., 266 Va. 564, 587 S.E.2d 711, 2003 Va. LEXIS 108 (2003).

CIRCUIT COURT OPINIONS

County law consistent with State law. — Spotsylvania County has opted out of the Virginia Public Procurement Act, § 2.2-4300 et seq., under § 2.2-4343, and has adopted its own procurement policy, which is consistent with State law, except the county extends a 10-day grace period for giving notice of intention to submit a claim. MCI Constructors v. Spotsylvania County, 62 Va. Cir. 375, 2003 Va. Cir. LEXIS 115 (Spotsylvania County 2003).

Sovereign immunity applied to fraud in the inducement claim. — Limited abrogation of a school board's sovereign immunity under the Virginia Public Procurement Act, § 2.2-4300 et seq, applied only to breach of contract claims, not to claims for damages for fraud in the inducement. Alexandria City Sch. Bd. v. Fox-Seko Constr., Inc., — Va. Cir. —, 2007 Va. Cir. LEXIS 256 (Alexandria July 27, 2007).

Notice of intent to file claim need not be separate and distinct from the claim itself in time or in form. RGA/SSA Architects, L.C. v. Va. Commonwealth Univ., 61 Va. Cir. 730, 2002 Va. Cir. LEXIS 441 (Richmond 2002).

Time and form of notice depend on circumstances. — By identifying more than one event that triggers the filing of an intent to file a claim, subsection A of § 2.2-4363 acknowledges that not all claims will arise under the same circumstances; for example, a dispute over payment under the contract may not arise until the work is completed, preventing a contractor from giving notice of an intent to file a claim for such payment at the beginning of the work upon which the claim is based. RGA/SSA Architects, L.C. v. Va. Commonwealth Univ., 61 Va. Cir. 730, 2002 Va. Cir. LEXIS 441 (Richmond 2002).

Trial court properly overruled museum's special plea where it argued a general contractor's lawsuit against it for not paying the entire amount due under the parties' contract had to be dismissed because the contractor did not give 60 days' notice of its intent to submit a claim under the contract; in cases such as this, where the contractor's claim was simply for payment under its contract, requiring the contractor to give notice of an intent to submit a claim before the contractor knew that payment under the contract would not be made made no sense. In such cases, the notice of intent to file a claim was the claim itself. F. T. Evans, Inc. v. Sci. Museum, 61 Va. Cir. 317, 2003 Va. Cir. LEXIS 238 (Richmond 2003).

Suit timely filed. — Architect complied with the Virginia Public Procurement Act, specifically § 2.2-4363, by filing suit within six months of the date the university president recommended to the Virginia Comptroller that a certain payment be made to the architect, which formed the basis of the suit. RGA/SSA Architects, L.C. v. Va. Commonwealth Univ., 61 Va. Cir. 730, 2002 Va. Cir. LEXIS 441 (Richmond 2002).

Suit not timely filed. — Any matter that a contractor submitted to a school board under a contract as part of the contractor's first claim, reasserted to the board in the contractor's second claim to the school board, and then sought to raise as part of a counterclaim the school board for breach of contract was time-barred under subsection E of § 2.2-4363 because the matter was not timely filed. Alexandria City Sch. Bd. v. Fox-Seko Constr., Inc., — Va. Cir. —, 2007 Va. Cir. LEXIS 256 (Alexandria July 27, 2007).

Suit barred for failure to notify. — Contractor's breach of contract claim was barred against a municipal water authority with regard to a water treatment plant construction project as the contractor breached the contract by failing to give notice of the conflicts in the contract documents and drawings prior to proceeding with the work and failed to give timely notice of its claim as required by the contract and by this section. Modern Cont'l South v. Fairfax County Water Auth., 70 Va. Cir. 172, 2006 Va. Cir. LEXIS 39 (Fairfax County 2006).

Aggrieved party not required to quantify claimed damages. — County's fourth plea in bar alleging that the corporation's notice of suit it sent to the county was defective was rejected, as the statute regarding contractual disputes with local government entities did not require that the corporation quantify its claimed damages by specifically alleging the dollar amount of its claim at the time it gave notice to the county of its suit against the county. Convista, Inc. v. Fairfax County, 63 Va. Cir. 384, 2003 Va. Cir. LEXIS 217 (Fairfax County 2003).

§ 2.2-4364. Legal actions. — A. A bidder or offeror, actual or prospective, who is refused permission or disqualified from participation in bidding or competitive negotiation, or who is determined not to be a responsible bidder or offeror for a particular contract, may bring an action in the appropriate circuit court challenging that decision, which shall be reversed only if the petitioner establishes that the decision was not (i) an honest exercise of discretion, but rather was arbitrary or capricious; (ii) in accordance with the Constitution of Virginia, applicable state law or regulation, or the terms or conditions of the Invitation to Bid; or (iii) in the case of denial of prequalification, based upon the criteria for denial of prequalification set forth in subsection B of § 2.2-4317. In the event the apparent low bidder, having been previously determined by the public body to be not responsible in accordance with § 2.2-4301, is found by the court to be a responsible bidder, the court may direct the public body to award the contract to such bidder in accordance with the requirements of this section and the Invitation to Bid.

B. A bidder denied withdrawal of a bid under § 2.2-4358 may bring an action in the appropriate circuit court challenging that decision, which shall be reversed only if the bidder establishes that the decision of the public body was not (i) an honest exercise of discretion, but rather was arbitrary or capricious or (ii) in accordance with the Constitution of Virginia, applicable state law or regulation, or the terms or conditions of the Invitation to Bid.

C. A bidder, offeror or contractor, or a potential bidder or offeror on a contract negotiated on a sole source or emergency basis in the manner provided in § 2.2-4303, whose protest of an award or decision to award under § 2.2-4360 is denied, may bring an action in the appropriate circuit court challenging a proposed award or the award of a contract, which shall be reversed only if the petitioner establishes that the proposed award or the award is not (i) an honest exercise of discretion, but rather is arbitrary or capricious or (ii) in accordance with the Constitution of Virginia, applicable state law or regulation, or the terms and conditions of the Invitation to Bid or Request for Proposal.

D. If injunctive relief is granted, the court, upon request of the public body, shall require the posting of reasonable security to protect the public body.

E. A contractor may bring an action involving a contract dispute with a public body in the appropriate circuit court. Notwithstanding any other provision of law, the Comptroller shall not be named as a defendant in any action brought pursuant to this chapter or § 33.1-387, except for disputes involving contracts of the Office of the Comptroller or the Department of Accounts.

F. A bidder, offeror or contractor need not utilize administrative procedures meeting the standards of § 2.2-4365, if available, but if those procedures are invoked by the bidder, offeror or contractor, the procedures shall be exhausted prior to instituting legal action concerning the same procurement transaction unless the public body agrees otherwise.

G. Nothing herein shall be construed to prevent a public body from instituting legal action against a contractor. (1982, c. 647, § 11-70; 1985, c.

164; 1994, c. 918; 1995, c. 527; 1997, c. 864; 1998, cc. 205, 753; 1999, c. 1008; 2001, c. 844.)

CASE NOTES

Editor's note. — Most of the cases below were decided under former § 11-35 et seq.

Appellate jurisdiction for action protesting decision to award contract. — For an action protesting the decision to award a contract brought under this section and not under the administrative appeals procedure authorized by § 11-71 (now § 2.2-4365), appellate jurisdiction lies with the Supreme Court and not the Court of Appeals. Allstar Towing, Inc. v. City of Alexandria, 231 Va. 421, 344 S.E.2d 903 (1986).

Statute overrides contract language. — This section overrides language in a contract in which a contractor agrees to submit to the administrative review procedures created by a public entity; the statutory language is controlling and the contractor can choose to proceed directly in court without utilizing the public body's administrative review procedures. W.M. Schlosser Co. v. Fairfax County Redevelopment & Housing Auth., 975 F.2d 1075 (4th Cir. 1992).

When special limitation is part of statute creating substantive right as it is in this section, namely appealing the written decision of the public body within ten days, the limitation is not merely a procedural requirement, but a part of the newly created substantive cause of action. Special limitation is a condition precedent to maintaining the claim, and failure to comply with it bars the claim. Sabre Constr. Corp. v. County of Fairfax, 256 Va. 68, 501 S.E.2d 144 (1998).

Subsection A is limited to challenges of public body decisions which "disqualified" a bidder or offeror from participating in the process in any manner. It applies to decisions which exclude the bidder from the process, not to decisions which exclude a particular bid. Sabre Constr. Corp. v. County of Fairfax, 256 Va. 68, 501 S.E.2d 144 (1998).

Subsection A does not provide bidder with remedy independent of the one created by subsection C and § 11-66 (now § 2.2-4360) to challenge a public body's finding that a bid was nonresponsive. Sabre Constr. Corp. v. County of Fairfax, 256 Va. 68, 501 S.E.2d 144 (1998).

Action by contractors. — While contract suits against the Commonwealth were permitted to a limited extent, a direct contractual relationship was contemplated; thus, the trial court did not err in denying the surety's motions for judgment against the state transportation department, which the surety filed in an attempt to collect on work it performed after it took over work for the original contracting party after that party defaulted on the underlying construction projects, as the surety did not have a direct contractual relationship with the state transportation department and the surety could not show any Virginia law which waived the Commonwealth's sovereign immunity regarding the surety's equitable subrogation claim. XL Specialty Ins. Co. v. Commonwealth, 47 Va. App. 424, 624 S.E.2d 658, 2006 Va. App. LEXIS 14 (2006).

CIRCUIT COURT OPINIONS

Construction with other law. — Ten day limitation period of § 2.2-4357, of the Virginia Public Procurement Act, § 2.2-4300 et seq., applies to an appeal of an agency decision, whether invoked by the administrative process or by legal action; thus, where university notified contractor that it was disqualified from the bidding process, and the contractor filed its declaratory judgment action more than 10 days after receipt of the disqualification letter, the contractor's appeal was time barred. Specialty Mech., L.L.C v. Va. Commonwealth Univ., 61 Va. Cir. 121, 2003 Va. Cir. LEXIS 241 (Richmond 2003).

Appeal before announcement of award not allowed. — Virginia Public Procurement Act, § 2.2-4300 et seq., did not permit an appeal before the public body's announcement of its decision; a contractor's protest, submitted in response to information that it would not be awarded a contract, was not capable of being appealed as it was filed before announcement of the award. John T. Moore & Assocs., P.C. v. Va. Commonwealth Univ., 69 Va. Cir. 200, 2005 Va. Cir. LEXIS 356 (Richmond 2005).

Failure to comply with invitational bid. — Because a bidder failed to submit a bid that complied with all of the requirements of a city's invitation to bid, it could not be considered a "bidder" for purposes of subsection C of § 2.2-4364, and therefore, lacked standing to bring a breach of contract action against the city; therefore, the city was entitled to summary judgment. Corr. Prods. Co. v. City of Alexandria, — Va. Cir. —, 2006 Va. Cir. LEXIS 278 (Alexandria Nov. 3, 2006).

§ **2.2-4365. Administrative appeals procedure.** — A. A public body may establish an administrative procedure for hearing (i) protests of a decision to award or an award, (ii) appeals from refusals to allow withdrawal of bids, (iii) appeals from disqualifications and determinations of nonresponsibility, and (iv) appeals from decisions on disputes arising during the performance of a contract, or (v) any of these. Such administrative procedure shall provide for a hearing before a disinterested person or panel, the opportunity to present pertinent information and the issuance of a written decision containing findings of fact. The disinterested person or panel shall not be an employee of the governmental entity against whom the claim has been filed. The findings of fact shall be final and conclusive and shall not be set aside unless the same are (a) fraudulent, arbitrary or capricious; (b) so grossly erroneous as to imply bad faith; or (c) in the case of denial of prequalification, the findings were not based upon the criteria for denial of prequalification set forth in subsection B of § 2.2-4317. No determination on an issue of law shall be final if appropriate legal action is instituted in a timely manner.

B. Any party to the administrative procedure, including the public body, shall be entitled to institute judicial review if such action is brought within thirty days of receipt of the written decision. (1982, c. 647, § 11-71; 1994, cc. 660, 918; 2001, c. 844.)

CASE NOTES

Editor's note. — The case below was decided under former § 11-35 et seq.

An employee of the governmental entity against whom a claim has been filed cannot be deemed a disinterested person within the intendment of subsection A of this section. W.M. Schlosser Co. v. Board of Supvrs., 245 Va. 451, 428 S.E.2d 919 (1993).

§ **2.2-4366. Alternative dispute resolution.** — Public bodies may enter into agreements to submit disputes arising from contracts entered into pursuant to this chapter to arbitration and utilize mediation and other alternative dispute resolution procedures. However, such procedures entered into by the Commonwealth, or any department, institution, division, commission, board or bureau thereof, shall be nonbinding and subject to § 2.2-514, as applicable. Alternative dispute resolution procedures entered into by school boards shall be nonbinding. (1995, c. 760, § 11-71.1; 2001, c. 844.)

Michie's Jurisprudence. — For related discussion, see 2A M.J. Arbitration and Award, § 4.

CIRCUIT COURT OPINIONS

Arbitration provisions. — Because the law during the relevant time period, former § 11-71.1, authorized public bodies to enter into agreements to submit contractual disputes to arbitration, an arbitration agreement in the parties' contract for the construction of a fire station was binding on a city. City of Portsmouth v. Cederquist Rodriguez Ripley, P.C., 72 Va. Cir. 405, 2007 Va. Cir. LEXIS 145 (Portsmouth 2007).

Article 6.

Ethics in Public Contracting.

§ **2.2-4367. Purpose.** — The provisions of this article supplement, but shall not supersede, other provisions of law including, but not limited to, the State and Local Government Conflict of Interests Act (§ 2.2-3100 et seq.), the

Virginia Governmental Frauds Act (§ 18.2-498.1 et seq.), and Articles 2 (§ 18.2-438 et seq.) and 3 (§ 18.2-446 et seq.) of Chapter 10 of Title 18.2.

The provisions of this article shall apply notwithstanding the fact that the conduct described may not constitute a violation of the State and Local Government Conflict of Interests Act. (1982, c. 647, § 11-72; 1987, Sp. Sess., c. 1; 2001, c. 844.)

Cross references. — As to orientation course for state filers, see § 2.2-3128. As to requirements for prequalification of prospective contractors, see § 2.2-4317.

§ **2.2-4368. Definitions.** — As used in this article:

"Immediate family" means a spouse, children, parents, brothers and sisters, and any other person living in the same household as the employee.

"Official responsibility" means administrative or operating authority, whether intermediate or final, to initiate, approve, disapprove or otherwise affect a procurement transaction, or any claim resulting therefrom.

"Pecuniary interest arising from the procurement" means a personal interest in a contract as defined in the State and Local Government Conflict of Interests Act (§ 2.2-3100 et seq.).

"Procurement transaction" means all functions that pertain to the obtaining of any goods, services or construction, including description of requirements, selection and solicitation of sources, preparation and award of contract, and all phases of contract administration.

"Public employee" means any person employed by a public body, including elected officials or appointed members of governing bodies. (1982, c. 647, § 11-73; 1987, Sp. Sess., c. 1; 2001, c. 844.)

§ **2.2-4369. Proscribed participation by public employees in procurement transactions.** — Except as may be specifically allowed by subdivisions A 2, 3 and 4 of § 2.2-3112, no public employee having official responsibility for a procurement transaction shall participate in that transaction on behalf of the public body when the employee knows that:

1. The employee is contemporaneously employed by a bidder, offeror or contractor involved in the procurement transaction;
2. The employee, the employee's partner, or any member of the employee's immediate family holds a position with a bidder, offeror or contractor such as an officer, director, trustee, partner or the like, or is employed in a capacity involving personal and substantial participation in the procurement transaction, or owns or controls an interest of more than five percent;
3. The employee, the employee's partner, or any member of the employee's immediate family has a pecuniary interest arising from the procurement transaction; or
4. The employee, the employee's partner, or any member of the employee's immediate family is negotiating, or has an arrangement concerning, prospective employment with a bidder, offeror or contractor. (1982, c. 647, § 11-74; 1985, c. 565; 1987, Sp. Sess., c. 1; 1997, c. 83; 2001, c. 844; 2003, c. 694.)

OPINIONS OF THE ATTORNEY GENERAL

Members of health regulatory boards. — It is not a violation of the State and Local Government Conflict of Interests Act or the Virginia Public Procurement Act for a member of a health regulatory board to vote to authorize the board to contract with or join an organization in the business of administering licensure examinations, where the Department of Health Professions reimburses the board member for per diem and expenses as allowable under state law and travel regulations. See opinion of Attorney General to Mr. Robert A. Nebiker, Director, Department of Health Professions, 05-029 (6/21/05).

It would be a violation of the State and Local Government Conflict of Interests Act or the

Virginia Public Procurement Act for a board member to vote to approve a contract or to join an organization where, at the time of the vote, there is an existing arrangement concerning prospective employment of such board member after departure from the board or the board member accepts the payment of monies in excess of allowable per diem payments and travel reimbursement allowances. See opinion of Attorney General to Mr. Robert A. Nebiker, Director, Department of Health Professions, 05-029 (6/21/05).

§ 2.2-4370. Disclosure of subsequent employment. — No public employee or former public employee having official responsibility for procurement transactions shall accept employment with any bidder, offeror or contractor with whom the employee or former employee dealt in an official capacity concerning procurement transactions for a period of one year from the cessation of employment by the public body unless the employee or former employee provides written notification to the public body, or a public official if designated by the public body, or both, prior to commencement of employment by that bidder, offeror or contractor. (1982, c. 647, § 11-76; 2001, c. 844.)

§ 2.2-4371. Prohibition on solicitation or acceptance of gifts; gifts by bidders, offerors, contractor or subcontractors prohibited. — A. No public employee having official responsibility for a procurement transaction shall solicit, demand, accept, or agree to accept from a bidder, offeror, contractor or subcontractor any payment, loan, subscription, advance, deposit of money, services or anything of more than nominal or minimal value, present or promised, unless consideration of substantially equal or greater value is exchanged. The public body may recover the value of anything conveyed in violation of this subsection.

B. No bidder, offeror, contractor or subcontractor shall confer upon any public employee having official responsibility for a procurement transaction any payment, loan, subscription, advance, deposit of money, services or anything of more than nominal value, present or promised, unless consideration of substantially equal or greater value is exchanged. (1982, c. 647, §§ 11-75, 11-77; 2001, c. 844.)

CASE NOTES

Constitutionality. — Section 11-75 (see now this section) is neither unconstitutionally vague nor overbroad. Vincent v. Commonwealth, Nos. 0416-95-1 and 0557-95-1 (Court of Appeals Jan. 30, 1996) (decided under prior law).

§ 2.2-4372. Kickbacks. — A. No contractor or subcontractor shall demand or receive from any of his suppliers or his subcontractors, as an inducement for the award of a subcontract or order, any payment, loan, subscription, advance, deposit of money, services or anything, present or promised, unless consideration of substantially equal or greater value is exchanged.

B. No subcontractor or supplier shall make, or offer to make, kickbacks as described in this section.

C. No person shall demand or receive any payment, loan, subscription, advance, deposit of money, services or anything of value in return for an agreement not to compete on a public contract.

D. If a subcontractor or supplier makes a kickback or other prohibited payment as described in this section, the amount thereof shall be conclusively presumed to have been included in the price of the subcontract or order and ultimately borne by the public body and shall be recoverable from both the maker and recipient. Recovery from one offending party shall not preclude recovery from other offending parties. (1982, c. 647, § 11-78; 2001, c. 844.)

§ 2.2-4373. Participation in bid preparation; limitation on submitting bid for same procurement. — No person who, for compensation, prepares an invitation to bid or request for proposal for or on behalf of a public body shall (i) submit a bid or proposal for that procurement or any portion thereof or (ii) disclose to any bidder or offeror information concerning the procurement that is not available to the public. However, a public body may permit such person to submit a bid or proposal for that procurement or any portion thereof if the public body determines that the exclusion of the person would limit the number of potential qualified bidders or offerors in a manner contrary to the best interests of the public body. (1997, c. 68, § 11-78.1; 2001, c. 844.)

Editor's note. — Acts 1997, c. 68, cl. 2, provides: "[t]hat the provisions of this act shall not affect the validity of any procurement contract entered into prior to July 1, 1997."

§ 2.2-4374. Purchase of building materials, etc., from architect or engineer prohibited. — A. No building materials, supplies or equipment for any building or structure constructed by or for a public body shall be sold by or purchased from any person employed as an independent contractor by the public body to furnish architectural or engineering services, but not construction, for such building or structure or from any partnership, association or corporation in which such architect or engineer has a personal interest as defined in § 2.2-3101.

B. No building materials, supplies or equipment for any building or structure constructed by or for a public body shall be sold by or purchased from any person who has provided or is currently providing design services specifying a sole source for such materials, supplies or equipment to be used in the building or structure to the independent contractor employed by the public body to furnish architectural or engineering services in which such person has a personal interest as defined in § 2.2-3101.

C. The provisions of subsections A and B shall not apply in cases of emergency or for transportation-related projects conducted by the Department of Transportation or the Virginia Port Authority. (1982, c. 647, § 11-79; 1993, c. 202; 1994, c. 882; 1996, c. 827; 2001, c. 844.)

§ 2.2-4375. Certification of compliance required; penalty for false statements. — A. Public bodies may require public employees having official responsibility for procurement transactions in which they participated to annually submit for such transactions a written certification that they complied with the provisions of this article.

B. Any public employee required to submit a certification as provided in subsection A who knowingly makes a false statement in the certification shall be punished as provided in § 2.2-4377. (1992, c. 761, § 11-79.1; 2001, c. 844.)

§ 2.2-4376. Misrepresentations prohibited. — No public employee having official responsibility for a procurement transaction shall knowingly falsify, conceal, or misrepresent a material fact; knowingly make any false, fictitious or fraudulent statements or representations; or make or use any false writing or document knowing it to contain any false, fictitious or fraudulent statement or entry. (1992, c. 761, § 11-79.2; 2001, c. 844.)

§ 2.2-4377. Penalty for violation. — Any person convicted of a willful violation of any provision of this article shall be guilty of a Class 1 misdemeanor. Upon conviction, any public employee, in addition to any other fine or penalty provided by law, shall forfeit his employment. (1982, c. 647, § 11-80; 2001, c. 844.)

Cross references. — As to punishment for Class 1 misdemeanors, see § 18.2-11.

CHAPTER 44.

Virginia Security for Public Deposits Act.

§ 2.2-4400. Short title; declaration of intent; applicability. — A. This chapter may be cited as the "Virginia Security for Public Deposits Act."

B. The General Assembly intends by this chapter to establish a single body of law applicable to the pledge of security as collateral for public funds on deposit in financial institutions so that the procedure for securing public deposits may be uniform throughout the Commonwealth.

C. All public deposits in qualified public depositories that are required to be secured by other provisions of law or by a public depositor shall be secured pursuant to this chapter.

D. This chapter, however, shall not apply to deposits made by the State Treasurer in out-of-state financial institutions related to master custody and tri-party repurchase agreements, provided (i) such deposits do not exceed ten percent of average monthly investment balances and (ii) the out-of-state financial institutions used for this purpose have a short-term deposit rating of not less than A-1 by Standard & Poor's Rating Service or P-1 by Moody's Investors Service, Inc., respectively. (1973, c. 172, §§ 2.1-359, 2.1-361; 1984, c. 135; 2000, cc. 335, 352; 2001, c. 844.)

Cross references. — As to security to be given by depositories holding state funds, see § 2.2-1815. As to the powers and duties of the Treasury Board, see § 2.2-2416. As to authority to allow a preference for community reinvestment activities in contracts for investment of funds, see § 2.2-4327.

Editor's note. — Acts 2008, c. 879, effective for the biennium ending June 30, 2010, in Item 208 K 2, provides: "Notwithstanding § 2.2-1802 of the Code of Virginia, Virginia Commonwealth University is authorized to maintain a local bank account in Qatar and non-U.S. countries to facilitate business operations the VCU Qatar Campus. These accounts are exempt from the Securities for Public Deposits Act, Title 2.2, Chapter 44 of the Code of Virginia."

§ 2.2-4401. Definitions. — As used in this chapter, unless the context requires a different meaning:

"Default or insolvency" includes, but shall not be limited to, the failure or refusal of any qualified public depository to return any public deposit upon demand or at maturity and the issuance of an order of supervisory authority restraining such depository from making payments of deposit liabilities or the appointment of a receiver for such depository.

"Eligible collateral" means securities of the character authorized as legal investments under the laws of the Commonwealth for public sinking funds or other public funds and securities acceptable under United States Treasury Department regulations as collateral for the security of treasury tax and loan accounts and Federal Home Loan Bank letters-of-credit that adhere to the guidelines as promulgated by the Treasury Board.

"Located in Virginia" means having a main office or branch office in the Commonwealth where deposits are accepted, checks are paid, and money is lent.

"Public deposit" means moneys of the Commonwealth or of any county, city, town or other political subdivision thereof, including moneys of any commission, institution, committee, board or officer of the foregoing and any state, circuit, county or municipal court, which moneys are deposited in any qualified public depository in any of the following types of accounts: nonnegotiable or registered time deposits, demand deposits, savings deposits, and any other transaction accounts, and security for such deposit is required by other provisions of law, or is required due to an election of the public depositor.

"Qualified public depository" means any national banking association, federal savings and loan association or federal savings bank located in Virginia, any bank, trust company or savings institution organized under Virginia law, or any state bank or savings institution organized under the laws of another state located in Virginia, that receives or holds public deposits that are secured pursuant to this chapter.

"Required collateral" of a qualified public depository means, (i) in the case of a bank, a sum equal to 50 percent of the actual public deposits not covered by federal deposit insurance held at the close of business on the last banking day in the month immediately preceding the date of any computation of such balance, or the average balance of all public deposits for such preceding month, whichever is greater, and (ii) in the case of a savings and loan association or savings bank, a sum equal to 100 percent of the average daily balance for the month immediately preceding the date of any computation of such balance of all public deposits not covered by federal deposit insurance held by such depository but shall not be less than 100 percent of the public deposits held by such depository at the close of business on the last banking day in such preceding month.

"Treasurer" and *"public depositor"* means the State Treasurer, a county, city, or town treasurer or director of finance or similar officer and the custodian of any other public deposits secured pursuant to this chapter.

"Treasury Board" means the Treasury Board of the Commonwealth created by § 2.2-2415. (1973, c. 172, § 2.1-360; 1984, c. 135; 1987, c. 718; 1996, c. 77; 1998, cc. 20, 21; 2001, c. 844; 2008, c. 7.)

Editor's note. — Acts 2008, c. 879, effective for the biennium ending June 30, 2010, in Item 275 F, provides: "F.1. The State Treasurer is authorized to charge qualified public depositories holding public deposits, as defined in §2.2-4401, Code of Virginia, an annual administrative fee of not more that one-half of one basis point of their average public deposit balances over a twelve month period. The State Treasurer shall issue guidelines to effect the implementation of this fee. However, the total fees collected from all qualified depositories shall not exceed $100,000 in any one year.

"2. Any regulations or guidelines necessary to implement or change the amount of the fee may be adopted without complying with the Administrative Process Act (§2.2-4000 et seq.) provided that input is solicited from qualified public depositories. Such input requires only that notice and an opportunity to submit written comments be given."

The 2008 amendments. — The 2008 amendment by c. 7, effective February 19, 2008, alphabetized the defined terms within the section and added the definition of "Located in Virginia"; in the definition of "Qualified public depository," inserted "or any state bank or savings institution organized under the laws of another state located in Virginia" and made a related change; and in the definition of "Required collateral," inserted "not covered by federal deposit insurance" twice and made a stylistic change.

§ 2.2-4402. Collateral for public deposits. — Every qualified public depository shall deposit with the State Treasurer, or, with the approval of the Treasury Board, with the Federal Reserve Bank of Richmond or any other bank or trust company located within or without the Commonwealth, eligible collateral equal to or in excess of the required collateral of such depository to be held subject to the order of the Treasury Board. Eligible collateral shall be valued as determined by the Treasury Board. Substitutions and withdrawals of eligible collateral may be made from time to time under regulations issued by the Treasury Board.

Each qualified public depository shall, at the time of the deposit of eligible collateral, deliver to the State Treasurer a power of attorney authorizing him to transfer any registered securities deposited, or any part thereof, for the purpose of paying any of the liabilities provided for in this chapter.

Notwithstanding any other provisions of law, no depository shall be required to give bond or pledge securities in the manner herein provided for the purpose of securing deposits received or held in the trust department of the depository and that are secured as required by § 6.1-21 or that are secured pursuant to Title 12, § 92a of the United States Code by securities of the classes prescribed by § 6.1-21.

No qualified public depository shall accept or retain any public deposit that is required to be secured unless it has deposited eligible collateral equal to its required collateral with some proper depository pursuant to this chapter. (1973, c. 172, § 2.1-362; 2001, c. 844.)

§ 2.2-4403. Procedure for payment of losses where depository is bank. — When the Treasury Board is advised by any treasurer or otherwise determines that a default or insolvency has occurred with regard to a qualified public depository that is a bank, it shall as promptly as practicable make payment to the proper treasurer of all funds subject to such default or insolvency, pursuant to the following procedures:

1. The Treasury Board and the treasurer shall ascertain the amount of public funds on deposit with the qualified public depository in default or insolvent that are secured pursuant to this chapter, either with the cooperation of the Commissioner of Financial Institutions or receiver appointed for such depository or by any other means available, and the amount of deposit insurance applicable to such deposits.

2. The amount of such public deposits ascertained as provided in subdivision 1, net of applicable deposit insurance, shall be assessed by the Treasury Board first against the depository in default or insolvent to the extent of the full realizable current market value of the collateral deposited by it to secure its public deposits, and second, to the extent that such collateral is insufficient to satisfy the liability of the depository upon its deposits secured pursuant to this chapter against each of the other qualified public depositories according to the ratio that the average daily balance for each month of the secured public deposits held by the depository during the twelve calendar months immediately preceding the date of the default or insolvency with respect to which the assessment is made bears to the total average daily balance for each month of all secured public deposits held by all qualified public depositories that are banks, other than the defaulting depository, during those twelve calendar months.

3. Assessments made by the Treasury Board shall be payable on the second business day following demand, and in case of the failure of any qualified

public depository to pay such assessment when due, the State Treasurer shall promptly take possession of the eligible collateral deposited with him or with the Federal Reserve Bank of Richmond or other bank or trust company pursuant to this chapter and liquidate the same to the extent necessary to pay such assessment and turn over such amounts received to the Treasury Board.

4. Upon receipt of such assessment, payments or the proceeds of the eligible collateral liquidated to pay such assessments from the State Treasurer, the Treasury Board shall reimburse the public depositors to the extent of the depository's deposit liability to them, net of any applicable deposit insurance. (1973, c. 172, § 2.1-363; 1978, c. 14; 1984, c. 135; 2001, c. 844.)

§ 2.2-4404. Procedure for payment of losses where depository is savings bank or savings and loan association. — When the Treasury Board is advised by any treasurer or otherwise determines that a default or insolvency has occurred with regard to a qualified public depository that is a savings bank or a savings and loan association, it shall as promptly as practicable make payment to the proper treasurer of all funds subject to such default or insolvency, pursuant to the following procedures:

1. The Treasury Board and the treasurer shall ascertain the amount of public funds on deposit with the qualified public depository in default or insolvent that are secured pursuant to this chapter, either with the cooperation of the Commissioner of Financial Institutions or receiver appointed for such depository or by any other means available, and the amount of deposit insurance applicable to such deposits.

2. The amount of such public deposits ascertained as provided in subdivision 1 net of applicable deposit insurance, shall be assessed by the Treasury Board against the depository in default or insolvent. The State Treasurer shall promptly take possession of such of the eligible collateral deposited by such depository with him, or with any other depository pursuant to this chapter, as is necessary to satisfy the assessment of the Treasury Board and shall liquidate the same and turn over the proceeds thereof to the Treasury Board.

3. Upon receipt from the State Treasurer of the payments or proceeds of the eligible collateral liquidated to pay such assessments from the State Treasurer, the Treasury Board shall reimburse the public depositors to the extent of the depository's deposit liability to them, net of any applicable deposit insurance. (1984, c. 135, § 2.1-363.1; 2001, c. 844.)

§ 2.2-4405. Powers of Treasury Board relating to the administration of this chapter. — The Treasury Board shall have power to:

1. Make and enforce regulations necessary and proper to the full and complete performance of its functions under this chapter;

2. Prescribe regulations fixing terms and conditions consistent with this chapter under which public deposits may be received and held;

3. Require such additional collateral, in excess of the required collateral of any qualified public depository, of any and all such depositories as it may determine prudent under the circumstances;

4. Determine what securities shall be acceptable as eligible collateral, and to fix the percentage of face value or market value of such securities that can be used to secure public deposits;

5. Require any qualified public depository to furnish such information concerning its public deposits; and

6. Determine when a default or insolvency has occurred and to take such action as it may deem advisable for the protection, collection, compromise or settlement of any claim arising in case of default or insolvency. (1973, c. 172, § 2.1-364; 2001, c. 844.)

§ 2.2-4406. Subrogation of Treasury Board to depositor's rights; payment of sums received from distribution of assets. — Upon payment in full to any public depositor, the Treasury Board shall be subrogated to all of such depositor's rights, title and interest against the depository in default or insolvent and shall share in any distribution of its assets ratably with other depositors. Any sums received from any such distribution shall be paid to the other qualified public depositories against which assessments were made, in proportion to such assessments, net of any proper expense of the Treasury Board in enforcing any such claim. (1973, c. 172, § 2.1-365; 2001, c. 844.)

§ 2.2-4407. Deposit of public funds in qualified public depository mandatory. — No public deposit that is required to be secured pursuant to this chapter shall be made except in a qualified public depository. (1973, c. 172, § 2.1-366; 2001, c. 844.)

§ 2.2-4408. Authority to deposit public funds. — A. All treasurers and public depositors are hereby authorized to deposit funds under their control in qualified public depositories securing public deposits pursuant to this chapter.

B. Local officials handling public funds in the Commonwealth may not require from a depository institution any pledge of collateral for their deposits in such institution which is in excess of the requirements of this chapter. (1973, c. 172, § 2.1-367; 1980, c. 538, § 2.1-234.5; 1998, cc. 20, 21; 2001, c. 844.)

§ 2.2-4409. Authority to secure public deposits; acceptance of liabilities and duties by public depositories. — All institutions located in the Commonwealth that are permitted to hold and receive public deposits are hereby authorized to secure such deposits in accordance with this chapter.

Any institution accepting a public deposit that is required to be secured pursuant to this chapter shall be deemed to have accepted the liabilities and duties imposed upon it pursuant to this chapter with respect to the deposit. (1973, c. 172, § 2.1-368; 2001, c. 844.)

§ 2.2-4410. Liability of treasurers or public depositors. — When deposits are made in accordance with this chapter no treasurer or public depositor shall be liable for any loss thereof resulting from the failure or default of any depository in the absence of negligence, malfeasance, misfeasance, or nonfeasance on his part or on the part of his assistants or employees. (1973, c. 172, § 2.1-370; 2001, c. 844.)

§ 2.2-4411. Reports of public depositories. — Within ten days after the end of each calendar month or when requested by the Treasury Board each qualified public depository shall submit to the Treasury Board a written report, under oath, indicating (i) the total amount of public deposits held by it at the close of business on the last banking day in the month, (ii) the average daily balance for the month of all secured public deposits held by it during the month, (iii) a detailed schedule of pledged collateral at its current asset value for purposes of collateral at the close of business on the last banking day in the month, and (iv) any other information with respect to its secured public deposits that may be required by the Treasury Board.

Each qualified public depository shall also furnish at the same time to each public depositor for which it holds deposits and that makes a written request therefor a schedule of the secured public deposits to the credit of such depositor as of the close of business on the last banking day in the month and the total amount of all secured public deposits held by it upon such date. (1973, c. 172, § 2.1-369; 1979, c. 154; 2001, c. 844.)

CHAPTER 45.

INVESTMENT OF PUBLIC FUNDS ACT.

§ 2.2-4500. Legal investments for public sinking funds. — The Commonwealth, all public officers, municipal corporations, other political subdivisions and all other public bodies of the Commonwealth may invest any sinking funds belonging to them or within their control in the following securities:

1. Bonds, notes and other evidences of indebtedness of the Commonwealth, and securities unconditionally guaranteed as to the payment of principal and interest by the Commonwealth.

2. Bonds, notes and other obligations of the United States, and securities unconditionally guaranteed as to the payment of principal and interest by the United States, or any agency thereof. The evidences of indebtedness enumerated by this subdivision may be held directly, or in the form of repurchase agreements collateralized by such debt securities, or in the form of securities of any open-end or closed-end management type investment company or investment trust registered under the Investment Company Act of 1940, provided that the portfolio of such investment company or investment trust is limited to such evidences of indebtedness, or repurchase agreements collateralized by such debt securities, or securities of other such investment companies or investment trusts whose portfolios are so restricted.

3. Bonds, notes and other evidences of indebtedness of any county, city, town, district, authority or other public body of the Commonwealth upon which there is no default; provided, that such bonds, notes and other evidences of indebtedness of any county, city, town, district, authority or other public body are either direct legal obligations of, or those unconditionally guaranteed as to the payment of principal and interest by the county, city, town, district, authority or other public body in question; and revenue bonds issued by agencies or authorities of the Commonwealth or its political subdivisions upon which there is no default.

4. Bonds and other obligations issued, guaranteed or assumed by the International Bank for Reconstruction and Development, bonds and other obligations issued, guaranteed or assumed by the Asian Development Bank

and bonds and other obligations issued, guaranteed or assumed by the African Development Bank.

5. Savings accounts or time deposits in any bank or savings institution within the Commonwealth provided the bank or savings institution is approved for the deposit of other funds of the Commonwealth or other political subdivision of the Commonwealth. (1956, c. 184, § 2-297; 1958, c. 102; 1966, c. 677, § 2.1-327; 1970, c. 75; 1974, c. 288; 1986, c. 270; 1988, cc. 526, 834; 1996, cc. 77, 508; 2001, c. 844.)

Cross references. — As to the purpose of the Local Government Investment Pool Act, see § 2.2-4601. As to the creation of the local government investment pool, see § 2.2-4602.

§ 2.2-4501. Legal investments for other public funds. — A. The Commonwealth, all public officers, municipal corporations, other political subdivisions and all other public bodies of the Commonwealth may invest any and all moneys belonging to them or within their control, other than sinking funds, in the following:

1. Stocks, bonds, notes, and other evidences of indebtedness of the Commonwealth and those unconditionally guaranteed as to the payment of principal and interest by the Commonwealth.

2. Bonds, notes and other obligations of the United States, and securities unconditionally guaranteed as to the payment of principal and interest by the United States, or any agency thereof. The evidences of indebtedness enumerated by this subdivision may be held directly, or in the form of repurchase agreements collateralized by such debt securities, or in the form of securities of any open-end or closed-end management type investment company or investment trust registered under the Investment Company Act of 1940, provided that the portfolio of such investment company or investment trust is limited to such evidences of indebtedness, or repurchase agreements collateralized by such debt securities, or securities of other such investment companies or investment trusts whose portfolios are so restricted.

3. Stocks, bonds, notes and other evidences of indebtedness of any state of the United States upon which there is no default and upon which there has been no default for more than ninety days; provided, that within the twenty fiscal years next preceding the making of such investment, such state has not been in default for more than ninety days in the payment of any part of principal or interest of any debt authorized by the legislature of such state to be contracted.

4. Stocks, bonds, notes and other evidences of indebtedness of any county, city, town, district, authority or other public body in the Commonwealth upon which there is no default; provided, that if the principal and interest be payable from revenues or tolls and the project has not been completed, or if completed, has not established an operating record of net earnings available for payment of principal and interest equal to estimated requirements for that purpose according to the terms of the issue, the standards of judgment and care required in Article 2 (§ 26-45.3 et seq.) of Chapter 3 of Title 26, without reference to this section, shall apply.

In any case in which an authority, having an established record of net earnings available for payment of principal and interest equal to estimated requirements for that purpose according to the terms of the issue, issues additional evidences of indebtedness for the purposes of acquiring or constructing additional facilities of the same general character that it is then operating, such additional evidences of indebtedness shall be governed by the provisions of this section without limitation.

5. Legally authorized stocks, bonds, notes and other evidences of indebtedness of any city, county, town or district situated in any one of the states of the

United States upon which there is no default and upon which there has been no default for more than ninety days; provided, that (i) within the twenty fiscal years next preceding the making of such investment, such city, county, town or district has not been in default for more than ninety days in the payment of any part of principal or interest of any stock, bond, note or other evidence of indebtedness issued by it; (ii) such city, county, town or district shall have been in continuous existence for at least twenty years; (iii) such city, county, town or district has a population, as shown by the federal census next preceding the making of such investment, of not less than 25,000 inhabitants; (iv) the stocks, bonds, notes or other evidences of indebtedness in which such investment is made are the direct legal obligations of the city, county, town or district issuing the same; (v) the city, county, town or district has power to levy taxes on the taxable real property therein for the payment of such obligations without limitation of rate or amount; and (vi) the net indebtedness of such city, county, town or district (including the issue in which such investment is made), after deducting the amount of its bonds issued for self-sustaining public utilities, does not exceed ten percent of the value of the taxable property in such city, county, town or district, to be ascertained by the valuation of such property therein for the assessment of taxes next preceding the making of such investment.

6. Bonds and other obligations issued, guaranteed or assumed by the International Bank for Reconstruction and Development, by the Asian Development Bank or by the African Development Bank.

B. This section shall not apply to funds authorized by law to be invested by the Virginia Retirement System or to deferred compensation plan funds to be invested pursuant to § 51.1-601 or to funds contributed by a locality to a pension program for the benefit of any volunteer fire department and rescue squad established pursuant to § 15.2-955.

C. Investments made prior to July 1, 1991, pursuant to § 51.1-601 are ratified and deemed valid to the extent that such investments were made in conformity with the standards set forth in Chapter 6 (§ 51.1-600 et seq.) of Title 51.1. (1956, c. 184, § 2-298; 1966, c. 677, § 2.1-328; 1980, c. 596; 1988, c. 834; 1991, c. 379; 1992, c. 810; 1996, c. 508; 1999, c. 772; 2001, c. 844; 2007, c. 67; 2008, c. 295.)

The 2007 amendments. — The 2007 amendment by c. 67 rewrote subsection B, which read: "This section shall not apply to retirement funds and deferred compensation plans to be invested pursuant to §§ 51.1-124.30 through 51.1-124.35 or § 51.1-601."

The 2008 amendments. — The 2008 amendment by c. 295 inserted "or to funds contributed by a locality to a pension program for the benefit of any volunteer fire department and rescue squad established pursuant to § 15.2-955" at the end of subsection B.

§ 2.2-4502. Investment of funds of Commonwealth, political subdivisions, and public bodies in "prime quality" commercial paper. — A. The Commonwealth, all public officers, municipal corporations, other political subdivisions and all other public bodies of the Commonwealth may invest any and all moneys belonging to them or within their control other than sinking funds in "prime quality" commercial paper, with a maturity of 270 days or less, of issuing corporations organized under the laws of the United States, or of any state thereof including paper issued by banks and bank holding companies. "Prime quality" shall be as rated by at least two of the following: Moody's Investors Service, Inc., within its NCO/Moody's rating of prime 1, by Standard & Poor's, Inc., within its rating of A-1, by Fitch Investor's Services, Inc., within its rating of F-1, by Duff and Phelps, Inc., within its rating of D-1, or by their corporate successors, provided that at the time of any such investment:

1. The issuing corporation, or its guarantor, has a net worth of at least fifty million dollars; and

2. The net income of the issuing corporation, or its guarantor, has averaged three million dollars per year for the previous five years; and

3. All existing senior bonded indebtedness of the issuer, or its guarantor, is rated "A" or better or the equivalent rating by at least two of the following: Moody's Investors Service, Inc., Standard & Poor's, Inc., Fitch Investor's Services, Inc., or Duff and Phelps, Inc.

Not more than thirty-five percent of the total funds available for investment may be invested in commercial paper, and not more than five percent of the total funds available for investment may be invested in commercial paper of any one issuing corporation.

B. Notwithstanding subsection A, the Commonwealth, municipal corporations, other political subdivisions and public bodies of the Commonwealth may invest any and all moneys belonging to them or within their control, except for sinking funds, in commercial paper other than "prime quality" commercial paper as defined in this section provided that:

1. Prior written approval is obtained from the governing board, committee or other entity that determines investment policy. The Treasury Board shall be the governing body for the Commonwealth; and

2. A written internal credit review justifying the creditworthiness of the issuing corporation is prepared in advance and made part of the purchase file. (1973, c. 232, § 2.1-328.1; 1974, c. 295; 1976, c. 665; 1986, c. 170; 1987, c. 73; 1988, c. 834; 1992, c. 769; 2001, c. 844.)

§ **2.2-4503:** Not set out. (2001, c. 844.)

Editor's note. — This section, relating to investment of public funds of Fairfax County, was enacted by Acts 2001, c. 844 (formerly by Acts 1980, c. 50 as § 2.1-328.2). In furtherance of the general policy of the Commission to include in the Code only provisions having general and permanent application, this section, which is limited in its purpose and scope, is not set out here, but attention is called to it by this reference.

§ **2.2-4504. Investment of funds by the Commonwealth and political subdivisions in bankers' acceptances.** — Notwithstanding any provisions of law to the contrary, all public officers, municipal corporations, other political subdivisions and all other public bodies of the Commonwealth may invest any and all moneys belonging to them or within their control other than sinking funds in bankers' acceptances. (1981, c. 18, § 2.1-328.3; 1988, c. 834; 2001, c. 844.)

§ **2.2-4505. Investment in certificates representing ownership of treasury bond principal at maturity or its coupons for accrued periods.** — Notwithstanding any provision of law to the contrary, the Commonwealth, all public officers, municipal corporations, other political subdivisions and all other public bodies of the Commonwealth may invest any and all moneys belonging to them or within their control, in certificates representing ownership of either treasury bond principal at maturity or its coupons for accrued periods. The underlying United States Treasury bonds or coupons shall be held by a third-party independent of the seller of such certificates. (1983, c. 117, § 2.1-328.5; 1985, c. 352; 1988, c. 834; 2001, c. 844.)

§ **2.2-4506. Securities lending.** — Notwithstanding any provision of law to the contrary, the Commonwealth, all public officers, municipal corporations, political subdivisions and all public bodies of the Commonwealth may engage in securities lending from the portfolio of investments of which they have custody and control, other than sinking funds. The Treasury Board shall develop guidelines with which such securities lending shall fully comply. Such guidelines shall ensure that the state treasury is at all times fully collateralized by the borrowing institution. (1983, c. 268, § 2.1-328.6; 2001, c. 844.)

§ 2.2-4507. Investment of funds in overnight, term and open repurchase agreements. — Notwithstanding any provision of law to the contrary, the Commonwealth, all public officers, municipal corporations, other political subdivisions and all other public bodies of the Commonwealth, may invest any and all moneys belonging to them or within their control in overnight, term and open repurchase agreements that are collateralized with securities that are approved for direct investment. (1985, c. 352, § 2.1-328.8; 1988, c. 834; 2001, c. 844.)

§ 2.2-4508. Investment of certain public moneys in certain mutual funds. — Notwithstanding any provision of law to the contrary, the Commonwealth, all public officers, municipal corporations, other political subdivisions and all other public bodies of the Commonwealth may invest any and all moneys belonging to them or within their control, other than sinking funds that are governed by the provisions of § 2.2-4500, in one or more open-end investment funds, provided that the funds are registered under the Securities Act (§ 13.1-501 et seq.) of the Commonwealth or the Federal Investment Co. Act of 1940, and that the investments by such funds are restricted to investments otherwise permitted by law for political subdivisions as set forth in this chapter, or investments in other such funds whose portfolios are so restricted. (1986, c. 170, § 2.1-328.9; 1988, c. 834; 1996, c. 508; 2001, c. 844.)

§ 2.2-4509. Investment of funds in negotiable certificates of deposit and negotiable bank deposit notes. — Notwithstanding any provision of law to the contrary, the Commonwealth and all public officers, municipal corporations, and other political subdivisions and all other public bodies of the Commonwealth may invest any or all of the moneys belonging to them or within their control, other than sinking funds, in negotiable certificates of deposit and negotiable bank deposit notes of domestic banks and domestic offices of foreign banks with a rating of at least A-1 by Standard & Poor's and P-1 by Moody's Investor Service, Inc., for maturities of one year or less, and a rating of at least AA by Standard & Poor's and Aa by Moody's Investor Service, Inc., for maturities over one year and not exceeding five years. (1998, cc. 20, 21, § 2.1-328.15; 2001, c. 844.)

§ 2.2-4510. Investment of funds in corporate notes. — A. Notwithstanding any provision of law to the contrary, the Commonwealth, all public officers, municipal corporations, other political subdivisions and all other public bodies of the Commonwealth may invest any and all moneys belonging to them or within their control, other than sinking funds, in high quality corporate notes with a rating of at least Aa by Moody's Investors Service, Inc., and a rating of at least AA by Standard and Poors, Inc., and a maturity of no more than five years.

B. Notwithstanding any provision of law to the contrary, any qualified public entity of the Commonwealth may invest any and all moneys belonging to it or within its control, other than sinking funds, in high quality corporate notes with a rating of at least A by two rating agencies, one of which shall be either Moody's Investors Service, Inc., or Standard and Poors, Inc.

As used in this section, *"qualified public entity"* means any state agency or institution of the Commonwealth, having an internal or external public funds manager with professional investment management capabilities.

C. Notwithstanding any provision of law to the contrary, the Department of the Treasury may invest any and all moneys belonging to it or within its control, other than sinking funds, in high quality corporate notes with a rating of at least BBB or Baa2 by two rating agencies, one of which shall be Moody's Investors Service, Inc., or Standard and Poors, Inc. With regard to investment securities rated below A, the Commonwealth Treasury Board shall establish strict investment guidelines concerning the investment in such securities and monitor the performance of the securities for compliance with the investment guidelines. (1987, c. 187, § 2.1-328.10; 1988, c. 834; 1994, c. 145; 2001, c. 844; 2002, cc. 18, 438; 2005, c. 30.)

§ 2.2-4511. Investment of funds in asset-backed securities. — Notwithstanding any provision of law to the contrary, any qualified public entity of the Commonwealth may invest any and all moneys belonging to it or within its control, other than sinking funds, in asset-backed securities with a duration of no more than five years and a rating of no less than AAA by two rating agencies, one of which must be either Moody's Investors Service, Inc., or Standard and Poors, Inc.

As used in this section, *"qualified public entity"* means any state agency, institution of the Commonwealth or statewide authority created under the laws of the Commonwealth having an internal or external public funds manager with professional investment management capabilities. (1994, c. 145, § 2.1-328.13; 1997, c. 29; 2001, c. 844.)

§ 2.2-4512. Investment of funds by State Treasurer in obligations of foreign sovereign governments. — Notwithstanding any provision of law to the contrary, the State Treasurer may invest unexpended or excess moneys in any fund or account over which he has custody and control, other than sinking funds, in fully hedged debt obligations of sovereign governments and companies that are fully guaranteed by such sovereign governments, with a rating of at least AAA by Moody's Investors Service, Inc., and a rating of at least AAA by Standard and Poors, Inc., and a maturity of no more than five years.

Not more than ten percent of the total funds of the Commonwealth available for investment may be invested in the manner described in this section. (1988, c. 461, § 2.1-328.11; 2001, c. 844.)

§ 2.2-4513. Investments by transportation commissions. — Transportation commissions that provide rail service may invest in, if required as a condition to obtaining insurance, participate in, or purchase insurance provided by, foreign insurance companies that insure railroad operations. (1988, c. 834, § 2.1-328.12; 2001, c. 844.)

§ 2.2-4514. Commonwealth and its political subdivisions as trustee of public funds; standard of care in investing such funds. — Public funds held by the Commonwealth, public officers, municipal corporations, political subdivisions, and any other public body of the Commonwealth shall be held in trust for the citizens of the Commonwealth. Any investment of such funds pursuant to the provisions of this chapter shall be made solely in the interest of the citizens of the Commonwealth and with the care, skill, prudence, and diligence under the circumstances then prevailing that a prudent person acting in a like capacity and familiar with such matters would use in the conduct of an enterprise of a like character and with like aims. (1996, c. 437, § 2.1-328.14; 2001, c. 844.)

§ 2.2-4515. Collateral and safekeeping arrangements. — Securities purchased pursuant to the provisions of this chapter shall be held by the public official, municipal corporation or other political subdivision or public body or its custodial agent who may not otherwise be a counterparty to the investment transaction. Securities held on the books of the custodial agent by a custodial agent shall be held in the name of the municipal corporation, political subdivision or other public body subject to the public body's order of withdrawal. The responsibilities of the public official, municipal corporation, political subdivision or other public body shall be evidenced by a written agreement that shall provide for delivery of the securities by the custodial agent in the event of default by a counterparty to the investment transaction.

As used in this section, *"counterparty"* means the issuer or seller of a security, an agent purchasing a security on behalf of a public official, municipal corporation, political subdivision or other public body or the party responsible for repurchasing securities underlying a repurchase agreement.

The provisions of this section shall not apply to (i) investments with a maturity of less than 31 calendar days or (ii) the State Treasurer, who shall comply with safekeeping guidelines issued by the Treasury Board or to endowment funds invested in accordance with the provisions of the Uniform Prudent Management of Institutional Funds Act, Article 1.2 (§ 55-268.11 et seq.) of Chapter 15 of Title 55. (1988, c. 834, § 2.1-329.01; 2001, c. 844; 2008, c. 184.)

The 2008 amendments. — The 2008 amendment by c. 184, in the third paragraph, substituted "31" for "thirty-one" and "Uniform Prudent Management of Institutional Funds Act, Article 1.2 (§ 55-268.11 et seq.)" for "Uniform Investment of Institutional Funds Act, Article 1.1 (§ 55-268.1 et seq.)."

§ 2.2-4516. Liability of treasurers or public depositors. — When investments are made in accordance with this chapter, no treasurer or public depositor shall be liable for any loss therefrom in the absence of negligence, malfeasance, misfeasance, or nonfeasance on his part or on the part of his assistants or employees. (1979, c. 135, § 2.1-329.1; 2001, c. 844.)

§ 2.2-4517. Contracts on interest rates, currency, cash flow or on other basis. — A. Any state entity may enter into any contract or other arrangement that is determined to be necessary or appropriate to place the obligation or investment of the state entity, as represented by bonds or investments, in whole or in part, on the interest rate cash flow or other basis desired by the state entity. Such contract or other arrangement may include contracts providing for payments based on levels of, or changes in, interest rates. These contracts or arrangements may be entered into by the state entity in connection with, or incidental to, entering into, or maintaining any (i) agreement that secures bonds or (ii) investment, or contract providing for investment, otherwise authorized by law. These contracts and arrangements may contain such payment, security, default, remedy, and other terms and conditions as determined by the state entity, after giving due consideration to the creditworthiness of the counterparty or other obligated party, including any rating by a nationally recognized rating agency, and any other criteria as may be appropriate. The determinations referred to in this subsection may be made by the Treasury Board, the governing body of the state entity or any public funds manager with professional investment capabilities duly authorized by the Treasury Board or the governing body of any state entity authorized to issue such obligations to make such determinations.

As used in this section, *"state entity"* means the Commonwealth and all agencies, authorities, boards and institutions of the Commonwealth.

B. Any money set aside and pledged to secure payments of bonds or any of the contracts entered into pursuant to this section may be invested in accordance with this chapter and may be pledged to and used to service any of the contracts or other arrangements entered into pursuant to this section. (2002, c. 407.)

§ 2.2-4518. Investment of funds in certificates of deposit. — A. Notwithstanding any provision of law to the contrary, the Commonwealth and all public officers, municipal corporations, other political subdivisions, and all other public bodies of the Commonwealth, each referred to in this section as a "public entity," may invest any or all of the moneys belonging to them or within their control in accordance with the following conditions:

1. The moneys are initially invested through any federally insured bank or savings institution selected by the public entity that is qualified by the Virginia Treasury Board to accept public deposits;
2. The selected bank or savings institution arranges for the deposit of the moneys in certificates of deposit in one or more federally insured banks or savings institutions wherever located, for the account of the public entity;
3. The full amount of principal and any accrued interest of each such certificate of deposit are covered by federal deposit insurance;
4. The selected bank or savings institution acts as custodian for the public entity with respect to such certificates of deposit issued for the public entity's account; and
5. At the same time that the public entity's moneys are deposited and the certificates of deposit are issued, the selected bank or savings institution receives an amount of deposits from customers of other financial institutions wherever located equal to or greater than the amount of moneys invested by the public entity through the selected bank or savings institution.

B. Moneys arranged to be invested by the selected bank or savings institution in certificates of deposit in one or more federally insured banks or savings institutions wherever located, for the account of the public entity in accordance with the conditions prescribed in subsection A shall not be subject to the provisions of Chapter 44 (§ 2.2-4400 et seq.), § 2.2-4515, or any security or collateral requirements that may otherwise be applicable to the investment or deposit of public moneys by government investors. (2008, c. 103.)

CHAPTER 46.

Local Government Investment Pool Act.

§ 2.2-4600. Short title; definitions. — This chapter may be cited as the "Local Government Investment Pool Act." (1980, c. 538, §§ 2.1-234.1, 2.1-234.3; 1996, c. 77; 2001, c. 844.)

Cross references. — As to the powers and duties of the Treasury Board, see § 2.2-2416.

§ 2.2-4601. Findings and purpose. — A. The General Assembly finds that the public interest is served by maximum and prudent investment of public funds so that the need for taxes and other public revenues is decreased commensurately with the earnings on such investments. In selecting among avenues of investment, the highest rate of return, consistent with safety and liquidity, shall be the objective.

B. The purpose of this chapter is to secure the maximum public benefit from the investment of public funds, and, in furtherance of such purposes to:

1. Establish and maintain a continuing statewide policy for the deposit and investment of public funds;

2. Establish a state-administered pool for the investment of local government funds; and

3. Authorize treasurers or any other person collecting, disbursing, or otherwise handling public funds to invest such public funds either in accordance with Chapter 45 (§ 2.2-4500 et seq.) of this title or through the local government investment pool created by the chapter.

C. The General Assembly finds that the objectives of this chapter will best be obtained through improved money management, emphasizing the primary requirements of safety and liquidity and recognizing the different investment objectives of operating and permanent funds. (1980, c. 538, § 2.1-234.2; 2001, c. 844.)

§ 2.2-4602. Local government investment pool created. — A. A local government investment pool is created, consisting of the aggregate of all funds from local officials handling public funds that are placed in the custody of the State Treasurer for investment and reinvestment as provided in this chapter.

B. The Treasury Board or its designee shall administer the local government investment pool on behalf of the participating local officials subject to regulations and guidelines adopted by the Treasury Board.

C. The Treasury Board or its designee shall invest moneys in the local government investment pool with the degree of judgment and care, under circumstances then prevailing, which persons of prudence, discretion, and intelligence exercise in the management of their own affairs, not for speculation, but for investment, considering the probable safety of their capital as well as the probable income to be derived. Specifically, the types of authorized investments for local government investment pool assets shall be limited to those set forth for local officials in Chapter 45 (§ 2.2-4500 et seq.) of this title.

D. A separate account for each participant in the fund shall be kept to record individual transactions and totals of all investments belonging to each participant. A monthly report showing the changes in investments made during the preceding month shall be furnished to each participant having a beneficial interest in the local government investment pool. Details of any investment transaction shall be furnished to any participant upon request.

E. The Treasury Board or its designee shall administer and handle the accounts in the same manner as bond and sinking fund trust accounts.

F. The principal and accrued income, and any part thereof, of each and every account maintained for a participant in the local government investment pool shall be subject to payment at any time from the local government investment pool upon request, subject to applicable regulations and guidelines. Accumulated income shall be remitted or credited to each participant at least quarterly.

G. Except as provided in this section, all instruments of title of all investments of the local government investment pool shall remain in the custody of the State Treasurer. The State Treasurer may deposit with one or more fiscal agents or banks, those instruments of title he considers advisable, to be held in safekeeping by the agents or banks for collection of the principal and interest or other income, or of the proceeds of sale. The State Treasurer shall collect the principal and interest or other income from investments of the investment pool, the instruments of title to which are in his custody, when due and payable. (1980, c. 538, § 2.1-234.8; 1984, c. 320; 1988, c. 834; 2001, c. 844.)

§ **2.2-4603. Investment authority.** — Subject to the procedures set forth in this chapter, any local official handling public funds may invest and reinvest any money subject to his control and jurisdiction in the local government investment pool established by § 2.2-4602. (1980, c. 538, § 2.1-234.4; 1988, c. 834; 2001, c. 844.)

§ **2.2-4604. Interfund pooling for investment purposes.** — Local officials handling public funds may effect temporary transfers among separate funds for the purpose of pooling amounts available for investment. This pooling may be accomplished through interfund advances and other appropriate means consistent with recognized principles of governmental accounting provided that (i) moneys are available for the investment period required; (ii) the investment fund can repay the advance by the time needed; (iii) the transactions are fully and promptly recorded; and (iv) the interest earned is credited to the loaning or advancing jurisdiction. (1980, c. 538, § 2.1-234.6; 1981, c. 583; 2001, c. 844.)

§ **2.2-4605. Powers of Treasury Board relating to the administration of local government investment pool.** — A. The Treasury Board shall have power to:

1. Make and adopt regulations necessary and proper for the efficient administration of the local government investment pool hereinafter created, including but not limited to:

a. Specification of minimum amounts that may be deposited in the local government investment pool and minimum periods of time for which deposits shall be retained in such pool;

b. Creation of a reserve for losses;

c. Payment of administrative expenses from the earnings of such pool;

d. Distribution of the earnings in excess of such expenses, or allocation of losses, to the several participants in a manner that equitably reflects the differing amounts of their respective investments and the differing periods of time for which such amounts were in the custody of the pool; and

e. Procedures for the deposit and withdrawal of funds.

2. Develop guidelines for the protection of the local government investment pool in the event of default in the payment of principal or interest or other income of any investment of such pool, such guidelines to include the following procedures:

a. Instituting the proper proceedings to collect the matured principal or interest or other income;

b. Accepting for exchange purposes refunding bonds or other evidences of indebtedness at appropriate interest rates;

c. Making compromises, adjustments, or disposition of matured principal or interest or other income as considered advisable for the purpose of protecting the moneys invested;

d. Making compromises or adjustments as to future payments of principal or interest or other income considered advisable for the purpose of protecting the moneys invested.

3. Formulate policies for the investment and reinvestment of funds in the local government investment pool and the acquisition, retention, management, and disposition of investments of the investment pool.

B. The Treasury Board may delegate the administrative aspects of operating under this chapter to the State Treasurer, subject to the regulations and guidelines adopted by the Treasury Board.

C. Such regulations and guidelines may be adopted without complying with the Administrative Process Act (§ 2.2-4000 et seq.) provided that input is solicited from local officials handling public funds. Such input requires only that notice and an opportunity to submit written comments be given. (1980, c. 538, § 2.1-234.7; 2001, c. 844.)

§ 2.2-4606. Chapter controlling over inconsistent laws; powers supplemental. — Insofar as the provisions of this chapter are inconsistent with the provisions of any other law, the provisions of this chapter shall be controlling and the powers conferred by this chapter shall be in addition and supplemental to the powers conferred by any other law. (1980, c. 538, § 2.1-234.9; 2001, c. 844.)

CHAPTER 47.

Government Non-Arbitrage Investment Act.

§ 2.2-4700. Authorization to Treasury Board to provide certain assistance. — A. This chapter shall be known, and may be cited, as the "Government Non-Arbitrage Investment Act."

B. The General Assembly authorizes the Treasury Board to make available to the Commonwealth, to counties, cities and towns in the Commonwealth, and to their agencies, institutions, and authorities or any combination of the foregoing assistance as provided in this chapter in making and accounting for such investments. (1988, c. 498, § 2.1-234.9:1; 1990, c. 516; 1991, c. 245; 2001, c. 844.)

Cross references. — As to exemptions, generally, from the Administrative Process Act, see § 2.2-4002.

§ 2.2-4701. Definitions. — As used in this chapter, unless the context requires a different meaning:

"Bonds" means bonds or other obligations issued by the Commonwealth, by counties, cities and towns, and by their agencies, institutions, and authorities or by any combination of the foregoing under the provisions of the Public Finance Act (§ 15.2-2600 et seq.), or otherwise, the interest on which is intended to be excludable from the gross income of the recipients thereof for federal income tax purposes.

"Depository institution" means any commercial bank, trust company, or savings institution insured by an agency or instrumentality of the United States government.

"Issuers" means the Commonwealth, counties, cities and towns in the Commonwealth, and their agencies, institutions, and authorities.

"Official handling public funds" or *"official"* means the treasurer of the issuer or, if there is no officer known as treasurer of the issuer, the chief financial officer of the issuer, and any person or entity described in § 58.1-3123. (1988, c. 498, § 2.1-234.9:2; 1990, c. 516; 1991, c. 245; 1996, c. 77; 2001, c. 844.)

§ **2.2-4702. Powers of the Treasury Board under this chapter.** — The Treasury Board shall have power to:

1. Provide assistance to issuers in the management of and accounting for their funds, including, without limitation, bond proceeds, reserves and sinking funds, and the investment thereof, any portion of the investment earnings on which is or may be subject to rebate to the federal government.
2. Manage, acquire, hold, trade and sell investment obligations, for and on behalf of issuers or a pool or pools, and not for its own account, that are authorized investments for issuer bond proceeds, reserves, sinking funds or other funds, as the case may be.
3. Establish one or more pools of the issuer bond proceeds, reserves, sinking funds or other funds that are placed in the custody of the State Treasurer for investment and reinvestment in authorized investments.
4. Adopt regulations necessary and proper for the efficient administration of the pools authorized by this chapter without complying with the Administrative Process Act (§ 2.2-4000 et seq.), provided that notice and an opportunity to submit written comments on such regulations be given to officials handling public funds.
5. Formulate policies for the investment and reinvestment of funds under management, including funds in the pool or pools, and the acquisition, retention, management and disposition of investments.
6. Delegate the administration of this chapter to the State Treasurer, subject to the regulations and guidelines adopted by the Treasury Board.
7. Retain employees and engage and enter into contracts with independent investment managers, accountants, counsel, depository institutions and other advisors and agents, as may be necessary or convenient.
8. Enter into contracts with issuers with respect to the performance of investment services.
9. Charge issuers for the costs of its investment services and for its expenses.
10. Do any and all other acts and things necessary, appropriate or incidental in carrying out the purposes of this chapter. (1988, c. 498, § 2.1-234.9:3; 1990, c. 516; 2001, c. 844.)

§ **2.2-4703. Powers of issuers.** — Any provision of any general or special law or of any charter to the contrary notwithstanding, issuers may use the investment services of the Treasury Board and for that purpose may enter into contracts with the Treasury Board and its agents. (1988, c. 498, § 2.1-234.9:4; 1990, c. 516; 2001, c. 844.)

§ **2.2-4704. Alternative method.** — This chapter shall be deemed to provide an additional, alternative method for the performance of actions authorized hereby and shall be regarded as supplemental and additional to powers conferred by other laws and shall not be regarded as in derogation of any powers now existing. (1988, c. 498, § 2.1-234.9:5; 2001, c. 844.)

§ **2.2-4705. Liberal construction; inconsistent laws inapplicable.** — A. This chapter, being necessary for the welfare of the people of the Commonwealth, shall be liberally construed to effect the purposes thereof.

B. Insofar as the provisions of this chapter are inconsistent with the provisions of any general or special laws or charters, or parts thereof, the provisions of this chapter shall control. (1988, c. 498, §§ 2.1-234.9:6, 2.1-234.9:7; 2001, c. 844.)

CHAPTER 48.

Virginia Debt Collection Act.

§ 2.2-4800. Policy of the Commonwealth; collection of accounts receivable. — This chapter establishes the policy of the Commonwealth as it relates to the accounting for, management and collection of all accounts receivable due to the Commonwealth. It shall be the policy of the Commonwealth that all state agencies and institutions shall take all appropriate and cost-effective actions to aggressively collect all accounts receivable. All state agencies and institutions shall be subject to this chapter and shall establish internal policies and procedures for the management and collection of accounts receivable that are in accordance with regulations adopted by the Department of Accounts and the Office of the Attorney General. (1988, c. 544, § 2.1-727; 2001, c. 844.)

Cross references. — As to the creation in the Department of Law of a Division of Debt Collection, see § 2.2-518. As to the effective date of payment of bills by state agencies when offset proceedings have been instituted under this chapter, see § 2.2-4350. As to payments withheld pursuant to the Comptroller's Debt Setoff Program being exempt from interest penalties, see § 2.2-4355.

§ 2.2-4801. Definitions. — As used in this chapter, unless the context requires a different meaning:

"Administrative offset" includes, but is not limited to, offsetting any monies, except those specifically exempted by state or federal law, paid by agency or institution for a debt owed to any other state agency or institution.

"Accounts receivable" refers to the classification of debts due the Commonwealth, including judgments, fines, costs, and penalties imposed upon conviction for criminal and traffic offenses, and as defined in the guidelines adopted by the State Comptroller.

"Discharge" means the compromise and settlement of disputes, claims, and controversies of the Commonwealth by the Office of the Attorney General as authorized by § 2.2-514.

"Past-due" means any account receivable for which payment has not been received by the payment due date.

"State agency and institution" means any authority, board, department, instrumentality, agency or other unit in any branch of state government. The term shall not include any county, city or town, or any local or regional governmental authority or any "nonstate agency" as defined in the appropriation act.

"Write-off" means a transaction to remove from an agency's financial accounting records an account receivable that management has determined to be uncollectible. (1988, c. 544, § 2.1-726; 1994, c. 565; 2001, c. 844.)

§ 2.2-4802. Responsibility for accounts receivable policy; reports. — The Department of Accounts shall be the primary state agency responsible for the oversight, reporting and monitoring of the Commonwealth's accounts receivable program.

The Department of Accounts shall adopt necessary policies and procedures for reporting, accounting for, and collecting the Commonwealth's accounts receivable. The Department of Accounts is also charged with adopting regulations concerning guidelines and procedures for writing off accounts receivable. (1988, c. 544, § 2.1-728; 2001, c. 844.)

§ 2.2-4803. Legal counsel. — The Office of the Attorney General shall be the primary agency responsible for the provision of all legal services and advice related to the collection of accounts receivable, pursuant to § 2.2-507.

The Attorney General shall adopt necessary policies and procedures pertaining to all accounts receivable legal matters and the litigation of past-due accounts receivable that shall be published together with the policies and procedures adopted by the Department of Accounts. (1988, c. 544, § 2.1-729; 2001, c. 844.)

Editor's note. — Acts 2008, c. 879, effective for the biennium ending June 30, 2010, in Item 63 B 1, provides: "The amounts provided in this Item include funds to support the Enterprise Applications Master Services Interim Agreement between the Commonwealth of Virginia and CGI Technologies & Solutions, Inc. (CGI). Notwithstanding any other provision of law except the limitations imposed by §2.2-518, §2.2-4803 and §2.2-4806, Code of Virginia, Executive Department agencies and institutions may enter into management agreements with CGI for debt collection and cost recovery services pursuant to Statements of Work 6 and 7 of the Enterprise Applications Master Services Agreement. Work on enhanced collections and recoveries shall not proceed if they commit the Commonwealth to expanding or significantly altering any existing federal or state program without the review and approval of the Governor and General Assembly."

§ 2.2-4804. Annual reports. — The Department of Accounts and the Attorney General shall annually report to the Governor, the Secretary of Finance and the Chairmen of the Senate Committee on Finance and the House Committee on Appropriations those agencies and institutions that are not making satisfactory progress toward implementing the provisions of this chapter and establishing effective accounts receivable programs. (1988, c. 544, § 2.1-730; 2001, c. 844.)

§ 2.2-4805. Interest, administrative charges and penalty fees. — Each state agency and institution may charge interest on all past due accounts receivable in accordance with guidelines adopted by the Department of Accounts and at the underpayment rate prescribed in § 58.1-15. Each past due accounts receivable may also be charged an additional amount that shall approximate the administrative costs, excluding attorneys' fees not authorized by contract, arising under § 2.2-4806. Agencies and institutions may also assess late penalty fees, not in excess of ten percent of the past-due account on past-due accounts receivable. The Department of Accounts shall adopt regulations concerning the imposition of administrative charges and late penalty fees. (1988, c. 544, § 2.1-732; 2001, c. 844.)

§ 2.2-4806. Utilization of certain collection techniques. — A. Each state agency and institution shall take all appropriate and cost-effective actions to aggressively collect its accounts receivable. Each agency and institution shall utilize, but not be limited to, the following collection techniques, according to the policies and procedures required by the Department of Accounts and the Attorney General: (i) credit reporting bureaus, (ii) collection agencies, (iii) garnishments, liens and judgments, (iv) administrative offset, and (v) participation in the Treasury Offset Program of the United States under 31 U.S.C. § 3716.

B. Except as provided otherwise herein, for collection of accounts receivable of $3,000 or more that are 60 days past due, each agency and institution shall forward those claims to the Office of Attorney General, Division of Debt Collection for collection. The Attorney General shall review forwarded accounts, determine the appropriate collection efforts, if any, for each account, and take such actions on the accounts as he may so determine.

C. Except as provided otherwise herein, for collection of accounts receivable under $3,000 that are 60 days past due, each agency and institution shall contract with a private collection agency for the collection of those debts. Prior to referring accounts receivable of less than $3,000, agencies and institutions may refer such accounts to the Office of Attorney General, Division of Debt Collection. The Attorney General may accept the account for collection or return it to the agency or institution for collection by a private collection agency.

D. Where an agency or institution has procedures to secure payment, or the debtor is paying a debt in periodic payments satisfactory to the agency or institution, it may elect to retain the claim in excess of 60 days, provided that such periodic payments are promptly paid until the account is satisfied. In the event the debtor is delinquent by 60 days in paying a periodic payment the account shall be handled in the manner provided by subsection C. (1988, c. 544, § 2.1-733; 2001, c. 844; 2004, c. 919; 2008, cc. 314, 637.)

Editor's note. — Acts 2008, c. 879, effective for the biennium ending June 30, 2010, in Item 60, provides: "A. All agencies and institutions shall follow the procedures for collection of funds owed the Commonwealth as specified in §§2.2-518 and 2.2-4806 of the Code of Virginia, except as provided otherwise therein or in this act.

"B.1. The Division of Debt Collection is entitled to retain as fees up to 30 percent of any revenues generated by it pursuant to paragraph A. to pay operating costs supported by the appropriation in this item.

"2. Upon closing its books at the end of the fiscal year, after the execution of all transfers to state agencies having claims collected by the Division of Debt Collection, the Division may retain up to a $400,000 balance in its operating accounts. Any amounts contained in the operating accounts that exceed $400,000 on the final day of the fiscal year shall be deposited to the credit of the general fund no later than September 1 of the succeeding fiscal year.

"3. The Director, Department of Planning and Budget, may grant an exception to the provisions in paragraph B.2. if the Division of Debt Collection can show just cause.

"C. The Division of Debt Collection may contract with private collection agents for the collection of debts amounting to less than $15,000."

Acts 2008, c. 879, effective for the biennium ending June 30, 2010, in Item 63 B 1, provides: "The amounts provided in this Item include funds to support the Enterprise Applications Master Services Interim Agreement between the Commonwealth of Virginia and CGI Technologies & Solutions, Inc. (CGI). Notwithstanding any other provision of law except the limitations imposed by §2.2-518, §2.2-4803 and §2.2-4806, Code of Virginia, Executive Department agencies and institutions may enter into management agreements with CGI for debt collection and cost recovery services pursuant to Statements of Work 6 and 7 of the Enterprise Applications Master Services Agreement. Work on enhanced collections and recoveries shall not proceed if they commit the Commonwealth to expanding or significantly altering any existing federal or state program without the review and approval of the Governor and General Assembly."

The 2008 amendments. — The 2008 amendment by c. 314 added clause (v) in subsection A; and made minor stylistic changes.

The 2008 amendment by c. 637, in subsection A, substituted "required" for "adopted"; in subsection B and C, substituted "60 days past due" for "60 days or more past due"; and in subsection D, substituted "provided that such periodic payments are promptly paid" for "pending results of such procedures, or" and added the last sentence.

§ **2.2-4807. Debtor information and skip-tracing.** — Each agency and institution shall collect minimum prescribed information from clients, debtors, and payees. Debtor information available from state agencies, credit reporting bureaus and other appropriate sources shall be used for the purpose of skip-tracing debtors, as specified in the guidelines of the Department of Accounts and the Attorney General. The minimum prescribed information to be collected shall include the federal employer identification number of partnerships, proprietorships, and corporate clients, debtors, and payees. This minimum prescribed information shall be included in the contract payment clause required by § 2.2-4354. The Department of Accounts may require that the minimum prescribed information be supplied on any request for payment, including invoices. (1988, c. 544, § 2.1-734; 1992, c. 110; 2001, c. 844.)

§ **2.2-4808. Provision of state services to delinquent debtors.** — Each state agency and institution shall develop internal policies and procedures, in accordance with accounts receivable policies of the Department of Accounts and the Attorney General, for delaying or withholding certain state services to those persons who refuse to pay their debts. (1988, c. 544, § 2.1-735; 2001, c. 844.)

§ **2.2-4809. Agreement authorized; setoff federal debts.** — A. The Comptroller is authorized to enter into an agreement with the United States to participate in the Treasury Offset Program pursuant to 31 U.S.C. § 3716 for the collection of any debts owed to state agencies. The agreement may provide for the United States to submit debts owed to federal agencies for offset against state payments similar to the procedures for offsetting debts owed to state agencies.

B. The Treasurer shall reduce any state payment by the amount of any federal debt submitted in accordance with the agreement authorized by this section, and pay such amount to the appropriate federal official in accordance with the procedures specified in such agreement. (2008, c. 314.)

CHAPTER 49.

Public Debt; Issuance of Bonds and Certificates of Indebtedness.

§ **2.2-4900. Authority of Governor to contract debts.** — The Governor may contract debts and issue obligations in evidence thereof upon the terms and conditions determined by the Governor to meet casual deficits in the revenue or in anticipation of the collection of revenues of the Commonwealth for the then current fiscal year within the amount of authorized appropriations, subject to the limitations and conditions of Article X, Section 9 (a) (2) of the Constitution of Virginia. The Governor may sell such obligations in a manner, either at public or private sale, and for a price as he determines to be in the best interests of the Commonwealth. (Code 1950, § 2-269; 1966, c. 677, § 2.1-303; 1971, Ex. Sess., c. 121; 2001, c. 844.)

Cross references. — As to exemption of the Innovative Technology Authority from personnel and procurement procedures, see § 2.2-2231. As to exemption of the Virginia Tourism Authority from personnel and procurement procedures, see § 2.2-2325.

§ 2.2-4901. Acts concerning issuance of bonds and certificates of indebtedness continued in effect. — The following sections of the Code of 1919 and the following subsequent acts, all relating to the issue and terms of, and provisions with respect to certain bonds or certificates of indebtedness of the Commonwealth, are continued in effect.

(1) Sections 2584 to 2602, inclusive, of the Code of 1919;

(2) Chapter 93 of the Acts of 1927, approved April 18, 1927;

(3) Chapter 91 of the Acts of 1932, approved March 3, 1932, codified as §§ 2641 (1)-2641 (11) of Michie Code 1942; and

(4) Chapter 203 of the Acts of 1936, approved March 14, 1936. (Code 1950, § 2-270; 1966, c. 677, § 2.1-304; 2001, c. 844.)

§ 2.2-4902. Ratings of bonds issued by governmental instrumentalities. — A. As used in this section, unless the context requires a different meaning:

"Bond" means any bonds, refunding bonds, notes, debentures, interim certificates, or any bond, grant, revenue anticipation notes or any other evidences of indebtedness, whether in temporary or definitive form and whether or not the interest thereon is exempt from federal taxation.

"Governmental instrumentality" means each department, institution, commission, public corporate instrumentality, or agency of the Commonwealth, including the Commonwealth itself, and each political subdivision thereof, including but without limitation each public authority and district and each county, city or town and each instrumentality thereof which under law has the power to issue bonds.

B. Notwithstanding any provision contained in any general or special law or in any charter of any county, city or town of the Commonwealth, any rating of bonds issued by a governmental instrumentality shall be provided by a bond rating agency approved by the State Treasurer.

C. In addition to all of his other powers and duties, the State Treasurer shall prepare a list of approved bond rating agencies and upon request provide a copy thereof to all governmental instrumentalities. (1997, c. 381, § 2.1-304.1:1; 2001, c. 844.)

§ 2.2-4902.1. Pledges and security interests created by governmental units. — Except for security interests, liens or pledges in goods or software, or the proceeds thereof, described in § 8.9A-109(e), the creation, perfection, priority and enforcement of a security interest, lien or pledge created, made or granted by the Commonwealth or a governmental unit of the Commonwealth, as defined in § 8.9A-102, to pay or secure any bonds, notes, obligations or other debt securities, herein collectively called "bonds," shall be governed by this section, the provisions of law under which the bonds were authorized, and the ordinance, resolution, trust agreement, indenture, financing agreement or similar instrument securing the bonds, herein called the "security interest." Property pledged or in which a security interest is created for the payment or security of any bonds, whether presently held by the governmental unit or as thereafter received by or otherwise credited to the governmental unit, shall immediately be subject to the lien of such pledge or security interest without any physical delivery, control, filing or further act. The lien of such pledge or security interest made or granted in the security instrument shall have priority over any other obligations or liabilities of the governmental unit, except as may be otherwise provided in the security instrument. The lien of each such pledge or security interest shall be valid, binding and enforceable as against all persons having claims of any kind in tort, contract, or otherwise against the governmental unit regardless of whether such persons have notice of such pledge or security interest. (2001, cc. 289, 296, § 2.1-304.1:2.)

Editor's note. — Acts 2001, cc. 289 and 296 enacted § 2.1-304.1:2, from which this section is derived. Pursuant to § 30-152, Acts 2001, cc. 289 and 296 have been given effect in this section as set out above.

§ **2.2-4903. Governor's consideration of tax-supported debt.** — Prior to the Governor recommending any new tax-supported debt, which is defined as debt for which the debt service payments are expected to be made, in whole or in part, from appropriations of the Commonwealth, the Governor shall consider the maximum amount of debt recommended as prudent for the subject biennium by the Debt Capacity Advisory Committee created pursuant to § 2.2-2712. (1994, c. 43, § 2.1-304.5; 2001, c. 844.)

§ **2.2-4904. Cooperation of the Commonwealth's instrumentalities.** — All Commonwealth debt-issuing agencies, institutions, boards, and authorities shall quarterly provide the State Treasurer with all information necessary to carry out the requirements of this chapter. The Departments of Accounts, Planning and Budget, and Taxation and other state agencies shall also provide the State Treasurer with the information and assistance the Debt Capacity Advisory Committee deems necessary. (1994, c. 43, § 2.1-304.6; 1997, c. 187; 2001, c. 844.)

§ **2.2-4905. Limitation of chapter.** — This chapter shall not limit or alter the rights of the Commonwealth or any of its instrumentalities to fulfill the terms of any agreements made with the holders of any bonds, notes, or other obligations of the Commonwealth or such instrumentality issued and outstanding prior to July 1, 1994, or to in any way impair the rights and remedies of such holders. (1994, c. 43, § 2.1-304.7; 2001, c. 844.)

§ **2.2-4906. How lost bond or certificate renewed.** — When any bond or certificate is lost or destroyed, the owner thereof may:

1. File in the office of the State Treasurer an affidavit, setting forth the time, place and circumstance of the loss or destruction; and
2. Execute a bond to the Commonwealth, with one or more sureties, approved by the State Treasurer, with condition to indemnify the Commonwealth and all persons against any loss in consequence of issuing a new bond or certificate in place of the one so lost or destroyed.

If the owner performs these acts, the State Treasurer may issue, at any time before the bond or certificate becomes due and payable, or at any time as to any such bond or certificate that has become due and payable on or after July 1, 1932, a new bond or certificate and register the same. (Code 1950, § 2-281; 1966, c. 677, § 2.1-313; 1997, c. 310; 2001, c. 844.)

Michie's Jurisprudence. — For related discussion, see 12A M.J. Lost Instruments and Records, § 9.

CHAPTER 50.

INTEREST ON CERTAIN OBLIGATIONS OF GOVERNMENT INSTRUMENTALITIES.

§ 2.2-5000. Governmental instrumentalities authorized to issue bonds, etc., at rates of interest in excess of legal limits; sale of such bonds. — A. Notwithstanding any limitation contained in any general or special law or in any charter of any city or town of the Commonwealth, a governmental instrumentality, which under law has the power to issue bonds, notes or other obligations (herein collectively called "bonds") to provide funds to carry out its public purposes, may issue such bonds at such rates of interest in excess of the rates now permitted by law as may be determined by the governing body empowered under law to authorize the issuance of bonds of such governmental instrumentality and to sell the bonds for a price it determines to be for the best interests of the Commonwealth and of such governmental instrumentality.

B. For the purposes of this chapter, *"governmental instrumentality"* means each department, institution, commission, public corporate instrumentality or agency of the Commonwealth and every political subdivision of the Commonwealth including, but not limited to, each public authority and district and each county, city or town or instrumentality thereof. (1970, c. 1, § 2.1-326.1; 1990, c. 712; 2001, c. 844.)

§ 2.2-5001. Manner of exercising authority. — The authority vested in governmental instrumentalities under the provisions of this chapter may be exercised by the body authorized to issue such bonds without securing the further approval of any other body, board or agency that may have approved the issuance of such bonds and, in the case of bonds approved by election, without a further election, unless a lower maximum rate of interest was stated in the approval of such other body, board or agency or was stated on the ballot of such election. (1970, c. 1, § 2.1-326.2; 1972, c. 735; 1974, cc. 82, 650; 1976, c. 522; 2001, c. 844.)

CASE NOTES

Editor's note. — The case below was decided under former Title 2.1 or prior provisions.

The effect of this section prior to the 1972 amendment was to remove the six percent interest ceiling on bonds issued by governmental entities until 1972. Miller v. Ayres, 211 Va. 69, 175 S.E.2d 253 (1970).

Issuance of bonds pursuant to election must be in conformity with terms and conditions of submission to voters. — Bonds approved by the voters of Prince William County and bonds approved by the voters of the city of Virginia Beach at a time when the Public Finance Act (see now § 15.2-2600 et seq.) provided a maximum interest rate of six percent cannot subsequently be issued at an interest rate of seven percent, although the General Assembly determined that a fiscal emergency existed and enacted a law authorizing counties and cities to issue bonds at higher interest rates. The rate of interest to be paid on the bonds was part of the "submission to the voters" and the issuance of bonds pursuant to an election must be in conformity with the terms and conditions of the submission. The terms of a bond cannot be changed so as to materially increase the burden on the voter after a vote that is constitutionally required. It was beyond the power of the General Assembly to authorize a higher interest rate on the bonds. Miller v. Ayres, 211 Va. 69, 175 S.E.2d 253 (1970).

After the approval by the voters of a bond issue in a constitutionally required election, the law which limited the interest to be paid on the bonds cannot be abrogated to remove such limit and thus increase the burden on the taxpayer beyond the maximum he approved. Miller v. Ayres, 211 Va. 69, 175 S.E.2d 253 (1970).

§ 2.2-5002. Power to issue obligations not to be denied because interest is subject to federal income taxation. — The power of any governmental instrumentality, to issue or have issued on its behalf for authorized purposes, bonds, shall not be construed to be restricted or limited solely because the interest thereon is subject, in whole or in part, directly or indirectly, to federal income taxes. (1986, c. 137, § 2.1-326.2:1; 2001, c. 844.)

§ 2.2-5003. Chapter controlling over inconsistent laws; powers supplemental. — Insofar as the provisions of this chapter are inconsistent with the provisions of any other law, the provisions of this chapter shall be controlling and the powers conferred by this chapter shall be in addition and supplemental to the powers conferred by any other law. (1970, c. 1, § 2.1-326.3; 2001, c. 844.)

CHAPTER 50.1.

MANAGEMENT STANDARDS.

§ 2.2-5004. Financial and administrative management standards for public institutions of higher education. — For purposes of this chapter:

"Public institution of higher education" means the same as that term is defined in § 23-38.89.

A. Every public institution of higher education in the Commonwealth shall take all appropriate actions to meet the following financial and administrative management standards:

1. An unqualified opinion from the Auditor of Public Accounts upon the audit of the public institution's financial statements;
2. No significant audit deficiencies attested to by the Auditor of Public Accounts;
3. Substantial compliance with all financial reporting standards approved by the State Comptroller;
4. Substantial attainment of accounts receivable standards approved by the State Comptroller, including, but not limited to, any standards for outstanding receivables and bad debts;
5. Substantial attainment of accounts payable standards approved by the State Comptroller including, but not limited to, any standards for accounts payable past due; and
6. Such other financial and administrative management standards as the Governor may establish, or as may be included in the appropriation act currently in effect.

B. Any public institution of higher education that does not meet all of the financial management standards in subsection A, including any established by the Governor, and such other financial management standards as may be included in the appropriation act currently in effect as determined in a written certification by the Auditor of Public Accounts pursuant to § 30-133.1 shall develop and implement a plan of corrective action for purposes of meeting such standards as soon as practicable. The Chairman of the Board of Visitors or other governing body of the public institution of higher education shall provide a copy of the written plan to the Auditor of Public Accounts and the Secretaries of Education, Finance, and Administration promptly upon completion of the development of the written plan.

C. In addition, any public institution of higher education that does not meet all administrative management standards specified by the Governor, and such standards currently in effect for such institutions as determined in a written certification by the Auditor of Public Accounts pursuant to § 30-133.1 shall develop and implement a plan of corrective action for purposes of meeting such standards as soon as practical. Copies of the corrective action plan shall be provided to the same persons included under subsection B upon completion of the development of the written plan. (2005, cc. 933, 945.)

§ **2.2-5005. Incentive performance benefits to certain public institutions of higher education.** — As used in this section, unless the context requires a different meaning:

"Fiscal year of implementation" means the first full fiscal year for which the financial and administrative management and educational-related performance benchmarks described under § 23-9.6:1.01 are effective, as provided in a general appropriation act.

Beginning with the fiscal year that immediately follows the fiscal year of implementation and for all fiscal years thereafter, each public institution of higher education that (i) has been certified during the fiscal year by the State Council of Higher Education of Virginia pursuant to § 23-9.6:1.01 as having met the institutional performance benchmarks for public institutions of higher education and (ii) meets the conditions prescribed in subsection B of § 23-38.88, shall receive the following financial benefits:

1. Interest on the tuition and fees and other nongeneral fund Educational and General Revenues deposited into the State Treasury by the public institution of higher education, as provided in the appropriation act. Such interest shall be paid from the general fund and shall be an appropriate and equitable amount as determined and certified in writing by the Secretary of Finance to the Comptroller by the end of each fiscal year, or as soon thereafter as practicable;

2. Any unexpended appropriations of the public institution of higher education at the close of the fiscal year, which shall be reappropriated and allotted for expenditure by the institution in the immediately following fiscal year; and

3. A pro rata amount of the rebate due to the Commonwealth on credit card purchases of $5,000 or less made during the fiscal year. The amount to be paid to each institution shall equal a pro rata share based upon its total transactions of $5,000 or less using the credit card that is approved for use by all state agencies as compared to all transactions of $5,000 or less using such card by all state agencies. The Comptroller shall determine the public institution's pro rata share and, as provided in the appropriation act, shall pay the institution by August 15, or as soon thereafter as practicable, of the fiscal year immediately following the year of certification.

The payment to an institution of its pro rata share under this subdivision shall also be applicable to other rebate or refund programs in effect that are similar to that of the credit card rebate program described in this subdivision. The Secretary of Finance shall identify such other rebate or refund programs and shall determine the pro rata share to be paid to the public institution of higher education.

4. A rebate of any transaction fees for the prior fiscal year paid for sole source procurements made by the institution in accordance with subsection E of § 2.2-4303, for using a vendor who is not registered with the Department of General Service's web-based electronic procurement program commonly

known as "eVA", as provided in the appropriation act. Such rebate shall be certified by the Department of General Services and paid to each public institution by August 15, or as soon thereafter as practicable, of the fiscal year immediately following the year of certification. (2005, cc. 933, 945.)

Editor's note. — Acts 2006, c. 124, provides: "§ 1. That the Department of General Services, in cooperation with the Virginia Information Technologies Agency, shall establish and publish in the vendor's manual a procedure for refunding the relevant eVa transaction fees in the event of a change order or cancellation of a contract by a vendor."

CHAPTER 51.

Virginia Investment Partnership Act.

§ **2.2-5100. Short title; definitions.** — A. This chapter shall be known and may be cited as the "Virginia Investment Partnership Act."

B. As used in this chapter, unless the context requires a different meaning:

"Average manufacturing wage" means that amount determined by the Virginia Employment Commission to be the average wage paid manufacturing workers in a locality or region of the Commonwealth.

"Average nonmanufacturing wage" means that amount determined by the Virginia Employment Commission to be the average wage paid nonmanufacturing workers in basic employment in a locality or region of the Commonwealth.

"Basic employment" means employment that brings new or additional income into Virginia and adds to the gross state product.

"Capital investment" means an investment in real property, personal property, or both, at a manufacturing or basic nonmanufacturing facility within the Commonwealth that is capitalized by the company and that increases the productivity of the manufacturing facility, results in the creation, development or utilization of a more advanced technology than is in use immediately prior to such investment, or both. In order to qualify as a capital investment, an investment in technology shall result in a measurable increase in capacity or productivity, a measurable decrease in the production of flawed product, or both. Expenditures for maintenance, replacement or repair of existing machinery, tools and real property shall not constitute a capital investment; however, expenditures for the replacement of property shall not be ineligible for designation as a capital investment if such replacement results in a measurable increase in productivity.

"Eligible company" means, for companies located in a Metropolitan Statistical Area with a population of 300,000 or more in the 2000 census, a Virginia employer that creates or causes to be created at least 400 jobs with average salaries at least 50 percent greater than the Prevailing Average Wage, and makes a capital investment of at least $5 million or $6,500 per job, whichever is greater. For all companies located elsewhere in Virginia, "eligible company" shall mean a Virginia employer that creates or causes to be created at least 200 jobs with average salaries at least 50 percent greater than the Prevailing Average Wage, and making a capital investment of at least $6,500 per job.

"Eligible manufacturer or research and development service" means an existing Virginia manufacturer or research and development service that makes a capital investment of at least $25 million that is announced on or after June 1, 1998, which investment does not result in any net reduction in employment within one year after the capital investment has been completed and verified. Any entity participating in any other production grant program in the Commonwealth shall not be an eligible manufacturer or research and development service.

"Eligible research and development service" means an existing Virginia research and development service that supports manufacturing and that makes a capital investment of at least $25 million, which investment does not result in any net reduction in employment within one year after the capital investment has been completed and verified. Any entity participating in any other production grant program in the Commonwealth shall not be eligible.

"Existing Virginia manufacturer" means a manufacturer that has a legal presence within the Commonwealth for at least five years prior to making the announcement of the capital investment that makes it an eligible manufacturer.

"Flawed product" means an irregular unit of goods that cannot be sold to an end user.

"Fund" means the Virginia Investment Partnership Grant Fund created pursuant to § 2.2-5104, comprised of (i) the Major Eligible Employer Grant subfund, (ii) the Investment Performance Grant subfund, and (iii) the Economic Development Incentive Grant subfund.

"Major eligible employer" means an existing Virginia manufacturer or any other nonmanufacturing basic employer that makes a capital investment of at least $100 million and creates at least 1,000 jobs, or corporate headquarters and other basic employers that make a capital investment of at least $100 million and create at least 400 jobs paying at least twice the prevailing average wage for the area.

"Manufacturer" means a business firm owning or operating a manufacturing establishment as defined in the Standard Industrial Classification Manual issued by the U.S. Office of Management and Budget or the North American Industry Classification System Manual issued by the United States Census Bureau.

"Net present value of benefits to Virginia" means the present value of the amount by which (i) the anticipated additional state tax revenue expected to accrue to the Commonwealth as a result of the capital investment and jobs created, over a period following the completion of the capital investment not to exceed 20 years, exceeds (ii) the value of all incentives provided by the Commonwealth, including any grant under this article, for such capital investment during that period.

"New job" means employment of an indefinite duration at the eligible facility, created as the direct result of the capital investment, for which the standard fringe benefits are paid by the firm for the employee, requiring a minimum of either (i) 35 hours of an employee's time a week for the entire normal year of the firm's operations, which "normal year" must consist of at least 48 weeks or (ii) 1,680 hours per year. Seasonal or temporary positions, positions created when a job function is shifted from an existing location in the Commonwealth to the facility, and positions with contractors, suppliers, and similar multiplier or spin-off jobs shall not qualify as new jobs under this article.

"Partnership" means the Virginia Economic Development Partnership.

"Prevailing Average Wage" means that amount determined by the Virginia Employment Commission to be the average wage paid workers in the city or county of the Commonwealth where the eligible company is located.

"Productivity" means the number of hours of labor required to produce a unit of goods.

"Research and development service" means a business firm owning or operating an establishment engaged in conducting research and experimental development that supports manufacturing in the physical, engineering and life sciences as defined in the North American Industry Classification System Manual issued by the United States Census Bureau.

"Secretary" means the Secretary of Commerce and Trade. (1999, cc. 875, 961, §§ 2.1-548.43:1, 2.1-548.43:2; 2000, c. 571; 2001, c. 844; 2003, c. 17; 2005, c. 431.)

§ 2.2-5101. Virginia Investment Performance Grants. — A. Subject to the appropriation by the General Assembly of sufficient moneys to the Investment Performance Grant subfund, any eligible manufacturer or research and development service that is not eligible for a major eligible employer grant under § 2.2-5102 shall be eligible for an investment performance grant as provided in this section.

B. The Partnership shall establish an application process by which eligible manufacturers and research and development services may apply for a grant under this section. An application for a grant under this section shall not be approved until the Partnership has verified that the capital investment has been completed.

C. The amount of the investment performance grant that an eligible manufacturer or research and development service shall be eligible to receive under this section shall be determined by the Secretary, based on the recommendation of the Partnership, and contingent upon approval by the Governor. The determination of the appropriate amount of an investment performance grant shall be based on the application of guidelines that establish criteria for correlating the amount of a grant to the relative value to the Commonwealth of the eligible investment.

D. The Partnership shall assist the Secretary in developing objective guidelines that shall be used in awarding investment performance grants. No grant shall be awarded until the Secretary has provided copies of such guidelines for review to the chairmen of the House Committee on Appropriations and the Senate Committee on Finance. The preparation of the guidelines shall be exempt from the requirements of Article 2 (§ 2.2-4006 et seq.) of the Administrative Process Act (§ 2.2-4000 et seq.). The guidelines shall require determinations regarding the amount of investment performance grants to address:

1. The number of new jobs created by the capital investment;
2. The wages paid for the new jobs and the amount by which wages exceed the average manufacturing wage for the locality or region;
3. The extent to which the capital investment produces (i) measurable increases in capacity, productivity, or both; (ii) measurable decreases in the production of flawed product; or (iii) measurable advances in knowledge, research, or the application of research findings for the creation of new or significantly improved products or processes that support manufacturing;
4. The amount of the capital investment;
5. The net present value of benefits to Virginia;
6. The amount of other incentives offered by the Commonwealth and the locality; and
7. The importance of the manufacturing or research and development facility to the economy of the locality or region.

The guidelines shall also address the eligibility of manufacturers or research and development services that make a capital investment in phases over a period of years, and limits on eligibility for multiple grants by the same manufacturer or research and development service within stated periods of time.

E. The amount of an investment performance grant to any eligible manufacturer under this section shall not exceed $3 million or 10 percent of the amount appropriated by the General Assembly to the Investment Performance Grant subfund in the year that the terms of a grant are determined. For all eligible projects awarded grants on or after July 1, 2005, the amount of an investment performance grant to any recipient under this section shall not exceed $1.5 million.

F. For all eligible projects awarded grants before July 1, 2005, the aggregate amount of investment performance grants approved under this section in any year shall not exceed $6 million, and the aggregate amount of grants outstanding to all eligible manufacturers under this section for all years shall at no time exceed $30 million. For all such grants awarded prior to that date, the annual obligations of the Commonwealth to make grant payments to individual eligible manufacturers under this section shall not exceed $600,000. For all eligible projects awarded grants on or after July 1, 2005, the aggregate amount of investment performance grants approved under this section in any year shall not exceed $3 million, and the aggregate amount of such grants awarded after that date and outstanding at any time shall not exceed $15 million. For all such grants awarded on or after that date, the annual obligations of the Commonwealth to make grant payments to individual recipients under this section shall not exceed $300,000.

G. Any eligible manufacturer or research and development service shall be eligible to receive a grant from the Fund in five equal installments beginning in the third year after the capital investment is completed and the Partnership has verified that the requirements applicable to such grant have been satisfied. Any eligible manufacturer or research and development service located in a fiscally distressed area of the State, as defined in the guidelines implementing this chapter, shall be eligible to begin receiving grants in the second year after the capital investment is completed and verified. (1999, cc. 875, 961, § 2.1-548.43:3; 2000, c. 571; 2001, c. 844; 2003, c. 17; 2005, c. 431; 2007, c. 384.)

Editor's note. — Acts 2007, c. 384, cl. 2, provides: "That the provisions of this act shall apply only to grants for new, eligible projects whose applications are approved on or after July 1, 2007."

The 2007 amendments. — The 2007 amendment by c. 384, in subsection G, substituted "third year" for "fourth year" in the first sentence and "second year" for "third year" in the second sentence.

§ 2.2-5102. Performance grant for major eligible manufacturers. — A. As used in this section, *"major eligible employer"* means any eligible manufacturer or other nonmanufacturing basic employer that makes a capital investment of at least $100 million that results in the creation of at least 1,000 new jobs. For corporate headquarters and other basic employers that make a capital investment of at least $100 million and create at least 400 new jobs paying at least twice the prevailing average wage for the area, the 1,000 job requirement may be reduced in proportion to the factor by which the wages for the new jobs exceed the prevailing average wage for the area. All other provisions of this chapter shall apply equally to major eligible manufacturers and major eligible nonmanufacturing basic employers, in this chapter collectively referred to as "major eligible employers."

B. Subject to the appropriation by the General Assembly of sufficient moneys to the Major Eligible Employer Grant subfund, any major eligible employer shall be eligible for a grant under this section of up to $25 million, to be payable from such subfund over a period of not less than five years and not more than seven years, commencing in the sixth year following the approval by the Secretary of the employer's grant application. Any major eligible employer located in a fiscally distressed area of the State, as defined in the guidelines implementing this chapter, shall be eligible to begin receiving grants in the fourth year after the capital investment is completed and verified.

C. The Partnership shall establish an application process by which major eligible employers may apply for a grant under this section. An application for a grant under this section shall not be approved until the Partnership has verified that the capital investment has been completed.

D. The Comptroller shall not draw any warrants to issue checks for grants under this chapter without a specific legislative appropriation as specified in conditions and restrictions on expenditures in the appropriation act. The payment of any grant under this section shall be in accordance with the terms and conditions set forth in a memorandum of understanding between a major eligible employer and the Commonwealth. These terms and conditions shall supplement the provisions of this chapter and shall include but not be limited to the terms of the payment of the grant. The payment of the grant shall be made in full or in proportion to a major eligible employer's fulfillment of the terms of the memorandum of understanding. The Secretary shall consult with the House Committee on Appropriations and the Senate Committee on Finance prior to entering into any memorandum of understanding. The House Committee on Appropriations and the Senate Committee on Finance shall have the opportunity to review any memorandum of understanding prior to its execution by the Commonwealth. (1999, cc. 875, 961, § 2.1-548.43:4; 2000, c. 571; 2001, c. 844; 2003, c. 17.)

§ **2.2-5102.1. Virginia Economic Development Incentive Grants.** — A. Subject to the appropriation by the General Assembly of sufficient moneys to the Economic Development Incentive Grant subfund, any eligible company that meets the requirements of this section and is not awarded a grant under § 2.2-5101 or 2.2-5102 for the same project shall be eligible to apply for an economic development incentive grant as provided in this section.

B. The Partnership shall establish an application process by which eligible companies may apply for a grant under this section. An application for a grant under this section shall not be approved for payment until the Partnership has verified that the applicable requirements of the memorandum of agreement have been satisfied.

C. The amount of the economic development incentive grant that an eligible company may receive under this section shall be determined at the sole discretion of the Governor based on the recommendation of the Secretary. The determination of the appropriate amount for an economic development incentive grant shall be based on the application of guidelines that establish criteria for correlating the amount of a grant to the relative value to the Commonwealth of the new investment and employment.

D. The Partnership shall assist the Secretary in developing objective guidelines that shall be used in awarding economic development incentive grants. No grant shall be awarded until the Secretary has provided copies of such guidelines for review to the chairmen of the House Committee on Appropriations and the Senate Committee on Finance. The preparation of the guidelines shall be exempt from the requirements of Article 2 (§ 2.2-4006 et seq.) of the Administrative Process Act (§ 2.2-4000 et seq.). The guidelines shall require determinations regarding the amount of investment performance grants to address:

1. The number of new jobs created by the capital investment;
2. The wages paid for the new jobs and the amount by which wages exceed the average wage for the locality or region;
3. The amount of the capital investment;
4. The net present value of benefits to Virginia;
5. The amount of other incentives offered by the Commonwealth and the locality; and

6. The importance of the facility to the economy of the locality or region.

The guidelines shall also address the eligibility of companies that make a capital investment in phases over a period of years, and limits on eligibility for multiple grants by the same company within stated periods of time.

E. The aggregate amount of economic development incentive grants payable under this section in any fiscal year shall not exceed $6 million, and the aggregate amount of such grants outstanding at any time shall not exceed $30 million.

F. Any eligible company shall be eligible to receive a grant from the Fund in no fewer than five installments beginning in the third year after the Partnership has verified that the requirements applicable to such grant have been satisfied. All such terms shall be negotiated and set forth in a memorandum of agreement.

G. The Comptroller shall not draw any warrants to issue checks for grants under this chapter without a specific legislative appropriation as specified in conditions and restrictions on expenditures in the appropriation act. The payment of any grant under this section shall be in accordance with the terms and conditions set forth in a memorandum of agreement between a major eligible employer and the Commonwealth. These terms and conditions shall supplement the provisions of this chapter and shall include but not be limited to the terms of the payment of the grant. The payment of the grant shall be made in full or in proportion to a major eligible employer's fulfillment of the terms of the memorandum of agreement. (2005, c. 431; 2007, c. 576.)

The 2007 amendments. — The 2007 amendment by c. 576 in subsection E, substituted "$6 million" for "$3 million" and "$30 million" for "$15 million" and deleted the last sentence, which read: "No more than three new economic development incentive grants can be awarded under this section in any one biennium"; and substituted "third year" for "fourth year" in subsection F.

§ 2.2-5103. Requirements for grants generally. — A. Any eligible manufacturer, eligible company, or research and development service eligible to apply for a grant under this chapter shall provide evidence, satisfactory to the Secretary, of the amount of the capital investment, the number of new jobs created as a result of the capital investment and such other evidence that requirements of this chapter have been satisfied. An eligible manufacturer, eligible company, or research and development service whose application has been approved shall continue to comply with the requirements for grant eligibility during the grant payment period. The Partnership shall verify that the conditions for approval of any grant have been satisfied.

B. Prior to any grant payment, the Partnership shall certify to (i) the Comptroller and (ii) each applicant the amount of the grant to which such applicant is entitled. Subject to the appropriation by the General Assembly of sufficient moneys to the appropriate subfund, payment of such grant shall be made from the subfund by check issued by the State Treasurer on warrant of the Comptroller within 60 days of certification.

C. As a condition of receipt of a grant, a major eligible employer or eligible company shall make available to the Partnership for inspection upon request all relevant and applicable documents to determine whether the requirements for the receipt of grants as set forth in this chapter have been satisfied. All such documents appropriately identified by the major eligible employer or eligible company shall be considered confidential and proprietary.

D. Within 30 days of each calendar quarter, the Secretary shall provide a report to the chairmen of the House Committee on Appropriations and the Senate Committee on Finance that shall include, but is not limited to, the following information: the name of the eligible manufacturer, eligible company, or research and development service determined to be eligible for a grant; the product it manufactures, the nature of the research, or the products it produces or services it provides, as applicable; the locality of the manufacturing, research and development, or other facility; the amount of the grant made or committed from the Fund; the number of new jobs created or projected to be created; the amount of the manufacturer's, eligible company's, or research and development service's capital investment; and the timetable for the completion of the capital investment and new jobs created or employment creation, as applicable.

E. The Secretary shall provide grants and commitments from the Fund in an amount not to exceed the dollar amount contained in the Fund. If funds are committed for years beyond the fiscal years covered under the existing appropriation act, the State Treasurer shall set aside and reserve such funds as have been committed, and such funds shall remain in the Fund for those future fiscal years. No grant shall be payable in the years beyond the existing appropriation act unless such funds are currently available in the Fund. (1999, cc. 875, 961, § 2.1-548.43:5; 2000, c. 571; 2001, c. 844; 2005, c. 431.)

§ 2.2-5104. Virginia Investment Partnership Grant Fund. — A. There is established a special fund in the state treasury to be known as the Virginia Investment Partnership Grant Fund. The Fund shall consist of the Major Eligible Employer Grant subfund, the Economic Development Incentive Grant subfund, and the Investment Performance Grant subfund. Each subfund shall include such moneys as may be appropriated by the General Assembly and designated for the respective subfund, and a "sinking fund" including some proportion of the marginal revenues derived from eligible companies receiving grants under this Act. The Fund shall be used solely for the payment of investment incentive grants to eligible Virginia business entities pursuant to this chapter. The Partnership shall administer the Virginia Investment Partnership Grant Fund.

B. The Partnership shall allocate, from the appropriate subfund, moneys in the following order of priority: (i) first to unpaid grant amounts carried forward from prior years because eligible manufacturers did not receive the full amount of any grant to which they were eligible in a prior year and (ii) then to other approved applicants. If the moneys in the Fund are less than the amount of grants to which approved applicants in any class of priority are eligible, the moneys in the appropriate subfund shall be apportioned pro rata among eligible applicants in such class, based upon the amount of the grant to which an approved applicant is eligible and the amount of money in the subfund available for allocation to such class.

C. If a grant recipient is allocated less than the full amount of a grant to which it is eligible in any year, it shall not be eligible for the deficiency in that year, but the unpaid portion of the grant to which it was eligible shall be carried forward by the Partnership to the following year, during which it shall be in the first class of priority as provided in clause (i) of subsection B.

D. The Partnership shall determine the amount of the grants to be allocated to eligible applicants by June 30 of each year. The Partnership shall then certify to the Comptroller the amount of grant an eligible manufacturer shall receive. Payments shall be made by check issued by the State Treasurer on warrant of the Comptroller.

E. All excess funds remaining in any given year shall be carried forward on the books of the Fund for use in subsequent years.

F. Actions of the Partnership relating to the allocation and awarding of grants shall be exempt from the provisions of the Administrative Process Act (§ 2.2-4000 et seq.) pursuant to subdivision B 4 of § 2.2-4002. (1999, cc. 875, 961, § 2.1-548.43:6; 2000, c. 571; 2001, c. 844; 2005, c. 431.)

CHAPTER 52.

Comprehensive Services Act for At-Risk Youth and Families.

§ 2.2-5200. Intent and purpose; definitions. — A. It is the intention of this law to create a collaborative system of services and funding that is child-centered, family-focused and community-based when addressing the strengths and needs of troubled and at-risk youths and their families in the Commonwealth.

This law shall be interpreted and construed so as to effectuate the following purposes:

1. Ensure that services and funding are consistent with the Commonwealth's policies of preserving families and providing appropriate services in the least restrictive environment, while protecting the welfare of children and maintaining the safety of the public;

2. Identify and intervene early with young children and their families who are at risk of developing emotional or behavioral problems, or both, due to environmental, physical or psychological stress;

3. Design and provide services that are responsive to the unique and diverse strengths and needs of troubled youths and families;

4. Increase interagency collaboration and family involvement in service delivery and management;

5. Encourage a public and private partnership in the delivery of services to troubled and at-risk youths and their families; and

6. Provide communities flexibility in the use of funds and to authorize communities to make decisions and be accountable for providing services in concert with these purposes.

B. As used in this chapter, unless the context requires a different meaning:

"CSA" means the Comprehensive Services Act.

"Council" means the State Executive Council for Comprehensive Services for At-Risk Youth and Families created pursuant to § 2.2-2648. (1992, cc. 837, 880, § 2.1-745; 2001, c. 844.)

Cross references. — As to the establishment of the State Executive Council for Comprehensive Services for At-Risk Youth and Families, see § 2.2-2648. As to public body purchasing services under the Comprehensive Services Act for At-Risk Youth and Families being exempt from the Virginia Public Procurement Act, see § 2.2-4345. As to appropriation and use of state pool of funds to provide basic foster care services for at-risk children, see § 63.2-410.

Editor's note. — Acts 1992, cc. 837 and 880,

which enacted former Chapter 46 of Title 2.1, from which this chapter was derived, provided in cl. 5, as amended by Acts 1993, cc. 232 and 283, cls. 1 and 2, that the chapter would become effective July 1, 1993.

Law Review. — For article, "Legal Issues Involving Children," see 35 U. Rich. L. Rev. 741 (2001). For article surveying developments in education law in Virginia, see 37 U. Rich. L. Rev. 89 (2002). For annual survey article on legal issues involving children, see 38 U. Rich. L. Rev. 161 (2003).

§ 2.2-5201. State and local advisory team; appointment; membership. — The state and local advisory team is established to better serve the needs of troubled and at-risk youths and their families by advising the Council by managing cooperative efforts at the state level and providing support to community efforts. The team shall be appointed by and be responsible to the Council. The team shall include one representative from each of the following state agencies: the Department of Health, Department of Juvenile Justice, Department of Social Services, Department of Mental Health, Mental Retardation and Substance Abuse Services, the Department of Medical Assistance Services, and the Department of Education. The team shall also include a parent representative who is not an employee of any public or private program which serves children and families; a representative of a private organization or association of providers for children's or family services; a local Comprehensive Services Act coordinator or program manager; a juvenile and domestic relations district court judge; and one member from each of five different geographical areas of the Commonwealth and who serves on and is representative of the different participants of community policy and management teams. The nonstate agency members shall serve staggered terms of not more than three years, such terms to be determined by the Council.

The team shall annually elect a chairman from among the local government representatives who shall be responsible for convening the team. The team shall develop and adopt bylaws to govern its operations that shall be subject to approval by the Council. Any person serving on such team who does not represent a public agency shall file a statement of economic interests as set out in § 2.2-3117 of the State and Local Government Conflict of Interests Act (§ 2.2-3100 et seq.). Persons representing public agencies shall file such statements if required to do so pursuant to the State and Local Government Conflict of Interests Act. (1992, cc. 837, 880, § 2.1-747; 2000, c. 937; 2001, c. 844; 2003, c. 499; 2004, c. 836.)

Law Review. — For 2003/2004 survey of family and juvenile law, see 39 U. Rich. L. Rev. 183 (2004).

§ 2.2-5202. State and local advisory team; powers and duties. — The state and local advisory team may:

1. Advise the Council on state interagency program policies that promote and support cooperation and collaboration in the provision of services to troubled and at-risk youths and their families at the state and local levels;
2. Advise the Council on state interagency fiscal policies that promote and support cooperation and collaboration in the provision of services to troubled and at-risk youths and their families at the state and local levels;
3. Advise state agencies and localities on training and technical assistance necessary for the provision of efficient and effective services that are responsive to the strengths and needs of troubled and at-risk youths and their families; and
4. Advise the Council on the effects of proposed policies, regulations and guidelines. (1992, cc. 837, 880, § 2.1-748; 2000, c. 937; 2001, c. 844; 2003, c. 483.)

§ 2.2-5203. Duties of agencies represented on state and local advisory team. — The state agencies represented on the state and local advisory team shall provide administrative support for the team in the development and implementation of the collaborative system of services and funding authorized by this chapter. This support shall also include, but not be limited to, the provision of timely fiscal information, data for client- and service-tracking, and assistance in training local agency personnel on the system of services and funding established by this chapter. (1992, cc. 837, 880, § 2.1-749; 2001, c. 844.)

§ 2.2-5204. Community policy and management team; appointment; fiscal agent. — Every county, city, or combination of counties, cities, or counties and cities shall establish a community policy and management team in order to receive funds pursuant to this chapter. Each such team shall be appointed by the governing body of the participating local political subdivision establishing the team. In making such appointments, the governing body shall ensure that the membership is appropriately balanced among the representatives required to serve on the team in accordance with § 2.2-5205. When any combination of counties, cities or counties and cities establishes a community policy and management team, the board of supervisors of each participating county or the council in the case of each participating city shall jointly establish the size of the team and the type of representatives to be selected from each locality in accordance with § 2.2-5205. The governing bodies of each participating county and city served by the team shall appoint the designated representatives from their localities. The participating governing bodies shall jointly designate an official of one member city or county to act as fiscal agent for the team.

The county or city that comprises a single team and the county or city whose designated official serves as the fiscal agent for the team in the case of joint teams shall annually audit the total revenues of the team and its programs. The county or city that comprises a single team and any combination of counties or cities establishing a team shall arrange for the provision of legal services to the team. (1992, cc. 837, 880, § 2.1-750; 2001, c. 844.)

Cross references. — As to coordination with the Delinquency Prevention and Youth Development Act, see § 66-35.

§ 2.2-5205. Community policy and management teams; membership; immunity from liability. — The community policy and management team to be appointed by the local governing body shall include, at a minimum, at least one elected official or appointed official or his designee from the governing body of a locality that is a member of the team, and the local agency heads or their designees of the following community agencies: community services board established pursuant to § 37.2-501, juvenile court services unit, department of health, department of social services and the local school division. The team shall also include a representative of a private organization or association of providers for children's or family services if such organizations or associations are located within the locality, and a parent representative. Parent representatives who are employed by a public or private program that receives funds pursuant to this chapter or agencies represented on a community policy and management team may serve as a parent representative provided that they do not, as a part of their employment, interact directly on a regular and daily basis with children or supervise employees who interact directly on a daily basis with children. Notwithstanding this provision, foster parents may serve as parent representatives. Those persons appointed to represent community agencies shall be authorized to make policy and funding decisions for their agencies.

The local governing body may appoint other members to the team including, but not limited to, a local government official, a local law-enforcement official and representatives of other public agencies.

When any combination of counties, cities or counties, and cities establishes a community policy and management team, the membership requirements previously set out shall be adhered to by the team as a whole.

Persons who serve on the team shall be immune from any civil liability for decisions made about the appropriate services for a family or the proper placement or treatment of a child who comes before the team, unless it is proven that such person acted with malicious intent. Any person serving on such team who does not represent a public agency shall file a statement of economic interests as set out in § 2.2-3117 of the State and Local Government Conflict of Interests Act (§ 2.2-3100 et seq.). Persons representing public agencies shall file such statements if required to do so pursuant to the State and Local Government Conflict of Interests Act.

Persons serving on the team who are parent representatives or who represent private organizations or associations of providers for children's or family services shall abstain from decision-making involving individual cases or agencies in which they have either a personal interest, as defined in § 2.2-3101 of the State and Local Government Conflict of Interests Act, or a fiduciary interest. (1992, cc. 837, 880, § 2.1-751; 1995, c. 190; 1999, cc. 644, 669; 2001, c. 844.)

§ 2.2-5206. Community policy and management teams; powers and duties. — The community policy and management team shall manage the cooperative effort in each community to better serve the needs of troubled and at-risk youths and their families and to maximize the use of state and community resources. Every such team shall:

1. Develop interagency policies and procedures to govern the provision of services to children and families in its community;

2. Develop interagency fiscal policies governing access to the state pool of funds by the eligible populations including immediate access to funds for emergency services and shelter care;

3. Establish policies to assess the ability of parents or legal guardians to contribute financially to the cost of services to be provided and, when not specifically prohibited by federal or state law or regulation, provide for appropriate parental or legal guardian financial contribution, utilizing a standard sliding fee scale based upon ability to pay;

4. Coordinate long-range, community-wide planning that ensures the development of resources and services needed by children and families in its community including consultation on the development of a community-based system of services established under § 16.1-309.3;

5. Establish policies governing referrals and reviews of children and families to the family assessment and planning teams or a collaborative, multidisciplinary team process approved by the Council and a process to review the teams' recommendations and requests for funding;

6. Establish quality assurance and accountability procedures for program utilization and funds management;

7. Establish procedures for obtaining bids on the development of new services;

8. Manage funds in the interagency budget allocated to the community from the state pool of funds, the trust fund, and any other source;

9. Authorize and monitor the expenditure of funds by each family assessment and planning team or a collaborative, multidisciplinary team process approved by the Council;

10. Submit grant proposals that benefit its community to the state trust fund and enter into contracts for the provision or operation of services upon approval of the participating governing bodies;

11. Serve as its community's liaison to the Office of Comprehensive Services for At-Risk Youth and Families, reporting on its programmatic and fiscal operations and on its recommendations for improving the service system, including consideration of realignment of geographical boundaries for providing human services;

12. Collect and provide uniform data to the Council as requested by the Office of Comprehensive Services for At-Risk Youth and Families in accordance with subdivision D 16 of § 2.2-2648;

13. Review and analyze data in management reports provided by the Office of Comprehensive Services for At-Risk Youth and Families in accordance with subdivision D 18 of § 2.2-2648 to help evaluate child and family outcomes and public and private provider performance in the provision of services to children and families through the Comprehensive Services Act program. Every team shall also review local and statewide data provided in the management reports on the number of children served, children placed out of state, demographics, types of services provided, duration of services, service expenditures, child and family outcomes, and performance measures. Additionally, teams shall track the utilization and performance of residential placements using data and management reports to develop and implement strategies for returning children placed outside of the Commonwealth, preventing placements, and reducing lengths of stay in residential programs for children who can appropriately and effectively be served in their home, relative's homes, family-like setting, or their community;

14. Administer funds pursuant to § 16.1-309.3;

15. Have authority, upon approval of the participating governing bodies, to enter into a contract with another community policy and management team to purchase coordination services provided that funds described as the state pool of funds under § 2.2-5211 are not used;

16. Submit to the Department of Mental Health, Mental Retardation and Substance Abuse Services information on children under the age of 14 and adolescents ages 14 through 17 for whom an admission to an acute care psychiatric or residential treatment facility licensed pursuant to Article 2 (§ 37.2-403 et seq.) of Chapter 4 of Title 37.2, exclusive of group homes, was sought but was unable to be obtained by the reporting entities. Such information shall be gathered from the family assessment and planning team or participating community agencies authorized in § 2.2-5207. Information to be submitted shall include:

a. The child or adolescent's date of birth;

b. Date admission was attempted; and

c. Reason the patient could not be admitted into the hospital or facility; and

17. Establish policies for providing intensive care coordination services for children who are at risk of entering, or are placed in, residential care through the Comprehensive Services Act program, consistent with guidelines developed pursuant to subdivision D 22 of § 2.2-2648. (1992, cc. 837, 880; 1995, cc. 396, 696, 699, § 2.1-752; 1997, c. 347; 1999, c. 669; 2000, c. 937; 2001, cc. 190, 206, 844; 2002, cc. 585, 619; 2003, c. 483; 2008, cc. 39, 170, 277.)

Cross references. — As to data reporting on children and adolescents, see § 37.2-308.

Editor's note. — Acts 1995, cc. 696 and 699, which amended § 2.1-752, from which this section was derived, provided in cl. 2: "That this act shall become effective January 1, 1996, if state funds are provided to carry out the purposes of the Virginia Juvenile Community Crime Control Act during the 1995 Session of the General Assembly." The appropriation for these acts was made under the Secretary of Public Safety, Department of Youth and Family Services, Acts 1995, c. 853, item 578 1c.

Acts 2001, cc. 190 and 206 amended § 2.1-

752, from which this section is derived. Pursuant to § 30-152, Acts 2001, cc. 190 and 206 have been given effect in this section as set out above. The 2001 amendments by cc. 190 and 206 deleted "and" at the end of subdivision 12, added "and" at the end of subdivision 13, and added subdivision 14.

Acts 2008, c. 879, effective for the biennium ending June 30, 2010, in Item 283 B 2 d, provides: "Pursuant to § 2.2-5200, Code of Virginia, Community Policy and Management Teams shall seek to ensure that services and funding are consistent with the Commonwealth's policies of preserving families and providing appropriate services in the least restrictive environment, while protecting the welfare of children and maintaining the safety of the public. Each locality shall submit to the Office of Comprehensive Services information on utilization of residential facilities for treatment of children and length of stay in such facilities. By December 15 of each year, the Office of Comprehensive Services shall report to the Governor and Chairmen of the House Appropriations and Senate Finance Committees on utilization rates and average lengths of stays statewide and for each locality."

The 2008 amendments. — The 2008 amendments by cc. 39 and 170 are identical, and added subdivision 16, which was subsequently renumbered as subdivision 17 at the direction of the Virginia Code Commission, and made related changes.

The 2008 amendment by c. 277, in subdivision 12, substituted "as requested by the Office of Comprehensive Services for At-Risk Youth and Families in accordance with subdivision D 16 of § 2.2-2648" for "on, but not limited to expenditures, number of youth served in specific CSA activities, length of stay for residents in core licensed residential facilities, and proportion of youth placed in treatment settings suggested by a uniform assessment instrument for CSA-funded services"; added subdivision 13 and redesignated the remaining subsections accordingly.

Law Review. — For an article, "Legal Issues Involving Children," see 32 U. Rich. L. Rev. 1345 (1998).

§ 2.2-5207. Family assessment and planning team; membership; immunity from liability. — Each community policy and management team shall establish and appoint one or more family assessment and planning teams as the needs of the community require. Each family assessment and planning team shall include representatives of the following community agencies who have authority to access services within their respective agencies: community services board established pursuant to § 37.2-501, juvenile court services unit, department of social services, and local school division. Each family and planning team also shall include a parent representative and may include a representative of the department of health at the request of the chair of the local community policy and management team. Parent representatives who are employed by a public or private program that receives funds pursuant to this chapter or agencies represented on a family assessment and planning team may serve as a parent representative provided that they do not, as a part of their employment, interact directly on a regular and daily basis with children or supervise employees who interact directly on a regular basis with children. Notwithstanding this provision, foster parents may serve as parent representatives. The family assessment and planning team may include a representative of a private organization or association of providers for children's or family services and of other public agencies.

Persons who serve on a family assessment and planning team shall be immune from any civil liability for decisions made about the appropriate services for a family or the proper placement or treatment of a child who comes before the team, unless it is proven that such person acted with malicious intent. Any person serving on such team who does not represent a public agency shall file a statement of economic interests as set out in § 2.2-3117 of the State and Local Government Conflict of Interests Act (§ 2.2-3100 et seq.). Persons representing public agencies shall file such statements if required to do so pursuant to the State and Local Government Conflict of Interests Act.

Persons serving on the team who are parent representatives or who represent private organizations or associations of providers for children's or family services shall abstain from decision-making involving individual cases or agencies in which they have either a personal interest, as defined in

§ 2.2-3101 of the State and Local Government Conflict of Interests Act, or a fiduciary interest. (1992, cc. 837, 880, § 2.1-753; 1995, c. 190; 1999, c. 644; 2001, c. 844; 2003, c. 483.)

Cross references. — As to creation, maintenance, and coordination of hospital and community-based multi-disciplinary teams to assist in identifying abused and neglected children, coordinating services for them, etc., which teams may be the family assessment and planning teams established pursuant to § 2.2-5207, see § 63.2-1503 J.

§ **2.2-5208. Family assessment and planning team; powers and duties.** — The family assessment and planning team, in accordance with § 2.2-2648, shall assess the strengths and needs of troubled youths and families who are approved for referral to the team and identify and determine the complement of services required to meet these unique needs.

Every such team, in accordance with policies developed by the community policy and management team, shall:

1. Review referrals of youths and families to the team;

2. Provide for family participation in all aspects of assessment, planning and implementation of services;

3. Provide for the participation of foster parents in the assessment, planning and implementation of services when a child has a program goal of permanent foster care or is in a long-term foster care placement. The case manager shall notify the foster parents of a troubled youth of the time and place of all assessment and planning meetings related to such youth. Such foster parents shall be given the opportunity to speak at the meeting or submit written testimony if the foster parents are unable to attend. The opinions of the foster parents shall be considered by the family assessment and planning team in its deliberations;

4. Develop an individual family services plan for youths and families reviewed by the team that provides for appropriate and cost-effective services;

5. Identify children who are at risk of entering, or are placed in, residential care through the Comprehensive Services Act program who can be appropriately and effectively served in their homes, relatives' homes, family-like settings, and communities. For each child entering or in residential care, in accordance with the policies of the community policy and management team developed pursuant to subdivision 17 of § 2.2-5206, the family assessment and planning team or approved alternative multidisciplinary team, in collaboration with the family, shall (i) identify the strengths and needs of the child and his family through conducting or reviewing comprehensive assessments, including but not limited to information gathered through the mandatory uniform assessment instrument, (ii) identify specific services and supports necessary to meet the identified needs of the child and his family, building upon the identified strengths, (iii) implement a plan for returning the youth to his home, relative's home, family-like setting, or community at the earliest appropriate time that addresses his needs, including identification of public or private community-based services to support the youth and his family during transition to community-based care, and (iv) provide regular monitoring and utilization review of the services and residential placement for the child to determine whether the services and placement continue to provide the most appropriate and effective services for the child and his family;

6. Where parental or legal guardian financial contribution is not specifically prohibited by federal or state law or regulation, or has not been ordered by the court or by the Division of Child Support Enforcement, assess the ability of parents or legal guardians, utilizing a standard sliding fee scale, based upon ability to pay, to contribute financially to the cost of services to be provided and provide for appropriate financial contribution from parents or legal guardians in the individual family services plan;

7. Refer the youth and family to community agencies and resources in accordance with the individual family services plan;

8. Recommend to the community policy and management team expenditures from the local allocation of the state pool of funds; and

9. Designate a person who is responsible for monitoring and reporting, as appropriate, on the progress being made in fulfilling the individual family services plan developed for each youth and family, such reports to be made to the team or the responsible local agencies. (1992, cc. 837, 880, § 2.1-754; 1995, c. 396; 1999, c. 669; 2001, cc. 437, 844; 2008, cc. 39, 170.)

Cross references. — As to foster care plans, placement of child, permissible plan goals, and court review of foster children, see § 63.2-906.

Editor's note. — Acts 2001, c. 437 amended § 2.1-754, from which this section is derived. Pursuant to § 30-152, Acts 2001, c. 437 has been given effect in this section as set out above. The 2001 amendment by c. 437 added present subdivision 3 and redesignated former subdivisions 3 through 7 as present subdivisions 4 through 8.

The 2008 amendments. — The 2008 amendments by cc. 39 and 170 are identical, and inserted subdivision 5 and redesignated former subdivisions 5 through 8 as subdivisions 6 through 9.

CASE NOTES

Editor's note. — The case below was decided under former Title 2.1 or prior provisions.

Court may compel provisions of services. — The trial court had authority to compel the family assessment and planning team and the community policy and management team to provide any necessary services. Fauquier County Dep't of Social Servs. v. Robinson, 20 Va. App. 142, 455 S.E.2d 734 (1995).

§ 2.2-5209. Referrals to family assessment and planning team or collaborative, multidisciplinary team process. — The community policy and management team shall establish policies governing the referral of troubled youths and families to the family assessment and planning team or a collaborative, multidisciplinary team process approved by the Council. These policies shall include that all youth and families for which CSA-funded treatment services are requested are to be assessed by the family assessment and planning team or an approved collaborative, multidisciplinary team process and shall consider the criteria set out in subdivisions A 1 and A 2 of § 2.2-5212. Except for cases involving only the payment of foster care maintenance that shall be at the discretion of the local community policy and management team, cases for which service plans are developed outside of this family assessment and planning team process or approved collaborative, multidisciplinary team process shall not be eligible for state pool funds.

Nothing in this section shall prohibit the use of state pool funds for emergency placements, provided the youth are subsequently assessed by the family assessment and planning team or an approved collaborative, multidisciplinary team process within 14 days of admission and the emergency placement is approved at the time of placement. In cases involving the denial of state pool funds resulting from parental refusal to consent to release of student records under federal law, where such refusal precludes the development of placement through the family assessment and planning team process or the approved collaborative, multidisciplinary team process, an appeal for good cause may be made to the Council. (1992, cc. 837, 880, § 2.1-755; 1999, c. 669; 2001, c. 844; 2003, c. 483.)

Editor's note. — Acts 2008, c. 879, effective for the biennium ending June 30, 2010, in Item 283 B 11, provides: "For purposes of defining cases involving only the payment of foster care maintenance, pursuant to § 2.2-5209, Code of Virginia, the definition of foster care maintenance used by the Virginia Department of Social Services for federal Title IV-E shall be used."

§ 2.2-5210. Information sharing; confidentiality. — All public agencies that have served a family or treated a child referred to a family assessment and planning team shall cooperate with this team. The agency that refers a youth and family to the team shall be responsible for obtaining the consent required to share agency client information with the team. After obtaining the proper consent, all agencies shall promptly deliver, upon request and without charge, such records of services, treatment or education of the family or child as are necessary for a full and informed assessment by the team.

Proceedings held to consider the appropriate provision of services and funding for a particular child or family or both who have been referred to the family assessment and planning team and whose case is being assessed by this team or reviewed by the community management and planning team shall be confidential and not open to the public, unless the child and family who are the subjects of the proceeding request, in writing, that it be open. All information about specific children and families obtained by the team members in the discharge of their responsibilities to the team shall be confidential.

Utilizing a secure electronic database, the CPMT and the family assessment and planning team shall provide the Office of Comprehensive Services for At-Risk Youth and Families with client-specific information from the mandatory uniform assessment and information in accordance with subdivision D 11 of § 2.2-2648. (1992, cc. 837, 880, § 2.1-756; 2001, c. 844; 2008, c. 277.)

The 2008 amendments. — The 2008 amendment by c. 277 substituted the present last paragraph for the former last paragraph, which read: "Demographic, service and cost information on youths and families receiving services and funding through this chapter that is of a nonidentifying nature may be gathered for reporting and evaluation purposes."

§ 2.2-5211. State pool of funds for community policy and management teams. — A. There is established a state pool of funds to be allocated to community policy and management teams in accordance with the appropriation act and appropriate state regulations. These funds, as made available by the General Assembly, shall be expended for public or private nonresidential or residential services for troubled youths and families.

The purposes of this system of funding are to:

1. Place authority for making program and funding decisions at the community level;

2. Consolidate categorical agency funding and institute community responsibility for the provision of services;

3. Provide greater flexibility in the use of funds to purchase services based on the strengths and needs of youths and families; and

4. Reduce disparity in accessing services and to reduce inadvertent fiscal incentives for serving children according to differing required local match rates for funding streams.

B. The state pool shall consist of funds that serve the target populations identified in subdivisions 1 through 5 of this subsection in the purchase of residential and nonresidential services for children. References to funding sources and current placement authority for the targeted populations of children are for the purpose of accounting for the funds in the pool. It is not intended that children be categorized by individual funding streams in order to access services. The target population shall be the following:

1. Children placed for purposes of special education in approved private school educational programs, previously funded by the Department of Education through private tuition assistance;

2. Children with disabilities placed by local social services agencies or the Department of Juvenile Justice in private residential facilities or across jurisdictional lines in private, special education day schools, if the individualized education program indicates such school is the appropriate placement while living in foster homes or child-caring facilities, previously funded by the Department of Education through the Interagency Assistance Fund for Noneducational Placements of Handicapped Children;

3. Children for whom foster care services, as defined by § 63.2-905, are being provided to prevent foster care placements, and children placed through parental agreements, entrusted to local social service agencies by their parents or guardians or committed to the agencies by any court of competent jurisdiction for purposes of placement in suitable family homes, child-caring institutions, residential facilities or independent living arrangements, as authorized by § 63.2-900;

4. Children placed by a juvenile and domestic relations district court, in accordance with the provisions of § 16.1-286, in a private or locally operated public facility or nonresidential program, or in a community or facility-based treatment program in accordance with the provisions of subsections B or C of § 16.1-284.1; and

5. Children committed to the Department of Juvenile Justice and placed by it in a private home or in a public or private facility in accordance with § 66-14.

C. The General Assembly and the governing body of each county and city shall annually appropriate such sums of money as shall be sufficient to (i) provide special education services and foster care services for children identified in subdivisions B 1, B 2 and B 3 and (ii) meet relevant federal mandates for the provision of these services. The community policy and management team shall anticipate to the best of its ability the number of children for whom such services will be required and reserve funds from its state pool allocation to meet these needs. Nothing in this section prohibits local governments from requiring parental or legal financial contributions, where not specifically prohibited by federal or state law or regulation, utilizing a standard sliding fee scale based upon ability to pay, as provided in the appropriation act.

D. When a community services board established pursuant to § 37.2-501, local school division, local social service agency, court service unit, or the Department of Juvenile Justice has referred a child and family to a family assessment and planning team and that team has recommended the proper level of treatment and services needed by that child and family and has determined the child's eligibility for funding for services through the state pool of funds, then the community services board, the local school division, local social services agency, court service unit or Department of Juvenile Justice has met its fiscal responsibility for that child for the services funded through the pool. However, the community services board, the local school division, local social services agency, court service unit or Department of Juvenile Justice shall continue to be responsible for providing services identified in individual family service plans that are within the agency's scope of responsibility and that are funded separately from the state pool.

Further, in any instance that an individual 18 through 21 years of age, inclusive, who is eligible for funding from the state pool and is properly defined as a school-aged child with disabilities pursuant to § 22.1-213 is placed by a local social services agency that has custody across jurisdictional lines in a group home in the Commonwealth and the individual's individualized education program (IEP), as prepared by the placing jurisdiction, indicates that a private day school placement is the appropriate educational program for such individual, the financial and legal responsibility for the individual's special education services and IEP shall remain, in compliance with the provisions of federal law, Article 2 (§ 22.1-213) of Chapter 13 of Title 22.1, and Board of

Education regulations, the responsibility of the placing jurisdiction until the individual reaches the age of 21, inclusive, or is no longer eligible for special education services. The financial and legal responsibility for such special education services shall remain with the placing jurisdiction, unless the placing jurisdiction has transitioned all appropriate services with the individual.

E. In any matter properly before a court for which state pool funds are to be accessed, the court shall, prior to final disposition, and pursuant to §§ 2.2-5209 and 2.2-5212, refer the matter to the community policy and management team for assessment by a local family assessment and planning team authorized by policies of the community policy and management team for assessment to determine the recommended level of treatment and services needed by the child and family. The family assessment and planning team making the assessment shall make a report of the case or forward a copy of the individual family services plan to the court within 30 days of the court's written referral to the community policy and management team. The court shall then consider the recommendations. However, the court may make such other disposition as is authorized or required by law, and services ordered pursuant to such disposition shall qualify for funding as appropriated under this section. (1992, cc. 837, 880, § 2.1-757; 1993, c. 567; 1994, cc. 854, 865; 1998, c. 534; 1999, c. 669; 2000, c. 914; 2001, c. 844; 2004, cc. 286, 631.)

Editor's note. — Acts 2008, c. 879, effective for the biennium ending June 30, 2010, in Item 133 A, provides: "The Department of Education, in collaboration with the Office of Comprehensive Services, shall provide training to local staff serving on Family Assessment and Planning Teams and Community Policy and Management Teams. Training shall include, but need not be limited to, the federal and state requirements pertaining to the provision of the special education services funded under § 2.2-5211, Code of Virginia. The training shall also include written guidance concerning which services remain the financial responsibility of the local school divisions. In addition, the Department of Education shall provide ongoing local oversight of its federal and state requirements related to the provision of services funded under § 2.2-5211, Code of Virginia."

Acts 2008, c. 879, effective for the biennium ending June 30, 2010, in Item 283 B 1 e, provides: "The Office of Comprehensive Services, per the policy of the State Executive Council, shall deny state pool funding to any locality not in compliance with federal and state requirements pertaining to the provision of special education and foster care services funded in accordance with § 2.2-5211, Code of Virginia."

Acts 2008, c. 879, effective for the biennium ending June 30, 2010, in Item 337, provides: "The Department of Social Services, in collaboration with the Office of Comprehensive Services, shall provide training to local staff serving on Family Assessment and Planning Teams and Community Policy and Management Teams. Training shall include, but need not be limited to, the federal and state requirements pertaining to the provision of the foster care services funded under § 2.2-5211, Code of Virginia. The training shall also include written guidance concerning which services remain the financial responsibility of the local departments of social services. Training shall be provided on a regional basis at least once per year. Written guidance shall be updated and provided to local Comprehensive Services Act teams whenever there is a change in allowable expenses under federal or state guidelines. In addition, the Department of Social Services shall provide ongoing local oversight of its federal and state requirements related to the provision of services funded under § 2.2-5211, Code of Virginia."

CASE NOTES

Editor's note. — The cases below were decided under former Title 2.1 or prior provisions.

Payment of juvenile's residential treatment. — The juvenile court judge had the authority to enter the decree ordering Social Services to provide treatment for the minor in a residential treatment facility. S.G. ex rel. v. Prince William County Dep't of Social Servs., 25 Va. App. 356, 488 S.E.2d 653 (1997).

Trial judge retains discretion over disposition. — Under the Comprehensive Services Act for At-Risks Youth and Families, the trial judge has discretion to make a disposition other than the one recommended by the family assessment and planning team. Fauquier County Dep't of Social Servs. v. Robinson, 20 Va. App. 142, 455 S.E.2d 734 (1995).

Evidentiary hearing required. — Comprehensive Services Act Office was entitled to an evidentiary hearing on order of juvenile and domestic relations district court directing it to provide residential placement for child found to be in need of supervision. Comprehensive Servs. Act Office v. J.M., No. 1620-98-2 (Ct. of Appeals Aug. 3, 1999).

§ 2.2-5211.1. Certain restrictions on reimbursement and placements of children in residential facilities. — Notwithstanding any provision of this chapter to the contrary or any practice or previous decision-making process of the state executive council, Office of Comprehensive Services, state and local advisory team, any community policy and management team, any family assessment and planning team or any other local entity placing children through the Comprehensive Services Act (CSA), the following restrictions shall control:

1. In the event that any group home or other residential facility in which CSA children reside has its licensure status lowered to provisional as a result of multiple health and safety or human rights violations, all children placed through CSA in such facility shall be assessed as to whether it is in the best interests of each child placed to be removed from the facility and placed in a fully licensed facility and no additional CSA placements shall be made in the provisionally licensed facility until and unless the violations and deficiencies relating to health and safety or human rights that caused the designation as provisional shall be completely remedied and full licensure status restored.

2. Prior to the placement of a child across jurisdictional lines, the family assessment and planning teams shall (i) explore all appropriate community services for the child, (ii) document that no appropriate placement is available in the locality, and (iii) report the rationale for the placement decision to the community policy and management team. The community policy and management team shall report annually to the Office of Comprehensive Services on the gaps in the services needed to keep children in the local community and any barriers to the development of those services.

3. Community policy and management teams, family assessment and planning teams or other local entities responsible for CSA placements shall notify the receiving school division whenever a child is placed across jurisdictional lines and identify any children with disabilities and foster care children to facilitate compliance with expedited enrollment and special education requirements. (2006, c. 781.)

Editor's note. — Acts 2006, c. 781, cl. 2, provides: "That the Board of Education, Board of Mental Health, Mental Retardation and Substance Abuse Services, Board of Social Services, and the State Board of Juvenile Justice shall promulgate regulations to implement the provisions of this act to be effective within 280 days of its enactment."

Acts 2006, c. 781, cl. 3, provides: "That the Board of Education, Board of Mental Health, Mental Retardation and Substance Abuse Services, Board of Social Services, and the State Board of Juvenile Justice shall also include in the emergency regulations required by the second enactment clause provisions to implement the requirements enacted by HB 2461 (2005) and SB 1304 (2005) [Acts 2005, cc. 358, 471]."

§ 2.2-5212. Eligibility for state pool of funds. — A. In order to be eligible for funding for services through the state pool of funds, a youth, or family with a child, shall meet one or more of the criteria specified in subdivisions 1 through 4 and shall be determined through the use of a uniform assessment instrument and process and by policies of the community policy and management team to have access to these funds.

1. The child or youth has emotional or behavior problems that:

a. Have persisted over a significant period of time or, though only in evidence for a short period of time, are of such a critical nature that intervention is warranted;

b. Are significantly disabling and are present in several community settings, such as at home, in school or with peers; and

c. Require services or resources that are unavailable or inaccessible, or that are beyond the normal agency services or routine collaborative processes across agencies, or require coordinated interventions by at least two agencies.

2. The child or youth has emotional or behavior problems, or both, and currently is in, or is at imminent risk of entering, purchased residential care. In addition, the child or youth requires services or resources that are beyond normal agency services or routine collaborative processes across agencies, and requires coordinated services by at least two agencies.

3. The child or youth requires placement for purposes of special education in approved private school educational programs.

4. The child or youth has been placed in foster care through a parental agreement between a local social services agency or public agency designated by the community policy and management team and his parents or guardians, entrusted to a local social services agency by his parents or guardian or has been committed to the agency by a court of competent jurisdiction for the purposes of placement as authorized by § 63.2-900.

B. For purposes of determining eligibility for the state pool of funds, *"child"* or *"youth"* means (i) a person less than eighteen years of age and (ii) any individual through twenty-one years of age who is otherwise eligible for mandated services of the participating state agencies including special education and foster care services. (1992, cc. 837, 880, § 2.1-758; 1994, c. 865; 1999, c. 669; 2001, c. 844.)

§ 2.2-5213. State trust fund. — A. There is established a state trust fund with funds appropriated by the General Assembly. The purposes of this fund are to develop:

1. Early intervention services for young children and their families, which are defined to include: prevention efforts for individuals who are at-risk for developing problems based on biological, psychological or social/environmental factors.

2. Community services for troubled youths who have emotional or behavior problems, or both, and who can appropriately and effectively be served in the home or community, or both, and their families.

The fund shall consist of moneys from the state general fund, federal grants, and private foundations.

B. Proposals for requesting these funds shall be made by community policy and management teams to the Office of Comprehensive Services for At-Risk Youth and Families. The Office of Comprehensive Services for At-Risk Youth and Families shall make recommendations on the proposals it receives to the Council, which shall award the grants to the community teams in accordance with the policies developed under the authority of § 2.2-5202. (1992, cc. 837, 880, § 2.1-759; 1995, c. 520; 2000, c. 937; 2001, c. 844.)

§ 2.2-5214. Rates for purchase of services; service fee directory. — The rates paid for services purchased pursuant to this chapter shall be determined by competition of the market place and by a process sufficiently flexible to ensure that family assessment and planning teams and providers can meet the needs of individual children and families referred to them. To ensure that family assessment and planning teams are informed about the availability of programs and the rates charged for such programs, the Council shall oversee the development of and approve a service fee directory that shall list the services offered and the rates charged by any entity, public or private, which offers specialized services for at-risk youth or families. The Council shall designate the Office of Comprehensive Services for At-Risk Youth and Families to coordinate the establishment, maintenance and other activities regarding the service fee directory. (1993, c. 110, § 2.1-759.1; 2000, c. 937; 2001, c. 844.)

CHAPTER 53.

Early Intervention Services System.

§ 2.2-5300. Definitions. — As used in this chapter, unless the context requires a different meaning:

"Council" means the Virginia Interagency Coordinating Council created pursuant to § 2.2-2664.

"Early intervention services" means services provided through Part C of the Individuals with Disabilities Education Act (20 U.S.C. § 1431 et seq.), as amended, designed to meet the developmental needs of each child and the needs of the family related to enhancing the child's development and provided to children from birth to age three who have (i) a 25 percent developmental delay in one or more areas of development, (ii) atypical development, or (iii) a diagnosed physical or mental condition that has a high probability of resulting in a developmental delay. Early intervention services provided in the child's home and in accordance with this chapter shall not be construed to be home health services as referenced in § 32.1-162.7.

"Participating agencies" means the Departments of Health, of Education, of Medical Assistance Services, of Mental Health, Mental Retardation and Substance Abuse Services, and of Social Services; the Departments for the Deaf and Hard-of-Hearing and for the Blind and Vision Impaired; the Virginia Office for Protection and Advocacy; and the Bureau of Insurance within the State Corporation Commission. (1992, c. 771, § 2.1-760; 1999, cc. 640, 684; 2001, c. 844; 2005, c. 695.)

Editor's note. — In light of Acts 2002, c. 572, at the direction of the Virginia Code Commission, the reference in the definition of "Participating Agencies" to the Department for Rights of Virginians with Disabilities has been changed to refer to the Virginia Office for Protection and Advocacy.

§ 2.2-5301. Secretaries of Health and Human Resources and Education to work together. — The Secretaries of Health and Human Resources and Education shall work together in:

1. Promoting interagency consensus and facilitating complementary agency positions on issues relating to early intervention services;

2. Examining and evaluating the effectiveness of state agency programs, services, and plans for early intervention services and identifying duplications, inefficiencies, and unmet needs;

3. Analyzing state agency budget requests and any other budget items affecting early intervention services;
4. Proposing ways of realigning funding to promote interagency initiatives and programs for early intervention services;
5. Formulating recommendations on planning, priorities, and expenditures for early intervention services and communicating the recommendations to the Governor and state agency heads;
6. Formulating joint policy positions and statements on legislative issues regarding early intervention services and communicating those positions and statements to the General Assembly; and
7. Resolving interagency disputes and assigning financial responsibility in accordance with Part C of the Individuals with Disabilities Education Act (20 U.S.C. § 1431 et seq.). (1992, c. 771, § 2.1-761; 2001, c. 844.)

§ **2.2-5302:** Repealed by Acts 2004, c. 38.

§ **2.2-5303. Duties of participating agencies.** — The duties of the participating agencies shall include:
1. Establishing a statewide system of early intervention services in accordance with state and federal statutes and regulations;
2. Identifying and maximizing coordination of all available public and private resources for early intervention services;
3. Developing and implementing formal state interagency agreements that define the financial responsibility and service obligations of each participating agency for early intervention services, establish procedures for resolving disputes, and address any additional matters necessary to ensure collaboration;
4. Consulting with the lead agency in the promulgation of regulations to implement the early intervention services system, including developing definitions of eligibility and services;
5. Carrying out decisions resulting from the dispute resolution process;
6. Providing assistance to localities in the implementation of a comprehensive early intervention services system in accordance with state and federal statutes and regulations; and
7. Requesting and reviewing data and reports on the implementation of early intervention services from counterpart local agencies. (1992, c. 771, § 2.1-763; 2001, c. 844.)

§ **2.2-5304. State lead agency's duties.** — To facilitate the implementation of an early intervention services system and to ensure compliance with federal requirements, the Governor shall appoint a lead agency. The duties of the lead agency shall include:
1. Promulgating regulations and adopting the policies and procedures as necessary to implement an early intervention services system and assure consistent and equitable access to such services, including, but not limited to, uniform statewide procedures on or before January 1, 2002, for public and private providers to determine parental liability and to charge fees for early intervention services in accordance with federal law and regulations, in consultation with other participating agencies; the regulations shall be adopted in accordance with the provisions of the Administrative Process Act (§ 2.2-4000 et seq.);
2. Contracting with local lead agencies for implementation of local early intervention systems statewide;
3. Providing technical assistance to local early intervention systems, including local lead agencies, local interagency coordinating councils, and early intervention service providers; and

4. Establishing an interagency system of monitoring and supervising the early intervention services system. (1992, c. 771, § 2.1-764; 2001, cc. 562, 844; 2005, c. 695.)

Editor's note. — Acts 2001, c. 562 amended § 2.1-764, from which this section is derived. Pursuant to § 30-152, Acts 2001, c. 562 has been given effect in this section as set out above. The 2001 amendment by c. 562, in subdivision 1, inserted "and adopting the policies and procedures as necessary" near the beginning, and inserted "and assure consistent and equitable access to such services, including, but not limited to, uniform statewide procedures on or before January 1, 2002, for public and private providers to determine parental liability and to charge fees for early intervention services in accordance with federal law and regulations."

§ 2.2-5304.1. Local lead agencies. — A. To facilitate implementation of local early intervention systems statewide, the state lead agency shall contract with local lead agencies selected by the local interagency coordinating council. If the local interagency coordinating council is unable to select a local lead agency, the state lead agency shall assist in making the determination.

B. The local lead agency shall have the power and duty to:

1. Establish and administer a local system of early intervention services in compliance with Part C of the Individuals With Disabilities Education Act (20 U.S.C. § 1431 et seq.) and all relevant state policies and procedures;

2. Implement consistent and uniform policies and procedures for public and private providers to determine parental liability and to charge fees for early intervention services pursuant to regulations, policies, and procedures adopted by the state lead agency in § 2.2-5304; and

3. Manage relevant state and federal early intervention funds allocated from the state lead agency for the local early intervention system, including contracting or otherwise arranging for services with local early intervention services providers.

C. Localities shall not be mandated to provide funding for any costs under this chapter, either directly or through participating local public agencies. (2005, c. 695.)

§ 2.2-5305. Local interagency coordinating councils. — A. The lead agency, in consultation with the Virginia Interagency Coordinating Council, shall establish local interagency coordinating councils on a statewide basis to advise and assist the local lead agencies and to enable early intervention service providers to establish working relationships that will increase the efficiency and effectiveness of early intervention services. The membership of local interagency coordinating councils shall include designees from the following agencies: community services boards, departments of health, departments of social services, and local school divisions. These designees shall designate additional council members as follows: at least one parent representative who is not an employee of any public or private program that serves infants and toddlers with disabilities; representatives from community providers of early intervention services; and representatives from other service providers as deemed appropriate. Every county and city may appoint a representative to the respective local interagency coordinating council.

B. The duties of local interagency coordinating councils shall include assisting and advising the local lead agency in the following:

1. Identifying existing early intervention services and resources;

2. Identifying gaps in the service delivery system and developing strategies to address these gaps;

3. Identifying alternative funding sources;

4. Facilitating the development of interagency agreements and supporting the development of service coalitions;

5. Implementing policies and procedures that will promote interagency collaboration; and

6. Developing local procedures and determining mechanisms for implementing policies and procedures in accordance with state and federal statutes and regulations. (1992, c. 771, § 2.1-766; 2001, cc. 562, 844; 2005, c. 695.)

Editor's note. — Acts 2001, c. 562 amended § 2.1-766, from which this section is derived. Pursuant to § 30-152, Acts 2001, c. 562 has been given effect in this section as set out above. The 2001 amendment by c. 562, in subsection B, deleted "and" at the end of subdivision 5, inserted "and" at the end of subdivision 6, and added subdivision 7.

§ **2.2-5306. Duties of local public agencies.** — Local public agencies represented on local interagency coordinating councils are responsible for:

1. Providing services as appropriate and agreed upon by members of the local interagency coordinating council;

2. Maintaining data and providing information as requested to their respective state agencies;

3. Developing and implementing interagency agreements;

4. Complying with applicable state and federal regulations and local policies and procedures; and

5. Following procedural safeguards and dispute resolution procedures as adopted by the Commonwealth. (1992, c. 771, § 2.1-767; 2001, c. 844.)

§ **2.2-5307. Existing funding levels.** — Any federal funds made available through Part C of the Individuals with Disabilities Education Act (20 U.S.C. § 1431 et seq.) and any state funds appropriated specifically for Part H services shall supplement overall funding for services currently provided under Part of the Individuals with Disabilities Education Act (20 U.S.C. § 1431 et seq.). (1992, c. 771, § 2.1-768; 2001, c. 844.)

§ **2.2-5308. Licensure as home care organization not required.** — Notwithstanding the provisions of § 32.1-162.9, no person who provides early intervention services in accordance with this chapter shall be required to be licensed as a home care organization in order to provide these services in a child's home. (1999, cc. 640, 684, § 2.1-768.1; 2001, c. 844.)

CHAPTER 54.

Community Action Act.

§ **2.2-5400. Short title; definitions.** — A. This chapter shall be known as the Community Action Act.

B. As used in this chapter, unless the context requires a different meaning:

"Community action agency" means a local subdivision of the Commonwealth, a combination of political subdivisions, a separate public agency or a private nonprofit agency that has the authority under its applicable charter or laws to receive funds to support community action activities and other appropriate measures designed to identify and deal with the causes of poverty in the Commonwealth, and that is designated as a community action agency by federal law, federal regulations or the Governor.

"Community action program budget" means state funds, federal block grants and federal categorical grants that are received by the Commonwealth for community action activities.

"Community action statewide organization" means community action programs, organized on a statewide basis, to enhance the capability of community action agencies.

"Designated agency" means the agency designated by the Secretary of Health and Human Resources pursuant to § 2.2-5401.

"Local share" means cash or in-kind goods and services donated to community action agencies to carry out their responsibilities.

"Low-income person" means a person who is a member of a household with a gross annual income equal to or less than 125 percent of the poverty standard accepted by the federal agency designated to establish poverty guidelines.

"Service area" means the geographical area within the jurisdiction of a community action agency or a community action statewide organization. (1982, c. 667, §§ 2.1-587, 2.1-588; 2001, c. 844.)

§ 2.2-5401. Designation by Secretary of Health and Human Resources of agency to administer act. — The Secretary of Health and Human Resources shall designate an agency to administer the Community Action Act and to work with community action agencies and community action statewide organizations to develop social and economic opportunities for low-income persons. (1982, c. 667, § 2.1-589; 2001, c. 844.)

§ 2.2-5402. Powers and duties of designated agency. — The designated agency shall have the following powers and duties to:

1. Coordinate state activities designed to reduce poverty.
2. Cooperate with agencies of the Commonwealth and the federal government in reducing poverty and implementing community, social and economic programs.
3. Receive and expend funds for any purpose authorized by this chapter.
4. Enter into contracts with and to award grants to public and private nonprofit agencies and organizations.
5. Develop a state plan based on needs identified by community action agencies and community action statewide organizations.
6. Fund community action agencies and community action statewide organizations and to adopt regulations.
7. Provide assistance to local governments or private organizations for the purpose of establishing and operating a community action agency.
8. Provide technical assistance to community action agencies to improve program planning, program development, administration and the mobilization of public and private resources.
9. Require community action agencies and community action statewide organizations to generate local contributions of cash or in-kind services as the agency may establish by regulation.
10. Convene public meetings that provide citizens the opportunity to comment on public policies and programs to reduce poverty.
11. Advise the Governor and the General Assembly of the nature and extent of poverty in the Commonwealth and to make recommendations concerning

changes in state and federal policies and programs. (1982, c. 667, § 2.1-590; 2001, c. 844.)

§ 2.2-5403. Community action boards. — A. Each community action agency shall administer its community action program through a community action board consisting of no less than fifteen members who shall be selected as follows:

1. One-third of the members of the board shall be elected public officials or their designees, who shall be selected by the local governing body of the service area, except that if the number of elected officials reasonably available and willing to serve is less than one-third of the membership of the board, membership on the board of appointed public officials may be counted in meeting the one-third requirement.

2. At least one-third of the members shall be persons chosen democratically to represent the poor of the area served.

3. The other members shall be members of business, industry, labor, religious, social service, education or other major community groups.

B. Each member of the board selected to represent a specific geographic area within a community shall reside in the area represented.

C. No person selected to serve on the board pursuant to subdivisions A. 2. and A. 3. shall serve for more than five consecutive years or more than a total of ten years.

D. Except as otherwise provided in subsection E, the board shall be responsible for the following:

1. Appointing and dismissing an executive director of the community action agency.

2. Approving grants and contracts, annual program budget requests and operational policies of the community action agency.

3. Having an annual audit performed by an independent auditor.

4. Convening public meetings to provide low-income and other persons the opportunity to comment upon public policies and programs to reduce poverty.

5. Annually evaluating the policies and programs of the community action agency. The board shall submit the evaluation and recommendations to improve the administration of the community action agency to the designated agency and to the local governing body or bodies within the service area.

6. Carrying out such other duties as may be delegated by the local governing body or bodies within the service area or by the designated agency.

7. Delegating responsibilities pursuant to the provisions of § 2.2-5404.

E. Where a local subdivision of the Commonwealth acts as or has designated a community action agency, the local governing body shall determine the responsibilities and authority of the community action board. (1982, c. 667, § 2.1-591; 1989, c. 273; 2001, c. 844.)

§ 2.2-5404. Delegation of responsibilities by community action agency. — If a community action agency places responsibility for major policy determination with respect to the character, funding, extent and administration of and budgeting for programs to be carried on in a particular geographic area within the community in a subsidiary board, council or similar agency, the board, council or agency shall be broadly representative of the area. (1982, c. 667, § 2.1-592; 2001, c. 844.)

§ 2.2-5405. Local participation. — Each community action agency shall consult neighborhood-based organizations composed of residents of the area it serves or members of the groups to be served to assist the agency in planning, conducting and evaluating components of the community action agency. (1982, c. 667, § 2.1-593; 2001, c. 844.)

§ 2.2-5406. Community action statewide organizations; structure; responsibilities. — A. A community action statewide organization shall be a nonprofit corporation whose charter, articles of incorporation and bylaws permit the corporation to operate in all jurisdictions of the Commonwealth.

B. A community action statewide organization shall be governed by a board. The board shall conform to requirements for the community action agency board.

C. Community action statewide organizations shall carry out all the planning, reporting, evaluation, fiscal and programmatic responsibilities required by the designated agency and other appropriate agencies of state government.

D. Community action statewide organizations shall receive and administer state, federal and private funds, render technical assistance and carry out activities that will enable community action agencies to solve local problems.

E. Community action statewide organizations shall work with community action agencies in areas served by those agencies and with community-based organizations, local governments, industry and other organizations in areas unserved by a community action agency to assist in carrying out the purposes of this chapter. (1982, c. 667, §§ 2.1-594, 2.1-595, 2.1-596; 1989, c. 273; 2001, c. 844.)

§ 2.2-5407. Designation of community action agencies; rescission of designation. — A. Each community action agency that has been designated by a unit of local government and funded pursuant to the Economic Opportunity Act of 1964 (Public Law 88-452) that was in operation on July 1, 1982, and is still in operation shall be deemed a community action agency for the purposes of this chapter.

B. No new community action agency shall be designated in any area of the Commonwealth that is served by an existing community action agency.

C. The Governor may designate a community action agency to serve any locality not currently served by an existing community action agency. This determination may be through the expansion of the service area of an existing community action agency or the designation of a new community action agency.

The designated agency shall receive and review requests for the expansion of existing community action agencies or the designation of new community action agencies and shall present to the Secretary of Health and Human Resources a recommendation for community action status and funding. The review and recommendation shall be in compliance with regulations developed by the board of the designated agency.

Upon completion of a satisfactory review of the request, the Secretary shall forward a recommendation to the Governor.

D. The Secretary of Human Resources may recommend that the Governor rescind the designation of a community action agency for cause or by mutual agreement.

If the rescission is for cause, the Secretary shall:

1. Receive from the designated agency a request to rescind the designation of the community action agency, including the causes for the request;
2. Notify the chief elected official of each local governing body in the service area of the intent to rescind the designation of the community action agency;
3. Provide the community action agency the opportunity for a hearing on the record; and
4. Meet any other provisions required by federal law.

If the rescission is by mutual agreement, the Secretary shall:

1. Receive from the designated agency a resolution, approved by the governing body of the community action agency, requesting the Governor to rescind its designation as a community action agency. The resolution shall include a proposed effective date for the rescission; and

2. Meet any other provisions required by federal law. (1982, c. 667, § 2.1-597; 2001, c. 844; 2007, c. 522.)

The 2007 amendments. — The 2007 amendment by c. 522 rewrote the section.

§ 2.2-5408. Administration of community action budget. — The designated agency shall adopt regulations detailing the formula for the distribution of community action program budget funds. The regulations shall take into consideration the distribution of low-income persons residing in the service areas of the community action agencies, the relative cost of living of the areas, as well as other factors considered appropriate.

Each community action agency and community action statewide organization annually shall develop and submit a program budget request for funds appropriated from the community action program budget. The designated agency shall publish annually guidelines detailing the nature and extent of information required in the program budget request for the succeeding fiscal year.

In order to carry out its overall responsibility for planning, coordinating, evaluating and administering a community action program, a community action agency may under its charter or applicable laws receive and administer funds pursuant to this chapter. The community action agency may receive and administer funds and contributions from private or public sources that may be used in support of a community action agency or program and funds under any federal or state assistance program pursuant to which a public or private nonprofit agency organized in accordance with this chapter could act as grantee, contractor or sponsor of projects appropriate for inclusion in a community action program. A community action agency or community action statewide organization may transfer funds so received between components and to delegate funds to other agencies subject to the powers of its governing board and its overall program responsibilities.

In accordance with the requirements of the federal Omnibus Budget Reconciliation Act of 1981 (Public Law 97-35), the designated agency in cooperation with community action agencies and community action statewide organizations, shall develop a state plan for submission annually by the Governor to the Secretary of Health and Human Services.

Community action agencies and community action statewide organizations shall provide the designated agency with quarterly financial and program reports.

Funds received in the Community Services Block Grant pursuant to the federal Omnibus Budget Reconciliation Act of 1981 (Public Law 97-35) shall be expended in support of the purposes of this chapter as follows:

1. Ninety percent of the funds received in the Community Services Block Grant shall be used for the development and implementation of programs and projects designed by community action agencies to serve poor or low-income areas of the Commonwealth in accordance with a formula approved by the Governor for the first year of the Community Services Block Grant and thereafter biennially by the General Assembly.

2. No more than five percent of the funds received in the Community Services Block Grant shall be used for administration of the duties required by this chapter of the designated agency.

3. At least five percent of the funds received in the Community Services Block Grant shall be used to support community action activities conducted by community action statewide organizations. (1982, c. 667, § 2.1-598; 2001, c. 844.)

CHAPTER 55.

VIRGINIA BIOTECHNOLOGY RESEARCH ACT.

§ **2.2-5500:** Not set out. (2001, c. 844.)

Cross references. — As to the duty of the Secretary of Commerce and Trade to implement the provisions of this act, see § 2.2-204.

Editor's note. — This section, pertaining to purpose, was enacted by Acts 2001, c. 844 (formerly by Acts 1994, c. 472 as § 2.1-769). In furtherance of the general policy of the Virginia Code Commission to include in the Code only provisions having general and permanent application, this section, which is limited in its purpose and scope, is not set out here, but attention is called to it by this reference.

§ **2.2-5501. Definitions.** — As used in this chapter, unless the context requires a different meaning:

"Affected localities" means the locality in which a regulated introduction is proposed to be made and any locality within a three-mile radius of the location where the regulated introduction is proposed to be made.

"Confidential business information" means information entitled to confidential treatment under subdivision A. 1. or A. 2. of § 2.2-5506.

"Coordinated Framework" means the federal Coordinated Framework for the Regulation of Biotechnology set forth in 51 Fed. Reg. 23,302 through 23,350 (June 26, 1986), as amended.

"Department" means the department designated by the Secretary of Commerce and Trade to implement the requirements of this chapter for certain types or classes of regulated introductions. Where possible, the Secretary shall designate the department whose purpose most closely resembles the purpose of the federal regulator that will be responsible under the Coordinated Framework for reviewing and authorizing the regulated introduction.

"Federal regulator" means a federal department, agency, or other instrumentality of the federal government, or a designee of such federal instrumentality, which is responsible for regulating an introduction of a genetically engineered organism into the environment under the Coordinated Framework.

"Genetically engineered organism" means an organism (any organism such as animal, plant, bacterium, cyanobacterium, fungus, protist, or virus), altered or produced through genetic modification from a donor, vector, or recipient organism using modern molecular techniques such as recombinant deoxyribonucleic acid (DNA) methodology, and any living organisms derived therefrom.

"Locality" means any county, city or town located within the Commonwealth.

"Planned introduction into the environment" means the intentional introduction or use in the Commonwealth beyond the de minimis level of a genetically engineered organism anywhere except within an indoor facility that is designed to physically contain the genetically engineered organism, including a laboratory, greenhouse, building, structure, growth chamber, or fermenter.

"Regulated introduction" means a planned introduction into the environment for which the Coordinated Framework requires that the person proposing to commence the introduction into the environment do one or more of the following:

1. Notify a federal regulator of the proposed introduction into the environment;

2. Secure the approval of or a permit or license from a federal regulator before commencing the introduction into the environment; or

3. Secure a determination by a federal regulator of the need for notification, approval, licensing or issuance of a permit by the federal regulator if the determination is part of a procedure specified in the Coordinated Framework. (1994, c. 472, § 2.1-770; 2001, c. 844.)

§ **2.2-5502. Exemptions from chapter to be determined by Department.** — A. The Department may waive part or all of the requirements under this chapter for a specified regulated introduction if the Department determines that the satisfaction of that requirement is not necessary to protect the public health or the environment.

B. The Department may exempt a class of regulated introductions from part or all of any requirement under this chapter if the Department determines that the satisfaction of those requirements or part thereof is not necessary to protect the public health or the environment.

C. Planned regulated introductions approved by a federal regulator pursuant to the federal Coordinated Framework prior to enactment of this chapter shall be exempt from the provisions of this chapter. (1994, c. 472, § 2.1-771; 2001, c. 844.)

§ **2.2-5503. Requirements for regulated introduction.** — Except as provided under § 2.2-5502, no person may commence a regulated introduction unless the person:

1. Provides to the Department all of the following information within seven days after the person submits or should have submitted the information specified in subdivisions 1. a. and 1. b. to a federal regulator, whichever is sooner:

a. A copy of all information that the person is required to submit to the federal regulator and that is not confidential information; and

b. A summary of any confidential information that the person submits or is required to submit to a federal regulator. The summary shall provide sufficient information to enable the Department to exercise its notice and comment functions under §§ 2.2-5504 and 2.2-5505, to provide public notice pursuant to § 2.2-5504, and to prepare comments pursuant to § 2.2-5505, and shall have minimal extraneous and irrelevant information. The summary shall also provide sufficient information to enable the locality in which the introduction is proposed to be made to exercise its comment function under § 2.2-5505.

2. Provides such additional information, if any, as is necessary to enable the Department to fulfill any functions it undertakes, on a case-by-case basis, under § 2.2-5505. (1994, c. 472, § 2.1-772; 2001, c. 844.)

§ **2.2-5504. Public notice of proposed regulated introduction.** — Within fifteen days after receiving the information required under § 2.2-5503, the Department shall publish notice and a brief description of the proposed regulated introduction. Notice shall also be provided to any affected locality and to any person who has filed a written request to be notified of regulated introductions. Notice shall be given by publication one time in a newspaper having general circulation in each locality where the regulated introduction is proposed to be made. In addition, subject to the provisions of this chapter regarding confidential business information, any documents submitted to the Department as required under § 2.2-5503 shall be available for public inspection or copying at or near the site of the proposed regulated introduction and at the offices of the Department. (1994, c. 472, § 2.1-773; 2001, c. 844.)

§ 2.2-5505. Comment on proposed regulated introduction. — A. The Department and any affected locality may prepare formal comments on the regulated introduction for submission to the federal regulator for that regulated introduction. The comments shall be submitted within the time established by the federal regulator for that regulated introduction, as determined by the applicable federal requirements or the Coordinated Framework. The comments shall address issues raised by application of the criteria for the granting of approval of a permit or a license under the applicable requirement in the Coordinated Framework and for the protection of the public health and the environment.

B. To assist in the preparation of comments, the Department may do any or all of the following:

1. Hold an informational meeting on the proposed regulated introduction;
2. Provide an opportunity for the public to comment on the proposed regulated introduction;
3. Request any additional information necessary on the proposed regulated introduction from the person providing information under § 2.2-5503;
4. Conduct a technical review of the proposed regulated introduction; and
5. Seek the assistance of the faculty and academic staff of any Virginia public institution of higher education, the Department of Health, the Department of Agriculture and Consumer Services, the Department of Environmental Quality, or any other appropriate state agency or organization, including but not limited to an institutional biosafety committee, in reviewing the proposed regulated introduction.

C. To assist in the preparation of comments, affected localities may do either or both of the following:

1. Hold an informational meeting on the proposed regulated introduction. When possible, that meeting shall be held in conjunction with an informational meeting held by the Department; and
2. Provide an opportunity for the public to comment on the proposed regulated introduction. (1994, c. 472, § 2.1-774; 2001, c. 844.)

§ 2.2-5506. Confidential business information; Department to establish procedures. — A. Except as provided in subsections B and C, the Department and any affected locality shall keep confidential any information received under this chapter if the person submitting the information notifies them that:

1. The federal regulator to whom the information has been submitted has determined that the information is entitled to confidential treatment and is not subject to public disclosure under the federal Freedom of Information Act, 5 U.S.C. § 552, as amended, or under the Coordinated Framework; or
2. The person submitting the information to the Department and any locality has submitted a claim to the federal regulator that the information is entitled to confidential treatment under the federal Freedom of Information Act or under the Coordinated Framework, and the federal regulator has not made a determination on that claim.

B. Subsection A shall not prevent the Department from using the information for the purposes of subdivision B. 4. or B. 5. of § 2.2-5505, subject to the requirements of subsection D.

C. The Department shall allow public access to any information that has been granted confidentiality under subsection A if either of the following occurs:

1. The person providing the information expressly agrees in writing to the public access of the information; or
2. After information has been granted confidentiality under subdivision A. 2., the federal regulator makes a determination that the information is not

entitled to confidential treatment under the federal Freedom of Information Act or under the Coordinated Framework.

D. The Department shall establish procedures to protect information required to be kept confidential under subsection A. Under the procedures, the Department shall not submit any information under subdivision B. 4. or B. 5. of § 2.2-5505 to any person who is not an employee of the Department unless that person has signed an agreement that satisfies the requirements of subsection E.

E. Any agreement under subsection D shall (i) provide that information that is the subject of the agreement shall be subject to confidential treatment; (ii) prohibit the release or sharing of the information with any other person except at the direction of the Department and in compliance with this chapter; (iii) acknowledge the penalties in § 59.1-338 of the Virginia Uniform Trade Secrets Act (§ 59.1-336, et seq.) and any other applicable law of the Commonwealth identified by the Department for the unauthorized disclosure of the information; and (iv) contain a statement that the person receiving the information, any member of his immediate family or any organization with which he is associated has no substantial financial interest in the regulated introduction that is the subject of the information.

F. Any person submitting the information under § 2.2-5503 may waive any of the requirements under this section. (1994, c. 472, § 2.1-775; 2001, c. 844.)

§ **2.2-5507. Enforcement.** — The Department shall enforce the provisions of §§ 2.2-5503 and 2.2-5506. Actions to enforce this chapter by injunctive and any other relief appropriate for enforcement may be filed in the Circuit Court of the City of Richmond or in any county or municipality where a violation occurred in whole or in part. In an enforcement action under this chapter, if it is determined that a person commenced a regulated introduction and did not comply with § 2.2-5503, the court may enter an injunction directing the person to cease the regulated introduction and may order any additional action necessary to protect human health and the environment. (1994, c. 472, § 2.1-776; 2001, c. 844.)

§ **2.2-5508. Penalties.** — A civil penalty of not more than $500 may be assessed by the Department against any person who violates any provision of this chapter. In determining the amount of the penalty, the Department shall consider the degree and extent of harm caused by the violation. No civil penalty may be assessed under this section unless the person has been given the opportunity for a hearing pursuant to the Administrative Process Act, (§ 2.2-4000 et seq.). Any continuing failure to notify under § 2.2-5503 shall constitute the same offense for purposes of imposing the penalty authorized by this section. (1994, c. 472, § 2.1-777; 2001, c. 844.)

§ **2.2-5509. Limitation on local regulation.** — No locality shall enact any regulation or ordinance regulating or prohibiting (i) the planned introduction of genetically engineered organisms into the environment or (ii) biotechnology research activities; however, the siting of biotechnology research activities shall be subject to the zoning and land-use laws and regulations of the localities in which such activities are conducted, the Uniform Statewide Building Code (§ 36-97 et seq.), the Statewide Fire Prevention Code (§ 27-94 et seq.), local public utility and public works ordinances and regulations of general application, and local tax ordinances of general application. (1994, c. 472, § 2.1-778; 2001, c. 844.)

CHAPTER 55.1.

Government Performance and Results Act.

(Expires July 1, 2013)

§ 2.2-5510. (Expires July 1, 2013) Strategic plan. — A. Each agency shall develop and maintain a strategic plan for its operations. The plan shall include:

1. A statement of the mission, goals, strategies, and performance measures of the agency that are linked into the performance management system directed by long-term objectives;
2. Identification of priority and other service populations under current law and how those populations are expected to change within the time period of the plan;
3. An analysis of any likely or expected changes in the services provided by the agency; and
4. An analysis of the impact that the aging of the population will have on its ability to deliver services and a description of how the agency is responding to these changes. Each agency shall report by November 15 of each year to the Department for the Aging its progress in addressing the impact of the aging of the population, according to guidance established by the Secretary of Health and Human Resources. Based upon information received, the Department for the Aging shall prepare a report summarizing the progress made by the agencies and submit such report to the Governor and the General Assembly by June 30 of the following year.

B. Strategic plans shall also include the following information:

1. Input, output, and outcome measures for the agency;
2. A description of the use of current agency resources in meeting current needs and expected future needs, and additional resources that may be necessary to meet future needs; and
3. A description of the activities of the agency that have received either a lesser priority or have been eliminated from the agency's mission or work plan over the previous year because of changing needs, conditions, focus, or mission.

C. The strategic plan shall cover a period of at least two years forward from the fiscal year in which it is submitted and shall be reviewed by the agency annually.

D. Each agency shall post its strategic plan on the Internet. (2003, c. 900; 2006, c. 54; 2007, c. 507.)

Editor's note. — Acts 2003, c. 900, cl. 3, as amended by Acts 2008, c. 240, provides: "That the provisions of this act shall expire on July 1, 2013."

The 2007 amendments. — The 2007 amendment by c. 507, in subdivision A 4, deleted the former second sentence, which read: "Based on guidance from the Secretary of Health and Human Resources, each agency shall report by October 1 of each year to the Governor and to the General Assembly its progress for addressing the impact of the aging of the population in at least five specific actions" and added the last two sentences.

§ 2.2-5511. (Expires July 1, 2013) Review of strategic plan information. — The Governor shall develop an implementation plan providing for each agency to develop a strategic plan. Such implementation plan shall provide for agency submission of individual strategic plans over a three-year period beginning December 1, 2003, and ending December 1, 2006, and require, at a minimum, one-third of state agencies each year to so submit. Thereafter, each agency shall submit, on a biennial basis by December 1 in even-numbered years, its strategic plan including goals, strategies, and performance measures for consideration and review by the Council on Virginia's Future. After review, the Council may submit comments to the Governor regarding any concerns about the strategic plan or recommendations to improve the plan. (2003, c. 900.)

Editor's note. — Acts 2003, c. 900, cl. 3, as amended by Acts 2008, c. 240, provides: "That the provisions of this act shall expire on July 1, 2013."

CHAPTER 55.2.

Competitive Government Act.

§ 2.2-5512. Definitions. — As used in this chapter:

"Commercial activity" means an activity performed by or for state government that is not an inherently governmental activity and that may feasibly be obtained from a commercial source at lower cost than the activity being performed by state employees.

"Commercial source" means any business or other private concern that is eligible for contract awarded in accordance with the Public-Private Education and Infrastructure Act of 2002 (§ 56-575.1 et seq.) or the Virginia Public Procurement Act (§ 2.2-4300 et seq.).

"State employee" means all persons employed by the Commonwealth to provide services, including both salaried and wage employees, and all persons engaged to perform work for or to provide services to the Commonwealth. (2004, c. 994.)

Editor's note. — Acts 2004, c. 994, cl. 2, provides: "That to implement the provisions of this act, no later than July 1, 2004, the Governor shall direct the Secretaries of Administration, Finance, and Technology to (i) develop a methodology for updating the inventory of commercial activities previously developed by the Commonwealth Competition Council; (ii) provide guidance in determining functions that should be performed by state employees because they are inherently governmental in nature, and those that may be suitable for cost comparison analyses; (iii) determine which commercial activities are suitable for consideration for outsourcing at the agency level and which should be the subject of enterprise-wide approaches; (iv) provide guidance to agencies and institutions in making realistic and fair cost comparisons for contracting with the private sector; and (v) recommend such other actions as may be necessary and appropriate to procure the services, and develop the reports provided for in the third enactment of this act."

Acts 2004, c. 994, cl. 3, as amended by Acts 2005, c. 566, provides: "That the initial examination required by this act shall result in a report being completed by the Secretary of Administration, in consultation with the Secretary of Finance and the Secretary of Technology, and presented to the Governor, the chairs of the House Committee on Appropriations and the Senate Committee on Finance, and such other entities as the Governor may designate no later than October 1, 2005. Thereafter, once in each biennium, the examination of commercial activities not already examined by a commercial source in a preceding report, shall be conducted and reported to the Governor, the chairs of the House Committee on Appropriations and the Senate Committee on Finance, and such other entities as the Governor may designate no later than October 1 of the second year of each biennium."

§ 2.2-5513. Responsibilities of Governor to ensure efficiency in government. — A. The Governor shall cause to be conducted an examination of the commercial activities that are being performed by state employees at state agencies and institutions to ensure such activities are being accomplished in the most cost-efficient and effective manner.

B. The examination required by subsection A shall be completed at least once in every two-year period and may be conducted entirely by a commercial source through a solicitation process as provided in the Virginia Public Procurement Act (§ 2.2-4300 et seq.) or the Public-Private Education Facilities and Infrastructure Act of 2002 (§ 56-575.1 et seq.).

C. The examination required by subsection A shall consider at least three commercial activities as the Governor or the commercial source may identify.

D. Upon determination that outsourcing a commercial activity may result in reduced costs or otherwise provide a measurable benefit to the Commonwealth and to assure such activities are being accomplished in the most cost efficient and effective manner, the Governor shall cause that commercial activity to be competed in accordance with the Virginia Public Procurement Act or by using the processes described in the Public-Private Education Facilities and Infrastructure Act of 2002 (§ 56-575.1 et seq.). (2004, c. 994.)

Part C.

Interstate Compacts and Agreements.

CHAPTER 56.

Southern States Energy Compact.

§ 2.2-5600. Form of compact. — The General Assembly hereby enacts, and the Commonwealth of Virginia hereby enters into, the Southern States Energy Compact with any and all states legally joining therein according to its terms, in the form substantially as follows:

Article I.
Policy and Purpose.

The party states recognize that the proper employment and conservation of energy and employment of energy-related facilities, materials, and products, within the context of a responsible regard for the environment can assist substantially in the industrialization of the South and the development of a balanced economy for the region. They also recognize that optimum benefit from the acquisition of energy resources and facilities require systematic encouragement, guidance, and assistance from the party states on a cooperative basis. It is the policy of the party states to undertake such cooperation on a continuing basis; it is the purpose of this compact to provide the instruments and framework for such a cooperative effort to improve the economy of the South and contribute to the individual and community well-being of the region's people.

Article II.
The Board.

A. There is created an agency of the party states to be known as the "Southern States Energy Board" (hereinafter called the Board). The Board shall be composed of three members from each party state, one of whom shall be appointed or designated in each state to represent the Governor, the State Senate and the State House of Representatives, respectively. Each member shall be designated or appointed in accordance with the law of the state which he represents and serving and subject to removal in accordance with such law. Any member of the Board may provide for the discharge of his duties and the performance of his functions thereon (either for the duration of his membership or for any lesser period of time) by a deputy or assistant, if the laws of his state make specific provisions therefor. The federal government may be represented without vote if provision is made by federal law for such representation.

B. Each party state shall be entitled to one vote on the Board, to be determined by majority vote of each member or member's representative from the party state present and voting on any question. No action of the Board shall be binding unless taken at a meeting at which a majority of all party states are represented and unless a majority of the total number of votes on the Board are cast in favor thereof.

C. The Board shall have a seal.

D. The Board shall elect annually, from among its members, a chairman, a vice-chairman, and a treasurer. The Board shall appoint an Executive Director who shall serve at its pleasure and who shall also act as Secretary, and who, together with the Treasurer, shall be bonded in such amounts as the Board may require.

E. The Executive Director, with the approval of the Board, shall appoint and remove or discharge such personnel as may be necessary for the performance of the Board's functions irrespective of the civil service, personnel or other merit system laws of any of the party states.

F. The Board may establish and maintain, independently or in conjunction with any one or more of the party states, a suitable retirement system for its full-time employees. Employees of the Board shall be eligible for social security coverage in respect of old age and survivors insurance provided that the Board takes such steps as may be necessary pursuant to federal law to participate in such program of insurance as a governmental agency or unit. The Board may establish and maintain or participate in such additional programs of employee benefits as may be appropriate.

G. The Board may borrow, accept, or contract for the services of personnel from any state or the United States or any subdivision or agency thereof, from any interstate agency, or from any institution, person, firm or corporation.

H. The Board may accept for any of its purposes and functions under this compact any and all donations, and grants of money, equipment, supplies, materials, and services (conditional or otherwise) from any state or the United States or any subdivision or agency thereof, or interstate agency, or from any institution, person, firm, or corporation, and may receive, utilize and dispose of the same.

I. The Board may establish and maintain such facilities as may be necessary for the transacting of its business. The Board may acquire, hold, and convey real and personal property and any interest therein.

J. The Board shall adopt bylaws, rules, and regulations for the conduct of its business, and shall have the power to amend and rescind these bylaws, rules, and regulations. The Board shall publish its bylaws, rules and regulations in convenient form and shall file a copy thereof, and shall also file a copy of any amendment thereto, with the appropriate agency or officer in each of the party states.

K. The Board annually shall make to the governor of each party state, a report covering the activities of the Board for the preceding year, and embodying such recommendations as may have been adopted by the Board, which report shall be transmitted to the legislature of said state. The Board may issue such additional reports as it may deem desirable.

Article III.
Finances.

A. The Board shall submit to the executive head or designated officer or officers of each party state a budget of its estimated expenditures for such period as may be required by the laws of that jurisdiction for presentation to the legislature thereof.

B. Each of the Board's budgets of estimated expenditures shall contain specific recommendations of the amount or amounts to be appropriated by each of the party states. One-half of the total amount of each budget of estimated expenditures shall be apportioned among the party states in equal shares; one quarter of each such budget shall be apportioned among the party states in accordance with the ratio of their populations to the total population of the entire group of party states based on the last decennial federal census; and one quarter of each such budget shall be apportioned among the party states on the basis of the relative average per capita income of the inhabitants in each of the party states based on the latest computations published by the federal census-taking agency. Subject to appropriation by their respective legislatures, the Board shall be provided with such funds by each of the party states as are necessary to provide the means of establishing and maintaining facilities, a staff of personnel, and such activities as may be necessary to fulfill the powers and duties imposed upon and entrusted to the Board.

C. The Board may meet any of its obligations in whole or in part with funds available to it under Article II (h) of this compact, provided that the Board takes specific action setting aside such funds prior to the incurring of any obligation to be met in whole or in part in this manner. Except where the Board makes use of funds available to it under Article II H, the Board shall not incur any obligation prior to the allotment of funds by the party jurisdictions adequate to meet the same.

D. The Board shall keep accurate accounts of all receipts and disbursements. The receipts and disbursements of the Board shall be subject to the audit and accounting procedures established under its bylaws. However, all receipts and disbursements of funds handled by the Board shall be audited yearly by a qualified public accountant and the report of the audit shall be included in and become part of the annual report of the Board.

E. The accounts of the Board shall be open at any reasonable time for inspection.

Article IV.
Advisory Committees.

The Board may establish such advisory and technical committees as it may deem necessary, membership on which to include but not be limited to private citizens, expert and lay personnel, representatives of industry, labor, commerce, agriculture, civic associations, medicine, education, voluntary health agencies, and officials of local, state and federal government, and may cooperate with and use the services of any such committees and the organizations which they represent in furthering any of its activities under this compact.

Article V.
Powers.

The Board shall have power to:

A. Ascertain and analyze on a continuing basis the position of the South with respect to energy, energy-related industries and environmental concerns.

B. Encourage the development, conservation, and responsible use of energy and energy-related facilities, installation, and products as part of a balanced economy and healthy environment.

C. Collect, correlate, and disseminate information relating to civilian uses of energy and energy-related materials and products.

D. Conduct, or cooperate in conducting, programs of training for state and local personnel engaged in any aspect of

1. Energy, environment, and application of energy, environmental, and related concerns to industry, medicine, or education or the promotion or regulation thereof.

2. The formulation or administration of measures designed to promote safety in any matter related to the development, use or disposal of energy and energy-related materials, products, installations, or wastes.

E. Organize and conduct, or assist and cooperate in organizing and conducting, demonstrations of energy product, material, or equipment use and disposal and of proper techniques or processes for the application of energy resources to the civilian economy or general welfare.

F. Undertake such nonregulatory functions with respect to sources of radiation as may promote the economic development and general welfare of the region.

G. Study industrial, health, safety, and other standards, laws, codes, rules, regulations, and administrative practices in or related to energy and environmental fields.

H. Recommend such changes in, or amendments or additions to the laws, codes, rules, regulations, administrative procedures and practices or ordinances of the party states in any of the fields of its interest and competence as in its judgment may be appropriate. Any such recommendation shall be made through the appropriate state agency with due consideration of the desirability of uniformity but shall also give appropriate weight to any special circumstance which may justify variations to meet local conditions.

I. Prepare, publish and distribute, (with or without charge) such reports, bulletins, newsletters or other material as it deems appropriate.

J. Cooperate with the United States Department of Energy or any agency successor thereto, any other officer or agency of the United States, and any other governmental unit or agency or officer thereof, and with any private persons or agencies in any of the fields of its interests.

K. Act as licensee of the United States government or any party state with respect to the conduct of any research activity requiring such license and operate such research facility or undertake any program pursuant thereto.

L. Ascertain from time to time such methods, practices, circumstances, and conditions as may bring about the prevention and control of energy and environmental incidents in the area comprising the party states, to coordinate the nuclear, environmental and other energy-related incident prevention and control plans and the work relating thereto of the appropriate agencies of the party states and to facilitate the rendering of aid by the party states to each other in coping with energy and environmental incidents.

The Board may formulate and, in accordance with need from time to time, revise a regional plan or regional plans for coping with energy and environmental incidents within the territory of the party states as a whole or within any subregion or subregions of the geographic area covered by this compact.

Article VI.
Supplementary Agreements.

A. To the extent that the Board has not undertaken any activity or project which would be within its power under the provisions of Article V of this compact, any two or more of the party states (acting by their duly constituted administrative officials) may enter into supplementary agreements for the undertaking and continuance of such an activity or project. Any such agreement shall specify its purpose or purposes; its duration and the procedure for termination thereof or withdrawal therefrom; the method of financing and allocating the costs of the activity or project; and such other matters as may be necessary or appropriate. No such supplementary agreement entered into pursuant to this article shall become effective prior to its submission to and approval by the Board. The Board shall give such approval unless it finds that the supplementary agreement or the activity or project contemplated thereby is inconsistent with the provisions of this compact or a program or activity conducted by or participated in by the Board.

B. Unless all of the party states participate in a supplementary agreement, any cost or costs thereof shall be borne separately by the states party thereto. However, the Board may administer or otherwise assist in the operation of any supplementary agreement.

C. No party to a supplementary agreement entered into pursuant to this article shall be relieved thereby of any obligation or duty assumed by said party state under or pursuant to this compact, except that timely and proper performance of such obligation or duty by means of the supplementary agreement may be offered as performance pursuant to the compact.

Article VII.
Other Laws and Relationships.

Nothing in this compact shall be construed to:

A. Permit or require any person or other entity to avoid or refuse compliance with any law, rule, regulation, order or ordinance of a party state or subdivision thereof now or hereafter made, enacted or in force.

B. Limit, diminish, or otherwise impair jurisdiction exercised by the United States Department of Energy, any agency successor thereto, or any other federal department, agency or officer pursuant to and in conformity with any valid and operative act of Congress.

C. Alter the relations between and respective internal responsibilities of the government of a party state and its subdivisions.

D. Permit or authorize the Board to exercise any regulatory authority or to own or operate any nuclear reactor for the generation of electric energy; nor shall the Board own or operate any facility or installation for industrial or commercial purposes.

Article VIII.
Eligible Parties, Entry Into Force or Withdrawal.

A. Any or all of the states of Alabama, Arkansas, Delaware, Florida, Georgia, Kentucky, Louisiana, Maryland, Mississippi, Missouri, North Carolina, Oklahoma, South Carolina, Tennessee, Texas, Virginia, West Virginia, the Commonwealth of Puerto Rico, and the United States Virgin Islands shall be eligible to become party to this compact.

B. As to any eligible party state, this compact shall become effective when its legislature shall have enacted the same into law; provided that it shall not become initially effective until enacted into law by seven states.

C. Any party state may withdraw from this compact by enacting a statute repealing the same, but no such withdrawal shall become effective until the governor of the withdrawing state shall have sent formal notice in writing to the governor of each other party state informing said governors of the action of the legislature in repealing the compact and declaring an intention to withdraw.

Article IX.
Severability and Construction.

The provisions of this compact and of any supplementary agreement entered into hereunder shall be severable and if any phrase, clause, sentence or provision of this compact or such supplementary agreement is declared to be contrary to the constitution of any participating state or of the United States or the applicability thereof to any government, agency, person, or circumstance is held invalid, the validity of the remainder of this compact or such supplementary agreement and the applicability thereof to any government, agency, person or circumstance shall not be affected thereby. If this compact or any supplementary agreement entered into hereunder shall be held contrary to the constitution of any state participating therein, the compact or such supplementary agreement shall remain in full force and effect as to the remaining states and in full force and effect as to the state affected as to all severable matters. The provisions of this compact and of any supplementary agreement entered into pursuant hereto shall be liberally construed to effectuate the purposes thereof. (1962, c. 364, § 2-306; 1966, c. 677, § 2.1-336; 1979, c. 295; 2001, c. 844.)

Compact cross references. — As to provisions of other member states, see:
Alabama: Code of Ala., § 9-18-1 et seq.
Arkansas: A.C.A., § 15-10-401 et seq.
Florida: Fla. Stat., §§ 377.71, 377.711.
Georgia: O.C.G.A., § 12-10-1 et seq.
Kentucky: KRS § 152.200 et seq.
Louisiana: La. R.S. 51:1001 et seq.
Maryland: Md. Ann. Code, art. 41, § 16-101 et seq.
Mississippi: Miss. Code Ann. § 57-25-1 et seq.
Missouri: § 18.060 R.S.Mo.
North Carolina: N.C. Gen. Stat. § 104D-1 et seq.
Oklahoma: 74 Okl. St. § 1051.
Puerto Rico: 1 L.P.R.A. § 201 et seq.
South Carolina: SC Code Ann., § 13-7-410 et seq.
Tennessee: Tenn. Code Ann. § 68-202-601 et seq.
Texas: Tex. Gov't Code, § 761.001 et seq.
West Virginia: W. Va. Code § 29-1E-1 et seq.

Editor's note. — Acts 1979, c. 295, added to Acts 1962, c. 364 a new § 5, reading as follows: "§ 5. The provisions of this Act shall become effective at such time as nine of the party states to the Southern Interstate Nuclear Compact approve substantially the same changes in the Compact as are provided for in this Act and the Congress of the United States consents to the Compact, substantially as amended by this Act." According to the Virginia Code Commission, the effective date of this chapter is 1979. Two states, the last two, enacted legislation in 1983: North Carolina on May 6, 1983, and Texas on August 29, 1983. Congress did not have to act.

§ 2.2-5601. Appointment, term, compensation and expenses of members of Southern States Energy Board. — The Commonwealth's representatives to the Southern States Energy Board shall be appointed in compliance with Article II of the compact as follows: one member of the House of Delegates appointed by the Speaker of the House of Delegates, one member of the Senate appointed by the Senate Committee on Rules and one nonlegislative citizen member appointed by the Governor. Legislative members shall serve terms coincident with their terms of office and shall not have the authority to designate an alternate in accordance with Article II of the compact. The gubernatorial appointee shall serve at the pleasure of the Governor. If any member appointed is the head of a department or agency of the Commonwealth, he may designate a subordinate officer or employee of his department or agency to serve in his stead as permitted by Article II A. of the compact and in conformity with any applicable bylaws of the Board. All members may be reappointed for successive terms.

Legislative members of the Board shall receive such compensation as provided in § 30-19.12 and shall be reimbursed for all reasonable and necessary expenses incurred in the performance of their duties as provided in §§ 2.2-2813 and 2.2-2825. The costs of compensation and expenses of the legislative members shall be paid from appropriations to the Virginia Commission on Intergovernmental Cooperation for the attendance of conferences. The nonlegislative citizen member of the Board shall receive such compensation and reimbursement for all his reasonable and necessary expenses in the performance of his duties as may be appropriated or made available for such purposes. (1962, c. 364, § 2-307; 1966, c. 677, § 2.1-337; 1979, c. 295; 2001, c. 844; 2003, c. 885; 2004, c. 1000.)

Editor's note. — Acts 2003, c. 885, cl. 7, provides: "That all current members of the collegial bodies whose terms have been modified by this act shall be eligible, if reappointed, to the full number of terms provided by this act regardless of prior service."

Acts 2004, c. 1000, cl. 5, provides: "That this act shall not be construed to affect existing appointments for which the terms have not expired. However, any new appointments or appointments to fill vacancies made after the effective date of this act shall be made in accordance with the provisions of this act."

§ 2.2-5602. Supplementary agreements. — No supplementary agreement entered into pursuant to Article VI of the compact and requiring the expenditure of funds or the assumption of an obligation to expend funds in addition to those already appropriated shall become effective as to the Commonwealth unless funds therefor are or have been appropriated as provided by law. (1962, c. 364, § 2-308; 1966, c. 677, § 2.1-338; 1979, c. 295; 2001, c. 844.)

§ 2.2-5603. Cooperation of departments, agencies and officers of Commonwealth. — All departments, agencies and officers of the Commonwealth and its political subdivisions may cooperate with the Southern States Energy Board in the furtherance of any of its activities pursuant to the compact. (1962, c. 364, § 2-309; 1966, c. 677, § 2.1-339; 1979, c. 295; 2001, c. 844.)

CHAPTER 57.

Southern Growth Policies Agreement.

§ 2.2-5700. Form of agreement. — The Southern Growth Policies Agreement is hereby enacted into law and entered into by the Commonwealth with all other states legally joining therein in the form substantially as follows:

Article I.

Findings and Purposes.

A. The party states find that the South has a sense of community based on common social, cultural and economic needs and fostered by a regional tradition. There are vast potentialities for mutual improvement of each state in the region by cooperative planning for the development, conservation and efficient utilization of human and natural resources in a geographic area large enough to afford a high degree of flexibility in identifying and taking maximum advantage of opportunities for healthy and beneficial growth. The independence of each state and the special needs of subregions are recognized and are to be safeguarded. Accordingly, the cooperation resulting from this agreement is intended to assist the states in meeting their own problems by enhancing their abilities to recognize and analyze regional opportunities and take account of regional influences in planning and implementing their public policies.

B. The purposes of this agreement are to provide:

1. Improved facilities and procedures for study, analysis and planning of governmental policies, programs and activities of regional significance.

2. Assistance in the prevention of interstate conflicts and the promotion of regional cooperation.

3. Mechanisms for the coordination of state and local interests on a regional basis.

4. An agency to assist the states in accomplishing the foregoing.

Article II.

The Board.

A. There is created the Southern Growth Policies Board, hereinafter called "the Board."

B. The Board shall consist of five members from each party state, as follows:

1. The governor.

2. Two members of the state legislature, one appointed by the presiding officer of each house of the legislature or in such other manner as the legislature may provide.

3. Two residents of the state who shall be appointed by the governor to serve at his pleasure.

C. In making appointments pursuant to paragraph B 3, a governor shall, to the greatest extent practicable, select persons who, along with the other members serving pursuant to paragraph B, will make the state's representation on the Board broadly representative of the several socioeconomic elements within his state.

D.1. A governor may be represented by an alternate with power to act in his place and stead, if notice of the designation of such alternate is given to the Board in such manner as its bylaws may provide.

2. A legislative member of the Board may be represented by an alternate with power to act in his place and stead, unless the laws of his state prohibit such representation and if notice of the designation of such alternate is given to the Board in such manner as its bylaws may provide. An alternate for a legislative member of the Board shall be selected by the member from among the members of the legislative house in which he serves.

3. A member of the Board serving pursuant to paragraph B 3 may be represented by another resident of his state who may participate in his place and stead, except that he shall not vote; provided that notice of the identity and designation of the representative selected by the member is given to the Board in such manner as its bylaws may provide.

Article III.

Powers.

A. The Board shall prepare and keep current a Statement of Regional Objectives, including recommended approaches to regional problems. The Statement may also identify projects deemed by the Board to be of regional significance. The Statement shall be available in its initial form two years from the effective date of this agreement and shall be amended or revised no less frequently than once every six years. The Statement shall be in such detail as the Board may prescribe. Amendments, revisions, supplements or evaluations may be transmitted at any time. An annual commentary on the Statement shall be submitted at a regular time to be determined by the Board.

B. In addition to powers conferred on the Board elsewhere in this agreement, the Board shall have the power to make or commission studies, investigations and recommendations with respect to:

1. The planning and programming of projects of interstate or regional significance.

2. Planning and scheduling of governmental services and programs which would be of assistance to the orderly growth and prosperity of the region, and to the well-being of its population.

3. Effective utilization of such federal assistance as may be available on a regional basis or as may have an interstate or regional impact.

4. Measures for influencing population distribution, land use, development of new communities and redevelopment of existing ones.

5. Transportation patterns and systems of interstate and regional significance.

6. Improved utilization of human and natural resources for the advancement of the region as a whole.

7. Any other matters of a planning, data collection or informational character that the Board may determine to be of value to the party states.

Article IV.

Avoidance of Duplication.

A. To avoid duplication of effort and in the interest of economy, the Board shall make use of existing studies, surveys, plans and data and other materials in the possession of the governmental agencies of the party states and their respective subdivisions or in the possession of other interstate agencies. Each such agency, within available appropriations and if not expressly prevented or limited by law, is hereby authorized to make such materials available to the Board and to otherwise assist it in the performance of its functions. At the request of the Board, each such agency is further authorized to provide information regarding plans and programs affecting the region, or any subarea thereof, so that the Board may have available to it current information with respect thereto.

B. The Board shall use qualified public and private agencies to make investigations and conduct research, but if it is unable to secure the undertaking of such investigations or original research by a qualified public or private agency, it shall have the power to make its own investigations and conduct its own research. The Board may make contracts with any public or private agencies or private persons or entities for the undertaking of such investigations or original research within its purview.

C. In general, the policy of paragraph B shall apply to the activities of the Board relating to its Statement of Regional Objectives, but nothing herein shall be construed to require the Board to rely on the services of other persons or agencies in developing the Statement of Regional Objectives or any amendment, supplement or revision thereof.

Article V.

Advisory Committees.

The Board shall establish a Local Governments Advisory Committee. In addition, the Board may establish advisory committees representative of subregions of the South, civic and community interests, industry, agriculture, labor or other categories or any combinations thereof. Unless the laws of a party state contain a contrary requirement, any public official of the party state or a subdivision thereof may serve on an advisory committee established pursuant hereto and such service may be considered as a duty of his regular office or employment.

Article VI.

Internal Management of the Board.

A. The members of the Board shall be entitled to one vote each. No action of the Board shall be binding unless taken at a meeting at which a majority of the total number of votes on the Board are cast in favor thereof. Action of the Board shall be only at a meeting at which a majority of the members or their alternates are present. The Board shall meet at least once a year. In its bylaws, and subject to such directions and limitations as may be contained therein, the Board may delegate the exercise of any of its powers relating to internal administration and management to an Executive Committee or the Executive Director. In no event shall any such delegation include final approval of:

1. A budget or appropriation request.

2. The Statement of Regional Objectives or any amendment, supplement or revision thereof.

3. Official comments on or recommendations with respect to projects of interstate or regional significance.

4. The annual report.

B. To assist in the expeditious conduct of its business when the full Board is not meeting, the Board shall elect an Executive Committee of not to exceed seventeen members, including at least one member from each party state. The Executive Committee, subject to the provisions of this agreement and consistent with the policies of the Board, shall be constituted and function as provided in the bylaws of the Board. One-half of the membership of the Executive Committee shall consist of governors, and the remainder shall consist of other members of the Board, except that at any time when there is an odd number of members on the Executive Committee, the number of governors shall be one less than half of the total membership. The members of the Executive Committee shall serve for terms of two years, except that members elected to the first Executive Committee shall be elected as follows: one less than half of the membership for two years and the remainder for one year. The Chairman, Chairman-Elect, Vice-Chairman and Treasurer of the Board shall be members of the Executive Committee and anything in this paragraph to the contrary notwithstanding shall serve during their continuance in these offices. Vacancies in the Executive Committee shall not affect its authority to act, but the Board at its next regularly ensuing meeting following the occurrence of any vacancy shall fill it for the unexpired term.

C. The Board shall have a seal.

D. The Board shall elect, from among its members, a Chairman, a Chairman-Elect, a Vice-Chairman and a Treasurer. Elections shall be annual. The

Chairman-Elect shall succeed to the office of Chairman for the year following his service as Chairman-Elect. For purposes of the election and service of officers of the Board, the year shall be deemed to commence at the conclusion of the annual meeting of the Board and terminate at the conclusion of the next annual meeting thereof. The Board shall provide for the appointment of an Executive Director. Such Executive Director shall serve at the pleasure of the Board, and together with the Treasurer and such other personnel as the Board may deem appropriate shall be bonded in such amounts as the Board shall determine. The Executive Director shall be Secretary.

E. The Executive Director, subject to the policy set forth in this agreement and any applicable directions given by the Board, may make contracts on behalf of the Board.

F. Irrespective of the civil service, personnel or other merit system laws of any of the party states, the Executive Director, subject to the approval of the Board, shall appoint, remove or discharge such personnel as may be necessary for the performance of the functions of the Board, and shall fix the duties and compensation of such personnel. The Board in its bylaws shall provide for the personnel policies and programs of the Board.

G. The Board may borrow, accept or contract for the services of personnel from any party jurisdiction, the United States, or any subdivision or agency of the aforementioned governments, or from any agency of two or more of the party jurisdictions or their subdivisions.

H. The Board may accept for any of its purposes and functions under this agreement any and all donations, and grants of money, equipment, supplies, materials and services, conditional or otherwise, from any state, the United States, or any other governmental agency, or from any person, firm, association, foundation, or corporation, and may receive, utilize and dispose of the same. Any donation or grant accepted by the Board pursuant to this paragraph or services borrowed pursuant to paragraph G of this article shall be reported in the annual report of the Board. Such report shall include the nature, amount and conditions, if any, of the donation, grant, or services borrowed, and the identity of the donor or lender.

I. The Board may establish and maintain such facilities as may be necessary for the transacting of its business. The Board may acquire, hold, and convey real and personal property and any interest therein.

J. The Board shall adopt bylaws for the conduct of its business and shall have the power to amend and rescind these bylaws. The Board shall publish its bylaws in convenient form and shall file a copy thereof and a copy of any amendment thereto, with the appropriate agency or officer in each of the party states.

K. The Board annually shall make to the governor and legislature of each party state a report covering the activities of the Board for the preceding year. The Board at any time may make such additional reports and transmit such studies as it may deem desirable.

L. The Board may do any other or additional things appropriate to implement powers conferred upon it by this agreement.

Article VII.

Finance.

A. The Board shall advise the governor or designated officer or officers of each party state of its budget of estimated expenditures for such period as may be required by the laws of that party state. Each of the Board's budgets of estimated expenditures shall contain specific recommendations of the amount or amounts to be appropriated by each of the party states.

B. The total amount of appropriation requests under any budget shall be apportioned among the party states. Such apportionment shall be in accordance with the following formula:

1. One third in equal shares,

2. One third in the proportion that the population of a party state bears to the population of all party states, and

3. One third in the proportion that the per capita income in a party state bears to the per capita income in all party states.

In implementing this formula, the Board shall employ the most recent authoritative sources of information and shall specify the sources used.

C. The Board shall not pledge the credit of any party state. The Board may meet any of its obligations in whole or in part with funds available to it pursuant to Article VI (h) of this agreement, provided that the Board takes specific action setting aside such funds prior to incurring an obligation to be met in whole or in part in such manner. Except where the Board makes use of funds available to it pursuant to Article VI H, or borrows pursuant to this paragraph, the Board shall not incur any obligation prior to the allotment of funds by the party states adequate to meet the same. The Board may borrow against anticipated revenues for terms not to exceed two years, but in any such event the credit pledged shall be that of the Board and not a party state.

D. The Board shall keep accurate accounts of all receipts and disbursements. The receipts and disbursements of the Board shall be subject to the audit and accounting procedures established by its bylaws. However, all receipts and disbursements of funds handled by the Board shall be audited yearly by a certified or licensed public accountant, and the report of the audit shall be included in and become part of the annual report of the Board.

E. The accounts of the Board shall be open at any reasonable time for inspection by duly constituted officers of the party states and by any persons authorized by the Board.

F. Nothing contained herein shall be construed to prevent Board compliance with laws relating to audit or inspection of accounts by or on behalf of any government contributing to the support of the Board.

Article VIII.

Cooperation with the Federal Government and Other Governmental Entities.

Each party state is hereby authorized to participate in cooperative or joint planning undertakings with the federal government, and any appropriate agency or agencies thereof, or with any interstate agency or agencies. Such participation shall be at the instance of the governor or in such manner as state law may provide or authorize. The Board may facilitate the work of state representatives in any joint interstate or cooperative federal-state undertaking authorized by this article, and each such state shall keep the Board advised of its activities in respect of such undertakings, to the extent that they have interstate or regional significance.

Article IX.

Subregional Activities.

The Board may undertake studies or investigations centering on the problems of one or more selected subareas within the region; provided that in its judgment, such studies or investigations will have value as demonstrations for similar or other areas within the region. If a study or investigation that would be of primary benefit to a given state, unit of local government, or intrastate or interstate area is proposed, and if the Board finds that it is not justified in undertaking the work for its regional value as a demonstration, the Board may undertake the study or investigation as a special project. In any such event, it shall be a condition precedent that satisfactory financing and personnel arrangements be concluded to assure that the party or parties benefited bear all costs which the Board determines that it would be inequitable for it to assume. Prior to undertaking any study or investigation pursuant to this article as a special project, the Board shall make reasonable efforts to secure the undertaking of the work by another responsible public or private entity in accordance with the policy set forth in Article IV B.

Article X.

Comprehensive Land Use Planning.

If any two or more contiguous party states desire to prepare a single or consolidated comprehensive land use plan, or a land use plan for any interstate area lying partly within each such state, the governors of the states involved may designate the Board as their joint agency for the purpose. The Board shall accept such designation and carry out such responsibility; provided that the states involved make arrangements satisfactory to the Board to reimburse it or otherwise provide the resources with which the land use plan is to be prepared. Nothing contained in this article shall be construed to deny the availability for use in the preparation of any such plan of data and information already in the possession of the Board or to require payment on account of the use thereof in addition to payments otherwise required to be made pursuant to other provisions of this agreement.

Article XI.

Compacts and Agencies Unaffected.

Nothing in this agreement shall be construed to:

1. Affect the powers or jurisdiction of any agency of a party state or any subdivision thereof.

2. Affect the rights or obligations of any governmental units, agencies or officials, or of any private persons or entities conferred or imposed by any interstate or interstate-federal compacts to which any one or more states participating herein are parties.

3. Impinge on the jurisdiction of any existing interstate-federal mechanism for regional planning or development.

Article XII.

Eligible Parties; Entry Into and Withdrawal.

A. This agreement shall have as eligible parties the states of Alabama, Arkansas, Delaware, Florida, Georgia, Kentucky, Louisiana, Maryland, Mississippi, Missouri, North Carolina, Oklahoma, South Carolina, Tennessee, Texas, Virginia and West Virginia, the Commonwealth of Puerto Rico and the Territory of the Virgin Islands, hereinafter referred to as party states.

B. Any eligible state may enter into this agreement and it shall become binding thereon when it has adopted the same; provided that in order to enter into initial effect, adoption by at least five states shall be required.

C. Adoption of the agreement may be either by enactment thereof or by adherence thereto by the governor; provided that in the absence of enactment, adherence by the governor shall be sufficient to make his state a party only until December 31, 1973. During any period when a state is participating in this agreement through gubernatorial action, the governor may provide to the Board an equitable share of the financial support of the Board from any source available to him. Nothing in this paragraph shall be construed to require a governor to take action contrary to the constitution or laws of his state.

D. Except for a withdrawal effective on December 31, 1973, in accordance with paragraph C of this article, any party state may withdraw from this agreement by enacting a statute repealing the same, but no such withdrawal shall take effect until one year after the governor of the withdrawing state has given notice in writing of the withdrawal to the governors of all other party states. No withdrawal shall affect any liability already incurred by or chargeable to a party state prior to the time of such withdrawal.

Article XIII.

Construction and Severability.

This agreement shall be liberally construed so as to effectuate the purposes thereof. The provisions of this agreement shall be severable and if any phrase, clause, sentence or provision of this agreement is declared to be contrary to the constitution of any state or of the United States, or the application thereof to any government, agency, person, or circumstance is held invalid, the validity of the remainder of this agreement and the applicability thereof to any government, agency, person or circumstance shall not be affected thereby. If this agreement shall be held contrary to the constitution of any state participating therein, the agreement shall remain in full force and effect as to the state affected as to all severable matters. (1973, c. 263, § 2.1-339.1; 1979, c. 633; 2001, c. 844.)

Compact cross references. — As to provisions of other member states, see:

Alabama: Code of Ala. § 41-18-1 et seq.

Arkansas: A.C.A. § 15-2-101.

Georgia: O.C.G.A. § 12-10-20 et seq.

Kentucky: KRS § 147.580.

Louisiana: La. R.S. 49:61.

Mississippi: Miss. Code Ann. §§ 57-33-1, 57-33-3.

North Carolina: N.C. Gen. Stat. § 143-490 et seq.

Oklahoma: 74 Okl. St. §§ 3501, 3502.

South Carolina: S.C. Code Ann. § 13-13-10.

Tennessee: Tenn. Code Ann. § 13-2-101 et seq.

§ 2.2-5700.1. Appointment, term, compensation and expenses of members of Southern Growth Policies Board. — The Commonwealth's representatives to the Southern Growth Policies Board in compliance with Article II of the compact shall consist of: the Governor; one member of the House of Delegates appointed by the Speaker of the House of Delegates; one member of the Senate appointed by the Senate Committee on Rules; and two nonlegislative citizen members appointed by the Governor. Legislative members shall serve terms coincident with their terms of office and shall not have the authority to designate an alternate in accordance with subdivision D.2. of Article II of the compact. The gubernatorial appointee shall serve at the pleasure of the Governor. All members may be reappointed for successive terms.

Legislative members of the Board shall receive such compensation as provided in § 30-19.12 and shall be reimbursed for all reasonable and necessary expenses incurred in the performance of their duties as provided in §§ 2.2-2813 and 2.2-2825. The costs of compensation and expenses of the legislative members shall be paid from appropriations to the Virginia Commission on Intergovernmental Cooperation for the attendance of conferences. Nonlegislative citizen members shall receive such compensation and shall be reimbursed for all reasonable and necessary expenses incurred in the performance of their duties as may be appropriated or made available for such purposes. (2004, c. 1000.)

Editor's note. — Acts 2004, c. 1000, cl. 5, provides: "That this act shall not be construed to affect existing appointments for which the terms have not expired. However, any new appointments or appointments to fill vacancies made after the effective date of this act shall be made in accordance with the provisions of this act."

§ 2.2-5701. Bylaws and amendments to be filed with Secretary of Commonwealth. — Copies of bylaws and amendments to be filed pursuant to Article VI J of the agreement shall be filed with the Secretary of the Commonwealth. (1973, c. 263, § 2.1-339.2; 2001, c. 844.)

§ 2.2-5702. Participation with other states not terminated. — Nothing contained in the Southern Growth Policies Agreement as enacted by this chapter shall in any event be construed to terminate the participation of the Commonwealth with any state which adopted the Southern Growth Policies Agreement prior to June 1, 1973, except that the provisions of Article XII C shall govern with respect to the continuance of states as parties thereto after December 31, 1973. (1973, c. 263, § 2.1-339.3; 2001, c. 844.)

CHAPTER 58.

Delmarva Peninsula Compact.

§ 2.2-5800. Formation of Delmarva Peninsula Compact. — The Governor of the Commonwealth may execute a compact or agreement on behalf of the Commonwealth and the states of Delaware and Maryland, joining with them to form the Delmarva Advisory Council. The Council's rights, duties and functions shall be substantially as follows within this chapter. (1985, c. 527, § 2.1-339.4; 2001, c. 844.)

Compact cross references. — As to provisions of other member states, see:
Delaware: 29 Del. C. § 11101 et seq.

§ 2.2-5801. Delmarva Advisory Council; membership; jurisdiction meetings; compensation. — A. Upon enactment of similar legislation by the states of Maryland and Delaware, the Delmarva Advisory Council shall be established as a regional advisory council for the Delmarva Peninsula. The Council shall be concerned with all of the Delmarva Peninsula south of the Chesapeake and Delaware Canal. Such jurisdiction shall include all of Kent and Sussex Counties and a portion of New Castle County in Delaware; all of the Counties of Kent, Queen Anne's, Caroline, Talbot, Dorchester, Wicomico, Worcester, and Somerset and a portion of Cecil County in Maryland; and all of Accomack and Northampton Counties in Virginia.

B. The membership of the Council shall consist of:

1. Five members appointed by the Governor of Delaware, five members appointed by the Governor of Maryland, and five members appointed by the Governor of Virginia; and

2. Such other members from county and municipal governments, and from the private sector as may be established from time to time in the bylaws of the Council.

C. Council members shall annually elect a chairman and such other officers as may be deemed necessary.

D. The Council shall hold quarterly meetings at a time and place designated by the Council, and shall hold additional meetings as are deemed necessary.

E. The Council shall hold not less than one meeting each year at which the public is given an opportunity to express views concerning regional issues.

F. The Council may adopt bylaws, rules and regulations for its governing and operation not inconsistent with this chapter or laws of the states of Delaware, Maryland and Virginia.

G. Members of the council shall serve without pay except that each shall be reimbursed for actual expenses incurred in the performance of their duties. (1985, c. 527, §§ 2.1-339.5, 2.1-339.6; 2001, c. 844.)

§ **2.2-5802. Duties and responsibilities of the Council.** — The duties and responsibilities of the Council shall include but are not limited to:

1. Assist in the identification of perceived regional problems and issues;

2. Assist in effective solutions for such problems and issues;

3. Assist in the resolution of such problems and issues in order to promote a balanced development to improve the economic conditions, quality of life, and environmental concerns of the people of the Delmarva Peninsula;

4. Advise the Governors, Secretaries, Legislatures and other local and state agencies on options to solve regional and interstate problems and issues as pertaining to the Delmarva Peninsula;

5. Prepare and submit quarterly reports and furnish such reports as well as any requested studies by the Governors; and

6. Serve in an advisory capacity only. (1985, c. 527, § 2.1-339.7; 2001, c. 844.)

§ **2.2-5803. Funding of the Council; staff.** — A. The Council may accept gifts and grants from any individual, group, association, or corporation, or from the United States Government, subject to such limitations or conditions as may be provided by law.

B. The Council shall employ the necessary personnel and consultants to perform the lawful duties required by this chapter.

C. The Delmarva Advisory Council shall receive such funding as is appropriated by law by the states of Delaware, Maryland and Virginia. (1985, c. 527, § 2.1-339.8; 2001, c. 844.)

CHAPTER 59.

Chesapeake Regional Olympic Games Compact.

Sec.

§ **2.2-5900. Form of compact.** — The General Assembly hereby enacts, and the Commonwealth of Virginia hereby enters into, the Chesapeake

Regional Olympic Games Compact with any and all states legally joining therein according to its terms, in the form substantially as follows:

CHESAPEAKE REGIONAL OLYMPIC GAMES COMPACT.

Article I.

Purpose and Findings.

A. The purpose of this compact shall be to create a regional authority to oversee the conduct of the 2012 Olympic Games, coordinated and managed by the local Organizing Committee for the Olympic Games (OCOG), and to assure that the region's guarantees and commitments accepted in conjunction with hosting the Olympic Games are fulfilled.

B. The General Assembly finds that:

1. For some time, the State of Maryland (including the City of Baltimore), the District of Columbia, and the Commonwealth of Virginia, through the nonprofit organization known as the Washington/Baltimore Regional 2012 Coalition (WBRC 2012), have been actively engaged in national competition to win the U.S. Candidate City designation and, subsequently, the Host City designation and the right to host the 2012 Olympic Games.

2. Hosting the Olympic Games will provide several major, lasting, and unique benefits for all of the citizens of the Chesapeake region, including:

a. Direct, positive economic impact on our regional economy;

b. An opportunity to showcase our region to the world;

c. A catalyst for regional action; and

d. A renewed sense of pride along with a tangible legacy (e.g. new and improved venues and enhanced transportation infrastructure).

3. Independent economic studies show that preparing for and hosting the Olympic Games will have a positive economic impact on the region, including:

a. Direct and indirect spending in excess of $5,000,000,000;

b. The creation of approximately 70,000 jobs;

c. Increased tax revenues resulting from Olympic-related economic activity in excess of $130,000,000, without raising or creating any new taxes; and

d. A lasting improvement in the region's competitive position within the travel/tourism industry, as well as the region's ability to attract new businesses.

4. The citizens of the region have responded positively to WBRC 2012's efforts and solidly embraced the cause to host the Olympic Games, expressed in part by the endorsement of scores of local business, civic, governmental, academic, and amateur sports organizations, and by survey results that show (i) eighty-two percent of the region's residents support the effort to bring the 2012 Olympic Games to this area and (ii) eighty-six percent of area residents believe that the Olympic Games will bring substantial economic benefits to our region.

5. Through the submission of the region's official bid proposal to the United States Olympic Committee (USOC) on December 15, 2000, WBRC 2012 reached a milestone in the process of capturing the Olympic Games by providing a 631-page logistical, operational, and financial blueprint for hosting the 2012 Games.

6. The bid proposal highlights the great venues and vistas found in our region and is developed around key principles, including (i) building less, not more and (ii) utilizing mass transit, and (iii) protecting the environment.

7. In addition to the region's bid proposal, the USOC and the International Olympic Committee (IOC) require certain government guarantees and commitments in conjunction with hosting the 2012 Olympic Games, should our region win the U.S. Candidate City designation.

8. Our unique regional approach to winning the right to host the Olympic Games creates the added complication of determining which entities will provide the necessary guarantees.

9. It is incumbent upon WBRC 2012 and government leaders to move forward together now to craft the solution that best "lives regionalism" and maximizes the region's chances of winning the 2012 Olympic Games, and reaping the many benefits that come with this honor.

10. Given that all four jurisdictions, Virginia, Maryland, the District of Columbia, and Baltimore, will host a significant number of events and reap substantial benefits, the most effective solution for all four jurisdictions is to enter into a single agreement that gives the USOC (and subsequently the IOC) a single focal point and a united front that reflects the regional nature of our bid.

Article II.

Definitions.

As used in this compact:

"Bid Proposal" means the bid formally submitted by WBRC 2012 to the USOC on December 15, 2000.

"Host City" means the entity that has been selected by the International Olympic Committee to host the 2012 Olympic Games.

"International Olympic Committee" and *"IOC"* means the International Olympic Committee, a body corporate under international law created by the Congress of Paris of 23 June, 1894, and having perpetual succession.

"Olympic Games" means any Olympic Games sponsored and governed by the International Olympic Committee and any other educational, cultural, athletic, or sporting events related or preliminary thereto.

"Organizing Committee for the Olympic Games," and *"OCOG"* means the Committee formed by WBRC 2012 to organize and conduct the Olympic Games, if WBRC 2012 is selected by the IOC as the host city in 2005.

"Signatories" means the Commonwealth of Virginia, the State of Maryland, the District of Columbia, and the City of Baltimore.

"U.S. Candidate City" means the entity that has received the United States Olympic Committee's endorsement to submit to the IOC the sole bid from the United States for the hosting of the 2012 Olympic Games.

"United States Olympic Committee" and *"USOC"* means the United States Olympic Committee, incorporated by Act of Congress on September 21, 1950, and having perpetual succession.

"WBRC 2012" means Washington/Baltimore Regional 2012 Coalition, a not-for-profit corporation organized under the laws of the State of Maryland, and its successors.

Article III.

Creation of Regional Authority.

A. The Signatories hereby provide the mechanism for the creation and termination of the "Chesapeake Regional Olympic Games Authority," hereinafter "Regional Authority," which shall be an instrumentality of the Commonwealth of Virginia, the State of Maryland, the District of Columbia, and the City of Baltimore, and shall have the powers and duties set forth herein, and those additional powers and duties conferred upon it by subsequent actions of the signatories.

B. The Regional Authority shall come into existence by the force of this compact when and if, and only if, the IOC awards the 2012 Olympic Games in year 2005 to WBRC 2012, as the U.S. Candidate City and the official representative of the Maryland, Virginia, District of Columbia, Baltimore region.

C. The Regional Authority shall, if ever brought into existence, cease to exist by the force of this Compact on January 1, 2014, unless extended by substantially similar future legislation passed by each of the Signatories.

D. Until such time as the Regional Authority comes into existence, the combined signatures of the Governors of Virginia and Maryland, and the Mayors of the District of Columbia and Baltimore, on any and all documents necessary and appropriate to the pursuit of the 2012 Olympic Games shall be deemed binding on future actions of the Regional Authority.

For the purposes of this subsection, (i) the above referenced signatures may be on the same document, on separate but materially and substantially similar documents, or any combination thereof; and (ii) no individual signature shall be deemed effective until such time as all four above referenced signatures are obtained.

Article IV.

Regional Authority; Composition; Terms; Accounting.

A. The Regional Authority shall be composed of eleven voting members, as follows: The State of Maryland shall be entitled to three voting members, to be appointed by the Governor of Maryland; the Commonwealth of Virginia shall be entitled to three voting members, to be appointed by the Governor of Virginia; the District of Columbia shall be entitled to three voting members, to be appointed by the Mayor of the District of Columbia; the City of Baltimore shall be entitled to one voting member, to be appointed by the Mayor of the City of Baltimore; and the Washington/Baltimore Regional 2012 Coalition, a not-for-profit corporation created for the sole purpose of bringing the Olympic Games to the region, or the OCOG, shall be entitled to one voting member, to be appointed in a manner consistent with its usual procedure.

B. The Regional Authority shall cause to be formed a Regional Authority Advisory Committee, which shall be comprised of representatives (Advisory Members) from each of the local jurisdictions substantially impacted by hosting the Olympic Games in the region, in a manner to be determined by the Regional Authority.

C. Reasonable efforts should be made to ensure that appointments of voting members and advisory members (i) are residents of the regional community with relevant and useful experience, and with sufficient time to devote to the duties of the Regional Authority, to help facilitate the successful hosting of the Olympic Games; (ii) reflect the geographical diversity inherent in the regional nature of WBRC 2012's bid proposal; and (iii) reflect the cultural, ethnic, and racial diversity inherent in the Chesapeake Region.

D. Voting members shall not be compensated for their service on the Regional Authority, but shall be entitled to be reimbursed by the Regional Authority for normal and customary expenses incurred in the performance of their duties.

E. The terms of the voting members of the Regional Authority shall be two years. Each voting member shall hold office until his successor shall be appointed and duly qualified. Any voting member of the Regional Authority may succeed himself. All vacancies in the membership of the voting members of the Regional Authority shall be filled in the manner of the original appointment for remainder of the unexpired term.

F. The Regional Authority shall elect from its membership a chair, a vice-chair, a secretary, and a treasurer. Such officers shall serve for such terms as shall be prescribed by resolution of the Regional Authority or until their successors are elected and qualified. No voting member of the Regional Authority shall hold more than one office on the Regional Authority.

G. Regular meetings of the Regional Authority shall be held on such dates and at such time and place as shall be fixed by resolution of the Regional Authority. Special meetings of the Regional Authority may be called by resolution of the authority, by the chairman or vice-chairman, or upon the written request of at least three voting members of the Regional Authority. Written notice of all meetings shall be delivered to each voting member, not less than three days prior to the date of the meeting in the case of regular meetings and not less than twenty-four hours in the case of special meetings.

H. A majority of the voting members of the Regional Authority shall constitute a quorum. A majority of the quorum is empowered to exercise all the rights and perform all the duties of the Regional Authority and no vacancy on the Regional Authority shall impair the right of such majority to act. If at any meeting there is less than a quorum present, a majority of those present may adjourn the meeting to a fixed time and place, and notice of the time and place shall be given in accordance with subsection G, provided that if the notice period required by subsection G cannot reasonably be complied with, such notice, if any, of such adjourned meeting shall be given as is reasonably practical.

I. The Regional Authority shall establish rules and regulations for its own governance, not inconsistent with this compact.

J. The Regional Authority shall make provision for a system of financial accounting and controls, audits, and reports. All accounting systems and records, auditing procedures and standards, and financial reporting shall conform to generally accepted principles of governmental accounting. All financial records, reports, and documents of the Regional Authority shall be public records and open to public inspection under reasonable regulations prescribed by the Regional Authority.

The Regional Authority shall designate a fiscal year, establish a system of accounting and financial control, designate the necessary funds for complete accountability, and specify the basis of accounting for each fund. The Regional Authority shall cause to be prepared a financial report on all funds at least quarterly and a comprehensive report on the fiscal operations and conditions of the Regional Authority annually.

Article V.

Funding of Regional Authority.

A. The OCOG shall provide reasonable funds for the operation of the Regional Authority and the conduct of its business in accordance with the provisions of this compact.

B. For the purposes of this article, payment of any insurance premiums incurred by the Regional Authority under the authority granted to it by Article VI shall not be considered operations funds referred to in subsection A. The OCOG shall pay only such insurance premiums as are reasonable.

C. The OCOG shall not be responsible for any financial liability that the Regional Authority may incur under Article VI.

D. The Regional Authority shall submit to the OCOG a planned budget for the Regional Authority's next fiscal year, adopted consistent with Article IV, no less than ninety days before the beginning of the next fiscal year.

Article VI.

Regional Authority Oversight of Organizing Committee of the Olympic Games; Additional Powers.

A. The Regional Authority, in recognition of its oversight responsibility over the OCOG, shall have access to (i) the quarterly financial statements of the

OCOG, (ii) the annual business plans of the OCOG, and (iii) all other OCOG documents necessary to achieve its oversight purpose.

B. The Regional Authority shall have the power to enforce OCOG budgetary and planning changes when review by the Regional Authority of the OCOG financial statements, annual business plans, or other documents contemplated in this article suggests (i) economic shortfalls that would possibly trigger the Regional Authority's liability outlined in this article; or (ii) the OCOG fails to host the Olympic Games in a manner that would satisfy the requirements of the USOC or the IOC; and such changes are supported by a majority of the voting members of the Regional Authority, notwithstanding the quorum requirements of Article IV.

C. The Regional Authority, in recognition of its duties as overseer of the OCOG, shall:

1. Be bound by the terms of, cause the OCOG to perform, and guaranty performance of the OCOG's obligations under all documents necessary and appropriate to the pursuit of the Olympic Games;

2. Certify the OCOG's performance of such obligations as requested by the USOC from time to time;

3. Accept liability for the OCOG, if any, as far as required by all documents necessary and appropriate to the pursuit and hosting of the Olympic Games; and

4. Accept liability, if any, with the OCOG, for any financial deficit of the OCOG, or the Olympic Games, as follows:

a. The OCOG shall be responsible for any amount up to twenty-five million dollars;

b. The Regional Authority shall be liable for any amount in excess of twenty-five million dollars, but not to exceed an additional $175 million; and

c. Except as set forth in existing applicable law, the OCOG and the Regional Authority shall not be limited in their choice of funding sources for covering possible financial losses, including but not limited to the purchase of insurance, if commercially available and reasonably priced.

D. The Regional Authority, in its financial oversight and safeguard role, shall ensure that no legacy programs, funds, or accounts shall be funded from any of the proceeds of the 2012 Olympic Games until all budgetary and operational financial obligations of the OCOG and the Regional Authority for hosting the Olympic Games are first met; and that no liability for any financial deficit resulting from the 2012 Olympic Games shall accrue to the Regional Authority (or the Signatories) until all budgetary and/or operational financial surpluses of the OCOG, if any, are applied to all outstanding financial obligations of OCOG and the Regional Authority, if any, accrued exclusively in connection with hosting the Olympic Games.

E. The Regional Authority, in order to facilitate its oversight responsibility over the OCOG, shall have the additional powers to:

1. Sue and be sued in contract and in tort;
2. Complain and defend in all courts;
3. Implead and be impleaded;
4. Enter into contracts;
5. Hire appropriate staff; and
6. Exercise any additional powers granted to it by subsequent legislation.

Article VII.

Indemnification.

A. Any liability incurred by the Regional Authority, not covered by insurance under Article VI, shall be further indemnified by the signatories to this compact, in proportion to the relative economic benefit currently expected to accrue to each signatory from hosting the Olympic Games, as follows:

1. The State of Maryland shall be liable for fifty-three percent;
2. The Commonwealth of Virginia shall be liable for nineteen percent; and
3. The District of Columbia shall be liable for twenty-eight percent.

B. Each of the signatories to this compact may provide for its share of any possible liability in any manner it may choose, as befits each signatory's independent commitment.

Article VIII.

Commitments of Signatories.

As appropriate to its individual jurisdiction and specific role in hosting the 2012 Olympic Games, each Signatory agrees to:

1. Ensure that necessary facilities are built and transportation infrastructure improvements take place, including government funding as appropriate;
2. Provide access to existing state/city-controlled facilities and other important resources as specified in WBRC 2012's bid proposal, in accordance with applicable law and contractual obligations; and
3. Provide adequate security, fire protection and other government-related services at a reasonable cost to ensure for the safe and orderly operation of the Olympic Games.

Article IX.

Compliance With Local Law.

The Regional Authority shall make every effort to comply with the local laws of each of the Signatories to this compact, regarding disclosure, appointment, and open meetings.

Article X.

Effective Dates.

None of the duties or responsibilities encompassed in this compact shall have effect until substantially similar legislation is passed by each of the signatories, at which time this compact shall immediately be effective. (2001, c. 824, § 2.1-818; 2002, c. 491.)

Compact cross references. — As to provisions of other member states, see:

District of Columbia: D.C. Code § 2-1131 et seq.

Maryland: Md. STATE GOVERNMENT Code Ann. § 9-2301 et seq.

Editor's note. — Acts 2001, c. 824 enacted § 2.1-818, from which this section is derived. Pursuant to § 30-152, Acts 2001, c. 824 has been given effect in this section as set out above.

§ 2.2-5901. Certain documents to be filed with Secretary of Commonwealth. — Copies of the Regional Authority's rules and regulations for its own governance required pursuant to Article IV shall be filed with the Secretary of the Commonwealth. (2001, c. 824, § 2.1-819.)

Editor's note. — Acts 2001, c. 824 enacted § 2.1-819, from which this section is derived. Pursuant to § 30-152, Acts 2001, c. 824 has been given effect in this section as set out above.